German

Quest for the Bavarian Cross

by

Brett Harriman

Harriman Books — Travel Publishing, 2006

ISBN: 0-9778188-0-2

Library of Congress information on file with publisher

Printed in the United States of America

Edited by the delightful and proficient Jazzy J. and Priscilla R. from Washington, D.C. Without there valuable input, their'd bee alota mustakes.

Hand-drawn maps © created by the author.

All other city maps © created by Peter "The Hunter" Jaeger, Darmstadt, Germany— refined and revised by the author and Denise Fortin.

Rhine, Mosel and Danube Valley maps ©, in addition to the Salzkammergut map, were created by the author and Denise Fortin.

Cover created by the author and Denise Fortin—denise@d2design.biz

Front-cover picture of the Brandenburg Gate (provided by the fab folks at Berlin Tourism, www.btm.de) was taken from Pariser Platz looking west towards the leafy Tiergarten. *To the right* (out of picture) is the French Embassy. *To the left* is the TI (look to red sign with white "i"), and behind that (out of picture) is the construction site for the new U.S. Embassy. For our do-it-yourself walking tour of Central Berlin, flip to page 360.

Back-cover pictures were taken by the author.

Left picture was snapped at the Rothenburg Christmas market.

Right picture overlooks the remarkably quaint town of St. Gilgen, Austria, with Lake Wolfgang(see) in background. Travelers familiar with the movie The Sound of Music will recognize this stunning scene as one of the fleeting shots in the beginning of the film. You can see St. Gilgen on our do-it-yourself Sound of Music driving tour (page 511).

Postmark canceling out stamp on front cover is dated (the European way) 09.07.06, or 9 July 2006. This is the final match of the FIFA World Cup soccer tournament to be played at Berlin's 74,000-seat Olympic Stadium (page 376). For more info on the tournament, flip to page 152.

All comments, tips, info, or whatever it is you want to get off your chest, please forward to author@ytcompanion.com

www.your-traveling-companion.com

After spending 12,000 mega-tedious hours basking in the glow of a computer screen writing this book, I frequently stand in amazement that it finally has found its way to you. Such an exhaustive effort deserves to be dedicated.

First, I would like to send a dedication "down under" to a good-natured Australian town called Newcastle. In this industrious, blue-collar community live honest people who work hard, speak their minds and can be counted on. My relatives live there and I want them to know how much they mean to me. There is not a day that goes by that I don't think of the wonderful times we've shared.

* * *

I would also like to pay homage to the brave soldiers who have paid the highest price in past wars so that we, as Americans, can live in a free society 365 days a year. I shall never forget the liberty they have bestowed upon us.

Without freedom, we are nothing!

I offer a token of gratitude in the chapter, *Lest We Forget* (see our Web site)

* * *

Additionally, I would like to pay tribute to the late Pat Tillman, along with the other selfless heroes who have recently fallen in the Middle East while upholding the liberty we cherish. Their sacrifices will never be forgotten!

* * *

And lastly, thank you, Mom, for flying to Germany and joining me in working at AFRC Chiemsee. Your untiring support gave me the opportunity to continue writing and a chance to fulfill my dream. Thank you, Dad, for your determined teamwork in the southern Nevada desert, speaking to social groups and knocking on doors to promote *"Your Traveling Companion."* You're my No. 2 fan, second to Mom, of course. And thanks, big brother, for lending me your credit card from time to time, it sure came in handy.

* * *

Last but not least, thanks to the real "Sydney." Without you as my model, enthusiastically discovering Europe, the book would not have been written.

C o n t e n t s (Adventure Novel)

Quest for the Bavarian Cross

C o n t e n t s (Travel Guide)

Germany & Austria

Prologue

I can't believe what a year it's been for a girl like me. One afternoon, on the way back from the student union, I experienced an overwhelming feeling as if a giant finger pierced the clouds and pointed at me. For what, I could only imagine.

The angelic experience transported me back to a conversation I had with an acquaintance from college, a radiant 40-year-old woman, who once imparted the details of her savings account. Every day her bank deposited 86,400 into the account, but by midnight whatever she didn't spend vanished. For most of her life she didn't think twice about the generous funds, as they were constantly replenished. Remarkably, she admitted, "On most days I failed to spend even half my allowance."

I stared at her in amazement and thought of what a fortunate woman she was. She explained further: "It wasn't until a visit to my doctor that I realized what a fool I had been for not spending every cent, every day." The doctor diagnosed her with cancer, and her wealth had an expiration date. She looked to the past and recognized her negligence. The woman then told me I had access to the same generous funds. The account she referred to was not full of money but time. There are 86,400 seconds in a day and every one that is wasted, she now understands, is a giant loss.

"There's no drawing against tomorrow," she said. "You can only live today's transactions. Just ask the student who failed a final exam the merit of a year, the value of a month to the mother who gave birth to a premature baby, the difference a day makes to lovers in waiting, the significance of a minute to someone who just missed his or her flight, or how vital a second is to a person who just survived an accident."

Yeah, absolutely it made me think, especially about my failing academics and the meaning of a year. I saw the opportunity before me as do-it-yourself destiny, something I couldn't deny. So, I did what any worn-out student would do, I said my goodbyes and set off to see the world.

The life I now lead seems a zillion miles away from the one I left back home. I moved into an apartment; it's not exactly the Ritz, but it has a certain charm. The interior is clean, smells freshly painted, the carpets aren't too stained, and my roommate seems amazingly normal. Now, I just need to learn the language.

P.S. When all is read and done, remember: *This is your time; make the most of it!*

I Need A Break

CHAPTER 1: PART I

Mid-November, Wednesday evening 7:35, Diplomaville USA

For a fleeting moment, I thought if I banged my head hard enough against the wall I could knock myself unconscious and have the perfect excuse for missing the exam. However, having enough guts to wallop myself that hard was certainly not in my gene pool. So I opened my psych book to Chapter One, "Introduction to Social Psychology," which might as well have read: Don't Even Bother! The psych exam would cover the first 10 chapters. So far, I had read the cover of the book and managed to scribble three pages of notes during the handful of lectures I'd attended.

My psychology class was 90 agonizing minutes three days a week with the most long-winded, self-important, mealy mouthed, pointy-headed, whiney-voiced, beady-eyed, anal-retentive, height-challenged, and badly dressed professor that I'd ever had the distinct displeasure of encountering in a classroom. It was going to take more than pretty persuasion for me to rise above my obstinate behavior, and, needless to say, a miracle to survive the mid-year evaluations. My pending collegiate failure seemed a forgone conclusion, and unless compelled I wouldn't give my troubles to a monkey on a rock.

The exam would begin at 8 a.m. tomorrow. It was now 7:37 p.m.

"Sydney...! Miss Sydney Endicott, are you in there?" I heard a choked shrill followed by a rap on my door and the slight nasal tones of my vivacious cohort, Heather. She was a bubbly redhead from Long Island who lived down the hallway in our dormitory and specialized in running with her sorority from one fraternity party to another while putting an enormous amount of energy into trying to get me to rush her house. Unfortunately for her, I lacked the inspiration to leap the epic hurdle of branding my clothes and advertising the fact that I was paying a few hundred bucks a semester for the privilege of going to private parties. I'd just as soon forage for my own booze and deal with the idiots at large.

"Yeah...Come in."

Heather stepped into the room and immediately her perfume hit me like a freight train, jostling my senses. "Whew, smells like you got something on the line tonight!"

"Yeah, I'm off to 'the Jungle' with a few sisters. I think some of the guys from the football team will be there. Wanna tag along?"

"No thanks, but I appreciate the thought."

I just wasn't up to it with all the academic pressure piling up on me. Plus, hanging with a group of jocks whose primary topics of conversation consisted of football and which girls they screwed last was not my idea of fun. Besides, I was positive that my respiratory system couldn't handle all the perfume and aftershave.

"Whatcha doing?" Heather asked while proceeding across the room and glancing curiously at the textbooks in front of me.

"Psych exam tomorrow morning."

"And you're only on Chapter One!?" She grimaced and shook her head. "Don't you think you're starting the semester a little late?"

"Please, don't remind me." If she only knew how badly I was really doing, but I didn't want to bother her with my problems. Reclining in my chair, I could only feign pleasantness. "Have fun tonight."

Heather shrugged and walked back to the door. "You know, Kiddo, life would be a whole lot easier if you'd either commit to school or commit to breaking the news to your folks that you're not committing."

Heather wasn't much better at studying than me, but she was a buckle-down-when-you-have-to kind of a gal. Her major was fashion design, which presented a slightly different academic perspective from liberal arts. Nonetheless, I was failing my classes and Heather wasn't.

"I don't know what's gotten into you lately, Sydney, but your dejection is creeping down the hallway and into the rooms of a few girls who are tugging on their vomit glands...including me!" With that judgment, she exited the room and pointedly slammed the door.

It was the middle of my sophomore year, and if I didn't shape up, my future would entail dragging home a handful of F's for the Christmas holidays. Needless to say, Mom and Dad were going to spit nickels.

It was time to get serious and regain my scholastic worth. I threw in some background music, "Mama Said," and made a cup of noodles before sitting down at my desk. Generally I studied with a cup of hot cocoa and the TV tuned to "The Simpsons" or something as wacky. The time I spent in high school absorbing unhinged network programming led to some academic accolades and admission to a decent university. Unfortunately, my academic success failed to follow me to its hallowed halls.

Sweeping the hair from my eyes, I stared down at the first page of the first chapter for the very first time all semester. Outside a low-pressure system had consumed the city and rain began softly tapping against the large window left of my desk. The tempo was a pleasant accompaniment to Lenny on CD. Lethargy set in and I put the book down while glancing at the clock. It was time to hop online and get my brain cooking again.

I'm not among those online enthusiasts who spill their guts to cyber-strangers or indulge in all-night sexual fantasies with aging, overweight, unhappily married men pretending to look like Brad Pitt. If I were to crave such a fantasy world, I would hardly go to one that used a keyboard as its primary mode of transportation.

I had found something more interesting and certainly more intriguing: puzzles. Not just any puzzles, not like jigsaws or anything. These were more like mysteries.

My first real-life mystery was labeled as a development study in psychology class. The course syllabus certainly had required reading, but one also had to volunteer for three lab experiments. So far, the only exercise I'd been involved in was a real mindbender. We all read the same convoluted story about a man who allegedly murdered his wife and hid the body in a forest near where he grew up. By taking apart the story, we were to decide where the body was buried and whether the husband was guilty. The experiment was essentially about group thinking and establishing the pecking order in social situations. I felt the project moving, but the other students didn't share the same passion. So most of the talking and all of the reasoning was left to me. The grad assistants never told us whether our conclusions were right or wrong, which was frustrating. Nevertheless, the whole idea of wading through the plot for clues and putting the puzzle together was captivating. The two hours we worked on it buzzed by like a Japanese bullet train. A week later, I bumped into one of the grad assistants who ran the experiment and I asked him where he'd gotten the story. That's when he mentioned the puzzle Web site.

The site was engaging, featuring brainteasers, intriguing quests, and any story with a twist. Most interesting was the subtopic: "Searches for Lost Relics."

Some of the guys hooked on the site regularly held treasure-hunt parties and cyber-geek get-togethers, which I backpedaled from as quickly as possible. But, a few mysteries leapt out like a 3-D movie — that's how I came across ShoSho12. We'd been chatting about relics stolen from noble landlords in Europe when he referred to a mystery involving his German ancestors, a lost crucifix, and a dead monarch. I read his story eagerly:

In the 19th century there was this king who had a ton of money, the love of the people, and a penchant for building castles. King Ludwig II of Bavaria constructed a number of storybook castles all over southern Germany, filling each with fanciful works of art and precious trinkets. The king suspiciously drowned in a lake the depth of a kiddie pool, but not before he allegedly doled out his treasures to celebrities and personal acquaintances. One of the lucky recipients was the son of a wine merchant from Chiemsee, a lake district in Bavaria, who on his 10th birthday received a bejeweled crucifix made of gold. The boy's family was indeed touched by the king's gesture; however, they were financially in dire straits and immediately made plans to sell it. A jeweler in the region took one look at the crucifix and just about coughed up a cat. He was so captivated by the relic that he gave the wine merchant all but the shirt off his back to purchase it. The wine merchant left delighted and much richer, while the jeweler rushed home with the cross to show his wife. She was impressed for sure, but not to the extent of handing over all their money. After a protracted episode of browbeating by his wife, the jeweler set out to get their cash back before the couple starved to death.

The jeweler traveled all night to reach the wine merchant's house, only to discover that it had gone up in flames; the entire family perished in the inferno. He had no choice but to turn around and head for Munich, where he intended to find another jeweler or anyone with money to take the crucifix off his hands. On his journey, four bandits robbed him. They took the crucifix, his horse, shoes and one gold tooth. They did, however, leave him alive — but stranded. As the jeweler began his long walk home, he realized that if the freezing temperatures of the Bavarian winter didn't kill him, his wife would. As fate would have it, the weather proved too overwhelming and he met his maker right there in the tranquil forest south of Munich — toothless, barefoot, and flat broke.

The thieves sold the crucifix to a wealthy old woman in another small town near Chiemsee. Overjoyed, they set off to spend their ill-gained wealth. Later that day the thieves themselves were robbed, dying in a shootout.

The old woman who had purchased the crucifix did so in the hope that her terminally ill husband would embrace death if he exemplified his devotion to the Almighty by sporting it around his neck. So heavy was the cross that it became impossible for her feeble husband to wear without collapsing from its weight. The old woman instead hung the sacred relic on the wall above his bed. The nail upon which it rested gave way and the crucifix came crashing down, killing the feeble man and making a mess of the sheets. Being superstitious, the old woman believed the relic to be a bad omen and consequently gave it to her manservant to pawn at the nearest jeweler.

In a strange array of coincidences, the jeweler in question was the widow of the one who originally purchased the crucifix from the wine merchant. Since that fateful event, she had become reliant on the charity of her brother and his intolerable wife to survive. Upon witnessing the rebirth of the cross, she went off her nut speaking of its evils and thrashing the manservant with a wooden candlestick. Injured, he hobbled back to his employer.

Upon his arrival, he told the old woman the tale of the cursed crucifix. Shocked, she ordered him to take the relic somewhere and bury it. Aware of the value, he instead carried the king's opulent cross to his quarters and locked it away. A month later came news that Ludwig had tossed himself in a lake. The old woman's trusty manservant, concluding that the time was ripe to capitalize on the king's death, immediately packed up the crucifix and headed into town to sell it. He never made it any farther than the end of the cobblestone lane where his horse began bucking wildly out of control, unceremoniously throwing the manservant onto the road and crushing his neck. When the crucifix was discovered on his body, the old woman seized it, wrapped it in wool, and placed it in a heavy lockbox. She wrote the tale of the cursed crucifix, set the pages inside and secretly took it to the shores of Lake Chiemsee. There she buried it deep within the soft earth, a stone's throw from King Ludwig's tribute to Versailles: Schloss Herrenchiemsee.

The old woman went to her grave without divulging its location, and the legend of the crucifix spread like wildfire. Many tried to find the king's treasure, but none succeeded. Some believed the crucifix would never be found, as Ludwig had reclaimed his gift from the earth.

* * *

The story was certainly fascinating, but if numerous fortune hunters had been sniffing the trails for so long — wouldn't someone have stumbled upon it by now? There is only so much shoreline, and a hundred years was plenty of time for every grain of sand to have been scrutinized once or twice. However, ShoSho12 reminded me that nobody ever found the Nazi gold, either. Maybe those folks are darn good at hiding things. But what about the crucifix's alleged curse? For a treasure seeker, I suspect this would be offset by the thrill of the chase.

Fantasyland devoured my time while reality stared me in the face. My psychology book remained open to the first page of the first chapter. Only one phrase came to mind: "Aw, screw it!" I could read all night and still fail the damn test. After grabbing my jacket, I slipped into some comfortable shoes and headed out the door. There was no way, regardless of weather, that I was going to stay in the rest of the night with a book I wouldn't absorb even if I ate it. The student union seemed the logical nocturnal setting to seek a cup of cocoa, a newspaper, and a distraction from my troubles.

Despite it being 11 p.m., the commons were full of people with their books, ill-fitting clothes, and strange, unkempt hairdos — I blended in fine. Most were in the lounge area conversing in small groups, contrasting the few who were quietly studying. To be honest, if one truly wanted to study on a Wednesday night, would one really be here? I was case in point. Anyway, over at the refreshment counter, I dumped a packet of cocoa into a cup, poured in some scalding water and filled the remainder with milk. After thoroughly stirring the contents, I bought a newspaper and sat down at a table near the television tuned in to the Travel Channel for the 10 or so people eating overpriced gourmet soups and frozen croissants. Opening the paper, I turned straight to the employment section and kept an eye out for the perfect job for me:

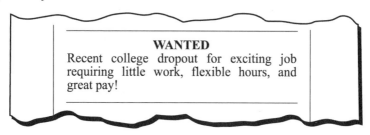

WANTED
Recent college dropout for exciting job requiring little work, flexible hours, and great pay!

Never found that one. At any rate, the fact that I wasn't exactly heading for *summa cum laude* made me think seriously about finding an alternative. Although, unearthing a job that would present such an enormous opportunity as to justify dumping my college education would be tricky at best.

I skimmed through some more ads. Many required prior work experience, but how does one get experience when...

Well, we're all familiar with that spiel. Nevertheless, my vocational skills have been limited to a summer of scooping ice cream at Baskin-Robbins and three weeks of shoveling fries at Wendy's. In high school, I didn't have to work much as I had reassured the folks that my invaluable study time after school would get me into a decent university.

Some two years later and I was no closer to finding my future than the night of high school graduation. I just seemed to be wasting vital discovery time sitting in class and telling professsors what they wanted to hear — not to mention squandering more of my parents' money. Of course, my looming failure in psychology class, along with two or three other subjects, had brought the whole grim affair sharply into focus. Failing was undeniably my fault, but I honestly couldn't think of a single reason to be all that concerned. Well, except for the fact that my parents were likely to kick my butt onto the street without so much as a used Chevy to live in. Moreover, homelessness held as little charm as did finishing the semester.

I meticulously scanned each ad on each page. Without losing focus, I reached for my cup of cocoa and took a swig. I nearly choked as an ad leapt off the page and slapped me in the face!

> **GOVERNMENT JOBS AVAILABLE**
> **AT EUROPEAN RESORTS**
> We are looking for energetic people to fill hotel positions at our resorts in Garmisch and Chiemsee, Germany. Waiters/waitresses, kitchen workers, room attendants, desk clerks, and recreation assts. Will receive airfare, subsidized meals and housing, competitive pay and benefits.

I couldn't believe what I was reading: the opportunity to travel to Europe, earn money, and get away from school — all *without* my parents.

An epiphany struck, my eyes quickly re-scanned the text. The resorts were located in Garmisch and Chiemsee, Germany. Could this be the same Chiemsee where the lost crucifix was buried? Was going all that way to track down a hundred-year-old legend justification for dropping out of college?

I had to confess: traveling an ocean away to work for the U.S. government did sound more substantial than washing dishes at the local diner. At the very least, I could see Europe before settling down and becoming submerged in life's obligatory car, rent, and insurance payments. I certainly couldn't tell Mom or Dad or even any of my friends about the quest for a lost crucifix; they'd all think I was nuts!

Nonetheless, these were all assumptions. First, a few phone calls were necessary to see whether the ad was genuine. Things that sounded too good to be true — usually were!

Chugging the rest of my cocoa, I tore the ad from the paper, stuffed it into my pocket and practically ran out of the student union. Outside, the light rain had turned into gently falling flakes. No snow had accumulated in the streets or on the boughs of the trees, but if it continued, *halle-lujah*...snow day!

Back at my desk, guilt made me skim over the unread chapters and useless notes for psych. At about two in the morning my eyes grew heavy and the text read like gobbledygook — that's when I found sanctuary between the sheets.

Thursday morning — the exam
PART II

The alarm *screeeeched* "Good morning!" in its usual maddening way — 7:30 came much too early. Following an uncoordinated shower, a frantic fumble through the clothes pile, and a glass of orange juice to wash down an unsavory burnt piece of toast, I grabbed my bag and landed a seat in the class auditorium by 8 a.m. I felt like I was dragging a piano behind me, but as usual I was denied the accompaniment.

Looking uninterested and lethargic, Professor Davis' grad assistants began passing out the exam booklets. I dreaded this test like no other. My fellow undergraduates appeared confident, sitting tall in their worn seats — they must have studied. When the professor finally announced that we could begin, I colored in the little circles so fast that I don't even remember reading the questions.

My mind drifted in a sea of emotional upheaval. The left half of my brain calculated the frightening consequences of academic failure and dropping out of school. My right brain held me motionless below the ceiling of the Sistine Chapel in Rome, staring upwards in wonderment at Michelangelo's Creation of Adam.

Thirty minutes later, I oozed down the stairs and outside the building, knowing I'd failed the exam miserably but relieved that the ordeal was over. If I never do that again, it'll be too soon!

Who am I? What am I doing here? Where am I going? My hands rested deep within the pockets of my jeans and my head hung low as I stared at the asphalt beneath my feet. I must have kicked every stone from the auditorium to Jefferson Avenue, eventually arriving in front of the dorms. Carpe diem, I convinced myself, seize the day. I pulled the wadded newspaper ad from my pocket and phoned the listed number.

I heard a steady drone: *b...e...e...p* — followed by silence and a second beep before a man answered. "Resort Europe, Human Resources, this is Jim...How may I help you?"

My voice countered some 5,000 miles away, "Is your ad for real?"

He assured me that the ad was legitimate, there were positions available, and yes, the resort was indeed on Lake Chiemsee. Additionally, they would give me a free plane ticket, partial reimbursement for extra baggage, discounted meals, and a roof over my head. All I had to do was fill out the application that he would fax. If accepted, the contract covered a 13-month period. Upon its completion they would fly me back home and into the loving arms of my folks. Unless I wished to stay longer, which could be worked out later. He also told me that a majority of the workforce were young people about my age, many of whom take advantage of their days off to travel around Europe. Who could ask for more?

I gave him the fax number at the student union, then ran over there as fast as possible — not caring about how uncool I looked. While waiting for the fax, I reflected upon how desperate I was for a change in my life, any change. Maybe this was it.

The buzzing of the fax machine roused me from my trance. I paid the clerk, sat at a table and filled out the application. It was pretty basic stuff, taking only 15 minutes to complete. The clock on the wall read 10:15 a.m.; I knew Germany was several hours ahead of local time and I decided any further action could wait until tomorrow. By then, the results of the exam would be up and I'd have the ultimate reason to seek other options.

Friday morning
PART III

Friday came, and as suspected, I failed! Not just barely, I went down like a kamikaze in the Pacific, scoring a mind-blowing 47 percent and officially qualifying for the most pathetic attempt to fake it through an exam. There was no point in showing up for classes on Monday; why delay the inevitable? Nevertheless, I was determined to finish out the day's lectures, arriving five minutes late for American Literature and promptly falling asleep 10 minutes later. That was the sign I required to warrant skipping my afternoon classes and progress to the dorms for some much-needed rest.

The cup of hot cocoa I brought back from the student union made lounging on my cool bed a little easier to take. Abruptly, in the corner of the room, my flower vase began to tremble in synch with the intimate pulse penetrating the thin wall.

"Oh no, not again!" I grumbled. If I'd known that my neighbor Cheryl was in her room with Gene, hormone extraordinaire, I would've remained in class and slept there.

Anticipating the love connection to climax multiple times, I got up from my bed and cranked up the radio to help drown out the merciless moaning.

My thoughts, challenged as they were, contemplated notifying ShoSho of my employment opportunity at Chiemsee. If I were to get the job, perhaps he would be willing to divulge information to a virtual stranger about a chunk of gold studded with jewels worth considerably more than either of us could earn in a lifetime. Yet, if I was afraid to ask, the consequences could mean that I spend more tedious hours trudging through the Chiemsee muck than necessary. Realistically speaking, I had nothing to lose, the worst that could happen was that he either ignores my query, or sues me if I were to get my hands on the crucifix first — which is assuming an awful lot.

I booted up the computer and logged on to the chat room with the hope of catching ShoSho12. He wasn't online. The next best option was to type him a tactful e-mail.

Subject: Potential Job in Germany

ShoSho–

This may sound odd, but I've decided that school
isn't where I want to be right now so I'm taking
a year off. For some reason, I've been stressed
out lately. ☺ Yesterday came a glimmer of hope;
I applied for a job at a hotel, and you'll never
guess where? On the shores of Lake Chiemsee,
Germany... That's right, I've got a line on a
job in the heart of your family history. I was
thinking that if my application is successful, I
might contribute some time to tracking down the
crucifix. I could sure use any info you would be
willing to impart. Of course, this is all hypo-
thetical; I'd have to get the job first. Anyway,
what do you think?

Endi

I clicked on send and the e-mail whisked away. While I remained seated and fretting for no reason, someone rapped vigorously on my door.

"Come in!" The door opened with a bang. I jumped in place and pivoted to see my neighbor Cheryl standing in the doorway wearing a bathrobe, an angry expression, and very little else. If she was shooting for modesty by donning a sheer white bathrobe, she missed the target by a long shot.

"Would you mind turning down your frigging radio? It's making my walls shake it's so gawd-damned loud!" Her arms were wrapped across her flat belly, just south of her equally flat chest, which was heaving with what she thought I would assume to be indignation. I knew for a fact that physical activity will also do the same thing to a young woman, and judging by the way the pictures on my wall had been swaying, I'd testify she had been pretty active in the next room. Needless to say, her screaming "Ride me harder, Gene," might also have given it away.

"Why, Cheryl, you *are* capable of walking upright. Isn't that hard to do with a bed strapped to your back?"

"Don't mess with me, Endicott!" Her eyes narrowed. "Turn down that radio or I'll rip out the speakers myself."

I was not intimidated. For starters, I was too absorbed with crash-and-burn academia to be concerned with the exasperation of an egotistical, bottled-blonde trollop. Cheryl was no great personality, either, but extremely popular with a large number of guys on campus, from what I'd heard.

Composed, I walked over to her at the doorway. We stood a mere two feet apart; mascara ran down her cheeks. Despite Cheryl's petite 5-foot-1 frame, she meant business. I couldn't believe this mindless episode of bickering was even occurring, but it was — and she deserved a verbal plateful.

"Look, you foul-mouthed freak show. I turned my radio on so I wouldn't have to listen to you and Gene trying to fornicate your way through my bedroom wall. Frankly, I don't care how big his dick is or how good it feels when he slaps you with it. What I do care about is getting a little peace and quiet in my own room. So if you want me to turn down the radio, why don't you take your stallion and go to his room at the fraternity? It's not like they haven't all seen you naked before."

A slap was tickling the palm of her hand, so I quickly slammed the door before she could give it a shot.

The computer then caught my eye; the e-mail icon alerted "incoming." I bounced into my chair and double-clicked "open." It was from ShoSho12.

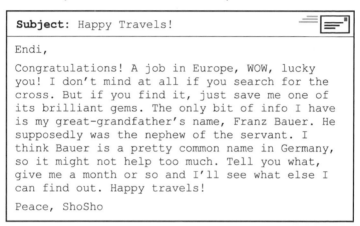

Subject: Happy Travels!

Endi,

Congratulations! A job in Europe, WOW, lucky you! I don't mind at all if you search for the cross. But if you find it, just save me one of its brilliant gems. The only bit of info I have is my great-grandfather's name, Franz Bauer. He supposedly was the nephew of the servant. I think Bauer is a pretty common name in Germany, so it might not help too much. Tell you what, give me a month or so and I'll see what else I can find out. Happy travels!

Peace, ShoSho

Fortunately he was congenial about the whole idea. However, he didn't seem to know much. But at least his great-grandfather's name was somewhere to start.

Meanwhile, I was beginning to feel guilty about yelling at Cheryl and maybe minutely frightened that she might be eagerly waiting outside my door to mash my melon with something mammoth. Although, considering how much energy she exerted helping Gene unload some excess fluids, I'd say she couldn't stand out there for very long without falling over.

Sunday afternoon
PART IV

The weekend flew by as I spent most of it researching the Chiemsee region in hopes of submitting a successful application. With any luck I'll be convincing my parents that the government job is an opportunity of a lifetime, and that Nazis don't wander the hills of Germany anymore.

My parents, of course, would be against my exodus and therefore wouldn't offer me a whole lot in the way of financial assistance. Cheap meals notwithstanding, I would still need some spending money in Germany, and I had very little of value that could be sold. The biggest-ticket items were my computer and stereo. My parents gave them to me as gifts for college, and assuming they took the news of my imminent departure as I predicted, these were probably to be the last donations I would receive this side of the grave.

Premonitions aside, I drew up a handful of flyers to advertise my things for sale. Heather and I spent the last hours of daylight traipsing all over campus tacking them to every bulletin board we could find. By the time we made it back to residence hall, I had almost persuaded her into being the proud new owner of my computer. But there's always that same lousy stumbling block for every college student — she didn't have the 400 bucks to spare.

She did, however, have more than enough friendly chitchat. "What are you gonna tell your parents? Mine would die of a heart attack if I were to tell them I was dropping out of school. My dad didn't talk to me for three days when he discovered my major was fashion design. When he finally did speak to me, he said: 'HEATHER, if you design any of that gay and lesbian bondage crap, I'll cut you off without a dime!' What a prince, huh?"

"At least you're still allowed to live. I'm thinking of telling my folks from the window of the bus as it pulls into the depot. That way my dad can't get a clean shot off in the transit confusion."

Heather rolled her eyes. "As if your dad's actually going to try to kill you. He'll probably give you an earful and then try to scare you back to school."

I somewhat agreed. "They'll try everything to talk me out of my decision, but when Dad hears how badly I'm doing, he'll want to re-examine his financial contribution to my career pursuit."

"What, you're not doing well?" Heather's eyes widened. "You mean you're failing some classes? The girl who's always studying?" The sarcasm was dripping from her tongue and sliding down her designer sweater onto her leather shoes.

"Go ahead, milk it for what it's worth." I wondered if I should help her assemble the gallows. "You know how it is... There are classes I like well enough, but I just can't believe that half the crap I'm expected to learn is going to help at all. To be perfectly honest with you, some professors don't give a damn whether you've learned anything useful or not. They just want to hear themselves talk. Anyway, my parents pressured me into college straight out of high school by relentlessly hounding me about getting a good education. Now I need some time to think and reassess my future... It's only for a year."

Heather accepted the fact that I needed some time off. She also took pity on my parents, whom she had met on several occasions. "You make your folks sound like such ogres."

"Aw, I know, but this time they won't understand. Plus I'm going home for Thanksgiving to drop this bomb on them. For the rest of my life, I'll be reminded that this was the holiday when I broke their hearts. Bet you a million dollars my mom will guilt me with tears, and there won't be any backup support. Except for the liquor cabinet; I guess I could always raid that."

Heather smiled. "That's where I'd go!" Her expression then changed to that of suggestion. "Listen, before you leave for Thanksgiving vacation, let's all get together for one last hurrah ...say Tuesday?"

"Okay, deal. But please don't tell anyone about my quitting school or of my plans to go to Europe."

Heather agreed. And on that note we parted ways. Job or no job, I was leaving college.

Happy Monday
PART V

The next morning I woke to outstanding news; it was as if I'd won the lottery. Jim from Resort Europe called to tell me that I'd been selected for a position as a hotel room attendant and that my ticket would be waiting for me at the airport on the day of departure.

I had to fill my shoes with lead to keep from floating into the air. I dropped the phone and danced to the window, where I bellowed to the whole campus, "Yippee! I'm going to Europe!"

My voice echoed from building to building, raced across Campus Square and bounced back through my window with such force that my hair stood on end.

Behind me, I heard a startled voice. "Syd, is everything okay?"

I swiveled to see my friend and neighbor, Kayumi, standing in the doorway wearing a perplexed look.

"Everything's great!" I exclaimed.

"What's all the racket about?"

"Oh, nothing." I replied.

She shook her head and began to leave.

"Ah, Kayumi, before you go."

"Yes."

"Are you free for drinks tomorrow night?"

"I'm not doing anything special." She double blinked. "Why, what's up?"

"Just tell the girls to keep it free and be here at seven."

"Oookaay," she curiously replied before reiterating her concern. "Are you sure you're feeling all right?"

"I promise, I haven't felt better. See you tomorrow night."

* * *

The idea of cleaning rooms or scrubbing toilets as a hotel room attendant wasn't in the slightest bit alluring, but more unappealing was failing my classes and living in shame with the folks until finding a job I was qualified for — which probably would have been cleaning rooms or scrubbing toilets. I hope while on room detail I don't come across anybody who has just discovered tequila for the first time.

It's amazing how piggish people can be when they know some minimum-wage schmuck will come in the next morning to wipe up whatever mess they make. A cleaning lady once gave me the gimlet eye at a motel outside Lincoln, Nebraska. My grandfather had passed, bringing the extended family together to grieve and sort things out, which required a few motel rooms to accommodate everyone. That night my parents, brother, and a few relatives went to Grandma Maple's house for a family discussion concerning post-funeral expenses, while my older cousins and I elected to stay at the motel. It just so happened that we stumbled across a bottle of tequila in my uncle's suitcase and ended up sampling a few shots.

Somehow, during the course of the evening, I fell into the bathroom and vomited all over the towels and floor. The next morning the folks caught on when I staggered into their room with bloodshot eyes, rotgut breath, and a ghostly complexion to ask if I could use their shower. Mom and Dad were curiously drawn to my squashed hair pressed flat on one side, where they recited the motel's logo from the fine impression left by the bathmat. They probably would have lectured me about underage drinking, but I told them it was an adverse effect from Grandfather's passing. That's when Mom broke down crying again and leaned into Dad's arms. I was off the hook for the time being, that is, until I went back to the vomit room just as the cleaning lady was exiting. She would have given me both barrels if that sort of behavior didn't mean getting fired with a jail sentence to boot. Job or no job, I don't think I would have cleaned that mess up. There had to be a Denny's nearby that was hiring.

As you can see, my burning desire in life wasn't to gain membership into a hotel room-attendant club. But if that's what it took to escape my current situation, that's what I was prepared to do. Europe was calling.

Tuesday, last period
PART VI

Closing the door on my collegiate curriculum channeled me through the administration office. I half expected someone to try to talk me out of it, but nobody so much as looked at me sideways. They really didn't appear to give a damn, except to be adamant that under no circumstances would my unused tuition be returned. I jokingly told them that my parents wouldn't be so worried about the tuition, since my funeral would be costing much, much more. This statement managed to evoke a slightly arched eyebrow in return for my sarcasm. These folks had heard all the sob stories before and didn't give two hoots either way. Unless I walked in with a visible limp and perhaps a lawyer, I doubted they would show me any signs of concern at all.

Other than the administration formalities, my last eight hours at school went somewhat smoothly. I sold both the computer and stereo, gave my ice chest to a freshman across the hall, and tossed "The Beast," my sometimes perilous toaster oven, in the garbage. Lastly, I packed all my belongings into boxes and hauled them to the post office to mail home.

As we had arranged, Heather came by with the girls at seven for my final sendoff. Saying goodbye was more difficult than I had imagined it would be. In the past, we spent most of our time together goofing around, shopping, or at happy hour. However, I broke the news of my departure while we were all stone sober and lounging on my sagging couch, which put me center stage to four befuddled faces.

"Well...aren't you girls going to say something?" I asked.

They sat in silence until Kayumi got up and left the room. This seemed to be the signal for the girls to launch into fits of whispering while ignoring my presence. A mild form of torture would have been more agreeable.

Kayumi suddenly returned to the room with a large box. A conspiracy appeared to be underway. Heather must have been the ringleader; she pivoted my direction and spoke first: "I'm sorry, Syd...but I already told the girls of your departure. I wanted to make sure we made a little contribution to your travels." She then handed me the box on behalf of the girls. "We hope you like it!"

I was as mesmerized as a deer in the headlights of an 18-wheeler. Nonetheless, excitement got the better of me and I opened the box at blinding speed. "Oh girls, you shouldn't have! A backpack?"

"It's a travel pack," Kayumi answered. "You're now officially a back-packer!"

"A backpacker?"

"Yeah, that's what everyone's doin' now. It's the cheap and easy way to travel." Kayumi continued enthusiastically. "Pack your belongings in here, zip it up, throw it on your back and presto, you're mobile."

"Great idea!" I said. "Beats the heck out of lugging around my two heavy suitcases." I put the backpack down and turned to the girls. "Thank you so much...This is exactly what I needed, something to kickstart my destiny." They got up one by one for a hug. A few tears were shed, until I broke the spell by reminiscing about the lighter times.

"Kayumi, remember last February at Heather's 'Come As You Dare' party and you came wearing that slippery toga?"

"Oh please, Endicott, don't bring that up again!"

"Sorry, Kayumi, just thinking about your public appearance makes me laugh."

"What...Whose appearance?" asked Abigail, my freshman-year room-mate.

The girls edged closer to hear the story one more time. "It was after midnight and several drinks later when Kayumi finally gathered the courage to ask Brad, The Body, for a dance. On her way over to him she bumped into Dexter, who was dressed as a tree, and as a result, one of his branches tugged at her safety pin just enough to loosen Kayumi's toga, exposing her left breast. About a half hour later, after Kayumi had danced with Brad and all his friends, Heather came over to hand her a drink and noticed the bare breast. Red as a beet, Kayumi ran off hastily and bumped into Dexter once again. This time the whole toga came loose, falling to the floor."

Kayumi, without wasting precious time, exacted her revenge. "Save your laughter, girls... What about you, Syd?"

"What?" I felt a diversionary tactic coming on. "Wait a minute, I have to go to the bathroom."

"Endicott, you sit your butt right back down!" The girls weren't game for any charades, neither was Kayumi, who stared me down and demanded sportsman-like conduct. "Remember first semester of freshman year when you had that big date with Brandon?"

"All right girls, you got me," I announced while raising a white tissue to surrender.

"Had an inkling you might remember," Kayumi said, savoring the moment. "It was such a crackup when Abigail, Heather, and I walked into your room to wish you a nice evening and found you practicing the 'make out' with your pillow."

As if that wasn't embarrassing enough, the girls continued with vigorous heckling. "More tongue Sydney... Mmm, bet that fabric tastes yummy!"

The stories materialized in abundance; no one got off lightly. We then proceeded to get drunk on dollar Coronas at the Casa Bar, which increased the amusement considerably. We got so smashed that we all started crying, whereupon the bouncers escorted us out for swaying the mood of the other patrons. At 2 a.m., we stumbled across the street to La Grande Tortilla and drowned our sorrows in burritos as big as your head. Thank goodness the cops blocked off Arlington Street or Heather would have tried to drive her dad's old Buick up the hill to the dorm. Then I'd possibly be breaking the news of my college departure to dear Mom and Dad from a hospital suite.

Wednesday morning,
one sheet in the wind
PART VII

I hauled my overstuffed bag onto the half-empty Greyhound bus, dragging it to the rear where I collapsed head first into a seat. There were a handful of girls in the back laughing and joking as if the seven-hour party bus to Mardi Gras had just begun. Anticipating the scolding I was to face at home, exuberance didn't ring a bell. The onboard exhilaration was making me wish I had decided to spare myself the $50 and walk instead. If it weren't for the bitter cold this time of year, I would have given it a shot.

Nevertheless, I was so exhausted from the goings-on of the past week that I slept through the entertainment and woke as the bus pulled into its final destination: home. I scanned the station for my parents to no avail. The depot resembled an extended food court in a shopping mall. There were eight different fast food counters running the length of the building, umpteen tables, two video games, and a decidedly clean bathroom that I was busting to use. It didn't look much like a depot at all. Maybe that was the point, the town planners wanted to attract a better clientele by discouraging vagrants from setting up camp. Although, one would think the homeless would prefer to wake up to the smell of Burger King than cigarette smoke and urine like perhaps in some bus stations.

There they were, Sid and Dolores Endicott, my lovely parents bouncing with anticipation as I stepped onto the pavement. Mom squeezed the stuffing out of me while Dad wrestled the bag off my shoulder. "Your bag is so heavy, Dear." Dad then glanced inside. "Books! Ah, you plan to study while you're home... That's my girl!" He smiled and hugged my guilty soul even tighter. I felt something inside me slither off into a dark corner.

Thanksgiving Day
PART VIII

The day of our forefathers came and went with the usual gluttony and shameless lounging around the house. The folks and relatives pretended to watch football, but they were really waiting for their stomachs to recover from the shock of over-gorging. I thought about taking the bull by the horns and telling everyone about my leaving school, but they looked so content. My proclamation meant shattering the evening, not only for the folks but also for my favorite aunt, uncle, and three cousins. Instead, I scooped the obligatory monster mound of whipped cream onto a piece of pumpkin pie and sat down to watch the football game, warm and secure at Father's side.

Before sliding between the sheets that night, I promised myself to face the music first thing in the morning. I knew it would be a long day and a rehearsed speech, or something semi-calculated, was essential. Lying restless in bed, I pondered all night the probabilities of zero hour, and with every infinitesimal rustle — I tossed and turned.

D-Day
PART IX

I rolled out of bed and peered into the mirror, my reflection was no ally in the cataclysmic day that lay ahead. Leaning into the sink, I cupped my hands and threw cold water over my face. "Miss Sydney Endicott...it's time."

Marching downstairs with absent courage, I went straight to where the voices of my parents echoed: the kitchen. "Dad!" I blurted.

Ignoring my tone, they countered with cordial 'Brady Bunch' smiles and pleasantries. "Good morning, Sydney...sleep well?"

"Mom." Be done with it, I thought.

"Yes, Dear."

A lump in my throat formed. "Ah...Can I help you with breakfast?" What a wimp, the diminutive courage I managed to muster left me as quickly as it came.

Dad and my brother, Alexander, were hovering over Mom, snatching scraps of bacon and slurping coffee while she flipped the pancakes and hash browns.

Breakfast was outstanding as always, but I had little time to enjoy it. My stomach churned, kinked, and coiled at the thought of breaking the news. We sat at the table nursing our coffee and handing praise to the chef. I took a deep breath and thought it was now or never. "Mom... The food was great!"

"Why, thank you, Darling." Mom always had that special way of letting her kids know they were loved. "It's such a treat to have you here with us again. We miss you so much, you know."

"I know, Mom, and a day at college wouldn't be the same if I didn't wonder what everybody was doing back home...especially lately."

"Oh, Honey." She reached over and stroked my hair with motherly love. "I made the hash browns exactly the way you like them."

"Mmm, I noticed. I love it when they are that extra bit crispy...I'm dropping out of school!" Bad timing prevailed; my hasty judgment coincided with Dad taking a sip of his coffee. It was time to get out of Dodge.

My stunned parents and confused brother sat quietly for a moment before Mom spoke slowly, as if speaking to a mentally challenged juvenile. "Honey... what ever do you mean? How... can you... leave... college? You... are... only... 20. If... you... leave, what...will...you...do?"

I allowed a scant smile to creep across my face as I tried to hide the terror I was beginning to feel. "Well, Mom, I'm just not getting anything out of it..."

Dad interrupted with an expected tirade. "Except an education! Let me tell you a secret, little girl, there's no career of any kind without a degree! Oh, I see now, you want to be a trash collector. Or is it a dishwasher? That's right, drop out of school, you can't even keep your room clean!" Dad was clearly not amused. I could see the rest of his arguments bubbling in his head. He was gathering momentum and would blow sooner or later. As a means of survival, I had to hurry and cut him off before we were all caught in the aftermath.

"I don't have to be at college to learn something. I just feel like I'm wasting my time and your money. I'm no closer to finding out what I want to do and it's been a year and a half. When Alex got out of high school, you gave him a year to decide his future. Just because I waited 18 months to ask, is it now too late for me to find out what I really want to do?"

I figured I was gambling there, but I thought it sounded good. My brother, Alex, had set the precedent by taking a year off after high school and doing odd jobs. He bounced from one employer to another because working put the pinch on his big plans to party. Dad just about had kittens he was so mad. Alex eventually caved and enrolled in the nearby community college and drank seldom. Things between Alex and Dad simmered down after that, but the whole debacle was a fairly sore subject around the house. Nonetheless, here I was nearly two years later and hitting Dad with similar trash. I was effectively taking college, wadding it up in front of him, and throwing it in the garbage.

Dad's rebuttal was exactly what I anticipated. "So you want to go from job to job for a year until you figure out what I already know...which is that college is a necessity and no one will hire you without a degree! Do you think your mother and I wore old clothes for 20 years so you could thumb your nose at the education we worked our butts off to pay for?"

Afraid to look him in the eye, I stared into my coffee and desperately continued my plea. "No, Dad. I'm not saying I'll never go to college, just not now. It's not the right time. I don't want to be merely spinning my wheels to find out years later I went for all the wrong reasons. I'm not planning on staying here living rent-free and running around with my friends from high school... I've got a job." I lifted my head to face everyone; Mom sat with an unsure smile while Dad wore that suspicious look he gets when he thinks someone is lying. Alex, on the other hand, resembled a 10-year-old boy trying his best to hold back an extreme case of the giggles. I suppose it was a nice change for him, watching someone else get the business end of Dad's ridicule.

"Doing what?" Mom chirped, wanting me to tell her a fairy tale and make things all better. I could see she was looking for a lifeline. She didn't handle family conflict well, especially over the breakfast table.

"Well, Mom, Dad... I saw an ad for a job in hospitality."

Without delay my father shot back: "And doing exactly what, Sydney?! I see you've managed to skirt that issue pretty well!"

I shifted in my chair. "I'll be a room attendant at a hotel."

"Is that another way of saying... someone who cleans roooooms?"

"Yes, Dad." I swallowed my tongue.

"Are you telling me that you're dropping out of college to make beds and vacuum carpets in some hotel around here!?"

"No... Actually the hotel is in Germany."

Suddenly, the room went still — except for the hypnotic hum of the refrigerator. A brief calm before the storm.

"Germany...?" My father's eyebrows disappeared into his hairline as his voice boomed to a level that made his temple veins appear ready to burst. "G-E-R-M-A-N-Y-!! Have you completely lost your mind?! You can't speak German! You've never been to Germany! Do you even know where the hell it is?! Do you?! I'll tell you where it is...It's a hell of a lot closer to the Middle East than it is to here! It's a hell of a lot more expensive than here, and it doesn't have your college education flapping in the wind! I... can't...believe...you'd pull a stunt like this!" He got up and brought the coffee pot to the table. "Now you have two days to work out whatever it was that made you decide throwing away your future was a good idea. Then you're going back to school, and that, young lady...is final!" He poured coffee into his cup and filled Mom's to the brim.

Mom looked pale and shaken; I could see tears welling in her eyes. "Europe? That's such a long way from home, Honey."

"I know, Mom, but I've always dreamed of traveling to Europe. The representative told me that plenty of people my age work there, and in their free time they travel all over the continent. I would get to see other countries like Austria, Italy and France. I will be able to witness first hand the different cultures and historical sites we learned about on the Travel and History channels. That alone is an education. Neither of you have been there, so please don't deny me the opportunity."

I looked at Dad, who had already left the discussion and was trying desperately to concentrate on the newspaper. Although, he couldn't be concentrating too hard as it was upside down. Reaching across, I pulled the paper down onto the table. "Daddy, you loved to tell Alex and me when we were kids about Grandpa's heroic exploits on D-Day, and how America mounted the greatest invasion force in the history of the world. You would name the beaches where the Allied soldiers landed...and to this day, I've never forgotten those names: Utah, Omaha, Gold, Juno and Sword. But, Dad, what you can't tell me is what it's like to walk those beaches and feel a Normandy breeze caress your face, or to scoop the once-crimson sand and watch it flow between your fingers, or to gaze over the rows of white-marble crosses that fill the cemeteries. I now have the chance if I take this job in Europe."

Before my parents could regain the floor, I took a quick sip of juice to wet my parched throat and continued my speech.

"Mom, you couldn't tell us enough about your beloved Mozart; the master musician who wrote his first piano composition at the age of 6, first symphony at 8 and opera at 12. Yeah, remarkable for someone as young as he, I know...but that's what the history books say. Mom, what you can't teach me is the impression the uneven cobblestones make as they weigh into the soles of my feet when walking the streets of his town, Salzburg. Or the tingling one feels when hearing Mozart's music in the house where he was born... I now have that chance." Knowing that my words were having an impact, I was gaining confidence.

"I've made up my mind. My things have been mailed home from school. I've withdrawn from my classes and signed out of the dorm. I'll pay you back for lost rent and tuition, I promise. In Germany I'll have a place to live and a steady job. My plane ticket will be waiting for me at the airport, and I've decided to go with or without your blessing. It's only for a year and then they'll fly me home. Maybe by then I'll know what it is I want to do."

Dad was trying hard not to look at me; he wasn't convinced. "Come on Dad. I want to make the next few months memorable with you, Mom, and Alex...please don't ignore me. On March 12th, I'll be on the plane and out of your hair."

He looked me squarely in the eyes. "I don't suppose we can stop you. You're old enough to make your own decisions, even if they are all wrong. You'd better be damned sure you know what you're doing and that this whole deal is kosher before you go. I'm not flying 5,000 miles to bail you out... GOT IT!?"

With a tremendous sigh of relief, I jumped from my seat and clutched Pops around his chest, giving him a big hug. "Got it! And if I have to...I'll bail myself out. I'll be fine, Dad... I will."

Bon voyage
PART X

The three months at home were spent catching up with family, working a part-time job, and preparing for my overseas move. When March 12th rolled around I found myself standing at the airport check-in with a small carry-on bag and my backpack comfortably adjusted. My nerves became cumbersome foes as deep down the same thoughts kept echoing in my head: "What if this whole thing is a big sham?"

Behind the check-in counter stood a tall, thin guy wearing a pilot's hat, blue suit, and the airline logo stitched to his breast pocket. "Hi! Your passport and ticket please."

"Here's my passport, but I was told my ticket would already be in the system. I'm on your 11:30 flight to Munich, Germany."

"Uh huh, I see... Miss Endicott, Munich, Germany," uttered the clerk as he keenly stared into the computer while his hands danced across the keyboard. "Endicott...Germany," he repeated, still gazing into the monitor. I stood in hopes of liberating the monkey off my back.

Finally he looked up. "Miss Endicott...Would you like a window or aisle seat?"

Whew. "Yes!"

"Was that a 'Yes' to the aisle seat or...?"

"I'm sorry, that was a 'Yes' to the window seat."

"Here you go Miss Endicott...Enjoy your flight."

My hand clenched the boarding pass as I pondered the forthcoming hours on a plane that would transport me countless miles from my family and home. Yet, despite last-minute jitters, everything seemed okay — until Mom's airport hysterics. She sobbed and hugged me until my ribs creaked, unleashing my own emotions. We dissolved into a pool of tears.

Dad cut in and handed me a small book. "Your Mother and I wanted you to have this, it's a travel journal. Someday you'll be thankful you kept an account of your experiences." He then reached out for a simple embrace and bid farewell. "Please always remember and don't ever forget...we love you, Sydney." Dad gave me a half smile, turned away and led Mom out of the terminal. They disappeared and, for the first time in my life, I was really on my own.

'Bye Mom, Dad, Alex...

'Bye America, *'bye home.*

WORK, STUDY in EUROPE

Resort Europe, as portrayed in Chapter 1, is the Armed Forces Recreation Centers (AFRC) Europe. It is, indeed, for real, and you, too, can acquaint yourself with Europe as Sydney did. To live and work in the Alps, go to the AFRC website (afrceurope.com) and click on employment.

Update: Since this book has been written, the Department of Defense (DOD) has closed the doors on AFRC Chiemsee because of downsizing U.S. military forces in Europe. There is a silver lining, however, AFRC freshly opened the 330-room Edelweiss Lodge and Resort (90-min west of Chiemsee) in the Bavarian ski-resort town of Garmisch, site of the 1936 Winter Olympics and home to Germany's highest peak: the Zugspitze (2963m/9718ft). Now is a good time to apply for a job! Go to the AFRC website (afrceurope.com) for details. Another DOD employment option that may be of interest, domestically as well as internationally, can be found at www.defenselink.mil/sites then click on Civilian Job Opportunities.

* * *

Another way to grasp the medieval reins of Germany or the Baroque curves of Austria is by correlating your studies with overseas programs.

Life-experience credits, document 'em! Alternative education, live it!

With your parents' support, you can skip off to Europe. Check with your university's study abroad programs. If you're not yet in college—and this topic interests you—consider going to one that has an appealing overseas curriculum. It's an easy and fun topic to explore and the opportunities have never been greater.

Here's an excellent address to get you started: www.studyabroad.com

For a peek into Germany's academic world: www.campus-germany.com

* * *

Or, try your luck with these jobs:

• Ski resorts are always looking for seasonal help. A good place to search is the Austrian state of Tyrol or anywhere-in-the-Alps Switzerland.

• Go where there are plenty of pubs and clubs, such as Amsterdam, Rimini, Costa Brava, or the holiday isles of Mallorca, Ibiza, Ios, Corfu, etc.

• Be an au pair in France, or a nanny in Great Britain.

• Try the hospitality industry. Youth hostels—including campgrounds—typically hire foreign help.

• And don't forget about the former Eastern-bloc nations, many of which are looking for people to teach English (TEFL certificate required).

CHAPTER 2: PART I

T he flight attendant directed me to a window seat and shortly thereafter the plane began reversing out of its bay; there was no turning back now. I stared out the window and watched the tarmac race by while the plane soared down the runway and powerfully lifted off; the earth dropped away beneath me. Below were the territories of a nation; its diverse ranges and multi-colored topography led to the rippling blue expanse of the Atlantic Ocean.

Our stewardess slowly navigated the narrow aisle with her cart while offering a list of beverages. When she approached me I asked for my usual with a perky smile. "Hot cocoa, please." My sparkle wilted when she told me the hot drinks consisted only of tea and coffee.

Some 20 minutes later our stewardess came by again, this time she handed us each a white tray wrapped in foil. It was lunch: chicken with peas, carrots and a mini container of vanilla pudding. What little appetite I had dissipated at the airport when leaving Mom and Dad. Nonetheless, I knew it was to be a flight of endurance and I'd better consume what nutrients I could.

Not long thereafter, the cabin darkened and the TV suspended above the aisle came to life. The focus seemed to be duty-free shopping until the main feature: "Mission: Impossible III." How appropriate.

I rested the pillow they gave me against the window to comfort my head while I pondered home and the future. It was hard to fathom that the time had come and I was actually en route, covering half the globe on a journey no one in my family had ever undertaken. My conclusions repetitively traveled in one direction; home was 13 months away and the future held new adventures. I felt an inner glow. Ripping open the complimentary plastic headset, I got comfortable with a jazzy music channel and the in-flight magazine.

Sleep on the plane proved more difficult than I had expected; for some strange reason I assumed airplanes rolled off the assembly line with bucket seats and generous legroom. Nevertheless, umpteen nonstop hours later we landed at Munich airport.

Grainy-eyed and lifeless, I waited in a monster line at Customs. I thought they'd ask a zillion questions, rifle through my bags, and look suspiciously when I showed them my passport. When it was finally my turn to face the blitz, the officer in the booth motioned for me to slide my passport and Customs declaration under the window. "How long vill you stay in Germany?" He asked while examining my documents.

"Thirteen months," I replied.

The officer looked baffled. "Zat lengz of time ist not authorized in Germany."

"But I'll be working here," I stated.

"Verrking...?! Do you have a verrk visa?"

"Oh, no, I have a contract with the U.S. government, Department of Defense." I produced my assignment letter with the DOD letterhead. With that proof, he stamped my passport and shoved it back under the window. "Auf Wiederseh'n."

I exited through the sliding doors behind Customs that led into the main terminal. Instantly I spotted an attractive girl with strawberry blonde hair wearing a blue sweatshirt and holding up a sign with my name neatly inscribed.

This was undoubtedly my contact. "Hi! You must be Melinda from the Chiemsee resort?"

Her eyes disengaged from the exiting crowds and turned my way. "Yes...and you must be Sydney Endicott?"

"That's me!" I reached out my hand for a welcoming shake.

Melinda reciprocated and our hands linked. "Nice to meet you. Did everything go okay?"

"Oh, yeah, everything went fine," I answered, before asking an essential question. "Is it far to Chiemsee?" I could feel my eyeballs rolling around in my head, and if I didn't find a horizontal surface to lie on soon, I'd start snoring standing up.

"It's about an hour and 15 minutes. Come on, the van's outside."

She escorted me to a white Volkswagen van, paid for parking, and sped away from the airport. Before I knew it, we were driving along a modern expressway with cars speeding past us like jets.

"This must be the world-famous autobahn?" I asked.

"Yep...Sure is."

Glancing at the speedometer, I noticed she was driving 120 kilometers per hour and cars were passing us as if we were standing still. I wondered where all of these people were going in such a hurry. Maybe they were late to their college lectures? The last thing I remember before falling asleep was wondering why I'd never heard of Ausfahrt, Germany. It seemed to be an unbelievably large city, because every exit marker pointed to it.

Melinda woke me as we drove past a security gate entering the hotel grounds. It was an overcast, bleak day. March proved to be unlike any of the pictures I had seen on the resort's Web site. The lake appeared steel gray and quite delicate with its small whitecaps standing up to the brisk winds that made the flags in front of the hotel snap smartly. In the foreground of a reasonably sized vanilla-colored structure, which Melinda said was the Lake Hotel, were manicured lawns, well-tended shrubs and leafless trees that stood like fragile skeletons. We turned left onto a short circular drive that brought us to the front entrance, where I saw a U.S.-style newspaper dispenser and an ATM. Seeing a bit of familiarity made me feel a tad more at home. As we walked up the steps to the hotel, I stopped just shy of the front doors to read a bronze plaque mounted on the wall.

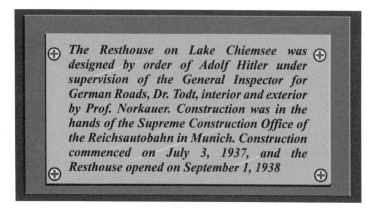

The Resthouse on Lake Chiemsee was designed by order of Adolf Hitler under supervision of the General Inspector for German Roads, Dr. Todt, interior and exterior by Prof. Norkauer. Construction was in the hands of the Supreme Construction Office of the Reichsautobahn in Munich. Construction commenced on July 3, 1937, and the Resthouse opened on September 1, 1938

Unfreaking believable! I hadn't really considered Hitler's whereabouts before; it was like living in my tenth-grade history book. Suddenly, a man emerged from the hotel in an outfit I had only seen on TV. He wore tall gray socks, knee-length brown leather pants with matching suspenders, and his handsome white shirt was embroidered down the front with small cream-colored spiky flowers; atop his head rested an emerald-green felt hat with a brush of animal hair pinned to the side.

Melinda pulled open the entrance door and smiled over her shoulder. "Oh, I almost forgot... Welcome to Bavaria!"

The Waldheim
PART II

Melinda offered the general tour of the hotel, introducing me to my boss, his boss and my co-workers. The orientation of the ground floor concluded in front of the tours office, where Melinda informed me that I could sign up for any of the posted tours for free. I watched the tour-desk guy, whom Melinda introduced briefly as Jesse, enthusiastically recommending a nearby restaurant to a gentleman buying a souvenir T-shirt. Jesse had wavy dark hair, brown eyes, zesty good looks, and an infectious smile. His hands waltzed around with dramatic flair while describing the meal he had eaten at the restaurant and the fine service tendered. By the time the gentleman had left the shop, I was yearning to eat there myself. I figured that employing Jesse was no accident; with his personality, one could probably sell air conditioning to the Eskimos.

The hotel might be 70 years old, but surprisingly it had an operational elevator. Melinda's office was on the upper floor next to the executive suites and Internet café. The second round of introductions began with the hotel manager's assistant and the head honcho himself, Mark. He was much more sociable than I had expected and appeared to keep things pretty casual, since everyone from Melinda down to a lowly chambermaid was on a first-name basis with him.

Interrupting the tour, a phone call from the States concerning employment was transferred into Melinda's office. I could hear familiar questions pouring in from the other end; Melinda did her best not to sound like a broken record. "Yes, the ad is for real..."

This was my cue to run next door and kick-start the Internet. I knew Mom and Dad would want to know I arrived safely. Plus, I had to check to see whether ShoSho12 had e-mailed anything regarding the crucifix. Melinda concluded the phone call and I shuffled back to her office. She had risen from her desk and was proceeding out the door when we crossed paths. "Ah, there you are," she said, "I'm sorry about the disruption. I get about 20 of those calls a day." Melinda turned to her desk and invited me to the chair opposite. "Now, where were we...?"

I got my first taste of life working for the government as I filled out more paperwork, had an ID card made, and set up a new bank account. This was all choreographed a half-hour away at Chiemsee's support center, otherwise known as Bad Aibling military base. In addition to the bank on base, there was a library, gas station, barbershop, post office, school, medical center, motor vehicles office, movie theater, bookstore, and a supermarket. It seemed a presentable place, a little America, where everyone spoke English and paid for their goods and services in U.S. dollars. Not exactly what I had come thousands of miles for, but handy just the same. If I absolutely had to have my Fruity Pebbles, I knew they would only be a yabba-dabba-doo away.

Back at the hotel, my eyes were weighing in like lead, but somehow I kept myself propped up. In consideration of my condition they gave me a day's reprieve to shake the jet lag before starting work. However, I had to hang my head somewhere and convalesce, which meant there was still the matter of housing to wrap up. My new home was to be in a building called the Waldheim, a few hundred yards from the Lake Hotel.

Melinda and I walked outside to a small vehicle parked in the circular drive. She tossed my backpack into the trunk, we buckled up, drove around the flagpoles and out past the security gate. Melinda paralleled the autobahn for a short distance while explaining that Hitler had it built some 70 years earlier. The autobahn looked good for a highway so old, but folks tended to build things better in those days. Now things only last until the warranty expires.

We drove past the Park Hotel and Melinda said that it, too, was part of the Chiemsee resort. The paved road we were traveling on turned to gravel and dead-ended at the edge of the woods. Nestled amongst the trees was the Waldheim, which fittingly translated to "Forest Home."

The Waldheim was a single-story, elongated building, and unless I was mistaken, it had a definite lean to the left. Melinda escorted me up the path and into the housing corridor. I was thankful my parents weren't here. In disagreement with the lean I'd noticed outside, the doorframes inside were skewing towards the right. The hallway carpet was several shades of green, most likely home to a multitude of foreign substances, and periodically a crack in the wall had been utilized as a cigarette receptacle, which told me that these coordinates did not exist on the housekeeping grid. Apparently, Hitler had these digs simultaneously built with the resort — obviously no one had bothered with any improvements since. The Lake Hotel's hallways and common areas were immaculate; I don't think that word had ever been used to describe a single area of the building I was about to call home.

Melinda waved me into apartment 428, where I met my roommate and housekeeping colleague, Janie. "Hi...Welcome to Germany!" she said.

"Thank you. I'm Sydney. It's nice to meet you." We shook hands.

Meanwhile, Melinda motioned towards the door. "Okay, well, I'll let you girls get acquainted... and Sydney, if you need anything, just give me a call or stop by. You know where my office is."

"Thanks, Melinda... Thanks for everything." She left and I dropped my backpack to the floor.

"Where are you from?" Janie asked.

"I'm from..."

There was a short knock at the door and Melinda popped her head back in. "Sorry. Forget to mention... Sydney, I had a double key to the room made. I'll drop it by tomorrow."

I thanked Melinda once again before returning to the conversation in progress. "So, where do you hail from, Janie?"

"Chicago! Born, bred, and schooled...the whole nine yards. I couldn't think of anywhere else I'd prefer to live," she paused, sweeping her pensive eyes over the various photos strategically placed near her bed.

This informed me there was more at stake in Illinois than just the folks. There appeared to be a young buck in her clutches.

Janie's pause became a recess, and I wasn't quite sure if the miracle of speech had been put on hold, or if she had simply forgotten what she was saying. I decided to interrupt the séance in progress. "I like your photo collection." I pointed to one in particular. "Is this your boyfriend?"

"Yes! That's Johnny." Judging by her tickled reaction, it was obvious I touched on her favorite subject. "We're engaged to be married when I return home in six months."

"Congratulations! I'm happy for you."

Staring into the photos, Janie sighed aloud. "Having a boyfriend like him is like opening a present every day."

She had fallen ass-over-tea-kettle in love, all right. However, one can't deny the dreamy feeling.

"Hey listen," Janie said, shaking herself out of a romantic haze. "I'll get out of your hair for a few hours so you can get some rest."

"Thanks, but don't worry about me."

"It's no problem. Really. This is about the time that I like to take a walk along the lake to think about home and my fiancé."

"OK. Sounds nice. I'll see you later then." She slid into a jacket and a pair of gloves before disappearing.

I glanced around my new home; it wasn't that spacious, a pink cracker box would have been a better description. There was hardly a place for the sink, but thank goodness the builders maximized their millimeters and muscled one in. Somehow the previous occupants had managed to squeeze two cumbersome wardrobes through the door. One rested against the wall at the foot of Janie's bed and its twin occupied the same position on my

half of the room. Outside our window naked trees cluttered the view and the cold ground was littered with gopher holes.
   Speaking of outside, the toilets and showers were down the hall. Unfortunately, there was no bathtub, which would've been lovely to soak in. But as tired as I was, I would have only fallen asleep and possibly drowned.
   In any case, my roommate seemed compatible and rather tidy from the state of our room. She had a van Gogh print neatly taped to the wall above her bed, a mini cube-like refrigerator perfectly tucked in the corner, and a broad shelf systematically swollen with books, cereal boxes, pastas, coffee cups, dishes, silverware, and a saucepan. On the nightstand adjacent to her bed sat a small arrangement of dried flowers along with several more photos of home. Lastly, the clock radio rested somewhere in between. Since we worked together, chances were we'd never forget to set the alarm.
   Preparing my side of things was going to be a mere formality. I was far too exhausted for anything ambitious. I hung my clothes in the wardrobe, stuffed all unmentionables in the two bottom drawers, parked my cosmetics bag above the sink, set a picture of the folks on the corner table, and made my bed with the sheets provided before passing out.
   Goodnight Waldheim... I look forward to the months ahead.

Sydney, International Chambermaid Extraordinaire
PART III

My first day of work began at 8 a.m. I reported to Roger, the executive housekeeper, who escorted me through a network of hallways to my workstation at the Lake Hotel, thus beginning my illustrious career as Sydney, international chambermaid extraordinaire.
   He assigned me to train with Sonya, a pretty Irish girl from Dublin, who spoke with the most melodious accent. "Gudd job, Luv." I hung on her every word as I emptied wastepaper baskets, made beds and scrubbed toilets.
   By the end of my shift, I was tired beyond belief, which I attributed to unshakable jet lag and vacuuming more rooms in one day than I had in my entire life.

The e-mail, Tuesday afternoon, eight days later
PART IV

The moment work finishes, my colleagues begin a race to the time clock in hopes of punching out first to secure one of the three Internet computers. Something kept telling me it was time to join the race and hasten the search for the crucifix. The fact that I hadn't heard anything from ShoSho bugged me — thus I commenced my own investigations.

Surfing the Web, I located a fair amount of information on King Ludwig II, which I expected, since he is such a notable figure in Bavarian history. However, a general search on relics unearthed no such crucifix or any similar tale. It became apparent that long, tedious hours knee-deep in lake water were the key to finding the proverbial "needle in a haystack."

Checking my mailbox one last time before logging off proved worthwhile; an e-mail from ShoSho12 had finally appeared. With curious expectations, I double-clicked "open."

Subject: Feeling Guilty

Dear Endi,

We share a mutual fascination, puzzles and quests. That is why I write you today. After guilty deliberations, I have to let you know that the crucifix does not exist! My buddies and I had been drinking that day in the chat room and we decided to have a little fun, at your expense. I can already hear your irritated reaction, so I'd best be going. That's all I have to say.

Peace, ShoSho

That's all he has to say! Yeah, he'd best be going. I guarantee he just threw himself a bad-karma boomerang.

What a disappointment! I felt as though I'd been punched in the stomach. I guess that's what I get for giving an Internet stranger instant credibility. Was Dad right? Maybe I should have listened more carefully to his arguments.

Wandering out of the hotel, I pondered the future: My college education hung in limbo, I live in a shoebox for two, and I'm in a country where I don't speak the language.

I think I'll go lie in bed and throw the covers over my head. With any luck, I'll fall asleep and be abducted by aliens.

The hallway pick-up
PART V

Is it possible that ShoSho was lying? Maybe he had second thoughts about letting someone else in on the quest?

Nevertheless, I do know one thing for sure — which is exactly what Dad would say — consider your actions before acting on them.

After entering the Waldheim at a swift pace, I glanced back to make sure the access door closed behind me. That's when it happened. Wham!

Upon turning the corner, I walked directly into a scantily clad man heading to the showers, temporarily dislodging the towel from around his waist and briefly exposing his nether region. He hastily managed to wrestle it back in place, anchoring it with both hands.

His face looked familiar. Then it came to mind. It was Jesse, the tour-desk guy, standing all but naked in front of me. My focus momentarily slipped away with his towel. I never once saw a naked man in the hallway of my dorm at college.

Tongue-tied, I could only utter: "Hi."

"Hey, don't I know you?" He double blinked and smiled.

I was a little surprised. I expected him to accuse me of trying to disrobe him right there in the hallway, or at least tell me to watch where the hell I was going. But here he was, turning on the charm while re-adjusting his towel.

·   The part of my brain responsible for intelligent conversation had been re-routed as I attempted unsuccessfully to hide my embarrassment. "Yeah, I, err... met you briefly in the tours office about a week ago...Melinda introduced us."

His eyes lit up. "Now I remember... You're Sydney, aren't you?"

He was infectious all right.

"Correct, Sydney Endicott."

"How's housekeeping treating you?"

I managed to clear my throat. "So far so good."

Looking down, he administered the final tuck to secure his towel.

"Have you ever been to Europe before?" he asked.

"No...this is my first trip overseas. How 'bout you?"

"I've been here a few times. I live to travel. Luckily, the hotel had a position open in their tours office and I jumped on it. That was nearly three years ago. I keep meaning to move on, but Chiemsee's so beautiful I'm drawn to it like a magnet to metal and can't pull away."

"Yeah, it certainly is beautiful. I'm eager to see as much as I can but I haven't yet had the time off. I'm free this Friday and Saturday, where do you suggest I go?"

"Salzburg! Why don't you tag along on our tour this Friday?"

I smiled and let out the breath I didn't realize I was holding. "I'd love to!"

The only tour I'd ever experienced was on our madcap family vacation when we walked around Washington, D.C., in 90-degree heat, listening to some blasé woman in an ill-fitting crimson blazer talk about the formal dining room at the White House. As a 10-year-old, I didn't care much about politics nor distinguished guests sitting around the presidential table.

"Great, it's a plan then." Jesse said. "And if you want, bring an overnight bag... I can recommend a little Salzburg nightlife."

"Yeah, why not?" Reckless thoughts came from my evil twin; please tell me he's available. Reality revisited. "Well, I'd better start making some dinner and call it an early night. I've had a hectic day."

"Ditto, I'm beat, too!" He grinned. "I was out late last night with my girlfriend."

Jesse was sincere, intriguing, alluring, and *not* available. He gestured toward the shower while bidding adieu. "Nice talking with you, Miss Endicott...I'll see ya Friday morning."

Jesse's Tour

CHAPTER 3

I woke abruptly as Janie slammed her hand down onto the alarm clock, silencing the Bee Gees – and my spicy dream. It's been a long time since I voluntarily got out of bed before 8 a.m. on a day off. I recall as a young, annoying snot of 9 years old putting my hair in little pigtails with red-velvet ribbons in preparation for church. God could hardly expect me to show much enthusiasm for dressing when I wanted nothing more than to go back to bed, curl beneath the quilt that Grandmother made, and snuggle up with Tipsy – my stuffed rabbit. Although, the smell of Mom's pancakes wafting through the house always succeeded in gravitating my butt to the breakfast table.

Things are much different now as a young woman working for the government in Europe. I can honestly say that dragging my bones out of bed at zero dark-thirty for a tour to Salzburg wasn't so tough.

It was a pleasant morning, the kind I'm readily accepting in Bavaria. Outside our bedroom window, feeble sunlight flickered through the morning mist languishing in the trees. A squirrel fidgeted across the cold ground and scampered up the white, parched trunk of a birch tree, whacking its head on the first branch. *Ouch!* I felt that one ruffle through my pajamas. I don't think I've ever seen a blind squirrel before. Anyway, as much as I'd like to find out where our fuzzy friend was going, a quick shower beckoned – towing me away from the Nature Channel.

Upon returning from the women's bathrooms, I glanced outside the window and happened to see Fuzzy nibbling on a golf ball. A blind squirrel that appreciates golf, huh? If this is an indication of the day's peculiarities to come, then it should be fascinating, to say the least.

Preparing for the next 36 hours might have been over-kill; I packed everything but the furniture in the room. The last thing I grabbed when heading out the door was my umbrella in case the rain promised by the weather bureau came our way.

Over at the hotel, the conditions appeared disheartening. There was no hint of the sun and the mist thickened into one of those foggy mornings that just seemed to hang around. The chill was amplified with every frozen breath. I had a few minutes to spare before the tour left, so I wandered into the cafeteria for a hot cup of cocoa. Once inside, I wish I could tell you the wafting smell of pancakes, bacon, and hash browns coming from the grill reminded me of home, but it just didn't equal Mom's.

Back outside, a group of about 20 hotel guests waited for someone to unlock the empty tour bus. A slightly built gentleman, sporting a brown mustache and a navy-blue jacket, walked up through the crowd, unlocked the bus and politely beckoned everyone aboard. I glanced back to see whether Jesse was coming, but there were only a couple of women in sweatpants, fleece jackets, and large shoulder bags making their way from the hotel. Directly in front of me stood a mildly irritating silver-haired couple bitching and moaning about everything from the weather to how rude the younger people were for not offering to let them board first. The pair in front of them, equal in age and guilty of being within earshot, heard every bickering word. They turned around and eyeballed the irritating couple with a piercing glare. Hopefully the warmth of the bus would simmer things down a touch.

My turn came to board and I patiently proceeded behind the irritating couple up the steps. For what seemed an eternity, I stood on the top step while they organized who would sit where and in which overhead compartment their coats would be stored. The silver-haired man, as if he were a bus-safety inspector, swiftly backed up two paces and bent over to examine the available space under the front seats. This shoved me in reverse motion, and like a human domino, I expected to fall lifelessly onto the women boarding behind me. Instead, I was propelled into a hard, angular object that dug into my left butt-cheek, registering the kind of pain that makes you call for Jesus. "Yeee...ooouuuuucccch!" Which, in turn, thrust me forward, knocking the silver-haired man into his seat face first.

Massaging my throbbing buttocks, I turned and stared accusingly at the angular object that dealt the pain. Meanwhile, my nemesis recovered from his plight and kicked off a series of scowling looks that provided great fodder for the thespians onboard. With a few stern expressions of my own I squeezed by his outstretched frame and took refuge in a seat halfway back, making myself as comfortable as possible considering the swelling of an egg-like formation on my posterior.

Within a few minutes everyone had settled and Jesse stepped onto the bus grinning from ear to ear. He said a couple of words to the driver, an exchange that was obviously much funnier to them than to the emotionally constipated passengers up front who sat stone faced and unamused, resembling guests at a funeral. Jesse then grabbed hold of the angular object and pulled it outwards, which opened into the tour guide's seat, dropped his bag to the floor and sat with his face all but plastered against the windshield.

A thirty-something brunette with enormous boobs that had to be fake, sitting a couple of rows behind the driver, yelled out to Jesse with eager curiosity. "Are you our tour guide?!"

He cranked his head around and answered charmingly: "Yes indeed, Miss, I'm your escort for the day." By her euphoric reaction, one could only presume that Cupid had materialized with a quiver of arrows and struck a bull's eye upon her heart.

Our escort blushed. He then signaled the driver with a snap of the fingers. Subsequently, the bus pulled away from the hotel like a train gathering steam. Jesse fiddled with the microphone and after a few seconds of tapping and thumping, his voice came booming through the bus: "GOOD MORNING, EVERYBODY!"

Startled by the volume, Jesse inadvertently won everybody's undivided attention. Wearing a sheepish grin, he quickly reached down and adjusted some buttons on the dash. "That better, everyone? Sorry, didn't mean to deafen you straight off."

Our driver lurched his bus past the guard gate and security pylons, taking the narrow, curvy road ahead in defiance of gravity. Jesse glanced back to his audience and began the pre-tour formalities. "Allow me to introduce ourselves: Your chauffeur today is Bernie from Cologne; he's been driving with the resort for more than 25 years...so let me assure you, folks, you're in safe hands. As for me, my name is Jesse and I hail from Southern California."

After a few hundred yards and the gravity struggle of releveling the bus, we entered onto Autobahn 8 southbound in the direction of Salzburg. Bernie merged into traffic jockeying for position in between a Danish 12-wheeler carrying a load of fish and an old Fiat towing a rickety camper displaying "Roma" license plates. With its engine sputtering and tailpipe spewing exhaust, Italy seemed like a long shot. In contrast to our lumbering bus, lead-footed speedsters were blazing past us in their sports cars leaving a vapor trail in their wake.

Jesse diverted our attention by beginning his tour:

"Ladies and gentleman...you are traveling on the world's first freeway system. Adolf Hitler, in a speech given on May 1, 1933, announced his ambitious autobahn construction plan. He appointed the competent Dr. Fritz Todt to equip Germany with an efficient, multilane transportation system. Work officially began that same year under the authority of the Reichs-autobahn bureau with ceremonies near Frankfurt on September 23. The initial crew assembled was that of a thousand men, and within a few years this increased to a workforce of 130,000 paving a vast network of asphalt to link the great cities of Hitler's infamous Third Reich. Without the knowledge of the German people, Hitler entertained secret plans for these high-speed expressways to hasten the mobilization of armies in case of war. Ironically, this logistical vision proved advantageous for the Allies as they raced across Germany to defeat the Nazis in 1945." Jesse paused briefly, scouring the crowd with enthusiastic eyes before striking the finale. "And since the autobahns were constructed with a dual purpose, swift as well as scenic, your Chiemsee resort is idyllically situated on the sandy shores of an alpine lake. Today, the resort is listed as a national landmark because it's the world's first hotel parked along an expressway."

Jesse seemed genuinely interested in the topic and not simply spewing descriptions with the jaded, bored monotone typical of many tour guides. His enthusiasm was sincere, even playful, and his guests wanted more. Jesse continued by gesturing out the window, naming the local villages and reciting their history. His charisma was magnetic, and without pausing he pointed to the rocky mountaintops and quoted the heights of their peaks.

Breaking from his tour, Jesse switched on the radio. "For your listening pleasure, folks, I'll tune in FM4, or 104.6 on the dial... incomparable radio this side of the Volga River. The morning personality, Stuart Freeman, broadcasts current events in English, gotta-know trivia and groovy tunes."

Meanwhile, the snow-covered Alps were traveling along with us, regularly changing shape from jagged peaks capped by a Latin cross to oversized hills stamped with ski runs. Every so often I could see a cable car lifting people over the fir trees to the summit. My eyes lowered to ground level, where tranquil beauty blanketed the farmers' fields and patches of melting snow. Charming villages dotted the valleys, each punctuated by a church spire jutting into the sky, looking heavenly against the fairy-tale landscape.

I gazed at the distinctive farmhouses; barns appeared to be crafted into the houses forming one residence for the farmers and their livestock. Several hundred years of sun, wind and snow seemed to have no lasting effect on these practical structures. The facades were warmly decorated in swirling trim outlining the windows and doorways. Local histories were painstakingly recorded onto the walls by what appeared to be old English typeface. Colorful murals depicted the scenes. Gables and support beams were exquisitely carved. Logs for the fireplace were evenly stacked waist high along three sides of the house, perfectly cut and true, testimonials to the cold winters. There was no doubt that Bavarians took extreme pride in their real estate.

Jesse interrupted these scenes of timeless tradition by pointing out a half-moon stone structure nestled into the left bank of the autobahn — just past the Bergen exit — that he presumed to be a former World War II anti-aircraft position. It was certainly interesting to see possible evidence of a war long since past, which had been little more than passages in my history book and Grandpa's stories relayed by Dad. I pondered the brave soldiers Dad always talked about, who fought for the liberty that many of us take for granted. Perhaps testimony of the war was sitting on this very bus. I wondered if the older gentleman behind me, or the irritating one up front, had been here before under less casual circumstances?

Moments later our tour guide was back in action. "How many fans of the movie 'The Sound of Music' do we have with us today?" Most everyone raised a hand or shot out of his or her seat enthusiastically. "I ask because Bernie and I think you've all been pretty groovy so far, and as a thank you, we'd like to make an extra-special stop to show you where one of the stars of the movie lives."

A few tour-goers seemed they would require resuscitation after that bargain.

"Plus, at this sojourn, there are FREE toilets...which in itself is worth the stop! How many of you folks have already had to break out the checkbook in Europe just to relieve yourself?"

Jesse's followers were eating out of his hand; he kept the offerings plentiful and they lapped it up.

The bus began descending into Berchtesgadenerland, placing the Salzburg valley in panoramic view.

"Gang, upon us is the Austrian border..." Jesse momentarily paused, lowering the mic to his chest to survey his guests before continuing. "Kids, that means keep your eyes open for kangaroos."

The adoring, middle-aged couple in front of me began whispering busily.

"Honey, did he say kangaroos?"

"Yes, Larry."

"Really...? That's great!"

"No Stupid, it's a joke!"

"What makes you say that, Darling?"

"Because we're in Austria, not Australia."

There was a pause. Obviously, this gent did not possess the brains in the family.

"Austria?" Larry sniveled.

The wife eyeballed her husband with disdain. "That's why he made the joke." Larry looked at her cockeyed. "Nevermind!" she snarled.

I couldn't help but giggle to myself. I'd heard that some tourists forget to pack their common sense when traveling, but apparently this guy didn't have any to start with. My ponderings were again interrupted when Jesse manned the mic.

"Welcome, ladies and gentlemen, to the Republic of Austria, comprised of nine states and eight million people, with Vienna as its capital. Thanks to the Schengen Agreement, the borders in Central Europe have been open since 1995 and we will scoot through the international boundary without stopping. The German autobahn has now ended, and the Austrian autobahn before us will split in two directions: The A1 heads east, accessing Vienna, Slovakia, Hungary and the Czech Republic. The other route is the A10, gateway to the south, accessing Italy, Slovenia, Greece and Turkey."

After having seen the movie "Midnight Express," set in a barbaric Turkish prison, I didn't have a strong desire to visit Turkey — let alone drive there. It was nice, however, to know that should the mood strike me, I could take off to somewhere like Istanbul for little more than time and gas money. I figured at the very least I'd have a working knowledge of which direction to point lost tourists.

Bernie veered onto the A10, exiting at the first "ausfahrt." Shortly thereafter, we rolled lazily through the village of Anif and arrived at the gates of a yellow palace called Schloss Hellbrunn. Jesse walked us beyond its golden walls and into the manicured gardens, where he stopped next to a seemingly out-of-place gazebo. An excited babble of voices erupted from the crowd: "Could it be...? The real one?"

"This is the extra bonus, folks," Jesse announced, "'The Sound of Music' star... the 'Gazebo.' Anyone care to entertain us with a song, perhaps 'Sixteen Going on Seventeen'? And, folks, before I lose your attention, behind us are the bathrooms."

A race ensued to see who would be first to get his or her picture taken with the famous gazebo. The hardcore 'Sound of Music' fans could hardly contain themselves, clutching at its panes and bursting into loud song. Two girls even brought along a life-sized paper cutout of their girlfriend from back home because she couldn't make it on the trip. They insisted: "This is the next best thing to having her here." Accordingly, Jesse played host to a mountain of photo requests.

Above and beyond the call of "The Sound of Music," my main goal here was self-relief number one — *desperately!* Several women were already pacing anxiously in line for the toilets; I guesstimated a 10-minute wait. Sometimes being a female isn't all it's cracked up to be, and this was one of those times. So I waited until the coast was clear and dashed into the men's bathroom, finding sanctuary within a stall.

Quickly I dropped my pants, squatting while being careful that no skin touched the seat, and let nature flow. Afterward, a stealthy exit was essential before a male decided to reoccupy his headquarters.

I pulled up my jeans and buttoned them snuggly to my waist, unlocked the stall door and began to exit with the finesse of a renowned Austrian: "Hasta la vista, Baby!"

I then heard approaching footsteps. "Oh shit!" I mutely cursed. Frantically, I jumped back into the stall and kept still.

The footsteps became louder — suddenly they halted and the men's room became as quiet as a confessional. The male had found what he came for. The tearing of a zipper pierced the silence; a steady gush of urine began its course while the depositor exhaled a sigh of relief against the wall tiles. I psyched myself into tolerance, knowing he'd be zipped up in a jiffy and I'd be a free girl. However, I did expect him to break wind a few times like a typical male — too late, before I could conclude my thought, guess what let itself out? ~~%~*~, and again, yet louder: ~%~^&~_*#~!

Meanwhile, I heard more footsteps enter the restroom. I couldn't believe the scene unzipping around me. The new male had the itch for a number two and camped out in the adjacent stall, pants to ankles. Back at the urinals, the farting cowboy zipped up and headed out. With one leaving and the other engaged on the neighboring throne, this was my cue to escape purgatory.

Then the unthinkable happened: Additional males sensed the urge to use their headquarters. The urinal flow began anew as there were now two or three more customers relieving themselves. One broke wind, encouraging the others to indulge in the same pleasure. The room graduated to a chorus.

Abruptly, the lock on my stall door jiggled aggressively. A male was trying to get in. I knelt down and saw his shoes in a holding pattern waiting their turn to land.

In a moment of desperation, I threw back the stall door and bolted by the befuddled patrons in a blue flash.

Lightheaded and ecstatic to be outside again, I rested momentarily on the nearest bench to break from sensory overload and admire the budding tulips.

*   *   *

Bernie and Jesse rounded up the gang to hit the road. Once underway, Jesse announced the time change. "Folks, we've just passed through the millennium warp. Please set your watches back 2,000 years."

We were soon swallowed up in the outskirts of Salzburg as the smooth roads narrowed into cobbled lanes. The city endorsed tidiness and cleanliness, and there was no trace of graffiti anywhere — nothing dirties a city more than graffiti. Moreover, everything appeared so authentic and old compared with the sleek and modern world I had left behind.

I glanced around to see whether any of the other passengers were as taken as I was and heard a child excitedly yelp, "Mom, look, it's a real castle!"
Then I noticed everyone perk up to what Jesse began describing ahead. "Ladies and gentleman...in front of us is the fortress of Salzburg, the largest preserved castle of its kind in Central Europe. It's been prominently perched above the townsfolk since the year 1077."
He was absolutely right, the history here is mind-boggling. Towering above the city, stark and imposing, on top of a bluff overlooking the expanse of Salzburg was a castle to rival none I had envisioned while listening to fairy tales as a child.
I visualized chapters of siege in the Middle Ages: local townsfolk backed up to their remaining defense posts while huddling behind massive ramparts for protection. I imagined them rubbing their hands together over open fires, chomping on enormous drumsticks of grotesque beasts under a canopy of stars while awaiting the invasion of enemy forces threatening from below.
The castle's ramparts formed an impregnable curtain of charcoal-gray stonework around the structure's pasty white facade and turrets, which stood out from the forested bluff it sat upon. Its magnitude was impressive for sure, looking every bit like the fortress it epitomized. How could such a colossal structure be built way back then? Perhaps several he-men, all having the physique of a Mack truck, took a break from their hobby of wrestling wild horses and maneuvered the gigantic stone blocks into place.
It seemed nothing could be so formidable, so impenetrable as that great hulk of stonework before us. Why hadn't I ever heard of it before? Something of such permanence must hold a place in history worth re-peating to those outside the boundaries of its country.
Before long, the bus slowed and Jesse's voice once more boomed over the intercom. "All right, folks, let's hop off this beaten pony and go for a little walk."
A handful poured out of the bus like prisoners being set free. As diligent as a wrangler, Jesse lassoed the ragtag bunch and herded them to a sizeable, tourist-friendly map of the city. He remained poised, waiting for the whole group to gather — an inquisitive few plodded sheepishly, absorbing every detail of their new surroundings. Once the last guest arrived, Jesse began explaining our route while pointing to the map. He told us to keep together and holler out if he was going too fast.
"Okay, folks, let's go!" Like an army sergeant, Jesse motioned everyone forward.
Judging by the elderly cluster following our guide, I was sure that if his gait were to exceed anything above slow, someone would certainly tug on the reins.
Jesse blitzkrieged ahead, periodically glancing back to see whether his troops were hot on the trail. Contrary to my initial assumptions, the twi-light assembly gamely kept up. At length we entered onto a broad expanse of asphalt, or as Jesse called it, Mozart Platz.

The thirty-something brunette with enormous boobs raised her hand and assertively inquired: "Is there a McDonald's in town?" According to the clock on the church tower, the time was 10:30 a.m. She was officially late for breakfast if that was her purpose.

"Yes, there is..." Jesse said, as he turned to face Boobs. "I'll let you know when we're close."

"When do you think that'll be?" she insisted.

He gave her just enough attention as not to be rude. "'bout an hour."

In the center of Mozart Platz stood a statue of its namesake. It was of considerable proportions, resembling a guy from the Planet of the Apes and liberally splattered in bird ca-ca. I was not impressed, and I'm sure Mozart wasn't either, most likely turning in his grave at the thought of this eternal tribute. At its base was the year 1842 stamped in Roman numerals.

My mother used to tell Alex and me, when we were little juveniles, bits of trivia from Mozart's life. One of those referred to the death of his wife, Constanze Weber, in that same year of 1842. Maybe she had something to do with the ugliness of the statue? Mom did mention their marriage was somewhat bitter.

Mom's Mozart narratives will remain with me for the rest of my life, and now that I'm here in his city, in his square, I couldn't think of a better time to reflect.

Wolfgang Amadeus Mozart, child prodigy born in 1756, wrote his first symphony at the tender age of 8 and his first opera at 12. In 1781, Mozart fell out of favor with Salzburg's ruling archbishop and moved to Vienna, where he married Constanze Weber. Tragically, given the antiquated medical procedures of the era, four of six children born to them died at birth or shortly thereafter. Mozart's lack of fiscal responsibility brought more heartache in the form of poverty. In 1791, he became fatally ill and died on December 5. Except for the gravedigger and the priest, no one showed up for his funeral, not even his wife. Wolfgang Amadeus Mozart, one of the greatest composers in history, was unceremoniously tossed into an unmarked commoner's grave for a large amount of people.

It was incredible to think that the musical maestro was born only a few hundred yards from Mozart Platz, where I now stood. Perhaps he played in this very square as a child, that is, if he had the time.

Getting back to his statue, I noticed the pen Mozart had clutched in his right hand looked like a Bic. That, I'm certain, did not exist in the 18th century.

In the meantime, my group had strayed from the asphalt expanse while Mozart held me mesmerized — I felt dreadfully alone. They were marching across the street into a gravel area. Stuffing my hands into my pockets, I hustled to catch up.

Jesse distanced himself a few feet from his guests, and like a circus ringmaster, he spread his arms out wide. Needing only to slip into a top hat and red tails to complete the image, he announced: "We are now standing in Residence Platz, the largest square in town..."

The prominent rectangular building at the far end of the square was the Residence, the former stately home of the archbishop. The three-story facade was loaded with windows, and the princely archway was just that. I pondered the thought of calling this place home, end of thought. I'd never make it past the first month's heating bill. I was thrilled at college just to have a single in the dorms outfitted with a giant spool for a coffee table, a sagging couch, and a double mattress on the floor.

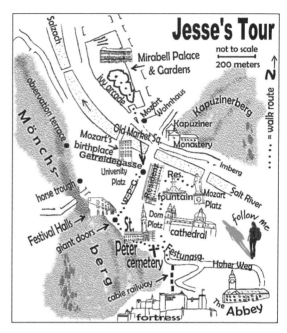

"...The jewel of the square is the Residence Fountain, built in 1661. It's one of the most impressive Baroque fountains north of the Alps, featuring four horses snorting water from their noses and mouths. The horse facing the 'Hypo' bank was made famous in the movie 'The Sound of Music' when Julie Andrews pranced through the square and splashed water in its face."

As fascinating as this was, our tour marched on — but now the humming of "The Sound of Music" soundtrack could clearly be heard echoing from our group, which I swore was on auto-replay.

In front of the Residence stood a handful of horse-drawn carriages offering rides through the Old Town.

A carriage ride began to look extremely attractive as I puffed to keep up with Jesse, who was all but sprinting ahead toward six tall archways opening onto yet another square. I glanced over to the older folks; they were keeping pace with gusto. Although, chances were they hadn't just postponed college, moved a world away, endured a depressing case of electronic deception, or been kept up late every night this week by a roommate keen to chat about how incredibly wonderful her fiancé is, either — so they had somewhat of an advantage.

In the next square — which was similar to the previous two, sparse but featuring a themed attraction — I followed the group past a statue of the Virgin Mary. The Cathedral of Salzburg stood magnificently before us as we craned our necks back to get the holy perspective.

"We are now standing in Dom Platz, or Cathedral Square. In front of us is the largest Baroque building north of the Alps, the Cathedral of Salzburg, having the capacity to hold more than 10,000 people. It was originally built in 774, and gutted by fire in 1598, to be rebuilt and reconsecrated in 1628. Some 300 years later it was heavily damaged during a World War II bombing raid in 1944; pictures at the back of the cathedral depict this awful day. The structure was again rebuilt and reconsecrated in 1959."

After his short sermon, Jesse pointed us across Dom Platz and inside the sacred confines of the cathedral. Along the main aisle, I noted the pews and kneeling benches, both of which looked uncomfortably hard. I reached the high altar where streams of light poured in from the massive octagonal dome, charging my body with newfound strength. Time seemed of no concern. I stood motionless, absorbing the entire spectrum. The cool, white interior was so elaborate, so awe-inspiring. Above me were heavenly frescos depicting scenes from the life and suffering of Christ. I felt humbled by the presence of such beauty, antiquity, and workmanship devoted to an undying faith. My eyes closed as I breathed the divine air and felt the past seep up through the floor and into my body. I sensed an unfamiliar permanence, and if it had been possible, I would've embraced the entire room.

Meanwhile, the twilight assembly had been silently milling around and conducting themselves in a similar manner — simply staring in wonderment. Most dipped their fingers in the basin of holy water before kneeling in front of the pews. Foreigners in a foreign land they may be, but home in any church.

By the main portal were pictures of conflict displaying the cathedral's tragic past. They revealed a dome that was no more; the bombing raid had all but destroyed it. The entire sanctuary was filled with wood and stone, the rubble of war. It seemed an abomination that evil hostilities would have touched this place dedicated to faith, love and hope. I was deeply moved by a power greater than any on Earth.

On the way out, I stopped at the main portal to drop a few coins into a contribution box that was manned by a priest distributing little remembrance cards to all who donated.

Outside, Jesse approached me. He wore a huge smile that seemed brighter than the sun, which shined curiously upon us. I'm sure I felt God tapping my shoulder with one of those vibrant rays, double-checking that I wasn't hitting on our shepherd right there on his front porch. Without disrupting his smile, Jesse managed to juice out a greeting: "Hi! How 're things?"

"Wunderbar! And what a church, huh?"

"Yeah, it's fantastic;" he double blinked. "You enjoying yourself so far?"

"Overwhelmed! I still find it hard to believe that I'm actually here."

"I know what you mean. I still feel the same way myself, and I've been here nearly three years. Hopefully the magic will never fade."

I nodded. "It would be tragic to tire of such a fascinating place. Frankly, I'm surprised not to see any stone gargoyles out on grocery runs."

"Wouldn't that be an exciting addition to the tour?!" Jesse then pulled a loose hair off my sweater before changing the subject. "As for tonight... You are staying, right?"

"Yep, I have everything I need in this daypack." I swiveled my upper body to remind Jesse of what rested upon my back. "You said...you've got a place in mind?"

"Sure do...It's a youth hostel that's cheap, clean, and hip!"

Fabulous! I had hoped my allowance of 60 euros would cover sleeping arrangements, dinner, and return train fare. I'd been assured that I had enough, but I was still grappling with a little overseas insecurity.

"I want to show the guests a few more things before we break," Jesse said, "then we'll have some free time and I can get you situated. Maybe I'll even head back down tonight and join you in painting the town red. I'm sure I'll find you in my favorite watering hole, 'Dos Dudes.' Everyone ends up there by midnight."

His words required no reply. A smile was sufficient.

The gang was again set in motion and a stringent hike ensued; this time we headed out the opposite set of arches and into the next square, where an awesome view of the fortress presented itself. Jesse moseyed across the square, leading us towards a narrow cobblestone lane. On the way we passed souvenir stands laden with Mozart mementos, useless knickknacks, colorful postcards, and T-shirts with catchy print: "No kangaroos in Austria" — "I met Mozart" — "Salzburgers do it sweetly." I also witnessed what must have been the world's biggest chessboard painted onto the asphalt; the pieces were the size of children.

Jesse stopped in front of the cable railway that ascended to the fortress. Precisely then an attractive redhead strutted past.

I could see that her all-natural beauty captivated our guide. Her timing couldn't have been more exact as she sauntered up the lane in the direction he pointed. Jesse, cool and coherent, began rendering a tale about Salzburg's locally sponsored beer restaurant, the Stiegl Keller, established in 1820. The group remained focused in the direction of his index finger, giving Jesse open rights to stare, gawk, and even ogle at every inch of the woman's voluptuous anatomy. His face read like a book:

Your auburn hair is a dream; how the curls playfully bounce past your luscious neck and onto your sassy, sheer-white blouse...

Luckily for him, I was the only one paying attention to his facial expressions. Miss Voluptuous disappeared out of view and Jesse concluded his narration, subsequently leading us through a nearby wrought-iron gate and into a cemetery.

Larry, the kangaroo specialist, happened to be walking next to me as we entered and commented with a chuckle: "Who said you can't quit smoking? All these people did!"

His wife scowled at him as if he were a life-sized turd. "Larry, you really are a nitwit! Stop bothering the poor girl and mind your own business...Now I don't want to hear another word out of you!"

"But, Honey, I..."

"Not another word," she exclaimed, jamming her finger into his brow. "Is that clear?!"

"Yes, dear," he answered meekly.

Larry demonstrated signs of being verbally tormented and abused for so long that it seemed second nature to him. He and his wife were the ideal specimens to prove that marriage can be a laborious affair. During the honeymooners' squabble, rhythmic sighs from the twilight assembly assured me something was up. Of course, I should have known, we were in the cemetery where the von Trapps hid during the escape scene in "The Sound of Music."

The cemetery proper was a mix of old and new graves, lopsided footpaths, vaulted tombs and a petite, frail church nestled in the middle — the date above its portal read 1491 and the bell tower showed every sign of its feeble age, ready to topple with each gust of wind. It's amazing to think that Europeans were already building cathedrals, fighting wars, and brewing beer when my government wasn't even yet conceived.

I noticed a few of the older headstones were leaning, awkwardly sunken into the rich, chocolate soil. The monument adjacent to me had a black-and-white picture of its occupant set in crookedly; otherwise the plot was immaculately cared for and highlighted by red begonias and burnt-orange marigolds. On each plot was a red candle, which must be a stunning sight when the bright light of day fades to darkness illuminating the graveyard to a red hue.

Jesse broke the silence by beginning his spiel on the Who's Who of gravesites. "As we stand here in the center of the burial ground, we see the plot of Harry J. Collins, an American World War II general attached to the 42nd Rainbow Division. After the war General Collins remained here in command of the occupying forces until 1955, when Austria became a republic and our boys were deployed elsewhere. By that time it was too late for the general to leave; he had fallen in love with Salzburg and one of its offspring. General Collins died in the early '60s and is buried here with his wife. His headstone reads: 'Honorary citizen of the cities of Salzburg and Linz.' Ironically, not far behind the general's grave is a World War II memorial dedicated to the Axis soldiers who fell in defense of the city."

Interrupting our narrator, Boobs verbalized a reminder that she was on the verge of starvation. "Is McDonald's near?"

Most of the group thought she was being rude, including Jesse. "I'll let you know!" he firmly replied.

"Okay," she said over her rumbling stomach, "...but don't forget."

Jesse continued the tour. "Going back a few years, before the general and World War II, are the catacombs in the cliffs to our left. These are dwellings dug out by Christians during the Roman occupation in the third century A.D. At its entrance are the graves of Michael Haydn, a celebrated composer in Salzburg and brother to the 'father of the symphony,' Joseph Haydn. The second grave is Mozart's sister, Maria Anna, a.k.a. Nannerl."

We exited the cemetery through an archway continuing our platz hop to St. Peter's Square.

"Ladies and gentleman, in the year 696, the Catholic Church sent Bishop Rupert from the German city of Worms to form St. Peter's Monastery, where we now stand, to bring peace and prosperity to the region.

From these roots, more than 13 centuries ago, came the first archbishop and the settlement's new name: Salzburg, or Salt Castle."

Jesse further explained that Bishop Rupert was entombed in the church to our right, and to our left was St. Peter's Stiftskeller, the oldest restaurant in Europe — dating from 803 A.D.

At that point a question rang out from the group. "Have the prices gone up since then?" That, I hate to say, came from Larry.

There was only one thing to do, shield my eyes from his upcoming punishment by Wifey. Regrettably, I forgot that other sense called hearing.

"Oooooooouuch... Let go of my ear, Honey!"

I removed my hands to see Larry being dragged off into the restaurant by his wife, probably to get personally acquainted with the prices.

The twilight assembly appeared to be aghast at this scene. No one could believe his or her eyes, but what could we do? Maybe that's how Larry and Wifey get their kicks.

Obviously, Jesse had seen and heard it all before; he simply continued: "I assume you're familiar with Hitler's 'thousand-year' Third Reich. Well, the court scribe, Alcuin, first recorded St. Peter's Stiftskeller into the history books during a visit in the year 803 by Emperor Charlemagne ...founder of the First Reich, which actually did last a thousand years under the Holy Roman Empire."

Before Jesse could continue, an elderly woman wearing a hot-pink jumpsuit, as if to impress us on her ability to count to three, blurted... "Was there a Second Reich between the first and the third?"

In a pleasant pitch, our knowledgeable guide responded, "Why, yes, there was. The Second Reich was the brainchild of Germany's 'Iron Chancellor,' Otto von Bismarck, who unified the German states into one empire in 1871, lasting almost 48 years."

Our faithful escort then marched us across the monastery grounds, paralleling the sheer cliffs that cradled the fortress, through yet another set of archways and into a secluded courtyard. Facing us were two giant-sized iron doors framed by six designer-like stone blocks; suspended above was an enormous, acidic-green organ. Using this locale as a backdrop, Jesse waited for everyone to catch up.

"This, gang, is the side of Salzburg's festival halls. From here they appear to be rather insignificant, but once around the corner you'll notice the building extends the entire length of the block. Within this massive 17th-century complex are three theaters: The second-largest theater is distinctively one of a kind because of its 96 arches hewn into the cliffs, which can be seen during the movie 'The Sound of Music' when the von Trapps perform their farewell songs before escaping to the cemetery."

The twilight assembly let out a gasp.

"Let's go and have a peek at the front of the building." Jesse waved us onward.

We paraded around the corner, where our group halted by a tree that partly obstructed my view of the main facade. As I pivoted to get a better angle, I suddenly felt the ground beneath my foot give way to mushiness. I peered down at the foreign matter and shrieked: "Oh...SHIT!" That's what it was all right, horseshit.

My outcry caught the attention of our group, as well as everyone within two blocks. In about the same amount of time it took to release my foot from the steaming goo, what appeared to be the "shit guy" from a municipal waste-disposal unit peddled up on his three-wheeled rickshaw. No kidding! He gallantly hopped off his ride and quickly pulled a white handkerchief from his back pocket. Lowering to one knee, he gently rested the goo shoe upon his thigh, wiping it goo-less. After releasing the immaculate shoe back to earth, he suavely grabbed a broom and shovel from his chariot and swiftly cleaned the street of its remaining waste. Coolly, the Shit Guy peered over his shoulder with a wink and a smile before riding humbly down the street. It was somewhat charming being the main character in a doo-doo fairy tale.

Our group assembled and marched to the next attraction. Along our route, I couldn't help but notice a gallery showcasing modern art. Billboards were plastered across its front facade promoting its latest exhibition: Nudes and Styrofoam. The ad caught my eye, as it featured the profile of a man and a woman naked from the waist up. The pair gazed seductively into one another's eyes while their hands caressed each other's body parts – a bare breast escaped the man's clutch.

As arresting as this was, it became evident that no one else noticed it. The gang had already stopped short of the next square and was patiently waiting for me. So, I hightailed it out of eroticville.

Jesse re-located our group to a platz he called Old Market Square; everything in this town seemed astonishingly old. Adjacent was Café Tomaselli, established in 1703, where allegedly Mozart played cards. At the other end of the square emerged Getreidegasse, the pedestrian shopping street and birthplace of the legendary composer. Nearby sat another beautiful church.

To our joy, Salzburg's many churches continuously rang their bells, seemingly competing for parishioners. On our way through the old square, Jesse challenged us: "Okay, folks, let's see if anyone can pick out the smallest house in Salzburg." Immediately the group embarked on their quest. I lagged behind, again.

Absorbing my thoughts were the classy facades encompassing our location – they approached six stories and were painted in soft pastels, perhaps suggesting the warmth of the square. To the right stood a fountain crowned by Saint Florian, patron of fire protection, pouring a bucket of water over a burning castle. And behind it was a sweets shop with nothing but chocolate in its front window. Boxes upon boxes, in all shapes and sizes, filled with little chocolate balls wrapped in shiny foil. I gladly plucked a sample from the lady standing outside offering passersby the tasty pleasure. Mmm. Abruptly, my attention was diverted to a chorus of sighs and people pointing. What could it be this time; did someone else step in horse dung?

Oh, of course, the smallest house in Salzburg. Not much of a house, more like a gap between two buildings. Add a door, a couple of windows, throw on a roof, nail in a gargoyle and call it the smallest house in town. Marvelous advertising for the present-day jewelry store.

At this pit stop I pulled ahead of the twilight assembly and milled around a cluster of market stalls while Jesse waited for the last of his guests to finish taking pictures. One stall in particular stood out — it was ornamented with religious trinkets and a menagerie of crosses: gold, silver and hand-carved. My interest roused, I walked over for a closer look. The stall owner must have sensed I was a tourist and offered her thoughts in English: "I see you are interested in my crosses. Can I help you make a choice?"

"Well, actually, I'm interested in a 19th-century gold crucifix covered with jewels that may have come from King Ludwig II."

The stall owner's face curiously tilted. "Sorry, there's nothing like that here. But a short time ago I did read a book that described a cross similar to the one you speak of."

Intrigued, I pressed the stall owner for the details. She said her book stated that a jeweled crucifix was dug up in the mid-1930s at a construction site along Hitler's new autobahn between Munich and Salzburg, but that's where the story ended. However, that was enough info to sway me to believe that ShoSho had second thoughts about letting someone else in on the quest.

Meanwhile, Jesse had his hands full. The obnoxious hot-pink jumpsuit lady had managed to bog down the gang who had otherwise adopted the motto: "Keep on truckin'." Her modus operandi effectively puppeteered the twilight assembly into photo shock. "Chuck, put your hand around Martha. Okay, smile, and...perfect!" *Click!*

Jumpsuit Lady searched for new recruits. "Ethel, I want you and your niece, Thelma, in this next one, just in front of the smallest house. Great, now a bit more to your left, a bit more... Stop! Okay, say 'peanut butter balls.'" *Snap!* "Good grief...I'm out of film! Hold your positions, everybody, this'll just take a second."

Ethel and Thelma stood impatiently while Jumpsuit Lady ripped open the foil packaging to a new 110-film cartridge and loaded it into her disco-like camera, complete with a turbocharged flashbulb-cube sitting on top.

Jumpsuit Lady, unfortunately, was back in business. "Okay, people, let's take a group photo. Now, Jesse, I want you standing up front with me!"

"Yes, Ma'am," Jesse replied, as if she were his mother and he the young obedient son.

Afterward, she rudely grabbed a passerby and asked him in English if he would take their photo. She put the camera in his hand and walked away before he could answer.

Uh oh, surely her posture gave credence to the term "ugly American."

The man politely took the photo; an embarrassed Jesse offered a courteous thank you in German, "Danke." That consequently wrapped things up on the photo front and the gang began marching onwards — without Jumpsuit Lady.

Our next move led us onto Getreidegasse, where throngs of shoppers scampered past. On the corner was a rather provocative lingerie shop, complete with window models flaunting the scant merchandise. If mannequins could speak, I wonder what they would say? Probably something like: "It's freakin' cold!" These girls were quite exposed; even a monk could easily see that temperatures teetered well below comfortable. Over here, nudity seemed to be accepted — much more than back home, anyway. I can honestly say that not many of the opposite sex have seen me as naked as these mannequins are, but the select few who have didn't complain.

If it were a government mandate to nominate one's best asset, I would have to choose my feet. They're not sexy or beautiful or anything like that, I simply mean they get me around with absolutely no problems. I frequently hear people complaining about their feet: a corn on the small toe, swelling, athlete's foot, uncomfortable shoes, or something. Fortunately, I've had no trouble and my feet are perfect just the way they are.

Yet, to the opposite gender, a girl's breasts or backside seem to be the main focus. Maybe there's nothing wrong with that, but I think there's something lacking in the way they go about it: "Hey, Honey...nice tits, nice ass!"

Come on guys, have some class. Treat a lady with respect, maybe give her flowers or spring for dinner once in awhile — there's more to a woman than tits and ass. You've got to take your time, give her long, slow caresses, define her curves with gentle strokes, hold her tight and feel how she radiates warmth. Look deep into her eyes — you'll see there's nothing sexier. And most importantly, listen to what she has to say. Gentlemen, do this, and I guarantee you will get what you want!

I'd better conclude there, because this time I'm lagging way behind. To catch up, I dodged and weaved the Getreidegasse furlong with Olympic finesse. Thankfully, Jesse had just begun counting heads as the group entered Mozart's birthplace and museum. I was last, but punctual.

"Good... Everyone's here!" Jesse faced us like a conductor to his orchestra. "Gang, this is where I say goodbye. I'm sure you're all ready to do your own thing and I do hope you've enjoyed our walk together. The museum is in English and there are bathrooms inside. If you have any questions, just stay behind, otherwise I'll see you at 3 p.m. on Mozart Platz. So, enjoy yourselves and... auf Wiederseh'n!"

The guests were all smiles, telling Jesse he had done a great job as they filed past him and into the museum. Well, that is, except for one. "Where's McDonald's?" By this time, Boobs' stomach was a shockwave of malnourishment; abdominal rumblings rocked the Mozart house to its foundations.

Without delay, Jesse pointed the way. Boobs pivoted and shot out of Mozart's place like a pair of melons launched from a catapult.

When I had a moment to collect my thoughts, my mother's convictions flooded in. How she would love to be here, to witness and feel the history. Yet, I would have to visit this shrine on behalf of my mother another day;

Jesse was heading in my direction and there was the issue of lodging to address.

"The guests are settled," he announced, "and we're free to do as you please." He shoved a stick of gum in his mouth and recycled the wrapper into his jeans pocket.

"How 'bout we grab a bite to eat before finding me somewhere to sleep?" I asked.

"Deal... I know just the place for some healthy grub."

Not far from Mozart's was a Japanese restaurant; Jesse's favorite. We ordered a sampler of California rolls — adding to each roll a scant portion of wasabi, a slice of ginger, and a dousing of soy before consumption. During the intervals, we sipped green tea and discussed the pros and cons of a backpack versus a suitcase. The backpack had no cons.

Shortly thereafter came our tempura dish with mixed vegetables and king prawns. I plucked a pair of chopsticks from the table and clumsily snapped at my share of the dish, hooking mere scraps. Jesse, in contrast, handled his chopsticks like an expert, smoothly transferring copious amounts of rice and nutritional substance from bowl to mouth. I managed to consume a few noodles while a few more slid onto my lap. Hopefully he didn't notice.

"So, what brings Sydney Endicott to Europe?"

"Ha! Where shall I begin? How 'bout a break from college, a sense of self-achievement, the quest for a golden crucifix, and the opportunity to travel and meet new people."

"Huh...? The quest for what?"

"A golden crucifix studded with precious gemstones that is supposedly buried in the Chiemsee area and came from the fairy-tale king, Ludwig II. Sound familiar?"

"Uh... No."

I didn't think so, but it was worth asking. Although, I'd better change the subject before he thinks I'm some kind of nut. "So, what brings you to Europe, Mister Tour Guide?"

"I guess you could say that I'm on a global mission for knowledge. It's the fuel that drives my engine. As a tour guide, I especially love to watch the expressions of people when I show them something they've never seen before. One guest, for example, was so overwhelmed by a cache of sacred relics that she actually fainted on tour."

"Serious...? Do tell!"

"We were in the heart of old Vienna admiring the main entrance of St. Stephan's Cathedral. Our hands shielded us from the sun as we gazed upwards beyond the stained-glass windows and gargoyles to the Heathen Towers. I then told my guests the tale of the cathedral: 'The peoples of the Romanesque era were here and built this divine structure, which improved in the Gothic age with ribbed vaults and pointy arches. In 1683, 200,000 Ottoman warriors rode in from the east to capture Vienna and the cathedral. Locked in mortal combat, the warriors were beat back from the city gates when the gallant Austrian general, Prince Eugene von Savoy, struck a counterblow with his army. Some 120 years later, Napoleon arrived with his modern cavalry and cannon, triumphing over Austria. In the 20th century, the bombs of World War II damaged the cathedral. Now we stand in memoriam of eight centuries of history, as if destiny brought us together to relish this very moment.'"

"And the fainted one," I inquired. "What about her?"

"Oh, right, yeah... I summoned the guests into the cathedral through the main entrance, along the left aisle and down the steps into the catacombs to witness piles of decayed bones and skulls from plagues past. That's when I lost her...She dropped like a sack of potatoes right there in the heart of old Vienna."

"No way! What did you do?"

"Well, I happened to have a piece of chocolate in my bag. I whipped it out, wagged it past her nose a few times and said if she didn't get up, the medieval trolls were going to come and whisk her away. And, boy, you should have seen her jump! She snapped to attention like a soldier in Patton's Third Army."

Jesse had whetted my appetite for travel. There's so much to see and do. Vienna had been just another grand city from the history books, but now the difference is — I'm here! Could a year possibly be enough time? I do know one thing for sure, out of the 86,400 seconds I get to spend daily, not one will be wasted.

After lunch, Jesse insisted on walking me through the Mirabell Gardens on the way to the hostel.

I was excited, all right, as this was my first of many adventures in European cities. Not to mention, my first night ever in a youth hostel.

The Mirabell Gardens were immensely beautiful, like a painting with tourists. At the entrance appeared to be two Greek-inspired statues of nude discus throwers in the after-release position, and beyond them were another two. We walked past the statues, as if being careful not to be struck, and noted countless flowers breaking through the earth, reaching for the sun. Jesse walked to the back center of the gardens and planted himself opposite a fragrant bed of roses.

From this spot, the splendor of the gardens, skyline of the Old Town, and the majestic Alps were all at my photographic disposal...*Truly a postcard-perfect picture.*

CHAPTER 4

W e exited the Mirabell Gardens via the "do-re-mi" steps portrayed in the movie "The Sound of Music," walked up a few streets and through the hostel's front door. Unknown to me, Jesse had called ahead and made a reservation. At the front desk, an Irish-sounding girl chatted to her colleague about nights past. Looking at Jesse, I shared a smirk and a subtle comment. "Sounds as if this place can get pretty wild."

The receptionist's peripheral vision then detected us. "Hi, can I help you?"

"Yeah, hi, I talked yesterday with Beena and made a reservation for my friend Sydney in a four-bed dorm." Jesse eyeballed the receptionist hoping she could verify his call.

"Sure, I remember." Jesse looked instantly relieved. "I'm Beena. You seemed a little concerned, so I took the opportunity and roomed her with some extra-pleasant girls." She then scrolled her finger down the roster in front of her. "Was that for one or two nights, Miss Endercut?"

"Just one night," I answered, not worrying about the name differential.

However, Jesse insisted on clearing up the discrepancy. "In case there's a problem of any sort," he turned to me with a cheeky grin, "...the name is Endicott."

"I'm sorry!" Beena apologized. "That does have a nicer ring to it."

"Oh, thank you." I accepted Beena's endorsement with a cheeky grin of my own.

She then handed me the room key and offered parting wishes. "Enjoy your stay! And just to let you know, happy hour in our bar is from 5 to 6:30."

Mister Tour Guide escorted me upstairs to the threshold of my room. I turned the key in the lock, pushed the door open, and swiveled to Jesse. "My first room in Europe. What do you think?"

By the look on his face, I knew something was wrong. Were the curtains a horrible color? Was there a dead body on the floor?

Pivoting to see for myself, I saw a rather bare room including two bunk beds, a sink, radiator, and my very first hostel roommates: two girls sitting on a bed and braiding their snow-white hair — wearing only their bras and panties. Unabashed, they got up in a relaxed, welcoming manner. "Hello. You must be our roommates," one of them said.

"Hi," I responded. "Actually, it's just me who is staying tonight." We entered the room and closed the door behind us. "My friend here will be leaving soon. Right, Jesse?" I gave him a double nudge to the ribs. "Jesse?!"

He appeared flushed and somewhat googly-eyed. "Oh right, yeah...I have ahh, err...some people, a tour to catch up with... soon!" Jesse mumbled, glancing at his watch. The two girls, lacking a shy bone, remained stationary with their enviable figures and suntanned skin on full display.

The room abruptly lit when the sun penetrated the afternoon clouds, emphasizing every detail of their bodies as the rays beamed through the curtainless window. Jesse offered his hand to divert from the obvious distractions. "Hiii I'mm...Jesse."

He struggled to maintain eye contact, the up-and-down motion of the handshake proved to be too overwhelming. His intense concentration dissolved and he introduced himself directly to their breasts. Jesse realized his dilemma and searched for an out. I dove in for the rescue, alerting him that the time was 2:45 and he needed to meet his group. Without hesitation, Jesse agreed and waved goodbye.

Embarrassed, I apologized on Jesse's behalf. "I'm sorry for my friend; he's not usually so...shy."

"No need to apologize," said one of the girls. They looked at each other and giggled. "He seemed very friendly," said the other.

"Ahh...yeah," I agreed, "friendly."

"Are you traveling around Europe?" questioned one of the girls as they began dressing for the evening.

"In a way, yeah. I'm working at a hotel just north of here for a year, and in that time I'd like to see as much as I can while searching for a golden cross. How about you two...?" I abruptly cut the sentence short and winced. "I'm sorry, I seem to have forgotten your names."

On that note they both thrust their hands at me. "Hi, I'm Liselott," said one.

"And I'm Britte," said the other. "We're university students from Sweden."

I couldn't thank my lucky stars enough. Beena had clearly made a clairvoyant decision to room me with these girls. Not only did I sense their sincerity, but maybe we had college frustrations in common.

"How long are you traveling for?" I asked.

"Well..." Liselott shrugged, "we wanted to take the semester off and tour Europe extensively, but our parents intervened and we were lucky to steal six weeks because of the Easter holidays."

Our ping-pong chatter lasted nearly two hours before we realized the time. During the conversation, the girls invited me to join them for dinner and a drink. I accepted, but first I decided to take a long, hot, relaxing shower.

The water was *freezing!* A short, frantic wash and a hurried scrub appeared to be my only option.

Upon returning to the dorm, I walked in on the Swedes talking to our new roommate, an attractive girl with honey-colored, shoulder-length hair that complemented her striking green eyes. She introduced herself as Onoma from Prague, Czech Republic.

"You have an interesting name," I stated. "Is that Czech for something?"

"That's a familiar question. My mother comes from Greece and she wanted to hand down something traditional. 'Onomastics' is the study of names and their origins; 'Onoma' is the Greek word for 'name.'"

"Now I really like your name." I said.

"Dekuji." Onoma stopped immediately when she understood her slip. "Sorry, that's Czech for what I wanted to say in English: 'Thank you.'"

"You're welcome. But, it's also interesting to hear your language."

"Britte and Liselott told me your name is Sydney. Is that after the Australian city?"

"That's also a familiar question. Actually, it comes from my grand-father and father. Because of how hard I was kicking in my mother's stomach, my parents assumed I was a boy and automatically had all the paperwork filled out as Sidney Lee Endicott III. So, of course, it was a shock for them when a girl popped out. Nevertheless, they left things as planned except for changing the 'i' to a 'y.'"

"Now I especially like your name," Onoma said, returning the compliment.

"Dekuji," I countered, hoping my memory served me correctly.

Onama's face lit up. "I'm impressed! I think you, Sydney III, have a gift for languages."

While the four of us were getting acquainted, I came to the conclusion that hostel life boasted many similarities to dorm life at college. The only differences were bunk beds, international camaraderie, and sharing your room with adventurers. I felt extremely fortunate to be here.

We all agreed that since none of us knew the city, happy hour should be our first stop and we would take the night from there. It was getting close to 5:45 and valuable time was slipping away.

The first drinks were poured and surprisingly the popular choice was beer. Our opening gesture of camaraderie was a toast to new friendships and the night ahead. I began: "Here's a little drinking ditty I learned in Bavaria. Okay, girls, are you ready? Raise your glasses and repeat after me...

Into each other's eyes we stare.
Our glasses engage with flair.
Down to the table for a tap.
We raise 'em up and throw 'em back.
Stomach and liver, have no fear,
This is how we drink our beer!"

Our sips became healthy gulps. We couldn't help but laugh at each other's little white moustaches and the teeny burps that followed. Conversation flowed, especially when the girls found out I took a freezing cold shower. An innocent giggle escalated to extreme laughter when they struck a visual of me running the soap up and down my body at lightning speed as if challenging the Guinness Book of Records for the world's fastest shower. They graciously informed me that sometimes when hostelling, one needs to buy hot-water tokens at reception, as was the case with our hostel. Next time I'll make sure I have plenty of tokens, with an extra to spare.

What a great experience! I was having so much fun talking to the people we met: Canadians, Australians, New Zealanders, British, Japanese, and other colorful travelers from faraway lands. It was much easier than I had anticipated — sharing a drink, discussing common interests, and exchanging travel tips to new adventures — everybody had a story to tell, a dream to grasp. Though, I must admit, no one was searching for a lost crucifix.

Happy hour wound down, but the night was still young. The word going around shifted the partygoers to Dos Dudes. I chuckled at the mention of this place; it reminded me of Jesse, which in turn reminded me of his earlier facial expressions when he awkwardly attempted to introduce himself to Britte and Liselott — he would've had better luck tackling a plate of spaghetti with chopsticks.

Although a liquid dinner was alluring, my new acquaintances and I elected to grab a bite to eat. A friend at Chiemsee had given me directions to a restaurant that shouldn't be missed, yielding tasty food and views of beautiful sunsets. The girls approved and we found our way by public transport.

We exited the bus and began walking up the hill towards our destination, Gasthaus Zur Plainlinde, which sat just below the Baroque church Maria Plain. The walk ascended through a quiet neighborhood that steadily lifted us above the Salzburg basin. Houses gradually disappeared and were replaced by plush, green fields that were home to cows playing tunes with the bells hanging from their necks. The church grew larger as the city became smaller beneath us. On the plateau, amid mouth-dropping scenery that included boundless views to the pointy Alps, sat the softly lit gasthaus. We arrived with ravaging bear hunger.

Once inside Zur Plainlinde, a gentleman swiftly came to our service. "Grüss Gott, Sie schauen aus, als hätten Sie einen Bärenhunger?"

We girls looked at each other wondering who was going to answer.

The host attentively acknowledged our language disability and switched to something more familiar. "Allow me to introduce myself, my name is Herr Boss. You girls look hungry!"

Boy, were we ever. He sat us at a table near the door and promptly handed us menus. After a quick flip through, I saw what my stomach craved. The others hardly took as much time.

Our wishes translated into four schnitzels, four beers, and one serving of asparagus cream soup with four spoons.

Herr Boss and a co-worker arrived a minute later with our drinks. We began the dinner toast the same as our happy-hour prost, but this time it went like clockwork. It had become our theme:

> "Into each other's eyes we stare.
> Our glasses engage with flair.
> Down to the table for a tap.
> We raise 'em up and throw 'em back.
> Stomach and liver, have no fear,
> This is how we drink our beer!"

We evidently caught the attention of all nearby as they stopped and listened to our toast.

Out the window, a natural wonder set before our eyes. The sun went down like a ball of fire, filling the horizon with golden rays. The fiery sphere continued its descent behind the mountains, painting the evening sky a deep red before disappearing into the arms of Mother Earth. The dazzling sunset electrified the mood in the restaurant. All were jovial as they ordered rounds of drinks and additional goodies, keeping Herr Boss and his staff moving at a brisk pace. The couple next to us commented in English on the beautiful sunset and introduced themselves as Karel and Silke. They said they got a kick out of our energy, as did the other patrons. Karel told us they were from Vienna and visiting Salzburg for a few days.

"Karel, are you originally Viennese?" Onoma asked. "Your name sounds more Slavic than Austrian."

"Actually, my grandparents are from the Sudetenland, so you could say I'm a little bit Czech, German and Austrian," he said.

"Can you talk the talk?" Onoma inquired, entertaining the notion of conversing with him in her native tongue.

We all stared and waited for an answer. It wasn't as if she was trying to hit on Karel; his girlfriend was sitting right next to him.

"I can get by," he modestly replied. This triggered a fluid conversation in Czech. At least that's what we thought we heard.

Britte and Liselott began chattering in Swedish, which left Silke and me with quizzical facial expressions. I felt like a green banana when it came to speaking German, and Silke wasn't much better in English.

Salvation came when Herr Boss arrived with our meals, interrupting the language debacle. "Mmm...That smells delicious," is how I interpreted everyone's expression. My hunter's schnitzel looked scrumptious: two slices of veal drenched in a chunky mushroom sauce accompanied by a house salad and homemade noodles called Spätzle.

"Bring another round of beers for myself and the traveling girls," Karel requested. "Oh, and Herr Boss..." he gestured as if he'd forgotten something, "Could you also pour me a soda for my friend here? Danke."

Uh oh, it was his girlfriend he had forgotten. We gave a hearty thank you to our admirer, much to the chagrin of Silke.

After finishing our yummy meals, we indulged in a round of short stories from our lives back home. Liselott began:

"Britte and I grew up in a small town in southern Sweden called Jön-köping. We've known each other since we were 3 years old, when in the mid-'80s our parents started an ABBA cover band: The Dancing Queens. The band was a local success, playing the country circuit on weekends. That is...until a very cold Saturday in November when they played to a sell-out crowd at Fernando's, the biggest club in town. The first two songs went smoothly. By the third song, their groove intensified and they belted out 'Mamma Mia,' bringing the crowd to its feet. That's when my father tripped over a power cord and fell off the stage and into the arms of a beautiful blonde in the front row. My father had the sympathy of the others in the band until it became apparent he was in no hurry to leave the comforting arms of the blonde. That's when my mother burst into tears. Backstage, our parents decided that life in a rock band was too demanding and from then on they'd spend their weekends raising sheep at their country homes. Even though we miss the old ABBA days, we really enjoy being with our parents and playing with the animals on their now very large and profitable farms they've created."

With the delighted look of a child being tucked into bed anticipating a story, Liselott rotated to Onoma and asked: "What do you miss about home?"

"My grandparents!" Onoma gushed before taking a sip of beer and positioning herself better to face us. "They're getting a bit older now, so I worry about them. They live in a two-story farmhouse in the Bohemian countryside with their rat-catching cat, Hanka. The estate dates from the 1700s and it needs regular assistance to keep the rodents at a minimum, the perfect job for Hanka. She's a bubbly creature that wanders the property licking the faces of the baby lambs and torments the cows by jumping on their backs and playing cowboy cat. About twice a week, during the early hours of the morning, Hanka will come to the bedroom window and scratch her paws against the glass, waking Grandpa and Grandma. Grandpa usually rolls over and insists: 'It's your turn to comfort the cat, Dear.' Grandma then gets out of bed, walks over to the window and affectionately says: 'Ahh, good cat...you caught a rat. Now you go run off and play, my darling.' Hanka leaves to play with her new toy and dear old Grandma and Grandpa go back to sleep."

"Cute story," Liselott chirped. Then the girls focused their attention on me. "It's your turn, Sydney."

"Well... I grew up in America with my brother, Alex, and two entertaining parents, Dolores and Sid. One summer about 10 years ago we took a family trip down to the southern states in our station wagon. It was getting late one evening in Alabama, so we decided to start looking for a motel. We got lucky and found a decent place for the night. Dad and I were first to take showers and slip into our pajamas. Alex then took his shower and spoiled the ambiance by making loud armpit farts instead of singing like most normal people do. Mother, on the other hand, as finicky as she is, decided to lift up the mattress and do a thorough inspection for cleanliness. She found a single dead bug, not a big deal, but to the finicky that's all it takes...and in one breath she roared: 'Pack up your things, we are leaving this minute!'

"'But we're in our PJs, and the room's paid for,' Dad said.

"'Sid...' Mom snapped in a huff, 'I don't care. I'll get our money back!'

"We kids could only sit and watch the antics unfold before our eyes.

"As we packed up our things, Mom marched straight into the motel office, which was adjacent to the motel's restaurant. Boy, was the manager in for a surprise. Mom elbowed the door open, stomped up to the desk and demanded our money back. 'Our room is infested with bugs crawling all over the beds and walls!'

"The manager nervously browsed around to see if any of the restaurant patrons had noticed the agitated woman. He gathered his composure and responded professionally. 'Madam, we pride ourselves in having a hygienic property... There must be some mistake. Besides, you've been in the room now for over 45 minutes.'

"Mother wanted our cash, and she wanted it no matter what. So, in a loud to screeching tone, she howled: 'We are not sleeping with your wretched insects, and we demand a refund NOW!'

"Mother's temple veins were throbbing. The manager saw this lady in front of him mutating through every color of the spectrum before the final phase, fiery red. His restaurant guests couldn't help but also notice, peering with the utmost curiosity. The manager knew a long-winded battle was on the horizon, and to concede victory was in his best interests. 'Ma'am, we are sorry for the inconvenience...Here's your $63 in full.'

"Dad was tired and not happy. When Mom returned to the car, us kids were in the back and Dad sat perturbed in the passenger seat. He exclaimed, 'Dolores, I'm sleepy...and you're driving!'

"She hopped in and floored it out of the parking lot. A half hour later we still hadn't found a hotel so Mom pulled into a quiet roadside park. We got as comfortable as humanly possible, using scrunched-up sweaters for pillows and towels for blankets. Suddenly we heard a gang of bikers motor in. Varoom. Varoom. Both Mom and Dad jumped in fright. 'We're outta here!'

"Once again we were on the road heading east. Soon we heard a repetitive clunking sound. 'What is that?' my jittery brother asked.

"'Oh no...' said our panic-stricken driver. 'I think we are on a bridge.'

"At that moment, we learned our mother was deathly afraid of long bridges over water, especially at night. Dad told Mom not to worry. 'Just keep driving straight!' A few uneasy miles later, we reached the other side...Florida.

"The time was approaching midnight and we agreed that anywhere on the side of the road to sleep would be wonderful. For the third time that evening, we got comfy in our sleeping positions. Dad and Alex were a little warm, so they cracked the windows for air. It was in everyone's best interests since they'd eaten bean burritos for dinner. Morning came and we woke to uncontrollable itching.

"We pulled into the first gas station to fill up. The attendant noticed our scratching. 'Looks like you've been bitten by the Noseeum.'

"'The what?' we asked.

"'In Florida we call them the 'No see 'um' bug...because you can't see 'um. But don't worry, we sell a powder here that'll fix y'all up in a jiffy!'

"The end."

The girls chuckled. "True story?"

"Every word!" I then offered a suggestion. "How about we finish our drinks and head into town?"

"As we say in Sweden," Britte said, "Sköl!"

"Our drinking theme girls: Eins, zwei, drei…..."

With frothy smiles we waved Herr Boss over so we could pay compliments to the chef and settle the bill. Karel made a proposal while Silke kept a watchful eye. "We're driving into the Old Town, if you girls would like a ride."

"Sure...if it's no problem," we innocently responded while trying not to look at Silke, knowing she was probably burning voodoo holes through us.

She seemed a pleasant girl, and there's absolutely no need for her to be jealous — unless she has reasons from the past. If that were the case, maybe she should feed Karel to Hanka, the rat-catching cat. Nonetheless, that's their deal and we weren't going to turn down a free ride into town.

Ten minutes later we turned onto Salzburg's old cobbled streets and were soon at the bar's front door. The girls and I bid farewell to Silke and Karel and entered Dos Dudes arm in arm. I felt as though we had been friends for years.

Once inside, it had the feel of a cantina from Mexico's past. The walls were a painted hodgepodge of Aztec symbols and little sombrero dudes resting against cacti.

"Andelé...andelé, arriba...arriba," I mumbled.

Liselott eyeballed me strangely.

When four girls walk into a bar unescorted, eyes will follow.

We went straight to the bar for a glass of white wine. With chardonnay in hand, we browsed the scene. A pair of musicians stood on a modest stage, one playing guitar and the other a hand-held accordion. They were performing the "Tequila" song, whipping everyone into a whirlwind as we danced our way past.

Up a few steps and farther back amidst the buoyant atmosphere, we saw an unattended table. Upon sitting down, four guys from our hostel came over to join us. Two were from Australia, and the other two were from Canada.

The waiter interrupted our salutations by delivering eight shots of flaming sambuca to the table.

The guys clearly had premeditated our meeting, and although I'm sure it was a ploy to get into our pants, free drinks on my already stretched euro budget were welcome. Besides, sometimes it's entertaining to take advantage of the male weaknesses.

The guys raised their sambuca up high and made a toast to new acquaintances.

The idea of flaming sambuca is to kill the flame and drink the sambuca. You do this by placing the palm of your hand over the shot glass, which kills the oxygen and extinguishes the flame. As a result, the glass will affix to your palm, like a leech to skin. Remove the glass and consume your heated beverage. Sounds simple, right?

Sure, until it was my turn to try it. As soon as I released my sautéed hand from the top of the shot glass, the sambuca spilled — spreading the flame with it. Panicked, I accidentally knocked the glass to the floor, where it smashed and created a mini firestorm. Luckily, the bar crew scurried over to help stomp out my little mishap.

Embarrassed, I began apologizing to our group. "I'm sorry, but... Hey, where did everyone go?"

At some point while the barkeeps mopped the floor and I picked glass bits out of my shoe, our group had shifted to the dance floor. So, I joined in the fun. With modest room to rumba, we all jumped and bumped into each other with little care.

During the next song, "Do You Love Me," the girls and I danced amongst ourselves. Not overly dirty, but apparently it was spicy enough to excite the guys, who were wiggling, jiggling and wriggling like gigantic sperm waiting for an opportunity to penetrate the egg.

This was curiously interrupted when we saw Karel enter the bar — without Silke. Britte, Liselott, and I swiftly rotated to Onoma.

"I had nothing to do with this!" she protested.

Onoma was somewhat annoyed that we appeared to have even considered such a thought. Feelings aside, she played the amicable hostess and walked over to say hi. The rest of us continued dancing, but our harmonious octet dwindled into an offbeat party of five. Liselott had interlocked with Dazza, one of the Australians. His hands glided up and down her body as their tongues did the tango. Without delay, Dazza's friends felt this was their cue to move in and mimic the action. Britte and I pried their hands from our buttocks.

Not that I am totally against extra fun once in awhile, but it was still possible that Jesse might show, which kept me from exploring other options. Britte also seemed disinterested, so we decided to take a break from the hormone overload and retreat to our table.

Britte signaled the waiter. At the same moment two guys sat down and made themselves comfy. "Ciao, yu girls a free?"

Luckily, the waiter arrived within nanoseconds. "Vhat kan I get you?"

"Two white wines, please," I answered.

"We a paya for yu girls," one of the guys said. "It's a no problema."

"Where do you come from?" Britte asked.

"Yu girls bella, beutiful." They each lit a cigarette. "Yua want smoke, I can giva yu?"

"No thank you." This time I asked the question. "Where do you come from?"

"We cuma from Italia, yua no thata place?"

"Oh, yes, of course..." Britte said, "I went last year to Rimini with my girlfriend, now my 'ex,' for a beach holiday. Nothing but sea, sand, and sex!"

"Oh si, si, yua meet lots Italian man."

"No man," Britte explained, "I went with my girlfriend!"

"Oh capito, si... yu and other girl make it weth Italian boy."

"Hier you ladiez are, two vhite vines." The waiter, thank goodness, had returned. "Zhat vill be zix euro, pleaz."

One of the guys reached for his wallet. "Rememba, we paya for yu beutiful girls." He handed the waiter a note. "Here, keepa the changa."

"Schönen Dank," said the appreciative waiter.

Meanwhile, Britte reached over and began stroking my hand. "This sensual woman is my current, monogamous partner."

Despite Britte's anti-male strokes, they persisted like animals. Her lesbian ploy had encouraged their arousal. It was like watching two male dogs drooling over prime rump roasts.

"Yu girls cuma weth us, we showa yu how real man maka luv...Italian-style."

If these guys would stop staring down our tops and listen, they might get the hint that we're not interested. Moreover, they look like the type of slime balls who try it on with every girl they meet. It was about time we put an end to this melee.

"Listen up!" I said. "We're not interested in having relations with you now, later, or ever...so put it back in your pants and save it for someone who's desperate enough to fall for your cheap talk." On that final note, we snatched our wine and waved arrivederci. I hated being so mean but they deserved it.

A woman's right to choose is a beautiful thing!

Still trying, the guys expressed their amore. "No ragazze, stai, stai, we luva yu!"

Before losing ourselves in the crowd, we turned to see the guys standing awkwardly. It was more than obvious that our charade had made them rise to the occasion.

On the other side of the dance floor, we mocked our wannabe lovers. "Oh baby, I giva yu spaghetti and vino, now we maka luv."

"Si, si, I showa you my pasta, you showa me yours."

It was time for another toast, this time to European travels as a theme:

"Here's to meeting different peoples;
Castles, cobblestones, and steeples.
Let's drink our white wine,
To escaping the swine!"

One drink and a few dances later landed us at 3 a.m. − time to call it a night. Britte went to retrieve Liselott, and I strayed in the direction of the front door to see how Onoma was doing. Sliding through the crowd, I arrived just in time to observe her reaching back with an open hand and slapping it forward. *Whack!* It was a sure bet that someone was ready to leave. She must have seen me approaching, because she rushed over immediately.

"Is everything okay?" I asked, grabbing both her jittery arms and looking her straight in the eyes.

"I'm fine!" Onoma insisted. However, she appeared rattled and her face glowed cherry red.

Translation of incident: Karel was giving her the sad story about how he and his girlfriend got into a fight, which brought him back to the bar for a cheerup. Onoma, being her polite self, tried to console him, but I could see in her eyes that she knew his game. He tried pulling a fast one by putting his lips on hers and that's when she gave him a complimentary outline of her hand across his face.

"Are the girls ready to go?" Onoma questioned.

Britte then walked up, followed by Liselott and Dazza.

I asked Liselott the question I'm sure we were all thinking: "Are you coming with us, or staying?"

"A foursome," she briskly responded, "is better than a threesome!"

"But..." Dazza reasoned, "...I thought we made a pretty good two-some." That was the smartest thing he could have said in his plea to sequester her.

"Maybe tomorrow night you'll get lucky?" Liselott proposed.

"What does that mean?" Dazza asked as he casually leaned against the doorway portraying the bad-boy image with his knotty hair, sweat-drenched T-shirt, and lipstick-smeared face while cocking his head and lighting a cigarette.

"Be here and find out!" Liselott replied.

Arm in arm, like our entrance hours earlier, we exited Dos Dudes. Onoma was bothered by her previous actions and began to apologize...

Britte instantly cut her off. "You need not explain a thing, we've all had bad experiences with the opposite sex."

Back at the hostel, we stripped from our smoke-rich clothing and snuggled deep into our beds. Dialogue soon petered to a soft snore as we drifted off to sleep.

Good night, Salzburg.

CHAPTER 5

Five weeks later, beginning of May

Jesse had been conducting some investigations of his own, as I found out when he excitedly burst into my room and explained that it's possible the crucifix was dug up right here beneath the Chiemsee resort. He said he'd been speaking with some older locals who had worked on the original construction of the Lake Hotel and admitted unearthing a golden crucifix. They weren't sure what happened to it after that as the on-site foreman, who was a high-ranking Nazi official, immediately spirited the cross away. What's more, each individual Jesse interviewed hinted that the hotel's cellar might hold a clue.

Upon hearing this, I grabbed my coat and we dashed out of the Waldheim for the Lake Hotel. At the reception desk, Jesse signed for a special key and grabbed two flashlights.

* * *

After a few hours of sleuthing, we were cotton-mouthed from the cellar's musty air. Lucky for us, it was karaoke night in the resort's bar! We rushed back to our rooms to change out of our cellar clothes and then joined our colleagues, who were already in the bar hoisting brews and murdering popular tunes.

These karaoke nights are often alluring, if not addicting. The locals come from neighboring villages to stimulate their voices and have a friendly drink with hotel guests and staff. Shyness is checked at the door and everybody sings a song. Some imitate Bon Jovi, others Elvis. The Bavarians especially love getting up on stage and losing themselves in Jimmy Buffett's "Margaritaville." By night's end there is always one extrovert who is half a drink from passing out and dabbles in the subtlety of Iron Maiden's "Run for the Hills."

Last drinks are called at 11:30 and the bar shuts at midnight, when sensible employees head back to their quarters. The unsensible migrate to a designated party room and continue the assault on their livers. On this particular evening in early May, I joined the glut. The designated party room belonged to Steve, 504 in the Annex, where about 20 of us diehards partied until dawn.

At 8:30 a.m., not exactly feeling chipper, I rolled out of bed and gingerly made my way to the Lake Hotel for work, almost certainly resembling a red-eyed zombie from a horror movie. I was supposed to have the day off but elected to fill in for someone who fleetingly decided on a trip to Berlin. I couldn't decline her karaoke wish.

After clocking in, I reported to Roger, the executive housekeeper. He handed me my work assignment, which consisted of nine checkouts and five stayovers on the ground floor of the Lake Hotel.

Upon arriving at my workstation, I was met by a very hearty "Gooood morning!" It was my roommate, Janie. She had gotten an early night's sleep.

I tried to equal her enthusiasm as best I could, "Mornin'."

"Have you seen Chad or Holly around?" Janie asked of our housekeeping colleagues.

"No, sorry I haven't. But I did see them last night partaking in karaoke festivities." They were in full swing mimicking John Travolta and Olivia Newton-John in a mesmerizing rendition of "Summer Nights." On stage they looked so cute together dancing, singing, and staring into each other's eyes. Maybe they finally got together like we'd all been hoping for, which would explain their tardiness.

Janie and I pulled our cleaning carts from the utility closet, arranged a time to meet for lunch, and went our separate ways down the hall.

The first room I had to clean was a stay-over. This entails transferal of trash, replacing towels and a general clean as necessary, which usually takes 15 minutes.

Operation Sanitize, as I call it for the lack of a better term, always begins at the door. ~ Knock ~ Knock ~ "Housekeeping," I announced.

There was no answer, so I said it again a tone louder: "HOUSE-KEEPING!" Still, no answer. Using the master key, I proceeded into the room. Inside I saw a half-naked guy passed out on the bed. In my professional work voice I offered, "Do you need any cleaning done in your room today, Sir?"

With sleep packed around his eyes and a string of drool connecting the corner of his mouth to the pillow, he raised his head with great difficulty and articulated: "No, I'm fi.." His head crashed back onto the pillow before he could finish. I recognized him from karaoke; Iron Maiden wasn't his best selection.

This first-rate example of employee-to-guest dedication gave me an extra 14 minutes for lunch. With the next room, a checkout, I should have parked my senses at the door. Upon entering, the smell of sex reached out and slapped me in the face. The former occupants undeniably got their money's worth — strewn everywhere were towels, sheets and condom packets. Instantly, I bolted to the window for fresh air.

Tucked in the corner of the room adjacent to the bed, partially hidden by an overhanging blanket, sat a black overnight bag. I was curious as to what was inside. On my way to open it, I stepped on something. *Squish!*

"Eeeeeeew...YUCK," I screeched until my lungs emptied, "That is so revolting!" I trampled the reservoir tip of a prophylactic with my sandal, pushing its contents out the other end.

I had to calm myself with pleasant thoughts. *Relax, I'm in Germany; I can readily travel on days off, tour medieval castles, shop European fashion, indulge on authentic schnitzel and strudel and chocolate-covered sweets.* Progressively, my plan worked, I picked up the rubber item with a towel and I didn't vomit.

Back to being a curious housekeeper, I lifted the blanket off the overnight bag and carefully pulled its zipper open.

"Yoowhza!" I exhaled as my eyes nearly popped out. It was a porno star's dream: a vibrator, whip, handcuffs, creams, edible undies, and assorted jellies. No wonder this place looked like Larry Flint threw a party here. I zipped up the bag and let it be. Its destiny was to grace the halls of Lost and Found. After that was anyone's guess.

In desperate need of a break, I plopped myself on the front corner of the bed and began lazily flipping television channels hoping for something other than music videos. I wasn't yet game for a repetitive beat.

One of the American Forces Network channels was showing "Gilligan's Island." On another was Oprah interviewing successful authors from her book club. FOX News had John Gibson and his legal-eagle sidekick Judge Napolitano discussing the ins-and-outs of the latest corporate fraud trial.

---------- *News Flash:* "A virus called 'You're Screwed' has just struck computers worldwide, causing billions of dollars in damage." ~ *click* ~ *click* ~ *click* ~

On a German channel I found an episode of the "Bold and the Beautiful." It seemed the logical choice to ease my hangover by focusing on how the rich playboy's housekeeper deep cleaned his bathroom.

~ *Knock* ~ *Knock* ~ Someone lightly tapped at the door. Quickly I jumped from the bed, turned off the television and pretended to dust. "Come in," I said, pivoting to see who it was.

A brunette in her mid-forties with schoolteacher looks entered. "Hello, I'm sorry to bother you" she said in a soft, pleasant voice, "...but I believe I left my overnight bag behind. By any chance have you seen it?"

Boy, had I ever!

"I did notice a bag in the corner," I answered politely, pointing in the direction of her treasure trove.

"Oh, thank you. I'd be lost without it." She pulled out a $5 bill from her purse and handed it to me. "Thanks again...and I'm sorry if the room was a bit of a mess." Offering an innocent smile, she turned and exited the room.

Well, I guess stranger things have happened. It was time to take a break and visit Janie to fill her in on the latest.

I found her sitting on a couch bawling her eyes out. "What's wrong?" I asked, rushing over to comfort her with a hug.

"My fiancé, Johnny, called. He said he'd been with another girl, and that our relationship...was over!" Tears cascaded down her face; she broke from my clutch and wept hysterically. "How could he do this to me? We've been together for three years and were planning on getting married and having children. This has got to be a mistake! I have to go back home and sort things out...I have to go immediately!"

"I am so sorry, Janie." I handed her a tissue before pulling her back into my arms. There wasn't much I could say to make her feel better; she was just too distraught. We've all been through it sometime or another, and the only cure is time.

However, to tell her that wouldn't have made any sense. I'm sure her mind was clouded by thoughts of desperation and anxiety. Most importantly, she needed a consoling shoulder to lean on.

One thing was for certain: I had to get that crazy idea of going home out of her head. Maybe it's easy for me to say, but if that jerk loved her as much as she said he did, she wouldn't have this problem! This sounds like a job for Hanka, the rat-catching cat. There are plenty of good men out there who would love to treat this pretty lady with respect.

"How about if we take our lunch break early and go outside for some fresh air?" I asked.

"Ookaay," she sadly replied.

We walked outside and took a seat on one of the benches facing the lake. I brought my sack lunch containing two quickly thrown-together peanut-butter-and-jelly sandwiches. Knowing she had to eat, I offered her a PB and J.

"No thanks, I'm not hungry." She seemed to be recovering.

"You've got to eat something," I insisted with my hand extended as though it were a silver platter, "even if it's a nibble."

She reluctantly accepted.

"I've got an idea that will help get your mind off things. In a few days I'm meeting up with two really fun girls I met five weeks ago in Salzburg. They told me about this health-spa town in the Black Forest called Baden-Baden, which is famous for its bathing palaces. Why don't you come along?"

"Oh, I don't know. It sounds nice..."

I interrupted her, realizing this was going to take some doing. "Just imagine Roman baths and saunas. Live the life of an empress for a few hours. Spoil yourself, Janie, you're allowed to once in a while, you know. Furthermore, it's near the Rhine River, which is the border between Germany and France." I just about had her convinced. She needed only a dash more pretty persuasion. "Come on, Janie, you're far better than that creep back home! You can't just mope around and watch the world go by, at least not in my presence you won't!"

"Maybe you're right, but..."

"But nothing!" I was starting to sound like my father. "We only live once, and you're coming along. I'll tell the girls our schedule and have them meet us at the train station."

I know I was rough on her, but no doubt she needed it.

"Sydney, you make me laugh when you deliver speeches that turn your face blue. How could I say no?" She shrugged, regaining her senses. "I'll talk to Roger or somebody and make sure I get the time off. After all...I think I'm suffering a midlife crisis."

"Hi girls! Beautiful day, isn't it?" Jesse appeared, hands tucked into his jeans pockets.

"Hi!" I countered, pleasantly surprised. "Sure is, it'd be an injustice to stay indoors. No tour today, Mister Guide?"

"It was cancelled, so I'm in the gift shop helping guests. So...anything new goin' on, any gossip, trips planned?"

"Matter of fact, yes!" He had no idea how perfect a question that was. "Janie and I are taking the train to Baden-Baden on Saturday for a girls' weekend away."

"Oh...you ladies will love it!" Jesse's face lit up. "It'll be a time to relax and forget about the world for awhile, a real bare-all experience."

"We're so looking forward to it," I replied. "How about you; anything new?"

"Funny you ask, I've just started the biggest undertaking in my life... and you're partly my inspiration."

"What!?" I exclaimed, genuinely shocked.

"It was your enthusiasm for traveling Europe that flipped the pages in my mind to the many unforgettable stories I hear from our guests and their journeys, and that's when it clicked! I decided to write a travel-adventure book."

"Sounds great! I wish you mountains of success."

"Thanks! But the downside of this grand plan is my social life will be nonexistent since I'll be chained to the computer. My girlfriend will freak when she finds out that we're locked in my room for other reasons than the usual."

"She'll get over it," I painlessly tendered. "Do you think I'll get a mention in the book?"

"It would be my pleasure, Ms. Sydney Endicott, Queen of Serendipity. And it wouldn't be complete without a mention of your attractive and witty roommate." Mister-Tour-Guide-Turned-Author pivoted to face the blushful girl at my side. "What do you think, Janie... Do I have your blessing?"

"Why of course, Jesse, of course," she replied, adoringly. I couldn't have paid him enough for that comment. She definitely needed some outside help in the cheering-up department.

Jesse saucered his head back to me. "I wanted to tell you... my best friend, Reuben McJiggy, from Cali is flying in next month for about a week and I'm taking him to Berchtesgaden for a visit. Would you like to come along?"

"I'd love to! Just let me know when." No doubt I wanted to see Berchtesgaden, but this would also be an opportunity to get to know Jesse better as well as to track down the crucifix.

"Great! I was hoping you'd join us. Besides, I think you'll find him on the cute side."

"We'll see about that."

"Gotta get back to the grindstone. See ya girls later, ciao."

"See you later, Jesse, don't work too hard," Janie responded, as her new favorite man sped off. "You know, Sydney," Janie wore a slight grin, "...he seems like a really neat guy."

"I know."

It was time we got back to work. One thing for sure, my head was no longer hurting from last night — only eager for the days ahead. Back in the porno room, I flipped the TV on to music videos for a little maid-groovin' pick up. Then it occurred to me, I never did tell Janie about my encounter with the loose brunette and her bag of tricks. Oh well, I'll save that story for a rainy day.

After work, I searched for Janie everywhere around the hotel with no luck. Eventually, I found her on the hallway phone in the Waldheim trying to work things out with her cheatin' fiancé.

Their conversation was about as mind-numbing as any one of the lectures given by my anal-retentive psychology professor. "Yeah, yeah, yeah...blah, blah, blah."

I'm sure The Cheater gave her the usual pathetic jargon: "Baby, it's not you, it's me." Followed by: "It's just that I'm here alone without you and it's making me do silly things."

Oh, PUH-LEASE! That crap's been around since the Bronze Age. It's only a ploy to keep a girl baited on the hook while the male casts his rod elsewhere. There's no good excuse; but most every male will try.

If it sounds like I'm male bashing, I'm sorry. But we do want her to be treated well, right guys? As for you girls out there, I already know what you think.

Janie's hallway banter was becoming quite the spectacle as she broadcasted her love mush with several Waldheimers in attendance. "I wuv you too, Schnooky Bear, and I'll wait for as long as you want me to. 'Bye, love you... 'Bye."

It wasn't until she hung up the phone that she noticed me. "Oh, hi! Guess you just heard: My boyfriend and I are back together. Isn't that great?!"

"I'm happy if you're happy." I replied with a pathetically fake smile. How could I tell her that she was making a big mistake? I decided to keep quiet, recognizing her love was blind. If I were to intervene, she would only end up hating me.

As we traipsed over the vomit-green carpet to our room, Janie glowingly added: "I knew it wasn't him speaking earlier... Now it's the real Johnny talking, and he wants me back! I'm sorry, but it's probably not a good idea that I go with you girls to Baden-Baden this weekend. I mean, what if he tries to call me and I'm not around?"

What is she saying? I think we would all agree that Janie should let Schnooky Bear stew in his own juice for a while. Anyway, I had to act swiftly before I lost her.

"You can't back out now, I've already contacted the girls and made the arrangements."

"Well..."

"Come on, Janie! How can you pass up a couple of fun, harmless days away?" I said with a devilish grin, having less innocent plans for her.

"Maybe you're right; what's it gonna hurt? I'll call Johnny back and tell him that I'm going away for two days. Do you have the number where we'll be staying in case he needs to contact me for some reason?"

"Sorry, I don't. The girls are making all the arrangements and I was lucky to catch them after lunch when I called, as they were just heading out the door. I only notified them of our arrival time on Saturday so they could meet us at the train station."

Janie was hesitant to respond. "I guess I'll just have to call him after we check into our room."

"Okay, it's settled then; you're going! Trust me, you won't regret a thing." I motioned towards the door. "I'm heading out for some fresh air; I'll see you a bit later on."

I was really off to the Lake Hotel to e-mail Britte and Liselott because I hadn't actually contacted them about any of this. Real sly of me I know, but I wanted to make 100 percent sure Janie was coming. Everything else was genuine. The girls were headed to Baden-Baden, and they did ask me to join them for a final farewell before flying back to Sweden. Besides, this was the perfect excuse to hit the road again. My last outing was so fantastic that I want nothing to change. It was time to summon the girls.

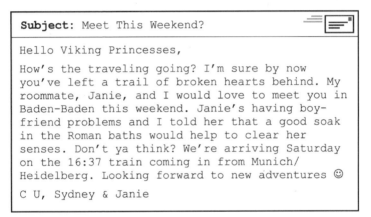

Subject: Meet This Weekend?

Hello Viking Princesses,

How's the traveling going? I'm sure by now you've left a trail of broken hearts behind. My roommate, Janie, and I would love to meet you in Baden-Baden this weekend. Janie's having boy-friend problems and I told her that a good soak in the Roman baths would help to clear her senses. Don't ya think? We're arriving Saturday on the 16:37 train coming in from Munich/Heidelberg. Looking forward to new adventures ☺

C U, Sydney & Janie

Work on Friday dragged by, because I could only think about the weekend. That night, Janie and I packed our bags and went to sleep early. On Saturday morning, Kevin, our neighbor, was nice enough to give us a ride to the train station.

The first stretch from Chiemsee to Munich took an hour. Our next connection was to depart some 40 minutes later. We spent our time on the upper level of Munich's main station getting a quick fix at Burger King and spying the guys below who were en route to their respective trains.

We got a few receptive looks, but most were too focused on keeping to a schedule to notice us. However, one guy was nothing but smiles and walked straight into a post. Talk about hilarious. Another guy, who we believe was related to heartthrob Orlando Bloom, caught our attention by wildly waving his arms as if he were stranded on an island and we were his rescuers. He jumped onto the escalator and began making his way up to us, but at that very moment Janie noticed the time: "Oh my gawd...Our train leaves in one minute!"

Over to the escalator and down we raced, unintentionally striking those before us with our backpacks. "Excuse us... Pardon me... Sorry!"

Like two hysterical mental patients on the loose, we darted around searching for the correct platform. Some sixty seconds later we found the right track but our train was in the process of pulling away. The conductor must have noticed our desperate expressions, because he held the doors open giving us a fighting chance to make an Olympic hurdle on board. I motioned for Janie to attempt the first door while I charged on to the second. With a running leap, Janie landed for a perfect 10.

I, on the other hand, was not as graceful. My legs collapsed like a house of cards somersaulting me into the door opposite. I got up immediately and brushed myself off to act as if nothing had happened, precisely when the conductor waltzed over. "Ticket pleaz." He was trying hard to keep a straight face.

After regaining my composure, Janie and I settled into second-class seating. Several stops, a change of trains, and five hours later we approached Baden-Baden. Janie had made the right decision to come along. It was written all over her face in a Shirley Temple kind of way as she peered out the windows. To our left, quaint towns were pressed into valleys, trees were bursting with the colors of spring, and the green rolling hills flowed into one another like the perfect, rhythmic heartbeat on a cardiograph score. To our right were the flatlands that lay before the Rhine River, and according to my map, the opposite bank was the Alsace region of France.

"France, Sydney...France!" Janie exclaimed. She grabbed me with both hands and gave me a spirited shake. That was enough; the weekend had already been worth it.

The train rolled into the leafy town of Baden-Baden. I shouted from the window as my Salzburg acquaintances were the first people I saw. "Liselott, Britte...HELLO!"

Their faces were beaming as they came running to the train door. I gave them both a hug and a Euro kiss, pecking each cheek lightly. Another round of greetings followed when I introduced my traveling companion.

The Swedes suggested our next move. "How about if we jump on the bus and head over to our room so you can drop off your packs and clean up? We reserved a four-bed dorm in a youth hostel, is that okay?"

"Excellent," I said. "We're ready when you are." Slinging the backpacks over our shoulders, we boarded the #201 bus into town.

The ride took about 10 minutes. We exited and the girls led us up a steep hill, which leveled off to a sizeable parking lot and the Werner-Dietz youth hostel. Inside was a generous seating area and the reception desk. Liselott recommended we pay for our two nights while the desk attendant was available and there was no line. Moreover, it would be nice to know how much money I'd have left over to splurge.

The desk attendant asked to see our HI cards.

"Our what?" Janie and I retorted.

Britte told us it was cheaper if we had a Hostelling International card. She obviously knew by our response that we weren't members, so she advised we make the investment.

"What if I don't want to pay extra to be a member?" Janie asked.

"You will still pay extra," courteously answered the desk attendant, "...but get nothing in return. If you foresee yourself hostelling around

Europe in the near future, then it's best to begin building up your temporary membership."

"Why didn't I have to pay extra at the hostel in Salzburg?" I asked, now baffled.

"It wasn't an HI hostel," Liselott replied.

"How about warm-water tokens," I inquired, "...is there an extra charge for those?" Britte and Liselott cracked up laughing at my earnest query.

The desk attendant looked at me blankly.

"They're not necessary here," Britte stated.

More puzzled than ever, I thought I'd speed up this hubbub. "Okay... Sell me temporary membership. I'd be delighted to join the world's tokenless, mobile crowd."

The desk attendant helped us fill in our membership cards. We then skipped upstairs to our room and threw down our gear. It looked comfortable and clean and had six beds — this extra space was probably a bonus for new members.

We proficiently made our beds with the sheets provided knowing that when we arrived back at late o'clock, we'd be too tired. Britte and Liselott were a change away from hitting town. Janie and I decided on showers.

This time hot water was as abundant as if our location resided in the middle of a geothermal reservoir. Afterward, Janie and I tried our best to match the Swedes stitch for stitch in tasteful evening attire.

Europeans seem to have their own modish dress style: understated tones, big shoes, excess denim, unkempt hair, little makeup, and elegant scarves. That's not to say Janie and I weren't fashionable, just more likely to throw on a pair of jeans and a T-shirt. Either way is vogue. The most significant thing I've learned since arriving in Europe is that it isn't about what you wear, but how you conduct yourself as a representative of your country in a foreign land.

*   *   *

After a deliciously filling geraucht Forelle — or smoked trout — dinner and an apple strudel for dessert, we decided to walk it off with a stroll around town. It was a balmy spring evening, temperate enough for a long-sleeved blouse and a knee-length skirt to show off my legs. Confidence is what makes a person, and no doubt we looked confident.

The city was waking to the season like a bear shaking off winter. Baden-Baden had all the telltale signs of a coming summer. Restaurants and cafés spilled onto the sidewalks, bringing the city and townsfolk out of hibernation. On every corner a vendor sold ice cream. Yet, it was a cheery bar just off the main pedestrian esplanade that pulled us in like a magnet. Feeling the moment, we ordered two bottles of white wine, specifically a German Riesling.

"So, Sydney, do you have a little rhyme for wine?" Liselott requested.

"Hmm...Let's see.

> We raise our glasses of this wine,
> Handpicked from vineyards of the Rhine.

> To an adventure bold and new,
> For this my friends I say... Thank you.
> So drink this drink with words of pleasure,
> One who finds a friend finds a treasure!"

The wine emptied promptly, compensating us with jovial feelings and a desire to wander. Arms interlocked, we chirped along our moonlit path like four contented nightingales on a springtime branch. "I think we've just found what we're looking for," tweeted Fledgling #1.

A transparent structure made largely of glass resembling an urban greenhouse advertised "*DISCO*" tonight. At the front door stood two buffoons trying to look smart in their posh suits.

"Hallelujah...Let's flap on in," peeped Frisky Chick #2.

"Sorry," said one of the buffoons, surprisingly in English. "It'll be an hour wait!"

"An hour wait!" squawked Hatchling #3. "But why?"

"Don't question our authority; you're just going to have to wait like all the rest," answered the other buffoon.

There was nobody behind us. "These guys are morons," Chickadee #4 couldn't resist, "...let's get the flock outta here!"

A bit farther down the road we came upon what appeared to be a colonial mansion; spotlights illuminated eight lofty pillars supporting the classy facade. In the foreground, a garden of flowers embraced a neatly trimmed lawn saturated with dewdrops that glistened beneath the full moon.

So far we only knew Baden-Baden externally; now it was time to peer inside for a closer look. We strolled through the mansion's main entrance and saw a broad staircase covered with emerald-green carpet, a gray-marble floor, a fine restaurant and ... a casino?

The hostess told us the building was called the Kurhaus, and indeed it was a casino. But nothing comparable to those in Vegas; this one was quite different. It happened to be the oldest and largest casino in Europe and was once dubbed by Marlene Dietrich as the most beautiful in the world.

We craved a peek inside. When I began to inquire whether it was okay, the hostess jumped in front of a man seeking to enter. We learned then that it was compulsory for men to wear a jacket and tie. She referred him to reception where he could rent the combo. I eagerly asked whether we could enter; without pausing she waved us through. Inside were sparkling chandeliers, walls draped in red velvet, and plenty of gold; it reminded me of a château I'd seen on the Travel Channel.

"How about a quick spin on the roulette wheel?" I asked, trying to coax the girls into a little adventure. "We are ladies and they do call it luck." I don't think they were thoroughly convinced, but they were game enough to play the odds.

I inspired them to chip in 10 euros each and let it ride on lucky black. A gentleman wearing a penguin suit sent the ball whizzing around the wheel. Round and round the ball rolled, mesmerizing us into a trance. I stood paralyzed with fear.

Even though it wasn't much money, if we were to lose, it was due to my persuasion. What if it spiraled into further losses, forcing us to hitch-hike home and beg for scraps at McDonald's all because I suggested gambling? Would I have to call home and ask Mom and Dad to bail me out? What was I saying? That would be the ultimate victory for them, especially for Dad. I could hear him now: "I told you so! If you'd listened to me, you wouldn't be in this mess...now would you?!"

And what about the girls? They would be my immediate threat. Would they send me into the Rhine with cement shoes?

The ball fell from the rim, causing it to bounce several times between slots — CLICK, *clink*, CLICK, *clink*, CLICK, *clink* — until it found its place. I closed my eyes and waited to hear the reaction from the others.

"Oh, no... I can't believe it!" Liselott shouted.

A shiver snaked down my spine. I opened my eyes. The numbered slot the ball sat in was a blur, but I recognized the color — lucky black!

"Yes! Yes! Yes!" Janie screamed as though an orgasm had struck. "Eighty euros, that's almost enough to pay for our Roman baths tomorrow ... Whoopeeeeeee!"

Janie gazed at the dealer with hungry eyes. "Let it ride!"

"Janie, no!" I shrieked frantically. "Are you crazy?! What's gotten into you?" I understood her enthusiasm, but we were lucky to escape with extra cash in our pockets. "Let's not get greedy," I begged her. Britte and Liselott echoed my sentiments.

However, it was too late. The ball had already been set in motion. I could have knelt down right then and there and ripped a chunk out of the table with my teeth. After the first few revolutions I had convinced myself that this time it wasn't my doing and Janie was to have three less friends if we lost.

What happened to that sweet, innocent girl I brought with me to Baden-Baden? Had I released the addict within? This was supposed to be a weekend to put our feet up. Instead, the evil of gambling had reared its ugly head. I silently promised God that if we escaped this moment, I would never, ever, gamble again.

CLICK, *clink*, CLICK, *clink*, CLICK, *clink* — This time it was Britte and Liselott with their hands over their faces. Janie's eyes reflected giant dollar signs. The palpitations of my heart bordered on cardiac arrest as I pondered the abyss of bankruptcy.

"Black! Black!" Janie roared. "We won!"

"Thank our lucky Swedish stars," Liselott exhaled.

Janie peered at the dealer with the same hungry expressions as before the last round. I gestured to the Swedes, beckoning a kidnapping. Britte and I grabbed Janie, while Liselott stifled her arguments until she was safely outside the building with our little fortune. We then marched her back to the hostel, giggling about our "gift from Herr Kurhaus." Once in our room, we counted the money like sheep, until we became very sleepy...

*   *   *

The next morning after breakfast we headed to the bathhouse. The whole idea of our time in Baden-Baden was relaxation and, of course, getting Janie's mind off of her so-called true love. Of the two main bathhouses in town, we decided on the Roman-Irish baths at the Friedrichsbad. I had no idea what Roman-Irish baths were, but it sounded like an interesting combination. Perhaps they were bubbling hot pools, surrounded by tall green columns made of marble. Maybe even some leprechauns to sooth the aches and pains.

Above the main door, three flags flapped in the light morning breeze. Once inside the foyer, we approached the reception desk. Although they offered several packages, we opted for the works.

"We'll take your pamper package designed to spoil," I said.

"That will be the 16-step, Roman-Irish treatment with soap-and-brush massage," replied the grinning receptionist, "...which will cost 29 euro and last three and a half hours."

By her air of confidence, I got the impression her customers were never disappointed.

"That is exactly what the doctor ordered," Britte proclaimed.

"Yeah...and the doctor's three-hour order came courtesy of Herr Kurhaus," Janie responded, giggling.

After receiving our entrance cards, we climbed a staircase fit for royalty that led to the women's changing rooms. Anticipation grew, as we had no idea what to expect. At least Janie and I didn't.

Inside the changing room, I eyeballed Janie with apprehension. She triple blinked, "Uh, oh!" Women were entering the baths stripped of all their worldly possessions. We undressed hastily so as not to be nervous. I hopped in place with a foot stuck inside my jeans while Janie struggled with lifting her shirt over her head.

"Is everything okay, girls?" Liselott asked.

"Well, actually," I confessed, "I've never been to a nude bathhouse before."

"Don't stress. Everyone is naked, you'll forget about it in no time. Besides, with a body like yours, you should take pride in showing it off."

I realize nudeness is natural, but to parade around in the buff with others isn't something your typical North American is accustomed to. However, I don't know anyone here, so what reason do I have to feel self-conscious? Perhaps the answer lies within the menacing norms put in place by countless puritans and phony beauty magazines that kept me bogged down in a quagmire of bodily insecurities. I have no problem with public nudity, as long as it isn't my own.

Step 1: The Virgin Mile to the Five-Minute Soap-and-Water Shower

Gracefully, I strolled to my premiere in the world of informal bathing. Within a few paces we were met by our host, Helga, and given towels.

"Maybe it's optional nudism," Janie said as we snuggly wrapped the towels around our bodies.

"We shouldn't worry anyway..." I replied, trying to make light of a bare situation. "It's only women here."
Britte and Liselott held the towels in their hands and entered the bathing world like all the rest, naked as babies.

Steps 2, 3 & 4: Just Like Italy

I followed the girls into the next arena: the dry-heat rooms. Step 2 proposed 15 minutes of unadulterated relaxation in the warm-air room. We each grabbed a lounge chair, stretched out and suspended all conversation.

Step 3 featured a similar room, only a tad hotter. Five minutes were suggested, talking recommended — and the towel was still intact.

"Where were you before Baden-Baden?" Janie asked, directing her thoughts to the Swedes.

"Cavallino," Liselott replied.

"Cavallino?" Janie responded, curiously.

"It's a not-so-crowded beach resort that is the side door into Venice."

"Ah, Italy..." Janie announced, "I can imagine it now in this soothing heat. If the ventilators offered the aroma of rigatoni... I'd be there."

Our five minutes were up and then we briefly soaked under a cascade of hot water at step 4, the rinsing shower.

Steps 5 & 6: No More Aching Muscles

It's now time for the fifth stage of our journey and a real spoiler, the complete soap-and-brush body massage. My host, Helga the masseuse, was a thick, stocky gal — something that proved advantageous. The strength of her huge hands allowed me to envision any male from the hulk class I desired. Perhaps I could have a member of the Chippendales materialize to rescue my tender back, or my very own Hollywood hunk.

Instead, I imagined myself as Cleopatra on a visit to Julius Caesar. His Roman garrison of menservants fulfilled my every desire. A cornucopia of males wearing sheer white robes squeezed juicy droplets from succulent grapes into my mouth. Gladiators fanned me with enormous feathers as I lay on a golden lounge. If anyone were to fail my requests, they would be ordered to their knees to lick my toes and plead for leniency. "You've - been - a - bad - boy!"

"Who's been a bad boy?" Janie chirped.

Whoops! Apparently I had drifted into Fantasyland, out loud. "Ah, err... I said 'bath toy,' you know, like rubber duckies and things." I quickly changed the subject. "So...are ya glad you came this weekend?"

"I'll let you know when I'm wearing clothes again," she insisted. "Right now I really miss my swimsuit and my fiancé!"

I couldn't understand why she would miss a guy who cheated on her only days before and was probably on a repeat performance. Love sure seems to have a short memory.

The massage and subsequent rinsing shower were blissful, and over too soon. At this point, Helga pried the security towels away from Janie and me — leaving us with nothing more than our bare expressions.

"Don't worry, girls," Britte said, offering her contingency plan. "What you don't have, you don't need." It appeared to be pure nakedness from here on in.

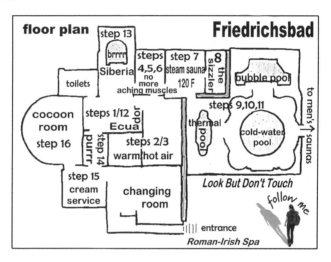

Step 7: *My First Nude Pow Wow*

...began with a 10-minute steam sauna at 120°F. It wasn't a large room per se, having a brown-tiled resting block in the middle that offered body-length, stepped tiers for varying levels of relaxation. There were already a few women basking when we arrived. One was sprawled out like a lounge lizard on the middle tier while chatting to her friend who stood proudly nearby as if she were the queen of saunas. On the top level were two French-speaking girls exposed to the maximum temperature in the upper heat zone. They looked as if they could take but a minute more of the pitiless steam. We mapped out a few brown tiles on the lowest tier and sat our cheeks down.

"Sydney, what kind of guy are you looking for?" Britte asked.

"Well, someone who is intelligent, funny, interested in traveling, and makes my heart thump."

"Sounds like someone I know," Janie claimed.

"I've had perhaps one unladylike dream about him."

"Who's this...anyone we know?" begged Britte and Liselott.

"No, just a guy we work with at Chiemsee. Wait! Actually, you have met him. His name's Jesse, the guy who came with me to the hostel in Salzburg."

"Oh, yeah," said Liselott. "The girls turned to each other and giggled. "The guy who introduced himself to our chests."

"That's the guy. Anyway, he has a girlfriend and I probably shouldn't even consider him a possibility... It's just that he's so edible, like man-candy."

Janie gave me a loopy grin. She then elected herself inspirational leader and rallied us off our behinds with a few claps of the hands. "Time to change to the hottest sauna of 'em all...five minutes at 126 degrees Fahrenheit. Come on, girls. Let's get moving, chop-chop!" Each sauna was hotter than the last, from sweltering to unbearable.

Step 8: The Sizzler! 126°F

We saw the same four women lounging in similar fashion as in the last sauna. But this time upon sitting down we felt obliged to say something, even if it was somewhat trivial. "Hot, isn't it?" Janie said, in broken German.

The French girls knew we spoke English from the previous sauna and their reply came the same. "Yes, very! Luckily our five minutes are over... We'll see you in the mineral pools." They stood up and proceeded out the door, followed by Lounge Lizard and Sauna Queen.

The condensed steam ran off our bodies in meandering rivulets. Janie held her right leg rigidly outwards, wiping collective beads of sweat off herself in long sweeping motions. I tilted my head back and rested my eyes.

"Hey, Sydney," summoned Britte, "...how's the search going for that golden cross you mentioned in Salzburg?"

"Oh, you remembered. Well, the other day Jesse and I went into our hotel's cellar. With flashlights, we illuminated numerous wall murals that were painted during the Second World War when frightened nurses, doctors, and patients gathered there to wait out the air-raid sirens. See, during the war our hotel was converted into a hospital to treat wounded German soldiers, so the basement became an air-raid shelter and make-shift infirmary." I paused briefly to change positions and wring more sweat from my limbs. The girls stared at me, patiently waiting.

"During our explorations, Jesse and I came across some amazing his-tory. In particular we found one very revealing wall mural, which showed carpenters, laborers and stonemasons building the hotel in the mid-1930s. Cleverly painted into the scene, we discovered a golden cross labeled 'das Bayernkreuz.'"

"What does that mean?" Liselott queried.

"The Bavarian Cross."

It was more than obvious that Janie was still deeply troubled by her problems with The Cheater. At times she just plain seemed out of it, more or less disoriented. This was one of those times; out of the blue she began narrating: "I have this friend, Sarah, who had been dating her boyfriend for almost two years, since they were seniors in high school. During this time she and a girlfriend of ours went to Europe for a month. Sarah missed her boyfriend tremendously, keeping in continuous contact with him by tele-phone. Even though the two girls were having the time of their lives, Sarah came home as planned at the end of the month. Meanwhile, her friend decided to stay a few extra weeks, as she had no lover to consider. When Sarah arrived home, her boyfriend wasn't there to greet her. Naturally she couldn't understand why. The next day she found out he was seeing another girl. When Sarah asked him if it was true, he replied: 'Sorry... It's over between us.' She freaked out! Partly because he didn't tell her while she was still in Europe. A few days later, Sarah bought a plane ticket back to Amsterdam to meet her friend." Janie, seemingly drained, halted the tale as she rested her head against the tiles.

Britte, Liselott, and I turned curiously to one another, hoping there was more to the story. "Well... Is that it?" Britte asked.

Liselott and I had inquiries of our own. "Did Sarah get even? Did she return to Europe?"

"Both!" Janie exclaimed. "On the way to the airport, she had one stop to make...and that was to do at least a plane ticket's worth in damage to her ex-boyfriend's brand-new Corvette. The last I heard of Sarah she was training to be a winemaker in Bordeaux, France."

Janie did a fabulous job of keeping our minds off the Vegas thermostat. Policing the minute hand, Britte notified us it was time to ooze out of here.

Outside the Sizzler, Britte pulled open the door leading into the mineral pools.

Step 9: *Look But Don't Touch*

"OH SHIT...!" I gasped. "Where did they come from?" There were men, lots of them — and all butt-ass naked!

"What do you mean?" Liselott asked. "There are always men, unless you go on a women-only day...which this is not, so the pool areas are communal."

My first instinct was to grab my towel. I had zilch to grab. My every detail was exposed with nothing left to the imagination. Dexterously, I crossed one arm over my breasts and placed my other hand down below in the position of a fig leaf.

Meanwhile, the Swedes had proceeded into the pool area. "Will both you girls come through this door right now?" Britte demanded with mock sternness.

We had no choice but to run the gantlet. Naked as a maple tree in December, I closed my eyes and held onto Liselott's shoulders as she led us out to the display pools.

"Sydney, you can open your eyes now," Britte insisted, tapping me on the shoulder. Even Janie played a role in the excess patter, "...Sydney!"

I turned to my roommate in astonishment before muttering like a whacked-out prude, "Aren't you worried about strange men seeing you in your birthday suit?"

Janie, undauntedly, replied: "Life is a roller coaster...get on and ride it!"

My jaw hit the floor. I couldn't believe what I was hearing. The Swedes stood next to me wearing nothing but cheeky grins. I had no alternative but to throw in the towel, so to speak. Plus, Janie was correct — strength comes from facing reality.

Chest out, shoulders back, head upright, legs firm — I boldly went where no other Endicott had gone before. Wading leisurely into a pool of poised men, I displayed my goods like a vendor at the markets.

"Hallelujah..." I bellowed under my breath, "I did it!" Glancing behind me, I saw the girls just standing there. "What are you waiting for? The water's wunderbar!" They stepped into the pool and dog paddled over to me.

"It's good to see you've gotten over your bashfulness," Liselott announced.

The experience seemed like a type of baptism. I was purified, initiated, and ready for the neighboring pools.

A mixture of people accumulated in the baths. Two guys in their mid-twenties of Italian appearance walked from pool to pool, not really accomplishing much, obviously spying the female populace. That reminds me; I must plan a trip to Pisa.

On the periphery, an adorable middle-aged couple debated their courage, which I could wholeheartedly identify with. He stepped cautiously as if minefield signs had been posted, while his better half tiptoed faithfully in his wake. This I would have to say reminded me of my parents, but Lord knows they'd never leave home destined for a nude bathhouse. Or would they?

This was an excellent opportunity to spy the male gender and their mannerisms. They were certainly not a shy bunch, displaying their doodads as if secret judges were handing out awards. Cheryl, my ex-neighbor at college, would no doubt have a VIP pass if the spas were within 100 miles of her bed.

Standing directly on the edge of our pool was an older, weight-challenged man with his hands resting upon his hips, belly out and pushed-in penis — not a pretty site. "Psst. Hey," I whispered to the girls, "...what's with this guy."

"What... Which guy?!" Janie countered in a booming voice.

"Nevermind." He presumably felt a draft because at that moment he retreated from his post, repositioning himself next to the center pool.

Since being generously exposed to the variety of male organs, I was curious about my discovery. "Have you girls noticed that the majority of these men are uncircumcised?"

"I certainly have," Janie said. "It's a good thing the sauna areas are segregated, I'd hate to see their baked noodles."

"They resemble a sleepy snake in a blanket," Britte contributed, giggling.

"Is it a fashion over here?" I asked the Swedes.

Britte and Liselott looked at each other, shrugging their shoulders.

"They look so...petite," Janie announced.

"Looks can be deceiving," Liselott claimed. "My ex-boyfriend, Sven, was the little acorn who turned into the major oak when aroused."

Britte raised a skeptical eyebrow — water cascaded off her fit body and onto the tiled floor as she exited the pool.

Step 10: *Fifteen Minutes of Bubbles*

"Ahh," Liselott exhaled, "...this is heavenly." Her eyes lay closed as she floated on her back in our new location, a pool of bubbles spawned by a network of air jets. "How about we stretch our time here to 20 minutes, girls?"

We were too busy floating in our own little dreamworld to respond.

Immersed up to her neck in a vortex of hydrating minerals, Janie admitted: "I've always thought of European women as having hairy armpits and body odor. But in my few months here, I've noticed the contrary."

Britte took the ball for Team Euro. "That's in the past. Modern times call for regular bathing and shaving. I think I'm a good example of both."

"No doubt about that," I asserted, referring to Britte's extra efforts to shave herself bare.

Meanwhile, I noticed one of the French girls rubbing shoulders with her boyfriend in the center pool. According to the list of steps, this was the cold-water bath, which I'm sure held matters at bay.

The central pool area was the traffic circle of the complex, resembling an enormous rotunda that culminated to a lavish dome. The focal point was the cold-water bath, surrounded by rose-marble columns that bolstered arched hollows — two having been outfitted into communal showers. Above stood statues of mermaids who appeared to supervise every virtuous move.

The playful French duet rose from the pool while each teasingly pursued the other's private parts, or in this case — public parts. Her short, dark hair and beautifully brown, toned body complemented her lover's fit muscles and Nordic blonde hair.

They frolicked into one of the arched hollows for a shower. It provided no refuge, yet the French couple persisted with their promiscuous recreation as if a curtain sheltered them from the growing audience. Sliding tongues hit all the bases; hands played a pivotal role. All men were already in, or scampering towards, the cold-water pool for safekeeping. The mermaids should have blushed.

Watching the romantic pair ignited distant memories: soft touches, cozy cuddles, sweet kisses, and long, caressing strokes that aroused my body. The bubbles floated me weightless like an astronaut in space. My sides, breasts, and inner thighs were at the mercy of the jets below. The sensations were tremendous; I wondered if my head was still attached to my body.

Step 11: *Cold-Water Pool, 300 Seconds Suggested*

It was frigid but refreshing. This I know we all needed; the overall scene was a little more than hot and spicy. For the moment, the French couple had wrapped up their show and progressed elsewhere — spectators weren't far behind. We passed the five minutes required here the best we could.

"Where were you before Cavallino?" Janie asked the Swedes.

"We were lucky," Liselott replied, "...because our Italian friend in Cavallino offered to drive us to Elba."

"Elba?" Janie questioned.

"It's an island off the coast of Italy, near the city of Pisa."

"Isn't Elba where Napoleon was exiled?" I inquired.

"Sure is," Britte answered. "He was lucky. I could think of worse places to be sent, like Siberia."

"Elba was beautiful," Liselott said. "Our room looked out across a sandy beach, and on the horizon was the island of Monte Cristo."

"Oh my gosh," Janie shrieked, "I love that book!"

At that moment, a stallion of a guy strutted in our direction.

"I had no idea Monte Cristo was so near," Janie proclaimed, "I've got to go."

"Unfortunately," Liselott announced, "no commercial boats travel there because it's a federally protected ecosystem. However, Moby Lines will get you close."

Meanwhile, Stallion stopped a few feet from our encampment. I must say, when God was handing out organs to men, this guy received special treatment.

"Moby Lines?" Janie repeated.

"It's the name of the boat company that shuttles people from the Italian mainland to Elba."

Stallion moved on, and fortunately so did the Moby issue.

"It's funny how nipples go hard when it's cold," Britte commented.

Liselott glanced down at hers. "It's not so funny. I noticed last week in Italy that a lot of men were staring at my breasts. I'll admit it was a bit cool outside, but by the way I was being stared at, they must have thought I was experiencing a deep freeze."

"Guys must get highly turned on by this act of nature," Britte said. "It's like the mannequin... Why are their nipples always extra pointy? I can't see a woman designing it that way."

I interrupted as a mental picture struck. "Imagine the person whose job it is to apply ice and oil to the models' bodies during photo sessions? The director shouts: 'Assistant, get some ice on Naomi's tits? We need a perk up!'"

"That's got to be every guy's dream job," Britte stated.

"Brr...It's freezing!" Janie affirmed. "Let's get outta here."

The concluding portions of the therapy cycle, steps 12 through 16, directed us back inside the women-only sections.

Steps 12 & 13: Eight Minutes in Ecuador, Two Minutes in Siberia

Step 12 offered a handful of showerheads budding from a tiled wall, expelling tremendously hot water. Opposite was step 13, a much-smaller and much-colder pool than step 11.

Taxing our brains, we analytically devised a tolerant multiphase plan to zip back and forth between steps.

Besides making us look like four crazies hopelessly trying out for the high-school relay team, our multiphase plan generated great feelings and unusual tingling sensations.

Step 14: Provided Us With Warm Towels. Bliss!
Four minutes of four girls purring like kittens wasn't nearly long enough, but heavenly just the same. Following the cuddly express, we put the towels into the basket provided and wandered into step 15, a room full of mirrors.

Step 15: Cream Service
Here the idea was simple: In this mirrored-room apply as much lotion to your body as you desire while watching your neighbors do exactly the same. Next to the mirrors on little shelves sat cream dispensers. A couple of pumps reward the benefactor with a mound of milky substance to further soothe the body.
Rubbing lotion between my hands, I massaged my forearms, stomach and breasts. It was so refreshing that several more pumps were essential.
After an unknown amount of time, we transfered our silky-smooth bodies to the last venue.

Step 16: Half Hour in the Cocoon Room
Helga reappeared and assisted us into the last area, a considerable room with raised beds similar to massage tables surrounding the perimeter. She guided us to separate beds and neatly spread out a large, white sheet on each, advising us to lie comfortably on our backs. Helga proceeded to wrap us one by one in the large sheet, together with thick blankets until we resembled cocoons. My thoughts drifted.
The room is silent; my body is bound. My eyes closed; my mind clear. I am drowsy. My spirit is tranquil, floating — an indescribable sensation. The ceiling is strange.
An hour passed. I must have fallen asleep. The girls were also dead to the world. Others had since been cocooned.
"Liselott, Britte... Janie," I whispered, giving each a nudge. "There's still 15 minutes remaining until our Roman-Irish affair expires. Let's head back to the sauna for a wake up?" Without saying a word, they unwrapped their naked bodies and followed.
At step 7 the sauna steamed conveniently empty, which meant freedom to lie where we pleased on the brown-tiled block.
Now seemed a good time to ask Britte the same question she had put to me earlier. "What kind of guy are you looking for?"
"A generous lover! One who's all about me."
"I have a confession to make," Liselott admitted, "my ex-boyfriend Sven is the best lover I've ever had. After I caught him cheating on me, though, I called off our relationship for good. Once a cheater, always a cheater, I say. But one thing I miss about him is after he'd orgasm his nipples would shrink rock-hard, which turned me on so much that my hormones begged for a second round!"
Janie piped up. "I've made love to only one person in my life and I've never noticed if his nipples were hard or not."

With the candidness of our situation and my inner emotions bursting to express themselves, I was compelled to share some otherwise private thoughts. "I think the most electrifying part of sex is the 'after-max,' the last sensual ingredient to lovemaking. When bodies are doused in sweat after simultaneously orgasming to a thunderous roar, it's magic to gaze into your partner's eyes while gently rubbing your nipples against his in a soft, climactic embrace. A lovely finale to an intimate experience."

Janie seemed shocked. Her upper body elevated, supported by her elbows; her petite breasts sat firm as she voiced doubt. "I believe I'm making myself sound like a case for Naiveté Anonymous, but I honestly didn't know."

Janie turned reflective, as if she was having a realization. "When Johnny and I made love, it was usually pants to the ankles followed by the two-minute drill. Since our passionate sessions peaked at 100 seconds and were completely exhausted by 120, I wanted to make love to him as often as possible to maintain the feeling of him. In my mind we were truly in love. Now I'm led to believe he was just using me. After weighing the events of this past week with the three years of what I thought was the perfect relationship, I now realize he cheated on me in more ways than one. He never once told me I looked nice, gave me a back massage, or even flowers. And he probably wouldn't even be at the airport to pick me up on account of 'Madam X.'

"That's it, my next phone call to Johnny will be my last! One day he'll come to his senses and realize what a special girl he lost."

Janie had detonated her pent-up tensions. It was a christening, a rebirth, a renaissance.

The Swedes and I wailed a mountain of hoorah! Janie had a gleam in her eye and concluded with gratitude: "I really want to thank you for sharing this liberating weekend with me. It's finally clear that I've got to let go of the past and look to the future. Today my vision is brighter than ever, and that...I owe to you girls."

One by one, we got up and gave our reborn friend a hug. We were in our own little world, four young women absorbing the thermal magic.

Back in the changing room, where insecurities were shed and virtues gained, Janie admitted, "I have never felt more relieved in my life! Kind of like an orgasm...I guess."

"What's a few euro for a naked romp through a German bathhouse?" Britte asked no one in particular.

"How about your next trip, Janie?" I asked. "Any inspirations?"

"Bordeaux, France...I owe a friend a visit."

Fully clothed and heading out the door, Liselott eyeballed me and commented, "That wasn't so bad, now was it?"

Funny she should say that, because until now I had forgotten I'd even been naked. In fact, it feels a tad strange wearing clothes. It makes me wonder what my friends back home would say. They'd never believe this one!

*   *   *

Baden-Baden really impressed me. The streets were clean, the restaurants chic, the hotels fancy, and the old Victorian homes quaint. The community was rich in culture, from music and theater companies to Europe's largest and most magnificent casino. Above all, it was an enriching thermal city boasting multiple hot springs that surged to the earth's surface from untold depths, replenishing us with its therapeutic properties.

Our time in Friedrichsbad was worthwhile, overwhelming in fact, 'cause today we all learned something new about ourselves — and maybe we were a little more independent because of it.

Good night, Black Forest.

A Quiet Village

CHAPTER 6

T he wind blew through my hair as Jesse's car zipped down the autobahn at speeds that were highly illegal back home. He spent almost the entire time in the fast lane passing columns of motor homes with Dutch license plates. I commented on how peculiar this appeared. Jesse merely replied, "This phenomenon is similar to bird migration. From the dikes of Holland to the docks of Palermo, the Dutch flock southward, offloading their euros in exchange for pizza and sun."

Educated on the relocation of Holland, I sat back and absorbed the names of the towns we passed: Marquartstein, Ruhpolding, Neukirchen, Teisendorf, Bad Reichenhall. I wondered if learning to spell took longer for German children, since each word has so many letters. Perhaps they feel the same way about Americans naming a state Mississippi.

It was a gorgeous blue-sky day in the middle of June. Geraniums in vibrant reds and pinks lit the balconies of rustic farmhouses, while bedspreads aired over windowsills. Cattle roamed freely in their pastures. Bales of hay sat five and six to a field, wrapped in white plastic and resembling giant marshmallows. One farmer mowed his pasture with a modern tractor, while his older, traditional neighbors clipped theirs by rocking a scythe back and forth in a motion similar to a pendulum on a clock. Beyond the farmers' fields, bulbous church towers shimmered in the morning sun. It was the perfect inauguration to summer, which couldn't have been better timing for Reuben's visit and our trip to Berchtesgaden.

The back seat was small but comfortable. Van Morrison reverberated from the rear speakers while Jesse and his buddy from California reminisced up front.

Abruptly, Jesse interrupted their conversation and eyeballed me through the rear-view mirror. "I have a feeling we're gonna find another clue regarding the crucifix today, since Berchtesgaden was formerly the base of operations for Nazi Southern Command."

"I hope you're right."

"Err, crucifixes and Nazis. What are you guys talkin' about?" Reuben asked, looking perplexed.

"Right now," I explained, "we're chasing old-wives' tales concerning a very old cross that could be worth a fortune."

"Fortune!" Reuben's face lit up. "Count me in."

"It's too bad you're here for such a short time," Jesse clarified, "...or else we might."

Reuben's smile collapsed. He'll get over it.

"Have you ever been to Berchtesgaden?" Reuben asked, apparently trying to learn a little more about the girl riding along in his best friend's car.

"Nope...Never!" Moving forward between the seats, I positioned my upper body into the front portion of the car. "I've ridden a bike around Chiemsee, Jesse introduced me to Salzburg, and a month ago I was in Baden-Baden with my roommate and two friends. Other than that...I'm pretty new at the sport of traveling.

"How about you...first time in Europe?"

"Sure is! And it's everything Jesse said it would be, and more... including you."

"Hmm...How shall I take that?" I replied, instantly meek.

"Take it as a compliment."

I rested my elbows upon either passenger seat getting comfy. "You seem like a nice guy yourself."

Jesse cut in. "I have an idea for you both...a tour of Munich, the capital of Bavaria. Unfortunately, my hectic work schedule won't allow me to take Reuben as planned, and he certainly could use a companion." He glanced at me again through the mirror. "If you could arrange some free time in the next few days...I'll do all the rest. How does that sound?"

"Sounds fine with me," I answered, surprised but delighted.

"Reuben?"

"Couldn't think of a better traveling companion!"

"Fine, it's settled then," Jesse said, concluding his matchmaking endeavor. "In the meantime, kick back and admire the edelweiss on the Alps."

"What's edelweiss?" Reuben inquired.

"It's a velvety snow-white flower that looks magical with its star-shaped symmetry and can only be found blossoming in the Alps, 6,000 feet and above."

"Have you ever seen one?" I asked.

"Several times. It is magical indeed."

"I heard edelweiss is Austria's national flower," I claimed.

"That's a myth," Jesse stated. "It is, however, the floral emblem of Switzerland, as well as for the Alpenvereine, or mountaineering clubs. Just remember, if you ever do cross paths with a cluster of edelweiss, it is a nationally protected flower and illegal to pick."

Subsequently, Reuben began a list of praise for his best friend. "Lucky for me, Jesse's a world traveler and a considerate one at that. I simply base my vacation every few years around his new whereabouts, and the rest is history. Sometimes, though, he can be a tough character to keep track of. His parents miss him a great deal, which gets me invited over for dinner once a week to fill them in on what's new with our crowd. I'm the next best thing to their walkabout son." Jesse took his eyes off the road for a nanosecond, aiming a smirk at Reuben.

"Sounds like you've known each other for some time," I said.

"Since we were two years old!" Reuben affirmed. "We grew up across the street from each other near the beach in Southern California. We've been through a lot together... kindergarten, catechism, Little League, high school. Occasionally, we even liked the same girls...which usually ended in disaster, but we're as good as brothers because of it. I remember our parents sending us out the door, with lunch boxes in hand, to school for the first time. We strolled to the bus stop, pausing every few feet to wave to our misty-eyed mothers. A couple of years later, our teacher tried separating us into different classrooms because our incessant chatter was upsetting the other students."

"What do you mean, tried?"

"Well...the classrooms we were moved into only got noisier, until the teacher decided to return things to the way they were. We weren't really all that bad, it's just...kids will be kids, and kids are noisy."

"One of the funniest episodes," Jesse chuckled, "was in second grade when Reuben got caught for the zillionth time blowing spit bubbles in class. The teacher got so mad that she sent him outside our portable classroom with a flowery Dixie Cup and told him not to resurface until it was filled to the brim with spit."

"Did you go to the drinking fountain to fill up the cup?" I asked Reuben.

"That would have been the easy way, but the teacher said I had to stay within the scope of the classroom windows."

"The whole class," Jesse claimed, "had a case of the giggles watching Reuben pace back and forth, like an oddball sentry pulling guard duty, trying to regurgitate enough spit to fill his little flowery cup."

"Okay, okay...I think she gets the picture!" Reuben huffed. He then snatched back the reins to finish his story. "Anyway, it started to rain an hour later, and as soon as the teacher turned her back to write on the chalkboard, I filled up the cup from a torrent of rainwater cascading off the roof...and I'm pleased to say, I haven't blown a bubble since."

"So I'm sitting with a pair of troublemakers, huh?" I announced from my perch between the driver and his best buddy.

After a few more childhood stories and about 40 minutes of pedal-to-the-metal German-style driving, we exited the autobahn.

Jesse began in his tour-guide voice: "We are now entering the town of Bischofswiesen, which means 'Bishop's Meadow.'" He pointed to the right. "There are the bishops now."

Two bronze statues stood poised in front of the most beautiful jade-green stream I had ever laid eyes on. We paralleled the watercourse for about a mile before making a left in the direction of Berchtesgaden.

Houses sat in the sun with plenty of distance from their neighbors; boxes bursting with flowers decorated the balconies. Cows rested peacefully in fields. One farmer took advantage of the good weather by hanging piles of grass on man-sized wooden stakes to dry. In the rural hamlet of Stangass, everything seemed tranquil.

Our tour guide pulled over and parked the car near a bus stop for a quick stretch of the legs.

"This narrow road to the right," Jesse recited, "leads to the former official headquarters of Nazi Southern Command and ex-residences of Wilhelm Keitel and Alfred Jodl, Hitler's chiefs of staff."

"It's incredible to be here," I declared, "...at the end of the line for the Allies, their strategic goal." Again I was delving back to my history books and Grandpa's stories relayed by Dad.

"You haven't seen anything yet!" Jesse yelped, shifting his body 90 degrees. "From this vantage point we can see two local landmarks. In front of us perched upon a pointy crest at 6,000 feet is Hitler's former Eagle's Nest, and to our right is the pride of Berchtesgaden, the Watzmann massif, Germany's second-highest mountain, at 8,900 feet. The Watzmann is comprised of seven peaks; legend refers to the largest as the 'king' and 'queen' and the smaller crests huddled in between as their children. Allegedly, in ancient times the king and queen were pitiless to the people, taxing them into poverty while ruling with an iron fist. The royal children weren't much friendlier, running through the farmers' fields and trampling their crops. The townsfolk prayed for an improvement of any kind. Then, one morning after a tremendous storm, the people awoke to see the royal family on the mountain, having been transformed into stone. Needless to say, the people lived happily ever after."

"You made that up, right?" said Jesse's best friend.

"What kind of question is that?!" Jesse snorted, appearing annoyed at Reuben's query. Then a wrestle broke out. They riveted together like two rams locking horns.

"Guys, break it up! Heeello!" I jumped in to stop the tussle, but it was too late. They were already laughing at my sincerity.

"Let's say we get a move on," Jesse proposed, as he brushed off his shirt. "I can tell you more on the road."

Seconds later we arrived in Berchtesgaden, passing the town-limits sign. Beyond the sign were two out-of-service hotels neighboring one another; Jesse said they belonged to our Chiemsee resort until 1995. The first one was the General McNair, and it was in reasonable shape. The adjacent hotel, separated from the McNair by a grubby dried-out pool, was the Berchtesgadener Hof. It appeared in dire need of a makeover. Huge sections of plaster had fallen off the walls and elsewhere the paint was peeling. A far cry from how I imagined the building to look after viewing its 1945 re-creation in "Band of Brothers," episode 10, "Points," when the boys of Easy Company entered and began lifting Hitler souvenirs.

Berchtesgaden seemed a quaint, admire-the-brook-and-cash-in-on-the-fresh-mountain-air kind of town. First, Jesse took us to the national park situated among a constellation of snow-peaked Alps for a breathtaking boat ride on the Königssee, Germany's cleanest lake, boasting drinking-quality water. We then visited the ultra-popular salt mines, where we donned authentic miner's uniforms and rode a mini railway one kilometer into the mountain face and slid down wooden chutes from one salty cavern to another. By the time we resurfaced from our subterranean adventure, it was nearly 1:30 and our stomachs were in competition for the loudest growl.

This brought us to the centrally located Hotel and Restaurant Watzmann, a handsome three-story gasthaus with a significant outdoor patio. Once inside, we noticed the décor was a balance between rustic, cozy and startling: coffee-colored wood rafters were splitting with age, classic

Bavarian furniture was tastefully arranged, and cream-painted walls were festooned with mounted antlers, old rifles and a medieval spear. Jesse introduced us to the decorators, Henry and Finny, who were also the owners. Henry told us he'd been in the German-American friendship association for 27 years. He was so proud. While making this remarkable statement, he interlocked his hands prayerfully and repeated himself: "I have bean foor tventy-zeven yearz mit die Amerikanz...und I luv zem!"

Since it was such a nice day, Henry and Finny showed us to a table on the outdoor patio. Our view of the Alps, including the Eagle's Nest, was prettier than a painting.

A personable lady took our order — it didn't take long; Jesse did it for us.

"So... What's on the grill?" Reuben asked, dying to know what his buddy had in store.

"You know I'm not going to spoil the surprise; just think Bavarian. I suggest you kick back, relax...and bask in the scenery."

Shortly thereafter our first course arrived: liver-dumpling soup for Jesse, cheese-onion for Reuben, and goulash for me. Judging by the guys' expressions, they were enjoying their fare as much as I was.

Next came the main meals. Our waitress placed them randomly on the table, commencing the festivities.

"Amen," I thanked the Almighty before digging into the mountain-climber's schnitzel: two slices of veal dipped in a cheesy-egg batter, sautéed and then smothered in a delicious tomato sauce. This surpassed the gastronomic boundaries of anything I'd ever consumed, and probably had originated from a medieval recipe composed by a culinary order of monks.

Reuben received the hunter's schnitzel: two slices of veal drenched in creamy mushroom gravy and served with crispy fries. Jesse ordered his favorite, Schweinshaxe: an entire pork knuckle, a bread dumpling, and a side of maroon-colored sauerkraut.

After Jesse cleared his plate, he disappeared for about 10 minutes. Reuben and I were too engrossed in our meals and the scenery to take much notice. When Jesse returned he gleefully announced: "I think I just found us our next clue. Follow me!"

Jesse had questioned Henry about the crucifix, asking him whether he'd heard anything about it. Amazingly he had, which led us behind Henry's restaurant to the entrance of a bunker that remained from the days of Hitler's Third Reich.

From the street running adjacent to his property, Henry escorted us through an inconspicuous, wooden portal that fronted a labyrinth of concrete tunnels dissecting the cavernous depths of Berchtesgaden. He walked us a short way in and explained that via the rumor mill he had learned the crucifix had been brought from the Chiemsee construction site and held in a tunnel system similar to this one at Obersalzberg, Hitler's neighborhood. Upon Hitler's next trip to Berlin, he personally took the crucifix with him and secured it in the vaults of the Reich's Chancellery. In April 1945, during the waning days of World War II, the Soviet Red Army entered the outskirts of Berlin and the vaults were hastily cleared with its contents transported to western Germany by truck convoys constantly under fire from Allied aircraft. Henry admitted things were unimaginably chaotic then and nobody knows for sure where the crucifix ended up, or if it even survived.

Although Henry's story didn't provide us with a solid lead, it did give us a reason to believe the crucifix existed.

"Come on, you two," Jesse announced to Reuben and me, "I want to show you something before we leave."

We nodded in agreement, then waved last adieus to our gracious hosts, Henry and Finny.

Jesse piloted us across the street and into a leafy church cemetery filled with an assortment of tall, dignified tombstones. The first grave on our right was that of a person named Anton Adner.

"Check out his living dates, 1705 to 1822," Jesse said, pointing to the monument.

After some quick number crunching, I verified, "That makes this guy 117 years old when he died. Is that possible?"

"It certainly is... He's Bavaria's oldest man, whose secret was walking. Adner's hobby was knitting warm garments and crafting wooden toys for kids. In those days, goods were taxed when crossing borders, unless they could be transported on your person. Thus Adner strapped a specially made wooden box to his back to carry his handiwork to distant markets to sell. During these journeys, Adner would knit socks or carve figurines as he went. The Bavarian king heard of Adner's remarkable story and at the tender age of 113 he was honored as one of the 12 worthiest men in the kingdom. According to tradition, this warranted a trip to the palace in Munich for the annual 'washing of the feet' by the king on Maundy Thursday, the Thursday before Easter, which is symbolic of Jesus washing the feet of his disciples. For the next four years, Adner was invited to Munich for a royal scrub until his death in 1822."

"Whoa, totally cool!" rolled Reuben's California tongue.

We were then led along a wall of remembrance opposite Adner's grave. Berchtesgaden's heroic sons were embedded in the mortar. Their names and dates spanned two world wars, written on the wall for all to see — where they fell in combat, what year, their age. Some had a poem; most featured a black-and-white photo of a proud soldier in uniform. Many families lost two young men, some lost three — one was father and son, Josef Ponn senior and junior.

I felt sad. I wished my Dad could be here.

"Their faces look so young...so innocent," Reuben noticed.

"Yes, you're right," Jesse agreed. "Endless names affixed to an endless wall. These men, like those of any nation, fought and died for their country. Many Wehrmacht, or German army, soldiers were regular guys drawn reluctantly into war. Today, we barely understand their times and troubles... Things were different then."

"Like how different?" I inquired.

"Well... Let's go back about 140 years and outline a simple German history lesson. Up to the year 1945 there are four main dates one needs to know: 1871, 1914, 1919 and 1933. Once you understand these dates, perhaps you'll have a better notion of why these young men are here on this wall."

"This should be good...yesteryear in a cemetery," uttered Reuben while folding his arms into his chest and leaning against a hearty pine tree in preparation for something longer than just a historical outline. The only things missing were a movie seat and popcorn. I did, however, have a fresh package of gummi bears. Mmm.

Jesse began: "In the year 1870, a Prussian statesman named Otto von Bismarck championed the idea of bringing together a related group of territories and forge an empire. Oiling the gears, he orchestrated a confrontation that became known as the Franco-Prussian War. At this time there was no Germany, only the southern states and the powerful northern confederation, or Prussians...kind of like the American Civil War, the North versus the South. But in this scenario there were other countries that could be exploited as a common enemy, shelving an interrelated bloodbath. Bismarck provoked a united German response against its neighbor and enemy, France, by publicly misrepresenting French documents, which induced heated dialogue and ultimately the Franco-Prussian War. The Prussian and southern-Germanic armies formed a military alliance and the so-called aggressor was swiftly defeated. Paris capitulated and on January 18, 1871, the King of Prussia, William I, was crowned emperor of the new, unified Germany in the Hall of Mirrors at Versailles, France. Thus began the Second Reich...with Otto von Bismarck as its first chancellor."

"What does Reich mean?" Reuben asked, chewing on a blade of grass. It was a valid query, but one I'd already learned from the Salzburg tour.

"It translates to empire, or kingdom." Jesse paused, brushing back the fringe of hair that kept dropping onto his brow.

"During the Second Reich, Germany became a mighty industrialized empire, and the factory worker embodied the nation's robust economy. Two decades after Germany's inauguration, Bismarck was dismissed by the new emperor, William II, grandson to William I and infamously known as 'Kaiser Wilhelm.' In 1914, Germany commenced its downward spiral with the beginning of World War I, which crippled an entire landmass for four years and stole the lives of millions of Europe's beloved sons. Germany lost this ghastly war, devastating its economy, people, and their will. The Kaiser fled to Holland and the Second Reich was kaput!"

"Who were the bad guys in World War I?" I inquired. "And why did it take the U.S. so long to enter the war?"

"Excellent questions. But keep in mind, the war was a European conflict, and the Atlantic Ocean was especially challenging to navigate in those days. Moreover, the U.S. didn't know who the bad guys were. See, World War I began as a local conflict between Austria and Serbia after the assassination of Archduke Francis Ferdinand, heir to the Austrian throne, in Sarajevo on June 28, 1914, by a Serb nationalist. Within weeks the various European countries took sides and by August the world was at war.

Germany and Austria were neighbors and natural partners, and with millions of immigrants from both sides of the conflict living in America, U.S. neutrality was reasonable. It wasn't until early 1917 that Germany became America's sworn enemy when it brought about a change to war policy with the commencement of unrestricted submarine warfare upon all vessels heading Britain's way. This meant the sinking of ships belonging to still-neutral countries, like the U.S. The Germans figured that by cutting off Britain's supply route once and for all, victory would be theirs within a year, or even months. This turned out to be a gross miscalculation because Germany was then seen as the aggressor and the U.S. declared war on April 6, 1917. The land battles raged on, but under a new light, the doughboys, or American soldiers, were on the field...and advancing. The roaring gunfire finally came to an end on the eleventh hour of the eleventh day of the eleventh month in the year 1918."

"What about World War II?" Reuben asked.

"We're getting there, Ruby... Be patient," Jesse said with a grin, knowing his audience was devouring the lesson.

"Remember the Hall of Mirrors at Versailles where our man William I was crowned emperor of the new, unified Germany? Well, to add further insult to Germany's demise, the victorious nations gathered near Paris to draft a peace treaty and decide the fate of the losers. The victors concluded that Germany must pay war retributions; ones that greatly exceeded the capabilities of a shattered nation. On June 28, 1919, the Treaty of Versailles was signed in that very same Hall of Mirrors."

"It's astonishing how history tends to repeat itself," I commented as I scanned more names on the remembrance wall.

"Yes, it truly is! And, Reuben...here begins the buildup to your previous query." At this point, Jesse walked us farther along the path.

"It later became evident that the Treaty of Versailles had a disastrous impact on Germany and was heavily to blame for the evils that brought forth the second European war of the century."

Reuben and I knew no more questions were required, as the finale was at hand. Our measured pace was halted in front of a large, featureless tombstone with the lone inscription: Dietrich Eckart. Jesse said he was Hitler's mentor.

"Post-war Germany had to produce a new government. Since Berlin, the nation's capital, was considered unsafe from revolution, the National Assembly moved some 200 kilometers southwest to the cultural town of Weimar. Thus began a new political era in Germany called the Weimar Republic. Within the first few years the German people were beset with unparalleled social, political and economic problems that spiraled the currency into a black hole. During these challenging times it literally took a briefcase full of money to buy a loaf of bread. Millions and eventually trillions of marks were necessary to equal just one U.S. dollar. Consequently, the victors seized Germany's industrial region, the Ruhr, for collateral on defaulted war payments. The streets were in chaos, generating the ideal climate to breed a broad range of political parties with each having a leader speaking of, yet again, a new, unified Germany. Their podium was the town square, the local beer hall, and even the circus. People came to these staged events to hear a way out of the mess their government had failed to alleviate; they congregated to hear solutions to the crisis. Germany's most impassioned speaker and political rising star was Adolf Hitler, a decorated World War I veteran who blamed the crisis on the Communists and the Jews.

"Economically, in the mid to late 1920s, things somewhat stabilized thanks to the resumption of foreign support. Until, that is, those nations revoked their assistance when the Great Depression struck in 1929, leaving Germany in a state of peril once again. The Weimar Republic was on the threshold of collapse. The following year, parliament held an election and the National Socialists, with Adolf Hitler as their leader, won second-most powerful party in the nation. As the world depression deepened, the stronger Hitler's party, the N.S.D.A.P., became."

Reuben interjected, "What does the N.S. blah, blah, mean?"

"The Nationalsozialistische Deutsche Arbeiterpartei, or the National Socialist German Workers' Party, or more commonly... the Nazis."

"Whoa...Dude!" said the amazed Californian.

Jesse rolled up his sleeves and continued: "Amid bitter political wrangling between the Social Democrats and the Communist parties, Hitler won control of the government and abolished all other political groups. The year 1933 marked the beginning of Hitler's so-called thousand-year empire, the Third Reich. During the thirties, the Germans regained their sense of pride under Nazi rule; jobs were created, the currency recovered, the Olympics came to Berlin, airports were built and mass-transit highways established. Once Germany got back onto its feet, Hitler avenged the Treaty of Versailles by reacquiring territories lost to the Great War victors while building up its armed forces well beyond what was necessary for a continent at peace. Hitler achieved this without so much as a whimper from its passive neighbors. How proud were the German people? Their Führer, or leader, Adolf Hitler, revived a deceased nation and produced a superpower within seven years, a feat unmatched in history. He led the country into war, and, of course, the people followed. That war, the Second World War, ripped apart continental Europe killing tens of millions of people, including those in the concentration camps, and leaving millions more homeless. The Third Reich was undeniably a scheme composed in hell."

Jesse wrapped up German History 101 and then pointed to the Alps. "Look to that mountain and you'll see a structure at the summit. A road leads there, and midway up that road lies Obersalzberg, the former seat of an empire — where the director once lived, walked his dog, bullied generals, intimidated statesmen, and shuffled massive armies from the English Channel to the borders of Asia. Come on... Let's go and have a look."

Craving more, Reuben posed one last question. Jesse and I were already exiting the churchyard.

"That was a groovy lesson and all, but..." Reuben then raised his arms outward, practically touching the snow-capped mountains themselves, "...can you teach me to yodel?"

This should be interesting! Jesse even had a laugh. Reuben stood eager, and so did I.

"Okay. I guess we got time. Are you ready?" Jesse began clearing his throat. "Now repeat after me... ANY ~ OLD ~ LADY'LL ~ DO." He insisted Reuben sing this three times rapidly with a Southern twang.

Reuben did, and he yodeled all the way from the cemetery gates to Hitler's former alpine getaway.

*   *   *

Upon turning right at a set of lights, Jesse pointed left. "This shack was the first of several security checkpoints up to Obersalzberg, Hitler's neighborhood. Above the door, where you see the sign advertising the pizzeria, once hung a wooden version of the Reich's iconic eagle, clasping the swastika with its talons."

Berchtesgaden sat nestled 1,700 feet above sea level. Where we were headed was nearly twice that elevation. The narrow road ascended at a seriously steep grade; on either side of us were lush maple trees, beech, and evergreens. We even passed a petite, multitiered waterfall. The beauty of God's work was overwhelming.

Jesse negotiated every bend in the serpentine road with diligence. After about two miles, and what was probably a quarter-tank of gas, we reached a green sign labeled "Obersalzberg."

Our guide was faithfully on cue, imparting his tour as he was so used to doing. "Obersalzberg translates to Upper Salt Mountain. We were in this mountain earlier when the mini railway delivered us deep within the salt mines. To our right is the driveway that led to Albert Speer's studio, the structure with the red terracotta-tiled roof. And beyond that, with the green roof, was his Obersalzberg address."

"Who was Albert Speer?" I asked, before popping a pair of gummi bears.

"He was an architect. Such a good one that Hitler took Speer under his wing and made him one of the Reich's primary designers. In Hitler's early years, he aspired to be an architect himself, but the Academy of Fine Arts in Vienna twice rejected him, saying he lacked talent. Speer was the architect Hitler dreamed of being: talented, intelligent, charismatic. In 1942 Speer was appointed Minister of Armaments and War Production, succeeding Fritz Todt, who died in a plane crash that year. Unfortunately for the Allies, Speer did his job too well, doubling, tripling, and sometimes quadrupling output. Later in the war, when the Allies were bombing the smithereens out of the manufacturing plants, Speer had them reassembled underground where they sustained 80 percent output until the end of 1944. During the opening months of '45, Hitler's Reich was on the verge of collapse and Speer did his best to stop the annihilation of the Germans themselves. Since Hitler believed his people had failed their mission to dominate Europe, he issued orders to 'scorch' Germany, leaving nothing for future generations. Defying the madness, Speer drove around much of the tattered nation persuading local leaders to disobey Hitler's orders."

"How come Hitler didn't have him executed?" Reuben asked from the back seat.

"For two reasons: First, Hitler was suffering from Parkinson's disease and his doctor prescribed a cocktail of drugs that more often than not left Hitler in Fantasyland. The second reason, and I'd say the main one, was that Hitler really admired Speer. He was among the rare few in the Reich who gained Hitler's unwavering trust.

"Speer's fanaticism to salvage whatever he could persisted to the very end. In the final days of the war, during the Battle for Berlin, Russian artillery pounded Hitler's command bunker knocking out all means of communication, except for one. Contact with the outside world fell to Hitler's personal pilot, Hans Baur, who flew daring missions in and out of the capital using a makeshift runway in the nearby Tiergarten park. To prepare the runway, Baur ordered his men to cut down the few remaining trees. This drove Speer mad. He yelled at Baur's men to stop the slaughter while grabbing the axes from their hands. An architect's purpose is to create, and at this point he'd seen so much destruction that every miniscule thing had a meaning of colossal importance. After the war, for his role in the Nazi regime, Speer was sentenced to 20 years in Spandau prison, Berlin."

"It's amazing," I commented, "how someone so intelligent could blindly follow the lead of a maniac like Hitler."

"My thoughts exactly...and Speer had two decades behind bars to reflect on that very question. His answer was as coherent as his character: 'One seldom recognizes the devil when he puts his hand on your shoulder.'"

"Whoa...Deep, man!" Reuben contributed.

"What happened with the trees in the Tiergarten park?" I inquired. "Did Speer save them?"

"Not a chance! He was nonexistent in an absent nation. Between Baur's men and, mainly, Russian artillery, nearly all living matter in the park was obliterated. After the war, new vegetation had to be planted, and today the trees in Berlin's Tiergarten are as old as the sum of years the war has been over."

Ahead we came to a junction where the main road curved right. Jesse continued straight onto a slender lane.

"We are now entering what used to be 'Adolf Hitler Strasse.' From this point we cross the former boundary that once accessed the sentimental heart of Nazi Germany, or as Sydney referred to earlier: the Allied goal. On the hill to the right is where Hitler lived in his three-story mansion, the 'Berghof.'"

Reuben leaned forward into the front part of the car. "What Berghof? There's nothing there."

"That's because on April 25, 1945, more than 300 British bombers flew overhead and royally pummeled this area into a lunar landscape. Later, in 1952, the local authorities had all remaining structures razed...blown up!"

Jesse continued our tour as we motored up the hill. "Only two properties that I can think of were allowed to be rebuilt after the 1952 demolitions. Ahead is one of them, the Hotel Türken. Because of the Türken's handy location next to the Berghof, the hotel was appropriated by the Reich's Security Service to safeguard Hitler. As the war progressed, a bunker system was excavated beneath the Türken that ran directly under the Berghof. Loaded with specially trained SS guards and laced with deadly machine-gun nests, Hitler could have retreated here and prolonged the war. Today, the tunnel system at the Türken is open to the public and we'll return later for a closer inspection."

"Woo hoo!" hooted Reuben.

"Would this be the tunnel network that Henry referred to earlier," I asked, "...where the crucifix was stashed after its discovery at Chiemsee?"

"You got it."

Continuing farther up the hill, the road leveled off. Here we saw at the peak of a grassy knoll a brand-new 140-room resort hotel, where Jesse said field marshal Herman Göring's house once stood. He commanded Hitler's terrifying Luftwaffe, or air force.

All around us were vacant lots wrapped in alpine flora that once prospered with structures devoted to a dictator's pursuit of world domination: administration buildings; archives and planning rooms; military barracks for Hitler's protection guard, the SS; an air-defense command bunker, which signaled the approach of enemy planes and alerted local anti-aircraft units; a kindergarten for the children of Obersalzberg personnel; and even a greenhouse.[1]

"A greenhouse?" Reuben asked.

"Hitler was a strict vegetarian who demanded his vegetables fresh. Additionally, Eva Braun used the greenhouse to hold Easter-egg hunts for the officers' children."

"Who was Eva Braun?" Reuben questioned, refusing to miss a trick.

"She was Hitler's longtime mistress, whom he married on April 29, 1945, only days before the end of the war, in Berlin's catacomb-like bunker system below the Reich's Chancellery. Hitler believed the German people had failed him, thus he divorced Germany to marry Eva. Some 40 hours after tying the knot, the wedding couple consummated their bond by committing suicide in the bunker. Honoring Hitler's wishes, both bodies were then carried outside to the chancellery garden by staff, doused in petrol and cremated. Lovely honeymoon, huh?"

"How did they do themselves in?" I asked.

"Sitting on a velvet sofa, Hitler opted for the foolproof poison-and-pistol method, biting down on a cyanide capsule and then shooting himself in the head. Sitting next to Hitler and wearing an elegant black dress, Eva

---

[1] For a reference map, turn to page 240

bit into her poison capsule at the sound of Hitler's gun...concluding her life with a simple but lethal pill."

"Killer!" Reuben grunted.

Our raconteur flipped the car around and retraced our route, descending past the Hotel Türken and Hitler's former estate to the junction, where we turned left and ascended another twisting road.

At the last curve, Jesse pointed to a heap of overgrown scrub on the right where the Kampfhäusl once stood, the cabin where Hitler in the mid-1920s finished revising his political manifesto, "Mein Kampf."

On the left side of the road was the Documentation Center, formerly Martin Bormann's administration office and VIP guest house. Today the structure accommodates a museum focusing on none other than the rise and fall of the Third Reich.

Farther ahead, Jesse hooked a left into a freshly paved parking lot and cut the engine, which concluded the automobile portion of our tour. From here we would explore Hitler's bygone neighborhood the old-fashioned way, by foot.

As we set off, Jesse explained that the parking lot used to be the location of the Platterhof, a grand Nazi hotel. We learned the hotel was bombed by the British, rebuilt by the Americans, and recently razed by the Germans to be blacktopped.

"What's that dwelling on the mountaintop?" Reuben inquired, rocking back on his heels looking skyward.

"That's the Eagle's Nest, where we're headed."

"Way up there?!"

Jesse dismissed his comment as sarcasm. We bought our tickets and waited for the bus that would deliver us to the summit.

In the distance, a red-and-white-striped boom gate opened and three buses returning from the Eagle's Nest motored in our direction. They made a wide, sweeping turn, each stopping momentarily to drop off its cargo before pulling forward into their predetermined loading bays.

"Which side has the best views?" Reuben queried with trepidation. I waited with enthusiasm.

"Merely pick a seat," Jesse responded. "Anywhere is fine with me." He was too occupied with talking to his friend, the bus driver, to notice Reuben's tense demeanor.

Again he questioned the seating arrangements: "No, really... which side has the best views?!" Reuben looked about as nervous as a long-tailed cat in a room full of rocking chairs. Possibly he was disguising the real reason, fear of heights.

We boarded the bus and Reuben aimed straight for the back. He then stopped just shy of the last row, twisted sideways and politely motioned for Jesse and me to pass. "It's okay," he said, "You guys can have the window seats." The acrophobia theory was proving correct.

Jesse squeezed by and slid over to the window. I stayed where I was to tease a reaction out of Reuben. "Thanks...but you go ahead and take the other window seat. I'll have plenty of opportunities to revisit."

Reuben's face contorted, as he appeared to be swallowing his tongue.

"What's going on? Is someone going to join me, or what?" snorted Jesse.

Reuben was visibly distraught; he deserved a break. "Since you're being so polite, I'll take the other window seat and you can have the middle."

"Well, okay...If you insist," Reuben confidently replied, his manhood still intact.

All three buses fired up their engines. The boom gate once again did its thing, and one by one the people-movers hammered out of their bays, forming a motorcade that rambled past the gate in one direction — *up*.

In a manner suggestive of a Hollywood thespian, Jesse dramatically explained our ascent. "We are about to embark on a four-mile-long stretch of road at a 22 percent grade to an elevation of 5,500 feet, more than one mile in the sky. From there we'll walk through a 400-foot tunnel blasted into the mountain face, where Hitler's former elevator will lift us another 400 feet directly into the heart of the Eagle's Nest." I felt deep within the pages of a Stephen Ambrose novel. Reuben sat motionless and pale.

Our bus wrestled through the trees, pursuing its alpine path. Eventually the dense tree line broke and superlative views developed in abundance. Reuben clutched the seat in front of him with both hands. There was no let up, his grip intensified as the driver played a game of cat and mouse with the guardrails. Higher and higher the bus climbed its narrow lane. Reuben's knuckles compressed to knots of ivory-bone as the objects on the earth's floor became minuscule. We passed through a few tunnels and suddenly Reuben's eyes bugged out as he braced the seat in front of him with all his might. What had been, for some, a long and nauseating road — abruptly disappeared.

"OoO...oOoo0...oOoOo0...hhhhhhhhhhhhh!" roared our fellow passenger brethren as the driver whipped around the 180-degree hairpin turn, no doubt scaring many into a change of underwear. The worry-free commuters on the left side of the bus now found themselves frightfully on the edge.

The driver raced even higher towards another tunnel. We were deeply camouflaged in the mountain face, becoming absorbed by the magnitude. A few scattered trees still held their roots, living life unabated in the dense mountain rock.

Jesse broke from his gaze out the window to express caution. "Oh! Guys, fasten your seatbelts... Here comes the shortcut to Salzburg."

The bus whipped around another provocative curve, exhausting the last of Reuben's bravado. He lowered his head into his lap. I thought he was going to be sick, or was he praying to the patron saint of bus catastrophes? This caught his best friend's eye. "Hey Mr. McJiggy...are you okay?!"

"Fine," he answered, in a less than fine voice.

While we studied the movements of our ill friend, the bus crept up to level ground and our destination of several thousand feet.

Jesse led us off the bus and over to the mouth of the 400-foot tunnel. Reuben was slow to react, but he made it. Small pockets of snow kept the clean air cool. I threw on a sweater, as did the others. A Baroque-style medallion crowned the tunnel entrance displaying its year of birth, 1938. Jesse pointed to a name etched into one of the mammoth-sized bronze security doors: "'Stellen Anderson — Rockford, Illinois — 1945 — 100th Division.' The boys were here!" he exclaimed, before shepherding us into the subterranean passageway.

"That's love!" Reuben was impressed and, apparently, business as usual.

The tunnel's interior, built out of roughly finished rose-marble blocks, was damp and cold. Our three bodies kept pace with the swelling crowds while Jesse imparted more of his inside info. "Hitler's chauffeur, SS Colonel Erich Kempka, would drive him down this confined passage to the elevator, where Hitler got out and Kempka was left to ponder a smoothly orchestrated return. Kempka carefully reversed Hitler's supercharged Mercedes out of the tunnel, where he turned it around and slowly reversed back to the elevator."

"Imagine if Kempka dented the front fender in the process." I visualized.

Reuben was quick to complete my vision. "Hitler would probably say: 'Okay Schultz...hand me the Luger!'"

Jesse laughed. "Yeah, really!"

"Wasn't this passageway a smidgen cold for the goofy-mustached man?" I asked through chattering teeth.

"Cold! Not at all... The goofy-mustached man had heating. Scope out the vents near the floor." Jesse pointed to the right, where we counted 11 along our path.

At the end of the tunnel we had no choice but to turn right into a rotunda-like vestibule where loads of people were spilling into a polished brass elevator.

"Kommen Sie herein bitte!" said the elevator man.

Jesse stepped across the threshold of the rock-solid vestibule into the already packed elevator. Now all the crammed people were staring at Reuben and me, including Jesse.

"What's going on?" Reuben questioned, a little testy.

"He told us to get in. So come on!" Jesse replied.

Reuben and I squeezed our way in and for once in my life I truly knew the real meaning of "sardine." We were face to face, shoulder to shoulder and butts against cheeks as the elevator doors closed and our cabin shot upward like a rocket. The predicament of 50 mashed individuals in a snug environment wasn't a picture of harmony. If I were to move any part of my body, my neighbor would more than likely sue for sexual harassment. Forty-five ear-popping seconds later, the elevator doors opened and we landed in the Nest.[2]

Jesse escorted us through the door on the right and into an oak-paneled banquet room. We followed him past the tables and chairs to the other end and down a few steps into a circular hall featuring stone-block construction, a red-marble fireplace, and five generous windows providing

[2] For an Eagle's Nest floor plan, turn to page 251

an abundance of light. Skirting the hall, he led us through a door on the left and down a few more steps into a quaint tea room. The walls were finished with knotted panels of pinewood that emitted a heady fragrance suggestive of an evergreen forest.

On the other side of the tea room was a large picture-frame window affording unforgettable views of the national park below: tender green valleys, the Königssee's arctic-blue water, and fluffy white clouds hugging the rugged peaks of the Alps. What a glorious sight! I felt as if I were in a capsule hovering above God's greatest creations.

"So, what did you think of the Eagle's Nest?" Jesse said.

Reuben and I eyeballed Jesse curiously. "What do you mean?" I asked.

"You've almost walked through the entire building. The only parts you haven't seen are the bathrooms, kitchen and former guards' room."

"Where did Hitler sleep?" Reuben queried.

"He slept at his house, the Berghof. Remember, we saw where it once stood, next to the Hotel Türken?"

Reuben rubbed his thumb and index finger against his chin trying to remember.

"This place must be tiny," I said.

"Not only is this place tiny...Hitler had a fear of heights and experienced claustrophobia in the elevator on the way up, thus he wasn't a huge fan of the property. Hitler officially visited the Nest 14 times between September 1938 and October 1940. The biggest function held here was a wedding reception in June 1944. The guests of honor were Eva Braun's sister, Gretl, and SS general Herman Fegelein. Hitler did not attend. A year later, Hitler had Fegelein killed in Berlin. But, that's another story."

"W~h~o~a...Nice guy!" Rueben exclaimed, rocking back on his heels again.

Jesse steered us out of the tea room, across the hall and over to the red-marble fireplace. "Allegedly this was a present from Benito Mussolini to Hitler on his 50th birthday, April 20, 1939."

"Not a bad rig," Reuben expressed. "I imagine it would warm the hall in a heartbeat."

"The edges and corners are drastically uneven." I noticed.

"That's because for years souvenir hunters have chipped away at the marble, giving it new dimensions."

Again Jesse motioned onward, retracing our steps through the oak-paneled banquet room and into the hallway connected to the elevator. Just as he said, it wasn't very spacious. We saw two bathrooms, a kitchen, and a petite room on the left before exiting the structure. Once outside, he turned left along the patio and stopped at the L-shaped corner made of granite blocks cemented knee high, where he pulled out a gray-colored book from his daypack. He thumbed through a few pages before holding up a picture of Hitler. "Where do you think he's standing in this photo?"

"Oh...my...gawd!" I gasped.

"He's standing exactly where we are now, isn't he?" Reuben declared.

"He sure is," answered our hobbyist.

"You mentioned earlier," I said, "that Hitler was a decorated World War I veteran. What did he do?"

"He was a courier running messages along the front-line trenches. Due to the hazards of the job, couriers were regularly killed in action. But not Hitler, somehow he survived. For his bravery, he was decorated with Germany's medal-of-honor equivalent: the 'Iron Cross.'"

Jesse escorted us around the corner and over to a wooden railing that was the only barrier between a spectacular panorama and a fatal tumble down the mountainside.

He continued from our new perspective: "Look at Obersalzberg 3,000 feet below. From there, roots nurtured beneath the soil developed into a ravenous tree feeding off its European neighbors. The Nazi regime contaminated an entire continent. And those men we saw earlier on the cemetery wall were the misguided leaves of a generation who fell off that tree in waste... ultimately fighting a war against their own liberation." Our host paused, facing us sincerely.

"Let's forget about Hitler and the Third Reich for a moment. Let's think about the bus ride up here, ascending through an ecosystem that could only be a supreme creation. That alone was worth the journey. Now we stand on top of a mountain and savor the miracles before us: gently flowing streams, the splendor of the Alps, and blossoming trees that fill the valleys. From here, you can see how lucky we are to be born in this generation of peace. The blood of many purchased our freedom...and we, as a nation of intellectuals, should never forget that."

Jesse's sermon withered to silence. We heard nothing but the wind's whistle and the caw of a crow somewhere high above.

How magnificent it is to stand here and relish this view of unparalleled beauty.

Reuben began yodeling, again...

The Letter

CHAPTER 7

8 a.m., late June: e-mail to the folks

Subject: Awesome Sights

Dear Mom & Dad,

A few days ago I got the royal tour of Berchtesgaden. Dad, you would have absolutely loved it!
We saw the Eagle's Nest and what was once Nazi
Southern Command. Today and tomorrow we are
touring Munich, the capital of Bavaria. I'll be
thinking of you both.

Love Syd, your prudent daughter

P.S. Hi to Alex

Reuben and I hauled our backpacks out of the trunk. Jesse walked us onto the correct platform, where he handed me an envelope. "Inside are a few things I jotted down that will help you get around, but don't open it until you arrive at Munich's Hauptbahnhof. Reuben, that means 'main train station.'"

The train blew its horn three times as it came screeching to a halt. I took the envelope, secured it in my pack and said good-bye.

"Thanks, man, see you tomorrow night," Reuben said. "Put a sock on the door if you're busy."

My travel partner and I hopped on board. The train doors shut and we were instantly moving in a northerly direction. We hoisted our backpacks onto the storage rack above and seized the two seats facing each other near the door.

"What's in the envelope?" Reuben asked

"I'm not exactly sure; Jesse only mentioned that he'd written down some stuff to do...and merely to have fun."

"What about our accommodations?"

"Good question. Let's just hope that it's part of the 'stuff to do!'"

"Fahrkarten, bitte?" The train conductor approached and aimed a sinister glare at Reuben's foot resting on my seat.

"What does he want?"

"He wants our tickets and for you to relocate your foot."

"Tickets...?" Reuben lowered his leg to the floor and felt his pockets while eyeballing me with a perplexed look. "What tickets?!"

The conductor became a tad perturbed. "Ven yuz have kein ticket, yuz musst die coal schovel'n'."

I nudged Reuben's knee with mine and muttered through my teeth: "Did you hear that?"

"Sure did! What are we going to do now?"

"Buy some tickets," I said.

"All right... If you insist."

"Do you have another idea?"

"Yeah, let's run. An international chase from car to car."

"Creative, but somehow I don't think that'll work."

The conductor must have understood Reuben because he widened his stance and blocked any chance of escape via the aisle.

I grabbed my bag from above and delved inside, yanking out my wallet. Jesse's envelope was wedged next to it; I noticed a pair of tickets paper-clipped to the back. "Cool! Look what I found."

"Excellent!"

"Here you go, Sir." I handed over the tickets with a jester's smile.

The conductor punched them and went humbly on his way. "Fahr-karten, bitte?"

"That was nice of Jesse," I said.

"Go ahead, while it's in your hand," Reuben pleaded, "Open the envelope."

"You heard what Jesse said: not until we reach Munich."

"Oh, come on...What's it gonna hurt? Plus, we need to know about our sleeping arrangements."

"Well..."

"Go on, Syd!"

I weaseled my index finger under the envelope's corner seal and slithered it partway across, ripping open a small section. "We really shouldn't be doing this... He stressed not until Munich!"

"Jesse's my best friend; he won't care."

My finger finished its dance across the seal; the envelope was open and its contents, several neatly folded sheets of paper, stared us passively in the face. I reached in and pulled out a piece of paper that was detached from the main bunch. It abrasively read: "I THOUGHT I TOLD YOU, NOT UNTIL THE HAUPTBAHNHOF!"

Swiftly, I stuffed the intimidating piece of paper back into the envelope. "I hope you're happy. We're gonna respect his wishes and leave well enough alone. After all, don't you remember Pandora's Box?"

"Hands up... You win." Reuben said, raising his arms pretending to surrender.

"Is there any place in particular you want to visit in Munich?" I asked.

"Yep, I'd like to visit a traditional beer hall."

"Sounds like a plan," I replied. "Jesse told me that Munich is the beer capital of the world and its name stems from the German word for 'monks,' who in medieval times mastered the art of brewing beer."

"Groovy!" Reuben wailed.

Suddenly, the conductor materialized and directed his spiel at Reuben and me. "Fahrkarten, bitte?"

"He must not recognize us," I whispered, nudging Reuben's knee again.

This was a good time to query my quest. "Excuse me, have you heard of das Bayernkreuz?"

"Fahrkarten, bitte?"

Perhaps he didn't hear me. I tugged on his blue jacket and repeated my query.

He wasn't concerned. "Fahrkarten, bitte?" Keenly he stared us down.

He definitely wasn't a friendly chap. I fished through my bag once more, snaring the tickets. "Here."

"Danke." He punched them as if he'd never seen them before.

Sauntering down the aisle, he continued his recording: "Fahrkarten, bitte...?"

"What's the latest with the cross, anyway?" Reuben asked.

"Good question. Not much. Jesse figured he'd keep pressing the locals for info while I surfed the Web. Since I'm on this overnight excursion, I thought I'd ask anybody and everybody."

"Something'll come up," Reuben replied.

The train drastically slowed as numerous tracks began converging. On our left we passed a stationary freight train packed with brand-new Porsches. To our right crawled an endless column of boxcars. Our train slightly jerked from side to side, conceivably changing tracks. On the horizon we approached a gigantic awning, one that could house a football stadium. It was the main train station.

"Great! Let's open the envelope." Reuben urged.

Our train tiptoed into its final destination: the Hauptbahnhof. All passengers began to exit; Reuben and I waited for the rush to subside.

We stepped onto the platform and rested our backpacks against a vending machine. Drawing the envelope from my pack, I handed it over. "You can do the honors."

"My pleasure!" However suave Reuben wanted to appear, his actions depicted quite a different mood. He handled the envelope like it was labeled "anthrax." With exaggerated care, he spread the envelope open using his thumb and forefinger. What he'd been craving the previous hour was now within his grasp. We kneeled to my backpack and Reuben unfolded Jesse's sheets of paper across its nylon surface.

The opening page read:

Rules

1) There are 10 pages in "The Letter"; however, you may only look at one page at a time.

2) When the assignment on that page has been fulfilled, you may then look to the next page.

3) Once you understand these rules, you have the green light to proceed.

We swiveled to each other and nodded in unison. Reuben promptly flipped to the next page.

Page 1

Once off the platform, exit out the left side of the train station to Arnulfstrasse. Cross the street via the crosswalk and continue straight into Pfefferstrasse. Make the next left on Hirtenstrasse and proceed a short distance to #18 on the right, the "4 You" youth hostel. This will be your humble abode for the evening. Your reservation is under "Einstein."

At the hostel's reception desk stood a brunette in her early twenties organizing keys into their correct room slots.

We set our packs down and Reuben confirmed the booking. "Hello, we have a reservation under the name...Einstein."

She gave us a fleeting glance and attentively ruffled through some paperwork. "Hier it is... Albert und Juliet."

"Err, yeah..." I unconvincingly responded, "...that's us."

"You're in a four-bed dorm on the second floor," our hostess explained, handing us each a key.

"Excuse me, have you heard of das Bayernkreuz?" I asked.

"Ah, the Bavarian Cross," she said.

This sounds positive. Perhaps she'll provide a clue. My optimism was curtly interrupted.

"Sorry, I'm not familiar with it."

Huh? That was a bit strange. Anyway, she taught me how to say my request in German, which might speed up the search. Well, that is, until the answer came back in German and I stood there like a mute potato. One of these days I'll master the language.

Our dorm room had four lockers, a sink, and two wood-framed bunks pushed against either wall. Reuben threw his bag down next to a bottom bunk while simultaneously keeling over onto its mattress. He completely stretched out his body, nudging his feet against the end support timbers and interlocking his hands behind his head. He couldn't have looked more comfortable.

After staking the bed above, I stood feverishly over Reuben. "Let's see what's on Page 2."

He waggled in delight. I whipped the Letter out and pulled off Page 1, filtering it to the back. Reuben's face warmed like an apple pie.

Page 2

Congratulations, Albert and Juliet, for achieving the mission outlined on Page 1. I hope you like the hostel and your new Munich identities. At the reception desk, have them show you how to get to Marienplatz. Make sure you're there by noon; that's when it starts. Upon completion of the mini-event, turn to the next page...

Back at the check-in counter, the receptionist gave us a map and pointed the way.

Boasting a bevy of sights, smells and sounds, Marienplatz was a gigantic plaza in the heart of the Old Town where throngs of people were buzzing around at a brisk pace. Along the square's perimeter, restaurant workers diligently set up outdoor tables in order to ensnare their lucrative prey. In the center of the plaza stood a lofty granite column on which stood a gilded statue of the Virgin Mary, who appeared to be blessing all those in her presence.

We arrived a minute before 12 and filtered among a crowd of camera-toting tourists huddled around the Virgin Mary and gazing skyward. The focus of their attention was an ornamental clock tower rising above an elongated Gothic structure dusted with black soot. It was obvious that something of significance was about to take place.

Loud bell chimes began ringing from the clock tower and all present ogled the lifeless figurines suspended within. Our hands shielded us from the bright sun as we stood poised for something to happen, but nothing did.

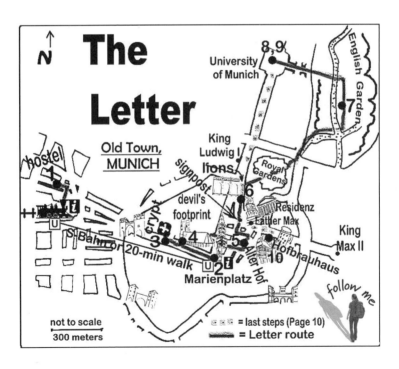

"Maybe we missed the event?" Reuben commented, the very moment the crowd sighed.

Suddenly, the lifeless figurines became animated as they moved around a king and queen perched upon a pedestal. A royal party had begun: musicians, jesters and jousting knights performed past the regal pair. Around again they acted a repeat performance: the musicians played, the jesters juggled, and the jousters dueled. The Bavarian knight, sporting the kingdom's blue-and-white colors, lunged forward with his lethal spear and stuck the Austrian knight deep in the belly, thrusting him backwards to his death. The crowd exhaled an immense moan.

The bells continued while the theatrical program changed to a dozen dancing men in traditional outfits twirling like ballerinas on a carousel. After a few minutes, the men halted motionless as if they had never begun. The bells continued to chime a few minutes more and the crowds dispersed. Those who remained heard the bells stop and a golden rooster crow three times, frightening nearby pigeons into premature flight.

"That was excellent!" Reuben declared. "Time for the next event."

Page 3

Cool show, huh? It's called the Glockenspiel (literally Bells Play), Germany's largest carillon.

Now, before we move on, note that there are toilets at the neo-Gothic town hall. Use 'em if you need 'em. To get there, go through the archway under the clock tower to the inner courtyard. The toilets, costing .50¢ to use, will be to your right.

Next, when facing the Glockenspiel, head left where the masses are converging. This pedestrian-only drag is Kaufingerstrasse, literally Shopping Street. Window-shop at your leisure — after about 250 meters you'll see (on right) a blue awning with a cuckoo clock; beyond that is Ettstrasse and on the corner is St. Michael's church. Inside you'll find the crypt of a famous person. Once you're both churched-out, return outside and read further...

The morning gray cloud had disappeared to a fine afternoon. As the sun climbed up the sky and intensified, we paused to remove our sweaters. Reuben must have been exceptionally warm in his velveteen pants and Levi's studded shirt.

The crowds flooded en masse along the pedestrian-only shopping street. We casually followed, passing department stores, fashion boutiques, and even a Gap. I hadn't yet saved enough money to spoil myself on European threads, but now seemed to be a good time to kick off that wish list I'd been dreaming about.

"There's the blue awning... There's Ettstrasse," Reuben reported with the Letter in hand, "and that must be the church."

In front of St. Michael's, I stopped and stared at a street entertainer standing on a wooden box posing as a statue. He was spray-painted silver from his floppy shoes to his top hat; he even held a silver cane. A little boy dropped a coin in his tips jar to get a reaction; the silver man bent over and smiled for a photo before returning to his rigid position.

"Juliet..." Reuben barked, "...Come on!" He stood at the entrance of the church, holding the door open, anxious to see the famous person.

The interior of St. Michael's was enormous, featuring barrel-vaulted ceilings and a high altar lavishly bedecked in gold. A few people milled around a black-and-white picture exhibition to our left. We walked over for a look and saw photos depicting the aftermath of a bombing raid during World War II. Some 60 years ago the church's roof had been blown off and where we stood was a pile of rubble.

We wandered midway up the central aisle, turning around to see an organ perched above the main portal. Like the altar, it, too, was gold-plated. Flanking us, along either side aisle, were private praying areas secured by wrought-iron gates. One gate to our right was open and inside burned dozens of donation candles beneath the blessed eyes of the Virgin Mary.

At the front of the church appeared to be two crypts below heavenly murals framed by rose-marble pillars. Could either of these belong to the person to whom Jesse referred? As we got closer to the right boundary, we saw wooden doors opened outward from the tiled floor providing passage into a cellar.

"There seems to be an entrance fee. Maybe this is where our famous one lies?" I said, standing in front of a sign that read: Eintritt, 2 Euro.

"Let's take a chance," gambled Reuben. "We can at least say we've seen the cellar of an ancient church."

"You've got a point. Let's check it out!"

At the bottom of the steps sat an older man at a desk swamped with paperwork and knickknacks. "Zwei Euro, bitte," he announced.

Here was a great opportunity to flaunt my newly learned German. "Entschuldigung, haben Sie schon einmal etwas über das Bayernkreuz gehört?"

"Keine Ahnung! Zwei Euro, bitte."

By his curt answer, I had to assume he either wasn't familiar with the cross or he didn't understand a word I said. My money was on the latter.

After handing him four euros between us, we ventured into a stunted hallway that led to a room the size of a studio apartment. Along the walls were crypts of the Bavarian royal family, Wittelsbach: dukes, kings, princes and princesses.

"I think we found our famous one?" Reuben stated as he led me to a crypt that was seemingly more noteworthy than the rest.

Yep, he was right. It belonged to King Ludwig II of Bavaria, better known as the slightly unhinged fairy-tale king. Somehow I thought his burial chamber would be as opulent as his castles, but it wasn't much to speak of. However, I can now say I've witnessed the last resting place of the famous monarch. Having already seen his Herrenchiemsee castle, all that's left for me to complete Ludwig's legacy is to visit his other two fantasy castles: Linderhof and Neuschwanstein, a.k.a. the Disneyland castle.

It appeared as if Reuben had seen enough. I figured this was a good time to shift gears. "Are you completely churched-out?"

"Completely!"

"Then we have our next task at hand. Let's go outside."

Page 4

Go back the way you came along the Shopping Street and make the first left at the Hunting and Fishing Museum, marked by a giant-sized wild boar and catfish. Shortly thereafter you will come to Frauenplatz — this is for you, Reuben; it translates to Women's Square. Here you'll find Munich's Old Town landmark, the enormous Frauenkirche, or Church of Our Lady. Go inside to find the devil's footprint. Once you're both completely and utterly churched-out, return outside and read further...

Reuben made a clucking sound of disapproval before objecting: "Another church!"

Although he wasn't thrilled, it didn't take much to sway him. "Come on, Reuben, it's history... Besides, don't the devil's footprint and Women's Square sound interesting?"

"Yeah, I guess."

The museum was easy to find; out front were hefty bronze figures of an open-mouthed catfish and a wild boar with funky teeth. Around the next bend was our square. "Where are the women?" Reuben asked curiously.

"It's just the name of the square. It doesn't mean women are standing on corners prostituting themselves."

"Pity."

"Albert!!" I scolded his Munich alias.

"Oh!" Reuben replied. "I'm sorry, did I say that out loud?"

The exterior of the church was ordinary, comprised of plain red brick devoid of fancy Baroque curves or intimidating Gothic gargoyles so common in Germany. Nonetheless, its two landmark clock towers made the building a focal point.

"They look like overflowing beer mugs," Reuben envisioned.

"I think they look phallic."

"Juliet!!" Reuben turned the tables and scolded my Munich identity.

The least I could do was use his material. "Oh! I'm sorry, did I say that out loud?"

We entered the holy structure through the main portal and instantly noticed two things: only one stained-glass window, which was set behind the high altar at the opposite end of the church, and directly in front of us a small group of tourists huddled around their guide, who was pointing at something on the floor. We were close enough to hear his narration:

"According to legend, this is the devil's footprint. Satan left it here more than five centuries ago when he came to inspect the completion of what he believed to be a one-window church. From this angle, due to an architectural trick, the stained-glass windows along the side walls are not visible. The devil was so thrilled about this dark and gloomy design rejecting God's light that his enthusiasm lifted him several meters off the ground. Upon coming down, Satan mightily landed on his right foot, permanently leaving an imprint in the floor tile."

At that intersection, Reuben backed up and made a swift exit.

"Albert," I called out in hopes of stopping him.

"Page 5!" he yelped on his way out the door.

Huh...What's his problem? Perhaps thoughts of Lucifer gave him the creeps. Anyway, the next page was calling.

Page 5

I would assume you're famished by now. Just bear with me through the next set of instructions:

Wander along the left side of the church until you reach Albertgasse. Take this alleyway to the pedestrian thoroughfare of Weinstrasse. Here you'll see numerous people scampering past; a reminder that you're in Germany's third-largest city. Cross over Weinstrasse and walk the length of Landschaftstrasse. A park will be to your left and the town hall to your right (other side of town hall is Marienplatz). Continue straight into the narrow lane, Altenhofstrasse. Near the end on the right you'll see a plaque dedicated to W.A. Mozart; the condensed version reads: "He lived here from Nov. 6, 1780, to March 11, 1781. Remember him and his music as you pass by."

At the end of the lane, make a left. Now you are standing at the castle gate of the Alter Hof. Dating from 1253, this was the original residence of the dynastic Wittelsbach family, rulers of the Bavarian kingdom for more than 700 years. Once inside, notice the so-called monkey tower on your left. The path will lead you through the medieval quad and back into modern society, where you'll turn left at the equestrian statue. Continue to the end of the block and turn left again. This is Dienerstrasse — you'll recognize the green park. Wander past the shop fronts until you come to the cigar window. Now that you've reached the home of the Dallmayr stogie, back up a few paces and enter through the two narrow doors.

Inside is a do-it-yourself culinary experience. You don't have to buy your food here; it can be pricey!

Another option is to head back to Marienplatz, which is to your right when facing Dallmayr's, and descend into the subway for a less-expensive selection. Nevertheless, pick up something, somewhere "to go" — you're in for a picnic. Once you've completed the food mission, return to Dienerstrasse and read further...

"Famished" was an understatement. Eagerly, we set course for our new destination: food.

Jesse was right about Weinstrasse being a hectic pedestrian thoroughfare. Here we had to dodge, dart, dip, and duck our way across. On the other side we paralleled the elongated, neo-Gothic town hall, and in the leafy park to our left we saw a carnival crammed with teeny tots. Traversing our way through a gaggle of cotton-candy brandishing kids, we navigated the assigned streets and rediscovered Mozart. To trace his whereabouts in Salzburg was fascinating enough; to rendezvous with him in Munich was unbelievable!

A few steps farther and we found ourselves facing the castle gate of the Alter Hof, where a modest tin shield denoted the year 1253. We entered through a medieval archway to reach the inner courtyard.

"That monkey tower has my interest," Reuben remarked while browsing the scene. "There, that could be it!" He pointed to a three-story bay window crowned by an emerald-green spire.

"I wonder how it got its name?" I questioned.

Reuben shrugged. "Perhaps monkeys were brought back from one of the king's African visits and kept here."

"Anything's possible," I said, "Hannibal once used his zoo of elephants to cross the Alps and attack Romans."

"Whoa!"

Exiting through the opposite gate, we left the age-old serenity of the Alter Hof behind and returned to the prosperous Munich of the 21st century — where police cars were BMWs and taxicabs were Mercedes.

Jesse wasn't kidding about the narrow wooden doors next to the stogie shop. Reuben and I were trying to squeeze through as a group of Hungarian weightlifters apparently had the same idea. The awkward tussle was rapidly forgotten once inside. The aroma from the food counters sent my stomach into a tizzy. Jesse had sent us into victuals heaven. From my lips to God's ears, thank you.

Food was Dallmayr's game and gourmet its specialty. Each counter was a boulevard of specialized fare, an edible odyssey of European cheese, German pastry, Munich sausage, Austrian torte, Wiener schnitzel, French quiche, exotic fruit, live crayfish, fresh pasta, elegant paté, robusta coffee, spicy tea, Chiemsee schnapps, and vintage wine. We must have bought a sample of everything.

Page 6

First, I must apologize for putting you through that gourmet drama at Dallmayr's, but it's a must-see on the tourist circuit because it is Munich's oldest deli and a delight to stroll through. So, with that being said and your picnic bags in hand, let's march on.

When facing Dallmayr's, go left and take Dienerstrasse to Residenzstrasse (where red bike lane begins). Farther ahead, at the streetcar tracks, look for the sign-posted corner of Residenzstrasse and Perusastrasse. Walk over to the signpost and stand next to it while facing in the direction you've been walking. From this hectic area you can see three noble members of the Bavarian royal family in statue form. You are obviously more than familiar with the most famous of the Wittelsbachs, King Ludwig II (a.k.a the fairy-tale king). To your distant right, at the other end of the boulevard, is his father, King Max II. After scoping Max II, rotate your eyes left until you see Father Max sitting on his favorite chair. He is King Ludwig II's great grandfather, and the founder of that neoclassical structure behind him, the Bavarian National Theater (to Father Max's right is the Residenz, where the Wittelsbachs moved to after outgrowing the Alter Hof). Gaze left again and look all the way down Residenzstrasse; you'll see the equestrian statue of King Ludwig I, the fairy-tale king's grandfather, and creator of the Oktoberfest. Don't worry if he's hard to see; he'll get closer as you forge ahead.

Continue your original course on Residenzstrasse, passing Father Max on the right and paralleling the Residence itself. Eventually you'll see four lions.

They represent the four seasons and are said to bring good luck when the nose of each lion is rubbed. Make a wish!

It was also here that on November 9, 1923, Hitler's Beer Hall Putsch came to a bloody end with 16 of his followers paying the ultimate price for the young Nazi Party. Opposite the third lion, atop the 10-foot side wall of the Feldhermhalle (General's Hall), a memorial was erected during the years of the Third Reich for those who died that day in the struggle — wreaths were laid, guards were posted, and all passersby had to hail the Nazi salute.

One couldn't miss our first stop. It was an extremely frantic intersection where the main road, bike lanes, pedestrian paths, and trolley tracks converged. In the midst of urban pandemonium, we saw the three nobles.

All of a sudden, Reuben hollered the approach of an oncoming truck: "Watch out!" Then I heard the blast of a horn followed by the spine-tingling screeches of a streetcar braking. Reuben grabbed my arm and yanked me clear of the trolley and straight into a bicyclist. I spun like a top and fell to the asphalt. The bicyclist lost his balance and rode into a post, leaving poor Reuben at odds for whom to attend to first. "I'll be fine," I insisted. "See if the bicyclist is okay."

Reuben raced over to help, "Are you all right?!"

"Ja, I zink so."

A passerby offered me a hand up. I thanked him and made my way over to Reuben and the shaken bicyclist. "I'm so sorry," I said. "It was my fault this happened and...Albert here saved my life."

The bicyclist brushed off his clothes. "Alles ist ok, don't vurry." He then maneuvered the ball cap he was wearing and his hair fell to her shoulders. He happened to be a she, and she was beautiful. By the expression on Reuben's face, you'd think he had just won the lotto.

"Ahh...," Reuben tried his college best, "Maybe I could buy you a drink later to make up for this most unfortunate incident?"

"I vould luv zat, but I musst go zu mein oma's haus in Dresden. How'z about next veek?" she adoringly asked.

This was turning out to be quite the love story. I pulled my hair back in a ponytail and watched on.

"I... I... fly back home in a few days." I could see by Reuben's immediate grief that a trip to the dentist to have teeth pulled would have been preferable.

"Vell... I give yu mein telefon nummer ins case yu stay." She snatched a pen from her bag, scribbled something on a piece of paper and handed it to Reuben. "Hier, it wuz nice meeting yu, Albert."

Bicycle Girl maneuvered into the Tour de Munich bike lane and rode off. Reuben wore a vacant stare as she cycled into the distance. He then anxiously glared my way. "She thinks my name is Albert!"

He was worried about nothing. But it was clearly my duty to ease the pain. "If you play your cards right, you'll get a second chance."

"I can't believe the love of my life just left me and she thinks my name is Albert."

"I think you'll survive. Besides, you've got her number. Why don't you postpone your flight home a week?"

"Yeah... Easy for you to say! I start work on Monday."

"You said she was the love of your life; doesn't that count for something?"

"I did say that, didn't I?" He frowned as if contemplating rocket science.

Obviously his fleeting attraction to me had passed and he was on to new frontiers, which made things less complicated.

"Hey, Albert, there's Father Max." I was trying to solicit a change of thought. "Doesn't he look ceremonial?"

"Oh, Father, you saw the twinkle in her eye, please offer some advice."

Well, that idea bit the dust. Reuben was now lobbying statues on his behalf. "Come on. We've got to catch up with some lions," I pleaded.

"That's right! Jesse did say they brought good luck."

The Residence adjacent to Father Max looked quite impressive with its extensive stone-block facade and three levels of arched windows rising to at least 80 feet overhead. Behind Father Max sat a classical structure that could have been mistaken for belonging to the Acropolis collection. According to Jesse, this was the Bavarian National Theater.

"Come on. The lions are waiting," Reuben insisted. Our previous stroll of leisure became a frantic walk-a-thon.

Reuben had a childish hankering for Bicycle Girl, and it was becoming quite the nuisance. We arrived at Lions' Row and he began furiously rubbing the nose of the first one. "If I ever needed luck, oh dear lion, I need it now! Please let my boss say I can stay a week longer... Please!" He finally looked relieved. But I then reminded him of the fable.

"Don't you remember that the lions represent the seasons, and a wish can't be cast unless all four noses are rubbed?"

Heeding my suggestion, Reuben sprinted to the remaining lions, rubbing each of their noses with a passion, until he reached the last lion, which was already occupied by a man who appeared to be suffering from a similar dilemma. Reuben stood behind the man, exhibiting the tolerance of a 5-year-old who had to pee. He bobbed up and down, danced the hokey-pokey, and jolted from side-to-side. From my angle, three lions down, it looked like the makings of a "Mister Bean" skit. The man eventually abandoned his position in favor of kneeling to the ground and bowing in what was probably the direction of Mecca. Reuben swiftly jumped in and embraced the last lion with a big hug, planting an even bigger kiss on the end of its nose.

Reuben's infatuation had gone too far. I had to come up with something to get this dog-and-pony show back on the road. "I have this tremendous feeling that your boss will have absolutely no problem with you staying a week longer...Perhaps even two!"

"How can you say that? You don't know my boss."

"Jesse and I were talking the other day about you, your job, and how lucky you were to have such a nice boss." I was lying through my teeth, hoping he wouldn't call my bluff.

"So Jesse mentioned my boss, huh?"

Oh no, here it comes.

"He's always appreciated what I do for a living, and has even gotten along with the nastiest of my colleagues." It looked as if Reuben might be coming around. "You're right...I'll call my boss later tonight when I know it'll be early afternoon there and he's in a good mood."

"Hey...There's the 10-foot wall!" I was fairly confident I could get him to do a 180 with this observation. "This must be where Jesse said 16 of Hitler's followers died in the 1923 Beer Hall Putsch."

"That's right, and all passersby had to hail the Nazi salute," Reuben said on his way over for a closer inspection.

I pulled the Letter out of my back pocket to quote Jesse. "A memorial was erected during the years of the Third Reich for those who died that day in the struggle; wreaths were laid and guards posted."

Meanwhile, Reuben had managed to scale the wall like Spiderman and gave a report from the top ledge. "Radical... This must be where the memorial rested."

I made my way up to him via the broad steps around the corner and saw a newer asphalt section that was clearly covering the remnants of something. I couldn't imagine having to raise my arm in recognition of Hitler every time I walked by here, saluting what I didn't believe in. I wonder if this has anything to do with the memorial my dad once told me about. Not all Germans believed in the Nazi way, and those who refused to salute turned left before reaching the memorial, utilizing a quiet lane to bypass it. In due course, the lane became locally known as Sidestepper's Alley.

Reuben and I stood atop the General's Hall reflecting on the hardships the locals endured during the dark days of Hitler's Third Reich. Subsequently, our stomachs persuaded us to move on to a banquet of champions.

Page 7

Now that you're doped up on luck, let's settle in the park for a picnic. When eyeing the plaza in front of the Feldherrnhalle, you'll see a considerable archway ahead on the right — venture through this to the Hofgarten, or Royal Gardens, landscaped in 1613 on orders of the king.

Once through the archway, angle left past the centrally located rotunda (Diana Temple, Renaissance-style) and out the other side of the gardens. Here, you'll see people heading down a path and into a darkened tunnel. Follow them into the abyss, leading into Germany's largest city park. Keep to the main trail, which will eventually cross over the picturesque stream. On the other side of the bridge, go left and stick to the left path. After about 200 meters, find a place at the brook's edge for your picnic. Relax and enjoy the views in the English Garden.

The sun shone brightly attracting throngs of people to the English Garden, where Reuben searched for the perfect picnic location. "What do you think about this spot?"

"Wunderbar!" As hungry as I was, anywhere would've done.

We tore open both bags of food and maneuvered the goodies into strategic positions. Reuben began cutting the bread rolls while I unwrapped the Emmenthaler cheese and soccer-ball ham. Our surroundings were ultra conducive to a picnic as we sat on the edge of a crystal-clear stream that split a giant grassy field, bordered by a wooded reserve. Opposite us, on the other side of the stream, were a few shrubs and umpteen sun worshippers staking a piece of prime Munich real estate for the afternoon.

Reuben peeled back the lid on the potato salad while bobbing his head and addressing his self-made sandwich: "You look sooo good... Mmm, I'm going to eat you all up!"

I jammed two plastic forks into the potato salad and dug in before Hungry Boy inhaled it all.

"Cowabunga!" Reuben's eyes inflated and his jaw dropped as he stared past me.

"What?!" I shrieked. "What?" Reuben had me worried.

I swiveled to my right to see what he was spying: Two girls blissfully wading in the water — wearing only their birthday suits! A naked guy who looked to be in his late twenties also entered the stream, following their lead. It appears Jesse sent us on a "clothing optional" picnic.

Reuben sat motionless. "Wake up, wake up," I chanted, accompanied by aggressive finger snapping. "Earth to Albert."

"Errr, yeah... Looks fantastic. I mean, what a tasty bread roll!"

"Sure is." I said, slapping another sandwich together and rearranging the deli items out of the charring sun.

"Do you want to jump in and cool off?" asked Reuben, a rather bare question.

"What do you mean?"

"I mean it's warm sitting here in the sun."

"We have no towels."

"I dare you!"

"You dare me!" I scoffed his appeal. "What do I get in return for this 'dare'?"

"I'll buy ya dinner."

"Deal..." I double blinked, "...but you're coming in with me."

"Deal!"

I stood up, unbuckled my belt, pulled off my jeans, lifted my top over my head and undid my bra. Four steps later and I was up to my thighs in stream water. "Ahh, so refreshing!"

Coincidentally, the Birthday-Suit Girls turned around and began wading in my direction, as was the Twenties Guy.

"Albert... We had a deal." I had to remind him, as he just sat there seemingly in shock that I carried out his dare. But nudity to me wasn't such a big deal anymore after touring the Friedrichsbad with the girls in Baden-Baden.

Reuben reluctantly got up, undressed to his boxers and jumped in. "You're right, the water is totally refreshing! Oh, by the way...nice boobs! I'm sorry, did I say that out loud?"

The Birthday-Suit Girls reached our water domain and Reuben couldn't help himself. "Hi...Do you girls come from around here?"

They waded past him with only a faint upwards bend of the lip as a sign of acknowledgement. Reuben's telling eyes scanned their bodies like a barcode. He tried his best to quell his feelings, but Mister Wobbly had other ideas.

"Hey, genius," I announced, "your brain has relocated down under and it appears to be...swelling!"

"Juliet!" He was embarrassed, I could tell.

I made a snappy exit before I had to hear a similar corny line from the Twenties Guy, who was a mere 5 feet away. The Birthday-Suit Girls also exited, leaving Reuben in his Bugs Bunny boxer shorts standing next to a perky, naked guy.

"Juliet?" Reuben called out awkwardly.

"Yes, Einstein."

"Page 8!"

Page 8

Wasn't that an eye-opener? I thought it might liven up your lunch. Nude bathing is accepted in Germany and one of the nation's prime settings for this bare-all experience is Munich's beloved English Garden.

Now, continue along the brook via the asphalt path; make your first left and cross over the bridge. Follow this straight for some distance, out of the park and onto Veterinarstrasse, ultimately arriving at the University of Munich. Here you'll find the major boulevard of Ludwigstrasse; cross it via the pedestrian walk on the right.

You are now on the side of the main university building. Go left and immediately turn right; follow the asphalt lane towards the university. A fountain will be to your left, and the eight columns supporting the entrance will be getting closer in front of you. Take up residence on one of the wooden-top benches to your left and face the fountain. Once you're cozy, read further...

"Great, the last wooden bench is available."

Page 9

I do apologize for the uncomfortable seats, but Page 10 will more than make up for it. The name of the square you are now in is Geschwister-Scholl-Platz — a strange name, I know, but not so strange once you understand its origin. The word Geschwister means "siblings," and the tragic story that follows dates to the nation's hellish past.

Hans and Sophie Scholl were simple students who lived defiant lifestyles. They attended studies at the university and walked the same cobblestones where your feet now rest. Both in their early twenties, Hans was a soldier and a medical student, while Sophie explored courses in philosophy. It was the early 1940s, Germany was at war and Hans had seen conflict at both fronts of the theater, the Western and Russian. Hans returned to Munich disturbed by the atrocities he had witnessed and began to doubt the policies of his government. Through social circles he came in contact with fellow students who had equal reservations about the Nazis, including a professor at the university, Kurt Huber. The newly formed alliance composed leaflets denouncing Hitler's regime, hoping to gain support for a popular uprising. Each new flyer was circulated a few thousand at a time, reaching all points in Germany, and some found their way abroad. Around this time (summer of 1942), Hans' sister, Sophie, found out about the clandestine operation and demanded to join the ranks.

To make the resistance movement appear larger than it really was, they arranged for flyers to be distributed from other cities in Germany, which would also divert attention from Munich, their head-quarters. For nearly a year the fledgling movement defied the system, as they tried to reclaim the basic civil rights that the Nazis had stolen. The moment of opportunity struck with the surrender of Germany's Sixth Army at Stalingrad; the nation's love affair with Hitler had come to an end. Beginning a new campaign against Nazi oppression, Hans and another activist, Alex Schmorell, set out with paintbrushes in hand and graffiti'd every wall in their path, condemning Hitler's Reich. The resistance movement seemed to be gaining momentum. Early on the morning of February 18, 1943, adding a new chapter to the annals of audac-ity, the labors of Hans and Sophie turned their most fearless corner yet. For unknown reasons, perhaps out of desperation, they openly distributed the movement's leaflets in the very building behind you, leaving them on windowsills, along corridors, and in front of lecture room doors. As if it were a final gesture, they fer-vently tossed what remained of their flyers over the balconies. The spirited words of the movement gently cascaded through the air, decorating the floor below with neatly trimmed pieces of paper. Among the curious students bending down to inspect the leaflets was the janitor, a Nazi sympathizer. Within minutes the university was in lockdown and the Gestapo (Secret State Police) were called to arrest the Scholl siblings. At first, the Gestapo felt they'd apprehended the wrong people, for Hans was a soldier in the Reich's army and Sophie was his young, ador-able sister. Nevertheless, the siblings stood defiant and admitted to their revolutionary actions. For their crimes they were sent to Stadelheim prison on the edge of town and beheaded by guillotine.

Now you know the meaning of the square in which you sit, and in Germany today there are many cities and towns with streets named in memoriam of the brother and sister Scholl. The resistance movement was called the "White Rose," and to your right, embedded between the cobblestones, are replications of the White Rose flyers.

We got up immediately to investigate. Sure enough, the White Rose flyers were exactly where Jesse said they'd be.

"Whoa, I can't believe it!" Reuben exclaimed while lowering to one knee and softly touching one of the inlaid tablets.

"How about if we take a quick look inside the university?" I asked.

He nodded, and we made our way between the massive columns supporting the building's entrance and past billboards pinned to the brim with various advertisements for guitar lessons, shared accommodations, items for sale, and a party next Thursday. Once inside the glass doors, the youthful college atmosphere yielded to an aged, uninspiring environment. Before us rose a staircase to the first level, where we discovered a generous view of the structure's interior. Sizeable windows lit the inner quad and the surrounding balconies. And then we saw it. Straight ahead on the left, a plaque flushed with flowers adorned the wall. This had to be a memorial to the White Rose.

The steps before us cascaded from our plateau to the main floor, which was cream-colored and ash gray in composition, consisting of little ceramic tiles similar to those used by ancient civilizations to create patterns and designs. Reuben and I walked over slithering snakes, neatly crafted squares, and half-moon arches before we reached the memorial.

On the wall were seven engraved names — I brushed the indentations with my forefinger — the last two were that of brother and sister Scholl.

Reuben and I gazed around the premises in reflection; I imagined Hans and Sophie hastily tossing the leaflets from the balconies above and watching them gently fall onto the very floor we stood. Perhaps it was also here that the Gestapo apprehended the siblings, before hauling them off to their brutal deaths.

Reuben broke his silence and pointed to the memorial. "These seven fighters are heroes in the name of humanity."

"My sentiments exactly. Hopefully in the next set of directions we'll have time to drink a toast to Geschwister Scholl and company."

"Cheers to that!"

Page 10

Whew... That was an emotional story. I'm glad you had the chance to experience the courageous actions of the White Rose.

Congratulations for reaching the last page in your 'Letter' escapade. I anticipate that you've enjoyed your jaunt through Bavaria's capital thus far. For your next installment of adventure, you'll be throwing on your research hat followed by grabbing a drink.

Exit Geschwister-Scholl-Platz right and head back into the old town via Ludwigstrasse — you'll recognize the Feldherrnhalle in the distance. Cross at the next traffic light and go right; from the other side of the boulevard you'll soon reach the Bavarian State Library, which is the second largest of its kind in Europe with more than 7 million books and 40,000 periodicals. Within this impressive building you're bound to find some info on the Bavarian Cross.

Lastly, after perusing the library, saunter over to the most famous beer hall in the world to experience some German culture — no doubt you deserve it! The tavern is called the Hofbrauhaus. Just ask anyone where it is; locals and tourists alike can point the way. Enjoy your evening and have a juice for me.

Your friend, Jesse

The library had an awesome collection of knowledge, indeed. While I researched the crucifix, Reuben kept himself busy by thumbing through a provocative array of German fashion magazines.

Jesse was right; I did find some info on the Bavarian Cross. In fact, I found much more than I had anticipated. The crucifix doesn't date from the 19th century, as previously thought — it dates back to the 14th century. It was hard to fathom. This venerable relic just went from mega-expensive to priceless in an afternoon.

In the year 1328, much of Central Europe had banded together to form the mighty and powerful Holy Roman Empire, which stretched from the North Sea to the Mediterranean. At this time the newly elected emperor to rule this vast territory was none other than Ludwig the Bavarian, the fairy-tale king's medieval grandfather. Apparently, Ludwig the Bavarian was an extremely pious individual who believed the prosperity of his empire lay with a particular jeweled crucifix made of gold given to him by an Augustinian monk upon his coronation.

Ludwig referred to the cross as "das Bayernkreuz" and traveled with it everywhere while his kingdom flourished. One day Ludwig went on a hunting trip outside Munich without the crucifix and mysteriously died. Consequently, das Bayernkreuz vanished for some 550 years until it reappeared at Chiemsee. By that time the Holy Roman Empire had gone the way of the buffalo and the ruler of the Bavarian kingdom was Ludwig II, better known as "Mad" King Ludwig or the fairy-tale king.

Ludwig II somehow found das Bayernkreuz but then gave it to a wine merchant's son for his 10th birthday, just as ShoSho had initially said. A month later, the king died. The official record of his death was drowning. But after doing more research, it didn't add up.

When it was Ludwig's turn to wear the Bavarian crown in 1864, he did a rather sloppy job, as ruling a nation state didn't come naturally. He first sided with the Austrians against the Prussians, or northern Germans, in the Seven Weeks' War, and then sided with the Prussians against the French in the Franco-Prussian War. Ludwig was more of a romantic, a pacifist, and a lover of the opera than a warmonger. His dream was to build the most beautiful, luxurious castles in the land, and he did. Ludwig furnished them with colorful murals of Wagnerian operas and medieval themes, showpiece bedrooms and glitzy thrones, gaudy chandeliers and intimate grottos. However, this high-maintenance lifestyle drained Bavaria's coffers. Add Ludwig's inept mode of leadership to the mix and you've got a recipe for murder.

Behind his back, Ludwig's cabinet conspired against him. On June 12, 1886, they declared the king mentally unfit to rule and exiled him with his doctor to Schloss Berg at Lake Starnberg, 25 kilometers southwest of Munich. The following day, both he and his doctor drowned in 3 feet of water. Not only did it seem amazing that two grown men simultaneously drowned, but even more amazing for Ludwig, who was 6 feet 5 inches tall.

There had to be more to the story than accidental drowning. And why did Ludwig hastily give away the crucifix? Perhaps he knew someone was after him, or more precisely, after the Bavarian Cross!

*   *   *

Reuben's body stood idle as he perused the cobbled lane. "There's the Hard Rock Cafe," he observed; his head saucered like a periscope, "and... There's the Hofbräuhaus, the world's most famous beer hall."

Inside the cavernous hall was noisy. The steady sound of clinking glasses and the chatter of voices came from hundreds of people sitting elbow to elbow at long, picnic-style tables busily conversing while quaffing tankards of golden-colored beer. Flanking the main aisle before us were four pillars rising to a ceiling splashed with colorful murals, and centrally located was a small stage laden with musical instruments that left hardly any room for their owners to play.

The only seats available were at a nearby table, occupied by six people gleefully attending to their colossal, liter-sized beer mugs.

"Excuse me, are these seats available?" I asked no one in particular, gesturing to the vacancy either side of the table.

"Ja, freilich!" said the closest guy with a rosy-cheeked grin.

We weren't quite sure what "freilich" meant, but by his friendly demeanor the answer had to be "yes."

While we were settling in, a buxom dirndl-clad waitress clutching fistfuls of frothy beers promptly marched over to our end of the table. "Was möchten Sie, bitte? Wir empfehlen Bier!" She delivered her spiel like bullets from a machine gun.

We must have looked perplexed, because our waitress rephrased her question: "Vhut you vant zu trink, pleez?"

"Zwei Bier, bitte." I replied, holding up two fingers to make sure my German translated. She lowered the beer to the table and released a pair of dimpled mugs dripping with suds.

"Oh my gawd...So much love!" wailed the funky Californian.

"Good cheer by the liter," I noted. Although, I wondered whether Reuben's euphoric mood had anything to do with his eyes being buried in our waitress' cleavage.

First things first, we elevated our gargantuan mugs in a toast to the others at the table: "Prost" — meaning "cheers" — we roared. It took both my hands and stark concentration not to chip a tooth or drop the mug on my lap. Afterwards, through introductions totaling almost a liter of beer, we met Fritz and Wolfgang from Berlin; Verena and Marietta from Innsbruck, Austria; along with Gemma and Katherine from Australia.

Now it was time to have that drink in honor of the White Rose. "Prost...To the White Rose!" I hoisted my glass once again.

Fritz, Wolfgang, Verena, Marietta, Gemma and Katherine must have been listening, because they, too, raised their mugs. "To the White Rose!"

The amber juice was undeniably making itself felt; things got nuttier by the hour. The Berliner boys were getting better acquainted with the Austrians and some guy from another table obnoxiously made himself comfortable next to Katherine. As for bonhomie Reuben, he made a play for her pretty pal. "Hey, Gemma, where do you come from in Australia?"

She got up and moved next to Reuben, who began to sparkle with delight. "Newcastle, it's 90 minutes north of Sydney," Gemma replied, emphasizing her harmonious accent.

"I think I've heard of that place."

"You have?!" She sounded thrilled.

"Yep, they have kangaroos there, right?"

Uh, oh, surely that didn't score him any points. He'll be lucky to get the rebound.

"We have a lot of wallabies in my area..."

Reuben unknowingly cut her off, "What's a wallaby?"

"They're ferocious creatures!" Gemma retorted, sarcastically. "...They have a tubby, long tail with monstrous hind legs, nimble feet and vicious forepaws."

"Wow!" He exclaimed with startled eyes.

"Excuse me, I've got to go to the loo," Gemma said before getting up and venturing in the direction of the toilet.

Reuben eyeballed me, sadly. "She's not interested," he said.

"How can you tell?"

"Oh, I can tell...and she's not interested!"

"She'll be back." I reassured him.

"Girls don't like me," he woefully claimed.

"What do you mean...girls don't like you?"

"Exactly that!"

"That's ridiculous!"

Interrupting our discourse, a folk band took the stage and began to play. I watched as rows of people linked arms and rocked back and forth. Others stood, swaying their mugs to the beat of the oompah-pah. An elderly gentleman with a green felt hat and handlebar moustache bought a pretzel from the mobile vendor to complement his beer. The frothy stuff flowed copiously and the mood was carefree. Some in the crowd decided to use the tabletop as a disco floor, including Reuben McJiggy, but were soon waved down by security.

"Prost!" Another round of cheers shook the table.

"Albert, look," I happily announced, "Gemma's back!"

"Yeah, with a player in tow," Reuben stated, jumping to conclusions. "I bet that guy gets more ass than a toilet seat!" He was clearly disappointed. "Girls just don't like me. I've tried everything from brushing my hair in the opposite direction to an assortment of deodorants."

"Don't be so hard on yourself," I said. "If it's any consolation, when we first met, I saw you as a type of...Reubeniser."

This statement seemed to boost his spirits.

"Really...!" he exclaimed. "You mean like a guy the chicks dig?"

I nodded.

His eyes shimmered, resembling giant eggs sunny-side up. "I guess you're right... This isn't my first rodeo!"

I wrapped my arm around Reuben's shoulders. "You see that pretty redhead over there?" I said, pointing to a girl sitting alone at a table full of revelers ignoring her company. He nodded. "Go over and cheer her up."

Reuben greeted this idea by jiggling his hand as if he'd burned his fingers with the flames of love. "Oh, baaaby!"

My suggestion took hold as he rose to his feet with the look of sheer confidence. Perhaps I had come to know my traveling companion almost too well, because as I watched his next move, I swore I could "hear" his thoughts.

Mmm, Sydney was correct; this chick's the cat's meow. Here comes the Reubeniser to hand out some sugar. "You mind if I sit here?"

"No, please do."

I situated myself next to her and began my spiel, "So..."

Not more than two nanoseconds had

transpired when the game was visibly over. A guy approached, he took her hand and whisked her away. Just my luck, she was probably waiting for him to come out of the pisser.

Refreshingly, I was plucked from the abyss. A girl from the next table must have noticed the Reubeniser because she made an effort to lean my way and pierce the rhythmic clamor. "What's your name?"

"Albert Einstein. What's yours?"

"Sarah."

"What?" I couldn't hear her because the folk band suddenly got louder. I tried to explain with a clutter of words and a plethora of hand expressions that I wasn't receiving her transmission.

She stretched herself even farther, reaching the vicinity of my ear and shouted. "My name is SARAH! Why don't you move over to my table?" As she spat out the last sentence, the music stopped and a nosy few whipped their necks in our direction with mischievous grins as if to say, 'Someone's gonna get lucky tonight!'

I nodded in response and redeployed to her table with my brew in hand. We lifted our mugs in recognition of a newly formed friendship. "Cheers."

Sarah seemed the talkative sort, an English chick from Cornwall, not one to set the world on fire — but hip just the same. We had a spirited conversation picking on each other's accents, my name, and peculiar British jargon. I must have really impressed her because she kept referring to me as King Wanker. I was flattered to be associated with royalty.

The minute hand had already swept once around the hour since our introduction, and a connection hadn't been made; it was time to close the deal: "Sarah, I'm going to the bar, and when I get back ... I'm gonna kiss you!"

I strutted to the john, unleashed Tommy Boy, zipped up Tommy Boy, casually exited past the toilet-cleaner guy sitting at the door collecting money for the pleasure, tracked down a waiter and swapped the change in my pocket for another beer. This was certainly enough time for Sarah to absorb my proposal.

When I got back, sucking face was not an option — she had split the scene sneaky-fast.

"Oh, there you are!" Sydney appeared with a liquored smile. "So, how ya doing with the ladies?"

"Not so good."

"Come on, you're a groovy guy." She put her arm around me again. "You know what we haven't done yet?"

"What?"

"Had a toast on behalf of our wonderful guide."

"You're right!" Without moving from our spot next to the souvenir stand, Sydney hoisted her mug to offer a toast. "Dear Jesse, thanks for your enter-taining letter; nothing could have enlightened us more... This is for you: Prost!"

I countered with a quote from Benjamin Franklin: "'Beer is proof that God loves us and wants us to be happy.' Prost!"

There was one last thing to do — call my boss. Sydney and I laughed our way over to the pay phone, traversing through a gaggle of tipsy patrons doing the Chicken Dance to the beat of the oompah-pah. It was exactly how I imagined walking through the cafeteria of a mental hospital.

The phone ate sickening amounts of coinage before I heard my boss' voice. "Joe's Mortuary, this is Joe, how can I help you?"

"Joe...it's Ruby!"

"Ruby, how are ya?"

"Good, Joe, good. Look, I gotta make this quick. I've got three horny Bavarian girls tugging at my Lederhosen...I can't come to work on Monday. I'll see ya the following week, auf Wiederseh'n!" Click!

I hung up the phone and glanced at Sydney, "How was I?"

"Splendid! Now let's get outta here!" She grabbed me and we whizzed out the door.

Back at the hostel, we tried to be as quiet as church mice — but to no avail. Sydney kept imitating the train conductor to an unfair advantage. In no way do I remember him having glistening hair that ceaselessly brushed against his breasts and a horrendously bad German accent with a beer-induced slur.

Before heading down the hallway in search of the john, I promised a swift return. When I came back, Sydney was fast asleep — tucked in like a baby. She looked prettier than ever.

*   *   *

"Albert, wake up... Albert!" His snoring was brutal, chasing away the other hostellers hours earlier.

"Huh, wha..., leave me alone!" Reuben brazenly pulled the covers over his head and continued snoring.

"Albert...We've overslept!" I shook him until a catastrophic 9 regis-tered on the Californian's Richter Scale.

The cleaning lady walked in, reminding me that it was 12:30 in the afternoon and, "If he doesn't get out of that bed in the next five minutes, management will have no choice but to enslave him on a remote island."

Then, as if smelling salts had been administered, there was life in the West Coast party owl. Reuben tiredly lifted himself up to his elbows and peeled open his sensitive, bloodshot eyes, resembling a vampire registering first light.

He then fell backwards onto the mattress as gracelessly as he'd raised himself up. "Oh, my aching head!" Reuben massaged his brow. Pillow creases defined his face.

"Are you okay?" I asked.

"I'll be fine; my head's just a little delicate."

Reuben tried desperately a second time to lift himself up. This time he laboriously succeeded. "You know, I just had the most bizarre dream. I was shipwrecked on a remote island with a gay Rastafarian who was frolicking on the beach holding two coconuts, wearing a pink Speedo and yodeling: 'ANY OLE MAN'LL DO.'"

That said, Reuben groggily exited the room and headed down the hallway to the bathroom. He looked quite the sight with his hair standing on end, mouth wide open, yawning, and only wearing his Bugs Bunny boxer shorts.

A minute later a frail man in his 70s or 80s with thin gray hair and a sagging face appeared at the door. He gave me a stern look, kind of freaky-like as if to say, 'It was you I came for.' Without breaking eye contact, the frail man reached into the pocket of his hand-woven sweater and pulled out a small piece of scratch paper that had been folded in half. The man then lifted the paper up and held it in front of his old face.

"This is for you," he said.

Okay, this was really weird. I hoped Reuben would return, soon, and join the fun.

The man slowly extended his hand outwards and gave me the paper. I opened it and read the contents:

What you can't see can easily be found.

I didn't understand; what could this have meant? I read it again. By the time I looked up, the man was gone. I bolted out the door to try to catch him, but the hallway was empty. He had vanished!

Bulwarks and Mysteries

CHAPTER 8

In some way, the Frail Man's note has to be connected to the Bavarian Cross. But how? Or maybe it's just me wanting to believe they're connected. I do know one thing for sure — this quest is beginning to drive me crazy. Totally crazy! I've paged through a mountain of old books, questioned what seems like half of Germany, worn fresh grooves into the cobbled lanes of nearby villages, burned the midnight oil surfing the Web, and I have nothing to show for it except strained eyes, sore feet and a cleavage-enhancing Bavarian dress called a dirndl that Sep, a local fisherman, gave me because he thinks I'll look "wunderschön" in it at next week's yodeling and beer-drinking festival. Well, at least my German is improving.

What you can't see can easily be found... What you can't see can easily be found... I must have run those words through my head a thousand times or more. And then, suddenly, it hit me. I dashed over to a neighbor's room who I knew had what I was looking for. She switched it on and, sure enough, the blacklight illuminated what could easily be found:

What you can't see can easily be found.
Dearest Investigators: Before a Brook and Forest Calculate Adventure 1010347000

The Frail Man's note was a clue within a clue. The second part was written with a UV pen. Now I knew it had something to do with the Bavarian Cross. The whole episode was too mysterious to be otherwise. But why would the Frail Man want to help me? Maybe he didn't. Maybe it's some kind of trap. Maybe there are others involved. Enough gibberish; I've come too far to be talking nonsense.

Just when I thought all leads had dead-ended, a riddle and some numbers appear. Now I had something to really sink my teeth into. Wait till Jesse sees this; he'll be ecstatic. Good thing Reuben's not here; he would've flipped out.

Reuben has been gone for almost a month. Although, I'm sure he'll be back sometime soon. Indeed he chased up that dream date with Bicycle Girl, or the love of his life, whichever you prefer. Jesse and I didn't see him until two days after the big rendezvous. We began to get worried and planned a full-scale search of Munich, then Reuben walked through my door grinning from ear to ear.

The day came when he had to fly home — and that was, to say the least, not a pretty sight. I thought my departure from Mother was a difficult one, but this exodus proved even more exhausting. Reuben had fallen ass-over-tea-kettle in love, all right. Jesse, Bicycle Girl, and I bid farewell to him under a hail of hugs and kisses. Reuben wept virtually the entire time in the arms of his love, while Jesse and I received periodic attention. I figured corralling a horde of wild boar would have been easier than saying goodbye to someone who could be The One. When I had told Jesse how they met, he could only utter: "That's when you know it was meant to be."

We knew Reuben would've loved to have hit the road with us — however, going in spirit would have to suffice. Jesse asked me if I wanted to take a drive up north with him for a few days. His girlfriend, for some reason, wasn't going. Reuben had mentioned something about "trouble in paradise." I could only hope. There was no way I was going to pass up such a serendipitous opportunity.

The trip was research for one of the chapters in his travel book, with emphasis on the Valley of the Loreley. This is the castle-studded stretch of the Rhine River from Bingen to Koblenz that recently joined the ranks of such unique and diverse places as the ancient pyramids of Giza and the Great Barrier Reef as an esteemed member of UNESCO's World Heritage List. Here we'd encounter picturesque hamlets and juicy vineyards adorning the riverbanks, as well as the famous Cat and Mouse castles, the bewitching legend of a maiden named Loreley, and a boat cruise likened to a mythical ride at Disneyland. I was especially looking forward to the latter, cruising back to a time when petty kings and ruthless robber barons occupied the magnificently medieval castles that crowned the unassailable bluffs. I even packed my bikini for the sundeck.

Then, despite the lure of the Loreley, our plans changed. The night before our departure I was dissecting the new clue, as usual, but this time I felt confident that I had flipped the numbers just the right way and possibly had solved the riddle. The only problem was that I wouldn't know for sure whether I had cracked the code unless I went to where the clue pointed. I immediately told Jesse about my discovery and he believed my findings carried enough weight to warrant a change in plans. Courtesy of the Frail Man, the Rhine River got relegated to another day and our next installment of adventure led Jesse and me to a new destination: Rothenburg ob der Tauber, a walled community dating from the Middle Ages situated on Germany's Romantic Road.

Jesse calculated our drive to Rothenburg would take about five hours. We decided to leave early to get a full day's sightseeing in along the way. Our first stop: Augsburg, 60 kilometers northwest of Munich.

It was a sunny and warm day in August with few clouds in a blue sky. The once snow-capped Alps revealed their solid-rock crests. Balmy summer gusts ruffled the sea-green grass carpeting the velvety pastures. Due to the proximity of Augsburg, the photographic backdrop began to become more urban. Golden fields of wheat yielded to endless lengths of sagging power lines supported by monstrous steel structures crisscrossing the landscape.

Commercialism prevailed over rural harmony while automobiles clashed at intersections. All northbound traffic merged onto the city streets. We knew the Old Town was close, but exactly where remained a mystery. The dizzying array of directional signs ultimately brought us to the periphery.

Jesse couldn't contain his enthusiasm. "Augsburg, a settlement that rings loudly in the history books! It's one of the three oldest cities in Germany and is named after its founding father, Roman Emperor Augustus, in 15 B.C."

How appropriate it was to be in Augsburg in August, since both were christened after the gallivanting Augustus. No doubt I wanted to know more; I could see Jesse waiting for the call. "What else can ya tell me?"

"Since you asked...Augsburg in the late 15th century, already having a population of 50,000, became a center for high finance. Nowadays we hear about the European Central Bank; then it was the Fuggers."

Here I had to giggle, the name sounded corny.

The traffic light turned green, Jesse motored ahead, and thick metropolitan air recycled through the car.

"The Fugger family was a dynastic authority commanding the wealth of an empire, financing the Habsburgs themselves. The Habsburgs frequently held the throne of the Holy Roman Empire, influencing power over Western Europe. In those days, imperial diets, or assemblies, of the kingdom were held here...for example, the Augsburg Confession and the Augsburg Peace."

I recall Jesse preaching the First Reich as being the Holy Roman Empire, but the Augsburg something or other was news to me. "What were the latter two?"

"You've heard of Martin Luther and the Reformation, right?"

"Right, but not in detail."

"Well, late in the Middle Ages, scholars began assessing translations of the Bible along with other documentation that shaped the foundations of church doctrine and ritual. In the mid-15th century, the printing press was invented, giving innovators a new mass media to work with to spread ideas quicker. One such innovator was Martin Luther, a theologian in the first half of the 16th century who popularized the theory of religious freedom when he nailed his Ninety-Five Theses to the door of the Castle Church in Wittenberg. To cut a long story short, the Church of Rome held a monopoly on the Christian faith. But Luther believed that it was the Bible, God's words...rather than the church...that should be the source of religious authority. Luther's liberal philosophy of guidance by faith alone struck a powerful chord with commoners, and in the thousands they began to sever their allegiance to the Church of Rome, which in turn spread rebellion across the northern parts of the empire. The rulers unsuccessfully tried to quell the people's uprising and the Augsburg Confession, a summary of the new Lutheran faith, was presented here in 1530 to German nobility. The convention was a landmark event. While nobles conferred within their swanky chambers, Luther's followers were protesting on the streets demanding freedom of religion. For this reason, Lutherans also became known as Protestants. Nevertheless, the emperor rejected Lutheranism as a faith, and consequently their struggles raged on." Jesse paused and I seized the opportunity for a question.

"Does that mean the battle for religious freedom was fought here?"

"No, that battle was fought throughout the land. In fact, it wasn't until some 25 years later that the emperor, due to diminishing support, felt obliged to declare the religious civil war over by instigating the Augsburg Peace. This finally meant that Protestants gained legitimate acceptance and the concept of a solitary Christian community in Western Europe under the supreme authority of the Pope...was abolished."

"Is it possible to see the signing chambers?"

"I read somewhere that they don't exist anymore..." he double blinked, "but we'll investigate."

"I wish my parents were here to witness the history." I eyeballed Jesse with a childish grin. "Do you think we could stop so I can pick up a postcard to send the folks?"

He must have been reading my mind, because at that moment Jesse pulled in front of a souvenir shop. Its windows displayed molded Martin Luther figurines, beer steins with pewter lids, and perky mannequins modeling T-shirts with the slogan: *Lose it the old-fashioned way, the Augsburg Diet — since 1530.*

Out front were revolving postcard stands. After I gave them a few squeaky twirls, the coveted postcard appeared at eye level. "Hey. What luck!"

"Oh, yeah...that's right! Mozart's father, Leopold, was born here."

This was excellent. I had found a card featuring Leopold as a youngster playing violin in the market square. I knew Mom would be thrilled to receive it. The shop lady, noticing our interest in the historical aspects of her stomping grounds, provided us with directions to points uptown, downtown and all around. The Fuggerei was one of those points, and the closest.

The architecture of the immediate area was indicative of contemporary design until we reached a gated community called the Fuggerei, which, I learned, dated to the early 1500s when Fugger the Rich decided to fund a welfare district to house the poor. With its row houses crawling with ivy and minuscule lanes, the Fuggerei registers as the world's first social housing project — and to this day its residents still benefit from what must be the lowest rent anywhere: 88 cents per year.

Our few hours tooling around Augsburg proved fruitful. We discovered original documentation pertaining to the Reformation in St. Anna's Church, in addition to a plaque next to the cathedral commemorating the spot where the Augsburg Confession was proclaimed. We also found triple the parking-meter inspectors of any normal city, and the Fugger lunch special: Bratwurst bathing in Senf, or mustard, and Sauerkraut.

When we returned to the car, we found that the city, to express its deepest appreciation of our visit, had left us a 30-euro parking ticket, payable at any police station. Compounding matters, when Jesse went to start his car, we made another discovery: the battery had lost its nerve. He subsequently called the ADAC, Germany's automobile club, to escort us to the nearest Pep Boys for a replacement.

Another 60 euros later, it was time to put misfortune behind us and concentrate on our destination: Rothenburg. On our way out of town, Jesse uttered faint undertones of concern. "I'm sorry we didn't have time to track down Leopold Mozart."

"That's okay...I'll be back. Besides, I'm already more than grateful for everything you're showing me."

"It's my pleasure." Jesse replied, saucering my way with his usual smile. "I have a question... Did your grandmother teach you that flattery will get you everywhere?"

"She sure did." I loved my sweet grandmother, who has since passed away, and I relish any chance for a memory. "Speak of angels and they shall enlighten your path."

We respectfully left the time-honored metropolis of Augsburg behind us. Our northerly route opened to a four-lane highway and wasn't much to speak of except for road construction, recently built houses, and congested traffic. This continued until we crossed the Danube at Donauwörth. The river flowed with moderate torque and its width was unremarkable. If you weren't paying attention, you'd easily miss one of the three great waterways of Europe.

The highway began to climb above Donauwörth, providing us with hurried glimpses of a community clinging to the banks of its commercial lifeline.

As we descended from the ridge, Donauwörth's pitched terra-cotta roofs and soaring church tower gradually dropped away and the four-lane highway narrowed into a popular country excursion. The geography ahead presented a delightful portrait of green rolling hills sprinkled lily white with sheep. The world of modern conveniences fell centuries to our rear and the Romantic Road was beginning to make sense.

Around the following bend, we saw a fortress perched upon the palisades. It was a stark reminder of the Middle Ages, when this road was a major trade route. Below its ramparts rested a picturesque hamlet split by a gently flowing stream. We motored up the hill and were met at the summit by a yellow sign marking the village limits of Harburg.

Townships napping in the afternoon sun flanked us. To our right, a meandering rivulet cut a channel through the shallow marshland. On the horizon materialized what Jesse and I dubbed Peak Peppermint Patty, a surreal knoll sporadically tattooed with stumpy pine trees.

The next settlement, Nördlingen, seemed to be a throwback from the Dark Ages, Asian style. Massive pagoda-like watchtowers with upward-curving roofs jutted into the baby-blue sky; imperial eagle crests were plastered onto the thick, ashlar stone. We paralleled the town's fortifications, moat, and modern sprawl until it again was subtle green fields. According to a reliable source, the area was struck some 15 million years ago by a meteorite discharging enough energy to equal 250,000 Hiroshima bombs, which penetrated a depth of three football fields and created a prehistoric crater 25 kilometers in diameter.

Our route took us through the next village, where a column stood in the middle of the road, almost as an obstruction. "That's a remembrance of plague," Jesse explained. "Many townships vowed to commemorate their deliverance from the deadly epidemic by erecting something of stature."

That was Wallerstein, another traditional hamlet we left behind in favor of a breathtaking vista. Farmers were active in these parts; adequate time had passed for them to safely go beyond their walled communities and cultivate the surrounding land. The smell of recently mowed grass lingered in the air. A slick tractor with rotary arms dispersed the young hay for drying, while a man in the neighboring pasture wearing black rubber boots, shabby jeans, a plaid shirt, and a peaked hat with a feather in its brim stood bent over, raking the grass by hand into piles.

A bit farther ahead a fertilizer truck spewed its contents onto the fields, reminiscent of a skunk dousing its victim. The ghastly odor triggered a desperate need to alter the topic.

We began discussing the crux of the Frail Man's code. His cryptic language was tough to crack.

Dearest Investigators: Before a Brook and Forest
Calculate Adventure 1010347000

I first explored the numbers as a possible telephone sequence, but that went nowhere. Then I scrutinized the numbers as a probable credit card or bank account. Still nothing, but I couldn't be sure. I had to delve further, so I put the digits aside and concentrated on the riddle, which appeared to be a pretty straightforward message. Wherever the clue pointed was likely to be near a brook and forest. But how did the rest translate?

Another option was to convert the riddle into digits, such as A equals 1, B equals 2, or the reverse sequence Z equals 1, Y equals 2, and so forth. Since there were so many alphanumeric combinations, I had to put emphasis on the capital letters, which seemed to be a logical call. When starting with the front-end of the alphabet, I got the configuration: 4922631. So I thought: great, more numbers to add to the ones I already have and don't know what to do with.

After fiddling with corkscrew reasoning that induced umpteen bouts of brain strain, I came up with something that seemed to make sense. However, in a blur of sleepless nights, everything seemed to make sense.

Anyway, I scoured numerous puzzle Web sites — all contributed tidbits of useful info, although, one site stood out: geocaching.com. These folks found hidden treasures via Global Positioning System, or GPS, which is a satellite-based navigation system. Apparently, some 12,000 miles above the planet, there are upwards of 24 satellites orbiting Earth twice daily that are used for determining precise points on a map. To lock into these satellites, all that is required is a hand-held GPS receiver, which essentially acts as a high-tech compass.

When comparing the digits I now had with those used for GPS, I still had nothing — unless, I dropped the last three zeros. Then the enigmatic sequence became explicit coordinates to four worldwide locations, depending on the directions used. For example, if the numbers were married with a point south of the equator and east of the prime meridian, the coordinates point to somewhere around South Africa. Digits wedded to south and west drown in the Atlantic Ocean, north and west land in Ireland, but when the Frail Man's digits were coupled with north and east, they point to not-so-far-away Rothenburg: N4922631-E1010347.

Either I treated the whole GPS coordinates mumbo-jumbo as a coincidence and continued to decipher the code, or I got off my duff and headed north to possibly solve this mind-numbing cloak-and-dagger affair. I had to consider that not only did the digits jibe, so did the riddle: Dearest could be likened to romantic, as in road, and Calculate to coordinates. What's more, Rothenburg's complete name is "ob der Tauber," meaning on the Tauber River, which could represent the Brook. In the end, all the telltale signs seemed convincing enough — thus we borrowed a GPS receiver from the hotel's engineering department and hit the road.

*   *   *

According to our map, the next community was Dinkelsbühl. The town's posted boundaries whizzed by, in addition to the "Reduce Your Speed" sign. Jesse slowed the car and we were instantly awestruck by the dreamy Hollywood-like movie set facing us. Authentic to its roots, this castle town was no doubt the embodiment of medieval drama and intrigue. Perhaps there was a damsel in distress waving a white hanky from one of the turrets, or was it home to the Holy Grail? We decided to take a closer look.

High sentry towers, solid in the making and broken only by manicured arrow slits, sat menacingly above Dinkelsbühl's fortified walls. Some defense positions were backed up by even thicker walls, creating a treacherous No Man's Land in between. Tucked within the fortifications was an impressive Gothic cathedral whose steeple towered above a sea of red-roofed dwellings that cluttered the skyline like ill-managed dominoes. Inside, the cathedral was vast and awe inspiring. Midway along the right aisle, we discovered the bones of St. Aurelius, who was executed because of his Christian faith nearly 2,000 years ago in Rome at the command of Emperor Nero. That concluded our history-drenched tour of Dinkelsbühl, and we exited via the longstanding Wörnitz Gate.

Today, the town battlements rest tranquilly. Well, almost. The only unfolding struggle was that of three ducks squawking over what appeared to be mating rights in the otherwise stagnant moat that brushed against the castle walls, shielding the populace from foreign invaders and, evidently, horny ducks.

We were to encounter two more towns before reaching our overnight destination. The first was called Feuchtwangen, which Jesse said translated to "moist cheeks." This made me wonder whether the town had odd-sounding street names, too, like Perspiration Avenue or Runny Nose Crescent. The next town had a less imaginative name: Schillingsfürst, or Prince Schilling. No wonder Dinkelsbühl had such prominent fortifications; with the likes of a royal Schilling and the Moist Cheeks as your neighbors — it would undeniably be a wise decision to keep your guard up.

Jesse laughed at my determination to make sense of all the oddities and then gave a fast-food analogy. "How about the city of Hamburg? Imagine the names of its streets: Mustard Road, Pickle Place, Cheeseburger Drive."

Damn, his voice could melt rock into lava. Suddenly the car jerked and I gripped the armrest as Jesse steered through a mini locust storm just outside Moist Cheeks.

The township came and went, with no more locust incidents. The Prince was somewhat kinder; there we only had a passing bout with disaster when a fox ran in front of the car causing Jesse to swerve onto an adjacent pasture. Otherwise, the times and troubles on Route 25 were simply wunderbar.

It was a true delight meandering through a countryside standing firm against the greedy desires of would-be property developers seeking to profit from shopping malls and apartment complexes.

Relaxing pauses in the land-scape were pleasantly inter-rupted by picture-perfect settle-ments along the way. Villages we passed were amazing, each hav-ing something unique to offer: a thin bell tower rising above a feeble church, a constellation of half-timbered houses, or a mighty citadel counting among its man-made treasures. More churches, more walled communities, more green fields — anywhere else and it could have been construed as an overdose of culture, but not here, this was the Romantic Road.

"Do you think you'll renew your work contract after the 13 months are up?" asked Mister Curious.

"That's a question I've been pondering myself lately," I said. "No doubt I've enjoyed my overseas break, and being a chambermaid certainly has had its moments, but I thought maybe it might be time to consider going back to school."

"In the States?" Jesse asked, looking stricken.

"No, I'm toying with the idea of attending a study abroad program over here. That way I can kill two birds with one stone. Dad will be happy that I'm in college...and I can stay in Europe!"

Jesse's grin returned. "That would be perfect. How about the University of Gibraltar?"

"Gibraltar?" I raised an eyebrow. "Why Gibraltar?"

"Well...you can go to Morocco whenever you want."

"Morocco? What's in Morocco?"

"Everybody's favorite: the Kasbah."

"That's it, sold!"

"Really?!" He sounded surprised. I was kidding, of course. So far, Vienna's academic program topped my list of prospects.

"There's another one," I chirped, pointing out the window. Rows of cornstalks in the sun-drenched field were at least 6 feet high, but there was no confusing the figure I saw amongst them: a guy tactfully peeing at the road's edge, which wasn't very tactful at all.

"Another one what?" Jesse asked.

"Another guy with a bursting bladder."

"Oh, that." Jesse then chuckled at my feminine outlook on this foreign custom before explaining: "It's legal, as long as your back is against traffic."

"Hmm."

Upon our approach to Rothenburg, images of peeing men were replaced by undulating crop fields, pockets of wooded areas, grazing cows, and a smorgasbord of buses on the road. This was a popular town to say the least; I'd never seen so many people-movers in one location. If German fortresses were royalty, I would have to say Rothenburg was king. We paralleled the town's extensive fortified wall before making a left turn at a junction with a quirky name: Vorm Würzburger Tor. Here we parked outside the main gate and agreed to see Rothenburg on foot.

Once inside the majestic walls, Jesse and I witnessed the Middle Ages magically preserved in the midst of a modern world. I expected to find peasants pouring buckets of refuse into the streets and victims of plague being carted away.

We wandered along cobblestone thoroughfares and crooked lanes flanked by flower boxes, bay windows and wrought-iron signs extending from lopsided, half-timbered houses. If one could realistically walk through a postcard, this was it.

In this must-see community, pedestrians were king of the road — cars were either parked or driving very slowly. Jesse and I couldn't believe our eyes; it was like being in an open-air museum, a thriving medieval settlement inside turreted walls. I walked in wonderment, just one of a procession of awed visitors.

It was minutes after 6 p.m., and our first goal was to find lodging. The flow of teeming vacationers anxious to spend their money led us past a gazillion shops to the main square, where we noticed an olive-green sign offering tourist information.

"I think we've found what we're looking for," I said.

Jesse entered through an archway and I followed. Inside was a vestibule with a pay phone and a locked door displaying the sign: Closed 6 p.m.

"What? Closed!" Jesse screeched. He then glanced at his watch, "Shit! It's 6:05!"

"Check this out," I motioned to a large map containing hotel information affixed to the opposite wall.

"Bingo...an accommodations directory with prices; perfect!" Jesse exclaimed.

I scanned the list of rates with my forefinger. They ranged from 40 to 200 euros a night.

"How about this place, Gasthaus Raidel?" Jesse asked, pointing, "...Fifty euros with breakfast, and it's just down the road."

In search of what we hoped to be our night's lodging, my sidekick and I exited the vestibule, turned right, scampered past the main square and proceeded down a sloping pedestrian street. Here we saw businesses advertising a multitude of fare: artwork, souvenirs, medieval weaponry, more souvenirs, sweets, and even more souvenirs.

Farther down, Jesse pinpointed the crossroad of our night's lodging, Wenggasse.

We sauntered through the old doorway of the half-timbered gasthaus and the manager, a personable soft-spoken fellow who introduced himself as Herr Raidel, offered to show us a room. He led us up a creaky staircase to the second floor, where Herr Raidel unlocked a door and waved us in. The room wasn't that big and the view wasn't that great, but it was cozy and clean. Furthermore, we were happy to have found something reasonably priced without a hassle.

We swiveled to Herr Raidel and told him we were sold. He smiled, handing us the key. Jesse asked him about parking and if he had any recommendations on restaurants. Herr Raidel responded by whipping out a map and showing us a nearby place to park, his favorite eatery, and a few local attractions, including where to meet the Night Watchman's tour. Boy, did we get our money's worth with this guy. Since it was getting late and the tourist to-do list sounded appealing, we decided to postpone our search for the Bavarian Cross until first thing in the morning. Moreover, our GPS receiver pointed the Frail Man's coordinates to a location in a non-populated, forested area outside Rothenburg's defense walls, which could be a tad spooky at night.

We offered Herr Raidel our thanks and left to pick up the car. Jesse then became sidetracked by what he saw in a shop window. "How 'bout we grab a bottle of wine for later?"

Meanwhile, I thought I noticed something peculiar: a person peering from street corners following our every move. "Jesse, look!" I pointed. "There... that person by the sweet shop?"

"What...Where?"

The mysterious person bolted and I ran to the corner of the shop for a closer look. I searched the alleyway but it was clear, as were the adjacent side streets. When I returned, Jesse had a perplexed look. "Is everything okay?"

"Yeah... I guess I'm just seeing things."

Jesse nodded and tried his question again. "How 'bout a bottle of wine? That'll remedy strained eyes."

"If it's a red...you've got a deal!"

Jesse and I got a little medieval lost on the way back to the car, not remembering which parapet we parked near. We must have looked pretty funny weaving past bulwarks, bastions and battlements while brandishing a bottle of burgundy.

We hopped in the car, but this time our drive was to take us through the main gate and onto Rothenburg's antiquated streets. Regardless of

Herr Raidel's assurance, it was still rather strange to cruise cobbled lanes that were once reserved for Teutonic knights.

Maneuvering through the droves of dawdling tourists wasn't easy — at times it seemed as if we were herding cattle. Dozens retreated to the sidewalks while the occasional disgruntled sightseer gave us a dirty look for the inconvenience. But what else could we do except drive slowly and smile?

Finding a parking space was relatively easy compared with reaching it. Jesse stopped briefly in front of the gasthaus to unload our gear; he then continued up the road to chase a space. He was soon back and I had our belongings situated in the room. Jesse suggested food and I couldn't have been happier. I was famished.

One of Herr Raidel's recommendations was a local Franconian wine house, which turned out to be a cozy restaurant tucked away on a side alley featuring a facade creeping with ivy and a wrought-iron sign hanging over the door publicizing its trade. The interior was engagingly rustic and bordered on hopelessly romantic, glowing with candlelit tables for two. Light strains of Mozart danced through the air.

The food was satisfying and following every scrumptious meal, Jesse said he traditionally preached: "Rub your tummy, lick your chops, and say thatwasdelicious!"

The time struck 7:45, and dusk began its course. The Night Watchman's tour kicked off on the hour in the Market Square. A few cobblestone streets later, we came upon numerous cliques of twosies and threesies waiting in the square. This was the English tour and we made sure not to be late; it just sounded like the perfect outing.

At the stroke of 8, the Night Watchman appeared. Jesse nudged me with his elbow; "Get a load of this guy!"

A lantern swayed from his fingertips as he approached, causing the flame to flicker with every footstep. The palm of his other hand clutched a deadly hatchet-head lance. His guise was dark and mysterious, consisting of a long, black cape; a black, long-sleeved shirt; black pants; black Doc Martens; a horn made from ebony tusk, and a medallion hanging from his neck. He was of average build about 6 feet tall with a full beard and dark brown, shoulder length, tousled hair that was partially covered by his pilgrim hat.

He introduced himself and explained that only the gravedigger and village executioner were lower on the community social scale than he was. Beneath the town hall are creepy dungeons, he said, where lawbreakers were tortured until they confessed, at which point they were brought up to the square, locked in stocks and pelted with rotten tomatoes. The Night Watchman then pointed to the Meister Trunk show that had just begun on the clock tower. This was the jovial Protestant story of Rothenburg's deliverance from total annihilation in 1631 during the Thirty Years' War, when the general of the invading Catholic army offered to spare the stronghold if a town councilor could chug a gallon of wine.

The mayor accepted the challenge and miraculously drank the tankard dry. Local hearsay suggested he was seen later that evening at the pillory tavern passed out on the "chair of nails" while the gravedigger danced his way past elated farmers, clerics, blacksmiths, bell ringers, merchants, seamstresses, fortune tellers, masons, maidens, wenches, and humble street cleaners feasting and celebrating their newly won independence.

The Night Watchman's tour traversed darkened streets, marched across a drawbridge, paralleled bulwarks, and finished at the entrance to Hell, a convivial wine tavern. On our trek we saw a medieval manhole, a Gothic doorbell, and a mask that coughed up hot oil.

The hour whizzed by faster than a Porsche on the autobahn and the final account in the Night Watchman's tour was wrapped up. The majority of the crowd dispersed while a few lingered to chat with the black-caped raconteur.

Jesse had other ideas. "What do you say we take care of that bottle of red?"

I agreed and we retraced the Night Watchman's route, down Herrngasse and into the Castle Garden. Along the way we politely asked a restaurant owner if he could open our bottle of wine. We didn't have the nerve to ask for paper cups as well.

The gardens afforded a breathtaking view of Rothenburg. If a photograph could express itself verbally, it would speak volumes here. A collage of turrets and towers and tilted roofs were silhouetted against the twilight sky. Rothenburg was the capital of medieval highlights — most I'd never heard of but I certainly won't forget them any time soon.

To take best advantage of the spectacular view, we hoisted ourselves onto a waist-high stone wall that was adorned by a coat of green moss spattering the lower sections for meters on end. We watched Germany's version of Camelot twinkle under a canopy of stars; it was exactly how I imagined sitting on your very own magic carpet. I wish I could have sent the reality home, but I couldn't. One has to taste it for themselves.

I sneaked a peek at Jesse and wondered if Mom would approve. Stupid notion; of course she would.

"I'd like to propose a toast," I said.

"Please do."

"I'd like to drink to Dolores and Sid, my lovely parents," I announced. "How can I convey to you, Mom and Dad, what I saw today in an e-mail or over the phone? Encountering millenniums-old castles and towns that look more like digitally created location sets for the movie 'Braveheart' than tangible reality... There is only one answer."

Jesse expressed the rest: "To Mr. and Mrs. Endicott." He raised the burgundy. "May your health be no less than that of an adventurous traveler so you may come here one day and revel in this very moment."

"Here...here!" I took the bottle and concluded, "Well done, Sire, I couldn't have said it better myself."

Beneath us, in the ravine, the Tauber River snaked a path around Rothenburg. The town was partly built on a plateau and the ledge upon which the fortifications rested fell briskly into the watercourse below.

Jesse lifted his head from staring into the river's current and asked, "What's big on your to-do list...I mean, besides the quest for the Bavarian Cross, does anything strike your fancy?"

"Yeah...I'd love to travel all over Europe. I'm especially looking forward to Budapest."

"The capital of Hungary." He stated, reacting as if it were a revelation, bobbing his head and gaping to the stars.

"I've heard the Danube River bisects the city, creating the hilly Buda and flat Pest," I said. "One has a royal palace and the other a mega-shopping boulevard."

"Yes. That's what I hear." Jesse was still profoundly absorbed in thought. A pleasant summer breeze patted the leaves of nearby trees. Then my handsome friend became animated again, enjoying a swallow of burgundy. "Any other big Sydney to-do's?"

"I'd like to swim with dolphins. I won a trip to Florida once, but then gave it away because a friend got sick."

"Sorry to hear that, although I'm sure one day you'll swim with Flipper."

Jesse pointed past our feet, which were dangling over the wall's edge, to the river below, where an arched, double-decker bridge made of stone crossed the Tauber. "Doesn't that look like one of those Roman-style viaducts?"

I didn't hear much of what he said because I had something on my mind. "I'd like to propose another toast," I ventured.

He handed the bottle over. "The stage is yours."

I took the wine and solemnly declared: "Here's to you, Jesse...You have been a very special friend, and I really want to thank you for everything you've done for me." I raised the bottle and summed up my last six months: "I couldn't have done it without you."

Jesse's aura was magnetic as he took his acceptance drink. His pheromones were tingling my innermost senses, making my heart thump.

He replied with an announcement of his own. "I guess you heard that my girlfriend and I broke up."

"Yes, Reuben mentioned it. You must be very sad."

"No, not really," Jesse said sincerely. "In fact, it was my idea. The truth is, I've become smitten with someone else... A certain chambermaid."

Then, as I looked into his eyes, he grasped my hand. In the radiant moonlight, our eager lips drew closer and locked passionately. I melted in his arms. At that moment, the patter of leaves fell silent and the river ran still.

* * *

The next morning, my fellow adventurer and I powered up the GPS receiver and exited Rothenburg in the direction it pointed through the Kobolzeller Gate. According to our high-tech compass, we were less than one kilometer from either realizing that I needed to re-examine the Frail Man's clue or unearthing a 600-year-old relic that could pay off in a lifetime of dreams.

The palm of my hand began to sweat as I gripped the receiver. It now indicated .63 kilometers as we walked over an ancient stone bridge spanning the Tauber. Off to the right were tremendous, eye-popping views of Rothenburg.

Our rural route led us past half-timbered farmhouses, horses trotting in paddocks, green meadows, and a Gothic church. As we got closer, our scenic path paralleled the river, which was more like a babbling brook. Up ahead, a wood-covered footbridge straddled the Tauber, where the receiver pointed to the opposite bank, estimating 100 meters farther to Pay Day.

We crossed the bridge and were directed left across a lush field dripping with dewdrops that had accumulated overnight. Jesse and I stared at the compass like two kids transfixed on a new video game as the distance lessened with every pace: 30 meters, then 20, 10, 5, until it zeroed-out beneath a cluster of trees. Jesse looked at me with nervous anticipation. I began to tremble.

The engineering department told us that GPS receivers were accurate to within 10 to 100 feet, depending on signal strength with orbiting satellites. Therefore, we still had our work cut out for us.

Nearby, I heard rustling noises coming from the bushes. I snapped my head in the direction of the sound but didn't see anything. "Did you hear that?!" I asked breathlessly. Jesse was too busy scanning the ground for unusual formations to notice. Perhaps my nerves were getting to me.

The cluster of trees hugged the riverbank and extended some 20 feet into the lush field. I concentrated on the task at hand and began kicking over leaves and branches looking for anything odd. We painstakingly combed every inch of the area, but nothing appeared out of the ordinary. Every now and then we did spot a few suspect patches of earth, which brought us to our knees like archaeologists hunched over and scratching at the dirt for that illusive find. Alas, our efforts always ended in disappointment and nursing sore fingers. Perhaps we were going about it wrong; maybe it was hidden up and not down. Therefore, we scoured the limbs and boughs of the trees. Still nothing.

Things weren't looking too hot. Nearly an hour had passed and all we'd accomplished was to successfully transform the once pristine area into a grid of deep cavities and heaped piles of leaves and twigs as if a band of gophers on speed had blown through.

It was obvious: I had failed at solving the clue and had led Jesse on a wild goose chase. We hung our heads low and began hoofing it back to Rothenburg. That's when Jesse detected an unnatural soil arrangement under his foot. "This doesn't quite feel right. Let's check it out."

We dropped to our hands and knees once again, clawing the earth with the tips of our fingers. Dirt piled up at our side as we dug deeper and deeper, until our elbows were lost in the hollow. Suddenly, my fingers touched metal. I yelped in excitement! We impatiently brushed the dirt away and scraped around the sides of the object. It appeared to be an old lockbox.

Jesse lifted the heavy container from its earthen grave to ground level. We struggled with the latch and then, without warning, it burst open. A box full of newspaper clippings stared us in the face, and beneath them was a layer of coarse fabric. Neither Jesse nor I had the faintest idea of what to make of it. After clearing out the contents, we discovered a wooden case, similar to one that would hold cigars.

Behind us, more rustling noises came from the bushes. This time Jesse heard them, too. As we turned around, a faceless figure darted from the dense shrubbery and snatched the wooden case. Jesse leapt to his feet and pursued the thief up a steep path that disappeared into a shadowy forest. I grabbed the lockbox and followed.

The path climbed steeply in the direction of Rothenburg's fortified walls. Jesse was somewhere up ahead, but nowhere to be seen. I jogged frantically to keep pace until my legs burned from over-exertion. I couldn't stop; I had to keep moving. I was alone, and in a dark forest. With the lockbox securely tucked under my arm, I forged ahead.

"Syd, are you all right?" I heard Jesse ask from a distance. I cranked my head around and saw him stomping out from a veil of trees. I've never been happier to see my faithful friend.

"Yeah, I'm fine." I insisted. "How 'bout you?"

Jesse looked relieved; he then held up the case. "I was within an arm's length of the thief..." he puffed, "...and as I reached out to grab his shirt, he tripped over a log and the case flew from his hand as he tumbled down the embankment."

"Did you get a look at him?" I asked.

"No... Once he got back on his feet, he took off running."

On that note we refocused our attention on the mysterious case. Kneeling to the ground, Jesse placed the case before us and gently levered it open with a pocketknife. I doubled blinked, not believing my eyes. Inside sat a crucifix studded with jewels that glinted in a rainbow of colors. It had to be das Bayernkreuz.

Jesse reached in to pick up the cross. As he did, he shifted his deep brown eyes to me and smiled that infectious smile.

"I think this belongs to you," he said, placing the cross gingerly in my hands.

I held it firmly and rose to my feet. It was much lighter and smaller than I had imagined.

Seemingly mesmerized by the relic, Jesse gently brushed the jewels with his forefinger. We looked at each other and I began to giggle uncontrollably; I cried tears of joy. Jesse wrapped his arms around me — and the Bavarian Cross — and lifted me a foot off the ground, laughing. I could not believe that I held an object that was centuries old and almost certainly worth a fortune, times two. I was thrilled, elated, and nervous as all heck. We had to make tracks, quickly, before the thief returned with backup.

Jesse gave me a soft kiss. "What now?" he asked.

"I don't know," I replied. "I never thought we'd actually find it. Maybe we can locate its rightful owner; maybe there's a reward."

"Oh shit," Jesse whispered, grabbing my shirt and towing me to the ground. He pointed into the trees. "Someone's coming..." [1]

---

[1] But who? And why? Find out where the Bavarian Cross takes Sydney in the next edition of "Your Traveling Companion."

TRAVEL GUIDE

GERMANY
(Deutschland)

Germany (357,000 sq km) is a little smaller than the U.S. state of Montana (381,000 sq km).

Capital: Berlin

Language: German, with varying dialect from state to state.

Population: approximately 82 million — divided into 16 Bundesländer, or federal states.
Baden-Württemberg: pop. 10 million — capital is Stuttgart
Bavaria: pop. 12 million — capital is Munich
Berlin: pop. 3.5 million — capital is Berlin
Brandenburg: pop. 2.7 million — capital is Potsdam
Bremen: pop. 700,000 — capital is Bremen
Hamburg: pop. 1.7 million — capital is Hamburg
Hessen: pop. 6 million — capital is Wiesbaden
Mecklenburg - W. Pomerania [Vorpommern]: pop. 1.85 million — capital is Schwerin
Lower Saxony: (Niedersachsen) pop. 7.5 million — capital is Hannover
North Rhine-Westphalia: (Nordrhein-Westfalen) pop. 18 million — capital is Düsseldorf
Rhineland-Palatinate: (Rheinland-Pfalz) pop. 4 million — capital is Mainz
Saarland: pop. 1.1 million — capital is Saarbrücken
Saxony: (Sachsen) pop. 5.6 million — capital is Dresden
Saxony-Anhalt: pop. 2.8 million — capital is Magdeburg
Schleswig-Holstein: pop. 2.7 million — capital is Kiel
Thuringia: (Thüringen) pop. 2.5 million — capital is Erfurt

Emergency Telephone Numbers: Known as a *Notruf* (pronounced note roof, meaning emergency call), the following numbers can be dialed free of charge Germany-wide.
Police (Polizei) = 110
Fire dept. (Feuerwehr) or general emergency = 112
Ambulance = 19222

Unemployment Rate: 11.2%, or 4.6 million (Dec. 2005)

Religion: Protestant 34%, Roman Catholic 34%, Muslim 3.5%, other 28.5%

Elevation: *Highest point:* Zugspitze—2962m/9715ft—is Germany's highest mountain, located in (Garmisch) southern Bavaria. *Lowest point:* Neuendorf bei Wilster, -3.5m/-11ft.

National Anthem: *Deutschlandlied* (Song of Germany). Only third verse is used—taken from the four-verse composition, "Deutschland über Alles."

Flag: Consists of three horizontal bands: black (top), red, gold.

Executive Branch:
President (Horst Köhler): Largely a ceremonial post; elected (in 2004) by a Federal Convention for a 5-year term.
Chancellor (Angela Merkel): Elected by popular vote for a 4-year term. On Nov. 22, 2005, Merkel was officially sworn into office—for the first time in German history a female has held the highest post in the land. With this historical realization came a second first: the traditional form of federal chancellor (Bundeskanzler) had to be changed to its female equivalent: Bundeskanzlerin. Mesmerized by the uniqueness of the word, the Society of German Language voted Bundeskanzlerin as the word of the year. You can check out Merkel at www.bundeskanzlerin.de

German National Tourist Office: 122 East 42nd Street, New York, NY 10168. *Tel.* # 1-212-661-7200 (www.visits-to-germany.com) or (www.germany-tourism.de)

German Rail Authority: www.bahn.de (For English, click International Guests.)

Calling Germany: (international country code: **49**)
For our example, let's say we are trying to call this tel. number in Munich: 089/123456.
Note: 089 is the city code; drop the 0 when dialing from outside of Germany. All area codes in this book are separated from the local number by a back slash (/).

To call Germany from another country in Europe you must first dial the international access code: 00 (from USA/Canada 011), then the country code: 49. From the USA and Canada you would dial the above number like so: 011-49-89/123456
From inside Europe, 0049-89/123456
From inside Germany, 089/123456
While in Munich, 123456

Country Codes: Australia 61 • Austria 43 • Belgium 32 • Canada 1 • Croatia 385 •

German (City) Telephone Codes: Berlin 030, Bremen 0421, Cologne 0221, Dresden 0351, Dortmund 0231, Düsseldorf 0211, Frankfurt am Main 069, Hamburg 040, Hannover 0511, Leipzig 0341, Munich 089, Stuttgart 0711.

DEUTSCHLAND

Deutsch: The word Deutsch originated sometime around the 7th or 8th century to label a particular language spoken. The term evolved to represent the speakers of this language and ultimately the region they lived in: Deutschland.

Germany: From Reich to Republic

First Reich: Holy Roman Empire; a collection of Germanic states in Central Europe founded by Emperor Charlemagne in the early 9th century, which lasted around 1000 years until Napoleon dissolved it in 1806.

Second Reich: (1871-1918) Germany's second empire was the brainchild of Otto von Bismarck—the Iron Chancellor—who unified the German states into one imperialistic empire in 1871, which roughly stretched from the present-day border in the west through to Poland and Latvia in the east. The Second Reich collapsed at the end of World War I, and much of Germany's territory in the east was lost.

Weimar Republic: (1919-33) Following Germany's devastating defeat in WWI, political gangs ruled the nation's city streets. In 1919, a provisional government convened in the central German town of Weimar to hash out a new constitution to establish Germany as a democracy—thus the Weimar Republic was born. Exacerbated by hyperinflation, mass unemployment, astronomical war reparations and the Great Depression, Germany's new republic struggled from the get-go. With Adolf Hitler's meteoric rise to power came the downfall of the Weimar Republic.

Third Reich: (1933-45) With grandiose visions of a rebirth of Charlemagne's 1000-year Reich, Adolf Hitler capitalized on the failures of the Weimar Republic, promising the people that Germany would rise again to its former glory. Hitler's National Socialist party, a.k.a. the Nazis, won control of parliament in 1933—thus began the reshaping of Germany. Hitler reacquired territories lost to the Great War victors and stimulated the economy via ambitious construction projects along with rebuilding the military. On Sept. 1, 1939, Hitler kick-started World War II by invading Poland—the first step of many to Nazify Europe, from the English Channel to the Asian frontier. With a catastrophic conclusion, the Third Reich barely lasted 12 years—the German nation was reduced to a smoldering ruin and Hitler committed suicide on April 30, 1945, in a beastly bunker beneath Berlin (page 362).

GDR: [German Democratic Republic] (1949-90) Upon the conclusion of World War II, Germany was divided into four zones of occupation administered by the so-called Allies: USA, UK, USSR and France. The Soviet Union (USSR)—whose government embraced a totalitarian-style regime through communistic indoctrination—ultimately sealed the borders of its newly acquired zone with landmines, barbed wire, tank traps, umpteen miles of fencing, guard towers and the infamous Berlin Wall. The forbidden territory officially became known as the GDR (1949), a.k.a. East Germany, which consumed roughly two-fifths of the landmass of (today's) Germany and had a population of about 16 million, with East Berlin as its capital. The GDR was dissolved in 1990 after a popular uprising and the collapse of the Marxist-style government.

FRG: [Federal Republic of Germany, a.k.a. West Germany—1949-90] In 1949, the western Allies unified their zones of occupation to create the FRG—a capitalistic counterweight to the communistic GDR—with Bonn as its capital. In 1990, the GDR dissolved and merged with the FRG, unifying all 16 states. Berlin succeeded Bonn as the nation's capital and the official date of German reunification, October 3, is celebrated as a national holiday: *Tag der Deutschen Einheit* (Day of German Unity).

FIFA WORLD CUP, 2006

The World Cup soccer (or, as it's called in Europe, "football") tournament, regulated by soccer's governing body—Fédération Internationale de Football Association, or FIFA (www.fifaworldcup.com)—is a competition between the world's best teams and occurs every four years. The last tournament, hosted by Korea-Japan in 2002, Brazil won! Now, four years later, 31 teams have their sights set on dethroning the world's No. 1 ranked team. However, no team will be more committed to the task than this year's host—Germany—who lost to Brazil in the 2002 final (2-0).

The teams will compete in a month-long soccer extravaganza, opening in Munich on June 9 and closing in Berlin on July 9. The games—or matches—will take place in 12 cities: Berlin, Cologne, Dortmund, Frankfurt, Gelsenkirchen, Hamburg, Hannover, Kaiserslautern, Leipzig, Munich, Nürnberg and Stuttgart. Eight of these venues will each host five matches, while Berlin, Dortmund, Munich and Stuttgart will each host an extra, sixth match. Additionally, during the group stage, no team will play in the same stadium twice. A global audience estimated at 1 billion viewers will watch the final, played in Berlin's 74,000-seat Olympic Stadium. That's about 1 out of every 6 people on Earth. Will you be one of them? Stay tuned to see which team will win bragging rights for the next four years.

For obvious reasons we couldn't list the schedules of all 32 teams in the tournament, so we went with the English-speakers, the reigning champs and, of course, the host.

Team **USA**, FIFA - *world ranking: 7

Date	Venue	Teams	Time
June 12	Gelsenkirchen	USA vs. Czech Republic	18:00
June 17	Kaiserslautern	USA vs. Italy	21:00
June 22	Nürnberg	USA vs. Ghana	16:00

Team **AUSTRALIA**, FIFA - *world ranking: 48

Date	Venue	Teams	Time
June 12	Kaiserslautern	Australia vs. Japan	15:00
June 18	Munich	Australia vs. Brazil	18:00
June 22	Stuttgart	Australia vs. Croatia	21:00

Team **ENGLAND**, FIFA - *world ranking: 9

Date	Venue	Teams	Time
June 10	Frankfurt	England vs. Paraguay	15:00
June 15	Nürnberg	England vs. Trinidad & T.	18:00
June 20	Cologne	England vs. Sweden	21:00

Team **BRAZIL**, FIFA - *world ranking: 1

Date	Venue	Teams	Time
June 13	Berlin	Brazil vs. Croatia	21:00
June 18	Munich	Brazil vs. Australia	18:00
June 22	Dortmund	Brazil vs. Japan	21:00

Team **GERMANY**, FIFA - *world ranking: 17

Date	Venue	Teams	Time
June 9	Munich	Germany vs. Costa Rica	18:00
June 14	Dortmund	Germany vs. Poland	21:00
June 20	Berlin	Germany vs. Ecuador	16:00

*World ranking at press time; the team's status may have changed by kickoff. Of course, concerning Brazil, this is not likely.

Note: If you're looking to buy a ticket to one of the matches, beware of unofficial solicitors, i.e. scalpers (trying to swindle an unsuspecting tourist). If you do purchase a ticket from one of these people (online or elsewhere), you will be out of pocket without a valid ticket! You see, to counter scalping and counterfeiting, FIFA has embedded each ticket with the original owner's personal details. If you're not the registered owner of the ticket, you will *not* be allowed entry into the stadium! The only avenue to procure tickets is via FIFA's official website: www.fifaworldcup.com

In case you're wondering what a ticket costs to see one of the matches, prices range from 35-100€ and 120-600€ for the Final in Berlin.

ROMANTIC ROAD
"Romantische Strasse"

Germany's most popular tourist route—the Romantic Road—meanders some 350 kilometers from the medieval walled towns of middle Bavaria, where time appears to have stood still for centuries, to the green foothills of the snow-peaked Alps bordering Austria, where hikers spot edelweiss and yodelers are welcome.

Boasting a bevy of scenic delights, the northern stretch of the Romantic Road, characterized by towers, turrets and half-timbered houses, complements the southern stretch typified by lush meadows, quaint farmhouses and bulbous church steeples.

Along this fabled route you'll meet Rothenburg's legendary night watchman; you'll witness the 2000-year-old bones of St. Aurelius in Dinkelsbühl's St. George Cathedral; you'll pass through the (Nördlingen) Ries impression where a meteorite struck the earth some 15 million years ago; you'll get acquainted with the Fuggers and the Fuggerei in Augsburg; and in Hohenschwangau you'll feast your eyes upon King Ludwig's fairy-tale castle, Schloss Neuschwanstein, Walt Disney's inspiration for his Sleeping Beauty castle.

To experience the whole of the Romantic Road, set aside three nights and four days—time-crunched tourists can do it in half the time. The main points of interest in the north are the cobbled communities of Rothenburg, Dinkelsbühl and Nördlingen—and in the south are Schloss Neuschwanstein and the Wieskirche. Whatever you do, spend at least one night in Rothenburg.

For more info on the Romantic Road, go to www.romantischestrasse.de

Railers: Most towns along this stretch are train-friendly. However, for a change of pace, considering utilizing the "Touring" bus company, which does the Romantic Road milk-run (April-Oct) once daily in each direction, between Frankfurt and Füssen. You can get off and on as you like. Reservations are not mandatory but suggested July-Sept. *Tel.#* (Frankfurt area code) 069/790-3230, or query TI for the nearest Touring office (—they have several throughout Germany). Holders of a German rail or Eurail (consecutive-day or dated Flexi/Select) pass receive a hefty 60% one-way discount on bus tickets. For example, Frankfurt to Rothenburg generally costs 35€ full price, or 14€ with rail-pass discount • to Dinkelsbühl 43€, or 18€ • to Nördlingen 48€, or 20€ • to Augsburg 60€, or 24€ • to Füssen 80€, or 32€. To receive this discount you *do not* have to use a travel day. It does, though, have to be within the pass' period of validation. Seniors, too, get a discount—typically 10%—query upon booking. Below is Touring's bus schedule. Times are subject to change; and only the main towns are listed. For the full, updated schedule, query TI or go to www.romantic-road-coach.de *Note:* At Wieskirche the stopover is only 15 min. Hardly enough time to wholly view this glorious church, thus you'll have to move double-time. If you miss the bus, a taxi won't be cheap. Lastly, notice Munich at the bottom of the schedule. If you're departing from (or heading to) Munich, you'll have to go through Füssen. Thus, depending on your situation, to take the train may be the best option. If you decide, however, to take the train from Munich to Augsburg to connect with the Touring bus—definitely reserve a seat. The Touring office is easily found in Munich's main train station opposite track 34. To rent a car, see next entry.

Romantic Road Bus Schedule, 2006

Daily, April-Oct	↓ Southbound ↓	↑ Northbound ↑
Frankfurt	Dep. 8:00	Arr. 21:00
Würzburg	Arr. 9:30	Dep. 19:35
Würzburg	Dep. 10:00	Arr. 19:20
Rothenburg	Arr. 12:15	Dep. 17:40
Rothenburg	Dep. 12:45	Arr. 17:10
Dinkelsbühl	Arr. 13:35	Dep. 16:25
Dinkelsbühl	Dep. 14:05	Arr. 16:05
Nördlingen	Arr. 14:45	Dep. 15:30
Nördlingen	Dep. 15:00	Arr. 15:15
Augsburg	Arr. 16:20	Dep. 14:00
Augsburg	Dep. 16:45	Arr. 13:15
Landsberg	Arr. 17:20	Dep. 12:35
Landsberg	Dep. 17:20	Arr. 12:20
Wieskirche	Arr. 18:10	Dep. 11:15
Wieskirche	Dep. 18:25	Arr. 11:00
Hohenschwangau	Arr. 18:50	Dep. 10:30
Hohenschwangau	Dep. 19:05	Arr. 10:15
Füssen	Arr. 19:10	Dep. 10:05
Füssen	Dep. 19:15	Arr. 10:00
Munich	Arr. 20:50	Dep. 8:15

Car Rental: AllRound car rental in Munich offers an affordable opportunity to hit the road—compacts from 35€/day (*300km) or 179€/week (*1500km), inclusive of taxes and insurance (1000€ deductible). Call or click for other rates and vehicle types. Minimum age 21 and one-year DL. (www.allroundrent.de) *Tel.#* 089/723-2343. English spoken. *Hours:* Mon-Fri 9:00-18:00, Sat 10:00-12:00. *Kilometers included in rental price—anything thereafter is 20¢ to 39¢ per km, depending on car-type.

Drivers: The Romantic Road is well marked with brown, waist-high signs that read "Romantische Straße." From Füssen to Augsburg the highway route is signposted as No. 17 — from Augsburg to Donauwörth No. 2, and from Donauwörth to Rothenburg No. 25. *Note:* Due to its size and ongoing construction, be prepared to get lost around Augsburg. Time-crunched drivers look to the A7 autobahn to expedite your trip between north and south (or vice-versa). • Regarding the walled towns of the north, pay attention to the two-way arrows signposted at narrow, medieval gates indicating dual passage. When a gate is only wide enough for one car, these arrows control the flow of traffic. If the red arrow is pointing in the direction you want to travel, you must give the right-of-way. If it's the opposite, and you're facing a black or white arrow, you have the right-of-way. • To park within the walled towns of Dinkelsbühl and Nördlingen, you'll need to use your "parking dial" (Parkscheibe), see page 450.

R O T H E N B U R G *ob der Tauber*

~ Population: 12,000   ~ Elevation: 425m/1400ft
~ Country/Area Code: +49-(0)9861

As far as German castle towns are concerned, Rothenburg is the jewel in the crown with an estimated 2 million visitors annually, making tourism the lifeblood of its economy. Easily seen on foot, you'll cherish this medieval gem.

In 1142, (Hohenstaufen) King Konrad III built a castle (where the Castle Garden is today) upon the bluff overlooking the Tauber River. This in turn attracted settlers who sought the protection of a fortification. A neighborhood developed around the castle, which flourished over the next century. In 1274, (Habsburg) King Rudolf I declared the new community of Rothenburg a free imperial city, or a state within a state. By the year 1400, Rothenburg had more than 6000 inhabitants, qualifying it as one of the largest cities in the kingdom.

During the Thirty Years' War (1618-48), Protestant Rothenburg was assaulted several times by the Catholic army and plundered. From the economic downturn of incessant war, Rothenburg spiraled into a state of destitution. The 18th century came and went with no reprieve. However, Rothenburg in the 19th century—preserved by poverty—was resurrected when it came under the spotlight for its old-world charm, becoming a haven for artists. Helping to promote this medieval romanticism was a playwright determined to amend the town's history to include a happy ending. And so he scripted a play that goes like this: During the assault of 1631, Rothenburg was spared the wrath of enemy troops when the besieging Catholic general offered to safeguard the community if a town councilor could chug a gallon of wine in one draft. The mayor heeded the call, and with tipsy success a legend was born into the history books as "der Meistertrunk" (Master Draft), the theme on the Market Square clock tower.

During the next century the god of war once again reared its ugly head when on March 31, 1945—due to a group of diehard Nazi soldiers who refused to surrender—16 Allied aircraft flew overhead and reduced 45% of Rothenburg to rubble. The townsfolk subsequently rebuilt what falling bombs had destroyed and today there couldn't be a more popular medieval hotspot in Germany than Rothenburg, deserving of any itinerary to Europe—an enjoyable place to visit and explore—a requisite for young and old alike. Couples will especially love the town's emptiness in the evening, making for a romantic hand-in-hand stroll along crooked lanes under a moonlit sky.

~ Rothenburg is worth a two-day stay. Mood permitting, divide your time like so,

Day 1: After checking into your digs, get orientated by toddling around town and absorbing the oldness. Walk a portion of the medieval wall, or all of it—don't forget your camera! Visit the Criminal Museum and face the torture. Pop your head into Käthe Wohlfahrt's Christmas store, even if you're not a shopper. Be on Market Square (Marktplatz) at 20:00 in time for the Night Watchman's tour, because he's bad. And conclude your history-packed day in Hell for a beverage. *Opinion:* The tantalizing snowballs (Schneebälle) you'll see in pastry-shop windows are somewhat dry and tasteless—we suggest you save your hard-earned cash. If you can't resist, however, split one with a friend. *Note:* Try to avoid Rothenburg's busiest times: weekends in summer (May-Oct) and all of Dec.

Day 2: Visit sights, attractions that you didn't have time for on day 1.

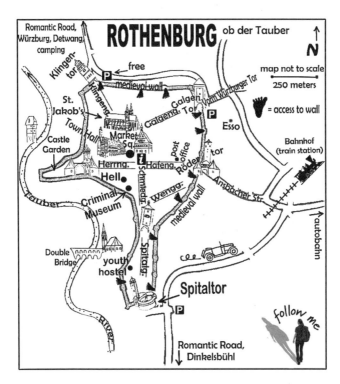

Tourist Information: [TI] (www.rothenburg.de) *Tel.#* 09861/404-800. Rothenburg's TI —located in the heart of town on Market Square—is well stocked with English literature and even has *free* Internet (one terminal). While there pick up the free, foldout "Map & Guide" brochure, which contains need-to-know info, history and a town map. If you don't make it to the TI, these same (or similar) maps are readily available around town, including at your accommodations. *Hours:* May-Oct Mon-Fri 9:00-12:00 & 13:00-18:00, Sat/Sun 10:00-15:00; Nov-April Mon-Fri 9:00-12:00 & 13:00-17:00, Sat 10:00-13:00. *Tours:* The TI sponsors a daily (April-Oct) 90-min English walking tour of the Old Town—meet at 14:00 on Market Square, 6€/person—minimum 10 people.

Emergency Tel. Numbers: [Germany-wide]
  Police (Polizei) = 110
  Fire dept. (Feuerwehr) or general emergency = 112
  Ambulance = 19222

Railers: (Transfer necessary in Steinach.) From Rothenburg's petite train station to the town center is an easy 15-min walk, or taxis at the ready will motor you in for about 5€. By foot, exit station left—at the forward traffic light turn right (Ansbacher Str.) following the brown "Altstadt" sign. Take this straight some 300 meters. Go through the medieval town gate (Rödertor) leading onto the cobbled streets Rödergasse and Hafengasse to Market Square. Once there, go right to find the TI—it's up ahead on the left. *Note:* There are storage lockers at the station (1€-2€/24hr). In the shopping mall across from the station is a post office (Mon-Fri 9:30-17:00, Sat 9:30-12:00) as well as a "Kaufland" supermarket (Mon-Sat 7:00-20:00). To reach the mall, exit station right and walk some 50 meters, then go left to its main entrance.

Drivers: Don't attempt to cruise through town; its narrow lanes packed with lollygagging tourists are enough to convert any sane driver into a trigger-happy motorist. *Overnighters,* drive straight to your digs via "Spitaltor" (*GPS:* N49° 22.231 - E10° 10.866) and have reception show you where to park. *Daytrippers,* park in one of the lots that parallel the outer periphery of the town wall and walk in, 1€/hr (or free in lot P5 outside Klingentor).

Post Office: There are two branches; one is across from the train station in the shopping mall (Mon-Fri 9:30-17:00, Sat 9:30-12:00) and the other can be found within the Old Town at Rödergasse 11 (Mon-Fri 9:00-13:00 & 14:00-17:30, Sat 9:00-12:00).

Internet: Begin your quest for the Web at the TI, where you can surf for *free*. If there's a line to use their one terminal, staff can point you to the nearest café. For example, Inter Play can be found at Milchmarkt 3 (1€/20min; open daily, 8:00-02:00).

SIGHTS

Night Watchman's Tour: Though technically not a "sight," to walk the candle-lit beat with Rothenburg's very own Night Watchman is an entertaining experience—therefore, he's listed first. Get the inside scoop on local histories while learning the lifestyles of nobles and peasants during the Middle Ages. The one-hour English tour (6€/person) departs daily April thru Christmas at 20:00 on Market Square (Marktplatz). *Note:* For the tour to go, a minimum of 10 people are required. On a cold and rainy night in November it's possible there won't be enough participants. However, under normal circumstances, there will be 50 to 100 people gathered in the square patiently waiting to do the medieval two-step with the black-caped raconteur. *Opinion:* Since the price is a bit stiff, be on the square at 19:55, watch him arrive, hear his intro, then decide whether you'd like to continue. Because the tour is informal and entirely outside, and the Night Watchman is a bit of a comedian, consider uncorking a bottle of wine with a friend to accompany your stroll. Afterwards, go to Hell (wine tavern).

Criminal Museum: A Rothenburg must-do is the "Mittelalterliches Kriminalmuseum," where you'll discover unpleasant contraptions (e.g. shame mask, finger screws) designed in the Middle Ages to crush, stretch, poke and humiliate lawbreakers. Allow at least two hours for a visit. Bring a camera to snap a photo of yourself (or a friend) in the shackles outside the front entrance. *Hours:* daily, April-Oct 9:30-18:00; Nov and Jan/Feb 14:00-16:00; Dec and March 10:00-16:00. *Price:* adult 3.50€, student 2.30€, senior 3€. *Getting There:* Museum is located at Burggasse 3, one block south of Market Square.

City Walls: (Stadtmauer) One of the joys of Rothenburg is to dawdle along its rampart promenade dating from medieval times. To ramble the whole length (from Spitaltor to Klingentor, or vice-versa) is more than a mile long and will take roughly 45-60 minutes. However, there are several access points so you can bounce on and off as you please. Don't forget to bring your camera, as the promenade provides a scenic platform to photograph Rothenburg's captivating collage of towers, turrets and tilted roofs. To get an even loftier perspective, climb the Rödertor tower (page 160) at the midway point. En route you'll see numerous plaques embedded in the stone, these represent people from all over the world who have donated money for the wall's upkeep, especially the rebuilding of sections blown apart by WWII bombs. In 1950, to symbolically "purchase" a meter of the wall (have your name honored on a plaque) cost 80dm (about $40). Today, the minimum donation is 1000€. *Note:* The promenade can be very narrow in places, and often has low-lying beams making it particularly annoying for tall people. Explore the 16th-century Spitaltor, a powerhouse bastion at the south end of town. Check out the adjacent cutesy-pie wooden bridge. Additionally, there is a short, walkable section of the wall situated behind the youth hostel (not necessary to visit if you're pushed for time).

Measuring Sticks: Before we explain what these are, let's find 'em first: Stand by the fountain at the south end of Market Square and face the Old Town clock (building TI is in). Now, go left and stop in front of the archway on the right, directly beneath the town hall tower (page 160). Left of the archway, attached to the wall, you'll see three rods. In medieval times these were used as tools to gauge measurements like we would use a yardstick or ruler today. The longest rod, 3.93 meters long (13 feet), is called a "rute" (or rod). Adjacent is a "shoe," the length of about a foot. The next one is an "elle," or nearly 2 feet. Step through the archway and on the left are the Historical Vaults...

Historical Vaults: Behind town hall you'll discover the "Historiengewölbe," featuring uniforms and weapons from the Thirty Years' War (1618-48) as well as a chilling look into the town's former dungeon and torture chamber *(step into the third cell and close the door to get the cold feeling of being an inmate in medieval Rothenburg)*. It was below ground level in this dark, clammy environment that Rothenburg's most powerful and famous mayor—Heinrich Toppler—died in 1408 after the discovery of his secret letters to the deposed king suggesting he retake the throne. The reigning king intercepted the letters and consequently had Toppler imprisoned in the dungeon as a traitor. *Hours:* Easter thru Dec, daily, 10:00-17:00 (closed Jan thru Easter). *Price:* adult 2€, student 1.50€. *Getting There:* The vaults can be found in the arcade behind the Rathaus (town hall). *Note:* Out the other end of the arcade is St. Jakob's Church...

St. Jakob's Church: This twin-towered structure belonging to the Lutheran faith is Rothenburg's principal church, built from 1311 to 1471. In medieval times St. Jakob's became a place of pilgrimage, as it claimed to have a drop of Christ's blood in crystallized form. The blood was set in a golden crucifix and mounted on the Altar of the Holy Blood (Heilig Blut Altar), a 35-foot-high altar meticulously carved out of wood (1499-1504) to provide a sacred seat for viewing the holy relic. The altar—crafted by Würzburg artist Tilman Riemenschneider—is arguably Germany's most exquisite wood carving, which depicts scenes from the Bible, e.g. Jesus on the Mount of Olives, his entry into Jerusalem, and the Last Supper. You can see the altar on the first floor (one level up) via a flight of stairs on left after entering church. To enter St. Jakob's will cost adult 1.50€, student 50¢. After paying, be sure to grab the church-info pamphlet in front of you against the pillar (it's free and in English). Take note of the 5000-pipe organ; the Altar of the Virgin Mary (1520); the chancel pews dating from 1514 and the above coats of arms; and the 14th-century stained-glass windows behind the Twelve Apostles Altar (high altar at head of church). *Hours:* April-Oct Mon-Sat 9:00-17:15, Sun 10:30-17:30; Nov and Jan-March 10:00-12:00 & 14:00-16:00; Dec 10:00-17:00. *Note:* An external bridge-like section of the church was built over the road. To get to the Klingentor (north end of town), one has to actually pass underneath the church.

Fountains: In the Middle Ages, most sizeable communities were typically comprised of narrow streets flanked by row houses made of wood. Thus, fire posed a constant threat. For the purpose of fire prevention, as well as water supply, numerous fountains were implemented. Having more than 40 fountains, Rothenburg is a prime example of this medieval trend. Located on the south end of Market Square, Rothenburg's largest example is St. George fountain (late-Renaissance, 1608), which is 8m/26ft deep and has the capacity to hold 100,000 liters (26,000 gal) of water. The metal gutters you see are moveable and were used to channel water into the villagers' buckets.

Herr Baumeister and Toppler: At the top of Obere Schmiedgasse (south end of Market Square) are the patrician houses formerly belonging to Rothenburg's Baumeister (or master builder) and its most famous mayor, Heinrich Toppler. The Baumeister's house (at No. 3) dates from 1596 and is the town's best example of Renaissance-style. On its facade are 14 statues allegedly representing the seven virtues and vices: Chastity/Lust,

Temperance/Gluttony, Hope/Envy, Charity/Greed, Courage/Sloth, Faith/Anger, Compassion/Pride. Step inside to find a casual restaurant nestled within a must-see, picturesque courtyard. Next door to the Baumeister's house (right side, No. 5, Goldener Greifen) are the former digs of Rothenburg's legendary mayor, Heinrich Toppler (see *Historical Vaults* above for his fate). Today, the building serves as a hotel and restaurant run by the Klingler family for five generations.

"Hell," Wine Tavern: (zur Höll) Besides a devilish wine bar, Hell qualifies as the oldest house in town because the back portion and foundation of the tavern dates from the 10th century. Pop in to warm your soul; Hell serves well-prepared food, Franconian wine, and a smooth beer in a snug and cozy atmosphere. For a good recommendation, go to Hell. *Hours:* daily from 17:00, kitchen open till 22:00. *Getting There:* Hell is located at Burggasse 8, one block south of Market Square (or continue some 75 meters past the Criminal Museum's main entrance, where—on the right-hand side of the road—you'll see a devil hangin' above Hell's front door).

Käthe Wohlfahrt: This themed store, which could easily be construed as a Disney-style attraction, is based around a village joyfully stuck in a Christmas wonderland—all year long. Here you'll discover every type of ornament, figurine and Saint Nick trinket conceivable (and for sale). Decorations adorning the village total more than 3 miles of Christmas garland and 80,000 lights. A visit here is worth your time, even for shopping skeptics. (www.wohlfahrt.com) *Hours:* Mon-Sat 10:00-18:00. *Getting There:* Käthe Wohlfahrt is located at the south end of Market Square. Look for the vintage bus parked out front and the giant nutcracker guarding the door. Across the street is another Käthe Wohlfahrt store. *Note:* Inside you'll also find the German Christmas Museum—excellent but an unnecessary expense for non-enthusiasts at 4€ per adult. Students, though, have a better deal at 2.50€.

English Conversation Club: Officially not a sight but engaging just the same; the English Conversation Club meets every Wednesday evening to shoot the breeze in English. This is a great opportunity for you to mingle with linguistically inquisitive locals. Conversations kick off around 19:00 at the Altfränkische Weinstube (wine tavern) situated two blocks north of St. Jakob's Church at Klosterhof 7 (lane off Klingengasse). *Tel.#* 09861/6404.

Best Views

Town Hall Tower: At the Rathaus (town hall) on Market Square enter through the middle arch and ascend more than 210 steps to reach the building's 197-foot-high, open-air observation level. *Hours:* April-Oct (daily) 9:30-12:30 & 13:30-17:00; Nov & Jan-March (weekends only) 12:00-15:00; Dec (daily) 12:00-15:00. *Price:* 1€.

Röder Tower: Dating from the 13th century, "Rödertor" is the only accessible tower along the city wall. Railers will recognize it as the medieval gate closest to the station. From street level, climb 135 steps to reach memorable views within the enclosed tower. In addition to the views, you'll be floored by a pictorial exhibition documenting Rothenburg's plight during WWII—black-and-white photos taken from the tower capture the ruinous aftermath of a 1945 bombing raid. *Hours:* irregular but typically 9:00-16:00. *Price:* 1.50€.

Events/Festivals, 2006

There are several festivals throughout the year. However, three stand out.

Imperial City Festival (Reichsstadt-Festtage), Sept 1-3 (Fri-Sun): This colorful three-day fiesta is the highlight of the festival calendar, when locals dressed as knights, musketeers, merchants and peasants reenact the history of Rothenburg. What's more, visitors will witness a medieval trial and a brilliant fireworks show (Sat night). *Note:* If you think you'll be in town around this time, book your accommodations well in advance.

Taubertal-Open-Air-Festival, Aug 11-13 (Fri-Sun): During this three-day bash some 30,000 fans will rock out to a host of bands in the Tauber Valley (beneath Rothenburg). Overnight revelers bring a tent. (www.taubertal-openair.de)

Christmas Market, Dec 1-22. If you thought (or heard) Rothenburg was busy during the summer, you should see it in December when the Christmas market is in full swing. Busloads of Germans and foreign tourists invade the turf from Market Square to Kirchplatz (square facing St. Jakob's Church), where vendors tending to their gift-wrapped stalls stocked with Christmassy wares and baked goods are ringin' up the holiday cheer. Don't forget to collect a Glühwein mug. And as for the Käthe Wohlfahrt store, expect a long wait to get in.

GOOD SLEEPS

There are numerous accommodations in Rothenburg to choose from, so we dissected the bunch and handpicked two lists to simplify choices for Railers and Drivers. Wrapping up this section, are good sleeps for a bit more money. *Note:* All below-mentioned entries come with breakfast and have facilities (shower/toilet) in the room, unless otherwise stated.

Good Sleeps, Railers

Railers: We've selected a handful of worthwhile places that will be easy for you to find. From the station, exit left—at the forward traffic light turn right (Ansbacher Str.) following the brown "Altstadt" sign. Take this straight some 300 meters. Go through the medieval town gate (Rödertor) leading onto the cobbled streets Rödergasse and Hafengasse to Market Square. Once at the junction of Obere Schmiedgasse and the environs of Market Square, STOP. — *The gingerbread house, Marien-Apotheke, should be in front of you and the Old Town clock to your right (in this brown building is the TI).* — You are now just steps away from your digs. From here to get to **Gästehaus Raidel**, go left down Obere Schmiedgasse three blocks and make a left on Wenggasse. To get to **Gästehaus Liebler**, continue straight (passing fountain and Marien-Apotheke) towards Herrngasse and make a left into Pfäffleinsgässchen—narrow lane just past the Käthe Wohlfahrt store. To get to **Gasthof Marktplatz**, angle right across Market Square and you'll see their yellow facade left of the clock. To get to **Gasthof zur Goldenen Rose** or the **youth hostel**, go left down Obere Schmiedgasse—straight through the tower and onto Spitalgasse. *Note:* For extra choices, consider the list for Drivers.

Gästehaus Raidel: Wenggasse 3 (www.romanticroad.com/raidel) *Tel.#* 09861/3115 These quaint, half-timbered digs won't disappoint. Herr Raidel—the owner—is a soft-spoken gentleman who crafted most all of the internal woodwork himself, including the bed frames. Check out his handiwork in the breakfast room, especially the pillar bearing his likeness—complete with handlebar moustache. *Price:* (cash only) Sgl without facilities (shower/toilet) in room 19€—with facilities 39€; Dbl without facilities 39€—with facilities 49€; Trpl with facilities 70€; quad with facilities 80€.

Gästehaus Liebler: Pfäffleinsgässchen 10. *Tel.#* 09861/709-215, fax. /709-216 Frau Liebler offers two comfy ground-floor (Dbl) rooms with kitchenettes. *Price:* (cash only) 35-50€ (per room—price depends on season), 10€/extra person.

Gasthof Marktplatz: *Tel.#* 09861/6722 (www.gasthof-marktplatz.de) Hidden in plain view on Market Square, Gasthof Markplatz offers no-frills accommodations in the heart of it all. *Note:* Church bells ring throughout night. *Price:* (cash only) Sgl without facilities in room 21€; Dbl without facilities 38€—with facilities 48€; Trpl without facilities 50€—with facilities 62€.

Gasthof zur Goldenen Rose: Spitalgasse 28 (www.zur-goldenen-rose.de) *Tel.#* 09861/4638. Easy-on-the-wallet prices combined with friendly staff and an appetizing, traditional-style restaurant make this historic hotel a pleasant stop. Pop in and say "How-dee-do" to Henny and Karin, your hospitable hosts. *Price:* Sgl without facilities (shower/toilet) in room 18-22€; Dbl without facilities 36€—with facilities 46-62€; Trpl without facilities 50€—with facilities 66-77€, four/five-bed with facilities 107-128€. *CC's:* VC, MC, AE, DC.

Hostel, Jungendherberge: [HI] *Tel.#* 09861/94-160 (www.djh.de) Located at the south end of town, Rothenburg's 500-year-old steep-roofed hostel accommodates 184 beds. Has laundry (5€/load) and cheap meals (5.40€). *Price:* (includes breakfast and sheets; same-sex dorms only) dorm bed 18.50€ (cheaper second night), Dbl 43€ (with shower/toilet). *CC's:* VC, MC. *Note:* Must be a member or an extra charge will apply. In Bavaria, government-supported youth hostels like this one still require their guests to be 25 years of age or under to stay. Families OK. *Getting There:* When coming from Market Square, turn right just past Gasthof zur Goldenen Rose at (lane) Rossmühlgasse.

Good Sleeps, Drivers

Drivers: We've selected a handful of affordable, comfy accommodations that are centrally located and easily reached via automobile—allowing for a smooth arrival. Once there, reception will give you the skinny on where to park.

Enter Rothenburg through the Spitaltor gate (*GPS:* N49° 22.231 - E10° 10.866) at the south end of town. Directions from the south, north and autobahn are spelled out below. *Note:* Spitaltor gate is closed Saturdays 14:00-18:00 and Sunday/holidays 11:00-18:00. If you have no choice but to arrive during the aforesaid times, enter Rothenburg through the Galgentor gate on (street) Vorm Würzburger Tor and ignore the following directions.

Arrival from the South, Romantic Road: Upon passing the Rothenburg city limits sign, turn left at the traffic light following the Spitaltor sign, then make the second (immediate) right leading under the Spitaltor gate. Out the other side is Spitalgasse—your digs will soon appear up ahead.

Arrival from the North, Romantic Road: Follow signs to Donauwörth. You'll pass several traffic lights. At about the eighth light turn right following the Spitaltor sign, then make the second (immediate) right leading under the Spitaltor gate. Out the other side is Spitalgasse—your digs will soon appear up ahead.

Arrival from the Autobahn: Follow signs to Rothenburg. After about 1.5km turn left direction Donauwörth. At the second traffic light turn right following the Spitaltor sign, then make the second (immediate) right leading under the Spitaltor gate. Out the other side is Spitalgasse—your digs will soon appear up ahead.

Hotel Gerberhaus: Spitalgasse 25 [on right]. (www.gerberhaus.rothenburg.de) *Tel.#* 09861/94-900. Rustic appeal and old-world charm make this is a popular choice. Has laundry. Free Internet for guests. *Price:* Sgl 50-70€, Dbl 62-84€, Trpl 99-109€, four-bed 114-130€, apartment available. *CC's:* VC, MC. *Note:* Pay cash and receive a 5% discount!

Gasthaus Raidel: Wenggasse 3 [go through forward tower and Wenggasse is the second right]. *Tel.#* 09861/3115. (www.romanticroad.com/raidel) These quaint, half-timbered digs won't disappoint. Herr Raidel—the owner—is a soft-spoken gentleman who crafted most all of the internal woodwork himself, including the bed frames. Check out his handiwork in the breakfast room, especially the pillar bearing his likeness—complete with handlebar moustache. *Price:* (cash only) Sgl without facilities (shower/toilet) in room 19€—with facilities 39€; Dbl without facilities 39€—with facilities 49€; Trpl with facilities 70€; quad with facilities 80€.

Gasthaus Am Siebersturm: Spitalgasse 6 [on left]. (www.siebersturm.com) *Tel.#* 09861/3355. This small inn offers a prime location and cozy digs. Most rooms have a view of the Tauber Valley. Oktay, the owner, says to show this book and you'll receive 5% off the listed price, and a further 5% if you pay with cash. *Price:* (before book, cash discount) Dbl 55-80€. *CC's:* VC, MC, AE.

Gasthof zur Goldenen Rose: Spitalgasse 28 [on left]. (www.zur-goldenen-rose.de) *Tel.#* 09861/4638. Easy-on-the-wallet prices combined with friendly staff and an appetizing, traditional-style restaurant make this historic hotel a pleasant stop. Pop in and say "How-dee-do" to Henny and Karin, your hospitable hosts. *Price:* Sgl without facilities (shower/toilet) in room 18-22€; Dbl without facilities 36€—with facilities 46-62€; Trpl without facilities 50€—with facilities 66-77€, four/five-bed with facilities 107-128€. *CC's:* VC, MC, AE, DC.

Hotel/Café Uhl: Plönlein 8 [go through forward tower and it's on the left]. *Tel.#* 09861/ 4895 (www.hotel-uhl.de) Reception is located behind a long counter loaded with mouth-watering pastries. Oh, the rooms are fine, too. *Price:* Sgl 30-45€, Dbl 50-68€, add 15€ per extra person. *CC's:* VC, MC, AE.

Camping: The following two campgrounds are situated near one another in the peaceful village of Detwang, 1.5km north of Rothenburg. Both offer bike rental and are open Easter thru Oct.

Camping Tauber Romantic: Apartments available (2-4 persons). *Tel.#* 09861/6191. (www.camping-tauberromantik.de)

Camping Tauber-Idyll: *Tel.#* 09861/3177

Good Sleeps, For a Bit More Money

Gotisches Haus: Herrngasse 13 (www.gotisches-haus.de) *Tel.#* 09861/2020. Enjoy the Middle Ages behind closed doors in these 4-star, 700-year-old accommodations. Each room at the "Gothic House"—spacious yet cozy—combines the romantic ambiance of medieval Rothenburg with modern conveniences. Centrally located, a short walk from Market Square, step into their traditional-style restaurant and ogle the old-world stone-and-timber charm. Go to the above-listed Gotisches Haus website and pick out your favorite room, two have a balcony. *Price:* Dbl from 86€, suite from 180€. *CC's:* VC, MC, AE, DC. *Getting There:* see directions below.

Burg-Hotel: Klostergasse 1 (www.romanticroad.com/burghotel) *Tel.#* 09861/94-890. This dreamy hotel is situated on the edge of Rothenburg, literally. Like a battlement, the Burg Hotel is perched upon the town's ramparts. The hotel offers 15 adorable rooms and suites, many with views of the Tauber Valley. If you're looking for a romantic getaway, this is the place. Free Internet for guests. *Price:* Dbl 90-170€, tower 150€; three-room family apartment (dating from 17C) also available, 155-215€ (depending on how many people, 2-7). *CC's:* VC, MC, AE. Free parking out front, or in their garage 7.50€. *Getting There:* see directions below.

Railers: Both the Gotisches Haus and Burg-Hotel are a short walk from Market Square. Wander down Herrngasse to find the Gotisches Haus on the left (by fountain) or continue straight to No. 26 on the right (Hotel Meistertrunk) and shoot through the lane just past it on the right to reach the Burg-Hotel.

Drivers: The Gotisches Haus and Burg-Hotel are situated near each other, thus the same directions apply.

Arrival from the Autobahn, or South (Romantic Road): Enter Rothenburg via the Galgentor gate from (street) Vorm Würzburger Tor. Follow "Stadtmitte" sign. On the other side of the gate continue straight all the way (through the packs of tourists). At the big church (St. Jakob's) stop at the crossroads of Kirchgasse and Klostergasse: Continue straight for the Burg-Hotel (end of lane on right) or turn left onto Kirchgasse for the Gotisches Haus (straight ahead and park other side of fountain).

Arrival from the North, Romantic Road: Enter Rothenburg via the ultra-narrow Klingentor gate and continue straight (on Klingengasse). After driving underneath the big church (St. Jakob's), STOP: Go right on Klostergasse for the Burg-Hotel (at end of lane on right), or continue straight ahead for the Gotisches Haus and park other side of fountain. *Note:* Klingentor gate is closed Sat 14:00-18:00 and Sun/holidays 11:00-18:00. If you arrive during these times, follow the above set of directions: *Arriving from the Autobahn, or South (Romantic Road).*

D I N K E L S B ü H L

~ Population: 11,500 ~ Elevation: 450m/1476ft
~ Country/Area Code: +49-(0)9851

Dating from 1188, Dinkelsbühl was first mentioned by Emperor Frederick Barbarossa as Burgum Tinkelspuhel. Having survived all the major wars unscathed, including WWII, Dinkelsbühl is arguably the Romantic Road's best-preserved walled town because it's home to more original structures than Rothenburg, its larger and more popular neighbor 45km to the north.

For photographers and bright-eyed daytrippers, Dinkelsbühl presents an abundance of captivating prospects. For example, you can explore the town's fortified walls that were completed by the citizens in 1450. You can visit St. George Cathedral and witness the bones of St. Aurelius, who was executed in Rome nearly 2000 years ago. For lunch or dinner, sink your teeth into a yummy trout. Sounds strange, we know, but the district maintains some 300 ponds and the locals specialize in the art of fish. Sticking with the culinary topic, have lunch on Gasthof Sonne's summer terrace (May-Oct), or experience dinner next door in Eisenkrug's historic vaulted cellar, or relish a meal in the Deutsches Haus under its 300-year-old, must-see ceiling splashed with murals of dashing knights, fearsome warriors and colorful crests.

Tourist Information: [TI] (www.dinkelsbuehl.de) *Tel.#* 09851/90-240. Situated on the corner across from St. George Cathedral, Dinkelsbühl's TI "Städt Verkehrsamt" is fairly easy to spot. Make sure to pick up their excellent town map (.30¢) with do-it-yourself walking tour. *Hours:* May-Oct Mon-Fri 9:00-18:00, Sat 10:00-13:00 & 14:00-16:00, Sun 10:00-12:00; Nov-April Mon-Fri 10:00-13:00 & 14:00-17:00, Sat 10:00-12:00.

Railers: Dinkelsbühl is not train friendly; its forlorn station died out years ago. Instead, the town can be reached via the "Touring" bus company's north-south route. Holders of a German rail or Eurail (consecutive-day or dated Flexi/Select) pass receive a hefty 60% one-way discount on bus tickets. For example, from Frankfurt to Augsburg—via Rothenburg, Dinkelsbühl and Nördlingen—will cost 60€ (or 24€ with a rail-pass discount). "Touring" buses do the Romantic Road milk-run (April-Oct) once daily in each direction (see page 155 for schedule). Reservations are not mandatory but suggested July-Sept. *Tel.#* (Frankfurt area code) 069/790-3230, or query TI for the nearest Touring office (— they have several throughout Germany). The following times are subject to change. For updates, query TI or go to www.romantic-road-coach.de

Bus departs Frankfurt heading south at 8:00 daily (April-Oct) arriving in Rothenburg at 12:15 and Dinkelsbühl 13:35.

Bus departs Augsburg heading north at 14:00 daily (April-Oct) arriving in Nördlingen 15:15, Dinkelsbühl 16:05 and Rothenburg 17:10.

Drivers: Use your "parking dial" (Parkscheibe; see page 450) to park on the street for one hour, applicable Mon-Fri 8:00-18:00 and Sat 8:00-15:00 (hotel guests refer to reception). *Note:* Dinkelsbühl is closed to traffic on Sundays (May-Sept) from 13:00-18:00, except for those who are checking into their lodgings.

Internet: You can surf a fast connection at "Fair Play," a somewhat smoky gaming parlor at Nördlinger Str. 9 (two-minute walk from cathedral). *Price:* 1€/15min, 4€/hr. *Hours:* daily 9:00-24:00. *Note:* Little English spoken. Easy-to-use system; put 1€ coin(s) in computer to pay as you go.

Cathedral, St. George: Consecrated in 1488, one can't miss Dinkelsbühl's marvelous Münster (cathedral) whose soaring steeple peers over a sea of lopsided, red-roofed dwellings. The cathedral's interior is vast and awe-inspiring. Walk through its massive stone portal and ogle the carved pews, ornate pulpit, webbed ceiling, Gothic dogs at your feet (beneath baptism receptacle), bold columns framing the main aisle, the impressive side doors and their silver locks. Midway along the right aisle rests the bones of St. Aurelius, who was executed because of his Christian faith nearly 2000 years ago in Rome at the command of Emperor Nero. St. Aurelius was brought here in 1748 from the catacombs in Rome and enshrined. The sign "Bitte nicht betreten" loosely translates: *Do not disturb or the soul of this martyr will haunt you for the rest of your natural life.* Yikes! We would advise not getting too close. St. Aurelius is part of the St. Sebastian Altar (early 16th century), whose mural depicts St. Sebastian being martyred because of his Christian faith. Before exiting, look at the size of the organ pipes above the portal. Below, you'll see the names of locals who died during WWII. To the right is a crucifix flanked by two angles (17C). In between are the names of WWI dead. *Hours:* April-Oct 9:00-12:00 & 14:00-19:00, winter same except closes 17:00. Climb the 60m/197ft high tower for heavy-duty views, May-Sept & Oct (weekends only) Sat/Sun 13:00-17:00.

Historical Museum: This modest museum—located adjacent to an old folks home that is part of the 15th-century hospital quarter, Spitalhof—exhibits the town's history on three levels; worthwhile for historians who Deutsch verstehen kann because the museum is in German. *Hours:* Tue-Sun 10:00-16:00. *Price:* adult 3€, student 2€. *Getting There:* When facing the cathedral's front entrance, go left a few hundred meters and the museum is on the right (at Dr.-Martin-Luther-Str. 6).

Museum, 3-D: Here you'll encounter three floors of illusion; however, what's really cool could fit into one room. Museum is overpriced at adult 8€, student 6€. *Hours:* April-Sept, daily, 10:00-18:00; Oct & 26 Dec thru 6 Jan 11:00-16:00; rest of year weekends only, 11:00-16:00. *Getting There:* Museum is located at the south end of Dinkelsbühl adjacent to the gate Nördlinger Tor.

Festivals, 2006:

Kinderzeche, July 14-23 (www.kinderzeche.de) This 10-day event weighs in at numero uno on Dinkelsbühl's festival calendar. Traditional costumes and dancing, historical re-enactments and performances, a brilliant fireworks show and a beer tent are a few of the ingredients that make the Kinderzeche a hit. The festival commemorates the feat of local children in 1632, when Swedish soldiers encircled Dinkelsbühl during the Thirty Years' War. The tale commences when the gatekeeper's young daughter—followed by a procession of local children—approached the besieging colonel and asked that the town be spared. The ploy worked and you, too, can play a role, just book your accommodations *well* in advance or simply stop by for a few hours during your delightful excursion along the Romantic Road.

Middle Ages' Festival, Sept 10 (Sun). By the title it shouldn't surprise you that the theme of this festival is "Life in an Old Town." The age of imperialism and chivalry revisits Dinkelsbühl when it transforms itself back to medieval times. An experience you won't want to miss.

Fish Harvest Week, Oct 28—Nov 5. Remember all those ponds we referred to earlier? Well, the fish are scooped up en masse and cooked to traditional recipes. Additionally, the town square will be awash with aquariums and makeshift ponds for your viewing pleasure.

Christmas Market, Nov 30—Dec 21. Packed with holiday cheer, Dinkelsbühl's Christmas market is a Romantic Road darling—located meters from St. George Cathedral in the center of town. Don't forget to collect a Glühwein mug.

Good Sleeps

There are some sweet digs next to the church, but we can't recommend them because the bells chime every 15 minutes—*all night long!* We woke the next morning in dire need of sleep. Urgh! The following pocket-friendly accommodations are hushed alternatives that we think you'll appreciate. The first two listings come with breakfast and have facilities (shower/toilet) in the room.

Hotel/Restaurant Eisenkrug: Dr-Martin-Luther-Str. 1. *Tel.#* 09851/57-700 (www.hotel-eisenkrug.de) The 16th-century Eisenkrug, or Iron Stein, is the best place in town for your money. Helmut and Patricia, the owners, pump large amounts of TLC into their individually decorated rooms to maintain a homely atmosphere. Hotel has elevator. Consider a knight's dinner (Rittermahl) in their historic cellar. *Note:* We must warn you, the Eisenkrug is still within earshot of the church bells. However, the coziness and hospitality offset the clanging. *Price:* Sgl from 40€, Dbl from 50€, apartment available. *Getting There:* When facing the cathedral's main entrance, go left 200 meters and your digs will be on the left. *GPS:* N49° 04.225 - E10° 19.117

Weib's Brauhaus: Untere Schmiedgasse 13 (www.weibsbrauhaus.de) *Tel.#* 09851/579-490. You'll no doubt sleep like a baby here. Besides shipshape accommodations, highlights include barley, hops and water. This is because Weib's Brauhaus is a microbrewery—the only one in Dinkelsbühl, in fact. In addition to fresh beer, yummy meals are served in their bistro. At Weib's, management—including the brewer—are women, hence the translation of its name: "Women's Brew House." *Note:* Weib's is closed Tuesdays—no check-in or bistro service available. Open Wed 18:00-01:00, Thur-Mon 11:00-01:00. *Price:* (cheaper without breakfast) Sgl 40€, Dbl 54€, Trpl 70€, extra bed 10€. *Getting There:* From the cathedral, head along Segringer Str. and turn right on Bauhofstr. The road will slightly curve to the right and change names to Untere Schmiedgasse, at which point Weib's Brauhaus will appear on the right. *GPS:* N49° 04.220 - E10° 19.013

Hostel, Jugendherberge: [HI] Koppengasse 10 (www.djh.de) *Tel.#* 09851/9509. Dating from 1508, this impressive half-timbered former grain store contains 148 beds. *Price:* (includes sheets, breakfast) dorm bed 15.50€ (cheaper second night), Dbl available. *Note:* Open March-Oct, closed Nov-Feb. Must be a member and under 26 years of age or an extra charge will apply. *Getting There:* From the cathedral, head along Segringer Str. and go right on Bauhofstr. Make the first left on Koppengasse and ascend cobbled lane to the top—look right. *GPS:* N49° 04.157 - E10° 18.881

DCC-Campingpark: *Tel.#* 09851/7817 (www.campingpark-dinkelsbuehl.de) Open all year. Located on the north side of town—turn off the Romantic Road onto Dürrwanger Str. following camping signs up hill.

N ö R D L I N G E N *im Ries*

~ *Population: 21,000* ~ *Country/Area Code: +49-(0)9081*
~ *Elevation: 430m/1410ft*
~ *Sister City: Wagga Wagga, (NSW) Australia; Markham, (Ont.) Canada*

Some 30km south of Dinkelsbühl, and 20km north of Harburg, you'll encounter Nördlingen, a fascinating walled town in the county of Ries. Upon your approach to Nördlingen, look for the sign denoting Ries county—capital letters spell "RIESIG" and in the background you'll see a blazing comet. In German, *Riesig* means enormous (or gigantic), which specifically relates to some 15 million years ago when a meteorite, one kilometer in circumference, impolitely slammed into a nearby plateau. The meteorite—traveling at a swift pace of 70,000kph (45,000 mph) when it struck—discharged enough energy to equal 250,000 Hiroshima bombs, which penetrated a depth of three football fields and created a prehistoric crater 25km/16mi in diameter. Many of Nördlingen's original structures were partly or wholly built with these extraterrestrial, Riesig boulders known as "Suevit." Although hardly noticeable to the general tourist, the vast Ries impression is regarded as one of the best-preserved craters on earth. For this reason, NASA sent astronauts from the Apollo space program to the Ries in 1970 on field exercises. As a "thank you" for the generous hospitality offered by the locals, the Apollo 14 team donated a moon rock to the town of Nördlingen, which can be seen today in the **Rieskrater-Museum**. For geologists and paleontologists, the Ries is a gold mine.

From several miles out, a visitor's first impression of Nördlingen is **Daniel**, the 90m/295ft high bell tower belonging to the late-Gothic cathedral, St. George. From this lofty perch a whopping 110 villages can be counted on a clear day. What's more, it is from this vantage point that Nördlingen's resident night watchman—the last full-time civil position of its kind in Germany—howls "So G'sell so." This legendary call dates from 1440 when the gatekeepers of the Löpsinger Tor were bribed by the powerful Count von Oettingen to leave the gate (Tor) unlocked for three nights so he could return with his troops and pillage Nördlingen. On the third night, while the count quietly approached with his army, a passerby coincidently noticed the gate door unlocked and shrieked, "So G'sell so!" (Ah ha, you've been caught!) The citizen guard was rallied and defensive positions were bolstered. Hence, the pending invasion was thwarted and the gatekeepers executed. From this incident forward, *So G'sell so* has been sounded through the ages by night watchmen as a caution to gatekeepers and tower sentries to be vigilant on their watch, as well as a reminder that traitors pay with their lives. To this day, you can still hear the night watchman howl *So G'sell so* from the top of Daniel every evening from 22:00-24:00 on the hour and half hour.

Another unique quality about Nördlingen is its 2.6km/1.5mi long **City Walls** (Stadt-mauer), which can be 100% circumnavigated (on foot) and register as the only remaining fortifications of their kind in Germany. To walk the rampart loop will take roughly 90 minutes—and if it rains, don't worry, the promenade is mostly covered. Don't forget your camera, and consider packing a picnic.

Tourist Information: [TI] (www.noerdlingen.de) *Tel.#* 09081/84-116. Folks interested in the aforesaid extraterrestrial Suevit can buy it here: small piece 2.50€, big 5€. Besides space rock, English tours of Nördlingen are possible (3€/person), call TI in advance to see whether one is scheduled. Drivers in need of a parking dial (Parkscheibe) should inquire here. If you ask nicely, you may get one for free. *Hours:* From Easter to the beginning of Nov, Mon-Thur 9:00-18:00, Fri 9:00-16:30, Sat and holidays 9:30-13:00; remainder of year, Mon-Thur 9:00-17:00, Fri 9:00-15:30. *Getting There:* TI is located in the heart of town, adjacent to the town hall (Rathaus) and near the cathedral. Follow "Information" signs.

Railers: (Transfer necessary in Donauwörth, or Aalen.) From Nördlingen's train station to the cathedral is a 15-minute walk.

Drivers: Within Nördlingen's fortified walls it can get a bit confusing with meandering lanes and numerous one-way streets. Follow the tourist "Information" signs into the center. Ninety-minute parking possible with use of your *parking dial (Parkscheibe) Mon-Fri 8:00-17:00, Sat 8:00-12:00, (hotel guests query reception about where to park). *Note:* Refer to (page 450) chapter *Traveler's Tips*—Drivers. Need a Parkscheibe? Ask TI—they may have an extra one.

Daniel: The first sight you'll see of Nördlingen is Daniel, the 90m/295ft high bell tower punctuating the skyline. Located in the center of town, Daniel belongs to the 15th-century St. George Cathedral, which—by the way—is mostly comprised of Suevit, the space rock. Scale 350 steps to the top of Daniel to properly see the whole of Nördlingen and the Ries basin, where some 110 villages can be counted on a clear day. *Hours:* daily, April-Oct 9:00-19:45, remainder of year 9:00-17:00. *Price:* 1.75€ (pay at top).

Rieskrater-Museum: At this geological museum you'll learn about, among other things, the meteorite that crashed into Ries county 15 million years ago and you'll see the moon rock donated by NASA. Although the museum is in German, an English translation guide can be obtained from the cashier (for 3€ after deposits and refund). *Hours:* Tue-Sun 10:00-12:00 and 13:30-16:30. *Price:* adult 3€, student 1.50€, senior 1.80€.

Hotel/Café Altreuter: Marktplatz 11 (hotel-cafe-altreuter@nordschwaben.de) *Tel.#* 09081/4319. Hidden in plain view, these clean digs are located in the heart of town adjacent to cathedral. You'll appreciate their sweet café. *Note:* No elevator; has some steps to negotiate. Little English spoken. *Price:* (cash preferred, AE accepted) Sgl 33-45€, Dbl 48-64€, Trpl 69-75€, family room from 90€. Free parking; inquire within.

HARBURG

~ Population: 6000   ~ Elevation: 471m/1550ft
~ Country/Area Code: +49-(0)9080

Some 20km south of Nördlingen, and 55km north of Augsburg, is Harburg, a quaint village with an unconquered fortress. Harburg's castle, dating from 1150 and formerly the home of Staufen kings, is one of the oldest and largest fortress complexes in southern Germany. Stop in for a taste of medieval times without the crowds.

While in the village—15-minute walk beneath the castle—wander onto the stone bridge spanning the Wörnitz River and admire the serenity, splendor and diligent ducks. Notice the two plaques cemented into the stonework. One remembers four local boys, ages 8 to 12, who died from landmines on April 25, 1945, less than two weeks before the end of WWII. The second plaque reads: *"The bridge still conforms to the original design from its christening in 1729. Partly renovated in 1784, the bridge was blown up, as a consequence of war, on April 24, 1945, against the will of the Harburgers. On September 10, 1945, the mayor, Friedrich Suser, organized a volunteer work program in con-junction with monetary donations to rebuild the bridge. For the love of home and their eagerness to overcome all difficulties, the townsfolk finished the bridge with their own hands on April 24, 1946."*

Railers: Harburg is train friendly—transfer necessary at Donauwörth, same line as Nörd-lingen.

Drivers: Follow Schloß Harburg signs off the Romantic Road and up to the castle; you won't be disappointed! Once at the parking area, drive some 100 meters farther up to a breathtaking view of the fortress and surrounding area. Great spot for a picnic.

Castle, Harburg: Breach the walls for a closer look; the courtyard is enchanting. Besides massive fortifications, you'll find a restaurant and hotel (*Tel.#* 09080/1504). *Tours of the castle run hourly, April-Oct, Tue-Sun 10:00-16:30. *Price:* adult 4.50€, student 3€. *<u>Note</u>:* Tours are in German, an English brochure will be provided. Call ahead to see if an English tour is scheduled: *Tel.#* 09080/96-860

AUGSBURG

~ Population: 265,000 ~ Elevation: 505m/1656ft
~ Country/Area Code: +49-(0)821 ~ Sister City: Dayton, Ohio

Augsburg is Bavaria's third largest city and ranks among the three oldest in Germany, along with Trier and Cologne. Augsburg inherited its name from the Roman emperor Augustus, who founded it in 15 B.C. as Augusta Vindelcorum.

Another name synonymous with Augsburg is Fugger, a local family of powerful financiers who commanded an empire of worldwide banking, trade and industry bringing all of Europe to Augsburg during the 15th and 16th centuries. The most renowned Fugger was Jakob the Rich (1495-1525), the wealthiest man in the world at the time. To give an idea of the Fugger wealth, you'd have to tally up today's top 100 German corporations to be in the ballpark. The Fuggers financed the imperial crown of the Holy Roman Empire, the Habsburgs; they minted the Pope's coins and paid the Vatican's Swiss Guard; loaned millions to the King of England and the Medici of Florence; brought Renaissance to Germany and founded the world's first social housing community, the **Fuggerei**.

Already having a whopping 50,000 residents by the 16th century, Augsburg played big-city host to a number of imperial diets—or assemblies—most famously the **Augsburg Confession** in 1530 and the Augsburg Peace in 1555, when Martin Luther's Reformation was legitimized spawning today's Lutheranism. Follow Luther's footsteps (free) in the **Church of St. Anna**, where he resided for two weeks in October 1518.

Records suggest Augsburg's cathedral (Dom)—St. Mary's—dates from as early as 823 A.D. Within its holy domain go to the main aisle and gaze upwards to see the prophets Jonah, Daniel, Hosea and Moses depicted on Germany's oldest examples of stained glass (12th century).

To commemorate the 1600-year anniversary of Augsburg's conception, three conspicuous, Renaissance-style fountains were erected. The oldest—dating from 1594 and located on Rathausplatz—is the Augustus Fountain, dedicated to the city's founding father. On each corner a figure symbolizes one of Augsburg's four rivers: Lech (oar), Wertach (grain mill), Brunnenbach (fishnet), Singold (cornucopia). Seductively affixed to the column beneath Augustus, one can't help but notice water spurting from the maidens' nipples. Within a few minutes on foot, descending the influential Maximilianstrasse, the other two fountains can be reached. First in line is the Mercury Fountain, which features its namesake: the god of merchants. Farther along is Hercules Fountain, where the Greek god is seen killing a Hydra, the second of the 12 "Labors of Hercules."

Facing Hercules Fountain is the 18th-century **Schaezler Palais**, home to one of Europe's glitziest Rococo ballrooms. While cruising around town you'll notice the ubiquitous pinecone, which is the city's emblem. The pinecone was originally brought to Augusta Vindelcorum by Roman legionnaires two millennia ago to symbolize fertility.

Augsburg's biggest example of a pinecone can be spotted on top of the **Rathaus** (town hall) from Rathausplatz.

Few realize that Augsburg is the birthplace of **Leopold Mozart**, the father of composer extraordinaire, Wolfgang Amadeus. Continuing on the topic of globally famous names, **Rudolf Diesel** assembled the world's first diesel engine in Augsburg from 1893-97. Visit the **M.A.N.** museum (free) to behold Diesel's first experimental engine. Another engineer and designer, *Wilhelm (Willie) Messerschmidtt established his legendary aircraft factory in Augsburg where his sleek "Me Bf 109" set the world speed record in 1939 (610kph/379mph) and later his "Flying Wing" (jet) reached the sound barrier. (*After WWII, aircraft production was banned in Germany and Willie was imprisoned for three years. Upon his release, Willie went to Spain to continue his passion for building aircraft until the ban was lifted in 1963, when he returned to his native land to once again work in the German aeronautic industry. Willie died in 1978.)*

On account of Messerschmidtt's aforementioned aircraft factory, Augsburg took a severe pounding from Allied bombers during WWII destroying much of the city's architectural heritage. Consequently, in the last 60 years, a dedicated rebuilding program has added a modern shine to the cityscape and today you'll almost certainly never associate Augsburg with ancient at first glance.

Drivers will notice billboards positioned on the city limits advertising Augsburg as Germany's "City of Renaissance," thanks to the Fuggers.

~ Although Bavaria's rich past is deeply rooted here, we only recommend a partial-day sightseeing in Augsburg.

Tourist Information: [TI] (www.augsburg.de) *Tel.#* 0821/502-070. Augsburg's TI offers free maps and brochures in English, including one that recalls the "historic sites of the Reformation." *Hours:* April-Oct Mon-Fri 9:00-18:00, Sat 10:00-16:00, Sun 10:00-14:00; Nov-March Mon-Fri 9:00-17:00, Sat 10:00-14:00. *Getting There:* TI is located on the sprawling, pedestrianized Rathausplatz (Town Hall Square) in the center of town. *Note:* Public toilets can be found two doors from TI.

Hauptbahnhof: [Hbf] From Augsburg's "main train station" to the city center is a five-minute walk—exit station straight into Bahnhofstr. and you'll soon reach the lively pedestrian zone. Trains from Augsburg leave regularly to Munich (trip time, 40min), Rothenburg (2.5hr, 2-3 changes), Berlin (6hr), Frankfurt (3.25hr).

Parking: Drivers, whatever you do, don't overstay your metered welcome in Augsburg—we've never seen so many parking inspectors patrolling the beat as in this city. For *street parking* pay at nearby automat and leave ticket on dashboard of your car. Price: (city center) 60¢/20min, max one hour, applicable Mon-Sat 10:00-18:00—free all other times. *Note:* For a less patrolled area and a much cheaper rate, automats near Leopold Mozart's birthplace (10-min walk from center) are only 60¢/hr, max two hours, applicable Mon-Sat 10:00-18:00. To print ticket, press "Bestätigung." *Parking garages* are abundantly located throughout the city.

Internet: You can browse the World Wide Web at the *Galeria Kaufhof* department store (3rd floor) in the pedestrian zone on Bgm-Fischer-Str. next to Königsplatz. *Hours:* Mon-Sat 9:30-20:00. *Price:* 50¢/10min or 3€/hr.

SIGHTS

Fuggerei: The Fuggerei, if you haven't already heard, is the world's first social housing project. The Fugger brothers—Ulrich, Georg and Jakob—established the Fuggerei in 1516. It is a community within a community, comprising 147 two-room (645sq.ft.) apartments, a fountain and a church. Founded on the premise of long-established Christian values, not much has changed in the community's 500-year history. For example, its

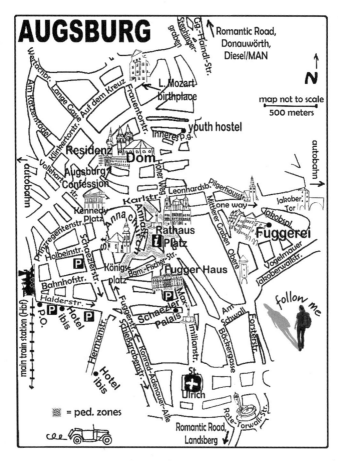

gates still close at 22:00 and latecomers are fined! Fines, just like the rent (we'll get to that in a moment), are on par with 16th-century tariffs. If the offender arrives between 22:00-24:00 the fine is 50¢, between 24:00-05:00 it doubles to 1€. Most laggards wait until 05:00 (when the gates reopen) to avoid the reprimand. The biggest WOW, however, can be heard when residents reveal how much they pay for rent annually: 88¢. An ultra-bargain! So we asked the caretaker how the average Fritz could sign up for this wonder rent. The answer will surprise you. To apply for residence you must be a morally sound, poor, married, Catholic native of Augsburg willing to pray daily for the good fortune handed down to you on behalf of the Fuggers. Do you qualify?

Worthy of your time is a stroll within the Fuggerei to ogle its quaint lanes flanked by coffee-colored facades crawling with ivy. At Mittlere Gasse 13 you can (and should) visit the **Fuggerei Museum** (1€), an age-old apartment preserved in its original condition. Next door lived W.A. Mozart's great grandfather. (www.fuggerei.de) *Hours:* daily, 9:00-18:00 (May-Oct till 20:00). *Tel.#* 0821/319-8810. *GPS:* N48° 22.137 - E10° 54.287—from these coordinates the museum is straight through the gate and to the right.

Fugger Haus: Dating from 1515, Jakob Fugger had the family's palace built along the moneyed Maximilianstrasse (36-38) at a cost of around 2€ million (in today's money).

Divided into separate houses, the urban palace is principally noted for its Italian Renaissance-style architecture and charming Damenhof (Ladies' Courtyard) that features a mosaic floor comprised of Tuscan marble and stones from the Lech River. In October 1518, Martin Luther held weeklong talks here with Cardinal Cajetan.

Augsburg Confession: For centuries, the Pope monopolized the religious beliefs of Western Europe. This abruptly changed in the early 16th century with the advent of Martin Luther, a theologian who challenged the Pope's gospel, sparking the Protestant Reformation. Luther's cutting-edge interpretation of the Bible inspired a grassroots movement that spread across the kingdom and culminated with the Augsburg Confession, a biased assembly of German nobility who rejected Protestant equality.

Alas, the chambers where the Augsburg Confession took place cannot be visited because they no longer exist. However, historians know the location and have marked it with a *plaque. To find it, go to the Residenz—former imperial palace of the bishop, today housing local government offices—adjacent to St. Mary's Cathedral (Dom). Once there, look below the tower and to the right you'll see the Reformation plaque, it reads: *"Here stood the provincial episcopal seat. In the Chapter Room on June 25, 1530, the Augsburg Confession was proclaimed."* On this spot the kingdom paused while Catholic nobility rejected Lutheranism, prolonging the battle for religious freedom another 25 years until the Augsburg Peace was signed, when Protestants gained legitimate acceptance and the antiquated concept of a solitary Christian community in Western Europe under the supreme authority of the Pope was abolished. *GPS:* N48° 22.339 - E10° 53.677. <u>Note:</u> Historians/Reformers, ask TI for their brochure on the "historic sites of the Reformation."

Church, St. Anna's: (Lutheran) Established in 1321 by Carmelite monks, St. Anna's Church provided refuge for Martin Luther during his two-week stay in October 1518. Here you'll discover the Luther Steps, "Lutherstiege" (dedicated in 1983 on Luther's 500th birthday), an exhibition of documents pertaining to the Reformation and Luther's whereabouts. Additionally, St. Anna's Church is home to the Fugger Chapel, "Fugger-kapelle" (1518)—the first example of Renaissance-style in Germany—including the burial site of the Fugger brothers: Ulrich, Georg and Jakob. To find the Fugger Chapel go left after entering the church and head to the front. To discover 14th-century Gothic wall frescos step into the "Goldschmiedekapelle" (continue straight after entering church). *Luther Steps:* Although this exhibition is in German, it is, nonetheless, remarkable and worth your time. What's more, you'll climb to a terrific view of the church's interior and the Fugger Chapel. The portal accessing the Luther Steps (Lutherstiege) can be found on the right a few meters after entering the church's outer door. *Hours:* Tue-Fri 10:00-12:00 & 15:00-17:00, Sat/Sun 15:00-17:00. *Price:* Free entry! *Getting There:* St. Anna's Church is located in the pedestrian zone on Annastr. across from the Foot Locker at No. 33. After crossing into Königsplatz from Bahnhofstr., veer left onto Annastr. and the church is midway along on the left (hard to see, enter "Im Annahof" through archway). *GPS:* N48° 22.048 - E10° 53.713

Rathaus: (town hall, 1620) In the core of the city you'll find Augsburg's signature landmark, the twin-towered imperial town hall. It is said to be the most significant secular Renaissance structure north of the Alps. On the second floor is the elaborate and enormous Golden Hall (Goldene Saal), dating from the 17th century (entrance fee applicable, or it's often illuminated at night allowing passersby a wowing look from Rathausplatz). *Hours:* (Rathaus) daily, 10:00-18:00. Inside the Rathaus are toilets—after entering go left, then right and the door is on the right.

Spread before the town hall is its namesake square: Rathausplatz, where you'll discover the TI, Emperor Augustus perched atop his fountain (and facing the Rathaus), the Christmas market from the end of November until December 24, and the Perlach Tower...

Parked next to the Rathaus is an even taller landmark, the **Perlach Tower**, rising more than 70m/230ft high. Climb the tower's 258 steps for the best view in town. On super clear days a yellow flag is flown to signify the Alps can be seen from the observation level. *Hours:* (tower) May-Oct, daily, 10:00-18:00. *Price:* (pay at top) adult 1€, student 50¢. *Getting There:* When standing before (and the facing the front of) the tower, go left around the corner to enter the "Perlachturm."

Leopold Mozart, Birthplace: Born on November 14, 1719, in a middle-class house at Frauentorstrasse 30, Leopold Mozart spanned two vocational worlds: his father's—a master bookbinder—and his son's—a master's maestro—creator of such timeless operas as The Marriage of Figaro, Don Giovanni and The Magic Flute. Since 1937, Leopold's birthplace has been a museum memorializing the Mozart family history, music and travels. It recently reopened (Jan. 27, 2006) after undergoing extensive renovations for the 250th anniversary of Wolfgang Amadeus Mozart's birth. *Hours:* Tue-Sun 10:00-17:00. *Price:* adult 3.50€, student 2€. *Getting There:* Frauentorstrasse is the road running north from the cathedral (Dom)—take this to the salmon-colored facade at number 30.

Schaezler Palais: Culture vultures shouldn't miss the Schaezler Palais, one of Germany's finest Rococo buildings. Dating from 1765, the palace is home to the German Baroque Gallery (Deutsche Barockgalerie) and the Municipal Art Gallery (Staatsgalerie)—the latter featuring south German artists from the early 1500s, e.g. Cranach, Holbein and Dürer. Most stunning of all, though, is the Rococo ballroom—outfitted with candelabras, ornate moldings, golden trim and a heavenly ceiling fresco—completed in 1770 to receive Marie Antoinette, the 14-year-old Austrian princess en route to France to marry its future king, Louis XVI. What a mistake that turned out to be. She literally lost her head! *Hours:* Tue-Sun 10:00-17:00. *Price:* (includes museums and ballroom) adult 7€, student/senior 5.50€. *Getting There:* Maximilianstr. 46—opposite Hercules Fountain.

Diesel, Rudolf: In February 1892, Rudolf applied for a patent for a technique he invented and described as "A working method and design for internal combustion engines." Exactly a year later, Rudolf was granted his patent. Next, he needed a sponsor. After approaching a number of companies, he signed a contract with the *M.A.N. group in Augsburg. From 1893, Rudolf began assembling and testing his revolutionary internal-combustion engine. Defying all the skeptics, his invention was brought to a successful conclusion four years later, in 1897, when the diesel engine ran for the first time (reaching a max. efficiency of 26.2% at a rated output of approx. 18 HP, a speed of 154 rpm with a fuel consumption rate [petroleum] of 238 g/HPh). Initially, diesel engines were used exclusively for stationary applications, i.e. in factories. By 1903, diesel engines were mounted in small vessels, and from 1910 in larger, ocean-going ships. Until the conclusion of WWI in 1918, the German monarchy funded the use of diesel engines for the propulsion of submarines. Of all the functions Rudolf had envisaged for his invention, it was the automobile engine that proved to be the most difficult to develop. It wasn't until 1923 that the M.A.N. group in Augsburg had successfully achieved direct fuel injection, paving the way for the high-performance automotive diesel engines of today. In a strange twist of fate, after accomplishing a lifetime of monumental achievements, Rudolf drowned in the English Channel on a voyage to England in 1913.

M.A.N.: (Machinenfabrik Augsburg-Nürnberg; www.man.de) It was at Augsburg's M.A.N. plant that the diesel engine ran for the first time. Here you can visit their museum that journeys through more than 200 years of engineering history, including original 19/20th-century flatbed and rotary printing presses and the first diesel engines of our time. *Note:* Rudolf's first *experimental* diesel engine (1893-95 type) is on display. However, the very first *operable* diesel engine (1897 type) has been transferred to the Deutsches Museum in Munich. The M.A.N. museum retains an exact replica. *Hours:* Mon-Fri

9:00-16:00. *Price:* Free entry! *Important:* Call in advance; the museum is located within the guard-gated M.A.N. compound: *Tel.#* 0821/322-3791. *Getting There:* M.A.N. is located at Heinrich-von-Buz-Str. 28. *Railers,* query TI for updated bus/tram connections. *Drivers,* head north out of town on Gg.-Haindl-Str, which changes to Sebastian Str.—at the first intersection turn left.

SLEEPS

Hostel, Jungendherberge: [HI] Beim Pfaffenkeller 3 (www.djh.de) *Tel.#* 0821/33-909. It's not the freshest building you'll ever see but the location is superb! — three minutes by foot to the cathedral (Dom) and five minutes to the city center. *Price:* (includes breakfast and sheets; same-sex dorms only) dorm bed 18€ (cheaper second night), Dbl available. *Note:* Must be a member or an extra charge will apply. In Bavaria, government-supported youth hostels like this one still require their guests to be under 26 years of age to stay. Families okay. *Hours:* (reception) 7:00-9:00 & 17:00-22:00. *Getting There: Railers,* exit station straight into Bahnhofstr. and continue to the major intersection (Königsplatz), where you'll cross into the pedestrian shopping district. From there, veer left onto Annastr. (you'll soon pass [on left] St. Anna's Church) and continue to Karlstr., then go right and stop at the forward traffic light. Now, go left and cross the intersection into Hoher Weg (you should be walking towards the cathedral). Continue on as if passing the cathedral and you'll see on the right-hand side the lane "Inneres Pfaffengäschen" just beyond the few parking spaces. Ramble down this lane and the hostel will soon appear on the left.

Hotel ibis: (www.ibishotel.com) In a city with meager accommodations, this is a great option. Hotel ibis has two central locations; neither is over 55€ per room and both charge 65€/room during conventions (Messe). *Note:* Parking, breakfast cost extra. Hotel code is compatible with ibis website, creating a shortcut to the property—type hotel code into middle left box and click "OK"; next page click on "The Hotel" (left side).

Hauptbahnhof: Halderstr. 25, tel.# 0821/50-160; hotel code 1438. Located near the main train station. Price: Sgl/Dbl 47-52€.

Königsplatz: Hermanstr. 25, tel.# 0821/50-310; hotel code 1092. Located around the corner (12-min walk) from the above property. Price: Sgl/Dbl 55€.

L A N D S B E R G *am Lech*

~ *Population: 27,000* ~ *Elevation: 600m/1968ft*
~ *Country/Area Code: +49-(0)8191* ~ *Sister City: Hudson, Ohio*

Some 45km south of Augsburg, Henry the Lion built a fort in the 12th century to better protect the Salzburg-Munich salt road—today's route 17, a.k.a. Romantic Road. The fort became known as Landsberg on the Lech River, a heavily fortified community that thrived from the salt trade.

Other than the town's rich history, Landsberg made national headlines in the early 20th century when Adolf Hitler was imprisoned here after his botched attempt to overthrow the Bavarian government in the so-called Beer Hall Putsch. From November 1923 to December 1924, Hitler lived in cell No. 7, where he spelled out his future plans in his book, "Mein Kampf" (My Struggle), which no politician in a democratic country bothered to read—until it was too late.

For drivers passing by, Landsberg is unquestionably worth a brief stop to ogle the old-world architecture on Hauptplatz (Main Square). For the general Railer, don't bother, as the train connections are not worth the effort.

Tourist Information: [TI] (www.landsberg.de) *Tel.#* 08191/128-246. Landsberg's TI is situated in the historic Rathaus (town hall) on Hauptplatz (Main Square). Ask for the "Guided Tour" brochure, which pinpoints Landsberg's sights in a do-it-yourself fashion. *Hours:* May-Oct Mon-Fri 8:30-17:30, Sat/Sun 10:00-12:00 & 14:00-17:00; Nov-April Mon-Thur 8:30-12:00 & 14:00-17:00, Fri 8:30-12:30.

Railers: Landsberg's station has been refreshingly renovated. Within its hall you can pick up the recommended "Guided Tour" brochure, rent a bike (see next entry) or buy food goodies. From the station to Hauptplatz (Main Square) is a short and scenic walk across a bridge spanning the Lech River. Exit station right, then go left at the main road.

Drivers: Divert off the Romantic Road direction Altstadt/Zentrum to ogle Landsberg's ultra-scenic Hauptplatz (Main Square). When your tires meet the cobblestones you've arrived at the Old Town, or Altstadt. *WWII buffs*, route 17 (Romantic Road) meanders right past the jail where Hitler was imprisoned (see *Prison, Landsberg* below).

Bike Rental: (Fahrradverleih) You can hire a bike daily from 8:00 at the train station—8€/day, 4€/half day.

Prison, Landsberg: (JustizVollzuganstalt) Landsberg's prison, built 1905-08, is arguably Germany's most notorious. Count von Arco-Valley, Kurt Eisner's assassin in 1919, occupied cell No. 7 before the future leader of Nazi Germany, Adolf Hitler, moved in on a cold day mid-November 1923. Rudolf Hess, Hitler's infamous right-hand man, also became an inmate not long thereafter, occupying an upper-floor cell. By the time of his release—December 20, 1924—Hitler had shrewdly converted his fellow inmates and many of the prison guards to National Socialism, even the warden: Herr Leybold. Subsequent to Hitler's assumption of power in 1933, delegations of Hitler-Youth groups from all over Germany planned pilgrimages (known as Adolf Hitler Marches) to Landsberg. They toured the prison compound, including hallowed cell No. 7, where their devoted Führer (leader) spent a year of his life for the resurrection of the fatherland. Baldur von Schirach, chief of the Hitler Youth, pushed the idea of converting the prison into the world's largest youth hostel, as well as building a stadium in a nearby field for mass rallies. Neither happened. Hitler tourism brought an economic boom to Landsberg, attracting an estimated 100,000 visitors annually to cell No. 7. The economic boom, however, faded when the Nazi war machine smashed across the Polish border on September 1, 1939, sparking World War II.

In 1946, after the defeat of Hitlerism, the commander of U.S. forces in Germany labeled Landsberg penitentiary as "War criminal prison No. 1." The jail eventually housed 110 persons sentenced during the Nürnberg trials, and more than 1400 convicted during the Dachau trials. Out of these, 248 were executed at Landsberg prison by 1951, marking the last year the death penalty was carried out in Germany. Many of these criminals, Hitler's "yes" men, were buried in the adjacent *Spöttinger cemetery, making this the largest cemetery for war criminals in the nation, and perhaps the world. Sparking a heated debate, the cost of the burials together with maintaining the graves was—and still is—paid by the Bavarian taxpayer. In an attempt to erase the past, all the names were removed from the burial markers in 2003. *The cemetery is some 200 meters left of (when facing) the prison's front entrance. Drivers, there is a gravel parking lot opposite.*

Note: There are no tours allowed of cell No. 7, or of the prison compound. You can, however, view the prison externally. Believe it or not, the compound and aforementioned Spöttinger cemetery are located directly along the Romantic Road (route 17). Today, the prison accommodates roughly 680 prisoners, all serving life sentences.

Getting There: **Railers,** from the station it's about a 20-min walk. Exit station right, then go left at the main road and go left again before the bridge. Follow the river. A short distance after the castle-like tower the path will ascend to the road. Follow the road and make the first left on Herbstweg. Ascend this lane and follow it right. When it merges with the next lane, Frühlingstr., go left. Proceed over the railway bridge and through the graffitied underpass. Go left up the stairs and the prison is on the right. **Drivers,** the prison is situated along the Hindenburgring (Romantic Road) on the north side of town—pull into the prison's U-shaped drive and park. *GPS:* N48° 03.218 - E10° 52.108

Band of Brothers: *(WWII Buffs)* For those of you who watched the second to last episode, part IX "Why We Fight," will remember the stomach-turning scenes when the boys of Easy Co. stumbled upon a concentration camp in the woods outside of Landsberg. This was no ordinary place; this was the end of the Holocaust. Landsberg hosted 11 concentration camps, or KZ-Lager, all with the same name: Kaufering (I-XI). Hitler required forced labor for a top-secret project code-named Ringeltaube—the construction of three gigantic, underground aircraft assembly plants to build the ME 262, the world's first mass-produced jet fighter. The plants were never completed and it is unknown how many workers died here, or on the death march in the last days of the war—some historians estimate 15,000. Today, there's not much left of the former camps. A few have been converted into gravel pits; lonely memorials mark some, while others have been masked by nature's wild growth. For more info, go to www.buergervereinigung-landsberg.de

WIESKIRCHE: Some 45km south of Landsberg, and 22km north of Hohenschwangau, you'll discover the Wieskirche, a gloriously scenic "Church in the Meadow." In 1740, a chapel was built to pay homage to a wooden likeness of Jesus allegedly seen weeping. The Christ-like figure, known as the "scourged Savior," became an object of worship for pilgrims Europe-wide. To handle the influx, a significant church was built in the meadow. Dating from 1754, the Wieskirche recently celebrated its 250-year anniversary. There's much to celebrate, as the church's heavenly interior is arguably Germany's most dazzling example of Rococo-style, earning a place (since 1983) alongside the Taj Mahal and the Acropolis as an esteemed member of UNESCO's World Heritage List. *Hours:* daily, 8:00-17:00 (summer till 19:00). *Note:* Visiting is limited during Mass. Regular services are held Sat 10:00, Sun 8:00, 9:30, 11:00 and every Wed (May-Oct) 8:15, 10:00, 11:00, 11:45, 15:15, 16:00. (www.wieskirche.de) *Getting There: Railers,* because of the church's isolation, connections are limited. Buses from Füssen are possible but not regular. The Romantic Road "Touring" bus is scheduled (daily, April-Oct) to stop here for 15 min. **Drivers,** turn off the Romantic Road at Steingaden and follow Wieskirche signs (uphill 5km) to the church. Parking 1€. *GPS:* N47° 40.943 - E10° 54.013

NEUSCHWANSTEIN (New Swan Stone)
in
Hohenschwangau (High Swan Land)

Fairy tales do exist because this one you can visit. Parked at the foot of the Alps at the southern end of the Romantic Road is Hohenschwangau, a nearly Austrian community of fabled castles. **Schloss Hohenschwangau**, built 1832-36 in neo-Gothic style, is where the fairy-tale king—Ludwig II—grew up. He especially loved playing in the garden and climbing the castle's turrets with his younger brother, Otto. At age 18, in 1864, Ludwig inherited Bavaria's throne and the title of king, enabling him to fulfill his childhood dream of building the most beautiful and luxurious castles in the land. He furnished them with murals of Wagnerian operas and medieval themes, showpiece bedrooms and gold-leaf fixtures, gaudy chandeliers and intimate grottos, and even a royal bathtub that could accommodate 20 of his guests comfortably.

The epitome of castles everywhere is **Schloss Neuschwanstein**—a Ludwig fantasy made real that resurrected the storybook style typically associated with chivalry and noble knights—now one of Germany's most visited tourist attractions accounting for some 1.3 million visitors annually. Ludwig commissioned its construction in 1869 on the scenic hillside opposite Schloss Hohenschwangau. Although Ludwig spent 17 years building Schloss Neuschwanstein and emptied Bavaria's coffers in the process, the castle was never completed and he lived in it only 170 days before his death in 1886, age 41. In the end, Ludwig's megalomania cost him the throne and his life after being declared mentally unfit to rule. In spite of a tragic conclusion, "Mad" King Ludwig II exemplifies true romanticism in modern times and gave Bavaria its moneymaking legacy of fairy-tale castles. So come along, and discover Walt Disney's inspiration for his Sleeping Beauty castle at Disneyland.

Note: Because Hohenschwangau is mega-touristy, consider avoiding the overpriced food outlets and pack a picnic to enjoy on the banks of the enchanting Alpsee, a nearby Alpine lake (rowboat rental available in summer).

Tourist Information: [TI] Hohenschwangau's convenient info kiosk is located at the people-busy junction spearheading the parking lots. *Hours:* Because of tight funding, hours are being scaled back and the following schedule may change: May-Sept 10:00-18:00, April & Oct 11:00-18:00, much less off-season. *Note:* Around the corner is the castle Ticket-Center; follow crowds up slope. TI has toilet; pay at turnstile, or for free use bathroom in restaurant across street from bus stop. The fountain left of the TI dispenses drinkable water; fill your bottle.

Railers: From Munich catch the train to Füssen (hourly, two-hour trip) and then a bus to Hohenschwangau, Königsschlösser (hourly, eight-minute ride, 3.10€ round trip, or 8.50€ one way by taxi). The bus drops off at the Hohenschwangau TI, around corner from castle Ticket-Center. *Note:* Buses and taxis depart from outside Füssen station. If you have time, stroll into the Old Town and browse around. You'll find a charming pedestrianized zone, a beautifully Baroque church and a medieval fortress (exit station left and continue straight three blocks).

Drivers: At the southern end of the Romantic Road—route 17—follow signs "Königsschlösser" (Royal Castles) to Hohenschwangau and Neuschwanstein. Upon arriving, park in any of the public lots, 4€. *Note:* Lots are open 8:00 till 20:00. From the lot, follow the other visitors to the TI or up the slope to the castle Ticket-Center (*GPS:* N47° 33.317 - E10° 44.377). Since you're so close to the border, consider crossing into Austria where gas prices are significantly cheaper. Along the way you'll pass medieval Füssen (5km) then Lechfall, a dramatic waterfall.

Ticket-Center, Castles: To visit either castle you have to go with a guided tour. Tickets must be bought at the Ticket-Center. Each ticket is printed with a fixed start time (or Einlasszeit); miss this time and you'll have to buy a new ticket!

Note: To avoid standing in a two-hour line to buy tickets in summer (worst case scenario you don't even get in), especially July/August, either arrive early (8:00) or *reserve your tickets at least 24hr in advance by phone (*tel.#* 08362/930-830) or online (www.ticket-center-hohenschwangau.de). *CC's:* VC, MC, AE.

*To reserve tickets in advance costs 1.80€ extra per person, per castle. Pick up your tickets at the Ticket-Center well before the tour departs (at least 30 minutes for Schloss Hohenschwangau and 60 minutes for Neuschwanstein). When there, do not stand in line. Instead, proceed directly to the window on the right handling reserved tickets. If you do not see this, head through the entrance on the right side of the building marked "Reiseleiter/Guides" and query staff (they speak good English).

Hours: (Ticket-Center) daily, April-Sept 8:00-17:00, Oct-March 9:00-15:00. Castle hours are synchronized with the Ticket-Center to open one hour later—for example—April-Sept 9:00 with last tour departing at 18:00, Oct-March 10:00 with last tour departing at 16:00. The duration of a tour at either castle is roughly 30 min.

Price: Each castle costs adult 9€ to tour, student/senior 8€, youth (17 or younger) are free. To tour both castles (on the same day), as most travelers do, purchase the "Königsticket"—adult 17€, student/senior 15€. *CC's:* VC, MC, AE. *Note:* With the Königsticket you will be scheduled to tour Schloss Hohenschwangau first and then Neuschwanstein, which is fine since chronologically you'd want to begin where Ludwig II grew up. After Hohenschwangau there will be roughly a two-hour interval before your Neuschwanstein tour begins. You will need about 50 min of that time to reach the tour starting point. With your 70 spare min, consider having a bite to eat (e.g. your picnic) and definitely visit Marienbrücke (page 179). Whatever you do, do not be late for your tour of Neuschwanstein.

Getting There: The Ticket-Center is located around the corner (left) from the TI— follow crowds up slope and it will soon appear on right. *GPS:* N47° 33.317 - E10° 44.377

Schloss Neuschwanstein: Arguably Europe's most famous castle, Schloss Neuschwanstein (like noy-shvahn-stein) is one of Germany's most visited tourist attractions netting some 1.3 million visitors annually (circa 6000 per day June-Sept). Because of its commanding position high upon the hillside, Neuschwanstein took nearly two decades to build. Now, more than a century later, it's your turn to negotiate the steep incline. For ticket prices, see above entry: *Ticket-Center, Castles.* To pick up a tour from Munich, see bottom of page.

Getting There: There are three ways to reach Schloss Neuschwanstein: by foot, horse-drawn carriage, and shuttle bus. Neither the carriage nor bus will drop you off at the castle entrance. The carriage drops off five min below the entrance and the bus 10 min above.

By foot from the Ticket-Center is a 35-min trek to reach the tour starting point.

The **horse-drawn carriage** departs regularly from in front of Hotel Müller (a bit farther along from Ticket-Center on right) and costs 5€ per person up and 2.50€ down. Pay driver. Not possible to reserve seats. *Note:* The ride up takes 20 min., then you'll need to walk five min to reach the tour starting point. If you're running late, the horse-drawn carriage is probably not your best bet so you'd better start running! Best idea; plan ahead so you're not rushed.

The **shuttle bus** typically departs every 20 min in front of Hotel Lisl (roughly 150 meters from Ticket-Center on left) and costs 1.80€ per person up and *1€ down. Pay driver. Not possible to reserve seats. *Note:* We do not recommend riding the bus down, as you will need to hike 15 min back up the hill to reach the departure area.

Suggestion: We recommend you take the shuttle bus up (1.80€) and either the carriage down (2.50€) or casually descend on foot (free). When the bus drops you off, wander over to Mary's Bridge (Marienbrücke, see next entry) for the ultra-popular, picture-perfect view of Neuschwanstein you see on all the travel brochures and postcards. Just be sure you leave early enough to make your castle start time. Allow at least 10 min to visit the bridge and add an extra 15 min for the walk down to the castle entrance.

Note: Tours of Schloss Neuschwanstein take roughly 30 min and you will need to negotiate more than 300 steps along the way. For more info and a virtual tour, go to www.neuschwanstein.de

Tours from Munich: If you're based out of Munich and don't feel comfortable making your own way to Neuschwanstein, we recommend the Radius tour. **Radius tours** (and bikes) is conveniently located opposite track (Gleis) 32 in Munich's main train station. Tours cost 25€/person with railpass (32€ without) and depart from mid-April thru mid-Oct, daily, at 9:30; less off-season. The tour begins at central station from Radius' office, where your guide will escort you onto a southbound train to Füssen; tour duration 9hr. Call or stop by for details: *Tel.#* 089/5502-9374, (www.radiusmunich.com)

Marienbrücke: (Mary's Bridge, 1866) No visit to Schloss Neuschwanstein is complete without a trudge over Mary's Bridge, rooted 90m/295ft above the Pöllat Gorge. Those who have a fear of heights (acrophobia) will find it difficult to reach the middle of the bridge, where the best photos of the castle are captured. Even Ludwig II said "The views are enchanting from here." Acrophobes, you need to relax, psych yourself and rambo the moment—you'll be glad you did! From the castle entrance up to the bridge is a steep, 15-min walk (follow signs), or better yet catch the shuttle bus from out front Hotel Lisl (near Ticket-Center) to the castle drop off area near the bridge.

Schloss Hohenschwangau: Dating from 1836, this neo-Gothic-style castle is where Ludwig II spent much of his childhood. Here, young Ludwig dreamt of storybook castles and mythical tales. *Getting There:* To reach Schloss Hohenschwangau's turrets is an easy 10-min climb from the Ticket-Center.

Ludwig II

Arguably Germany's most famous monarch, Ludwig II was born on August 25, 1845, in Munich to Crown Prince Max II (King of Bavaria 1848-64) and Princess Marie of Prussia. Max II often took little Ludwig to his castle—Hohenschwangau—for a break from big-city Munich to play in a peaceful, idyllic setting with his younger brother, Otto. When it was Ludwig's turn to wear the Bavarian crown (1864), he did a rather sloppy job, as ruling a nation state did not come naturally. He first sided with the Austrians against the Prussians, or northern Germans, in the Seven Weeks' War and then sided with the Prussians against the French in the Franco-Prussian War. Ludwig was more of a romantic, a pacifist, and a lover of the opera than a warmonger. His dream was to build the most beautiful, luxurious castles in the land, and he did. However, this weird and wonderful lifestyle bankrupted Bavaria's economy. Add Ludwig's unorthodox leadership style to the mix and his cabinet decided they had no choice but to conspire against him. On June 12, 1886, they declared Ludwig clinically insane and exiled him with his doctor to Schloss Berg at Lake Starnberg, 25km southwest of Munich. The next day, both he and the doctor drowned in 3 feet of water. Not only did it seem amazing that two grown men simultaneously drowned, but even more amazing for Ludwig, who was 6 feet 5 inches tall. Maybe Mad King Ludwig wasn't so "mad" after all. Within months of Ludwig's death, tourists were paying to see his castles. Today, a large wooden cross rising from the shoreline of Lake Starnberg marks the spot of the king's death.

Good Sleeps: *Railers*, your best bet is to overnight in Füssen. *Drivers*, this region is rife with pensions and the like, especially in the neighborhoods of Hohenschwangau and Schwangau. To cut the choices down, we found a pair of pension-style accommodations that are clean and conveniently located within yodeling distance of the castles. Both places accept cash only, have facilities (shower/toilet) in room, come with breakfast, and (most) all of their rooms have a balcony exploiting the enchanting views. Reserve well in advance! Add an extra 1.35€ per person per night for local taxes (Kurtaxe).

Romantic Pension Neuschwanstein: (www.romantic-pension.de) Pfleger-Rothut-Weg 2, Hohenschwangau. *Tel.#* 08362/81-102. Well-kept facilities and a charming hostess (Frau Strauss) make overnighting here a joy. *Price:* (cash only) Sgl from 35€, Dbl 38-78€, add an extra 3€/person if staying three nights or less. *Getting There:* From the Hohenschwangau TI, head down Colomanstr. and make the second right on Pfleger-Rothut-Weg. Your digs will appear on the right. *GPS:* N47° 33.589 - E10° 44.530

Gästehaus Weiher: (www.hotel-ami.de/pension/haus-weiher) Hofwiesenweg 11, Hohenschwangau. *Tel.#* 08362/81-161. Located around the corner from the above-mentioned pension, Haus Weiher has all the comforts of home in addition to a royal view. *Price:* (cash only) Sgl 30€, Dbl 50-55€, Trpl 65-70€. *Getting There:* From the Hohenschwangau TI, head down Colomanstr. and make the second right on Pfleger-Rothut-Weg then first left on Hofwiesenweg. Continue around the bend and your digs will soon appear on the left. *GPS:* N47° 33.625 - E10° 44.650

Camping Bannwaldsee: (www.camping-bannwaldsee.de) *Tel.#* 08362/93-000. Campers will appreciate this outdoor oasis idyllically situated on Lake Bannwald, 5km from the castles. Apartments available. Office hours 8:00-12:30 & 14:30-20:00. *Getting There:* Campground is located on the right-hand side of the Romantic Road when approaching Schwangau from the north.

"Mad" King Ludwig's Other Fantasy Castles

Schloss Linderhof: Located some 45km from Schloss Neuschwanstein, and 12km from the Christmassy, woodcarving village of Oberammergau near Garmisch-Partenkirchen, Schloss Linderhof is the only one of Ludwig's castles he lived to see completed. Dating from 1870, Linderhof is perhaps better described as an ultra-lavish mansion than a castle. Before Linderhof was converted into a Rococo masterpiece, the property existed as an unpretentious hunting lodge called "Königshäuschen," or the King's Little House, belonging to Max II, Ludwig's father. Due to Linderhof's isolation in the plush Bavarian hinterland, the property could afford several acres of manicured gardens. Wear comfy shoes and explore its beauty. Don't miss the erupting fountain that spouts (every 30 min, April-Sept, 9:00-18:00) some 70 feet into the air and the Venus Grotto located on the upper gardens beyond the fountain. To visit Linderhof you must go with a (25-min) guided tour.

(www.linderhof.de) *Hours:* daily, April-Sept 9:00-18:00 (last tour 17:15); Oct-March 10:00-16:00 (last tour 15:15). *Price:* adult 7€, student 6€, (1€ less in winter because palace grounds are closed), youth (17 or younger) are free. *Note:* Reservations are typically not necessary. Flash photography not allowed; video cameras questionable. *Tel.#* 08822/920-30. *Getting There:* **Railers,** (from Hohenschwangau is a hassle and not worth the effort), from Munich catch the train to Oberammergau (hourly, transfer necessary, two-hour trip) and then bus #9622 to Linderhof (hourly, 30-min ride). **Drivers,** from Hohenschwangau head towards Füssen, then Reutte (Austria). Don't go into Reutte—at Reutte Süd follow signs to Schloss Linderhof. The next stretch is a stunning alpine route that parallels a crisp lake ("Plansee," a perfect picnic stop) before crossing back into Bavaria and on to petite Linderhof (Ludwig often took this route in his carriage). Parking 2€ ("pkw" = car). *GPS:* N47° 34.186 - E10° 57.424. After visiting Linderhof, consider driving on to Oberammergau to see the famous woodcarving shops (Holzschnitzerei) and the picture-worthy houses splashed with storytelling murals. If required, there are plenty of first-rate Zimmer (Bed & Breakfast) in this area.

Schloss Herrenchiemsee: Located on Lake Chiemsee—Germany's second principal lake, known as the Bavarian sea, some 200km from Schloss Neuschwanstein and 75km from Munich—Schloss Herrenchiemsee is the largest of Ludwig's castles. As far as kings were concerned, Ludwig II regarded Louis XIV of France, the "Sun King," as the quintessential monarch. During two trips to Paris, 1867 and 1874, Ludwig studied Louis XIV's most ostentatious architectural achievement: the palace of Versailles.

Ludwig fell in love with the serenity of Herreninsel, one of two islands on Lake Chiemsee. On this island, Ludwig chose to build his new Versailles, a creation he called Schloss Herrenchiemsee. The foundation stone was laid on May 21, 1878. Construction costs ballooned and Ludwig's tribute to Versailles became his most costly project to date, pushing the Bavarian economy to the brink of bankruptcy. Indifferent to the privilege of having the royal equivalent to a limitless credit card, Ludwig demanded more gold, more candelabras, more chandeliers, more marble, and more rooms. In the fall of 1885, Ludwig inhabited Schloss Herrenchiemsee for the first time, but only for nine days. By early summer of the following year, while Bavaria's financial woes continued, Ludwig's cabinet declared him mentally unfit to rule bringing about his death shortly thereafter. Today, hundreds of thousands of tourists annually cruise across the idyllic Bavarian blue waters of Lake Chiemsee to see Ludwig's biggest and most expensive palace: Schloss Herrenchiemsee.

(www.herren-chiemsee.de) *Tel.#* 08051/688-70. *Hours:* daily, April thru mid-Oct, 9:00-18:00 (last tour 17:00); mid-Oct thru March, 9:40-16:15 (last tour 15:40). *Price:* (includes 30-min palace tour and entrance into museum) adult 7€, student 6€, youth (17 or younger) are free. *Note:* Tours in English depart hourly. Reservations are typically not necessary. No photography allowed; video cameras questionable. Once on Herreninsel, you can either walk (20 min) to the palace or (mid-April thru Oct) take the horse-drawn carriage, 3€/person. Fountains on the palace grounds are operational May-Sept. *Getting There:* **Railers**, from Munich catch the train to Prien am Chiemsee (hourly, one-hour trip) and then either hail a cab (waiting outside station) to the boat dock or walk (30 min) or ride the historic steam train *"Chiemsee-Bahn" dating from 1887 (*runs weekends in May and daily June-Sept. Ticket booth open 9:00-15:00. Price, round trip, 8€/adult for steam train + boat to Herreninsel). *Note:* Next door to the station is a Lidl grocery store (Mon-Sat 8:00-20:00); a good place to buy picnic supplies. **Drivers**, exit the A8 autobahn at Prien am Chiemsee and head in the direction of Prien—after about 3km turn right at the traffic circle. Your scenic country drive will conclude at the boat dock.

Boats Rides: Boats ferry tourists (hourly) over to the islands from Felden and Prien (both are off autobahn A8) or Gstadt (other side of lake, closest to Fraueninsel). **Railers**, the only train-friendly town here is Prien am Chiemsee. *Note:* When purchasing a boat ticket to Ludwig's palace on Herreninsel, pay 1€ more to include Fraueninsel. The boat from Prien to Herreninsel costs 6€/adult (round trip) and takes 15 min each way; from Herreninsel to Fraueninsel takes 10 min. Be sure to study the boat schedule to neatly plan your connections.

The Islands: On Lake Chiemsee are two islands, Herreninsel and Fraueninsel, both are worth visiting. **Herreninsel**, or Isle of Men, gets its name from a monastery that existed centuries ago on the island. Today, Ludwig's French-inspired palace sits smack-dab in the middle of the island surrounded by a state-protected nature reserve. Expect a visit to take three hours—this includes the boat ride, castle tour and strolling around. **Fraueninsel**, or Isle of Women, obtained its name from the existing 8th-century convent of nuns, who are known for their popular brand of Chiemsee schnapps. Other than the long-standing convent, Fraueninsel is home to a picture-book fishing village with a few shops and beer gardens and restaurants (specializing in smoked fish from the lake). We recommend a visit here if time is on your side—add two hours to your trip. **WWII Buffs:** Buried on Fraueninsel (in the church cemetery, adjacent to convent) is General Alfred Jodl, former operations chief for Hitler's armed forces (Wehrmacht). Jodl was sentenced to death by hanging at the 1946 Nürnberg trials. For more info on Jodl, see page 464.

Note: The resort hotel Sydney and Jesse worked at in the adventure novel, *Quest for the Bavarian Cross*, can be seen on the southern shore of Lake Chiemsee—look for the elongated, vanilla-colored structure. Alas, the resort hotel (AFRC Chiemsee) ceased operations as a recreational facility for U.S. servicemen and women in the fall of 2003 and is presently closed.

FÜSSEN

~ Population: 14,000 ~ Elevation: 700m/2296ft
~ Country/Area Code: +49-(0)8362 ~ Sister City: Helen, Georgia

Situated 5km from the royal castles of Neuschwanstein and Hohenschwangau, Füssen is the last Bavarian enclave before crossing the Austrian border. Commanding Füssen's skyline is Hohes Schloss, a landmark fortress securing the frontier since the Middle Ages. In its shadow is Füssen's quaint Old Town, accented by medieval architecture and crooked lanes. Although Füssen recently celebrated its 700th birthday, the town really dates from Roman times when Emperor Claudius forged the north-south trade route, Via Claudia Augusta, and garrisoned his troops here. Funnily, the name Füssen translates to "Feet"—perhaps suggestive of the emperor's legions of boots on the ground.

Tourist Information: [TI] (www.fuessen.de) *Tel.#* 08362/938-50. Füssen's TI is centrally located a few blocks from the train station. Out front of the office you'll see a cluster of columns capped by rotating rock boulders that compose a mesmerizing arrangement of fountains, which at night are even more entrancing to ogle. *Hours:* (may change, call ahead to verify) May-Sept Mon-Sat 9:00-18:00, Sun 10:00-12:00, less off-season. *Note:* Folks arriving after hours use the 24hr self-service info kiosk out front to find a room or pick up a brochure.

Railers: Most of you are here for one reason: to visit Schloss Neuschwanstein. To get there, buses (hourly, eight-minute ride, 3.10€ round trip) and taxis (8.50€ one way) depart from outside the station. If you have time, though, stroll into the Old Town and browse around. Exit station left and continue straight three blocks to reach the TI and main pedestrian drag (Reichen Str.). If you're planning on staying the night, query TI for best options and vacancies. Station has storage lockers, 1€-2€/24hr. Bike rental available at end of track. Across the street is the post office (Mon-Fri 8:30-17:15, Sat 8:30-12:00).

Drivers: Surprisingly, traffic can get quite congested in Füssen. To avoid the snarl, park in one of the handful of garages and survey the Old Town on foot. Garages cost roughly 1€/hr, or "P2" (off Kemptener Str.) is typically free (10-min walk into town).

Post Office is across from the train station (Mon-Fri 8:30-17:15, Sat 8:30-12:00).

Sights: Besides a charming Old Town and cobbled pedestrianized zone, Füssen boasts a glorious monastery, a medieval castle and a wondrous waterfall called Lechfall. At the southern end of the main shopping street (Reichen Str.) is the **Benedictine Monastery St. Mang**, dating from the 8th century but renovations 1000 years later reflect its Baroque character. Within this holy complex of structures is the **heritage museum** (2.50€/adult, April-Oct Tue-Sun 10:00-17:00, Nov-March Tue-Sun 13:00-16:00) exhibiting the history of Füssen, including Bavaria's oldest Dance of Death painting cycle (Totentanz, 1602). Literally towering above St. Mang is **Hohes Schloss**, a powerhouse fortress and former summer residence of the prince bishops of Augsburg. To reach its picturesque inner courtyard, ascend the path running past St. Mang monastery and church. The bishop's former living quarters now accommodate a painting gallery displaying late-Gothic and Renaissance works from regional artists. In the corner climb the tower (free, April-Oct 11:00-16:00). About a 15-min walk southwest of St. Mang monastery and church is the must-see **Lechfall** (*GPS:* N47° 34.131 - E10° 41.890). Drivers heading to Austria to fill up the tank will pass Lechfall on the way.

MUNICH

~ Population: 1.3 million ~ Elevation: 530m/1740ft
~ Country/Area Code: +49-(0)89 ~ Sister City: Cincinnati, Ohio

Munich (München)—Germany's third largest metropolis, after Berlin and Hamburg—is one of those appealing cities that inspire long-lasting memories and a sense for a return visit. Often referred to as "the village of one million," Munich is the proud capital of Bavaria (Bayern), as well as the head-quarters of BMW (Bavarian Motor Works); it was voted "the city most Germans would prefer to live in," and is the capital of beer—thanks to the monks.

In the 8th century, monks from a nearby monastery formed a settlement on the Isar River. From this evolved "Zu den Mönchen" (literally, By the Monks) and today's modern-day name: München. Monks are the masters of brewing beer, and Munich, a settlement of monks, evolved into an intoxicating hub.

In the 12th century, Bavaria was one of several hundred satellite states within Charlemagne's Holy Roman Empire—the First Reich—established in the year 800. Then-Emperor Fredrick I (Barbarossa) gave the territory of Bavaria to his cousin, Henry the Lion. In 1158, Henry traveled to the settlement of monks and built a bridge (today's Ludwigsbrücke) over the Isar River to tax the salt merchants heading north from the salt mines of Salzburg. Shortly thereafter, on June 14, the city of Munich was officially born.

As a result of internal quarrels, Henry fell out of favor with Barbarossa in 1180 and was consequently replaced by Otto I (Wittelsbach), the new duke of Bavaria. So begins the reign of the Wittelsbachs, rulers of the Bavarian throne for 738 years—including Germany's most famous monarch, the "fairy-tale" king, Ludwig II. Interestingly, the House of Wittelsbach ruled 93 years longer than Europe's most renowned royal family, the Habsburgs.

By the 13th century, Munich was booming from the salt trade, and the fourth member to wear the Bavarian crown, Ludwig der Strenge, shrewdly moved the House of Wittelsbach in 1253 to the city of monks, where he built the first royal residence known as the Alter Hof. However, it was the reign of the next member to wear the Wittelsbach crown, Ludwig the Bavarian, which proved to be one of the most significant in Munich's history. In 1328, Ludwig the Bavarian became emperor of the Holy Roman Empire, and since Munich was his seat of power, the eyes of Europe focused on the imperial city of monks. Ludwig brought about great change to the region, transferring the crown jewels to Munich in addition to securing market and salt rights (this meant salt had to be exclusively transported through Munich); he revamped the empire's new capital by adding immense city walls (now replaced by the existing ring road) that could be entered through four gates (Isartor, Karlstor, Sendlingertor, Swabingertor); and he gave Munich his imperial colors—black and yellow—which still decorate the city streets.

Despite Munich's red-hot economy and political importance, it remained rather small in the year 1500 with 13,000 inhabitants compared to other cities in the kingdom, such as Nürnberg with 30,000 residents and Augsburg—the largest German city—with 50,000. Munich had neither the commerce or woodcraft industry of Nürnberg, nor the helping hand of the Fuggers (Europe's richest family) who lived in Augsburg, but Munich did possess special skills in the trendy industry of brewing beer. On April 23, 1516, the Wittelsbach sovereign, Duke Wilhelm IV, introduced the Reinheitsgebot, or Purity Decree, a law to control the ingredients in beer. This new regulation stated that beer could only consist of barley, hops and water—qualifying the *Reinheitsgebot as the first ever food and drug law. The new law was such a success that Duke Wilhelm V, grandson of Wilhelm IV, commissioned the first state brewery in the Alter Hof in 1589.

(*The function of yeast in fermentation was unknown in the 16th century, thus the Reinheitsgebot has since been amended to include yeast as a beer-making ingredient and dictate that all barley be malted.)

Perhaps due to an increase in alcoholism among the House of Wittelsbach, the state brewery was moved in 1644 to a new location, where the Hofbräuhaus (or Royal Brew House) stands today (page 202).

During the following centuries, some insane monarchs wore the Bavarian crown, some not so insane, and some wonderfully creative. Around the turn of the 20th century, Albert Einstein wandered the streets of Munich collecting his thoughts, the Glockenspiel put on its first show, Max Friz launched BMW, and a world war struck.

With the conclusion of World War I in 1918, the House of Wittelsbach came tumbling down and the Socialist Red flag of the fleeting Räterepublik flew over the Rathaus (town hall). The Freikorps (Free Corps, small right-wing paramilitary groups) quashed the Reds, or Bolsheviks, in 1919, paving the way for the democratic Weimar Republic. Hyperinflation paralyzed the country, facilitating the political triumph of a crazed Nazi who saw himself as a prophet sent from the trenches of WWI to lead Germany back to its former glory. Consequently, a second world war ensued and Munich became the target of more than 70 Allied bombing raids. After the defeat of Nazi Germany, post-war Munich saw massive reconstruction, a new currency, the restoration of religious and royal traditions, and its millionth resident in 1957.

Munich is truly a fabulous city with umpteen attractions for visitors to see or experience, such as the world-famous Glockenspiel (page 192), or an orgy of beer at the Oktoberfest (or Hofbräuhaus), or FIFA World Cup soccer action (page 204), or Munich's magnificent Pinakotheks (art galleries, page 196), or our Hitler's Munich do-it-yourself tour (page 219), or surfing in the English Garden (page 193)—found at these GPS coordinates: N48° 08.609 - E11° 35.263

~ **Munich is worth at least a three-day stay. To optimize your time, plan ahead to arrive on a Friday.** *This permits travelers to take advantage of reduced admission (1€) into state-run museums on Sunday, while eliminating Monday from the itinerary—the only day the Dachau concentration camp memorial is closed.*

Day 1: (Friday) Begin your Munich adventure at 11:00 (or 12:00) on Marienplatz to the gyrations of the Glockenspiel (page 192). Upon completion of the mini-event, turn to Page 3 of "The Letter" (page 110, chapter seven of the *Quest for the Bavarian Cross*) and experience the remaining 7 Pages in the footsteps of Sydney and Reuben. (When on Page 9, look for the White Rose museum "Gedenkstätte" in the university bldg.: Mon-Thur 10:00-16:00, Fri till 15:00).

Day 2: (Saturday) Tour the Dachau concentration camp memorial (page 212) and/or other sights of interest.

Day 3: (Sunday) Culture vultures will save on Sundays in Munich, as the state-run museums offer hugely reduced admission: 1€ (see *Museums*, page 195).

Day 4: WWII buffs can use this extra day to experience Hitler's Munich do-it-yourself tour (page 219). _Railers,_ you'll need to rent a bike. _Drivers,_ you can do this tour in half a day. _Note:_ For those who are interested but don't have a full (fourth) day to spare, split Hitler's Munich between day 2 and day 3.

Tourist Information: [TI] (www.muenchen-tourist.de) _Tel.#_ 089/2339-6500
Munich has two TIs and the EurAide office. The latter office and one TI can be found in the _Hbf_ (main train station); the other TI is centrally located on _Marienplatz_ (Mary's Square). City maps can be purchased for 50¢ at either location (or they're usually free at your accommodations).

TI: Hbf (located outside front entrance; turn right upon exiting station). Hours: Mon-Sat 9:00-19:00 (open longer April-Oct), Sun 10:00-18:00.

TI: Marienplatz (beneath Glockenspiel). Hours: Mon-Fri 10:00-20:00, Sat 10:00-16:00.

EurAide: Another info option is the EurAide office, located within the main train station. (A stop here would negate the need to visit a TI.) EurAide is partnered with the German rail authority—Deutsche Bahn—and is staffed by native English-speakers. **Railers,** take advantage of this source to ask any questions concerning travel by rail, e.g. connections, routes, ticket purchase, reservations (incl. overnight couchettes/sleepers), and EurAide can help with any queries you may have regarding your railpass—they can even validate it. Additionally, they sell city maps, the Bavaria- (discount rail) Ticket, and book tours. _Getting There:_ EurAide is positioned next to track (Gleis) 11. _Hours:_ (tend to vary) daily, 8:00-12:00 & 13:00-16:00 (summer till 18:00).

Emergency Tel. Numbers: [Germany-wide]
Police (Polizei) = 110
Fire dept. (Feuerwehr) or general emergency = 112
Ambulance = 19222

Post Office: A post office can be found next to the Internet café across from the main train station's front entrance (Mon-Fri 7:30-20:00, Sat 9:00-16:00). Another P.O. is located at Residenzstr. 2, near Father Max at the corner of Maximilianstr. and Residenz-str. (Mon-Fri 8:00-18:30, Sat 9:00-12:30).

Hauptbahnhof: [Hbf] Munich's "main train station" is an easy-to-navigate, urban terminus. Here, eateries abound, including a Burger King on the upper level. For handy, city info head to the EurAide office adjacent to track (Gleis) 11 or to the TI out the front entrance (and a few doors to the right). For _train info_ or _itinerary printouts,_ see the DB Service desk opposite tracks 18-19. _U- and S-Bahn_ lines are situated on either side of the main transit area (to reach the _airport,_ ride the S1 or S8 located opposite track 25. To reach the _Oktoberfest,_ ride the U4 or U5 located opposite track 11, below Coca Cola sign). _Storage lockers_ are opposite track 25, or follow signs "Schließfächer" (2€-4€/24hr, depending on size of locker). The _post office_ can be found across the street from the station's front entrance, right of Internet café. The _Deutsche Touring_ (buses to Romantic Road) office is located in the hallway opposite track 34 (Mon-Fri 8:30-18:00, Sat 8:30-12:00). _To Marienplatz_ (Mary's Square) from the station is a cushy 20-min walk, or take the S-Bahn two stops. By foot, exit station straight and cross the street—left of Internet café take Schützenstr. straight to the major intersection and cross over to Karlsplatz. Walk under Munich's oldest gate, Karlstor (dating from 1302), leading onto Neuhauser Str. (main shopping street) and eventually into Munich's living room—Marienplatz.

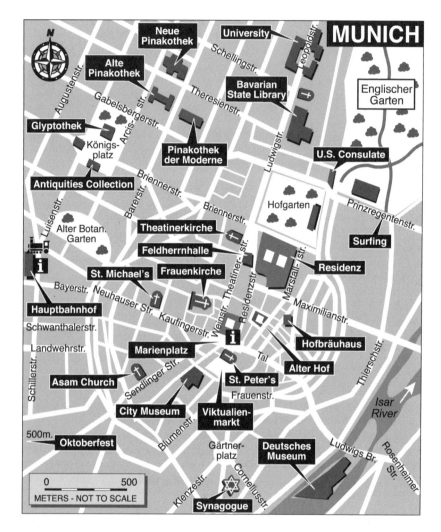

Bavarian Speak (Boarisch)

Grüss Gott: To greet one another most Germans use the standard "Guten Tag" (good day), but not in Bavaria. Here, it's quite different, natives say "Grüss Gott"— literally, "God greet thee," but colloquially it means "greetings" or "hello." So, unless you want to be branded as a northerner, use the familiar "Grüss Gott."

Servus: This dual-purpose hello-goodbye greeting is Bavaria's equivalent to Italy's "Ciao" or Hawaii's "Aloha." That said, Servus is chiefly used informally with friends or people in casual situations. Interestingly, Servus means "slave" in Latin.

Lederhosen: This is Bavaria's answer to the Scottish kilt; a knee-length pair of "leather pants" with suspenders worn by men in traditional costume.

Dirndl: This is the traditional Bavarian dress for women, often having a cleavage-enhancing front.

Subway/Bus/Tram: Munich's integrated and efficient transportation authority—MVV (www.mvv-muenchen.de)—offers a multitude of destinations and ticket options to choose from. The MVV network is divided into four color-coded zones: white, green, yellow and red. The white zone, or metro area, has a wide scope and will suffice for most travelers. The green zone encompasses the next sphere of Munich, notably the Dachau concentration camp memorial and the Flugwerft aviation museum at Oberschleissheim. The yellow zone reaches Ammersee and Starnberger See, two idyllic Bavarian lakes. And, lastly, the red zone lands at the airport (Flughafen). Now that you're familiar with each color zone, MVV has packaged them into four fare categories: **Innenraum** (white zone); **XXL** (white and green zones); **Außenraum** (green, yellow and red zones); *Gesamtnetz* (all 4 zones). The below-listed tickets cover every mode of transportation in the MVV network—prices range according to fare categories and zones of travel. Stop by an MVV info point for your free U-Bahn (underground)/S-Bahn (suburban rail) network map.

Note: All ticket types can be purchased at vending machines marked MVV-Tickets. Stamp ticket in blue box to validate, watch locals. (Bus/tram tickets are pre-stamped.) Travelers riding without valid ticket risk a 40€ fine, on the spot! Plain-clothed officials patrol trains regularly. Holders of a Eurail consecutive-day or dated Flexi/Select pass ride *free* on the S-Bahn.

Basic: (Einzel-Fahrkarte) One-way travel ticket—for use within any one zone and valid three hours—within any two zones (or more) and valid four hours. *Price:* one zone 2.20€, two zones 4.40€, three zones 6.60€, Gesamtnetz 8.80€.

Short Trip: (Kurzstrecke) Valid for one hour up to two stops on the S- and U-Bahn, or four stops on a bus/tram. *Price:* 1.10€.

Day Ticket, Single: (Tageskarte) For individual use within a zone(s) from time of validation until 6 a.m. *Price:* Innenraum 4.50€, XXL 6€, Außenraum 4.50€, Gesamtnetz 9€.

Day Ticket, Partner: (Tageskarte Partner) Excellent deal, valid for up to 5 people within a zone(s) from time of validation until 6 a.m. *Price:* Innenraum 8€, XXL 10.50€, Außenraum 8€, Gesamtnetz 16€.

3-Day Ticket, Single: (3-Tageskarte Innenraum) For individual use within the white zone, or Innenraum, from time of validation until 6 a.m. the fourth morning. *Price:* 11€.

3-Day Ticket, Partner: (3-Tageskarte Partner Innenraum) Another dynamite deal, valid for up to 5 people within the white zone, or Innenraum, from time of validation until 6 a.m. the fourth morning. *Price:* 18.50€.

7-Day-Ticket: (IsarCard or Wochenkarte) Great value for longer stays. Ticket is transferable (between people) and is valid Mon to Sun 24:00. *Price:* within one zone 14.60€, two zones 23.60€, three zones 33€, Gesamtnetz 42€.

Bike Ticket: To transport a bike on board the subway will require the purchase of an extra ticket: Tageskarte, 2.50€.

Airport: (*Flughafen*; code MUC; www.munich-airport.de) Munich's welcoming airport, Franz Josef Strauß, lies 30km northeast of downtown Munich and is the second busiest in Germany (eighth in Europe), moving 25 million passengers annually (Heathrow 67 million, Frankfurt 51 million). Taxis are waiting patiently outside if you require the service (roughly 50€ to central Munich), but the most common mode of transportation is the *S-Bahn located on the lower level. For rental cars, follow sign "Mietwagon."

*Note: S-Bahn (S1 or S8) runs regularly (every 20 min) from early morning to late evening and takes roughly 35 minutes into the city. Purchase ticket (8.80€) from vending machine and be sure to validate it before hopping aboard. To maximize savings, consider buying the Welcome Card (page 188) or Day Ticket Single/Partner—Gesamtnetz (see above *Subway*).

Parking: For *street parking* pay at nearby automat and leave ticket on dashboard of your car. To park downtown costs 50¢/12 min (max 1-2hr), Mon-Sat, 8:00-19:00—otherwise free. The farther you are from the center, the cheaper it is, typically 20¢/12 min (no max). *Note:* Munich is parking-dial (Parkscheibe) friendly (page 450); look for applicable signs, which are especially prevalent along Ludwigstr. either side of the university. *Parking garages* (denoted by blue-and-white "P" signs) are abundant throughout the city, usually costing 3€ for the first hour and 2€ for every hour thereafter. To avoid driving into the city, look for the P+R (Park + Ride) signs on the outskirts of Munich (off autobahn A99). These P+R are (typically free) parking lots set up adjacent to a subway or bus line so you can conveniently park and ride public transportation into Munich.

Share Ride: *(Mitfahrzentrale; a concept matching passengers with drivers, and vice-versa.)* Those who are not traveling with a railpass, "Mitfahrzentrale" is the cheapest and most social option of getting from one city to another. There is one Share Ride office in Munich. *Tel.#* 089/19-440. *Hours:* daily, 8:00-20:00. *Price:* approx. cost per passenger, for example, from Munich to Frankfurt 24€, Berlin 32€, Amsterdam 43€. *Getting There:* located on Lämerstr. 6—exit the main train station on its Arnulfstr. side and cross into Pfefferstr., then go left on Hirtenstr. and it's a short distance on the right.

   Note: Those who have a working knowledge of German will want to first refer to this website (www.mitfahrgelegenheit.de) for an opportunity to contact the driver directly, i.e. cutting out the middleman for an even cheaper Share Ride.

Bike Rental: Munich is about as bike-friendly as a city can get, having its own network of traffic lanes, signs and signals. Conveniently located opposite track (Gleis) 32 in the main train station, *Radius* bikes offer a wide range of bicycles to choose from, in addition to walking tours of the city and rail tours to Dachau concentration camp memorial as well as to King Ludwig II's Neuschwanstein castle. *Hours:* (Radius) May thru mid-Oct, daily, 10:00-18:00. *Price:* (**bike rental**) from 3€/hr, 14€/day (10% discount with Welcome Card). *Note:* Must have ID and 50€ (cash or CC) for deposit. *Price:* (**tours**) City Highlights [walking, dur. 2hr] 10€; Third Reich [walking, dur. 2.5hr] 10€; Dachau [rail, dur. 5hr] 19€; Neuschwanstein [rail, dur. 9hr] from 25€; save money by combining a second tour. (www.radiusmunich.com) Call or stop by for details: *Tel.#* 089/5502-9374

Car Rental: AllRound car rental offers an affordable opportunity to hit the road—compacts from 35€/day (first 300km free) or 179€/week (first 1500km free), inclusive of taxes and insurance (1600€ deductible). *CC's:* all accepted. Call for other rates, vehicle types, and directions to their office (located a handful of U-Bahn stops from central Munich). *Note:* Minimum age 21 and one-year DL. (www.allroundrent.de) *Hours:* Mon-Fri 9:00-18:00, Sat 10:00-12:00. *Tel.#* 089/723-2343 (English spoken).

Internet: There are oodles of call shops around the main train station offering cheap Internet (roughly 1.50€/hr) and international dialing.

   One popular hangout is easyeverything.com, across the street from the station's front entrance, which has more than 500 Internet terminals. *Hours:* 24/7. *Price:* 1.20€-4€/hr (depending on time of day)—pay automat (requires exact change), take ticket to computer and log in. *Note:* Most computers are downstairs.

   Another online possibility is Munich Internet Service Center, located at Tal street 31 (near Isartor). Besides the World Wide Web, the service center offers faxing, printing, CD/DVD burning (including digital pix), etc. *Hours:* 24/7. Price: (Internet) 1€/30min, 2€/hr, 3€/2hr. *Tel.#* 089/2070-2737

Welcome Card: Munich's Welcome Card offers a slew of city-wide discounts for individuals or small groups ("partner card," great value! valid for up to 5 people) from one to three days, awarding the holder unlimited use of public transport within the metro area (Innenraum, white zone) and up to 50% discount on select attractions, tours and museums. Additionally, you have the option of upgrading the Welcome Card to include all four transportation zones (Gesamtnetz) in the MVV network (page 187) accessing outer Munich—e.g. Dachau concentration camp memorial and the airport. The Welcome Card is valid until 6:00 a.m. the morning after for the day card or on the fourth morning for the 3-day card. Welcome Cards can be purchased at the Airport Service Center, the EurAide office in the main train station, or at either TI. _Price:_ **Individual** day card (metro area) 7.50€; day card Gesamtnetz 13€; 3-day card (metro area) 17.50€; 3-day card Gesamtnetz 32€. **Partner** day card (metro area) 12.50€; day card Gesamtnetz 22.50€; 3-day card (metro area) 25.50€; 3-day card Gesamtnetz 48€. _Opinion:_ Excellent card for small groups. Individuals should scan the brochure to see whether your movements will compensate the price of the card. Purchase Gesamtnetz upgrade if you're traveling to/fro airport and planning a trip to Dachau.

American Express: Munich has two Amex branches in the city and a few service centers at the airport. — _**Neuhauser Str. 47**_ [zip: 80331]; situated on the main shopping street, in building adjacent to Karlstor. (fes.munich.neuhauserstrasse@aexp.com) _Tel.#_ 089/2280-1387 _Hours:_ Mon-Fri 9:30-18:00, Sat 10:00-13:00. — _**Promenadeplatz 6**_ (Bayerische Hof) [zip: 80333]. _Tel.#_ 089/2280-1465 (fes.munich.promenadeplatz@aexp.com) _Hours:_ Mon-Fri 9:00-17:30, Sat 9:30-12:30. — _**Munich Airport**_, offices are located in terminal 2, gates G and H. _Hours:_ daily, 7:00-21:00. _Tel.#_ 089/9758-4433

CONSULATES:

USA: Königinstr. 5 (located at southern end of Englischer Garten, left side). _Tel.#_ 089/28-880 (munich.usconsulate.gov) _Hours:_ Mon-Fri 8:00-11:00. (consmunich@state.gov)

Canada: Tal 29 (west of Marienplatz). www.canada.de _Tel.#_ 089/219-9570. (munic@international.gc.ca) _Hours:_ Mon-Fri 9:00-12:00, and by appointment 14:00-16:00. _Note:_ Emergency 24-hour (toll-free) number for Canadians in distress: 00-800-2326-6831

_UK_: Bürkleinstr. 10 (U4/U5 Lehel). www.british-embassy.de (then click Munich under "local offices" on left). _Tel.#_ 089/211-090. (info.munich@fco.gov.uk) _Hours:_ Mon-Fri 8:30-12:00 & 13:00-17:00 (Fri till 15:30).

Australia: No office in Munich; refer to chapters _Berlin_ or _Frankfurt_.

English Cinema: There are two theaters in Munich that feature English-speaking movies: _The Cinema_ and _Museum Lichtspiele_. By far the more popular venue is The Cinema, as it's called. _Note:_ Here, equate your movie ticket to that of a ballpark ticket; first you are required to sit in your assigned seat: row (Reihe) / seat (Sitz). Once the action begins, if the venue is not full, you can move seats.

**The Cinema** has one theater maintaining 427 seats, located a few blocks from the sudsy Löwenbräu Keller (beer hall). _Price:_ adult 7€, student 6€ (only ISIC card is accepted for discount). Seating chart right of cashier. _Specials:_ (except holidays) Mon/Tue 5€; Mon-Fri before 17:30 4€. Every Friday 23:00 is the "sneak preview"—a surprise film screened before its national release. To reserve tickets (wise choice) or check movie schedule, go to www.cinema-muenchen.com or call _tel.#_ 089/555-255. _Getting There:_ The Cinema is located at Nymphenburger Str. 31 — U1 Stiglmaierplatz, exit Nymphenburger Str. and continue a few blocks to The Cinema on the left. _Note:_ The Löwenbräu brewery is located on Stiglmaierplatz (intersection above station). Consider arriving a few hours early to enjoy a schnitzel and beer at the Löwenbräu Keller (beer hall/restaurant on corner). _WWII Buffs:_ During the 1923 Beer Hall Putsch, the Löwenbräu Keller was the staging area for Röhm's SA, including Himmler, before marching on the War Ministry (see page 223, chapter _Hitler's Munich_).

Museum Lichtspiele is a petite theater hidden in plain view, near the Deutsches Museum. (www.museum-lichtspiele.de) *Price:* adult 6.50€, student 5.50€ (except Sat). Specials: all movies on Mondays are 5€ and every Thursday from 22:00 is the "sneak preview" 5€—surprise film (usually in English). For movie schedule, tel.# 089/489-1296—for ticket reservations, tel.# 089/482-403. *Getting There:* Theater is located at Lilienstr. 2, between Ludwigsbrücke and Rosenheimer Str. *Note:* Consider arriving early and have dinner and drinks (half liter beer 3.30€, liter [Maß] 6.40€) at the traditional Bavarian-style *Wirtshaus in der Au*, two blocks from the theater at Lilienstr. and Paulanerplatz. Hours: Mon-Fri 17:00-01:00, Sat/Sun 10:00-01:00. Good idea to reserve: *Tel.#* 089/448-1400. *GPS:* N48° 07.738 - E11° 35.181

Books: Central Munich's biggest bookstore—"Hugendubel" (yes, you read it right)—stocks the city's largest collection of *English-language books. You can find Hugendubel's 6-floor mega-store on Marienplatz opposite the Glockenspiel; look for the company's *Die Welt der Bücher* (The World of Books) slogan outside its entrance. Inside, grab a book(s) and a seat on one of their comfy couches and read the afternoon away (works well on a rainy day). If it's 11:00 or 12:00 (or 17:00 May-Oct) take the escalator to an upper floor for a bird's eye view of the Glockenspiel show. On the top floor is a café. *Hours:* (store) Mon-Sat 9:30-20:00. *Note:* Although the Marienplatz branch has a plethora of books to choose from, Hugendubel's nearby (5-min walk) Salvatorplatz branch contains Munich's most extensive collection of English-language books (open Mon-Sat 10:00-20:00).

Holidays in Munich, 2006

1. January, Sunday – New Year
6. January, Friday – Epiphany (Three Kings' Day)
14. April – Good Friday
17. April – Easter Monday
1. May, Monday – May Day (Labor Day)
25. May, Thursday – Ascension Day
5. June – Whit Monday
15. June, Thursday – Corpus Christi
15. August, Tuesday – Assumption Day
3. October, Tuesday – Day of German (East-West) Unity
1. November, Wednesday – All Saints' Day
25. December, Monday – Christmas
26. December, Tuesday – St. Stephen's Day (Christmas Day No. 2)

What to do on a Sunday

Sundays are a good time to be in Munich because many of the city's best museums offer drastically reduced admission, 1€ (see *Museums*, page 195).

Church Service, "Gottesdienst"

Note: Hours may have changed—check with staff at your accommodations or at the TI for the latest info, as well as for other religious denominations.

Roman Catholic: (English service) Berchmannskolleg (located at Kaulbachstr. 33, street behind US consulate) — Sun 10:30

Roman Catholic: (English service) Kreuzkirche (located at Kreuzstr. 10, street behind Asamkirche) — Sun 18:00

United Methodist: (English service) Friedenskirche (located at Frauenlobstr. 5, few blocks south of Sendlinger Tor) — Sun 11:45 (www.peacechurch.de) *Tel.#* 089/2602-3677

Lutheran: (German service) Matthäuskirche (located at Sendlinger-Tor-Platz and Lindwurmstr.) — Fri 18:30, Sun 8:30, 10:00 and 18:00
    Judaism: For info, tel.# 089/201-4960 — synagogue is located at Reichenbachstr. 27.

FREE Munich

1) Behold the world-famous **Glockenspiel** (page 192).
    2) With the help of **"The Letter"** (chapter seven of the *Quest for the Bavarian Cross*), explore Munich in the footsteps of Sydney and Reuben.
    3) WWII buffs will want to discover **Hitler's Munich**, do-it-yourself tour (page 219).
    4) **Dachau concentration camp** (memorial), the Nazi's first interment camp, is free to enter—closed Monday (page 212).
    5) Check out the relaxing green expanse of the **Englischer Garten** and the locals **surfing** the Eisbach (pages 192-93).
    6) Tag along on a free **BMW** factory tour (page 197) and survey the assembly of one of the world's finest automobiles. Book at least a month in advance.
    7) Catch up with the world's most famous beer hall: the **Hofbräuhaus** (page 202). Entertaining is to arrive around 22:15, about an hour before closing, to see smashed patrons flappin' to the Chicken Dance and boogying to the Macarena.
    8) For a do-it-yourself culinary experience, pop into Munich's oldest delicatessen, **Alois Dallmayr** (page 206).
    9) Ogle Munich's **museum-like churches** (page 199), especially the Asamkirche. Witness the bones of Mundita in St. Peter's.
    10) Although not technically free, culture vultures will save on Sundays because the **state-run museums** offer hugely reduced admission, 1€ (see *Museums*, page 195).
    11) Hang out with your favorite novel at **The World of Books** in Munich's living room: Marienplatz (page 190—*Books*).
    12) Wander through the dramatic (and free) exhibition of the **Nibelungen (-säle) Halls** illustrating the destruction and reconstruction of the Residenz (page 193—Residenz).

SIGHTS

Marienplatz: (Mary's Square) Affectionately referred to by the locals as their "living room," Marienplatz in medieval times was Munich's commercial and entertainment center, hosting a lively open-air market as well as colorful festivals and jousting tournaments featuring chivalrous knights. It was also on Marienplatz that Duke Wilhelm V and his bride Renate were married in 1568, the theme of the Glockenspiel.
    In the 19th century, the abovementioned open-air market moved to the other side of St. Peter's church and is known today as the *Viktualienmarkt* (**Victuals Market**, open Mon-Sat, morning till 18:00, depending on weather). The Viktualienmarkt, Munich's largest outdoor market, is an appetizing place for self-catering locals, travelers seeking picnic goodies, romantics searching for an evening wine, or recommended for a casual, sit-down lunch.
    The fountain on Marienplatz was stocked with fish in former times; the reason this part of the plaza was known as the fish market. Today, the **Fish Fountain** is a popular meeting place and a source for temporary relief on sweltering summer days.
    The namesake of Marienplatz is represented on its centerpiece, the 14-meter-high **Mary's Column** *(Mariensäule)*, which was erected in 1638 during the Protestant-vs-Catholics Thirty Years' War and features a gilded Virgin Mary keeping a blessed eye on Munich's citizens.

The dominant structure on the square is the neo-Gothic **New Town Hall** *(Neues Rathaus)*, built 1867-1909. Every day throngs of people cram before its soot-stained facade to watch the world-famous Glockenspiel (see next entry). ***Toilets anyone?*** *For the pleasure will cost 50¢. Walk through the central archway beneath the clock tower to the back courtyard and look right.*

Next to the New Town Hall is the **Old Town Hall** *(Altes Rathaus)*, dating from the late-15th century. Inside the Disneyland-like structure is a superb Gothic hall used for stately functions, and within its clock tower is the city's Toy (Spielzeug) Museum, from where you hear the periodic clanging.

Glockenspiel: The famous Marienplatz carillon, known as the Glockenspiel (literally Bells Play), is the animated attraction on the clock tower of the New Town Hall (Neues Rathaus). It is Germany's largest carillon, having 43 bells (weighing from 20lbs to 25 tons) and housing 32 life-sized figures, each made of copper. The Glockenspiel springs to life thrice daily in summer and twice in winter, attracting thousands of spectators for the 10-minute-long extravaganza split into two spirited acts.

The first act represents the wedding of Duke Wilhelm V and his bride Renate that took place on the square in 1568. The royal couple can be seen in the background spectating the festivities before them. *(Note: Watch the blue-and-white Bavarian knight joust the red-and-white Austrian knight. Nudge your neighbor and bet a beer on the Bavarian knight. You don't have much time; the joust is decided on the second revolution.)*

The second act represents the dancing Schäffler, who were the coopers—or barrel makers—in the Middle Ages. After enduring a devastating outbreak of plague in the early 16th century, the townsfolk refused to emerge from their dwellings since they did not believe the worst was over. The coopers, nonetheless, emerged from their houses in joyous song while dressed in their traditional, colorful costumes to celebrate the end of pestilence. History proved them right and this custom is still repeated every seven years to keep plague away. (Their next performance is scheduled for 2012.)

The finale of the Glockenspiel occurs after most of the onlookers have dispersed. Stick around a few minutes longer until the bells silence, when the golden rooster above the Glockenspiel crows three times (frightening nearby pigeons into premature flight). *Glockenspiel Show Times:* daily, 11:00 and 12:00 (also 17:00 May-Oct).

Dachau: Infamous Nazi concentration camp; page 212.

Hofbräuhaus: The world's most renowned tavern; page 202.

St. Michael: Munich's most touristed church—burial place of the fairy-tale king, a.k.a "Mad" Ludwig II (page 199).

Frauenkirche: Munich's Old Town landmark; page 200.

BMW: see page 197.

Englischer Garten: The English Garden, also known as the "green lung" because it stretches (some 5km) north-south along the Isar River, is one of the largest urban parks in the world, humbly upstaging London's Hyde Park and New York's Central Park. Originally, the 18th-century garden was a royal hunting reserve for the House of Wittelsbach. However, an influential American minister—Benjamin Thompson from Massachusetts—swayed the monarchy to donate the green lung to the city. For the people and landscaped by the people, the English-style garden was officially opened to the public in 1792 and millions of visitors have been flocking to it since. Today, the garden accommodates a recreational lake, idyllic horse trails, bike routes, walking paths, four beer gardens, several waterways, and umpteen sunbathers who are known for wearing a lot less than a bikini, or to be more precise, Superman-style underwear. Bottoms up—

popular beer-hall jargon—takes on a whole new meaning here. (*Note:* Many nudists at the garden are men who seem to enjoy exposing their wursts to the world, which, as the picture in your head already illustrates, can be a startling experience. Consider yourself forewarned.) On a lighter note, read the next entry and get tubed.

Surfing: What's this...Surf's up in Munich? Yeah, dude, killer swell south end of the Englischer Garten—bring your board, wetsuit and chicks if ya got 'em! The steady-flowing alpine water of the Eisbach—Ice Creek—hustles through the garden creating a very surfable wave off Prinzregentenstr., beneath bridge between the Haus der Kunst and the Bavarian National Museum. *GPS:* N48° 08.609 - E11° 35.263

Residenz: For more than four centuries, from 1508 to 1918, the titanic-sized Residenz functioned as the royal palace and seat of government for the House of Wittelsbach, rulers of Bavaria. Alas, WWII bombs wrecked the imperial dwelling, requiring decades of meticulous restoration to return it to its former grandeur. Take the recommended tour and wander past epochs of history, from Renaissance to neoclassical. Ogle busts of historic emperors and 16th-century murals of Bavarian villages in the lavish, 66m/216ft long Antiquarium (the largest Renaissance hall north of the Alps). Behold the Court Chapel where the fairy-tale king, Ludwig II, was put to rest after his mysterious death in 1886 and where his grandfather, Ludwig I, was married in 1810 before rushing off to the reception, now celebrated annually as the Oktoberfest. The Residenz is so big (more than 130 rooms) that the self-guided tour is split into two routes, morning and afternoon, when different rooms are open to view. The afternoon tour (from 13:30 in summer, 12:30 in winter) is best since it offers more rooms to view (such as the aforesaid Court Chapel). However, since tickets to the Residenz are valid all day, your best bet is to arrive before 13:00 (12:00 in winter) and do both tours. Expect each respective tour to take approx. 90 min. *Hours:* daily, April to mid-Oct 9:00-18:00, mid-Oct to March 10:00-16:00. *Price:* (includes audio guide) adult 6€, student 5€, combo-ticket with Treasury 9€/8€, Welcome Card holders receive 1€ off adult or combo-ticket price. *Note:* After buying your ticket, pick up the included audio guide from the attendant around the corner. To keep on track with the tour, follow signs "Rundgang" and "Führungslinie." Oh, and "Ausgang" means exit. After turning in the audio guide and exiting the building, don't miss the dramatic exhibition of the **Nibelungen (-säle) Halls**, located about 20 meters from the Residenz entrance. Here you'll see spacious rooms and mythological scenes as well as petite rooms plastered with photos depicting the destruction and reconstruction of the Residenz. The Nibelungen Halls are *FREE* for all to enter. *Getting There:* Residenz can be entered from Max-Joseph-Platz or off Residenzstr., three blocks north of Marienplatz.

Treasury, Residenz: (Schatzkammer) Under one heavily secured roof in the Residenz is the priceless treasure collection of the Bavarian royal family, Wittelsbach. If you've ever wondered what an imperial crucifix or ceremonial sword looks like, you'll find a millennium's worth of regal knickknacks in the Residenz Treasury, some before Munich existed. The Wittelsbachs loved to impress and therefore compiled a vibrant array of jewels, crystal and ivory, among other riches. In the first room don't miss the oldest English crown in existence, dating from 1370. In the third room, the holy relic of St. Georg (1586)—patron saint of the Wittelsbachs—will dazzle you. *Hours:* daily, April to mid-Oct 9:00-18:00, mid-Oct to March 10:00-16:00. *Price:* (includes audio guide) adult 6€, student 5€, combo-ticket with Residenz 9€/8€, Welcome Card holders receive 1€ off adult or combo-ticket price. *Getting There:* Treasury is situated in the Residenz—enter from Max-Joseph-Platz or off Residenzstr., three blocks north of Marienplatz. *Suggestion:* For those of you buying the combo-ticket, visit the Treasury first and use your photographic memory to record the significant pieces of jewelry. With these images stored, step into the Residenz and see how many pieces of jewelry you can spot the monarchs wearing in the ancestral picture gallery (room 4).

Cuvilliés-Theater: Part of the sprawling Residenz complex, this most sumptuous theater (1755) will be closed for renovations until (presumably) 2008.

Zoo, Munich: A pleasant day out can always be had at the zoo, and Munich's wildlife contribution is a further testament to the zoological premise. The Munich Zoo—established in 1911—is idyllically situated on the banks of the Isar River, 3km south of the city center. Arrive early and grab the daily program listing the animal shows, feeding times and camel rides. *Hours:* daily, April-Sept 8:00-18:00, Oct-March 9:00-17:00. *Price:* adult 9€, student 6€, senior 6.50€, Welcome Card holders pay student price. *Feeding Times: ("Fütterungszeiten")* Animals are not fed on Fridays!—Tuesday is also meager. Otherwise, the feeding festivities begin with the penguins at 11:00 and conclude with the lions, monkeys and polar bears 15:30-16:00. *Getting There: By subway,* take the U3 to Thalkirchen and it's a few-minutes walk from there. *Drivers,* from the autobahn head towards Munich. Eventually, you'll come across (or merge with) the so-called the Mittlerer Ring—take this to the southern suburbs while keeping an eye out for the "Zoo" signs. Parking 3€.

Olympia Park: Munich's Olympic Park is the largest sports and recreation park in Europe, having more than 210 acres. Before it became the Grand Pooba of European leisure parks, it was a training ground for the Royal Bavarian army in the early 20th century. In 1909, the first zeppelin landed here and from 1925 it was converted into Munich's first civil airport, Oberwiesenfeld. After WWII, Oberwiesenfeld became a massive dumping ground for the rubble accumulated by more than 70 bombing raids that pasted the city. In the 1960s, Munich put in a bid to host the Olympics—thus mammoth construction projects began citywide. Munich's present-day subway system was excavated and the former Oberwiesenfeld was landscaped into a world-class sports venue for the 1972 Summer Olympic Games. Today, Olympia Park attracts several million visitors annually to its recreational facilities, sporting events, summer festivals, and sky-high Olympic Tower.

The world-famous Olympic Stadium, resembling a giant-sized circus tent and having the capacity to hold 70,000 spectators, hosts A-list concerts and (hosted for 33 years, until they moved in 2005) Munich's champion soccer team, Bayern München. Literally soaring above the park is the 291m/954ft high **Olympic Tower** (page 200), which features an observation level and revolving restaurant. Other park attractions include the Olympic Hall (capacity 13,500) • Olympic Swim Complex (50m competition pool; dive pool—10m board; teach and warm-up pool; fitness rooms and saunas) • Olympic Ice Center, hosting in-line and ice skating • Olympic Cycling Hall, capacity 5,000 • Olympic Lake, 21 acres • and an open-air theater.

Tours: April thru October, park guides offer a variety of tours, from the Adventure Tour (1.5hr, 7€/5€) to scaling the dizzying heights of the Olympic Stadium on the Tent Roof Tour (2hr, Mon-Fri 25€, Sat/Sun 30€). *Note:* It's a good idea to reserve in advance. Welcome Card holders ask for discount. You can always browse the Olympic Stadium on your own year round for 2€. *Tel.#* 089/3067-2414. (www.olympiapark-muenchen.de)

Getting There: By subway, take the U3 to Olympiazentrum, then a few-minutes walk. *Drivers,* from the autobahn head towards Munich. Eventually, you'll come across (or merge with) the so-called Mittlerer Ring—take this to the northern suburbs and Olympia Park.

Empress Elisabeth: Though not really a "sight," some readers might be interested in seeing the facade of Empress Elisabeth's birthplace. Who's Empress Elisabeth, you ask? Largely she is known as "Sisi," and often regarded as the Princess Diana of the 19th century. Born into Bavarian royalty on Dec. 24, 1837, Sisi was the beautiful daughter of Duke Maximilian and the cousin of the fairy-tale king, Ludwig II. She gained international celebrity status when Austria's Habsburg emperor, Franz Josef I, chose her to be his wife—when she was just 16 years old! Although Sisi was the First Lady of Europe's most influential dynasty, she lived a sad life with an uncaring and absent husband. After four decades of discontent, Sisi was murdered in Switzerland on Sept. 10, 1898, at the age of 60. Today, she is buried in Vienna's Imperial Crypt (page 573). _Getting There:_ at Ludwigstr. 13, two blocks north of the Feldherrnhalle, you'll come across the Bavarian Central Bank building (on left), formerly the Herzog-Max-Palais, where Sisi was born. _Note:_ Only the facade can be seen; there are no tours. A plaque on the wall commemorates her birth.

MUSEUMS

Note: All museums listed in this section are run by the state of Bavaria and offer drastically reduced admission on Sundays (with the last two museums being _FREE_ on Sunday). Additionally, all museums in this section are **closed Mondays!** with the exception of the Neue Pinakothek, closed Tuesday.

It's always a good idea to have a 1€ coin handy when visiting museums because it is often required that you store your belongings in one of the in-house security lockers (coin will pop back out when locker is reopened).

For the latest info regarding Bavaria's cultural heritage, including its castles and palaces, visit the newly opened and neatly designed Info Point in the Alter Hof. _Hours:_ Mon-Fri 10:00-18:00, Sat 10:00-13:00. _Tel.#_ 089/2101-4050 (www.infopoint-museen-bayern.de)

Excluding the three Pinakotheks, there is little English to be seen or heard within the below-listed museums.

Königsplatz: (King's Square) Munich's largest plaza was commissioned by Ludwig I, the fairy-tale king's grandfather, in the early-19th century as a Greek arrangement of temples modeled after the Acropolis. The central structure on the square is the Propylaen, a magnificent gateway leading nowhere. Flanking the Propylaen are two classic state-run museums, the Glyptothek and Antiquities Collection. After your visit, cut through the park behind the Glyptothek to reach the nearby Pinakotheks (see next entry). **Getting There**: By subway, take the U2 to Königsplatz. By foot from the main train station, exit the front entrance and go left—cross at the traffic light and proceed three blocks north on Luisenstr. **GPS:** N48° 08.736 - E11° 33.969. **WWII Buffs:** refer to (page 226) chapter Hitler's Munich.

Glyptothek: Dating from 1830, this temple-like structure qualifies as Munich's oldest museum, which maintains one of the finest collections of Greek and Roman sculptures, sarcophagi and busts in the world. The Glyptothek's most prized possession is a 2500-year-old marble panel belonging to the Greek temple of Aphaia from the island of Aegina. Take a break from inspecting sculpted muscles and fractured body parts and chill in the Glyptothek's out-of-doors café. Useful translation booklet available at cashier, 1€. Outside, stroll the building's exterior to behold the larger-than-life statues peering from niches. _Hours:_ Tue-Sun 10:00-17:00 (Thur till 20:00). _Price:_ adult 3€, student 2€, Sundays 1€.

Antiquities Collection: (Antikensammlungen) Across from the Glyptothek is its neoclassical twin—the house of antiquities (built 1845)—showcasing King Ludwig I's collection of Greek, Roman and Etruscan artifacts, including vases, bowls, gold, jewelry and porcelain. No English. _Hours:_ Tue-Sun 10:00-17:00 (Wed till 20:00). _Price:_ adult 3€, student 2€, Sundays 1€.

Pinakotheks: (www.pinakothek.de) Located one block north of Königsplatz, the following three museums are among the finest in the world. Since each Pinakothek contains masterpieces from heavy-hitters of its particular genre, expect to spend a decent chunk of your day ogling artwork.

Alte Pinakothek: Under the Alte Pinakothek's lengthy roof you can wander through the artistic genius of the Middle Ages through to the Rococo era feasting your eyes on more than 700 works from European masters, including Rembrandt, da Vinci, El Greco, Dürer, Raphael, and one of the largest collections of Rubens on Earth. *Hours:* Tue-Sun 10:00-17:00 (Tue till 20:00). *Price:* (includes audio guide) adult 5.50€, student 4€. Sundays 1€—audio guide 4€ (optional). *WWII Buffs:* On the Arcisstr. side of the museum you'll find a copper horse with its belly ripped open by shrapnel and a Plexiglas shield that reads, Wounds of Remembrance. Look beyond the horse to the museum and you'll notice enormous brick sections repaired post-WWII.

Neue Pinakothek: Across the Alte Pinakothek's broad green lawn is its younger sibling, the Neue Pinakothek, where you'll behold treasured art collections from the 18th to 20th centuries, including works from van Gogh, Cézanne, Klimt, Toulouse-Lautrec, Gauguin, Picasso, Goya, Degas, Manet, Monet and Renoir, as well as sculptures by Rodin. During WWII the artwork was sensibly transported out of town before the original 19th century building copped it sweet by falling bombs—its contemporary replacement dates from 1981. *Hours:* Wed thru Mon 10:00-17:00 (Wed till 20:00), closed Tue. *Price:* (includes audio guide) adult 5.50€, student 4€. Sundays 1€—audio guide 4€ (optional).

Pinakothek der Moderne: Within this concrete fortress you'll discover Germany's largest modern-art museum, divided into four areas of interest: contemporary art, graphics, design and architecture. This new member of the Pinakothek family opened its doors September 2002 to a whopping 250,000 visitors in the first six days—the line extended for blocks. *Hours:* Tue-Sun 10:00-17:00 (Thur/Fri till 20:00). *Price:* adult 9.50€, student 6€, Sundays 1€, (audio guides are planned for 2006).

Bavarian National Museum: This phenomenal, three-story museum retains a wealth of Bavarian history within a 19th-century architectural wonder—even the entry door is more than 100 years old. Inside, you'll literally be flabbergasted by the maze of rooms preserving the region's rich historical past. Themed exhibitions rush you back in time, from the Romanesque era to Baroque. Among the incalculable items on display are intricate locks, pious relics, medieval weaponry, rare porcelain, stained glass, Wittelsbach tapestries, hand-carved furniture, prized clocks, three-dimensional sculpture, traditional steins, musical instruments, city models, ceremonial dress, exquisite ceramics, and a breathtaking Nativity scene—which is the most precious and extensive example on Earth, dating from the early 1700s (a collective masterpiece so rare that it is infrequently on display, inquire in advance, tel.# 089/211-2401). While touring the Bavarian National Museum, ponder the umpteen room attendants who diligently patrol their confined area hour upon hour—you've got to admire their stamina. *Hours:* Tue-Sun 10:00-17:00 (Thur till 20:00). (www.bayerisches-nationalmuseum.de) *Price:* adult 5€, student 4€, Sundays 1€. *Note:* Unfortunately, in this vast complex, there are no English descriptions. *Getting There:* BNM is located at Prinzregentenstr. 3, on the southeast corner of the English Garden—meters from the surfers rippin' up Ice Creek.

Egyptian Art Museum: (Ägyptischer Kunst) The name says it all, except ultra-ancient. From the great land of the pyramids, you'll unearth the art and afterlife of a B.C. culture, including an eerie collection of mummies. *Hours:* Tue-Fri 9:00-17:00 (Tue also 19:00-21:00), Sat/Sun 10:00-17:00. *Price:* (includes audio guide) adult 3.50€, student 2.50€. Sundays 1€—audio guide 2€ (optional). *Getting There:* EAM is situated in the Residenz and can be entered from the Hofgarten.

Ethnology Museum: (Völkerkunde) Without leaving this stately building, constructed 1859-65, you can wander around the world and discover a multitude of traditions and cultures. With 150,000 objects, the Ethnology Museum is the second largest of its kind in Germany. Ogle African woodcarvings, South American artifacts, Asian temples, and American Indian wares—including the world's oldest preserved kayak (1577). *Hours:* Tue-Sun 9:30-17:15. *Price:* adult 3.50€, student 2.50€; Sundays 1€. *Getting There:* EM is located at Maximilianstr. 42, corner of Th.-Wimmer-Ring.

State Archeological Museum: (Archäologische Staatssammlung) At this museum you'll encounter examples of Bavaria's colonization from the first settlement in the Stone Age through the days of the Roman Empire to medieval times. *Hours:* Tue-Sun 9:00-16:30. *Price:* adult 2.50€, student 1.50€; Sundays 1€. *Getting There:* SAM is located at Lerchenfeldstr. 2, behind the Bavarian National Museum.

City Museum: (Stadtmuseum) Founded in 1888, the City Museum exhibits Munich's heritage from the medieval walled city to the modern-day metropolis. On the upstairs carnival floor, watch out for the "Smash Hitler" arcade game and an animated version of King-Kong. For WWII buffs, a stop here is a must, as the annex museum (across courtyard) offers a wowing section on National Socialism in Munich—"capital of the movement." Before entering the museum, visitors will see the very unusual "Kugel-bunker," a concrete air-raid shelter designed during WWII in the shape of a ball to protect 3-4 people. No English in museum, except for orientation pamphlet near cashier. *Hours:* Tue-Sun 10:00-18:00. *Price:* adult 4€, student 2€. *FREE* Sunday! *Getting There:* CM is situated two blocks southwest of St. Peter's church (off Marienplatz); enter midway along building on Oberanger (street).

State Coin Collection: (Münzsammlung) Do you like money, very old money? Be sure to cash in on this museum's exclusive collection of German coins, including currencies from the Goths, Vandals, Celts and ancient Greeks. *Hours:* Tue-Sun 10:00-17:00. *Price:* adult 2€, student 1.50€. *FREE* Sunday! *Getting There:* SCC can be found in the Residenz—enter from Residenzstr.

MUSEUMS, Other

BMW: (Bayerische Motoren Werke, or Bavarian Motor Works) One of Munich's prized possessions is the BMW factory and museum. The company's roots go back to the First World War, when the peoples of Europe were engulfed in venomous hostilities against one another, which required the German nation to tirelessly churn out armaments to sustain its military might. During this chaotic time, BMW was awarded a government contract (in 1917) to manufacture aircraft engines. Subsequent to Germany's demoralizing defeat and the termination of its air force, BMW began producing motorcycles. It wasn't until 1929 that BMW assembled its first automobile, the 3/15 PS DA 2, a.k.a. the "Dixi," which evolved into a successful touring car. Alas, the Second World War demanded that BMW once again build aircraft engines in conjunction with the progressive task of testing rockets, which consequently attracted swarms of Allied bombers resulting in a ruined factory. After the war, BMW regressed to building motorcycles again with the added task of repairing Allied vehicles. In 1951, BMW built its first post-WWII automobile, the full-bodied 501 "Baroque Angel." From the 501 spawned the 504, which was outfitted with the world's first V8 light-alloy engine. In 1972, BMW hatched the modern-day 5-Series, followed by the 3-Series in 1975, and the 7-Series in 1977. The rest is history, which can only be seen in Munich. (www.bmw-welt.com) *GPS:* N48° 10.592 - E11° 33.470

   BMW's headquarters is located in northern Munich, opposite Olympia Park—look to the 1000-foot-high Olympic Tower to get your bearings. As you get closer, you'll see a four-cylinder-shaped high-rise building. This is BMW headquarters, completed in 1972. Below are the factory and (former) museum. *BMW-Welt,* a world-class convention center and showroom, is currently under construction across the street (its completion date is set for summer 2006).

Museum: BMW's outmoded, 30-year-old museum was finally closed in 2004 for a newer look—completion 2007. Meanwhile, a BMW exhibition (daily 10:00-20:00, 2€) will be open to visitors next to the Olympic Tower.

Factory Tour: The *FREE* 90-min behind-the-scenes factory tour is a must-do experience, which delves into all facets of the BMW assembly line. *(Many people on the tour have preordered a model from overseas and are there to pick it up—a complimentary factory tour is part of the sale package. The customer then drives his/her new vehicle on their European vacation before returning it to BMW to be shipped home.)* To sign up for a tour, a month's advance notice is suggested; call: 089/3822-3306 or email: produktionsmeile@bmw.de. When the big day arrives, bring small change for the locker they offer to store your belongings—your guide will provide you with protective clothing and goggles to wander through every detail that goes into the making of a BMW.

Facts, Munich Plant: Built in 1922 • roughly 12,000 employees (10k in production, 2k in admin.) • more than 750 automobiles (3-Series) manufactured daily • it takes 30 hours to produce a vehicle, which is then tested at 191mph • each car requires 8kg/17.5lbs of paint and seven hours to dry at temps upwards of 150°C.

Getting There: The factory and (uncompleted) museum are located next to each other, which are adjacent to BMW's four-cylinder high-rise HQ building across from Olympia Park. *By subway,* take the U3 to Olympiazentrum, then short walk. *Drivers,* parking available in their garage.

Deutsches Museum: Established in 1903, the Deutsches Museum is the largest technological museum in the world and one of the first institutions of its kind. The museum—hauling in a whopping 1.4 million visitors annually—exhibits most every invention from trains and planes and cars to hands-on innovations and high voltage. However, don't expect to see everything in one visit—the Deutsches Museum has more than 40 sections comprising a circuit of 20km on eight levels, housing some 15,000 exhibits. To put this voluminous collection into perspective, if you were to look at every exhibit for just one minute—it would take 10 straight days! *Hours:* daily, 9:00-17:00. (www.deutsches-museum.de) *Price:* adult 8.50€, senior 7€, student 3€, (Welcome Card holders pay senior price), planetarium 2€, combo-ticket with Flugwerft Museum 10€. *Getting There:* DM is situated on Museumsinsel (Museum Island) behind the Imax Theater (25-min walk from Marienplatz). *By subway,* U1/U2 to Frauenhoferstr., or tram #18. *Drivers,* park in the Gasteig (Rosenheimer Str.) or across the street in Hochstr.

Flugwerft Museum: This is the aeronautical branch of the Deutsches Museum, located 15km north of downtown Munich in the leafy suburb of Oberschleissheim. The museum's historic buildings are among the oldest surviving airport structures in Germany, as the adjacent airfield was landscaped in 1912 for the Royal Bavarian Flying Corps. During WWII, it was used as a Luftwaffe airbase and then (post-Nazism) by the Americans. In 1992, the tattered airport structures were lovingly restored and converted into 8000sq.m./86,000sq.ft. of exhibition floor space for the Flugwerft Museum —even the original control tower is accessible as an observation platform. Inside the main hanger are jet aircraft (some military), helicopters, hang gliders, sailplanes and a flight simulator. There is plenty to do, from walking through an aircraft and sitting in a cockpit to controlling a model airplane. *Hours:* daily, 9:00-17:00. *Price:* adult 3.50€, student 2.50€, (Welcome Card holders pay student price), combo-ticket with Deutsches Museum 10€. *Getting There: By subway,* S1 to Oberschleissheim, then 15-min walk (take Mittenheimer Str. direction Schloss Schleissheim). *Drivers,* from the A99 autobahn exit Neuherberg and follow signs to Flugwerft. From downtown Munich, get to Ludwigstr. and then go straight, its name changes to Leopoldstr. and Ingolstädter Str. before ultimately arriving in Oberschleissheim—follow signs to Flugwerft.

Jewish Museum: (Jüdisches Museum) Since WWII the Jewish Museum has been, in fact, homeless. Temporarily it is being housed on Reichenbachstrasse before moving next year (March 2007) to its new, permanent home adjacent to the City Museum, where a synagogue and Jewish center are also planned. For now, this small museum does its best to showcase the life-and-times of Jewry in Munich from the first persecutions in the 13th century to their brutal 20th-century expulsion and willing return. _Hours:_ Tue 14:00-18:00, Wed 10:00-12:00 & 14:00-18:00, Thur 14:00-20:00, closed Fri thru Mon. _Price:_ FREE entry! _Getting There:_ JM is located at Reichenbachstr. 27—due south of Marienplatz and Gärtnerplatz. _Tel.#_ 089/2000-9693 _Note:_ Bring ID for security purposes.

Museum-like Churches

Asam Church: (Asamkirche) This must-see church is a Baroque masterpiece, built from 1733 to 1746 by the tremendously wealthy Asam brothers for their personal use. Years later, due to unwavering demand by the people, the brothers were obliged to go public with their consecrated treasure. Upon entering, notice (midway up wall on right) the Grim Reaper (evil skeleton) cutting the angel's lifeline. Yikes! _Getting There:_ Church is located midway along Sendlinger Str. (at No. 34), some 300 meters southwest of Marienplatz. Across the street is a sweets shop selling gummi bears in bulk quantities.

St. Peter's: (Alte Peter, or Old Peter) Between Marienplatz and Viktualienmarkt is St. Peter's church, Munich's oldest. So old, in fact, Alte Peter dates from the mid-11th century, 100 years before Munich was officially founded! In the 18th century, St. Peter's was refashioned in Baroque-style, evident by the curvaceously striking interior. Upon entering, notice the ruinous pictures (on nearest pillar) of the church post-WWII. From there, mosey along the left aisle to the second chapel where you'll witness the 1700-year-old bones of the holy Mundita, "die Heilige Mundita," who was martyred in Rome for her Christian beliefs. The Catholic Church gave Mundita to St. Peter's in 1677 as a gift for their good work in staving off the reforming ways of Protestant northerners. Outside, at the top of St. Peter's, you'll see the wrought-iron railing enclosing the observation level, from where jaw-dropping views can be had of the Old Town and beyond to the Alps. Notice how packed this elevated perch is prior to Glockenspiel show times (11:00 and 12:00). For more info on St. Peter's observation level, look to page 200.

St. Michael's: This is Munich's most touristed church, not because it is located on the main shopping street, but because Germany's most famous monarch—the "fairy-tale" king, or "mad" Ludwig II—is interred here. Built in Renaissance-style and consecrated in 1597, Duke Wilhelm V (founder of the Hofbräuhaus) commissioned St. Michael's in celebration of Catholicism during the Counter Reformation—the Wittelsbachs were staunch supporters of the Church of Rome and a dozen or so members of the imperial family can be seen posing on the heavenly facade.

Upon entering St. Michael's, go left and examine the photos depicting its destruction from WWII bombs. With your back to the wall, face the high altar and look up to see the largest vaulted ceiling north of the Alps (20m/65ft wide). Left of the high altar, in the corner, is the tomb of Eugéne Beauharnais, Napoleon's stepson by marriage to his first wife, Joséphine. Now, take a few steps forward and go right to the kneeling bench before the rows of remembrance candles and the Virgin Mary. When ready, walk left to the end of the aisle; here you'll find a staircase descending into the royal crypt, where some 40 members of the Wittelsbachs are interred, notably the fairy-tale king and Duke Wilhelm

V and his wife Renate—the couple seen in the background of the Glockenspiel. *Hours:* (royal crypt) Mon-Fri 9:30-16:30, Sat 9:30-14:30. *Price:* 2€.

Frauenkirche: (Church of Our Lady) The Frauenkirche's twin *99-meter-high onion-domed towers are recognized as Munich's old-town landmark and can be seen from miles away. (*One tower is actually 1 meter taller, rising to 100m. To climb it, see page 201.*) The Frauenkirche dates from 1488 and the aforementioned onion-domed towers—mounted some 40 years later—set the precedent for church design throughout Bavaria. When facing the front portal, to your left next to the granite block wall is a model of Munich for visually impaired people, who use their hands as their eyes.

Enter the Frauenkirche via its elaborate front portal made of oak wood to witness the so-called devil's footprint. According to legend, Satan left it behind more than five centuries ago when he came to inspect the completion of what he believed to be a one-window church. From the location of the footprint, due to an architectural trick, the stained-glass windows along the side walls are not visible. The devil was so thrilled about this dark and gloomy design rejecting God's light that his enthusiasm lifted him several meters off the ground. Upon coming down, Satan mightily landed on his right foot, permanently leaving an imprint in the floor tile. (Right of footprint, against the wall, are photos of the church post-WWII.)

As you move farther into the church, you'll see (right) the tomb of Ludwig the Bavarian, king of Germany (1314-47) and Holy Roman Emperor (1328-47). Ludwig is one of Bavaria's greatest rulers. His imperial colors, black and yellow, still decorate the city streets.

Now look up, where the tops of the support pillars meet the webbed ceiling, you'll see petite figures molded in memory of the original workmen who constructed the church. Adorning the Frauenkirche's exterior walls are headstones salvaged from the old church cemetery of prominent citizens.

Theatinerkirche: To simplify pronunciation, we'll refer to this house of worship as Tina Turner's church. Obviously Munich is far from Nut Bush, but the church's curvaceous exterior screams Tina. Featuring an exquisite golden facade, two stylish clock towers and a buxom dome, Turner's church is one of Munich's most impressive. In 1675, the church was consecrated in Italian Baroque-style, reflected by its sumptuous interior. In the cellar are several crypts belonging to Bavaria's royal family, Wittelsbach. Since the church neighbors the Feldherrnhalle, it has witnessed numerous public gatherings, nationalistic marches, and even the bloody ending to a putsch. *Hours:* (royal crypt) Mon-Fri 10:00-16:30, Sat 10:00-15:00. *Price:* 2€.

Best Views

For a memorable view of the Bavarian capital, negotiate one of three towers.

St. Peter's: The best vantage point above the Old Town, or Altstadt, is atop St. Peter's tower, positioned between Marienplatz and the Viktualienmarkt. Climb 306 leg-burning steps to reach the narrow, outdoor observation level (at 96m/314ft high), where you'll be rewarded with magnificent views of the Glockenspiel, old-town Munich and beyond to the Alps. *Hours:* Mon-Sat 9:00-17:30, Sun 10:00-17:30 (one hour longer in summer). *Price:* adult 1.50€, student 1€. *Getting There:* Tower entrance is located outside church, around corner.

Olympic Tower: This is the big daddy of towers, soaring above metropolitan Munich to the dizzying height of 291m/954ft—that's more than three times the height of the Statue of Liberty! Visitors' levels are between the elevations of 174-192m/570-629ft, which feature indoor/outdoor observation decks, a revolving restaurant with some 230 seats, and an exhibit on the 1972 Olympic Games. At a cost of 11€ million, the Olympic Tower opened to the public in 1968. Today, high-speed elevators (7m/second) whisk 1 million visitors per year up to heart-skipping views of Munich and beyond. _Hours:_ daily, 9:00-23:30 (last entry). _Price:_ adult 4€, student 2.50€, Welcome Card holders pay 3€. _Getting There: By subway_ take the U3 to Olympiazentrum, then it's a few-minutes walk. _Restaurant:_ Full revolution every 53 min. Open daily, 11:00-23:30. Lunch menu is reasonable; evening menu is understandably pricey. Reservations, _tel._# 089/3066-8585.

Frauenkirche: (Church of Our Lady) Head to the top of Munich's old-town landmark via 86 steps and an elevator ride. Tickets can be obtained at the one-person souvenir kiosk, right of Frauenkirche's front portal. _Hours:_ April-Oct, Mon-Sat 10:00-16:30 (last entry). _Price:_ adult 3€, student 1.50€.

Shopping

Kaufingerstrasse: In medieval times, Munich thrived on the steady flow of merchants who passed through the heart of town via the east-west trade route flanked by inns and marketers. Today, the tradition continues and this pedestrian-only thoroughfare is aptly known as Kaufingerstrasse, or Shopping Street. Here you'll discover throngs of locals and tourists strolling past shop-front windows while admiring smartly dressed manne-quins and a variety of street performers. Kaufingerstrasse begins on the west side of Marienplatz and extends roughly one kilometer past department stores, fashion boutiques and telecommunications shops before reaching Karlsplatz (plaza one block from the main train station). _Note:_ midway along Kaufingerstrasse its name changes (without inter-ruption) to Neuhauser Str.

Max Krug: Marked by a blue awning with a yellow cuckoo clock, midway along Kaufingerstrasse, is Max Krug, a popular souvenir outlet carrying most everything Germanic a tourist would desire, from beer steins to nutcrackers to Black Forest cuckoo clocks—global shipping available. All _CC's_ welcome. _Tel._# 089/224-501 (www.max-krug.com) _Hours:_ Mon-Sat 9:30-20:00.

Maximilianstrasse: This A-list boulevard—three blocks north of Marienplatz—is Munich's Rodeo Drive equivalent, patronized by moneyed shoppers picking up the latest Versace, Chanel, Cartier and Christian Dior fashions.

Goethestrasse: This ethnically charged avenue is situated on the south side of the main train station and is the first leg en route to the Oktoberfest grounds. Goethestrasse—and its neighboring streets—offers a wide variety of merchandise and services from low-cost knickknack shops to peep shows to mouth-watering Döner Kebaps (on Landwehrstr.).

WWII Buffs: Check out Werner Winning's shop specializing in war medals and rare coins. _Hours:_ Mon-Fri 11:00-18:00, Sat 10:00-13:00. _Tel._# 089/299-351. _Getting There:_ Bräuhausstr. 10—behind Hofbräuhaus.

ENTERTAINMENT

Night owls: After the beer halls and beer gardens close around midnight, head to Kultfabrik—a former complex of gritty warehouses transformed into an urban village of pubs, clubs and eateries. Kultfabrik is located 250 meters from Ostbahnhof—take the subway U5 or any S-Bahn.

Beer Halls, Gardens
The epitome of Bavarian culture

One fact every sharp-eyed traveler will notice while touring Germany is that beer is often cheaper than a soft drink in restaurants and cheaper than bottled water in convenience shops—and Munich is no exception to the observation. Referred to as the beer-drinking capital of the world, Munich is famous for its mass-guzzling beer halls and summertime beer gardens where *Gemütlichkeit*—or homegrown coziness—is king. These intoxicating establishments are unique to this south-German capital and millions of tourists each year consummate their relationship with Munich's amber brew under a decorative ceiling splashed with Bavarian-themed murals or beneath the cooling leaves of a chestnut tree (only grown in traditional beer gardens). In this informal setting, it is customary to share your table with people you don't know—jovial moods allow for quick friendships.

Find A Seat: Upon arriving in a beer hall or beer garden, it can often be a challenge to find somewhere to sit. To communicate your desire to take a load off, say *"Ist hier Platz frei?"* (Is this seat available? [also used for plural form]). Positive responses are *"Ja. Bitte."* (Yes. Please [take a seat]), *"Freilich!"* or *"Sicher!"* (Of course!). And whatever you do, don't sit where it says *"Stammtisch"*—this table is reserved for regulars!

Order A Beer: Now that you have a seat, let's order a beer: *"Ein (zwei) Bier, bitte"* (One [two] beer[s], please). To order your next beer, say *"Noch eins (zwei), bitte."* (Another one [two], please). **Suggestion:** Don't pay with a credit card—on-the-go waiters/waitresses get uptight! *Note:* Often at beer gardens and festivals, a **Pfand**, or deposit, is required with the purchase of your beer. Return the glass and get your Pfand back.

BEER: In German, beer is **Bier** (same pronunciation). The Bavarian standard is the golden-colored "**Helles**," a lager-style brew. If you order a beer, plain and simple, a Helles is what you'll get. Other popular beer-types are "**Dunkels**," a dark smooth brew, and "**Weissbier**," a cloudy wheat beer warranting an acquired taste. (Note: *Weissbier* is only served in half-liter quantities). Also available anywhere is the "**Radler**," a half-half mix of beer and lemon soda. With drink in hand, say *Prost*—German for "cheers."

The traditional size of a Bavarian beer is called a "**Maß**" (pronounced Moss), a liter-sized mug weighing 2.3kg/5lbs (when full). The term Maß translates to "measure" and dates from medieval times when the non-specific volume of a tankard was simply referred to as a Maß, or measure. Today, the average price around town for a Maß is 6€—excluding Oktoberfest.

Historically, beer dates from the ancient world—thousands of years before Christ. However, it was the German monks who perfected the all-natural brewing process in medieval times to formulate an economical alternative to wine as well as a nutritional food substitute during Lent. The monks' recipes have endured the ages bringing social cheer to every-day people. Per capita, Germans drink around 120 liters of beer annually, which ranks third in the world behind the Czechs and Irish.

Bavarians sure do love their beer—affectionately known as "liquid bread"—and often quote the following adage: *Durst ist schlimmer als Heimweh* (Thirst is worse than homesickness). With respect to Bavarian ritual, and your needs, we've listed a few popular beer establishments to get you started on the amber path that the monks forged. And just as the monks did, kick back with your brew, relax and count your blessings.

Hofbräuhaus: Filled with tipsy tourists and numbed locals, the Hofbräuhaus is undeniably the most famous beer hall in the world—a trip to Munich wouldn't be complete without at least a walk-through. What's more, grab one of their paper menus (Speisenkarte) as a souvenir—they're readily lying on tables. The lederhosen-wearing oompah-pah band kicks off around 11:00 and plays sets until closing. Here is your chance to learn traditional Bavarian drinking songs, such as "Oans, zwoa, g'suffa!" (One, two, chug-a-lug!), get reacquainted with John Denver's "Country Roads," and perform the chicken dance in front of a live audience. Expect to pay 6.20€ for a liter of beer.

Beer steins that belong to the *Stammtisch* elite are secured in the various wrought-iron racks. To be a member of this regulars' club one has to be accepted, pay dues (few euro), and drink often in the 'haus.

(www.hofbraeuhaus.de) *Hours:* daily, 9:30-23:30. *Heimatabend:* Traditional Bavarian show, inclusive of whip cracking and spoon clanging, is held daily in the Festsaal at
19:30 (doors open at 18:30, dinner buffet begins at 19:00). Show duration, 2.5hr.
Admission with dinner buffet 19.50€, without dinner 5.20€. Reservations recommended
July-Sept. *Tel.#* 089/2901-3610. *Getting There:* Hofbräuhaus is located at Am Platzl 9,
opposite Hard Rock Café. To reach the Festsaal, ascend broad stairway left of main
entrance. For those of you who can't make it to Munich any time soon, Las Vegas opened
its own authentic Hofbräuhaus (Jan. 2004) at 4510 Paradise Rd., across from the Hard
Rock Hotel & Casino. (www.hofbrauhauslasvegas.com)

Augustiner Bräu: First documented in 1328, Augustiner Bräu is Munich's oldest
brewery and arguably pours the city's finest Helles, which is still tapped fresh from
wooden kegs. The Augustiner brewery is situated 1km west of the main train station on
Landsberger Str., where they draw their own premium water from a spring 230m/754ft
beneath the premises. There are numerous Augustiner inns around town boasting old-age
traditions and scrumptious Bavarian fare. Three of the most popular inns are the
Augustiner Bräustuben, Augustinerkeller and *Augustiner Großgaststätten.*

Augustiner Bräustuben: Positioned on the site of the brewery itself, this atmosphere-
soaked Augustiner establishment is about as genuinely Bavarian as their Lederhosen-clad
brewers. With unbeatable prices and large portions, a visit here is a must! For 15€ you
can eat and drink yourself merry. A liter of beer here—arguably the cheapest (and
tastiest) in the land—will only set you back 4.50€. Oh, and their scrumptious
Schweinshaxe (half pork knuckle, 7.50€), Schweinsbraten (roast pork, 6€) and Schnitzel
(8.60€) will convince you to move in. *Hours:* daily, 10:00 till late. *Getting There:*
Landsberger Str. 19—either ride the S-Bahn to Hackerbrücke and walk a few minutes or
from the Bayerstr. side of the main train station catch tram 18 (direction Gondrellplatz) or
19 (direction Pasing) and ride it a handful of stops to Holzapfelstr. (where you'll find the
Bräustuben on the corner).

Augustinerkeller: On the other side of the sprawling railroad tracks from the
Augustiner Bräustuben is the Augustinerkeller, where you'll discover thousands of locals
savoring their time in Munich's oldest beer garden (first mentioned in 1812) quaffing
tankards of golden-colored beer under a cool forest of chestnut trees while consuming a
grilled chicken, pork knuckle or fish-on-a-stick ("steckerl-fisch" [smoked mackerel]).
Expect to pay 6.40€ for a liter of beer (Maß). *Hours:* daily, 10:00 till late. *Getting There:*
Arnulfstr. 52—either ride the S-Bahn to Hackerbrücke and walk a handful of minutes or
from the main train station catch tram 16 (direction Romanplatz) or 17 (direction
Amalienburgstr.) and ride it a few stops to Hackerbrücke (after the stop Hopfenstr. look
right and you'll see the 'keller).

Großgaststätten: Dating from the late-19th century, this immensely popular
restaurant-and-beer-hall hangout is certainly *Groß* (big), containing a multilevel maze of
historic rooms including an in-house bakery, confectionary, butcher shop, and a leafy
beer garden. What's more, the Großgaststätten is conveniently located on Kaufingerstrasse, or Shopping Street—thus you won't have to travel far to reach their classic
wooden-barreled beer and award-winning regional cuisine. Expect to pay 6€ for a liter of
beer (Maß). *Hours:* daily, 10:00 till late. *Getting There:* Neuhauser Str. 27—from St.
Michael's church, head towards Karlstor and you'll see it on the left.

Chinese Pagoda: (Chinesischer Turm) Planted in the heart of the Englischer Garten is a
unique and historical landmark, the 5-tiered Chinese pagoda—dating from 1791. Huddled
around this open-air attraction is one of Munich's most beloved beer gardens, maintaining some 7000 places to rest your saddle. In summer, most every seat is taken by a
colorful cross-section of people from students to tourists to bankers, largely savoring an
oven-fresh pretzel, a frothy beverage, spirited conversation, and traditional music (brass

band Wed, Fri-Sun afternoons). Expect to pay 6€ for a liter of beer (Maß). For kids there is a wooden carousel—open from 14:00 in good weather—dating from 1913, the oldest in Bavaria. *Hours:* (depending on weather) April-Oct 10:00-19:00 (summer till 23:00). *Getting There:* From the south end of the English Garden, mosey into the central area and follow the path left of the neoclassical rotunda (upon grassy knoll) to the Chinese pagoda.

Hirschgarten: With more than 8000 seats, the oh-so-cozy Hirschgarten is the largest beer garden in Germany, and probably the world. This shaded oasis gets its name from a herd of fenced-in Hirsch (deer), which is a mesmerizing attraction for children and a welcomed reprieve for their parents from 24-hour babysitting duties. *Hours:* (depending on weather) April-Oct 10:00-23:30. *Getting There:* Hirschgarten is situated in the Hirschgarten, an enormous park just south of Schloss Nymphenburg. Take the S-Bahn to Laim—exit station onto Wotanstr. and turn right on Winfriedstr. (first road); follow this into the park and to the beer garden. *GPS:* N48° 08.965 - E11° 30.673

Headline Concerts, Munich 2006

<u>Note</u>: *Prices, dates, concerts may have changed or been added — query TI or ticket agency for latest details.*

<u>Depeche Mode</u>: February 14-15, 20:00 at the Olympic Hall. Price 35-63€
　　<u>Eros Ramazzotti</u>: May 6-7, 20:00 at the Olympic Hall. Price 47-57€
<u>Santana</u>: May 27, 20:00 at the Olympic Hall. Price 47-57€
　　<u>Bon Jovi</u>: May 28, 18:00 at the Olympic Stadium. Price 58-74€
<u>Live</u>: June 22, 20:30 at Georg-Elser-Halle. Price 30€
　　<u>Tracy Chapman</u>: July 4, 20:30 at the Circus Krone. Price 45€
<u>Madness</u>: July 6, 19:00 at the Tollwood Festival. Price 38€
　　<u>Art Garfunkel</u>: July 7, 19:00 at the Tollwood Festival. Price 41€
<u>Rolling Stones</u>: July 16, 19:00 at the Olympic Stadium. Price 86-190€
　　<u>James Blunt</u>: July 17, 20:00 at the Olympic Hall. Price 38€
<u>Eric Clapton</u>: July 22, 20:00 at the Olympic Hall. Price 59€
　　<u>Robbie Williams</u>: August 1-3, 18:30 at the Olympic Stadium. Price 73-87€
<u>B.B. King</u>: September 12, 20:00 at the Olympic Hall. Price 65-101€
　　<u>Pink</u>: October 7, 20:00 at the Olympic Hall. Price 35-53€
<u>James Last</u>: November 3, 20:00 at the Olympic Hall. Price 43-74€

Events/Festivals, 2006

Munich's Birthday Celebration (Stadtgrundüngsfest), June 10-11 (Sat-Sun): Thrown by *Münchner* for *Münchner*, Munich celebrates its 848th birthday party. Aditionally, this year Mozart's 250th birthday will be included in the celebrations. Between Marienplatz and Odeonsplatz (Feldherrnhalle) you'll discover heaps of food, fun and festivities—even a makeshift village on Odeonsplatz exhibiting local crafts.

Blade Nights: Every Monday evening May-Sept thousands of in-line skaters meet, mingle and skim through town like a solid mass of marathoners on wheels. Bring your skates (or borrow someone's) and join in the fun. Query TI for exact route and time. Typically skaters start congregating around 19:30 by the Hackerbrücke (Arnulfstr. side) and depart 21:00.

World Cup Soccer: Munich has six matches scheduled: Friday **June 9** (World Cup opener), *Germany vs Costa Rica* • Wednesday **June 14**, *Tunisia vs Saudi Arabia* • Sunday **June 18**, *Brazil vs Australia* • Wednesday **June 21**, *Ivory Coast vs Serb./Mont.* • Saturday **June 24**, *Round 16* • Wednesday **July 5**, *Semi-Final*. The matches will be played at Munich's 66,000-seat Allianz Arena, located in the northern suburb of Fröttmaning. Ride subway U6 direction Garching and get off at Fröttmaning (11 stops from Marienplatz, 16-min trip). Your travel will require a normal white zone, or Innen-raum, ticket—see *Subway*, page 187. At a cost of 340€ million, the state-of-the-art Allianz Arena took three years to build and opened to the public May 2005. At night you'll be wowed by the arena's exterior, which is brilliantly illuminated in various shades of red, white and blue by more than 25,000 lamps that are connected by a 100km/60mi long network of cables.

Summer Festival, Tollwood, June 14 — July 9: This popular, annual event features loads of art, food, market stalls and music—acts include Golden Earring, Herbie Hancock, Madness, Art Garfunkel. (www.tollwood.de) *Hours:* Mon-Fri 14:00-01:00, Sat/Sun 11:00-01:00. *Getting There:* Tollwood is set up at Olympia Park. *By subway,* U3 to Olympiazentrum; from there it's a few-minutes walk.

Annual Fun Run, June 25 (Sun): Joggers unite! Beginning and ending on Marienplatz, trot through town and the English Gardens. Joggers have two options: the 10km fun-run or the 21km half-marathon. Query TI for registration details.

Munich Marathon, October 8 (Sun): Besides a 42km leg-burning marathon, this year's program will also include a 10km fun-run. Starting point is Olympia Park, 10:00. For details query TI or go to www.muenchenmarathon.de

Oktoberfest, Sept 16 — Oct 3: "O'zapft is!" roars the Bürgermeister (mayor of Munich) after he taps the ceremonial first keg to officially kick-start the world's biggest beer party: the Oktoberfest, 18 days of drinking, singing and carnival rides (see page 209, chapter *Oktoberfest*).

Winter Festival, Tollwood, Nov 31 — Dec 31: To close out the year, the organizers of Tollwood (www.tollwood.de) are at it again, this time they will hold their festival on Theresienwiese—same fairgrounds as the Oktoberfest.

Christmas Market, Dec 1-23: *Mmm...* This is a wonderful time of year when the delightful scent of lebkuchen (gingerbread) and Glühwein (mulled wine) wafts through the air. To find Munich's traditional Christmas market, head to Marienplatz. Sample the Glühwein and keep your mug as a souvenir; you've already paid for it with the deposit. Daily, around 17:30, Christmas music will be played from the balcony of the Rathaus (town hall).

GOOD EATS

Note: Prices quoted in this section may have changed since publication.

Augustiner Bräustuben: In this traditional Bavarian institution you can eat big, drink big and pay little; head to the Augustiner Bräustuben (page 203—*Augustiner Bräu*). *Note:* Informal (shared) seating.

Donisl: This Bavarian-style restaurant is so convenient and cost-effective that all budget-minded travelers should check it out. Donisl's motto is *München muss nicht teuer sein* (Munich doesn't have to be expensive). Standing by their word, Donisl serves no meal over 6.95€! Not one cent more. No matter if you order the woodcutter steak with fried onions and roasted potatoes or a half, oven-fresh chicken with potato salad or the goulash with noodles. To liven things up, an accordion player belts out tunes every evening from 18:30. *Hours:* daily, 9:00-24:00. *Getting There:* Donisl is located on Marienplatz (on left when facing the Glockenspiel). *Toilets* are upstairs.

Weisses Bräuhaus: This establishment is so traditionally Bavarian that northern Germans often have difficulty translating the menu and refer to the simpler, English version. Find a table with spare seats (it's customary to share your eating space at informal restaurants), snare a pretzel from the basket in front of you and soak up the hearty atmosphere. Oh, and spy a neighbors dish to see what looks good to order. Popular homegrown dishes are the *Schweinshax'n mit hausgemachtem Kartoffelknödl und Speckkrautsalat* (12.50€, [meat-lovers] pork knuckle with a homemade potato dumpling and cabbage salad sprinkled with bacon) or the *Spinatspätzl, Käsnockerl mit Parmesan überbacken, Grilltomate und Rahmchampignons* (9€, [vegetarian] spinach noodles, baby cheese dumplings with Parmesan cheese baked on top, grilled tomatoes and mushroom sauce). To wash it down, try the house specialty: the locally brewed Schneider Weisse (wheat beer; half liter 3.20€). *Hours:* daily, 9:00-23:30. *Getting There:* located at Tal street 7, across from McDonald's and Burger King—two-minute walk west of Marienplatz.

Dallmayr, Alois: Alois Dallmayr, dating from the early 18th century, is Munich's oldest delicatessen and proudly tied to Bavarian royalty. Before entering, check out the plaque by the door stating their imperial legacy: *Koenigl(ich) Bayer(ischer) ~ Hoflieferant*; ("Deliverer to the Bavarian king and his court"). Even if you're not hungry, allocate five minutes of your time to shuffle past Dallmayr's counters laden with mouth-watering cuisine from French quiche to exotic fruit to rich chocolates. *Hours:* Mon-Fri 9:30-19:00, Sat 9:00-18:00. *Getting There:* Dallmayr is located at Dienerstr. 15—two-minute walk from Marienplatz. When facing the Glockenspiel, Dienerstr. is the street running along the right-hand side of the (town hall) building.

Haxnbauer: For a good look at one of the staples of Bavarian cuisine, head to Haxnbauer's window-front and ogle their rotisserie as it slowly rotates crispy Schweinshaxe (pork knuckle) over beech-wood coals. To purchase a knuckle will set you back 14€, but it's worth it. While you're savoring your meal, you should know that the building dates from the 14th-century and the meat is specially selected and prepared by Haxnbauer's in-house butcher. *Hours:* daily, 11:00-24:00. *Tel.#* 089/216-6540. *Getting There:* Haxnbauer is located at Sparkassenstr. 6, a few-minutes walk from Marienplatz and two blocks from the Hofbräuhaus.

Münchner Kartoffelhaus: Crazy for potatoes? "Munich's Potato House" offers a plethora of potato-types to choose from, for example Greek, gourmet, Hawaiian, Hungarian, vegetarian, tuna, steak, Mexican, asparagus, French and Indian—dishes range from 8-17€. *Hours:* Mon-Sat 12:00-23:00 (Fri/Sat till 24:00), Sun 17:30-23:00. *Tel.#* 089/296-331. *Getting There:* Kartoffelhaus is located at Hochbrückenstr. 3 (off Tal street, west of Marienplatz).

Imbiss Shoya: Decorative platters of seaweed rolls and raw fish coupled with soy sauce, ginger and hot wasabi displayed in their window-front lure passersby to this petite Japanese sushi bar meters from the Hofbräuhaus. Imbiss Shoya does a booming "to-go" business, but for those who wish to eat on premises can do so in their ultra-cozy restaurant that has seating for just a few. *Hours:* daily, 11:00-23:30. *Tel.#* 089/292-772. *Getting There:* Imbiss Shoya is located at Orlandostr. 5, meters from the Hofbräuhaus. *Note:* Imbiss Shoya has a second location at Frauenstr. 18, southern end of the Viktualien Markt (similar hours).

Riva Pizzeria: Crave a pizza? At this hip ristorante you'll dig their woodfired pizza, from sushi 12€ to chicken curry 10€ to the standard margarita 7€. Pasta dishes 8€. If the weather is fine, opt for a table outside—inside can be smoky. *Hours:* daily, 9:00-24:00. *Tel.#* 089/220-240. *Getting There:* Riva is located at Tal street 42, near Isartor.

GOOD SLEEPS

The following accommodations—listed from the least expensive to the most—come with breakfast and have facilities (shower/toilet) in the room, unless otherwise stated.

Note: All room rates rise dramatically during the Oktoberfest (third Sat in Sept until the first Sunday in Oct). And you can expect to see inflated prices or the "no vacancy" signs out during the World Cup soccer tournament, chiefly June 7 thru July 7 in Munich. Soccer fans in desperate need of a room check out this website: www.host-a-fan.de

Railers: Most of the below-listed selections are near the main train station.

Drivers: Most inner-city hotels have no internal parking and refer their guests to the nearest parking garage, costing roughly 15€/24hr. Outside of the following hours—Mon-Sat 8:00-19:00—street parking is free (that is, if you can find a space). To park for free, consider staying at Hotel Marienbad. If you're arriving late without a room reservation, consider Hotel ibis Messe on the outskirts of Munich.

Hostel/Hotel, "4 You": Hirtenstr. 18 (www.the4you.de) *Tel.#* 089/552-1660
Located some 200 meters from the main train station, the "4 You" hostel and hotel is a convenient and friendly choice for your Munich holiday. Show this book and receive a **10% *discount*** if you pay with cash (*discount does not apply during Oktoberfest or World Cup). *Note:* All below-listed prices include buffet breakfast and linen. Add 1.50€-3€ for those who are 27 years or older. Prices drop a tad during the low season: Nov-March.

Hostel: (shower/toilet in hallway) 12-bed dorm 18.50€, 8-bed 20.50€, 6-bed 21.50€, 4-bed 23.50€, Sgl 35.50€, Dbl 51€. During Oktoberfest and World Cup add 3€ per person, per night.

Hotel: (shower/toilet in room) Sgl 44.50€, Dbl 70.50€, Trpl 95.50€. Prices increase upwards of 45% during Oktoberfest and select conventions.

CC's: VC, MC. *Getting There: Railers,* exit main train station on the Arnulfstr. side of the station (left off platform) and cross at the pedestrian crossing. Continue straight into Pfefferstr. and then go left on Hirtenstr.—"4 You" is ahead on the right.

Hostel, Wombats: Senefelderstr. 1 (www.wombats-hostels.com) *Tel.#* 089/5998-9180. Brand new on Munich's hostel scene, Wombats has fresh amenities and a hip bar. All rooms include linen and have built-in facilities, shower/toilet. *Price:* (cash only) 6- to 10-bed dorms 19-22€, Sgl 31€, Dbl 62€, breakfast 4€. *Note:* Room rates will rise around 50% during Oktoberfest and 40% during the World Cup (chiefly June 7 thru July 7). Prices are drastically reduced over the winter months. *Getting There: Railers,* exit main train station on the Bayerstr. side of the station (right off platform). Cross at the traffic signal to the other side of Bayerstr. and go left; the first street you come to is Senefelderstr., go right. Wombats will soon appear on the left.

Hostel, Meininger: Landsberger Str. 20 (www.meininger-hostels.de) *Tel.#* 089/8563-7700. Another hostel to burst onto Munich's cheap-sleeps scene (since 2005) is Meininger, boasting modern rooms with an upmarket sense. Although it's a long walk from the main train station, Meininger is located near the Oktoberfest grounds and directly opposite the best eats and drink establishment in Munich: *Augustiner Bräustuben.* All rooms include linen and have built-in facilities, shower/toilet. Hostel has kitchen, Internet, laundry and bike rental (12€/day). *Price:* [cash only] (buffet breakfast included in price) 7- to 12-bed dorms 16.50-21.50€, 4- to 6-bed dorms 21-24.50€, Sgl 44-55€, Dbl 62-88€, family room available. *Note:* Book online and save 10%. *Getting There:* Either ride the S-Bahn to Hackerbrücke and walk a few minutes or from the Bayerstr. side of the main train station catch tram 18 (direction Gondrellplatz) or 19 (direction Pasing) and ride it a handful of stops to Holzapfelstr. and your digs. *Drivers,* parking 5€.

Hostel, A&O: Bayerstr. 75 (www.aohostel.com) *Tel.#* 089/4523-5760 or toll free within Germany 0800/222-5722. The Berlin-based A&O hostel group recently acquired this Munich property, which opened Jan 2005. Here you'll find standardized digs at economical prices. Private rooms (Sgl/Dbl) come with breakfast, linen and balcony. Dorm beds require a *one-time* 3€ linen fee and breakfast is an optional 4€. All rooms have shower/toilet. Bike rental 10€/day. *Price:* dorm bed from 12€, Sgl from 29€, Dbl from 32€. *CC's:* VC, MC, AE. *Getting There:* A&O is a 10-min walk from the main train station. Exit station on the Bayerstr. side (right off platform) and cross at the traffic signal. On the other side go right and continue straight to your digs.

Pension Locarno: Bahnhofplatz 5 (www.pensionlocarno.de) *Tel.#* 089/555-164. These pocket-friendly digs offer the basics and a bit more in the heart of it all. *Note:* Shower/toilet in hallway. Reception on third floor; has elevator. *Price:* Sgl 38-46€, Dbl 51-89€, Trpl 72-130€. *CC's:* VC, MC, AE. *Getting There: Railers,* exit the front entrance of the main train station and go left to the traffic light. Cross the street and a few meters in front of subway escalators you'll see the door for Pension Locarno on the left—push button to open. *Drivers,* parking 9€.

Hotel Eder: Zweigstr. 8 (www.hotel-eder.de) *Tel.#* 089/554-660. Located on a not-so-busy street near the main train station, this quaint mom-and-pop hotel offers very small but endearing rooms. *Price:* Sgl 50-85€, Dbl 60-130€, Trpl 90-145€—cheaper options available without shower/toilet in room. *CC's:* VC, MC, AE. *Getting There: Railers,* exit main train station on the Bayerstr. side of the station (right off platform). Cross at the traffic signal to the other side of Bayerstr. and go left. Continue along Bayerstr. passing Senefelderstr. and Schillerstr. to Zweigstr., go right. Hotel Eder will soon appear on the right. *Drivers,* park in nearby garage (14.50€) or on the street (free) outside of these hours: Mon-Sat 8:00-19:00.

Hotel ibis: (www.ibishotel.com) Standardized comfort for your convenience, the ibis chain has two amiable Munich hotels worth mentioning. **Note:* Hotel code is compatible with ibis website, creating a shortcut to the property — type hotel code into middle left box and click "OK"; next page click on "The Hotel" (left side).

ibis City: Dachauer Str. 21, tel.# 089/551-930; *hotel code 1450. Price:* (during Oktoberfest 129€, otherwise) Sgl 66-72€, Dbl 81-87€, breakfast 9€. *Getting There: Railers,* exit the front entrance of the main train station and go left to the traffic light. Cross into Dachauer Str. and continue a ways to No. 21 on the left. *Drivers,* parking 15€.

ibis Messe: (Convention Center) Otto-Lilienthal-Ring 2, tel.# 089/939-290; *hotel code 3292. Located outside of town, this ibis property is an easy option for drivers. *Price:* Sgl/Dbl 59-64€ (during conventions 129-149€), breakfast 9€. *Getting There: Drivers,* from the A99 autobahn orbiting Munich, take the Munich "Ost" interchange and merge onto the A94 towards Munich—exit at Feldkirchen Ost to reach your digs.

Hotel Marienbad: Barer Str. 11 (www.hotelmarienbad.de) *Tel.#* 089/595-585. Dating from 1850, Hotel Marienbad has accommodated a host of prominent personalities, including Sigmund Freud. The hotel offers older-style rooms situated in a pleasant, leafy neighborhood—just far enough away from the urban hubbub to preserve peace and quiet, yet close enough for guests to enjoy the city by foot. In the evening, before you crawl between the sheets, stroll through the nearby Königsplatz when it's brilliantly illuminated. *Note:* Hotel Marienbad is especially ideal for drivers, who can park for free on site. *Price:* Sgl 75-95€ (←cheaper options available without shower/toilet in room), Dbl 105-125€, apartment available 135-155€, extra bed 20€. *CC's:* VC, MC. *Getting There: Drivers,* look for Hotel Marienbad sign pointing into (concrete) lane at Barer Str. 11. *Taxi* from train station 6-7€. *Railers,* (15-min walk) exit the front entrance of the main train station and go left to the traffic light. From there, cross into Luisenstr. and continue straight through Elisenstr.—then make first right. Follow this lane as it curves along with the park. Take the next left (Meiserstr.). Make next right (Karlstr.) and then left (Barer Str.)—some 100 meters farther on the left your digs will appear (hotel sign points into lane at No. 11). Take the concrete lane, not the gravel one. *GPS:* N48° 08.624 - E11° 34.101

Alpen Hotel: Adolf-Kolping-Str. 14 (www.alpenhotel-muenchen.de) *Tel.#* 089/559-330. European ambiance coupled with stylish flair make these historic, 4-star digs a popular overnight stay. *Price:* Sgl 95-135€, Dbl 115-195€, Trpl 155-225€, junior suite 175-245€. *CC's:* VC, MC, AE. *Getting There: Railers,* exit main train station on the Bayerstr. side of the station (right off platform). Cross at the traffic signal to the other side of Bayerstr. and go left. Continue along Bayerstr. passing Senefelderstr. to Schillerstr., go right. The first street ahead on the left is Adolf-Kolping-Str, go left and the Alpen Hotel will soon appear on the left. *Drivers,* park in nearby garage (14.50€, see reception) or on the street (free) outside of these hours: Mon-Sat 8:00-19:00

Mandarin Oriental: Neuturmstr. 1 (www.mandarinoriental.com) *Tel.#* 089/290-980, toll-free reservations from USA/Canada 1-866-526-6567 or within Europe 00800-2828-3838. For travelers who can afford wallet-busting prices, stay at the Mandarin Oriental positioned within yodeling distance of Marienplatz. This premier property features spacious rooms with extraordinary amenities, including a rooftop swimming pool and terrace boasting 360-degree views. *Price:* rooms from 295€, suites from 530€.

OKTOBERFEST

September 16 (Sat) thru October 3 (Tue), 2006

If it's September, it must be Oktoberfest!

In a nutshell, the Oktoberfest is the world's biggest beer festival—an orgy of drinking, eating and singing. It all began on a joyous autumn day in October 1810, when Crown Prince Ludwig, later King Ludwig I (the fairy-tale king's grandfather), married his bride, Princess Therese von Hildburghausen. The wedding reception was such a big hit that it materialized into a weeklong party and an annual celebration—the Oktoberfest—which now attracts some 6 million beer-swilling visitors from all over the world during the two-week festival. The average price for a liter of beer—or Maß—is 7.10€.

The Oktoberfest is held on the Theresienwiese (Therese's Meadow)—locally referred to as the "Wies'n"—fairgrounds named in honor of Princess Therese, located 1km southwest of the Hauptbahnhof, or main train station. Today, the fest could really be called the Septemberfest because it's been moved up a month to take advantage of the better weather. To figure out the formula for future Oktoberfest dates is easy: It begins on the third Saturday in September and ends on the first Sunday in October (although, this year the fest has been extended two days because of a national holiday on Tuesday).

Day 1: Leading up to the official start of the Oktoberfest is the traditional opening-day parade, known as the Festival of Innkeepers, which begins in the *city at 10:45 and finishes in front of the beer tents at 11:45 *(*for good viewing, stake out an elevated spot along Schwanthalerstr.).* The parade is an hour-long procession of horse-drawn brewer wagons transporting the ceremonial first beer kegs to the fairgrounds. Riding on these wagons are the brewery owners along with their friends, family and staff (many of whom are full-bosomed fräuleins donning provocative dirndls). Additionally, you'll see the Bürgermeister—or mayor of Munich—who will tap the first keg. Once the wagons arrive at the fairgrounds, the climax is not far off. At the stroke of 12 noon—in the Schottenhamel tent—the Bürgermeister clobbers the very first keg of Oktoberfest beer with a wooden mallet and proclaims, "O'zapft is!" (It's tapped!) At that moment a cannon rings out across the Wies'n officially signaling the start of Oktoberfest and that beer can be served—precisely when determined barmaids begin the mad dash of carrying fistfuls of frothy mugs to dry-mouthed patrons crying out for beer like nesting chicks begging their mother for food. The rest of the day is a blur!

Day 2: The prelude to the second day of the Oktoberfest is another traditional parade, but this one happens to be the largest and most beautiful and historically rich folk-costume parade in the world, comprised of some 6500 participants marching in a 6-kilometer-long spectacle from Ludwigstrasse (10:00) through the city to the fairgrounds. The participants are members of folk clubs from all parts of Germany, and

Europe, proudly displaying their regional colors. This is truly a spectacle not to be missed—don't forget your camera! For a closer look at the costumes, the participants will either be drinking in the Schottenhamel tent or wandering around the Wies'n.

Facts, Oktoberfest: It takes two months for construction workers to transform the fairgrounds from an enormous asphalt expanse to a pulsating city of beer tents and roller coasters—and one month to disassemble it. • Some 6 million people will visit the fairgrounds during the 16-day event and together they will consume the same figure in liters of beer as well as 400,000 roasted chickens and 200,000 pairs of sausages. • How many steins can a waitress carry at one time? In 2002 a world record was set when a waitress carried 18 full beer steins that totaled 41kg/90lbs (a full stein weighs an average of 2.3kg/5lbs). • Within the city limits of Munich there are six breweries: Augustiner, Hofbräu, Löwenbräu, Spaten, Paulaner and Hacker-Pschorr. Primarily, each brewery is represented on the fair grounds by two tents. The word "tent," however, is wildly misleading since these massive structures are actually well-constructed beer-drinking halls that hold upwards of 5000 people. The largest of these is the Schottenhamel tent (belonging to Spaten), which holds some 10,000 people. (www.oktoberfest.de)

Tips, Oktoberfest: 1) Tents are usually full by 16:00 on weekends. If there is a line to get in, try the side and back entrances. If you still can't get in, you can usually always get a beer at Käfer Wies'n Schänke beneath Lady Bavaria.

2) You have to be seated to order a beer (with the exception of the central part of the Hofbräu tent).

3) Beer is served from 10:00 (Mon-Fri, from 9:00 Sat/Sun) and last call for alcohol is 22:30; tents start closing at 23:00 (Käfer stays open till 0:45).

4) The word "Vorsicht" the wait staff keeps shouting is a warning for you to "watch out" or "move" because they're "coming through!"

5) Ride the Ferris wheel (4€) for a sweeping view of the fairgrounds and Munich—don't forget your camera!

6) Food can be quite pricey at the Oktoberfest; consider eating at one of the delicious and pocket-friendly Turkish eateries on nearby Landwehrstr.

7) And most importantly, DO NOT wear open-toed shoes (no sandals)! Those big liter mugs are continually being broken by inebriated persons toasting a belligerent "cheers" resulting in thick glass chunks falling to the ground, which—as you can imagine—is VERY dangerous!

> *Singing:* Here's a little ditty that's the toast of the fest: *Ein prosit, ein prosit der Gemütlichkeit, (repeat) ... Oans, zwoa, drei, g'suffa!* ("A toast, a toast to your health ... One, two, three, chug-a-lug!") *Zicke, zacke, zicke, zacke, oi, oi, oi.* (Again, louder.) *Zicke, zacke, zicke, zacke, oi, oi, oi. Prosit!*

Lady Bavaria: Dating from 1850, Lady Bavaria is the glorious statue made of bronze towering 18m/59ft above the fairgrounds. Ascend the broad steps to reach her feet and a dynamite view. Or, for 2€, you can climb to the observation platform in her head (enter at back side of statue). During the Oktoberfest, Lady Bavaria is open daily from 9:00-20:00. The neoclassical structure behind her is the Ruhmeshalle—or Hall of Fame—celebrating distinguished Bavarians for their contributions to the arts, sciences or politics.

Lost & Found, Police and First Aid: Behind and above the Schottenhamel tent you'll see a white balloon with a red cross (west side of fairgrounds); the balloon is tethered to the command center for police, medical personnel and Lost & Found. **GPS:** N48° 07.945 - E11° 32.853

Getting There, Oktoberfest: **By subway,** take the U4 or U5 to Theresienwiese (one stop from the main train station, enter opposite track 11). Or, it's an easy 10-minute walk from the station—exit on the Bayerstr. side of the station (right off platform) and cross at the traffic signal into Goethestr. Continue along Goethestr. two blocks and make a right onto Landwehrstr. Behind the magnificent church in front of you is the Oktoberfest.

Drivers, from the autobahn head towards Munich. Eventually, you'll come across (or merge with) the so-called the Mittlerer Ring—take this to either the western suburbs and exit at Landsberger Str. or to the southwestern suburbs and exit at Plinganserstr. From either exit, head towards the city—the fairgrounds are within a mile. Be patient in the traffic—park in a garage or wherever you can. To beat the traffic, consider pulling into a Park + Ride (P+R) located near the autobahn. Make sure it is connected with public transportation, i.e. the subway.

DACHAU

Concentration Camp Memorial (KZ-Gedenkstätte)

Dating from 805 A.D., the picturesque market town of Dachau—elevated upon a bluff—is so pleasant that in the 16th century the Wittelsbach royal family built a Renaissance palace here to take advantage of the far-reaching views of the Bavarian capital some 20km to the south.

Fast-forward four centuries and a cluster of munitions factories were constructed a few miles outside of town to sustain the German army during World War I. In 1918, the government collapsed, Germany surrendered, and the factories were abandoned. In January 1933, the German people voted for a new chancellor—the winner was a blue-eyed Austrian named Adolf Hitler, who had sinister plans for Dachau's abandoned factories.

Hitler converted the derelict buildings into an internment camp for enemies of the Nazi state, such as Communists and Monarchists. Later these enemies were to include gypsies, anti-socials, homosexuals, Jews, political dissidents, members of the clergy, and so-called racially inferior individuals. On March 21, 1933, the following announcement appeared in the Munich newspaper, setting the precedent for what was to come: "Tomorrow, the first concentration camp, with accommodations for 5000 detainees, will open in the neighborhood of Dachau. We have adopted this measure in the certainty that our actions will help to restore stability to our nation and it is in the best interests of our people. — Heinrich Himmler, Chief of Munich Police."

By 1937, the influx of detainees expanded well beyond the camp's capacity of 5000 and the SS (camp administrators, watchdogs or thugs) ordered the inmates to build a new, larger camp. The project was completed in the summer of 1938 and the camp remained this way until after the war. During the camp's 12-year existence—1933-45—files show that upwards of 200,000 prisoners passed through its main gate emblazoned with the deceiving words, *Arbeit Macht Frei* (Work Will Set You Free).

When American troops liberated the camp on April 29, 1945, they witnessed a ghastly scene of horror. Emaciated corpses lay everywhere—the stench of death permeated the camp. Of the 30,000 inmates still alive—1230 of these were too weak and died shortly thereafter from starvation or disease. All told, more than 43,000 prisoners died at Dachau and its satellite camps.

On April 29, 2005—the 60th anniversary of the camp's liberation—the above-mentioned *Arbeit Macht Frei* gate was reopened and is now the camp's official entrance in which you will walk through. Anniversaries here are special, marked by remembrance, reverence and reconciliation, but in 2005 the ceremonies were extra poignant because the survivors wanted to return and be the first to walk through the gate as free men. And they did!

To the Nazis, Dachau was symbolic, as it was their first concentration camp and the model for all future camps in Hitler's Reich, or empire. Many of Hitler's top henchmen were trained at Dachau, such as Adolf Eichmann (chief executioner of the Holocaust), Rudolf Hoess (commandant of Auschwitz), and Theodor Eicke (first commandant of Dachau, promoted to Inspector of Concentration Camps. Eicke systematized the inhumane treatment of prisoners in conjunction with the creation of the feared SS Death's Head units).

By mid-1939, six main camps existed in Germany, containing some 20,000 detainees. Once the war began—September 1939—the Einsatzgruppen (or special action squads) amassed scores of new prisoners from the conquered territories, allowing Theodor Eicke to expand his infamous network of concentration camps to the east, mainly Poland. By 1944, nearly 300 camps were in existence, some specifically for the sole purpose of extermination, e.g. Auschwitz, Sobibor, Belzec and Treblinka. By war's end, some 40,000 SS guards were engaged in upholding this part of Nazi Germany.

On account of Hitler's unspeakable crimes, this resurgent 1200-year-old suburb of Munich will forever be associated with spineless murder and emaciated bodies locked behind steel gates. Nonetheless, the population of Dachau today is 40,000 strong and growing. New housing and commercial developments are wildly springing up and the concentration camp—formerly miles from town—is now part of Dachau proper. Amazingly, as you stroll the grounds, you'll see newish townhouses abutting the memorial. Imagine how glum backyard cookouts must be.

To experience the camp at Dachau—while solemn—is worth your time. Expect to spend between two and three hours here. Prior to entering, stop in at the visitor's info kiosk (portable) to pick up the memorial site pamphlet-guide (Wegweiser, 50¢) containing a map and brief descriptions. You can also arrange a tour here, see _Tours_ below. Toilets are also here.

On the memorial grounds themselves there are only two barracks left standing, and both have been reconstructed—one is closed and the other we recommend you walk through. Originally, the camp had 34 barracks. Today, only the foundations remain representing the other 32. Multilingual info boards are posted throughout the camp. (www.kz-gedenkstaette-dachau.de)

Hours: (closed Monday) Tue-Sun 9:00-17:00. _Price:_ Free entry!

Museum: The German-English museum, set in the former administration building, documents the camp's history as well as atrocities committed. At the beginning of the museum is the bookshop and midway through is a theater that screens a thought-provoking, 22-minute documentary: Tue-Sun, English, 11:30, 14:00 and 1530 (confirm times upon arrival)—in summer, start lining up 10 min prior to show time.

Tours: For a complete, do-it-yourself tour of the camp, rent an audio guide (available at visitor's info kiosk prior to entering memorial site): adult 3€, student 2€. _Note:_ Must leave ID as deposit. Tours average between two and three hours; the length of time is up to you. Guided tours with a camp representative are also possible, generally Thur & Sat/Sun 12:00 (orientation tour, 1.50€/30min) and 13:00 (comprehensive, 3€/2.5hr)—times are seasonal, verify prior to, or upon, your arrival. Inquire about—or pay for—tours within the abovementioned visitor's info kiosk. Another recommended tour option is to book one in Munich with **Radius tours** (and bikes), located opposite track (Gleis) 32 in the main train station. Tours depart in the morning Tue-Sun year round from their office in the station. The cost is 19€/person including transportation (train and bus); duration five hours. (www.radiusmunich.com) Call or stop by for departure times and/or further details: _Tel.#_ 089/5502-9374

Getting There: To reach the memorial camp at Dachau will take roughly 45 minutes from central Munich (first subway, then bus). _Railers,_ take the S-Bahn (S2) direction Petershausen and get off at Dachau. (_Note:_ This will require an XXL ticket; buy the day ticket, or Tageskarte, which will cover the entire trip, subway+bus both ways [for ticket types see page 187—_Subway_]. Holders of a Eurail consecutive-day or dated Flexi/Select pass ride _free_ on the S-Bahn.) Outside the Dachau train station, veer left to catch bus #726 to KZ-Gedenkstätte (camp memorial) [7-min ride—bus departs every 20 min; on Sundays every 40 min]. _By foot,_ from Dachau station it's possible to walk into the "Altstadt"—or Old Town—(to the Wittelsbach royal palace) or to the camp memorial. Outside the station a red-and-white sign points the way: to the camp memorial (KZ-Gedenkstätte, 50 min); to the Altstadt/Schloss (Old Town/royal palace, 20 min). _Drivers,_ from central Munich take Dachauer Str. (north of train station) several kilometers—

eventually you'll see signs pointing KZ-Gedenkstätte (camp memorial); follow these to the parking lot. • From the A99 autobahn exit at Ludwigsfeld and head towards Dachau. • From the A8 autobahn (northwest) exit at Dachau and follow the KZ-Gedenkstätte (camp memorial) signs to the parking lot. *Note:* To park in lot costs 2€. Beware—they lock it at 17:45! *GPS:* N48° 15.962 - E11° 28.249

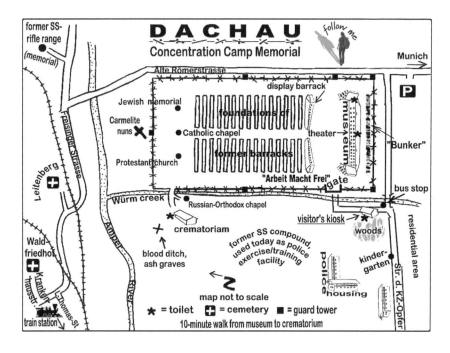

Dachau, *KZ-Lager*, 1945

Konzentrationslager (concentration camp), abbr. KZ-Lager

We frequently get asked how the camp appeared during the days of its hellish past, thus we drew up a dated map together with some descriptions (listed below). Additionally, for those who have wheels, we've included a few sites near the camp worth visiting.

Barracks: Originally, there were 34 barracks (also called *blocks*). Two of these exist today as reconstructions, but only one is open to the public. Within its confines, visitors get a decent idea of how prisoners slept and washed. Each barrack was built to house 208 inmates (with the exception of the first four blocks, which were used as a canteen, morgue and infirmary). Near the end of the war, the Nazis relocated thousands of prisoners to Dachau from camps in the east. With nowhere to put these new arrivals, the Nazis grossly overcrowded the barracks with upwards of 2000 prisoners each. In fact, when the Americans liberated Dachau on April 29, 1945, members of the 45th "Thunderbird" Division came across 39 boxcars belonging to a transport train that had been neglected by the Nazis—inside were the rotting corpses of some 2310 prisoners.

Post WWII, the camp and barracks were used to accommodate displaced persons and refugees from the war until the 1960s, when the barracks were pulled down for hygienic reasons and the camp was opened as a memorial.

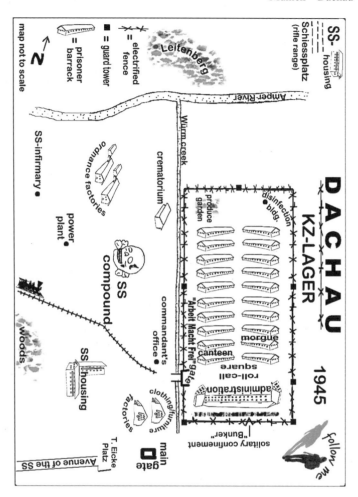

Crematorium: Initially there were two ovens—another four were added with the influx of prisoners after the war began, including a gas chamber disguised as showers (never used). The ovens could convert bodies to ash in roughly 90 minutes at temperatures upwards of 1000°F. The ashes were then dumped behind the building. Today, these ash graves are marked by cenotaphs for all to see.

Roll-Call Square: In the camp's wide gravel expanse prisoners were forced to assemble twice a day for roll call, typically 6 a.m. and 6 p.m. Evening roll call often took longer because the guards made absolutely sure that all prisoners were present and accounted for. If the number of prisoners did not match the morning's tally, they had to remain standing—regardless of weather—until the correct number was reached or the missing person was found; sometimes this took hours, even over night in freezing conditions. It wasn't uncommon during one of these episodes that a prisoner(s) collapsed and his dead body carried off the plaza. Conditions were so unbearable that some prisoners put an end to their suffering by purposely stepping into the prohibited zone—narrow perimeter surrounding the camp directly in front of the electrified fence—to draw deadly fire from the guards.

Bunker: Behind the museum, formerly the camp administration building, is the so-called Bunker, built in 1938 during renovations to the original site. The Bunker—now open as part of the museum exhibition—was the center of terror within the camp; an island of detention, or solitary confinement, where SS guards mistreated and tortured prisoners for indefinite amounts of time—extra-thick walls and double doors were implemented to prevent cries from being heard outside. Prisoners were fed meagerly for the day, if at all, while kept in complete darkness for weeks or months on end. An unknown number of prisoners were driven to commit suicide. In 1944, another form of torture was introduced: standing cells, which were only a few feet wide and installed to prevent select prisoners from lying or sitting (up to 72 hours at a time). When it was decided to execute a prisoner, he was dragged into the courtyard by guards and shot. For more than five years, Georg Elser—man accused of trying to assassinate Hitler in the Bürgerbräu Keller (on Nov 8, 1939)—was jailed in the Bunker as a so-called privileged prisoner. Days before the camp's liberation in 1945, he was murdered. Post-WWII, the US military used the Bunker to confine Nazis who were on trial for war crimes, notoriously those charged with the Malmédy massacre (when 84 US POWs were taken to a field in Malmédy, Belgium, during the Battle of the Bulge on Dec 17, 1944, and machine-gunned by troops belonging to Col. Joachim Peiper's SS division). Forty-three of the accused, including Peiper, were sentenced to death. However, in a rare reversal of justice, none of the death sentences were carried out and all of the accused were released by 1956. (Justice eventually caught up with Peiper in 1976 when alleged French communists firebombed his house with him trapped inside—the perpetrators were never caught.)

SS Compound: An electric fence, a pair of guard towers, a moat, and a swiftly flowing creek separated the SS garrison from the prisoners. Within the SS compound, guards were schooled in their sadistic profession and warehouses were crammed with the personal belongings of their victims, e.g. spectacles, shoes, clothing. Additionally, the prisoners were used as a cheap labor force to work within the on-site ordnance factories to supply Hitler's war machine. The former SS compound, three times larger than the prison camp, is used today as a police training facility. Many of the original buildings still remain and can be seen through the fence just past the kindergarten on Strasse der KZ-Opfer (Street of the Concentration Camp Victims).

SS Rifle Range: Located some 2.5km from the Dachau camp memorial is the former SS rifle range, where guards executed between 4000 and 6000 Soviet prisoners in 1941-42. The firing lanes are still present, including a concrete bunker peppered with bullet holes. The former SS housing is still partially intact, inhabited by renters capitalizing on cheap accommodations (if not offered free by the state). Expect a visit to take 15 min. *Getting There: Drivers,* from the Dachau camp memorial, take the road (Alte Römerstrasse) north paralleling the camp to the junction, where you'll turn right and then left following the white sign "Gedenkstätte Schießplatz." *GPS:* N48° 17.126 - E11° 27.639

Leitenberg: In April 1945, scores of Allied planes continuously flew over the camp and the rattle of gunfire could be heard in the distance. The prisoners knew liberation was imminent, but many were weak. The Leitenberg cemetery is the final resting place to more than 7400 unknown prisoners who died only days—even hours—before freedom arrived. The cemetery is a lonely place located some 4km from the Dachau camp memorial. Expect a visit to take around 30 min. From the cemetery parking lot, a path running adjacent to the utility building leads to a number of steps ascending to the cemetery (5-min walk). At the top, follow the gravel path left. Once through the pointy gate opening into the cemetery you'll see (left) a remembrance to the Polish prisoners buried here. The path solemnly meanders past graves marked only by numbered bricks. Out the other side of the cemetery, follow the path straight to an Italian memorial guarded by stone tigers. From there, retrace your steps and make the first right. This route descends past the stages of the cross and ends in the parking lot. *Getting There: Drivers,* Leitenberg is located some 4km from the Dachau camp memorial. From there, take the road (Alte Römerstrasse) north paralleling the camp to the junction and turn left—1.5km farther turn right on Leitenweg (following small white sign *"KZ-Friedhof auf der Leiten"*). Make the next left into the spacious gravel parking lot. *GPS:* N48° 16.526 - E11° 26.738

Waldfriedhof: This "Forest cemetery" is actually the Dachau town cemetery, the final resting place to the 1230 prisoners who died from starvation or disease shortly after the camp's liberation. After entering the cemetery, go right and ascend the path to an elongated, white building. Opposite this are the graves; in the background you'll see the quaint St. Stephan's church. Expect a visit to take 15 min. *Getting There: Drivers,* Waldfriedhof is located some 6.5km from the Dachau camp memorial. From there, take the road (Alte Römerstrasse) north paralleling the camp to the junction and turn left. A few kilometers farther you'll pass over train tracks; continue straight nearly a kilometer and turn right on Krankenhausstr.—the cemetery is at the end of this road. *GPS:* N48° 16.024 - E11° 25.857

Adolf Hitler

Adolf Hitler absorbed the world with his fanatical ideology as Germany's dictator for 12 long years, 1933 to 1945. The architect of the infamous Third Reich came not from the Junker class associated with land-owning Prussian aristocracy but from very humble Austrian roots.

Adolf was born on April 20, 1889, in Braunau am Inn, Austria, to Alois (Schickelgruber) Hitler, a customs officer, and to Klara Pölzl, a farmer's daughter, who was Alois' niece and former nursemaid to his ailing wife.

Alois was born the illegitimate son of Maria Schickelgruber on June 7, 1837, in a rural community 100km northwest of Vienna. (Even today the mystery remains as to who fathered Alois. At the time he was conceived, Maria Schickelgruber worked for a wealthy Jewish man who allegedly had a frisky son, spawning rumors that Adolf's grandfather had Jewish blood). Nevertheless, five years later, Maria Schickelgruber married Georg Hiedler, a drifting mill worker. Maria died a few years after the wedding and Georg resumed his vagabond lifestyle, leaving young Alois to be raised by his brother, Johann Hiedler.

Curiously, in 1876—some 30 years later—Johann insisted that Alois change his name from Schickelgruber to Hiedler. As a result, when making the change, Alois' birth certificate was altered from "illegitimate" to "legitimate," as records did show that a Herr Hiedler indeed married a Frau Schickelgruber. Although interesting, it was the next part of the name-changing procedure that made the history books. The administering official misspelled Hiedler as Hitler, and amazingly this blatant mistake was of no concern to Alois or his stepfather—Johann—and thus the name Hitler stuck.

After the death of Alois' second wife, he married Klara Pölzl, his 24-year-old niece (granddaughter of Johann Hiedler). The wedding took place in Braunau am Inn on the morning of January 7, 1885—by lunchtime Alois was back at work and Klara was left to care for his two children from his previous marriage. Four years later, after giving birth to three children who died shortly thereafter, Klara gave birth to their fourth child: Adolf.

As a customs officer in a border town, Alois was always busy at work, which left Klara to raise young Adolf. Within a few years, Alois was promoted at work and transferred to another office in the town of Leonding, a suburb of Linz, where he later died in 1903 after settling into retirement.

In the spring of 1906, Klara allowed her 17-year-old son to visit Vienna, the capital of art, music, opera and the Habsburg dynasty. Adolf fell in love with the city's charm and decided to move there permanently. On December 21, 1907, tragedy struck—Adolf lost his mother to breast cancer. This was a devastating blow to the young 18-year-old, who had already lost his father.

It was the next five and a half years that radically shaped Adolf's racist views. He became disillusioned with Vienna, concluding that the empire's capital was filled with Jews who soaked every cent from his wallet. In another blow dealt to Hitler, his dream of becoming a famous artist was quashed when the Academy of Fine Arts turned him down a second time. He was devastated, living penniless like a bum on the streets, freezing cold without proper clothing or food. Eventually, he found his way into a men's shelter where he lived in a room no bigger than a jail cell. Here, Adolf painted postcards of Viennese landmarks to sell to tourists. Unsuccessful, he developed a passion for politics and an unshakable case of anti-Semitism. Vienna served its purpose for the history books and Adolf—a poor, parentless soul, searching for his calling in life—boarded a train for Munich on May 24, 1913. It wasn't until 25 years later that Adolf Hitler would return to Vienna, but this time as the Führer of the Third Reich and the master of its people.

HiTLER'S MUNiCH, 1914-1945

Do-It-Yourself Tour

Hitler regarded Munich a true German city. It was here that the Nazi party was born and the Beer Hall Putsch catapulted a rebellion into an empire. During his stay, Hitler developed a magnetism that mesmerized the masses and convinced the cynical, inspiring their immediate loyalty. (Concerning the latter, we wonder if people would have reacted with the same fervor if he carried his original family name: Adolf Schickelgruber).

So that history buffs can witness and learn the whereabouts of an aspiring dictator— as well as the rise of the Nazi party—we have compiled the following chronological journey through Hitler's Munich, from 1914 to 1945.

Note: If you get the chance, check out the enthralling collection of National Socialist regalia in the City Museum (page 197); free admission on Sunday.

Elisabethplatz: On the west corner of "Elisabeth's Square" you'll see a turn-of-the-century clock tower building, where Hitler took basic military training after the outbreak of World War I. The building is now a vocational school.

Early 1914, while living in his first Munich accommodations—an ordinary room on the third floor at Schleissheimerstrasse 34—there was a knock on the door. It was a police officer ordering him to the station. Hitler's native land, Austria, required him for military duty. He reported to the nearest post, Salzburg, and was found "unfit for service." Disenchanted, Hitler returned to Munich and continued life as a struggling artist. On June 28, 1914, however, the world changed forever. Francis Ferdinand, heir to the Austro-Hungarian throne, was assassinated in Sarajevo, Bosnia, sparking the First World War. Already rejected by the Austrian army, Hitler requested permission to join the Bavarian army. On August 16th, he was accepted into the 16th Infantry Regiment. Filled with emotion, Hitler forever celebrated this date as if it were his birthday. For on this "soldier's birthday" in mid-August, Hitler could finally devote his life to duty and discipline for a united Germany.

After Hitler was elected chancellor of Germany, August 16th became a day of celebration. Old army buddies would stop by Hitler's office to wish the former corporal a happy "soldier's birthday" while others hoisted the iconic red, white and black Nazi battle flag over his old regiment's headquarters that was aptly renamed, Adolf Hitler Barracks.

Loth Street Barracks: (*GPS:* N48° 09.477 - E11° 33.626) After World War I, Hitler was posted to the barracks on Lothstrasse with the Royal Bavarian 2nd Infantry Regiment. While living at these digs, Hitler discovered the DAP (German Workers' Party) in 1919—the precursor to the Nazi party—and became a seasoned public speaker before moving back into civilian life on March 31, 1920. Although the former barracks have been renovated into office buildings, the original fence posts remain either side of the main structure, which is located on the bend in the road where Lothstr. and Winzererstr. meet. Across from the former barracks is an old weathered obelisk honoring the fallen members of the 2nd Infantry Regiment from 1682-1918.

Sternecker Bräu: (*GPS:* N48° 08.146 - E11° 34.843) This is where it all began, the birthplace of the Nazi party. After World War I, Hitler's army unit assigned him to investigate the radical political parties that were multiplying in Munich. In September 1919, Hitler was ordered to attend a meeting of the DAP (Deutsche Arbeiterpartei, or German Workers' Party) at the Sternecker Bräu, an old beer hall located within a stone's throw from one of Munich's medieval city gates: the 14th-century Isartor.

Once the guest speaker finished his talk on Bavaria's succession from Prussia, Hitler decided to leave the meeting and report the DAP as a harmless fly-by-night party. At that

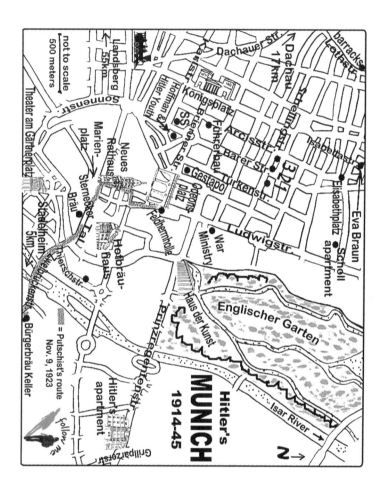

moment, a free discussion period was announced and Hitler readily volunteered. His impassioned speech of a united Germany so impressed the party's founder, Anton Drexler—a toolmaker with the state railroad—that he shoved some DAP literature in the blue-eyed Austrian's hand and invited him to the next meeting.

At the second gathering, Anton eagerly petitioned for Hitler's membership. In response, Hitler asked the handful of members the party's goals. Their answers were vague at best. He learned the DAP was more of a social club than a political party to better the future of Germany. Although initially disappointed, Hitler considered that perhaps the DAP was exactly what he had been searching for: a party looking for leadership. Hitler approached his army unit with the membership proposition and they encouraged him to join. Thus, Hitler's destiny was decided for him, and in the back room of the smoke-filled Sternecker Bräu, Adolf Hitler received party membership No. 7.

Within a few months of joining, Hitler took command of the adolescent DAP and established a party HQ in the Sternecker Bräu. His first office was a small, dimly lit room with a lamp, telephone, desk, a pair of cabinets, and a few chairs dragged in from the beer hall. In the late summer of 1920, Hitler changed the party's name from DAP to the NSDAP, "Nationalsozialistische Deutsche Arbeiterpartei," or the National Socialist German Workers' Party, or universally: the Nazis.

The former Sternecker Bräu can be found at Tal street 38. Today, it is a bedroom design store—other than a fresh paint job, the original facade is much the same.

Hofbräuhaus: As you probably already know, the Hofbräuhaus is the world's most famous beer hall. Here, in Bavaria, beer halls are a novelty for tourists and a tradition with locals. Consequently, they do a lucrative trade. Some 80 years ago, these same beer halls were the nerve center of revolutionary credos—the ideal venue for leaders of political groups to spread their party's message to throngs of working-class citizens.

During the Third Reich, Hitler's regime torched synagogues, ransacked Jewish stores, looted art galleries, raided churches, renamed or relocated age-old landmarks, and stamped out confessional schools—but it went to great lengths not to interfere with Germany's institutionalized beer halls.

It was in the Hofbräuhaus that the Nazis held their first large-scale meetings. On October 16, 1919, one month after Hitler joined the DAP, or German Workers' Party, the political group sent out flyers announcing a public gathering at the Hofbräuhaus—70 people attended. The second such meeting at the same venue attracted an enormous standing-room-only crowd, packing more than 2000 people into the Festsaal (where the Heimatabend is held today). The momentous date was February 24, 1920, and Hitler outlined the party's new 25-point program, in which he centered on Lebensraum for Germany (extra territory for its people); due justice to undesirables and criminals of the fatherland; retraction of the Versailles Treaty; a united Germany similar to Bismarck's Second Reich; and finally, Hitler proposed if Germany were to be revitalized back to its glory days the government must not yield to outside pressures, instead it must unite as one centralized body and rule with an iron fist. When Hitler finished his semi-calculated speech, he wiped the perspiration from his brow and exited the Hofbräuhaus to thunderous applause. As the Nazi party grew, Hitler returned every year to the Hofbräuhaus on the anniversary of the 25-point program to stand atop a table and informally preach of a greater Reich. His visits lessened after becoming chancellor and eventually stopped after the Nazi boot stepped into Poland kick-starting WWII.

Thierschstrasse: (*GPS:* N48° 08.191 - E11° 35.256) The same day Hitler was discharged from the army to become a civilian—March 31, 1920—he moved into a tiny room at Thierschstrasse 41. His accommodations were dark and dingy and no bigger than his room at the men's shelter in Vienna. It was here that Hitler lived as an unknown World War I veteran; where he premeditated the Beer Hall Putsch in 1923; and moved back in as a hero of the movement after completing his jail term in December 1924. By the time Hitler moved out in September 1929, he was the leader of the second most powerful party in the nation. Today, the building has been renovated and can only be viewed externally (located one block south of the King Max II statue on Maximilianstrasse).

Bürgerbräu Keller: On the evening of November 8, 1923, the Bürgerbräu Keller—an enormous beer hall—was the scene of the famous Beer Hall Putsch (coup d'état). The smoke-filled Bürgerbräu Keller was jam-packed with 4000 citizens who had come to hear the three leaders of the Bavarian government speak about the problems plaguing the nation. The meeting of this "triumvirate" was a golden opportunity for Hitler to ensnare the main power brokers of the state government in one swoop. *The following is a summary of what happened that evening as well as the cast of characters.*

Key Nazi Putschists: **Adolf Hitler**; **General Erich von Ludendorff** (Hitler's trump card, who was a greatly respected WWI hero); **Hermann Göring** (also a respected WWI hero; later Reichsmarschall of the Luftwaffe, or German air force); **Rudolf Hess** (Hitler's deputy, who made international headlines when he flew to Scotland in 1941 to forge a peace plan with the British. He spent the rest of his life in Spandau prison, Berlin); **Ernst Röhm** (leader of the SA, storm troopers or brown shirts—military arm of the Nazi party. Hitler had Röhm killed in 1934); **Heinrich Himmler** (loyal to Röhm in 1923; Himmler later became the chief of all Nazi police forces, including the Gestapo, SD and SS).

Heads of Bavarian State Govt., a.k.a the "Triumvirate": **Gustav von Kahr** (Minister President); **General Otto von Lossow** (head of the Bavarian army); **Colonel Hans Ritter von Seisser** (chief of police).

Beer Hall Putsch: On November 8, 1923, Hitler arrived at the Bürgerbräu Keller just after 8 p.m. with a small entourage. He leaned against a pillar while the crowd listened to the first speaker, Gustav von Kahr. Although a non-drinker, Hitler ordered a beer to blend in to the alcohol-soaked atmosphere. Since Germany was grappling with a hyperinflation crisis at the time, Hitler's beer cost one billion marks.

A half hour after Hitler's arrival—at 8:30 p.m.—the action began. Truckloads of Nazi storm troopers surrounded the building while Hermann Göring rushed in with a team of men armed with guns. Hitler dropped his beer, brandished a pistol and headed for the podium. Panic set in, tables were overturned and beer mugs smashed onto the floor. Hitler waved his pistol and appealed for calm; when the chaos continued, he fired a shot into the ceiling. The crowd went silent and Hitler announced, "The national revolution has broken out! The hall is surrounded!" Hitler subsequently instructed that nobody leave the building and then escorted the triumvirate into the back room.

The first part of Hitler's putsch, or coup, was going according to plan. Now, he just needed to convince the triumvirate to side with his party before marching on Berlin. After receiving passive support from his three captives, Hitler went back into the hall and spoke to the concerned crowd, proclaiming the triumvirate was in agreement with his plan to oust the central government in Berlin. Within minutes the crowd was shouting "Ja" in support of his putsch. Meanwhile, as planned, Ernst Röhm's storm troopers were seizing the Bavarian War Ministry. Hitler was ecstatic!

Hitler then received word that a group of his putschists were running into some troubles downtown. Hitler—his heart racing—had to think quickly. He decided to leave the Bürgerbräu Keller and handle the problem in person. Before his departure, Hitler left General Ludendorff in charge. The moment Hitler exited the beer hall, the triumvirate promised to support the putsch and asked if they could be excused to start setting up the new government. Ludendorff, an honorable Prussian, believed the men and subsequently released them. When Hitler returned a short time later, he nearly coughed up a cat upon hearing the news that his political prisoners had been set free. The general explained to Hitler that their release would benefit the movement. The time was around 10:30 p.m.

In the course of the next eight hours, stories flooded in to Hitler's camp that the triumvirate had broken their promise and army units from neighboring cities were on their way to quell the putsch.

Dawn broke to a frosty winter's morning on November 9. Time was running short and Hitler's Nazis had to devise a counter move. The focus centered on Ernst Röhm—accompanied by Heinrich Himmler—and the captured War Ministry. (Story continued, see next entry—*War Ministry.*)

Bürgerbräu Keller & Georg Elser: After Hitler was elected Germany's chancellor in 1933, he returned annually to the Bürgerbräu Keller on November 8 to reenact the putsch by making a speech and walking the route they took on the morning of the 9th in memory of those who died for the movement on that historic Nazi day. It was during one of these reenactments that the Bürgerbräu Keller became the location of another historic event. On November 8, 1939, Georg Elser planted a bomb next to the podium to assassinate Hitler. Alas, Hitler cut his speech short and left the building earlier than usual. The bomb exploded shortly thereafter, severely damaging the hall and killing seven. Elser was apprehended and sent to Dachau concentration camp. Once there, he was accused of working with British spies in a plot to kill Hitler. Curiously, in light of these treasonous charges, Elser was treated as a privileged prisoner (many were executed on the spot for far less crimes in the Reich), which leads many historians to speculate that the plot was actually devised by the Nazis so the blame could be placed on the British, thus gaining public support for a war against Britain. Nevertheless, Elser's fate was almost certainly sealed well before the assassination attempt and he was murdered days before the liberation of Dachau, April 1945.

The Bürgerbräu Keller has since been torn down and is now the Gasteig, an enormous brick structure housing the City Library; Munich's Philharmonic Orchestra along with a 2400-seat clam-shaped theater; the Richard Strauss Conservatory; and an adult education center, all for the cheap price of 150€ million.

At the side of the Gasteig is a *plaque embedded in the ground to commemorate Georg Elser's sacrifice (*on Hilton hotel side of building follow two white stripes on ground leading from horn fountain. *GPS:* N48° 07.837 - E11° 35.539). It reads: "At this location, in the former Bürgerbräu Keller, Johann Georg Elser, a carpenter, tried on November 8, 1939, to assassinate Adolf Hitler. He wanted to put an end to the Nazi terror regime. The plan failed and he was consequently jailed at Dachau concentration camp for 5½ years before being murdered on April 9, 1945."

War Ministry: Ernst Röhm and his 150-man SA detachment stormed into the War Ministry compound to little opposition and immediately seized General Otto von Lossow's headquarters. (Röhm formerly worked at the ministry and new the layout.) Röhm ordered his men to secure the premises with barbed wire and machine-gun emplacements. Amazingly, after locking down just about every inch of the War Ministry, he neglected the building's lifeline: the switchboard. This left an operator loyal to the government to relay General von Lossow's orders to dispatch all army units from neighboring cities to Munich. It wasn't until several hours later that Röhm realized his mistake and arrested the operator, but the damage had been already done!

By early next morning, Röhm and his SA found themselves under siege by the Bavarian army and state police. (Story continued, see next entry—*Feldherrnhalle*.) The War Ministry is now the Bavarian State Archives and can be found three blocks north of the Feldherrnhalle, at the corner of Ludwigstr. and Schönfeldstr.

Feldherrnhalle: (General's Hall) Late morning November 9, 1923, Hitler and his men received word at the Bürgerbräu Keller that Röhm's forces were surrounded. Hitler had two options: 1) either head 40km south to Rosenheim (next largest city and birthplace of Hermann Göring) and try to revive the putsch from there before they, too, were surrounded, or 2) march on the War Ministry and rescue Röhm.

Hitler, Ludendorff, Hess, Göring, and other key Nazis decided on the latter, to rescue Röhm. Just before noon, Hitler and 2000 of his followers donned their battle gear and assembled in parade formation. Hitler led the swastika-draped formation—a tide of men shouldering rifles and sporting either their work clothes or steel-gray army uniforms—through the streets of Munich to the War Ministry. (Nazis would emulate this historical march for the following 20 years.)

As the procession headed along Rosenheimer Str. and onto Zweibrückenstr., throngs of Nazi supporters lined the streets and waved swastikas; many joined the march. Their route led them past the Isartor (14th-century city gate) and onto Tal street passing the

Sternecker Bräu, birthplace of the Nazi party. The putschists then marched through Marienplatz, where they looked up and saw swastikas waving from the windows either side of the Glockenspiel. Subsequently, they turned right onto Weinstr. continuing for three blocks before turning right on Perusastr. and then, finally, left on Residenz str. Here, only a few blocks shy of the War Ministry, their march would come to a grinding halt.

At the point where Residenzstr. meets the Feldherrnhalle, the state police had set up a roadblock with barbed wire and a multitude of men. The putschists could go no farther. Röhm appeared stranded. Eye to eye, bayonets fixed, the putschists and police squared off. Suddenly, a shot rang out, triggering both sides—everyone scattered to evade the hail of bullets. When the firing stopped, the putsch was over and the body count began: 16 Nazis and 4 policemen had been killed. Hitler and Hess were sent to prison in Landsberg am Lech; Hermann Göring was badly wounded and avoided arrest by fleeing the country; and General Erich von Ludendorff was pardoned.

In front of the Feldherrnhalle you'll find a plaque embedded in the cobblestones (post-Third Reich; left side when facing the structure) memorializing the four policemen who died that day in the struggle. It reads: "The members of the Bavarian State Police who gave their lives in the skirmish against the Nazi putschists on Nov. 9, 1923: Friedrich Fink, Nikolaus Hollweg, Max Schobert, Rudolf Schraut."

During the Third Reich, the Nazis created their own memorial here, which was erected on the Residenzstr. side of the Feldherrnhalle—wreaths were laid, guards were posted, and all passersby had to hail the Nazi salute.

Landsberg Prison: refer to (page 175) chapter *Romantic Road*—Landsberg am Lech.

Schellingstrasse: From the mid-1920s until the early '30s, Hitler spent a great deal of time on Schellingstrasse, a few blocks west of the university.

1) Let's start at the pumpkin-colored facade at Schellingstrasse 50 (*GPS:* N48° 09.047 - E11° 34.417). Heinrich Hoffman's photography studio was located here, where in 1929 Hitler first met Eva Braun, his future wife. Above the door you'll see the very-worn forerunner to the iconic Third Reich eagle. In the back of the building the Nazis held their party's headquarters from 1925-31.

2) Face the eagle then walk left and cross at the traffic light. On the corner is the five-story Schelling Salon, an early Hitler favorite. The Salon, still run by the Mehr family (original owners), is the last bistro of its kind from the 19th century (1872) in the trendy university suburb of Schwabing. What used to be one of the finest eateries in town has simmered to students playing pool in between classes and pensioners chatting about days past while nursing their beers. Consider stopping in for lunch, the food's not bad and the prices are just right—be sure to check out the original, turn-of-the-century toilets.

3) Continue along Schellingstrasse in the same direction and on the next corner you'll discover the Osteria Italiana, Munich's oldest Italian restaurant (est. 1890) and another Hitler favorite. He spent many hours here preaching to his disciples over a fine meal. The Osteria Italiana (formerly "Osteria Bavaria") doesn't look like much from the outside but it's a cozy gem from Munich's past on the inside—(pricey; can be smoky; romantic courtyard). Schellingstr. 62. *Hours:* Mon-Sat 12:00-14:30 & 18:30-23:00. *Tel.#* 089/272-0307

Hitler's Apartment: (*GPS:* N48° 08.339 - E11° 36.450) After a decade of impassioned public speaking—from beer halls to major auditoriums—Hitler rose the political ranks from a loner with a message to the leader of the nation's second most powerful party. With this awesome responsibility came new digs. In 1929, Hitler left his shabby room at Thierschstrasse 41 and moved across the Isar River to an upmarket part of town, where he settled into a nine-room apartment that spanned the entire first floor (one level up) at Prinzregentenplatz 16.

Hitler provided rooms for the domestic help and one for his half-sister's 21-year-old daughter, Geli Raubal, who was pursuing a medical career in Munich. Like his father, Hitler had romantic feelings for his niece. Geli was the only woman in Hitler's life, other than his mother, that he truly loved. The two went out on dates together but Hitler refused to show her any public affection. Moreover, Hitler assigned guards to escort her every move; Geli felt smothered and considered Hitler her jailor. As a result, she experienced chronic depression. This came to an abrupt end in the early hours of September 18, 1931, when she was found in her room with a pistol in her hand and a bullet through her heart. Hitler never entered her room again. It is still debated whether they ever had sexual relations. John Toland—in his book "Adolf Hitler"—doubts they ever did. In Ernest Pope's book—"Munich Playground"—he writes, according to a reliable source, "Geli shot herself after an unwilling incestual night with her wild-eyed uncle."

In September 1938, another momentous occasion took place at Prinzregentenplatz 16—Hitler and Neville Chamberlain, Britain's prime minister, signed a historic peace agreement. An exuberant Chamberlain flew back to Britain and gave his famous speech in front of No. 10 Downing Street: "I believe it is peace in our time!" Less than a year later the German army smashed across the Polish frontier and Chamberlain was a cooked goose.

Hitler's former apartment building, at the corner of Prinzregentenstr. and Grill-parzerstr., is now a district police station.

Eva Braun: Eva Braun—the daughter of a schoolteacher—was born in an apartment building at *Isabellastrasse 45 on February 6, 1912. (*GPS: N48° 09.582 - E11° 34.384). Braun's claim to fame was her 15-year affair with Germany's Caesar equivalent—Adolf Hitler—whom she later married before committing suicide.

Braun first met Hitler in 1929 at Heinrich Hoffman's photo studio, where she worked. Their meeting came at a time when Hitler was already infatuated with another girl, Geli Raubal, his niece.

Either Hitler was the amorous James Bond-type who the babes couldn't live without or he preferred to date extremely insecure women because they all had the uncanny urge to commit suicide. First it was Raubal in 1931, who succeeded. Then it was Braun's turn in 1932, and again in 1935—both times were unsuccessful; and finally, Lady Unity Mitford, daughter of an English lord and a close acquaintance of Hitler, successfully committed suicide in 1939 by putting a gun to her temple.

During Braun's 15-year relationship with Hitler, not many people knew she existed. Hitler believed a strong leader should only show love for his country. This had a profound effect on Braun, a high-spirited girl who loved to be the center of attention—hence the suicide attempts. According to Braun herself, she was a prisoner in a gilded cage.

In 1936, Braun moved into Hitler's alpine estate—the Berghof—at Obersalzberg, where she remained until March 1945, when she insisted on being with her man in the Reich's chancellery bunker, Berlin, till the bitter end. One month after her arrival, the Soviet Red Army had reached the center of Berlin and encircled the bunker. At this point, Hitler decided to divorce Germany and marry Braun. The marriage lasted a whole 39.5 hours before they committed suicide together at approximately 3:30 p.m. on April 30, 1945. Eva Braun was 33 years young—10 days prior Hitler had turned 56.

Dachau Concentration Camp: Shortly after Hitler became chancellor of Germany in 1933, he opened the gates to the Dachau concentration camp (page 212).

Haus der Kunst: Where the English Gardens meet Prinzregentenstrasse you'll find the Haus der Kunst (House of Art, formerly the House of "German" Art). This is Hitler's first significant example of Nazi architecture, completed in 1937. Due to its multicolumn pseudo-Greek facade and provocative nude statuettes inside, many locals secretly referred to their new "House of Art" as the School Gymnasium, Athens Train Station, or the House of German Tarts.

This so-called temple of Nazi art took four years to complete; inside featured an art gallery, restaurant, night club and, of course, a beer hall.

Hitler laid the cornerstone to the Haus der Kunst on October 15, 1933, in front of a large audience of commoners and dignitaries. Before striking the stone with a specially designed silver hammer, Hitler exclaimed, *"May this House of German Art be a symbol of perpetual indestructibility of German creative effort. A new and flourishing era in German art commences with the laying of this cornerstone."* Hitler concluded by robustly striking the hammer against the cornerstone. The enthusiastic faces in the crowd quickly turned to open-mouthed disbelief when the specially designed hammer broke! Hitler was so embarrassed that he turned pale and swiftly exited the ceremony for his apartment, where he withdrew from society for two days. The incident proved to be an ominous sign for the project's architect, Paul Ludwig Troost, who fell ill two days later and died within three months.

After the war, the Haus der Kunst was utilized by the U.S. army as an officers' club till 1955, when it was restored back to an art gallery. Today, the structure accommodates a café and revolving art exhibitions.

Königsplatz: (*GPS:* N48° 08.736 - E11° 33.969) "King's Square" is the largest in Munich, originally commissioned by King Ludwig I (fairy-tale king's grandfather) in the early 19th century as a Greek arrangement of temples modeled after the Acropolis.

After Hitler and his Nazis nabbed power in 1933, the party HQ did not move to Berlin—the nation's capital—as normally would be the case, but instead it stayed in Munich, the capital of the Nazi movement. In 1929, Hitler purchased the three-story Barlow Palace (a.k.a. "Brown House"; now torn down), located meters from Königsplatz on Brienner Str, and renovated it into the party's headquarters. After this acquisition, the party began snapping up properties in the neighborhood and by 1939 they had accumulated more than 50 buildings, shaping a nerve center for Nazi totalitarianism with Königsplatz as its core. Unofficially, Königsplatz was consecrated as a holy Nazi site on May 10, 1933, when it became the setting for the infamous burning of books that the regime avowed were written by "undesirable authors."

During the 1930s, Hitler gave the square a facelift, paving over the refreshing grass areas with more than 22,000 granite slabs to create a parade ground. Hitler then commissioned the focal point of the square, the Greek-style pantheons. These were two open-air temples built to honor the 16 putschists who died during the bloody ending of the Beer Hall Putsch. Each pantheon, permanently guarded by SS sentries, accommodated eight crypts. Today, the foundations of the pantheons can still be seen (on either corner) at the intersection of Arcisstr. and Brienner Str. In 1987, the square was restored back to its original design with sidewalks and grass areas. *Note:* Also at the intersection of Arcisstr. and Brienner Str. you'll find an excellent info board detailing the cityscape of the Nazi party in Munich.

Führerbau: (*GPS:* N48° 08.760 - E11° 34.020) This gray, sterile "Hitler Building" on the northeast side of the intersection at Brienner Str. and Arcisstr. could easily be confused with its twin on the opposite corner. Both buildings were constructed to augment the epicenter of Nazi administration. On September 29, 1938, the Führerbau was the chosen venue for the historic signing of the Munich Pact, an agreement that sealed the fate of Czechoslovakia. To appease Hitler and preserve world peace, Prime Minister

Neville Chamberlain of Great Britain and Premier Edouard Daladier of France signed an agreement stating that Germany could legally annex the *Sudetenland two days later on October 1. (*The Sudetenland was a strip of land on the fringe of Czechoslovakia occupied largely by Sudeten Germans loyal to Hitler).

In accordance with the pact, Germany seized the Sudetenland. Within five months—symbolizing the dangers of appeasement—Hitler nullified the pact by invading the whole of Czechoslovakia (March 1939), which began the slide toward the outbreak of World War II.

After the war, the Führerbau was used as the first HQ for the occupying U.S. forces, and later the central collection point for plundered Nazi art Europe-wide. Today, the Führerbau houses a music conservatory and its twin across the intersection is an art academy. On the backsides of each building notice the innumerable wounds of war resulting from the Allied bombing raids. Additionally, behold the patched-up cavities above the Führerbau's main entrance where the eagle and swastika hung.

Neues Rathaus: (New Town Hall on Marienplatz; building that houses the Glockenspiel) Hitler was in Munich every year on Nov. 8 and 9 for the anniversary of the Beer Hall Putsch—and 1938 was no exception. While Hitler was holding a meeting at the Neues Rathaus on Nov. 9, he received word that a young Jew—Ernst von Rath—had assassinated an official at the German Embassy in Paris. This was the moment Hitler had been waiting for; he unleashed his army of thugs upon what he considered to be the universal pest, encouraging a nationwide "pogrom" (an organized massacre of helpless people, i.e. Jews), in which all synagogues in Germany, including some Jewish shops, were set on fire. The infamous night landed in the history books as Kristallnacht, or The Night of Broken Glass.

SS, Hoffman & Hitler Youth: Formerly at the south end of Barer Strasse, now empty blocks of land, were the offices of the Hitler Youth and *Heinrich Hoffman's photography studio. Across the street, now an insurance firm, were the head offices of the SS. (*Originally a portrait photographer, Hoffman became rich from being Hitler's personal photographer. Most all photos of Hitler bear the name Hoffman at the bottom. The two met soon after Hitler joined the DAP.)

Theater am Gärtnerplatz: Hitler's great joy in life was the theater. Even in Vienna when he was flat broke and living in his first dwelling he always had enough cash to see an opera, in fact, several a week. He would press his pants by putting them under his mattress and even starve himself just so he could attend the theater. In Munich, he visited all the theaters, but the one closest to his heart was the Theater am Gärtnerplatz, where he'd regularly attend his favorite production: "The Merry Widow," a comic operetta with plenty of Viennese waltzing and Parisian Can-Can. Hitler watched with a cheeky grin as the chorus girls saluted "Heils" with elevated right legs.

Gestapo: (*GPS:* N48° 08.634 - E11° 34.317) The most feared building in Munich belonged to the Geheime Staatspolizei (Gestapo)—or Secret State Police—the eyes and ears of Hitler's terror regime. Gestapo headquarters looked splendid from the outside, since it was the Wittelsbacher Palais, former royal palace of King Ludwig I (fairy-tale king's grandfather). However, looks can be deceiving and on the inside party hardliners conducted cruel business. It was within these fear-provoking confines that Hans and Sophie Scholl were interrogated on February 18, 1943, after being apprehended for distributing White Rose flyers at Munich University. Shortly after the interrogation, they were sent to Stadelheim prison and beheaded. During the war, Allied bombs destroyed the former palace in late 1944. Today, it is a modern five-story financial building.

Eternal Flame: Half a block from the former headquarters of the Gestapo, where Brienner Str. meets Oskar-von-Miller-Ring, an eternal flame burns bright on the Platz der

Opfer des Nationsozialismus (Victims of the Nazis Square) in memory of those victims who perished during Hitler's reign of terror, 1933-45.

Scholl, Hans & Sophie: (For full story, turn to Page 9 of "The Letter," chapter seven of the *Quest for the Bavarian Cross*.) Not far from where Eva Braun was born and Hitler completed basic military training, lived Hans and Sophie Scholl, key members of the White Rose resistance movement.

On the front facade of a graffiti-clad apartment building at Franz-Joseph-Strasse 13 (*GPS:* N48° 09.460 - E11° 34.892), you'll find a plaque in memory of the brother and sister Scholl. It reads: "Sophie and Hans Scholl, who led the White Rose resistance movement against the Third Reich, lived here in the back building from June 1942 until their execution on 22 February, 1943."

To reach the former Scholl residence, or "back building" as described on the plaque, can be difficult. To your left (when facing the plaque) is a gate that leads to their former residence, a modest house-style apartment building. If you catch it just right, someone will be coming or going through the gate and you may get a glimpse of the Scholl's former residence.

Stadelheim Prison: Stadelheim to *Münchner*, or the citizens of Munich, is what San Quentin is to Californians, a notorious high-security prison—even Hitler spent nearly five weeks within its walls for provoking an anti-Bolshevik riot in 1922. Serving as a place of execution during the Third Reich, many key members of the White Rose resistance movement were put to death here, i.e. Hans and Sophie Scholl, Christoph Probst, Alexander Schmorell, Prof. Kurt Huber, Willie Graf and Hans Leipel. In the Perlach cemetery, adjacent to the prison, you'll find some very old and interesting graves, including those of the Scholl family (Hans and Sophie and their parents), Christoph Probst and his mother, and Alexander Schmorell. *Getting There:* Stadelheim prison is located some 5km south of downtown Munich.

M A R K T L *am Inn*

~ Population: 2700   ~ Elevation: 360m/1180ft   ~ Country/Area Code: +49-(0)8678

Pope Benedict XVI

Some 67km north of Salzburg, and 110km east of Munich, is the Bavarian village of Marktl, nestled on the Inn River 15km upstream from the Austrian border. First mentioned in 1386, deeply religious Marktl grew up in the shadow of its 13th century church, St. Oswald. Centuries passed and petite Marktl hardly changed; villagers went about their daily routine of baking bread, farming the land and tending to their livestock, living a simple but fruitful life in relative obscurity. However, on April 16, 1927, a single event occurred in town that would make headlines 78 years later, touching tens of millions of people across the globe and forever changing the unassuming village on the Inn River.

In the spring of 1927, the Ratzingers—Joseph, a police officer, and Marie, a homemaker about to give birth—lived on the market square in a large, two-story residence formerly the customs house dating from 1745. The day of anticipation arrived on April 16; Marie Ratzinger gave birth to a healthy baby boy. The newborn was escorted across the village to St. Oswald's Church and, like his father, baptized as Joseph.

Young Joseph had an influential relationship with God that guided him safely through the horrors of WWII and into a course of religious studies in Munich. In 1951, he graduated and entered priesthood. Sadly, in 1959, Joseph senior died, followed by the death of his mother four years later. But, as a child and servant of God, Ratzinger knew that the Almighty had called for his parents to serve a greater purpose.

In 1977, after years of teaching theology as a professor in Bonn and Regensburg, Ratzinger was named the archbishop of Munich. Then, three months later, the country boy from Marktl was elevated to the status of cardinal, the second highest rank in the Roman Catholic Church.

On October 16, 1978, John Paul II, a native of Poland, was elected to the papacy, the first non-Italian pope in more than 450 years. As one of the pope's most trusted and influential advisers, Ratzinger was tasked with many paramount duties, but the duty he carried out on April 8, 2005, was incomparable to anything already on his resume: He gave the eulogy for Pope John Paul II at his funeral. Eleven days later, on April 19, Joseph Ratzinger, son of Joseph and Marie, a Bavarian, a cardinal, a child of God, a disciple of Jesus, was elected the Catholic Church's 265th pope. He took the name Benedict XVI. (*Note:* You can keep up with all things Vatican at this site: www.vatican.va)

Since Ratzinger's papal election, the sleepy village of Marktl has been injected with a heavy dose of tourism, from religious pilgrims to heady locals to bus tours. Exhausted from the onslaught, the owner of Ratzinger's birth house decided to put it on the market. Its normal appraisal value is 150,000€, but more than 400 offers have inflated the price upwards of 5€ million. For less money, though, the owner is likely to sell to a church group with plans of converting the pope's birthplace into a museum. Until then, the house can only be viewed externally. The frenzy is not unique to Ratzinger's birth house, however, his former 1999 VW Golf sold for 200,000€ one month after becoming pope. The owner, a 21-year-old Bavarian, had purchased the vehicle in January 2005 for 9500€ from a used-car salesman. After reading through the car's documents he noticed the previous owner was one Cardinal Joseph Ratzinger. Hallelujah! (We presume he shouted.) And where does one go these days if one has something of value to sell? Answer: eBay. Actually, the 21-year-old would have gotten truckloads more money if eBay hadn't crashed 40 minutes prior to the end of the auction. Yikes!

Getting There: *Railers*, trains depart hourly from Munich (2hr trip, transfer necessary). *Drivers*, from Salzburg pick up route 20 on the German side of the border at Freilassing and continue straight all the way to Marktl. First, follow signs to Laufen, then Burghausen, then Passau, (consider visiting Oberndorf along the way, see page 493). Once in Burghausen, Marktl is 12km farther. When you reach the (Inn) river, Marktl is on the other side. (The white church steeple soaring above the village belongs to St. Oswald's.) Now, cross the river and after some 300 meters turn left on Pfarrstr. Continue straight and the pope's birth house is in front of you at the end of the street. Once there, go left for the market square. *GPS:* N48° 15.232 - E12° 50.505. From Munich, head east on the A94, then route 12 to Marktl.

TI: (www.marktl.de) *Tel.#* 08678/748-820. Across from the pope's birth house is the TI. Straight inside are clean (free) toilets. Hours (may change, call ahead to verify) daily, 11:00-17:00.

Note: Ironically, only 15km downstream, on the Austrian side of the river, is Braunau am Inn: the birthplace of Adolf Hitler, born 38 years prior to Joseph Ratzinger.

Oh, and lastly, in case you were wondering, there are about 26 million members of the Catholic Church in Germany. These figures are relatively easy to calculate since each citizen must register his or her faith with the authorities to pay church tax.

BERCHTESGADEN

~ Population: 8000   ~ Elevation: 530m/1740ft
~ Country/Area code: +49-(0)8652

After the founding of Salzburg in 696 A.D. came the first mention of many settlements in the area, including the forest in front of the snow-peaked Watzmann, Germany's second-highest mountain at 2712m/8900ft.

In the 11th century, Lord Perther arrived and established a finely tuned hunting lodge for himself that he referred to as Perther's Gaden. From this moniker evolved the name Berchtesgaden.

In 1102, the Augustinian monks settled here and began building a monastery — look for the twin spires rising above town. They were determined to achieve this symbolic feat as they had first proclaimed Perther's Gaden "a terrifying forest, constantly covered with ice and snow; a vast solitude inhabited by wild beasts and dragons."

Frederick Barbarossa, Holy Roman Emperor and king of Germany from 1152-90, was delighted to hear of this fruitful monastery that neighbored the ever-annoying archbishops of Salzburg who boasted abundant deposits of salt. Barbarossa was quick to grant the monks extra rights to hunt, fish, forest, cultivate, and develop mines to excavate the "white gold" on their side of the border. Salt was the key resource in these parts that assured Berchtesgaden unusual power for such a small enclave, securing a political voice in the Reichstag (parliament) and ultimately the right to become an independent principality ruled by prince-provosts.

The following centuries brought social woes to the Catholic settlement: salt squabbles continued with Salzburg, the Thirty Years' War raged across Europe, and Protestant ways became covertly trendy.

In 1803, Napoleon dashed in with his battle-hardened Le Grand Armée and seized Berchtesgaden in one swoop. The monastery was consequently disbanded and church administration secularized. In the years to follow, Berchtesgaden was tossed around like a political football. First it was annexed to Salzburg under Habsburg rule before finally being restored to Bavaria in 1810.

The 20th century produced two world wars. The first was fought in the distant trenches of France and Belgium, but the second came knocking at Perther's front door. Adolf Hitler became chancellor of Germany in 1933 and decided to throw up his tent in the Gaden, calling it home. Hitler began the Second World War that the Germans grossly lost. Thankfully, the Allied band of brothers safeguarded the hallowed Augustinian seat, securing its prosperity for centuries to come.

Tourist Information: [TI] (www.berchtesgadener-land.info) *Tel.#* 08652/9670
Berchtesgaden has one TI, located opposite the train station on Königsseerstr. *Hours:* (summer) Mon-Fri 8:30-18:00, Sat 9:30-17:00, Sun 9:00-15:00 — (winter) Mon-Thur 8:30-17:00, Fri 8:30-15:30, Sat 9:00-12:00.

Tours: If you're interested in a tour of the Eagle's Nest, Obersalzberg, WWII bunker system, or the Sound of Music, there's only one company to consider: **Eagle's Nest Tours**. The company's owners, David and Christine Harper, are a lovely (American) husband-and-wife team who have called Berchtesgaden home for decades. The Harpers' booming success is attributed to their warm personalities, in-depth tours, and wealth of local knowledge. To inquire about their tours or anything historically on your mind, call or stop by—Eagle's Nest Tours is located within the TI, opposite the train station. *Tel.#* 08652/64-971 (www.eagles-nest-tours.com) Their *Eagle's Nest package* includes a guided tour of the Eagle's Nest, Obersalzberg and a WWII bunker system — duration four hours. Tour is offered daily at 13:30 mid-May thru Oct. *Note:* Reservations required. *Price:* adult 40€, student 37.50€. *CC's:* VC, MC, AE. The *Sound of Music tour* revisits the sights in Salzburg made famous by this movie classic — duration four hours. Tour is offered Mon-Sat at 8:30. *Note:* Reservations required. *Price:* 30€. *CC's:* VC, MC, AE.

Emergency Tel. Numbers: [Germany-wide]
Police (Polizei) = 110
Fire dept. (Feuerwehr) or general emergency = 112
Ambulance = 19222

Railers: Berchtesgaden is train-friendly but you'll have to transfer in Freilassing (German border town next to Salzburg). Another way to arrive is via bus—#840 departs hourly (from 8:15 until early evening) from Salzburg's main train station at bay (Stand) 4, across parking lot from P.O. (or from Mirabellplatz a few minutes later). The cost is 4.40€ one-way; consider purchasing the day ticket (*Tageskarte*) from the driver for 8€, which will cover all your bus transportation for the day, including to/fro Salzburg and Obersalzberg (bus departure area for Eagle's Nest). From Berchtesgaden's train station buses depart roughly every half hour to Obersalzberg. For more info regarding the Eagle's Nest, flip to page 248.

Berchtesgaden's train station was built in 1937 at a blinding pace in harmony with Third Reich improvements for a nation that had planned to dominate the western world. As the gateway to Hitler's neighborhood, Berchtesgaden received numerous foreign dignitaries—therefore the train station was designed to impress. After its completion, Berchtesgaden—an alpine community with just a few thousand residents—had a train station that was larger than the one in Athens, Greece. When Hitler would steam into town, on his train curiously called "Amerika," the mood bordered hysteria; Swastikas billowed from every window and flower-wielding children stood at the forefront of mesmerized crowds. Such was a typical scene in Nazi Germany when the Führer came to town. Today, things have quieted down dramatically—just 21 trains chug through the station daily and the only time local crowds get worked up is when *Krampus* (page 235) whips through the market square.

When facing the station's front facade, to your left are the local buses heading to all the Sights (listed in below section), including Salzburg. In front of you, sprouting from the facade, are two rusty flagpoles—here the iconic flag of Germany's fascist era flapped with every alpine breeze; and behind you, across the street, is the TI.

Drivers: *Street parking* pay at nearby automat and leave ticket on dashboard of your car. Price: 50¢/hr, max 2hr, applicable Mon-Fri 10:00-17:00, and Sat 10:00-13:00 with parking dial (page 450), free all other times. There are plenty of parking possibilities throughout town. Free spaces can be had on the west side of town between the gas station and traffic circle facing the Berchtesgadener Hof.

Shops: In Berchtesgaden most shops keep the old-fashioned hours with builtin siestas and short Saturdays. The following schedule generalizes the opening times for shops in town: Mon-Fri 9:00-12:30 & 14:00-18:00, Sat 9:00-12:00 (until 16:00 on first Saturday of every month).

SIGHTS

Eagle's Nest: see page 248.

Obersalzberg: *(WWII Buffs)* Hitler's former neighborhood, flip to page 238.

Salt Mines: (Salzbergwerk) On average 370,000 visitors descend upon the salt mines each year. Embarking on a subterranean adventure, tourists love throwing on a miner's uniform (navy-blue overalls), riding the narrow-gauge railway deep into the mountain, swooshing down slick slides, navigating a salty lake, and licking the walls of sodium-rich tunnels that resemble taffy.

A tour of the mine takes an hour, but that's once you get inside. Expect to wait anywhere from 15 minutes during the off-peak season and up to two hours in peak season (July/Aug). *Suggestion:* If you're faced with a long wait, ramble along the river and check out the Watzmann Therme. Drivers can avoid waiting by purchasing tickets in advance, or at least drop someone off at the ticket booth while the car is being parked. Or, buy tickets for a later tour before spending a few deserving hours in the Watzmann Therme (page 234).

(www.salzwelt.de) *Hours:* (salt mines) daily, May thru Oct 15, 9:00-16:45 (last entry); Oct 16 thru April, 11:30-14:45 (last entry).

Price: 3€; discount available with valid Salzburg Card. After tour you can buy pictures of yourself on the train or slide—4€ each, or US$4.

Note: The mines are not for people who are claustrophobic; confined spaces abound. Outside, if you see either of two German shepherds (Leika & Ascan), don't be alarmed, they're friendly and belong to the photographer.

GPS: N47° 38.248 - E13° 01.028

Getting There: The salt mines are nestled along a pretty jade-green stream on Bergwerkstrasse, which runs off the main road connecting Berchtesgaden with Salzburg. **Railers**, from the train station buses leave hourly for the mines, or it's a 30-min walk. From Salzburg's train station take bus #840. **Drivers**, *from the center of Berchtesgaden* pass the pedestrian shopping zone (on left) and follow the road as it curves right. At the bottom of the hill is a traffic light, turn left (direction Kehlstein)—this is almost a U-turn. Now you're on Bergwerkstr. Pass the second set of lights and follow Salzbergwerk signs (left) into their parking area (if it's high season, then turn right at the second set of lights and drop someone off to buy tickets while the car is being parked). **Drivers**, *if you're coming from Salzburg,* follow signs to Berchtesgaden. As you approach town follow Salzbergwerk signs (right) into the parking lot.

Königssee: (King's Lake) The cool, blue Königssee is Germany's cleanest lake, spectacularly positioned in the heart of Berchtesgaden's 210sq.km/81sq.mi national park. What's more, Königssee is the nation's deepest lake at 190m/620ft; it is 8km/5mi long and hemmed in on three sides by the Alps, including the snow-peaked Watzmann. Königssee is so clean that it boasts drinking-quality water, and the locals are intent on keeping it pure—thus no swimming is allowed and the boats that cruise across it are electrical.

The Königsseer fleet of 17 electrical boats ship more than 700,000 people annually across the lake's arctic-blue waters. During the cruise, the captain stops the boat to blow his trumpet—the tune dances along the sheer cliffs performing the Alp echo. Königssee is truly wunderbar; come see it for yourself! (www.seenschifffahrt.de) *Hours:* Boats run daily every 30 minutes May thru mid-Oct 8:00-17:00 and mid-Oct thru April 9:45-15:30.

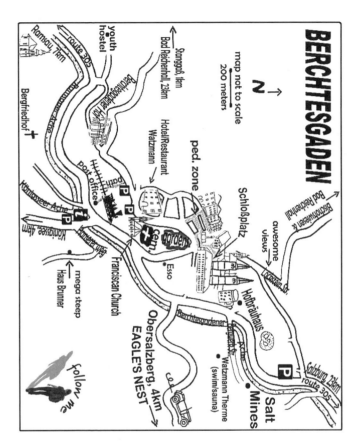

Price: (for round trip to the 12th-century chapel of St. Bartholomew—35-min ride each way) adult 11€, family 28.50€. *Getting There: Railers,* from the train station buses leave roughly every 50 min. *Drivers,* from Berchtesgaden you'll find the road to Königssee opposite the train station. Once at the lake, you'll have to pay for parking. *Suggestion:* If you're hungry when on the peninsula of St. Bartholomew, try the smoked trout ("geraucht forelle") at the shoreline shack (served from 11:00, mid-April thru Oct). *S.O.M. Fans:* Königssee can be briefly seen during the aerial shots in the beginning of the film.

Schloßplatz: Beneath the twin spires rising above town is Schloßplatz, or Palace Square, a spacious plaza that is home to the *Stiftskirche, Königliches Schloss,* and a memorial to Berchtesgaden's war dead. When standing in the gravel square, face the mural above the arches; it reads (left): "The fallen sons of Berchtesgaden" (right) "They gave their lives; their sacrifice will always be remembered." Now walk up to the arches to view the names of the dead on the wall—they are under the watchful of the Eagle's Nest (behind you) peering down from the mountaintop. On a more festive note, return here in December when the square is ornamented with the gingerbread-scented Christmas market. Mmm.

Stiftskirche: (Collegiate Church) The Augustinian monks established Berchtesgaden with this hallowed structure more than 900 years ago.

Königliches Schloss: (Royal Palace) Adjoined to the Stiftskirche is the former Augustinian monastery, dating from 1122. The significant structure was later converted to the seat of Berchtesgaden's prince-provosts and from 1818 to 1918 used as the summer palace by Bavaria's royal family, the Wittelsbachs—thus the fairy-tale king, Ludwig II, spent many childhood summers in Berchtesgaden. Today, the palace remains stuffed with historic trinkets and is still used by members of the Wittelsbach clan when in town.

Tours of the palace are possible but in German, duration 50 min. *Hours:* Easter thru mid-Oct, Sun thru Fri 10:00-12:00 & 14:00-16:00—rest of year Mon-Fri 11:00-14:00. *Price:* adult 7€, student 3.50€, discount with valid Salzburg Card.

Watzmann Therme: Bergwerkstr. 54. *Tel.#* 08652/94-640. The Watzmann Therme is Berchtesgaden's new bathers' paradise, offering a plethora of invigorating options, such as a therapeutic soak indoors or a waterfall massage outdoors—relax on a lounge chair or zip down an 80m/262ft long waterslide—stuff yourself in the restaurant or get steamed in a bare-all *sauna. *Hours:* daily, 10:00-22:00. *Price:* adult 8€/2hr, 11€/4hr, 15€/day pass; sauna area is 3.30€ extra, or included with day pass; discount available with valid Salzburg Card; classic full-body massage 29€/40min (other options available, call in advance: tel.# 08652/946-450). *Getting There:* Therme is located on the same road as the salt mines. **Note:* Mondays are reserved for women-only in the sauna.

Hofbrauhaus: Bräuhausstr. 15. *Tel.#* 08652/96-640. Established in 1645, this internationally famous house boasts more than 350 years of brewing tradition. Drown your thirst with liter jugs of beer (called "Maß," 4.60€), gorge yourself on regional cuisine, and/or enjoy a "Heimatabend" (traditional Bavarian show, inclusive of whip cracking, table dancing and spoon clanging) every Saturday evening at 20:00 mid-May thru mid-Oct. *Price:* (Heimatabend) 5€. *Hours:* (Hofbrauhaus) daily, 10:00-24:00.

Grassl Enzianbrennerei: (distillery) *Tel.#* 08652/95-360. Over 100,000 visitors a year stop by for a *free* tour of Germany's oldest Enzian distillery, established in 1602. Enzian is a type of mountain flower and the distillers at Grassl use it as the essential ingredient to produce several varieties of liqueur and schnapps. One of their most popular blends is Berg Feuer, or Mountain Fire, containing 57% alcohol. Whew! This is likely to put hair on your chest. *Hours:* Mon-Fri 8:00-17:00 (May-Oct till 18:00), Sat 8:30-12:00 (May-Oct till 14:00). *Getting There: Railers*, take bus #840 from town or Salzburg's train station. *Drivers*, Grassl is located 4km from Berchtesgaden (on left side of road) and 18km from Salzburg (right side) on route 305 running between the two towns.

Berchtesgadener Hof: *(WWII Buffs)* Most of you are familiar with the Berchtesgadener Hof from its portrayal in the television miniseries "Band of Brothers," episode 10, "Points," when the boys of Easy Company entered the hotel and began lifting Hitler souvenirs.

Originally called the Grand Hotel from its inauguration in 1898, these digs once pampered European nobility. When the Nazis acquired the Grand Hotel in the 1930s, they renovated it and changed the name to Berchtesgadener Hof. The property fast became the preferred hotel of Hitler's guests, including General Irwin Rommel ("Desert Fox"), British Prime Minister Neville Chamberlain, Heinrich Himmler, Joachim von Ribbentrop, Josef Goebbels, and Eva Braun before she moved in with Hitler on Obersalzberg at his chalet-style mansion: the "Berghof."

After the war, the hotel was acquisitioned by U.S forces as an AFRC resort. It was turned back to the Germans in 1995. Today, the building remains unoccupied and for sale.

Hitler, Paula: *(WWII Buffs)* Adolf's little sister, Paula, was interred in Berchtesgaden's Bergfriedhof until mid-2005, when cemetery administration allowed her remains to be buried over (presumably because nobody paid the "rent" due on her grave, which in Germany, as well as in Austria, means *Hasta la vista, Baby*).

Events/Festivals 2006

May Day, May 1 (Mon): This day is special throughout Bavaria because numerous communities (visit TI to find out which ones) will be raising their Maypole. May Day festivities include folk dancing, pole-climbing events, traditional costume and customary drinking. Amen! *Note:* Some communities postpone festivities a week or two. Thus, if you plan it right, you can follow the celebrations all month.

Pentecost (Whit) Monday, June 5: In Berchtesgaden, the salt miners have adopted this holiday. (*Consequently, the salt mines will be closed.*) Led by members of the Stiftskirche (Collegiate church), the salt miners wear traditional costume and parade through the decorated streets of town to the church where a service will be held. Afterward, the procession continues.

Almabtrieb: This is the German term for when the cows are led from the summer pastures to their winter stalls, which transpires in the latter half of September. Milkmaids and cowherders adorn their livelihood with flamboyant headdresses and parade them along village streets to their homes. During this procession the milkmaids call out *"In God's name move on, my cow, in health and joy—St. Anthony will herd you."* Truly a colorful and memorable spectacle to witness. It's especially interesting to see the cows being loaded onto the Königsseer boats to be shipped across the lake to their distant homes. Don't forget your camera. Inquire at the TI for exact dates—these vary depending on weather.

Krampus: Exclusive to these parts is Krampus, the local tradition that kicks-off the Christmas season. The Krampus are a group of wicked-looking creatures (Kramperl, Buttnmandl and Gangerl) who accompany St. Nicholas before Christmas to frighten misbehaved children. What really happens, however, is the creatures run wild through Berchtesgaden's pedestrian zone whipping and terrorizing the populace at large. Although, legend does vow that a generous whipping ensures good health and prosperity for the coming year, in addition to expelling all the demons from your body. Yikes!

The whips the Krampus carry are nothing to laugh at, each one is handmade from a bundle of slender and flexible branches firmly woven, tied and taped together for maximum effect. Each creature will arm itself with three to four whips in case one comes apart, or even more troubling, one gets snatched by a cunning member of the public. The Krampus creatures are *Kramperl:* Young boys wearing self-made fur costumes with handcrafted masks and modest bells attached to their belts. *Buttnmandl:* Men wearing hand-carved masks, 3-6 large cowbells tied to their backs, and straw outfits that take an hour to don. *Gangerl:* This is the Devil and the leader of the pack. He wears horns, a black stocking over his face, and a fur jacket. Be afraid boys and girls—*be very afraid!* *Hours:* You can see the Krampus at the beginning of December—typically the 5th and 6th, early evening. Check dates with TI. *Suggestion:* Because the Krampus creatures tend to administer a painful whipping, wear ski pants (if you have them) or two pairs of jeans to help absorb the sting. For a memorable experience, and a great souvenir, snatch one of the creatures' handmade whips. We dare you!

GOOD SLEEPS

<u>Hotel Watzmann:</u> *Tel.#* 08652/2055 (www.hotel-watzmann.de) Positioned in the center of Berchtesgaden, the Hotel Watzmann is an excellent, convenient choice. Besides comfortable accommodations, the Watzmann also boasts a well-respected restaurant patronized by locals and tourists alike. Here you can enjoy a scrumptious meal indoors amid traditional Bavarian décor or on the outdoor patio immersed in majestic views of the Alps. *Price:* (includes buffet breakfast, room with facilities) Sgl 42€, Dbl 78. *CC's:* VC, MC. *Note:* Watzmann is closed from Nov thru Christmas. *Getting There:* Hotel Watzmann is located on the main road through town, opposite Franciscan church—10-min walk above train station. *Drivers,* inquire at reception about free parking. *GPS:* N47° 37.794 - E13° 00.059

<u>Haus Brunner:</u> Hansererweg 16, tel.# 08652/61-886. Perched high above Berchtesgaden, Haus Brunner is run by Herr and Frau Lösel who offer clean rooms with a balcony and memorable view—facilities (shower/toilet), though, are in the hallway. Little English spoken. *Price:* (includes breakfast) Sgl 16€, Dbl 32€. *Getting There:* across from TI is Hansererweg—follow this road *up* to No. 16. At first the road is flat, then it curves sharply to the right and climbs at a grueling 24% grade! Jeepers, Hansererweg has got to be Germany's steepest neighborhood street. *Drivers,* beware—it's two-way! *Railers,* call and they may pick you up. *GPS:* N47° 37.570 - E13° 00.157

<u>Hostel, Strub:</u> [HI] Gebirgsjägerstr. 52 (www.djh.de) *Tel.#* 08652/94-370. This older-style hostel dates from the late 1930s and hasn't seen many renovations since. Older-style house rules remain, too. In Bavaria, government-supported youth hostels still require their guests to be under 26 years of age to stay. A sizable building containing more than 300 beds, the hostel is situated on the outer rim of town—2km from the train station. From the hostel's front door is a sharp view of the Eagle's Nest, which is a great angle justifying why British bombers missed their target on April 25, 1945. A stone's throw from the hostel is Strub Kasern, former military base for Hitler's elite "Edelweiss" mountain troops. *Hours:* (reception) 7:00-9:00 & 17:00-19:00 (but there's usually someone always around). *Price:* (linen and breakfast included) dorm bed 15.50€, bed tax is an extra 1.80€ per person, per night. *Note:* Hostel is closed from Nov thru Christmas. *Getting There:* From the train station it's a 35-min walk. Exit station right and take the main road (Ramsauerstr.) roughly 1km and make the first right, direction Strub. Follow the youth hostel (Jugendherberge) signs left up the hill. After a (600 meter) hike that will make you feel fit for the elite mountain units, you'll see the youth hostel on the left. *GPS:* N47° 37.449 - E12° 58.774

The following two farmhouse-style accommodations are located 10km from Berchtesgaden, outside of *Ramsau. Alas, there is no public bus service to this area, essentially cutting off Railers *(although, if you're willing to stay at least a few days at the Leyererhof, call and they'll pick you up from the Berchtesgaden train station).* *In this town be sure and view the postcard-perfect Ramsauer Kirche (picturesque church along jade-green river).

Here you'll experience the classic Alpine dream: grazing cows, idyllic meadows, clanging bells, babbling brooks, pine-fresh air, solid-rock mountains close enough to touch, snow-capped peaks, men donning lederhosen, girls sporting pigtails, women wearing dirndls, hikers clutching ornamented sticks, quaint farmhouses, and a meandering road. The latter road is route 305, or more famously, the Deutsche Alpenstrasse (German Alpine Road)—the most scenic in the land. This is the same road portrayed in the television miniseries "Band of Brothers," episode 10, "Points," when the boys of Easy

Co., destination Obersalzberg, try adamantly with grenades and bazookas to clear huge mounds of avalanche rubble left by retreating Nazis.

Getting There: **Drivers**, *from Berchtesgaden* take the main road (route 305) direction Ramsau, which leads to the "Deutsche Alpenstrasse" and your pastoral digs. **Drivers,** *from the Munich-Salzburg autobahn (A8)* exit at Siegsdorf/Inzell. Follow signs to Inzell, then Berchtesgaden. After Inzell the road becomes route 305, which rambles along a tremendously scenic and curvy and narrow route. (*Note:* Avoid this route at night.) Some 20km later you'll reach your digs; both are on the left-hand side.

Leyererhof: Alpenstrasse 114 (www.leyererhof.de) *Tel.#* 08657/371. The Leyererhof is immaculate and ideal for a rustic Bavarian sabbatical. Michael and Martina Votz, your hosts, only have seven rooms available—six doubles and one triple, the latter is without a balcony—therefore they are often full. Book well in advance for the summer months. *Note:* Smoke-free house. Little English spoken. *Price:* (includes breakfast, room with facilities) 25€ per person, per day. Cheaper from 3 nights. *Railers*, if you're staying at least a few nights, call and they'll pick you up from Berchtesgaden's train station. *GPS:* N47° 37.725 - E12° 52.554

Haus Oberwegscheid: Alpenstrasse 60. *Tel.#* 08657/250. Haus Oberwegscheid is run by a sweet lady who has five rooms available, most have a balcony. Originally built in 1414, these historic digs are more worn than the Leyererhof and less advertised, thus you have a chance for a vacancy. Travelers on a budget will find great value here because the facilities (toilet/shower) are in the hallway. *Price:* (includes breakfast) 12-16€ per person. *Note:* No English spoken. Smoke-free house. Roughly 100 meters away is the federally protected 1200-year-old Hindenburg linden tree, measuring some 15m/49ft round at the base. *Getting There:* Haus Oberwegscheid can be found along the Alpenstrasse opposite the 14km marker; nearby a narrow driveway ascends to the house. *GPS:* N47° 36.945 - E12° 53.250

OBERSALZBERG

(Upper Salt Mountain)

~ Elevation: 970m/3181ft ~ Population: Just a rare few

Before 1933, Obersalzberg was a peaceful alpine farming community with a breathtaking view of Salzburg, Austria. Hitler decided this was the idyllic spot on the doorstep of his native land to call home. Dietrich Eckart—a literary connoisseur; a coarse individual who drank to stay sober; a raging anti-Semite, and Hitler's mentor—was the one who introduced young Adolf to this heavenly locale in the early '20s. When Hitler's heavy-handed tactics won his party, the Nazis, enough votes in the Reichstag (parliament) to seize power in 1933, Obersalzberg lost its innocence forever.

During the mid '30s, Hitler's personal secretary and right-hand man, Martin Bormann, kicked out the locals in Obersalzberg and transformed their alpine treasure into a massive construction site, housing up to 6000 workers in temporary barracks. Bormann was responsible for every building project in the region, including the Eagle's Nest on Mount Kehlstein. His plan was to create a cozy neighborhood for his boss while constructing a Nazi command center. In doing this, Bormann separated Obersalzberg into three security zones by implementing a nine-foot-high barbed-wire fence. Albert Speer referred to the Führer Gebiet (Hitler's main security zone) as an "open-air enclosure for wild animals."

Bormann ultimately acquired all land from the entry road connecting Berchtesgaden with Obersalzberg to the top of Mount Kehlstein, which completed the first in a long list of FHQs (Führerhauptquartier, or Hitler's headquarters, the most famous of which are Obersalzberg, Wolf's Layer and the Berlin bunker).

Ultimately, Obersalzberg was royally plastered during a massive air raid by some 300 British bombers on April 25, 1945. With the exception of a few buildings, the Bavarian government razed all remnants of Hitler's Third Reich on the "Upper Salt Mountain" in 1952.

Since Obersalzberg played a major role during WWII, this chapter has been widely extended and divided into four sections: **Obersalzberg Today; Obersalzberg 1933-45; WWII Bunker**—do-it-yourself; and **Eagle's Nest**—do-it-yourself.

OBERSALZBERG Today

The main reason tourists ascend the narrow, curvy road from Berchtesgaden in the valley to Obersalzberg at 3000 feet is the opportunity to hop on a specially modified bus and ascend even higher to behold gargantuan views from the world-famous Eagle's Nest. Obersalzberg, a former community at the helm of an empire, has been wiped clean but continues to pulse via tourism. Other than freshly paved parking lots, a motor pool of buses, and the newly built InterContinental resort hotel, there are few attractions to note. *Railers,* catch bus 849 or 838 from Berchtesgaden's train station (10-min ride).

<u>Bunker System:</u> see pages 242 and 245.

<u>Eagle's Nest:</u> see page 248.

<u>Documentation Center:</u> Set up in Martin Bormann's former administration office and VIP guest house, the Documentation Center is a worthy exhibition focusing on the rise and fall of the Third Reich, including a section of the subterranean bunker system. (www.obersalzberg.de) *Hours:* April-Oct, daily, 9:00-16:00 (last entry); Nov-March Tue-Sun 10:00-14:00. *Price:* adult 2.50€, students (with ID) are *FREE. Note:* Center is in German, thus we recommend the English audio guide for 2€. Wooded path behind property leads to Hitler's former estate—on a clear day the views into Austria are breathtaking.

Zoo: Privately run by an animal-loving local, this petite zoo has been in operation for years and presently accommodates turtles, owls, snakes, fish, marmots, a bald eagle, vulture and a falcon. The zoo is open to all who wish to visit—donations (to help feed the animals) are gladly accepted. *Hours:* (tend to vary, use as general reference) May-Oct 10:00-12:00 & 13:00-16:00—closed during bad weather and from Nov-April. *Getting There:* Walk past private apartments (white bldg. beneath Hotel InterContinental) to the zoo.

Hotel InterContinental: Believe it or not, the InterContinental hotel group just finished construction (July 2005) on a 138-room resort hotel on the hilltop where Hermann Göring formerly had his country estate. This oddly placed but exquisite resort affords panoramic Alpine views, two restaurants, a bar, wine room, beauty and fitness centers, heated indoor and outdoor pools, banquet and conference rooms. *Tel.#* 08652/97-550, or toll-free reservations from USA/Canada 1-888-424-6835. *Price:* Standard 280-340€, Executive 300-360€, Panorama Suite 410-630€, Duplex Suite 1000-1830€, Presidential Suite 2500€. (www.intercontinental.com)

OBERSALZBERG 1933-45

After Hitler assumed power in 1933, Obersalzberg went from small-town obscurity to front-page headlines. With uncompromising resolve, Martin Bormann reshaped the Upper Salt Mountain into a center for Nazi Southern Command. Ultimately, it was all for naught—the command center was pasted by bombs and Bormann met his maker courtesy of Soviet bullets on a Berlin street in 1945. The following list of entries help recount the way it was at Obersalzberg during the days of the Third Reich. To orientate yourself, refer to the map on the next page.

Drivers, entries are listed in the order they will be reached from Berchtesgaden (to reach Obersalzberg, follow signs Kehlstein). A few tips and suggestions are offered along the way.

Railers, catch bus 849 or 838 from train station to Obersalzberg—buy ticket inclusive of ride to Eagle's Nest (page 248—price, tickets).

> *From Berchtesgaden the road to Obersalzberg ascends at a demanding pace; after about 2.5km you'll reach the green Obersalzberg sign—just beyond it (on right) is the driveway that led to Speer's former haus and studio.*

Haus Speer: (briefly seen from road; green roof) Albert Speer was Hitler's favorite architect, who joined the Nazi party in 1931 as member No. 474,481. Hitler was so impressed by Speer's charisma and architectural flair that he rewarded him with his grand plan to reconstruct Berlin into Germania (never completed), capital of the so-called master race. Other monumental projects awarded to Speer were the Reich's Chancellery in Berlin and the Rally Grounds (Reichsparteigelände, i.e. Zeppelin Field) in Nürnberg, including the fanatically celebrated 1934 party rally. After the death of Fritz Todt in '42 (plane crash over Russia), Speer was appointed his ministerial position overseeing "armaments and war production." This gained Speer exclusive access to the Führer and further bonded a unique relationship. Consequently, Speer had to be available at a moment's notice and was therefore furnished with this modest chalet-style house.

After the war—during the 1946 Nürnberg trials—Speer was sentenced to 20 years in Spandau prison, Berlin. While reflecting on his relationship with Hitler, Speer declared: "One seldom recognizes the devil when he puts his hand on your shoulder." Albert Speer died in 1981 and is buried in the Bergfriedhof, Heidelberg.

Studio Speer: (red terracotta-tiled roof) Albert and Adolf spent many hours in this roadside studio mulling over fancy models and intricate drawings. After the war, Speer's studio was converted into the Evergreen Lodge, suite-style accommodations belonging to AFRC's General Walker resort (closed 1995). Today, both former Speer properties are privately owned.

Gutshof & Pig Stables: (Accessible via road on left, opposite studio Speer.) Bormann constructed the Gutshof and pig stables to serve as the model farm for Nazi Germany. However, his concept didn't exactly outshine any real farm because Bormann evicted the local farmers in 1933—and generals, including politicians, don't make good farmers! Instead, the Gutshof became more of a hobby for Bormann to keep Haflinger mountain ponies and colonies of bees. Today, it serves as a restaurant as well as a clubhouse for the 9-hole golf course. Nothing remains of the pig stables.

Drivers, continue up the road and at the junction go straight—this was the entrance to Adolf-Hitler-Strasse, where another guard post was stationed. Look left and a fabulous view into Salzburg will emerge. On the hill to the right is where Hitler lived in his three-story mansion, the Berghof. His driveway will appear shortly on the right. Ahead on the ridge is the Hotel Türken, where you'll find the WWII Bunker (Bunkeranlagen).

Haus Hitler: (Berghof) In 1927 Hitler moved into Haus Wachenfeld, an unpretentious chalet. By 1936, Haus Wachenfeld had received a monstrous overhaul deserving of the nation's chancellor. Hitler designed the new look himself, transforming the unpretentious chalet into the Berghof, a three-story mansion boasting more than 30 rooms. The Berghof's architectural highlight was an enormous picture-frame window (4m x 8m/13ft x 26ft) in the living room that could be hydraulically lowered into the windowsill adding a natural, airy quality to an already awesome view into Austria, his country of birth. Albert Speer, in his book "Inside the Third Reich," commented on how Hitler's design of the Berghof was substandard and if a professor had to evaluate the work (without the threat of being shot) he probably would have given it a D grade. Albert used the picture-frame window as the prime example in his assessment, saying Hitler curiously designed the massive window above the garage, which allowed gasoline fumes to waft throughout the house.

Before the war, the Berghof became an alternative center of government, where Hitler held important meetings rather than in Berlin or Munich. Some prominent visitors were Benito Mussolini ("Il Duce"), British Prime Minister Neville Chamberlain, Britain's Foreign Minister Lord Halifax, King Boris of Bulgaria, and Duke (Edward) and Duchess of Windsor—*in a whirlwind of controversy, King Edward VIII chose to abdicate the British throne in 1936 to marry Wallis Simpson, a divorced American. Subsequently Edward received the title of duke. The public had their doubts whether or not they were Nazi sympathizers.*

As the war dismally progressed and the incessant aerial bombardment of German cities became a harsh reality, Hitler retreated to the Berghof not for a holiday but to hide from the grim reality of Germany's future. In the end, the Berghof was flattened by a storm of bombs on April 25, 1945, and today the only parts remaining are the driveway and remnants of the back wall.

Hotel Türken: The age-old Hotel Türken did not fall prey to Bormann's bulldozers but instead it was annexed by the Reich's Security Service (Reichssicherheitsdienst)—being next door to the Berghof, it was too convenient a location. For the history of the Hotel Türken, flip to page 245.

Bunker System: (Bunkeranlagen) It is easy to understand in the beginning of the war why terms such as "air raid" or "underground shelter" were taboo in Hitler's peaceful neighborhood. By the middle of 1943, however, the Allies increased the air war over Germany to daily sorties and the Nazi war machine had suffered great defeats on the Eastern front, e.g. Stalingrad and Kursk. Hitler had no choice but to agree on a new construction project for his alpine command center. Engineers scrambled to devise plans, which were drafted, evaluated, modified, disapproved, redrafted, and finally approved to relocate Nazi Southern Command underground in an attempt to prolong the fight. By war's end, the bunker system was estimated to be 5km/3mi long. All tunnels were interlinked, except Herman Göring's air-raid shelter with Martin Bormann's because of an internal rivalry.

As for the construction of the bunkers, you'll have to imagine thousands of craftsmen and laborers rotating every eight hours in overly cramped working conditions. While a mason cemented the ceiling of an entrance, for example, plumbers, electricians and handymen had to crawl between his legs to get to their positions. The excavated dirt was trucked miles away so aerial reconnaissance could not detect the clandestine operation.

For a do-it-yourself subterranean adventure, flip to page 245.

Haus Bormann: (Formerly located on bluff across road from Hotel Türken.) Martin Bormann lived in a large, two-story cottage that externally appeared rustic Bavarian while internally it was outfitted with state-of-the-art amenities and luxurious furnishings, even the children's rooms were fit for royalty. Bormann acquired the house from Dr. Seitz, who locally ran a children's medical clinic. The acquisition was meticulously planned. Since it overlooked the Berghof, he could observe Hitler's every move. Bormann had the unusual ability to influence Hitler when others couldn't. As a result of Bormann's tireless energy and obsessive nature to serve his master, he was always informed of Hitler's state of affairs, and even on matters that were none of his business. He frequently traveled with Hitler while his wife and nine children lived permanently at Obersalzberg. It was during these times that Mrs. Bormann, the children, and Eva Braun regularly visited the Eagle's Nest—the property that Bormann insisted on building for his boss, who he must have known was afraid of heights! Bormann died on the streets of Berlin shortly following Hitler's suicide. Today, nothing remains of Haus Bormann.

Kindergarten, Archives & Admin: Situated above the Hotel Türken, the administration building belonged to the SS barracks. Adjacent were the archives—a studio containing models of future projects for the neighborhood—and the kindergarten, which was instituted for the children of Obersalzberg personnel. Today, nothing remains of these structures.

SS Barracks: To guarantee Hitler's protection, barracks for an SS battalion ("Schutz Staffel," or protection detachment) were constructed near his house. These consisted of residence quarters, a motor pool, mess hall, and (to ensure tranquility on Obersalzberg) an underground rifle range.

In 1952, the barracks were razed and redeveloped into a soccer field. A few years ago, in preparation for the new Eagle's Nest bus departure area, the soccer field was dug up. During this project much of the past was unearthed: ammunition, movie reels, official documents, SS porcelain wares, numerous bottles of wine seized during the occupation of France, and many other knickknacks needed to sustain 600 SS troops. Today, buses departing for the Eagle's Nest drive right through the site of the former SS barracks.

Greenhouse: Hitler was a strict vegetarian and the greenhouse supplied ample produce for his cravings as well as a fresh supply of flowers for the homes of high-ranking officers. What's more, Eva Braun found the greenhouse the perfect location to organize Easter-egg hunts for the officers' children. Today, nothing remains of the greenhouse.

Air-Raid Warning Center: While Hitler and his top brass were managing the war from Obersalzberg, the air-raid warning center was on high alert. Entrenched within the hill behind the greenhouse, this cavernous bunker featured the most modern technical equipment known, which detected air traffic over Nazi-occupied Europe by relaying signals from the various radar stations positioned throughout the territories. If enemy planes were headed for Obersalzberg, the 11 anti-aircraft units in the Berchtesgaden district would then be contacted and ready for action within five minutes.

Additionally, the air-raid center governed the smoke-screen department. This was comprised of three batteries, with each having more than 250 smoke-screen devices loyal to the districts of Obersalzberg, Königssee, Bad Reichenhall and Salzburg. If the order was given, the entire region could be blanketed by smoke within 20 minutes making it virtually impossible for the enemy to achieve a successful bombing run.

With all these preventative measures in place—we hear you asking—how is it possible that Obersalzberg was bombed at all?

What made the British bombing raid on Wednesday, April 25, 1945, such a success was by this late stage in the war the Germans had lost so much territory that the bombers flew most of their mission over friendly terrain. By the time functioning German radar stations actually picked up the signal of approaching enemy aircraft, the bombers were only 70km/44mi away. Thus, Hitler's neighborhood and command center were blown to smithereens. Today, nothing remains of the air-raid warning center.

Haus Göring: (The new InterContinental resort was built on the site of Haus Göring.) Born south of Munich in Rosenheim, Hermann Göring was a full-blooded Bavarian who loved everything about his heritage. He would often don tailor-made lederhosen and go deer hunting in the local forests. Göring became a hero to most Germans during WWI as a flamboyant fighter pilot. In 1918—upon the death of Germany's internationally famed ace of aces, Manfred von Richthofen, a.k.a. the Red Baron—Göring was honored with the command of Richthofen's legendary fighter squadron, the Flying Circus.

In the early 1920s, Hitler met Göring through his writer friend Dietrich Eckart. As a struggling politician, Hitler rode the social wave of Göring's celebrity. Germany's chancellor-to-be and the WWI hero teamed up as partners with a purpose, attending numerous public rallies and private functions together. Thus Göring became one of the original Nazis; he even participated in the 1923 Beer Hall Putsch. During the latter failed coup, Göring was seriously wounded and he subsequently fled the country until an amnesty allowed him back in 1927.

Years later, during the Third Reich, Hitler awarded Göring many titles, such as police chief of Prussia; original head of the Gestapo; commander of the Luftwaffe (German air force); and, ultimately, he was given the jeweled baton that came with the title of Herr Reichsmarschall (field marshal).

When Göring moved to Obersalzberg he had an elongated Bavarian-style house built with a California touch added to the front lawn: a swimming pool. Göring owned the estate for a decade before fleeing Germany at the end of the war. He was eventually picked up in Austria by U.S. troops and subsequently sentenced to death by hanging at the Nürnberg trials. Hours before his scheduled execution on October 15, 1946, Göring cheated the hangman by taking a hidden capsule of poison.

The foundations of Göring's house, along with the cellar and front-yard pool, remained somewhat intact right up until the turn of the new millennium, when work began on the 140-room InterContinental resort hotel.

Göring's Adjutant: In this white apartment building lived General Bodenschatz, Göring's chief of staff, as well as a few other officers and their families. Today the building still serves as apartments, seven in fact, and you'll walk by them if you visit the zoo.

Coal Bunker: Not far away, a huge concrete edifice was constructed to store tons of coal. Trucks would fill the internal storage units by unloading their cargo into the top of the structure via the above access road. Today, the coal bunker remains largely intact.

Drivers, when ready turn around and head back past the Hotel Türken and Hitler's former estate to the junction, where you'll turn left (direction Obersalzberg) and ascend the windy road to the next sites. To the right of the final curve, marked by a gravel pullover area and a yellow directional sign, stood the Kampfhäusl and where a path leads to the theater ruins.

Kampfhäusl: Hitler moved into this petite log cabin after serving his 13-month jail sentence at Landsberg prison (Nov 1923—Dec '24). It was here that in 1925 he wrote the second and final part of his political manifesto, Mein Kampf (My Struggle). In 1927, he moved a few properties over to Haus Wachenfeld, which later morphed into the Berghof mansion and the nucleus of Nazi Southern Command. Today, nothing remains of the Kampfhäusl.

Theater: Catering to the morale of the personnel at Obersalzberg, a 2000-seat theater hall was constructed. Here appeared the latest films and stage productions, as well as propaganda newsreels from the front. Hitler seldom visited. During the April '45 air raid the theater collapsed; some of the enormous concrete support pylons still remain. *Getting There:* At the curve in the road ascend the dirt path paralleling the earthen embankment on left (Kampfhäusl stood behind this). At the top, the path will veer right and flatten out—*(do not take narrow path that continues to ascend)*—follow this to the ruins.

VIP Guest House: Originally part of Pension Moritz, the cottage was aquired by Martin Bormann and renovated into his administration office and a VIP guest house to accommodate the businessmen with whom he had dealings. Today, the structure is the Documentation Center. *Note:* Wooded path behind property leads to Hitler's former estate; on a clear day the views into Austria are breathtaking.

Volkshotel Platterhof: Obersalzberg tourism began right here in the 19th century when a visionary named Mauritia Mayer, called Moritz by her friends, bought a ranch and developed the property into Pension Moritz. Profiting from Obersalzberg's clean air, Mayer marketed her pension as a healthy vacation. The rich and famous caught wind of this natural wonderland and filled the rooms. Distinguished guests included Sigmund Freud, Johannes Brahms and members of the Bavarian, Prussian and Austrian ruling families. Pension Moritz even entertained Dietrich Eckart, who in turn brought his protégé, Adolf Hitler.

In the 1930s Hitler's regime acquired the pension and renovated it into the 150-bed Volkshotel (People's Hotel) Platterhof. Initially, for 1 Reich's mark a night—roughly U.S. 33¢—party members could book a room to be near their beloved Führer. This concept soon went the way of the buffalo and the Volkshotel Platterhof only catered to bigwigs.

After the war, the U.S. repaired the damage from the April 25 bombing raid and the former Nazi hotel reopened as an AFRC resort (Armed Forces Recreation Center) under the moniker "General Walker." For more than 40 years the General Walker was a bustling resort hotel until the U.S. government closed its doors in 1995 as a result of military downsizing and sold it to the Germans. Ultimately, the 19th-century clean-air pension turned plush Nazi hotel was bombed by the British, rebuilt by the Americans, and razed by the Germans to become a revenue-making parking lot in the 21st century.

Post Office: Across from the Volkshotel Platterhof was a general store and post office for the convenience of Obersalzberg personnel. Today it's a traffic circle.

Haus Eckart: Dietrich Eckart often found himself in trouble with the law and would therefore go into hiding at his isolated residence miles from Obersalzberg. Eckart died in 1923 shortly after the failure of the Beer Hall Putsch. He is buried in the Old Cemetery (next to the Franciscan church in Berchtesgaden) along with Mauritia "Moritz" Mayer and Anton Adner (oldest Bavarian). Today, Eckart's former abode is known as the Hinterbrand lodge and used by the U.S. government as a youth education facility.

Eagle's Nest: see page 248.

WWII BUNKER

The bunker is located beneath the Hotel Türken. To fully understand its origin, we have outlined a basic history.

Our story begins in the 17th century with a soldier's return from the Turkish siege of Vienna in 1683. The Turks lost the battle and the allies who fought to defend the Austrian capital came home victorious. Upon the green alpine pastures of Obersalzberg the veteran found himself a homestead that became known as "Zum Türken."

Two centuries later, Herr Schuster—a local fireman—bought the Türken with his wife in 1911 and refurbished it to a hotel. Together with the nearby Platterhof Inn (former Pension Moritz), Hotel Türken entertained prominent members of the royal family and celebrities of the era.

In the early 1930s, the area around the Türken buzzed with optimistic nationals shunning the Great Depression. The previous decade had been much worse for the German people, who had seen their currency massively devalued, 40 percent unemployment, and perilous politics. The time was ripe for a new beginning. Germany's savior was Herr Schuster's new next-door neighbor, Adolf Hitler.

In January 1933, Hitler was elected chancellor of Germany and within a month he enabled parliament (on account of the Reichstag fire) to sanction him with special powers comparable to absolute dictatorship. At this time, the Nazis, Hitler's party, insisted on buying the Hotel Türken. However, Herr Schuster's answer was blunt: "Tell Herr Hitler, I won't sell!"

Schuster didn't agree with the brash ways of his new neighbor and did the unthinkable—he publicly spoke his mind. The brown shirts, Hitler's army of thugs, consequently arrested Schuster and organized a picket line in front of the Türken to ward off any possible commerce. One of the boycott signs read: "A good German would never do business with a traitor!" Schuster's new address was Dachau, an internment camp for enemies of the state.

The Schuster family was subsequently exiled from Berchtesgaden. They fled 50km north to Seebruck, a town on the Bavarian blue waters of Lake Chiemsee. Herr Schuster was released from Dachau a month later. He never fully recovered from the ensuing traumas and died at age 56 the following year, but not before the Nazis forced him to sell the Hotel Türken for a fraction of its value.

When the Nazis got their greasy hands on the Türken they converted it to a branch of the Reichssicherheitsdienst (RSD, or Reich's Security Service) under Heinrich Himmler, head of Nazi police forces. Being situated above the Berghof, Hitler's home, the Türken provided the perfect outpost from which to safeguard their chancellor. Ultimately a tunnel system was constructed beneath the Türken that ran directly under the Berghof—loaded with specially trained SS guards and laced with deadly machine-gun nests, Hitler could have retreated here and prolonged the war.

The tunnel system at the Türken provides us with a unique opportunity to delve into a WWII bunker—an underground labyrinth that leads directly into the Wolf's den. Come on, let's go and have a peek.

Hours: daily, 9:00-15:00 (April-Oct 7:00-18:00). *Price:* 2.70€/person.

Opinion: A trip to the bunker is worth your time, even if it's only to meet the owner, Frau Scharfenberg—Herr Schuster's granddaughter.

Besides the bunker, the property is also a hotel. For more info, go to www.hotel-zum-tuerken.com *Tel.#* 08652/2428

Note: There are a large number of stairs to negotiate within the bunker, which can be taxing to those who are in bad health.

Do-It-Yourself, WWII Bunker

Duration 20-45 min—amount of time depends on whether you're in a hurry or not. Time-crunched tourists can move through pretty fast; the only slowdown will be the flights of stairs. Visitors with time will want to move at a slower pace and possibly climb into the machine-gun nests for a gunner's perspective (see *Step 10*). Okay, let's start…

Step 1) Go through the gate and begin descending the spiral staircase. Keep an eye out for the first left. Turn here (toilet on left) and go to the dead end. These are Gefängnis-zellen, or "jail cells." No need to conjure harsh visuals, not much actually happened here. The so-called villains they were meant for didn't frequent Obersalzberg. If there were such criminals or conspirators, they would have been most likely found and detained in the village of Berchtesgaden by Polizei. The real horror stories that you're familiar with, "Vee have vays of making zu tawk," took place at Prinz-Albrecht-Strasse 8, Berlin—headquarters to the Gestapo and Heinrich Himmler (the latter HQ is now the Topography of Terror exhibition; see page 360).

Notice the black soot, it's left over from the fire that broke out as a result of the British bombing raid on April 25, 1945.

Step 2) Continue down the spiral staircase. At the bottom is an excellent opportunity to see the way the tunnels were constructed. Two layers of bricks accompanied by concrete, insulation, two more rows of bricks and more concrete—generally a meter thick until natural rock is reached.

Step 3) Continue forward to the junction. Left or right, which will it be? — *If you were to go left, you'd come to a bricked-off dead end. This formerly connected with the rest of the tunnel network, e.g. Martin Bormann's house, administration, the kindergarten, SS barracks, and so on.* — Go right to the next staircase but pay close attention to the concrete floor; the ceiling light will illuminate the "jackboot" footprints left behind by scurrying German officers.

Step 4) At the top of the staircase you'll see an inscription on the wall (post war) explaining that at this point you are 10m/30ft underground. Notice the concrete lids to your right; these covered the hot-air duct. The above brackets secured the water pipe. Walk down the steps to the bottom and stop. Don't turn the corner!

Step 5) Look back up the stairs and imagine this: It's May 4, 1945, and your company has just secured everything above ground. The task at hand is to expel any last-stand Nazis from the bunker system. You're a private and the job has landed in your lap. The only way out is to weasel a pardon. "Wait, I've got a wife and kids!" But there's nothing you can do, it's your turn. You hand over your wallet and the farewell letter you wrote your family weeks earlier in case you cop it sweet somewhere on the battlefield.

To get back to where you're standing—if there were Nazis still at their posts, our private wouldn't have made it any farther than the top of the stairs. That's because you're standing in front of a machine-gun nest. The Seh-Schlitz is the peephole and the other slots are to shoot through: Schiess.

Step 6) Walk the next few feet and stop at the top of the steps, <u>don't go down them!</u> While standing there, <u>without bending over</u>, what do you see? You see a sloping ceiling. If somehow our private had made it past the first welcoming party, then the second group of die-hards would have just sliced him in two at the waist. Go down the steps and you'll be faced with another machine-gun nest.

Step 7) Navigate the corridor and stop just before entering into the vestibule.

Step 8) Notice the concrete frame where a watertight iron door was implemented. If our private had miraculously made it this far, he would've been trapped between the locked iron door and welcoming party number three behind him. Turn around to see another machine-gun nest.

Step 9) Walk into the vestibule. Congratulations, you've just made it into Hitler's foyer—70m/230ft underground. From here you'll notice a few things. Let's start with what looks like another prison cell. If Hitler were to have taken up residence below ground, then the prison cell would've been the home (kennel) for his dog, Blondie.

Above the entrance you came through you'll see a gas duct (Schleuse); these were installed throughout the bunker system to prevent the airways from being used forcibly. The writing on the wall to the right reads: "Construction of the bunker system began mid-August 1943, it's described in the book 'Obersalzberg' that is available upstairs in the kiosk."

Hitler's personal bodyguards known as "Leibwache" occupied the vestibule. Hence the two openings left of the bricked-off doorway, which were used as domestic facilities. Within the second entrance it looks like our private heard some noises and let his rifle rock 'n' roll.

We see more writing to the right of the bricked-off doorway, it reads: "Behind this door were the rooms of Hitler, Eva Braun, and Dr. Morell."

Adolf had 19 rooms in his bunker and most were lavishly decked out with marble, wood paneling, tapestries, chandeliers, parquet floors, and carpeting. The equivalent of millions of dollars were spent putting all this together while the nation had to ration even the most basic foods in addition to melting church bells for the war effort. How many times did Hitler stay here, you ask? Not even once!

Step 10) You have a choice of two stairways; they both lead to the same place. Face the aforementioned gas duct and descend the one on the right.

At the bottom of the staircase you have the opportunity (on right) to *climb up and into those three machine-gun nests that we passed on the way in. It's worth the climb, even if your hands smell like rust afterwards. Bring your camera. *Suggestion:* Shoot a photo from the gunner's perspective as a private belonging to your company tries to breach the premises. *Note:* Before climbing, finish our tour since it's almost over and then come back.

To the left of the staircase you'll see three things: another bricked-off wall that formerly led under Hitler's house; a cubical designated "maschinenraum" (machine shop), which facilitated the heating, lighting and ventilation in the bunker; and you'll see a short corridor, head down this.

Step 11) At the junction you can go left or straight, either way you end up in the same place. However, let's go straight.

To your immediate left is the inside of another gunner's nest. A few feet farther and you'll be inside yet another nest; here you can witness the ramifications of repeated bazooka blasts by our private. This provides a unique opportunity to see firsthand how the Nazis reinforced their fortifications, such as the Atlantic Wall. The barred passage led out the side of the mountain—depending on the situation, this could have been utilized as a secret entrance or an escape route.

That wraps up our tour, folks! We hope you enjoyed yourselves and continue to do so. Take your time and remember…all paths lead up and out.

And to conclude the final entry in the journal of our brave private: He never encountered any resistance that afternoon, surviving to once again breathe the fresh air that we take for granted everyday.

Then what were those bazooka blasts for? Why the hell not!

EAGLE'S NEST

~ "Kehlsteinhaus" ~ Elevation: 1834m/6015ft

The Eagle's Nest—or Kehlsteinhaus as it's referred to in Bavaria—is a petite structure built from massive granite blocks cemented into the summit of Mount Kehlstein at 6015 feet. The views are stunning from its perch and the bus ride there is a marvel in itself. From Obersalzberg at 3100 feet the road zigzags its way 4 miles up the mountain face to the entrance of a 400-foot tunnel blasted into the dense rock, where visitors walk the remaining leg to Hitler's former elevator that lifts its occupants into the heart of the Eagle's Nest.

In just 13 months 3500 workers from 1937-38 completed the entire Eagle's Nest project: access roads, tunneling, elevator and the structure itself. To facilitate such swift results the mountainside was illuminated throughout the night allowing construction to continue nonstop. While several work crews were forging the road, others were simultaneously building the Nest with the aid of a cable-car system hauling up materials. Even by today's standards the Eagle's Nest project is seen as a remarkable engineering feat.

It is said that Hitler had a fear of heights and experienced claustrophobia in the elevator on the way up, thus he wasn't a great admirer of the property. Hitler officially visited the Nest 14 times between September 1938 and October 1940. Unofficially there are only a handful of visits noted. The biggest function held in the Nest was a wedding reception in June '44—the guests of honor were Eva Braun's sister, Gretl, and SS general Herman Fegelein. Hitler did not attend. To dispel the myth, there are no bedrooms in the Eagle's Nest and Hitler never spent the night. There were, however, a few bunk beds situated in the basement for guards stationed on premises (this area is off limits to visitors).

Fortunately, during the immense bombing raid on April 25, 1945, the British missed the Eagle's Nest and it therefore remains in original condition—minus most of the original furnishings. Today, around 300,000 tourists per season visit the mountaintop structure, which is maintained by the Berchtesgaden historical society and marketed as a casual restaurant.

Hours: Nest is open daily from (depending on weather) mid-May thru October. It is closed the rest of the year due to mammoth amounts snow.

Price: 13.50€—includes round-trip bus fare from Obersalzberg to the Eagle's Nest and entry into the structure. 17.50€—includes round-trip bus fare from Berchtesgaden's train station to Obersalzberg, then to the Eagle's Nest and entry into the structure.

Tickets can be bought at the Eagle's Nest departure area at Obersalzberg or from the ticket counter at the bus terminal adjoining Berchtesgaden's train station. From the bus terminal the price will be 17.50€, which includes the added *fare of 4€ from Berchtesgaden to Obersalzberg and back. *_Note:_ This added fare will not be charged to holders of a valid day ticket *(Tageskarte)* [you would have bought this when coming from Salzburg] or the Bavaria Ticket *(Bayern-Ticket)* [you might have bought this when coming from anywhere in Bavaria, i.e. Munich].

Buses: The first bus to leave from Obersalzberg to the Eagle's Nest is around 7:35 (mostly Nest employees take this bus); the second bus leaves about 8:25—after this, buses depart every 25 minutes until the last one at 16:00. *Note:* Times are from last year's schedule and should be used as a general reference.

Tours of the Eagle's Nest in English (duration 40 min) meet outside the tunnel entrance at 10:50 and 11:40. Anyone can tag along for 5€. To make either tour you'll need to catch the 10:30 or 11:20 bus from Obersalzberg.

Note: Once bus arrives at the Eagle's Nest, stand in line at the window on the right to have your ticket stamped with your desired return time. As a head's up, you'll notice the available return times are located behind the bus driver. Consider a departure time of at least 70 minutes after your arrival. If the weather is nice and you're a history buff, allow 90-120 min. Calculate whether you're going to eat at the restaurant or enjoy a beverage. Additionally, standing in line for the elevator can sometimes take 15 min.

Weather: Complement your journey to the Eagle's Nest with good weather by planning days in advance, i.e. stay on top of the weather reports! If you're short on time and get caught on a bad weather day, then no more than an hour is necessary for your visit, as the views will be stifled—unless you are a WWII buff, then it doesn't matter.

Suggestion: Instead of taking the elevator back down from inside the Nest, consider walking to the bus area via the scenic path (allow at least 20 min), which can be found on the right side of the structure when facing it from outside on the patio.

Restaurant is very casual, reasonably priced, and serves Bavarian-style cuisine. Inside can be crowded and stuffy, consider enjoying your beverage or meal on the out-door patio.

Band of Brothers: For those who caught the last episode "Points," you'll see that Hanks and Spielberg did a superb job of re-creating the Eagle's Nest. The only giveaway is when Dick Winters comes up a stairway from Eva Braun's tea room (not possible) and onto the sun terrace to tell the boys to hold their positions.

Getting There: **Railers,** the first bus to leave Berchtesgaden's train station for Obersalzberg is 7:15 (mostly Nest employees take this bus); the second bus leaves about 8:10—after this, buses depart roughly every half hour until the last one at 15:00. **Drivers,** *from the center of Berchtesgaden* pass the pedestrian shopping zone (on left) and follow the road as it curves right. At the bottom of the hill is a traffic light, turn left (direction Kehlstein)—this is almost a U-turn. At the next set of lights turn right—upon turning notice the shack to your left, this was the first of many check points up to Hitler's former neighborhood, Obersalzberg. **Drivers,** *if you're coming from the Austrian-Bavarian border at Marktschellenberg,* continue towards Berchtesgaden and after about 5km look for the sign Obersalzberg/Kehlstein—follow this left. (If it's a clear day you'll be rewarded with a surreal view of Germany's second highest mountain, the Watzmann. Just before the left turn is the Grassl Enzianbrennerei [distillery] on the right).

Parking: There are two parking lots neighboring the Eagle's Nest departure area at Obersalzberg. The cost is a one-time fee of 2.50€, payable at the "Parkschein-Automat." *Note:* Automat does not give change, bring exact amount! Push "PKW" button, this means "car."

Do-It-Yourself, Eagle's Nest

You've just endured a riveting bus ride up the side of an alpine mountain to the Nest landing zone at 1695m/5500ft. Bravo! Now get your ticket stamped with your desired return time at the window to the right. Afterward, proceed to the tunnel.

Tunnel: Before entering the 124m/400ft long tunnel, notice the Baroque-style medallion crowning the entrance, it reads: Erbaut (built) 1938. Now check out the inscribed names on the mammoth bronze portal—many of these soldiers fought their way across Europe from Normandy to the Nest.

The tunnel's interior is outfitted with roughly finished rose-marble blocks, which ring with moisture and seem to encourage the cold. Hitler's chauffeur, Erich Kempka, drove him down this confined passage to the elevator, where Hitler got out and Kempka was left to ponder a smoothly orchestrated return. Kempka carefully reversed Hitler's dark-blue, 7-liter Mercedes out of the tunnel, where he then turned the car around and slowly reversed back to the elevator.

Notice the vents near the floor, which total 11. The tunnel had central heating. At the end of the 124-meter stretch is an elevator that will lift visitors another 124 meters into the heart of the Eagle's Nest—45 people in 45 seconds.

~ *Upon exiting the elevator notice the snow-packed picture on the right—that's why the Eagle's Nest is closed from November thru mid-May. Now go through the adjacent door into the...*

Oak-Paneled Banquet Room: As the name suggests, people would gather here for a meal. Originally, a long rectangular table spanned the length of the room and could accommodate up to 30 guests. Adorning the table was a lavish hand-made tablecloth that cost upwards of $12,000 to make. The large oak buffet (on right) is the only original piece of furniture left in the Nest. All other furnishings were removable and could easily "go walkabout."

~ *Out the other end of the banquet room steps lead into the...*

Former Conference Hall: Spearheading the Eagle's Nest is the former conference hall, noticeably the largest room in the structure, featuring five generous windows providing an abundance of light and eye-popping views. The red-marble fireplace is original and still in working order, stoked by more than six decades of occupants—look inside for its birth year: 1938. The floor in the hall was primarily covered with a luxurious, hefty carpet weighing 600kg/1300lbs. After the war, the carpet was cut into small squares and taken home as souvenirs by the liberating soldiers.

~ *Eva Braun would often visit the Nest; her favorite place is said to be the cute and cozy tea room that adjoins the hall.*

Eva Braun's Tea Room: Within this intoxicating room the walls are finished with knotted panels of pinewood, polished and light in color. Upon entering through the narrow doorway, the visitor is immediately jostled by a heady fragrance suggestive of an evergreen forest. The window at the far side of the room affords spectacular views of Königssee's sparkling glacier-blue water and of the Watzmann massif, second highest mountain in Germany at 2712m/8900ft. The doorway on the left connects onto the sun terrace. *Note:* In Eva Braun's tea room some of the chairs depict the letters H+B. Does this stand for Hitler and Braun? Is there a drinker amongst you?

~ *When you're ready, head back the way you came. Upon exiting the oak banquet room go right into the...*

Hallway: The hallway and the rooms running off it are exactly as they were in 1938, except that the kitchen has been refitted to serve a multitude of tourists. For those who have the urge, toilets are on the left.

~ *A few doors farther down on the left is the...*

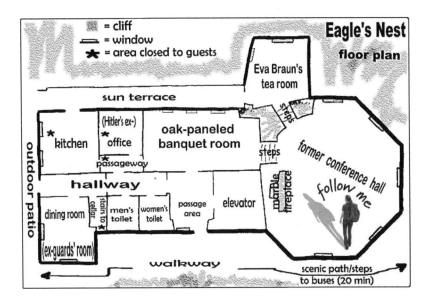

Ex-Guards' Room: Today this room with its Bavarian feel is part of the restaurant and referred to as a Stube. During the Third Reich, sentries would occupy this area before and after their patrols. When it came to sleeping, the guards would head down to the basement where a few bunks were set up.

~ *At the end of the hallway a door leads onto the...*

Outdoor Patio: Upon stepping outside, move to the left (off the beaten path) for an orientation. With your back to the Nest, *to your left* and around the corner begins the scenic path/steps down to the buses—highly recommended if weather permits (allow 20 min). *To your right* is an arched portal that leads onto the sun terrace (this is where the "Band of Brothers" scene was portrayed when Dick Winters tells the boys to hold their positions). From the terrace, a doorway connects back into Eva Braun's tea room. *In front of you* on the peak is a cross, which has nothing to do with the Nazis—it was implemented by the local mountaineering club as a remembrance to those who have died while exploring nature. *Note:* Walk up the stepped path towards the cross to snap a fine photo of the Nest. The farther up the path you go, the better the shot.

BADEN-BADEN

~ Pop: 50,000 ~ Elev: 180m/590ft ~ Country/Area Code: +49-(0)7221

Situated 16km/10mi from the French border on the lower slopes of the Black Forest, Baden-Baden—literally Bath-Bath—was first settled some 2000 years ago by the Romans, who championed the health-spa movement. In the 19th century, Baden-Baden became a hotspot for emperors, aristocrats and artists who convened here to gamble, elegantly stroll about, and bathe in the town's curative mineral waters.

Today, Baden-Baden is a showcase for litter-free streets, chic restaurants, fancy hotels, and quaint Victorian homes. The community is rich in culture, from music and theater companies to Europe's largest and "most beautiful of all casinos," according to Marlene Dietrich. What's more, Baden-Baden embraces 12 hot springs (between 12,000 and 17,000 years old) that continuously surge to the earth's surface from depths of up to 2000 meters, replenishing visitors with its therapeutic properties. To fully appreciate the latter, be sure to experience Friedrichsbad's 16-step, Roman-Irish treatment —with soap-and-brush massage—designed to spoil (page 253).

~ Baden-Baden is worth a two-day stay—divide your time like so,

Day 1: Arrive early — get orientated, check into your digs, soak in the baths, and crown your day with a satisfying dinner. *Note:* Make sure to begin your (Friedrichsbad) bathing experience no later than 4 hours prior to closing.

Day 2: Tour the casino (before noon), stroll along Lichtentaler Allee, and ramble up the "Schloßstaffeln" (page 257—*Marktplatz*) for the best views in town. ***Railers:*** Instead, you could head to Triberg (page 263) for the day. Or, if you're ready to exit Baden-Baden, consider buzzing south to Freiburg (page 271). Trains depart hourly for either destination and take about an hour. ***Drivers:*** Consider an afternoon excursion on the Black Forest High Road (page 260) or Baden Wine Road (page 266), or both.

Tourist Information: [TI] (www.baden-baden.com) *Tel.#* 07221/275-200
Baden-Baden has two TIs; both are open daily. One is centrally located near the casino and the other branch is outside of town, catering to drivers.

TI: The downtown branch is situated in the *Trinkhalle*, adjacent to the Kurhaus (casino). *Hours:* daily, Mon-Sat 10:00-17:00, Sun 14:00-17:00.

TI: Baden-Baden's second TI caters to drivers, as it's situated on the right-hand side of route 500 when approaching town from the autobahn (or France). Set up in a modern structure spanning the Oos-bach (-stream), this TI offers a free room-finding service during biz hours and an after-hours hotel info board outside with free phone to call your chosen digs. You'll find clean toilets on the left after entering through the first door. *Hours:* daily, Mon-Sat 9:00-18:00, Sun 9:00-13:00.

Note: At either TI be sure and pick up the free (monthly) Baden-Baden events program: "Aktuell," which contains a city map, daily happenings (*Veranstaltungen*), as well as a list of church services (*Gottesdienst*), emergency doctors (*Notfalldienst*), and discounts with the Kurkarte (you'll receive the latter "visitor's card" when checking into your accommodations, excluding the youth hostel).

Railers: This pleasant and clean train station (Bahnhof) is located in the suburb of Oos, some 5km from central Baden-Baden. Storage lockers (depending on size) cost 1.50€/3€ 24hr. Taxis and buses are out front. A taxi to central Baden-Baden will approximately cost 12€. Bus #201 does a regular milk-run from the station to downtown (15-min ride; 2€/person, buy ticket from driver), get off at Leopoldsplatz (Stadtmitte), or at Grosse Dollenstrasse for the youth hostel (eight-minute ride)—hostelers should consider buying the 24hr ticket (*Tageskarte*) 4€. *Note:* Validate bus ticket in onboard box, watch locals.

Drivers: Baden-Baden can be tricky to drive through. Just remember, the signposted *Thermen* (and hotel) route is a great slide from one end of town to the other, often leading you through lanes that appear as auto-free zones.

Parking: To park on the street in town, most automats cost 1€/hr with a max time of one hour between 8:00-19:00, applicable seven days. Parking garages usually run 1.50€/hr, 15€/24hr.

Bike Rental: To rent a bike in Baden-Baden is a very informal experience: Head to the underground garage at the Kurhaus (casino) and notify the attendant. The bicycles are not in the best shape but they're mega-cheap: 1€/2hr, 2.50€/6hr—show your Kurkarte to receive a 50% discount. *Hours:* daily 8:00-18:00; can return bikes until 20:00. *Note:* Must bring ID! Arrive early; they only have a handful of bikes to choose from. If they're sold out, check the Festspielhaus garage or query TI for other options.

Internet: For a surf, head to the Internet café "Weblounge" at Eichstr. 3, located off Lichtentaler Str.—a few-minutes walk south of Leopoldsplatz. *Hours:* Mon-Sat 10:00-24:00, Sun 12:00-24:00. *Price:* 2.40€/hr. *Tel.#* 07221/397-868.

What to do on a Sunday or holiday

Both the Friedrichsbad and Caracalla spa are open on Sundays and holidays, with the exception of Good Friday and December 24/25.

Consider joining the casino tour in the morning followed by a stroll around town and then a Roman-Irish soak in the Friedrichsbad. Another Sunday idea is to hike or drive to the Altes Schloß. Drivers have the added option of cruising the Black Forest High Road (page 260) or Baden Wine Road (page 266), or both.

FREE Baden-Baden

1) Explore the 11th-century ruins of the Altes Schloß (page 257).

2) Sample Baden-Baden's curative mineral water bubbling from underground springs—fountains can be found in the Caracalla spa (first floor, one level up) as well as in the Trinkhalle.

3) With the *Kurkarte (or visitor's card) you're entitled to a free 90-minute tour—called a Stadtrundgang—of Baden-Baden. These tours are usually in German; query TI to see whether an English tour is scheduled.

*When you spend the night in Baden-Baden you'll receive the Kurkarte from your accommodations, excluding the youth hostel.

SIGHTS

Friedrichsbad: Römerplatz (www.carasana.de) *Tel.#* 07221/275-920. Let's cut to the chase, there are two types of baths in this world, some that are totally nude and some that are not. Dating from 1877, the classic-style Friedrichsbad is of the totally nude variety. But we believe you already knew that, thus you are still reading. Unrivaled in Germany, Friedrichsbad offers thermal and therapeutic facilities prescribed by doctors, preferred by natives and adored by tourists. Look But Don't Touch—chapter five in YTC's novel, *Quest for the Bavarian Cross*—typified a North American's experience in Friedrichsbad. Will your encounter be different?

Friedrichsbad's signature treatment is the 16-step Roman-Irish pamper package designed to spoil, consisting of mineral pools, steam rooms, soothing showers, cream therapy, and a soap-and-brush massage. Posted at each step is a sign recommending how much time should be allowed; however, you can allocate your time how you please. In all, you will spend between 3 and 3.5 hours pampering yourself.

What exactly is Roman-Irish therapy? "Roman" refers to thermal steam saunas, and "Irish" represents hot/dry air rooms. Combine these elements with Friedrichsbad's mineral pools and you've got a healthy fusion to cure, relieve and prevent colds, nerves and rheumatism as well as stimulate your skin, blood circulation and respiratory system. In fact, Mark Twain visited here in the latter part of the 19th century and penned the following words in his adventure novel—A Tramp Abroad—referring to his Fried-richsbad experience: "I had the twinges of rheumatism unceasingly during three years, but the last one departed after a fortnight's bathing there, and I have never had one since. I fully believe I left my rheumatism in Baden-Baden. Baden-Baden is welcome to it. It was little, but it was all I had to give."

Suggestion: Bring clean socks and undies! After you've pampered yourself for more than three hours and are feeling squeaky clean, you won't want to throw on your previously worn undergarments.

Note: Begin your bathing experience no later than four hours prior to closing. (Ideally, start early afternoon and crown your day with a satisfying dinner.) Bath slippers are included in the price, along with lockers to secure your clothes and valuables. All you need to bring is money, clean socks and underwear, and an open mind. For folks who are looking for alternative treatments, Friedrichsbad offers a variety of wellness programs, from sea-algae scrubs to facial Shiatsu to full-body massages (the latter roughly costs 45€/50 min)—see reception for details or call for an appointment.

Keep in mind Mondays and Thursdays are reserved for same-sex bathing, labeled as "getrennt" *(the exception to the rule here is the central pool, although possible to avoid, remains open to both sexes).* The remaining five days of the week are mixed, or "gemischt," meaning both sexes enjoy each other's company in the pool areas. If you're having second thoughts about visiting Friedrichsbad on a day that is mixed (gemischt), heed this piece of advice: In steps 1-8 you're introduced to nudity amongst your own gender. By the time you reach the "mixed" pools in steps 9-11, you should be comfortable enough with your body to thwart feelings of self-consciousness.

Hours: daily, Mon-Sat 9:00-22:00, Sun and holidays 12:00-20:00.

Price: (Ask at your accommodations if they happen to have a discount coupon.) There are two main treatments to consider, the Roman-Irish 15-step and 16-step. The 15-step treatment costs 21€ and lasts three hours. The 16-step treatment *(recommended)* costs 29€, lasts 3.5 hours, and includes the soap-and-brush massage. If you decide to stay longer, or time just slips away, the cost is 3.50€ per extra half hour. *CC's:* VC, MC, AE, DC.

Getting There: Friedrichsbad is located in the center of town. *Drivers,* follow signs "Centrum-Thermen." After climbing the hill (Leopoldstr.) and passing through the tunnel, make your second right onto Rotenbachtalstr. Soon after the first traffic light, pull into the "Bädergarage" on your right. Visitors to Friedrichsbad park for *free the first two hours and pay 1€ for each additional hour. *Receptionist must validate your ticket. *GPS:* (front door) N48° 45.774 - E8° 14.545

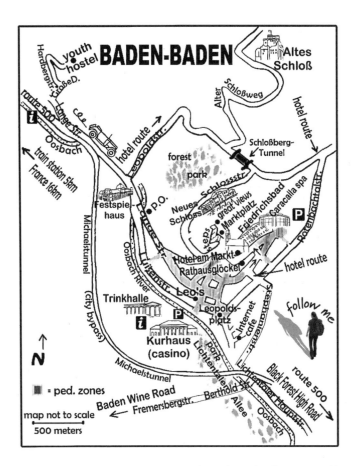

Caracalla Spa: Römerplatz 1 (www.carasana.de) *Tel.#* 07221/275-940. Although they are neighbors and both have the same owner, the Caracalla spa couldn't be more different from the Friedrichsbad. The Caracalla spa is a contemporary bathing complex where you'll keep your privates under wraps.

    The walls are not made of marble here, as were the original Caracalla baths in Rome, but if the emperor were still alive he would be most impressed with this modern indoor/outdoor aquatic center, or bathers' paradise. Even though the Caracalla spa is loads of fun, it has similar amenities found throughout Germany. Thus we recommend the Friedrichsbad experience. Ideally, you could visit both places. For a closer look, wander inside the Caracalla spa and up to the first floor—here you can also taste test three of Baden-Baden's thermal springs. *Hours:* daily, 8:00-22:00 (last entry 20:00). *Price:* 12€/2hr, 14€/3hr, 16€/4hr. If there's a long line at the cashier, consider using the "Verkaufsautomat" opposite or the one on the first floor—button for English. *Note:* Price includes entry to all areas, even the saunas, which are upstairs and typically nude (log cabin saunas are outside). Bring your own towel or you'll have to rent one, 5€ plus deposit. *Getting There:* The Caracalla spa is located in the center of town. *Drivers,* follow signs "Centrum-Thermen." After climbing Leopoldstr. and passing through the tunnel, make your second right onto Rotenbachtalstr. Soon after the first traffic light, pull into the "Bädergarage" on your right. Visitors to the Caracalla spa park for *free the first two hours and pay 1€ for each additional hour. *Receptionist must validate your ticket.

Kurhaus: Centrally located and dating from 1821, this neoclassic temple is the heart and soul of Baden-Baden's social life—hosting concerts, exhibitions, recitals, afternoon tea, late dinner, grand balls, and the château-style casino (see next entry). Management here told us the world is invited! *Note:* Toilets are straight inside and to the left; continue past them for the slot machines ("Automatenspiel"), which are right and downstairs.

Outside the Kurhaus stand at the top of the steps with your back to the door. In front of you to the right is a bandstand where free concerts are held in summer. Directly in front of you and extending left along the promenade are six old-fashioned gas lamps, which are still lit by hand every evening at dusk. While casting an eye to the left you'll see (behind the row of chestnut trees) the side of the Trinkhalle (page 257). And like a real-life portrait spread before you is Baden-Baden—the pink spire belongs to the Catholic church situated on Marktplatz; adjacent (left) are the prominent gables belonging to the Neues Schloss, and farther left on the hillside are the must-see ruins of the Altes Schloß.

Casino: Within Germany there are upwards of 60 casinos. However, the largest and "most beautiful of all casinos," according to Marlene Dietrich, is the one in Baden-Baden, exhibiting a lavish French-style interior. Following its grand opening in 1824, Baden-Baden gained the reputation of being the summer capital of Europe. Emperors, nobles and artists gathered here to gamble, enjoy social events and bathe in the thermal magic. Yet every party must come to an end, and in 1872—one year after the christening of the Second Reich—the casino was shut down. How things teeter-totter, in 1933 came the Third Reich and the casino was keenly reopened. By 1944, after 5 years of war, Germany's high life had withered into the gutter and the casino's doors were once again padlocked. In 1950, a rebirth occurred under the nation's new democratic republic bringing prosperous days for worldly patrons to try their luck in Europe's most beautiful casino. Today, it averages 600 gamblers per day—although, peak summer can attract up to 2500 visitors. About 90% of the takings—roughly 30€ million per year—must be given to the state, Baden-Württemberg. However, a decent portion comes back to Baden-Baden for reinvestment.

(www.casino-baden-baden.de) *Tel.#* 07221/30-240 *Hours:* daily, 14:00-02:00 (black jack from 17:00; poker from 18:00—Fri/Sat from 20:00). *Price:* (entry into casino) 3€ or 1.50€ with Kurkarte. Minimum bets in the casino, depending on the game, are 2€ and the maximum is 10,000€. *Note:* Must be 21 years of age to enter, ID required. *Attire:* Men must wear a jacket and tie; rental is available at desk *(jacket 8€, tie 14€ but you get 11€ back upon its return, and 16€ for a shirt—but you keep it)*. Ladies, just look appropriate. No jeans or tennis shoes allowed. *Lady's Day:* Every 2nd Tuesday of the month is Lady's Day, which means ladies get free entry into the casino, a free cocktail, a 2€ chip, and are allowed four free spins on the wheel of fortune for cash/prizes (one spin at 16:00, 18:00, 20:00 and 22:00). *Slot Machines:* (Automatenspiel) 50¢ slots can be found downstairs— 1€ entry (or free with paid admission into the casino), no dress code, same hours as casino. *Tours:* The daily, multilingual tour is a great alternative to dressing up and risking your Euro budget to see the casino. Tours cost 4€ and depart at 30-min intervals in the morning, beginning from 9:30 in summer (Nov-March from 10:00) until last tour at 11:30. *Gaming Brochures:* Descriptive brochures in English (free) explaining the rules of each individual game (roulette, black jack, baccara, etc) are available at reception. *Getting There:* Casino is located in the center of town in the Kurhaus (see above entry).

Trinkhalle: (Pump Room, 1842) During the mid-19th century when Baden-Baden was enjoying its heyday, the Trinkhalle—with its enclosed promenade almost a football field long, bolstered by 16 Corinthian-style columns and featuring 14 prominent frescos depicting dreamy nymphs and provincial legends—was considered a stroller's delight and a place to be seen. Inside the Trinkhalle is a TI, a chic café, and a faucet expelling endless, warm, restorative, mineral-rich spring water for your healthy consumption— tastes yucky! _Hours:_ (Trinkhalle & TI) Mon-Sat 10:00-17:00, Sun 14:00-17:00. The café is open till late in the evening; enter via left side of Trinkhalle.

Lichtentaler Allee: This tree-lined path is a dawdler's joy, especially in fall when the leaves are burning with color. Lichtentaler Allee extends some 2km (from Goetheplatz adjacent to the Kurhaus) through beautiful gardens and along the Oos stream to Kloster Lichtental, a 13th-century convent. At about the halfway mark you'll reach Berthold Str. _(drivers note that this road leads to Varnhalt, the first town on the Baden Wine Road)_, cross the crosswalk and continue straight passing the tennis courts on the right—traverse the river via the forward bridge to discover the *Gönneranlage, a fragrant garden featuring more than 100 varieties of roses. *_GPS:_ N48° 45.185 - E8° 14.443

Marktplatz: To visually find the "Market Square" is easy since it's located beneath the salmon-colored church spire rising above town. The spire belongs to the **Stiftskirche**, a Catholic church; parts still original from the 13th century. Behind the church you'll discover the three-story, Toscana-style **Altes Dampfbad** (Old Steam Bath—dating from 1848), which today houses regularly changing art exhibitions. The huge edifice next door belongs to the Friedrichsbad. Facing the church is the **Rathaus**; since 1862 this structure has served as the town hall. To the right of the church—on the corner—is the quaint **Hotel am Markt** (page 259), one of our recommended accommodations. On the leafy side of the church is a four-spouted fountain gushing endless Black Forest (drinkable) water. Nearby, you'll spot a telephone booth; head towards this and ascend the adjacent staircase "Schloßstaffeln" to the **best views** in town (143 steps). About one-third of the way up, follow the sign right. At the top, go right and hop onto the observation terrace. After you're done admiring the gigantic views, look behind you to the Neues Schloss (see next entry). Its main entrance is on the right past the handful of parking spaces. Hopefully the arched gateway will be open so you can get a glimpse into the courtyard.

Neues Schloss: Dating from the 14th century, the "New Palace" was built as a residence for the margraves of Baden. Some 200 years later a Renaissance palace replaced the original residence, which was destroyed in 1689 during the city fire. Ultimately, in 1847, the structure was rebuilt to the _exterior_ you see today. Exterior is the operative word here because the last descendant of the margraves of Baden, a nice fellow, privately owns the Neues Schloss. He said the palace has 110 rooms but he only lives in four of them, noting that the price of heating and general upkeep can be astronomical. After peering through the gates, notice the quaint streets descending back to town.

Altes Schloß: (Old Castle) Time well spent is a visit to the Altes Schloß, an 11th-century ruined burg cemented in the hillside above Baden-Baden. Here you can live out your childhood fantasy of playing in a real castle. In addition to the remains of a medieval burg, the property consists of a reasonably priced restaurant and hotel (page 259).

Between the 11th and 16th centuries the castle was the seat of the margraves of Baden, who named it Hohenbaden. During this time the margraves modified it to a formidable bastion featuring enlarged fortifications, multiple turrets, 30-meter-high walls and a tower that soared an additional 30 meters defining the skyline. Alas, centuries worth of modifications went up in smoke in the late 1500s when a firestorm swept through the premises. By the year 1627, locals condemned Hohenbaden labeling it the "old withered schloss." However, that didn't stop the wicked Frau Margrave from eternally combing the ramparts and local scrub for her son who fell from the tower to an unkind death. Her chilling screams often haunt the ruins, scaring little boys and girls into a change of underwear. Putting ghostly matters aside, the Altes Schloß commands sweeping vistas of Baden-Baden, the Rhine basin, and the Alsace region of France—196 steps will get you to the top of the tower, the last 15 are extra steep. If the wind is howling during your visit, take a break from scaling the bulwarks and listen to the soothing melody of the 120-string wind harp, currently the largest in Europe at 13-feet tall (located on the second tier in the main quad). *Hours:* ruins are open daily, usually till 22:00. *Price: FREE* entry! *Toilets* can be found immediately on the left after entering through the gate. *Getting There: Railers,* there are no regular bus connections, except twice on Sundays. Other ways of getting there would be to hike (worthwhile, 90 min one-way from Neues Schloss), catch a cab (roughly 13€ from city center), or befriend someone with wheels. *Drivers,* when coming from Leopoldstr. turn left just before the Schlossberg-Tunnel at the top of town (or turn right just after the tunnel when coming from Rotenbachtalstr.) and follow signs to Altes Schloß (3km). *GPS:* N48° 46.596 - E8° 14.590. *Note:* Once you begin your climb towards the castle, just after 1km notice the fountain on the left-hand side of the road—this is a good opportunity to fill your water bottles. The water originates deep within the Black Forest and is so pure that locals often come to fill their multi-gallon containers, hence the two woodboards. The fountain is called the *Eberbrun-nen and dates from 1861. The words on the bench—"bitte sauber halten"—are urging patrons to please keep the area clean. *GPS:* N48° 46.307 - E8° 14.851

Entertainment

There's not much to speak of when it comes to evening entertainment for the young and zealous in Baden-Baden. Here's what a few locals had to say: "This town is totenhosen (dead pants)," said the cashier at the Caracalla spa. "We go clubbing in Karlsruhe," asserted an acquaintance. So our list of hot spots will include just one, where Sydney and the girls drank two bottles of Riesling: **Leo's Restaurant-Café-Wine Bar**, Luisenstr. 10, near Leopoldsplatz; *tel.#* 07221/38-081. Open daily 08:00-02:00 (www.leos-baden-baden.de)

Culture vultures who are into the ballet, opera, or concerts should check out the **Festspielhaus**, or Playhouse. Refurbished in 1998 from the old train station (Alter Bahnhof), the Festspielhaus is one of the world's largest opera houses seating upwards of 2500 guests with an additional, smaller theater accommodating 1500 guests. For info regarding upcoming performances, go to www.festspielhaus.de

GOOD SLEEPS

In addition to the prices listed below—with the exception of the youth hostel—all accommodations in Baden-Baden are required by law to charge an extra 2.80€ per person, per night in the name of the so-called **Kurtaxe,** or Spa Tax, for the upkeep of the town's spa facilities. This isn't a complete waste of your money, as each person will in turn receive a **Kurkarte,** or visitor's card, entitling you to select discounts around town, including 50% off the casino tour, 50% off bike rental, and a free city tour.

Drivers: To reach the below-listed accommodations, follow the signposted "Thermen" route. When exiting the A5 autobahn (or coming from France), follow signs to Baden-Baden (route 500). After about 6km, you'll see signs to "Thermen." Follow this route, which will soon guide you left on Leopoldstr. This road will ascend 1km to a tunnel—if you're headed to the **Altes Schloß**, turn left before the tunnel, otherwise continue straight—through the tunnel and make your second right onto Rotenbachtalstr.

Descend this street; you'll pass a traffic signal and soon another leading into the shopping district. This is where it gets tricky—go slow—you need to get onto the pedestrian zone itself. *Turn right* (at Sonnenplatz) where the small white sign points *"Rathaus."* Persist slowly while being careful of pedestrians; veer right and then left. Now, there should be a large edifice in front of you, this is the Friedrichsbad. At the T-intersection: go right for the **Hotel Bischoff** (on right); turn left and drive up the cobbled lane for the **Rathausglöckel** (on left) or for the **Hotel am Markt** at the top (on right).

Both the **Hotel am Markt** and **Rathausglöckel** are charming choices, centrally located, and should be considered first when determining your Baden-Baden digs. Book well in advance! *Note:* Hotel am Markt has an elevator; the Rathausglöckel does not.

Hotel am Markt: Marktplatz (www.hotel-am-markt-baden.de) *Tel.#* 07221/27-040. This quaint hotel, run by (sisters) Mrs. Jung and Mrs. Schindler, is situated on the Market Square (Marktplatz) adjacent to the church—bells ring every quarter hour from 06:15-22:00. As disturbing as this may sound, the delightful owners and location make up for the clamor. *Price:* Sgl with facilities (shower/toilet) 42-47€, Sgl without facilities 30-32€; Dbl with bath or shower and toilet 75-80€, Dbl with toilet 60-64€. Parking 2.50€/day; notify reception when booking. *CC's:* VC, MC, AE. *Getting There:* **Railers,** from Leopoldsplatz walk over to McDonald's and ramble your way along the adjacent pedestrian lane—continue straight and climb the steps passing the giant statue of Bismarck, the "Iron Chancellor." At the top, 43 steps later, go left and your digs are on the right. *Drivers,* see directions above outlined under Good Sleeps. *GPS:* N48° 45.766 - E8° 14.458

Rathausglöckel: Steinstr. 7 (www.rathausgloeckel.de) *Tel.#* 07221/90-610 Situated on a cobbled lane running into the Market Square (Marktplatz), the Rathausglöckel is one of Baden-Baden's oldest guest houses, dating from the 16th century. Has respected restaurant. The church bells mentioned above for Hotel am Markt affect here, too. *Price:* Sgl 70-80€, Dbl 77-80€, extra bed 30€. Parking 6€/day; notify reception when booking. *CC's:* VC, MC. *Getting There:* Railers, see directions above for Hotel am Markt—only difference, go right at the top of the stairs to your digs on the right-hand side. *Drivers,* see directions above outlined under Good Sleeps. *GPS:* use same coordinates listed for Hotel am Markt.

Hotel Bischoff: Römerplatz 2; *tel.#* 07221/22-378, *fax.* /38-308. These average digs have an above-average location, directly across from the Friedrichsbad spa. *Price:* Sgl 45-55€, Dbl 65-85€. Parking 8€/day; notify reception when booking. *CC's:* VC, MC, AE. *Getting There: Drivers,* see directions outlined under Good Sleeps.

Altes Schloß: (Old Castle) Alter Schloßweg; *tel.#* 07221/26-948, *fax.* /391-775. Perched high above Baden-Baden where far-reaching views extend into France, the historic Altes Schloß offers five spacious rooms to rest your head. Closed Jan/Feb. *Price:* (5€/extra person if staying only one night) Sgl 30€ (facilities [shower/toilet] in hallway), Dbl 55€ (facilities in hallway), Dbl 65€ (facilities in room), Trpl-Quad 96-128€ (facilities in room). *CC's:* VC, MC, AE. *Note:* For an additional fee, management can arrange a romantic breakfast on the castle wall with super views to France. Furthermore, management can orchestrate most any event that you wish to celebrate within the castle confines. *Getting There: Railers,* not worth an overnight—there are no regular bus connections and a taxi (one-way) from the city center will roughly cost 13€. *Drivers,* see directions outlined under Good Sleeps. *GPS:* N48° 46.596 - E8° 14.590

Hostel, Werner-Dietz Jugendherberge: [HI] Hardbergstr. 34 (www.djh.de) *Tel.#* 07221/52-223. Midway between central Baden-Baden and the railway station, you'll find the only hostel in town. Closed occasionally in winter. *Price:* (includes breakfast and sheets; same-sex dorms only) dorm bed 18€ first night—15€ second night, Dbl 46€

(shower/toilet in room). <u>Note:</u> Must be a member and 26 or under to stay, or an extra charge will apply. Reception is open for a few hours in the morning, then for a short time every hour on the hour during the day until it reopens from 17:00 to 23:00. A walk from here into town is roughly 40 min, and to the Altes Schloß three hours. <u>*Getting There:*</u> ***Railers**,* from the station take *bus #201 (departs every 10 min) and get off at Grosse Dollenstr. (Jugendherberge). From there cross street and follow Jugendherberge signs up the hill, 15 min. **Note:* Purchase bus ticket from driver. A one-way ticket costs 2€ but we recommend you buy the 24hr ticket (*Tageskarte*) for 4€. **Drivers:** When approaching Baden-Baden from the autobahn (or France) on route 500, make the first left at the lights (which you'll reach after about 6km)—this is virtually a U-turn, then veer right (onto Lange Str.). Before the bus stop turn right on Grosse Dollenstr. following Jugendherberge signs up the hill to hostel. *GPS:* N48° 46.626 - E8° 13.533

Schloss Hotel Bühlerhöhe: *Tel.#* 07226/550 (www.buehlerhoehe.com)
Located 15km from Baden-Baden off the Black Forest High Road, the Schloss Hotel offers ultra-exclusive digs frequented by the rich and famous. *Price:* Sgl (standard) 160€, with view to Rhineland plains 260€; Dbl (standard) 260€, with view to Rhineland plains 360€; suite (junior) 490€, suite (Japan) 1400€, suite (presidential) 2150€.

the BLACK FOREST

Centuries ago, Germanic peoples found sanctuary within a deep, shadowy forest that protected them from their enemies. This sweeping green belt was a jungle rich with thick fur and oak and beech trees, an impenetrable, living wall. Before long, tales spread across the kingdom of this dark, flourishing mass. From the density of these woods originated its name: Schwarzwald, or Black Forest.

The Black Forest stretches along a range of undulating hills extending 160km/100mi north-south from Pforzheim to the Swiss border and 60km/37mi east-west from Donau-eschingen—the source of the Danube River—to the Baden vineyards along the French border.

The two major cities of the Schwarzwald are Freiburg in the south and Baden-Baden in the north. Both are uniquely different. Freiburg is the capital of the Black Forest, old but cosmopolitan. Baden-Baden is the capital of Roman-Irish spas, naked but delightful.

In this chapter are a handful of alluring subcategories, each escorting you on a journey through time and tradition. You'll discover the mysterious glacial lake of Mummelsee on the **Black Forest High Road**, and the world's largest cuckoo clock on the **German Clock Road,** as well as the juicy, sunburnt town of Staufen on the **Baden Wine Road**. What's more, a former WWII battlefield awaits you across the border in (Colmar) France, where Audie Murphy's courageous actions earned him the highest American and French distinctions: the Medal of Honor and Croix de Guerre.

Railers: Excluding the main towns, the Schwarzwald (and this chapter) is difficult to navigate via rail. Your best Black Forest bet is a jaunt to Triberg. Or, if it's financially possible, rent a car for a few days to fully experience the Schwarzwald (for ideas, flip to page 440).

Black Forest High Road
"Schwarzwaldhochstraße" (route 500)
This is an easy and idyllic run from Baden-Baden, lifting serendipitous sightseers to an elevation of 1000m/3280ft where rolling hills clad with fragrant pine trees stretch to the horizon. Freudenstadt, the farthest point, is only a 50-minute drive. Pack a picnic lunch;

the route offers a plethora of pull-over opportunities accompanied by eye-popping vistas, including those of which sweep across the Rhineland plains into France. *Note: For a more comprehensive drive, see page 267—Day Trip From Baden-Baden.*

The Black Forest High Road, one of the most beautiful drives in Germany, can be picked up in the southeast part of Baden-Baden—follow signs Schwarzwaldhochstraße (route 500). The below-mentioned towns and sights are listed in the order they will be reached when coming from Baden-Baden. After a lengthy ascent you will arrive on the Bühlerhöhe, noted for its exclusive hotel.

BüHLERHöHE, Schloss Hotel: Nestled amongst 45 acres of pristine parkland—15km from Baden-Baden—the Schloss Hotel's restorative spa treatments and sumptuous amenities are favorites of the rich and famous. Those who wish to see for themselves, it's no problem to park in the hotel's lot and browse around. *Price:* Sgl (standard) 160€, with view to Rhineland plains 260€; Dbl (standard) 260€, with view to Rhineland plains 360€; suite (junior) 490€, suite (presidential) 2200€. *Getting There:* At the traffic light turn right. On the corner there'll be a grayish, brown sign that reads: Bühlerhöhe. *Tel.#* 07226/550 (www.buehlerhoehe.com)

~ A few kilometers farther along route 500 you'll reach...

MUMMELSEE: This dark and mysterious glacial lake—encompassed by a thick collage of fur trees—is 800m/2624ft in circumference, 17m/56ft deep, and sits at an elevation of 1036m/3400ft. To stroll around the lake is a delight, allow 20 min. Spearheading Mummelsee is the busy but comfortable Berg Hotel, which offers food and beverages and accommodations as well as paddleboats for hire (4€/30min).

Mummelsee Legend: On full-moon nights, nymphs emerge from the dark, mystic waters to sing and dance until their father, the king of Mummelsee, appears to steal them back to the depths of the lake.

Note: In the colonnade of Baden-Baden's Trinkhalle, you'll behold a mural depicting the Mummelsee nymphs.

~ Farther along the route is a turn off to Allerheiligen—hikers and howlers will want to take time here to do some exploring. Those who are not interested, simply continue along the blissful route direction Freudenstadt.

ALLERHEiLiGEN: (Klosterruine) Roughly 8km off route 500 are the 12th-century ruins of a (Premonstratensian) monastery and a mesmerizing waterfall. At the monastery ruins, known as Klosterruine, you'll find a restaurant/café and a forested path leading to the waterfall. The Klosterruine is located just off the road, but the waterfall is a hike. For a short cut, hop back in your car and descend to the lower parking lot at the "Wasserfälle" entrance. From here it's a breathtaking trek (25 min, 232 steps) to the top of the (83m/272ft) falls.

~ Along the Schwarzwaldhochstraße (route 500) direction Freudenstadt, you may have noticed vast bald sections of forest—seemingly isolated and plucked by a higher being. These bald sections are largely the destructive work of a violent tempest that ripped through the region in December 1999, when terrifying winds howled up to 150kph/93mph. While sections of woodlands are in regenerating mode, we are still blessed with flourishing reserves of fragrant pine forests—a panorama of Christmas trees—that continually fill the air with an addicting bouquet.

FREUDENSTADT: In Freudenstadt—the "City of Joy"—you'll often see the medieval game Nine Man's Morris. This is attributed to Duke Friedrich von Württemberg, who in 1599 had the town designed after the game's layout—squares within squares tapering to the main square, or Marktplatz. Registering an elevation of 732m/2400ft, Freudenstadt's main square is the largest in Germany—measuring more than two football fields long and two football fields wide. On this massive square you'll find the church, TI, museum of local history, and just about every other business in town. Freudenstadt is also home to one of Germany's oldest golf clubs, dating from 1929.

German Clock Road (Deutsche Uhrenstraße)
Everyone's going cuckoo in the Black Forest

(Round trip: 320km/200mi) Since 1664, when the first Black Forest clock was crafted, locals have carved out a niche in the global marketplace by keeping time. Clockmakers originally distributed their products by carrying them in hand-made boxes strapped to their backs. Sales skyrocketed and—as early as 1840—businesses of the Black Forest clock traders existed in 23 countries on four continents. To give an idea of demand, in 1845 there were some 600,000 clocks produced. More than a century later (1989) that figure multiplied by 100, reaching 60 million units produced. Today, it is estimated that 12,000 people work in the Black Forest clock industry and—for the most part—the handcrafted traditions of clockmakers and woodcarvers have not changed.

Although it is a true delight to tour the German Clock Road, expect to repeatedly get lost. The "Deutsche Uhrenstraße" sign marking the route is small and tends to vanish at times. It is not necessary to drive the entire 320km route; pick instead a section of interest to explore. Especially pleasant is the scenery around Triberg, Schonach, Waldau, St. Märgen and St. Peter—you'll find the green rolling hills "wunderbar" and the architecture reminiscent of Switzerland. Those who wish to spend the night along the way will find plenty of Gästezimmer to choose from. And don't forget to stop somewhere to buy a slice of that famous, heart-warming, calorie-filled Schwarzwald Kirschtorte: Black Forest cherry cake.

Below are a handful of words you may see on the German Clock Road, along with a list of places to discover. (www.deutsche-uhrenstrasse.de)

Words you may see on the Deutsche Uhrenstraße

Gästezimmer = Bed & Breakfast
Ferienwohnung = Accommodations for long-term vacationers
Zimmernachweis = Info on accommodations for tourists
Belegt = No vacancy!
Luftkurort = Doctors prescribe this town for its extra-clean air
Uhrenmacher = Clockmaker who usually has product for sale
Kuckucksuhr = Cuckoo clock
(Uhren)Verkauf = (Clocks) For sale

ROTTWEiL: (pop. 25,000) Rottweil is the oldest town in the Black Forest as well as in the state of Baden-Württemberg. The Romans settled the area some 2000 years ago, calling their camp Arae Flaviae. During this time the Romans introduced herding dogs to help guard their camps and drive cattle. The custom continued and throughout the Middle Ages a descendant of this dog was widely used in the Rottweil region—hence the breed, Rottweiler.

Visitors to Rottweil will appreciate a stroll along **Hauptstrasse**—the main drag cutting through the Old Town—and the 360-degree view from atop the **Hochturm**, a cultural relic from the 13th century.

TI: (www.rottweil.de) *Tel.#* 0741/494-280. TI has excellent, free town maps (in English) with history and attractions. *Hours:* May-Oct Mon-Fri 9:30-17:30, Sat 9:30-

12:30; Nov-April Mon-Fri 9:30-12:30 & 14:00-17:00. *Getting There:* TI is located on the higher end of Hauptstr. at No. 21. *GPS:* N48° 10.055 - E8° 37.526

Railers: Station is a 10-min walk from the Old Town.

Drivers: Use your "parking dial" (page 450) to park in lot *P2—max three hours. From here it's an easy stroll into the Old Town. *GPS:* N48° 10.186 - E8° 37.437

Hauptstrasse: Dating from medieval times, "Main Street" pulsates with the thump of locals wearing grooves in the cobblestones as they browse the shop fronts and market stalls for the best deals. As you ascend Hauptstrasse the TI will appear on your right. At the top end of this main drag you'll encounter the Black Gate (Schwarzes Tor), a former bastion dating from 1230. Left of the gate is Hübscher Winkel, or Good-Looking Corner, an unusual and cute three-story structure that registers as one of the last original citizen (Bürger) dwellings in Rottweil. One block away, behind the TI, is the Gothic-style Heilig-Kreuz-Münster, the most impressive of Rottweil's three churches.

Hochturm: Punctuating the top of town at an elevation of 640m/2100ft, the Hochturm, or High Tower, has stood vigilantly over Rottweil since its conception in the 13th century. In medieval times it served as a prison and watchtower, where guards could spy the panoramic view for approaching enemies while detaining them at the same time. Today, the guards have gone, along with the threat of invading armies, but the sweeping views are idyllic as ever. Thus the town of Rottweil would like to make a unique offer: For just 1€ you can rent the key to the tower. No kidding! Go to the TI, hand them 1€, a photo ID, and in return they'll give you the key to a 13th-century relic. The tower is a five-minute walk from the TI. Once inside, notice the red sign on your left, it reads: *"Don't forget to turn out the light upon exiting."* The other sign, in front of you, *asks that you please respect this cultural and historic structure during your visit. Additionally, you are liable if anything happens. Proceed at your own risk. Smoking is prohibited. Parents keep an eye on your children.* There are 173 wooden steps to the top, where you'll discover splendid vistas and the word "Gefängniszelle": jail cell.

SCHONACH: (pop. 4300) In this rural community you'll find the world's *second largest cuckoo clock (*until 1997 it was the largest), measuring in at 3.50m wide x 3.30m high *(the largest today is on the other side of Triberg, listed in the next entry).* The workshop belonging to the clockmaker, Herr Dold, is the cuckoo clock. On the outside of the structure you can watch the clock sound the hour, signaled by a lumberjack chopping timber and a boisterous bird popping out from behind a wooden door. Inside the workshop you'll encounter the clock's machinery along with Herr Dold working on new cuckoos to sell. Herr Dold is not the friendliest chap in the world; that is until you ask the price of a clock, which is when he leaps from his work stool and turns on the charm, "Hi there!" *Hours:* daily, 9:00-12:00 & 13:00-18:00. *Price:* 1€. *Getting There:* located 1km from Triberg, follow signs Schonach then l. Weltgrösste kuckucksuhr. *GPS:* N48° 08.169 - E8° 12.844

TRiBERG: (pop. 5600) Less than a mile from the world's largest cuckoo clocks, you'll come upon Germany's highest waterfall, situated in the touristy town of Triberg. The main street through town is long and ascends at a tiring grade. Most attractions are located at the top end, including the waterfall, Black Forest Museum, and a number of clock shops.

Railers: Triberg provides an exceptional look into the Schwarzwald, with its clocks, waterfall, and embracing pine forest. The train unloads at the bottom of town, more than a kilometer from the waterfall at the top of town.

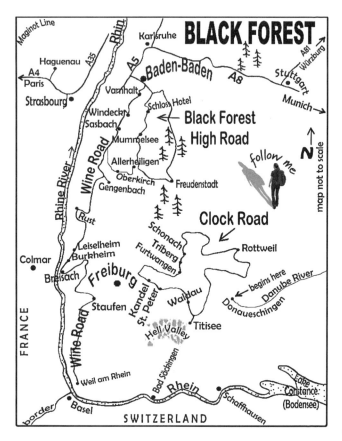

Drivers: Parking in Triberg is largely along the main road. To reach the waterfall, park at the top of town—other parking opportunities for the falls exist on the road climbing towards Schönwald.

Waterfall: Cascading through a forest of spruce trees and past nature trails teeming with fidgety squirrels, Germany's highest waterfall bounces 163m/534ft between multiple ledges before gushing into the valley. The privilege to witness this natural wonder will cost adult 1.50€, student 50¢. Bags of peanuts—snacks for the squirrels—are usually sold at the ticket booth for 50¢ each. *Hours:* daily, 9:00-19:00 (less winter). *Note:* If you arrive after sundown, don't despair, the waterfall is brilliantly lit at night.

Black Forest Museum: Another attraction in Triberg is the regional museum presenting the economic and cultural life of the Black Forest peoples, past and present—including costumes, carvings and customs. *Hours:* daily, 10:00-17:00. *Price:* adult 4€, student 2.50€.

Clock Shops: There are several to choose from here; a popular choice is "House of a 1000 Clocks." By the shop's name it's obvious they have a medley of clocks to mull over. In view of the latter, management employs numerous staff—all of whom speak English—to help you make an informed purchase. *Hours:* Mon-Sat 9:00-17:00 (Sundays also from Easter till Oct 10:00-16:00). *Tel.#* 07722/96-300. *CC's:* VC, MC, AE. *Getting*

There: House of a 1000 Clocks is located at the top end of town. Or, from the comfort of your own home, go to www.houseof1000clocks.com

World's Largest Cuckoo: Measuring in at 4.50m wide x 4.50m high, the clock at Uhren-Park was entered into the Guinness Book of World Records in 1997 as the world's largest cuckoo clock, relegating Herr Dold's specimen in Schonach off the top perch. Besides the big cuckoo, Uhren-Park maintains a wide range of clocks for sale. (www.uhren-park.de) *Hours:* Mon-Sat 9:00-18:00, Sun 10:00-18:00 (less in winter). *Price:* 1.50€/person. *Getting There:* Uhren-Park is situated just outside of Triberg—at the bottom of town, by the train station, turn left on route 33 direction Hornberg. Shortly thereafter, Uhren-Park will appear on the right.

FURTWANGEN: (pop. 10,000) From tracing the sun's course across the sky to the development of the atomic clock, man has measured time through the epochs in a variety of ways. In Furtwangen's German Clock Museum—which boasts the nation's largest collection—you'll learn the history and technology of the clock, plus solve the mystery as to how the cuckoo got inside. *Hours:* daily, 9:00-18:00 (Nov-March 10:00-17:00). *Price:* adult 3€, student 2€. Tours in English are possible with at least 5 people (duration 45min, 1.50€/person)—call in advance if you have a group, or to see whether an English tour is scheduled: *Tel.#* 07723/920-2800.

Visitors in August, consider timing your visit to Furtwangen to correspond with Europe's largest antique clock fair "Antik-Uhrenbörse" on the last weekend of the month (Aug 26-27, 2006; www.antik-uhrenmesse.de). *Hours:* Sat 9:00-18:00, Sun 10:00-16:00. What's more, on the Saturday, the town festival and flea market kick off at 9:00. (www.furtwangen.de)

TiTiSEE-NEUSTADT: (pop. 12,000) Boasting a magical lake in the midst of an invigorating reserve of coniferous trees, this twin town headlines as one of the most popular tourist destinations in the Schwarzwald. Titisee, the more arousing of the twin communities, is most likely named after the Roman general Titus, who once camped with his troops along the shoreline of Lake Titi (Titisee) nearly two millennia ago. Today, route 31 runs through town connecting Titisee-Neustadt with its eastern neighbor, Donaueschingen (33km)—the source of the Danube—and with Freiburg (35km) in the west via Hell's Valley (Höllental). Keeping to the Deutsche Uhrenstraße, the themed road lazily meanders some 8km northward to Waldau then St. Märgen.

WALDAU: (pop. 350) The countryside around the villages of Waldau and St. Märgen couldn't get any more picturesque as you drive along a road that toddles past green rolling hills, forests of fur trees, dairy cows grazing on idyllic pastures, and ultra-quaint houses with pitched roofs accentuating the harsh winters. Besides beautiful scenery, Waldau stepped into the history books in 1664 when two locals—the Kreutz brothers—assembled the first Black Forest clock at the Glashof farm, situated just outside town. Alas, there's no exhibition here presenting this history-making fact. However, for those who would like to see where the Black Forest clock industry began can punch in these GPS coordinates (N47° 59.273 - E8° 08.862) leading to a fine view overlooking the Glashof farm (the elongated cottage facing you is the original structure). It's privately owned so please keep your distance.

If you're thinking of stopping for the night in Waldau, Gasthof zur Traube is the nicest but priciest—roughly 40€/person. *Tel.#* 07669/2290 (www.traube-waldau.de) If the price exceeds your budget, other places in town run about 25€/person a night.

The following two towns are 7km apart and epitomize tranquility via their doctor-prescribed air ("Luftkurort"), sweet idleness, deep-rooted tradition, aged trees, and onion-shaped church steeples.

ST. MäRGEN: (pop. 1900) Some 9km from Waldau, St. Märgen is another charming community along a delightful route. The town began its existence in 1118 when Augustinian monks built a monastery here. In 1716, a trendy twin-steepled Baroque church replaced the monastery after invading armies destroyed it. Inside the Rathaus—adjacent to the church—is the TI.

ST. PETER: (pop. 2500) Crowned by a twin-towered church and a former Benedictine monastery, St. Peter is another enviable Luftkurort in the midst of lush meadows and aromatic conifers. The former monastery maintains a fanciful Rococo library and the final burial place of the dukes of Zähringen, founders of Freiburg.

Drivers: Those who are ready to exit the German Clock Road, heed the following instructions escorting you via a must-see sight some 10km (uphill) from St. Peter.

From St. Peter, take the road to Waldkirch via "Kandel." It's a windy ascent but the views up top are worth the curves. Once at the Kandel summit (*GPS:* N48° 03.930 - E8° 00.954) park your car and relish the fresh air and views. OK, now, let's head to the real summit. Behind the restaurant follow the sign "Kandel Gipfel" leading you up a 400-meter path to the peak (1244m /4080ft) and heavy-duty vistas.

Back at the car, continue in the direction of Waldkirch. The road will descend some 11km. At the bottom an express route can deliver you to Freiburg, the A5 autobahn, or the Baden Wine Road—the choice is yours.

Baden Wine Road (Badische Weinstrasse)

From toying with cuckoos to sampling the local grape juice…

There are 13 wine-growing regions in Germany, totaling some 247,000 acres of vineyards—about 78% of this land is dedicated to white grapes. Estimated at 38,000 acres, the Baden vineyards rank as the third largest in the nation. Per capita, Germans drink 30 bottles of wine annually. In the Baden region, that figure leaps to 53 bottles. The locals are a hearty bunch, who abide by an age-old maxim: *Das Leben ist viel zu kurz um schlechten Wein zu trinken* (Life is way too short to drink bad wine).

From Baden-Baden, the Wine Road pleasantly staggers 180km/112mi past vineyard-draped villages on the lower slopes of the Schwarzwald to the Swiss border. Since the road tends to branch off in many directions, it's not worthwhile to drive the whole stretch. Pick a section that suits your itinerary and begin sampling what the locals do best. Especially enjoyable are the areas west and south of Freiburg—for example, Breisach and Staufen.

For a gratifying taste of the Wine Road, with the added mystique of the Black Forest High Road, consider our below-mentioned do-it-yourself day trip from Baden-Baden.

Words you may see on the Baden Wine Road	
Weingut = Winery (usually has tasting)	
Winzergenossenschaft = Winegrowers' society (usually has tasting)	
Weinverkauf = Wine sales	
Weinprobe = Wine tasting	Zimmer frei = Vacancy
Gästezimmer—= Bed & Breakfast	Belegt = No vacancy!

Day Trip From Baden-Baden, Do It Yourself

Expect a journey of around 130km, taking 4.5hr.

<u>Drivers:</u> Below is a fun and flavorsome day trip escorting you along a juicy section of the Wine Road before returning to Baden-Baden via the aromatic and ultra-scenic Black Forest High Road (Schwarzwaldhochstraße). *Note:* Go easy on the wine tasting as the road ahead has more curves than Anna Nicole Smith. Instead, buy a bottle to savor in the evening. Pack a picnic.

~ Let's begin our drive by taking Lichtentaler Str. in the south of town to Berthold Str.to Fremersbergstr. to Varnhalt, the first town on the Wine Road.

VARNHALT: This cute community 5km from Baden-Baden has some 350 registered winegrowers nurturing 210 acres of grape stock. In case you were wondering, 80% of their yield is dedicated to Riesling, and 95% of their vines are more than 25 years old, with some pushing the ripe age of 50.

*~ From Varnhalt ramble through the forthcoming Hansel-and-Gretel towns of **Steinbach, Neuweier, Bühl-Eisental** (go left at little intersection, even if sign looks to be pointing straight), **Altschweier,** (don't drive direction Bühl), **Bühlertal, Bühlertal-Obertal,** then **Obertal.** Continue on this main road and after a few kilometers turn right direction **Neusatz.** Eventually, the road will descend several kilometers through Neusatz—on the other side of town turn right on Burg-Windeck-Str.; ascend this curvy road some 2.5km and park in Burg Windeck's lot (GPS: N48° 40.316 - E8° 09.499). This is a slight detour off the wine route to visit a former 13th-century castle.*

<u>Burg Windeck:</u> This is a great place to stretch your legs and absorb a fine view. Explorers can wander through flourishing vineyards and the ruins of an 800-year-old fortification. Those who wish to relax awhile can enjoy something to eat or drink on the outdoor terrace. Besides a popular restaurant, Burg Windeck is also a reputable hotel. Interested parties ask to see a room; they're adorable. (www.burg-windeck.de) *Tel.#* 07223/94-920. *Price:* Sgl 77-87€, Dbl 113-123€ (cheaper the longer you stay). *CC's:* VC, MC, AE.

~ After your visit, head back to the Wine Road and resume your route in the same direction: follow signs Ottersweier. At the lights, continue straight to Hub; then turn left at the forthcoming T-intersection, direction Achern (6km; Sasbach 5km).

*Upon arriving in **Sasbach**—we are going to once again make a slight detour off the main road—pass through the traffic light and make your first left on Obersasbacher Str., followed by the second right on Turenne Weg to the historical *monument explained in the text below (*GPS: N48° 38.147 - E8° 05.794).*

SASBACH: Marshal Henri Turenne, second only to Napoleon as France's greatest war-time commander, died here when a cannonball struck him during the Battle of Sasbach in 1675. You'll find an obelisk (fourth reconstruction) on the spot of his death. The first monument built in honor of Turenne was battered by a storm in 1786 and collapsed. Napoleon, a great admirer of Turenne, ordered the shrine to be rebuilt. However, before its completion, Napoleon was exiled. The third tribute, a 12-meter obelisk, was constructed in 1829 on the orders of King Charles X of France. The memorial somehow survived WWI but had no chance of outlasting WWII. The Nazis believed that the monument boosted French morale and therefore Hitler's resident gauleiter, Robert Wagner (no relation to the actor), razed it in 1940. Shortly after the war ended, Charles de Gaulle had the monument rebuilt—he arrived to personally inaugurate it in October 1945. The neighboring Turenne Museum is open Sun and Wed 14:00-18:00. Price: 1€ (50¢ with your Baden-Baden Kurkarte).

~ *After your visit, head back to the main road and resume your route in the direction of Achern. Once there, watch closely for signs to your next destination: **Oberachern** (turn left on the traffic circle, then right).*

*Part way through Oberachern go left at the junction and then soon you'll be turning right direction **Oberkirch**—12km. (The Oberkirch region is known for its groves of fruit trees.)*

*At Oberkirch head into the town center and follow signs to **Oppenau** (via Lautenbach)—10km. This concludes the Wine Road.*

*For the home stretch ascend the windy road from Oppenau deep into the Black Forest to **Allerheiligen**—10km.*

*For the final segment, refer to the Black Forest High Road (page 261). Start with the **Allerheiligen** "Wasserfälle" and work your back to Baden-Baden: Klosterruine (12th-century monastery ruins), **Mummelsee**, **Bühlerhöhe**—Schloss Hotel.*

More Sites on the Wine Road

GENGENBACH: Defining church spires, retired battlements, medieval walls, half-timbered houses and a Rococo Rathaus make Gengenbach a popular tourist destination. In fact, in 1955, Gengenbach's Old Town was placed under federal Denkmalschutz, or historic preservation. Snap a village view from the Swedish Tower or soak up the past on Engelgasse (Angel Lane) or Höllengasse (Hell's Lane).

RUST: With more than 3 million visitors annually, this corrosive-sounding town is home to Germany's largest amusement park: Europa-Park. Recently (Dec 2004) the theme park was the site of a new world record when the most Santas ever (2797) congregated in one place. A record previously held by a town in Sweden with a flock of 2685 Santas. *Hours:* (Europa-Park) April-Oct, daily, 9:00-18:00 (longer in peak summer). *Price:* adult 28.50€, child (4-11) 25.50€. (www.europapark.de)

BREiSACH: (pop. 12,000) Capping the right bank of the Rhine, a 12th-century sandstone basilica belonging to the frontier town of Breisach stands tall in the morning sky as it casts a shadow upon its French neighbors across the river. Some 1700 years ago the Romans recognized Breisach's strategic importance and used it as a base to garrison their troops. Following in the sandaled footsteps of the Caesar's legionnaires, nomadic tribes and imperial armies fought bitterly to possess Breisach. Whoever occupied this outpost, held the key to the Reich and controlled the Rhine. Needless to say, much of original Breisach was destroyed, and most recently 85% of the town was pasted by Allied artillery during WWII. In fact, the wounds of war can still be seen on the basilica's external walls. Today, international relations have warmed and the two largest euro-zone economies are connected here by a bridge—absent of border guards—spanning the Rhine to France and Breisach's sister city, Neuf-Brisach (5km). A visit to this part of the world is a delight, as are the views across the river to the French province of Alsace from the ramparts embracing the basilica. *(Note: Around the basilica are multilingual info boards expounding on local histories. Inside the basilica, notice the 15C wall frescos by the entrance portal.)* See TI for an excellent town map in English with history, illustrations, and a trio of DIY walking tours to explore.

TI: (www.breisach.de) *Tel.#* 07667/940-155. *Hours:* Mon-Fri 9:30-12:30 & 13:30-17:00 (till 18:00 April thru Dec), Sat 10:00-13:00 (Sat closed Jan-March). *Getting There:* located on the market square, 10-min walk from train station.

Railers: There are regular connections (2/hr) between Freiburg and Breisach, 25-min trip (4.80€ o.w. or [recommended] buy the "Regio24" *24hr ticket, 9.60€ [or 14.40€ for up to 5 people], valid for bus, tram, train. *Must validate 24hr ticket before first use).

Station has storage lockers, depending on size, 1.50€-3€/24hr. The TI and Old Town are a 10-min walk from the station—to get there, exit station left and continue straight.

Drivers: Use your "parking dial" (page 450) to park in town.

LEiSELHEiM: If you're passing through this village, you'll love their cute fire hydrants.

BURKHEiM: Wonderfully wrapped in vineyards, this charming town sits on a gently rising knoll just off the Wine Road. Half-timbered houses, a Renaissance Rathaus, and a congenial Market Street make this picturesque town worthy of a visit.

STAUFEN: Admirers of Italy's Toscana region will be at home here amongst the sunburnt flora, undulating geography, and full-bodied wine. Stop in for a stroll around town to ogle the quaint houses, cute marketplace, 16th-century Rathaus, and late-Gothic church. Entrenched some 90m/295ft above Staufen rests a ruined castle—trek through the vineyards to reach a grand view. *Railers:* Regular connections between Freiburg and Staufen, 30-min trip — 3.40€ o.w. or (recommended) buy the "Regio24" *24hr ticket, 9.60€ [or 14.40€ for up to 5 people], valid for bus, tram, train. *Must validate 24hr ticket before first use.

Other Locations On The Black Forest Map

DONAUESCHiNGEN: In these parts you'll often come across the word *Donau* (pronounced Doe-now), referring to the Danube River. And the town of Donaueschingen is home to the renowned "Donauquelle," the official source of the Danube spring. In other words, here begins the second longest river in Europe, flowing east 2840km/ 1775mi through eight countries, including the capital cities of Vienna, Bratislava, Budapest and Belgrade before dumping into the Black Sea via Romania. Besides an economic lifeline, the historic watercourse became an excuse to dance in the 19th century when Johann Strauss II tagged it as the beautiful "Blue Danube," a musical score that waltzed across the imperial ballrooms of Europe. Although the Donauquelle is the official source of the spring, the Danube actually becomes the famed river 2km east of town at the confluence of the streams Breg and Brigach. The Donauquelle is located in the Schloss Park, where you'll find a 19th-century monument encasing a crystal-clear pool of water periodically burping rhythms of air bubbles from the earth's sandy floor. Throw a coin in for good luck. The sculpture spearheading the monument portrays the Danube as a compassionate woman fostering the young Brigach and baby Breg. *GPS:* (Donauquelle) N47° 57.109 - E8° 30.154

In case you were wondering, the Volga (Russia) is the longest river in Europe, flowing 3700km/2300mi; the Ural (Russia) is third longest, flowing 2400km/1500mi; and the Rhine ranks seventh, flowing 1320km/820mi.

SCHAFFHAUSEN, Switzerland: In this Swiss city you can ogle the Rhine Falls ("Rheinfall"), where a 183m/600ft wide section of the Rhine River wildly plunges 23m/75ft to the rocks below, creating Europe's most spectacular waterfall. To feel the spray and snap a close-up picture from the observation perch will cost 1€.

BAD SäCKiNGEN: Facing the Swiss frontier on the German side of the Rhine River, Bad Säckingen grew from two monasteries and a church in the 7th century to a matter-of-fact town of 17,000 residents preserving the continent's most valuable collection of trumpets (exhibited in Schloss Schönau) and its longest wood-covered bridge. Worthwhile is a stroll across the latter bridge—midway along its timber frame you'll reach Switzerland.

HAGUENAU, France: Many of you may remember the name of this town from its portrayal in the television miniseries Band of Brothers, episode 8, "The Last patrol," when the boys of Easy Co. embarked on a prisoner-seeking mission in the Nazi-occupied town.

Maginot Line: (Schoenenbourg, France) Built in the 1930s and named after its creator—the French war minister André Maginot—the Maginot Line was a defensive chain of bunkers that extended along the French border, from the province of Alsace to Belgium, designed to prevent another bloody, WWI-style engagement with Germany. In May 1940, disrespecting Belgian neutrality, Hitler strategically maneuvered his men and machinery around the Maginot Line by sweeping through Belgium, rendering France's billion-dollar defensive plan insignificant. Those who would like to tour a real Maginot bunker should consider Le Fort de Schoenenbourg. It'll be chilly inside, so wear something warm. *Hours:* May-Sept, daily, Mon-Sat 14:00-16:00, Sun 9:30-11:00 & 14:00-16:00. April and Oct, Sun and holidays only. (www.lignemaginot.com) *Tel.#* +33-(0)3/8880-9619

STRASBOURG, France: (pop. 260,000) Positioned 55km from Baden-Baden, Strasbourg is the 7th largest city in France: home to European parliament; Petite France (charming half-timbered houses and delicious pastry); the canal bateaux (cruise the Ill River on these idyllic boats, daily 60-min excursions from Palais des Rohan, 7€); the Cathedral of Notre Dame (astrological clock runs daily, tickets 1€—enter south portal no later than 12:20); and the most modern tram system you'll probably ever see. What's more, beer lovers should note Strasbourg is home to Kronenbourg—call in advance to see if an English brewery tour is scheduled: *Tel.#* +33-(0)3/8827-4159.

Folks looking to spend the night in Strasbourg should consider *Hotel Suisse*, centrally located near the market square, cathedral, and Palais des Rohan. Behind the hotel's reception desk you'll find Beatrice, an effervescent gal who's worked there more than 20 years, but by her fresh enthusiasm you'd think it was her first day. Price: Sgl 55-74€, Dbl 69-90€, Trpl 99-109€. Breakfast 7.50€, parking 9€/day. CC's: VC, MC, AE. *Tel.#* +33-(0)3/8835-2211. Address: 2 rue de la Râpe. (www.hotel-suisse.com)

Travelers not interested in the aforesaid accommodations can query other options at either of Strasbourg's two tourist information offices, one at the main train station and the other on the cathedral square. Across from the station is a *Hotel ibis*. Price: (per room) Sgl/Dbl 62-75€. Breakfast, parking cost extra. www.ibishotel.com (hotel code 3018). *Tel.#* +33-(0)3/8823-9898

COLMAR, France: (pop. 63,000) Less than an hour from Freiburg—across the French border—is its blood relative, Colmar. The Germans occupied this part of France after the Franco-Prussian War in 1871 until the defeat of Germany in WWI (1918), and once again during WWII (1940-1945). Colmar has a fascinating, must-see Old Town! Consider staying a night in the Hotel ibis (Centre)—from there, Colmar's half-timbered pedestrian zone and historic center is a short stroll away. *Tel.#* +33-(0)3/8941-3014. *Price:* Sgl/Dbl 45-75€, breakfast and parking are extra. www.ibishotel.com (hotel code 1377).

WWII Buffs: At 5 feet 5 inches tall, **Audie Leon Murphy** wasn't a big man but his heroic deeds were larger than life. In the woods just outside the town of Holtzwihr (8km northeast of Colmar), Audie Murphy—a farm boy from Kingston, Texas, who became the most decorated soldier in American history—won the Congressional Medal of Honor. On the spot where the battle raged is a memorial depicting him in *action and a plaque commemorating the liberation of Holtzwihr. It reads:

> *This memorial is dedicated to the soldiers of the 3rd U.S. Infantry Division and Combat Command 4 (CC4) under the 1st French Army who liberated Holtzwihr on January 27, 1945, after a bloody struggle under horrendous conditions.*

Additionally, the memorial represents the heroic actions of Lieut. Audie L. Murphy with the 15th U.S. Infantry Regiment, when on this spot January 26, 1945, he repulsed an enemy counter-attack. For this feat he was decorated with the highest American and French distinctions.

In passing, respect this memorial and don't forget these soldiers who have died so that you may live in freedom.

Holtzwihr, January 29, 2000

*Note: Murphy stood on a burning tank and single-handedly held off six German tanks and some 250 enemy soldiers while being shot at from three directions. The memorial itself is of Murphy standing on an American tank.

Getting There: To reach the memorial take route D4 from Colmar to Holtzwihr—once there, make the first main left (Rue Principale). Soon, make another left at the church clock tower and pass the school, "Ecole." Follow the road right at the crucifix and continue straight past the soccer (sports) field. Just beyond the green-and-white "Forêt Communale de Holtzwihr" sign is the memorial. *GPS:* N48° 07.363 - E7° 25.247

F R E I B U R G *im Breisgau*

~ Population: 210,000   ~ Elevation: 275m/900ft
~ Country/Area Code: +49-(0)761   ~ Sister City: Madison, Wisconsin

As the cultural and economic center of the Black Forest, this cosmopolitan hub will impress you with its modern infrastructure, old-world charm and—arguably—Germany's best tap water. Freiburg is a colorful city buzzing with life, including the country's highest concentration of bicyclists. For extra-clean air and dynamite views of France, hike Schlossberg (Castle Hill) rising above the Altstadt (Old Town). The Altstadt is a world unto itself, passionately preserved to showcase its historic architecture, climbable cathedral, colorful marketplace, sprawling pedestrian zone, and umpteen fountains. Notice that many buildings have their name and birth year inscribed on the facade in Gothic typeface—one example reads: Zum roten Stiefel, 1379 ("the red boot"). Contrary to age-old Freiburg, the city has an array of avant-garde street performers and a college-type atmosphere with its youthful contingent of 35,000 students. Besides being a hangout for academics, puddle-stomping kids are mesmerized by the Altstadt's signature "Bächle"—once a medieval remedy for flushing sewage is today a 6km network of "tiny streams" that flow in trench-like gutters begging for a lawsuit. Together with the Bächle, the sidewalks, too, are an attraction. When rambling through the pedestrian zone notice the unique designs embedded beneath your feet—these patterns were created by using Rhine stones unearthed from the river. *Note:* Without window shopping it takes 10 minutes to walk across the Old Town.

TI: Rotteckring 14 (www.freiburg.de) *Tel.#* 0761/388-1880. TI offers heaps of info (mostly free) on the Black Forest, as well as a room-finding service for a 3€ fee. Free city maps available, or for 1€ they offer a (worthwhile) foldout map with descriptions and history. *Hours:* daily, June-Sept Mon-Fri 9:30-20:00, Sat 9:30-17:00, Sun 10:00-12:00; Oct thru May Mon-Fri 9:30-18:00, Sat 9:30-14:30, Sun 10:00-12:00. *Getting There: Railers,* exit station straight into Eisenbahnstr.—on the right you'll soon pass the main post office (Mon-Fri 8:30-18:30, Sat 9:00-14:00; 24hr stamp machine out front). Cross at the next traffic intersection and the TI will be on the left, or continue straight for the Old Town. *Drivers,* even though the TI is located on the main ring road that orbits the Old Town, it can be tricky to spot. When driving clockwise (north) on Rotteckring, the TI is on the right—metered parking in front; inspectors patrol often. ***GPS:*** N47° 59.805 - E7° 50.813

Railers: The station is within easy reach of the TI and Old Town—by foot, see directions listed (above) under *TI, Getting There.* Or, trams into the Old Town depart from the upper level, 2€/person. Freiburg station is well connected to outlying towns in the region with reasonable fares to get there. The 24hr ticket, known as "Regio24," is great value, valid for all buses, trams and trains within the regional (RVF) network. *(Note: You must validate this 24hr ticket before first use).* Regio24 is sold at RVF ticket automats in two price categories consisting of three zones of travel: *zone 1* is Freiburg, 4.80€/person or 7.20€ for up to 5 persons; *zones 2 and 3* reach towns outside of Freiburg (e.g. Staufen, Breisach) and costs 9.60€/person or 14.40€ for up to 5 persons. ***Note:*** If you stay at the Hotel Schwarzwälder Hof (page 273) your transportation in Freiburg and in the region is free.

Drivers: Freiburg is not car friendly; the inner city is heavily pedestrianized and the one-way streets are enough to make anyone scream! Either take the train to Freiburg, or park in town where possible and walk from there. In general, parking meters read "Parkschein Automat" and are applicable Mon-Sat 9:00-19:00, 1€/30 min. Plenty of parking garages are also available.

Internet: A good surf can be had at the café and call shop at Kartäuserstr. 3, a few-minutes walk from the Schwabentor (medieval town gate) in the southeast part of the Old Town. *Price:* (surf) 1.80€/hr. *Hours:* Mon-Sat 9:00-22:00, Sun 11:00-22:00. *Tel.#* 0761/389-0745.

Schlossberg: Butting against the Old Town's east side is Schlossberg, or Castle Hill, an elevated and trekking-friendly section of the Black Forest boasting views to France. Formerly the location of a powerful fortress built in the 17th-century by the French during their occupation of Freiburg, Schlossberg today is affectionately referred to by locals as the "green nose" due to its wooded reserve. Schlossberg can be reached via the free elevator (Aufzug) located across from the Schwabentor (medieval town gate)—use wooden bridge to cross road and access elevator. The elevator lets out beneath the "Schlössle" restaurant (open daily 11:00-24:00), which has great views and a Munich-style beer garden (half liter 3€, liter 5.50€). When the elevator doors open, you can either ascend the path to the Schlossberg viewpoint or go right to the next elevator lifting you into the restaurant.

Cathedral: Punctuating the skyline and referred to as "das Münster," Freiburg's long-standing cathedral miraculously survived the horrific WWII bombing raids that flattened much of the city in 1944. Built over three centuries from 1200-1513, the cathedral is one of Germany's finest examples of Gothic-style architecture. Additionally, das Münster features mesmerizing stained-glass windows dating from the 13th to 16th centuries as well as 123 representations of the Virgin Mary (some are outside). Inside, look for the four organs—together they comprise 10,800 pipes. *(You've found three but can you locate the fourth? Hint: look to the choir.)* Spearheading the cathedral is the must-see Vorhalle (restored 1998-2003) displaying scenes from the life and suffering of Christ. From here, notice the two portals leading into the cathedral—the left one dates from 1606 and the right 1724 (renovated 1907). The climbable spire ("Turm")—329 steps to the top—is as tall as the cathedral is long: 116m/380ft. "Hosanna," the oldest of 16 bells in the belfry, dates from 1258. *Hours:* (Münster) Mon-Sat 10:00-17:00, Sun 13:00-19:30. *Hours:* (Turm; entrance outside) Mon-Sat 9:30-17:00, Sun 13:00-17:00. *Price:* (Turm) adult 1.50€, student 1€.

Münsterplatz: This, as you may have already guessed, is the square surrounding the cathedral (Münster)—certainly the pulsating heart of Freiburg, where you'll stumble upon throngs of locals and wowed tourists absorbing old-town ambience together with the thriving (green and craft) market (Mon-Sat, early morning to early afternoon).

Augustiner Museum: In this esteemed museum—Freiburg's largest—you'll find rare, regional exhibitions of stone sculptures and pious relics from the Middle Ages housed in a former Augustinian monastery. Because of the current, ongoing renovations admission is *FREE*! Museum is in German. *Hours:* Tue-Sun 10:00-17:00. *Getting There:* Museum is located two short blocks south of Münsterplatz. If arriving by tram #1, get off at "Oberlinden." From there, parallel the mustard-colored building and make the first left, then left again to enter.

Good Sleeps: Folks looking for a respectable hotel in the heart of town—two-minute walk from the cathedral—stay at the *Schwarzwälder Hof.* Backpackers choose the *Black Forest Hostel.*

Hotel Schwarzwälder Hof: Herrenstr. 43 (www.shof.de) *Tel.#* 0761/38-030. Before it became a hotel, this 500-year-old structure was the town mint. In 1806 it became an inn, and today the traditional-style Schwarzwälder Hof is warmly run by the Engler family. Has elevator and appetizing restaurant. Additionally, the Englers have a special *offer for their guests: for each night you stay, you will receive a card allowing you free transportation in the region. For non-railpass holders, this is an amazing deal! Base yourself here for a few days, take advantage of the card and see the sights region-wide. *Note:* double-check in advance that offer is still valid. *Price:* Sgl 38-60€ (←cheaper rooms have toilet/shower in hallway→) Dbl 65-90€, Trpl 100€; parking 8€/24hr. *CC's:* VC, MC. *Getting There:* **Railers,** from the train station take tram #1 direction Littenweiler and get off at "Oberlinden" (3rd stop). Exit tram left and cross the cobbles to the fountain. The lane on your left is Herrenstr.—continue along this lane and your digs will soon appear on the right. Once there, the hotel's entrance can be found midway along the lane on the right. **Drivers,** follow signs into the Altstadt, then the green hotel signs—unload out front and reception will show you where to park (8€/24hr). *GPS:* N47° 59.670 - E7° 51.231

Hostel, Black Forest: Kartäuserstr. 33 (www.blackforest-hostel.de) *Tel.#* 0761/881-7870. Close to the Old Town and vineyard-draped slopes of Schlossberg, backpackers will appreciate this former speedometer factory now friendly digs offering Internet, cosmic space-capsule showers, washer/dryer, do-it-yourself kitchen, chill-out room with ready-to-play instruments, and no bunk beds. The sound of running water from the neighboring creek makes for a pleasant sleep—unless, that is, someone's snoring in your (dorm) room. *Price:* (cash only) 6- to 8-bed dorm 17€, 10-bed dorm 16€, 20-bed dorm 13€, Sgl 28€, Dbl 46€, linen 3€ (one-time fee)—or free with own sack. *Getting There:* From the train station take tram #1 direction Littenweiler and get off at "Oberlinden" (3rd stop). Exit tram left; follow the tracks in the same direction you were riding and pass underneath the clock tower. On other side continue straight (Schwabentorring) and make the next left—this is Kartäuserstr. Continue straight and after a few minutes your digs will appear on the left. *GPS:* N47° 59.522 - E7° 51.473

Hostel, Jugendherberge: [HI] Kartäuserstr. 151, tel.# 0761/67-656. These accommodations are the only other hostel in town and listed in case of necessity. Not recommend for Railers because it is too ordinary, too expensive, and too far (3km) out of town. *Note:* Must be a member and 26 or under to stay, or an extra (3€) charge will apply. *Price:* (includes breakfast and sheets) dorm bed 20.30€ (second night 17.10€). *CC's:* VC, MC.

MOSEL VALLEY — KOBLENZ to TRiER

190km/119mi—allow 1 full day for time-crunched tourists, 2-3 days for avid historians, 4-5 days for historically minded wine-sippin' nature-lovin' enthusiasts. Note: during the off-season, Nov thru March, touristy things slow to a crawl or are completely closed.

From its source in the Vosges, a French mountain chain, the Mosel River gushes north and subsequently forms the border between Luxembourg and Germany, where midway along the territorial frontier it slices east and flows through ancient Trier. From this 2000-year-old metropolis, the Mosel lazily meanders a serpentine-like course between the Eifel and Hunsrück ranges to Koblenz emptying into the Rhine. Twisting and turning with the river is the Mosel Wine Road (Weinstrasse), where juicy vineyards and picturesque hamlets adorn the riverbanks while muscle-flexing castles stand guard from the Riesling hilltops. This former route of industrious Celts, Roman Legionnaires and Charlemagne's Franks—a melting pot rich with history—is simply *wunderbar*! Comparable to a lazy picnic, the Mosel affords a blood-pressure friendly air to enjoy one of Germany's most stunning destinations. Especially revered is the stretch between the towns of Cochem and Bernkastel-Kues. As you set off, note this Mosel adage: *Wein ist Würze des Lebens* (Wine is the spice of life).

Railers: Only a limited number of towns are train-friendly. Base yourselves in medieval Cochem—centrally located, it's a great starting point for Burg Eltz, Beilstein, the Calmont Klettersteig and a river cruise.

Drivers: Similar to Railers, base yourselves in Cochem—although, there are plenty of alluring Zimmer (B&B) along the wine route. For a shortcut to the Rhine, go to Brodenbach (8km downstream from Burg Eltz). From there, follow sign to Ehrenburg. After some 50 meters turn left and ascend road to Boppard. On Sunday June 11, 2006, the Mosel Wine Road will be closed to motorists between Cochem and Schweich (10km downstream from Trier) between the hours 9:00-19:00 in an effort to create a smog-free, environment-friendly zone for cyclists, Inline skaters and pedestrians. This annually sponsored auto-free day is known as "Happy-Mosel"—total roads closed equal 140km, the largest one-time closure of its kind in Europe. *Note:* route 53 straddles both banks of the river from Trier to Zell, then it becomes route 49 from Zell to (near) Moselkern, when route 49 runs exclusively along on the right bank and route 416 parallels the left bank to Koblenz.

Boaters: Only a few towns along the Mosel are accessible via sightseer boats. The best waterborne excursion is Cochem to Beilstein (1hr). For those using the K-D line, their fleet only cruises between Cochem and Koblenz.

Hikers: Don't miss the steepest vineyard trek in Europe, the Calmont Klettersteig (page 283), located between Bremm and Eller.

Bicyclists: Highly recommended is a healthy, enjoyable, eco-ride along the Mosel. If it seems the distances are too great, cycle one-way and return via train or boat. When bringing a bike on the train, get on the carriage displaying the bicycle symbol. *Note:* Upon renting a bike, pick one that has at least a few gears—this will come in handy between towns. Additionally, always ask which side of the river is best to ride on. *Suggestion:* A pleasant, short ride is from Cochem to Beilstein (9km). From Cochem, cyclists looking for a longer ride should head the other direction to Burg Eltz (20km) and tour the castle.

Picnickers: The region offers countless picnic opportunities, whether along the river facing a medieval castle or high above the valley on a trail flanked by grapevines—always be prepared with a daypack full of goodies.

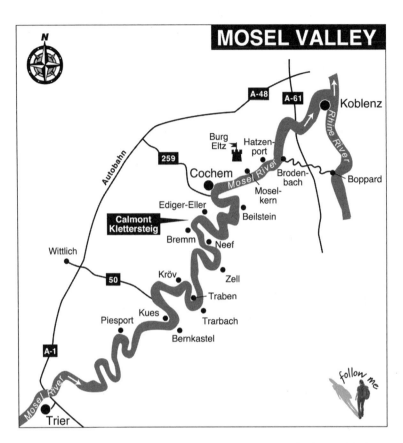

MOSEL VALLEY

Car/Passenger Ferry: (Fähre) Bridges along the Mosel can be few and far between, thus ferries cover the bald spots. Price per jaunt: (approx.) adult 1€, bicycle 50¢, auto 3€. On regional brochures and maps, AF means auto ferry and PF pedestrian-only ferry.

Fishing: Local permits (day, week or month) are available for a small fee; inquire at TI or Rathaus (town hall). Present your stateside fishing license if you have one—this may help to speed up German paperwork. Fish you are likely to catch: pike, carp, perch, bream, tench or bass.

Mosel-Saar-Ruwer (MSR)

There are 13 wine-growing regions in Germany, totaling 247,000 acres of vineyards—about 81% of this land is dedicated to white grapes. With 31,000 acres, the MSR wine region ranks as the nation's fourth largest, behind Rheinhessen, Rheinpfalz and the Baden vineyards.

MSR is the acronym for the rivers Mosel, Saar and Ruwer. The Saar and Ruwer rivers flow into the region's main artery, the Mosel, where the majority of vineyards are cultivated. Happy-go-lucky motorists can savor every twisting turn along the Mosel Wine Road as it staggers its way some 200km between Trier and Koblenz.

Words you may see on the Mosel Wine Road	
Winzer = Winegrower	Verkauf+probe = Sales+tasting
Weingut = Winery (usually has tasting)	Wein verkauf = Wine sales
Weinprobe = Wine tasting	Flasche(n) = Bottle(s)
Stuben = Consumption room (eat/drink)	Vom fass = On tap
Historische Ortskern = Historic part of town	DU/WC = Shower/toilet
Gästezimmer = Bed & Breakfast	Belegt = No vacancy!
Zimmer = Bed & Breakfast	Frei = Vacancy
Ferienwohnung = Accommodations for long-term vacationers	

The major crop in the MSR is the Riesling grape, accounting for 60% of the yield. The hillside terraces are ideally suited for growing this white variety, allowing for plenty of sun exposure while providing adequate protection from the occasional, not-so-friendly winds. Wine experts often agree that Riesling is the king of white grapes, considering its cellar longevity and flexible flavor from dry to racy. Adding to the palatable taste, marketing savvy winegrowers have merged local folklore with old-school design to create saucy labels, such as the Black Cat (Schwarze Katz) from Zell or the Naked Ass (Nacktarsch) from Kröv. The MSR boasts some 6500 winegrowing operations in 125 towns, which manage more than 80 million vines between the elevations of 100-380m/ 328-1246ft. Picking grapes on these slopes is backbreaking work and there are few mechanical aides to help with the harvest. The highest of the aforementioned elevations (380m/1246ft) is where you'll find Europe's steepest hillside wine estate, Bremmer Calmont, located in the picturesque Mosel town of Bremm. Hikers should experience the Calmont Klettersteig (page 283). <u>Note:</u> Travelers in September and October look out for Federweißer, the new harvest of wine that is typically fizzy and low in alcohol. Traditionally a glass of Federweißer is consumed with a slice of Zwiebel Kuchen (onion cake). Really!

<u>Mosel Wine, *Facts*</u>
• The MSR is Germany's oldest wine-growing district; Romans brought the craft with them 2000 years ago.
• In 1987 the first "red" vines (blue grapes) were planted—previously it was strictly *verboten*!
• Mosel wine is typically filled in green bottles; Rhine wine in brown bottles.
• Picking season is late-Sept/October; festivals abound.
• To get a job as a grape picker, one must be a European resident or have a valid work visa. Those who qualify should begin their inquiries (to winegrowers) in June/July to ensure the necessary paperwork (legal & insurance) can be filled out and processed in time. Pickers usually work 8-hour days during the 3- to 6-week season (time depends on size of property). Payment is roughly 5€ per hour, inclusive of room and board.
• When a wine grower goes into retirement at 65, he/she can only keep 1875sq.m (half acre) of his/her crop, no more. The remainder must be sold, leased or returned to the wild. (Look around, occasionally you'll see an overgrown parcel amongst cultivated vineyards, i.e. no one had the money to acquire it and the younger generation is moving on to other careers.)
<u>Mosel Wine, *What Local Doctors Say*...</u>
• Two glasses of red wine per day assists blood circulation and helps reduce the risk of heart disease by combating the bad (LDL) cholesterol.
• White wine is a remedy for acne (not consumption, apply directly to blemish).
• To soak ailing feet in wine is a proactive measure assisting recovery.

KOBLENZ: For history/sights of Koblenz, refer to (page 323) chapter *Middle Rhine, Valley of the Loreley.*

TI: (www.koblenz.de) *Tel.#* 0261/31-304. Koblenz has two TIs: *Bahnhofplatz* (outside main train station) and *Rathaus* (in the Old Town), both have a free room-finding service, offer an excellent free (fold-out) city map with description of sights, and keep similar hours: April-Oct, daily, 9:00-18:00; Nov-March Mon-Fri 9:00-18:00, Sat 10:00-14:00 (Rathaus till 16:00). *Note:* Culture vultures ask for their handy Museums brochure; but everyone ask for their "Koblenz — 2000 years of history" pamphlet, then visit the History Column (Historiensäule) near TI in the Old Town.

Railers: Koblenz's newly renovated train station is a 30-min walk from the Old Town and K-D boat dock, or from out front take bus #1 direction Deutsches Eck/Altstadt (2/hr). Taxis are also out front—6-7€ to the Old Town or K-D boat dock; roughly 10€ to the fortress (Festung). In the station's main hall is the DB service desk, which also offers a free city map when TI is closed. Exit station right, pass McDonald's, and the **TI** is in the building on the left. Exit station right for the **post office** (Mon-Fri 8:00-18:30, Sat 8:30-13:30; 24hr stamp machine "Briefmarken" outside, button for English) and farther right around the corner is a Lidl **grocery store** (Mon-Sat 8:00-20:00). Trains from Koblenz leave regularly to Trier (trip time 1.5-2hr), Cochem (40min), St. Goar (30min), Bacharach (40min), Cologne and Bingen (1hr).

Boaters: The K-D fleet (Köln-Düsseldorfer, www.k-d.com) offers Mosel excursions only as far as Cochem—*one per scheduled day. Their boat dock is located on the Rhine side of Koblenz, some 100 meters from Deutsches Eck. The spirited gal who runs the K-D ticket kiosk is Martina; tell her we said "Hi!" *Note:* Boats moored on the Mosel side of Koblenz are for overnight excursions, e.g. Viking River Cruises (vikingrivercruises.com)

Koblenz to Cochem [22.40€ o.w.] (dep.) 9:45→15:00 (arr.), stopping at Moselkern (Burg Eltz) 13:00. Times applicable Fri thru Mon April 29 to June 6, and then daily from June 16 to Oct 3. *Note:* June 7-15, 2006, boat traffic to/fro Cochem will be closed due to sluice (lock) closure. You'll cruise through two locks on the way to Moselkern and a third to Cochem.

K-D Discounts: Holders of a German rail or Eurail (consecutive-day or dated Flexi/Select) pass cruise for *FREE!* If it's your birthday, you cruise for *FREE!* Students 26 years of age or under with valid student ID receive a 50% discount, and seniors (60+) travel half price Mondays and Fridays.

BURG ELTZ: *(35km upstream from Koblenz, situated behind the town of Moselkern).* Witness centuries of history in this mint-condition, must-see 12th-century citadel, jam-packed with medieval wares. Burg Eltz is idyllically perched upon a rocky crag above a mellow stream flowing through an enchanting forest. Because of its stealth-like location, Burg Eltz evaded 800 years of European conflict and remained intact. It survived the pillaging of the Thirty Years' War, dodged the Sun King's (Louis XIV) powerful armeé, and eluded WWII bombs. Even today, in the 21st century, it can be tricky to find—unless you're GPS savvy, of course. *Hours:* April-Oct, daily, 9:30-17:30 (last admission). *Price:* adult 6€, student 4.50€. (www.burg-eltz.de)

Tours: Admission price includes tour, duration 40 min. Unfortunately, tours are in German. You have two options for English: (1) 50¢ translation sheet available at ticket counter; buy this and go with a German tour departing every 10-15 min. (2) English tours are possible, but with groups of at least 15-20. Call ahead to see if an English tour is scheduled (tel.# 02672/950-500) or try to organize your own group by snaring the new arrivals, as well as corralling those who have already paid and are waiting in the inner courtyard for the next tour (follow signs "Burgführung")—English speakers will be in possession of the translation sheet. Once your group is complete, alert staff member (be persistent).

Railers: Get off at Moselkern; exit right out of station and follow the hard-to-find Burg Eltz signs—80-min walk! There are no buses or taxis to the castle. *Note:* From Moselkern station, trains leave hourly in the direction of Koblenz 43 min past the hour—and in the direction of Trier 4 min past the hour. A one-way ticket Cochem ↔ Moselkern costs 3.30€ (20-min trip), purchase at automat on platform. Storage lockers are not yet installed in the station, and the service counter is rarely attended.

Drivers: There are two ways to reach the castle after turning off the Mosel Wine Road (route 416): **(1)** *9km drive (mostly uphill), 1.50€ to park, and a 15-min walk or 1.50€ on shuttle bus.* ~ **Turn off route 416** at Hatzenport direction Münstermaifeld, then Wierschem to parking area—*GPS:* N50° 12.741 - E7° 20.374. **(2)** *circa 2km drive (flat), 2€ to park, and a pleasant 40-min walk through a forest.* ~ **Turn off route 416** at Moselkern and drive through a section of town and woods, eventually reaching a café and parking area—*GPS:* N50° 12.074 - E7° 21.171 (coordinates are actually to the forested trail farther ahead, but these will get you to the parking area nonetheless). *Note:* Drivers coming from the direction of Beilstein take the overland shortcut Bruttig to Treis-Karden. Once there, follow signs to Cochem on narrow road through town. After crossing the river, turn right at the traffic lights. In about 5km you'll arrive at the turn off for option 2—if you prefer option 1, continue to the Hatzenport turn off.

Boaters: From the dock follow (infrequent) signs to Burg Eltz—80 min.

Bicyclists: Cycling from Cochem (20km), keep to the left (north) bank. After Müden turn left at Moselkern and follow Burg Eltz signs; from this point it's still a few kilometers farther. You'll ride through a section of town and woods, eventually reaching a café and parking area. Continue straight and cycle all the way to the *steps ascending above the creek leading deeper into the forest—lock your bike up at the steps and continue on foot, 30-min walk. *GPS:* N50° 12.074 - E7° 21.171. If you're tired after the ride and the walk and the castle tour, return to Cochem by train. Cycle to Moselkern station and get on the carriage displaying the bicycle symbol (there is no charge to transport bike). Train departure times are listed above under *Railers*.

Good Sleeps: There's no better place in Moselkern to lay your head for the price than the charming, half-timbered **Gästehaus Grolig**—20-min walk from train station—located at Elztal 27 (along route to castle). *Tel.#* 02672/1567 (www.grolig-moselkern.de.vu) *Price:* (cash only) Sgl 19€, Dbl 37€. *GPS:* N50° 11.501 - E7° 21.854

COCHEM: *(52km upstream from Koblenz, 138km downstream from Trier. Note: These distances are by boat; by car they are 49km and 88km respectively.)* [pop. 5800] Dating from 866 A.D., Cochem is the Mosel's best option for tourists—it's not too big, not too small, centrally located, and has all the necessary services a traveler requires, as well as an inviting old town, a storybook castle, and graceful (but aggressive) swans waddling by the riverbank. The majestic Reichsburg castle is the valley's trademark, perched upon a vineyard-draped bluff overshadowing the village and dominating the skyline. Consider making Cochem your home base for a few nights, touring the town and surrounding areas. Cochem is within comfortable striking distance of Burg Eltz (17km downstream, five train stops); Beilstein (9km upstream, bike-friendly); and the Calmont Klettersteig [page 283] (one train stop away at Ediger-Eller). Visitors on the last weekend in August will arrive in time for the wine festival, when Cochem swells with wine stands and musical bands. Be sure and check out the fountain on the market square, which spouts wine during the festival. The highpoint is Sunday when at 14:00 begins the parade through the old town and at 22:00 explodes a spectacle of fireworks.

TI: Endertplatz (adjacent to old bridge) www.cochem.de *Tel.#* 02671/600-40. *Hours:* May-Oct Mon-Sat 9:00-17:00 (Fri till 18:00, also Sun July-Oct 10:00-12:00); Nov-April Mon-Fri 9:00-13:00 & 14:00-17:00. Free town maps available, which include a (decent) walking tour. Outside TI is a panel listing room vacancies with free telephone connection.

Railers: From the train station the TI and old town are a 10-min stroll. To get there, exit station straight to the river and go right towards the old bridge—in the square before the bridge is the TI, beyond the bridge begins the old town. To get orientated, you'll find a map of Cochem on the right after exiting the station. Storage lockers by exit, 1.50€-2.50€/24hr. Hourly train connections to both Trier and Koblenz—trip time roughly an hour.

Drivers: parking before and after the new bridge (north end of town) is free. Parking by the old bridge (in heart of town) costs 1€/hr, max 2hr (applicable, daily, 8:00-19:00; free all other times).

Bike Rental: The Tour de Mosel begins here! See our German-Canadian pal Jürgen for a bike. He's the pleasant chap working in the K-D ticket kiosk adjacent to the old town and bridge. Jürgen has about 25 bikes for rent, both 3- and 7-speed, costing 4€/4hr or 7€/24hr (prices are for 3-speed, add 1€ for 7-speed). *Note:* Must leave DL or passport as deposit. *Hours:* Easter thru Oct, daily, 9:30-18:00. For other bike-rental options, e.g. mountain bike, go to Rad Sport Schrauth at Endertstr. 41 (some 300 meters up hill from old bridge, on left opposite Sesselbahn [chairlift]). *Hours:* Mon-Fri 9:30-18:00, Sat 9:00-13:00, Sun 9:30-12:00. *Tel.#* 02671/7974 or *cell.#* 0171-385-4242. *Suggestion:* The 9km ride to Beilstein is a must-do. For the better bike lane and photo opportunities keep to the left bank. Ultimately, for the last leg of your jaunt into Beilstein, you'll need to hop on a ferry and cross the Mosel (ferry, 1.50€/person with bike, hours 10:30-12:00 & 13:00-17:30). Another suggestion is to cycle to Burg Eltz, 20km each way (consider riding train back). Keep to the left bank; right bank is not complete! For directions, see page 278— *Bicyclists.*

Boat Rides: A cruise on the merry Mosel is a summer joy. Ticket kiosks are adjacent to the old bridge. Consider the delightful excursion to Beilstein (1hr each way), 9€ o.w./12€ r.t. Boats **depart Cochem** (May-Oct daily) 10:30, 12:00, 13:30, 15:00, 16:15 (we don't recommend this last boat because you'll have to return immediately on the 17:30 boat with no time to visit Beilstein). Boats **depart Beilstein** 12:00, 13:30, 15:00, 17:30. *Note:* Holders of a valid Eurail pass ask our friend Jürgen (in K-D ticket kiosk) for a (10%) discount.

Internet: You can surf at the café two doors from the post office on Ravenéstr. *Price:* 3.50€/hr. *Hours:* Mon-Fri 7:00-18:00, Sat 10:00-18:00, Sun 13:00-18:00. Another place is "Log In," a hangout for gamers, located on Brückenstr. (2nd building on right when coming from old bridge). *Price:* 4€/hr. *Hours:* daily, 11:00 till early morning (may open earlier in 2006).

Post Office: Located at the corner of Ravenéstr. and Josefstr. (near TI). *Hours:* Mon-Fri 9:00-17:00, Sat 9:00-12:00. *GPS:* N50° 08.975 - E7° 09.982

Supermarket: Across from the post office is a clothing store, behind that (up sloping lane) is a grocery store. *Hours:* Mon-Fri 8:30-18:30, Sat 8:00-15:00. Another option is the mini shopping center containing an Aldi market, located 700m beyond the youth hostel and just past the swimming center. *Hours:* (Aldi) Mon-Fri 8:00-20:00, Sat 8:00-18:00. *Note:* At either store notice how cheap a bottle of wine is.

Reichsburg Castle: One of the biggest attractions along the Mosel is Cochem's 11th-century Reichsburg castle. In 1689, the medieval stronghold was destroyed by Louis XIV's armeé and has since been meticulously restored according to original plans. It is well worth the 15-min (steep) walk to reach the castle's ramparts (the vista from where the canon is positioned is stunning)—take Herrenstr. running off the market square; it's flat at first then you'll soon go right and climb Schloßstr. Or you can catch the shuttle bus from either the market square or departure area outside TI (bus departs roughly every 20 min, May-Oct, 2€/person—buy ticket from driver). Tours of the castle interior are in German only—English translation sheet available. Inside, notice how the door locks were crafted in the Hunter's Room so the key effortlessly slides into the hole (ingenious idea aiding drunks and farsighted nobility). Travelers who have a fear of heights beware of the suspended balcony affording paralyzing views 100m/328ft above the Mosel. (www.reichsburg-cochem.de) *Hours:* mid-March thru Oct, daily, 9:00-17:00 (last tour); Nov 1 thru Nov 15 & Dec 26 thru Jan 1, 10:30-15:00 (last tour). *Price:* (includes 40-min tour) adult 4.50€, student 4€. *CC's:* (are accepted with a purchase of 25€ or more) VC, MC, AE. *Tours* are in German and run about every 15 min. To get an English tour, a group of at least 20 is required—call ahead to see if one is scheduled: tel.# 02671/255. Time your visit to coincide with one of the falcon shows (3€/person): Tue-Sun 11:00, 13:00, 14:30 and 16:00. Show is roughly 30 min and in German; if you have a question, ask after show. *Toilets* can be found on the right after entering through the castle gate—"H" for men, "D" for women.

Mustard Mill: Visit Cochem's historic "Senfmühle" dating from 1810; there are only two of its kind in Germany, seven in Europe. Wolfgang is the mill's mustard maestro and he's offering free samples to prove the quality and individuality of his craft. You don't have to be a mustard (Senf) connoisseur to appreciate Wolfgang's seven unique blends: **Mühlen-Senf** (this is the best, reminiscent of Christmas and boasting 11 spices, chiefly cinnamon) • **Riesling-Senf** (yes, you guessed it, mustard infused with the local grape juice—a popular choice) • **Waben-Senf** (yummy…this is honey-mustard) • **Historischer-Senf** (original recipe from 1820) • **Knobi-Senf** (garlic mustard, enough said) • **Cayenne-Senf** (hot, hot, hot) • **Indisch-Senf** (curry lovers, this is your magic). Interested? Wolfgang sells his Senf in ceramic, 250ml jars for 6.50€. Although not conducive to traveling, his mustard is so good it's worth the burden. Buy one to complement your on-the-road picnics or to spice up the kitchen back home. (www.senfmuehle.net) *Hours:* daily, 10:00-18:00. Tours available, 2€/person: 11:00, 14:00, 15:00 and 16:00. *Tel.#* 02671/607-665. *Opinion:* The 45-minute tour (really an oral explanation of mustard in German) is not worth 2€. *Getting There:* The mustard mill (Senfmühle) is located at Stadionstr. 1—adjacent to old bridge, across river from TI.

Swimming Center: (Moselbad; Freizeit Zentrum) Feel like chillin' out at the pool, gettin' steamed in a sauna, or whizzin' down a 55m/180ft long water slide? Take a day off from your travel schedule and head to the Moselbad, located 500 meters past the youth hostel; follow signs Freizeit Zentrum. *Hours:* daily, 10:00-19:00. *Price:* 7.50€/3hr, 11€/day, 12€ for *sauna but this price includes day ticket for whole complex. Students with ID get discount. Bring your own towel or rent one for 2€. For a muscle-relaxing massage (generally 20€/45min), call one day in advance: tel.# 02671/97-990. *Note:* Sauna is totally nude—Tuesday is women-only day.

Good Sleeps: The following accommodations have been selected for their charming disposition, homelike feel and memorable view of Cochem. All come with breakfast. *Railers,* call ahead and they may pick you up.

Villa Schönblick: Kelbergerstr. 40 (villa_schoenblick@yahoo.de) *Tel.#* 02671/7168 Perched high above the old town, 19th-century Villa Schönblick boasts lovely apartment-style accommodations and jaw-dropping views. At these unforgettable digs, Hans and Ursula will be your hosts. *Price:* (cash only) Dbl, small apt. 70€, large apt. 110€ (3-4 people possible). *Getting There: Railers,* call and they may pick you up—otherwise it's a 25-min walk or a taxi is about 6€. *Drivers,* ascend Endertstr. (street running off the old bridge) above Cochem. After 1km turn left following the sign Oberstadt. Continue on this steep and windy road about 2km, eventually it will descend back towards Cochem and your digs will appear on the left. *GPS:* N50° 08.821 - E7° 09.679

Haus Ostermann: Kaasstr. 11 (haus-ostermann@t-online.de) *Tel.#* 02671/1601. The Ostermann's, Erna and Werner, run an adorable five-room B&B across the Mosel from the old town and castle—three rooms have view, two don't (all have facilities). Little English spoken. *Price:* (cash only) 24€/person (cheaper the longer you stay). Apartment with balcony is also available (great deal—book well in advance for *at least* a 2-night stay; 55€ double occupancy, 65€ with 4 persons—add 26€ at the end of your stay for sheets cleaning; breakfast offered for 5€/person.). *Getting There: Railers,* call and they may pick you up, otherwise it's a 25-min walk—head towards town and cross over the river via the old bridge; on the other side descend stairway to river and go left (Uferstr.), when you're even with the castle look left. *Drivers,* from Cochem cross the old bridge and go right towards Beilstein—after a few hundred meters turn right on Talstr. and descend to the river. From there go left (Uferstr.); when you're even with the castle turn left and park—Erna and Werner have rights to eight spaces. Let them know where you parked in case the space isn't theirs. *GPS:* N50° 08.575 - E7° 10.237

Villa Burgblick: Bergstr. 14. *Tel.#* 02671/915-916, fax. /916-696. This B&B charges a higher price for large rooms featuring superb views. Closed Dec/Jan. Little English spoken. *Price:* (cash only) Dbl 70-100€, Trpl available. *Getting There: Railers,* call and they may pick you up, otherwise it's a 15-min walk—head towards town and cross over the old bridge. Once across, go left (Bergstr.). *Drivers,* from Cochem cross the old bridge and go left (Bergstr.). *GPS:* N50° 08.897 - E7° 10.214

Hotel/Restaurant Hieronimi: Uferstr. 14 (www.weinstuben-hieronimi.de) *Tel.#* 02671/7271. These wine-flavored digs are idyllically situated on the Mosel's right bank, across from the old town and castle. The owners (Fuhrmann family) also possess the generations-old Fuhrmann-Burg wine estate, which is expressed in Hieronimi's country-style décor. *Price:* (cash only) Sgl 42-50€, Dbl 76-100€, (add 5€/person if only staying one night). *Getting There: Railers,* call and they may pick you up, otherwise it's a 20-min walk—head towards town and cross over the river via the old bridge; on the other side descend stairway to river and go left (Uferstr.). *Drivers,* from Cochem cross the old bridge and go right towards Beilstein—after a few hundred meters turn right on Talstr. and right again at the river (Uferstr.). Your digs will soon appear on the right. *GPS:* N50° 08.664 - E7° 10.190

Hostel, Jugendgästehaus: [HI] Klottener Str. 9 (www.djh.de) *Tel.#* 02671/8633. Hostelers will appreciate this brand-new addition to the HI family, located 20 min by foot from the old town on the Mosel's right bank. Catering to a welcome mix of German families and international travelers, the hostel offers a game room, BBQ area, sun terrace (boasting remarkable views), small bar, and a cafeteria (for the price you can't beat their 6€ dinners, served between 18:00-19:00). As of yet, there are no Internet or laundry facilities. *Price:* (includes linen, breakfast) dorm bed 17.50€, Sgl 33€, Dbl 46€, (all rooms have facilities). *CC's:* VC, MC. *Note:* Must be a member or an extra charge will apply. *Getting There: Railers,* exit station straight to the river and go left, eventually you'll reach the bridge's graffiti'd stairwell—climb this and cross the bridge to reach the hostel. *Drivers coming from Trier:* pass the heart of Cochem on route 49 and at the end of town cross the (new) bridge by following sign (left) to Cochem-Cond—other side of bridge is hostel. *Drivers coming from Koblenz:* upon passing the Cochem town limits follow sign (right) to Cochem-Cond leading you across the (new) bridge—other side is hostel. *GPS:* N50° 09.283 - E7° 10.347

Campground am Freizeitzentrum: *Tel.#* 02671/4409. Open Easter thru Oct; office hours 8:00-21:00 (July/Aug till 22:00). Located on the Mosel's right bank, this "camping-platz" is an extension of the swimming complex. *Getting There: Drivers,* continue 700 meters past the above-listed hostel and then follow camping sign (left at Aldi). *Note:* To reserve a space will cost 3€. Guests of the campground get 15% discount at the swimming center.

BEILSTEIN: *(61km upstream from Koblenz, 9km from Cochem)* Enormously quaint and tremendously romantic, Beilstein is a picture-perfect community of a few hundred residents living in lopsided, half-timbered houses overshadowed by the scant 12th-century remains of Burg Metternich, once an intimidating fortress. Bisecting the village is Bachstrasse, a cobbled lane journeying past the medieval market square and worn, arched portals leading into vaulted wine cellars. During the high season Beilstein's population more than triples, filling with stress-free tourists—most buildings in town cater to this crowd, offering eats, drinks and sleeps. *(Note: During the off-season—mid-Nov thru March—everything is closed.)* Beilstein is a true gem deserving of your presence; have lunch on a fragrant riverside terrace or a glass of wine in a centuries-old candlelit cellar. What's more, wander to the top of town (via Bachstrasse) and up to a fabulous Mosel view (see *Burg Metternich* below).

Getting There: Beilstein is accessible via car, bus, boat or bike—although, arrival by bike or boat is most interesting. If your approach into Beilstein is from the left bank, you'll need to take the ferry across the Mosel—the ferry generally runs 10:30-12:00 & 13:00-17:30 and costs 1.50€ per adult + bike, 3€ per auto.

Burg Metternich: Getting to the ruined fortress is worth the short hike to flirt with history and absorb a predictably stunning view—entrance 2€, students 1.50€, hours April-Oct 9:00-18:00 (July/Aug till 19:00). To get there wander up Bachstrasse to the back end of the village, go right up the steps following the brown sign "Burgruine Metternich." *Suggestion:* Cost-conscious travelers looking for a stunning view but not an entrance fee, walk as far as (stopping in front of) the posted sign "Aufgang zur Burg Metternich" found at the bottom of the steps leading to the cashier's shack. Now, turn around, walk back down some eight meters, and follow the dirt path veering left—you won't be disappointed! *GPS:* N50° 06.567 - E7° 14.334

Good Sleeps: Beilstein is perhaps too small to warrant an overnight. That said, the medieval hamlet does offer a few enticing accommodations worthy of consideration. All accept *cash only*!

The delightfully charismatic **Hotel Haus Lipmann**, nestled alongside the Mosel and boasting a perfumed garden terrace, is the best! *Tel.#* 02673/1573 (www.hotel-haus-lipmann.de) *Price:* (cash only) Sgl 75-85€, Dbl 85-95€. *GPS:* N50° 06.633 - E7° 14.327

The half-timbered, riverside **Altes Zollhaus** and the ultra-rustic **Hotel Am Klosterberg** are sister properties sharing the same tel. 02673/1850, website (www.hotel-lipmann.de) and price: (cash only) Dbl 60-80€. The *Altes Zollhaus* is small but comfortable—all rooms have Mosel view (use same GPS coordinates as Hotel Haus Lipmann). The *Hotel Am Klosterberg* is roomier, snuggled against the hillside at the top of town featuring views to the fortress ruins. *GPS:* N50° 06.579 - E7° 14.443.

A cute hotel hidden in plain sight is the family-run **Hotel Burg Metternich** (when facing Beilstein, look to the structure at the far right side of town with the step-gabled roof). *Tel.#* 02673/1756. *Price:* (cash only) Sgl 36€, Dbl 62€. *GPS:* N50° 06.603 - E7° 14.300

EDIGER-ELLER: *(72km upstream from Koblenz, 20km from Cochem)* Separated by some 400 meters of undeveloped land, this twin town is located on the left bank of the Mosel, one train stop from Cochem. Ediger is bigger and quainter, flushed with 17th-century wood-beamed houses. Adjacent to the train station and the Calmont Klettersteig (Europe's steepest wine trail, page 283) is Eller, home to the parish church St. Hilarius (12C). Take advantage of your visit to Ediger and have one of the calming gals at the Kreuzberg pharmacy (Apotheke) check your (total) cholesterol level for 3€. It only takes a few minutes. Pharmacy is next to TI and open Mon/Tue and Thur/Fri 8:30-13:00 & 14:30-18:30, Wed 8:30-13:00, Sat 8:30-12:00.

TI: Tourist information can be found in a lopsided, 17th-century half-timbered house that is neat to walk through. Outside, you'll see markings denoting the high-water levels of historic floods. The TI only has brochures and info auf Deutsch, in German. Just inside the door is a makeshift post office with very short hours: Mon-Fri 8:30-10:00, Sat 9:00-10:00. TI is situated on the Mosel Wine Road, midway along Ediger—adjacent is the pharmacy and a mini food mart. (www.ediger-eller.de) *Tel.#* 02675/1344. *Hours:* July-Oct Mon-Fri 10:00-12:00 & 16:00-18:00 (except closed Wed afternoon), Sat/Sun 16:00-18:00. Winter less hours. *Note:* Public toilets can be found right of TI's entrance (around corner), in front of fountain.

Railers: Those who wish to hike the Klettersteig, get off at Ediger-Eller and descend towards the main road. Go right under the train bridge and the trail begins on the other side (*GPS:* N50° 06.163 - E7° 08.296). Upon completing the hike, it's a 30-min walk along the river back to the station.

Good Sleeps: **Gästehaus am Klettersteig**, a cute house with apartment-like rooms, is a good option for budget-minded hikers traveling by rail and looking for a base camp near the Klettersteig. *Tel.#* 02675/1290 (gaestehaus-wolber@gmx.de) *Price:* (cash only) 18€/person. *Getting There:* Gästehaus am Klettersteig is a two-minute walk from the station at Ellerbachweg 7. After exiting station descend towards the main road; then make a left followed by another left at the blue house (Ellerbachweg)—the house with balcony located across grass area is your objective. *GPS:* N50° 06.195 - E7° 08.385

BREMM: *(75km upstream from Koblenz, 23km from Cochem)* Situated on one of the tightest bends in the Mosel's meandering course is the utterly charming village of Bremm, home to 1000 residents and Europe's steepest wine estate: Bremmer Calmont. Sure-footed hikers can trek through the vines on the Calmont Klettersteig, a dizzying path high above the valley floor. When tackling such heights, one realizes the beauty beneath them—a true slice of heaven!

Railers: no station in Bremm, closest is a 30-min walk along the river to Ediger-Eller (1 stop from Cochem). Railers who wish to hike the Calmont Klettersteig, get off at Ediger-Eller and descend towards the main road. Go right under the train bridge and the trail begins on the other side. *GPS:* N50° 06.163 - E7° 08.296.

Drivers: If you're looking for a parking place to hike the Klettersteig, try the service road paralleling route 49 (Mosel Wine Road) adjacent to the train bridge at Eller—the path begins here (*GPS:* N50° 06.163 - E7° 08.296). To walk between Bremm and Eller along the river takes 30 min.

Calmont Klettersteig: This is the famous 3km trek through Europe's steepest vineyards—380m/1246ft at a 55% grade—situated on the cliffs at the river bend between Bremm and the Ediger-Eller train station. Here you'll teeter high above the Mosel River while traversing narrow footpaths pressed against the sheer hillside. The dizzying trek presents a handful of ladders to be negotiated and the occasional section bolstered by safety ropes. If you're still reading, the path levels out over long stretches, allowing ample time to relax and enjoy the scenery. (If it's October, you'll see winegrowers picking their livelihood.) Expect your journey to take between 2 and 3 hours. Pack a picnic, and do not forget your camera—the views are astonishing! *Note:* Only serious, sure-footed hikers need apply. Those who are afraid of heights or suffer from vertigo—*do not attempt this trek!* Wear shoes conducive to hiking. And lastly, hike with a partner.

Kloster Stuben: This is the name for the vineyard-besieged ruins across the river, which is a former nunnery in Romanesque-style dating from the 12th century. On occasion the ruins are used for open-air events, such as a warm summer evening of Dixieland jazz under a blanket of stars.

Good Sleeps: There are many Gästezimmer (B&B) possibilities in Bremm, especially on Calmontstr. Since they are small-town mom-and-pop accommodations, there is little to no English spoken, they only accept cash and are open April-Oct. The following three options are downright adorable and have facilities (shower-toilet) in the room. Book well in advance.

Margret Schmitz, Calmontstr. 7, tel.# 02675/468. *Price:* Dbl rooms only, from 32€. *GPS:* N50° 06.008 - E7° 06.984. Ascend any narrow lane at bottom of town and it will connect with Calmontstr.

Weingut Helmut Treis, Calmontstr. 11/16, tel.# 02675/401. *Price:* Sgl 21€, Dbl 36€. Located a few doors from the above-listed Margret Schmitz.

Willi Pellenz, Moselstr. 44, tel.# 02675/576. *Price:* 21€/person. Situated along route 49 (Mosel Wine Road) at the south end of town—look for an off-white facade featuring a petite terrace adorned by flower boxes and creeping grapevines. *GPS:* N50° 05.991 - E7° 07.149

NEEF: This tranquil and tourist-free hamlet across the Mosel (2km) from Bremm incorporates 560 residents and 10 wineries. For drivers, Neef adds to the accommodations pool and offers a panoramic view of the valley via Petersberg (Peter's Ridge), including a wide-angle perspective of the Bremmer Calmont, Europe's steepest wine estate.

Railers: station is centrally located—1 stop from Ediger-Eller, 2 from Cochem. Considering the town's isolation for pedestrians, it's not recommended to stop here—although, hiking trails are plentiful (35 min to Bremm or Petersberg—for more info on the latter, see *Drivers* below).

Drivers: Follow signs Petersberg(kapelle) for a must-see hilltop perspective of the Mosel. The 2km scenic drive ascends a tight lane through terraced vineyards to St. Peter's chapel (1138) and cemetery (1152). *GPS:* N50° 05.892 - E7° 08.093. Once at the petite parking lot, discover the area by foot. From here you have a bird's-eye view of the Ediger-Eller train station. Left of the tracks begins the Calmont Klettersteig, and right of the station is the town of Eller (Ediger is farther right, where you see the 2nd church steeple). The closer church is St. Hilarius (12C), belonging to Eller. Now wander to the back end of the cemetery following the sign Eulenköpfchen. Ascend the trail to breathtaking views of the valley and the river bend accommodating the Bremmer Calmont, Europe's steepest wine estate.

Good Sleeps: Stay with local vintners—the following two households subsidize their wine estates by offering accommodations. Little to no English spoken. Cash only. Breakfast included.

Weingut-Pension Markert is centrally located at Fährstr. 4, short walk from station and 35 min from the Calmont Klettersteig. Closed Nov-Easter. *Price:* 22€/person, cheaper the longer you stay. All rooms have facilities. (www.pension-markert.de) *Tel.#* 06542/2829. *GPS:* N50° 05.481 - E7° 08.267

At the south end of town is **Gästezimmer Nelius-Kirch**, run by a retired couple, Bernhard and Thea, who still harvest the crop framing their house. Because Nelius-Kirch is situated slightly off the main road and Bernhard doesn't advertise, you're bound to always find a vacancy here. Open all year. Call one day in advance (if possible): tel.# 06542/2637. *Price:* 21€/person in room with facilities, 18€/person without facilities. *Drivers:* Nelius-Kirch is located at Bachtalstr. 30. From Bremm head direction Trier and then Neef. Cross the Mosel via the bridge and continue to the end of town; make the last possible left and drive through the short tunnel into Bachtalstr.—Nelius-Kirch is the 5th house on the left. *GPS:* N50° 05.080 - E7° 08.407

ZELL: *(87km upstream from Koblenz, 35km from Cochem)* From the Latin "Cella," this little pedestrian-friendly jewel boasts 16 wine estates comprising 627 hectares (1550 acres) of vineyards, which accommodates some six million Riesling stock—qualifying Zell as the largest wine-growing community on the Mosel. Among the town's wineries is the internationally celebrated Schwarze Katz (Black Cat) estate; more than 80% of the label is exported. In the early 13th century the town's fortified wall was completed, numerous watchtowers and three gates secured the riverside municipality. By the mid-1800s the wall proved obsolete and was consequently recycled into building materials, the Square and Round towers were spared and the latter is the town's landmark—a splendid view can be had from its hillside perch, adjacent to the cemetery. A modern pedestrian bridge connects Zell with its partner neighborhoods (Kaimt and Barl) across the Mosel.

TI: in Rathaus (www.zellmosel.de) *Tel.#* 06542/96-220. *Hours:* (summer) Mon-Fri 9:00-17:00, Sat 10:00-15:00; (winter) Mon-Thur 9:00-12:30 & 13:30-17:00, Fri 9:00-13:00. Meters from TI is the Black Cat fountain.

Railers: no train station, line ends in Bullay—hourly buses run from there (10-min ride). *Opinion:* For most Railers, Zell is not worth the effort.

TRABEN-TRARBACH: *(109km upstream from Koblenz, 57km from Cochem)* Traben-Trarbach represents twin communities adorning either bank of the Mosel. Traben, on the left (north) bank, is bigger and accommodates the sleepy train line, the modern TI, the poorly signposted badly located youth hostel [HI], and vestiges of Louis XIV's power-house fortress: Mont Royal. Trarbach, on the right (south) bank, maintains a quaint old town, the ruined 14th-century Grevenburg castle entrenched on the ridgeline, and the turn-of-the-century Brückenschänke: romantic restaurant that is the double-tower gate securing the bridge.

TI: found in Traben on the plaza before the railway line. (www.traben-trarbach.de) *Tel.#* 06541/83-980. *Hours:* (May-Oct) Mon-Fri 9:00-18:00, Sat 11:00-15:00; (Nov-April) Mon-Fri 9:00-12:00 & 14:00-17:00.

Railers: A privately run train line maintained by Trans-Regio connects Traben-Trarbach with the Deutsche Bahn (DB) Trier-Koblenz line—transfer at Bullay (hourly connections), 20-min ride to last (third) stop. *Opinion:* For most Railers, Traben-Trarbach is not worth the effort.

Good Sleeps: To visit Traben-Trarbach is worth it for drivers just to stay at **Christine Ferienappartments** and eat at Christine's rustic restaurant next door: the Alte Zunftscheune. Christine and her husband are a hard-working couple whose efforts commencing decades ago have earned them one of the Mosel's most respected restau-rants along with their adorable apartment-style accommodations. Couples looking for a charming residence to call home will find it at Christine Ferienappartments. Only four rooms available, all of which are self-contained. Minimum two nights stay; book well in advance. *Tel.#* 06541/9737. (www.zunftscheune.de) *Price:* (cash only) 44-67€. Breakfast not included in price, but Christine can prepare something if desired for 6€/person and leave it in your fridge. *Getting There:* Christine's Ferienappartments are centrally located at Neue Rathausstr. 13, Traben. Look for the ivy-covered facade. *GPS:* N49° 57.068 - E7° 06.922. *Drivers,* parking is tight, inquire beforehand.

Hostel, Jugendherberge: [HI] Hirtenpfad 6, Traben. (www.djh.de) *Tel.#* 06541/9278. *Price:* (includes linen, breakfast) dorm bed 16.50€, Sgl/Dbl available. Must be a member or an extra charge will apply. *Railers:* The 80s-style hostel is a 20-min walk (badly signposted) from the rail line. From platform ascend steps following sign Ausgang Bismarckstrasse; parallel tracks some 300 meters to the end of the street. From there ramble through the pedestrian lane (on left) between the houses and continue a ways farther to (street) Hirtenpfad—then left up the hill. *GPS:* N49° 57.550 - E7° 07.608

KRöV: *(112km upstream from Koblenz, 60km from Cochem)* A few kilometers from Traben on the Mosel's left bank is the extremely delightful hamlet of Kröv, home to the famous Naked Ass wine. This rather provocative name for a wine has several interpretations recounting its origin. The most popular tale is told like so: *A local wine-grower entered his cellar—rich with dusty bottles of Riesling and oak casks ready for the tapping—to find three sneaky boys sampling the goods. The winegrower caught the adolescents and handed each an old-fashioned whippin', smacking their naked ass(es).*
    Town highlights (2006) include the Naked Ass wine festival (Oct 13-14) and the traditional costume festival (June 30—July 3), the latter having folk dancing, fireworks, crowning of the wine queen, and music on the Mosel's only floating stage. And antique markets on June 24-25, July 29-30, Sept 2-3.
    TI: you'll find it situated on the Mosel Wine Road (route 53), midway along town on the river side. (www.kroev.de) *Tel.#* 06541/9486. *Hours:* Mon-Fri 8:00-12:00 & 14:00-17:00, Sat 10:00-12:00.
    Railers: no station, line ends in Traben-Trarbach—buses run from there.
    WWII Buffs: Baldur von Schirach is buried in Kröv; refer to (page 465) chapter *Tomb-Lovers, Who's Buried Where? WWII Buffs.*
    Sleeps: Plenty of enticing Zimmer (B&B) throughout town.

BERNKASTEL-KUES: *(129km upstream from Koblenz, 70km from Cochem, 61km downstream from Trier)* [pop. 6000] Bernkastel-Kues is another rural gem pressed against the riverbanks by green rolling hills laden with flavorsome grape stock, a breathtaking sight so commonplace along the Mosel Wine Road. Like Cochem, Bernkastel-Kues is a mega-tourist magnet, boasting old-world charm with an exclusive collection of ill-proportioned half-timbered houses, a medieval marketplace and a (ruined) castle. In Kues, on the Mosel's left (north) bank, white-wine lovers will cherish the Vinothek, a hospice cellar jam-packed with regional wines for your taste approval. Bernkastel, on the Mosel's right bank, possess the TI and main touristy sights. The dual community's most boisterous festival takes place on Aug 31—Sept 4, '06: Thur 18:00 kickoff, Fri 18:00 celebration of wine queen, Sat 21:00 fireworks show, Sun 14:00 winegrowers' parade, Mon party continues.
    TI: (main road) Gestade 6, Bernkastel (www.bernkastel.de) *Tel.#* 06531/4023. *Hours:* Easter thru Oct Mon-Fri 8:30-12:30 & 13:00-17:00, Sat 10:00-17:00, Sun 10:00-13:00 (in winter, weekends are closed and Fridays open till 15:30). Internet, bike rental available—inquire at TI for current locations.
    Railers: no train station, transfer in Wittlich—buses run from there (20-min ride) or from Trier (2-hr ride).
    Drivers: Parking available all along Bernkastel's main road, use your "parking dial" (page 450), applicable Mon-Sat 8:00-18:00, max one hour. If the latter area is full, you can park on either side of the Cochem end of town without the dial. To park in the lot on the waterfront where the touristy boats depart will cost 1€/hour, max nine hours, applicable Easter thru Oct, daily, 8:00-19:00. However, if you only want to stay an hour or less, it's *FREE!* At the ticket automat, press the "parkschein anfordern" button and your free one-hour ticket will pop out. Put this on the dashboard of your car.
    Boat Rides: A cruise on the merry Mosel is a summer joy (May-Oct). Ticket kiosks "Schiffskarten" can be found along the waterfront on the Bernkastel side, near TI. Consider the delightful excursion to Kröv (1.25hr each way, 9€ o.w./13€ r.t.), or a bit farther to Traben-Trarbach (1.45hr each way), 10€ o.w./14€ r.t. Or hop on the one-hour sightseer boat for a "Moselrundfahrt" departing regularly from 11:00, 7€/person. *Note:* Holders of a valid Eurail pass ask for a 10% discount with Gebr. Kolb.

Post Office: located in Kues at Mozartstr. 25, a few streets in front of Vinothek. *Hours:* Mon-Fri 9:00-17:00, Sat 9:00-12:00—24-hour stamp automat ("Briefmarken") available. *GPS:* N49° 54.976 - E7° 04.037

Medieval Marketplace: Arguably the region's most unique town square, "Markt" is situated in Bernkastel and is routinely buzzing with camera-toting tourists. (To get there, follow cobbled lane opposite bridge.) Here you'll discover **St. Michael's fountain** (1606) spouting off in front of the **Rathaus** (town hall, 1608). Face the Rathaus then look left three facades—notice how the five-story half-timbered dwelling (dating from 1613) appears to be falling over. Yikes! Now walk over to the Rathaus and have someone snap a photo of yourself wearing the shackles pegged to the left corner. While shackled, face the fountain then look left to see the adorable **Spitzhäuschen** (1416), the narrow wood-beamed structure shaped like the tip of a spear. Inside you can buy wine. To exit the square and delve farther into Bernkastel, walk over to the dwelling that appears to be falling over and wander along Römerstr., the main drag. If you make it as far as Römerstr. 81 you'll see old typeface on the facade, it reads: "I was once young and beautiful."

Vinothek: Exclusive are the vaulted cellars of the 15th-century St. Nikolaus Hospital, stacked with more than 150 wines for your taste approval. The cellars today are called the Vinothek, and for 9€ you can taste till ya drop. This is strictly for "white" connoisseurs; red lovers will find little value here. Alas, there are no English descriptions—just remember: trocken = dry and halbtrocken = half dry. *Hours:* daily, mid-April thru Oct 10:00-17:00, Nov thru mid-April 14:00-17:00. *Note:* They require that you leave your bag(s) at the front desk. More importantly, there is no charge to browse the wine assortment. To reach the cellar, descend the stairs midway along on the right. To reach the toilet, continue past the stairway to the back of the building. ***Getting There:*** Vinothek is located in Kues, adjacent to the bridge—when crossing from Bernkastel it's on the right in the historic complex.

Wine Museum: entrance 2€. For the general traveler, the Wine Museum next door to the Vinothek is not worth the effort.

Burg Landshut: Positioned high above the southern end of Bernkastel is the 13th-century carcass of Landshut castle, testimony to the town's feudal past. Visitors are welcome to wander the historic ruins, climb the tower (1€—pay within café), absorb the sweeping views, and/or grab a snack at the café. Next door is the Bernkastel-Kues youth hostel [HI]—dorm 14.50€, Dbl 37€. *Tel.#* 06531/2395 (www.djh.de). *Getting There: Railers,* there is a bus that runs to the castle, or it's a 40-min hike. *Drivers,* on the Bernkastel side go through the tunnel and ascend the hill some 2km following signs to the burg and hostel (Jugendherberge). *Note:* From the parking lot it's a 5-min walk to the castle, 10-min back.

Good Sleeps: There are numerous options to choose from; here are a charming few. Little English spoken.

Hotel Binz: Am Markt 1, Bernkastel. (www.hotel-binz.de) *Tel.#* 06531/2225. This 3-star hotel is centrally located, meters from the medieval marketplace and bridge to Kues. *Price:* Sgl 40-50€, Dbl 65-75€, Dbl Komfort 70-85€, Trpl 80-110€. *Note:* Komfort room is recommended for the extra euro. *CC's:* VC, MC. *Drivers,* parking 2€/day. *GPS:* N49° 54.923 - E7° 04.509

Gasthaus Burkard: Burgstr. 1, Bernkastel. (www.gasthaus-burkard.de) *Tel.#* 06531/2380. From the medieval marketplace, stroll to the end of Römerstr. to find the ever delightful, femininely rustic scarlet-colored Gasthaus. *Price:* (cash only) Dbl 46-70€. *GPS:* N49° 54.911 - E7° 04.663. *Drivers,* free parking—see website for most direct route.

Hotel-Garni Alter Posthof: Burgstr. 26 (www.bernkastel-posthof.de) *Tel.#* 06531/ 91-257. Pleasant wood-beamed digs offering comfy rooms outfitted with a modern touch. *Price:* Sgl 30-45€, Dbl 55-70€; apartment available. Bike rental 6€/day. *CC's:* VC, MC, AE, DC. *Getting There:* Hotel is located up street from Gasthaus Burkard, 10-min walk from river. *Drivers,* free parking—see website for most direct route, click English then Route. *GPS:* N49° 54. 827 - E7° 04.685

~ *Drivers* who prefer a spontaneous choice will find oodles of cute pension-type Zimmer (B&B) in the north section of Kues. From the main road turn left onto Beethovenstr. and follow the green signs, each one represents a Zimmer or hotel. For more choices, check the historic part of Kues in the south end of town along Weingartenstr.

~ *Campers* will enjoy **Campingplatz Kueser-Werth**, tel.# 06531/8200, idyllically set on a peninsula in the southwest part of Kues, between a tranquil harbor and the merry Mosel. Fishermen will rub shoulders with fellow hobbyists here. *GPS:* N49° 54.561 - E7° 03.170

PIESPORT: *(148km upstream from Koblenz, 96km from Cochem, 42km downstream from Trier)* [pop. 2500] This community is not unlike the other gems along the Mosel, tranquil and effervescent. Piesport is mentioned here for keen fisherman, a great place to cast a line. Start by checking out the riverfront and talking to the locals hangin' at the petite bar of the Gasthaus Moselloreley; have them show you their trophy room in the back. The locals are a curious bunch and appreciate the company of fellow enthusiasts from foreign shores. Picknickers will love the riverside serenity Piesport offers. Gasthaus Moselloreley can be found at the following coordinates, opposite the Mosel's own Loreley cliff face: *GPS:* N49° 52.423 - E6° 55.692

Good Sleeps: Located in an ultra-quaint part of town, the **Landgasthof Alt Piesport** are cozy digs housed in an 18th-century building practically touching the Mosel. Little English spoken. *Price:* (cash only) Dbl 54€ (cheaper the longer you stay). *Tel.#* 06507/ 6506. *Note:* Ask for a room with a view of the Mosel ("Zimmer mit Mosel Blick"). *Getting There:* Follow autobahn signs direction Salmtal, leading you to the river. Halfway across the bridge, look left to discover your digs. *GPS:* N49° 53.160 - E6° 54.946

TRIER: refer to chapter *Trier*, beginning next page.

T R I E R

~ Population: 105,000   ~ Elevation: 140m/460ft
~ Country/Area Code: +49-(0)651   ~ Sister City: Fort Worth, Texas

Spearheading the Mosel Valley is Germany's oldest city, Augusta Treverorum (later Treveris, then Trier), founded by Roman emperor Augustus in 16 B.C. Although, a slightly different and much older tale of the city's establishment is inscribed above the

door of the Rotes Haus on the market square: "Ante Romam Treviris Stetit Annis Mille Trecentis" (Trier existed 1300 years before Rome).

By 150 A.D., Augusta Treverorum had become a bustling metropolis on the banks of the Mosel River with approximately 25,000 residents—hence the commission and construction of the Barbara Baths, amphitheater, and even a circus. With the looming threat of a Germanic invasion, the Romans constructed a 4-mile defense wall around the city, which ultimately had five gates— each being 100-feet high and made of enormous sandstone blocks. Of these five ancient portals, the north gate, Porta Nigra (or Black Gate), still exists.

From humble beginnings, Trier became a provincial capital and eventually the administrative center for the Western Roman Empire (roughly modern-day Germany, France, Spain and Britain) on account of Emperor Diocletian (ruler 284-305 A.D.) who reorganized his overstretched empire into four manageable sections.

The first half of the 4th century brought monumental change to the newly inaugurated capital. The population swelled to a whopping 80,000 and Constantine the Great (ruler 306-337 A.D.)—the Roman emperor responsible for ending the persecution of the Christians and legalizing all religious worship via the Edict of Milan—made Trier his residence and commissioned many of the city's legendary sites before shipping off to his freshly renovated eastern capital, Constantinople (present-day Istanbul).

By 465 A.D. the once mighty Roman Empire had lost its muscle and Trier fell into the hands of the Franks, a Germanic tribe. Centuries later, Trier was absorbed into what became known as the Holy Roman Empire, Charlemagne's 1000-year Reich. In 1512, during this new empire, the first public exhibit of the Holy Robe—Christ's seamless shroud (brought back to Trier from Jerusalem by Constantine's mother, Helena)—took place in the cathedral. By the early 18th century the Holy Roman Empire was neither holy, Roman, nor a real state and Trier's population dwindled to a staggering 3000, reaching a 1700-year low from chronic outbreaks of plague and war. In 1794 France annexed Trier, and after the fall of Napoleon in 1814 it became part of Prussia. Near the end of the 19th century, Trier's population had increased to 37,000 and in 1891 a million pilgrims came via the newly built railroad to admire Christ's Holy Robe.

Following the successful D-Day invasion of Normandy, France, the Allies marched into a record-cold winter and the bloodiest campaigns yet seen in Western Europe. On December 16, 1944, the Nazi war machine smashed across a 50-mile front of the

American sector in the Ardennes forest with some 250,000 troops, kick-starting Hitler's last great offensive in the west: a.k.a the Battle of the Bulge. The Führer's bid for victory failed and Nazi forces retreated east, leaving the Mosel and Rhine rivers as the last natural barriers between the Allied juggernaut and the interior of Germany. U.S. General George S. Patton—a history buff—relished the opportunity to liberate Trier. German troops regrouped and dug in around the city, bringing Patton's men to a grinding halt. The German's blew all bridges in the area except the Römerbrücke, the nation's oldest bridge dating from 144 A.D. On March 1, 1945, Patton decided to rambo his troops across the Römerbrücke and seize Trier. That evening, Patton received orders from Allied HQ to bypass the city since it was believed that at least four divisions were necessary for its capture. Patton allegedly replied: Have taken Trier with two divisions. What do you want me to do…give it back?!

Today, more than 3 million people visit Trier annually to witness the largest collection of ancient Roman buildings outside of Italy. So culturally unique, these (eight) sites were voted onto UNESCO's World Heritage list. Additionally, Trier maintains two sacred relics, Christ's Holy Robe and the bones of Matthias, the Twelfth Apostle, which attracts pilgrims from all over the world. What's more, Trier is a wine metropolis, ideally situated in the heart of the Mosel-Saar-Ruwer (MSR) wine region, the nation's fourth largest. Geographically, Trier neighbors Luxembourg (16km/10mi) and France (35km/22mi), and is closer to London (630km/394mi) and Paris (370km/231mi) than it is to Berlin (729km/455mi), the capital of Germany.

~ Trier is worth a two-day stay. Mood and weather permitting, divide your time like so,

Day 1: Visit the first five Roman attractions listed in the section UNESCO Sites, Trier (page 292): Porta Nigra, Cathedral, Church of Our Lady, Amphitheater, and Basilika. The five sites won't take very long to visit, leaving extra time for other interests. On your way from the Porta Nigra to the Cathedral, notice the House of the Three Magi (page 299) midway along Simeonstrasse—and a bit farther ahead is the Market Square (page 298). After ogling the Church of Our Lady, proceed to the Basilika—behind it is the Electoral Palace (page 299) and gardens (snap a palace view from the knoll in front of the Archaeological Museum, page 301). Consider visiting the Imperial Baths (page 296) on your way to the amphitheater. If time allows, trek through the vineyards to reach sweeping vistas of Trier from the Petrisberg (hill above amphitheater).

Day 2: Tour sights/museums of interest that weren't on the agenda for day 1, e.g. Karl-Marx-Haus, Roman Bridge, Matthias' tomb (Twelfth Apostle), or Archaeological Museum.

Tourist Information: [TI] (www.trier.de) *Tel.#* 0651/978-080. There is only one TI in Trier and you can't miss it because it's located next to the Porta Nigra and is usually packed with people. Free city maps available. Do-it-yourself folks may be interested in the "Trier walking tours" booklet for 2.90€. Visually minded folks might want to take Trier home with them in the new DVD format, 10€ (grab NTSC version for USA). *Hours:* April-Oct Mon-Sat 9:00-19:00, Sun 10:00-17:00; Nov/Dec Mon-Sat 9:00-18:00, Sun 10:00-15:00; Jan/Feb Mon-Sat 10:00-17:00, Sun 10:00-13:00. *Note:* Across the street from TI, at Simeonstrasse 8, lived Karl Marx from 1819-35. Midway up the building's facade (left) is a plaque commemorating the fact.

Tours: TI offers an English walking tour May-Oct every Sat at 13:30 for 6€, duration two hours. *(Note: If you are in town on a Saturday [May-Oct] we recommend the aforesaid walking tour over the following multilanguage motorized tours that impart only a fraction of the historical info.)* Those who are looking for a Trier quickie, hop on either the open-air **City Tour** bus or the **Römer-Express** (little choo choo on wheels)—

both tours last 35 min, are multilanguage, pickup at Porta Nigra, run regularly every day March-Nov 10:00-17:00 (April-Oct till 18:00) and cost 6€/person.

Emergency Tel. Numbers: [Germany-wide]
   Police (Polizei) = 110
   Fire dept. (Feuerwehr) or general emergency = 112
   Ambulance = 19222

Hauptbahnhof: [Hbf] Don't expect Grand Central here, Trier's "main train station" is rather small for a city topping 100,000 residents. Situated in the entrance hall, the train *info desk* (open daily 7:00-22:00) can offer a free city map and answer general touristy questions—if desk is unattended, a (DB) representative won't be too far away. *Storage lockers* are around the corner and cost 1.50€-2.50€/24hr. A *post office* can be found outside and to the right (Mon-Fri 8:30-18:00, Sat 8:30-13:00). *Bike rental* is on platform 11 Süd (mid-April thru Oct, daily, 9:00-19:00; Nov thru mid-April Mon-Fri 10:00-18:00). *Trains leave regularly for* Koblenz (1.5-hr trip) and Cochem (40-min trip). *Getting to* the TI and Porta Nigra (Germany's most significant Roman relic) is a 10-min walk; exit station straight onto Bahnhofstr. and continue through the forward intersection (Theodor-Heuss-Allee). After a few minutes the Porta Nigra will appear on the left (along the way is a chance to go online, see *Internet* below); other side of Porta Nigra is the TI. From there, Simeonstr. (main shopping street) leads to the market square and cathedral within seven min.

Buses: Most of Trier's attractions are within walking distance of the market square, rendering public transportation for the general traveler unnecessary. However, for those who require the service: a single ticket (**Einzelfahrscheine**) for 1-2 zones costs 1.50-2€, valid for 60 min (not valid for return travel). A day ticket (**Tageskarte**) costs 4-5€. The best deal is the **Minigruppen** ticket, valid for up to 5 people, 7.50-9€.

Parking: *Drivers,* prepare to get lost—road signs are somewhat erratic! Head towards "Centrum." To *park on the street* across from the Porta Nigra will cost 20¢/12 min, max 2hr, applicable Mon-Fri 8:30-19:00, Sat 8:30-15:00—free all other times. Or pull into a side street for a cheaper price and longer max time. The following inner city *parking garages* — City-Parkhaus, Hauptmarkt, Basilika, Konstantin, Viehmarkt — cost 1.20€/hr, 2.40€/2hr, 9.50€/24hr. All other inner-city garages charge a bit more. **Note:** When you're ready to drive downstream along the Mosel, take route 53 direction Bernkastel-Kues.

Bike Rental: Located at the train station on platform 11 Süd is *Radstation*, renting 7-speed bikes for 7.50€/day or 27-speed 10€/day. Little English spoken. They have several excellent brochures (although in German) on bike routes in the area. *Hours:* mid-April thru Oct, daily, 9:00-19:00; Nov thru mid-April Mon-Fri 10:00-18:00. *Tel.#* 0651/148-856. Radstation is not privately owned but instead it's operated by the city as an initiative for the unemployed. *Note:* Enthusiasts consider cycling to Koblenz (195km/121mi) on the Moselradweg (Mosel Bicycle Trail)—a breathtaking journey. Allow at least five days to properly fulfill your sightseeing obligations. Weekly rate: 38€/7-speed, 50€/27-speed. It's possible to leave bike in Koblenz; query staff at Radstation for details.

Internet: Across from the Porta Nigra on Theodor-Heuss-Allee is a little computer shop offering Internet (Mon-Fri 11:00-19:00, Sat 10:00-18:00) for 1€-1.50€/60 min and coffee/cappuccino 1€, tea 50¢. Literally around the corner on Paulinstr. (next to the Norma grocery store) is a call shop, offering cheap Internet (1€/hr) and international telephoning. *Hours:* daily, 9:00-22:00. *Tel.#* 0651/991-4207

Post Office: exit the main train station and go right to find a P.O. *Hours:* Mon-Fri 8:30-18:00, Sat 8:30-13:00. Another P.O. can be found at Fleischstr. 60 (opposite white fountain), a few minutes south of the market square. *Hours:* Mon-Fri 9:30-18:00, Sat 9:30-13:00. *Note:* at both locations there is 24-hour stamp machine (Briefmarken) available, button for English.

Trier-Card: The Trier-Card is valid for three consecutive days, inclusive of free use of public transportation, 50% discount on Roman (UNESCO) monuments and 25% concession on several museums, select tours, and bicycle hire. *Price:* adult 9€, family 15€— available at TI. *Note:* Grab brochure and mull over details; perhaps the Trier-Card will save you money in the long run. Couples consider the "family" card to increase savings. *Opinion:* For the general traveler, the card isn't worth it—public transportation won't play a big role (if at all), the Roman monuments are only 2.10€ full price (only three are worth paying for), and the museums don't add up.

Roman Sites Combo-Ticket: Around town you'll see a little square foldout brochure advertising the Roman UNESCO sites combo-ticket (Römisches Trier Erleben) for adult 6.20€, *student/seniors 3.10€. The pictures and map inside the brochure are nice but the ticket—available at participating sites—is not really worth it (for the adult price). Have a look at the brochure then read our *UNESCO Sites, Trier* section to see whether you'd like to visit the five sites on offer. Actually, one of the sites, Barbara Baths, is closed— leaving only four sites that charge admission, but only three (Porta Nigra, Imperial Baths and amphitheater) are worth visiting for non-buffs. The full admission price for each site is 2.10€, equaling 6.30€ for the three suggested sites—10¢ more than the adult combo-ticket. Oh, and the free guided tours the brochure advertises for ticket holders are in German. *_Note:_ The student/seniors price is the best deal for those who qualify, serving up 1.70€ in savings for three sites or 3.30€ for all four.

Supermarket: Across from the Porta Nigra on Paulinstr. (next to the call shop) is a "Norma" grocery store—open Mon-Sat 8:00-20:00.

What to do on a Sunday or holiday

The pedestrian shopping avenues of Simeonstr., Fleischstr. and Brotstr. will be empty. All attractions and most eateries will be business as usual.

FREE Trier

1) Witness the **sacred tomb of Matthias** (page 297), the Twelfth Apostle. He is the only one of Christ's original 12 disciples buried north of the Alps.

2) The **Cathedral**, **Church of Our Lady** and **Basilika** are UNESCO World Heritage sites, *FREE*, and worth visiting.

UNESCO Sites, Trier

The following eight World Heritage sites date from the days of the Roman Empire and are listed in order of visitor appeal, from the most interesting to the least. *Note:* For most every site an informative English booklet is available (at cashier, 2.50€) describing each individual monument.

> *UNESCO: The United Nations Educational, Scientific and Cultural Organization was established at the end of 1945 to encourage partnerships among nations in the areas of education, science, ethnicity and communication. Additionally, since 1972, UNESCO began protecting the natural and cultural properties of exceptional worldwide importance against the threat of damage in a rapidly developing world so that future generations can inherit the treasures of the past. Through such unified endeavors, UNESCO hopes to encourage universal respect for traditions, human rights and fundamental freedoms. Headquartered in Paris, France, 180 nations belong to UNESCO. As of July 2005, the World Heritage List stands at 812 sites.*

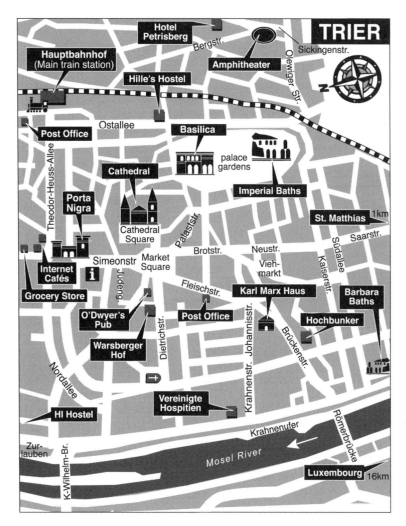

Porta Nigra: (Black Gate, 160-180 A.D.) Midway through the 2nd century A.D., when prophets were predicting a grandiose future for Trier, a 4-mile-long fortified wall—including five gates—was swiftly built around the riverside settlement to protect the inhabitants from hostile incursions. Of these five ancient portals, the north gate, Porta Nigra (Black Gate), still exists. The gate's colossal dimensions—built without the use of mortar by layering huge sandstone blocks on top of one another fastened with iron clamps—continue to amaze historians and onlookers. In medieval times the iron was hewn from the sandstone for recycling and as a result several cavities can be seen where clamps once held the blocks together. Porta Nigra is the only gate to have survived the dismantling of the city's Roman fortifications during the Middle Ages, when it was converted into a two-story church honoring St. Simeon—a spiritual hermit who took up residence in the gate. Upon Simeon's death in the 11th century, many miracles occurred—thus the former recluse entered into sainthood. After Napoleon conquered Trier, he secularized the city and ordered the Black Gate to be restored to its former Roman grandeur—only the Romanesque apse is preserved from St. Simeon church (look to the section butting against Simeonstr.). Although weather beaten and sullied by centuries of pollution, the Porta Nigra still portrays a structure of enormous strength and significance. *Hours:* daily, 9:00-17:00 (April-Sept till 18:00)—last admission half hour prior to closing. *Price:* adult 2.10€, student/seniors 1.60€, child (up to 18) 1€, family 5.10€. *GPS:* N49° 45.557 - E6° 38.701 *Opinion:* There's not a lot to see inside but it's worth the entrance fee to ramble through the most important Roman relic on German soil—and the upper-level view is terrific. Expect a visit to take around 20 min.

Cathedral: The present-day cathedral, or Dom, the oldest in Germany, stands on top of a former Roman palace once belonging to Emperor Constantine, who donated his estate on the 20th anniversary of his reign in 326 A.D. to build the largest Christian church of its era, roughly four times the size of today's structure. Reinforcing Constantine's enormous church were four granite columns called Domstein, each standing 12m/39ft tall and weighing 64 tons. For the most part these columns have disintegrated, except for one—a decent portion of a Domstein can be seen lying adjacent to the main portal before entering. Inside the cathedral, the only parts remaining with Roman origins are the impressive 26m/85ft high walls. After reasonable deterioration and destruction from fire, the cathedral was renovated in the 11th century in Romanesque-style. A more recent addition to this sacred structure is the "swallow's nest" (1974), a glorious neo-Baroque organ suspended midway along the nave, weighing 30 tons and featuring 5602 flue pipes, the tallest being 5.4m/18ft. The cathedral's most prized possession, however, is the seamless Holy Robe of Christ, which is kept in a chapel behind the altar—(to get there, see *Holy Robe* below). Info pamphlets (10¢) containing the cathedral's history and *floor plan can be picked up straight inside the main portal and on the right, where remembrance leaflets of the Holy Robe are also available (15¢). *Note:* The floor plan illustrates the enormity of Constantine's church; look for the light-colored pavers outside in the plaza (Cathedral Square) marking the corners.

Holy Robe: (Heilige Rock) First evidence of Christ's Holy Robe dates from 1196, when it appeared in the cathedral's west choir. It is thought that Empress Helena, mother of Emperor Constantine, brought the seamless robe to Trier after a pilgrimage to Jerusalem and donated it to the Dom in the early 4th century. In 1512, at the request of Kaiser Maximilian I, the Holy Robe was displayed publicly for the first time. During the two-month exhibition thousands of mesmerized believers paid homage. The Kaiser was so impressed by the turnout that he proclaimed the sacred relic be displayed annually. This transpired for five consecutive years until the pope overruled the kaiser and decreed the robe be displayed every seven years. This continued until wars ravaged the land and exhibitions became irregular. The four most recent exhibitions date from the industrial revolution, when in 1891 a million devotees steamed into Trier via the new railroad to admire Christ's Holy Robe. The exhibitions of 1933 and 1959 each attracted 2 million pilgrims. The latest exhibition, in 1996, brought 1 million visitors to the cathedral for the 800-year jubilee of the robe's discovery. It has not yet been decided when the next exhibition will be, perhaps in 2046 for the 850-year jubilee? ***Getting There:*** You can access the Holy Robe chapel via the stairway in the front right part of the cathedral. After the first flight of stairs you'll see pictures of the robe and reliquary on the right. The second flight of stairs leads to the Dom Treasury and gift shop. From here, steps on the left ascend through a narrow portal to the chapel area (free entry; open same hours as *Dom Treasury*, see below). Through a golden gate the lavish reliquary encasing the Holy Robe can be seen beneath a suspended gold-plated crucifix. When retracing your route back downstairs, walk through the door on the left at the bottom of the steps. This leads into the Dom's restful cemetery encompassed by wowing Gothic architecture.

Lopsided Steeples: Outside, face the cathedral and you'll notice the design of the right tower is different from the left. The reason for this dates from the early 16th century when St. Gangolf—the parish church overshadowing the market square—was built. Upon St. Gangolf's completion in 1507, its castle-like tower—tagged with the Latin inscription: "Watch and pray"—soared 62m/203ft high topping the city's skyline as the tallest structure in Trier. For obvious reasons this infuriated the bishop, who immediately commissioned the extensions of the cathedral towers to rise above St. Gangolf. The bishop, however, only half succeeded in his endeavor because he ran out of money. The taller right tower exudes the bishop's one-story Gothic-style addition, whereas the shorter left steeple still exhibits the original height in Romanesque-style. The bishop, though, did scrape up enough cash to add his own gilded Latin inscription (above clock), continuing St. Gangolf's verse: "For it is unknown when our Lord will arrive."

Hours: (cathedral) daily, April-Oct, 6:30-18:00, winter till 17:30. *FREE* entry! Visiting restricted during Mass: Mon-Sat 7:00 & 9:00, Sun 7:00, 10:00, 11:30 & 18:00.

Getting There: Cathedral joins the east side of the market square via the pedestrian lane, Sternstrasse.

Note: Long after the cathedral shuts its doors—when the evening sky twinkles high above—spotlights flood the sacred structure making it a luminescent sight not to be missed.

For more on the cathedral, see page 298—*Cathedral City.*

Dom-Information: This is the cathedral's tourist center, located across from the Church of Our Lady—enter through the Baroque-style arch. Stop by if you have a question about the cathedral or church, or would like an info brochure (or book) in English, or if you desire a 60-min tour of the cellar (4€/person). The cellar is circa 100 years older than the cathedral itself. Tours are in German; phone ahead to see if an English tour is scheduled. *Tel.#* 0651/979-0790. *Hours:* April-Oct Mon-Sat 9:30-17:30, Sun 12:00-17:30—similar hours off-season but closed Sundays. *Note:* Toilets are on left after entering—50¢ for a stall.

Dom Treasury: (Domschatzkammer) Here you'll discover significant works of pious art and holy relics—including the 10th century St. Andrews altar and a nail allegedly from the Crucifixion (brought back by Empress Helena; same journey as Holy Robe). *Hours:* April-Oct Mon-Sat 10:00-17:00, Sun 14:00-17:00; Nov-March Mon-Sat 11:00-16:00, Sun 14:00-16:00. *Price:* 1.50€.

Church of Our Lady: Adjoined to the cathedral is the "Liebfrauenkirche," the oldest Gothic church in Germany. Construction began around 1235 A.D. with a French design in mind. In the early 13th century the southern part of the cathedral was razed (destroying all remnants of Roman origin) and replaced by the Church of Our Lady. The interior is small in comparison to the cathedral; although, the brilliant blend of colorful light beaming through the stained-glass windows gives the impression of extra space while setting a distinctly medieval atmosphere. Unique are the rounded altar niches that encompass the cross-shaped floor plan. When facing the altar, on the left you'll see vestiges of the original wall murals and to your right are the names of soldiers belonging to the church's congregation who died during WWI. *Hours:* daily, 8:00-12:00 & 14:00-18:00. *FREE* entry!

Amphitheater: The arena was built in the 2nd century A.D. on the eastern boundary of the Roman city wall, doubling as an entertainment center and defense post, which explains the lack of entrances. During Roman times popular entertainment meant blood-sport sacrifices, humans fighting to the death and gladiators clashing with wild beasts. The amphitheater had seating for 20,000 spectators and they poured through the entrances like baseball fans skimming through turnstiles to enjoy a day at the park. The crowd was nonetheless demanding, and to appease them cruelty reigned supreme. Surrounding the arena floor are hollowed enclosures that served the gladiators as a quasi locker-room. Beneath the amphitheater was an elaborate staging area, where a moveable platform could usher the stars of the show up to the arena floor for their deadly performance. The amphitheater today—with its fine acoustics and pleasant location amid juicy vineyards—serves as a major tourist attraction and a venue for the occasional open-air concert. Expect a visit to take 20-35 min. *Hours:* daily, 9:00-17:00 (April-Sept till 18:00)—last admission half hour prior to closing. *Price:* adult 2.10€, student/seniors 1.60€, child (up to 18) 1€, family 5.10€. *Getting There:* Amphitheater is located some 600 meters east of the Imperial Baths on Olewiger Str., 10-min walk. *Drivers,* follow signs Olewig. *Note:* Wineries are located 1km farther east on Olewiger Str; follow sign Olewig. *GPS:* N49° 44.805 - E6° 38.959

   Suggested Tour: After paying admission, ascend stairs on left to the observation terrace. Here you can survey the arena, vineyards and bleachers from a lofty prospective *(you'll also notice a map illustrating how Trier looked in Roman times)*. Continue along path. After passing the remnants of Roman columns (behind the two benches), turn left—descend path and follow it right to enter the arena like a mighty gladiator. *(Imagine the roar of the crowd, the blowing of trumpets.)* Ascend the stairs before you to the bleachers. Here you can take a seat and express your desire to show mercy to the defeated contestant by raising a white hanky or give the thumbs down for death. After absorbing a bleacher view, head back down the steps and through the portal (on left) to the arena floor. Once there, pop your head into one of the hollowed enclosures. Conclude your tour by cruising the boardwalk through the now barren subterranean cellar (via stairway) that was once an elaborate staging area. Before leaving the grounds, you'll see toilets adjacent to the exit: "D" for women, "H" for men.

Basilika: Once Constantine's lavish throne room and a palatial reception hall for Roman emperors, the so-called Basilika stands today as the largest surviving single-room structure from Roman times: 27m/89ft wide, 33m/108ft high and 67m/220ft long. With such colossal dimensions, Constantine could express the splendor and supremacy of the empire. It was at this time in the early 4th century A.D. that Trier became known as the second Rome. Although, in reality, Rome's authority was already diminishing and Trier was in all likelihood the more important of the two capitals. Since the mid-19th century, the Basilika has been a Protestant church in Catholic Trier. Upon entering the main portal, one is immediately struck by the vastness of the unadorned brick interior—which could keep a team of decorators employed for years. Where the altar rests, at the far end of the structure, Constantine had his throne. Expect a visit to take 5-10 min, unless you are a decorator. *Hours:* April-Oct Mon-Sat 10:00-18:00, Sun 12:00-18:00; Nov-March Tue-Sat 11:00-12:00 & 15:00-16:00, Sun 12:00-13:00. *FREE* entry! *Note:* Adjoined to the Basilika is the Electoral Palace (page 299). *Getting There:* Basilika is a five-minute walk south of the cathedral. When facing the cathedral, go right (on Liebfrauenstr., passing Dom information on right)—at the end of this street follow it left (An der Meerkatz). At the end of this short road you'll see the Basilika's mammoth, brick facade on the right. Enter at far end, left around corner.

Imperial Baths: The imperial bathing complex, known as the "Kaiserthermen," was enormous in its heyday, large enough to contain more than seven U.S. football fields. The reason for this enormity was the integration of military barracks accommodating 1000 legionnaires, their horses, and a sports ground. Still standing are two levels of massive arches that formed the southern and eastern apse of the main bathing hall—bounded by useful ruins, these massive arches were reinforced in medieval times and molded into the city's fortified wall. When Napoleon captured the city in the late 18th century, he entered via this point and joked how he conquered Trier through a bathroom window. Interesting to see is the subterranean labyrinth where slaves would have operated the heating and circulation facilities for the hot and cold pools. The conditions below ground were damp, dirty, and the only light came from the burning embers used to heat the baths. *Hours:* daily, 9:00-17:00 (April-Sept till 18:00)—last admission half hour prior to closing. *Price:* adult 2.10€, student/seniors 1.60€, child (up to 18) 1€, family 5.10€. *Getting There:* Imperial Baths are a few-minutes walk south of the Basilika, through the gardens of the Electoral Palace.

Roman Bridge: Here you'll discover the oldest bridge north of the Alps—the "Römer-brücke"—dating from 144 A.D. It's a third generation Roman prototype, which replaced the two former wooden designs. Notice the red-and-black color contrast. The black basalt pillars disappearing into the water are original and come from the nearby Eifel region— the red stone arches and roadway date from the 18th century. The bridge played a vital role in Trier's expansion through the epochs, and in 1945 it stood as the lone conduit for General Patton's 10th Armored Division (Third Army) to assault the city. Early on the morning of March 1, U.S. troops captured the ancient bridge intact due to the heroism of Lieutenant J. J. Richardson, who was riding in the front vehicle of his battalion when he saw wires leading to demolition charges. Springing from his jeep, J. J. raced across the bridge under heavy enemy fire and cut the wires—Richardson saved the day but sacrificed his life! *Getting There:* Römerbrücke spans the Mosel River at the southwest part of town, which is a 17-min walk from the market square—from there take Fleischstr. to Brückenstr. (passing Karl Marx's house) to Karl-Marx-Str. to the Roman Bridge.

Barbara Baths: (Barbara Thermen) Public baths were a significant part of Roman culture, a social center for both sexes. Here one could be massaged with oil, sprayed with perfume, have body hair removed, or receive a pedicure. In the beginning of the Roman health-spa movement, men and women bathed naked in separate facilities. The latter hedonistic stages of the empire called for mixed bathing and quite often the facilities became the scene of amorous affairs. The Barbara Baths date from the 2nd century A.D. and qualify as Trier's oldest and largest bathing complex, which could accommodate eight U.S. football fields. Recently, the Barbara Baths have been closed due to excavations. Nevertheless, to most visitors, there's not a lot to see amid the wide expanse of ruins, making a trip here uneventful. Interested party's can get a decent look from the street. Enthusiasts check with TI for the grand reopening—hours/prices will be the same as the Porta Nigra. *Getting There:* Barbara Baths are situated on Südallee in the south-west part of town, two minutes from the Roman Bridge.

Forum Baths: (Thermen am Viehmarkt) Although technically not a UNESCO World Heritage site because of its recent discovery, the Forum Baths are still considered part of the package. During excavations for an underground parking garage in 1987, construction workers were stunned to find the vestiges of Trier's third Roman bathing facility. Albeit the discovery and history of the Forum Baths is astonishing, it's not worth visiting— excellent toilets, though. *Hours:* Tue-Sun 9:00-17:00. *Price:* adult 2.10€, student/seniors 1.60€, child (up to 18) 1€, family 5.10€. *Getting There:* Forum Baths are a 10-min walk from the market square; take Fleischstr. to Stresemannstr., where you'll go left to Vieh-marktplatz and the baths.

SIGHTS

St. Matthias: This majestic Benedictine abbey originated as the memorial chapel St. Eucharius built upon a Roman cemetery of Christians. In the early 4th century Empress Helena—mother of Emperor Constantine—returned to Trier from a pilgrimage to Jerusalem and brought back the bones of Matthias, the Twelfth Apostle (after Judas betrayed Jesus, Matthias replaced him). The relics were rediscovered 800 years later in an altar when St. Eucharius was undergoing renovations to become a multi-church complex. Since the Middle Ages, pilgrims have flocked to St. Eucharius (now St. Matthias) to worship the Twelfth Apostle—the only apostle buried north of the Alps. Today, St. Matthias is a significant monastic complex, home to 20 active monks and several acres of pristine parkland (only accessible to the monks). *Getting There:* Matthias' tomb can be found 2km due south of the market square; opposite the monastery's main gate is a parking lot (free) and bus stop (Railers ride bus #3 to St. Matthias Basilika). Pass through gate and continue straight across the vast courtyard. Inside the church's magnificent facade you'll discover the tomb of the Twelfth Apostle. *GPS:* N49° 44.316 - E6° 37.864. *Hours:* daily, 6:00-19:30 (Sundays visiting is restricted). Monastery gift shop (right side of church before entering): Mon-Fri 9:00-12:00 & 14:30-17:45 (no lunch break in summer), Sat 9:00-12:00, Sun 11:00-12:45.

Market Square: (Hauptmarkt) After the Vikings sacked Trier in 882 A.D., it was decided to move the marketplace off the riverbank to its present location. The raising of the *Market Cross (column in middle of square) in 958 commemorates this event. *(*Note: The original cross, the oldest of its kind in Germany, is in the Municipal Museum.)* As the commercial center and heart of Trier, the market square is colorful and full of activity, teeming with locals, tourists, vendors selling flowers, fruits and vegetables, newspapers and magazines. Now, for a marketplace orientation, stand by the Market Cross and face the Porta Nigra, which (for the sake of this exercise) we will say is 12:00 on a clock dial. To your right, **at 3:00**, is Sternstrasse, the lane leading to the cathedral—1000 years ago, a gate stood here marking the entrance into Cathedral City (see next entry). **At 2:00**, the handsome pink building on the left corner of the lane, is the bishop's former palace (notice ecclesiastical seal above door). Today, the bishop would be pleased to know that his former digs have been renovated into an H&M fashion store—some of the best (and most reasonable) shopping in the land. Really! **At 5:00** is St. Peter's Fountain, dating from 1595. Perched atop its ornate frame is the city's patron saint, Peter. Below, maidens symbolize the four cardinal virtues: justice (scales), courage (snake), temperance (wine and water), and wisdom (broken column). **At 6:00**, overshadowing the marketplace, is St. Gangolf, a parish church dating from the 15th century. You'll see it's castle-like tower soaring 62m/203ft into the sky; above the clock is a Latin Bible verse (for its meaning, see page 295—*Lopsided Steeples*). To reach St. Gangolf, venture (past beggar[s] and) through the Baroque portal left of yellow, half-timbered building. **At 8:00**, on the corner of the square, is the Steipe, a unique 15th-century edifice resembling a four-story castle turret crowned by a sheer roof. Propped upon its facade, flanking the ground-floor arches, are representations of Trier's patrons (l. to r.): St. James the Elder, St. Helena, St. Peter and St. Paul. Above them, on either corner, are two knights standing guard over the marketplace in full battle armor. The one on the left dutifully watches over his citizens while the other faces the bishop and cathedral with his visor down and hand on his sword, symbolizing the people's struggle for independence from the bishop's gripping powers. The Steipe building has played multiple roles in its history, from a festival hall to a council tavern to community offices. Today it contains a restaurant/café, of course. Adjacent to and behind the Steipe is the **Rotes Haus** (Red House), where you'll find the Latin inscription declaring Trier is 1300 years older than Rome (gold typeset one level above main door). Inside the Rotes Haus is a café (same one as in the Steipe) and the upper floor is dedicated to the city's Toy Museum (Spielzeugmuseum).

Cathedral City: One thousand years ago an extensive fortified wall was built around the Dom, essentially creating a city within a city—the district was fittingly called Cathedral City. Pedestrian lanes and auto-friendly streets such as Palaststr., Simeonstr., Glockenstr. and Flanderstr. now mark the former walled boundaries. The main gate into Cathedral City was erected opposite the Market Cross, hence today's Sternstrasse passage funneling visitors onto the cathedral's threshold. Noteworthy are the age-old lanes behind the Dom, flanked by high walls built from recycled Roman materials and typified by washed-out inscriptions above longstanding portals before houses of former church hierarchy. ***To get to*** the aforesaid lanes take Windstrasse (when facing Dom, lane on left side) to Hinter dem Dom (veer right and right again). Along the way, notice examples of the high walls on the left and the multifaceted blend of brickwork on the right representing different epochs of cathedral construction, some sections dating from the first millennium A.D. Shortly you'll see a decorative yellow-and-white building on the right; peek through its burgundy doors to see the cathedral's cemetery encompassed by mesmerizing Gothic architecture (along walls in arcade is evolution of Dom, even in war). Head back to the road and continue in the same direction—then go left on Predigerstr. and right on Große Eulenpfütz. Notice the sandstone archway on the corner sporting a worn crest and (below) an unknown date 16??—adjacent is a long-forgotten portal. Continue ahead to exit the former Cathedral City. Once at main road, go left for Hille's hostel/train station or go right and the road will soon curve left to the Basilika (page 296).

House of the Three Magi: (Dreikönigenhaus) Don't miss this decorative and unusual tower-like house situated 150 meters from the Porta Nigra (on left side when heading to market square) on the pedestrian-only Simeonstr. The Romanesque-style house was built around the year 1230, during a time when Trier's upper class had to safeguard their residences by constructing the front door midway up the facade (you'll see it on the right) so that it was only accessible via a retractable ladder. The street-level entrance you see today is a modern addition, opening to a lucrative bakery and café. If you're in need of a *free* toilet, head to the rear of the café. *Note:* The oldest of these unusual residences is Franco's Tower (Frankenturm), dating from the 11th century. Alas, Franco's Tower is worn and forsaken—located on Dietrichstr., across from the Warsberger Hof (hostel).

Electoral Palace: Behind the Basilika are fanciful gardens spread before an exquisite Rococo palace. The original wing of the palace dates from 1615 when prince electors, powerful rulers who were part of the voting process to elect the Holy Roman emperor, decided to build a new royal residence. Today, the palace is the seat of local government and generally not open to the public. The gardens parallel the former medieval city wall (on left) to the Archaeological Museum (Landesmuseum) and finish at the ruins of the Imperial Baths. *Note:* Snap a palace view from the knoll in front of the museum's pink entrance (go through stone archway, then right and up steps).

St. Irminen: During Roman times the Mosel River flowed heavy with merchant traffic, as a result large-scale warehouses called "Horrea" were constructed near the river to store goods off-loaded from the boats. By the 7th century the Horrea had long been abandoned and many were converted into the convent St. Irminen. During the Napoleonic-era, the French altered the function of the Horrea, modifying them into civil welfare facilities— e.g. hospital, old-age nursing home, learning center and rehabilitation clinic—a role they still primarily play today. Besides St. Irminen and the aforesaid facilities, the complex accommodates the Vereinigte Hospitien…

Vereinigte Hospitien: The "United Hospitals" winery is important because it includes Germany's oldest wine cellar—here you can sip, swirl and spit the region's famed Riesling in a monastic cellar composed of Roman brickwork dating from 330 A.D.— *minimum 15 people required*. Book in advance. *Tel.#* 0651/945-1210 or e-mail: weingut@vereinigtehospitien.de *Hours:* (typically) Mon-Thur 8:00-12:30 & 13:30-17:00, Friday 8:00-12:30 & 13:30-16:00. *Getting There:* Vereinigte Hospitien is located at Krahnenufer 19, a 15-min walk west of the market square. From there, take Fleischstr. to the end of the pedestrian zone—at the intersection cross into Johannisstr. (on right) and continue to the end of Krahnenstr., where you'll ascend the footpath on the right. Go straight (paralleling the *boulevard) and make the first right into the Hospitien grounds. Continue straight, then left, then right passing the rose-colored building (on your left) to the "Ältester Weinkeller Deutschlands." *GPS:* N49° 45.409 - E6° 37.876. **Note:* Across the boulevard, adjacent to the river, is the older of the two historical cranes (see next entry).

Historical Cranes: North of the Roman Bridge on the Mosel's right bank are two former loading cranes, standing as evidence to the bygone days when the river catered to an armada of merchant vessels. The northerly crane, opposite the Vereinigte Hospitien winery, was built in 1413; the crane closest to the Roman Bridge dates from 1774. The riverside path running past the cranes makes for a refreshing stroll and is popular with joggers.

Hochbunker: *(WWII Buffs)* In the southwest corner of town, next to the Rathaus (or town hall), is an enormous structure resembling a defensive bastion from the Middle Ages. This concrete giant is called the Hochbunker and was actually built in more recent times, during WWII (1941-42), in fact, for use as an air-raid shelter. It stands today as part of Trier's skyline, a stark reminder of Germany's hellish past. In case you were wondering, it's too big to implode. The Hochbunker is not open to the public, only for external viewing. *GPS:* N49° 45.110 - E6° 37.983

MUSEUMS

Karl-Marx-Haus: (birth house and museum) Karl Marx—the son of Jewish parents Heschel (Heinrich) and Henrietta Marx—was born on May 5, 1818, in the quaint three-story house at Brückenstrasse 10. Dating from the Baroque era, the Brückenstrasse residence was built in 1727 and qualifies as one of the most attractive burgher (middle-class) houses in Trier, inclusive of a courtyard and a surprisingly large garden. This excellent, newly renovated and comprehensive museum spans three floors, featuring the life of Karl Marx and the evolution of Marxism. (www.fes.de/marx) Allow at least 40 min for a visit. *Hours:* (last admission half hour prior to closing) daily, April-Oct Mon 13:00-18:00, Tue-Sun 10:00-18:00; Nov-March Mon 14:00-17:00, Tue-Sun 10:00-13:00 & 14:00-17:00. *Price:* (includes audio guide) adult 3€, student 1.50€. *Getting There:* Karl-Marx-Haus is a 10-min walk from the market square—from there take Fleischstr. to Brückenstr. and it's the fifth building on the right. *Note:* No furniture from the Marx family has survived. *WWII Buffs:* Marx's birth house was seized by the Nazis in 1933 and used as their party HQ.

History, Karl Marx: The political ideology that Hitler loathed, the Red philosophy that stimulated the Cold War, and the social fear that compelled Senator Joe McCarthy to imagine "pinkos" infiltrating Capitol Hill originated right here in Trier on May 5, 1818, with the birth of Karl Marx.

When Karl was 1 year old, the Marxes moved to Simeonstrasse 8 (marked by a commemorative plaque)—a stone's throw from the Porta Nigra—where Karl lived until he finished high school in 1835. The Marxes were a family with rich Jewish traditions, which proved difficult to sustain in a country polluted by anti-Semitism. When Karl was 6 years old, Heschel Marx, Karl's father—an attorney—was forced to convert his family's religion because of professional reasons. Heschel changed his name to Heinrich and Karl was baptized as a Protestant. In 1835, Karl left Trier (at age 17) after high school to study in Bonn, then Berlin, and ultimately at the University of Jena, where in 1841 he received a Ph.D. in philosophy. After college, Marx took a job in Cologne as the editor of the newspaper "der Rheinische Zeitung." His writings for the paper were controversial, as he criticized the government's political and social position, which landed him in deep poop with the authorities. He subsequently resigned and the newspaper was obliged to cease operations. Now unemployed, Marx decided to marry his longtime love, Jenny von Westphalen, and move to Paris, France (1843). It was here that he met up with Friedrich Engels and began nurturing the seeds for a working-class movement with Communistic principles. Two years later, in 1845, Marx was expelled from France on account of his revolutionary activities. The married couple packed their bags and moved to Brussels, Belgium, where he formed a network of left-wing committees. In 1847, the committees were amalgamated to form the Communist League with Marx and Engels as their first chairmen. The newly formed revolutionary group needed a set of guidelines and objectives; thus Marx drafted the Communist Manifesto, which identified a class struggle between the capitalists and the proletariats (laboring class) while predicting a revolution and the downfall of the capitalistic state. The year 1848 brought a period of political instability leading to a series of rebellions that began in France and spread across much of Europe. Belgium's government feared the wave of revolution would roll across its border and consequently evicted Marx from Brussels. He headed back to Cologne and revived his old newspaper to spread forward-looking propaganda. The authorities weren't keen on the reappearance of Marx and swiftly arrested him. They revoked his citizenship and respectfully expelled him from the country. This landed Marx in London, England, where he lived the remaining 33 years of his life. During these three decades Marx found work as a European correspondent for the New-York Daily Tribune from 1852-1861 and completed his trademark publication, Das Kapital, in 1867. Karl Marx—philosopher, author, leader, visionary, father of modern Communism—was a man who didn't influence many people during his lifetime, but posthumously he changed the world. Marx died (at the age of 64) on March 14, 1883, and is buried at Highgate Cemetery, London. _Note:_ Marx's influence is still strong in countries like China, Cuba and several in Africa. The Chinese, in particular, count for a large percentage of the museum's visitors, who view their trip as a quasi-pilgrimage.

Archaeological Museum: Here at the "Rheinishes Landesmuseum" you'll trudge across some 3000sq.m/32,000sq.ft of floor space dedicated to exhibiting artifacts from the Celtic age to medieval times, as well as the most extensive compilation of Gallo-Roman antiquities in Germany—including the world's largest Roman coin collection. The museum has so many artifacts (approx. 10 million) that it's not possible to exhibit them all. _Hours:_ May-Oct, daily, Mon-Fri 9:30-17:00, Sat/Sun 10:30-17:00; Nov-April same hours except closed Mondays. _Price:_ (includes audio guide) adult 2.50€, student 1.50€. _Note:_ Sections presently closed for renovations, which should finish June 2007, thus the reduced price. _Getting There:_ Museum is located between the Electoral Palace and Imperial Baths; go through archway in medieval city wall. _Note:_ Nice view of Electoral Palace can be had from knoll in front of museum's pink entrance—ascend steps.

Municipal (Städtisches) Museum, housing Trier's history from the 5th century to modern times, is closed for renovations until 2007. The museum is located in the two-story Romanesque complex adjoining the Porta Nigra and TI.

Best Views

Porta Nigra: This 1800-year-old Roman relic offers the best inner-city view—see page 293.

Petrisberg: (Mount Petris) The crest above the amphitheater offers outstanding vistas of Trier—accessible by car, bus or foot (40-min walk from Old Town). Take these views to bed with you, see page 303—_Hotel Petrisberg._

St. Mary's Column: (Mariensäule) Look to the west and you'll see the Virgin Mary keeping a watchful eye over Trier from atop a 40m/131ft tall pillar entrenched upon the 1000-foot sandstone ridge. The column was built with the help of donations in 1866. Getting there is possible by car, bus or foot (50-min trek from Old Town)—pack a picnic.

Entertainment

No need to rush to get a bar stool in Trier, the locals tend to get a late start—especially on weekends. The most interesting way to make pub-and-club discoveries is by venturing through the Judengasse portal, accessing the former Jewish quarter (near market square on Simeonstr.—enter below attractive half-timbered facade and protruding clock).

For an older, chic crowd, a great place to chill is at **Walderdorff's** (opposite Dom, right of governmental pink building). Next door is a club that kicks off in the heat of the night, usually Fri/Sat. And if you happen to meet the love of your life, the Standesamt (marriage registry) is in the same complex. Guinness connoisseurs will find a home at **O'Dwyer's Irish pub**, located at Jakobstr. 10 (accessible via market square or Judengasse). O'Dwyer's frequently offers live music/DJs and karaoke Mondays. *Hours:* daily, 11:00 till late. Guinness 4€.

Events/Festivals 2006

Annual Fun Run, May 21 (Sun): Run with history on your side—4km (fun run), 10km, or 21km (half marathon). Entry fee applicable, prize money feasible. Must pay by May 20—the earlier you pay, the cheaper the fee. www.triererstadtlauf.de (in German). *Tel.#* 0651/42-222

Antiquity Festival, June 17—July 16: Traditional indoor theater moves its stage and props outdoors to the ancient playgrounds of the Romans: amphitheater and Imperial Baths.

Old City Festival (Altstadtfest), June 23-25 (Fri-Sun): A rockin' weekend! The Old Town is amplified with live music, wine-tasting booths, knickknack stands, a festival tent, and regional cuisine dished from sidewalk vendors.

Wine Festival, August 4-7 (Fri-Mon): Countless bottles of Riesling will be uncorked to the delight of many. "Red" connoisseurs need not apply. The festival is located in Trier's wine-growing district, Olewig (1km past amphitheater)—follow signs Olewig.

Roman Festival, August 11-13 (Fri-Sun): Delve back 2000 years to a time when men were warriors and women were vestal virgins. The theme is "Bread and the Circus," performances scheduled at the Imperial Baths and amphitheater.

Christmas Markets, Nov 27—Dec 22: *Mmm*, this is a wonderful time of year when gift-wrapped stands come to town to sell hot-spiced wine (Glühwein), roasted chestnuts, baked apples, gingerbread goodies, grilled sausages and tree decorations. Trier's Christmas markets are small but charming, romantically set on the medieval market square as well as in the plaza facing the cathedral. Don't forget to collect a Glühwein mug.

GOOD SLEEPS

Hostel, Hille's: Gartenfeldstr. 7 (www.hilles-hostel-trier.de) *Tel.#* 0651/710-2785 or cell 0171/329-1247. Respectable accommodations; practical self-service kitchen; washer/dryer and Internet available; eateries/pubs and bakery nearby as well as a grocery store (exit hostel left and it's on the corner). *Price:* (includes linen) dorm bed from 14€, Sgl from 28€, Dbl from 38€. *CC's:* VC, MC. *Note:* Late check-in, between 16:00-18:00—if arriving earlier, call ahead to arrange baggage storage or you can hang out in the kitchen. *Getting There:* Hille's is a 10-min walk from the market square or main train station. From the station, exit straight to the main intersection (Ostallee) and go left. Continue straight and at the second traffic light (Gartenfeldstr.), go left. Your digs are a few doors along on the left (enter through big wooden door). *GPS:* N49° 45.211 - E6° 38.851

Hostel, Warsberger Hof: Dietrichstr. 42 (www.warsberger-hof.de) *Tel.#* 0651/975-250. Even though the Warsberger Hof is a former 18th-century palace for nobles, its quarters are average, no rooms have a toilet or shower and the nights can be noisy when revelers come home—but its location is *phenomenal*, 1-min walk from market square. Say "Hi" to our friend Roland, if he's on duty. *Note:* Hip bar on premises. Drivers, free parking in courtyard. *Price:* dorm bed from 15€, Sgl 19-26€, Dbl 32-44€, linen 3€, breakfast 5€. *CC's:* VC, MC. *GPS:* N49° 45.440 - E6° 38.348

Hostel, Jugendgästehaus: [HI] An der Jugendherberge 4 (www.djh.de) *Tel.#* 0651/146-620. Standard German youth hostel—same-gender dorms commonly patronized by hyper school kids rampaging through hallways—for use by backpackers in a pinch, drivers on a budget. *Price:* (includes linen, breakfast) dorm 17.50€, Sgl/Dbl available—all rooms have shower/toilet. *Note:* Must be a member or an extra charge (of 3.10€) will apply. *Getting There:* Hostel is located in the northwest part of Trier, adjacent to the Mosel, 20-min walk from market square or 30 min from main train station. *GPS:* N49° 46.062 - E6° 38.340

Hotel Petrisberg: Sickingenstr. 13 (www.hotel-petrisberg.de) *Tel.#* 0651/4640. Idyllically situated above the amphitheater and overlooking the city, Hotel Petrisberg offers its guests the best, family run digs in town. Non-smoking rooms • yummy buffet breakfast • romantic strolls through vineyards • ogle dreamy sunsets. Allow the astute and mature owners—(brothers) Helmut and Wolfgang—to be your attentive maître d's and valuable info sources. *Price:* Sgl 60-65€, Dbl 90-95€, Trpl 135-145€. *CC's:* VC, MC. *Note:* Reserve a room with a balcony and city view. *Getting There: Railers,* from the station a taxi roughly costs 7€, or it's a 30-min walk (use same walking directions to get to Hille's hostel. Continue straight past Hille's to Bergstr. and go right. At the top of this residential road, go left (Sickingenstr.). Ahead you'll see the hotel's Baroque-style wrought-iron gate—walk straight through it to the end. Rest assured. *Drivers,* follow signs to Olewig then amphitheater. Once there, make a left on Sickingenstr. to Petrisberg—after 500 meters you'll see the hotel's Baroque-style wrought-iron gate. Drive straight through it to the end. Rest assured. *GPS:* N49° 45.022 - E6° 39.275

The following three turn-of-the-century hotels are similar in price, comfortably outfitted, and centrally located next door to one another—steps from the Porta Nigra. **Getting There:** *Railers, exit station straight onto Bahnhofstr. and continue through the forward intersection (Theodor-Heuss-Allee). After a few minutes the hotels and Porta Nigra will appear on the left. Drivers, follow signs to Centrum, then Porta Nigra. GPS: N49° 45.557 - E6° 38.701*

Zum Christophel: *Tel.#* 0651/979-4200 (www.zumchristophel.de) *Price:* Sgl 55-60€, Dbl 85-90€, Trpl available. Parking 3€.

Römischer Kaiser: *Tel.#* 0651/97-700 (www.hotels-trier.de) *Price:* Sgl from 67€, Dbl from 98€, Trpl from 128€. *CC's:* VC, MC, AE, DC. Free parking, enter on Rindertanzstr.

Altstadt-Hotel: Sister property of Römischer Kaiser; same prices, website and free parking—except different tel.# 0651/145-560.

MiDDLE RHiNE, Valley of the Loreley — BiNGEN to KOBLENZ

60km/38mi—allow at least one full day, and a night if you have time

Beginning in the Swiss Alps and streaming west from Lake Constance, the Rhine River forms Germany's border with Switzerland and subsequently the frontier with France as it surges north from Basel eventually spilling into the North Sea via Rotterdam, an extensive journey spanning 1320km/820mi through four countries. Although not the longest river in Europe (the Danube is more than twice its length, and the Volga nearly three times as long), the Rhine is one of the most important and renowned commercial rivers in the world, greatly influencing the culture, history and economy of Europe for two millennia, from the earliest days of the Roman Caesars to modern times.

Today, the Rhine is awash with 2000-ton barges hauling freight—and usually the captain's car—to their destinations. Along the banks of Germany's autobahn of rivers are black-and-white kilometer markers denoting the distance from Basel, Switzerland, where Europe's busiest waterway becomes navigable. The Upper Middle Rhine, incorporating some 120,000 residents living in 30 towns on either riverbank, is known to merchant captains as kilometers 528 to 588 from Bingen to Koblenz and is recognized by tourists as the Romantic Rhine or Valley of the Loreley. It is this world-famous section of the Rhine River that has recently (since June 2002) taken its place alongside the ancient pyramids of Giza and the wilds of East Africa's Serengeti as an honored member of UNESCO's World Heritage List. The banks along this 60-kilometer stretch of the Rhine are adorned by terraced vineyards yielding succulent Riesling stock and by magnificently medieval castles crowning impregnable ridgelines. Nowhere in the world are there so many fortifications on a river as the Rhine. Like a mythical ride at Disneyland, hop on a boat and imagine cruising through the Middle Ages when ruthless robber barons and petty kings reigned supreme. During these times powerful fortresses were routinely erected adjacent to—or even in—the river as customs stations to levy excessive tolls on passing merchant vessels. Squabbles broke out and battles raged between alliances.

Lured by the Loreley, intoxicated by thirst-quenching vineyards, charmed by quaint villages, and spellbound by the Baumeisters' bastions—it's time you, too, fell under the Rhineland's magical spell. *The Romantic Rhine is a must for any itinerary to Europe!*

In this chapter the towns and attractions are listed sequentially according to the black-and-white kilometer markers, beginning with Bingen and heading downstream to Koblenz. Those who are planning to spend a night (or two), choose Bacharach or Boppard 1st and St. Goar 2nd.

~ *Suggested Itineraries*

Time-crunched tourists: Rambo a Rhine tour by heading to Bacharach (543km) and hopping on a *boat to St. Goar. This cruise only takes 40 min and covers the most famous castles as well as the curvaceous Loreley. With a few hours to spare, tour Burg Rheinfels (557km) towering above St. Goar.

Tourists with 1 day, night: Start early and experience the whole of the Romantic Rhine. From your accommodations head upstream by train to Bingen—from there hop on a *boat to Koblenz (3.4-hr cruise). *(Note: Train station at Koblenz is a 30-min walk from the boat landing; if it does not interest you to see the confluence of the Rhine/Mosel [Deutsches Eck], disembark at Boppard [570km] to catch the train back).* When time is best suited, allow 90-120 min to tour Burg Rheinfels (557km) above St. Goar.

Tourists with 2 days: Utilize your second day for general sightseeing. Consider visiting the birds-of-prey flight show at Burg Maus (559km) or touring the formidable

Marksburg castle (580km). If you choose the latter, do it on day 1 during your whole-of-the-Romantic-Rhine cruise (since you're cruising by) and tour Burg Rheinfels on day 2.

*The K-D cruise line departs daily May-Sept (less April & Oct) from...

Bacharach (heading downstream) at 10:15, 11:15, 12:15, 15:15, *17:15 (*departure time of "Goethe" paddle-wheel steamship, add 1.50€/person). *Price* to St. Goar 9.20€ o.w./11.30€ r.t. Holders of a Eurail (consecutive-day or dated Flexi/Select) pass cruise for *FREE!* For other K-D discounts, see next entry—*Boaters. Note:* Those who don't qualify for a K-D discount, the Bingen-Rüdesheimer cruise line is the cheaper option here.

Bingen (heading downstream) at 9:30, 10:30, 11:30, 14:30, *16:30 (*departure time of "Goethe" steamer, add 1.50€/person). Between points you may get off and on as you please. *Price* to Koblenz 25.40€ o.w. (3.4hr) — to Boppard 17.80€ o.w. (2.2hr). Holders of a Eurail (consecutive-day or dated Flexi/Select) pass cruise for *FREE!* For other K-D discounts, see next entry.

Boaters: A cruise on the Rhine is a traveler's delight! Besides that, the best views are had from the river because you can ogle both banks equally. The prominent K-D line (Köln-Düsseldorfer, www.k-d.com) is typically the most expensive option; however, they have a much bigger fleet and by far the best discounts (see *K-D Discounts* below). The Bingen-Rüdesheimer line is cheaper but only cruise between Bingen and St. Goar.

Note: Boats cruise the Rhine regularly from May thru Sept, less April and Oct. • Mornings on the Rhine can be foggy; if this is the case, opt out of the early boat (and hop on a later one) to give nature a chance to burn things off for better views. • If you plan on getting off and on during your cruise to visit towns/sites (which many people do), don't let the boat conductor take your ticket until your last connection. • Folks looking to experience a multiday cruise package should check out Viking River Cruises at www.vikingrivercruises.com

Suggestion: The Rhine's current is very strong. Don't lose valuable time by cruising upstream against the current. Instead, cruise downstream by boat and upstream via train. (The only case where the reverse order would be okay is the upstream stretch from St. Goar to Bacharach, taking 70 min. Some travelers may see the 45-min downstream version to the latter option [Bacharach → St. Goar] as too short a trip). *Romantics,* hop aboard the 90-year-old *Goethe* paddle-wheel steamship departing May-Sept, 1.50€ per person extra.

K-D Discounts: Holders of a Eurail (consecutive-day or dated Flexi/Select) pass cruise for *FREE! (But you still need to obtain a ticket.)* If it's your birthday, you cruise for *FREE!* Students 26 years of age or under with valid ID receive a 50% discount, and seniors (60+) travel half price Mondays and Fridays. What's more, those who have bought a train ticket to get to the K-D boat dock can present it for a 20% discount off the cruise price.

Railers: Hourly trains do the milk-run between Koblenz and Bingen, stopping at every town. From the left (west) bank you'll get the best perspective, including a view of the Loreley. *Note:* Those who buy a train ticket to get to the K-D boat dock can present it for a 20% discount off the cruise price.

Drivers: Keep to the left bank—route 9—because it passes the most popular towns and has the best perspective of the Loreley. Better yet, park the car at Bingen or Bacharach and ride the boat downstream, return by train. *For a shortcut to the Mosel River:* Drive to Boppard—from there, follow blue A61 (autobahn) signs. After railway underpass, turn left following signs to Buchholz. When there, continue straight—following signs to Brodenbach (16km trip). *Note:* On Sunday June 25, 2006, route 9 and 42 (highways either side of the Rhine) will be closed to motorists between Koblenz and Bingen/Rüdesheim during the hours 9:00-19:00 in an effort to create a smog-free, environment-friendly zone for cyclists, Inline skaters and pedestrians. This annual auto-free day is known as Tal to Tal (Valley to Valley) and represents 120km of road closures.

Bicyclists: Enjoy a healthy, eco-ride along the Rhine. Bike lanes either side of the river (from Bingen to Koblenz) are well maintained—although, the left (west) bank is best. If it seems the distances are too great, cycle one-way and return by train or boat. To bring a bike on the train is free (after 9:00 Mon-Fri or anytime Sat/Sun) but get on the carriage displaying the bicycle symbol. To transport a bike aboard the K-D line will cost 1.50€. When renting a bike, pick one that has at least a handful of gears. *Suggestion:* Gratifying is the scenic, 13km stretch between Bacharach and St. Goar. Another idea is Bacharach to Burg Reichenstein, 9km (a bit farther along is Burg Rheinstein).

Car/Passenger Ferry: (Fähre) There are no bridges between Bingen and Koblenz, thus ferries control a lucrative business. Price per jaunt: (generally) adult 1€, bicycle 50¢, auto (PKW) + driver 3€. On brochures and maps you'll see the acronyms AF and PF: AF means auto ferry, PF pedestrian ferry.

Rhine in Flames: On four occasions between July and September, the Valley of the Loreley basks in the brilliance of multicolored Bengal lights illuminating hilltop castles while fireworks burst overhead showering spectators, church steeples and medieval turrets with a dazzling glow.

   Note: Plan your time accordingly to catch one of these explosive (Saturday) evenings—book accommodations well in advance. To maximize your options, stay in another town. If interested, query TI about securing seats on a boat to view the fiery spectacle; meal packages also available.
   • *Bingen/Rüdesheim:* July 1, 2006, "Night of Fire Magic."
   • *Koblenz to Braubach:* Aug 12, 2006, "Mega Night on the Rhine."
   • *Oberwesel:* Sept 9, 2006, "Night of a 1000 Fires."
   • *St. Goar:* Sept 16, 2006, "Night of the Loreley."

Castle "Burg" Ticket: For enthusiasts swept away by turrets, towers and bulwarks, this ticket has your name on it. It allows the holder access to 10 of the Rhine's most impressive medieval strongholds for one price: adult 14€, child (6-14) 7€—valid for 24 months upon receipt but it can only be used once per burg (not applicable for special events). Tickets available at participating castles: Burg Rheinfels, Marksburg, Pfalzgrafenstein, Rheinstein, Sooneck, Lahneck, Ehrenbreitstein (Koblenz), Stolzenfels, Brömserburg (Rüdesheim).

Let's begin our journey through the Valley of the Loreley

528km, BINGEN: [left bank] (pop. 26,000) Strategically developed at the confluence of the Rhine and Nahe, Bingen thrived on the lucrative river trade. As a consequence, Bingen was the target of numerous attacks and ultimately defeated eight times during the last millennium. Originally, the Romans constructed a fortress here in 11 B.C., calling it Castellum Bingium. The Roman legions may have long since vanished but their legacy lives on through the town's modern-day name and celebrated wine culture. Bingen's vineyards belong to the Rheinhessen region, the largest of Germany's 13 wine-growing districts, possessing some 25,000 hectares (61,000 acres) from Bingen to Worms, largely filling the pocket between the Rhine and Nahe rivers. Highlights of Bingen's events calendar are the wine festival (Sept 1-11, 2006) and the pyrotechnic extravaganza "Night of Fire Magic" (Rhine in Flames), which is always held jointly with Rüdesheim on the first Saturday in July.

TI: Rheinkai 21 (www.bingen.de) *Tel.#* 06721/184-205. The TI is centrally located near the "Stadt" train station and boat docks. *Hours:* Easter thru Oct Mon-Fri 9:00-18:00, Sat 9:00-12:30, Sun 10:00-13:00; Nov thru Easter Mon-Thur 9:00-12:30 & 13:30-16:00, Fri 9:00-13:00.

Railers: There are two stations in Bingen, "Hbf" and "Stadt"—get off at *Stadt* (which is near the boat dock and TI). If you end up at the Hbf without a connection, it's a 10-min walk into town and to the boat dock.

Boat Rides: Boats from the K-D fleet depart Bingen, May-Sept (less April and Oct), heading downstream at 9:30, 10:30, 11:30, 14:30, *16:30 (*departure time of the 90-year-old *Goethe* paddle-wheel steamship, add 1.50€/person). Between points you may get off and on as you please (just don't let the boat conductor take your ticket until your last connection). *Price* to Koblenz 25.40€ o.w. (3.4hr) — to Boppard 17.80€ o.w. (2.2hr). *Note:* Holders of a Eurail (consecutive-day or dated Flexi/Select) pass cruise for *FREE!* *(But you still need to obtain a ticket.)* For other K-D discounts, see page 305—*Boaters.* *GPS:* (boat dock) N49° 58.213 - E7° 53.889

Burg Klopp: Built on Roman foundations atop a hill in the center of town, the multi-restored Burg Klopp is the seat of local government. Within the burg's fortifications you'll discover a 52m/171ft deep well shaft thought to date from Roman times as well as a climbable tower (open till 17:00, 50¢ entrance) boasting panoramic views of the Rhine and Nahe rivers, old-town Bingen, and the *Rheingau* wine region (on opposite bank) including the neighborhoods belonging to Rüdesheim.

528km, Niederwald-Monument: [right bank] High above the Rhine on a sun-drenched hill is the 37m/122ft tall Niederwald-Monument, erected from 1877-83 to symbolize the reestablishment of the German empire (Second Reich) following the defeat of France during the Franco-Prussian War (1870-71). The monument's main figure—dubbed the Prussian Madonna, or Germania—is 35-feet tall, weighs 31 tons and has a slimming 20-foot waist. She bears the imperial sword in her left hand while raising the emperor's laurel crown with her right hand. Flanking Germania are two 10-foot-high winged statues: "War" is holding a sword and blowing a trumpet while on the opposite corner "Peace" is offering a cornucopia signifying prosperity. In the center of the monument—between War and Peace—is a bronze relief depicting nearly 200 life-sized figures with the focal point being Emperor William I on horseback and Chancellor Bismarck standing at his side. The monument can be reached via car, gondola in Rüdesheim, or chairlift from Assmannshausen. The views are awesome and the hiking trails are pleasingly abundant.

530km, Burg Ehrenfels: [right bank] This twin-towered carcass is all that remains of an early 13th-century fortress built to enforce tariffs on the passing river trade. The burg was left a ruin after Louis XIV's armée steamrolled through the Rhineland in 1689.

The vineyards surrounding Burg Ehrenfels belong to the Rheingau region—one of the smaller but more historic of Germany's 13 wine-growing districts—which stretches along the Rhine's right bank from Wiesbaden to Assmannshausen/Lorch. The vineyards you'll see farther downstream toward Koblenz belong to the Mittelrhein region, a reasonably small wine-growing district that is continually shrinking due to population encroachment.

530km, Mouse Tower: (Mäuseturm) Petite and regal—standing opposite Bingen Hbf on a sliver of land in the middle of the Rhine—is the Mouse Tower, a former toll station (and sentry post) belonging to Burg Ehrenfels, and more recently a navigation tower to guide river traffic. According to legend, the archbishop—fat Hatto—hoarded stockpiles of food while his people starved. Hatto's dwelling became so mouse infested that he fled to the petite tower, where he was pursued by the mice and eaten.

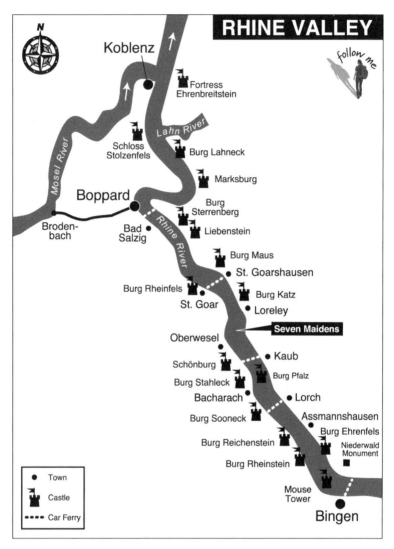

532km, <u>ASSMANNSHAUSEN</u>: [right bank] Listed as a suburb of Rüdesheim, the picturesque village pressed between terraced vineyards is renowned for its full-bodied Spätburgunder (Pinot Noir) red wine.

533km, <u>Burg Rheinstein</u>: [left bank] Perched upon on a rocky massif across from Assmannshausen is Burg Rheinstein, dating from the early 10th century. By the time Louis XIV's armée arrived nearly 800 years later, Burg Rheinstein was already in tatters and therefore ignored by the French. In 1823, a Hohenzollern prince acquired the burg and refurbished it to exude Rhine romanticism. Today, Burg Rheinstein is open to the public as a museum. To reach the burg, a footpath ascends from the road (10 min trek) where drivers will find a petite parking lot—slow down or you'll pass it.

Hours: (end times are last admission) mid-March thru mid-Nov, daily, 9:30-17:30; rest of year Mon-Thur 14:00-17:00, Sun 10:00-17:00, Fri/Sat closed. *Price:* 3.80€, or free with Castle Ticket. Additionally, Rheinstein has two apartment-style accommodations for 125€/night (either apartment), including breakfast—tel.# 06721/6348

534km, <u>Burg Reichenstein</u>: [left bank] First mentioned in 1213, Burg Reichenstein is the mighty castle you'll see entrenched above the village of Trechtingshausen. Formerly inhabited by robbers, royalty and regents, the castle was destroyed several times during feudal conflicts and ultimately restored in 1902 to original designs. Today, Burg Reichenstein—a popular locale for wedding parties—is open to the public as a museum (fine collection of hunting trophies, antique furniture, medieval armor). *Hours:* March thru mid-Nov Tue-Sun 10:00-18:00. *Price:* 3.40€. *Tel.#* 06721/6117. *Getting There:* Reichenstein is located 500 meters off route 9; follow signs up hill.

537km, <u>Burg Sooneck</u>: [left bank] Dating from the 11th century, Burg Sooneck was the lair of robber barons—feudal lords who stole, plundered, and sometimes kidnapped people to get what they wanted—thus the castle was twice destroyed and rebuilt within 300 years, only to be shattered by the French in 1689. Reconstructed in the 19th century, Burg Sooneck is today open to the public as a museum. *Hours:* (end times are last admission) April-Sept, closed first day of the workweek, otherwise 9:00-17:00; Oct/Nov & Jan-March 9:00-16:00; December closed. *Price:* adult 2.60€, student 1.30€, or free with Castle Ticket. *Drivers:* From route 9, ascend narrow road 1km to the parking lot. *Note:* Middle Ages festival at Burg Sooneck July 1-2, 2006.

543km, <u>BACHARACH</u>: [left bank] No relation to Burt, originally from Celtic origin: *Baccaracus*. Evolution produced Bacchus, the God of Wine, who took the shape of a stone altar in the Rhine (removed in the 19th century to aid river flow) and now occasionally rolls through town (in human form) on a wine barrel during festivals wearing a tiara made from grapes while hoisting a wine goblet. Times are good when Bacchus comes to town.

Cobbled lanes, candlelit Weinstuben, and cozy half-timbered inns flaunting vibrant flower boxes epitomize this adoringly cute, must-see Rhineland village. Victor Hugo—the French romantic novelist who penned Les Misérables—stopped here in the early 19th century and wrote: "Bacharach is the most antiquated settlement that I have ever seen in my life…a storybook village, sown from fables and legends." (Le Rhin, 1842)

Bacharach is a wonder, steeped in history and bound by Riesling stock rising from the banks of the mighty Rhine. Here you can stroll the former **city fortifications** where sentries stood watch in medieval times, scale the **Postenturm** for a village view, peer into the 13th-century skeleton of **St. Werner's Chapel** to remember a martyr, snap a picture of the wobbly **Altes Haus**, and marvel at the Loreley valley from the ramparts of the Steel Corner (**Burg Stahleck**).

Wine enthusiasts, mark June 16-18, 2006, in your calendar, when Bacharach and neighboring village Steeg join forces to host the lively wine festival "Weinblütenfest" in a scenic valley embraced by a collage of grapevines. What's more, food fanatics shouldn't miss the last weekend in August (25-27) when Bacharach provides the perfect backdrop for an array of culinary delights served up by 14 vintners and five restaurants from the Middle Rhine. Entertainment ranges from modern live music and dance hits to comedy and variety theater—Saturday evening (around 21:30) a stunning fireworks display will set the town aglow.

TI: Oberstr. 45 (on main drag; ramble through archway beneath wrought-iron sign displaying "Posthof" and a golden horn). TI has Internet 2€/hour and a free room-finding service. Free town map available; Rhine guidebook 4.50€; few brochures on castles. *Tel.#* 06743/919-303 (www.bacharach.de) *Hours:* April-Oct Mon-Fri 9:00-17:00, Sat/Sun 10:00-14:00; Nov-March Mon-Fri 9:00-12:00. *Getting There: Railers,* from station the TI is a five-minute walk—exit station right and mosey up the few meters to the main drag cutting through town; turn right. Continue straight about four blocks and TI is on the left. *Drivers,* TI is meters from the towering church. Parking is illegal in this area.

    Post Office: Oberstr. 37 (six doors from TI). *Hours:* Mon-Fri 9:00-12:00 & 15:00-18:00, Sat 9:00-12:00.

    Railers: At Bacharach's non-descript station, trains leave hourly in the direction of Koblenz/St. Goar 20 min past the hour—and in the direction of Bingen 30 min past the hour. A one-way ticket Bacharach to Koblenz costs 7.60€ (40-min trip), Bacharach to St. Goar 2.80€ (11-min trip), Bacharach to Bingen "Stadt" 3.50€ (25-min trip). *Note:* If you buy a train ticket to get to the K-D boat dock you can present it for a 20% discount off the cruise price. Purchase your ticket at the "Fahrkarten" machine. Press "Einfache Fahrt" for one way or "Hin- und Rückfahrt" for round trip, then punch the number corresponding to your destination using the adjacent chart. Once completed, the amount of the fare will appear.

    Drivers: To park within Bacharach's town walls is tight and mostly illegal. Opposite the church and traffic light on the Bingen side of town is a free parking area (found at these *GPS* coordinates: N50° 03.429 - E7° 46.235). Otherwise coin automats govern the foreshore along the highway: applicable, daily, 9:00-18:00 (free all other times), 50¢/hr or 3€/day (*Tagesticket*).

    Boat Rides: Boats from the K-D fleet depart Bacharach, May-Sept (less April and Oct), heading downstream at 10:15, 11:15, 12:15, 15:15, *17:15 (*departure time of "Goethe" paddle-wheel steamship, add 1.50€/person). Reservations not necessary. **Price** to St. Goar 9.20€ o.w./11.30€ r.t. *(45-min trip one-way. If this seems too short, either buy the round-trip ticket or take the train [or ride a bike] to St. Goar and cruise boat back [upstream] which takes 70 min).* Questions? Ask Christel, the neat gal selling tickets at the K-D kiosk. **Note:** Holders of a Eurail (consecutive-day or dated Flexi/Select) pass cruise for *FREE! (But you still need to obtain a ticket.)* For other K-D discounts, see page 305—*Boaters.* Those who don't qualify for a K-D discount, the Bingen-Rüdesheimer cruise line is the cheaper option here.

    Bike Rental: Available from Hotel Hillen, Langstr. 18, tel.# 06743/1287. *GPS:* N50° 03.495 - E7° 46.134. **Hours:** open from 9:00; see Erich at hotel reception desk. **Price:** 8-12€/day. Erich has bikes with 3 to 21 gears, as well as bikes for children. **Note:** Show this YTC book for a 10% discount. **Distances:** Cycling from Bacharach to Bingen is 15km • to Burg Pfalz 4km • to Oberwesel 6km • to Loreley 11km • to St. Goar 13km. If distances seem too great, cycle one-way and return by train or boat. To bring a bike on the train is free (after 9:00 Mon-Fri or anytime Sat/Sun) but get on the carriage displaying the bicycle symbol. To transport a bike aboard the K-D line will cost 1.50€. **Suggestion:** Gratifying is the scenic, 13km stretch to St. Goar (consider taking boat back), as well as the 9km cycle to Burg Reichenstein (a bit farther along is Burg Rheinstein).

    Mini Food Mart: Opposite the Altes Haus, some 50 meters from the church, you'll find a grocery store. *Hours:* Mon-Fri 8:00-12:30 & 14:00-18:00, Sat 8:00-12:30.

    Beer Steins: The Jost family has been wheeling and dealing in affordable beer steins, cuckoo clocks and memorabilia bringing warmth to the hearts of countless tourists for almost as long as Bacchus has been the wine god of Bacharach. What's more, show this book and receive 10% off any cash purchase of at least 10€ worth of merchandise (discount not valid for items "on sale"). Tax-free discounts available; ask shop attendant. Overseas shipping no problem. *CCs:* VC, MC. Phil Jost has two stores; one across from church on market square and the other is around the corner at Rosenstr. 16 (not always open). *Tel.#* 06743/1224 (www.phil-jost-germany.com) *Hours:* April-Oct Mon-Fri 8:30-18:30, Sat 8:30-17:00, Sun 10:00-17:00; Nov-March Mon-Fri 10:00-12:30 & 14:00-17:00, Sat 10:00-16:00. *Note:* For emergency after-hours shopping, ring bell to alert Jost family (who live upstairs).

Burg Stahleck: see *543km, Burg Stahleck*—page 313.

St. Peter's Church: Dating from the 1100s, this Evangelical house of God rests in the middle of town with its steeple prominently rising above the village's rooftops. Inside, at the head of the left aisle, you'll see a topless gal (left of steps) with snakes gnawing at her nipples—a warning to those who commit adultery. The medieval mural of Jesus behind the slithery scene belongs to the church's original collection of wall frescos. Outside, 352 steps ascend to Burg Stahleck—along the way you'll pass St. Werner's Chapel (Wernerkapelle).

St. Werner's Chapel: (Wernerkapelle) These are the skeletal ruins (on hillside beyond church steeple) you'll pass while trekking to Burg Stahleck. The former chapel is dedicated to a slain boy named Werner. His murder was blamed on a Jewish cult that allegedly used his blood for a sacrificial ceremony. Society honored Werner into sainthood and construction began on the Wernerkapelle in 1294. Allegations pertaining to blood rituals and Jewish involvement in the boy's murder were later proven to be false. Consequently, Werner was removed from the Catholic Church's calendar of saints. In 1689, St. Werner's Chapel took on its present shape when French forces ruined it upon the demolition of Burg Stahleck. The views are tremendous from the chapel site, and even more so from Stahleck's battlements above.

Altes Haus: Dating from 1368, the "Old House" is precisely that, the oldest in town. Located a stone's throw from the church and TI, be sure and snap a picture of its adorable, wood-beamed facade ornamented by colorful flower boxes and creeping ivy. Today, the Altes Haus serves food and wine, but mainly wine.

City Fortifications: (Stadtbefestigung) Many of Bacharach's medieval fortifications still exist, allowing tourists the rare opportunity to wander an age-old section of wall once paced by sentries on guard duty. A walkable section of wall parallels Langstr. and the train tracks, between Zollstr. and Münzestr. (allow 5-10 min). Entry points are readily found.

Postenturm: To visit the "Sentry Tower" is a must-do attraction while in Bacharach. An observation turret dating from the Middle Ages, the Postenturm has just been renovated and is now equipped with four ultra-sturdy levels boasting fabulous views of the Rhine, medieval Bacharach and its crowning castle—Burg Stahleck—now a youth hostel (see *Good Sleeps* below). ***Getting There:*** Ascend steps past Rosenstr. 4 (behind ancient well; on third step look right to see a wall mural of Bacharach in 1632). Continue up path and slate steps and through a harvest of grapevines to the tower. The view will develop into a wonder. After climbing the tower, return to town via the following picturesque route: Take sloping trail past the next tower and onto the street. From here, ramble left under the tower. Be mindful of cars; it's a tight squeeze. Head downhill, paralleling the half-timbered house on your right. Stop when you reach the house's weary front facade and look to the caption painted above the door. It reads: *"I've seen centuries pass, and through God's generosity I am still here."* Now wander left down the cobbled lane to the cutsey-pie bridge spanning the babbling brook. This charming quarter is called Malerwinkel (Painter's Corner). In front of you is the gingerbread facade belonging to pension Im Malerwinkel (listed in *Good Sleeps*), which can be reached via the stubby stone archway (right). To get back to town, step over the bridge and mosey left along the brook. On this route, note the shortcut (steps) ascending to Burg Stahleck on the right.

Military Buffs: On the Rhine promenade, opposite Kranenturm, is a notable memorial to the Great War.

Good Sleeps: A special village such as Bacharach deserves special accommodations, which are listed below in order of price: from the most expensive to the least. All come with breakfast except the last two entries.

Altkölnischer Hof: Blücherstr. 2 [market square]. (www.altkoelnischer-hof.info) *Tel.#* 06743/1339. Situated in the heart of town, this 16th-century half-timbered charm run by the Scherschlicht family (Gernot, Elke, Thomas and Bärbel) is overwhelming with its rustic décor and historic wood-paneled dining hall. Couples engaged to be married should test drive the Hochzeitszimmer (HZZ) "wedding room." Four (reasonably priced holiday) apartments are also available—breakfast costs extra and the laundering of sheets is added to the bill—see reception for details. *Note:* Closed Nov thru March. Hotel has elevator, and some rooms have balconies. *Price:* Sgl 48-70€, Dbl (basic) 65-80€, Dbl (comfort) 85-105€, HZZ 95-110€, Trpl 95-110€. *CC's:* VC, MC. *Getting There:* Altkölnischer Hof is located across from church and some 40 meters right of TI. *GPS:* N50° 03.603 - E7° 46.081

Rhein Hotel: Langstr. 50 (www.rhein-hotel-bacharach.de) *Tel.#* 06743/1243. Dating from the 14th century, this 3-star hotel is part of the medieval town wall. For six generations the Rhein Hotel has been in the family, and sticking to traditions are Andreas and Sabine Stüber, your proud hosts. The rooms are ultra-cozy having been recently refurbished, featuring a modern touch—even air-conditioning—and a fine view. In fact, each room is named after its unique view. The hotel's restaurant is a popular choice in town and Andreas, also the head chef, specializes in regional fare, especially Riesling braten. *Note:* Hotel is located adjacent to train tracks; double soundproof windows implemented. Free bikes for guests. *Price:* (cheaper the longer you stay) Dbl 76-88€, apartment available. *CC's:* VC, MC, AE. *Getting There: Railers,* pass the TI and turn right on Marktstr.—adjacent to the tower are your digs. *Drivers,* from route 9 turn into Bacharach beneath the tower midway along town following the sign "Tourist Information." Once through the underpass, the Rhein Hotel is on your left. *GPS:* N50° 03.583 - E7° 46.132

Im Malerwinkel: (pension) Blücherstr. 41 (www.im-malerwinkel.de) *Tel.#* 06743/1239. Im Malerwinkel is idyllically (and romantically) situated adjacent to a babbling brook, juicy vineyards and medieval bulwarks. *Note:* Little English spoken. Closed Nov thru March. *Price:* (cash only) Sgl 36€, Dbl 59€, Trpl 75€, (cheaper the longer you stay). *Getting There: Railers,* 10-min walk from station—pass TI, church then turn left on Blücherstr. Other side of forward tower are your digs (on left). If you have loads of luggage, call ahead and they'll pick you up. *Drivers,* from the town's main drag turn at the church into Blücherstr. Other side of forward tower are your digs (on left). Park in their private lot. *GPS:* N50° 03.566 - E7° 45.873

Hotel Hillen: Langstr. 18 (e-mail: hotel-hillen@web.de) *Tel.#* 06743/1287. Warmly run accommodations by Erich and Iris, Hotel Hillen is situated upon the age-old city fortifications. Rooms have views either of Burg Stahleck or the Rhine—views of Rhine come with some train noise (soundproof windows implemented). *Note:* Show this book and receive a 10% discount! Bike rental also available. *Price:* Sgl 28-36€, Dbl 42-57€, Trpl 65-75€, (cheaper the longer you stay). *CC's:* VC, MC, AE. *Getting There: Railers,* exit station right and mosey up the few meters to the main drag cutting through town; turn right. Continue straight some 100 meters to Zollstr. and go right. Before the tunnel turn left; this is Langstr.—your digs are in front of you on the right. *Drivers,* from route 9 turn into Bacharach beneath the tower midway along town following the sign "Tourist Information." Once through the underpass, turn left (Langstr.)—your digs will soon appear on the left. Unload outside their door and Erich/Iris will direct you where to park. *GPS:* N50° 03.495 - E7° 46.134

Hostel, Jugendherberge Burg Stahleck: [HI] (www.djh.de) *Tel.#* 06743/1266. A heck of a trek but worth the visit as well as an overnight stay. Couples will find Burg Stahleck's 12th-century bulwarks dreamy; singles will find adventure. *Price:* (includes linen, breakfast) dorm bed 16.50€, Sgl 32€, Dbl 45€. *CC's:* VC, MC. *Note:* Must be a member or an extra charge will apply. Has bar, laundry, 22:00 curfew, no Internet. *Getting There: Railers,* 25-min walk from station. A few doors from TI, adjacent to church, the trail begins its tiring ascent (352 steps). *Drivers,* begin on Blücherstr. Eventually you'll see signs Jugendherberge, which lead to the parking area: *GPS:* N50° 03.445 - E7° 45.797. From there, it's a few-minutes walk to the hostel/burg.

Holiday Apartments, Bunke-Eichner: Blücherstr. 75 (www.rhein.ferienwohnung-online.de/bacharach) *Tel.#* 06743/1831. Heidi offers three self-contained apartments in her cute house a few minutes walk from town. Each apartment affords a cozy atmosphere having a TV, couch, kitchen, microwave, toaster, garden and more. If you ask nicely, Heidi (or her hubby) may escort you through town on a mini wine-tasting tour. *Note:* Minimum two nights stay required. No breakfast served here. *Price:* (cash only) Apt. 1 (345 sq.ft.) 1 to 2 persons 37.50€ • Apt. 2 (450sq.ft.) 2 to 3 persons 42.50€ • Apt. 3 (750sq.ft.) 2 to 5 persons 57.50€. *Getting There: Railers,* 10-min walk from station—pass TI and church and then turn left on Blücherstr. Continue through forward tower to your digs. If you have loads of luggage, call ahead to arrange a pick up. *Drivers,* from the town's main drag turn at the church into Blücherstr. Continue through forward tower to your digs. Parking available on property. *GPS:* N50° 03.566 - E7° 45.873 (coordinates to tower).

Campingplatz Sonnenstrand: open April to mid-Oct. This campground is refreshingly situated on the Rhine, inclusive of a beach. *Tel.#* 06743/1752. (www.camping-sonnenstrand.de) *GPS:* N50° 03.213 - E7° 46.362

543km, Burg Stahleck: [left bank] The castle above Bacharach is known as Burg Stahleck—meaning Steel Corner—first mentioned in 1135. The burg was twice sacked, both times in the 17th century—first by the Swedish and then the French. Stahleck remained a ruin until 1926, when it was reincarnated as a youth hostel (see *Bacharach* above—Good Sleeps). A steep trail running off Bacharach's main drag (Oberstr.) ascends to Stahleck's superb viewing terrace (20-min trek, 352 steps; trail begins a few doors from TI, adjacent to church).

546km, Burg Pfalz(grafenstein): This is the valley's trademark castle, seen on numerous postcards and all the travel brochures. Burg Pfalz—an island citadel rising from the center of the Rhine—was built from 1325 to impose tolls on the river trade. By raising cables across the traffic lanes, Burg Pfalz forced merchant vessels to a standstill until they paid the agreed duty, when the cables were lowered and safe passage guaranteed. Marauding French forces did not destroy the water castle during past wars and it therefore remains in original condition. Burg Pfalz can be visited via shuttle boat from Kaub, town on right bank (those who are on the left bank can crossover by ferry 100 meters downstream from the castle). *Hours:* (Burg Pfalz) April-Sept, closed first day of workweek, otherwise 9:00-13:00 & 14:00-18:00 (last entry one hour prior to closing); off-season same hours except open till 17:00. *Price:* adult 2.10€, student 1.10€, or free with Castle Ticket. *Shuttle boat to Burg Pfalz:* (from Kaub) 1.60€. *Ferry to Kaub:* adult 1.20€, bicycle 50¢, auto (PKW) + driver 3€.

546km, KAUB, Gutenfels & Blücher: [right bank] Opposite Burg Pfalz is the elongated village of Kaub, from where terraced vineyards creep up to the 13th-century fortress, Burg Gutenfels. Today, the fortress is part ruin and part hotel. Kaub, with its picturesque disposition and romantic lanes, is nationally renowned for being General Blücher's chosen location to advance 90,000 troops across the Rhine to outflank Napoleon and expel his Grand Armée from Deutschland. You'll see a statue of the triumphant general standing tall on the riverside promenade. On the left bank, facing Burg Pfalz and crowning a pleasant viewing point, is a blocky memorial to Blücher's gallant maneuver. It reads: *"From this spot, around midnight in the year of our Lord December 31, 1813,*

Prince Blücher von Wahlstadt, field marshal, advanced his courageous troops over the Rhine resurrecting Prussia, and the German Fatherland." (Erected November 1853). Eighteen months later, Blücher helped defeat Napoleon at Waterloo. For drivers and bicyclists touring the left bank, you'll meet the memorial site at these *GPS* coordinates: N50° 04.870 - E7° 45.854

550km, OBERWESEL: [left bank] Known as the "town of towers and wine," the muscle of medieval Oberwesel is apparent from the get-go—hefty bulwarks and forbidding turrets line the riverside promenade while an imposing fortress ("Schönburg," see next entry) flaunts its might from the heights above. Oberwesel's fortifications qualify as the valley's most complete and best-preserved defense system, standing as they did during the Middle Ages (parts accessible by foot). From the town's original 22 towers, 16 still remain. Obvious to any visitor are the colossal dimensions of the Oxen Tower (Ochsenturm) overshadowing the north end of Oberwesel—at 40m/131ft tall and 12m/39ft wide it registers as one of the largest defense posts in the Rhineland. These bullying battlements provide the perfect backdrop for Oberwesel's most thrilling weekend (Sept 8-10, 2006), when simultaneously the town's wine festival and fireworks extravaganza "Night of a 1000 Fires" are held (Rhine in Flames—Sat night, Sept 9). What's more, April 30 is known as Wine Witch Night (Weinhexennacht), which marks the season's first wine festival. On this evening the focus of the ceremony is a giant wine barrel, which is rolled onto the market square. After everyone has gathered around, the newly elected *Wine Witch pops out like a jack-in-the-box punctuating her presence. (*The Wine Witch represents Oberwesel much the same way as the Wine Queen symbolizes other wine-growing communities.)* Fueled by plenty of goodwill and flavorsome grape juice, celebrations continue into the wee hours of the morning.

TI: Rathausstr. 3, tel.# 06744/1521 (www.oberwesel.de) *Hours:* April-Oct Mon-Fri 9:00-18:00, Sat 10:00-14:00; Nov-March Mon-Thur 9:00-13:00 & 14:00-17:00, Fri 9:00-14:00.

549km, Schönburg: [left bank] Ensconced above Oberwesel is the enclosed community of Schönburg (Beautiful Castle), dating from the 11th century. In 1166, Emperor Frederick Barbarossa passed the property onto one of his trusted servants who added von Schönburg to his name, suggesting lordship. During the 14th century there were upwards of 24 von Schönburg families—some 250 people—residing in the Beautiful Castle. The lords of Schönburg were ousted in 1689 upon the arrival of French forces, who torched the Beautiful Castle reducing it to ruins. In 1885, an American—aptly named Rhinelander—purchased Schönburg and had it restored to original designs. In 1950, Rhinelander's son sold the estate to Oberwesel, and today it is a dreamy hotel (Sgl 85-105€, Dbl 150-210€, suite 215€). *CC's:* VC, MC. *Tel.#* 06744/93-930 (www.hotel-schoenburg.com) *Note:* Hotel does not have a shuttle service to/fro Oberwesel. From the hotel's parking lot (or taxi drop off point) it's a two-minute uphill walk to reception. Call ahead if you require a porter to meet you with a baggage cart. *Drivers,* to reach Schönburg ascend road running adjacent to towering church opposite train station.

552km, Seven Maidens: More treacherous and less apparent than the Loreley are the Seven Maidens, perilous reefs prompting numerous wrecks in medieval times now marked by colored buoys. Boaters, notice how carefully your captain maneuvers away from them.

According to legend, seven maidens lived in Schönburg castle and had dual personalities: They were beautiful and sincere on the outside while conceited and mischievous on the inside. Handsome knights and affluent nobles competed for their hand in marriage. Unbeknownst to the dashing gents, the maidens exploited them for their riches. The time had come for the maidens to announce their choices and all the bachelors were summoned to the castle. After entering the reception hall, the bachelors discovered seven female figures—each stuffed with straw and propped upon chairs rattling to the beat of the wind howling through the open windows. Bewildered, the men rushed across the hall to close the windows, when they saw the maidens cruising downstream on the Rhine. The women spotted the men and began mocking them, laughing and waving farewell. Suddenly, their laughter turned to cries for help as a gust of wind blew violently capsizing their boat, tossing the maidens into the river's unforgiving current. Their bodies were never found but a short time later seven jagged rocks appeared at the place they were last scene.

554km, The Loreley: [right bank] Steeped in legendary folklore is the curvaceous yet modest cliff face at kilometer 554 (two flags atop), where the Rhine is squeezed to its narrowest and deepest point. According to myth, a maiden named Loreley sat upon the jagged cliff combing her golden hair and bewitching the hearts of sailors with her melodious singing. Mesmerized by the irresistible siren, the sailors disregarded their turbulent course and slammed into the deadly rocks below her dangling feet.

Centuries later, sailors got wise to the lure of Loreley. Instead of ogling the diva they responded to the captain's three-bell warning system by dropping to their knees in solemn prayer for safe passage. Moreover, the cliff face comprised of slate is known to generate spin-chilling echoes thought to be the ghostly voices of drowned sailors. Today, strategically placed radar and light towers (on left bank) have replaced the captain's three-bell warning system. Consequently, shipwrecks are a thing of the past.

Reachable by footpath or car, the plateau atop the Loreley cliff face (132m/433ft high) hosts a visitor's center, campground, hotel, and an open-air theater dating from the Third Reich. To reach the footpath from the K-D boat dock at St. Goarshausen is a 25-min walk along the river. The footpath—signposted "Treppenweg," climbs steeply to the top (15 min, 386 steps)—begins at the base of the cliff (next to souvenir stand and by parking area), from where the statue of Loreley is also accessible (see next entry). Another way of getting to the plateau is by bus, which runs hourly (mid-morning to early afternoon, circa 10:15-16:30) from St. Goarshausen.

555km, Statue of Loreley: [right bank] Just past the Loreley cliff face begins a sheltered harbor. On the forested spit of land at the harbor's entrance is a statue of the fabled seductress.

556km, Burg Katz: [right bank] In 1245, Count von Katzenelnbogen built the most powerful castle on the Rhine (Burg Rheinfels) above St. Goar and subsequently raised the river taxes on passing merchant vessels. This angered provincial monarchs, who in turn formed a small army and besieged Burg Rheinfels for more than a year. The army lost hundreds of men in a futile struggle. As a result of their stunning victory, the Katzenelnbogens built a partner fortress across the river to solidify their position on the Loreley passage. Thus, in 1371, Burg Neukatzenelnbogen was erected. To eliminate any tongue-twister mishaps, the burg simply became known as "Katz" (Cat). Ultimately, Burg Katz was conquered by Napoleon's forces in 1806 and was rebuilt a century later. Today, the Cat is privately owned.

556km, ST. GOAR: [left bank] Named after a miraculous monk from Aquitania (south-western France), St. Goar represents the faith of a 6th-century holy man who lived as a hermit where the two-tone collegiate church now stands on the town square. In medieval times, the square was often the venue for punishing criminals or humiliating wrongdoers; one example recounts an abusive housewife who was sentenced to ride around the plaza on a donkey.

With the region's most powerful fortress (Burg Rheinfels) overshadowing the pros-perous riverside tax haven, St. Goar was the most envied and detested community in the

Rhineland—thus it was besieged no less than 15 times. Today, St. Goar is frequently referred to as the "crown of the Rhine."

Not to miss is Sept 16, 2006 (same date as the opening day of the Oktoberfest), when St. Goar co-hosts the enchanting "Night of the Loreley" (Rhine in Flames) with St. Goarshausen. Around 80,000 spectators will converge on the twin towns, including some 70 sightseeing boats. Interested parties, book your accommodations months in advance. *Note:* On this weekend most hotels require a minimum of four nights stay. Best idea is to stay in another town and book one of the evening boat tours to St. Goar (with the option of an onboard meal), or simply (and cheaply) take the train into town.

TI: Heerstr. 86, located on pedestrian shopping street, some 150 meters from K-D boat dock and train station. (www.st-goar.de) *Tel.#* 06741/383. Free room-finding service. Has some brochures in English. If you ask nicely, Heike will look after your baggage for the day. *Hours:* May-Sept Mon-Fri 9:00-12:30 & 13:30-18:00, Sat 10:00-12:00; Oct-April Mon-Thur 9:00-12:30 & 14:00-17:00, Fri 9:00-14:00.

Railers: St. Goar's neglected—but heavily trafficked—train station is a sorry sight for arriving tourists. This (including Bacharach's station) is a prime example of corporate mismanagement, i.e. Deutsche Bahn. Since there are no storage lockers at the station, the TI will do the honors (see *TI* above). **To get to Burg Rheinfels**, exit station left and you'll see it on the hill as you forge ahead (15-min trek). **To get to the TI or K-D boat dock**, exit station straight and skirt the two-tone church via steps on left—for K-D walk to the Rhine—for the TI go left on Heerstr. (pedestrian shopping street) and it'll appear some 50 meters along on the right.

Trains leave hourly in the direction of Koblenz 30 min past the hour—and in the direction of Bingen/Bacharach 20 min past the hour. A one-way ticket St. Goar to Koblenz costs 5.60€ (30-min trip), St. Goar to Bacharach 2.80€ (11-min trip), St. Goar to Bingen "Stadt" 4.60€ (35-min trip). Purchase tickets at automat on platform. *Note:* Those who are buying a train ticket to get to the K-D boat dock can present it for a 20% discount off the cruise price.

Drivers: Parking is available along the foreshore for a price (payable at nearby coin automat)—applicable Mon-Sat 9:00-18:00, Sun 12:00-18:00—1€/hr (price varies) or 3.50€/day "Tagesticket." Free parking can be had in the lot where the ferry docks, located on the Oberwesel side of town at these *GPS* coordinates: N50° 08.993 - E7° 43.079

Boat Rides: Boats from the K-D fleet depart St. Goar, May-Sept (less April & Oct), heading upstream to Bacharach at 10:20, *12:20, 14:20, 15:20 and 17:20. Reservations not necessary. *Price* 9.20€ o.w./11.30€ r.t. (70-min cruise, one-way). *Departure time for the much-adored, 90-year-old *Goethe* paddle-wheel steamship (1.50€/person supplement applicable). *Note:* Holders of a Eurail (consecutive-day or dated Flexi/Select) pass cruise for *FREE! (But you still need to obtain a ticket.)* For other K-D discounts, see page 305—*Boaters.* Those who don't qualify for a K-D discount, the Bingen-Rüdesheimer cruise line is the cheaper option here.

Ferry to St. Goarshausen: adult 1.20€, bike 50¢, auto (PKW) + driver 3€. *Note:* If you're cruising with the K-D line, synchronize your jaunt across the Rhine with their schedule to save paying the ferry.

Cuckoo Clock: Hand carved from linden wood, the world's largest free-hangin' cuckoo clock can be found at Heerstr. 131 (castle end of pedestrian shopping street). Pretty cool how the cuckoo bird pops out on both sides. Look below the address to see markings denoting the high-water levels of historic floods. *Note:* Other side of street (at No. 128) they claim to have the world's largest beer stein (35ltr). But if you visited Brau Welt in Salzburg you'd know that's not entirely true since they have a 43-liter stein on display. To this shop's credit, though, their stein is much nicer.

Burg Rheinfels: see *557km, Burg Rheinfels*—page 317.

Loreley Visitor Center: Situated atop the Loreley cliff face, the visitor's center showcases the history, myth, flora and culture of the area through multimedia exhibits. *Hours:* April-Oct, daily 10:00-17:00. *Price:* adult 2.50€, parking 1€. *Tel.#* 06771/599-093 (www.loreley-touristik.de)

WWII Buffs: In the wee hours of March 26, 1945, the first wave of the 89th Infantry Division (Third Army) began crossing the Rhine at St. Goar into a storm of enemy fire stemming from dug-in positions around St. Goarshausen. GIs were sitting ducks as bullets whizzed around violently, hissing like snakes as they shredded the air and the assault boats they were riding in. Many boats sank; the few that did make it across to the east bank landed downstream—off course. Casualties mounted—upward of 250—more than 50%. The Rhine ran red with American blood. GIs assembling on St. Goar's shoreline to begin the second wave were driven behind walls and houses to seek refuge. As dawn broke, U.S. mortar and artillery crews were able to direct fatal blows on enemy strongholds. By that evening St. Goarshausen was secure, including the ridgeline supporting the Cat and Mouse castles.

Good Sleeps: All come with breakfast.

Hotel am Markt: Am Markt 1 (www.hotelammarkt1.de) *Tel.#* 06741/1689. A favorite hotel that's hidden in plain sight, located on the corner of the town square and pedestrian shopping street—meters from the K-D boat dock, train station, two-tone church and TI. Most rooms have Rhine view. The owners (Velich family) have recently opened a second, slightly more modern property—Rheinhotel—a few doors away for a few euros more. Check in at Hotel am Markt. Hotels are closed mid-Nov thru Feb. *Price:* Sgl 35-43€, Dbl 59-75€, Trpl from 82€. *CC's:* VC, MC. *GPS:* N50° 09.059 - E7° 42.911

Hotel Hauser: Heerstr. 77 (www.hotelhauser.de) *Tel.#* 06741/333. Situated across from the K-D boat dock and Hotel am Markt (use same GPS as above), Hotel Hauser possess worn accommodations at a terrific location on the Rhine promenade. Room choices are with/without facilities and balcony/Rhine view. *Price:* Sgl 22-32€, Dbl (no facilities) 44€, Dbl (with facilities/no balcony) 52-56€ (*50-54€), Dbl (with facilities & balcony) 62-65€ (*56-58€). *CC's:* VC, MC, AE. *Note:* You can get these prices by paying cash and showing this book.

Romantik Hotel Schloss Rheinfels: (www.schloss-rheinfels.de) *Tel.#* 06741/8020. Here you'll experience 4-star luxury in a ruined 13th-century castle: Burg Rheinfels. Even if you're not staying here, you're welcome to enjoy a drink on their outdoor terrace boasting eye-popping views. *Price:* Sgl 90-140€, Dbl 130-185€, suite 160-265€. *CC's:* VC, MC, AE. *Getting There:* Railers, 15-min walk or 5€ by taxi. *Drivers,* follow signs Burg Rheinfels. Once there, drive across wooden bridge to unload. Reception will explain free parking. *GPS:* N50° 09.202 - E7° 42.285

Hostel, Jugendherberge St. Goar: [HI] Bismarckweg 17 (www.djh.de) *Tel.#* 06741/388. This stout building perched above town and below the castle offers basic amenities and a marvelous vista. When booking, ask for a room with a Rhine view: "Zimmer mit Rhein Blick." *Price:* (includes linen, breakfast) dorm 13.50€, Dbl 27€. *CC's:* VC, MC. *Note:* Must be a member or an extra charge will apply. *Getting There:* Railers, 12-min walk from station—exit station left and continue straight (toward Burg Rheinfels). After passing under the train bridge, turn right on Bismarckweg. *Drivers,* follow signs Burg Rheinfels. After passing under the train bridge, turn right on Bismarckweg. Parking limited. *GPS:* N50° 09.198 - E7° 42.453

Campgrounds are available on either side of the Rhine (St. Goar, St. Goarshausen), as well as on top of the Loreley bluff.

557km, Burg Rheinfels: [left bank] Constructed in 1245 as the largest and mightiest castle on the Rhine, Burg Rheinfels dominated the skyline above St. Goar from where it could enforce outrageous levies on the passing river trade. To pacify this massive stone menace, an army led by an alliance of Rhineland states surrounded Burg Rheinfels. The castle held its ground—repelling the attackers—and the outrageous levies continued. In 1692, Louis XIV was determined to conquer Rheinfels and assaulted the burg with 28,000 French troops. The battle raged for 10 days. Inside the castle 3000 men held their positions, firing cannon and musket as fast as could be reloaded. When the smoke cleared, the French had suffered a bloody defeat, counting 4000 dead and some 6500 wounded—eight times the defenders' casualties. A century later the French were at it again, but this time the burg commander surrendered without a fight and the attackers took revenge on past sacrifices by demolishing the castle, converting it to a quarry. During the mid-19th century, the rubble was excavated and used to rebuild Fortress Ehrenbreitstein in Koblenz. Although still enormous, only one-third of the ruined burg remains. Today, Rheinfels is open to the public and fun to explore, attracting more than 100,000 visitors annually. For the general traveler, allow 60-90 min for a visit. *(Spooky are the subterranean passages known as Minengängen.)* The burg also serves as a 4-star hotel (see above: *St. Goar*—Good Sleeps, *Romantik Hotel Schloss Rheinfels*). For a fine drink and a fab view, step into the hotel's reception area to discover a popular outdoor terrace.

(www.burg-rheinfels.com) *Hours:* (end times are last admission) mid-March thru Sept, daily, 9:00-17:00, Oct till 16:00; Nov thru mid-March weekends only 11:00-16:00. *Price:* (includes castle museum) adult 4€, family 10€, or free with Castle Ticket. *Note:* To explore the subterranean passages (Minengängen) bring a flashlight *(or you might be able to purchase a mini one from the cashier, 3€—candles available, 50¢). Burg Tour:* An English tour is possible with 10-15 people; gather your own group or call ahead to see whether any are scheduled, tel.# 06741/7753. Alternatively, consider the castle booklet (2€) with history and illustrations. *Castle Museum:* Be sure and visit the museum, inclusive of burg model. After paying admission into the castle, ramble straight ahead and up to the museum (open mid-March thru Oct 10:00-12:30 & 13:00-17:00). *Getting There: Railers/Boaters,* the burg is a (steep) 15-min trek, a 5€ taxi ride, or hop on the cheesy "BurgExpress" (train on wheels, 2€ o.w./3€ r.t.), departing every 20 min (April-Oct) from the town square (plaza between two-tone church and K-D boat dock). *Drivers,* follow signs Burg Rheinfels; parking 50¢/hour. *GPS:* N50° 09.202 - E7° 42.285

559km, Burg Maus: [right bank] Perched above the riverside hamlet of Wellmich, an extension of St. Goarshausen, is Burg Maus (Mouse). The Archbishop of Trier had the burg constructed in 1356 under the name Thurnburg, which was fittingly changed to Maus 15 years later after the completion of its daunting neighbor, Burg Neukatzenelnbogen (Katz, or Cat). In 1806, Napoleon's forces sprung a trap and killed the Maus as part of his plan to exterminate the Rhineland. Fortunately, the Maus was resurrected in 1906 and today it is home to Europe's foremost breeding facility for various birds of prey (mainly eagles), where flight demonstrations are held within a unique medieval environment. *Hours:* (bird shows) mid-March to beginning of October, Tue-Sun twice daily, 11:00 & 14:30 (Sun/holidays also 16:30). Show duration one hour—reasonable info in English. *Price:* 6.50€/person. *Tel.#* 06771/7669. Some birds displayed are the peregrine falcon, red kite (fork-tailed hunter), eagle owl, sea eagle and the golden eagle.

566km, Burg Liebenstein & Sterrenberg: [right bank] This castle duet is known as the Feindlichen Brüder (Feudal Brothers)—think of the American folklore saga pertaining to the Hatfield and McCoy's, but imagine this feud between brothers, over a woman, and in medieval times. When spying the fortified duo, Sterrenberg is on the left with the whitewashed turret. You won't see any saber rattling, though, as the brothers' families have since made amends and happy times once again reign upon the idyllic ridgeline. Today, Burg Liebenstein is one of the best deals in the Rhineland concerning millennium-old castle hotels. Rooms are easy on the pocketbook and intimately decorated in Gothic-style, including arched doorways, beamed ceilings, and stone-framed windows. *Price:* Dbl 85-98€, suite 120-195€. *Tel.#* 06773/308 (www.castle-liebenstein.com)

566km, <u>BAD SALZIG</u>: [left bank] This village, a suburb of Boppard, was first mentioned in the year 922. Bad Salzig—meaning Salty Bath—is home to the valley's only mineral springs, Barbara and Leonora, which continually spout curative waters from depths of up to 445m/1460ft.

570km, <u>BOPPARD</u>: [left bank] Often referred to as the "pearl of the Rhine," Boppard—pronounced *Bo-part*—exudes big-town charm with its 8000 residents. (*Note:* At this point on the Rhine, the Mosel River is a mere 16km/10mi to the west.)

Some 1700 years ago the Romans built **Bodobrica** here, an immense fortress secured by massive curtain walls more than 8m/26ft high. Protruding from these stone ramparts were 28 semicircular towers positioned within arrow-shot distance of each other and outfitted with catapults for hurling boulders at the enemy. Much of Bodobrica remained as part of the town's defense system well into the Middle Ages, when every evening at 10 p.m. a bell rang from the church tower on the market square signaling those who were laboring outside the walls to return home before the nightly lockdown—a medieval custom that can still be heard. Maintaining age-old tradition, the local council insists that (most) all rooftops be comprised of black slate to preserve the town's character.

Wine production is a serious affair in Boppard; some 500,000 vines are cultivated on 185 acres, of which 80% is Riesling stock. Attracted to Boppard's juicy ambiance, **Engelbert Humperdinck**, the celebrated composer best known for his opera Hänsel and Gretel (1893), lived here from 1897-1901. To rise above the valley floor, head to the Koblenz side of town and hop on a chair (**Sesselbahn**) lifting you (240m/787ft) to a bird's eye perspective of the Boppard bend—the sharpest curve along the Rhine—and the Vierseenblick (four lakes view), a panoramic illusion created by the various twists in the river. If elevations don't get you high, perhaps shed a friendly tear with the locals during the Onion Market (Sept 13-14, 2006), a traditional bazaar dating from the Middle Ages. Riesling lovers shouldn't miss the town's intoxicating wine festivals, Sept 22-25 & Sept 29–Oct 1, 2006. On either Saturday at 21:00 the evening sky will explode with fireworks. Folks visiting on a summer Sunday, head to the Rhine Pavilion on the foreshore (around 10:30) for free music. Lastly, check out the **Boppard Museum** to witness the town's history along with homegrown furniture styles that widely influenced the industry's modern design. To enjoy Boppard at its best, there's no better place to hang your hat for the evening than **Hotel Günther** (page 321—*Good Sleeps*).

TI: Located on the market square, "Marktplatz," *(in former Rathaus [town hall] building between fountain and twin-steepled church)*, the TI is well stocked with English info and friendly staff. *Tel.#* 06742/3888. *Hours:* May-Sept Mon-Fri 8:00-17:30, Sat 9:00-13:00; Oct-April Mon-Fri 8:00-16:00. (www.boppard.de) *Getting There:* TI is a five-minute walk from the train station—exit station right and head straight into the pedestrian mall, where you'll soon reach the market square.

Internet & Bike Rental: Surf or cycle, both can be had at Hotel Günther, located steps from the K-D boat dock on the Rhine promenade. Internet, 1€/20min. Bike rental, 6.50€/day. *Tel.#* 06742/89-090. *Hours:* daily, 8:30-21:00.

Railers: To get to the K-D boat dock is a five-minute walk. Exit station straight, cross at the crosswalk, go right, then left and through the arch—at the bottom is the river, go right.

Trains leave hourly in the direction of Koblenz 45 min past the hour—and in the direction of Bingen/Bacharach/St. Goar 5 min past the hour. A one-way ticket Boppard to

Koblenz costs 4.20€ (17-min trip), Boppard to Bingen "Stadt" 7.60€ (50-min trip), Boppard to Bacharach 4.60€ (25-min trip), Boppard to St. Goar 2.70€ (13-min trip). Purchase tickets at automat on platform. *Note:* Those who buy a train ticket to get to the K-D boat dock can present it for a 20% discount off the cruise price.

Drivers: Even though Boppard is a decent size town, it's still pretty easy to get around and park. The following coordinates lead to the K-D boat dock and foreshore: *GPS:* N50° 13.968 - E7° 35.432. To park on the foreshore will cost 20¢ for the first 30 min and 10¢ for every 12 min thereafter, or 2.50€/day "Tagesticket." *Note:* From Boppard, the Mosel River is a 16km/10mi drive—follow blue A61 (autobahn) signs. After railway underpass, turn left following signs to Buchholz. When there, continue straight—following signs to Brodenbach.

Boaters: From Boppard's K-D boat dock to the train station is a five-minute walk — to the market square and TI is two min. Upon landing, if you have some local questions don't hesitate to ask bonhomie Jürgen, who works at the K-D ticket kiosk and speaks great English. Or, a few meters farther, you can find jaunty Jim, co-owner of Hotel Günther, who hails from the USA. What's more, Hotel Günther offers reasonable Internet and bike hire.

Boats from the K-D fleet depart Boppard, May-Sept (less April and Oct), heading upstream to St. Goar/Bacharach at 9:00, *11:00, 13:00, 14:00 and 16:00. *Price* to St. Goar 9.20€ o.w./11.30€ r.t. (75-min cruise, one-way) — to Bacharach 14.90€ o.w./17.30€ r.t. (2.25hr cruise, one-way). In order to save valuable time, the latter upstream cruise (to Bacharach) is not recommended. Instead, ride the train upstream and cruise downstream (show your train ticket to receive 20% discount on K-D cruise). Holders of a Eurail (consecutive-day or dated Flexi/Select) pass cruise for *FREE! (But you still need to obtain a ticket.)* For other K-D discounts, see page 305—*Boaters.* *Note:* Departure time for the much-adored, 90-year-old *Goethe* paddle-wheel steamship (1.50€/person supplement applicable).

Bodobrica: Sizeable sections of this 4th-century Roman fort were recently unearthed during the construction of a multilevel parking garage on Kirchgasse (lane opposite market square). Accordingly, plans for the garage were abandoned and the Archaeological Park was created to showcase Boppard's Roman heritage. These findings are arguably the best examples of Roman bulwarks north of the Alps. Additionally, the excavations exposed more than 30 early Christian graves dating from the 7th century— three of these burial plots are marked. The info boards posted throughout the site are in German but the illustrations are understandable. *Hours/Price:* The Archaeological Park is always open and free to enter, located at the top of Kirchgasse. *Note:* TI has excellent English brochures regarding Bodobrica, including a town walking tour.

Boppard Museum: Housed in a 14th-century bastion, the Boppard Museum is utterly stuffed with the town's historical treasures, including age-old artifacts stored in the three-story tower and an exhibition of 19th-century Thonet furniture in the main building. One of Boppard's favorite sons, Michael Thonet (1796-1871), designed easy-to-assemble bentwood furniture that became an industry standard for mass-produced café-style chairs and hat stands. By the 1850s, Thonet's bentwood furniture was being exported across Europe. Chairs, for example, were easily transported because they were lightweight and made from a handful of pieces screwed together, which could be tightly packed into crates and effortlessly assembled on the receiving end. Thonet's avant-garde cabinet-making techniques widely influenced the style behind the classic look of today's contemporary design. See for yourself! His furniture was identified by one and two digit numbers, for example chair No. 14—arguably the most popular in history—was used by the likes of Tolstoi, Picasso, Chaplin and seen by millions in Liza Minnelli's movie "Cabaret."

Upon entering the museum's courtyard you'll instantly notice weathered headstones dating from the 16th and 17th centuries. The stairs on the left ascend into the three-story tower (exhibits in German). But, for now, march straight ahead to the Thonet exhibition up the stairs on the first floor. The cashier/curator has some leaflets in English as well as the key to the toilet located on the second floor, if needed. The orange info boards you see have the English translation on the bottom right. Opposite the cashier notice stool No. 52 with its handy boot remover (Stiefelzieher). Two meters from the sofa check out the cool smoker's stool (Raucherstuhl)—men would sit on it backwards, rest their elbows on the leather cushions and extract a cigar from the left compartment and ash it in the right one. Look to the adjacent chair in front of the desk; the Austrian emperor Kaiser Franz Josef sat on it in September 1897. You're not allowed to, though. In the second to last room pore over the "production flow" chart from 1929; here you can follow the manufacturing process. In the last room check out the "Stahlmöbel" (steel furniture) from 1931—similar to chairs used today. Expect a visit to take about an hour. The next time you're chillin' in a coffeehouse and you see a Thonet-like chair, turn it over to see whether it's real. www.thonet.de (site to their factory in Frankenberg/Eder). *Hours:* (Boppard Museum) April-Oct Tue-Sun 10:00-12:30 & 13:30-17:00. *Price: FREE* entry! *Getting There:* Museum is located on the Rhine promenade at the ferry landing, a few hundred meters from the K-D boat dock. *Note:* The odd-looking fountain on the market square depicts various parts comprising Thonet chairs. Thonet's former factory in Vienna was acquired by Hundertwasser and is now KunstHausWien (page 568).

Chair Lift: Glide above the valley floor on the "Sesselbahn" (20-min ride, nearly 1km long) to a bird's eye perspective of the Boppard bend—the sharpest curve along the Rhine—and the Vierseenblick (four lakes view), a panoramic illusion created by the various twists in the river. Additionally, hikers will discover numerous nature trails to wander. A pair of casual restaurants offer visitors a place to relax and admire the sweeping vistas. *Hours:* (chair lift) April-Oct, daily, 10:00-17:00. *Price:* 4.20€ o.w., 6.20€ r.t. *Getting There: Railers,* few buses run from town to the Sesselbahn. Consider hopping on the touristy Rhein Express, a sightseeing tram resembling a choo choo train (runs regularly April-Oct, 3.50€/person r.t.). *Drivers,* either park in the nearby lot and take the chair lift or drive the following directions to the lookout point (*GPS:* N50° 14.633 - E7° 34.316): From the Koblenz side of town, turn off route 9 following the sign Vierseenblick. After 1km veer right and ascend the ultra-narrow road another 2km to reach the parking areas for the Vierseenblick and Boppard bend.

Engelbert Humperdinck: During his time in Boppard (1897-1901), Engelbert composed the Moorish Rhapsody and worked on the Königskinder opera. His former house, known as the Humperdinck Schlößchen, was converted into private apartments and is closed to the public.

Good Sleeps: **Hotel Günther:** Rheinallee 40 (www.hotelguenther.com) *Tel.#* 06742/ 89-090. Cozy, convenient and cost effective, Hotel Günther offers the best accommodations in town. Motherly run by the Sunthimers—Jim, Doris, Scott and Sonya—Hotel Günther is ideally situated on the Rhine promenade meters from the K-D boat dock and market square. Most rooms have a balcony boasting memorable views of the Rhine. For budget-minded travelers, the Sunthimers have a cheap-sleeps guest house next door with no view but similar amenities (including toilet/shower in room) and the same generous buffet breakfast offered in the main building. _Note:_ Free Internet for guests! Main building has elevator. Bike rental, 6.50€/day. Moreover, jaunty Jim and sprightly Scott hail from the USA and will be pleased to answer in North American English whatever questions you may have regarding the local culture, wine or sights. _Price:_ Sgl 28-82€, Dbl 47-98€ (cheaper the longer you stay). _CC's:_ VC, MC, AE. _Getting There: **Railers,**_ exit station straight, cross at the crosswalk, go right, then left and through the arch—at the bottom is the river, go right a few hundred meters to your digs. **Drivers,** off route 9 turn into Boppard at the south end of town following the sign "Autofähre" (car ferry). After some 300 meters follow the sign right and at the end of the road turn left into Rheinallee. A relaxing park and the romantic Rhine will be to your right. Continue straight and your digs will appear on the left after 700 meters. Parking 2.50€/day. *GPS:* N50° 13.968 - E7° 35.432

580km, <u>Marksburg</u>: [right bank] Dominating the skyline above the village of Braubach are the whitewashed bulwarks and towering keep of Marksburg, an impressive 12th-century fortress that was never conquered—qualifying it as the Rhineland's most original castle. *(Fittingly, Marksburg is home to the German Castles' Association.)* Well worth a visit, guided tours run regularly through the fortress and feature, among other things, instruments of medieval torture, cannons targeting the Rhine, suits of armor (rare collection), a herb garden from the Middle Ages *(beware of "Schierling"! This herb is the same type of poison hemlock used to execute Socrates)*, and a 40-meter-high keep employed as an observation tower, dungeon and a defenders' last refuge. *Hours:* (end times are last admission) daily, Easter-Oct 10:00-17:00, Nov-Easter 11:00-16:00. *Price:* adult 4.50€, student 4€, or free with Castle Ticket. *Tours* run regularly in German (less regular in winter), duration 50 min—a basic info sheet in English is provided. English tour possible with 20 people—call ahead to see whether any are scheduled, tel.# 02627/ 206. See website for virtual tour: www.marksburg.de (click Welcome, then Circuit). *Getting There: Boaters,* a 20-min trek from dock. Or, hop on the Marksburg Express— cheesy choo choo on wheels (3.50€ r.t., Easter thru mid-Oct). *Drivers,* parking 1.50€ in summer—five-minute walk from lot.

585km, <u>Burg Lahneck</u>: [right bank] Built in 1226 to defend nearby silver mines, you'll see Burg Lahneck perched upon a bluff overlooking the town of Lahnstein and the confluence of the Lahn and Rhine rivers. The burg later assumed a greater role as the northernmost bastion safeguarding the territory governed by the electors of Mainz. In the 15th century, the castle's fortifications were extended and improved to withstand the vigor of modern weaponry. However, the modifications proved ineffective against French artillery in 1688 when Burg Lahneck was besieged and reduced to rubble. The burg lay in ruin the following two centuries until a wealthy Scotsman, who fancied himself as a medieval knight, rebuilt it in neo-Gothic style using the original foundations and stonework. Today, Burg Lahneck is open to the public—guided tours leave on the hour, April-Oct 10:00-17:00. *Price:* 3€, or free with Castle Ticket. (www.burg-lahneck.de) *Tel.#* 02621/2789. *Note:* There is a restaurant on the premises (closed Monday) and not far away is a campground boasting gargantuan views—tel.# 02621/2765 (campground).

585km, <u>Schloss Stolzenfels</u>: [left bank] Across the river from Burg Lahneck, vibrantly protruding from the wooded hillside, is the enormous mustard-yellow Schloss Stolzenfels. In the 14th century, both the aforementioned castles simultaneously levied taxes on the passing river trade. After the destruction of Stolzenfels by French troops in 1689, the medieval burg was transformed (1836-42) into a lavish palace (Schloss) exuding Rhine romanticism. From the bluff upon which it sits, the castle offers a fine view towards Koblenz and Fortress Ehrenbreitstein. Today, Schloss Stolzenfels is open to the public exhibiting its sumptuous décor. *Note:* Photos not allowed inside. Toilets on left before cashier. *Hours:* April-Sept, closed first day of the workweek, otherwise 9:00-18:00 (last admission one hour prior to closing)—off-season same hours except open till 17:00. *Price:* (includes German tour; translation sheet provided) adult 2.60€, student 1.30€, or free with Castle Ticket. *Drivers,* park in lot along route 9. From there a path ascends to the castle—enchanting, 10-min walk. In the beginning leg notice the chapel off to the right that includes a memorial for the fallen soldiers of WWI & II.

588km, <u>KOBLENZ</u>: *(~ Pop. 108,000 ~ Country/Area Code: +49-(0)261 ~ Sister City: Austin, Texas)* Most travelers at some time or another will pass through Koblenz, located at the confluence of the Mosel and Rhine rivers. Deriving from the Latin "confluentes," Koblenz has 2000-year-old Roman origins. Those who are traveling by boat can't miss the **Deutsches Eck** (German Corner), the tip of Koblenz accommodating a colossal equestrian statue of Emperor William I (1871-88) marking the confluence. Not too far away is the beloved *Schängelbrunnen*, a fountain punctuated by a "little rascal" who spits a stream of water every two minutes dousing unsuspecting tourists. Strategically entrenched above Koblenz, the formidable **Fortress Ehrenbreitstein** presents marvelous views, the provincial museum, and a youth hostel [HI]. Koblenz will literally explode on Aug 12, 2006, during one of the nation's biggest firework shows, attracting around half a million spectators and 70 ships for Rhine in Flames: "Mega Night on the Rhine."

Although Koblenz is a nice city, plan a brief stay (few hours). Your time is better spent discovering the ultra-quaint wine villages that line the Mosel or the robber-baron castles perched above the Romantic Rhine.

TI: (www.koblenz.de) *Tel.#* 0261/31-304. Koblenz has two TIs: *Bahnhofplatz* (outside main train station) and *Rathaus* (in the Old Town), both have a free room-finding service, offer an excellent free (fold-out) city map with description of sights, and keep similar hours: April-Oct, daily, 9:00-18:00; Nov-March Mon-Fri 9:00-18:00, Sat 10:00-14:00 (Rathaus till 16:00). *Note:* Culture vultures ask for their handy Museums brochure; everyone ask for their "Koblenz — 2000 years of history" pamphlet, then visit the History Column (Historiensäule) near TI in the Old Town.

Tours: For a Koblenz quickie, hop on the *Altstadt-Express* (little choo choo on wheels). The 30-min tour, in German and English, departs April-Oct, daily, 10:00-17:00 on the hour from the Deutsches Eck and costs 4€/person.

Railers: Koblenz's newly renovated train station is a 30-min walk from the Old Town and K-D boat dock, or from out front take bus #1 direction Deutsches Eck/Altstadt (2/hr). Taxis are also out front—6-7€ to the Old Town or K-D boat dock; roughly 10€ to the fortress (Festung). In the station's main hall is the DB service desk, which also offers a free city map when TI is closed. Exit station right, pass McDonald's, and the **TI** is in the building on the left. Exit station right for the **post office** (Mon-Fri 8:00-18:30, Sat 8:30-13:30; 24hr stamp machine "Briefmarken" outside, button for English) and farther right around the corner is a Lidl **grocery store** (Mon-Sat 8:00-20:00). Trains from Koblenz leave regularly to Trier (trip time 1.5-2hr), Cochem (40min), St. Goar (30min), Bacharach (40min), Cologne and Bingen (1hr).

Boaters: The Rhine's current is very strong. Don't lose valuable time by cruising upstream against the current. Instead, cruise downstream by boat and upstream via train. Both of the below-listed schedules are upstream and therefore not recommended. *Note:* The main K-D boat dock (100 meters from the Deutsches Eck on the Rhine side) is a 35-min walk from the train station—bus #1 shuttles to/fro twice hourly. May thru Sept K-D has a second dock open, which is roughly a 10-min walk from the station but boats departing from there only head south direction Bingen. To get to the second K-D dock exit station straight to Marken-Bildchen-Weg—continue on this street to the river. The spirited gal who runs the main K-D ticket kiosk is Martina; tell her we said "Hi!" You'll meet Heike at the second K-D dock. *K-D Discounts:* see page 305—*Boaters.*

Koblenz direction Bingen, May-Sept boats depart *9:00, 11:00, 14:00—April and Oct 9:00, 14:00. *Note: Departure of 90-year-old Goethe paddle steamer.

Koblenz direction Cochem [22.40€ o.w.] (dep.) 9:45→15:00 (arr.), stopping at Moselkern (Burg Eltz) 13:00. Times applicable Fri thru Mon April 29 to June 6, 2006, and then daily from June 16 to Oct 3. *Note:* June 7-15 boat traffic to/fro Cochem will be closed due to sluice (lock) closure. You'll cruise through two locks on the way to Mosel-kern and a third to Cochem.

Suggestion: Consider hopping aboard a one-hour (5€) Rhine-Mosel "Rundfahrt," which is a boat ride skirting the Deutsches Eck, essentially cruising both rivers. Rundfahrts depart hourly from the Rhine promenade.

Schängelbrunnen: This unique spitting fountain—dating from 1941—can be found in the Old Town (five-minute walk from K-D dock), steps from the Rathaus and TI. Don't get wet. *GPS:* N50° 21.618 - E7° 35.893

Deutsches Eck: Stand on the tip of the "German Corner" and be a part of the Rhine-Mosel confluence. Here you'll clearly see the different colors of the merging rivers. Resembling the bow of a ship, the Deutsches Eck is punctuated by a 14-meter-high equestrian statue of Emperor (Kaiser) William I, dating from 1897. In 1945, units of Patton's Third Army blasted the kaiser off his pedestal. Nearly 50 years later, the emperor reappeared when Europe's largest floating crane hoisted a 60-ton bronze replica onto the empty platform. If you think the views are cool from the confluence, walk around to the backside of the kaiser and ascend the stairs to the top of his pedestal to an even better view. (Once there, look up to see the horse's hoof just feet away.) *Note:* When facing the kaiser, walk to the beginning of the steps and stop. Now go left and swivel the handle in the lion's mouth (but before you do, make a wish). When ready, wander over to the Mosel promenade to check out three sections of the Berlin Wall, each labeled by a plaque representing (l. to r.) *"Victims of the Wall"* — *"17 June, 1953"* (date of workers' uprising in East Germany when some 50 citizens were killed and thousands arrested; until the fall of the Wall the date was honored as a public holiday in the west, and it is the namesake of the western axis running from the Brandenburg Gate) — *"9 Nov. 1989"* (fall of the Wall). *Getting There: Railers,* from the train station the Deutsches Eck is a 35-min walk, or bus #1 shuttles to/fro twice hourly. *Drivers,* follow signs "Altstadt" then Deutsches Eck. Once there, ample parking is available—coin automat applicable, generally 50¢/hr. *GPS:* N50° 21.902 - E7° 36.392

Fortress Ehrenbreitstein: Strategically entrenched (120m/393ft) above Koblenz, this powerhouse citadel governed the Rhine-Mosel confluence from its birth in the late 10th century until its destruction by French forces in 1799. After Napoleon's defeat in 1814, the Prussians reacquired the fortress and used the ruins of Burg Rheinfels (in St. Goar) to rebuild it. Today, the fortress is an open-air museum that will certainly impress history buffs. Inside its walls are the provincial (Landes-) museum and a youth hostel (see below). Needless to say, the views are tremendous from the fortress' battlements. *Hours:* open year round. *Price:* adult 3.10€, student 2.10€. *Getting There: Drivers*, from the Rhine's right bank (route 42) follow signs Ehrenbreitstein. *GPS:* N50° 21.974 - E7° 36.959 (coordinates to parking lot). *Railers*, fortress is located on Rhine's right bank 4km from the main train station (Hbf)—reachable via bus or train, then by foot (steep, 25 min) or chairlift (Sesselbahn: April/May and Oct 10:00-16:45, June-Sept 9:30-17:45, 4.20€ normal or 2.50€ for hostel guests). To reach the chairlift, hop on bus 9 or 10 and get off at Obertal. If you prefer to walk, catch either bus 8 or a train (from main station: Hbf) to Ehrenbreitstein. From there, exit bus left and after 250 meters ascend footpath to fortress (from Ehrenbreitstein train station exit left, cross road and ascend footpath to fortress). *GPS:* N50° 21.849 - E7° 36.700 (coordinates to footpath). *Note:* The ferry shuttling peo-ple from near the K-D dock across the river departs regularly May-Oct, 1.20€/person o.w.

Hostel, Jugendherberge Ehrenbreitstein: [HI] (www.djh.de) *Tel.#* 0261/972-870. Lay your head on top of the world! This hostel has a premier location in a millennium-old fortress overlooking Koblenz and the Rhine-Mosel confluence. *Price*: (includes linen, breakfast) dorm bed 16.50€, Sgl 31€, Dbl 44€. *Note*: Must be a member or an extra charge will apply. Excellent dinners available for 6€, usually served 18:00-19:00.

C O L O G N E (Köln)

~ Population: 1.05 million   ~ Elevation: 60m/196ft
~ Country/Area Code: +49-(0)221   ~ Sister City: Indianapolis, Indiana

Köln is Germany's fourth most-populated city. And since Berlin, Hamburg and Munich are nowhere near the Rhineland, Cologne is the largest community on the nation's commercial lifeline: the Rhine River. The city's "toilet water," Eau de Cologne, has made the riverside metropolis a household name, and Köln's world-famous Gothic Dom (cathedral) is Germany's most visited site with 20,000 people paying their respects daily.

The city's English name still bears witness to its roots nearly 2000 years ago when it was a Roman colony. In 50 A.D., Emperor Claudius gave the swelling community the rights of a Roman city as well as its new name, "Colonia" (Latin for colony). In the 4th century, Emperor Constantine, the first Roman ruler to convert to Christianity, declared the colony a bishopric.

Nearly 500 years later, Charlemagne—king of the Franks—upgraded the diocese of Cologne to an archbishopric. The archbishops became important advisers to the emperors and by 1180 they were exercising their papal authority over Cologne's 40,000 inhabitants, which qualified the former Roman colony as the largest city in the new empire. The Germanic mega-metropolis was an important cultural and religious center, and by controlling the (Rhine) river trade, Cologne's economy thrived throughout the Middle Ages. Academically Cologne excelled too, establishing the first municipal university in 1388. As a result, journalistic and literary trades flourished and it was here that Karl Marx—founder of modern communism—began his career as a newspaper editor in 1842.

During WWII Cologne endured horrific times: 262 air raids destroyed 90% of the city center—miraculously the Dom was left intact—and its population declined from 800,000 to 40,000, setting back the clock 750 years. In the final, desperate months of the war, Hitler's commander of Cologne—Josef Grohés—ordered the "absolute defense of the city to the last man." On March 5, 1945, the U.S. 3rd Armored "Spearhead" Division began its attack on Cologne. By early afternoon on March 6, the city was free.

Post-WWII, all able-bodied citizens—mainly women, nicknamed Trümmerfrauen—banded together to clear the rubble from the war-torn streets. Thanks to their dogged determination and the ingenuity of those who followed, Cologne has since grown into one of the most exciting hubs in the nation. Partygoers will go nuts during Karneval, Cologne's "fifth season" and Europe's most boisterous pre-Lenten festival. Beer enthusiasts will appreciate the Brauhäuser and the pleasingly persistent Köbes (waiters) who serve the locally brewed Kölsch. Pyrotechnic fans will love KölnerLichter, an explosive night in July when fireworks are hurled into the sky, bathing Cologne in brilliant light. Homosexuals can't beat Europe's largest gay event: Christopher Street Day parade. Pious folk will worship the Dom, as well as the city's Romanesque past. Chocoholics will go cocoa in the chocolate museum. Soccer fans will get a kick out of the FIFA World Cup action (page 336), for which Cologne has five matches scheduled. And cost-conscious travelers will splurge on *FREE* Cologne (page 329). Anyone coming to Germany should stop in for a few days to experience this magnetic and pleasantly scented Rhineland metropolis for themselves. These GPS coordinates—N50° 56.510 - E6° 57.403—will get you downtown to a world-famous site.

~ Cologne is worth a two-day stay. Mood permitting, divide your time like so,
  Day 1: Start early—visit the awe-inspiring Dom, climb the tower. Afterwards, begin touring points of interest. Consider Haus 4711 followed by Gestapo HQ and the Romanesque churches St. Gereon and St. Ursula. Or, after the Dom, head south via Hohe Str. (shopping street) to the Romanesque churches St. Maria im Kapitol and St. Maria Lyskirchen, followed by the chocolate museum. Folks who savor olives, try the "Oliven-Seele" (baguette loaded with olives, 1.60€) at the Kamps bread shop on the corner of Marzellenstr. and Komödienstr. (when facing TI, go right and cross the street).
  Day 2: Tour sights/museums/churches of interest that you missed on day 1. (Consider renting a bike and cycling to the attractions as well as along the Rhine—it's healthy, fun and productive. Pack a picnic).

Tourist Information: [TI] (www.stadt-koeln.de/en) *Tel.#* 0221/2213-0400. Cologne's newly renovated TI is stocked with books, brochures, city maps (20¢ ea.) and helpful staff. Downstairs you'll find a souvenir shop selling everything Cologne as well as a service desk for booking accommodations (3€/booking) and tickets to shows and concerts. *Getting There:* TI is located at Unter Fettenhennen 19 (when facing the Dom's main entrance, the TI is behind you on the corner). *Hours:* daily, Mon-Sat 9:00-21:00 (till 22:00 July-Sept), Sun 10:00-18:00.

Emergency Tel. Numbers: [Germany-wide]
  Police (Polizei) = 110
  Fire dept. (Feuerwehr) or general emergency = 112
  Ambulance = 19222

Hauptbahnhof: [Hbf] Cologne's smoke-free "main train station" is a delight in comparison to other Hauptbahnhofs. It's motherly clean, has a smorgasbord of food options—from Pizza Hut to fish & chips, Mexican to Chinese—and is conveniently located in the heart of the Old Town. Upon exiting, it's an impressive sight to see the Dom's Gothic magnitude staring you in face.
  The *luggage storage* system is a modern marvel. It is a series of baggage islands, blocky automats that are situated (near DB Service desk by track 1) on the Dom side of the station and crowned by a blue cube that reads: Gepäck - Luggage - Baggage. Deposit 3€ (for 24hr) and pop your bag into the compartment. A conveyer belt will deliver it to a central storage area so you can collect it from any baggage island any time. For *train info* or *itinerary printouts*, see "DB Service" desk (which faces exit on Dom side and usually hosts a long line of people). The *post office* can be found in the "Ludwig" newspaper shop opposite tracks 8 and 9 (north end). Hours: Mon-Sat 6:00-22:00, Sun 8:00-22:00. Around the corner from the P.O. are *toilets* ("WC"), and just past them you can drive model trains for 50¢. Woo-hoo!

Subway/Bus: Most of Cologne's attractions are within walking distance of the Dom, rendering public transportation for the general traveler unnecessary. However, here is the list of ticket prices for those who require the service (bus & U-Bahn): *Kurzstrecke* (short trip) 1.20€, valid for up to 4 stops within 20 min. *Einzelticket* (one-way, one-direction) 1.70€, valid for use within 90 min in the city. *Tagesticket* (Day Ticket) 4.40€, valid throughout the city till 03:00. Small groups buy the *Minigruppen* city ticket 6.70€, valid for up to 5 people Mon-Fri 9:00 till 03:00 or all day on weekends. **Airport:** If you're headed to Cologne (-Bonn) airport, the S-Bahn leaves every 15 min from track 10 and costs 2.10€ (15-min trip). Holders of a Eurail consecutive-day or dated Flexi/Select pass ride for *free* on the S-Bahn. *Note:* All ticket types offer alternative travel combinations, which can be purchased at multilingual automats. Tickets from automats are already time-stamped (validated).

Parking: For *street parking* pay at nearby "Parkschein Automat" and leave ticket on dashboard of your car. Price: 1€/30min, max/4hr, applicable (automats vary) Mon-Sat 9:00 to 18-23:00—free all other times. *Parking garages* are abundantly located throughout the city and cost on average 1.30€/hr. For the most popular garage (located beneath the Dom), follow signs Dom/Rhein (1.80€/hr or 18€/day). *GPS:* (Dom garage) N50° 56.510 - E6° 57.403. *Note:* For Drivers who wish to avoid the city entirely, leave your car at a P+R (Park+Ride) on the outskirts and catch bus/subway in.

Share Ride: *(Mitfahrzentrale; a concept matching passengers with drivers, and vice-versa.)* Those who are not traveling by Eurail, "Mitfahrzentrale" is the cheapest and most social option of getting from one city to another. You'll find the Share Ride office at Maximinenstr. 2 (exit main train station into Breslauer Platz [by track 10], go left some 150m and it's across the street). *Tel.#* 0221/19-440. *Hours:* daily, 9:00-19:00. *Price:* approximate cost per passenger from Cologne to Munich or Berlin 31€, Frankfurt 14€, Amsterdam 17€, Prague 38€. *Note:* Those who have a working knowledge of German will want to first refer to this website (www.mitfahrgelegenheit.de) for an opportunity to contact the driver directly, i.e. cutting out the middleman for an even cheaper Share Ride.

Airport: *(Flughafen;* code CGN; www.airport-cgn.de) Cologne's modern (Köln-Bonn) airport, located 17km southeast of Cologne and 22km north of Bonn, is the 4th busiest in Germany, moving some 8.5 million passengers annually. The TI is located in the arrivals area terminal 2 (open daily [generally] 9:00-20:00). Beneath the airport is a train station that conveniently connects all of Germany, with frequent departures to Cologne and Bonn. To reach central Cologne jump on any train headed direction Köln Hbf (Hauptbahnhof). The trip will take 15 min and cost 2.10€—purchase ticket from vending machine. By taxi to Cologne is roughly 25€, to Bonn 35-40€. For deep discounts in air travel, Köln-Bonn airport is the hub of the low-cost airline German Wings (www.germanwings.com), which flies to most major destinations in Europe. Its bread-and-butter route is Cologne–Berlin (SXF), departing several times daily. (*Note:* If you plan ahead and book online you'll only pay between 30-45€ one way to Berlin.) Another airline making a big landing in Cologne is Continental, which plans to fly daily non-stop between Cologne and Newark, New Jersey, starting May 2006. Oh, and just so you know, *Abflug* means departure and *Ankunft* means arrival.

Bike Rental: Because of Cologne's uncongested streets and scenic position on the Rhine River, the best way to see the city is by bike. And the best place to rent a bike is from the "Radstation," across the street from the main train station. See Ralf, who is usually working and speaks good English. Possibly you've seen Radstation before, most major German cities have one connected to the Hauptbahnhof. It's a convenient and safe place for locals to store their bikes (.70¢/day or 7€/month) while they're at work or on vacation. *Getting There:* To find the Radstation, exit the main train station into Breslauer Platz (by McDonald's) and follow signs across street. *Hours:* Mon-Fri 6:00-22:30, Sat/Sun 8:00-20:00. *Price:* 5€/3hr, 10€/24hr. *Note:* Need ID and 50€ deposit.

Internet: Two minutes from the main train station are a few call shops offering reasonable Internet (roughly 2.50€/hr) and telephone services connecting the globe (15-20¢/min to N. America). *Hours:* daily, early till late. *Getting There:* exit station on the Dom side (by track 1), veer right and ascend road paralleling the taxis. Once at the turning circle you'll see the call shops across the street on the left.

Boat Rides: If Cologne is your only opportunity to cruise the Rhine, hop on. The prominent K-D fleet (Köln-Düsseldorfer, www.k-d.com) offers the snappy Panorama tour (6.80€/person) four times daily (April-Oct 10:30, 12:00, 14:00 and 18:00). Consider a cruise to Bonn (one way 11.40€, round trip 13.70€), a scenic alternative to the train. Those who wish to cruise the merry Mosel or romantic Rhine, take the train (or drive) to Koblenz and consider your next move (refer to chapters *Mosel Valley* or *Middle Rhine, Valley of the Loreley*). *K-D Discounts:* Holders of a German rail or Eurail (consecutive-day or dated Flexi/Select) pass cruise for *FREE* (← normal routes →). If it's your birthday, you cruise for *FREE!* What's more, students 26 years of age or under with valid student ID receive a 50% discount, and seniors (60+) travel half price Mondays and Fridays.

Post Office: P.O. in the Hauptbahnhof (main train station) can be found in the "Ludwig" newspaper shop, opposite tracks 8 and 9 (north end). *Hours:* Mon-Sat 6:00-22:00, Sun 8:00-22:00. Another P.O. is located at Hohe Str. 1 (far end of main shopping street). *Hours:* Mon-Fri 9:00-18:00, Sat 9:00-13:00 (opposite front door is a 24-hour stamp machine labeled "Briefmarken").

Welcome Card: Cologne's Welcome Card offers free use of public transportation, plus discounts on select tours and museums. *Price:* 24-hour card 9€, 48hr/14€, 72hr/19€; double the price for groups of three. *Opinion:* For the general traveler, the card isn't worth it.

American Express: Located at Burgmauer 14 (zip: 50667), up cobbled lane from TI. (fes.cologne@aexp.com) *Hours:* Mon-Fri 9:00-18:00, Sat 10:00-13:00. *Tel.#* 0221/257-5186. *Note:* Folks using American Express products (e.g. traveler's checks, credit card) can use their offices Europe-wide to receive letters—small packages okay!

Holidays in Cologne, 2006

1. January, Sunday – New Year
14. April – Good Friday
17. April – Easter Monday
1. May, Monday – May Day (Labor Day)
25. May, Thursday – Ascension Day
5. June – Whit Monday
15. June, Thursday – Corpus Christi
3. October, Tuesday – Day of German (East-West) Unity
1. November, Wednesday – All Saints' Day
25. December, Monday – Christmas
26. December, Tuesday – St. Stephen's Day (Christmas Day No. 2)

What to do on a Sunday or holiday

Shops will be closed but most attractions will remain open, along with most eateries and touristy shops. Keep in mind the **Dom** will be engaged with Mass, especially in the morning. For those interested in a tour, only 14:30 is offered.

If the weather is nice, **consider renting a bike** and cycling along the Rhine as well as through the hushed city streets taking in a few urban sights.

Cologne's zoo is always a delight to visit. Hours: daily, 9:00-17:00 (last entry 16:30), April-Oct till 18:00 (last entry 17:30). Price: adult 12€, student 8.50€—adults pay student price on Mondays. (www.zoo-koeln.de)

For those looking to be rejuvenated—consider a swim, soak in a Jacuzzi, or getting steamed in a sauna—head to the **Claudius Therme** across river from zoo. *Hours:* daily,

9:00-24:00. *Price:* 2hr/13-15€, 4hr/18-20€, day/23-25€; 30-min massage 27€, 45min/41€. *Tel.#* 0221/981-440 (www.claudius-therme.de)

Church Service (Gottesdienst)

Note: Check with staff at your accommodations or at TI for up-to-date info, including other religious denominations.

St. Andreas: (Catholic) English service, Sat 18:30 — around corner from TI.

St. Mauritius: (Catholic) English service, Sat 18:30 — Mauritiuskirchplatz 9 (five-minute walk southwest of Neumarkt).

FREE Cologne

1) The awe-inspiring **Dom** is free and a must-do, as well as splashing yourself with authentic "toilet water," Eau de Cologne, at **Haus 4711** (page 331).

2) Pop into the glass-constructed **Dom Forum** (page 331), opposite Dom, for the latest on free organ and gospel concerts, or simply to people watch while hashing out the day's game plan.

3) The city's **Romanesque churches** (page 333) are free and recapture Cologne's medieval heritage.

4) **Ride a bike—or walk—along the Rhine**.

5) Generations have enjoyed the **Flora & Botanical Gardens**—28 acres of fragrant parkland situated 2km north of the Dom, adjacent to zoo. Known to the locals as "Die Flora," the park's overwhelming popularity is verified by the 1 million visitors who stroll its idyllic paths each year. Here you'll see themed horticulture, exhibition greenhouses, cultivated gardens, and some 10,000 plant varieties from all over the world. Die Flora is free to enter and is open daily: 8:00 till dusk, greenhouses 10:00-16:00 (later in summer).

6) Dating from the Middle Ages, Jewish ritual baths (excavated 1957) can be seen through a glass pyramid-shaped structure in front of the Rathaus (town hall). Formerly located in the heart of the Jewish quarter, the baths, called **Mikwe**, are 16m/52ft deep but a closer look is possible by retrieving the entrance key (*free* from clerk just inside door of Rathaus, leave passport as deposit. Hours: Mon-Thur 8:00-16:00, Fri 8:00-12:00, or on weekends you can try asking at the Römisch-Germanisches Museum). The key will open the little gate adjacent to glass pyramid as well as the iron door at bottom of stairs.

SIGHTS

Dom: The Kölner Dom is Germany's biggest cathedral, soaring 157m/515ft into the sky and measuring 144m/472ft from front to back. It has a total window surface of 108,000sq.ft. and a roof that spans nearly 3 acres. No wonder this breathtaking structure took 632 years to complete (1248-1880). The Kölner Dom is also the nation's most visited attraction with roughly 20,000 people paying their respects daily. During WWII, much of Cologne was destroyed. Miraculously, the Dom survived. In 1998, the Kölner Dom was added to UNESCO's World Heritage List, a United Nations register of the world's most unique and precious places.

The Dom's must-see interior is enormous and jam-packed with history, but before you enter, check out the real-size replica of the cathedral's spire located across the plaza adjacent to the steps, some 50m opposite the Dom's double-wide front portal. Once there, look up to see the original spire(s) 515ft above you. Neighboring the replica spire (left when facing cathedral) are the remnants of an ancient gate dating from Roman "Colonia." The Romans built a chapel where the Dom now stands and the gate provided access to the settlement's north-south trade route: Cologne's 2000-year-old High Street (Hohe Str.; to your right when facing cathedral), which still upholds lively commerce as the city's main shopping street.

Hours: (Dom) daily 6:00-19:30 (visiting is restricted during Mass: Mon-Sat 6:30, 7:15, 8:00, 9:00, 18:30 & Sun 7:00 thru 10:45, 12:00, 17:00, 18:30).

Dom Highlights: Among the cathedral's many highlights are the **Chapel of the Three Magi** (Three Kings, or Wise Men of the East, who paid homage to baby Jesus—chapel is located at far end of Dom) • Above the chapel is the Dom's oldest stained-glass window (center; 1265 A.D.) • **Shrine of the Three Magi** (1190-1225), which allegedly holds the bones of the Three Kings (gold casket can be seen behind main altar, opposite Chapel of the Three Magi) • **Gero-Crucifix** (976 A.D.), oldest surviving monumental crucifix of the Western world (found mid-section of Dom, left side beyond wrought-iron gate). *Note:* If wrought-iron gates are open you are allowed to walk to the back end of the Dom and view the abovementioned objects up close. If the gates are locked, come back in a few hours and they should be open.

Tower: Just inside the front/right portal is the ascent to the tower—509 heavily worn, dizzying steps lead to the 97-meter-high observation platform offering a paralyzing view of Cologne. It takes 15 minutes to reach the top, however you're allowed to catch your breath at the Glockenstube, a chamber housing the tower's bells. A few of these date from the Middle Ages; although it's the newer massive-sized bell, "decke Pitter" (Fat Pete), which grabs all the attention—at 24 tons, it's the world's heaviest swingin' bell. *Hours:* (tower) daily, 9:00-16:00 (May-Sept till 18:00). *Price:* adult 2€, student 1€. *Note:* The climb is very taxing—folks who have health problems should reconsider.

Guided tours in English are offered twice daily, except once on Sunday. They are approx. 45 min long and can be met inside the front/right portal—enter straight then look left for the info board marked Domführungen or Cathedral Tours. *Tour times:* Mon-Sat 10:30 & 14:30, Sun 14:30. *Price:* adult 4€, student 2€—price includes a 20-minute film entitled "Faszination Kölner Dom" shown at the Dom Forum after tour.

Self-guided tours, (although not as comprehensive), are also possible—go to where the guided tours meet and you'll see brochures of the cathedral (70¢) in several languages. Brochures are also available at the Dom Forum.

Dom Treasury: (Schatzkammer) The Dom's purpose-built subterranean vaults are filled with sacred treasures dating from the 10th century. They can be entered (from either inside or outside) on the Hauptbahnhof side of the Dom, mid section. *Hours:* daily, 10:00-18:00 (last entry 17:30). *Price:* adult 4€, student 2€. To beat down the price, consider the combo-ticket (treasury + tower) adult 5€, student 2.50€.

Dom Forum: Across from the Dom's main entrance is the Forum, a visitor's center offering info on Cologne's Catholic community, in particular the Dom. This building made of tall glass windows is a great place to take a break, inquire about free organ/gospel concerts, grab a coffee/tea (70¢), and/or people watch while hashing out the day's game plan. Toilets downstairs—bring small change. *Hours:* (Forum) Mon-Fri 10:00-18:30, Sat 10:00-17:00, Sun 13:00-17:00. Additionally, the Dom Forum hosts the 20-minute movie "Faszination Kölner Dom," outlining the history of the Dom. *Screening times:* (English) Mon-Sat 11:30 & 15:30, Sun 15:30. *Price:* adult 1.50€, student 1€ (or included with Dom tour).

Haus 4711: This property on Glockengasse single-handedly made Cologne a household name. In the 18th century a secret formula containing Cologne water was believed to have medicinal properties and used as a drinkable curative. In 1792 a Carthusian monk presented the newly wedded Mülhens couple with a special gift: The secret formula to "aqua mirabilis," later called Eau de Cologne. Wilhelm Mülhens soon realized the value of this formula and began producing Eau de Cologne out of his residence on Glockengasse. During the French occupation of Cologne in 1796, the Napoleonic system ordered the consecutive numbering of houses and Mülhens received the address 4711. Ultimately, the address became renowned throughout Europe as the place to buy the aromatic curative. Thus, 4711 was registered as the company's trademark in 1875.

The original building still stands and today it is a chic fragrance shop marketing the whole range of 4711 products. A visit is worthwhile to see the mini-museum (upper floor) and to splash yourself with the real Eau de Cologne from the running fountain (next to entrance—*beware*, potent!). Time your visit to correspond with the chiming of the carillon outside, located in the gable—every hour on the hour, 9:00-19:00, historical figures waltz to the melody of the Marseillaise, the French national anthem. (www.4711.com) *Hours:* (shop/museum) Mon-Fri 9:00-19:00, Sat 9:00-18:00. *Price: FREE* entry! *Gift Ideas:* Consider the small bottle (25ml/0.8fl.oz) of Eau de Cologne, 4.75€ — or the nicely wrapped gift pack (soap and 25ml bottle), 10€. *Getting There:* Glockengasse 4711 is located southwest of the Dom, 15 min by foot. Expect a visit to take around 15 min. *GPS:* N50° 56.301 - E6° 57.138

Gestapo HQ: (EL-DE-Haus) The Geheime Staatspolizei ("Gestapo," or Secret State Police) HQ building was the most feared in Cologne. The Gestapo were the eyes and ears and strong-arm of Hitler's despotic regime—Jews, Communists, Social Democrats, monarchists, homosexuals, anti-socials, and even some church clergy were considered enemies of the state. These so-called enemies were commonly detained and beaten in the basement of Gestapo HQ, where prison cells still bear handwritten evidence of their despair. You'll witness hundreds of inscriptions (ask cashier for translations), including calendars, poems, testimonies of innocence/defiance, and even a portrait of a drag queen.

The building is also known as the EL-DE-Haus, referring to the initials L. D. of its former owner, Leopold Dahmen, a jeweler whom the Nazis appropriated the building from.

Since the defeat of Nazism and the reconstruction of Germany, Cologne has turned this former four-story terror institution into a documentation center presenting a look back to the city as it was during its dark era. However, other than the prison cells, the exhibition is somewhat of a disappointment, as there is very little English throughout. Expect a visit to take 30-60 min. (Buffs will enjoy browsing through the library on the second floor—open Wed/Thur 10:00-16:00 & Fri 10:00-13:00.)

Hours: Tue-Fri 10:00-16:00, Sat/Sun 11:00-16:00. *Price:* adult 3.60€, student 1.50€. *Getting There:* Former Gestapo HQ (EL-DE-Haus or NS-Dokumentationszentrum) is located at Appellhofplatz 23-25, 15-min walk west of Dom—U-Bahn Appellhofplatz. *Note:* Black Madonna (see next entry, St. Maria) is only one block away—exit EL-DE-Haus right.

St. Maria (in der Kupfergasse): This early 18th-century church won't attract many tourists with its unimaginative brick facade, but through the front portal is a heavenly statue of the Black (Schwarzen) Madonna—the focus of many visitors. Upon entering the church (either door), the Black Madonna is in the adjacent payer room. *Getting There:* St. Maria is located on the corner of Neven-DuMont-Str. and Schwalbengasse (one block from Gestapo HQ). Two local hobos looking for handouts usually flank the church's street-side portal.

MUSEUMS

Note: Museums are *closed on Mondays!* To get the skinny on Cologne's cultural institutions, ask for the museums brochure at the TI. Or, get a head start from home, go to www.museenkoeln.de

For culture vultures, consider the *Museum Card*—valid for two days, inclusive of *free travel on all public transportation within the metro area and entry into most museums (not valid for chocolate museum or Gestapo HQ) *Price:* 12.20€—available at participating museums. *Note:* Oddly, free travel is only valid for the first day.

Chocolate Museum: (a.k.a. Imhoff-Stollwerck-Museum) A must-do for chocoholics—young and old alike simply love this modern three-level museum neatly situated on the Rhine. Here you'll learn the cultural history of chocolate, observe how it's produced, and even walk through a mini rainforest. *Did you know that the cacao tree, which bears the cocoa bean, is cultivated in the tropics by so-called third-world countries (e.g. Ivory Coast, Ghana, Nigeria, Cameroon) accounting for 95% of their exports?*

What's more, you can sample real cocoa beans to savor the bitterness as well as visit the choco fountain—everyone's favorite, where delicate wafers are dipped in melted chocolate for your consumption (don't be shy, recycle yourself back in line for a second helping). Additionally, you'll see exquisite Meissen porcelain aristocrats sipped chocolate from in the 18th century. Expect a visit to take at least 70 min. *Hours:* Tue-Fri 10:00-18:00 (last entry 17:00), Sat/Sun 11:00-19:00 (last entry 18:00). *Price:* adult 6€, student 3.50€. *Getting There:* Chocolate museum is a 15-min walk south of the Dom. When approaching the museum via the riverfront promenade, you'll see the gilded cone-shaped choco fountain through the contemporary facade of windows. *Note:* Combine your trip here with a visit to the Romanesque church St. Maria Lyskirchen, located across the boulevard (entrance An Lyskirchen).

Römisch-Germanisches Museum: Here you'll discover Germany's most extensive collection of Roman artifacts. *Hours:* Tue-Sun 10:00-17:00. *Price:* adult 5€, student 3€, (or free with Museum Card). *Getting There:* To reach the museum, cross the plaza on the south (right) side of the Dom.

Museum Ludwig: This mega-popular museum features an extensive gathering of 20th-century art, including works from Dali to Warhol as well as one of the world's largest Picasso collections (more than 600 pieces). *Hours:* Tue-Sun 10:00-18:00. *Price:* adult 7.50€, student 5.50€, (or free with Museum Card), audio guide available (3€). *Getting There:* Museum Ludwig is located behind the Dom, south (right) side.

Wallraf-Richartz-Museum: Rubens to van Gogh, this museum hosts a superb collection of paintings on three floors from the old masters to post-impressionists. *Hours:* Tue 10:00-20:00, Wed thru Fri 10:00-18:00, Sat/Sun 11:00-18:00. *Price:* adult 6€, student 3.50€, (or free with Museum Card), audio guide available (2.50€). *Getting There:* Museum is located south of the Dom at Martinstr. 39, opposite Mikwe (at Rathaus), 10-min walk.

Museum Schnütgen: Housed in the unique surroundings of the former 12th-century Romanesque church, St. Cäcilien, Museum Schnütgen features mainly Christian art from the Middle Ages. *Hours:* Tue-Fri 10:00-17:00, Sat/Sun 11:00-17:00. *Price:* adult 3.20€, student 2€, (or free with Museum Card). *Getting There:* St. Cäcilien is a few-minutes walk east of Neumarkt—U-Bahn Neumarkt.

Kölnisches Stadtmuseum: Here at the "City Museum" you'll unearth Cologne's history from the Middle Ages to the 21st century. *Hours:* Tue-Sun 10:00-17:00 (Tue till 20:00). *Price:* (includes audio guide) adult 4.20€, student 2.60€, (or free with Museum Card). *Getting There:* Stadtmuseum is located due west of the Dom, 10-min walk. Enter at Zeughausstr. 3. *Note:* Walk along Zeughausstr. and peer through the windows for a free view into the museum's ground-floor exhibits.

Romanesque Churches

Cologne has a dozen houses of worship that date from the 11th to mid-13th century. This divine ensemble from the Middle Ages, unrivaled in the Germanic-speaking world, forms a half-moon crescent around the Old Town. They attest to the pious heritage of Cologne's forefathers, sanctimoniously keeping evil and immorality off the city streets. Alas, many of the churches were destroyed during WWII—now, a refurbished shine often dominates their facades and interiors. In view of the latter, visiting all 12 properties would be overkill—hence the following abridged list outlining the Romanesque churches worth a visit. For obvious reasons, avoid Sundays if possible.

St. Gereon: This church, by far, feels the most Romanesque of Cologne's 12 and is well worth a visit. Upon entering the foyer you're confronted by a portrayal of Jesus' burial (sandstone, early 1500s). Resting upon plinths either side of the portal leading into the church are a pair of carnivorous creatures (lion on right dates from 12C). Step through the portal to behold fascinating architecture nearly 1000 years old. St. Gereon's inner core, magnificent indeed, is comprised of ten vaulted recesses defined between giant pillars to form a decagon. Above are thin columns supporting dramatic arches, and above them vibrant stained-glass windows rise to a collage of teardrops raining from the parachute-like ceiling.

    Back to eye-level, look right of the altar until you see a (late-Gothic) figure of Madonna holding baby Jesus. Farther right, a few meters, is the entrance into the striking Taufkappelle (Chapel of Christening). The faint wall murals in this room date from the 12th and 13th centuries. The church's crypt (left of altar) contains the venerated Samson Mosaic (circa 1070 A.D.) depicting scenes of Samson and King David from the Old Testament. Notice the bones hanging on the left wall after entering. Before exiting the church, look up to see the organ ominously perched above the door. Yikes! *Hours:*

Mon-Sat 10:00-12:00 & 15:00-17:00, Sun 15:00-17:00. *Getting There:* St. Gereon is located at Gereonskloster & Christophstr., 1km west of the Dom.

St. Maria im Kapitol: Built from 1040-1065, this is Cologne's oldest and largest Romanesque church. Upon entering the premises from Kasinostr., notice the pictures (ahead on right pillar) depicting this place of worship post-WWII. After entering the church, ramble around the right corner to discover a former portal in retirement. This astonishing 16-foot relic was handcrafted in the year 1065. The artist carved 26 scenes (one is missing) from the life of Christ on walnut and mounted them on oak wood planks. At the heart of the church is the altar; to either side are entrances into the crypt, which is the second largest in Germany after the crypt in the cathedral of Speyer. Left of the altar you'll see the 6-foot Limburger Madonna (13C) made from oak. Mary is holding baby Jesus in her left arm while gripping an apple in her right hand—it is not known whether the apple was part of the artist's original creation or added after its restoration.

Above the altar are 16th-century reliefs sculpted from marble and limestone tablets depicting images of prophets and biblical subjects. Perched above the tablets is the church's newest organ (1985). Along the north (left) wall are four stained-glass windows, the two middle examples date from 1510: the deep-blue Crucifixion (middle left) and St. Ursula (next window on right). The remaining windows encompassing the interior are contemporary works. At the head of the church, left side of choir, is a Madonna (circa 1180 A.D.) with real apples at her feet. Legend has it that Saint Hermann Josef as a child used to admire the holy figure on his way to school and as thanks for the fruits of life he'd place the apple he received for breakfast at her feet. Local worshippers still keep the tradition alive today. Behind the apple Madonna is the so-called Plague Crucifix (circa 1300 A.D.) *Hours:* daily, Mon-Sat 9:00-18:00, Sun 12:00-16:30. *Getting There:* St. Maria im Kapitol is located on Pipinstr. (15-min walk south of Dom), enter from Kasinostr.

St. Ursula: Built in the 12th century on top of a Roman cemetery, this church is a popular stop on Cologne's sightseeing circuit. Here began the legend of St. Ursula, a devout maiden. According to ancient script, sometime during the 4th century A.D., Ursula and 11,000 of her chaste companions embarked on a pilgrimage to Rome. Upon their ill-timed return to Cologne they were met by invading Huns and murdered. As a remembrance of the massacre, a chapel was erected and its walls were lined with the skulls and bones of the "virgins." Today, the room containing the calcium-deficient relics is known as the Golden Chamber (Goldene Kammer, 17C)—found within St. Ursula's church. In the Middle Ages Ursula was canonized as the patron saint of maidens and the martyrdom of her 11,000 companions is represented on the city's coat of arms by eleven teardrops. *Golden Chamber:* Upon entering the church, the Golden Chamber can be entered (for 1€) via the old door on the right. If it's locked, look around for the caretaker and ask nicely (basically you're begging here) to see the Golden Chamber (you came thousands of miles, no?). *Hours:* Mon-Sat 10:00-12:00 & 15:00-16:30, Sun 15:00-16:30. *Getting There:* St. Ursula is located on Ursalaplatz, roughly 700 meters northeast of the Dom (take Marzellenstr.).

St. Maria Lyskirchen: (Combine a visit here with a tour of the chocolate museum.) St. Maria Lyskirchen is the smallest of Cologne's Romanesque churches. Before entering, notice the line above the door marking the Rhine's water level on February 28, 1784. Now, calculate the age of the door—you'll find the date of its creation (1614) left of the face with wings. Once inside, look up—the ceiling frescos, dating from 1250, are wonderfully divine. Back at eye level, gaze right into the corner to see the eight-sided marble basin formally used for baptisms (13C). Left of the entrance you'll see two stained-glass window scenes dating from 1520: the Crucifixion of Jesus (with Mary Magdalene at his feet while Mary and Joseph of Arimathea flank him) and the three saints

Helena, Maternus and Gereon (third window, far end). *Hours:* daily, 10:00-12:00 & 15:00-17:00. *Getting There:* St. Maria Lyskirchen is located An Lyskirchen—a petite lane between Gr. Witschgasse and Filzen-graben—across the boulevard from the chocolate museum.

St. Aposteln: This church has a significantly large, rather sterile interior that boasts modern ceiling murals and 13 attention-grabbing figures of saints (in corner by Mary's Altar)—notice St. Dionysius (1st figure from left) holding his head. *Hours:* Wed thru Mon (closed Tue) 10:00-12:00 & 15:00-17:00. *Getting There:* St. Aposteln is located at the west end of Neumarkt.

ENTERTAINMENT

A prerequisite for any visit to Cologne is to patronize one of the city's numerous multilevel, half-timbered **Brauhäuser**, a traditional Germanic brasserie offering regional cuisine, flavorsome brew and smoke-enriched Gemütlichkeit. The local beer is called Kölsch, served in a slender 200ml glass called a "Stange." Although, where Cologne lacks in size, it is made up in service. In a traditional Kölsch establishment the waiter (*Köbes*) darts from table to table doling out beers from a 10-glass tray known as a "Kranz," which resembles the cylinder of a western-style revolver. There are numerous Brauhäuser in Cologne, two of the most popular are situated near the Dom: **Früh am Dom** and **Alt-Köln** (head upstairs for Dom views). A Stange of Kölsch roughly costs 1.45€.

Less traditional and more avant-garde, the **university scene** can be found in the southwest part of town, where budget eateries and watering holes inundate the area around Zülpicher Str. and Luxemburger Str.

The **Köln-Arena**, which opened in 1998 and has 18,000 seats, is Germany's largest and most modern multifunctional hall. As well as being home to Cologne's hockey team, "Kölner Haie" (the Sharks), the Arena hosts big-name concerts, e.g. Madonna, U2, Springsteen. The Köln-Arena is located on the east bank of the Rhine, near Köln-Deutz train station.

Hard Rock Café fans go to Gürzenichstr. 8 (from the Dom head five minutes along Hohe Str. [shopping street] to find Gürzenichstr., then make a left and it's some 50m on the right). *Hours:* daily — merchandise shop from 10:00 / restaurant from 12:00. *Tel.#* 0221/272-6880 (www.hardrock.com)

Caffeine addicts looking for a **Starbucks** will find one opposite Früh am Dom Brauhaus. *Hours:* daily, 9:00-22:00. *Price:* Caffé Mocha (tall) 3.50€, Latte (tall) 3€, Cappuccino (tall) 3€. *Getting There:* When facing Dom, go right along Hohe Str. (shopping street) and make first left.

Headline Concerts, Cologne 2006

Note: Prices, dates, concerts may have changed or been added — for the latest details query TI (ticket agency downstairs, tel.# 0221/2212-6129) or Köln Ticket (tel.# 0221/2801, www.koelnticket.de)

Eros Ramazzotti: May 19, 20:00 at the Köln-Arena. Price 41-55€
Santana: May 23, 20:00 at the Köln-Arena. Price 61€
James Blunt: July 11, 19:00 (open air) Am Tanzbrunnen. Price 38€
Eric Clapton: July 13, 20:00 at the Köln-Arena. Price 58-70€
Rolling Stones: July 23, 19:00 at Rhein-Energie Stadium. Price 87-207€
Robbie Williams: August 8-9, 18:30 at Rhein-Energie Stadium. Price 71-81€
Pink: October 19, 20:00 at the Köln-Arena. Price 44-53€
James Last: November 24, 20:00 at the Köln-Arena. Price 40-72€

Events/Festivals 2006

Karneval, February 23-27 (Thur-Mon): A time of fools and fun, Karneval is Germany's answer to Brazil's Carnival in Rio (known as "Fasching" in southern Germany and Austria). More than a million visitors converge on Cologne for the five-day fest, fervently referred to as the "fifth season" or "crazy days." The crazy season officially kicks off at 11:11 on November 11 and culminates on Rosenmontag (Monday before Lent, main carnival day) with mounds of music, beer, sausages, schnapps and kissing. The latter indulgences begin with Weiberfastnacht, Thursday before Lent, when women rule the city chopping men's ties off without the possibility of retribution. Merriment of this sort will continue over the weekend to Rosenmontag, when miles of ornamented floats, marching bands, disciplined horses, and costume-clad dancers make their way past a million people shouting for candy and flowers. Interested? Reserve your accommodations a year in advance.

World Cup Soccer: Cologne has five matches scheduled: Sunday **June 11**, *Angola vs. Portugal* • Saturday **June 17**, *Ghana vs. Czech Rep.* • Tuesday **June 20**, *England vs. Sweden* • Friday **June 23**, *France vs. Togo* • Monday **June 26**, *Round 16*. The matches will be played at Cologne's 46,000-seat Rhein-Energie Stadium, located 7km west of the Old Town.

Christopher Street Day (CSD), July 14-16 (Fri-Sun): Cologne's CSD carnival and parade is the largest "queer" event of its kind in Europe, where you'll witness colorful fantasy costumes and scores of male hard bodies and women on women. This sizzling event opens (Fri 18:00) with a street festival offering music, food, drink and knickknack stands, and climaxes high noon on Sunday with the commencement of the gay-pride parade. Approximately 750,000 people will attend the three-day bonanza.

Kölner-Lichter (Cologne Lights), July 29 (Sat): Mega candle and sparkler and firework party, illuminating Cologne. Nearly 1 million people will take part in this spectacle of light, including some 50 tour ships from the Rhine fleet lit up like Christmas trees. One of the evening's many highlights is when the thousands of spectators gathered upon the bridges greet the arrival of the Rhine fleet by tossing sparklers over the railings giving the impression of a luminous waterfall. Capping off Kölner-Lichter is an explosive firework show synchronized with music.

Ringfest Köln, August 25-27 (Fri-Sun): During this three-day event around 150 bands will perform on multiple stages across the city for more than 1 million people, qualifying the Ringfest as the world's largest open-air music festival. *FREE* entry!

Bierbörse (Beer Exchange), August 25-27 (Fri-Sun): For beer lovers, this event is glorious—imagine a gigantic beer garden where you can sample several hundred varieties of brew from all over the globe. The Bierbörse will be held in the shopping/pedestrian area of Neumarkt. For more info, or other cities hosting a Bierbörse, or the history of beer, go to www.bierboerse.com

Cologne Marathon, October 8 (Sun): More than 20,000 participants will take part in this year's 42km leg-burning marathon. Interested applicants go to www.koeln-marathon.de for details on how to register (Anmelden).

Christmas Markets: Typically the last week of November until December 21-23—hours, daily, 11:00-21:00. Don't forget to collect a *Glühwein* mug.

There are several markets in Cologne to talk about. The most visited is *Markt am Dom,* set up around the cathedral. Another Christmas bazaar is at the *Alter Markt,* adjacent to the Rathaus. The next two markets are unusual to say the least. Along the Altstadt Rhine promenade a ship will be docked offering a *floating Christmas market—*

2€ admission. And lastly, head to the chocolate museum to experience a _medieval market_; it's small but worth a visit—2€ admission. _Hours:_ Tue-Sun 11:00-21:00.

Those who wish to escape the city crunch and venture out to a castle, consider the historical Christmas market at _Burg Satzvey_, Advent weekends only—4€ admission. Burg Satzvey is located 55km southwest of Cologne.

GOOD SLEEPS
From youth hostel fare to hotels extraordinaire

Note: Expect to see inflated room rates or the "no vacancy" signs out during the World Cup soccer tournament, chiefly June 9-28 in Cologne. Fans in desperate need of a room check out this website: www.host-a-fan.de

Hostel, Station: Marzellenstr. 44-48 (www.hostel-cologne.de) _Tel.#_ 0221/912-5301. Backpackers will appreciate Station hostel, as it's conveniently situated around the corner (two minutes) from the main train station and offers a washer/dryer, self-service kitchen, and _free_ Internet! Beer, soda, a-la-carte breakfast, and other knickknacks available at reception. _Price:_ (includes linen) dorm bed 16-19€, Sgl 28-35€, Dbl 42-50€. _Note:_ Cash only! _Getting There: Railers_—exit station on the Dom side (by track 1), veer right and ascend road paralleling the taxis. Turn right at the traffic circle and the hostel is roughly 130m on the right. _GPS:_ N50° 56.629 - E6° 57.355

Hostel, Köln-Deutz Jugendherberge: [HI] (www.djh.de) _Tel.#_ 0221/814-711. This stellar property, revamped for the 21st century, is a must-see for youth-hostel enthusiasts. All 157 rooms—totaling 506 beds—have a shower and toilet. _Price:_ (includes linen, breakfast) dorm bed 23.30€, Sgl 40€, Dbl 60€. _CC's:_ VC, MC. _Note:_ Must be a member or an extra charge will apply. _Getting There: Railers,_ hostel is located across from the Köln-Deutz train station. Or, from the main train station, walk across the railway bridge (Hohenzollernbrücke), 15 min. _Drivers,_ secure parking available—enter at back of property.

Hotel Heinzelmännchen: (Hotel of the Elves) Hohe Pforte 5-7. _Tel.#_ 0221/211-217. (www.hotel-heinzelmaennchen.com) Here you'll find a wonderfully quaint inner-city dwelling, run by the Schmahl family. Ute Schmahl, master of the elves, will be your attentive hostess. She takes great pride in her comfortably cute rooms, which all have toilet and shower. Additionally, Internet is free for guests. _Price:_ (breakfast buffet included) Sgl 40-45€, Dbl 65-70€, Trpl 80-85€ (during conventions add 15-40%). _CC's:_ VC, MC. _Getting There: Railers,_ from the main train station it's a 15-min walk. Pass Dom and ramble to other end of Hohe Str. (shopping street). Continue straight through the intersection at Pipinstr. to Hohe Pforte and the Heinzelmännchen will soon appear on your right. Or, by bus from the station, catch bus #132 direction Meschenich and get off at Waidmarkt. Exit bus right, go straight across intersection and your digs are on the left. _Drivers,_ parking is near hotel and free; query reception. _GPS:_ N50° 55.984 - E6° 57.375

Hotel ibis: (www.ibishotel.com) Clean, reasonably priced and well located, the ibis chain has two amiable Cologne hotels worth mentioning. _Note:_ Parking, breakfast cost extra. *Hotel code is compatible with ibis website, creating a shortcut to the property—type hotel code into middle left box and click "OK"; next page click "The Hotel" (left side).

ibis am Dom: _Tel.#_ 0221/912-8580; *hotel code 0739. Snugly situated in the main train station (Dom side—near track 1), this property couldn't have a better, more convenient locale. _Price:_ Sgl 77€, Dbl 92€—during conventions 109€/129€.

ibis Messe: Brügelmannstr. 1, tel.# 0221/989-310; *hotel code 3744. This newly opened property (Nov. 2003) is situated on the east bank of the Rhine, 10-min walk from the Köln-Deutz train station. _Price:_ Sgl/Dbl 47-56€—during conventions 119-139€.

Hilton: Marzellenstr. 13-17 (www.hilton.com) *Tel.#* 0221/130-710, toll-free reservations from USA/Canada 1-800-445-8667 or within Europe 00800-4445-8667. This refurbished property is situated in the heart of the city; the proverbial stone's throw from the Dom and main train station. *Price:* Sgl from 149€, Dbl from 179€—parking 22€, breakfast 19€. *Getting There: Railers*—exit station on the Dom side (by track 1), veer right and ascend road paralleling the taxis. Turn right at the traffic circle and the Hilton is across the street. *GPS:* N50° 56.600 - E6° 57.355

Dom Hotel: (www.lemeridien-domhotel.com) *Tel.#* 0221/20-240, toll-free reservations from USA/Canada 1-800-543-4300 or within Germany 0800-294-4000. Nestled on the footsteps of the Dom, this upmarket hotel exudes comfort and sophistication, having been ensconced in Cologne's culture as one of the top European addresses for more than 140 years. Recently, the Dom Hotel underwent renovations worth 8.5€ million and all rooms are now expensively outfitted with plasma flat-panel TVs, high-speed Internet, and Italian-marble bathrooms. *Price:* Sgl from 150, Dbl from 170€ (Internet rate), suite 450-1200€—breakfast 20€, parking 18€ (public garage under Dom).

EXCURSIONS

Bonn: *(Pop. 310,000 ~ Area Code: -0228)* Dating from Roman times, Bonn has a rich history, famously as the birthplace of Ludwig van Beethoven and more recently (1949-90) as the Cold War capital of West Germany. Located 27km upstream from Cologne, Bonn is easily reached by car, boat, or via the interconnected suburban rail (S-Bahn). Within the Old Town, points of interest include the 13th-century Romanesque Münster (cathedral) and the Beethoven Haus (adult 4€, student 3€. Open daily, Mon-Sat 10:00-17:00 [April-Oct till 18:00], Sun 11:00-17:00). The TI, P.O., WC, Beethoven Haus, Beethoven monument, cathedral, and entertaining street musicians can all be found on or near the sizeable Münsterplatz, minutes from Bonn's main train station. Beethoven's mother is buried in the nearby Alter Friedhof; Ludwig van is buried in Vienna (page 458). *TI:* Münsterplatz, tel.# 0228/775-000 (www.bonn-region.de) *Hours:* Mon-Fri 9:00-18:30, Sat 9:00-16:00, Sun 10:00-14:00.

Remagen: *(Pop. 7000 ~ Area Code: -02642)* This unassuming settlement on the Rhine's left (west) bank is 42km upstream from Cologne, 20km from Bonn. Recently (in 2001) Remagen celebrated its 2000th birthday. However, it's the history of the town's 20th-century railroad bridge that caught the world's attention, spawning numerous books and a Hollywood movie: "The Bridge at Remagen" (MGM 1969; George Segal, Robert Vaughn, Ben Gazzara).

By the early months of 1945, Hitler's armies had been widely routed on both fronts, the Eastern and Western. After a series of bloody offensives, the Russians beat the Germans from the gates of Moscow to the outskirts of Berlin. The story was much the same in the west, the Allies liberated France following the invasion of Normandy and the Germans continued their retreat with their backs to the borders of the Reich—the Rhine River stood as the last natural barrier between the Allied juggernaut and the interior of Germany. Strategically, there was only one option: Hitler ordered all bridges be destroyed on the Rhine. Without delay, the order was fanatically carried out and all river crossings were blown—except for one.

On March 7, 1945, forward elements of the U.S. 9th Armored Division (First Army) couldn't believe their eyes when, through a pair of binoculars, they witnessed remnants of the German army fleeing across the Rhine on an intact bridge. Wasting no time, the Americans swarmed Remagen surprising the defenders. In a Herculean effort under withering enemy fire, specialist GIs ran like hell across the bridge cutting demolition cables. The Germans only had enough time to ignite two charges; both failed to collapse the bridge. Consequently, U.S. forces secured a bridgehead and some 8000 troops crossed within the first 24 hours, gaining a foothold on the Rhine's east bank—a feat no enemy had achieved since Napoleon in 1805. When news reached Nazi central command that the bridge had been captured intact, Hitler flew into a sadistic rage and sentenced the five responsible officers to death. The Germans were bent on rectifying their blunder and employed desperate attempts to destroy the bridge by means of field artillery, suicide pilots, and even underwater frogmen. On March 17, 10 days after the initial battle, the bridge at Remagen succumbed to external pressurcs and collapsed, killing 28 American soldiers. By this time pontoon bridges had been set up and the Allied juggernaut was already sweeping across the German heartland, hastening the end of the war in Europe. The "Miracle of Remagen" was globally hailed as one of the single greatest events of WWII. Eisenhower summed up the universal mood when he stated, "The bridge is worth its weight in gold." Today, all that remains of the bridge at Remagen are four support towers, two on either bank. The twin towers on the west bank have been converted into the *Friedensmuseum* (Peace Museum), an exhibition of war and peace worthy of your time—follow signs "Brücke von Remagen."

Getting There: Auto: Remagen is an easy drive from Cologne. *Boat:* Not recommended. *Train:* There are regular train connections between Remagen and Cologne (45-min trip, 9.10€ one way). Remagen's station is centrally located, meters from the main pedestrian zone, five-minute walk from the TI, and a 20-min walk from the battle-scarred Brücke von Remagen. *Note:* Upon exiting the train station, the road to the right is Geschwister-Scholl-Str. Do you remember this "White Rose" duo?

TI: Kirchstr. 6 (www.remagen.de) *Tel.#* 02642/20-187. *Hours:* Mon-Thur 8:30-12:00 & 14:00-16:00, Fri 8:30-12:00, Sat/Sun 11:00-14:00. *Getting There: Railers* (five-min walk)—exit station straight into Josefstr., at the end go left on Marktstr. Once the pedestrian zone ends, the TI is on the right.

Friedensmuseum: "Peace Museum" is well described in English—expect a visit to take at least 60 min. (www.bruecke-remagen.de) *Hours:* March-Nov, daily, 10:00-17:00 (May-Oct till 18:00), closed winter. *Price:* adult 3.50€, student 1€. *Getting There: Railers* (20-min walk)—exit station straight into Josefstr., at the end go right on Marktstr. and then first left on Postgasse. Once at the Rhine, go right along the riverside promenade to reach the bridge's landmark towers. *Drivers,* follow signs Brücke von Remagen. *GPS:* N50° 34.689 - E7° 14.645

Schwarzen Madonna: One kilometer south of the bridge (off Goethestr.) is the six-pointed "Black Madonna Memorial Chapel," commemorating the site where 300,000 German POWs were detained from April to July 1945. *GPS:* N50° 34.348 - E7° 15.322

WWII Buffs: Adolf Galland is buried in Oberwinter (4km north of Remagen, 10km south of Bonn)—page 463.

Aachen: *(Pop. 255,000 ~ Area Code: -0241 ~ Sister City: Arlington, Virginia)* History buffs who will be in the Benelux region should plan a jaunt through Aachen. This historical city lies 70km west of Cologne, sharing borders with Belgium and the Netherlands. It was here that Karl der Große (Charlemagne), king of the Franks, chose as his imperial seat in the 8th century, when he ruled Western Europe in the name of the Carolingian dynasty and initiated the Holy Roman Empire. For that reason, Aachen, or Aix-la-Chapelle as the French call it, saw some 30 emperors of the Holy Roman Empire crowned between the 9th to 16th centuries.

During the French Revolution (1789-99), Aachen was occupied by revolutionary forces and later ceded to France. After the defeat of Napoleon in 1815, Aix-la-Chapelle became a possession of Prussia. In 1940, it was from this sector that Hitler launched his legendary blitzkrieg into Belgium and northern France. Five years later, Aachen was the first German city captured by U.S. forces.

In all honesty, greater Aachen is nothing to rave about—its Old Town, though, is somethin' special. Sites of interest include the **Dom** (cathedral) and the 14th-century Rathaus built on the ruins of Charlemagne's palace. The Dom is a must-see site, so extraordinary that it's been added to UNESCO's World Heritage List. Prior to the year 800, Charlemagne commissioned the widely celebrated **Pfalzkapelle** (Palatine Chapel, a.k.a. the Octagon), now the Dom's central axis and a masterpiece of Carolingian architecture. In 814 A.D. the Pfalzkapelle became Charlemagne's final resting place. For more on Charlemagne, flip to page 455.

<u>*TI*</u>*:* Friedrich-Wilhelm-Pl. (10-min walk from main train station), tel.# 0241/180-2960 (www.aachen.de) *Hours:* Mon-Fri 9:00-18:00, Sat 9:00-14:00, (open Sundays in summer).

<u>*ABMC*</u>*:* (American Battle Monuments Commission) U.S. readers refer to our website—your-traveling-companion.com—for info on the two nearby ABMC cemeteries: "Netherlands" and "Henri-Chapelle."

BERLIN

~ Population: 3.4 million   ~ Elevation: 35m/114ft
~ Country/Area Code: +49-(0)30
~ Total area 892 sq. km (slightly bigger than Dallas, TX)
~ Sister City: Los Angeles, CA • Charleston, SC • London, England

Before you die, visit Berlin! It's a fascinating old city. A place where you don't just see the history, it's happening before your very eyes. Berlin is constantly reinventing itself, and if you stand still long enough, you'll miss the latest changes. Berlin is a dream, and to many it is a miracle. It has a unique past unparalleled in history: medieval Berlin, imperial Berlin, Huguenot Berlin, the Kaiser's Berlin, industrial Berlin, Weimar Berlin, Bauhaus Berlin, Nazi Berlin, bombed-out Berlin, Cold War Berlin, and reunified Berlin — a modern reincarnation of its former glory.

Unlike other important cities, Berlin did not develop on the banks of a major river like the Rhine or the Danube nor did it succeed a former Roman colony.

Berlin was first mentioned in 1237 as Cölln, a settlement of merchants (encamped on what is today Museum Island) scraping out a living via the east-west trade route on the insignificant Spree River. From these humble beginnings grew one of the great cities of Europe.

From 1618 to 1648 the Thirty Years' War ruined Berlin, sinking its remaining population of 6000 into poverty. Berlin rebounded in the latter part of the century when Frederick William—member of the Hohenzollern royal family—fortified the community and established it as a major center for trade and finance. Equally as significant, in 1685, Frederick William welcomed large numbers of Huguenots, French Protestant refugees, to help develop Berlin's struggling economy with their much-needed skills. When the flood of immigrants subsided, one out of every five Berliners would be a French Protestant. In 1701, Frederick I—son of Frederick William—became the first king of Prussia, a kingdom fused together from various Germanic and eastern European territories inherited by the Hohenzollerns. Under Frederick I, Berlin became the capital of Prussia and the seat of the Hohenzollern royal family. During the reign of the next Hohenzollern monarch, Frederick II (the Great), Prussia emerged as a powerful empire and Berlin's economy thrived with an industrious population of 150,000.

In 1806, Napoleon's Grand Armée invaded Prussia and French forces occupied Berlin. Upon Napoleon's defeat in 1814, Prussia was reestablished as one of the leading powers among the German territories. These territories aligned in 1870 and easily conquered France in the Franco-Prussian War (1870-71). The Prussian king, William I, and a Prussian statesman, Otto von Bismarck, convinced the rulers of the German territories to band together to form a single, unified nation. Thus began the Deutsches Reich, or German empire, with Berlin and its 1 million inhabitants as Germany's capital.

The industrial age heartily gripped Berlin and its population exploded, attracting some 270 new residents daily. By the turn of the 20th century, the German capital was accommodating a whopping 3.5 million citizens. In 1914 World War I began, paralyzing the nation and the continent. Four years later, Germany lost the war and consequently its last Hohenzollern king, William II, or infamously Kaiser Wilhelm, when he was forced to abandon the throne and Berlin—ending the Deutsches Reich.

Post-war Germany had to produce a new government. The Weimar Republic was born (1919-1933) with Berlin once again as the nation's capital. During the 1920s, despite economic turmoil plaguing the country, Berlin prospered via the arts: architecture, film, theater and literature.

During the next decade, Berlin—and Germany—took a woeful turn with the election of the National Socialists to power. In 1933, Berlin would literally be blown away by the Nazi menace: Adolf Hitler. The goofy-mustached dictator banned all political parties and axed Berlin's successful artistic community. Hitler believed in reviving the Deutsches Reich and reestablishing Germany as a military power while regaining territories lost to the victors of World War I. Amazingly, the victors—Britain, France, USA—watched while Hitler did exactly that. Little did they know, Hitler planned his Reich to last 1000 years.

In 1936, the Olympics came to Berlin. The stadium (page 376), which still stands, was built especially for the games. Hitler—with help from his primary architect, Albert Speer—planned to redevelop Berlin into a mega-metropolis of more than 10 million residents that he would call "Germania," the capital of Fascist Europe. (Prior to World War II, Berlin's population was 4.5 million—about 1 million more than today.)

Rejecting Hitler's scheme, U.S. and British strategic bombers engaged in round-the-clock saturation bombing transforming Berlin into an urban wasteland. In April 1945, the Soviets unleashed more than 1 million soldiers into the capital sparking the Battle for Berlin, the final battle of World War II in Europe. Hitler committed suicide in his bunker (page 362) on April 30 and the war concluded a week later on May 8, 1945, when Nazi Germany capitulated in the suburb of Karlshorst. (The signing chamber can be viewed in its original condition; see page 380—*German-Russian Museum*.)

Following the Nazi surrender, Berlin—and Germany—was divided into four zones of occupation by the war victors. The Soviets controlled the eastern part of Berlin/ Germany while the Allies (USA, Britain and France) governed the western part of Berlin/ Germany. By mid-1948 tensions were high between the Soviets and Allies, resulting in the Soviets blockading their zone—the eastern part of Germany—from the Allies, essentially cutting off Berlin. The Allies responded with the Berlin Airlift, 1948-49 (page 346—*Tempelhof*). Upon the conclusion of the airlift, two ideologically different countries emerged. In September 1949, the three Allied zones of occupation in the democratic west collectively became the Federal Republic of Germany (FRG, or West Germany) with Bonn as its capital. The following month, the totalitarian rule of the Soviet Union responded with the establishment of the German Democratic Republic (GDR, or East Germany) and East Berlin as its capital. With the two sides firmly entrenched, the Cold War began in earnest.

In the wee hours of August 13, 1961, GDR soldiers encircled West Berlin with makeshift barriers that infamously became known as the Berlin Wall. Fear gripped the city. All power, gas, water, telephone, subway and road connections stopped dead at the east-west boundary. From the mid-'60s, the GDR stepped-up its containment program with high-tech defenses and a reinforced concrete wall—13-feet high and rounded at the top so it couldn't be gripped—replacing the original bricks-and-mortar barrier. Making escape impossible, behind the new wall a wide area of land was bulldozed—likened to no-man's land but nicknamed the "death strip"—and landscaped with antitank defenses, self-firing guns, barbed wire, minefields, spotlights and watchtowers positioned before another concrete wall deeper in East Berlin (page 354—*The Wall*).

When John F. Kennedy came to Berlin in 1963, he was celebrated like a rock star. The president brought hope to the citizens of West Berlin who were living in a city sealed-off from the free world, deep within Soviet-backed East Germany and only 40 miles from Communist Poland. Times were difficult—even desperate—and hundreds of thousands of people came to hear the leader of the free world speak. Kennedy delivered a poignant speech, one that made history: "…All free men, wherever they may live, are citizens of Berlin, and, therefore, as a free man, I take pride in the words *Ich bin ein Berliner*." (page 375)

The Berlin Wall was the demarcation line between the West and East, democracy and communism, economic prosperity and grinding repression, good and evil. Germany was essentially two countries sharing the same language, history, and traditions but torn apart by political creed.

In 1987 another American president came to Berlin, this time it was Ronald Reagan. He boldly stood before the Brandenburg Gate and declared: "…General Secretary Gorbachev, if you seek peace, if you seek prosperity for the Soviet Union and Eastern Europe, if you seek liberalization: Come here, to this gate. Mr. Gorbachev, open this gate. Mr. Gorbachev, tear – down – this – wall!" (Taken from the *Do-it-yourself walking tour—Central Berlin* beginning on page 360.)

Two years later, in 1989, the East German regime collapsed and the Wall indeed fell, disappearing under a sea of revelers celebrating "die Wende": the end of Socialism. The two Germanys officially reunited on October 3, 1990—thus the Day of German Unity became a national holiday.

The reunified German government chose the sentimental favorite, Berlin, to be the nation's capital. Administration offices were either newly constructed or totally refurbished. An ultramodern chancellery building was erected and parliament moved into the must-see Reichstag (page 357). During the shuffle, the new government realized that 40 years of separate development had created a number of technical headaches in the East that had to be resolved. Not just the dismantling of the Wall, but phone lines had to be updated to handle the flow of modern fax and data traffic; power cables, gas lines, streets and the subway had to be reconnected; maps redrawn; electrical grids refitted to supply normal amperage to keep clocks running on time; and sewers had to be unblocked that were sealed to prevent escapes.

On the upside, Berlin found itself with the unique problem of having three opera houses, two zoos, several museum quarters, three airports, two commercial districts, a pair of central rail stations, and so on.

Post-reunification, Berlin qualified as Europe's biggest construction zone, and over the past 15 years more than $1.25 trillion has been poured into the former Communist East, with most of the cash landing in Berlin's lap.

As you can imagine, Berlin's cultural landscape is rivaled by few cities. Moreover, the air is like cocaine: addictive and euphoric. Come here, and indulge in a feast of historic sites and fascinating experiences. To say you made a wise decision would be an understatement! And since the city's budget is busted, Berlin will be your cheapest metropolitan stop in Germany.

Keep in mind, state-run museums (page 377) are closed Mondays and free to enter every Thursday four hours before closing and Sundays are terrific for bric-a-brac bazaars (page 387—*Flea Markets*). What's more, this year Berlin is hosting six World Cup soccer matches (page 389), including a quarter-final and the final. Oh, and with this book our buddy Ahmet will dish you up a thick, juicy Döner Kebap for a mere 1.25€! Yes, that's right, 1.25€ (page 388—*Döner Kebap*).

Berlin is simply humongous, a real metropolis with umpteen attractions to visit. To spend a month here would hardly be enough time to see everything. However, the average tourist doesn't have the luxury of an open-ended schedule—thus the following cut-to-the-chase itinerary nails the significant sites on the premise of a four-day stay. Maximize your time and start early!

~ Mood and weather permitting, divide your time like so,

<u>*Day 1:*</u> [**Orientation**] First things first, acquire an ultra-essential city map—either from your accommodations or the TI. Next, to familiarize yourself with Berlin, choose a tour that best suits your taste (page 349—*Tours*). Upon the conclusion of your tour, begin visiting attractions of interest listed in any of the four *Sights* sections, or check out a *World-Class Auto Showroom* (page 383), or if it's a Thursday take advantage of free entry into a state-run museum (last four hours before closing—see *Museums, State* page 377), or head over to one of the *Best Views* (page 384) and admire the beauty of Berlin as the sun slips away for the evening.

<u>*Day 2:*</u> [**Heart of Berlin**] Now that you're better acquainted with the layout of Berlin, spend a day taking in the sights from the Reichstag to Alexanderplatz to Potsdamer Platz (page 357—*Sights, Central Berlin.* DIY tour begins on page 360).

<u>*Day 3:*</u> [**The Wall**] A trip to Berlin would not be complete without visiting a preserved section of the infamous Berlin Wall (page 354). This won't take all day so combine other activities here.

<u>*Day 4:*</u> [**Culture Vultures**] Berlin abounds with world-class museums; devote at least one full day for this activity (see *Museums* beginning on page 377). *Note:* State-run museums are closed Mondays and free to enter every Thursday four hours before closing.

<u>*Day 5:*</u> [**Excursion**] Travelers who have extra time, spend a day outside of Berlin and visit Potsdam and Wannsee (you can do both but leave early) or visit Sachsenhausen (concentration camp memorial)—see *Excursions* beginning on page 392, Potsdam follows. For an unforgettable sporting experience, consider going to a soccer game in the Olympic stadium (page 376).

<u>**Tourist Information:**</u> [TI] (www.btm.de) *Tel.#* 030/250-025
There are three TIs (and one EurAide) in Berlin, covering east to west. Info sources such as these are priceless in such a vast city. Since the TIs in Berlin are privately owned they refer to their branches as "info-stores," which act essentially the same as a normal TI but with just more opportunity to purchase souvenirs and T-shirts. They also sell city maps (1€), concert tickets, book tours, and have a room-finding service (3€). *Note:* TI hours are further extended April thru Oct from what's written below. Railers arriving at "Zoo" station see EurAide.

<u>*TI:*</u> *Europa-Center,* (main branch, five-minute walk from Bahnhof Zoo). *Hours:* Mon-Sat 10:00-19:00, Sun 10:00-18:00. *Getting There:* exit "Zoo" train station into Hardenbergplatz; from this lively area go right and cross Hardenbergstr.—to your left you'll see the famous church (with severed steeple) still remaining from the shattered ruins of WWII Berlin. Just beyond the church is the Europa-Center shopping mall (with rotating Mercedes icon on roof)—the TI is below, enter on Budapester Str.

<u>*TI:*</u> *Brandenburg Gate* (you can see the TI sign [red square, white "i"] on the front cover of this book, left side). *Hours:* daily, 10:00-18:00.

<u>*TI:*</u> *Fernsehturm.* This TI is located at the base of the sky-high disco ball ("TV-Tower") on Alexanderplatz. *Hours:* daily, 10:00-18:00.

<u>*EurAide:*</u> Another option for valuable information is the EurAide office, located within the "Zoo" train station (a stop here would negate the need to visit a TI). EurAide is partnered with the German rail authority—Deutsche Bahn—and is staffed by native English-speakers. ***Railers,*** take advantage of this source to ask any questions concerning travel by rail, e.g. connections, routes, ticket purchase, reservations (incl. overnight couchettes/sleepers), and EurAide can help with any queries you may have regarding

your railpass—they can even validate it. Additionally, they sell city maps, subway/bus tickets, and book tours. *Hours:* (tend to vary, may differ from what's written) June-Oct, daily, 8:00-12:00 & 13:00-18:00; rest of year Mon-Fri 8:00-12:00 & 13:00-16:45. *Getting There:* In "Zoo" station, EurAide is positioned in the DB Reisezentrum, facing Hardenbergplatz.

Emergency Tel. Numbers: [Germany-wide]
    Police (Polizei) = 110
    Fire dept. (Feuerwehr) or general emergency = 112
    Ambulance = 19222

Hauptbahnhof: [Hbf] Presently, Berlin doesn't have one "main train station" per se, instead the city divides its attention between two long-distance rail hubs: **Zoologischer Garten** (a.k.a. Bahnhof Zoo) located in West Berlin—or the more modern **Ostbahnhof**, located in East Berlin. If you're not sure where to disembark, shoot for trendy East Berlin. However, either station is well connected to the rest of the city via the subway (U-/S-Bahn). *Note:* The construction of Berlin's Lehrter Bahnhof, Europe's largest train station, is due to be completed in May 2006, eventually busting the aforesaid stations.

Parking: Berlin's public transportation system is so handy and efficient that the best option here is to park your car and leave it. Prices vary on street parking citywide but generally 50¢/30min Mon-Fri 9:00-19:00, Sat 9:00-14:00—otherwise free. Pay at nearby "Parkschein Automat" and leave ticket on dashboard of your car. To park in a garage, follow the blue-and-white "P" signs (roughly 1.50€/hr, 13€/24hr). To avoid the city entirely, leave your car at a P+R (Park+Ride) on the outskirts and ride the subway in.

Subway/Bus: Berlin's integrated and efficient transit authority (BVG, www.bvg.de) governs an enormous urban network — the largest in Europe, in fact, consisting of 13,000 employees, umpteen buses, 151km of U-Bahn (Underground) tracks and 321km of S-Bahn (Suburban) tracks — utilized by nearly 1 billion commuters per year. Stop in at any BVG info point for your free map of the network.

The BVG network is divided into three zones: A, B and C. Zone (**A**) is the city proper, framed by the orbiting S-Bahn lines S41 and S42. The middle zone (**B**), extending a bit farther outside of Berlin, includes such noteworthy stops as Wannsee, Spandau, Magdalenenstr. (Stasi HQ), Olympic Stadium, and the airports TXL and SXF. The outer zone (**C**), extending to the fringes of greater Berlin and beyond, reaches Sachsenhausen (concentration camp memorial) and the city of Potsdam.

The following tickets cover every mode of transportation in the BVG network; prices range according to zones of travel.

Short Trip: (Kurzestrecke) Valid for up to three stops on S- and U-Bahn, or six stops on a bus/tram. Price: 1.20€.

Single Ticket: (EinzelTicket) For use within two hours. Can get on/off as you like but only in the same, one-way direction—zones AB 2.10€, ABC 2.60€.

Day Ticket: (Tageskarte) For use from time of validation until 3 a.m. the following morning—zones AB 5.80€, ABC 6€.

7-Day-Ticket: Great value for longer stays, plus the ticket is transferable so others can use it. For use from time of validation until midnight on the 7th day—zones AB 25.40€, ABC 31.30€. *Note:* This ticket is not available for purchase on buses or trams.

Small Group Ticket: (Kleingruppenkarte) Excellent deal! Valid for up to 5 people from time of validation until 3 a.m.—zones AB 14.80€, ABC 15€.

City Tour Card: This is similar to the Welcome Card (page 347) except that it's only valid for zones AB. If you have no excursions planned for any sites in zone C, buy this card—otherwise the Welcome Card is recommended. Price: AB 15€/48hr, AB 20€/72hr.

Note: All ticket types can be purchased at vending machines marked Fahrscheine/ Tickets, button for English. *Tickets must be stamped in yellow (or red) box to validate, "hier entwerten," watch locals.* (For buses, buy ticket from driver.) Travelers riding without valid ticket risk fines upwards of 60€, on the spot! Plain-clothed officials patrol subway constantly! Holders of a Eurail consecutive-day or dated Flexi/Select pass ride *free* on the S-Bahn.

Suggestion: If you're lost in Berlin, bus stops typically post a detailed map of the city with the local area circled.

Airport: (Flughafen; www.berlin-airport.de) Berlin may be one of the world's major capital cities, but there are few direct flights into the metropolis from overseas. To arrive in either of Berlin's two commercial airports (TXL or SXF), the chances are you're going to have to first land elsewhere in Europe (e.g. FRA, LHR, AMS) and catch a connecting flight.

Tegel [TXL]: Located 8km northwest of the city center, Tegel is the main airport serving the majority of Berlin's air traffic. Regular buses run to/fro the city. The TXL express bus is the quickest connection to the Brandenburg Gate (30 min) or Alexander-platz — the X9 express shuttles to/fro Bahnhof Zoo (20 min). Or short bus connections to/fro U7 Jakob-Kaiser-Platz, U6 Kurt-Schumacher-Platz. A taxi into the city will cost circa 18€.

Schönefeld [SXF]: Located 18km southeast of the city center, Schönefeld airfield was employed by the Soviets post-WWII to serve the then GDR, including East Berlin. Today, it is the preferred airport for smaller carriers like RyanAir (www.ryanair.com) and EasyJet (www.easyjet.com). With either carrier from London, Schönefeld is usually the cheapest avenue into the German capital. Within Germany (i.e. from Cologne or Stuttgart) fly the domestic airline GermanWings(.com). The nearby S-Bahn (S9) and railway (DB) station connect Schönefeld with Berlin (station is a five-minute walk from the airport, or ask for the free shuttle bus). A taxi into the city will cost circa 27€. Or, depending on where you're headed in Berlin, hop on bus #171 (departs out front of terminal) and take it several stops to Rudow (U7)—don't worry about missing the stop, most people on board will be getting off here.

Tempelhof [THF]: Located 6km south of the city center, Tempelhof is the oldest of Berlin's three airports (1923) and registers as the largest single building in Europe (length 1.23km; floor space 300,000sq.m./74 acres). Besides its age and size, Tempelhof is chiefly recognized for its role during the Berlin Airlift (1948-49)—when the Soviets blockaded East Germany from the western Allies, essentially cutting off Berlin. The Allies responded by organizing a massive system of air transport to supply the western sectors of Berlin, which became known as the Berlin Airlift (or Luftbrücke in German). So-called "raisin bombers" (DC-3) landed at Tempelhof every 90 seconds in an unprece-dented effort to deliver the several million tons of food and relief supplies necessary to sustain the cut-off sectors. Today, Tempelhof is largely closed to commercial traffic and won't play much of a roll for the general tourist. For aviation buffs, stop by and marvel at history. If you travel between the stations Tempelhof and Hermannstr. on the S41/42 you'll get a good look at the enormity of the airfield. *Tours* of the structure are usually possible but in German, 6€/person. Call ahead to inquire: tel.# 030/6091-1660. Air tours from THF are also possible (page 351). *Getting There:* U6 Platz der Luftbrücke (Airlift Square). *Note:* Outside the U-Bahn station is a park dedicated to the airlift. The large, claw-like memorial reads: "They gave their lives for the freedom of Berlin during the airlift of 1948-49." Adjacent are the 71 names of the Allied personnel who died.

Share Ride: *(Mitfahrzentrale; a concept matching passengers with drivers, and vice-versa.)* Those who are not traveling with a railpass, "Mitfahrzentrale" is the cheapest and most social option of getting from one city to another. Berlin has two Share Ride offices, each keeping similar hours: Mon-Fri 9:00-20:00, Sat/Sun 10:00-18:00. *Price:* approx. cost per passenger from Berlin to Prague 26€, Amsterdam 33€, Dresden 12.50€, Munich or Frankfurt or Cologne 29€.

Mitfahrzentrale 'CityNetz': Joachimstaler Str. 14 (U9 Kurfürstendamm; exit Rankeplatz, cross the street and it's on the left). *Tel.# 030/19-444.*

Mitfahrzentrale: inside Bahnhof Zoo station, on platform U2 direction Pankow. *Tel.# 030/19-440* or 030/883-1313.

Note: Those who have a working knowledge of German will want to first refer to this website (www.mitfahrgelegenheit.de) for an opportunity to contact the driver directly, i.e. cutting out the middleman for an even cheaper Share Ride.

Bike Rental: Query TI or staff at your digs for the nearest bike rental location. *Note:* It's possible to bring a bike on the subway. To do this you must supplement your transit ticket with a reduced-fare—or ermäßigung—ticket.

Taxi: Cabs are commonplace in Berlin and easy to hail. One local custom you should be aware of is the *3€ Kurzstrecke*—a special, discounted fare for no more than two kilometers and only valid when hailing a cab from the street. So, if you're not heading far, say to the cab driver upon getting in: "Kurzstrecke, drei Euro, bitte."

Welcome Card: This card is your key to Berlin (and Potsdam) for 48 or 72 hours. During this 2- or 3-day period, the Welcome Card allows one adult (and up to three children to the age of 13) free use of the BVG transportation network in all three zones (A,B,C—see *Subway*, page 345), plus discounts (usually 25%) on select tours, theaters and museums (e.g. Checkpoint Charlie, Jewish Museum, Konzerthaus, and all three opera houses). The Welcome Card is available at all TIs (also EurAide) and BVG kiosks. *Price:* 16€/48hr, 22€/72hr. *Opinion:* The Welcome Card is a good value *for non-students— scan brochure to see whether your movements will compensate the price of the card. **Note:* Most all discounts apply to adult admission price, therefore the Welcome Card is not recommended for I.D.-carrying students.

Internet: Since Berlin is so vast, have staff at your digs point you to the nearest café. Otherwise here are a few 'net providers with handy locations: **EasyEverything** has terminals within Dunkin' Donuts at Hardenbergplatz (outside Bahnhof Zoo) and on Potsdamer Str. (behind Sony Center). Open early till late. • **Surf-Point-Charlie** screams its location—Zimmerstr. 79 (by Checkpoint Charlie). Open Mon-Fri 9:00-18:00.

Post Office: There are numerous branches in Berlin, so we narrowed the list to three—all are near major transportation hubs. • *Joachimstaler Str. 7* (near Bahnhof Zoo). Hours: Mon-Sat 9:00-20:00. • *Koppenstr. 3* (by Ostbahnhof). Hours: Mon-Sat 8:00-20:00, Sun 10:00-18:00. • *Georgenstr. 12* (by Friedrichstr. station). Hours: Mon-Fri 6:00-22:00, Sat/Sun 8:00-22:00.

American Express: There are two branches in Berlin, both maintain the same hours: Mon-Fri 9:00-19:00, Sat 10:00-14:00. • *Bayreuther Str. 37* (zip 10787), tel.# 030/2147-6292 — U1/U2 Wittenbergplatz. • *Friedrichstr. 172* (zip 10117), tel.# 030/2045-5721 — U6 Französische Str. *Note:* Folks using American Express products (e.g. traveler's checks, credit card) can use their offices Europe-wide to receive letters—small packages okay!

Embassies

Normal office hours listed—times for other departments may vary.

USA: Neustädtische Kirchstr. 4 [three blocks E. of Brandenburg Gate; high security—street blocked off] (www.usembassy.de) Tel.# 030/832-9233 [general inquiries] or /83-050 [emergency only]. (consberlin@state.gov) The U.S. consulate is located at Clayallee 170—southwest Berlin, near Allied Museum—U3 Oskar-Helene-Heim. Hours: Mon-Fri 8:30-12:00.

Australia: Wallstr. 76-79 (www.australian-embassy.de) Tel.# 030/8800-880 (info@australian-embassy.de) Hours: Mon-Thu 8:30-17:00, Fri 8:30-16:15

UK: Wilhelmstr. 70 [around corner from Brandenburg Gate] Tel.# 030/204-570. (www.british-embassy.de) Hours: Mon-Fri 9:00-12:00 & 14:00-16:00 (consular@british-embassy.de)

Canada: Leipziger Platz 17 [by Potsdamer Platz; look for Canadian flag] Tel.# 030/203-120. (www.canada.de) Hours: Mon-Fri 8:30-17:00. (berlin@canada.de) *Note:* The Canadian Embassy moved into this newly built complex in 2005 and staffers have done a heck-of-a-job beautifying it. Everyone is invited to discover the splendor and diversity of Canada at the embassy's one-of-a-kind multimedia learning center (Marshall McLuhan Salon) where you can explore interactive touch-screens and watch a vivid travelogue on a plasma TV. Enter at Ebertstr. 14 and have your ID ready for security. After your visit, continue through the arcade—called the Northwest Passage—to Leipziger Platz (embassy's official front entrance) and behold a grassy expanse previously no-man's land during the Cold War. Here you'll see a section of the Wall and a double row of stones marking its former path.

Holidays in Berlin, 2006

1. January, Sunday – New Year
14. April – Good Friday
17. April – Easter Monday
1. May, Monday – May Day (Labor [riot] Day)
25. May, Thursday – Ascension Day
5. June – Whit Monday
3. October, Tuesday – Day of German (East-West) Unity
25. December, Monday – Christmas
26. December, Tuesday – St. Stephen's Day (Christmas Day No. 2)

What to do on a Sunday or holiday

Most all sights and attractions will be open. Retail shops will be closed, but that doesn't mean you can't go shopping—Berlin awakes to weekend markets bursting with bric-a-brac (see *Shopping,* Flea Markets, page 387).

FREE Berlin

1) Free of charge and full of emotion is the **Berlin Wall Documentation Center** — page 356.

2) **State-run museums** are free to enter every Thursday four hours before closing — see *Museums, State*, page 377.

3) Extremely interesting and 100% gratis are the following three museums: **German-Russian Museum**, **Allied Museum**, and the **German Resistance Memorial** — see *Museums, Free Admission,* page 380.

4) **Automobile aficionados** have a golden opportunity in Berlin to get behind the wheel of their favorite German sports (or luxury) car free of charge — see *World-Class Auto Showrooms*, page 383.

5) **Grave seekers** will unearth the following names in Berlin: *Dietrich, Marlene* • *Grimm, Brothers* • *Stauffenberg, Claus von* — refer to chapter *Tomb-Lovers, Who's Buried Where? Germany* (page 455 or *WWII Buffs* flip to page 466 for Stauffenberg).

6) Reaching back to Hitler's ghastly regime, the Final Solution (Holocaust) was formulated at the **House of the Wannsee Conference**, now a memorial and educational site — page 393.

7) A sobering sight north of the capital is the **Sachsenhausen Concentration Camp Memorial** — page 392.

Central Berlin

8) **Reichstag** (page 357) is well worth a visit and free to enter, as is the open-air **Topography of Terror** exhibit (page 360).

9) Part of the section *Sights, Central Berlin* (page 360) has been written as a **do-it-yourself walking tour**—from the Brandenburg Gate along Unter den Linden to Alexanderplatz—allow at least two hours.

10) Amble around **Gendarmenmarkt** and pop into the **Deutscher Dom**, which houses an in-depth exhibit (free) relating to the history of German parliament (see *Gendarmenmarkt*, page 365).

11) The ultramodern Sony Center at **Potsdamer Platz** is free and a must stroll-through (page 359).

Eastern Berlin

12) Dawdle along the **East Side Gallery**, a former section of the Berlin Wall (now the world's largest open-air exposition of art) and farther up the road you'll reach the forested **Treptower Park**, home of the must-visit Soviet memorial. For both sites, flip to page 370.

Western Berlin

13) The locals refer to it as the "hollow tooth" — you'll discover it as the **Kaiser Wilhelm Memorial Church** — a world-famous landmark reminding us of the horrors of war (page 371).

14) For presidential history buffs and JFK fans, here's your chance to visit **Rathaus Schöneberg** (page 374), town hall made famous by JFK when he delivered his famous speech: "Ich bin ein Berliner." Additionally, climb the town hall tower to ogle a dynamite view of the western suburbs as well as a replica of the Liberty Bell and rows of boxes containing some 16 million signatures belonging to Americans pledging the right to freedom for all Berliners.

15) Shoppers and people-watchers head over to the continent's largest department store: **KaDeWe** (page 385)—arrive via the must-see, turn-of-the-century U-Bahn station (U1/U2) "Wittenbergplatz."

TOURS

Upon arriving in Berlin, book a tour to orientate yourself with the city's alluring boroughs and attractions. There are several types of tours and companies to choose from—take your time and sift through this section for the tour that best suits your body, budget and taste. Additionally, to facilitate your decision, brochures are readily available at the TI or EurAide office. No matter what the decision, you're in a win-win situation!

<u>Walking Tours:</u> For a healthy introduction to Berlin, join one of the tailor-made walking tours. There are three main companies to choose from, all dedicated to guiding you on a historical and cultural journey through the ever changing landscape of contemporary Berlin. Generally, tours run twice daily May-Oct, morning/afternoon (less off-season), and meet at (depending on the company) Hackescher Markt, Friedrichstrasse station,

outside Bahnhof Zoo, or in the lobby of your accommodations. *Note:* Buy ticket from guide. No reservation necessary—be at the meeting point five minutes prior to departure. Comfortable shoes imperative; tours range from four hours to all day! Confirm times before setting off for the meeting point.

Insider Tours: This hip co. offers mountains of need-to-know info with their specialized, insider tours. **Insider Walk** 4hr, classic Berlin, (adult 12€, student 9€); departs daily April-Oct 10:00 & 14:30 at (A) or 10:30 & 15:00 at (B) — also Nov-March daily 10:00 at (A) or 10:30 at (B). **Insider Bike Tour** (adult 22€, student 19€) departs April thru mid-Nov daily 11:00 at (B) — June-Aug also 16:00 at (B). **Third Reich Tour** 3hr, (adult 12€, student 9€); departs May-Oct Tue/Fri/Sun 10:00 at (A) — also Nov-April Fri & Sun 10:00 at (A). **Bar and Club Crawl** (10€) 5hr; departs May-Oct Tue-Sun 20:30 at (B) — also Nov-April Tue & Thur-Sat 20:30 at (B). *Meeting Point:* **(A)** in front of McDonald's opposite Bahnhof Zoo or **(B)** in front of coffeemamas outside Hackescher Markt S-Bahn station. *Note:* Welcome Card holders receive 25% discount. *Tel.#* 030/692-3149. (www.insidertour.com)

Brewer's Tours: Veteran guide Terry Brewer has been leading tours through Berlin since the Cold War and has handpicked a dedicated team to help share his wisdom. (www.brewersberlintours.com) **All Day Berlin** 8hr (12€), departs daily 10:00 at (A) or 10:30 at (B). **Tuesdays with Terry** 8hr (10€), departs 10:00 at (A) or 10:30 at (B). **Classic Berlin** 4hr (10€), departs May thru mid-Oct, daily, 14:00 at (A) or 14:30 at (B). **Cold War Tour** 4hr (10€), departs May thru mid-Oct, Wed/Fri/Sun 14:00 at (A) or 14:30 at (B). **Third Reich Tour** 4hr (10€), departs May thru mid-Oct, Mon/Thur/Sat 14:00 at (A) or 14:30 at (B). *Meeting Point:* **(A)** by main entrance of Kaiser Wilhelm Memorial Church or **(B)** Friedrichstrasse station, corner of Georgenstr. and Friedrichstr. outside the Australian ice-cream shop.

Berlin Walks: Another popular choice, Berlin Walks offers a handful of info-packed tours: **Discover Berlin** 4hr; departs, daily, April-Oct 10:00 & 14:30 at (A) or 10:30 & 15:00 at (B) — also Nov-March, daily, 10:00 at (A) or 10:30 at (B). **Third Reich Tour** 3hr; departs May-Sept Wed & Sun 10:00, Sat 14:30 at (A) — also March/April and Oct Sat 14:30, Sun 10:00 at (A). **Jewish Berlin** 3hr; departs May-Sept Mon 10:00 at (A) or 10:30 at (B). **Discover Potsdam** 6hr; departs May-Sept Sun 9:45 at (A). **Sachsenhausen Concentration Camp Memorial** 6hr; departs May-Sept Tue & Thur-Sun 10:15 at (A) or 9:50 at (B) — also March/April and Oct Tue/Fri/Sun 10:15 at (A) or 9:50 at (B) — and Nov-Feb Tue & Sun 10:15 at (A) or 9:50 at (B). *Meeting Point:* **(A)** taxi stand outside Bahnhof Zoo or **(B)** in front of Häagen-Dazs café outside Hackescher Markt S-Bahn station. *Price:* (for first three listed tours) 26 years old and over/12€, under 26/9€. Discover Potsdam 15€/11.50€; Sachsenhausen 15€/7.50€. Welcome Card holders receive 25% discount off full price. Printable, 1€-off coupon available on website. *Tel.#* 030/301-9194. (www.berlinwalks.com)

Bus Tours: Little time, sore feet? Plop yourself on an open-air double-decker bus and enjoy the highlights of Berlin as the wind brushes through your hair. Buses keep to a regular schedule throughout the year with running commentary in multiple languages. *Hours:* daily, April-Oct 10:15-15:45, Nov-March 10:15-14:45 (time shown is last departure for complete tour, which takes roughly 2hr). Other tour types available; click on website or pick up brochure. Welcome Card holders receive a 25% discount with either tour operator.

City Circle Tours: Hop-on and -off as you please at 15 different points across Berlin—e.g. Brandenburg Gate, Alexanderplatz, Checkpoint Charlie. Price: 20€, tickets valid all day. (www.sightseeing.de)

Berlin City Tours: This bus company cruises the sightseeing circuit in 105 min with live narration—hop on at the Brandenburg Gate or Tauentzienstr. 16 (Europa-Center shopping mall). Price: adult 15€, student/senior 12€. (www.berlin-city-tour.de)

Boat Tours: Change your pace and sunbathe on the Spree River while absorbing Berlin's celebrated architecture and exclusive landscape. The **Reederei Riedel** boating co. offers a 60-min tour departing (mid-March thru Oct 11:00-19:15) from Alte Börse/Burgstr. (between Museum Island and the S-Bahn station Hackescher Markt). *Price:* 7€, seniors 1€ off Mon thru Fri. Welcome Card holders receive 25% discount. (www.reederei-riedel.de) *Tel.#* 030/693-4646. *Note:* Other tour types available. Tours are usually in German; English info sheet provided. Another possibility is **Reederei Hadynski:** one-hour tours on the Spree, 5€/4€, depart regularly from Museum Island (by Berliner Dom) April-Nov 11:00-17:00.

Trabi Tours: What the heck is a Trabi, you ask? Trabi is short for Trabant—East Germany's answer to the West German Volkswagen—a mass-produced two-stroke 26-horsepower get-around vehicle made out of plastic, recognizable by its trailing exhaust cloud and lawnmower-like stroke. The nearly extinct—now classic—Cold War automobile has been revived by the folks at **Trabi-Safari**, who offer guided tours in their adorable Trabi's with you as the driver. You will be briefed, tested, and even given your very own photo Trabi license before taking to the streets in a procession of Trabants with informative commentary beaming through your radio from the lead car—a tour that will no doubt be a trip highlight. *Hours:* March-Nov, daily, 10:00-18:00 (less off-season). *Price:* 90-min tours (called safaris) cost between 25€ and 35€ per person (depending on attendance—2 people 35€, 3/30€, 4/25€). *Meeting Point:* Gendarmenmarkt and Markgrafenstr.—call ahead for English tour: *Tel.#* 030/2759-2273. (www.trabi-safari.de)

Air Tours: (Air Service Berlin) Here's your chance to take off from historic Tempelhof airfield in a vintage 1944 DC-3 (a.k.a C-47, same model the 82nd/101st Airborne parachuted from on D-Day). Air tours lift off March thru Nov and soar 35 minutes over Berlin and southwest towards Potsdam for a once-in-a-lifetime flight above the former Prussian heartland. *Price:* 99€. Tours are usually full, book well in advance. Air Service Berlin's office can be found in the main hall of Tempelhof airport, behind counter No. 28. *Tel.#* 030/5321-5321 (www.air-service-berlin.de) *Note:* Tours are in German, but the miracle of flight goes beyond speech. Helicopter rides also possible, 123€/15 min. Air Service Berlin is the same company that operates the Hi-Flyer balloon (page 384) near Checkpoint Charlie.

Tunnel Tours: (Berliner Unterwelten, "Underworlds") Those who are looking for a real down-to-earth experience should slip under Berlin's skin for a subterranean adventure. Moreover, WWII buffs will appreciate this cavernous maze—excavated under Hitler's watch—where air-raid protocol is stenciled on the walls and Nazi relics are on display along with a hand-cranked ventilation system that's still operational. When exploring the tunnels it's not hard to envision hundreds of terrified Berliners huddled together while Allied planes dropped 1000-pound demolition bombs onto the city above shattering blocks at a time. During the Cold War, the tunnels were used as nuclear fall-out shelters, warehouses to store food, and a stealthy avenue for Stasi agents to relay top-secret communiqué across town. Even though it's literally under their feet, most visitors overlook this part of the German capital. The Berlin Underworld Assoc.—a non-profit org. founded to preserve this unique part of the city's history—offers weekly, 90-min tours. (www.berliner-unterwelten.de) *Tour #1* (in English): *Dark Worlds* departs year round Sat and Mon 11:00 & 13:00. *Tour #2* (in German; chilly inside, bring jacket/sweater; wear shoes with good traction): *Flak Towers to Mountains of Rubble* departs April-Oct Sat/Sun 11:00, 13:00 & 15:00. *Tour #3* (in German): *Subways, Bunkers* *and the Cold War* departs Sat/Sun 12:00, 14:00 & 16:00. *Price:* (all tours) adult 9€, student 7€. Welcome Card holders receive 25% discount. *Note:* Folks interested in tour #2 or #3, call ahead to see whether any English groups are scheduled. *Tel.#* 030/4991-0517. Reservations not necessary. *Meeting Point:* Gesundbrunnen (U8) station. Because each tour meets at a different location, arrive at least 15 min early at their ticket office located in the southern hall of Gesundbrunnen (U8) station—exit Humboldthain Park and Brunnenstr.

Do-It-Yourself: The DIY option is always a crowd pleaser, because it's cheap and not spoon-fed. There are two "un-narrated," public transportation choices that qualify: the S-Bahn and bus #100—either option is a generalized orientation of Berlin and not to be considered a traditional tour. For either below-listed *excursion you'll need to buy a BVG Single Ticket (Einzel-Ticket, 2.10€—see *Subway* on page 345). *Note:* For the bus, you can buy a ticket from the driver. For the S-Bahn, buy your ticket from an automat and then stamp it in a yellow (or red) box to validate, "hier entwerten"—watch locals. Holders of a Welcome Card or day/multi-day BVG ticket ride for free. Holders of a Eurail consecutive-day or dated Flexi/Select pass ride free on the S-Bahn.

Suggestion: With extra time, do both excursions (total trip time 45 min). Begin by riding the S-Bahn from Ostbahnhof to Bahnhof Zoo (15 min)—from there, hop on bus #100 (30 min). In this case, you will need to purchase another Single Ticket at Bahnhof Zoo, or at Ostbahnhof buy the Day Ticket (Tageskarte), which covers all public transportation until 3 a.m.

S-Bahn: Enjoyable is to ride the S-Bahn (S5, S7, S9) from Ostbahnhof to Bahnhof Zoo (or vice versa). This 8-stop, 15-minute ride is entirely above ground allowing for a visually fascinating journey from east to west while gliding over the rooftops of Berlin. You'll emerge from the working-class districts of the former Soviet sector, cut through Alexanderplatz to trendy Hackescher Markt and glide past the bullet-peppered cultural buildings belonging to Museum Island before navigating the Spree River and through the leafy, upmarket western suburbs to Bahnhof Zoo. *Note:* Holders of a Eurail consecutive-day or dated Flexi/Select pass ride *free* on the S-Bahn.

Bus #100: Board the much-loved bus #100 in front of Bahnhof Zoo (on traffic island between Hardenbergplatz and McDonald's) and ascend steps to the upper deck—low ceiling, tall people watch your head! *Bus departs regularly, which is jam-packed in summer with tourists.* Your excursion will take 30 minutes, escorting you from Bahnhof Zoo to Alexanderplatz past many of Berlin's most famous attractions. ***Note:*** *Since Berlin is continuously under construction, it's possible the below-written bus route has been slightly altered.*

OK, off we go…As the bus sweeps left you'll see (on left, then ahead) the bombed-out remains of the **Kaiser Wilhelm Memorial Church** (page 371), a world-famous landmark—referred to by locals as the "hollow tooth"—reminding us of the horrors of war. After a short distance, the Europa-Center TI is immediately on the right. As the bus comes to a stop, look left to the Elephant Gate—main entrance into the **Berlin Zoo** (page 373); farther ahead (left) you'll spot the entrance into the zoo's sister attraction: the Aquarium.

Soon, after the bus rambles a few blocks more, you'll turn left and motor towards the **Tiergarten** (page 372—central Berlin's largest park, comprising some 400 acres) and past the angel-tipped **Siegessäule** (Victory Column—rising 67m/220ft above the Tiergarten—the Siegessäule was erected in 1873 to commemorate Prussian military triumphs. To access the column, step into any of the four temple-like structures on the perimeter of the traffic circle and descend to the underground tunnel).

Beyond the traffic circle (left) is the beautifully Baroque Schloss Bellevue, residence of the German president—whose post is largely ceremonial. Now we turn right and drive briefly along the Spree River, soon passing (left) the House of World Cultures (dubbed the "pregnant oyster") and the bell tower, or Carillon, donated by Daimler-Benz in 1987 to commemorate Berlin's 750th birthday.

Through the trees on the left you'll see the federal chancellery, or Kanzleramt—nicknamed the "washing machine" because of its cube-like design—where Chancellor Angela Merkel holds court. Adjacent to the chancellery is the Swiss Embassy. Next stop: **Reichstag** (left; page 357). Notice the long line of people waiting to get in, usually an hour. After the bus pulls away from the stop, look right to see the famed **Brandenburg Gate** (page 360).

(Note: Directions in this paragraph may be off due to the construction of the new U-Bahn line—U55, connecting the Brandenburg Gate with the Lehrter Bahnhof.) The bus will turn right and you'll see the French flag belonging to their embassy. Straight ahead is the British Embassy, protected by a noticeable amount of police and barricades blocking off Wilhelmstrasse. As the bus turns left you'll have a great view of the Brandenburg Gate (right) and a better view of the British Embassy. You're now on the mile-long **Unter den Linden** boulevard (page 363), flanked by full-bodied linden trees. The TV-Tower (giant disco ball) you see in the distance pinpoints your end station.

On the right is the palatial-style Russian Embassy along with the Russian national airline, Aeroflot, on the next corner. Opposite (left), across the other side of the boulevard, is the U.S. Embassy—the whole street is blocked off. The next intersection is the prominent **Friedrichstrasse**, formerly a dreary street in Communist East Berlin now a moneyed shopping avenue accommodating (right) upscale names like Gucci, Louis Vuitton and Yves Saint Laurent, to name a few. On the immediate right corner you'll see **Volkswagen World**—VW's mall-like dealership housing their latest models in addition to their extended family of cars: Bentley, Bugatti, Seat and Skoda.

Coming up—in the middle of the road—is the equestrian statue of Frederick the Great, King of Prussia (1740-1786). On the left is **Humboldt University** (page 366), Berlin's most distinguished, founded in 1810 (usually its front courtyard is the scene of a popular secondhand book market). On the right is **Bebelplatz** (page 366), a square bounded by beloved buildings such as the German State Opera (left side), former state library (right side), and the domed St. Hedwig's church behind the opera house. However, Bebelplatz gained notoriety on May 10, 1933, when a horde of Nazi activists congregated in the center of the square and burned books written by critics of Hitler's regime—works by Einstein, Freud and Marx topped the list. Marking the spot is the Book Burning Memorial, a pane of glass embedded between the cobblestones casting light into a symbolic library with empty shelves.

On the left—next to Humboldt University—is the temple-like **Neue Wache** (page 367), a memorial to the victims of war. The neighboring structure with the peach facade extending the entire block is the **German History Museum** (page 382). Continuing eastward you'll cross the Spree River via the elegant statue-lined Castle Bridge, dating from 1824, leading onto the culturally unique **Museumsinsel** (page 378), or Museum Island—voted onto the UNESCO World Heritage List in 1999. At the forefront of Museum Island (left) is the green Lustgarten sprawled out before the **Berliner Dom** (page 367) and elongated **Altes Museum** (page 378). On the opposite (right) side of the boulevard is the **Palast der Republik**—former home of East German parliament called the Volkskammer, or People's Chamber, recently renowned for its asbestos-filled interior—now facing the wrecking ball. Demolition is slated for completion by early 2007 at a cost of around 12€ million, that's on top of the 70€ million already spent after the fall of the Wall by the government to strip it of the cancer-causing fibers. Politicians, historians, architects and Berliners are presently locked in a heated debate as to what should take the building's place: park or palace?

After crossing the second leg of the Spree River, you'll see (left) the **Radisson Hotel** (page 392)—its lobby features the world's largest cylindrical aquarium (82ft tall, 36ft wide), which is part of the **AquaDom** Sea Life attraction (page 368). On the right side of the road is Berlin's red town hall, punctuated by a soaring clock tower. And above you is the **Fernsehturm** (TV-Tower, page 368), pinpointing where you get off: **Alexanderplatz** (page 369). From here, all transportation types connect to the rest of Berlin. To ride bus #100 back in the direction you came, cross the street to its departure area.

Besides Alexanderplatz, consider checking out nearby **Karl-Marx-Allee** (page 369), and with extra time visit the former headquarters of **Stasi** (page 369)—East Germany's secret state police.

SIGHTS, The Wall

One of the first things a tourist does upon arriving in the German capital is ask directions to the Berlin Wall. Even though it's been more than a decade since its fall, sightseers are astonished to hear that the Wall (die Mauer) has gone the way of the buffalo and few sections remain.

In this section—*Sights, The Wall*—we will tell you how to find die Mauer as well as dish out the basics regarding its history…

Germany was largely defeated in World War II by a pincer movement from four national armies: the Soviet Union in the east and the Allies (USA, Britain and France) in the west. The Soviets captured Berlin and everything beyond it to the Elbe River, while the Allies liberated all territory west of the Elbe. Post WWII, May 1945, the proverbial line in the sand was drawn across the German heartland dividing the nation into four zones of occupation—the Soviets controlled the eastern part of Germany and the Allies the west. Although deep in the Soviet zone, Berlin, too, was divided into four zones—the Soviets governed the eastern sector of the city and the Allies the western sectors. However, by mid-1948, tensions were high between the Soviets and Allies resulting in the Soviets blockading their zone—the eastern part of Germany—from the Allies, essentially cutting off Berlin. The Soviets figured the Allies would concede to the pressure and abandon their sectors in the western half of the city. Instead, the Allies responded with Operation Vittles (June 1948—May '49), a massive system of air transport to supply the stranded sectors, which famously became known as the Berlin Airlift. Planes took off every few minutes from airfields across the western part of Germany, delivering nearly 2.5 million tons of relief supplies to the cut-off sectors throughout the 11-month effort. Tensions eased between the two sides and the Soviets shelved the blockade in May 1949.

At this pivotal point in history, the tone was set for decades to come when two ideologically different countries emerged. In Sept. 1949, the three Allied zones of occupation in the democratic west collectively became the Federal Republic of Germany (FRG, or West Germany) with Bonn as its capital. The following month, the totalitarian rule of the Soviet Union responded with the establishment of the German Democratic Republic (GDR, or East Germany) and East Berlin—or the Soviet-controlled sector of the city—as its capital. With the two sides firmly entrenched, the Cold War began in earnest.

By 1961, the oppressive GDR state was grappling with a fading economy as a result of a mass exodus of its workforce. Essentially voting with their feet, more than 2.5 million East Germans had fled to the democratic west during the 12-year period (1949-1961, largely through West Berlin). If the socialist East German regime did not act quickly, there would be nobody left in the so-called workers' paradise to turn out the lights.

To the Communist hardliners ruling East Germany, the solution was simple: keep the population captive. In the wee hours of August 13, 1961, GDR soldiers encircled West Berlin with makeshift barriers that were swiftly replaced by a 6-foot bricks-and-mortar wall topped by barbed wire. Fear gripped the city. All power, gas, water, telephone, subway and road connections stopped dead at the east-west boundary. Nowhere in Berlin was the scene more chaotic, desperate or surreal than on **Bernauer Strasse**, where the back walls of the apartment buildings formed the boundary. The residents woke that morning behind the Iron Curtain while their flower boxes hung over freedom. West Berliners—congregating several stories below on the street—encouraged the residents to jump out of their windows and into the fire tarps they held tight. One by one the residents jumped while GDR soldiers tried to pull them back inside. Embarrassed by such scenes, the East German government evicted the residents and bricked up the buildings. Families, friends, lovers—only streets away—were literally forced apart.

The hellish reality of the situation became evident 11 days later when GDR guards shot dead a young East Berliner (Günter Litfin, age 24) trying to escape. Although the stakes were high, Berliners continued to invent new ways to cross the border. For example, tunnels were dug and when GDR guards intervened, friends and relatives on the other side began digging from west to east. Less labor-intensive efforts included hiding one to two people in pint-sized vehicles that guards didn't feel the need to search. Occasionally, even the guards themselves escaped—until guards were posted on guards.

From the mid-'60s, the GDR stepped-up its containment program with high-tech defenses and a reinforced concrete wall—13-feet high and rounded at the top so it couldn't be gripped—replacing the original bricks-and-mortar barrier. Making escape impossible, behind the new wall a wide area of land was bulldozed—likened to no-man's land but nicknamed the "death strip"—and landscaped with antitank defenses, self-firing guns, barbed wire, minefields, spotlights and watchtowers positioned before another concrete wall deeper in East Berlin. The GDR regime claimed all this was necessary to defend itself against West Germany's aggressive military posture. However, many people found this announcement hard to believe since all the defenses were pointing east, suggesting they were constructed solely to suppress its own people. Moreover, the modest garrison of Allied troops stationed in West Berlin was certainly no match for the some 250,000 battle-ready Soviet soldiers positioned in and around the city.

During this time, the Cold War was at its peak and Communist countries were increasing in numbers. Although it was a psychological war fought on a global scale, the front lines were meticulously carved through the heart of Berlin. Despite being 100 miles in East German territory—essentially an island of democracy behind enemy lines—West Berlin thrived like any major city, having trendy movie theaters, a spirited nightlife and shopping malls with the latest fashions. Unlike other cities, however, West Berlin's only lifeline to the free world was served by one road, one train line and a lone air corridor. Geographically, West Berlin was closer to communist Poland than it was capitalist West Germany. Also hard to fathom, while West Berliners strolled along the shop-lined Kurfürstendamm—West Germany's answer to California's ritzy Rodeo Drive—residents in the eastern half of the city, separated by the Wall, were on food rations and forbidden to travel. The Wall, however, wasn't just a divisional bulwark separating a city, it was the worldwide boundary between two staunchly different ideologies: communism vs. capitalism, totalitarianism vs. democracy. As long as the Wall stood, the global struggle between the East and the West—between oppression and freedom—would continue.

The year 1989 marked the 40th anniversary of the GDR state—leader Erich Honecker celebrated his oppressive regime by claiming it would last another 100 years. He couldn't have been more wrong. Wildly unpopular with his people, Honecker had rejected Soviet President Mikhail Gorbachev's liberalized political and economic reforms (known as Glasnost and Perestroika) that were already sweeping through neighboring Eastern bloc countries. Protest movements strengthened and by the autumn of 1989, East Germans figured out a way to circumvent the Wall by slipping into Czechoslovakia and through Hungary—whose government had embraced liberal reforms—where they were allowed to cross the Iron Curtain into Austria.

On November 9, 1989, GDR officials held a live televised press conference to help defuse the political unrest gripping the nation. Formally prohibited in the GDR, the head official announced that East Germans would be allowed to travel. At that moment, a journalist shouted the question on everyone's minds, "When?" The head official—not used to being questioned—fumbled to find his notes. He then looked up and with extreme uncertainty replied: "Immediately." Gasps of astonishment echoed in living rooms across the land. The official had no idea the implications his reply would have. Without delay, East Germans flocked to the Wall by the hundreds, then thousands. It was normally forbidden to approach the border, but the people pressed forward. The GDR guards didn't know what to do and orders from above were unclear. No longer able to contain the throng, guards opened the border around 10:15 that evening and a sea of jubilant East Germans flooded west. Berliners—weeping and cheering in front of the Brandenburg Gate—reunited after four decades of separation. Euphoria gushed through the streets of West Berlin like a flash flood. Hundreds danced on the Wall itself while hundreds more fervently chipped away at it, trying to sever Communism from their lives. The era of the Wall had come to an end. The GDR regime collapsed the following month, and in true domino fashion so did the remaining Eastern bloc governments, culminating in 1991 with the fall of the Soviet Union—former superpower and champion of the Marxist doctrine.

All told, the Berlin Wall stretched some 155km/97mi across the city and more than 150 people died trying to cross it—the last victim: Chris Gueffroy, Feb 1989, age 20. Crosses honoring the victims can be found at the corner of Scheidemannstr. and Ebertstr., between the Brandenburg Gate and Reichstag.

Soon after the fall of the Wall on November 9, 1989, the first sections of the infamous barrier were dismantled, and by the official reunification of Germany on October 3, 1990, the Wall had largely disappeared from the Berlin cityscape. Today, a double row of cobblestones—labeled "Berliner Mauer"—mark its route. The only remaining sections of the Berlin Wall can be found at the following five locations.

Bernauer Strasse 111: Not far up the road from the Nordbahnhof station (S1/S2) is the official **Berlin Wall Documentation Center** (Dokumentationszentrum), which opened to the public on Nov 9, 1999—the 10th anniversary of the fall of the Wall. The center focuses on the history of the Wall and the division of Germany via multimedia and hands-on exhibits. Their souvenir shop has excellent postcards, posters, maps and books concerning the Wall. *Hours:* Tue-Sun 10:00-17:00 (April-Oct till 18:00). *GPS:* N52° 32.126 - E13° 23.408. (www.berliner-mauer-dokumentationszentrum.de) *Note:* Entry is *free* and exhibition (on 1st floor) is in English. Before leaving, climb steps to the top level to reach the observation platform. From here, you can see the center of Berlin as well as the other two parts of the Documentation Center: the Memorial (Gedenkstätte Berliner Mauer) and the oval-shaped Chapel of Reconciliation (die Kapelle der Versöhnung). Located opposite the Documentation Center is the **Memorial**, a section of the Wall— complete with death strip—that has been sealed by flanking 25-foot-high steel walls to preserve the memory of those who suffered and died during its period of influence. Walk behind the Wall and peer between the gaps in the concrete inner wall to get the basic idea of what an East Berliner would have been confronted with if attempting to escape. A bit farther up Bernauer Strasse is the **Chapel of Reconciliation**, the successor to the Church of Reconciliation that fatefully resided in the death strip—hence inaccessible to its congregation. Choked and left to rot, the GDR regime heartlessly razed the church in 1985. Today's memorial chapel was built in its place—upon entering the grounds you'll see (on left) the original church bells suspended within a timber frame. Around the back of the chapel look through the grate in the floor—the bomb you see was dropped by U.S.

aircraft in 1945 and found and defused in 1999. Now turn around, peer through the wooden beams, and you'll see another section of the Wall. *Hours:* (chapel) Wed-Sun 10:00-17:00. Mass: (Evangelical) Sun 10:00. Four days a week, Tue-Fri at 12:00 (for 15 min), the chapel holds an open memorial service (Andacht) for the victims of the Wall. *Getting There:* (Documentation Center) Take the S1 or S2 to Nordbahnhof station. From there, exit Bernauer Str. Once outside, cross the road and ascend Bernauer Str. Soon you'll parallel remaining sections of the Wall. You're actually on the western side of the Wall and everything beyond it to the right is former East Berlin where freedom was measured in meters across the death strip. After a few minutes you'll reach the memorial—opposite it is the Documentation Center. A short distance farther is the Chapel of Reconciliation and if you were to continue straight another 15-20 min you'd reach Mauer Park (see next entry).

Bernauer Strasse, Mauer Park: At the eastern end of Bernauer Strasse—a kilometer from the Documentation Center (20-min walk)—you'll discover a recreational area called Mauer Park, where a long graffitied section of the Wall remains. The best time to visit Mauer Park is on a Sunday 8:00-16:00, when the flea market is open (page 387). Concert goers and boxing fans will be interested to know that part of Mauer Park includes the 10,000-seat Max-Schmeling-Halle (auditorium), named after the legendary boxer who once knocked out the invincible Joe Louis (in 1936). Schmeling, at age 99, died in Feb 2005. *Note:* If you want to visit both Mauer Park and the Documentation Center at Bernauer Strasse 111, then start from Nordbahnhof station (S1/S2) and work your way up the street, stopping at the Documentation Center, Memorial, Chapel, then Mauer Park. If you only want to visit Mauer Park, take the subway U8 to Bernauer Strasse station and exit Bernauer Str.—at top of steps go right, then 7 min walk.

Mühlenstrasse: On this street, located near Ostbahnhof, is the longest remaining stretch of the Wall (1km) known as the East Side Gallery (page 370).

Niederkirchnerstrasse: At the corner of Niederkirchnerstr. and Wilhelmstr. you'll find a souvenir-devoured section of the Wall adjacent to the Topography of Terror open-air exhibition (page 360).

Erna-Berger-Str.: At the corner of Erna-Berger-Str. and Stresemannstr. is a sweet-and-petite section of the Wall that you should not miss. Its dreary concrete face is masked with vibrant murals and protected by a fence. Walk to the end of Erna-Berger-Str. to see an example of a former GDR guard tower (city officials are/were contemplating razing it, thus it may already be gone). To find Erna-Berger-Str. is easy: you can find it across from Potsdamer Platz or let the above-listed Niederkirchnerstrasse section of Wall lead you to Stresemannstr., where you'll go right and find Erna-Berger-Str. on the next corner.

SIGHTS, Central Berlin

Most of the sights listed in this section are located in the "Mitte" district, which during the Cold War was in East Berlin. The first four sights (Reichstag, Potsdamer Platz, Checkpoint Charlie, Topography of Terror) are not coupled with the other sights in this section, which have been arranged as a do-it-yourself walking tour—from the Brandenburg Gate along Unter den Linden to Alexanderplatz. For now, heading the list is the must-see...

Reichstag: *Dem Deutschen Volke* (To The German People) are the words you'll see emblazoned on the structure's front facade. The Reichstag—cradle of German democracy, symbolizing the past, present and future of Berlin—was inaugurated in 1894 as Germany's parliament building under Kaiser Wilhelm's Second Reich (or empire). The word Reichstag dates from the 11th century, during Charlemagne's First Reich, and was associated with imperial diets, or assemblies. Since the fall of Hitler's Third Reich, the term Reichstag has been ostracized and is only used here in the historical sense.

Less than a month after Hitler took office in 1933, the Reichstag was mysteriously gutted by fire (and remained a charred shell until the 1990s). The Nazis blamed the Communists and shrewdly used the catastrophe to justify the persecution of political opponents while shelving constitutional freedoms. There is still debate whether the Nazis were responsible (Göring and Goebbels in particular) because the timely tragedy promoted a nationalistic charge lifting Hitler one level closer to securing his dictatorial powers that ultimately decimated the nation. Twelve years later, the final battle of WWII in Europe—the Battle for Berlin—culminated on the eaves of the Reichstag when a Red Army soldier raised the Soviet flag above the war-torn city on April 30, 1945. Stalin had ordered the city be taken by May 1, Labor Day.

Upon the erection of the Berlin Wall in 1961, the Reichstag barely remained in the western sector, as its rear butted against the Wall. Four decades later, the Reichstag reopened in 1999 after extensive renovations to accommodate the lower house of German parliament, now referred to as the Bundestag (Federal Assembly). On account of the building's new observation terrace and climbable glass dome boasting memorable views of Berlin, the Reichstag has become a must-do tourist attraction and literally the world's most public federal building. Spiked in the heart of the new dome is a cone of mirrors reflecting natural light onto the parliamentary floor and providing a unique over-the-shoulder view of Germany's legislative body hard at work.

(www.bundestag.de) *Hours:* daily, 8:00-24:00 (last admission 22:00, but arrive no later than 21:00 to account for the hour-long wait to get in). *Price: FREE* entry! *Note:* Expect to wait in line for at least 60 min. Once inside, there will be an airport-like security check—leave anything behind that could be conceived as threatening! After the security check, an elevator will lift you to a fabulous view. Expect to spend at least an hour on the observation terrace: study the photo exhibition; ascend the dome; savor your location.

To beat the hour-long wait in line you have three options: 1) Arrive early, 8:00-8:45. 2) A yummy option, allowing you to skip the line but requires money, is to make reservations at the Roof Garden restaurant located on the observation terrace—see *Roof Garden* below for details. 3) If you come bearing a baby and buggy you can skip the line—notify one of the officials usually roaming around and wearing red.

Avoid visiting the Reichstag on a Monday—since many of the museums are closed, the line is that much longer. Additionally, the glass dome will be closed for cleaning during the following dates: March 20-26, July 17-23, Aug 7-11, Aug 14-18 and Oct 9-15. During these dates, the observation terrace will remain open—only the glass dome will be closed.

Roof Garden (Dachgarten) Restaurant: Meals served with a view—reasonable prices considering location—and great way to avoid the line into the Reichstag. For dinner expect to spend 40€-50€/person (average price: main meal 26€, soup 11€)—for lunch expect to spend 25€-35€/person (average price: main meal 16€, salad 13€, soup 7.50€, apple strudel with vanilla sauce 4.20€). *Hours:* daily, 9:00-24:00. *Reservations:* Tel.# 030/226-2990. kaeferreservierung.berlin@feinkost-kaefer.de *Getting There:* If you've reserved a table, enter the Reichstag via the disabled access. To find it, either ask one of the officials usually roaming around and wearing red or follow these directions: face the main entrance of the Reichstag, then go right and walk around the sloping waist-high wall—then the hedgerow and follow the wheelchair access ramp to the door.

Potsdamer Platz: In 1838, a modern miracle came steaming into Berlin: the train. The newly formed rail authority built the Potsdamer Bahnhof, attracting people from far and away to ride the rails—thus the Platz was born. In the beginning of the 20th century,

Potsdamer Platz became the busiest plaza in Europe. So busy, in fact, that the continent's *first traffic lights* were installed. Alas, the Nazis came into power bringing with them a world war. Consequently, the people-packed plaza became a heap of rubble. Following the war, Potsdamer Platz suffered another setback when it was divided onto the wrong side of freedom. Socialist East Germany erected the Berlin Wall and bulldozed the Platz in favor of the infamous death strip, or no-man's land. The former chic plaza took on a new look, featuring antitank defenses, barbed wire, deadly minefields, and beaming spotlights attached to hideous guard towers. On the western side of the Wall, at the intersection of Bellevuestr. and Potsdamer Platz, a viewing grandstand was erected affording locals and tourists the unsettling perspective into the ugliness of Communism.

A shortened replica of the green traffic light can be seen near the signposted corner of Stresemannstr. and Potsdamer Platz (GPS: N52° 30.557 - E13° 22.569). Adjacent to the light is a multilanguage info board. While there, notice the double row of cobblestones tracing the route of the Berlin Wall. Follow these across the street to original sections of the Wall. As you forge ahead, look for the Canadian flag flying above Canada's new embassy (page 348).

In 1993—three years after the fall of the Wall—an enormous building program transformed the former death strip into Europe's largest construction zone (where numerous artifacts were unearthed, even the body of a German soldier). From this hyper-initiative, Potsdamer Platz morphed into an ultramodern commercial quarter unlike anywhere on Earth. The unprecedented development concluded with a fireworks extravaganza on October 2, 1998—the eve of the 8-year anniversary of German reunification.

Today, Spearheading Potsdamer Platz is the must-see futuristic Sony Center, an arena-like atrium accommodating a cluster of glass and steel office buildings, cafés, an Imax theater, Sony's European headquarters (including a 4-level store), and a one-of-a-kind sunroof featuring a halo of sails, which are brilliantly illuminated at night.

The neighboring DaimlerChrysler development also boasts a bevy of entertainment: a shopping mall, theater, hotels, restaurants, and Berlin's casino—"Spielbank"—attracting some 2000 visitors per day. *Tel.#* 030/255-990. (www.spielbank-berlin.de) *Hours:* slots 11:30-03:00, gaming tables 15:00-03:00. *Price:* 2€ entry—free for Welcome Card holders. *Minimum Bet:* slots 50¢, roulette 2€, black jack 10€. *Note:* Casino is located on Marlene-Dietrich-Platz, across from the Hyatt hotel, Tony Roma's restaurant, and Starbuck's coffee. *Note:* To see an excellent section of the Berlin Wall at Potsdamer Platz, see page 357—*Erna-Berger-Str.*).

Checkpoint Charlie: Although not much remains of the legendary border checkpoint, a visit here is still recommended to see (and have your picture taken in front of) the *replica guardhouse as it appeared in the early '60s, complete with sandbags. (*Original is on display at the Allied Museum, page 381).* Posted above the street is a billboard framing the head and shoulders of a young American soldier (facing east) and a Soviet soldier (facing west), signifying the tense Cold War showdowns experienced here when American and Soviet tanks faced-off. Many people ask if Checkpoint Charlie was named after a person. Actually, it was named after the third such American border crossing situated on the East-West frontier—for example "Alpha" was located at Helmstedt (near Wolfsburg) and "Bravo" at Dreilinden (near Potsdam). Checkpoint Charlie, however, was the only crossing where foreigners could pass, including the exchange of spies. *Getting There:* Checkpoint Charlie is situated at the intersection of Friedrichstr. and Zimmerstr., 1.5km southeast of the Brandenburg Gate. Ride the subway U6 to Kochstraße and exit Haus am Checkpoint Charlie. At street level you'll be faced with a Soviet soldier staring at you from the end of the block. Proceed straight to reach the replica guardhouse and museum (right). *Note:* The neighboring Checkpoint Charlie museum (page 381) is expensive (9.50€) but worthwhile for historians and enthusiasts.

~ *Combine your jaunt to Checkpoint Charlie with a visit to the Topography of Terror exhibit—seven-minute walk. At the *intersection of Friedrichstr. and Zimmerstr. a double row of cobblestones mark the route of the Berlin Wall (Zimmerstr. was actually in East Berlin and formed no-man's land).*

*When facing the sandbagged guardhouse, from the aforementioned intersection, the cobblestones begin some 20 meters to your right. Follow this cobbled route the length of the block and across Wilhelmstr. to a souvenir-ravaged section of the Wall and the...

Topography of Terror: This open-air exhibition on Niederkirchnerstrasse (formerly Prinz-Albrecht-Strasse) narrates the history of the terrain that once accommodated the headquarters of Hitler's secret police. From May 1933 till the end of WWII (May 1945), Prinz-Albrecht-Strasse 8—previously an arts school—was the administrative center of Hitler's state-sponsored terror organizations, e.g. Gestapo, Kripo, SD and SS (the eyes and ears of the Third Reich), i.e. the most feared address in Nazi Germany. On the first floor (above ground floor) of the turn-of-the-century building at Prinz-Albrecht-Strasse 8 was the desk of Heinrich Himmler (chief of all Nazi police departments), from where the notorious mass-murdering special action squads (Einsatzgruppen) were created, the Final Solution (Holocaust) was drafted, and National Socialist crimes were authorized and executed. Opponents of the Nazi regime were regularly brought to Prinz-Albrecht-Strasse for interrogation—thus the basement of the building was converted into a prison, known as the Hausgefängnis. In these cells numerous people died, either via torture or suicide. It is to these individuals—guilty of no crime, only of human morality—that the terrain on Niederkirchnerstrasse is dedicated. Due to Soviet artillery and Allied bombs, the complex was pulverized and only the excavated foundations remain. Nonetheless, to visit the Topography of Terror—although unsettling—is an enlightening memorial worthy of your time.

(www.topographie.de) Upon arriving, head to the office (portable) at the west end of the site to pick up your free English audio guide for the permanent exhibition (leave ID as deposit). *Hours:* daily, 10:00-18:00 (or until dark), May-Sept till 20:00. *Price: FREE* entry! Expect a visit to take 60-90 min. *Note:* Paralleling the site is a souvenir-devoured section of the Berlin Wall. Across from the Wall (extending the entire block along Wilhelmstr. to Leipziger Str.) is the Federal Finance Ministry, formerly the ministry of the Luftwaffe (air force) during WWII. This stark, monolithic ministerial complex—which once directed paralyzing aerial attacks across Europe, now stuns the locals with dismal economic figures—is one of the last surviving examples of Nazi architecture in Berlin (other significant examples are the Olympic stadium and Tempelhof airport).

Do-it-yourself walking tour — Central Berlin

*The remainder of sights in this section have been arranged as a DIY walking tour: **from the Brandenburg Gate along Unter den Linden to Alexanderplatz**—allow at least two hours; this does not include time spent at the attractions. (Note: Since Berlin is continuously under construction, it's possible that some directions in this section will be slightly off.) Let's start at the...*

Brandenburg Gate: Built from 1788-91 in timeless Doric-style, Berlin's most recognizable landmark—and the scene of Germany's biggest annual New Year's bash—is the last of 14 gates that were once part of the old city wall. The gate's design is based on the Propylaea, the ceremonial entrance to the Acropolis in Athens. Surmounting the gate (and

facing east) in Hellenistic glory is Nike, goddess of victory, riding a (quadriga) chariot drawn by four horses. In an act of thievery, Napoleon Bonaparte stole Nike and her stallions after marching on Berlin in 1806, transporting them to Paris. The homesick quintet was rightfully returned upon Napoleon's downfall in 1814. The Brandenburg Gate, named after the state in which Berlin is bound, is situated in the heart of the city bridging the east-west axis between the boulevards of Unter den Linden and Strasse des 17 Juni. Throughout the gate's history it has been a staging area for rallies, ceremonies, and even a symbolic backdrop for a presidential speech (Ronald Reagan, June 1987). During WWII, British and American pilots used the gate as a marker to guide their bombs, and more recently (1961-1989) it was sealed off in no-man's land as part of the Berlin Wall. The Brandenburg Gate, emblematic of Berlin's division during the Cold War—and epitome of the city's reunification upon the fall of the Wall—was reopened on December 22, 1989. After two centuries of celebration and conflict, the world-famous attraction stands once again, liberated and unsullied, at the epicenter of one of the great capital cities on Earth. What's more, the Brandenburg Gate is featured on three of Germany's (eight) euro coins: 10¢, 20¢, 50¢. *GPS:* N52° 30.981 - E13° 22.761

~ Before we head along Unter den Linden towards Alexanderplatz, we are going to make a slight detour. When standing on the west—or leafy—side of (and facing) the Brandenburg Gate, go right one block to the...

Holocaust Memorial: One block south of the Brandenburg Gate, construction workers recently completed the 28€ million Holocaust memorial, bluntly called the "Memorial to the Murdered Jews of Europe." After 17 years of debate and delay, the memorial finally opened on May 12, 2005 (following the 60th anniversary of Nazi Germany's surrender ending the war in Europe). The five-acre site contains an undulating field of more than 2700 multisized, tombstone-like pillars (from surface level to over 15ft tall) called "stelae," commemorating the victims of the Holocaust. Simulating a wave-like impression, the irregular stelae were designed to generate emotions of isolation and insecurity; feelings experienced by many Jews who were sent to concentration camps. The subterranean visitor's center can be found in the southeast (back right) corner of the site (open Tue-Sun 10:00-20:00, last entry 19:15), which documents personal stories of victims and where staff will be on hand to answer your questions. (www.stiftung-denkmal.de) *Hours:* (memorial) open 24/7. *Note:* Guided tour in English every Sun 16:00—adult 3€, student 1.50€—minimum 3 people, max 25.

*~ Two blocks southeast of the memorial is where Hitler committed suicide, explained in the next entry… *To get there continue in the direction you were headed—away from the Brandenburg Gate—and make the first left (Hannah-Arendt-Str.), then go right on Gertrud-Kolmar-Str. (which is across the street from the Holocaust memorial's visitor center) and stop some 100 meters farther at the red-and-white boom gate opposite (street) In den Ministergärten. Now read the next entry, Hitler's Bunker. (*If you're not interested, walk back to the Brandenburg Gate via the next set of directions.)*

The Bunker, Hitler: (exact location unknown) mid-January 1945, Adolf Hitler descended below the New Reich's Chancellery on Voßstrasse into a catacomb-like bunker system that was to be his last earthly address. This self-imposed subterranean endurance test would last some 105 days more than 40 feet below the chaos-swept streets of Berlin, beneath several tons of sandy soil and a 16-foot-thick concrete roof—a world where the elements were non-existent and the artificial light of day flickered with every external explosion. Besides being the "Führerbunker," it was also the Führerhauptquartier, or supreme Nazi command—the last (and smallest) of several headquarters (e.g. Wolf's Lair, Vinnytsya, Wolfsschlucht) where Hitler and his staff conducted the strategies and struggles of WWII. In the depths of this reinforced urban cave, Hitler spent many hours with his generals poring over maps and repositioning nonexistent army units, as well as discussing the carefree times on Obersalzberg and the reconstruction of Berlin upon Germany's forthcoming victory. High on the intoxicating bunker air, Hitler wed his long-time mistress, Eva Braun, in the final days of the war—they consummated their marital bond by committing suicide some 40 hours later on April 30, 1945. Sitting on a velvet sofa, Hitler opted for the foolproof poison-and-pistol method, biting down on a cyanide capsule and then shooting himself in the head. Sitting next to Hitler and wearing an elegant black dress, Eva Braun bit into her poison capsule at the sound of Hitler's gun—concluding her life with a simple but lethal pill. Honoring Hitler's wishes, both bodies were then carried outside the bunker to the chancellery garden by staff, doused in petrol and cremated.

The chancellery occupied the entire block at Wilhelmstrasse and Voßstrasse, where today multilevel housing tenements dominate the area. After the war Hitler's bunker was sealed, becoming completely inaccessible in 1961 when the Soviets erected the Berlin Wall. Today, the bunker's exact location is difficult to say. Generally, it is said to be off Gertrud-Kolmar-Str. beneath the parking lot opposite (street) In den Ministergärten. *Note:* The red marble that once lined Hitler's football-field-long palatial hallway in the chancellery was pilfered by the Soviets and used to garnish the nearby Mohrenstrasse U-Bahn station (across Wilhelmstr.). The Soviets also used the marble for their memorial in Treptower Park (page 370).

~ From in front of the Holocaust memorial, walk back to the Brandenburg Gate the way you came; along the route you'll pass the future site of the new U.S. Embassy (right) and notice the double row of cobblestones (left; other side of road) marking the course of the

Berlin Wall. You are—and have been—walking in what was formerly known as the "death strip," or no-man's land.

Continue straight and when you reach the second of the Brandenburg Gate's six giant columns, STOP (be careful of zippy bicyclists)—stand next to the column and between the two gray pods sprouting from the cobbles and face the glass dome belonging to the Reichstag in front of you. To your left is the boulevard Strasse des 17 Juni, flanked by the Tiergarten—central Berlin's largest park, embracing some 400 acres—and in the distance is the angel-tipped Siegessäule (Victory Column, erected in 1873 to commemorate Prussian military triumphs. The column originally stood in front of the Reichstag before Hitler moved it to adorn this western artery into Berlin). A few hundred meters along the boulevard on the right-hand side (just in front of yellow directional sign) are a pair of T-34 tanks marking a Soviet monument, the last resting place of 2500 Red Army soldiers who died here at the end of WWII, April-May 1945. (Note: The aforesaid places of interest are listed in Sights, Western Berlin—Tiergarten.)

Reel your eyes back in along Strasse des 17 Juni to the immediate intersection and where the double row of cobblestones arc through the traffic. In June 1987, Ronald Reagan stood on the west side of that boundary in the center of the boulevard (in front of traffic lights) and delivered a presidential speech: "...General Secretary Gorbachev, if you seek peace, if you seek prosperity for the Soviet Union and Eastern Europe, if you seek liberalization: Come here, to this gate. Mr. Gorbachev, open this gate. Mr. Gorbachev, tear – down – this – wall!"

When clear of cyclists, go right and walk beneath the Brandenburg Gate. Once through you'll see the TI on your immediate right and to your left, opposite TI, is the Raum der Stille (Room of Silence)—a non-denominational room for anyone who is interested in taking a seat to ponder life, pray for world peace, mull the day's touring opportunities, or whatever. Go ahead, step inside, you'll get a free brochure.

Now, back to our tour, the disco ball you see hogging the skyline at the other end of the boulevard belongs to the Fernsehturm, or TV-Tower, and pinpoints the end of our walk. In front of you begins...

Unter den Linden: Berlin's most prestigious boulevard stretches "under the linden trees" from the Brandenburg Gate east to the Berliner Dom on the Spree River. This broad, mile-long thoroughfare has been the praise of royalty, the conquest of a French emperor, the playground of cabaret icons, the treeless parade ground of a dictator, and the responsibility of a Communist state. Unter den Linden, the invention of Prussian monarchs from the 16th to 18th centuries, became the tree-lined east-west axis of imperial Berlin. Often gilded carriages carting members of the dynastic Hohenzollern family rolled past adoring crowds as they headed west to enjoy a day in their private nature reserve, Tiergarten, or a week in their country palace, Schloss Charlottenburg. In the roaring 1920s, the former royal avenue became synonymous with glitzy gatherings and smartly dressed dandies and was often compared to Paris' fashionable Champs-Élysées. During the dark years of the Third Reich, Hitler widened the boulevard by *cutting down the 200-year-old linden trees to plant Nazi flags. Forget the blatant massacre of trees, by the end of WWII—May 1945—Berlin's historical main street was unrecognizable, a surreal heap of rubble. (*The lindens were replanted by Socialist East Germany in the '50s.) Since the reunification of Germany in 1990, the nation's grand avenue is back in business—revitalized by the reopening of embassies, commercial enterprises and the resurrection of tourism.

~ Continue straight and keep to the right-hand side of the boulevard. On the left is the French Embassy (look for the French flag), and on the right is another view of the future site of the U.S. Embassy. (At this point you're near the spot where the front cover of this book was photographed.) Ahead on the right is the...

Hotel Adlon: The hotel dates from 1907 when Lorenz Adlon built his dream property to accommodate overnight guests. Lorenz set high standards for service and filled the interior with sumptuous décor. Word buzzed across international boundaries and the Hotel Adlon became a place to see and be seen. Many of the world's A-list personalities have since stayed at the Adlon, such as Einstein, Edison, Ford, Rockefeller, Strauss, Chaplin, Marlene Dietrich, as well as European royalty. Miraculously, the Adlon survived WWII without any major damage and was converted into a military hospital (April 1945) to treat the wounded. After the war, only meters behind the Iron Curtain, the Adlon suffered economically—and physically—under the oppressive East German regime and was eventually razed in 1984. With the reunification of Germany (1990) came the reconstruction and renaissance of the historically charming Hotel Adlon (1997). The Adlon's first-class flair and service were revived to replicate Lorenz's vision of high standards and imperial grandeur that made the hotel so famous all those years ago. More recently (2002) the Adlon was thrust into the international spotlight when Michael Jackson recklessly—and thoughtlessly—dangled his child over the balcony for the throng of fans below. For hotel prices, flip to page 392.

~ Beyond the Hotel Adlon you'll see that Wilhelmstrasse (right) is barricaded to better protect the British Embassy. Continuing along Unter den Linden, on the next block (right) is the...

Russian Embassy: Heading away from the Brandenburg Gate you'll come across what was once the most influential building in East Berlin, the Russian Embassy. Prior to WWII, the modest structure hosted delegates representing an economically challenged nation barely surviving off its collective ideology. Post WWII, the diplomatic mission lay in ruin and the Red victors—conquerors of Eastern Europe—had the perfect excuse to rebuild the former czarist post three times the size in true neo-Stalinist fashion as a symbol of Soviet supremacy. Inside the block-long palace-like embassy, ornate chandeliers hung from molded ceilings, doorknobs shimmered in gold, and luxurious velvet curtains dressed Muscovite windows. Once a magnet for KGB operatives, the Russian Embassy has relegated its Soviet past to the cellar and is duly exercising a more centrist approach to 21st-century politics.

~ At the next intersection (Glinkastr.) gaze left across the boulevard to see a curtain of police and cement obstacles barricading the present U.S. Embassy, located midway down the street. (This'll give you a good idea of how Checkpoint Charlie would have looked in the '70s and '80s.) Continue in the direction you've been walking and at the next intersection (Friedrichstrasse) you'll see the unofficial mascot of Berlin, the...

Ampelmännchen: Tourists often ask: "How do I know when I'm in the former Soviet sector of the city, East Berlin?" Since the dismantling of the Wall and the completion of most renovation/building projects, it can be hard to distinguish the East from the West. However, there is one easy way to tell—spot the Ampelmännchen, or "traffic light little man," a Cold War relic born in 1961 that resides exclusively in the former East. To find the Ampelmännchen, look at the pedestrian crossing light at a traffic intersection. If you see a stern-looking red character wearing a flying-saucer-shaped hat with the outstretched arms of an anal traffic cop urging you to stop, or a spunky green guy wearing a man-about-town hat who appears to be walking at a brisk pace—then you've found the "traffic light little man" and you're officially in former East Berlin.

This colorful traffic man nearly went the way of the buffalo in the mid-1990s due to an anxious government eager to rid Berlin of its Socialist past. Countering the government's position, historically minded activists leading an exhaustive campaign saved the traffic man from certain extinction while elevating him to a tourist attraction in his own right. Love for the Ampelmännchen has become infectious and purchasable mementos are abundant, from "traffic light little man" table lamps to T-shirts, candies to coffee mugs, and postcards to pens. What's more, you can ogle him from home at this address: www.ampelmann.de (German). *Note:* The Ampelmännchen can also be seen in cities all over the former GDR (East Germany), e.g. Dresden. But, more importantly, you'll see him at our next stop: Friedrichstrasse.

~ He's pretty neat, huh? ... Much cooler-lookin' than his skinnier cousins in the west. Shifting gears, automobile aficionados will want to pop into Volkswagen World on the corner, where Europe's biggest automaker—VW—houses their latest models in a mall-like dealership. (Note: Toilets inside!) After browsing, head south (go right) along...

Friedrichstrasse: Once the center of Berlin's shopping and entertainment district, Friedrichstrasse was transformed into a ruin by the end of World War II (1945). The Soviet victors reshaped the rubble into a socialistically drab street, lined with cookie-cutter office and housing blocks dead-ending at Checkpoint Charlie. Today, this north-south avenue racing through the heart of Berlin typifies the city's reinvention post reunification. The dull, gray, monotonic socialist design—amplified by decades of neglect—has been substituted with a plethora of modernistic, lively buildings accommo-dating premier auto dealerships and upscale shopping (e.g. Galeries Lafayette, Hugo Boss, Gucci, Hermés, Louis Vuitton, Yves Saint Laurent) where trendsetters and trend followers come to score the latest fads and hottest styles.

~ Continuing along Friedrichstrasse, on the next corner you'll see another auto showroom—this one belonging to the Bavarian carmaker, Audi. One block farther you'll see the American Express office (on right at No. 172; in case you need it). In two blocks you'll reach Mohrenstrasse—turn left here. If you were to continue along Friedrich-strasse, you'd encounter the famed Checkpoint Charlie in a handful of minutes (listed at the top of this Sights section). But for now, let's ramble east along Mohrenstrasse. Ahead on the (right) corner is a very sweet place...

Fassbender & Rausch: Satisfying customers for more than 140 years, this family owned chocolate shop is Europe's largest. Step inside to absorb their mouth-watering selection. Savor a sample and say "lecker!" (German for "tasty"), and ogle their giant-sized chocolate *recreations of the Titanic, Reichstag and Brandenburg Gate. *Hours:* Mon-Fri 10:00-20:00, Sat 10:00-19:00, Sun 12:00-18:00. *Tel.#* 030/2045-8440. *Getting There:* U6/U2 Stadtmitte—corner of Mohrenstr. and Charlottenstr.

~ From the chocolate shop, continue along Mohrenstr. Pass the Hilton hotel and go left at Markgrafenstr. (the building on your left is the Deutscher Dom; free exhibition inside, see below). The adjoining plaza is Berlin's most charming...

Gendarmenmarkt: This French-sounding plaza is undeniably Berlin's most beautiful square, originally laid out in the late 17th century. Its name, however, derives from the 18th century when a military regiment "Gens d' armes" took up quarters here. Gendarmen-markt features three eye-catching buildings constructed in neoclassical-style: The core of the classic ensemble is the Konzerthaus (1820), home to the Berlin Symphony Orchestra. Flanking the Konzerthaus are twin churches, the Französischer Dom (French Cathedral) on the north side of the square and the Deutscher Dom (German Cathedral, 1708) on the south side. The Französischer Dom, interestingly enough, was initially built 1701-1705 to indulge Berlin's Huguenots (French Protestant immigrants)—hence the cathedral's name. During WWII, Gendarmenmarkt was heavily damaged. Since Germany's East-West reunification (1990), it has been superbly recreated. Today, luxury hotels and fine restaurants neighbor Gendarmenmarkt. Classical music fans will appreciate orchestras under the stars when Gendarmenmarkt is transformed into a dreamy concert arena: July 6-9, 2006. What's more, the joy-ridin' Trabi Tours (page 351) depart from here—look for the East German (Cold War classic) vehicle drawing a crowd. *Getting There:* U6/U2 Stadtmitte.

The **Deutscher Dom** houses an outstanding exhibition recounting the history of German parliament and democracy on five floors, entitled "Milestones, Setbacks, Sidetracks" (Wege, Irrwege, Umwege). *Note:* The exhibition is in German, but a free audio guide in English is available at the info desk (leave ID as deposit). Expect a visit to take 60-90 min. *Price:* Free entry! *Hours:* Tue-Sun 10:00-18:00 (May-Sept till 19:00).

~ *From Gendarmenmarkt your journey moves on—continue along Markgrafenstr. for a short distance and go right on Französische Str., then make the next left (Hinter d. Katholischen Kirche) and go left again around the domed church into...*

Bebelplatz: Located on Unter den Linden boulevard, across from Humboldt University, you'll find Bebelplatz—a spacious square framed by distinguished buildings dating from the 18th century. In the center of the square is a panel of glass fixed into the ground; walk over to this and face the boulevard (Unter den Linden). In front of you is *Humboldt University*, your next stop. To your left is the *Alte Bibliothek* (Old Library); to your right is the *Staatsoper*, or State Opera House (Richard Wagner was conductor/director here from 1898-1919); behind you is the domed *St. Hedwig's Church*, the most important Catholic structure in Berlin. When convenient, step inside and ogle its Socialist-style interior outfitted by the former GDR regime (open Mon-Sat 10:00-17:00, Sun 13:00-17:00). But before you do, read on…

Alas, Bebelplatz has a dark side: On May 10, 1933, a horde of Nazi activists congregated in the center of the square and threw shelves of books written by Jewish-Germans, Communists, and critics of Hitler's regime into a raging bonfire—works by Marx, Einstein and Freud topped the list. Marking the spot is the Book Burning Memorial, a pane of glass embedded between the cobblestones casting light into a symbolic library with empty shelves. A few meters in front of the glass is a plaque that reads: "In the middle of this square on May 10, 1933, National Socialist [Nazi] students burned the works of hundreds of freethinking authors, publishers, philosophers and scientists." The adjacent plaque bears the words of Heinrich Heine, a German-Jewish poet: "That was merely a prelude. Where books are burned, in the end, people will burn."

~ *From Bebelplatz skip across Unter den Linden to Humboldt University. Along the way you'll see (left, center of boulevard) the equestrian statue of Frederick II "the Great," Prussia's most celebrated monarch (1740-86). Later, we'll pass where his palace stood.*

Humboldt University: [HU] Wilhelm von Humboldt established Berlin's most distinguished university here in 1810 with support from his famous brother, Alexander von Humboldt, naturalist and explorer. Statues of both brothers adorn the front courtyard. HU's first semester featured four subjects: law, medicine, philosophy and theology—256 students were in attendance, instructed by 52 teachers. Since then, a long list of prominent names have been associated with HU in the capacity of either professor or student, such as Albert Einstein, Karl Marx, Otto von Bismarck, Brothers Grimm, and 29 recipients of the Nobel Peace Prize. The university hit an all-time low during the Nazi era when several students and professors participated in the infamous Burning of the Books across the boulevard on Bebelplatz, May 10, 1933. Other professors were shocked by the Nazi wave rolling through campus and wisely resigned their positions, while some (like Einstein) took it one step further and left the country. During the Cold War—torn between ideologies—teaching staff from the university set up an independent campus in the American sector and appropriately named it the Free University of Berlin. Since the reunification of Germany, HU has strengthened its commitment to "humanity and knowledge." This year some 225 courses will be offered at the university's 11 facilities, educating a student body of some 35,000 (of which 13% come from abroad). Complementing HU's international fellowship is the campus' new addition: the Center for British Studies — Jägerstr. 10, tel.# 030/2093-5379. (gbz@gbz.hu-berlin.de)

Today, the university's front courtyard is often the scene of a popular secondhand book market, where bookworms can usually find a Schnäppchen (bargain).

~ As we were doing earlier, let's continue east along Unter den Linden and head towards the giant disco ball in the sky. Next door to HU is the…

Neue Wache: Adjacent to Humboldt University is the Prussian-built war monument, "New Guardhouse," dating from 1818. Until 1945 it served as a memorial to the fallen of past wars. In 1969, the temple-like structure—bolstered by Doric-style columns—became the final resting place of the Unknown Soldier and the vestiges of an unnamed prisoner from a Nazi death camp. From the '70s until the collapse of the GDR in 1990, East German soldiers were posted here and ceremonially goose-stepped the changing of the guard. Today, the Neue Wache represents the reunified German nation, commemorating the victims of war and tyranny. Inside is the poignant statue, "Mother with her dead son."

~ The next building we come to—with peach facade, extending the entire block—is the German History Museum, displaying more than 700,000 objects (open daily 10:00-18:00; entry 2€). Design students and architects will want to make a left at the side of the Neue Wache and ramble through the leafy plaza to check out the museum's new spiraling glass addition by star architect I. M. Pei—creator of the Rock 'n' Roll Hall of Fame in Cleveland, the J.F.K Library in Boston, and the Louvre's glass pyramid in Paris. (For more info on the museum, flip to page 382.)

Continue east along Unter den Linden and cross the Spree River via the elegant statue-lined Castle Bridge, dating from 1824. On the other side is the culturally unique Museumsinsel (page 378), or Museum Island—voted to the UNESCO World Heritage List in 1999. At the forefront of Museum Island is the green Lustgarten (left) sprawled out before the elongated Altes Museum and the…

Dom, Berliner: (Cathedral) At the eastern end of Unter den Linden—one mile from the Brandenburg Gate—stands the heavenly Berliner Dom on Museum Island. Dating from 1905, the imposing cathedral was inaugurated by Kaiser Wilhelm II as Berlin's Protestant answer to Rome's St. Peter's Basilica. The Dom was the Hohenzollern's (Prussian royal family) exclusive church, which explains why the crypt contains their remains (nearly 100 tombs). To climb the dome is possible, counting 270 tiring steps to the apex. *Hours:* April-Sept Mon-Sat 9:00-19:00 (←last entry→) Sun 12:00-19:00, (less Oct-Mar). *Price:* adult 5€, student 3€. Welcome Card holders pay 3.50€.

~ Across the boulevard from the Berliner Dom is Schlossplatz, former location of the Hohenzollern palace and ex-digs of Frederick II "the Great." On this plaza, during GDR times, the Socialist regime built the…

Palast der Republik: Situated on Schlossplatz—across the boulevard from the Berliner Dom—is (was) one of the city's most pretentious eyesores, the "Palace of the Republic," former home of East German parliament called the Volkskammer, or People's Chamber—now facing the wrecking ball since Feb 2006 *(concluding a heated debate that lasted more than a decade. Demolition is slated for completion by Easter 2007 at a cost of some 12€ million).* Before it became the legislative center of a communistic regime, Schlossplatz was home to the centuries-old Hohenzollern (Prussian royal family) palace. Alas, the palace was heavily damaged during WWII. Instead of renovating it, the then Soviet-backed GDR government demolished the palace and later built the copper-tinted Palast der Republik. Besides the Volkskammer, the enormous governmental structure housed an entertainment complex unusual for an Eastern-bloc nation that included several restaurants, bars, a bowling alley, auditorium, theater, and a wedding hall where many East Berliners were married. Funnily, because of an inordinate amount of (more

368 Your Traveling Companion

than 1000) light fittings and chandeliers hanging in the foyer, the Palace of the Republic acquired the nickname "Erich's lamp shop," referring to Erich Honecker, the leader of East Germany. After the regime's collapse in 1990, the West moved in and discovered the building was contaminated with asbestos. Yikes! At a cost of circa 70€ million, the cancer-causing fibers were removed. So what will take the place of the Palace of the Republic? Fiscal conservatives are hoping for a park; sentimentalists are calling for the reconstruction of the Hohenzollern palace—but if the latter were to happen, funds for the billion-euro project wouldn't become available for a decade, at least.

~ *From the Berliner Dom, cross the second leg of the Spree River (as you do, notice—on left—that boat tours leave from here). On the other side is the Radisson Hotel—slither past the doorman and into the lobby, where you'll witness the world's largest cylindrical aquarium, part of the...*

AquaDom: ("Sea Life") Fish lovers should plunge into the new (Dec 2003) Sea Life center, which follows the life cycles of thousands of underwater inhabitants in more than 30 natural marine environments, from the Spree River to the depths of the Atlantic Ocean. Here, you can get face to face with a moray eel, virtually walk through the ray tank, or poke around with sea anemones in the finger pools. Did you know male sea horses give birth, not the female. And a shark's skin is so rough that it could be used as sand paper. Visitors get a fish-eye view of the exotic undersea world from inside a specially designed glass *elevator rising through the middle of the world's largest cylindrical aquarium (25m/82ft high, 11m/36ft wide—containing 900,000 liters of water). Your aquatic adventure concludes on the rooftop level for a fine view of the aquarium and parts of Berlin. (www.sealife.de) *Hours:* daily, 10:00-18:00 (last entry— one hour later April-Sept). *Price:* 13.50€, Welcome Card holders receive a 25% discount. *Getting There:* S5, S7, S9 Hackescher Markt. The main entrance of Aqua Dom is at Spandauer Str. 3 (from the Radisson, walk east to the intersection and go left to find the entrance on the left). *_Note:_ Claustrophobes may find elevator unnerving.

~ *From the Radisson Hotel, cross the boulevard to the park and cobbled plaza featuring the larger-than-life statues of two German revolutionaries: Karl Marx and Friedrich Engels (the latter is standing). Relics from the former GDR, the statues were erected in honor of the two grandfathers of Communism, who defined scientific socialism through their published works, the Communist Manifesto (1848) and Das Kapital (1867).*

As you can see, Marx and Engels have a million-dollar view of the sky-high disco ball, crowning the Fernsehturm, or TV-Tower. We're only minutes from our destination: Alexanderplatz. Walk towards the tower and cross the street—as we forge ahead—you'll pass Berlin's 19th-century red town hall (right), punctuated by a soaring clock tower. Within this structure, Klaus Wowereit, Berlin's openly gay mayor, manages the city's welfare.

From everywhere in town you could see it, now you can whisk to the top of it and see everywhere in town... (From the tower's concrete base to the tip of the candy-cane spire is 368m/1207ft.)

Fernsehturm: (TV-Tower) Without a doubt the giant disco ball dominating Berlin's eastern skyline offers the most impressive, heart-skipping views in town. Completed in 1969 as a television transmission tower, it became East Germany's most innovative design—perhaps inspiring the feverish '70s dance craze. People are so fascinated by the high-altitude disco ball that it's become a trendy venue to exchange wedding vows. Additionally, 1 million thrill-seekers annually cram into the elevators for the 40-second ear-popping ride to the viewing level at 203m/665ft. The floor above the viewing level contains Berlin's highest restaurant, the revolving "Telecafé" (30-min full revolution)— tel.# 030/242-3333—approx. price per person: breakfast (10:00-12:00) 6-12€; lunch (from 11:00) 13-20€; soda 2.50€, beer 3€, cappuccino 3.60€, chocolate torte 3€. (www.berlinerfernsehturm.de) *Hours:* daily, 9:00-24:00 (Nov-Feb from 10:00). *Price:* (elevator to viewing level) 7.50€, Welcome Card holders pay 6€. *Note:* expect 30-min wait for elevator. *Getting There:* Tower is located at Alexanderplatz—S5, S7, S9 or U2, U8.

~ *From the TV-Tower, walk beneath the train tracks (via station) into Alexanderplatz (see below—Sights, Eastern Berlin), where we conclude our walking tour.*

To extend your adventure, consider checking out nearby Karl-Marx-Allee and/or visit the former headquarters of Stasi—East Germany's secret state police (see Sights, Eastern Berlin below)—or hop on the subway U2 (direction Ruhleben) and ride it seven stops to Potsdamer Platz (page 359).

SIGHTS, Eastern Berlin

Alexanderplatz: This renowned plaza is named after Czar Alexander I, who visited Berlin in 1805 and allied himself with Prussia against Napoleon. Fittingly, the Czar's namesake square became the centerpiece and commercial heart of Soviet-occupied Berlin, i.e. the public arena of the GDR nation. Referred to locally as "Alex," the upwardly mobile plaza was destroyed during WWII. In the 1960s, Alex received a first-class communistic makeover, complete with tons of concrete, unimaginative design, and cookie-cutter office blocks. Although Alex has had a face-lift since the reunification of Germany (1990), most visitors here can still capture the vibe of a bygone Socialist era. One object that draws attention in the vast square is the World Time Clock (in front of Sparkasse building)—once regarded as an East German technological masterpiece, it is now hailed as a great meeting place by locals and Hollywood celebrities alike. You may remember in the movie "Bourne Supremacy" that Matt Damon chose to meet Julia Stiles at the clock. Since Alexanderplatz is a major transportation hub, most everybody will pass through the famed plaza at one time or another.

Karl-Marx-Allee: Running off Alexanderplatz is the monumental Karl-Marx-Allee—formerly Stalin's Avenue—a multilane boulevard leading into the depths of eastern Berlin and eventually arriving at the Polish frontier. The broad boulevard was rebuilt after WWII as a Marxist utopia, showcasing the idealistic lifestyle afforded to the working class—ration stores, a cinema, hotel, and proletarian apartment buildings lined the sidewalks.

Suggestion: For a retro-journey into the GDR era (Socialist East Germany), stroll from Alexanderplatz to the roomy roundabout at Strausberger Platz (20-min; 1km). Even though the apartment buildings along the route have recently undergone a face-lift, you'll still experience a time warp on the ex-boulevard of Socialist dreams. Be sure to check out the dreary Schillingstr. U-Bahn station with its lackluster green tiles. Just past the fountain on Strausberger Platz is the U5, where you can ride the subway either two stops back to Alexanderplatz or five stops to "Magdalenenstr." for Stasi HQ.

Stasi HQ: ("Normannenstrasse" memorial site) Spy wannabes or students of political subjugation should tour the former headquarters of the devious East German political police known as Stasi (Staatsicherheit, or State Security). The Grand Poo-ba of Stasi—Erich Mielke (1957-89)—claimed his network of oppression to be the "sword and shield of the [Socialist] party." Modeled after the Russian CHEKA (Special Commission to Counter Revolution and Sabotage), Stasi evolved from a collection of post-WWII "information agencies" within the German Communist Party (KPD) to a vast, centralized spy network infiltrating West Germany, as well as its own populace to the degree of instilling an environment of suspicion and distrust where family and friends had to rethink their conversations. Stasi was everywhere. In 1985, the number of full-time Stasi agents peaked at 83,000—include the number of "unofficial" informers and State Security numbered into the millions.

As extensive as this clandestine agency was, its grip on the nation weakened to the charm of democracy. By the end of 1989, the repressive East German government was history and—on January 15, 1990—Stasi HQ was stormed by a mob of angry citizens demanding to see their personal files, as well as the names of informants *(even today files are being uncovered that reveal prominent members of German society as being former Stasi moles, tarnishing their character and career)*. However, at the time, the matter was lawfully put to rest and the doors to Stasi HQ were sealed shut—official stamps and sealing tape can still be seen (upon reaching the 1st floor, go right and close the hallway doors). Also on the 1st floor, you'll see Stasi chief Mielke's office and desk, which accommodates the death mask of his role model: Vladimir Lenin. What's more, the original socialistically sterile décor still hangs from the walls and dulls the offices as if time seemingly froze in the '70s. Before leaving the floor, consider making a pit stop in one of the Communist-era's finest toilets. On ground level (near cashier), don't miss the prisoner transport vehicle (left of stairway)—step inside and sit in one of the mini holding compartments. The vehicle's purpose was to shuttle detainees to the Stasi prison (Gefängnis) at Hohenschönhausen (tours of prison available [in German]—interested parties ask cashier for brochure and directions).

(www.stasimuseum.de) *Hours:* Mon-Fri 11:00-18:00, Sat/Sun 14:00-18:00. *Price:* adult 3.50€, student 2.50€. Expect a visit to take around 30 min. *Note:* Exhibits in German—helpful guidebook in English available, 3€. The best option, however, is to call ahead to see whether any English tours are scheduled, tel.# 030/553-6854. *Getting There:* Take subway U5 to Magdalenenstr. and exit Ruschestr. Upon ascending the steps to street level, go right (u-turn) and make an immediate left, following the arrow pointing "Normannenstrasse"—you have just entered the Stasi compound—this lane ascends between ex-Stasi buildings before spilling into the main parking lot. The tallest building you see (right, center) is Stasi HQ. *Drivers,* Stasi HQ is located at Ruschestr. 103. *GPS:* N52° 30.866 - E13° 29.215

East Side Gallery: Before the fall of the Berlin Wall, graffiti artists fervently used the west side of the infamous concrete barrier as if it were their own personal canvass. Immediately after the fall of the Wall, the graffiti trend jumped to its east side. No where is this more apparent than in the Berlin suburb of Friedrichshain, where some 115 artists from 20 countries have created the *East Side Gallery—the largest open-air exposition of art in the world—by painting a menagerie of murals on a kilometer-long stretch of the Wall in the former Soviet sector. (*The first half has been restored; the second half is in poor condition.)* The most famous mural is Dmitri Vribel's "Bruderkuss," which depicts the former Soviet leader Leonid Brezhnev and his East German counterpart, Erich Honecker, embraced in a passionate kiss. *Getting There:* From Ostbahnhof, exit Stralauer Platz (front of station) to Mühlenstr., where the Wall begins. The East Side Gallery is 1km long, taking 20 min to walk. The Wall ends at Warschauer Str. and the marvelous twin-towered Oberbaumbrücke (bridge). *GPS:* N52° 30.498 - E13° 26.084. *Note:* There is a well-connected S-Bahn station up Warschauer Str. Travelers looking to continue on to Treptower Park (next entry), you have two options: from the intersection of Mühlenstr. and Warschauer Str. *1)* continue straight (30 min) by foot and cross the Spree River at the next bridge leading to the park, or *2)* walk up Warschauer Str. to the station and take the S9 two stops to Treptower Park, saving 1.5km on the feet.

Treptower Park: The gritty multicultural district of Treptow retains a significant chapter of Berlin's intriguing history as well as its contemporary future. The Berlin Wall once cut through here obstructing freedom for 28 years. Since its fall, a number of novel creations and new developments have emerged. One fashionable example is the Molecule Man, sculptured figures rising from the Spree River (spotlights rigged at the feet brilliantly illuminate the artwork at night. Look for Molecule Man from the S-Bahn). Near Molecule Man is a group of modern high-rise buildings known as the Treptowers. The largest of these (125m/410ft high) belongs to the global insurance and financial service provider, Allianz (NYSE symbol: AZ), which maintains 3000 employees and a modern-art collection. Across from the Treptowers begins Treptower Park, exhibiting the district's unique past. This forested oasis was laid out in the 19th century and is one of Berlin's largest public reserves. In 1896, the park became the home of the **Archenhold Observatory**, Germany's oldest structure from where astronomers could view celestial objects—such as stars, planets and galaxies. What's more, the observatory owns the world's longest, moveable refractor telescope (21m/69ft), and it was here that in 1915 Albert Einstein first publicly presented his Theory of Relativity—the 300-seat lecture hall where he spoke has been renamed in his honor.

Near the observatory is an even bigger attraction, the **Soviet Memorial** (Sowj. Ehrenmal). On this soil, the Soviets buried their dead concluding the final volleys of World War II. Flanking the memorial's entrance are two Soviet soldiers on plinths bowing in reverence—behind them are gates resembling massive bookends comprised of red marble pilfered from Hitler's chancellery. (Notice the hammer and sickle up top.) Descend the steps to the rectangular grass sections crowned by brass wreaths, the final resting place of thousands of Soviet warriors. The path either side of the burial ground wanders past heroic battle scenes chiseled onto stone blocks. Check out how equality in a collective society is portrayed in the near identical facial features of all those depicted. The appended *inscriptions are propaganda quotes from Stalin *(*if you walk the left path the inscriptions are in Russian—right path German)*. Spearheading the memorial is a gigantic Stalinesque statue representing the champion of the Soviet Union, a Red Army soldier cradling a motherless child while clutching a Braveheart-type sword and resting his foot upon the crushed remains of a Swastika. At the base of the statue is a mausoleum—reachable via 55 steps—accented by a vivid mosaic depicting the peoples of the Soviet Union honoring their dead. Above is the red star of the CCCP (Russian for USSR). During the painfully proud days of the GDR, visitors to East Berlin were required to pay their respects at the memorial, including school kids on field trips and tour buses from the West. Behind the memorial is a pleasant lake—check it out if the gate isn't locked.

Getting There, Memorial & Observatory: S8, S9, S41, S42 Treptower Park. From the station the Soviet memorial is a 10-min walk, and the Archenhold Observatory is 10 min beyond the memorial. Exit station on the park side and go right to the busy road (Puschkinallee). Cross with the signal and go left, paralleling the road. After about 7 min you'll see a stone archway on the right—walk through this to the memorial. For the observatory (or *Sternwarte*), continue straight on Puschkinallee for circa 10 min—just past the Burger King you'll see its main entrance on the right (open Wed thru Sun 14:00-16:30; adult 2.50€, student 2€—exhibits in German). To get back to the S-Bahn station, either retrace your steps or hop on the bus or stroll the scenic riverside promenade.

SIGHTS, Western Berlin

Kaiser Wilhelm Memorial Church: Preserved to remind us of the horrors of war, the world-famous landmark church—referred to by locals as the "hollow tooth"—exhibits hideous wounds sustained during a bombing raid on Nov 23, 1943. The church was built in 1895 to posthumously honor the Hohenzollern Kaiser, Wilhelm I. The former entrance has been converted into a memorial displaying holy relics, archival photographs, and a marvelous mosaic ceiling. Adjacent to the historical structure is a smaller, contemporary church (1961, designed in the shape of an octagon) boasting some 10,000 little blue windows brilliantly illuminating the interior (visit on a sunny day). *Hours:* (memorial) Mon-Sat 10:00-16:00 — (contemporary church) daily, 9:00-19:00. *Price: FREE* entry! Expect a visit to take 15 min. *Getting There:* Churches are located on Breitscheidplatz, a lively square at the eastern end of Kurfürstendamm, near the Europa-Center shopping mall and TI. From Bahnhof Zoo, exit into Hardenbergplatz. From this peppy platz go right and cross Hardenbergstr.—to your left you'll see the church's severed steeple. Just beyond the church is the Europa-Center shopping mall (with rotating Mercedes icon on roof)—the TI is below. If you're arriving via subway take the U1 or U9 to Kurfürstendamm—exit Breitscheidplatz.

Kurfürstendamm: Popularly known as "Ku'damm," this swanky shopping boulevard runs 3.5km/2mi from the Kaiser Wilhelm Memorial Church to the exclusive villa neighborhoods of the western suburbs. Laid out in the latter half of the 19th century, Ku'damm entertained the rich and pompous. During the Cold War, the showpiece boulevard became the social center of West Berlin. While its counterpart (Friedrichstrasse) in East Berlin struggled with rationing and decay, Ku'damm boasted well-stocked shops and prosperity. For those who experienced the harsh reality of an ideologically divided city bolstered by a 13-foot-high concrete barrier, Ku'damm confirmed capitalistic superiority over communism. *Getting There:* U1, U9 Kurfürstendamm.

Tiergarten: Literally "Animal Garden," the Tiergarten is central Berlin's largest green space, embracing some 400 acres—beginning in front of the Brandenburg Gate and extending west to Bahnhof Zoo. Bisecting the park, the multilane *Strasse des 17 Juni* boulevard scoots past a few of Tiergarten's many attractions, e.g. the *Siegessäule, Soviet monument*, and a *flea market* on weekends. Generations have enjoyed the forested park, which was originally planned in the 18th century as a private hunting reserve for Prussian royalty. During WWII, aimless bombs and artillery ravaged the Tiergarten—automobile-sized craters inundated the landscape, groomed vegetation became unrecognizable debris, and once full-bodied trees stood like raw skeletons against a smoky, red-tinged sky. Destitute Berliners seeking to survive the winter of 1945 cut down what few trees remained—the park resembled a barren wasteland. Post-WWII, a massive reforestation program took place, and today the trees in the Tiergarten are essentially as old as the sum of years the war has been over. The parkland has since regenerated to its original splendor, boasting amiable walkways and waterways, lush meadows and trees and colorful flowerbeds—ideal terrain for a relaxing stroll, lazy picnic, game of football, healthy jog, or (nude) sunbathing.

The **Siegessäule** (Victory Column)—erected in 1873 to commemorate Prussian military triumphs—is the angel-tipped monument soaring (67m/220ft) above the central part of the Tiergarten. Crowned by a gilded Nike, goddess of victory, the Siegessäule originally stood (60m/197ft tall) in front of the Reichstag before Hitler increased the column's size and moved it in 1939 (to its present location) to adorn the western artery into Berlin. *Note:* When facing the column, notice the umpteen bullet holes and shrapnel wounds from WWII scarring its body. For a splendid panoramic view of Berlin, ascend the column's dizzying 285-step staircase to the observation platform. *Hours:* daily, 10:00-17:00 (April-Oct 9:30-18:30). *Price:* (includes museum) adult 2.20€, student 1.50€. *Getting There:* Hop on the touristy bus #100. To access the column, step into any of the four temple-like structures on the perimeter of the traffic circle and descend to the underground tunnel.

Beyond the Siegessäule—on the western horizon—is *Teufelsberg*, or Devil's Peak, Berlin's highest landmass (120m/393ft), compiled from the rubble of bombed-out Berlin. During the Cold War, Teufelsberg was the ideal location for the western allies to conduct intelligence operations on their eastern neighbors—hence the futuristic white globes mushrooming from the summit. Today, instead of playing I spy, Teufelsberg is popular for family outings and flying kites.

A few hundred meters before the Brandenburg Gate (along Strasse des 17 Juni) are a pair of T-34 tanks marking a **Soviet monument** (Sowj. Ehrenmal), the last resting place of 2500 Red Army soldiers who died here at the end of WWII, April-May 1945. The monument was erected after the war and dedicated on Nov 11, 1945, to the Soviet Union's victory over National Socialism. At the center of the monument is a giant statue of a Soviet soldier standing triumphant atop a lofty column. During the Cold War, tourists often stood open-jawed before the statue of Ivan, wondering how he got into the enemy sector. Allegedly, the two tanks are the first Soviet armor to enter Berlin in April 1945, kick-starting the final battle of the war in Europe. *Note:* Before you leave, check out the excellent pictorial exhibition in the white building behind the monument. Pic#1: German troops (1939) marching along Strasse des 17 Juni. Pic#8: House where Germans signed the surrender of WWII Europe; today this is the German-Russian Museum (page 380). Pic#7: Signing of the surrender. Pic#9: Tiergarten post-WWII—(unbelievable, huh?) notice the Soviet monument in the background and to its right the Reichstag in ruins. Pic#19: President JFK driving past Soviet monument. Pic#22: Tourist snapping photo of monument. Notice the two Soviet guards posted before it. Pic#20: Shows one of the guards in a hospital bed after being shot by a protester who disapproved of the Soviet occupation of East Germany. Pics#26-34 are of the Soviet memorial in Treptower Park (page 370).

If you're visiting on a Sat/Sun 10:00-17:00, rummage through the Tiergarten's weekly **flea market** (Trödelmarkt)—located outside the "Tiergarten" S-Bahn station: S5, S7, S9. Berlin's largest and most renowned bazaar (and the priciest) has just about everything, from treasures to trinkets.

Zoo, Berlin: Caged in the Tiergarten's southwestern corner, Berlin's prized zoo—or Zoologischer Garten—is Germany's oldest wildlife park, established in 1844 (9th oldest in Europe). Today, the Berlin Zoo is spread across 86 acres and accommodates some 13,500 animals representing 1400 species, which qualifies as the richest collection of wildlife on Earth! However, this wasn't always the case. Before the madness of WWII, the zoo accounted for nearly 2000 animals—only 91 of these survived the war. Thanks to thousands of volunteers and dollars donated, the zoo promptly recovered and now attracts a staggering 2.6 million visitors annually, making Berlin's zoo the busiest on the continent. If you're ever to visit a wildlife park in Europe, this is the one—especially since it's the proverbial hop, skip and a jump away from an ICE train at Bahnhof "Zoo." Additionally, animal-adoring tourists can visit the Aquarium, a multilevel habitat containing fish, amphibians and the Crocodile Hall (crocs are usually fed on Mondays at 15:00, sharks Mon & Thur 13:30). *Hours:* daily, 9:00-17:00 (March to mid-Oct till 18:30). *Price:* (for zoo or aquarium) adult 11€, student 8€, combo-ticket (both zoo and aquarium) 16.50€/13€, Welcome Card holders pay student price, family discount available. *Tel.#* 030/254-010. *Feeding Times: "Fütterungszeiten"* (use as general guide, times may have changed) polar bears 10:30, pandas 11:30 & 15:00, seals 10:30 & 15:15, penguins 13:45, monkeys 12:00/14:00/16:00, lions/tigers 14:30 (summer) ↔ daily except Mon & Thur ↔ (winter) 15:30. *Getting There:* The zoo has two gated entrances: the *Lion Gate* is off Hardenbergplatz at Bahnhof Zoo, or the *Elephant Gate* at Budapester Str. 34 (across street from Europa-Center shopping mall). The Elephant Gate—featuring two outstretched elephants—is the more exotic of the two entrances, where you'll also find the Aquarium.

Rathaus Schöneberg: If there is one "town hall" you should visit while in Germany—it's Schöneberg, located in southwest Berlin. For four reasons we consider Rathaus Schöneberg a must-see site: *1)* the Freedom Bell, *2)* John F. Kennedy, *3)* a flea market, *4)* during the Cold War the town hall was the political and administrative center of West Berlin. *Getting There:* U4 Rathaus Schöneberg—then five-minute walk. Exit subway "Rathaus"; at top of steps look (right) for Berlin's red-and-white flag flapping atop the town hall tower (where soon you'll be). Now, angle right and follow Freiherr-von-Stein-Str. two blocks to the Rathaus (main entrance on left in front of building). *GPS:* N52° 29.119 - E13° 20.680. ***Note:*** Time your arrival just prior to noon to hear the...

Freedom Bell: On the heels of a Soviet blockade and the Berlin Airlift, the citizens of the United States gave a replica of their Liberty Bell as a gift to the people of Berlin to symbolize their unity with democratic West Germany. Berliners called their new bell the "Freiheitsglocke," or Freedom Bell. But before the bell reached Schöneberg, it traveled across the United States and 16 million Americans signed the "Declaration of Freedom," a document pledging the right to freedom for all Berliners. The bell was mounted in Rathaus Schöneberg's 70-meter-high tower and at noon on October 24, 1950, some 500,000 Berliners crammed into the square opposite to hear their Freedom Bell chime the sound of liberty. This began a tradition that can still be heard every day at noon. Thus we recommend you time your visit to coincide with this monstrous midday melody. As you stand there absorbing the thunderous beat, imagine the square packed with people in 1950 and again in 1963 for JFK (see below). The bell rings for five minutes; afterwards climb the tower to see the Freedom Bell along with the rows of boxes containing the 16 million signatures. When viewing the boxes through the glass door, push the button to the right to hear a recording of the Freedom Bell (if you didn't hear it live at noon). On the wooden door is a German translation of the Declaration of Freedom (an example of the document can be seen in front of you, but we recommend you spy the readable [pink] copy behind you on one of the display boards). Climb the final set of stairs to reach the bell and a predictably awesome view. **Hours:** Tower is open most days April thru mid-Oct 10:00-16:30 (and also during good weather in the off-season), call ahead to confirm: Tel.# 030/7560-2200 (little English spoken). **Price:** FREE entry! **Getting There:** Upon entering the main hall of the Rathaus, go right to the elevator, push 3rd floor and then ascend stairs following "Zum Turm" (to the tower).

John F. Kennedy: On August 13, 1961, East German soldiers encircled West Berlin with what infamously became known as the Berlin Wall. Fear gripped the city and angst weighed heavily in the air. Located deep within Communist East Germany, West Berliners went to bed every night wondering if the Soviets would come to engulf the remainder of the city. During these trying times, America stood faithfully by the side of West Berliners, defending their freedom. This meant the world to them, especially since it came from a former enemy. To further endorse America's conviction, the President of the United States, John F. Kennedy, came to West Berlin on June 26, 1963. West Berliners were ecstatic—they chanted his name as if he were a rock star. Once again, hundreds of thousands of people crammed into the square (Rudolph Wilde Platz) opposite Rathaus Schöneberg. And perched upon a terrace in front of the mayor's office, JFK faced a sea of euphoric people and delivered one of his most famous speeches:

"There are many people in the world who really don't understand, or say they don't, what is the great issue between the free world and the Communist world. Let them come to Berlin. And there are some who say that communism is the wave of the future. Let them come to Berlin. And there are some who say in Europe and elsewhere we can work with the Communists. Let them come to Berlin. And there are even a few who say that it is true that Communism is an evil system, but it permits us to make economic progress. _Lass' sie nach Berlin kommen._ Let them come to Berlin. Freedom has many difficulties and democracy is not perfect, but we have never had to put a wall up to keep our people in, to prevent them from leaving us...While the wall is the most obvious and vivid demonstration of the failures of the communistic system, for all the world to see, we take no satisfaction in it, for it is, as your mayor said, an offense not only against humanity, separating families, dividing husbands and wives and brothers and sisters, and dividing people who wish to be joined together. ...Freedom is indivisible, and when one man is enslaved, all are not free. When are all free, then we can look forward to that day when this city will be joined as one and this country and this great continent of Europe in a peaceful and hopeful globe. ...All free men, wherever they may live, are citizens of Berlin, and, therefore, as a free man, I take pride in the words _Ich bin ein Berliner._" (I am a Berliner.)

And just like that, the leader of the free world departed after an eight-hour visit. A short trip maybe, but it had a profound affect on the citizens of West Berlin. Inspired by his speech, the people could take comfort in knowing that the remainder of the western world were Berliners just like them on the front lines in the struggle against Communism. Mournfully, JFK was gunned down in Dallas, Texas, less than five months later. The German people were devastated, and the nation stopped to mourn his loss. They honored their friend—the President—by naming streets, avenues, and even bridges after him. And as a final and fitting tribute, Berliners renamed Rudolph Wilde Platz—the square facing Rathaus Schöneberg—to John-F.-Kennedy-Platz. **Note:** To hear the speech, go to www.jfklibrary.org and "search" Berliner speech.

Flea Market: Ideally, you want to visit Rathaus Schöneberg on a weekend (Sat/Sun 8:00-16:00) when John-F.-Kennedy-Platz, the square facing the town hall, is awash with vendors selling their reasonably priced goods at the flea market. *Note:* Call ahead to make sure the tower is open so you can also visit the Freedom Bell (see *Freedom Bell* above).

Olympic Stadium: This neoclassic coliseum is Germany's largest stadium and Berlin's best example of Nazi architecture. Built in the mid-1930s, the stadium's architect—Werner March—submitted plans for a grandiose arena seating 100,000 spectators for the 1936 Summer Olympiad. Hitler threatened to disassociate himself from the games when he found out March's plans for the arena included partition walls made of glass, resembling a transparent egg. The plans were quickly redrafted substituting the glass with natural stone—thus, the 11th Olympiad began on schedule with Germany's anal-retentive dictator in attendance. Meanwhile, the Nazis rekindled the Olympic Flame from traditional ceremonies held at Olympia by the ancient Greeks and initiated the first-ever torch relay to journey across several countries before reaching the host city. During the games, Hitler was pleased to flaunt to the world a utopian-like lifestyle spawned by Aryan supremacy and National Socialist ideology. Hitler's jovial disposition quickly changed to disillusionment in front of swastika-waving Germans when a gifted African American—Jesse Owens—won four gold medals, set two world records, and, of course, stole the show. Post WWII, in honor of one of the greatest track-and-field athletes of all time, the street running into the "Olympia Stadion" S-Bahn station has been renamed Jesse-Owens-Allee. Beginning the 21st century, the stadium underwent a four-year 242€ million modernistic overhaul (while keeping the historical shell) to cater to Berlin's premier soccer club (Hertha) and the 2006 World Cup, as well as A-list concerts and other sporting events. Today, the stadium can seat upwards of 74,000 people. When there, walk around to the west (open) end of the stadium to see Jesse Owen's name and the rest of the medal winners from the 1936 Olympics. *Getting There:* S5, S75, U2 Olympia Stadion. *Soccer Tickets:* We urge you to see a game (especially if you've never been to one before); it will be a trip highlight, guaranteed! Berlin's Hertha soccer club plays a few times monthly from Aug thru May. Tickets cost 10-55€ (students, seniors receive discount) and can be purchased at the stadium, via ticket agencies in Berlin, or go to their website at www.hertha-bsc.de *Note:* Huge bonus, the ticket is valid for public transportation to/fro game—zones ABC (see page 345 *Subway/Bus*)—starting three hours before stadium opens until 03:00. If you require a European delivery address, have tickets sent to your respective Berlin hotel/hostel. *Reichssportfeld:* Developed for the 1936 XI Olympiad, the 326-acre Reichssportfeld was the blanket term for the entire Olympic complex. At the heart of the former Reichssportfeld is the federally protected Olympic Stadium. *Maifeld:* The grassy 28-acre pitch on the west side of the stadium is known as the Maifeld, used during the Olympics as a staging area and polo field. After the war, the Reichssportfeld landed in the British sector and, therefore, the Maifeld was officially introduced to rugby and cricket. *Glockenturm:* (Bell Tower) Soaring (77m/252ft) into the sky at the west end of the Maifeld is the Glockenturm, the famous stone tower from which the Olympic bell rang to signal the opening of the 1936 games. The bell can be reached, as well as an outstanding panoramic view of western Berlin, via the express elevator in 25 seconds. However, the 4.5-ton bell in the tower is a replica—the original 9.6-ton Olympic bell is damaged and displayed by the stadium's south gate (Südtor). On its cast-iron body are the words, "I summon the youth of the world — Olympic Games 1936." *Hours:* (Glockenturm) April-Oct, daily, 9:00-18:00. *Price:* 3.50€. *Suggestion:* Upon your arrival to the stadium, ascend the Glockenturm first to gain an overview of the entire Olympic complex—catch either the S5 or S75 and get off at Pichelsberg, one stop past Olympiastadion. *Waldbühne:* (Forest Stage) Originally named after Hitler's close friend, Dietrich Eckart, the open-air Waldbühne was designed to emulate a crescent-shaped amphitheater dating from the ancient Greeks. It is located in the woods behind the Glockenturm and belonged to the Olympic complex, hosting gymnastic competitions and cultural events. The amphitheater was constructed in a (30m/98ft) hollow, boasting excellent acoustics and seating for 22,000 spectators—down and front Hitler eyed the bendy performances from his VIP box. Post-Olympics, the Waldbühne became the stage for numerous boxing matches. Today, during the summer, the Waldbühne presents movies in the moonlight as well as premier classical and pop concerts (page 388—*Headline Concerts*).

Schloss Charlottenburg: Berlin's finest Baroque palace—Schloss Charlottenburg—is the former home to Hohenzollern royalty, built from 1695 as a summer residence for the Prussian king's wife: Sophie Charlotte. Although the Schloss—or palace—is easily reached today by bus from central Berlin, it took several hours on a horse-drawn carriage in the 17th/18th centuries. Since there's oodles to do in Berlin, and many of you are already palace'd out, you're excused if you were to give Schloss Charlottenburg a miss. However, for palace enthusiasts, Charlottenburg belongs to the Prussian Palaces and Gardens Foundation and therefore the Park Sanssouci (in Potsdam) day or premium ticket is also valid here. The premium ticket is the better buy but only available for purchase at Sanssouci—thus you should visit there first. Visitors to Charlottenburg will love the Schloss' magnificent gardens. Tuck a bag of breadcrumbs in your daypack for the slap-happy ducks and graceful swans. *Hours:* (Charlottenburg) Tue-Sun 9:00-17:00. *Price:* (includes tour, usually in German) adult 8€, student 5€; Park Sanssouci day ticket 12€/9€ (includes all Prussian palaces except Schloss Sanssouci), premium ticket 15€/10€ (includes Schloss Sanssouci)—both tickets (day/premium) are valid for two consecutive days! *Getting There:* Since the nearest U- and S-Bahn station is a 15-min walk from Schloss Charlottenburg, your best bet is to hop on bus #145 (direction Spandau) from Bahnhof Zoo and ride it to the palace's front gate.

MUSEUMS: Since there are numerous museums in Berlin, 128 in fact (according to the bureau of Berlin statistics), it is not feasible to list them all. Thus, we have composed an abridged list separated into subcategories: *museums run by the state, museums that offer free admission,* and *all others.* The most visited museums are run by the state—therefore, they shall be listed first.

    Tickets: Culture vultures should consider the Museum Pass (3-Tage-Karte), which offers free admission for three consecutive days into many of Berlin's important museums—pass available at participating museums (or TI) for adult 15€, student 7.50€. *Note:* Pass does not include special exhibitions (Sonderausstellungen), or the Checkpoint Charlie museum.

MUSEUMS, State

The state museums of Berlin (**SMB**) attract more than 3 million visitors annually, which attest to the world-class status of its collections. The SMB society has incorporated their collected works into five museum quarters—the most popular being the *Museumsinsel* and *Kulturforum.*

    (www.museen-berlin.de) ***Tickets:*** There are three ways into the SMB:

    1) Purchase a ticket for the museum quarter you're interested in. For example, if you want to see the Pergamon Museum and Alte Nationalgalerie then buy the ticket valid for the Museumsinsel (available from museum). This ticket is valid for the entire day and allows free entry into all museums in the quarter. *Note:* Get an early start to see as many collections as you can. Prices vary per museum quarter and are therefore listed individually in their respective group.

2) If you're interested in seeing museums from different quarters, buy the easy-on-the-wallet Museum Pass (3-Tage-Karte) for adult 15€, student 7.50€. This pass is valid for three consecutive days and allows free entry into all SMB as well as many of Berlin's important museums. *Note:* Pass *does not* include entry into special exhibitions (sonderausstellungen).

3) FREE admission! If you're only interested in seeing one or two museums, arrive on a Thursday four hours before closing and admission is *FREE!*

Note: *1)* All SMB museums listed in this section are closed Mondays, and all are open late (till 22:00) on Thursdays except the Coin Cabinet.

2) FREE admission (into the permanent collection) is permitted into all SMB every Thursday four hours before closing. However, there will be a charge for the audio guide (if applicable).

Museumsinsel: (Museum Island) Packed onto the tip of an island splitting the Spree River at the eastern end of Unter den Linden boulevard—one mile from the Brandenburg Gate—is a neoclassic ensemble of buildings so culturally unique that they were voted to the UNESCO World Heritage List in 1999. Featuring archeological treasures and 19th-century art, the state-run island complex is without a doubt the cultural heart of Berlin, which emerged in the mid-1800s and capped its completion with the Pergamon Museum in 1930. Alas, the museums suffered extensive damage during WWII—and since the island was situated behind the Iron Curtain—the wounds of war are still present while renovations continue during a billion-dollar project that is slated to finish around the year 2011. Four museums on the island are presently open: *Pergamon Museum, Alte Nationalgalerie, Coin Cabinet* and the *Altes Museum with Egyptian Museum.* (*Note:* A fifth museum—the Bode-Museum—will open summer 2006.) **Price:** Museumsinsel day-ticket—allows free entry into all museums on the island—adult 12€, student 6€ (available from museum). **Getting There:** S5, S7, S9 Hackescher Markt. **Suggestion:** Consider having a picnic (or a relaxing break) in the Lustgarten, the alluring green space flanked by the Altes Museum, Spree River and Berliner Dom.

Pergamon Museum: Regarded as a temple of the arts, the Pergamon Museum attracts nearly 1 million visitors annually. The museum's star attraction is arguably the Pergamon Altar dating from the 2nd-century B.C. that features the 113-meter-long sculptured frieze of the Battle Between the Gods and Giants. Other museum highlights are contained within its three main collections: Antiquity Collection (shared with Altes Museum) • Museum of Ancient Near-East Art • Museum of Islamic Art. Don't miss the walled facade of the Mshatta Palace (8th century Jordan) or the brilliantly blue-tiled Ishtar Gate (6th century B.C. Babylon). Expect to spend anywhere from 75 min to all day in this enormous museum. **Hours:** Tue-Sun 10:00-18:00 (Thur till 22:00). **Price:** Museumsinsel day-ticket—adult 12€, student 6€—audio guide included. Free entry Thursday evenings from 18:00. Free admission with Museum Pass (3-Tage-Karte). **Getting There:** To reach the Pergamon Museum—head to the west side of the island, follow the river and cross the bridge. **Note:** If they've run out of audio guides (due to recharging), keep checking back or head to the exit and plead for one just turned in. Another way to obtain the facts is to pick up the informative pamphlets placed near select exhibitions—definitely grab the pamphlet on the Pergamon Altar, which illustrates the Gods and Giants. Upon entering the museum, daypacks and coats must be checked—this can be done by depositing a euro coin into a locker (downstairs in corner; if occupied give your stuff to the attendant), coin pops back out when locker is reopened.

Altes Museum & Egyptian Museum: This elongated structure bolstered by a row of bullet-peppered Ionic-style columns was built from 1823-30 at the forefront of Museumsinsel, facing the Lustgarten, Berliner Dom and Unter den Linden boulevard. The Altes Museum—an extension of the Pergamon Museum—houses the Antiquity Collection

(Antikensammlung), a significant compilation of artwork from the ancient Greeks, Romans and Etruscans. Don't miss the battle helmets from Olympia, 6th century B.C. Not too long ago (Aug 2005), much to the delight of many, the ultra-popular and critically acclaimed Egyptian Museum moved its collection here, including its prized possession: the bust of Queen Nefertiti (check out her remarkable facial features), dating from about 1340 B.C.—New Kingdom, 18th Dynasty. *Hours:* Tue-Sun 10:00-18:00 (Thur till 22:00). *Price:* Museumsinsel day-ticket—adult 12€, student 6€—audio guide included. Free entry Thursday afternoons from 18:00. Free admission with Museum Pass (3-Tage-Karte).

Alte Nationalgalerie: Completed in 1876, the "Old National Gallery" exhibits one of Germany's largest collections of art from the 19th century. Distinguished German painters such as Max Liebermann as well as works by celebrated French Impressionists—Paul Cézanne, Edgar Degas, Edouard Manet, Claude Monet, Auguste Renoir, and sculptures by Auguste Rodin—grace the halls of this gallery. *Note:* Start on the top floor and work your way down. *Hours:* Tue-Sun 10:00-18:00 (Thur till 22:00). *Price:* Museumsinsel day-ticket—adult 12€, student 6€. Free entry Thursday evenings from 18:00. Free with Museum Pass (3-Tage-Karte). *Getting There:* Alte Nationalgalerie is situated behind and to the right of the Altes Museum—enclosed by a curtain of pockmarked Greek-style columns.

Coin Cabinet: (Münzkabinett) At the tip of Museumsinsel is the Bode-Museum, which houses Germany's largest coin collection with around 500,000 pieces dating from 600 B.C. to modern times (remainder of museum is closed for renovations till summer 2006). The Coin Cabinct also houses medallions, paper money and historical seals. *Hours:* Tue-Fri 10:00-16:30. *Price:* Museumsinsel day-ticket—adult 12€, student 6€. Free entry Thursday afternoons from 12:30. Free admission with Museum Pass (3-Tage-Karte).

Kulturforum: During the Cold War, the cultural heart of Berlin lay in the eastern half of the city behind the infamous Berlin Wall—thus the "Culture Forum" was developed in the western half of the city from 1968. Today, the Kulturforum is Berlin's second most popular museum quarter and the largest, maintaining several museums—the most notable collections are in the *Gemäldegalerie* and the *Neue Nationalgalerie*. The Kulturforum is situated a few minutes west of Potsdamer Platz, neighboring the Tiergarten, Berlin's Philharmonic concert hall, the enormous State Library, and the German Resistance Memorial (page 380). *Price:* Kulturforum day-ticket—allows free entry into all museums belonging to the quarter—adult 8€, student 4€ (available from museum). *Getting There:* S1, S2, U2 Potsdamer Platz—then walk west along Potsdamer Str.

Gemäldegalerie: This gigantic "Picture Gallery"—totaling 72 rooms covering nearly 2 kilometers—possesses one of the world's finest collections of European art from the 13th thru 17th centuries. Italian, German, Flemish and Dutch masters are all present: Botticelli, Titian (Tizian), Raphael (Raffael), Dürer, Holbein, Brueghel, Rubens and van Dyck. Most significant are the some two dozen Rembrandt masterpieces on display, which ranks as one of the planet's top collections of the famed Dutchman. Expect to spend anywhere from 90 min to most of the day in the Gemäldegalerie. *Hours:* Tue-Sun 10:00-18:00 (Thur till 22:00). *Price:* Kulturforum day-ticket—adult 8€, student 4€—audio guide included. Free entry Thursday evenings from 18:00. Free admission with Museum Pass (3-Tage-Karte).

Neue Nationalgalerie: Referred to as the "temple of light and glass," the "New National Gallery" features 20th-century art ranging from Cubism to Expressionism and Bauhaus to Surrealism. Featured artists include Max Beckmann, Salvador Dali, Ernst Ludwig Kirchner and Pablo Picasso. The New National Gallery is located at Potsdamer Str. 50, across from the supersized State Library. *Hours:* Tue-Sun 10:00-18:00 (Thur till

22:00). *Price:* Kulturforum day-ticket—adult 8€, student 4€. Free entry Thursday evenings from 18:00. Free admission with Museum Pass (3-Tage-Karte). *Note:* Before visiting, double check that the permanent collection is on display.

MUSEUMS, *FREE* Admission

German Resistance Memorial: (Gedenkstätte Deutscher Widerstand) A must for WWII buffs; the memorial and museum recounts the German resistance movement via a maze of exhibits—more than 5000 photographs and documents illustrate the motives, actions and goals of individuals and groups involved in resisting the Nazis. What makes this memorial extra poignant is its location: the Bendlerblock, a historical group of buildings on the former Bendlerstrasse that accommodated Germany's War Ministry. It was here that Hitler first spoke of Lebensraum ("living space," a.k.a. German resettlement in the east—Feb 1933) and where the invasion of Poland was planned, as well as the assault on France and the offensive against Russia. Yet Bendlerblock is best remembered for its central role during the July Plot, when a senior German officer—Claus von Stauffenberg—tried to assassinate Hitler (at the Wolf's Lair in today's Ketrzyn, Poland) on July 20, 1944, and overthrow the National Socialist government. The plan failed and several hundred Germans were condemned to death as accomplices, starting with the execution of Stauffenberg in the building's courtyard. After the war, on the 10-year anniversary of the July Plot, Bendlerstrasse was ceremoniously renamed "Stauffenbergstrasse."

Upon entering the memorial you'll see (right) the following inscription on the wall: *"Here in the former Army High Command, Germans organized the attempt to overthrow the lawless National Socialist regime on July 20, 1944. For this they sacrificed their lives."* Amble forward into the courtyard of honor. To your left is the entrance into the museum. Farther ahead on the left (against wall) is a wreath and a plaque memorializing the masterminds of the July Plot who paid the ultimate price for their actions, it reads: *"They died here for Germany on the 20th of July 1944: Colonel-General Ludwig Beck; General of the Infantry Friedrich Olbricht; Colonel Claus von Stauffenberg; Colonel Albrecht Ritter Mertz von Quirnheim; 1st Lt. Werner von Haeften."*

The memorial's permanent exhibition—German Resistance to National Socialism—is presented on the second floor in the historic offices of the ill-fated July Plot, including Stauffenberg's office. <u>Hours:</u> Mon-Fri 9:00-18:00 (Thur till 20:00), Sat/Sun 10:00-18:00. (www.gdw-berlin.de) <u>Price:</u> FREE entry and English audio guide (leave ID as deposit). Informative book for sale (3€) at reception counter. <u>Getting There:</u> The memorial is located at Stauffenbergstr. 13—a 10-min walk west of Potsdamer Platz, behind the Kulturforum. <u>Note:</u> For more info on Claus von Stauffenberg and the July Plot, refer to (page 466) chapter *Tomb-Lovers, Who's Buried Where? WWII Buffs.* At the Tiergarten end of Stauffenbergstr. are the Austrian and Egyptian embassies. <u>*WWII Buffs:*</u> From the museum, mosey around the corner to No. 4 Sigismundstr. and check out the war-torn facade—it has been preserved as a remembrance to the "wounds of war."

German-Russian Museum: Situated deep in the former Soviet sector of Berlin is the suburb of Karlshorst, where on May 8, 1945, Nazi Germany signed a declaration of surrender officially ending the war in Europe. The building (now museum) selected for this historic event was erected in 1938 as an officers' club for the German army's Pioneer School. During the Battle for Berlin (April-May 1945) it was overrun by the Soviets and commissioned as the headquarters for their Fifth Assault Army. Since central Berlin was a heap of rubble, it was here that Marshal Zhukov—Supreme Soviet Commander—chose to accept the signatures of German generals (Keitel, Friedeburg and Stumpff) for the unconditional surrender of Nazi Germany. It was also here that on October 10, 1949, East Germany officially became the German Democratic Republic (GDR). In May 1995, on the 50th anniversary of V-E Day, the building opened as the German-Russian Museum, which steps the visitor through the Russian front (1941-44) and the original signing chamber where the war ended. Also on display is an astonishing collection of pictures, weapons, uniforms, medals, propaganda posters, and heavy armor (in back garden). To be blunt, the German-Russian Museum is a WWII buff's wet dream! Expect a visit to take at least 90 min, but allow a minimum of 4 hours to include travel time to/fro Berlin. Since you're on that side of town, consider visiting some sites in Eastern Berlin, i.e. Stasi HQ (page 369). _Note:_ exhibition is in German—buy the 2€ translation guide as part souvenir and donation. When in the museum, follow signs "Rundgang" guiding you between rooms. (www.museum-karlshorst.de) _Hours:_ Tue-Sun 10:00-18:00. _Price:_ FREE entry! _Getting There:_ Museum is located at Zwieseler Str. 4, a good hour from central Berlin! Ride the subway S3 to Karlshorst and exit Treskowallee (then *20-min walk, or catch bus #396 outside station)—*walk away from train bridge and head north some 20 meters on Treskowallee (follow brown sign) and turn right on Rheinsteinstr.; at the end of this street is the museum. _GPS:_ N52° 29.169 - E13° 32.339

Allied Museum: (Alliiertenmuseum) This intriguing museum proudly recounts West Berlin's occupation by the Allies (USA, UK and France) from July 4, 1945, to Sept 4, 1994. Housed in the neighborhood of the former HQ of the U.S. military government and Supreme Command of the legendary Berlin Brigade, the exhibition spans nearly five decades tracking the Allies as they move into their predetermined sectors of occupation in 1945, manages the ups and downs of the Berlin Airlift, calculates Cold War espionage, defuses tense standoffs with Soviet troops, and neatly marches along the grand boulevard of Strasse des 17 Juni for their teary-eyed going-home parade in 1994. Of the many historical items on display, the largest include a British "Hastings" airplane _(used in the Berlin Airlift by the RAF)_ — A railroad car from the French military train _(each of the three Allied powers ran a daily military train between West Germany and Berlin. Besides supplying the city with goods, the train also served as a tool to monitor Soviet movements)_ — A restored segment of the famous 'spy tunnel' _(built by American and British intelligence agencies in 1953/54 to tap Soviet lines of communication)_ — And the most adored exhibit is the original Checkpoint Charlie guardhouse. _Tel.#_ 030/818-1990. (www.alliiertenmuseum.de) _Hours:_ (closed Wed) Thur thru Tue 10:00-18:00. _Price:_ FREE entry! _Getting There:_ Museum is located in southwest Berlin at Clayallee 135 (street named in honor of Lucius Clay, U.S. military governor of Germany 1947-49 and mastermind of the Berlin Airlift). Ride the subway U3 to Oskar-Helene-Heim, then 10-min walk. _Note:_ Between museum and U-Bahn station is the Truman Plaza and U.S. Consulate (at Clayallee and Hüttenweg). Further evidence denoting the area's Cold War prominence are the names of neighboring streets: Taylor, Flanagan, Marshall, Tom Sawyer, and the nearby U-Bahn station Uncle Tom's Hütte (Cabin).

MUSEUMS, All Other

Checkpoint Charlie Museum: (Mauermuseum Haus am Checkpoint Charlie) Most everyone is checking out Charlie; the lines at the cashier attest to the museum's mega-popularity. Here a comprehensive gathering of exhibits transport you over, under and through the Berlin Wall in various attempts—some desperate, some coolly calculated—to escape from behind the Iron Curtain. The museum is situated opposite the legendary Checkpoint Charlie border crossing. The original checkpoint guardhouse has long since been removed (on display at the above _Allied Museum_) and replaced with a replica as it appeared in the early '60s, complete with sandbags. The Checkpoint Charlie museum is expensive (9.50€) but worthwhile for historians and enthusiasts—expect a visit to take between 90 min and 4hr. _Hours:_ daily, 9:00-22:00. (www.mauermuseum.de) _Price:_ adult 9.50€, student 5.50€, audio guide 3€. Welcome Card holders receive 25% off adult price.

Getting There: The former Checkpoint Charlie is situated at the intersection of Friedrich-str. and Zimmerstr.—1.5km southeast of the Brandenburg Gate—and the museum is located a few doors south at Friedrichstr. 43. Ride the subway U6 to Kochstraße and exit Haus am Checkpoint Charlie. At street level you'll be faced with a Soviet soldier staring at you from the end of the block. Proceed straight to reach the replica guardhouse and museum (right). *Note:* To get to the Jewish Museum (next entry) from the Checkpoint Charlie museum is a 20-min walk—exit left out of museum and head south on Friedrich-str. to E.T.A.-Hoffmann-Promenade (after Besselstr.) and make a left—at the end of the lane you'll see the Jewish Museum across the street.

Jewish Museum: Europe's largest Jewish museum—spanning more than 15,000sq.m./ 161,500sq.ft.—features an overwhelming collection dedicated to 2000 years of German-Jewish history and culture. Enter the museum via the 18th-century Baroque building next door and descend into the subterranean "Axes," each of these offering a distinct passage. The initial and longest journeys to the main exhibition via the Axis of Continuity. The second leads outdoors to a pensive garden symbolic of the exile and emigration of Jews from Germany. The third axis dead-ends at the Holocaust Tower, an isolated and thought-provoking space lit by a hole in the ceiling.

With a price tag of U.S. $40 million, the museum opened Sept 9, 2001, and has since attracted more than 3 million visitors. The building's design is one of Berlin's architectural highlights, interpreted by visitors as a lightning bolt striking the city, or defined by the architect himself—Daniel Libeskind—as a burst Star of David. The zigzagging fortress-like structure features a unique zinc-plated facade and a series of windows slashing through its skin. New York-based Libeskind has achieved worldwide acclaim for his architectural projects ranging from the Imperial War Museum in Man-chester, England, to the Jewish Museum in San Francisco, and in February 2003 he won the prized competition for the most renowned building project: New York's World Trade Center site. *Hours:* daily, 10:00-20:00 (Mon till 22:00), last admission one hour prior to closing. *Price:* adult 5€, student 2.50€, free with Museum Pass (3-Tage-Karte), Welcome Card holders receive 30% off adult price. (www.jmberlin.de) *Getting There:* Museum is located at Lindenstr. 9—subway U1 Hallesches Tor or U6 Kochstraße. From Checkpoint Charlie the museum is a 20-min walk.

New Synagogue: Upon its consecration in 1866, the New Synagogue qualified as the largest Jewish temple in Germany, affording 3200 seats and a landmark golden dome reaching a height of 50m/164ft. During the 20th century, the New Synagogue suffered immensely under Hitler's anti-Semitic rule—first on Kristallnacht (Night of the Broken Glass) Nov 9, 1938, and throughout the war years via Allied bombs. Rebuilt (partially) and reopened by 1995, the New Synagogue exhibits the history and vestiges of the original structure as well as Jewish life in Berlin. *Hours:* April-Sept Sun/Mon 10:00-20:00, Tue-Thurs 10:00-18:00, Fri 10:00-17:00, (less Nov-March)—last admission 30 min prior to closing. Dome is open in summer. *Price:* (dome + exhibition) adult 4.50€, student 3€. *Getting There:* New Synagogue is located at Oranienburger Str. 28—subway S1, S2 Oranienburger Str.

German History Museum: Treasures of Germany's past will pleasingly overwhelm enthusiasts in the "Historisches Museum"—the oldest edifice on Berlin's grand avenue, Unter den Linden. In this peach-colored building—formerly the city's arsenal (18C)—more than 700,000 objects are stored, e.g. art, weapons, flags, medallions, uniforms, and trophies of war from the sword-wielding Middle Ages to the workers' paradise of the GDR. Bookworms will want to study the museum's library containing roughly 200,000 titles (library hours Mon-Fri 9:00-16:30). What's more, in 2003 a 54€ million exhibition hall with spiraling glass entrance was added to the museum by star architect I. M. Pei—

creator of the Rock 'n' Roll Hall of Fame in Cleveland, the J.F.K. Library in Boston and the Louvre's glass pyramid in Paris. To find the new addition, go down (street) Hinter dem Gießhaus next to the temple-like Neue Wache. (www.dhm.de) *Hours:* daily, 10:00-18:00. *Price:* 2€, *FREE* Mondays. *Getting There:* GHM is located at Unter den Linden 2, between the Neue Wache and Spree River.

Natural History Museum: Admirers of extinct reptiles or shooting stars should visit the "Naturkunde," or Natural History Museum, featuring Germany's most extensive collection of meteorites (third biggest in Europe) and the world's largest mounted dinosaur skeleton, which is some 150 million years old (brachiosaurus—12m/39ft high and 23m/75ft long). *Another 30-odd skeletons dating from the Triassic, Jurassic and Cretaceous periods are on display in the dinosaur hall. *__Note:__ The dinosaur hall is largely closed for renovations till 2007 and only the head and spine of the largest mounted dinosaur skeleton can be seen. *Hours:* Tue-Fri 9:30-17:00, Sat/Sun 10:00-18:00. *Price:* (includes audio guide) adult 3.50€, student 2€, free with Museum Pass (3-Tage-Karte), Welcome Card holders pay 2.10€. *Getting There:* NHM is located at Invalidenstr. 43—subway U6 Zinnowitzer Str.

World-Class Auto Showrooms

What would a trip to Deutschland be without getting behind the wheel of a coveted German driving machine? Well, here's your chance to get personal with the nation's latest and greatest automobiles in flagship showrooms. What's more, there's no pressure to buy and entry is *FREE!* Of the following five museum-like dealerships, four are located on Friedrichstrasse. Without a doubt, Mercedes operates the most exciting showroom in town—therefore, it shall be listed first.

Mercedes World: Mercedes went all-out in the nation's capital and constructed (July 2000) the world's most modern dealership, resembling an ocean liner made of glass. This enormous multilevel structure—consisting of 14,000sq.m/150,700sq.ft. of exhibition floor space—not only boasts a myriad of luxury vehicles but also two 17-meter-high rock-climbing walls, a 20-meter wall of water, a Formula 1 simulator, a restaurant, a playpen for kids (featuring electric go-carts), valet parking and exotic flora, including an olive tree from southern Italy almost as old as Berlin itself. No doubt a visit to Mercedes World would be a trip highlight. Check out their website for a 360-degree perspective (www.mercedes-welt.de). *Hours:* Mon-Fri 6:00-24:00, Sat 8:00-22:00, Sun 10:00-22:00. *Note:* Call ahead to see whether any English tours are scheduled, tel.# 030/390-100. *Getting There:* MW is located at Salzufer 1 (west end of Tiergarten, off Strasse des 17 Juni)—S5, S7, S9 Tiergarten, then eight-minute walk. *GPS:* N52° 30.850 - E13° 19.848

Volkswagen World: Under the roof of Volkswagen's mall-like dealership you'll not only discover the new Beetle, Golf and the ultra-economical Lupo, but also models from Volkswagen's extended family: Bentley, Bugatti, Seat and Skoda. *Hours:* Mon-Fri 9:00-20:00, Sat/Sun 10:00-18:00. *Tel.#* 030/2092-1200. *Getting There:* VW is located at Unter den Linden 21 (corner of Friedrichstr.).

Audi Forum: At this showroom you'll discover the newest and hottest behind the four rings of Audi on two floors. *Hours:* Mon-Fri 9:00-20:00, Sat/Sun 10:00-18:00. *Tel.#* 030/2063-5200. (www.audi.com) *Getting There:* Audi is located at Friedrichstr. 83—other end of block from VW. *History:* In 1904, August Horch established the Horch motor vehicle company. Some five years later, ongoing squabbles within management compelled August Horch to leave the company. Already a popular brand name in Germany, the Horch motor vehicle company applied for no fewer than 26 trademarks to insure that August Horch had no chance of starting a new company using his name. August Horch lived automobiles and indeed he founded a new motor vehicle company, but this one could not bear his name. He contested the trademarks in court, but lost the battles. In 1910, August Horch called an urgent meeting with his associates to brainstorm a new name. After hours of tossing around a bevy of unremarkable ideas, an associate's son sitting quietly in the corner of the room doing his homework—or that's what everyone thought—suddenly turned to his father and said: "Audiatur et altera pars *[Latin: Also the other party has to be heard]* … wouldn't it be a good idea to call it 'Audi'?" It was a hit! In 1932, Audi joined forces with three top car manufacturers (DKW, Horch and Wanderer) creating the "Auto Union." This friendly foursome required a new insignia to stamp on their vehicles, something neutral and unifying. The result: four intersecting rings symbolizing the inseparable bond between the new alliance. Today, Audi's base of operations is in the Bavarian city of Ingolstadt, 75km north of Munich.

Opel: Internationally, Opel is arguably Germany's least known car manufacturer—however, within Deutschland, it's big business. Adam Opel began his multifaceted production line with a version of the sewing machine in 1862 and progressed into bicycles two decades later (on display in showroom). In 1899, the Opel family continued the tradition of wheeled transportation by building their first automobile. Fritz Opel (Adam's son) was behind the helm of the RAK2 ("the Rocket"; on display) when it reached the speed of 238kph/148mph in 1928. The following year, Fritz set a world speed record of 254kph/158mph with the RAK3 in Frankfurt. In the 1970s, Opel gained more than 20% of the market share, qualifying it as Germany's biggest automobile manufacturer. Since the pubescent days of sewing machines and rocket engines, Opel has sold more than 55 million vehicles. Opel's showroom consists of two floors highlighting the company's past and present. The in-house café (Adam's) offers free Internet. *Hours:* Mon-Fri 10:00-20:00, Sat/Sun 10:00-18:00. *Tel.#* 030/2061-44500. *Getting There:* Opel is located at Friedrichstr. 94—north end of Friedrichstr. on the right-hand side just before the train bridge belonging to Friedrichstrasse station.

MINI: Steeped in British culture, this petite vehicle has been Germanized by the Bavarian workhorse, BMW, and is currently enjoying a renaissance. Assembled in Oxford, England, MINIs are shipped globally to customers who are seduced by its boffo body and intimate interior. (www.mini.com) *Hours:* Mon-Fri 10:00-19:00, Sat 10:00-16:00, Sun 12:00-16:00. *Tel.#* 030/3498-35100. *Getting There:* MINI is located at Friedrichstr. 191—across from Starbucks and the U-Bahn station Stadtmitte (U6/U2).

Best Views

Reichstag: (page 357) Rise above German parliament for a must-see panoramic view of central Berlin. *FREE* entry! daily, 8:00-24:00.

Rathaus Schöneberg: (page 374) At this must-visit "town hall" in the suburb of Schöneberg you'll discover a stunning view, a liberty bell, and the memory of a president. *FREE* entry!

Balloon Ride, "Hi-Flyer": Hop aboard the multicolored Hi-Flyer helium balloon and hover (150m/492ft) above Checkpoint Charlie for a unique, hair-raising view of downtown Berlin. Reservations not necessary. *Hours:* May-Oct 10:00 till late, Nov-April 11:00-18:00. *Price:* adult 19€, student 10€, free for children 6 or under; Welcome Card holders receive 30% off adult price. *Note:* Balloon does not fly when windy. Wind hotline: *Tel.#* 030/2266-78811. *Getting There:* Balloon is located at Wilhelmstr. and Zimmerstr.

Fernsehturm: (TV-Tower) Without a doubt the giant disco ball dominating Berlin's eastern skyline offers the most impressive, heart-skipping views in town. One million thrill-seekers annually cram into the elevators for the 40-second ear-popping ride to the viewing level at 203m/665ft. The floor above the viewing level contains Berlin's highest restaurant, the revolving "Telecafé" (30-min full revolution)—tel.# 030/242-3333—approx. price per person: breakfast (10:00-12:00) 6-12€; lunch (from 11:00) 13-20€; soda 2.50€, beer 3€, cappuccino 3.60€, chocolate torte 3€. _Hours:_ daily, 9:00-24:00 (Nov-Feb from 10:00). _Price:_ (elevator to viewing level) 7.50€, Welcome Card holders pay 6€. (www.berlinerfernsehturm.de) _Note:_ expect 30-min wait for elevator. _Getting There:_ Tower is located at Alexanderplatz—S5, S7, S9 or U2, U8.

Siegessäule: (Victory Column) For a splendid panoramic view of Berlin, ascend the monument's dizzying 285-step staircase to the observation platform. _Hours:_ daily, 10:00-17:00 (April-Oct 9:30-18:30). _Price:_ (includes museum) adult 2.20€, student 1.50€. _Getting There:_ Hop on the touristy bus #100. To access the column, step into any of the four temple-like structures on the perimeter of the traffic circle and descend to the underground tunnel. _Note:_ For more on the Siegessäule, see page 372—_Tiergarten_.

SHOPPING

Who doesn't relish a little retail therapy once in a while? And there's no better German city than Berlin to do the rounds. Generally, bargains can be found in the eastern suburbs—the former Soviet sector is coming-of-age and drawing people by the busloads. The classic Berlin shopping experience can be had on—and around—the store-lined _Kurfürstendamm_. Militaria and antique hunters check out the _Berliner Antikmarkt_. Weekenders will treasure rummaging through the city's loaded _flea markets_ (Flohmärkte). _Note:_ Shops will be open (generally) 12:00-17:00 on the following Sundays in 2006: April 30, Oct 1 and Nov 5. Additionally, shopping hours in Berlin will be widely extended during the World Cup soccer tournament—June 9 thru July 9—opening Mon-Sat 6:30-24:00, Sun 14:00-20:00.

Kurfürstendamm: During the Cold War, swanky "Ku'damm" was _THE_ shopping boulevard in Berlin. Since the German reunification in 1990, the trend has slowly migrated east—Friedrichstrasse is back in fashion and Friedrichshain is good for a bargain (Schnäppchen). Nonetheless, the customary Berlin shopping excursion still makes its way onto glossy Kurfürstendamm to experience the former Rodeo Drive of West Germany. Specialty shops and cheaper prices can be found on the side streets. At the top of Ku'damm, the Kaiser Wilhelm memorial church intersects Tauentzienstr., where at No. 24 you'll find KaDeWe, the continent's largest department store.

KaDeWe: (Kaufhaus des Westens) This mega "Department Store of the West" has nearly half a million goods for sale, dispersed between 646,000 sq. ft. (or 15 acres) of floor space on 8 levels. KaDeWe opened its doors in 1907 featuring an impressive 258,000 sq. ft. (or 6 acres) of floor space on 5 levels. During the Cold War, the fully stocked department store took on a political role as the retail nirvana of a democratic state. Today, apart from the broad-spectrum of goods for sale, KaDeWe boasts a wide variety of services from childcare to shoe repair. While browsing, don't be surprised to see a customer shopping with his or her dog in tow. Europeans consider this normal. Animals aside, on the ground floor you'll see women getting makeovers and men testing free samples of cologne. Head over to the elevator and press 6; the scenic ride will conclude on the 6th floor where you'll begin an appetizing odyssey through Europe's largest delicatessen (don't visit on an empty stomach). This enthralling food emporium offers—among other items—1300 kinds of cheese, 1200 sorts of sausage/ham, 400 types of bread, an intoxicating array of sweets, shelves of international beers, and an ocean's worth of fishy foods. Hundreds of cooks, pastry chefs and service attendants are at the

ready to satisfy your palate—even a pianist playing classical tunes to enhance your shopping experience. On the level above (top floor) there are tables available (with a non-smoking section) for you to savor your goodies along with a somewhat pricey cafeteria. *Hours:* Mon-Fri 10:00-20:00, Sat 9:30-20:00. *Getting There:* KaDeWe is located at Tauentzienstr. 21-24. Arrive via the must-see, turn-of-the-century U-Bahn station "Wittenbergplatz" (U1/U2)—exit Tauentzienstr. and KaDeWe is the building across the street taking up the whole corner block. Opposite is a Deutsche Bank and at the other end of the boulevard you'll cop a great view of the Kaiser Wilhelm Memorial Church. *Drivers:* 1000-space parking garage available.

Friedrichstrasse: Once a mecca for lively cafés, taverns, nightclubs and burlesque theaters, Friedrichstrasse became a decimated war zone in 1945 and ultimately a socialistically drab street, lined with cookie-cutter office and housing blocks dead-ending at Checkpoint Charlie. Today, this north-south avenue racing through the heart of Berlin typifies the city's reinvention post reunification with a plethora of modernistic buildings accommodating premier auto dealerships and upscale shopping (e.g. Galeries Lafayette, Hugo Boss, Gucci, Hermès, Louis Vuitton, Yves Saint Laurent) where trendsetters and trend followers come to score the latest fads and hottest styles.

Berliner Antikmarkt: Part of the historic Friedrichstrasse subway station (Georgenstr. side) is home to the Berliner Antikmarkt, a rich cluster of antique shops. Inside, a browsing-friendly walkway connects all the dealers. *Hours:* Wed thru Mon 11:00-18:00. Militaria (WWII) buffs check out AKM-Depot's petite (and pricey) shop (inside door) at 191 Georgenstr.—tel/fax. 030/204-1842 (little English spoken). *GPS:* N52° 31.185 - E13° 23.377

Street Vendors: If you encounter these guys selling souvenirs or Soviet-era memorabilia (usually replicas), be sure to haggle the price down. Browse the different stalls for the best deal. Commonly, the price will drop the less interest you show—especially when you walk away. Bottom line: Be patient and prudent!

Flea Markets (Flohmärkte)

Bursting with bric-a-brac, Berlin hosts more flea markets than any other German city. Weekend bazaars abound and you never know what you might uncover: a treasure from a past empire, Soviet-era memorabilia, a Bauhaus lamp, a trinket from a half-forgotten era, or perhaps Hitler's tiara. To update your German vocabulary, here are a few words you'll see during your search for that elusive find: *Trödelmarkt* (secondhand market), *Antiquitäten* (antiques), *Schnäppchen* (bargain). Below we've listed a handful of markets to get you started on the path to secondhand treasures and trinkets. _Note:_ Generally the prices are negotiable, so exercise your haggling skills.

Tiergarten: Arguably Berlin's best—and biggest—flea market is teeming with tourists, dealers, speculators, and locals competing to find a bargain. However, the word bargain is probably too generous, as prices aren't usually negotiable and they can be steep, too. Here you'll uncover a myriad of exclusive objects from old dolls to porcelain wares and collectible paintings to antique furnishings. _Hours:_ Sat/Sun 10:00-17:00. _Getting There:_ Market is located outside the S-Bahn station, Tiergarten S5, S7, S9. _GPS:_ N52° 30.823 - E13° 20.108

Potsdamer Platz: To be honest, folks, this market just opened late 2005, thus we haven't visited it and can't tell you much about it other than what our sources have said: "It's worth mentioning to your readers." There you have it. Okay, our view: Potsdamer Platz is fashionable and the market prices here probably reflect that. You can be sure we'll be there in 2006 to get the lowdown. Maybe we'll see ya there? _Hours:_ Sun 9:00-16:00 (maybe Sat too; check beforehand). _Getting There:_ Market is located outside the U-Bahn station, Mendelssohn-Bartholdy-Park U2.

Rathaus Schöneberg: At this flea market on John-F.-Kennedy-Platz you can pick through stalls as well as discover a dynamite view, a liberty bell, and the iconic words of a president (page 374). _Hours:_ Sat/Sun 8:00-16:00. _Getting There:_ subway U4 Rathaus Schöneberg—then five-minute walk. _GPS:_ N52° 29.119 - E13° 20.680

Arkonaplatz: As far as hand-me-down markets go, the one at Arkonaplatz is tops—items range from old knickknacks to cheap jewelry to cool clothes. Since it's located in former East Berlin, prices are reasonable and negotiable. Near the center of the market, look for Constantine—the guy selling retrostyle Americana. He loves North Americans and would be happy to make you a deal or point you to one. _Note:_ When visiting Arkonaplatz, also pick through Flohmarkt am Mauerpark (next entry). _Hours:_ Sun 9:30-16:00. _Getting There:_ Take subway U8 to Bernauer Strasse and exit station Bernauer Str. At top of steps go right and make the first right (Ruppiner Str.)—as you do this you'll step over a double row of cobblestones; these represent the path of the Berlin Wall. Notice the vacant lots either side of you—this was the former "death strip"—less than 20 years ago you would have been shot for being here! OK, enough of this glum talk, let's go find a bargain; continue straight two blocks and you'll see the market on the left. _GPS:_ N52° 32.233 - E13° 24.119

Flohmarkt am Mauerpark: This "Flea Market at Wall Park" has similar knickknacks as its neighbor—Arkonaplatz—but historically it's located in a heck-of-a-place adjacent to a lengthy section of the Berlin Wall at the eastern end of Bernauer Strasse, where many desperate attempts to escape were documented. (For a history of the Wall, flip to page 354.) _Hours:_ Sun 8:00-16:00. _Getting There:_ Take subway U8 to Bernauer Strasse and exit station Bernauer Str. At top of steps go right and walk east along Bernauer Str. about 7 min to Mauerpark (on left). *GPS:* N52° 32.409 - E13° 24.152

Antik Market: This worthwhile bazaar in former East Berlin has a lot of old books, postcards, coins, records and, of course, pre-loved treasures. It's really easy to get to so you have no excuse not to go! Oh, we should probably tell you, though, that the prices here are slightly higher than the two above-listed markets in the east but much lower than those, say, at the Tiergarten in the west. *Hours:* Sun 9:00-16:30. *Getting There:* Market is located at the back of Ostbahnhof—S3, S5, S7, S9. *Note:* Out front of Ostbahnhof begins the East Side Gallery (page 370).

Markstrasse: If you're looking for junk, nothing but junk, ultra-cheap junk, stop by Markstrasse and join much of Berlin's Turkish population in sifting through oodles of junk. *Hours:* Sat/Sun 8:00-16:00. *Getting There:* subway U8 Franz-Neumann-Platz—then walk to McDonald's on Markstrasse, where you'll find the market next door. *GPS:* N52° 33.630 - E13° 21.894

ENTERTAINMENT

Under this category there are three topics: *Events/Festivals, Headline Concerts,* and *Döner Kebaps.* Huh, Döner what?

Döner Kebap: After an evening (or day) out on the town, a popular coming-home bite is the Döner Kebap—the unofficial street food of Berlin—pita bread stuffed with lettuce, tomatoes, onions (optional), lamb or chicken shavings, and a choice from three sauces: garlic, chili or yogurt. (We recommend yogurt.) Kebap shops (typically Turkish) are everywhere and open all hours. The price for a Kebap in Berlin ranges from 2€-3€, but we know where you can score a fat-and-juicy one for 1.25€. Yes, that's right, 1.25€! Just show this book to our pal, Ahmet, who runs the *Safari-Bistro* at Brunnenstr. 25. *Hours:* daily, early till late. *Getting There:* To reach Safari-Bistro take subway U8 to Bernauer Strasse and exit station Brunnenstr. At top of steps go left and cross the street. Continue straight and midway along the second block you'll find Ahmet at No. 25. *Note:* Safari-Bistro is near the Arkonaplatz flea market (page 387); about a 15-minute walk from the Berlin Wall Documentation Center and Mauer Park (page 356-57), and about a seven-minute walk north of the Circus hostel (page 390). *GPS:* N52° 32.015 - E13° 23.897

Headline Concerts, Berlin 2006

Note: Prices, dates, concerts may have changed or been added — query TI or ticket agency for latest details.

Paul Weller: April 23, 20:00 at Huxley's Neue Welt. Price 31€
   Erasure: April 27, 20:00 at the Universität der Künste. Price 40-44€
The Buzzcocks: April 27, 21:00 at KATO Kulturbahnhof (Kreuzberg). Price 19€
   Ray Davies: April 28, 20:00 at the Universität der Künste. Price 30-43€
Santana: May 17, 20:00 at Kindl-Bühne Wuhlheide. Price 61€
   Van Morrison: May 19, 20:00 at the Tempodrom. Price 37-51€
Ted Nugent: May 25, 20:00 at the Columbia Club. Price 36€
   Metallica: June 6, 18:30 at the Waldbühne. Price 57€
Eric Clapton: June 7, 19:00 at Kindl-Bühne Wuhlheide. Price 67€
   Rogers Waters: June 8, 19:30 at Kindl-Bühne Wuhlheide. Price 65€
Howard Jones: June 19, 20:00 at the Columbia Club. Price 32€
   Arctic Monkeys: June 24, 20:00 at Columbia Halle. Price 25€
Live: June 27, 20:00 at Columbia Halle. Price 31€
   Depeche Mode: June 28 & July 12, 19:00 at the Waldbühne. Price ??€

The Black Eyed Peas: June 28, 20:00 in front of the Reichstag. Price 38-44€
   James Blunt: July 7, 19:00 in front of the Reichstag. Price 39-41€
The Who: July 12, 19:30 at Kindl-Bühne Wuhlheide. Price 69€
   Madness: July 14, 20:00 at the Zitadelle Spandau. Price 42€
Billy Idol: July 18, 20:00 at the Zitadelle Spandau. Price 49€
   Rolling Stones: July 21, 19:00 at the Olympic Stadium. Price 93-175€
Robbie Williams: July 27-28, 18:00 at the Olympic Stadium. Price 66-88€
   Simply Red: August 16, 19:30 at the Museum Island Festival. Price 54€
B.B. King: September 7, 20:00 at the Convention Center (Messe). Price 59-102€
   Pink: October 10, 20:00 at the Max-Schmeling-Halle. Price 44-55€
James Last: November 12, 19:00 at the Velodrom. Price 39-74€
   Chris de Burgh: November 28, 20:00 at the Max-Schmeling-Halle. Price 50-73€

Events/Festivals 2006

Carnival of Cultures, June 2-5 (Fri-Mon): Roughly 100 music bands and 4000 residents will represent some 80 countries in this colorfully energetic carnival reflecting Berlin's cultural diversity. Festivities center on Blücherplatz (U6 Hallesches Tor—south end of Friedrichstr.), where international cuisine, cocktails and crafts will be for sale. The highlight of the carnival is the street parade on June 4 (12:30-21:00)—route begins on Hermannplatz and rolls along Hasenheide to its conclusion at Gneisenaustr. and Yorckstr. Officials are expecting upwards of a million spectators.

World Cup Soccer: Berlin has six matches scheduled: Tuesday **June 13**, *Brazil vs. Croatia* • Thursday **June 15**, *Sweden vs. Paraguay* • Tuesday **June 20**, *Germany vs. Ecuador* • Friday **June 23**, *Ukraine vs. Tunisia* • Friday **June 30**, *Quarter-Final* • Sunday **July 9**, *Final!* The matches will be played at Berlin's 74,000-seat Olympic Stadium (page 376). Tours of the stadium are possible, query TI for price and times.

Love Parade, July 15 (Sat): Ravers unite! After a two-year hiatus, the Love Parade—Europe's largest rave party—is back. Head to the Tiergarten.

Christopher Street Day (CSD), July 22 (Sat): This outrageously multi-sexual event is part demonstration march and part gay-pride celebration. Some 400,000 scantily clad homosexuals, bisexuals and transsexuals will parade through the inner-city streets to voice their concerns about equal rights while celebrating gay-pride. To kick-start the colorful procession will be Berlin's openly gay mayor, Klaus Wowereit, at high noon on Kurfürstendamm. From there the pageant bounces onto Tauentzienstr. to Potsdamer Platz to the Brandenburg Gate, culminating at 17:00 by the phallic-looking Siegessäule (Victory Column)—the center piece of the Tiergarten.

German-American Volksfest, July 28–Aug 20: This year marks the 46th annual German-American friendship festival, presenting cowboys, Indians, southern belles, live music, mechanical bull riding, rodeo, and corn-on-the-cob, among other things. The Volksfest will be held daily (typically 14:00-23:00, Fri/Sat till 24:00) for three weeks at the "American Village" in southwest Berlin. Combine a visit here with the nearby Allied Museum (page 381). Entry into the festival usually costs 1.50€/person; Wednesdays are Family Day (half price on rides) and Fridays are Ladies Day (1€ rides). *Getting There:* Volksfest is held at Truman Plaza—Clayallee and Argentinische Allee—which is easy to reach because it's outside the U3 station Oskar-Helene-Heim.

Berlin Marathon, Sept 24 (Sun): Roughly 40,000 runners, power walkers, and wheelchair competitors from 100 nations are expected to participate in this year's 42km marathon, scheduled to start and finish on Strasse des 17 Juni (between the Brandenburg Gate and Siegessäule). Live music and 1 million spectators line the route, inspiring the athletes' endurance. *Note:* Entry fee is 50€ to 90€, depending on when you register: 50€ Jan-April, 70€ May-June, 90€ thereafter until the **deadline:** August 4! (Unless limit of 40,000 is met prior to this date.) Interested applicants should make arrangements a.s.a.p.: tel.# 030/3012-8810 or www.berlin-marathon.com

GOOD SLEEPS
From cheap to steep!

<u>Note</u>: Expect to see inflated room rates or the "no vacancy" signs out during the World Cup soccer tournament, June 9 thru July 9. Fans in desperate need of a room check out this website: www.host-a-fan.de

Hostel, CIRCUS: Weinbergsweg 1 (www.circus-berlin.de) *Tel.#* 030/2839-1433. Anyone who has ever considered staying in a hostel should overnight here, there's hardly a better equivalent in town—or in urbanized Germany for that matter. The Circus is fresh and clean and wonderfully located near cultural institutions, Cold War spectacles, the subway, delicious eateries and inexpensive Laundromats. *(Note: Because nearby Laundromats only charge 3€/load with powder, save your washing for Berlin.)* What's more, the Circus offers 24-hour reception, Internet, a lively bar, café, bike rental (May-Oct 12€/day), friendly staff and a very resourceful front desk that can organize your onward hostel reservation *free of charge*. <u>Price:</u> (cash only) 7/8-bed dorm 17€, 4/5-bed 19€, 3-bed 21€ (←add 2€ *one-time* linen charge→) private rooms (facilities in hallway) Sgl 33€, Dbl 50€. Private rooms (with facilities and linen) Sgl 46€, Dbl 62€. Apartment-style rooms (with kitchen/facilities/linen, *minimum two-day stay*) Dbl 77€, Quad 134€. Breakfast 2€ to 4.50€. Book your accommodations here as soon as you have dates! Oh, almost forgot, seven-minutes up the road is the Kebap king, Ahmet (page 388—*Döner Kebap*). <u>Note:</u> Front desk has access to money-saving discounts Berlin-wide as well as to a ticket center for concerts, theater or sporting events (like Berlin's soccer club, Hertha, whose home stadium is the site of the 1936 Olympics. This a great opportunity to see a German "football" match). *Suggestion:* Call ahead (with your C.C.#) for whatever event you're interested in and Circus will try to arrange this and have the tickets waiting for you upon check in. <u>Getting There:</u> subway U8 Rosenthaler Platz; exit Weinbergsweg and at the top of the steps you'll see the hostel's yellow facade on the right. <u>GPS:</u> N52° 31.809 - E13° 24.093

Hostel, CIRCUS II: Rosa-Luxemburg-Strasse 39. This is the sister property to the abovementioned Circus hostel, thus it shares the same website, tel.#, prices, and tourist-friendly qualities. Circus II is more homely and suggested for the quieter type. <u>Getting There:</u> subway U2 Rosa-Luxemburg-Platz, exit station in the opposite direction your train came and the hostel is 15 meters on right. Or it's roughly an eight-minute walk from the Circus hostel.

Hostel, Heart of Gold: Johannisstr. 11 (www.heartofgold-hostel.de) *Tel.#* 030/2900-3300. Often referred to by employees as an interplanetary vehicle, this new hostel (2003) even serves alien drinks at the bar. Besides far-out lingo, the Heart of Gold is clean, modernistic and a superb choice for your Berlin sojourn. Hostel has Internet, pool table, laundry, 24-hour bar, cosmic staff, and bands often play in the common room. Oh, and you have a choice of DVDs to watch on their big-screen TV. <u>Price:</u> (includes linen) dorm beds 13-19€. Private rooms: Sgl 36-40€, (lower price mean facilities in hall→) Dbl 46-56€. Breakfast 3€. <u>CC's:</u> VC, MC. <u>Note:</u> Stay 7 nights in a dorm, pay 6! <u>Getting There:</u> subway U6 or S-Bahn to Friedrichstrasse, then 10-min walk—cross river and continue on Friedrichstr. Make the second right on Johannisstr. and the hostel is 150m farther on left. <u>GPS:</u> N52° 31.466 - E13° 23.503

Hostel, A & O: This outfit has three well-located hostel/hotels in Berlin, providing reasonable digs for a convenient stay. Private rooms (Sgl/Dbl) come with breakfast, linen and have facilities. Dorm beds require a *one-time* 3€ linen fee. *Price:* dorm bed from 10€ (must book at least 24hr in advance to get this rate, otherwise expect to pay about 15€), Sgl/Dbl 40-70€. *CC's:* VC, MC. Properties have Internet (3€/hr), bike rental 10€/day (50€ deposit), and breakfast buffet 5€. If staying a few nights, ask whether a discount rate is available. (www.aohostel.com) *Tel.#* 030/297-7810, or toll free within Germany 0800/222-5722

A&O Bhf Zoo: Joachimstaler Str. 3. This hostel is a very convenient choice for anyone arriving into Berlin at Bahnhof Zoo early morning or late evening without reservations. *Getting There:* exit "Zoo" train station into Hardenbergplatz; from this lively area go right and cross Hardenbergstr. into Joachimstaler Str.—hostel is up the stairs.

A&O Mitte: Köpenicker Str. 127. *Tel.#* 030/809-470. This is the most recently acquired property of the A&O group, situated in a former elevator factory southeast of the city center—a handy option for those who are arriving into Berlin at Ostbahnhof early morning or late evening without reservations. *Getting There:* S5, S7, S9 (or DB) Ostbahnhof—via the main exit head to the river and cross the bridge (Schillingbrücke), then turn right (Köpenicker Str.) and it's about 100 meters on left. *Note:* nearby is the East Side Gallery (page 370).

A&O Friedrichshain: Boxhangener Str. 73. Because of its location deep in the former Soviet sector of Berlin and its large 19th-century warehouse-style accommodations, this A&O property will usually have a vacancy when other hostels in Berlin are full. Nearby is a cluster of bars and, amazingly—as if the water system is connected to the Fountain of Youth—the average age in this district seems to be about 22. *Getting There:* S-Bahn to Ostkreuz, exit station into Sonntagstr. and make the next right on Lenbachstr.—at end of street is Boxhangener Str. and the hostel. *Drivers:* plenty of parking. *Note:* hostel occasionally gets teenie-boppin' school groups—can be annoying!

Accor Hotel Group: This multinational conglomerate has some 4000 hotels in 90 countries (e.g. Motel 6, red roof inns, Dorint, Mercure) and has recently invested in Berlin (Oct 2004) big time, purchasing an entire block of Anhalter Strasse—within a 10-minute walk from Potsdamer Platz and Checkpoint Charlie—to outfit with three name hotels (adjacent to each other) offering several hundred rooms and a range of prices, from cheap to reasonable (prices increase during conventions). *CC's:* VC, MC, AE, DC. All rooms are furnished with modern amenities and facilities (shower/toilet). Breakfast can be purchased extra per person. ***Getting There:*** S-Bahn (S1/S2) Anhalter Bahnhof. *Drivers:* parking available inside (10€), or outside. *GPS:* N52° 30.290 - E13° 23.057. *Note:* Hotel ibis is the only one of the three properties that has a restaurant. *Hotel code is compatible with the Etap and ibis websites, creating a shortcut to the property—type hotel code into middle left box and click "OK"; next page click on "The Hotel" (left side).

Hotel Etap: www.etaphotel.com (*hotel code 5058) *Tel.#* 030/257-6770. Basic-service, budget hotel with (217 rooms and) everything a traveler needs, including a TV. Beds are generally a one-piece (triple) unit with a double on the bottom and a single bunk-like bed above for a child. *Price:* Sgl 45-48€, Dbl 55-58€, Trpl 55-58€ (only with child 12 or under), breakfast 5€.

Hotel ibis: www.ibishotel.com (*hotel code 3752) *Tel.#* 030/261-050. Standardized hotel comfort (having 146 rooms) at an affordable price: Sgl 64-74€, Dbl 79-89€, (Trpl available), during events 99-119€, breakfast 9€.

Suite hotel: (www.suite-hotel.com) *Tel.#* 030/200-560. Stepping up the comfort a notch, the Suite hotel prides itself on their 229 3-star suites all having 30sq.m./323sq.ft.

of floor space. *Price:* Dbl suite 89€ (Trpl possible), breakfast 8€. If staying more than three nights, ask if discount rate applies.

Hotel Luise: Luisenstr. 19 (www.luise-berlin.com) *Tel.#* 030/284-480. These fun, imaginative, outrageous, endearing digs have been individually designed by a host of European artists. Visualize sleeping in a gallery. We recommend you go to Hotel Luise's website and reserve your favorite room in advance. What's more, Hotel Luise is centrally located in a federally protected building dating from 1825, roughly an eight-minute walk from the Brandenburg Gate. All rooms have wireless Internet access. Mike is the owner and your friendly host. Say "Howdy!" for us. *Price:* Sgl 48-115€ (←lower price means facilities in hall→) Dbl 79-150€, suite 135-175€, buffet breakfast 8€. *Getting There:* subway U6 or S-Bahn to Friedrichstrasse, exit Albrechtstr. (cross river) then go left on Marienstr. to Luisenstr. and your digs. *Drivers:* private or street parking available, query reception. *GPS:* N52° 31.302 - E13° 22.793

Radisson Hotel: Karl-Liebknecht-Str. 3 (www.radisson.com/berlinde) *Tel.#* 030/238-280, toll-free reservations from USA/Canada 1-800-333-3333 or within Europe 00800/3333-3333. Adjacent to the Berliner Dom, Scandinavian Airlines has recently opened (2004) this 5-star hotel featuring rooms with ocean views. In the lobby you'll witness the AquaDom, the world's largest cylindrical aquarium (25m/82ft high, 11m/36ft wide—containing 900,000 liters of water). Besides rubbing shoulders with sharks and clown fish, the Radisson is centrally located in the heart of Berlin, meters from Museum Island, Alexanderplatz and Unter den Linden boulevard. *Price:* Sgl/Dbl 140-280€. When booking, inquire about possible special rates, such as government, seniors or hot deals. *Getting There:* S5, S7, S9 Hackescher Markt. *Note:* For more on the AquaDom flip to page 368.

Hotel Adlon: (www.hotel-adlon.de) *Tel.#* 030/22-610, toll-free reservations from USA/Canada 1-800-426-3135 or within Europe 00800/4263-1355. As far as hotels are concerned, the Adlon is the most historically exclusive address in town. Within a horse's gallop of the Brandenburg Gate, the 5-star Hotel Adlon has more than 300 luxury rooms and 70 suites available for tourists with deep pockets yearning to be pampered in the heart of Berlin. *Price:* (when booking, inquire about special weekend rates or seasonal packages) Rooms begin at 380€ and max out at 8500€ for the Presidential Suite, whose balcony many of you saw when (2002) Michael Jackson dangled his child over the railing for the throng of fans below. *Getting There:* subway U55 Brandenburg Gate. *GPS:* N52° 30.981 - E13° 22.761

EXCURSIONS

Potsdam: refer to chapter *Potsdam*, page 394.

Sachsenhausen, Concentration Camp Memorial: While swastika-waving Germans watched the so-called Aryan super athletes compete against the world at the 1936 Summer Olympics in Berlin, slave laborers were constructing the notorious Sachsenhausen concentration camp just outside the town of Oranienburg, some 30km to the north. During the camp's 9-year existence, more than 200,000 people were imprisoned here—these ranged from critics of Hitler's regime to Jews to homosexuals to Soviet soldiers. On April 21, 1945—the day prior to Sachsenhausen's liberation by Red Army soldiers—33,000 of the camp's remaining 38,000 inmates were forced by the Nazi (SS) guards to march northwest away from the advancing Soviet troops. Many prisoners died of cold, starvation, physical exhaustion, or by the hand of their captures. As American and Soviet units closed in, the SS guards disappeared and the surviving prisoners were rescued. Today, few of the camp's original barracks or structures remain. Nonetheless, a visit here—although somber—is highly worth your time. Because of the memorial's comprehensive, multimedia exhibition (in English), allow at least two hours for a visit—do not come with little time—and add another two hours to your excursion for travel to/from Berlin. (www.gedenkstaette-sachsenhausen.de) Be sure and pick up the excellent (and free) foldout memorial brochure with brief history and site map. And definitely walk through the museum building on your right after entering the camp. *Hours:* (camp memorial) Tue-Sun 8:30-16:30 (mid-March thru mid-Oct till 18:00). *Price:* Free entry. *Getting There:* **Drivers,** from Oranienburg follow signs Gedenkstätte (Sachsenhausen). **Railers,** from Berlin take the S-Bahn (S1) to Oranienburg (last stop), 50 min. From the station, either catch the bus (4 stops) or walk (20 min). **By bus,** hop on #804 out front to Gedenkstätte (memorial)—bus departs hourly Mon-Fri, bi-hourly Sat/Sun. Upon arriving, check the bus schedule to time your return. **By foot,** exit station right and dutifully follow the signs Gedenkstätte/Memorial Sachsenhausen. *Note:* Railers, if you don't already have a comparable ticket, purchase the public transportation (BVG) day ticket (*Tageskarte*) covering your travel in all three zones (ABC), 6€. Holders of a Eurail consecutive-day or dated Flexi/Select pass ride *free* on the S-Bahn.

Tours, you have a few options here: **1)** The camp memorial offers a thorough audio guide for 3€. Consider renting one and splitting the cost with a friend. **2)** Call ahead to the memorial to see whether any English-speaking tours are scheduled, tel.# 03301/2000. **3)** or join Berlin Walks whose six-hour memorial tour departs 2-5 times weekly: May-Sept Tue & Thur-Sun 10:15 at (A) or 9:50 at (B) — also March/April and Oct Tue/Fri/Sun 10:15 at (A) or 9:50 at (B) — and Nov-Feb Tue & Sun 10:15 at (A) or 9:50 at (B). **Meeting Point: (A)** taxi stand outside Bahnhof Zoo or **(B)** in front of Häagen-Dazs café outside Hackescher Markt S-Bahn station. *Note:* Buy ticket from guide. No reservation necessary—be at the meeting point five minutes prior to departure. *Price:* 26 years old and over/15€, under 26/7.50€; Welcome Card holders receive 25% discount off over-26 price. Printable, 1€-off coupon available on website. (www.berlinwalks.com) *Tel.#* 030/301-9194

Wannsee Conference, (House of the): On January 20, 1942, 15 high-ranking Nazis and civil servants met at a stately villa nestled on the shoreline of (lake) Wannsee 20km southwest of Berlin. Chaired by Reinhard Heydrich, second in charge of Nazi police forces after Heinrich Himmler—and the minutes recorded by the infamous Adolf Eichmann—the conference was arranged to plan the "final solution" (Endlösung) to the "Jewish question" (Judenfrage). The impeccably dressed men tallied Europe's Jews from more than 30 countries and territories to the sum of 11 million, with the Soviet Union accounting for more than half. Heading the extermination campaign against the Jews, Adolf Eichmann had them systematically rounded up and installed in concentration camps, where many were literally worked to death. Transport trains brought a seemingly endless flow of new arrivals. Ultimately, poison-gas chambers were constructed and disguised as showers to hasten the "liquidation" process. Camps such as Auschwitz, Sobibor, Belzec and Treblinka (all in Poland) were constructed for the sole purpose of fulfilling the "final solution" devised at the Wannsee Conference. Before Hitler's regime could be defeated, some 6 million Jews were murdered in what universally became known as the Holocaust.

Less than four months after the conference—May 1942—resistance fighters gunned down Reinhard Heydrich on the streets of Prague. Adolf Eichmann, on the other hand, survived the war and escaped to South America, where he was eventually tracked down in 1960 by Israeli secret agents. Following a lengthy trial, Eichmann was sentenced to death by hanging.

Today, the House of the Wannsee Conference is a memorial and educational site showcasing an excellent exhibition (in English) entitled "The Wannsee Conference and the Genocide of the European Jews." Expect a visit to take about 90 min. For history buffs, a trip here is well worth your time. Since it's on the way, plan your visit to coincide with a trip to Potsdam; leave early! (www.ghwk.de) *Tel.#* 030/805-0010 *Hours:* daily, 10:00-18:00. *Price:* Free entry. *Getting There:* House of the Wannsee Conference is located Am Großen Wannsee 56, roughly 50 min from central Berlin. **Railers,** from Berlin catch the S-Bahn (S1/S7) to Wannsee, or ride the regularly scheduled Regional Express (RE) train departing from Bahnhof Zoo (10-min ride), Friedrichstrasse station, Alexanderplatz or Ostbahnhof. From Wannsee station, cross the street and hop on bus #114 to "Haus der Wannsee Konferenz" (10-min ride). Upon arriving, check the bus schedule to time your return. *Note:* Railers, if you don't already have a comparable ticket, purchase the public transportation day ticket (*Tageskarte*) covering all your travel—e.g. RE, S-Bahn, U-Bahn, tram, bus—in all three zones (ABC; Berlin to Potsdam) for a mere 6€ (see page 345—*Subway/Bus*). Holders of a Eurail consecutive-day or dated Flexi/ Select pass ride *free* on the S-Bahn and RE.

POTSDAM

~ Population 145,000 ~ Country/Area Code: +49-(0)331
~ Sister City: Sioux Falls, South Dakota

Located within easy reach (30km southwest) of Berlin, Potsdam has been the summer playground for Prussian royalty for centuries. First mentioned in 993 A.D. as the Slavic village Poztupimi ("beneath the oaks"), Potsdam is over 200 years older than Berlin. During the Thirty Years' War (1618-1648) Potsdam was virtually wiped out, leaving only 50 taxable residents on the books in 1660. Framed by lakes and rivers on three sides, Potsdam screams the kind of natural beauty beloved by the in-crowd. Frederick William, member of the Hohenzollern royal family, chose idyllic Potsdam as his second residence, after big-city Berlin. The royal tradition continued when Frederick II (the Great), famed Prussian king (1740-86), built the magnificent tourist-swamped **Schloss Sanssouci** ("without a care"; 1745-47) and Neues Palais (New Palace, 1763-69) on the grounds of a 700-acre landscaped park that as a whole has been voted onto UNESCO's World Heritage List.

In 1912, Babelsberg film studio—Germany's oldest and most distinguished—was founded in Potsdam. Since then the studio's production lot has been the scene of more than 3000 cinema and TV movies. Marlene Dietrich began her film career here in the talking movie "The Blue Angel" (1930), and more recent A-list movies include Kevin Spacey's "Beyond the Sea," "The Bourne Supremacy" with Matt Damon, and the Oscar-winning film "The Pianist" with Adrien Brody. Across town in the lakeside park Neuer Garten (New Garden)—also voted onto the coveted World Heritage List—you'll discover **Schloss Cecilienhof**, site of the 1945 Potsdam Conference attended by the anti-Hitler coalition: Truman, Stalin and Churchill. Post-WWII, Potsdam became a hotspot during the Cold War because the East-West boundary ran along the northeast edge of town. Separated by a river and the Berlin Wall; Americans and Soviets faced each other across the **Glienicker Brücke**, a.k.a. "the bridge of spies."

Besides palaces, parks and bridges, Potsdam preserves a matchless patchwork of grand villas, Dutch row houses and Russian farmsteads engaging to most any tourist—even you! *Note:* Don't visit Potsdam on a Monday, when many of the palaces are closed, including Sanssouci.

Tourist Information: [TI] (www.potsdam-tourism.com) Brandenburger Str. 3. *Tel.#* 0331/275-580. The TI offers few brochures in English, handy tours (in English) of Schloss Sanssouci, foldout city map 1€ (they may have a free version by the time you get there), free room-finding service, and a Potsdam guidebook for 12€ (yikes, that's nearly the price of this book). *Hours:* daily, April-Oct, Mon-Fri 9:30-18:00, Sat/Sun 9:30-16:00; Nov-March Mon-Fri 10:00-18:00, Sat/Sun 9:30-14:00. *Getting There:* The TI recently moved and is now a neighbor of Potsdam's very own Brandenburg Gate, named after the federal state in which Potsdam is the capital. From Potsdam's train station (Hbf), exit Friedrich-Engels-Str. and ride tram 96 (five stops direction Schloss Charlottenhof) [or bus 695] to Luisenplatz, then short walk.

Railers: To reach Potsdam from Berlin either catch the S-Bahn (S1, ca. 30 min) or the snappy, regularly scheduled Regional Express (RE) train departing from Bahnhof Zoo (17-min ride), Friedrichstrasse station (25 min), Alexanderplatz (30 min) or Ostbahnhof (35 min). Potsdam's clean mall-like station is loaded with shops and eateries, including the enormous has-everything "Kaufland" supermarket (by exit Babelsberger Str., open Mon-Sat 6:00-20:00) that is perfect for picnickers. Internet can be found on street level by exit Babelsberger Str. and storage lockers (2€-3€/24hr) are located by exit Friedrich-Engels-Str. *Note:* If you don't already have a comparable ticket, purchase the public transportation (BVG) day ticket (*Tageskarte*) covering all your travel—e.g. RE, S-Bahn, U-Bahn, tram, bus—in all three zones (ABC; Berlin to Potsdam) for a mere 6€. Holders of a Eurail consecutive-day or dated Flexi/Select pass ride *free* on the S-Bahn and RE.

Drivers: Directional signs to Potsdam's parks and gardens are well marked. Expect to pay for parking, e.g. 2€/hr or 6€/day at Park Sanssouci. If you're coming from Berlin on Hwy 1, once you cross the Glienicker Brücke—the bridge of spies—you're in Potsdam.

Tours, Potsdam: From Berlin consider the *Berlin Walks Discover Potsdam Tour* (6hr), which departs May-Sept Sun 9:45 at the taxi stand outside Bahnhof Zoo. *Price:* 26 years old and over/15€, under 26/11.50€; Welcome Card holders receive 25% discount off over-26 price. Printable, 1€-off coupon available on website: www.berlinwalks.com *Tel.#* 030/301-9194. *Note:* Buy ticket from guide. Price does not include tour of Schloss Sanssouci. No reservation necessary—be at the meeting point five minutes prior to departure.

Dutch Quarter: Built 1732 to 1742, the "Holländisches Viertel" was assembled for Dutch craftsmen who were invited by King Frederick William I to help develop Potsdam. The quarter (about four blocks) consists of some 150 Dutch-style three-story row houses made of red bricks and having uniform up-and-down gables. Besides family residences, you'll discover inviting cafés and shops here. For this slice of Holland, go to Mittelstrasse in the heart of town—take tram 90, 92 or 95 and get off at Nauener Tor.

Russian Colony: On the north side of town you'll find a Russian colony of farmhouses built in 1826 on the orders of King Frederick William III in memory of his deceased friend, Czar Alexander I. In 1999, the colony was elected onto the Potsdam group of UNESCO's world heritage sites. To find this diverse landscape take tram 90, 92 or 95 and get off at Puschkinallee.

Glienicker Brücke (Bridge): For more than three centuries the Glienicker Bridge over the Havel River connected Potsdam with Berlin. However, when the Berlin Wall went up in 1961, the East-West boundary ran through the middle of the bridge bringing traffic to a halt. The American sector of West Berlin terminated at the foot of the bridge and the cross over to Potsdam was branded as No Man's Land. Far from prying eyes, the Americans and Soviets used the bridge as a corridor for covert activity—namely the exchange of spies. The most famous exchange occurred on February 10, 1962, when American U-2 spy plane pilot (Francis) Gary Powers was swapped for KGB agent Rudolf (Ivanovich) Abel. *Getting There:* Glienicker Bridge is located on the northeast edge of town. *Railers,* from Potsdam's train station (Hbf), exit Friedrich-Engels-Str. and take tram 93 to the bridge (last stop). *Drivers,* coming from Berlin on Hwy 1 you will cross the bridge into

Potsdam. <u>*Note:*</u> From Glienicker Bridge to Schloss Cecilienhof (next entry) is a *25-min walk *(*this allows time for getting lost)* through a pleasant park.

Schloss Cecilienhof: Situated within the lush Neuer Garten (New Garden) and flanked by two lakes—Maiden and Holy—Schloss Cecilienhof was the last palace (actually a half-timbered mansion, 1914-17) built by the Hohenzollern royal family. History was made here when Truman, Stalin and Churchill—leaders of the "big three" nations: USA, USSR and the UK—met from July 17 to August 2, 1945, to draft the final plans for the supervision of postwar Germany and Europe. Specifically, the agenda tackled zones of occupation, the denazification and education of the German people, reparations by the vanquished, and the judging of alleged Axis war criminals, e.g. at the Nürnberg trials (1945-1946). In addition to the conference itself, two historic events occurred: *1)* Soon after the meeting got underway, Churchill was voted out of office and Britain's new prime minister, Clement Attlee, replaced him. *2)* On President Truman's first full day in Potsdam—July 16—he received word that an atomic bomb had been successfully tested in New Mexico. Shortly thereafter, he made the decision to use it against Japan. <u>*Hours:*</u> (Schloss Cecilienhof) Tue-Sun 9:00-16:00 (April-Oct till 17:00). <u>*Price:*</u> (includes 35-min tour, in German) adult 5€, student 4€—pay 1€ less without tour and Nov-March. <u>*Note:*</u> Borrow English text from cashier for 5€ deposit. Your Park Sanssouci day or premium ticket (see next entry, *Schloss Sanssouci*—Tickets) will cover the admission price. From Schloss Cecilienhof, the Glienicker Bridge is a *25-min walk *(*this allows time for getting lost)* through a pleasant park. <u>*Hotel:*</u> Part of the historic complex has been renovated into upmarket digs, "relexa Schlosshotel Cecilienhof" (tel.# 0331/37-050): Sgl 80-135€, Dbl (standard) 100-175€, Dbl (deluxe) 155-215€, suite 185-255€, Hohenzollern suite 550-610€. <u>*Getting There:*</u> Schloss Cecilienhof is located in the north part of Potsdam at the top end of the Neuer Garten, 5km from the train station (Hbf). **Railers**, from Potsdam's train station (Hbf), exit Friedrich-Engels-Str. and take tram 90 or 92 to Rathaus, then change to bus #692 to Schloss Cecilienhof.

Schloss Sanssouci: Prussia's most celebrated monarch, Frederick II (the Great), spent many a moon in his favorite Schloss—or palace—he designed with grandiose visions of Versailles, naming it Sanssouci: "without a care," built 1745-47. It is here the great monarch rests eternally—without a care. Voltaire, the French writer and philosopher and fleeting friend of Frederick's, lived here off-and-on for three years—if you're lucky, you'll get to sneak a peek at the Voltaire Room. On the other side of the enormous 700-acre Park Sanssouci (the park grounds in which the palace resides)—featuring botanical gardens, Roman baths, the Orangerie, a historic windmill, and a painting gallery (housing Caravaggio and Rubens, among others)—Frederick built a second palace: Neues Palais (New Palace, 1763-1769).

<u>*Note:*</u> Entrance into Park Sanssouci is free. Photography is allowed in the park but not in either palace. Both palaces (separated by a 30-min stroll) are open to visitors, but you'd better arrive early at Schloss Sanssouci to guarantee a walk-through—arrivals after 11:30 (July-Sept) may not get in. Generally, tours leave every 20 minutes. In peak summer, though, some 1700 people visit the palace daily as a tour departs every 10 minutes in groups of 30-40 visitors.

<u>*Tickets:*</u> Forget the prices mentioned below for both palaces (and the same goes for Schloss Cecilienhof listed above) because these historic structures (including Schloss Charlottenburg in Berlin) all belong to the Prussian Palaces and Gardens Foundation. Simplifying things, the foundation offers a pair of easy-on-the-pocket tickets allowing humble tourists (like yourself) admission into all of their properties, which are several besides the ones listed here. (For the foundation's list of properties, either log onto their website—www.spsg.de—or grab their brochure in the palace TI mentioned below). **Price:** The two best deals are the "day" and "premium" tickets. 1) The <u>*day ticket*</u> (adult

12€, student 9€) includes entrance into all Prussian palaces except Schloss Sanssouci. 2) The _premium ticket_ (adult 15€, student 10€) includes entrance into all Prussian palaces as well as Schloss Sanssouci —but this "premium" ticket must be purchased at Schloss Sanssouci. *Note:* Both ticket-types are valid for two consecutive days! Family ticket also available. *Suggestion:* If you want to tour Schloss Sanssouci, buy the _premium_ ticket. If you do not care about touring Schloss Sanssouci, buy the _day_ ticket.

TI, Palace: To purchase tickets or ask questions, pop into the palace TI located behind the historic windmill—adjacent to Schloss Sanssouci. *Hours:* daily, March-Oct 8:30-17:00, Nov-Feb 9:00-16:00.

Hours: (Schloss Sanssouci) Tue-Sun 9:00-16:00 (April-Oct till 17:00)—end times are last tour. *Price:* (includes 40-min German tour—English-speakers get translation sheet) adult 8€, student 5€.

Hours: (Neues Palais) Sat thru Thur (closed Friday) 9:00-16:00 (April-Oct till 17:00)—end times are last tour. *Price:* 5€—or 6€ for 60-min tour in German—1€ cheaper over winter (Nov-March) because, apparently, the palace isn't heated.

Getting There: Park (and Schloss) Sanssouci is easily reached from Potsdam's train station (Hbf)—exit station Friedrich-Engels-Str. and catch bus #695 (direction Bhf Pirschheide, departs every 20 min) to Schloss Sanssouci. Or, for an enjoyable combination of city sightseeing and walking (ca. 30 min), take tram 90 (direction Viereckremise) or tram 92 (direction Kirschallee) a handful of stops to Nauener Tor. From there, check out the Dutch Quarter on Mittelstrasse. Then, walk back the way the tram came along Friedrich-Ebert-Str. and go right on Brandenburger Str. At the other end of this pedestrian zone is the TI and (Potsdam's) Brandenburg Gate. Behind the gate follow signs into Park Sanssouci. You'll soon pass toilets.

Tour: For an English-speaking tour inside Schloss Sanssouci, join the Potsdam TI on their 3.5-hour city tour, 26€ (Welcome Card holders receive a 25% discount). Tour leaves April-Oct—Tue-Sun—at 11:00 from their office at Brandenburger Str. 3 (Luisenplatz). Buy your ticket at the office; try to reserve 24hr in advance, 48hr in peak summer. *Tel.#* 0331/275-580. *Note:* From Nov thru March (three-hour) tours leave Fri/Sat/Sun at 10:45.

DRESDEN

~ *Population: 480,000* ~ *Elevation: 113m/370ft*
~ *Country/Area Code: +49-(0)351* ~ *Sister City: Columbus, Ohio*

Situated in the eastern German state of Saxony, Dresden is actually closer to the capital of the Czech Republic, Prague, than it is to the capital of Germany, Berlin. More unusual is the fact that a Polish king once ruled the Saxons, and their Prussian neighbors in the west were considered a deadly foe. Be-
fore all that, however, Dresden began as a tiny enclave on the Elbe River established by missionaries. First documented in 1206, Dresden was the chosen location for the margraves of Meissen to build a castle to enforce their authority on the river traffic. The year 1485 proved instru-mental for the future Saxon capital, when the margraves bequeathed their assets to the royal house of Wettin, who ultimately reigned over the Saxon territories until 1918. The most significant Wettin ruler was Augustus the Strong, elector of Saxony and king of Poland (1694/97-1733). Under his direction the Zwinger and Frauenkirche were built and he approved major renovations to the palaces Pillnitz and Moritzburg. Additionally,

Augustus established the world-famous Meissen porcelain works as well as the collections of the Old Masters' Galley and the treasures of the Green Vault. It was during his rule that Dresden became a European cultural center and a Baroque masterpiece, often referred to as the "Florence on the Elbe." Economic and social development was so robust that the population swelled to 65,000 by the early 18th century. However, during the opening salvos of the Seven Years' War in 1756, Prussian troops sacked the city. It took nearly half a century before the residents returned. This coincided with Napoleon's armies marching on Dresden and allying Saxony with France in 1806. Napoleon achieved his last significant victory here—at the Battle of Dresden in 1813—when 100,000 French soldiers defeated 150,000 coalition troops (Prussian, Austrian and Russian).

   In the decades that followed, Dresden progressed into the industrial age with the completion of Germany's first long-distance railway connecting it with Leipzig. People gravitated to Dresden in droves encouraging a new phenomenon, the urban sprawl: city fortifications were dismantled, factories were implemented, a port was constructed along with bridges, transportation lines, a city hall, a zoo, a romantic riverside terrace, and an elegant opera house: the Semperoper. By the turn of the 20th century, Dresden was the fourth largest city in the newly unified German nation with half a million residents. The November revolution in 1918 forced the abdication of the last Wettin monarch and the Free State of Saxony was formed. The assumption of power by the Nazis in 1933 dissolved any progress the city had achieved post-WWI by banning political freedom, infiltrating the church, supporting the deportation of Jews, and replacing democracy with a strictly controlled centralized state. This new form of government damned the German people to an apocalyptic finale, nearly erasing Dresden off the map. Three months before the end of WWII, a series of Allied air raids over Dresden (Feb. 13-14, 1945)—comprising more than 1000 planes—unleashed a firestorm of incendiary bombs that landed on the metropolis in a feverish rage, sucking the oxygen from the air and sending mountains of debris racing toward the sky. After the smoke cleared, roughly 80 percent of the city was destroyed and 35,000 bodies were recovered from the rubble. *(In memoriam to those who fell, special church services—along with special performances at the Semperoper and philharmonic—are held annually on Feb 13-14.)*

In October 1949, some four years after the war, the German Democratic Republic (GDR), or East Germany, was established under the auspices of hard-line Soviet authority. The Allies may have won the war, but the victory celebrations were short-lived for the citizens of Eastern Europe—one dictatorial ideology was simply replaced by another: from Hitler to Stalin, Fascism to Communism. Life for Dresdeners was surreal; they lived like puppets, their strings manipulated by party-loyal puppeteers. This new form of collective government eliminated private enterprise and made basic goods available to the workers, or general public, as needed. Owning a luxury car was not possible, listening to broadcasts from the West was outlawed, and a Dresdener had a better chance of seeing a prehistoric dinosaur on the city streets than a briefcase-toting businessman wearing a suit and tie. Colorful neon billboards advertising brands like Mercedes or Levi's did not exist; instead dull, gray, monotone signs offered bread and milk. The only things that had color were the flowers in summer and trees in autumn and, of course, propaganda rallies. Such was life in Socialist Dresden.

In the early 1950s, reconstruction began with residential and governmental structures as well as on select monuments. Work was slow-going and the Zwinger was the first monumental structure to be completed (1964). The Semperoper and Albertinum were next to celebrate their grand reopenings, some four decades after the conclusion of WWII. Since the collapse of the GDR and the reunification of Germany in 1990, the rebuilding of Dresden has moved at a blinding pace, with emphasis on the famed Frauenkirche (page 411). The Saxon capital is once again a weighty beacon inspiring tourism. Pouring in from across the globe, vacationers are heeding the call. A testament to the fact is Dresden's record-breaking 2.9 million overnights stays in 2005, and forecasts for 2006 expect that figure to climb even higher.

Baroque monuments of yesteryear twinkle under the midday sun while affording a unique contrast of gilded trim and thick soot. Tourists anxiously line up along the banks of the Elbe to catch a ride on a 19th-century paddle steamer belonging to the world's largest and oldest fleet. Night owls converge on the Neustadt quarter, which has more than 130 pubs, clubs and restaurants to accommodate, entertain and indulge. High-tech corporations, too, are investing in the Saxon capital. Infineon Technologies and Advanced Micro Devices (AMD) have since moved in and established multibillion dollar computer-chip manufacturing facilities that are creating thousands of new jobs in a region quickly becoming known as "Silicon Saxony." What's more, an 18km stretch from Dresden southeast along the Elbe River to Schloss Pillnitz has recently (July 2004) joined the ranks of such unique and diverse places as the Kathmandu Valley of Nepal and the tropical rainforest of Sumatra as an esteemed member of UNESCO's World Heritage List.

Lastly, since Dresden was first documented in 1206, this year means the city is celebrating its 800th birthday. During those eight centuries, Dresden has more than proven its right to legendary status—from Wettin royalty to Prussian aristocracy, from Baroque mode to the Napoleonic code, from Nazi totalitarianism to Red communism—its people are survivors who have learned to celebrate each day as it comes. Dresden defines resilience, and once again it is the quintessential city of grandeur. Unsurprisingly, the Saxon capital deserves a top-priority listing on any itinerary to Germany. *Note:* Make sure your visit to Dresden includes a Saturday; this will enable you to rummage through one of Germany's best flea markets (page 415).

~ **Dresden—including its environs—is worth at least a three-day stay. Mood and weather permitting, divide your time like so,**

Day 1: Start early at Theaterplatz and complete our Do-It-Yourself Orientation Tour, 60 min (page 405). Afterwards, tackle the museums (page 407). Start at the Hausmannsturm in the Dresdener Schloss (page 409), where you can purchase the Museum Day-Ticket (adult 10€, student 6€) and get an overview of the Old Town. *Note:* Another option to the museum ticket is to purchase either of the two city cards (see *Dresden City Card*, page 402).

Day 2: Those who have purchased a Dresden City Card can visit what museums they missed on day 1. Others should rent a bike and cycle around town touring "Sights" of interest, e.g. Pfund's Molkerei, Golden Rider and Kunsthofpassage in Neustadt; the Slaughterhouse-Five area 2km west of the Old Town; and/or the Blue Wonder 6km east along the Elbe — it's healthy, fun, and productive! Pack a picnic.

Day 3: Explore the Saxon Switzerland national park (page 418) — take the train there and a paddle steamer back. Or, porcelain fans, take the S-Bahn to Meissen (page 420) for the day.

Day 4: Consider staying an extra day to realize both opportunities listed for day 3. Or, national-park goers, turn your day into an overnight allowing for more time to explore the region with the option of crossing the border into the Czech Republic (don't forget your passport).

Tourist Info: [TI] (www.dresden-tourist.de) *Tel.#* 0351/491-920. There are two TIs in Dresden: one is near the main train station, or Hauptbahnhof, and the other ("Schinkelwache") is centrally located in the Old Town. At either location basic city maps are free or you can buy a foldout city guide with map for 30¢. TI also has a room-finding service for 3€/person and a ticket agency. Ask about their new city audio-guide tour, 10€/day.

TI: The "Schinkelwache" TI is located on Theaterplatz adjacent to the Zwinger. *Hours:* Mon-Fri 10:00-18:00, Sat/Sun 10:00-16:00.

TI: Prager Strasse (main shopping street, five-minute walk from Hauptbahnhof (Hbf). *Hours:* Mon-Fri 10:00-18:00, Sat 10:00-16:00. *Getting There:* exit Hbf "Ausgang City" and follow the flow of people one block to Prager Str., the pedestrian-only shopping street. Continue past the Mercure Hotel and the TI's stand-alone portable is just ahead on the right.

Emergency Tel. Numbers: [Germany-wide]
Police (Polizei) = 110
Fire dept. (Feuerwehr) or general emergency = 112
Ambulance = 19222

Hauptbahnhof: [Hbf] Dresden has two main rail stations: the "Hbf" services the Old Town, and "Dresden-Neustadt" services the New Town across the Elbe River — tram 11 connects the two. *(Note: If your accommodations are in the New Town, get off at Dresden-Neustadt.)*

The **Hbf** is presently under construction and therefore lacks many of the usual amenities. Storage lockers (1.50€-2€/24hr) are next to track 13 or beneath track 17. You'll find a supermarket (Mon-Sat 7:00-20:00) in the City Center Passage across the street from track 1 at the back side of the station. Trams: To pick up a tram, exit station "Ausgang City" — tram 7 is directly out front; tram 8 departs to the right at the side of the station; and tram 11 departs from Hbf Nord, which is located off Prager Strasse by the TI. Getting there by tram: To reach *Dresden-Neustadt* take tram 7 (direction Weixdorf) or tram 8 (direction Hellerau). To get to the *Old Town* take tram 8 (direction Hellerau) and get off at Theaterplatz. To reach the *Dresden- (Bahnhof-) Neustadt train station* take tram 11 (direction Bühlau). By foot *into the Old Town* is a 10-min walk. Exit station "Ausgang

City" and follow the flow of people one block to Prager Str., the pedestrian-only shopping street—continue straight to the Old Town. <u>Trains</u> from the Hbf leave regularly for Berlin (trip time 2hr) • for Prague (trip time 3hr) • for Frankfurt (trip time 5hr).

Dresden-Neustadt—locally known as Bahnhof Neustadt—is a comfortable station with all the necessary amenities, even a Burger King. <u>Storage lockers</u> cost 1.50€-2€/24hr. <u>Bike rental</u>, see *Bike Rental* below. <u>Supermarket</u> (Lidl) is next door—exit station right (open daily Mon-Sat 8:00-21:00, Sun 8:00-19:00). <u>Share Ride</u> is across the street; see *Share Ride* below.

Note: From either station the S-Bahn departs every half hour for Meissen as well as Schöna (in the national park) — one-way ticket (*Einzelfahrt*) costs 5.10€. Best buy is the total network (*Verbundraum*) day ticket (*Tageskarte*) valid till 04:00: adult 10€, family 13€ (*Familientageskarte,* couples purchase the latter ticket to increase savings). Small groups purchase the *Kleingruppenkarte* 21€, valid for up to 5 people till 04:00. Holders of a Eurail consecutive-day or dated Flexi/Select pass ride *FREE* on the S-Bahn.

Bus/Tram: For the most part, Dresden is walkable—however, if you find yourself out of the historic core you may want to use local transportation, which, by the way, is painted black and yellow—the city's medieval colors. Prices are as follows: *Einzelfahrt* (one-way ticket) 1.70€ • *Tageskarte* (Day Ticket, valid till 04:00) 4.50€. Ticket automats ("Fahrausweise") are commonplace at major stops and explained in English. *Note:* Stamp ticket in appropriate box to validate or run the risk of an on-the-spot fine.

Parking: For *street parking* pay at nearby automat and leave ticket on dashboard of your car. Price: (applicable daily 8:00-20:00) Mon-Sat 50¢/20min, Sun 50¢/60min, or day rate (Tagestarif) 6€/24hr. Note: Automats do not give change. *Parking garages* are abundantly located throughout town, look for blue-and-white "P" signs. Price: (typically) 1.50€/hr, 15€/24hr. To reach downtown, enter these GPS coordinates: N51° 03.145 - E13° 44.434

Share Ride: *(Mitfahrzentrale; a concept matching passengers with drivers, and vice-versa.)* Those who are not traveling by Eurail, "Mitfahrzentrale" is the cheapest and most social option of getting from one city to another. There is one Share Ride office in Dresden. *Tel.#* 0351/19-440. *Hours:* Mon-Fri 9:00-20:00, Sat/Sun 10:00-16:00. *Price:* approx. cost per passenger from Dresden to Prague 8€, Berlin 12€, Munich/Frankfurt 26€. *Getting There:* Located on Dr.-Friedrich-Wolf-Str. 2, which is opposite Dresden-Neustadt train station. Exit station and cross street, go through green gate, up steps, through door and it's on the left. *Note:* Those who have a working knowledge of German will want to first refer to this website (www.mitfahrgelegenheit.de) for an opportunity to contact the driver directly, i.e. cutting out the middleman for an even cheaper Share Ride.

Bike Rental: To cover more ground, reasonable bikes with seven gears can be rented for 7€/day at Dresden-Neustadt train station — look for "Fahrradvermietung" at the DB office (near Burger King). *Hours:* Mon-Fri 6:00-20:00, Sat/Sun 8:00-20:00. *Note: Must bring passport!* Bikes are equipped with handy little baskets to cradle your daypack and picnic goodies.

Within the city limits are more than 250km of bike paths to enjoy, especially along the Elbe River. Below are two popular options:

Ride along the Saxon Wine Road to Meissen (25km, start early and take train back): From Neustadt head downstream on north side of river; or from the Old Town cycle the south bank of the Elbe for about 12km and cross over river on Niederwarthär bridge, continuing to Meissen on north side.

Route into the Sächsische Schweiz National Park (37km to Königstein, or 51km to Czech border—Schöna) [start early and take train back]: From the Old Town head upstream along the south bank of the Elbe to Königstein. Once there take ferry (Fähre) over to north bank and cross back again at Bad Schandau via the bridge—route continues direction Schöna and the Czech border. *Note:* Bring your passport if you plan to cross the border into the Czech Republic. For more on the national park, see page 418.

Boat Rides: Paddle steamers first began ushering passengers along the Saxon stretch of the Elbe River in 1836—so it's not surprising that Saxony's state capital, Dresden, accommodates the largest and oldest fleet in the world. Today, the Dresden steamer fleet welcomes some 700,000 passengers aboard its vessels each year. Steamer season is April thru Oct. Trips on offer include the 90-minute city tour (called *Rundfahrt*), Dixieland and Summer Night cruises, as well as excursions into the Saxon Switzerland national park. Additionally, all boats can be chartered for private events (tel.# 0351/866-0918).

Here are a few particulars about Germany's floating history; (steamers are named after regional communities): **Stadt Wehlen** built 1879, oldest paddle steamer in the fleet; length 59m; capacity 300 passengers, 284 seats; operates mainly the City Tour • **Diesbar** built 1884, driven by the world's oldest steam engine (1841) still on active duty. Boat length 53m; capacity 175 passengers, 160 seats; operates mainly on the Saxon wine route (Meissen) and under charter • **Meissen** built 1885, camouflaged during WWII and used to evacuate refugees from Hamburg; length 65m; capacity 350 passengers, 270 seats; operates mainly on the Saxon Switzerland route • **Pillnitz** built 1886; length 65m; capacity 350 passengers, 254 seats; operates mainly on the Saxon Switzerland route • **Krippen** built 1892; length 56m; capacity 221 passengers, 221 seats; operates mainly on the Saxon wine route (Meissen) and under charter • **Kurort Rathen** built 1896; length 57m; capacity 300 passengers, 267 seats; operates mainly on the Saxon Switzerland route • **Pirna** built 1898; length 56m; capacity 300 passengers, 265 seats; operates mainly on the Saxon Switzerland route through to Bohemia (Czech Rep.) • **Dresden** built 1926; length 68m; capacity 610 passengers, 400 seats; operates mainly on the Palace Tour and Dixieland cruises • **Leipzig** built 1929, youngest paddle steamer in the fleet; length 70m; capacity 610 passengers, 439 seats; operates mainly on the Palace Tour and Dixieland cruises.

Price: (The following list of cruises and prices may have changed, query ticket office below west end of Brühlsche Terrasse for the latest details.) *City Tour* (*Rundfahrt,* 90 min) 11€ • one-way ticket (*Einfache Fahrt*) to Meissen 11€ • one-way ticket (*Einfache Fahrt*) from Königstein (downstream, 3hr) to Dresden 15.30€ • Day Ticket (*Tageskarte*) 20€, valid for all regular steamer routes • *combo-ticket,* 25.50€, valid for all regular steamer routes and public transportation for the day, including S-Bahn • *Dixieland Cruise* (May-Oct, Fri/Sat 19:30-22:30) 17€ • *Summer Night Cruise* [incl. buffet] (May-Sept, Sat 20:00-24:00) 32€. *Note:* Steamers run April-Oct. Every Monday fares are reduced by 20% (except for City Tour and on holidays). Bikes are transported free of charge when space is available.

Dresden City Card: The *City Card* (19€, available at TI) is valid for 48 hours, awarding the holder unlimited use of public transportation as well as discounts on select attractions/ tours and free admission into all the museums listed in the "Museums" section.

Another option is the *Dresden Regio-Card* (29€), which incorporates the City Card benefits and is valid for 72 hours, inclusive of discounts on select regional attractions and free transportation within the Oberelbe region, which embraces Meissen and the Saxon Switzerland national park.

Note: Validate card yourself by writing in time and date of first use.

Opinion: The *City Card* is worthwhile for those who have the time to visit the museums over a 48-hour period. Those who are determined to visit all the museums in one day (except Green Vaults), purchase instead the Museum Day-Ticket (see *Museums,* page 407). The *Regio-Card* possibly retains its value (excluding holders of a consecutive-day Eurail pass)—scan brochure to see whether your movements will compensate the price of the card. If you're planning on visiting a number of museums as well as Meissen and the Saxon Switzerland national park, the *Regio-Card* is for you.

Internet: See TI for latest access points. If you're in Neustadt, a good café to surf is at Böhmische Str. 3 (just off Alaunstr.), 2€/hr—daily, 10:00-24:00.

Post Office: Königsbrücker Str. 21, Neustadt. *Hours:* Mon-Fri 9:00-19:00, Sat 10:00-13:00, or 24hr stamp machine outside ("Briefmarken"). Another P.O. is located at the Altmarkt Galerie shopping mall. *Hours:* Mon-Sat 9:00-20:00.

Supermarkets: *In Neustadt* next door to the train station is a "Lidl"—open daily, Mon-Sat 8:00-21:00, Sun 8:00-19:00. Or, a few blocks away, there's a "Plus" at the intersection of Louisenstr. and Königsbrücker Str. (in front of tram stop and opposite P.O.)—open Mon-Sat 8:00-20:00. *In the Old Town* go to the Altmarkt Galerie shopping mall (adjacent to Altmarkt); on one end of the lower level is an "Aldi" and at the other end is a "Rewe"—both supermarkets are open the same hours as the mall, Mon-Sat 9:00-20:00. The better market of the two is Rewe—in fact, it's way better! *Note:* At any supermarket in Germany and Austria notice how cheap a bottle of wine is.

Holidays in Dresden, 2006

1. January, Sunday – New Year
14. April – Good Friday
17. April – Easter Monday
1. May, Monday – May Day (Labor Day)
25. May, Thursday – Ascension Day
5. June – Whit Monday
3. October, Tuesday – Day of German (East-West) Unity
31. October, Tuesday – Day of Reformation
22. November, Wednesday – Buß- und Bettag (Day of Repentance & Prayer)
25. December, Monday – Christmas
26. December, Tuesday – St. Stephen's Day (Christmas Day No. 2)

What to do on a Sunday or holiday

Stores will be closed; most eateries will be open along with the touristy kitsch shops/stands. Sunday presents a good opportunity to explore Dresden's most important museums. Start early, buy the museum day-ticket—this will keep you busy from a.m. till p.m. (see *Museums*, page 407). Contrary to a museum crawl, consider visiting Meissen (page 420) or taking a nature trip into the Saxon Switzerland national park (page 418), or rent a bike and cycle along the Elbe and through the hushed city streets—pack a picnic.

FREE Dresden

1) For a bargain tour of the city, complete our **Do-It-Yourself Orientation Tour, Dresden** (page 405). Dawdle through the gardens and along the upper-level promenade of the Zwinger; admire its beauty and peek into the museums. If you time it just right, you'll hear the chiming of the Glockenspielpavillon.

2) Mosey along Dresden's romantic river esplanade—the **Brühlsche Terrasse** (page 411)—and marvel at the city's Baroque past as well as the world's oldest paddle-steamer fleet (page 402).

3) Tours—in German—are gratis at the **Hofkirche** (page 410). What's more, this Roman Catholic church also offers a free organ recital every Wed and Sat 11:30-12:00.

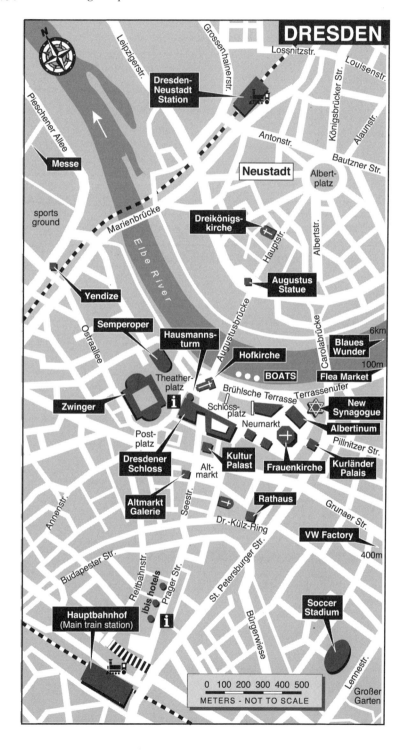

DRESDEN

Lossnitzstr.

Leipzigerstr.

Grossenhainerstr.

Pieschener Allee

Dresden-Neustadt Station

Antonstr.

Königsbrücker Str.

Louisenstr.

Alaunstr.

Bautzner Str.

Messe

Neustadt

Albertplatz

sports ground

Marienbrücke

Dreikönigs-kirche

Hauptstr.

Albertstr.

Elbe River

Augustus Statue

Yendize

Augustusbrücke

Carolabrücke

6km

Semperoper

Hausmanns-turm

Hofkirche

Blaues Wunder

100m

Ostraallee

Theatherplatz

BOATS

Flea Market

Terrassenufer

Brühlsche Terrasse

New Synagogue

Zwinger

Schloss-platz

Neumarkt

Albertinum

Post-platz

Dresdener Schloss

Alt-markt

Kultur Palast

Frauenkirche

Pillnitzer Str.

Kurländer Palais

Annenstr.

Altmarkt Galerie

Seestr.

Rathaus

Grunaer Str.

Dr.-Külz-Ring

VW Factory

400m

Budapester Str.

Reitbahnstr.

Prager Str.

St. Petersburger Str.

ibis hotels

Soccer Stadium

Hauptbahnhof (Main train station)

Bürgerwiese

Lennestr.

0 100 200 300 400 500

METERS - NOT TO SCALE

Großer Garten

4) Explore the district that inspired Kurt Vonnegut's antiwar novel, **Slaughter-house-Five**, or watch cars being assembled at the glass-encased **VW Transparent Factory** (pages 413-14). Neighboring the VW factory is a pleasant opportunity for a picnic and a leafy stroll in the extensive **Großer Garten**, which offers a 17th-century palace, the city zoo and a mini railway.

5) Art aficionados will adore the **Regenwasserspiel**, a network of aluminum pipes, funnels and guttering attached to the decorative facade of an apartment block, creating the unique "rain water fountain" (see *Kunsthofpassage*, page 412).

6) To get an idea of what downtown Dresden looked like after the firebombing of Feb. 13-14, 1945, check out the remains of the **Kurländer Palais** one block southeast of the Frauenkirche. The Kurländer Palais dates from 1718, but it gets its name from Prince Carl—Duke of Kurland and son of the Saxon King August III—who acquired the palace in 1773.

Do-It-Yourself Orientation Tour, Dresden—60 min

Let's begin our jaunt through Dresden at *Theaterplatz*, an immense cobbled plaza in the heart of the Old Town. In the center of the square is an equestrian statue of Saxon King Johann, who ruled from 1854 to 1873. Stand behind him and face the horse's buttocks. From this unflattering perspective let's get acquainted with the Old Town by pretending the horse's backside is high noon (12:00) on a clock dial.

Looking slightly left, or counterclockwise, to 10:00 is the **Hofkirche**'s (page 410) sullied and curvaceous facade—if you were to walk around the edifice and count each holy figure you'd total 78.

At 9:00 is the elongated **Italienisches Dörfchen** (or Little Italian Village—see *Entertainment, Eats* on page 415), featuring white-arched windows, eight Ionic-style columns (at main entrance) and a mouth-watering cluster of gastronomic possibilities, e.g. café, bistro, beer garden, and a restaurant.

At 6:00, behind you, is the city's signature landmark, the **Semperoper** opera house (page 410).

Turning to 3:00 is Dresden's renowned museum quarter, the **Zwinger** (page 407).

At 1:00 is the neoclassic Schinkelwache, former Altstadt guardhouse, where you'll find a café, the **TI** and the Semperoper's box office.

Punctuating our 360-degree spin is the pointy **Hausmannsturm** (page 409), soot-stained clock tower seen beyond the statue—notice the gilded balustrade enclosing the observation terrace; this'll be your vantage point after this tour is over.

Now let's turn our attention back to 3:00. Walk through the arched passage to familiarize yourself with the **Zwinger** (page 407), the famed museum quarter.

Midway through the passage are two portals, the one on the left leads into the **Armory** (Rüstkammer), on your right is the **Old Masters' Gallery** (Gemäldegalerie). Continue straight and descend five steps, stopping on the wide landing. If you were standing here a few years ago, rising floodwaters would have been splashing at your toes. In August 2002, the Elbe River reached a record height of 31ft and the Zwinger narrowly avoided a third-millennium washout.

Now continue down the remainder of the steps and walk into the middle of the grounds—stop between the four fountains and face the direction you were walking.

Welcome to the Zwinger's lively gardens, encompassed by four world-class museums (page 408—*Armory, Old Masters' Gallery, Mathematics-Physics Salon, Porcelain Collection*), an intimate grotto and an upper-level promenade.

(Using the same clock-dial analogy as on Theaterplatz:) In front of you, at 12:00, is the suitably named Kronentor, or Crown Gate, a beautifully Baroque gateway capped by a golden crown. Intersecting its arches is a section of the abovementioned upper-level promenade—a stroller's delight.

Follow your eyes slightly to the right, or clockwise, to 2:00 to find the stairway leading into the **Mathematics-Physics Salon**. Its second floor is stuffed with ornate clocks that are a part of the Salon's exhibition, accessible via the museum or the upper-level promenade.

In case you were wondering, you can reach the upper-level promenade via the stairway at 3:00 ascending beneath the bulbous, two-story pavilion.

Cast your eyes farther right to 5:00—later, when you come back, climb this staircase to a must-see grotto, where 16 nymphs in niches encompass an intimate fountain. (From here steps also ascend to the upper promenade.)

Swivel right again to 6:00 and you'll see where you entered the Zwinger complex—here you should have King Johann neatly framed within the middle arch.

Finally, rotate right once more to 9:00 to the harmonious **Glockenspielpavillon**, which features a gilded clock and a mesmerizing melody originating from 40 bells made of Meissen porcelain. They're hanging either side of the clock and chime every 15 min as well as play a classical tune thrice daily: 10:15, 14:15, 18:15. The first tune (10:15) is always a rendition of Vivaldi's Four Seasons. What's more, the Glockenspielpavillon is where you'll find the entrance into the **Porcelain Collection**.

Now, let's head through the Glockenspielpavillon to exit the Zwinger complex. As you do this you will get a closer look at the 40 Meissen bells as well as a peek into the Porcelain Collection.

Upon exiting the Zwinger go left, cross the road when clear and turn right on (street) Taschenberg. Stop. In front of you, left of arched passageway over street, is the **Dresdener Schloss**, entrance into the **Green Vaults** (Grünes Gewölbe*)* and **Hausmannsturm** (page 409). Remember this location for when you visit later with your Museum Day-Ticket or Dresden City Card.

This is a good time to consider which Ticket/Card to buy. If you decide on the Dresden City Card (page 402), then go left and purchase it at the TI (building across the street, beyond bus stop, with six Ionic-style columns at entrance). If you decide on the Museum Day-Ticket (see Museums, page 407), purchase it at the cashier of the first museum you visit.

Continue straight on Taschenberg. On your immediate right is the 5-star Grand Hotel Taschenberg Palais, which dates from 1705 when Augustus the Strong had the palace built for his favorite mistress, Countess Cosel. Today, royalty is not a requirement to reside here—you only need a fat wallet *(Sgl from 235€, Dbl from 275€; tel.# 0351/49-120; www.kempinski-dresden.de)*. Ahead on the left you'll see people streaming in and out of the Dresener Schloss (page 409), largely owing to the popularity of the Green Vaults (Grünes Gewölbe).

Stroll beneath the arched passageway and continue straight some 60 meters until the cobbled road turns left; stop here. We will follow the road left in a few minutes; for now, go right and stand in front of the faded mural stamped onto the upper level of the elongated, modern building. The structure is called the **Kulturpalast**, or Palace of Culture, built by the former East German regime from 1967-1969 as a theater and concert hall for the great citizens of Dresden, or as they were more commonly referred to as *Arbeiter und Bauer* (workers and farmers). The peoples are collectively represented on this propaganda mural known as *Der Siegeszug der Rotten Fahne* (The Victory Parade of the Red Flag). It is a stark reminder of the city's socialist past. At the time of its construction this temple of culture was an architectural triumph; today, it is similarly used as a theater hall, with the addition of a multifunctional business center and lecture rooms. At the heart of the building is a tiered concert hall that has seating for more 2400 persons. With the mural in front of you, to your right is the Altmarkt, or Old Market Square. In the buildings to the right of the square is the **Altmarkt Galerie** (page 415), a popular shopping mall. If you were to continue straight through the Altmarkt, you'd reach Prager Str., the pedestrian-only shopping street, and at the other end of that is the Hauptbahnhof, or main train station.

For now, retrace your steps and head towards the church steeple. The building complex in front of you is the central part of the Drcsdener Schloss, still under repairs from the '45 firebombing.

Continue straight into the covered passage; midway through (on right) is the entrance into the Stallhof, one of the palace's courtyards. Visitors in December will be treated to the **Advent Spektakel**, a must-see historical Christmas market (pages 416-17).

Once through the covered passage you'll arrive into Schlossplatz, or Palace Square. From your new location, in front of you, at 12:00, is Augustusbrücke, or Augustus' Bridge, spanning the Elbe River—on the other side you'll be greeted by the **Golden Rider** (page 412), who spearheads the Dresden suburb of Neustadt.

At 9:00 is the entrance into the **Hofkirche**. Ahead and to the right at 2:00 is a wide staircase ascending onto the **Brühlsche Terrasse** (← pages 410-11 →) To your right, at 5:00, begins the **Fürstenzug**, animated figures of Saxon royalty depicted on Meissen porcelain tiles. If you were to follow the tiles they would lead you to the freshly restored **Frauenkirche** (page 411), or Church of Our Lady, and one block beyond that is the remains of the **Kurländer Palais** (page 405).

Okay, folks, that's a wrap. We hope you enjoyed the tour and now have a better feel for Dresden. If you're at odds at what to do next, head back to the entrance into the Dresdener Schloss and climb up the Hausmannsturm to get an overview of the city and a bevy of panoramic views.

MUSEUMS

Everything listed in this section (<u>except Green Vaults</u>) is *FREE* with the **Museum Day-Ticket** (adult 10€, student 6€—available for purchase at all below-mentioned museums). It is not recommended to pay the individual entrance fee at each museum, as you'll see when calculating the prices written below. Another option to cover all the museums is the **Dresden City Card** (page 402), worthwhile for travelers with two days.

Dresden's main museums are housed in two prominent complexes: the *Zwinger* and *Dresdener Schloss*. The Old Masters' Gallery, Green Vaults, and the Hausmannsturm are musts! Museums website: www.skd-dresden.de

<u>Note:</u> The Albertinum museum complex will be closed for renovations in 2006. Zwinger museums are closed Monday; Dresdener Schloss museums are closed Tuesday. When visiting, bring a 1€ coin for the locker you'll be required to use to store your daypack/personal items (1€ coin is returned upon reopening locker). *Suggestion:* At the Zwinger complex drop your daypack/items at the Old Masters' Gallery (downstairs; toilets are adjacent) and pick them up after visiting the complex/museums—but bring your camera for outside shots!

<u>**Zwinger:**</u> With more than several million visitors pouring through its premises each year, the Zwinger is Dresden's most visited attraction. Constructed between 1710 and 1728, the Zwinger's original buildings were designed as the royal palace's entertainment center to host concerts and festivals. However, the development of the Baroque complex took a different course and became one of Europe's finest museum quarters. The name Zwinger dates back several hundred years, meaning an area between the outer and inner zones of the city's former fortified walls. Alas, the complex was severely damaged during the air raids of 1945—the locals feared the Zwinger would forever remain a ruin. Fear gave way

to perseverance and a dogged determination to safeguard Dresden's future. In due time, the museum quarter was meticulously restored. Since WWII, the rising waters of the Elbe River have replaced aerial bombardment as the city's number one enemy. During the devastating floods of August 2002, the Elbe reached a record height of 9.40m/31ft and the Zwinger narrowly avoided a third-millennium washout. On a more harmonious note, don't miss the mesmerizing melody of the Glockenspielpavillon, chiming a classical tune thrice daily: 10:15, 14:15, 18:15—look to the pavilion featuring a clock, including 40 bells made from Meissen porcelain. *Getting There:* Take any tram to Postplatz, the Altstadt's transportation hub, or tram 8 to Theaterplatz. *Hours:* Within the Zwinger's Baroque walls are four museums, all keep the same hours: *Tue-Sun 10:00-18:00, last entry 17:30!*

Old Masters' Gallery (Gemäldegalerie Alte Meister) is king at the Zwinger having one of the most significant collections of paintings in the world, displaying more than 750 artworks on three floors. Here one can spend hours ogling over masterpieces from the 16th to 18th centuries. Highlights include Rembrandt's self-portrait with Saskia (on his lap; circa 1635) and Raphael's (or Raffael's) Sistine Madonna (circa 1513) with two angels at bottom. After entering the museum and climbing to the top of the stairs, the immediate room and hallway in front of you exhibits a series of Canaletto paintings of Dresden from the mid-1700s. The last painting is of the Zwinger courtyard. Notice the outside fountains and the 40 Meissen bells on the Glockenspielpavillon as well as the building you are now standing in are all absent. This is how the Zwinger complex originally looked and the aforesaid parts missing were added more than a century later. Hours: Tue-Sun 10:00-18:00. Price: (includes entry into the Armory) adult 6€, student 3.50€.

Armory: (Rüstkammer) More than 1300 exhibits are displayed on 950 sq.m/ 10,225sq.ft of floor space representing weapons of glistening steel, e.g. sharp sabers, flintlock pistols, and musket rifles as well as ceremonial suits of armor—even suits made for kids. Non-buffs expect a visit to take 30 min. *Note:* This exhibition will soon move to the Dresdener Schloss. Hours: Tue-Sun 10:00-18:00. Price: adult 3€, student 2€.

Porcelain Collection: (Porzellansammlung) This famed collection originated in the early 18th century because of one man's obsession with porcelain. Augustus the Strong, elector of Saxony and King of Poland, described his passion for the precious and fragile material as his "maladie de porcelaine" (porcelain sickness). In 1710 he established the Meissen porcelain factory, which enhanced his already unprecedented collection from Asia with local products—by 1721 the Porzellansammlung comprised more than 14,000 examples of the "white gold." During WWII the collection was wisely moved out of town and therefore survived the war—although, in Soviet hands. The porcelain was transported back to Dresden from Moscow in 1958, and since 1962 the Zwinger has housed Augustus' white gold. Without a doubt the most renowned part of the collection is its 18th-century Meissen porcelain; roughly 8000 pieces are on display from the factory's earliest products. Other treasures of the bi-level Porzellansammlung include examples of ancient Chinese ceramics and priceless pieces from the Ming dynasty. Non-buffs expect a visit to take around 40 min. Hours: Tue-Sun 10:00-18:00. Price: adult 5€, student 3€. *Note:* After your visit, consider exiting onto the outdoor promenade and walk the upper-level circuit to the other side of the Zwinger, descending the steps to the grotto—where 16 nymphs in niches encompass an intimate fountain.

Mathematics-Physics Salon: This specialty museum has been housed in the Zwinger since 1728, debuting with more than 1000 exhibits in its collection. Here you'll discover a room full of terrestrial globes, telescopes, compasses, geometric instruments, calculators from the 16th century, and an upper-level exhibition of ornate clocks, including an astronomical clock commissioned for the Dresden court in the mid-1500s. Non-buffs expect a visit to take around 35 min. Hours: Tue-Sun 10:00-18:00. Price: adult 3€, student 2€.

Dresdener Schloss: (Residenz) Adjacent to the Zwinger and Hofkirche is the Schloss, first mentioned in the 13th century. It was enlarged 200 years later in Renaissance-style and a grand palace began to take shape. In 1701 fire gutted the complex, and the incumbent ruler, Augustus the Strong, wasted no time in building a superior version. The Schloss is once again enduring major renovations, which are slated for completion this year (2006)—synchronized for Dresden's 800th birthday celebrations. The Schloss is home to a handful of museums and rotating exhibitions, which keep the same *hours*: Wed thru Mon 10:00-18:00 (last entry 17:30), closed Tuesday. The most popular attractions within the Dresdener Schloss are the Hausmannsturm and Green Vaults—note that in the latter museum pictures are not allowed. The Münzkabinett, or Coin Collection, is also located here but its permanent home is undergoing renovations, which will be finished April/May this year (2006). ***Getting There:*** Enter the Dresdener Schloss at the corner of Sophienstr. and (street) Taschenberg.

Hausmannsturm: This is the 100-meter-high tower you see rising above the Schloss with people reeling in the views from its observation level. Take the elevator to the second floor and hoof it up a few levels until you come to a room presenting very sobering pictures of the February '45 firebombing, when the city was transformed into a smoldering heap of rubble. Exhibition is in German, but the pictures speak for themselves. Continue up the spiral staircase to the observation level; the bevy of panoramic views is not to be missed! *(Opinion: Those who have a fear of heights don't deny yourself this opportunity, it's a rather mild affair.)* On the way up you'll pass an intriguing time mechanism reset in 1996. It controls all four clocks belonging to the tower and rang from 1746 till February 13, 1945. Expect a visit to take around 30 min. Hours: April to mid-Nov, Wed thru Mon 10:00-18:00, closed Tue and mid-Nov thru March. Price: adult 2.50€, student 1.50€.

Green Vaults: (Grünes Gewölbe) Here you'll discover Europe's most spectacular treasure collection, a cache (of gold, diamonds, rubies and emeralds) dating from the 16th to 18th centuries. Augustus the Strong, elector of Saxony and King of Poland, began collecting valuables in the early 1700s from all over the world and housing them in the Schloss. Augustus put the valuables on display and referred to the exhibition rooms as The Secret Chambers. Because the rooms were green, visitors began calling them the Green Vaults. During WWII, the collection became homeless and it wasn't until 1974 that it found accommodations in the Albertinum complex. Recently, in 2004, the collection moved back to the Dresdener Schloss, where it was originally housed. *(Only half of the collection is on display—the absent half will make its grand reopening on Sept 15, 2006.)* Within the first treasure room, notice the meticulous craftsmanship that went into the riches of the Mikro-Kabinett (back, left corner). In the Dinglinger Saal (6th room) don't miss the 132 petite figures that adorn the Throne of the Grand Mogul, dating from 1708. Expect a visit to take between 90-180 min. Hours: Wed thru Mon 10:00-18:00, closed Tue. Price: adult 6€, student 3.50€. Audio guide available for 2€—exhibits, though, are in English. ***Note:*** Pictures are not allowed in the Green Vaults. *Prices, hours, procedure may change due to new exhibitions making their way into the museum.*

Münzkabinett: The "Coin Collection" was minimally displayed in the Hausmannsturm throughout 2005 while its new home was built, which will be finished April/May this year (2006). On display were cases loaded with fascinating coins dating from the 4th century B.C. (Greek Hellenistic period) to Roman times (3rd century A.D.), including coins featuring Julius Caesar, Caligula, Nero, Augustus, and Alexander the Great.

SIGHTS, Old Town

Zwinger: see *Museums*, page 407.

Green Vaults: (Grünes Gewölbe) see *Dresdener Schloss*, page 409.

Hausmannsturm: see *Dresdener Schloss*, page 409.

Semperoper: One of Dresden's grand landmarks is its opera house, called the Semperoper, completed in 1841 by the celebrated architect, Gottfried Semper—designer of several elaborate buildings on Vienna's beloved Ring strasse. The Semperoper opened with great fanfare to three world premiers by Richard Wagner: Rienzi (1842), Der Fliegende Holländer (1843), and Tannhäuser (1845). Alas, the opera house was gutted by fire in 1869. Gottfried's son, Manfred, finished the reconstruction eight years later in Italian Renaissance-style. The opera house was yet again reduced to ash during the February 1945 firebombing—and brought back to life in February 1985, on the 40th anniversary of the Allied attack. Today, the Semperoper features leading opera and ballet productions as well as classical concerts. *Show Tickets:* Call 0351/491-1705, or go to the "Opernkasse" (box office) at the Schinkelwache TI — 5-9€ for "Stehplatz" (standing room), 20-85€ for seats, or 8.50€ for "Höreplatz" (hear seat; you have a seat but you can only hear the performane, not see it). You can buy tickets (if available) directly at the opera house up to one hour before the show starts. *CC's:* VC, MC, AE. *Note:* Generally there are no performances for the last two weeks of July and most of August. Go to their website for updated info: www.semperoper.de *Tours:* ("Führungen") Another way to ogle the sumptuous interior of the Semperoper is to take a tour (in German with English translation sheet. For a tour in English, ask TI if one is scheduled.): adult 6€, student 3€—duration one hour. Enter on Elbe side (when facing opera house from Theaterplatz, the entry doors are on right side under arched passageway). Tour times frequently change according to the season—for current schedule inquire at the TI, or call 0351/491-1496, or go to the abovementioned website. Purchase tickets at entrance prior to tour.

Hofkirche: Across from the Semperoper is the Hofkirche, also referred to as the Kathedrale, built from 1739-51 in Baroque-style. Inside this Roman Catholic church is vast and impressive. Perched above the rear of the central nave is the 3000-pipe Silbermann organ (1755), named after its creator and made from pine and oak wood. *(FREE recitals every Wed & Sat 11:30-12:00.)* Left of the altar, beneath the Sakramentskapelle, is the crypt accommodating 47 sarcophagi of the Saxon royal family, Wettin, including a vessel containing the heart of Augustus the Strong (his remains rest in Krakow, Poland). Ornamenting the Hofkirche's curvaceous exterior are 78 holy figures perched upon balustrades, and rising 86 meters into the sky is its three-tiered wedding-cake-like steeple (an even more spectacular sight at night when it's floodlit). *Hours:* (church) Mon-Thur 9:00-17:00, Fri 13:00-17:00, Sat 10:30-16:00, Sun 12:00-16:00. *Note:* Visits into crypt are only possible with *FREE* German tour; times are posted outside entrance door (donations welcome).

Fürstenzug: This "Procession of Nobles" is the gilded, 102-meter-long mural you'll see on Augustusstrasse, the cobbled lane running between the Hofkirche and Frauenkirche. The animated figures depict successive generations of Saxony's dynastic family, Wettin, as well as other provincial icons, e.g. artists and scientists. In 1907, Wilhelm Walther completed the mural on 25,000 tiles of Meissen porcelain. The process required that the tiles be heated three times to extreme temperatures, circa 1000ºF. His hard work paid off—the Fürstenzug survived the WWII bombing raids nearly unscathed, only a few hundred tiles needed replacing. While walking with the procession toward the Frauenkirche, look for Augustus the Strong (Augustus II), the authoritative figure seen atop a powerful horse rearing up on its hind legs. At the far end of the mural you'll see its creator, Wilhelm Walther.

Frauenkirche: (Church of Our Lady) Masterfully built in just 17 years (1726-43) as a monument to Protestant faith, this divine structure's magnificent bell-like Baroque dome—reaching 95 meters—dominated the city skyline for more than two centuries. *(At 1.5 meters thick, the Frauenkirche's dome was often referred to as the "Bell of Stone"—look to the mammoth-sized section out front, which remains from the '45 firestorm.)* Alas, the Frauenkirche was reduced to a smoldering ruin in the fiery aftermath of the (WWII) Allied air campaign over Dresden. The East German socialists, whose GDR government chronologically followed Hitler's fascists, left the church a ruin as a so-called memorial to the victims who died in the bombings. In 1991, after the collapse of Eastern-bloc Communism and the reunification of Germany, it was decided to rebuild the Frauenkirche. Full-scale renovations began; many of the original stone blocks were sorted, numbered and—with the help of computer imaging—put back in their correct positions. Resembling a freckled face, the Frauenkirche's facade is a tidy blend of original, soot-stained blocks and a majority assortment of new, tan-colored ones. With donations (mostly private) from around the world ringing up to the total of 150€ million, the Frauenkirche was finally completed mid-summer 2005 and consecrated a few months later with terrific fanfare on October 30. To show unity, the newly handcrafted cross atop the church was shaped by the son of a Royal Air Force pilot (who had bombed the city) and donated by Britain's "Dresden Trust." *Hours:* (for visitors, but may change) Mon-Sat 10:00-12:00 & 13:00-18:00. (www.frauenkirche-dresden.com) *Price:* (to ascend dome; first elevator then steep steps) adult 8€, student 5€. *GPS:* N51° 03.145 - E13° 44.434

Brühlsche Terrasse: In 1739, minister Brühl transformed part of the city's fortified wall facing the Elbe River into a self-serving aristocratic promenade. Some 75 years later, in 1814, a broad stairway was added from the street to make the terrace accessible to the public. Ecstatic, locals referred to their new riverside promenade as "Europe's balcony." Located in the heart of the Old Town and affording memorable views of the Elbe and Neustadt, a trip to Dresden wouldn't be complete without a stroll along minister Brühl's delightful terrace. A good entry point is the wide staircase facing the Hofkirche.

Underneath the promenade are vaulted cellars and casemates from when it was part of the city's fortifications during the Renaissance period—possible to view is the Jung-fernbastei, where the alchemist Johann Böttger uncovered the secret to Chinese porcelain in 1707. In more recent times, parts of the subterranean labyrinth were used as air-raid shelters during WWII. *Hours:* (cellars/casemates) daily, 10:00-16:00 (April-Oct till 17:00). *Price:* (includes audio guide) adult 3.10€, student 2€. City Card holders receive 50¢ discount. *Getting There:* When facing the Albertinum (from Brühlsche Terrasse) go right and descend stairway to find the "Kasematten/Festung."

New Synagogue: Gottfried Semper, first architect of the opera house, designed the original synagogue in 1838. Exactly a century later the Nazis set fire to the hallowed structure, during what became infamously known as Kristallnacht, or Night of Broken Glass (Nov 8, 1938), in a multiphase plan to eradicate Dresden's 6000-member Jewish community. Sixty-three years later (Nov 2001), on the anniversary of its destruction, the 11€ million New Synagogue was unveiled. The modest cube-like structure, consisting of giant-sized stone blocks, is modeled after the first Israelite temples with architectural angles pointing east in the direction of prayer. The only original artifact that survived the Semper synagogue is the golden Star of David, which was saved by Dresden firefighter Alfred Neugebauer in 1938 and is now mounted at the main entrance. Standing opposite the New Synagogue is the Gemeinde Haus, the administration center of Dresden's existing 550-member Jewish community. In the courtyard between the two buildings is a steel frame fixed into the ground marking the original site of the Semper synagogue. *Tours* of the New Synagogue (duration 60-70 min; adult 4€, student 2.50€; arranged by HATiKVA, www.hatikva.de) are possible in German, call ahead to see if there is one in English: *tel.#* 0351/656-8825. *Getting There:* Synagogue is located at the southeastern end of the Brühlsche Terrasse—reach it by foot or take tram 3 or 7 to Synagogue. While there, notice the typical Soviet-style apartment blocks (now renovated) across the busy traffic intersection.

SIGHTS, Neustadt

Neustadt (New Town) isn't all that new. The borough on the north bank of the Elbe was ravaged by fire in 1685 and subsequently rebuilt with the adopted name "Neue Stadt bei Dresden" (New Town near Dresden). The borough was granted city rights as early as 1403, however it was always in the shadows of the royal palace (Dresdener Schloss) on the south bank. Today, the once neglected borough has been transformed into a vital part of Dresden, maintaining its own history, sprawling cityscape, and nightlife fever. Neustadt boasts more than 130 pubs, clubs and restaurants, principally on Louisen, Alaun and Görlitzer streets.

Golden Rider: (Goldener Reiter) On the north side of Augustusbrücke and spearheading Neustadt is the larger-than-life gilded equestrian statue of Augustus the Strong, the Saxon ruler who is responsible for bringing porcelain to Europe and making Dresden an architecturally grand city. The statue was ceremoniously unveiled in 1736, three years after Augustus' death. The Golden Rider is facing Hauptstrasse, Neustadt's main pedestrian promenade flanked by shops, cafés, restaurants and the Church of the Three Kings.

Church of the Three Kings: Dating from 1739, the Baroque-style "Dreikönigskirche" situated on Neustadt's Hauptstrasse (Main Street) is worth a visit. Refurbished since its destruction during WWII, the church's fresh interior resembles that of a theater with its two tiers of balconies above rows of neatly aligned chairs. The sandstone altar is original and partially intact, a grim reminder of the horrors of war. Above the entrance portal is the startling *Totentanz,* The Dresdener Dance of Death, a 13m/42ft long stone relief dating from 1535. *Hours:* daily, 10:00-18:00. *Note:* It's possible to climb the church's 87m/285ft high tower, see page 415.

Kunsthofpassage: This rather long German word is actually three rolled into one, meaning "passageway through the courtyard of art." This Laguna Beach-style quarter hidden in the midst of Neustadt is a must-see for art aficionados and anyone with a sense of the unusual. It features groovy galleries, bubbly boutiques, fancy facades and the Regenwasserspiel. The what? (We hear you ask.) The Regenwasserspiel is the "rain water fountain," an exceptional artistic creation involving a network of aluminum pipes, funnels and guttering strategically attached to the hand-painted facade of an apartment block to fancifully direct water off the eaves of the roof. Synchronize a visit to Neustadt to correspond with a wet performance by the Regenwasserspiel—you can see it in action from spring thru fall Mon-Fri 13:00-19:00, Sat/Sun 10:00-20:00 on the hour and half hour, and, of course, when it rains. *Getting There:* Kunsthofpassage is located between Görlitzer Str. and Alaunstr.—enter either at Alaunstr. 70 or Görlitzer Str. 25, both entrances are marked by a large blue sign featuring a golden cow springing into the air. If you enter at Görlitzer Str. 25, ramble through the short covered passage and feast your eyes on the dazzling yellow facade, then turn around to discover the Regenwasserspiel. *GPS:* N51° 04.071 - E13° 45.266

Pfund's Molkerei: (Dairy) In 1997, this unique milk shop entered the Guinness Book of Records as the most beautiful in the world. With 2669sq.ft. of hand-painted tiles from Villeroy and Boch, it's not hard to understand why. The Pfund brothers established the *molkerei,* or dairy, more than a century ago and business subsequently boomed—milk production peaked at 60,000 liters per day with Europe-wide deliveries consisting of cream, butter, cheese, yogurt, milk powder, and even milk-based soap. Business may have declined from its heyday, but there's no doubt you'll ever see a more beautiful milk shop in the world! Cheese lovers will appreciate the extra dairy selection to choose from, inclusive of heady aroma, pungent smell. Interior designers note the specially designed (frieze) wall tiles for sale (10€/ea.)—a decorative addition to the kitchen. *Hours:* Mon-Sat 10:00-18:00, Sun 10:00-15:00. (www.pfunds.de) *Getting There:* Pfund's Molkerei is located at Bautzner Str. 79, Neustadt—20-min walk from the Bahnhof or take tram 11 (direction Bühlau) to Pulsnitzer Str. *GPS:* N51° 03.821 - E13° 45.591

Old Jewish Cemetery: (Alter Jüdischer Friedhof) This is the oldest maintained Jewish cemetery in Saxony, established in 1751 and closed to burial since 1869. Witness more than 1000 gravestones of all shapes and sizes, unevenly resting in the rich coffee-brown soil. The gate will be locked but a fine view can still be had. Those who are keen for a closer look, inquire at the HATiKVA office in the adjacent building on right (Pulsnitzer Str. 10)—push HATiKVA button and say "Friedhof Schlüssel" (cemetery key). You'll subsequently be buzzed in and a member of the Jewish community will then open the cemetery gate for you (just notify him/her when to return to lock up). *Note:* Men are required to wear a skullcap, available at HATiKVA office. Also available at the office are brochures for 80¢, and they can arrange a tour of the New Synagogue for you. (www.hatikva.de) *Hours:* Mon-Thur 9:00-12:00 & 13:00-16:00 (Thur till 17:00), Fri thru Sun closed. *Getting There:* Cemetery is located on Pulsnitzer Str. in Neustadt, near Pfund's Molkerei. *GPS:* N51° 03.866 - E13° 45.496

More SIGHTS

(All of the below-listed sights are on Elbe's south bank, Old-Town side.)

Yendize: In the west end of the Old Town you'll notice a piece of the Orient, a mosque-like edifice soaring into the sky. The Arabesque structure dates from 1907 and was originally used as a tobacco warehouse by the Yendize cigarette company. The building, today, is still referred to as the Yendize but business offices and a restaurant have replaced the stockpiles of Turkish blend.

VW Transparent Factory: (Gläserne Manufaktur) This state-of-the-art Volkswagen factory complex, which maintains some 800 employees (including numerous robots) and produces upwards of 150 cars per day, is a newly added architectural highlight to Dresden's cityscape, costing 186€ million to build. Transparent is not only a fancy word in the title, the factory features nearly 7 acres (27,500sq.m./296,000sq.ft.) of floor-to-ceiling glass panels rising up to 40m/131ft high. On the first floor (one level up) is an interactive exhibition where you can virtually walk through the assembly process via touch-screen terminals and literally watch white-coated personnel piece together VW's luxury-class sedan, the Phaeton, as it glides through the production line. Auto-buffs can expect a visit to take 60-90 min; non auto-buffs can walk through in 10-15 min. After entering the building you'll see lockers located in the back corner (toilets are adjacent). Put your things in a locker (bring a 1€ coin; you get it back upon your return—like at museums), then ascend steps to the exhibition floor above. *Hours:* daily, 8:00-20:00. (www.glaesernemanufaktur.de) Free *tours* of the factory are possible but in German. You must reserve at least 48 hours in advance—when reserving, ask if an English tour is scheduled. Email: infoservice@glaesernemanufaktur.de or tel.# 0180/589-6268 (12¢/min within Germany). *Getting There:* Factory neighbors the Großer Garten (see next entry) at Straßburger Platz, one mile southeast of the Frauenkirche. Take tram 1, 2, or 4 from Postplatz; tram 10 from the main train station; or tram 13 from Neustadt; and get off at

Straßburger Platz. *Drivers:* Visitor's parking lot (Besucher-Parkplatz) is adjacent to factory complex off Lennéstr. *GPS:* N51° 02.685 - E13° 45.220

Großer Garten: Located in the southeast part of town—behind VW's Transparent Factory—is the "Grand Garden," Dresden's biggest and most beautiful park, initially landscaped in 1676 as a royal hunting ground. Today, the Großer Garten encompasses 363 acres, including the zoo (see next entry), a Baroque palace (1683), an open-air theater, and a mini steam-railway for big and little kids alike. Hauptallee, the main drag bisecting the park, is busy with walkers, joggers, cyclists and in-line skaters. It's as if all of Dresden has come out to play. The railway scoots its way through the gardens daily from mid-April thru Oct (times vary slightly, but mainly) 10:00-18:00. Price: (depending on how many stops) adult 2€-3€, student 1€-1.50€. Those who will be visiting the zoo, consider the zoo + train Kombi-ticket—(roughly) adult 8.50€, student 5.60€, child 4.60€. *Note:* next to VW's Transparent Factory is a railway stop. Because of the park's enormity, to go for a ride on the railway is a good idea.

Zoo, Dresden: Established in 1861, the Dresden Zoo is the fourth oldest in Germany. During WWII the animal park was destroyed and a year after the war ended the doors were once again open. In 1961 the zoo celebrated its 100th birthday and 1.2 million visitors showed up for the party. Today, the zoo maintains around 3000 animals representing 400 species. *Hours:* daily, 8:30-16:30 (May-Oct till 18:30), last entry 45 min before closing. *Price:* adult 7€ (Mondays 5€), student 5€. *Feeding Times:* "Fütterungszeiten" (use as general guide, times may have changed) elephants 12:00; penguins 15:00; lions/leopards 13:00 & 15:00 (cats are not fed on Mondays, thus the cheaper entrance fee). *Getting There:* Zoo is located in the Großer Garten (see previous entry). Take tram 9 or 13 to Zoo, or the mini-railway within the garden.

Blue Wonder: Six kilometers upriver from the Old Town, along an enchanting stretch of terrain recently voted onto UNESCO's World Heritage List, is Dresden's most famous bridge, the so-called "Blaues Wunder." Upon its completion in 1893, the steel suspension bridge really was a wonder, built without any piers and considered to be "hanging"—a remarkable engineering feat of its time. But the real wonder was yet to come: Not long after the opening-day fanfare, the original green paint turned blue!

In addition to the Blue Wonder, the architects constructed two railways nearby on the north (right) bank: The suspended railway (Schwebebahn), built 1898-1901, is the oldest of its kind in the world. The funicular railway (Stand Seilbahn, 1895) ushers passengers to a restaurant 100 meters above the river (daily, one way 2€, round trip 3€). *Getting There:* (Blue Wonder) *By tram,* take #6 from Neustadt or #12 from Postplatz to Schillerplatz. *Cyclists*, worthwhile ride—keep to the south (left) bank (pack a picnic). *Drivers*, also keep to the south (left) bank—start from Terrassenufer.

Slaughterhouse-Five: The WWII bombing of Dresden inspired Kurt Vonnegut to write his antiwar (interplanetary) novel, "Slaughterhouse-Five." Vonnegut was an American GI captured by the German army in 1945 and held as a POW on the outskirts of Dresden, where he worked in a slaughterhouse and witnessed the horrific firebombing. Much of the district Vonnegut spent his POW days has been developed into the city's convention center ("Messe"); however, a small area still remains as it did in '45. *Getting There:* The Messe is located 2km northwest of the Semperoper. Catch bus #82 from Postplatz and get off at "Parkplatz Ostragehege" (6th stop); the pre-war now-being-renovated complex begins on the next corner some 30 meters farther. *Cyclists,* from Semperoper follow riverside route downstream to the Marienbrücke (bridge)—cross underneath it with the traffic and turn right onto Pieschener Allee. After a few minutes the "Parkplatz Ostragehege" bus stop will appear on the right, along with the pre-war now-being-renovated complex on the next corner some 30 meters farther. *Note:* From "Parkplatz Ostragehege" follow the cobblestones paralleling the old and dilapidated structures to the next bus stop "Ostragehege Messehalle 1," where you'll see (on the freshly renovated pre-war buildings opposite) many representations of cattle from the days when it was part of the slaughterhouse. *GPS:* N51° 04.088 - E13° 43.204

Best Views

Hausmannsturm: Dating from 1674 and rising 100m/328ft, the Hausmannsturm (page 409) is the highest of Dresden's historical towers and is absolutely worth a visit. *Hours:* April to mid-Nov, Wed thru Mon 10:00-18:00, closed Tue and mid-Nov thru March. Price: adult 2.50€, student 1.50€.

Rathaus Turm: Dating from 1910 and standing 98m/321ft tall, the "Town Hall Tower" affords a fine view of the Old Town. *Hours:* April-Oct, daily, 10:00-18:00 (last entry 17:30). *Price:* adult 2.50€, student 1.25€. *Getting There:* Tower is located one block south of Altmarkt, enter off Kreuzstr. through archway to "Turmaufzug."

Church of the Three Kings: (Dreikönigskirche) Reaching 87m/285ft high, this church's neo-Baroque tower offers an exalted perspective of Dresden's New and Old Towns. *Hours:* March-Oct Tue-Sun 11:30-16:00 (Wed-Sat till 17:00); Nov-Feb Wed 12:00-16:00, Thur/Fri 10:00-16:00, Sat 10:00-17:00, Sun 11:30-16:30. *Price:* adult 1.50€, student 1€. *Getting There:* located at Hauptstr. 23, Neustadt; enter at back of church.

Frauenkirche: (page 411) The newly opened Church of Our Lady boasts heavenly views of Dresden, but it'll cost ya: adult 8€/student 5€.

Shopping

Shopping Mall: It seems that most Dresdeners are milling around inside the city's spiffy new three-level shopping mall, **Altmarkt Galerie** (open Mon-Sat 9:00-20:00), located adjacent to Altmarkt (Old Market Square). Toilets are situated on each floor; bring small change. On the lower level is a pair of grocery stores; on one end is an "Aldi" and at the other end is a "Rewe"—both stores are open the same hours as the mall. The better of the two is Rewe, way better.

Main Shopping Street: One block from Altmarkt Galerie begins the city's main shopping street—**Prager Strasse**—an open-air pedestrian thoroughfare flanked by department stores, fashion boutiques, banks, three ibis hotels, a pair of H&M's and a TI. At the southern end of Prager Strasse is the Hauptbahnhof, or main train station.

Flea Market: For one of Germany's best flea markets, be in Dresden on a Saturday. Here you'll find vendors from Dresden, and surrounding communities, who have seemingly cleaned the old wares from their attics to sell at the market. Get there early, allow 2 to 4 hours to browse (it's a large market), and bring the maximum amount of money you can afford to spend. Space in your suitcase won't be a problem because you packed light, right? *Suggestion:* If you found a good price on an item, buy it—you'll regret it later if you don't! *Hours:* Sat, 6:30-16:00 (all year)—and typically every third Sunday of the month. *Getting There:* The market is set up along the south (left) bank of the Elbe River, adjacent to the Albertbrücke (old stone bridge). Take tram 6 or 13 to Sachsenallee. *GPS:* N51° 03.361 - E13° 45.362

Entertainment, Eats

Just about every type of cuisine, watering hole, club and pub is situated in Neustadt, approximately 130 establishments registered. Cruise the area around Louisen, Alaun and Görlitzer streets for the most choices. Restaurants usually display their menu outside (adjacent to the front door) for easy viewing. For a few more euros, consider the Italienisches Dörfchen (Little Italian Village) located on Theaterplatz in the Old Town.

The Dörfchen came about in the mid-18th century when Italian tradesmen inhabited the complex while erecting the Hofkirche. Today, the Dörfchen offers a unique cluster of gastronomic possibilities: café, bistro, beer garden, Italian restaurant—all boasting pleasant views of the Elbe River, Zwinger, Semperoper and Hofkirche.

Headline Concerts, Dresden 2006

Note: Prices, dates, concerts may have changed or been added — query TI or ticket agency for latest details.

> Arctic Monkeys: May 9, 20:00 at the Alter Schlachthof. Price 22€
> Tracy Chapman: June 29, 20:00 at the Freilichtbühne Großer Garten. Price 40€
> Robbie Williams: July 10-11, 18:30 at the Fairgrounds (Ostragehege). Price 71-88€
> Scorpions: July 29, 20:00 on the banks of the Elbe River. Price 41€
> Simply Red: August 20, 20:00 at the Freilichtbühne Großer Garten. Price 53€
> James Last: October 24, 20:00 at the Kulturpalast. Price 38-73€

Events/Festivals 2006

Steamboat Parade, May 1 (Mon): A floating spectacle not to be missed! The steamboat armada shoves off from their moorings in front of the Brühlsche Terrasse at 10:00, returning approx. 14:00. Consider renting a bike and following the armada upstream to Schloss Pillnitz.

(36th Annual) **Dixieland Festival**, May 10-14 (Wed-Sun): Europe's oldest and most traditional jazz festival will host numerous bands and performers from Europe and North America to the delight of thousands of music fans during the 5-day event. For more info, go to www.dixieland.de

Elbhangfest (Riverside Festival), June 23-25 (Fri-Sun): Dresden's longest festival stretches 7km along the Saxon Wine Road from the Blue Wonder (page 414) to Schloss Pillnitz. You'll find stands selling arts and crafts, food and wine, and perhaps some former GDR memorabilia. This is another perfect excuse to rent a bike and get the blood pumping.

City Festival Week, (Stadtfestwoche) July 14-23: This year Dresden celebrates its 800-year birthday. No doubt the festivities will be grand.

Marathon: Runners have two opportunities this year to compete in Dresden: April 30 and October 22, both are Sundays. On April 30 participants begin in Königstein (Sächsische Schweiz national park) and jog a scenic route along the Elbe River to Dresden—10km and half marathon are also possible. Route is easily accessible by train. (www.oberelbe-marathon.de)

On October 22 the starting blocks are moved to Dresden for the city marathon, which orbits the Old Town—10km and half marathon are also possible. www.dresden-marathon.de (in German).

Christmas Markets: This is the time of year (from the end of November until Christmas Eve) when your senses will tingle thanks to the aroma of hot-spiced wine, roasted chestnuts, baked apples and gingerbread wafting through the streets of Dresden. The "Christmas mile" begins with the market on Prager Strasse, continues through the Old Town and concludes in Neustadt with the market on Hauptstrasse. Most impressive are the two markets in the Old Town: the **Advent Spektakel** in the Stallhof (Schloss Courtyard) and the **Striezelmarkt** on the Altmarkt (Old Market Square). Skaters looking for an ice rink will find one at the Tascheberg Palais (across from TI at Theaterplatz). It's typically open December thru February, Mon-Fri 15:00-22:00, Sat/Sun 11:00-20:00—5€ during week, 7€ weekend, skate rental 3€.

Advent Spektakel is a must-see historical market where visitors can experience Christmas as it existed during the Renaissance era—handmade products, wood-fired cuisine, live performers, and period costume. *Hours:* Nov 24 thru Dec 22, daily, 11:00-20:00. *Price:* usually free entry during the week and 3€ on weekends.

Striezelmarkt is the oldest Christmas market in Germany, founded in 1434. (Open end of Nov till Dec 24, daily, 10:00-20:00.) During the four-week event some 2 million visitors will converge on the Altmarkt, where 220 vendors surround a glimmering 22m/72ft tall Christmas tree. One of the highlights of the Striezelmarkt is the appetizing **Stollenfest** (usually first Sat in Dec), when approx. 80,000 spectators will be in town to gawk at the world's largest sugar-dusted fruitcake, or "stollen," which weighs in at around 7600lbs (3.5 tons), 15ft long and 6ft wide. The fruitcake is so large that it has to be prepared by more than 60 bakers and cut with a specially made knife 5 feet long weighing 26lbs. Some ingredients used are 3300lbs (ca.1.5 tons) of flour, approx. 10gal of Jamaican rum, 1000lbs of sugar and 1750lbs of butter. That's some fruitcake! And you can share in the sweetness for 3€ a piece after the cake-cutting ceremony at 12:30. The Stollenfest kicks off at 10:30 around the Zwinger, followed by the unveiling of the giant stollen at 11:00 and the parade at 11:15 (procession of bakers, pastry chefs, horse-drawn carriages, and the stollen maiden), which ends at the Striezelmarkt about 12:00. Some 20 minutes later the stollen is cut and the consumption begins.

GOOD SLEEPS
Accommodations on Elbe's north bank, Neustadt

Neustadt is where the majority of accommodations are, and where the nightlife is, thus the recommendations begin here. *Note:* When traveling to Dresden by train, be sure to get off at "Dresden-Neustadt" train station, otherwise from the "Hauptbahnhof" (Hbf) catch tram 7 or 8 to your Neustadt digs.

Both of the following hostels are clean and have friendly staff as well as respectable self-service kitchens. **Louise20** is more homely and suggested for the quieter type. **Mondpalast** has a hip bar and generous lounge areas facilitating a more social atmosphere.

Getting There: (for either hostel) exit Dresden-Neustadt station left, cut through parking lot and continue along cobbled road passing bombed-out buildings on right (this is how much of Dresden looked after the war). After a few blocks you'll reach a railway underpass on the left, *go right* (Lößnitzstr.) and at the next intersection begins Louisen-strasse. Continue straight and on the right (after two minutes) is Louise20—about another eight minutes farther is Mondpalast on the left.

Note: If your train does not stop at Dresden-Neustadt, you'll need to catch a tram from the Hauptbahnhof (main train station)—out front catch tram 7 direction Weixdorf, or at the side of the station catch tram 8 direction Hellerau, and get off at Louisenstrasse (exit tram left and then go right on Louisenstrasse to your digs).

Hostel, Louise 20: Louisenstr. 20 (www.louise20.de) *Tel.#* 0351/889-4894. *Price:* 20-bed dorm 10€, 5-bed dorm 15€, 3/4-bed dorm 16€, Sgl 26€, Dbl 37€, comfort Dbl 40€, (apartments available), linen 2.50€ (one-time charge), buffet breakfast 4.50€. *CC's:* VC, MC. *Getting There:* Follow directions above; 12-min walk from Neustadt train station. Once at Louisenstr. 20, go through covered passage to petite courtyard where you'll find entry into the Planwirtschaft (very popular restaurant)—adjacent is a stairway ascending to your digs. *GPS:* N51° 04.036 - E13° 45.002

Hostel, Mondpalast: Louisenstr. 77 (www.mondpalast.de) *Tel.#* 0351/563-4050. Has Internet access. Rents bikes, 6€/day. *Price:* dorm beds 13.50-18.50€, Sgl 29-39€, Dbl 37-50€, buffet breakfast 5€, linen 2€ (one-time charge). *CC's:* VC, MC. *Getting There:*

Follow directions above; 20-min walk from Neustadt train station. *GPS:* N51° 03.941 - E13° 45.393

Guest House, Mezcalero: Königsbrücker Str. 64 (www.mezcalero.de) *Tel.#* 0351/810-770. Mezcalero is an excellent choice for anyone who appreciates Aztec-Mexican design, individually decorated rooms, is seeking a quieter stay, or couples looking for a Latin-themed, amorous getaway. *Price:* dorm beds from 17€ (linen 2.30€—one-time charge), Sgl *33-50€, Dbl *54-64€, Trpl *63-69€, breakfast 6€, (*cheaper price is without shower/toilet in room). *CC's:* VC, MC. *Getting There:* **Railers,** Mezcalero is a 15-min walk from Dresden-Neustadt train station. Exit station left, cut through parking lot and continue along cobbled road passing bombed-out buildings on right (this is how much of Dresden looked after the war). After a few blocks you'll reach a railway underpass on the left, *go right* (Lößnitzstr.) At next intersection turn left, this is Königsbrücker Str.—continue straight to No. 64 on right (go through passage to your digs). *If you're coming from the Hauptbahnhof,* take tram 7 or 8 to "Bischofsweg" and walk back roughly 50 meters. **Drivers,** free parking available in their courtyard. *GPS:* N51° 04.231 - E13° 44.994

Accommodations on Elbe's south bank, Old-Town

Hotel ibis: (www.ibishotel.com) Clean, reasonably priced and centrally located, the ibis chain has three concrete-block hotels neighboring each other on the GDR-influenced pedestrian shopping mall (Prager Strasse), five-minute walk from the Hauptbahnhof and Old Town. Each property, virtually identical, has the same number of rooms (306) and charges the same rates: Sgl 53-66€, Dbl 68-81€, during conventions 76-91€. *CC's:* VC, MC, AE, DC. *Note:* Breakfast 9€/person, extra bed 15€, parking available. *Hotel code is compatible with ibis website, creating a shortcut to the property—type hotel code into middle left box and click "OK"; next page click on "The Hotel" (left side).

ibis Bastei: tel.# 0351/4856-5447; *hotel code 1578. Rooms have Internet access.
ibis Lilienstein: tel.# 0351/4856-7447; *hotel code 1579
ibis Königstein: tel.# 0351/4856-6447; *hotel code 1580

Hilton: (www.hilton.com) *Tel.#* 0351/86-420, toll-free reservations from USA/Canada 1-800-445-8667 or within Europe 00800/4445-8667. Located in the heart of the Old Town, this exclusive property can be found opposite the Frauenkirche. *Price:* Sgl from 130€, Dbl from 150€. Parking, breakfast extra. *GPS:* N51° 03.145 - E13° 44.434

EXCURSIONS

Meissen: see page 420.

Saxon Switzerland National Park: (Sächsische Schweiz) This rather odd name for a German national park miles from the Swiss border dates from the 18th century, when two artists from Switzerland fell in love with the region's undulating landscape, mystical forests, sandstone plateaus, deep canyons, and fascinating rock spires. The two artists, Anton and Adrian, referred to the region as Switzerland and the name stuck. Throughout the centuries, the region's much-adored sandstone has been used to construct many of Dresden's architectural highlights, such as the Zwinger and Frauenkirche, as well as the Brandenburg Gate in Berlin and the royal palace in Copenhagen, Denmark. The national park covers 92sq.km on the north (right) bank of the Elbe starting at Stadt Wehlen (32km upstream from Dresden) and—almost without interruption—stretches to the Czech border (another 20km). With umpteen natural wonders and more than 1200 hiking trails, Saxon Switzerland is well worth a visit, and perhaps an overnight. (www.sax-ch.de)

Getting There from Dresden: Trains (S-Bahn) leave every half hour from the stations—Hauptbahnhof and Neustadt—direction Schöna (70-min journey; sit on upper level and enjoy the scenery). *Price:* From either station a one-way ticket (*Einzelfahrt*) costs 5.10€. Best buy is the total network (*Verbundraum*) day ticket (*Tageskarte*) valid till 04:00: adult 10€, family 13€ (*Familientageskarte,* couples purchase the latter ticket to increase savings). Small groups purchase the *Kleingruppenkarte* 21€, valid for up to 5 people till 04:00. *Note:* Holders of a Eurail consecutive-day or dated Flexi/Select pass ride *FREE* on the S-Bahn. <u>*Paddle steamers*</u> head upstream a few times before noon; although, this is not recommended—just to get to Königstein takes 5.5hr. To return via Königstein, downstream, only takes 3hr (consider taking the last steamer at around 17:00 [15.30€]; summer schedule, applicable May-Sept). <u>*Drivers*</u>, from the Old Town take the Terrasscnufer (road paralleling river) upstream along the coveted stretch recently voted onto UNESCO's World Heritage List—after 6km you'll arrive at the Blue Wonder (page 414), cross bridge and continue direction Pirna (this is the Saxon Wine Road) passing Schloss Pillnitz. At Pirna cross the Elbe River once again and connect onto road 172 direction Königstein. The road will cross the Elbe at Bad Schandau and after some 10km arrive at the Czech border (total journey 55km).

<u>*Suggested Day Trip*</u> *into the national park and Czech Republic—bring your passport:* Take the train (S-Bahn) from Dresden to Schöna—70-min journey (but you'll reach your first stop after 40 min at Kurort Rathen). The first 25 minutes of the journey are nothin' special, then from Pirna the tracks scenically follow the Elbe River. After the town of Stadt Wehlen keep an eye on the sheer sandstone cliffs on the left, eventually you'll see the Bastei, a 76m/250ft long sandstone bridge. This is a federally protected monument and your first destination. Get off the train at the next stop, Kurort Rathen, a cutesy-pie village of 460 residents on the opposite bank (www.kurort-rathen.de). *At the station look for the train departure schedule that reads "Abfahrt: Dresden – Schöna." Note the departure times so you can neatly plan your connection to Schöna.* Take the ferry across the river—runs regularly, 1.30€ round trip—to reach Kurort Rathen and the Bastei. Once on the other side, walk straight into the village and go left and left again following signs Bastei. The hike will take 40 minutes to reach the sandstone bridge; if you're in a hurry and don't mind sweating you can do it in 15-20 min. Whatever your pace, you will be greatly rewarded at the top with tremendous views of the Elbe valley and the miracles of nature. After your explorations, hop back on the train to Schöna. Soon you'll see the massive 13th-century fortress Königstein perched upon the ridgeline (fortress is open year round to visitors; April-Sept 9:00-20:00, Oct-March 9:00-17:00; adult 5€, student 3€, audio guide 2.50€). As you arrive at Schöna station, the market stalls you see on the opposite bank are in the Czech Republic. A ferry will transport you across the river (90-second trip, 1.30€ each way). *Note:* If you're looking for traditional goods from the Czech Rep. you won't find them here. The umpteen market stalls are run by Asians who are selling typical products from Asia at ultra-cheap prices. To give you an idea of how cheap, 30 pairs of socks were selling for 5€. The preferred currency is the euro and the spoken language is German—you'll hardly find any English speakers in these parts.

Saxon Wine Road: Out of the 13 wine-growing regions in Germany, the Saxon wine district is the smallest with 425 hectares/1050 acres—about 90% of this land is dedicated to white grapes. The Saxon Wine Road stretches 55km along the north bank of the Elbe, from Pirna (23km upstream from Dresden) to Diesbar-Seusslitz (10km downstream from Meissen). Although, the best stretch is from Radebeul to Diesbar-Seusslitz. In these parts, porcelain and wine go hand in hand—grapes have been cultivated here for more than 800 years along with the production of Augustus the Strong's "white gold" for nearly three centuries. <u>*Getting There:*</u> To experience the Saxon vineyards drive the wine road along the Elbe, or take a paddle steamer, or bike and hike (start early; pack a picnic). <u>*Note:*</u> Wine enthusiasts should note festivals are in full swing during the grape-pickin' month of September. Query TI for fest schedule.

Moritzburg Palace: Situated on a petite island 10km from Dresden, the luxurious 18th-century Moritzburg palace was Augustus the Strong's hunting estate. The palace museum contains an enormous variety of antlers and the world's largest collection of Baroque leather wall coverings as well as period furniture, paintings and porcelain. *Hours:* April-Oct, daily, 10:00-17:30 (last entry 17:00). Nov/Dec and Feb/March Tue-Sun, tours on the hour from 10:00 till 16:00. Jan open weekends only. *Price:* (museum and Feather Room) adult 6€, student 4€. *Note:* Palace gardens are free to meander. *Getting There:* from Dresden-Neustadt train station hop on the bus direction Radeburg/Großenhain and get off at Schloss Moritzburg. *Drivers,* take Großenhainer Str. from Dresden-Neustadt train station to Moritzburg.

MEISSEN

~ Population: 29,000   ~ Elevation: 107m/351ft
~ Country/Area Code: +49-(0)3521   ~ Sister City: Provo, Utah

The world-famous porcelain town dates from 929 A.D. and is gracefully reaching its 1080th birthday (in 2009). In fact, Meissen is nearly 300 years older than Dresden. Long ago, in medieval times, the Wettin royal family—whom we associate with reigning over the Saxon capital—actually originated in Meissen, marking the beginning of the state's history.

Located 25km downriver (northwest) from Dresden, Meissen is charmingly wrapped around a Gothic cathedral (Dom) and the 500-year-old Schloss Albrechtsburg—both attractions are perched upon a hill flaunting their imperial past. However, the main reason tourists pull into town is porcelain. The Chinese were first to invent the "white gold" in the 13th century, and until the early 1700s Europeans were scratching their heads trying to figure out its secret composition. Augustus the Strong, Saxony's most celebrated Wettin ruler, had a passion for porcelain and demanded its ingredients be uncovered.

In 1708, the moment of jubilation arrived when the alchemist Johann Böttger discovered the recipe—hence the birth of Europe's first porcelain factory. Production began in Meissen's Schloss Albrechtsburg in 1710, and within a few decades its beloved porcelain decorated royal palaces and aristocratic villas across the continent. After banking 154 years of international success, authorities moved the factory across town to its present location, Talstrasse 9. Today, Meissen is synonymous with the finest porcelain, and its trademark—(cobalt blue) crossed swords—guarantees excellence.

Opinion: If you're crunched for time and not porcelain friendly, don't bother visiting Meissen. Sure it's beautiful, but so are countless other German communities. For porcelain-friendly tourists, Meissen is a must!

~ Travelers visiting between May-Oct, divide your time like so:
Be at the town square by 11:30 to hear the chiming of the Frauenkirche's 37 porcelain bells—afterward march up to the Dom by noon to catch the organ recital from 12:00-12:20 (except Sunday)—at 13:00 begins the first tower tour. To walk from train station to the Dom, or porcelain factory, is circa 25 min.

Getting There from Dresden: *Trains* (S-Bahn) leave every half hour from the stations Hauptbahnhof and Neustadt to Meissen, 30-min journey (sit on upper level and enjoy the scenery). *Price:* From either station a one-way ticket (*Einzelfahrt*) costs 5.10€. Best buy is the total network (*Verbundraum*) day ticket (*Tageskarte*) valid till 04:00: adult 10€, family 13€ (*Familientageskarte,* couples purchase the latter ticket to increase savings). Small groups purchase the *Kleingruppenkarte* 21€, valid for up to 5 people till 04:00. *Note:* Holders of a Eurail consecutive-day or dated Flexi/Select pass ride *FREE* on the S-

Bahn. _Boat:_ Another option is to ride the *train there and hop on the 14:45 paddle steamer back (11€, arrives in Dresden 18:00). *With this itinerary catch the early train to be at the porcelain factory by 9:00 when it opens and the town square by 11:30, followed by the Dom (see above, _Travelers visiting between May-Oct, divide your time like so:_). _Auto:_ For those with wheels, drive the Saxon Wine Route to Meissen (25km, north bank).

Tourist Information: [TI] (www.touristinfo-meissen.de) _Tel.#_ 03521/41940
Hours: April-Oct Mon-Fri 10:00-18:00, Sat/Sun 10:00-16:00; Nov-March Mon-Fri 10:00-17:00, Sat 10:00-15:00. _Getting There:_ TI is located on the market square. From the Meissen train station exit left then go right towards the Old Town (at the bridge is a nice photo opportunity). On the other side of the river begins the Old Town (Altstadt); continue straight to market square.

Porcelain Manufacturer: Talstrasse 9 (www.meissen.de) _Tel.#_ 03521/468-700
Meissen's porcelain factory is not possible to tour, instead they have two in-house attractions: The **Exhibition Hall** and **Demonstration Workshop**. The factory complex increased its size in June 2005 with the opening of a three-story 90€ million annex, which includes a "special exhibition" and a restaurant where you can eat off the fine porcelain plates made on the premises. The concept of the new annex was heartily welcomed by the board since worldwide sales were in the neighborhood of 40€ million (60% within Germany, 40% elsewhere) and more than 300,000 visitors had passed through the turn-stiles (in 2004) to experience either of the two aforementioned attractions. _Hours:_ daily, 9:00-17:00 (May-Oct till 18:00), last entry 40 min before closing.

Getting There: **Railers**, from Dresden take S-Bahn to Meissen-Triebischtal (rail 35 min, foot 7 min). Exit station via sloping path, go left under rail tracks and over creek—continue straight to T-intersection, then right (Talstrasse) to factory ahead on right. _(Note: Have your camera ready! After train pulls out of Meissen station [Bhf] headed for Triebischtal, you'll be treated to a fabulous view of Meissen on the right.)_ **Drivers,** parking by factory available. _GPS:_ N51° 09.411 - E13° 27.884

Price: adult 8€, student 4€—this includes admission into both the Exhibition Hall and Demonstration Workshop, plus the new "special exhibition."

Exhibition Hall: (Schauhalle) Here you'll find around 3000 items from the Meissen collection on display, dating from 1710 to the present day. Walk through on your own—expect a visit to take about an hour.

Demonstration Workshop: (Schauwerkstatt) This is a unique tour set within a hand-ful of rooms where artists will demonstrate to you the process of making porcelain, from the initial turning and molding to embossing and hand painting each delicate piece. Tours leave every 10 min, duration 35 min. Audio guide included.

Gift Shop: Interesting is to browse the porcelain on sale, ranging from a doable 30€ to an outrageous 20,000€.

Note: Enthusiasts have the opportunity to become a Meissen club member and/or join a seminar, e.g. 3-day porcelain decoration course 345€—see website. Those who would like to browse Meissen porcelain without leaving Dresden, visit the Meissen shop next door to the Hilton hotel, a stone's throw from the Frauenkirche. Hours: (shop) daily, Mon-Fri 9:30-19:00, Sat/Sun 9:00-16:00.

Dom: (Cathedral) Perched high above town boasting splendid views of Meissen, the Dom dates from 1250 with final construction being completed some 150 years later. WWII bombs didn't rain on Meissen, like in many other German communities, thus the Dom remains largely in original condition. The interior of this hallowed structure is just as impressive as its exterior and is recommended for a visit. Interesting is the Fürsten-kapelle (Princes' Chapel, 15C), the last resting place of the early Wettin rulers. It is found at the rear end of the nave, from where a heavenly photo can be captured looking back towards the altar. Time your visit to include the midday organ recital, May-Oct, Mon-Sat 12:00-12:20.

Hours: (Dom) daily, April-Oct 9:00-18:00, Nov-March 10:00-16:00. *Price:* (entry into Dom) adult 2.50€, student 1.50€—add an extra 1.50€ for tower tour and 50¢ for midday organ recital (both are worthwhile), combo-ticket with Albrechtsburg 5.50€/3.50€. *Tower Tour:* April-Oct, daily, tours of the tower cost 1.50€/person and depart on the hour from 13:00 till 16:00. Here you will climb 304 steps to the top of the Dom, where you'll be one with the gargoyles enjoying stupendous views. Your guide will break the climb into segments to explain the history. Those who are afraid of heights, give it your best shot. Try and make it to the 8-ton Johannes bell; it's nearly the top and the views are, nonetheless, stunning!

Albrechtsburg: Neighboring the Dom is Albrechtsburg; dating from 1525 it is considered to be the first castle designed as a royal residence in Germany. Today it houses a museum. Expect a visit to take 60 min. *Hours:* daily, 10:00-17:00 (March-Oct till 18:00), last entry 30 min before closing. *Price:* adult 3.50€, student 2.50€, combo-ticket with Dom 5.50€/3.50€.

Frauenkirche: Dating from 1457, the adorable Gothic-style Church of Our Lady is a commanding presence on the market square, especially since it maintains the world's first church bells made from porcelain. The 37 bells were a gift from the Meissen factory in 1929 for the town's 1000th birthday. From the market square look up to the church tower and below the clock you'll see the bells (notice the big bell, bottom center, having the signature Meissen swords). The porcelain bells are a delight to hear, chiming 8:30, 11:30, 14:30, 17:30 and 20:30. Above the bells is an open-air viewing terrace, implemented centuries ago for the night watchman to keep an eye out for fires and the approach of enemy forces—the last watchman to oversee this post was in 1907. The tower, today, is open to the public and may be climbed for a fine view (ask inside church for key). *Price:* adult 2€, student 1€. *Hours:* May-Oct, daily, 10:00-12:00 & 14:00-16:00 (less off-season).

FRANKFURT *am Main*

~ Population: 650,000   ~ Elevation: 98m/321ft
~ Country/Area Code: +49-(0)69   ~ Sister City: Toronto, Canada

Frankfurt on the Main (pronounced Mine) River was settled by the Romans in the 1st century A.D. and received its first official mention in 794 by Charlemagne, king of the Franks. The king and his people discovered a fordable (Furt) section of the Main, crossed there and set up camp—hence the name Frankfurt.

During the reign of Charlemagne (founder of the Holy Roman Empire, and its first emperor 800-814) numerous imperial councils were held here, and the decree of 1356, known as the Golden Bull, established Frankfurt as the seat of imperial elections. Thus the riverside community thrived as a free imperial city, or a state within a state, allowing merchants generous trading liberties.

Centuries later Frankfurt saw the birth of two literary phenomenons, Goethe in 1749 and Anne Frank in 1929—both are buried elsewhere. Much of Frankfurt's old-age flair vanished during WWII when Allied bombers delivered their explosive cargo, paving the way for a sleek skyline. Today, Frankfurt is a global marketplace and the financial center of Europe, acquiring such nicknames as Mainhattan and Bankfurt. It is home to the European Central Bank (ECB), the €uro, and the world's third busiest stock exchange—die Börse (est. 1585). For many travelers Frankfurt will be their introduction to Germany, as the city's airport is the second busiest in Europe (behind Heathrow) and the continent's main hub. Thus the airport has an excellent rail system offering regular connections to regional and long-distance destinations.

Those who wish to tour Frankfurt, there are enough attractions in town to keep any resolute traveler busy for a day or two. For example, you can discover our do-it-yourself Anne Frank Reflective Walk, JFK's presence at St. Paul's Church, fine views at Galeria Kaufhof, or spy the mechanics of a multibillion dollar monetary institution at die Börse (for more on the aforesaid list see *FREE* Frankfurt—page 427).

Soccer fans will be interested to know that five matches of the 2006 World Cup will be played at Frankfurt's Waldstadion (Forest Stadium), 5km south of the city center. **June 10**, England vs. Paraguay • **June 13**, S. Korea vs. Togo • **June 17**, Iran vs. Portugal • **June 21**, Argentina vs. Netherlands • **July 1**, Quarter-Final.

AIRPORT: (*Flughafen*; code FRA; www.frankfurt-airport.com) Frankfurt's airport, located 15km southwest of the city center, is the 7th busiest in the world and No. 1 on the European continent, moving 51 million passengers per year—or 137,000 passengers per day. The airport is split into two terminals: #1 (Hall A, B, C) and #2 (Hall D, E). By far the biggest terminal is #1, where you'll find rail stations for regional and long-distance destinations, the majority of services and airline counters, as well as the Sheraton Hotel. On the upper floor of each terminal is the "Sky Line," a people mover continuously running between both terminals. Since many of you will be transiting through Frankfurt airport, useful services and suggestions are outlined below. And just so you know, *Abflug* means departure and *Ankunft* means arrival. *Note:* Luggage carts are free!

Post Office: Centrally located in both terminals, open daily 7:00-21:00.

Internet: T-Mobile Internet terminals are located throughout the airport; 10¢/minute. For cheaper options, head to the FAC communications lounge in terminal 1.

Sleeping: Those on a **budget** and looking to spend the night at the airport will find in terminal 1 the only seating possible for stretching out—seats without armrests can be found two and three together. Best places are had by 22:00. For **reasonably priced** digs see Hotel ibis, page 435. Those who are **not on a budget** can find the Sheraton Hotel (page 435) near the "Fernbahnhof" train station in terminal 1.

Luggage Storage: Baggage depositories are situated in both terminals, either location 3€/7hr or 3.50€/24hr. Terminal 1, arrivals hall B (level 1), open 24/7. *Tel.#* 069/6907-3277. Terminal 2, arrivals hall D (level 2), daily 6:00-22:00.

Showers: (6€) Available 24/7 in terminal 1, departure hall B.

Taxi: From the airport into the city, taxis roughly cost 25€.

Trains, inter-city: From the plane to the train, exit Frankfurt by following signs "Bahnhöfe" (train stations). Hop on a train headed to your city/country of destination (or vice versa, arrive directly into Frankfurt airport from anywhere in Europe). Both the regional (Regionalbahnhof) and long- distance (Fernbahnhof) train stations depart from terminal 1. Shuttle busses run regularly between the train stations and terminal 2. By train to Vienna roughly takes 7.5hr, Amsterdam 4hr, Munich 3.5hr, Cologne 1.5hr, Koblenz 1.5hr, Rothenburg 3hr—change in Würzburg and Steinach.

S-Bahn: Suburban rail into the city takes 15 minutes and costs 3.30€ one-way— before departure consider buying the Frankfurt Card 7.80€ (1 day) or 11.50€ (2 days). Suburban rail runs regularly from the Regionalbahnhof; jump on any train headed direction Frankfurt Hbf (Hauptbahnhof).

Frankfurt Card: see page 426. *Opinion*: The card is worth it for the active tourist, especially with airport connection.

Hotel Reservations: In terminal 1—arrival hall B—you'll find the "Hotelreservierung" counter, where you can buy the Frankfurt Card or have a room booked (commission applicable). Open daily 7:00-22:00.

Meeting Points: (suggested ideas) *Terminal 1)* Meet at the seating area in front of the P.O. *Terminal 2)* Meet at the McDonald's Food Plaza (upper floor), a great place to hang out while observing aircraft.

Killing Time: (suggested ideas) *1)* Head to the McDonald's Food Plaza on the upper floor of terminal 2, where you can grab something to eat/drink and observe powerful views of aircraft coming and going. *2)* If you have at least three hours to spare, consider heading into the city. Allow 30 minutes travel time each way by rail.

Tax, Value Added: [VAT] Reclaiming German VAT can be done via the "Global Refund" counter. Upon checking in, notify service personnel of your "duty free" items and they'll inform you of what to do and where to go. *Suggestion:* To eliminate any hassles at the Global Refund counter, make sure that the following info is clearly written on your receipts: description of goods, monetary amount, your address and passport number. *Note:* U.S. duty-free personal exemption is now $800. For latest info, go to www.customs.gov For more info on Global Refund, go to www.globalrefund.com

History, Airport: In the early part of the 20th century the area that is now the Frankfurt airport was used as a landing zone for the enormously large hydrogen- and helium-gas dirigibles (or airships), such as the Graf Zeppelin. In 1936 the landing zone became a commercial airport, catering to airplane traffic. By mid-1940 Germany was involved in a world war and the airport was acquired by the Luftwaffe (or air force) for military purposes. After WWII the airfield was appropriated by the U.S. air force and became known as Rhein-Main Air Base, "The Gateway to Europe." The air base played a principal role in Operation Vittles (June 1948—May '49) when the Soviets blockaded East Germany from the western Allies, essentially cutting off Berlin. The Allies responded by organizing a massive system of air transport to supply the western sectors of Berlin, which famously became known as the Berlin Airlift. Planes took off every few minutes, delivering nearly 2.5 million tons of relief supplies to the cut-off sectors throughout the 11-month effort. In 1959, the U.S. air force opened part of the air base for the German government to once again operate as a commercial airport. Since the end of the Cold War, Rhein-Main Air Base has been downsizing and in December 2005 it was officially passed back to Germany. Fraport, the company that manages the airport, plans to build a third terminal here, which includes docking areas for the new double-decker super Airbus A380.

Frankfurt-Hahn: (www.hahn-airport.de) Don't get this airfield confused with Frankfurt airport. Frankfurt-Hahn airport—chiefly used as a low-cost-carrier hub for flights within Europe—is actually closer to Trier and the country of Luxembourg than it is to downtown Frankfurt nearly two hours away. Hahn, by the way, means rooster in German and is a village of a few hundred residents. Buses leave for Hahn airport on the south side of Frankfurt's main train station and cost 12€/person one-way; total trip time 1.45 hr.

Tourist Information: [TI] (www.frankfurt-tourismus.de) *Tel.#* 069/2123-8800. Frankfurt has two TIs: *Hauptbahnhof* (Hbf) and *Römer* (town hall). City maps 50¢ (or free at your digs) — hotel bookings available for a 3€ fee (or free through TI website). Bus tours of city depart daily from either TI.

TI: Hauptbahnhof (Hbf), located at the main entrance (right side before exiting station). Hours: Mon-Fri 8:00-21:00, Sat/Sun 9:00-18:00.

TI: Römer (when looking at the prominent step-gabled flag-waving town-hall building, TI is to the right on the corner). Hours: Mon-Fri 9:30-17:00, Sat/Sun 10:00-16:00.

Note: Info/service counters are also located at the airport. The counter near the post office in terminal 1 is usually always open.

Emergency Tel. Numbers: [Germany-wide]
Police (Polizei) = 110
Fire dept. (Feuerwehr) or general emergency = 112
Ambulance = 19222

Hauptbahnhof: [Hbf] Frankfurt's "main train station," Germany's busiest, is located 20 min by foot from the Old Town—mosey along Kaiserstr. to reach the Römerberg (market square). If you've had enough of walking, hop on either the U4 or U5 and take it two stops to Römer. Within Frankfurt's Hauptbahnhof you'll find the *post office* (Mon-Fri 7:00-19:30, Sat 8:00-16:00) next door to McDonald's, opposite tracks 22-23. *Storage lockers* are adjacent to track 24, 1.50€-3€/24hr (if full, other lockers are available by exits). *Food:* Opposite track 5 you'll find an arcade rich with appetizing selections, including a Burger King. Nearby, opposite track 2, you can kill time by driving model trains, 50¢ for about six revolutions ("Fahrten"). For *train info* or *itinerary printouts*, see "DB Service" desk opposite track 12. To find the *S-Bahn*, head towards "Tiefbahnhof" — *U-Bahn* is nearby. *Touring bus to Romantic Road:* For tickets and info, exit train station "Südausgang," go right and cross the street to their office. Eurailpass holders receive a hefty 60% discount. Tel.# 069/790-3300. (www.romantic-road-coach.de)

Subway/Bus/Tram: Frankfurt has four types of public transport: S-Bahn (Suburban rail; green "S"), U-Bahn (Underground rail; blue "U"), bus or tram. The following list of tickets cover all four transit-types within central Frankfurt. ***Kurzstrecke*** (short trip) 1.25€, valid up to a distance of 1.5km. *Einzelfahrt* (one-way, one-direction) 1.80€, with airport 3.30€. *Tageskarte* (Day Ticket) 4.80€, with airport 7.30€, valid till 02:00. *Gruppen-Tageskarte* (Group Day Ticket) 8€, with airport 13€, valid for up to 5 people till 02:00.

All ticket types can be bought at automats marked Fahrkarten, button for English. Those who require a one-way bus ticket can buy it directly from driver. _Note:_ Holders of a valid Frankfurt Card are already covered for all travel within the city network. Holders of a Eurail consecutive-day or dated Flexi/Select pass ride the S-Bahn for *FREE!*

Parking: For _street parking_ pay at nearby automat and leave ticket on dashboard of your car. Price: (commonly) 1€/30min, max 1hr, applicable (automats vary) Mon-Fri 8:00-18:00, Sat 8:00-14:00, otherwise free. _Parking garages_ are abundantly located throughout the city. An outdoor, secure parking lot is situated on the south side of the Hauptbahnhof (Mannheimer Str. and Karlsruher Str.), 2.50€/hr, 20€/24hr.

Boat Rides: From the heart of the Old Town hop aboard a boat (by History Museum at the Römerberg) and cruise the Main for a unique perspective of Frankfurt. See riverside kiosk for tickets and tour options. The 100-minute sightseeing cruise departs May to mid-Oct daily every hour from noon, July/Aug from 11:00. *Price:* 7.80€.

Share Ride: *(Mitfahrzentrale; a concept matching passengers with drivers, and vice-versa.)* Those who are not traveling with a railpass, "Mitfahrzentrale" is the cheapest and most social option of getting from one city to another. There is one Share Ride office in Frankfurt. *Tel.#* 069/236-127 or /19-440. _Hours:_ Mon-Fri 8:00-18:30, Sat 8:00-16:00, Sun 10:00-16:00. _Price:_ Approx. cost per passenger from Frankfurt to Munich 22€, Berlin 30€, Amsterdam 27€. _Getting There:_ Office is located at Stuttgarter Str. 13, six-minute walk from Hauptbahnhof. Exit station "Südausgang" and go right, then second left on Stuttgarter Str. and it's a few blocks ahead on the right.

Note: Those who have a working knowledge of German will want to first refer to this website (www.mitfahrgelegenheit.de) for an opportunity to contact the driver directly, i.e. cutting out the middleman for an even cheaper Share Ride.

Internet: There are numerous call shops around town offering inexpensive Internet and telephone services connecting the globe. Some of these shops can be found opposite the Hauptbahnhof on Kaiserstr. as well as on the streets of Sachsenhausen behind the Haus der Jugend (youth hostel).

Frankfurt Card: Valid for either one or two days, this city card entitles the user free use of public transportation (including to/fro airport), plus 50% discount on several museums and up to 25% on regularly scheduled tours. The Frankfurt Card is available from either TI in town or at the airport (Hotel Reservations desk, terminal 1—arrival hall B). *Price:* 1-day card 7.80€, 2-day card 11.50€. *Opinion*: Worth it for the active tourist, especially with airport connection.

Post Office: In the main train station you'll discover a P.O. next door to McDonald's—opposite tracks 22-23. Hours: Mon-Fri 7:00-19:30, Sat 8:00-16:00. Another branch is located on the main shopping street at Zeil 90 (inside the Karstadt dept. store). Hours: Mon-Fri 9:30-20:00, Sat 9:30-16:00.

American Express: Kaiserstr. 10 (zip: 60311), near Hauptwache. *Tel.#* 069/2193-8860 (fes.frankfurt.kaisserstrasse@aexp.com) Hours: Mon-Fri 9:30-18:00, Sat 10:00-13:00. *Note:* Folks using American Express products (e.g. traveler's checks, credit card) can use their offices Europe-wide to receive letters—small packages okay.

Consulates

USA: Gießener Str. 30, tel.# 069/75-350 (http://frankfurt.usconsulate.gov) Passport section, tel.# 069/7535-2100 or 7535-2280. Hours: Mon-Fri 7:30-11:30. The Frankfurt consulate is the fifth largest diplomatic mission in the world and the largest of all U.S. consular posts, which employs 750 staff (450 U.S., 300 local) and services roughly 250,000 U.S. citizens in four German states, including members of the Armed Forces.

Australia: Grüneburgweg 58-62 (www.dfat.gov.au/missions) *Tel.#* 069/905-580.

Canada: No office in Frankfurt, refer to chapters *Berlin* or *Munich.*

UK: Consular office closed; refer to chapters *Berlin* or *Munich.*

Church Service, "Gottesdienst"

Note: Hours may have changed—check with staff at your accommodations or at the TI for the latest info, as well as for other religious denominations.

St. Leonhard: (Roman Catholic) English service—Sat 17:00, Sun 10:00. This 13th-century church is one of the oldest and most important in Frankfurt, located at Alte Mainzer Gasse (one block west of the Römerberg, along Main River). *Church Hours:* Tue-Sat 10:00-12:00 & 15:00-18:00 (Wed till 20:00), Sun 9:00-13:00 & 15:00-18:00.

FREE Frankfurt

1) A handful of **museums** (page 432) have particular days earmarked for free admission. For example the Jewish museums, along with the Film Museum, Liebieghaus, and Historisches Museum are free on the last Saturday of each month. The Money Museum is always gratis.

2) Speaking of money and museums, head to Kaiserstr. 30 and step inside the most beautiful bank you'll ever see. It belongs to the **Commerzbank** and dates from 1905. Hours: Mon-Fri 9:00-15:30 (Tue/Thur till 18:00).

3) **St. Paul's Church** (page 428)—home of German democracy—is free and worth a buzz through to examine the pictorial exhibition outlining the building's tremendous history, including a visit by JFK.

4) Do you remember **Alzheimer**? He's buried at the Hauptfriedhof in the northern suburbs. *GPS:* N50° 08.021 - E8° 41.434

5) The **Cathedral** (page 428) is free and worth a visit, as well as **Galeria Kaufhof** (page 433) for invigorating city views.

6) Let's not forget Anne Frank; you can view (from outside) her birth house and second family residence on the **Anne Frank Reflective Walk** (page 430).

7) **Oskar Schindler**, portrayed in Spielberg's movie "Schindler's List" (1993), lived in Frankfurt from 1965 to 1974, the year of his death. There is a memorial plaque outside the apartment house where he lived; you can find it next door to the Irish pub across from the main train station.

8) **Das Hostel Frankfurt** (page 435) offers their guests a free orientation walk of the city as well as a free spaghetti dinner every Saturday.

9) **Die Börse**—the German stock exchange—offers a free presentation (in German) that is particularly interesting for industry professionals, brokers, or enthusiasts who understand Deutsch. The German-language presentation is offered thrice daily Mon-Fri: 10:00, 11:00 and 12:00. For security purposes you must bring your passport and reserve at least a day in advance by phone 069/2111-1515 or email: visitors.center@deutsche-boerse.com *Note:* When reserving, inquire if any English tours are scheduled. If none are going, ask to see the "visitor's gallery." This will bypass the German presentation so you can get straight onto the observation level to watch the (lethargic) trading floor (ruled by computerized trading networks) and where English brochures on Die Börse are available.

10) **Red-Light District:** For those who have heard about Frankfurt's erotic quarter, an honest description would be somewhat seedy, shifty and drug-infested. As long as you remain vigilant, it's a reasonably safe area to stroll through—just keep moving or you risk getting spanked! Since this erotic quarter is near the Hauptbahnhof, it might be an

interesting venue to kill time between trains. For an exotic escapade, wander into one of the multistory brothels called "Eros Center." Here women seductively stand in doorways waiting for the pleasure of your introduction; usually 30€ buys the john a quick ride on the train o' love. *Note:* Those who are visualizing Amsterdam's red-light district, stop—there's no comparison. *Getting There:* From the Hauptbahnhof venture along Taunusstr. two blocks to Elbestr.

SIGHTS

Römerberg: This is Frankfurt's historical center, where Charlemagne once constructed his fort. Römerberg was the scene of numerous Carolingian trade fairs and a bustling marketplace during medieval times. The square is still the pulsating core of Frankfurt and a great place to begin your explorations. The Römer—Frankfurt's town-hall complex—is located on the western side of the square. It is made up of 11 interconnected patrician houses, including the town hall, TI and Kaisersaal (see next entry). *Getting There:* U4 or U5 Römer.

Kaisersaal: Here in the "Emperor's Room" you'll find the former imperial banquet hall, featuring 52 portraits of German kings and emperors, beginning with Charlemagne (crowned 800 A.D.) and ending with Kaiser Franz II (abdicated 1806). *Hours:* daily, 10:00-13:00 & 14:00-17:00. *Getting There:* U4 or U5 Römer. Face the step-gabbled town hall (one with clock) and go left around corner on Limpurgergasse. Continue along this lane some 40 meters to the arched portal on the right. Once through you'll see a ticket machine on the wall. After purchasing your entry ticket (2€), ascend spiral stairway.

Cathedral, St. Bartholomew: Dominating the eastern end of Römerberg is the so-called "Kaiserdom." Construction on this magnificent cathedral began around 1235 to replace a dilapidated 9th-century Carolingian church on the same spot. From 1356 the cathedral served as the electoral site for German kings, and from 1562-1792 as the coronation site for emperors of the Holy Roman Empire—thus the hallowed structure acquired the name Kaiserdom, or Emperor's Cathedral. In 1867 a fire gutted the interior, and during the reconstruction phase the tower (dating from 1415) was extended to a height of 92m/301ft. Of the cathedral's many highlights are the Sleeping-Mary-Altar (1438; left of high altar behind iron gate), Bartholomew-frieze (circa 1410; flanking high altar), Dom Museum (2€/1€), and the 328 steps to the tower's observation level (closed for renovations perhaps until 2007). *Hours:* (cathedral) Mon-Thur 9:00-12:00 & 14:30-18:00, Fri 14:30-18:00, Sat 9:00-12:00 & 14:30-17:00, Sun 14:30-17:00. *Getting There:* U4 or U5 Römer.

Goethe-Haus: Situated on Große Hirschgraben—an inner-city lane—one discovers the birth house of Johann Wolfgang Goethe, Germany's literary legend and Frankfurt's most famous son. Out of Goethe's 82 years of life (1749-1832), he spent 26 of them in this four-story dwelling, where he wrote his most celebrated work, "Faust." On the third floor you'll find the Geburtszimmer, Goethe's birth room. (www.goethehaus-frankfurt.de) *Hours:* daily, 10:00-17:30. *Price:* adult 5€, student 2.50€, audio guide 2€. Free admission with Museumsufer Ticket. *Getting There:* U4 or U5 Römer. When facing the step-gabbled town hall, walk right past St. Paul's Church and cross Berliner Str. into Sandgasse, then left on Weißadlergasse to Große Hirschgraben on the left (Goethe-Haus will appear on the right).

St. Paul's Church: (Paulskirche) For German history buffs and JFK admirers, this is a must. The interior of this church no longer exists, in its place is a spacious foyer flanked by a pictorial exhibition outlining the building's history. On the upper level (closed to the public) is an assembly hall frequented by the mayor, and on occasion by the federal chancellor.

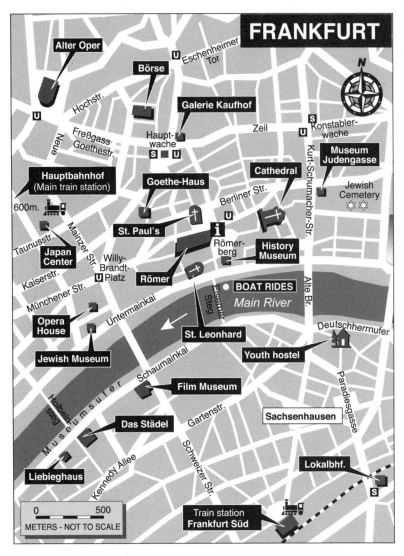

St. Paul's Church stands today as a symbol of, and memorial to, German democracy. It was here, not the Reichstag in Berlin, that on May 18, 1848, Germany's first freely elected parliament (National Assembly) held session. Within 10 months the National Assembly passed the first democratic constitution, together with the Fundamental Rights of the German Nation, a document that significantly influenced the structure of the Weimar Republic in 1919 and the Federal Republic of Germany in 1949. Alas, the constitution led to a revolt and the National Assembly was abolished, convening for the last time (a year later) at St. Paul's on May 30, 1849. Three years thereafter the church was again used as a place of worship.

During WWII, an air of hopelessness fell upon the church and the final service was held on March 12, 1944; shortly thereafter the holy structure was smashed by a storm of bombs. Immediately following the war, donations were gathered to restore the structure in a simplified, contemporary form. St. Paul's Church was reconsecrated and declared a national memorial on May 18, 1948—the 100th anniversary of the National Assembly's first meeting. It was also here, at this symbol of democracy, that John F. Kennedy spoke to Germany and the world on June 25, 1963—on the church's outside wall is a plaque commemorating his visit. The wildly entrancing mural decorating the foyer is titled the "Procession of the People's Representatives to St. Paul's Church" (1991). *Hours:* daily, 10:00-17:00. *Price: FREE* entry! *Getting There:* U4 or U5 Römer. When facing the TI, go right and cross the street.

Anne Frank: For those who are not familiar with Anne Frank, she is essentially the face of the Holocaust—an unimaginable business designed by the Nazis to exterminate the Jews from Europe.

(Before continuing, read the condensed version of Anne Frank's life story in the chapter Tomb-Lovers, Who's Buried Where? Germany—page 456.)

Now that we know Anne Frank was born right here in Frankfurt, we will soon see that the two former Frank family dwellings *(Ganghoferstrasse and Marbachweg)* reveal very little to complement the universal legacy which evolved.

Anne Frank Reflective Walk

Do-it-yourself: Railers, allow two hours, inclusive of subway time. The total distance by foot is roughly 2km—wear comfortable shoes. *Drivers,* you can complete the tour in around 40 minutes (includes drive from city).

Note: The two former Frank family dwellings (at Ganghoferstrasse and Marbachweg) are privately owned and can only be viewed from the outside.

Midway along Marbachweg—a busy street in middle-class suburbia (4 km north of downtown Frankfurt)—stands a cream-colored apartment house identified by the number 307 headlining the left fence pillar. Oddly, there are no distinguishing features—such as a remembrance plaque or memorial—to indicate that this is the birthplace of Anne Frank.

Shortly after Anne was born, the Frank's moved to **Ganghoferstrasse** 24, an upper middle-class house a mile northwest of Marbachweg. They only resided here a few years before fleeing Germany in 1933. Nothing remains inside the house from the days of the Frank family—the plaque on the front facade is the only reminder of Anne's place in history.

~ *OK, are you ready? Our first stop is Ganghoferstrasse 24*

Railers: Take either the U1, U2 or U3 to "Hügelstraße" (7th stop from Hauptwache). Once you arrive at Hügelstraße exit right and after a short distance go right crossing the tracks and street. From there, go left and walk back toward the city 100 meters (this is Eschersheimer Landstr.) and turn right into Ganghoferstr.—walk another 120 meters to No. 24 on right.

GPS: N50° 08.718 - E8° 39.910

Drivers: From the city head north on Eschersheimer Landstr. After passing the Am Dornbusch/Marbachweg intersection, Ganghoferstr. is about the sixth left.

Ganghoferstrasse 24: *(private property, please keep out!)* As mentioned above, nothing remains inside the house from the days of the Frank family—the only reminder here of Anne's place in history is the plaque on the front facade. It reads: *"'In this house lived Anne Frank, born June 12, 1929, Frankfurt am Main. She died as a victim of National Socialistic persecution in 1945 at the concentration camp Bergen-Belsen. Her life and death are our devotion.' (signed) The children of Frankfurt."*

~ *Our second stop is the Anne Frank middle school*

Railers: Head back to Eschersheimer Landstr. and go right—at the forward traffic lights cross the street. On the other side go right; at the next set of lights go left on Fritz-Tarnow-Str.—200 meters ahead on the left (at No. 29) is the Anne Frank middle school.

GPS: N50° 08.573 - E8° 40.371

Drivers: This next set of directions is somewhat tricky because of one-way streets. Bear with us and we'll get you through. Head back to Eschersheimer Landstr. and go right. Continue straight through the first set of traffic lights and turn left at the second set; go straight into Fritz-Tarnow-Str. Some 200 meters ahead is the school but midway along it turns into a one-way street, so turn right on Carl-Goerdeler-Str. and we'll make a loop around the block before reaching the school. At the end of Carl-Goerdeler-Str. follow the one-way sign left. At the end of this street is Mierendorffstr., go left *(if you want to skip the school and head to Anne's birth house, go right to the lights and pick up the directions in the next Drivers entry).* At the end of Mierendorffstr. go left (this is Fritz-Tarnow-Str.) and the school will be on the right. If you're interested in getting a closer look at the school, park the car and wander back by foot for a snoop around.

Anne Frank Middle School: Named in honor of the high-spirited teenager who penned a global best seller—this educational facility stands as one of the only reminders Anne Frank hailed from the area. It's logical to assume that she attended school here, since the facility is located handily between the two former Frank residences. Anne, in fact, never attended school in Frankfurt, or anywhere in Germany. Young Anne was escorted out of the country to Amsterdam at 4 years old and educated in the Netherlands—thus, her internationally famous diary was written in Dutch.

~ Our third and last stop is Anne Frank's birth house, Marbachweg 307

Railers: After your explorations, take Mierendorffstr. to the forward traffic lights (this is Marbachweg). From there, cross the street and go left two blocks (to Ebersheimstr.) to find Anne Frank's birth house at No. 307 on the corner.

GPS: N50° 08.418 - E8° 40.592

Drivers: To exit the neighborhood follow the same one-way route (via Carl-Goerdeler-Str.) to Mierendorffstr., where you'll turn right to the traffic lights. Continue straight through the intersection; ahead make the first left on Ammelburgstr. and the second left on Ebersheimstr. At the end of this street is Marbachweg 307 (on right): Anne Frank's birth house.

Birth House, Anne Frank: Amazingly, there is nothing to commemorate the fact. Thousands pass by daily without the slightest clue. However, you now have a better perspective about the creative 15-year-old girl who captured the hearts of millions of people the world over.

~ Wondering where to go next? Here are three suggestions:

1) The *Geldmuseum* (page 432) is located 1km away. Go west along Marbachweg. *(In other words, Railers head back in the direction you came, Drivers turn left out of Ebersheimstr.)* Marbachweg will turn into Am Dornbusch, then Wilhelm-Epstein-Str.—museum will appear on the left.

2) Do you remember *Alzheimer?* (page 455) The doctor is located 1.5km away. To find him, go east along Marbachweg — *(Railers continue in the direction you were walking; Drivers turn right out of Ebersheimstr.)* — to the main intersection at Eckenheimer Landstr. and turn right; the Hauptfriedhof (cemetery) will appear 1km farther on the left. *GPS:* N50° 08.021 - E8° 41.434

3) *Railers,* to return to the city continue on Marbachweg in the direction you were walking. At the main intersection ahead is the U5 on the right. This U-Bahn line connects with the Hauptbahnhof and "Römer" (see *Römerberg,* page 428).

MUSEUMS

Several of Frankfurt's museums are clustered on the south bank of the Main River, locally known as the Museumsufer. Many museums are **closed Mondays** and some offer *FREE* entry days. For a more comprehensive look, go to www.kultur.frankfurt.de or ask TI for the museums booklet.

Culture vultures should purchase the 2-day **Museumsufer Ticket** (adult 12€, student 6€, family 20€; couples purchase the latter to increase savings). This 48-hour ticket is valid for all of the city's noteworthy museums (including the Goethe-Haus), available at museum or TI. *Note:* Ticket is valid for permanent collections only, not for special exhibitions.

Das Städel: Here you'll spend several hours discovering an important and wide-ranging collection of European art containing more than 600 masterpieces from the 15th century to the present, including works from Dürer, Rembrandt, Monet, Renoir, van Gogh and Picasso. *Hours:* Tue-Sun 10:00-19:00 (Wed/Thur till 21:00). *Price:* adult 8€, student 6€. *Getting There:* Das Städel is located at Schaumainkai 63, Museumsufer. *GPS:* N50° 06.201 - E8° 40.373

Liebieghaus: This exclusive sculpture museum exhibits works from ancient Egypt, Greece and Rome through to the Middle Ages to neoclassicism. Collection highlights include Egyptian wood sarcophagi from the 13th-century B.C., a rose-granite statue of Alexander the Great from 400 B.C., and a marble bust of Emperor Augustus from the year 27 A.D. *Hours:* Tue-Sun 10:00-17:00 (Wed till 20:00). *Price:* adult 4€, student 2.50€. *FREE* entry on last Saturday of month, and always free with Museumsufer Ticket. *Getting There:* Liebieghaus is located at Schaumainkai 71, Museumsufer.

Film Museum: Trace the evolution of film from its roots in the 19th century to the early 1970s. Within the museum are models illustrating how original special effects were shot, mechanisms giving the illusion of moving pictures, director's props, and walk into die camera obscura to see Frankfurt's skyline upside down. Foreign movies are shown in their cinema, adult 5.50€, student 4.50€; for the latest schedule ask cashier for the "Kino-programm." *Note:* Museum is in German, ask cashier for free English brochure outlining the permanent collection. *Hours:* Tue-Fri 10:00-17:00 (Wed till 19:00), Sat 14:00-19:00, Sun 10:00-19:00. *Price:* adult 2.50€, student 1.30€. *FREE* entry on last Saturday of month, and always free with the Museumsufer Ticket. *Getting There:* Film Museum is located at Schaumainkai 41, Museumsufer.

Historisches Museum: Standing tall outside the "History Museum" is a statue of the great Charlemagne. Inside the building, exhibitions highlight Frankfurt's history on three floors—an English translation sheet is available upon request (upstairs). Cross the courtyard to see models of the town's evolution (view 15-min documentary, 1€); paralyzing is the rubble model, a look at the Altstadt (Old Town) after WWII—behind it is the oldest room in Frankfurt, part of the emperor's palace dating from the 12th century. *Hours:* Tue-Sun 10:00-17:00 (Wed till 20:00). *Price:* adult 4€, student 2€. *FREE* entry on last Saturday of month, and always free with Museumsufer Ticket. *Getting There:* History Museum is located in the southwestern corner of the Römerberg, near river. *Note:* For the sweet taste of Frankfurt, step into the pastry shop (Konditorei) Hollhorst located meters away in a charming half-timbered building. On the back wall you'll see a picture of JFK when he was in town.

Geldmuseum: (Money Museum) With an interactive touch, this neat exposition helps to explain Europe's new currency, the €uro, including the mastery of counterfeiting. Before leaving, check out the "bricks" of shredded cash for sale in the gift shop. *Hours:* Sun thru Fri 10:00-17:00 (Wed till 21:00), closed Sat. *Price: FREE* entry! *Getting There:* Geld

Museum is located at the Deutschen Bundesbank (German Federal Bank) in Frankfurt's northern suburbs. Take either the U1, U2 or U3 to "Dornbusch" (5th stop from Haupt-wache). From there take Am Dornbusch west toward the space needle and cross into Wilhelm-Epstein-Str, where the museum will appear on the left.

Jewish & Judengasse Museums: These two museums are situated on either ends of the Old Town, each offering something different.

The *Jewish Museum* represents Jewish culture and history in Frankfurt, located at Untermainkai 14 (north bank of the Main, opposite Museumsufer).

Museum Judengasse exhibits well-preserved relics that are former dwellings from Frankfurt's Jewish ghetto, "Judengasse," located at Kurt-Schumacher-Str. 10.

Hours: (both museums) Tue-Sun 10:00-17:00 (Wed till 20:00). *Price:* (JM) adult 2.60€, student 1.30€; (MJ) adult 1.50€, student 70¢; combo-ticket (both museums) 3€/1.50€. *FREE* admission into either museum on last Saturday of month, and always free with the Museumsufer Ticket.

Goethe-Haus: see page 428.

Best Views

In German the word for skyscraper is *Hochhaus*, literally "high house," and there's no city in Europe with a skyline of *Hochhäuser* like Frankfurt.

Main Tower: (locally known as "Helaba," short for Hessische Landesbank) Whiz up to the 54th floor in 45 ear-popping seconds for the best view in town (open air). At 200 meters high, the Main Tower is the fourth tallest office building in Frankfurt (one with candy-cane spire). For highfliers craving a bite to eat or a beverage, the 53rd floor is an exclusive restaurant/bar. *Hours:* (viewing platform) daily, 10:00-19:00 (longer in summer). *Price:* adult 4.50€, student 3€. *Hours:* (restaurant) Tue-Sat 17:30 till late — tel.# (res.) 069/3650-4777. *Getting There:* Main Tower is located at Neue Mainzer Str. 52.

Galeria Kaufhof: On the top (7th) floor of this department store is a self-service cafeteria with good food and a great view! Even if you're not starving or cringing for caffeine, get your saddle up there to enjoy urban vistas from the outdoor terrace. *FREE* entry! *Hours:* Mon-Sat 9:30-20:00. *Getting There:* Galeria Kaufhof is located on the corner of Hauptwache and Zeil (pedestrian shopping street). U-/S-Bahn Hauptwache.

Japan Center: For a budget version of the Main Tower, head to the top of this 25-story financial district office building. Its observation level is actually a self-service restaurant open to the public—lunch only, Mon-Fri 11:30-14:30. The prices are a bit stiff and the food is average, so if you want to stay awhile to absorb the dizzying views, consider kicking back with just a beverage. Japan Center is located at Taunustor 2, which abuts Taunusanlage.

~ *Frankfurt's five tallest buildings are…*

1) *Europaturm:* EuropaTower (space needle in northern suburbs) is 331m/1085ft. Not open to tourists.

2) *Commerzbank:* Europe's tallest office building—258m/846ft, built '94-97

3) *Messeturm:* (Convention Tower) 256m/840ft, built 1989-91.

4) *Bürohaus Westendstraße:* 208m/682ft, built 1990-93.

5) *Main Tower:* (Helaba) 200m/656ft, built 1996-1999 (see *Best Views* above).

SHOPPING

Zeil: Stretching some 600 meters between Konstablerwache and Hauptwache is Frankfurt's main shopping drag, Zeil. Flanked by shops and split by lush maple trees, Zeil is to shoppers what a ballpark is to sports fans.

Goethestrasse & Freßgass: In the heart of the banking district, moneyed shoppers can count on Goethestrasse for big-name fashion, namely Gucci, Tiffany & Co., Armani, Versace, Hermés and Chanel. Even if your money belt isn't stuffed with euros, get down there for a look. Don't miss nearby Gr. Bockenheimer Str. (pedestrianized), locally known as "Freßgass", or Pig-Out lane because of its lively trade of deli's, bistros and sidewalk cafés.

Euro Info Center & Bookshop: If you want lots of money, you can get it here. When the long-established German *d-mark* became a thing of the past, replaced by the fancy euro, it was relegated to the trash heap and shredded. Today you can literally buy blocks of the former currency, 100,000 dm for just 9€. Not a bad deal since the changeover rate was 2 to 1. Besides shredded banknotes, coin and currency enthusiasts will find a cache of euro collectibles. *Hours:* Mon-Fri 9:00-18:30, Sat 10:00-14:00. *Getting There:* located at Kaiserstr. 29, within the European Central Bank building. *Tel.#* 069/2440-4798. *Note:* While there, go across the street to Kaiserstr. 30 and step into the most beautiful bank you'll ever see. It is a branch of the Commerzbank, dating from 1905. Hours: Mon-Fri 9:00-15:30 (Tue/Thur till 18:00).

Flea Market: Every Saturday (8:00-14:00) year round you can find a flea market along Museumsufer, between the pedestrian bridges Eiserner Steg and Holbeinsteg.

Trade Fairs

The German word for convention (or fair) is "Messe," and Frankfurt has umpteen throughout the year. For more info, go to www.messefrankfurt.com The two most notable are the Buchmesse (Book Fair) and Motor Show (IAA). *Getting There:* The Messe (or convention) center is a 10-min walk northwest of the Hauptbahnhof — U-/S-Bahn Messe.

Buchmesse: (early Oct) This is the world's largest gathering of publishing professionals and authors—nearly 300,000 people visited the five-day event in 2005. (www.frankfurt-bookfair.com)

Motor Show: (mid-Sept, bi-annually—rotates with Hannover) The IAA (Internationale Automobil Ausstellung) is the largest International Motor Show on Earth and takes place in Frankfurt every two years. (www.iaa.de)

Entertainment

Especially entertaining is the most popular drink in town: apple wine, locally known as *Ebbelwei*. It's similar to cider but with a putrid taste. A Frankfurter told us over dinner that Ebbelwei tastes better by the third glass. With this philosophy in mind, and a loss of count, we were seeing purple elephants before Cinderella's buggy turned into a pumpkin. To find out for yourself there are numerous watering holes on the Main's south bank in the suburb of Sachsenhausen. Look to the pedestrian lanes—Große and Kleine Rittergasse—located behind the Haus der Jugend (youth hostel).

Headline Concerts, Frankfurt 2006

Note: Prices, dates, concerts may have changed or been added — query TI or ticket agency for latest details.

Santana: May 18, 20:00 at the Festhalle. Price 62-73€
  Eros Ramazzotti: May 21, 20:00 at the Festhalle. Price 52-65€
Eric Clapton: June 3, 20:00 at the Festhalle. Price 70€
  50 Cent: June 4, 20:00 at the Festhalle. Price 51-62€
Billy Joel: July 2, 20:00 at the Festhalle. Price 74-102€
  Rolling Stones: July 14, 19:00 at Commerzbank Arena. Price 87-207€

GOOD SLEEPS

Note: Room prices increase upwards of 50% during major conventions, which seem to happen a lot. And you can expect to see inflated prices or the "no vacancy" signs out during the World Cup soccer tournament, chiefly June 8 thru July 3 in Frankfurt. Fans in desperate need of a room log on here: www.host-a-fan.de

Airport: Ultra-budget sleeps in terminal 1. Those on a **budget** and looking to spend the night at the airport will find in terminal 1 the only seating possible for stretching out—seats without armrests can be found two and three together. Best places are had by 22:00.

Airport: Middle price range digs with free shuttle bus to/fro airport; see *Hotel ibis* below.

Airport Sheraton: From your bed straight onto the plane (or vice-versa), these exclusive soundproof digs are located within the airport, terminal 1 (near "Fernbahnhof" train station). *Price:* Sgl/Dbl from 220€ — Internet and weekend rates are typically cheapest, inclusive of breakfast. *Tel.#* 069/69-770, toll-free reservations from USA/Canada 1-888-625-5144 or within Europe 00800-3253-5353. (www.sheraton.com/frankfurt)

Hostel, Das Hostel Frankfurt: Kaiserstr. 74 (www.room-frankfurt.de) *Tel.#* 069/247-5130. You can't beat this hostel's low prices, stupendous location (across from main train station) and great deals for guests, e.g. free spaghetti dinner on Saturdays; free city walking tour; daily "happy hour" at their bar, 20:00-21:00. On premises is an Easy Internet café, generally 1.30€/hour. *Price:* (includes linen) dorm bed 18€, Sgl 40€ (←both have facilities in room→) Dbl 50€. Check-in from 15:00. Check out 11:00. *Note:* Prices increase upwards of 50% during conventions. *CC's:* VC, MC. *Getting There:* Exit main train station (Hauptbahnhof) straight into Kaiserstrasse; continue some 20 meters farther to their door on the left. Reception is on 3rd floor; take elevator.

Hostel, Haus der Jugend: [HI] Deutschherrnufer 12 (www.jugendherberge-frankfurt.de) *Tel.#* 069/610-0150. Handy location! Haus der Jugend has the Main River on its doorstep, the nightlife of Sachsenhausen at its rear, and the museum district a short walk downriver. *Price:* (includes linen, breakfast) 8/10-bed dorm 16€, 4-bed dorm 20€ (with shower 25€), Sgl 35€ (←both have facilities in room→) Dbl 60€. *CC's:* VC, MC. *Note:* Must be a member and under 26 years of age or an extra charge (4€) will apply. Check-in from 13:00. Check out 9:30! *Getting There: Railers,* from the main train station take bus 46 (out front and to the right) to Frankensteiner Platz (12-min ride) and walk back 40 meters. Bus leaves roughly every 25 min until typically 22:30.

Hotel ibis: (www.ibishotel.com) Clean, reasonably priced and well located, the ibis chain has two Frankfurt hotels worth mentioning. *Note:* Parking, breakfast cost extra. *Hotel code is compatible with ibis website, creating a shortcut to the property—type hotel code into middle left box and click "OK"; next page click on "The Hotel" (left side).

ibis Friedensbrücke: Speicherstr. 4, tel.# 069/273-030; *hotel code 1445. Within a 10-min walk from the main train station, this ibis property is pleasingly set on a quiet city street opposite the river. *Price:* Sgl/Dbl 59-72€, during conventions 149-169€. *Getting There:* Exit main train station right into Baseler Str. and before bridge turn right into Speicherstr.

ibis Airport: *Tel.#* 06107/9870; *hotel code 2203. Favorably situated five minutes from the airport. Free shuttle bus available (to/fro) 6:00-23:00; at airport go to *Pendelverkehr* (commuter traffic) area. *Price:* Sgl/Dbl 59-72€, during conventions 129-149€.

Hilton: Hochstr. 4 (www.frankfurt.hilton.com) *Tel.#* 069/133-80, toll-free reservations from USA/Canada 1-800-445-8667 or within Europe 00800-4445-8667. This contemporary, 12-story hotel is centrally located near the opera, main shopping street (Zeil), stock market, and a pleasant park. *Price:* Sgl/Dbl from 179€. Parking, breakfast extra. *Note:* Internet and weekend rates are typically cheapest, inclusive of breakfast.

TRAVELER'S TIPS

Within this chapter are several topics and sections. The opening section begins with **General Tips** for both Railers and Drivers. Following General Tips are individual sections listing tips for **Railers** and **Drivers**; we also have an **Itinerary**, the **Euro**, **Measurements & Temperatures**, **Epochs and Art Styles**: a feel for time, and the modest **Glossary**.

General Tips

How To Use This Book: The first part of this book is the adventure novel, *"Quest for the Bavarian Cross,"* which will (hopefully) motivate you off the couch and onto the road. That's where the second part of the book—the travel guide—comes in. A typical city chapter in the travel guide consists of a historical introduction • an orientation (including tourist info, local transportation, bike rental, post office, Internet, etc.) • what's *FREE* to do • sights • museums • entertainment • good sleeps • excursions. Bigger cities such as Munich, Berlin and Vienna will have added segments listing annual holidays, what to do on a Sunday or holiday, church services, and headline (rock/pop) concerts.

For the most part, restaurants and bars/clubs are absent from the travel guide chapters. The reason for this is because we found that management and/or cooks often change, making it difficult for us to nail down a solid recommendation. The people who know this topic best—the hippest club and tastiest grub in town—is the TI or staff at your accommodations. We have, instead, elected to spend our time researching the best deals and pertinent info to enhance your European adventure. You will, however, notice that in a few cities (e.g. Munich and Salzburg) there are some Good Eats recommended that we know are a sure thing to satisfy your palette.

Concerning accommodations, they are listed in the Good Sleeps section either in order of price—from cheap to steep—or (especially in the smaller towns) by preference. Many times you'll notice a price range for a room, like so: Dbl 55-95€. In most cases the reason for this is because the price fluctuates according to season and/or the cheaper price means the facilities (shower/toilet) are in the hallway (in which case this is noted adjacent to the price).

You will notice in this guidebook that the acronym *TI* is always used for "tourist information" and the word *facilities* (referring to shower/toilet) may be used when discussing a hotel room, as in the facilities are in the hallway. And most importantly, travelers with wheels are labeled as *Drivers* and those using the rails are identified as *Railers*. Lastly, all times are written using the 24-hour clock (see chart below).

Europeans write & speak the 24-hour system. Here is a refresher course.			
1:00 = 1 a.m.	7:00 = 7 a.m.	13:00 = 1 p.m.	19:00 = 7 p.m.
2:00 = 2 a.m.	8:00 = 8 a.m.	14:00 = 2 p.m.	20:00 = 8 p.m.
3:00 = 3 a.m.	9:00 = 9 a.m.	15:00 = 3 p.m.	21:00 = 9 p.m.
4:00 = 4 a.m.	10:00 = 10 a.m.	16:00 = 4 p.m.	22:00 = 10 p.m.
5:00 = 5 a.m.	11:00 = 11 a.m.	17:00 = 5 p.m.	23:00 = 11 p.m.
6:00 = 6 a.m.	12:00 = 12 p.m.	18:00 = 6 p.m.	24:00 = midnight

Date, Europe: Europeans write the date contrary to Americans, like so: day/month/year — for example, 9.7.06 = 9 July 2006, which happens to be the date of the final match of the FIFA World Cup soccer tournament to be played at Berlin's 74,000-seat Olympic Stadium (page 376). For more info on the tournament, flip to page 152.

Daylight Savings: Don't forget to change the clock one hour if you are in Europe on the last Sunday in March (spring forward) or on the last Sunday in October (fall back).

Passport/Visa: Citizens of North America, Australia and New Zealand only require a valid *passport to enter Germany and Austria. Without a specific work- or study-related visa/permit, your stay will be limited to 90 days every six months. **Note:* Your passport must be valid for at least three months beyond your intended stay.

Adaptors and Voltage Converters: Like the rest of Europe, voltage in Germany and Austria is 220/240, enough to fry any 110V North American appliance. Thus Americans and Canadians will require a **converter** ($20, to convert the voltage) and an **adapter** (set $10, or typically $3 for the piece specific to Europe, so you can plug it into the socket). Some appliances are dual-voltage, like laptop computers which only require the adapter, but double-check instructions to prevent what could be an expensive blowout. *Note:* If you're only looking to plug in, let's say, a hairdryer, then consider buying a local product at a discount store (which may only cost 10€). Australians and Kiwis already subscribe to the 220V system and will only require an adaptor.

Packing List: For a suggested packing list, go to our website at www.your-traveling-companion.com *Note:* Anything you absolutely must have upon landing (e.g. prescription drugs, toiletries, extra pair of undies/socks) pack into your carry-on bag.

Bathrooms: In most cases it costs to use the toilet in Europe. Always keep small change on hand for those necessary breaks (especially the ladies)—typically 20¢ for the attendant's dish, or 50¢ for coin-operated stalls.

International Dialing: To call another country you must first dial the international access code (IAC). If you're inside Europe, the IAC is 00 — from inside USA/Canada, the IAC is 011. Next, punch in the country code (see next entry).

For our example, let's say we are trying to call this tel. number in Salzburg, Austria: 0662/123456. (*Note:* 0662 is the city code; drop the 0 when dialing from outside of Austria. All area codes in this book are separated from the local number by a back slash [/].) From the USA/Canada you would dial the number like so: 011-43-662/123456.

From inside Europe, 0043-662/123456
From inside Austria, 0662/123456
While in Salzburg, 123456

Country Codes: Australia 61 • Austria 43 • Belgium 32 • Canada 1 • Croatia 385 • Czech Republic 420 • Denmark 45 • Estonia 372 • Finland 358 • France 33 • Germany 49 • Greece 30 • Hungary 36 • Iceland 354 • Ireland 353 • Italy 39 • Latvia 371 • Liechtenstein 423 • Lithuania 370 • Netherlands 31 • Norway 47 • Poland 48 • Portugal 351 • Slovakia 421 • Slovenia 386 • Spain 34 • Sweden 46 • Switzerland 41 • UK 44 • USA 1

The following emergency numbers are individually referred to as a "Notruf" (pronounced note roof, meaning emergency call) and can be dialed within their respective countries (from a payphone or wherever) free of charge.

Nationwide Emergency Tel. Numbers within GERMANY:
Police (Polizei) = 110
Fire dept. (Feuerwehr) or general emergency = 112
Ambulance = 19222

Nationwide Emergency Tel. Numbers within AUSTRIA:
Fire dept. (Feuerwehr) = 122
Police (Polizei) = 133
Ambulance/Rescue = 144

Telephones: Public telephones in Germany and Austria use either coins or calling cards, but mainly the latter. Calling cards are handy to have (to make reservations or confirm the ones you have) and can be purchased for typically 5€-10€ from newspaper and tobacco stands/shops. The price of a call, depending on the time of day and how long you're on the phone, begins with a nominal fee and then incrementally compounds as you talk. Outside of business hours, the price is cheaper. *Note:* Telephone books are a quick source for a local area/city map.

Cell Phones: If you're planning on staying awhile in Germany or Austria, buy a cell phone locally (called a "Handy")—they're inexpensive, you'll always be contactable, and your family will have piece of mind.

Ask at the TI for the best retailer to purchase a "Handy" that uses a pre-paid card. *(In Germany, Vodafone shops have easy-to-choose-from selections—look for their "CallYa" Handy.)* A pre-paid card phone means no contract, no strings. They're cheap (from 50€) and come with a starter card worth 10€—while you're in the shop buy a second card, 15€-25€. **It costs nothing to receive a call in the phone's home country.** If you're roaming outside the country you bought the phone in, then it'll cost big time to receive a call! *Note:* Buy the phone in whichever country you plan on spending most of your time. To use your "Handy" to frequently make calls will empty its pre-paid card in no time. The phones are perfect for emergencies, receiving calls, or to send a text message ("SMS"). Most important is that you have a number your family can reach you on while overseas. As your European journey comes to an end, you can either sell your phone to a fellow traveler, hold on to it for your next visit, or keep it as a memento.

Credit Cards: Ideally you want to bring a second credit card on your trip in case your primary card gets lost, stolen, demagnetized, or for some reason the transaction won't go through. Plastic is a convenient way to carry purchase power while providing an itemized record of your expenses. Use your credit card to charge accommodations, tours, train tickets, general services, etc. *(Note: Depending on the card company, you will pay 3% on foreign transactions vs. 1% with a debit card.)* If you charge a rental car or your plane ticket to the card, you may be rewarded with significant insurance coverage (check your paperwork or call the issuer for details). Avoid using your credit card for a cash advance, which will burden you with a sky-high APR, accrued immediately (hence you brought your debit card, see next entry). Also, avoid using your credit card in fast-paced service environments, such as a beer hall in Bavaria, which will only incur a nasty frown from the wait staff. Use a credit card with a low, fixed APR or one that benefits you with a rewards program, e.g. cash back or air miles. *Note:* Not every place accepts credit cards in Europe; query service provider before initiating purchase. To eliminate any confusion back home, notify your lender that you will be using your credit card overseas (customer service number is on back of card). If you do not notify them, chances are the lender will block your account when they see transactions coming in from abroad.

Debit Cards: To access cash while abroad, bring a debit card linked to your bank account. Nowadays, with ATMs blanketing Europe and offering low exchange rates, traveler's checks are old hat and your humble debit card is the most cost effective way to retrieve funds while overseas. *(*To avoid frequent withdrawal fees—which can total upwards of $7.50 per transaction—consider taking out a few hundred euro at a time.)* Ideally you want to bring a second debit card in case your primary card gets lost, stolen or demagnetized. You can arrange for a back-up card by calling the customer service number on your card. Always carry cash for emergencies or for the many places that do not accept credit cards. **It is very important that you know your numeric PIN because European keypads *do not* have letters on them.** When the ATM is located indoors, use your card to gain access if the door is locked (slide card into slot by door). An ATM in Germany/Austria is called a "Bankomat," or "Geldautomat." Look for one displaying the bank symbol (Plus, Star, Interlink, Cirrus, or whichever is) compatible with your card. Typically, ATMs do not dispense a receipt. And sometimes, because of a glitch, it won't even give you money (don't worry, your account is not charged). If this is the case, and no money was dispensed, wait about two minutes before trying again and/or enter a different amount, or try a different ATM. *Note: Call the customer service number on the back of your card to ask whether they have an arrangement with any banks in Europe (Germany, Austria) that do not charge a withdrawal service fee—for example, Bank of America customers can use Deutsche Bank ATMs fee-free. To eliminate any confusion back home, notify your bank that you will be using your debit card overseas (customer service number is on back of card). If you do not notify them, chances are the bank will block your account when they see transactions/withdrawals occurring abroad.

Traveler's Checks: These days, with the advent of the ubiquitous ATM offering low exchange rates, traveler's checks have lost their luster. However, in case there's a problem with your debit card—and since we don't want you to take out a cash advance with your credit card—it's probably not a bad idea to bring $200-$300 as extra security (but it's easier and more cost effective to bring this amount in cash rather than traveler's checks, which cost about 2% to purchase and are vulnerable to high commission rates when exchanged). For folks who prefer to bring traveler's checks because of their replacement guarantee if lost or stolen, consult your bank for options. Arguably the most recognized issuer, American Express checks can be cashed at their overseas offices commission-free, and if you do have a problem with the checks (lost/stolen) you can talk to someone in person to swiftly sort out the crisis. (Note: Amex locations are listed in their respective city chapters.) Working on a similar premise to traveler's checks, American Express has created the Travelers Cheque Card, which is a pre-paid card—not to be confused with a credit or debit card linked to an account—that you load funds onto to withdraw as needed. To query American Express about the Travelers Cheque Card, call toll-free (within USA/Canada) 1-888-412-6945.

Discounts, Students & Youths: Youths under 18, and college students with a valid International Student Identity Card (ISIC), typically get a handsome discount on tours, attractions, public transportation, etc. Your price category will be listed next to the German word "Ermäßigt" (meaning reduced) or "Studenten." If you do not see either word, present your ID card to the cashier and ask if a discount applies (especially in Austria, where reduced prices are often not listed). Note: To get the discounted price, you must show your ID card (or Ausweis in German). Carry it all times! Oh, and concerning students, many cashiers only accept a valid ISIC—otherwise, your uni. card will be fine.

Discounts, Family: Discounts are regularly given to families for tours, attractions, public transportation, etc.; always ask for the Family Ticket, or if a concession applies.

Discounts, Healthy Working-Class Adults Over 25: If this is your category, forget it, you're dreaming! No discounts applicable. It's a nice thought, though.

Trip Costs: The following figures are a generalized low-end summation of a daily budget in Germany and Austria. Backpackers can expect to pay on average 18€ per person per night for accommodations (hostel) and those who wish to stay in a hotel (private room) can expect to pay 30-40€ per person per night. Budget 12€ per day for food, 10€ for sights/attractions, and 5€ for local (public) transportation—equaling a minimum of 45€ per day. Drivers can calculate a fair bit more into their budget since gas is upwards of $6.50/gallon and parking can be expensive as well as a hassle in big cities.

Flight Costs: Flights from New York to Frankfurt, depending on the season, generally run $400-750, and from Los Angeles $500-950. Surf the Web for the best deal. Begin shopping about five weeks prior to liftoff. Good sites to check are orbitz.com, expedia.com and hotwire.com (Note: Although hotwire is typically the cheapest, they do not offer frequent flyer miles, a choice of airlines or departure times.)

Backup Your Documents: To be extra prudent, take digital photos of your valuables and important documents—e.g. airline ticket (if applicable) and the first two pages of your passport—and email them to yourself. This will speed replacement if lost or stolen as well as facilitate an insurance claim.

Train or Car?: Travelers 25 years of age or younger receive hard-to-pass-up discounts on rail travel in Europe (↔ compare prices at railpass.com and raileurope.com for a wide range of options ↔) Over 25 year olds pay a steeper price but will get first-class seating. Trains are easy-to-use in Germany/Austria, zipping you smoothly and scenically between cities and dropping you (typically) in the heart of the Old Town near a TI, post office, food court, accommodations, and/or local transportation connections. By rail is the way to go for first-timers and travelers who are sticking to main routes. With a car, however, you have freedom to roam and it carriers your bags for you. You will, though, pay ridiculously high gas prices (upwards of $6.50/gallon) and possibly a road toll, and sometimes encounter a traffic jam (called a "Stau"). Moreover, cars are a pain to have in the big cities, like Vienna and Berlin. That said, it's still nice to have wheels to take you wherever, whenever. In our city chapters in the travel guide we've tried to accommodate Drivers by listing the local parking situations as well as a convenient place to park outside of the major cities where you can take the subway in to avoid traffic (if you wish), and/or a pick of Good Sleeps that are easily accessible by car. *Note:* Combine the benefits of both modes of transportation by purchasing a railpass as well as renting a car. This is easily done with a well-defined itinerary. Rent a car to visit all the difficult-to-reach-by-train destinations, such as the Black Forest, Romantic Road, Mosel Valley and use the railpass between major cities. (Between cities in Germany, however, you may want to substitute the train with *Share Ride*—see next entry.)

Share Ride: *(Mitfahrzentrale; a concept matching passengers with drivers, and vice-versa.)* For an alternative to the train in Germany, "Mitfahrzentrale" (like Mitt-far-zen-trolley) is the cheapest and most social option of getting from one city to another. **This applies to Germany only**—Austria does not yet have Share Ride—locations are listed in the German city chapters. *Note:* Those who have a working knowledge of German will want to first refer to this website (www.mitfahrgelegenheit.de) for an opportunity to contact the driver directly, i.e. cutting out the middleman for an even cheaper Share Ride.

Car Rental: Plan ahead and arrange your car rental from home; it's cheaper than doing it in Europe. A good place to start is www.kemwel.com (toll-free 1-877-820-0668), who deal with all the major companies to get you the best price. On their website, when selecting your pick-up and drop-off points, note that picking up a car in one country and dropping it off in another will incur a substantial surcharge. Your best bet is to pick up and drop off the car in Germany (in different cities is not a problem and will cost little or nothing to do so). Besides being centrally located on the continent with numerous cities to choose from, Germany only requires that you have your D.L.—an international driver's license is recommended but not obligatory. If you were to pick up and drop off in Austria, for example, an international driver's license would be required and you'd have to pay a hefty road tax (about $5/day compared to Germany's $1/day). To get the cheapest rate, do not pick up the car at an airport or a train station—either place will increase your rate by about 20% (to drop off at either place does not incur a charge). Instead, pick up the car at the downtown office, which is usually close to the train station. Secure the booking/rate with your credit card but don't worry if your dates change; Kemwel is flexible so you can either drop the car off early (and be credited) or keep it longer (and continue on the same weekly rate). Credit card holders check with your lender to see whether the CDW insurance is covered when you pay for the rental with your card. If you're covered, you just saved around $10/day. *Note:* Keep in mind that gas prices are outrageously high in Europe, upwards of $6.50/gallon. Ouch! To trim that price, request a diesel (saving you about 10%). Lastly, the more passengers you have, the cheaper the end cost will be.

Accommodations: The following are a few general tips concerning accommodations.
(1) To guarantee your first night in Europe is hassle-free and cozy, reserve a room/bed as soon as you have an arrival date.
(2) Under normal circumstances make reservations 24-48 hours in advance. In peak summer (July/Aug), depending on the destination, reserve several days/weeks in advance.
(3) July/Aug is the hotelier's best time to do business; be prepared to pay the *highest* price.
(4) In peak summer (July/Aug) ready yourself for seeing the "Belegt" (no vacancy) sign on the door. Also, most rooms are *not* equipped with AC/fans to thwart the summer heat!
(5) To travel in August can be a nightmare because this is when many Europeans plan their vacation.
(6) Sometimes you will be charged an extra 3-5€ for staying only one night.
(7) Many hoteliers take their due break and close for the months of Jan/Feb.
(8) Avoid using hotel-room phones; otherwise you will pay exorbitant rates.

Youth Hostels: They're not just pocket-friendly digs but a place to meet people of all nationalities. A place to socialize, formulate ideas, share experiences, and exchange travel tips. There are plenty of hostels listed in this guidebook, but if you stay within the government-backed network of Hostelling International (HI) hostels you must be member or an extra charge will apply (typically 3-4€/night). If you're going to be staying awhile at an HI hostel or others in the network, query reception about taking out membership. But beware; HI hostels often cater to (menacing) kids on school-group outings (weekdays during the school year and many weekends in summer). On the upside, breakfast and sheets are included in the price and as a courtesy (reception) staff can phone ahead to make your next HI booking. In Bavaria, you must be under 26 years of age to stay at an HI. *Note:* Dorm rooms in HI hostels are gender-segregated; in most independent backpacker hostels the dorms are mixed.

Tipping & Restaurants: No need to go overboard on tipping in Germany or Austria. In restaurants the service is included in the price of your meal; however, it's common to leave a small tip by rounding the amount up (e.g., a bill that comes to 11.10€, pay 12€, or 23.50€, pay 25€). Rather than leaving the tip on the table, pay it when settling your bill. For example, if you were to hand the waiter 30€ for a 23.50€ meal, you would say 25€ and the waiter would automatically hand you 5€ back.

To tip taxi drivers, follow the same (rounding-up) procedure as mentioned above. Porters in hotels typically receive 1€/bag.

Restaurants: Many restaurants display their menu outside (next to front door). This is optimal for travelers on a budget, who can study the menu before making a decision.

Asking for water: If you ask the waiter for water, it is automatic that bottled water will arrive at a cost of about 2€/bottle. If you want tap water, ask for Leitungswasser (pronounced lie-toongs-vasser).

Apfelschorle is a nice alternative to Coke/Pepsi, containing about 55% apple juice and 45% carbonated water.

Smoking: Next to Spain and Greece, Germany has the highest rate of smokers in Europe. If you're planning on hitting a pub or club, prepare yourself for smoke-filled rooms and your clothes reeking of cigarettes.

Inexpensive Clothes: If you're looking for trendy Euro fashion at pocket-friendly prices, pop into an "H&M" store. Each city has one (or three) H&M that is generally located in the pedestrian shopping zone in the Old Town. *Note:* To find the changing room to try on an article of clothing, look for the word "Anprobe" (meaning, try on).

Going to the Cinema: When browsing the movie listings in Germany or Austria keep an eye out for films labeled "OV" (original version) or "OmU" (original version with subtitles). However—as a word of warning—this doesn't always mean the movie will be in English. For example, if you unknowingly paid to see "Crouching Tiger, Hidden Dragon" labeled "OmU," you'd get a Chinese-speaking movie with German subtitles.

Finding The @ Button: Making toys is to Santa's elves what the @ button is to tech-savvy travelers. No matter how easy it is at home, writing e-mail is tricky business when trying to find your way around a German/Austrian keyboard. Have no fear, press the *Alt Gr* button while pushing the @ button. Presto, Aunt Betty is just a click away.

Laundry: Cost-conscious travelers do your laundry in Berlin, where Laundromats are cheapest (roughly 3€/load, incl. powder). In the meantime, hit a Laundromat when necessary but realistically you can wash (socks, undies, T-shirts) in your room by using the sink (or bathtub) and the tube of liquid soap you brought from home (or bought on the road). In case of a plugless sink, which is common, either buy a plug in advance or stuff the drain with a plastic bag. Hang your clothes to dry on radiator heaters, shower-curtain rods, or wherever convenient. A hairdryer works well in a pinch if it's close to checkout time. *Note:* Washers/dryers are very small in Europe; put in items hard to wash by hand, e.g. towel, jeans. Bring a plastic bag to separate your dirty clothes from the clean ones.

Common Sense: The biggest chunk of advice we can offer to travelers is to use common sense! Part of that logic is to remember that you are an ambassador to your country wherever you go—the locals will judge your nation on your actions.

ITINERARY

To travel is the world's greatest education, period. Here's your chance to see Europe; don't miss this opportunity! Save your money and embark on the journey of a lifetime. You'll have few regrets. Below are three suggested itineraries to choose from. Just remember: *This is your time; make the most of it!* So come along, and discover Europe with YTC.

Note: Each itinerary can be traveled with either a car or train or a combination of both. Although a car is always handy, it's an expensive proposition in Europe considering costly parking (and hassles) in big cities and wallet-busting gas prices. There's really no need to rent a car for Quest One or Two, but for Quest Three wheels would enhance sightseeing en route. For more details on either mode of transportation—including how to rent a car and where to buy your railpass—see *General Tips* and *Railers* in this Traveler's Tips chapter. **Railers,** upon arriving at each destination ask at the train info counter the best connection to your next destination. This is vital because on long stretches there can be numerous options with an hour or so difference in travel time between them. **Drivers,** the autobahns and highways in Germany and Austria are a thorough network that will usually get you to your destination without too much fuss. The biggest hurdle is the gas price—upwards of $6.50/gallon—and then there's the X-factor: the traffic jam, called a "Stau" (pronounced like "wow" but with "st" instead of "w").

Quest One:
The Quickie — Sydney's Adventure, in 11 days

Day	Where	Sleep
1	Arrive in Vienna	Vienna
2	Explore Vienna	Vienna
3	Vienna to Salzburg	Salzburg
4	Explore Salzburg; do-it-yourself SOM tour?	Salzburg

5	Explore Berchtesgaden	Salzburg
6	Salzburg to Munich	Munich
7	Explore Munich	Munich
8	(get an early start) Munich to Baden-Baden	Baden-Baden
9	Baden-Baden to Rothenburg	Rothenburg
10	Explore Rothenburg	Rothenburg
11	Rothenburg to Frankfurt Airport	Airplane

To extend this trip consider adding an extra day after Vienna to travel to nearby Melk in the Danube Valley (page 543). There, rent a bike and cycle along the Danube River. Sleep in Melk.

Another trip-extension idea is to add 1-2 days after Rothenburg to cruise the Rhine River (page 304).

Note: **Day 6:** On the way from Salzburg to Munich you'll pass the Chiemsee (AFRC) resort portrayed in the adventure novel. Remember, though, it's since been closed by the U.S. Department of Defense due to the downsizing of military forces in Europe. *Drivers,* you'll see it on the right just prior to the Felden exit. *Railers,* after the Bernau stop you'll briefly see it in the distance on the right nestled on the shore of the lake (Chiemsee). **Day 8:** This is a 4hr drive or rail. (Railers, picnic on train.) Get an early start so you can spend your afternoon soaking in the baths. **Day 9:** Railers, prepare for a long trip (4-5.5hr with up to three changes). Drivers, it's pretty clear-cut: take the A5 north (Karlsruhe-Heidelberg), then the A6 east (Heilbronn-Nürnberg), then the A7 north (Würzburg).

Quest Two:
Your Life-Changing Experience, in 21 days

Day	Where	Sleep
1	Arrive in Frankfurt	Frankfurt
2	(get an early start) Frankfurt to Rothenburg	Rothenburg
3	Rothenburg to (Ludwig's) Neuschwanstein	near castle
4	Neuschwanstein to Munich	Munich
5	Explore Munich	Munich
6	Munich to Salzburg	Salzburg
7	Explore Salzburg; do-it-yourself SOM tour?	Salzburg
8	Explore Berchtesgaden	Salzburg
9	(get an early start) Salzburg to Innsbruck	Innsbruck
10	Explore Innsbruck	Innsbruck
11	Innsbruck to Baden-Baden (long journey)	Baden-Baden
12	Relax, soak in Baden-Baden	Baden-Baden
13	Baden-Baden to Rhine River	Rhine River
14	Cruise the Romantic Rhine	Rhine River
15	Rhine River to Cologne	Cologne
16	Cologne to Berlin (read note for Day 16)	Berlin
17	Explore Berlin	Berlin
18	Explore Berlin	Berlin
19	Berlin to Dresden	Dresden
20	Explore Dresden	Dresden
21	Dresden to Frankfurt Airport	Airplane

<u>Note:</u> **Day 1:** Or you could go straight from the airport to Rothenburg for an extra night there—if you do this, disregard Day 2. **Day 2:** Get an early start to maximize your time in Rothenburg. **Day 3:** Railers, ride the "Touring" bus (page 154-55) along the Romantic Road to Schloss Neuschwanstein (page 176). **Day 4:** Railers, ride the train from Füssen to Munich. **Day 6:** *Bank of America debit card holders withdraw enough money in Munich from a Deutsche Bank (DB) ATM (fee-free) to last you through Austria (there are no DBs in Austria). If you use an unfriendly ATM anywhere—Germany or Austria— it will cost you upwards of $7.50 in fees per transaction. *(*Customers of other banks call the number on the back of your card and ask if they have an arrangement with any banks in Germany or Austria that do not charge a withdrawal service fee.)* On the way from Munich to Salzburg you'll pass the Chiemsee (AFRC) resort portrayed in the adventure novel. Remember, though, it's since been closed by the U.S. Department of Defense due to downsizing military forces in Europe. *Railers,* shortly after the Prien stop you'll briefly see it in the distance on the left nestled on the shore of lake Chiemsee. *Drivers,* you'll see it on the left after the Prien am Chiemsee exit. (Prior to the exit the autobahn will descend into the valley affording a fantastic view of the lake district.) **Day 9:** Although it's only a 2hr train ride, leave early so you can get a good jump on touring the sights in town using your two-day Innsbruck Card (page 518). **Day 11:** Get the last few sights in before embarking on a long journey (6hr by train) to Baden-Baden. *Railers,* picnic on the train— visit the supermarket in Innsbruck's central station for lunch/dinner items before departing. ***Drivers,*** consider heading west on the autobahn to Feldkirch, then Lindau. From there, parallel Lake Constance (on route 31) to Friedrichshafen, Überlingen and ultimately the autobahn. After a short while on the A81, follow signs to Villingen and cut through the Black Forest on route 33 to Offenburg. From there, take the A5 north to

Baden-Baden. **Day 16:** *Drivers,* *drop rental car off at the Hauptbahnhof in Cologne because you won't need it anymore; this also allows you to fly to Berlin—read Railers. (*If you arrive early enough and it works to your benefit, drop car off on Day 15—or Day 26 for Quest Three readers.) ***Railers,*** for a very reasonable price you can book a one-way flight on the Web (at least a week in advance) with GermanWings(.com) from Cologne to Berlin (flip to page 327, Airport). **Day 19:** Although Berlin to Dresden is an easy 2hr journey by train, consider the cheaper and more social option: Share Ride (page 347). **Day 21:** Depending on your flight departure time, you may need to sleep in Frankfurt (or its airport) on Day 20 (or Day 32 for Quest Three readers). Remember that trains can (and do) arrive directly at the airport. Another option is Share Ride (query drivers headed to Frankfurt if, for extra money, they'll stop at the airport)—hopefully the person's car won't break down on the way. Yikes!

Quest Three:
The Whole Strudel, in 33 days

Day	Where	Sleep
1	Arrive in Frankfurt (preferably on a Tue.)	Frankfurt
2	(get an early start) Frankfurt to Rothenburg	Rothenburg
3	Rothenburg to (Ludwig's) Neuschwanstein	near castle
4	Neuschwanstein to Munich	Munich
5	Explore Munich	Munich
6	Explore Munich	Munich
7	Munich to Salzburg	Salzburg
8	Explore Salzburg; do-it-yourself SOM tour?	Salzburg
9	Explore Berchtesgaden	Salzburg
10	Either explore Werfen or Salzkammergut	Salzburg
11	Salzburg to Melk (Danube Valley)	Melk
12	Melk to Vienna	Vienna
13	Explore Vienna	Vienna
14	Vienna to Graz	Graz
15	Explore Graz	Graz
16	Graz to Innsbruck (long, scenic journey)	Innsbruck
17	Explore Innsbruck	Innsbruck
18	Explore Innsbruck	Innsbruck
19	Innsbruck to Baden-Baden (long journey)	Baden-Baden
20	Relax, soak in Baden-Baden	Baden-Baden
21	Baden-Baden to Trier	Trier
22	Trier to Cochem	Cochem
23	Explore Cochem and environs	Cochem
24	Cochem to Rhine River	Rhine River
25	Cruise the Romantic Rhine	Rhine River
26	Rhine River to Cologne	Cologne
27	Cologne to Berlin (read note for Day 27)	Berlin
28	Explore Berlin	Berlin
29	Explore Berlin	Berlin
30	Explore Berlin	Berlin
31	Berlin to Dresden	Dresden
32	Explore Dresden	Dresden
33	Dresden to Frankfurt Airport	Airplane

Note: **Day 1:** Preferably arrive on a Tuesday so you can generally keep to the suggested itinerary outlined in Munich beginning on Friday (page 184). **Day 2:** Since you have more time with this tour, you could stay an extra night in Rothenburg and cut a day elsewhere—or you could just go straight from Frankfurt airport to Rothenburg. **Day 3:** Railers, ride the "Touring" bus (page 154-55) along the Romantic Road to Schloss Neuschwanstein (page 176). **Day 4:** Railers, ride the train from Füssen to Munich. **Day 7:** Read Day 6 listed under Quest Two. Additionally, you'll notice you have several days allocated for Salzburg and side trips—you can cut one of these days if you wish. **Day 9:** Prospective Drivers, consider picking up your rental car in Berchtesgaden (Königsseer Str. 47; gas station up road and on left from TI). **Day 10:** If you choose Salzkammergut, you could overnight there. **Day 11:** (If the weather's nice…) Get an early start so you'll have enough time to rent a bike and cycle along the Danube River (page 543). Railers, from Salzburg you'll need to change trains in Linz or Amstetten. **Day 16:** Although this is a long journey (6hr by train), it is very scenic—steaming past green rolling hills sprinkled with livestock and through popular winter ski resorts like St. Johann and Kitzbühel. Because you'll be arriving late into Innsbruck, begin touring the sights first thing in the morning using your two-day Innsbruck Card (page 518). Railers, picnic on the train—visit the supermarket in Graz's central station for lunch/dinner items before departing. **Day 19:** Railers, this is another long (6hr) train journey (visit the supermarket in Innsbruck's central station for lunch items before departing). Drivers, read Day 11—Drivers—listed under Quest Two. **Day 21:** Railers, this is around a 4.5hr journey with up to three changes—plan another picnic on the train. Drivers, consider cutting through France and filling up your tank in Luxembourg with Central Europe's cheapest gas/diesel (plan to arrive on an empty tank): Cross the Rhine River (border) into France and at the freeway head towards *Haguenau. Skirt the town via the ring road and connect onto the N62 direction Mertzwiller, Phillipsbourg, Bitche then Sarreguemines. From here, cross into Germany—head towards Saarbrücken and connect onto the (autobahn) A620 direction Saarlouis. Drive this route (via the A8) to the Luxembourg border (Schengen), where you'll connect onto the scenic N10 paralleling the Mosel River (on Lux. side) to Remich; farther ahead pick up the autobahn to Trier. *WWII buffs,* you're not far from General Patton's grave in Luxembourg Cemetery (go to your-traveling-companion.com then *Lest We Forget*). At Remich take the N2 towards Luxembourg City—past Sandweiler is Hamm (by freeway). From here, follow signs "Cimetieres Militaires" to the cemetery (open daily 9:00-17:00). After your visit, take the adjacent freeway to Trier—if you haven't already, you can fill up at the huge gas station at the border crossing: Wasserbillig. *(*This country route via Haguenau is much slower but free. The alternative is the tollway—called the Péage—that will cost about 6€ to Saarbrücken, Germany. If you prefer the Péage, head direction Metz then Saarbrücken and connect onto the A620 autobahn after the border. From here, follow directions above to the Luxembourg border…).* **Day 27:** Read Day 16 listed under Quest Two. **Day 31:** Read Day 19 listed under Quest Two. **Day 33:** Read Day 21 listed under Quest Two. *Note:* With extra time explore Dresden one more day and/or jump over to nearby Prague, Czech Republic, for a few nights. You'll love it!

EURO

On January 1, 2002, Europeans were not only nursing their hangovers, they were taking part in the most ambitious currency swap in history. Twelve nations—incorporating some 300-million people—threw their historic monies into the kiln to forge a common currency: the euro (symbol: € — 1€ = 100 cents), a legal tender that will enhance established trade, encourage new deals, and rival the U.S. dollar. At press time: 1€ = $1.20.

The first trading session of the euro was New Year's Day (Tuesday) January 1, 2002, and all the shops and banks were closed for the holiday. People rushed to the ATMs in their respective countries to get their hands on the new euro. Some machines ran out of cash or mysteriously broke down, while others simply spewed out the old currency. On Wednesday, January 2, the banks opened and they were immediately flooded with people who were anxious to exchange the old for the new. It was a historic day that called for something special and some banks, such as the Sparkasse Bank in Bad Aibling, Germany, served champagne to those who were queuing in the monstrous lines that extended out the door and into the parking lot.

Today, the euro-zone countries are Austria, Belgium, Finland, France, Germany, Greece, Ireland, Italy, Luxembourg, Netherlands, Portugal and Spain. *Note:* Denmark, the United Kingdom and Sweden are also members of the European Union (EU) but have elected not to use the euro as their common currency. In May 2004, 10 more countries joined the EU block: Cyprus, Czech Republic, Estonia, Hungary, Latvia, Lithuania, Malta, Poland, Slovakia and Slovenia. These countries will not be using the euro for a few years yet until certain bureaucratic requirements are met.

All euro notes are shared by the 12 participating lands and are neutrally designed the same. The set includes seven denominations: 5€, 10€, 20€, 50€, 100€, 200€ and the 500€ note.

All coins are shared just the same as the notes; however, their backsides are designed individually by country. The set includes eight denominations: 1¢, 2¢, 5¢, 10¢, 20¢, 50¢, 1€ and the 2€ coin. (1€ = 100 cents.)

Since the coins are individually designed, many people find it interesting to check out the different nations they have in their pockets. For hobbyists, the coins can be worth much more than their face value; such is the case with the specially minted Vatican euro coins featuring Pope John Paul II. Also, enthusiasts may swap a higher-value coin for a lesser-value coin to complete their collection, like Belgium's 20-cent coin with funny-looking guy for Italy's 5-cent coin featuring the Roman Colosseum.

Many coins are not engraved with their country's name, so here are a few hints to help you identify what land you have in your hand. Try to find...

A big flower (2€), flying geese (1€), or a lion wielding a sword for **Finland**

RF (Republic of France) for **France**

An eagle, the Brandenburg Gate, or oak leaves for **Germany**

The words ΛΕΝΤΑ (cent) or ΕΥΡΩ (euro) for **Greece**

The harp for **Ireland**

RI (Republic of Italy) for **Italy**

Lëtzebuerg for **Luxembourg**

Nederlanden for **Netherlands**

Portugal for **Portugal**

España for **Spain**

Funny-looking guy wearing glasses for **Belgium**

The Edelweiss (2¢) or Mozart (1€) for **Austria**

RAILERS

Railpasses: Many travelers in Europe these days are seeing the sights with railpasses suited to their itinerary. That said, don't buy a railpass because everybody else is. Make sure it complements your travel plans and you are going to make the most out of it. If you are not planning frequent travel by rail, it may be cheaper for you to purchase tickets individually at the train station. (*Note:* Those 25 years of age and younger receive generous discounts.) However, if you feel you're going to be a busy bee on the rails, order the pass that best suits your preplanned itinerary. What's more, you will get plenty of other discounts by being a railpass holder (explained online and also within the info kit you'll receive with your pass in the mail). Surf these sites (railpass.com, raileurope.com, eurail.com) for a wide variety of options and the best price. All three sites sell the same product; only some of the combinations and prices vary. From YTC to you: *Gute Reise.*

(1) Your railpass is considered an open ticket until it is validated, which is done by an official from the rail authority (not by you). Before boarding your first train, go to a ticket counter and present the railpass with your passport. Arrive well before your train is due to depart (about 30 min for smaller stations, 60 min for larger stations) in case there's a long line or an unforeseen hassle. *Note:* EurAide offices (in Munich and Berlin) can also validate your railpass (see next entry).

(2) If you find yourself in Munich's main train station or in Berlin's "Zoo" station, stop by the EurAide office to have all your rail questions answered in fluent English. They also validate railpasses. Details on EurAide are listed in the Munich and Berlin chapters under TI (tourist information).

(3) Treat your railpass like it's cash because if you lose it, there's no refund. If you're insured you may be able to recoup your losses at a later date, but you'll still need to purchase another pass (or individual tickets) for the time being.

(4) If you're traveling on a Flexi or Select railpass, fill out the date of travel on your ticket before the conductor approaches—he/she can get testy otherwise.

(5) To reserve a seat (3€) is a good idea on busy routes within the ICE, IC, and EC train network (it is mandatory on overnight trains, 4-9€, or a bunk from 17€). You can reserve over the counter at the station's Reisezentrum (Travel Center).

(6) When traveling on European trains, don't embarrass yourself—keep your feet off the seats. The conductors will confront you.

(7) If you ever feel confused about a particular train journey—what connections to catch on which track and when—ask a staff member at the station's info desk to kindly print out your itinerary (this is free of charge).

(8) Check out train schedules in addition to local specials and current deals for overseas travelers offered by Germany and Austria's national rail authority — Germany: www.bahn.de — Austria: www.oebb.at

(9) At most train stations you'll find day lockers. These are a good alternative to lugging your pack around in search of food, sights or whatever it is that you want to do. Locker sizes vary as do their prices, generally 2€-3€/24hr.

(10) Lastly, German and Austrian trains leave on time; *don't be late!*

Rail Discounts, Germany: The German rail authority "Deutsche Bahn" offers a plethora of discounts to get people to ride the rails. Price categories include 25 years of age and younger and everyone else up to seniors. The youthful folks filling the former category receive such cheap rates that the following discounts will not be of particular interest.

If you're traveling as a pair (or up to four people), you pay full price for the first ticket and only 50% for subsequent tickets. If you book your trip at least three days in advance, you will receive a healthy discount. Book your train travel via the German rail authority's website (www.bahn.de) or over the counter at the station's Reisezentrum (Travel Center) situated in every busy train station.

Länder-Ticket: Germany also offers the attractive Länder-Ticket (or State-Ticket), valid within the boundaries of the state it was purchased. Ticket prices vary between states but generally cost *24€, which covers up to five people in 2nd-class seating on *regional* trains (IRE, RE, RB, S-Bahn and local transportation, i.e. bus, tram)—valid during the week, Mon-Fri from 9:00 until 03:00 the following morning. Parents can use the ticket to travel with unlimited kids under the age of 14. In many cases, the ticket will also get you beyond the boundaries of the state; such is the case with the Bavarian state ticket (or *Bayern-Ticket*), allowing the holder access to Ulm, Salzburg and Kufstein. **Note:* If you're traveling alone, often a cheaper price is available for single-person use, for example, the Bavarian state ticket (*Bayern-Ticket*) costs 25€ full price and 18€ for singles. Purchase the Länder-Ticket either via the Internet (www.bahn.de) or at a ticket automat in the station (automats accept all credit cards and are multilingual). If bought over the counter there will be a 2€ surcharge.

Schönes-Wochenende-Ticket: With this railpass (literally Happy-Weekend-Ticket) all the same details apply as the above Länder-Ticket, except that it's valid for either Sat or Sun and it's effective from midnight (rather than 9:00) and, most importantly, it's good for all of Germany and within some parts of Poland and the Czech Republic. The price per ticket is 30€ (when bought at an automat or 32€ if purchased over the counter or 33€ on board the train) and covers up to five people in 2nd-class seating on regional trains: IRE, RE, RB, S-Bahn and local transportation, i.e. bus, tram. *Note:* The only setback to this wonderfully priced ticket is that the aforesaid regional trains are the slow ones and if you're traveling a great distance it'll take *all* day. Really!

Words You May See At The Train Station	
Bahnhof (Bhf) = Train station	Abfahrt = Departure
Hauptbahnhof (Hbf) = Main train station	Ankunft = Arrival
Zug = Train	Erwachsene = Adult
Gleis = Platform	Kind(er) = Child(ren)
Hin- und Rückfahrt = Roundtrip	Ermäßigung = Reduced price
Einfache Fahrt = One way	Fahrtziele = Destinations
Fahrkarten (or Fahrscheine) = Travel tickets	Haltestelle = (train/bus) Stop

Trains & Laptops: Trains in Germany and Austria that offer outlets—for laptops and other handy gizmos—are the ICE (Inter City Express) and often the IC (Inter City) and EC (Euro City).

Trains & Picnics: Before embarking on a long journey, visit a grocery store and buy the makings for a feast. It's a delight to kick back and savor European cuisine while admiring the beautiful countryside pass by your window like a moving painting. Grocery stores are either in—or near—main train stations. While most trains offer a catered food service (guy pushing cart), the items for sale are typically overpriced and less than appealing.

First Class vs. Second Class: Typically Trains in Germany and Austria are immaculate and the only real difference between the classes is the seats and the people sitting in them. While the people in second class tend to be more interesting (or animated), the seats in first class are that little bit comfier and if the train is full, chances are first class will be half empty.

Share Ride: (page 440) Backpackers over the age of 25 traveling through Germany, or those using Germany as a base, consider using "Mitfahrzentrale" between cities instead of the train.

DRIVERS

Road Map: Buy/bring a road atlas of Germany/Austria to accompany your journey.

Miles & Kilometers: 1 mile = 1.61 kilometers • 6 mi = 10 km • 100 mph = 161 kph. *Note:* You could be driving 161 kph on the German autobahn and still have a car pass you as if you were driving miss daisy.

Unleaded, or "Bleifrei": 1 gallon = 3.79 liters (1 liter is similar to a quart). Because it's heavily taxed, a liter of *Bleifrei* (or unleaded gas) in Germany costs roughly 1.32€, or about $6.50/gallon. Ouch! Gasoline is notably cheaper in Austria, costing roughly 1.15€/ liter, and it's even cheaper in Luxembourg. Fill up there if you have the chance.

Austrian Autobahn: The maximum speed limit on the Austrian autobahn is 130 kilometers per hour (kph). And to drive on this efficient motorway you are required to have what's called a *Vignette*, or toll sticker. You can obtain this little decal at most any gas station approaching the border. *Price:* 10 days 7.60€, two months 22€, one year 73€. *Note:* Affix the Vignette to the inside corner of your windshield or behind the rear-view mirror. (Your rental car may already have a toll sticker from the previous renters, but don't be fooled—it's most likely expired.) If you happen to get pulled over without a Vignette, the fine will be upwards of 150€, on the spot!

German Autobahn: On this, the world's fastest freeway, there are no tollbooths to slow down for or a tax sticker to procure. Occasionally—more often now with the advent of some horrific crashes—there will be sections of the autobahn that have speed limit signs posted. Whatever you do, however, do not lollygag in the passing lane—keep right or you may get run over by a speedster in a sports car. It only takes a nanosecond for something to happen. *Note:* Emergency call boxes are located about every mile along the autobahn in case you have car trouble. On the shoulder—if you don't see a call box— look to the top of the road marker (reflector) and you will see an arrow pointing in the direction of the closest box.

Words You May See While Driving	
Ausfahrt = Exit	Bleifrei = Unleaded gas
Geschwindigkeit = Speed	Nur bei nässe = Only when wet
Stau = Traffic jam	Bitte folgen = Please follow (police)
Unfall = Accident	Autobahn = Expressway
Umleitung = Traffic detour	Messe = Convention center
Stadt(mitte) or Zentrum = City center	
Nord = North • Süd = South • Ost = East • West = West	

Bicycles Have Right-Of-Way! Be careful with this one. It's very easy to think that your car is bigger and therefore you should have the right-of-way. Bicycles always have the right-of-way in normal traffic conditions. Bottom line: Pay attention to your surroundings —especially when making a turn.

One-Way Street: Get acquainted with the following words or you could very easily find yourself staring down the hood of a racy BMW, Alfa Romeo, or Peugeot. *Einbahn(strasse)* = one-way street in German • *Senso Unico* = one-way street in Italian • *Sens Unique* = one-way street in French.

Parking Dial: Before hitting the road, make sure you have the nifty parking dial: a small, 24-hour (blue) cardboard disk that is manually rotated and called a "Parkscheibe," or often "Parkuhr" in Austria. The dial will allow you to park in designated areas for *FREE*. There should be a dial in the glove box (or in the side-door pocket) of your rental car. If your car did not come with a dial, and you haven't left the rental agency, go back in and ask for one. If it's too late, you can purchase a dial cheaply at a gas station or paper shop.

How to use the dial: In cities and towns look for the parking sign that displays a diagram of the dial. The sign will also display a maximum time limit, which is usually an hour. Rotate the dial to the time when you pulled into the space (*Ankunftszeit*, or arrival time) and put it on the dashboard—this way the parking inspector can see when you arrived and if you've overstayed your welcome.

Parking Meters, Automats: Carry exact change, because these do not give change.

Tight Parking: Beware; regardless of what the signs say, if you park on a narrow lane and your vehicle hinders the access of public transportation (i.e. a bus) you will be towed, then ticketed! Really! As is the case with most everything in this guidebook, we speak from experience.

Two-Way Arrows: When approaching the narrow gate of a medieval town—or a bridge that's suitable for only one car—you will see a sign with two arrows indicating dual passage. Instead of implementing a traffic light, Europeans have put up this sign to control the flow of traffic. One arrow will be red; the other will be either black or white. If the red arrow is pointing in the direction you want to travel, you must give the right-of-way. Just sit tight until the other side is clear of approaching vehicles. If it's the opposite, and the black or white arrow is pointing in the direction you want to travel, you have the right-of-way and the cars on the other side will stop for you. **Put simply: red = yield.**

Measurements & Temperatures

Today, most of the world—including Europe—uses the decimal-based metric system, originating from France in the late-18th century. Here are a few conversions to help you stay in tune with Europe's digits.

1 kilometer (km) = .62 miles (10 km = 6.2 mi)
1 meter (m) = 3.28 feet (think of a meter as a yard)
1 liter = 1.05 quarts
4 liters = 1.05 gallons (40 liters = 10.5 gal)
1 kilogram (kg) = 2.2 lbs (10 kilos = 22 lbs)
2.5 centimeters (cm) = 1 inch (25 cm = 10 in.)

Did You Know: In one mile there are 5280 feet, 63,360 inches and 1,609,344 millimeters.

Celsius & Fahrenheit: If you're confused by the Celsius temperature system, here's a simple formula that will get you close to Fahrenheit: double the Celsius and add 30, e.g. 20° C x 2 = 40 + 30 = 70. By looking at the chart below, you can see we were pretty close. Now you try.

0° Celsius (C) = 32° Fahrenheit (F)
4° C = 40° F
10° C = 50° F
16° C = 60° F
21° C = 70° F
27° C = 80° F
32° C = 90° F
38° C = 100° F

Epochs and Art Styles: a feel for time

Architecture and artwork in Europe are expressed in the style of the era they were produced. But what does that mean?

Late Antiquity: This is the era associated with the final stages of the Roman Empire (circa 350 A.D.) to about the late-6th century.

Middle Ages: This is the term given to the period of time from the latter part of Late Antiquity to the Renaissance (circa 550 A.D. to the 1500s). The Middle Ages is best described as an era between the classical and modern world. The people living in "medieval times" did not know, per se, that they were living in the Middle Ages.

Romanesque: A period of art and architecture during the Middle Ages from the 11th to 13th centuries. Or you can think of Romanesque as the period from the turn of the 2nd millennium to the Gothic-era.

Gothic: The last period of art and architecture of the Middle Ages, flourishing from the 13th to 15th centuries. Arguably, Europe's most intriguing architecture is Gothic-style.

Renaissance: Now we enter the new age of humanism—a way of life centered on human values—which began in Italy during the 14th century and spread through Europe in the 15th to 16th centuries, when Latin literature, Greek ideology, Classical styles and the sciences were all rediscovered. The Renaissance was a belief that the new age rivaled the great worlds of ancient Greece and Rome.

Baroque: This is a period of art and architecture characterized by undulating curves and dramatic flair from the 1590s until the mid-18th century. Probably from the Portuguese *Barucca* (or irregular pearl), Baroque-style originated in Italy and likely spread to other parts of Europe with the help of such painters as Caravaggio and Carracci.

Rococo: Originating in the latter part of the 18th century, Rococo is a style of painting and decoration that is typified by rich ornamentation, soft colors and gilded figures.

Neoclassical: This bold style, applied from about 1760 through to 1850, replicates the popular and decorative elements of Greco-Roman structures, paintings and sculptures. Neoclassical works in Britain are referred to as Georgian-style, and in the United States as Federal-style.

Biedermeier: This post-Napoleon style of middle-class furniture and interior design became fashionable in Germany and Austria from 1815 to about 1860.

Art Nouveau: French for "New Art"; a style of decorative patterns and dazzling floral design at the turn of the 20th century. In Germany the movement is known as *Jugendstil* (Youth Style) and in Austria as *Sezessionstil* (Secession Style). The best examples of art nouveau in this guidebook can be found in Vienna; look to Sezessionstil on page 569.

The modest GLOSSARY

German is a difficult language to master, even the Germans have coined a catchphrase for its complexity: *Deutsche Sprache, schwere Sprache* (The German language is a difficult one).

Think of the German language as a jigsaw puzzle—once you have the main pieces together, the subject matter becomes apparent.

Example: "Wenn ich dir eine Kopie des Briefes faxen soll, so bitte ich dich, mir deine Faxnummer mitzuteilen."

Word for word translation: "If I you a copy of the letter fax should, so please I you, me your fax number inform."

Actual translation: "If you would like me to fax you the letter, please send me your fax number."

As you can see by our example, German is, indeed, a challenge. However, don't let that discourage you; it is a great language to learn and know. Below are some words to get you started. At the very least, you could initiate dialogue with the polite, *Sprechen Sie Englisch?* (Do you speak English?) For the most part, Germans and Austrians speak pretty good English because they are introduced to it in grade school. But by applying the age-old adage, when in Rome do as the Romans, immerse yourself in the culture the best you can, which includes mustering enough chutzpah to spit out some foreign words. The locals will appreciate you for it. Remember: Nobody's perfect; just do your best.

* * *

Yes = **Ja** • No = **Nein** (pronounce like nine)
Thank you = **Danke** (dahn-keh)
You're welcome = **Bitte schön** (bit-teh shuhn)
Please = **Bitte** (bit-teh)
Sorry/excuse me = **Entschuldigung** (ent-shool-dee-goong)
I love you = **Ich liebe dich** (ikh lee-beh dikh)

Emergency = **Notfall** (like note-fall) Emergency phone call = **Notruf** (like note-roof) Emergency doctor = **Notarzt** (like note-artst) Emergency exit = **Notausgang** (like note-aus-gong)

Today = **Heute** (hoy-teh)
Tonight = **Heute abend** (hoy-teh ah-bend)
Yesterday = **Gestern** (ghes-tern)
Tomorrow = **Morgen** (mohr-gen)
Good morning = **Guten morgen** (goo-tehn mohr-gen)
Good night = **Gute nacht** (goo-teh nahkt)
Good day = **Guten tag** (goo-tehn tahg; expressed as a greeting)
Goodbye = **Auf wiedersehen** (or more sincere, "Leb wohl")

Where is…? = **Wo ist** (voh ist) …the post office = **…die Post** …the tourist information = **…das Verkehrsamt** …the train station = **…der Bahnhof** (commonly seen acronym, Bhf)

Main train station = **Hauptbahnhof** (commonly seen acronym, Hbf)
How much is it? = **Wieviel kostet es?** (vee-feel kostet es)
Cheap = **Billig** • Expensive = **Teuer** (like toy-er)
Open = **Offen** or **Geöffnet** • Closed = **Geschlossen** (ge-shlossen)
Push = **Drücken** • Pull = **Ziehen**
Left = **Links** • Right = **Rechts**
Entrance = **Eingang** (by foot) or **Einfahrt** (by car)

PRONOUNCE: "**w**" like "**v**"	"**ei**" like "**i**" in wine
"**v**" like "**f**"	"**ie**" like "**ee**" in meet
"**j**" like "**y**" in yes	"**äu**", "**eu**" like **oi** in toy

City center = **Stadtmitte** or **Zentrum**
Church = **Kirche**
Cemetery = **Friedhof**
Castle, palace = **Schloss** or **Schloß** (ß = ss—it's old German)
(medieval) Castle = **Burg**
Fortress = **Festung**
Street = **Strasse** or **Straße** (ß = ss—it's old German)
Lane = **Gasse** or **Gässchen** (little lane)
Old town = **Altstadt**
Water *not* for drinking = **Kein trinkwasser** (before you drink from the cute town fountain, look for these words).
Bakery = **Bäckerei**
Snack bar = **Imbiss** (fast-food eatery)

Money = **Geld**
Bank = **Bank** (like bonk)
Postage stamp = **Briefmarke**
Inquiries/info = **Auskunft**
Toilet = **die Toilette** (commonly seen acronym, WC [pronounced VC]—a British term for "water closet")
 Do you mind if I drive your Porsche around the block? = **Darf Ich mir deinen Porsche für eine Runde durch die Nachbarschaft leihen?**
And lastly, you'll often hear this word: **Scheisse!** = Shit!

DAYS OF THE WEEK

Monday = **Montag** (mohn-tahg)	Friday = **Freitag** (frei-tahg)
Tuesday = **Dienstag** (deens-tahg)	Saturday = **Samstag** (sahms-tahg)
Wednesday = **Mittwoch** (mit-vokh)	Sunday = **Sonntag** (zohn-tahg)
Thursday = **Donnerstag** (dohn-nehrs-tahg)	

RESTAURANT/TAVERN: (**Gasthof** or **Gasthaus**)
Rest day = **Ruhetag** (in other words, closed)
The bill = **die Rechnung**
The menu = **die Speisekarte**
I would like…? = **Ich hätte gern**
…a beer, please = **…ein Bier, bitte**
…tap water = **…Leitungswasser** (like lie-toongs-vasser)

NUMBERS

One = **Eins** (like wines without the "w")

Two = **Zwei** (like why but zvhy)	Seven = **Sieben** (zee-bn)
Three = **Drei** (like dry)	Eight = **Acht** (ahkht)
Four = **Vier** (like fear)	Nine = **Neun** (like coin but noin)
Five = **Fünf** (fuhnf)	Ten = **Zehn** (like cane/cain but tszain)
Six = **Sechs** (like sex but zex)	Eleven = **Elf** (think Santa's helper)

ACCOMMODATIONS: (**Unterkunft**)
No vacancy = **Belegt**
Bed & Breakfast = (posted signs read) **Zimmer** or **Gästezimmer**
Do you have a room available? = **Haben Sie ein Zimmer frei?**
Single = **Einzelzimmer**
Double = **Doppelzimmer**
The key = **der Schlüssel** (shluhs-sehl)
Shower = **Dusche** (like doo-sheh)
Bathtub = **Bad** (also used for restroom—pronounce like the fish cod but with a "b")
Towel = **Handtuch** (hahnd-tewk)
Blanket = **Bettdecke** (bet-deh-ke)
Breakfast = **Frühstück** (frew-shtook)
Kurtax = Visitor's tax
Hotel-Garni = Bed & breakfast in a hotel-like atmosphere
Fremdenzimmer = Small hotel
Pension = Small, family-run digs
Ferienwohnung = Accommodations for long-term vacationers
Gasthof & **Gasthaus** = Can be a restaurant, tavern, inn or a hotel (for the latter two look for the word "Zimmer" out front)

TOMB-LOVERS, WHO'S BURiED WHERE?

GERMANY

Alzheimer, Dr. Alois: (b.) June 14, 1864 — (d.) Dec. 19, 1915. Considered a medical guru, Dr. Alzheimer specialized in brain research and neuropathology and was widely recognized as the authority on dementia after reporting his studies at a medical seminar in 1906. He proposed that abnormalities of the brain—in particular the cerebral cortex— were responsible for the malfunctioning of brain cells, causing memory loss, hallucinations, disorientation, and even death. Dr. Alzheimer is buried with his wife in the Hauptfriedhof, Frankfurt am Main. *GPS:* N50° 08.021 - E8° 41.434

Bach, J. S.: (b.) March 21, 1685 — (d.) July 28, 1750. Composer, church musician, and organ virtuoso—often regarded as one of the world's greatest. Johann Sebastian Bach was born in the central German town of Eisenach and in 1723 he moved (160km northeast) to Leipzig, where he spent the rest of his life. In Leipzig, Bach took a position as a teacher and musical director at Saint Thomas' theology school and was later promoted to choirmaster. Although the modern world recognizes Bach as a musical genius, the Baroque-era in which he lived saw him as a conservative relic who stubbornly refused to let go of "outdated" music styles. After his death, Bach became a favorite among many of the contemporary composers, e.g. Mozart and Beethoven, which fueled a revival and a new admiration for his works. Johann Sebastian Bach is buried in St. Thomas' Church (Thomaskirche), Leipzig.

Benz, Karl: (b.) Nov. 25, 1844 — (d.) April 4, 1929. Karl Benz was an engineer co-credited with building the first automobile. Initially, he introduced the Benz 3-wheeler— a vehicle powered by a water-cooled internal combustion engine—to the streets of Mannheim in 1885. The following year his prototype received patent #37435. Later, Benz converted the 3-wheeler to a 4-wheel design and subsequently teamed up with Gottlieb Daimler, becoming Daimler-Benz, or more commonly: Mercedes-Benz. The latter name originated from one of Benz's business partners, Emil Jellinek, who had a daughter named Mercedes. In 1899, Benz had 430 workers who churned out 572 cars for the year. By 1904, demand for the automobile increased dramatically and his production swelled to nearly 3500 vehicles. Unlike Gottlieb Daimler, who died in 1900, Karl Benz lived long enough to see the evolution of the automobile grow beyond his wildest dreams. Karl Benz is buried in Ladenburg, 7km northwest of Heidelberg.

Charlemagne: (b.) 742 ~ [circa] ~ (d.) 814. Charlemagne—a.k.a. Karl the Great—was the quintessential emperor, setting the example for all future monarchs in the second millennium. He assumed the title king of the Franks (landlords of present-day France) in 768 A.D. and was later pronounced emperor of the Romans after being crowned by the pope on Christmas Day in the year 800. Charlemagne conquered most of Europe, uniting Christian lands to bolster church power, which paved the way for the 1000-year Holy Roman Empire, or First Reich. Unique to history, Charlemagne was successful in concurrently ruling an empire while acting as head of the church. He unified the Roman, Germanic and Christian cultures that were the necessary building blocks for Europe's progression through the coming centuries. Charlemagne's legacy will undoubtedly live for another 1000 years, and as a testament to his contemporary greatness, several Slavic languages have revised their word for "king" to "Karl"—as in Charlemagne the great. Charlemagne is enshrined in the Dom of Aachen, a truly awesome cathedral!

Dietrich, Marlene: (b.) Dec. 27, 1901 — (d.) May 6, 1992. Actress, singer, entertainer, and mega-movie star in the 1930s and '40s. During the golden years of film production, Hollywood churned out a plethora of real-people icons with class, integrity, and a patriotic love for their country, e.g. Clark Gable (B-17 gunner, who engaged in numerous death-defying missions over Hitler's Germany) • Jimmy Stewart (bomber pilot, who flew umpteen missions over Nazi-occupied Europe) • Bob Hope (founder of the USO and, since 1941, dedicated his life to entertaining GIs) • Marlene Dietrich (entertained U.S. troops, endorsed war bonds, and broadcast anti-Nazi propaganda to Hitler's soldiers). What's ironic about the latter is that Marlene is a German, born in Berlin. Marlene got her start in the local theater and progressed into silent movies. The exotic and alluring starlet with bedroom eyes received her big break in 1929, when she landed a major role in the movie "The Blue Angel." This led Marlene to Hollywood where she often starred as a barmaid or cabaret singer. Some of her movies include "Morocco" (1930) • "The Blonde Venus" (1932) • "Shanghai Express" (1932) • "Destry Rides Again" (1939) • "Follow The Boys" (1944) • "A Foreign Affair" (1948) • and "Judgment at Nuremberg" (1961). During WWII, Dietrich became a powerful propaganda tool for the war effort, selling bonds and performing the song "Lili Marleen" for the GIs. For her efforts to help defeat Nazi Germany, she was awarded the U.S. Medal of Freedom and the Chevalier of the French Legion of Honor. In the 1950s, as Dietrich began to lose roles to younger stars, the film diva added another chapter to her resume by becoming a Las Vegas headliner. Eventually she took her glitzy gowns and fashionable furs all over the world, performing until she was 74. Marvelous Marlene spent the remaining years of her life in Paris, France, where she died in her sleep. She is buried in the Berlin suburb of Friedenau at Stubenrauchstr. 45 (in section 34 of the cemetery)—take subway S41, S42 or U9 to Bundesplatz. Her grave reads: "Here I stand at the end of my days." *Note:* For more of Marlene, the Berlin Film Museum (Deutsche Kinemathek) has a large collection of her personal belongings on display—located at Potsdamer Str. 2, Sony Center. Tel.# 030/ 300-9030. Hours: Tue-Sun 10:00-18:00, Thur till 20:00. Price: adult 6€, student 4€.

Frank, Anne: (b.) June 12, 1929 — (d.) March 1945. A young German-Jew who became world renown for her living-room diary. Anne Frank's grim situation in Nazi-occupied Europe typified the near hopeless plight of the Jews, putting a face on the Holocaust. Anne, the youngest daughter of Edith and Otto Frank, was born in Frankfurt am Main. In 1933, after Hitler's rise to power, the Franks fled Germany to escape the anti-Semitic National Socialist regime—they arrived in Amsterdam hoping the worst was over, Anne was 4 years old. In 1940, Hitler's troops smashed across the Dutch frontier and seized Amsterdam; the Jewish persecution in Holland is about to begin. The following two years were traumatic and frightening as the Nazis tightened the noose around Holland's Jewish population by imposing numerous anti-Semitic laws and initiating surprise roundups. Anne's only mental escape was the diary she received on her 13th birthday from her father, into which she penned her teenage feelings about her family, friends, future and budding adolescence. To elude deportation, the Frank family went into hiding in early July 1942—Anne brought her diary. Months before, Otto Frank had created a "secret annex" above his office (center of Amsterdam, 263 Prinsengracht) to conceal his wife and two daughters if the situation arose. For 25 months, the Franks and another four Jews were holed up in the secret annex, which could only be accessed via a cleverly built revolving bookcase. Their only lifeline was a small group of confidants and Miep Gies— a family friend and one of the central figures in Anne's diary. The Franks fugitive-like status came to an end on August 4, 1944, when their hiding place was betrayed. They were subsequently corralled onto a cattle train bound for Auschwitz (Anne and her sister were later deported to Bergen-Belsen while their mother remained at Auschwitz). After their arrest, Miep Gies searched the secret annex and found Anne's diary. She saved it with the hope of returning it to Anne after the war. Alas, Otto was the only member of the Frank family to survive the Nazi death camps. Upon his return, Miep Gies handed the precious diary to a shattered Otto Frank. "Here is your daughter Anne's legacy to you," Miep said.

Anne Frank was an inquisitive, intelligent, and sparkling child. She was all of 15 years old when she perished (from typhus) in the Bergen-Belsen concentration camp, some three weeks before its liberation. Anne's life has been immortalized through her embracing diary and the preservation of the secret annex as a museum—the "Anne Frank House," with nearly a million visitors per year, is one of Amsterdam's biggest attractions. The diary of Anne Frank has been translated into more than 50 languages, selling some 25 million copies worldwide—in 1959 her story became an award-winning film.

Excerpt from Anne's diary, October 1, 1942: "We are as quiet as baby mice. Who, three months ago, would ever have guessed that Quicksilver Anne would have to sit still for hours—and, what's more, could?"

Anne Frank is buried in a mass grave at Bergen-Belsen concentration camp, 23km northwest of the medieval town of Celle. Her sister, Margot, is with her. _Note:_ To see where Anne was born, flip to page 430—Anne Frank Reflective Walk (do-it-yourself tour).

Frank, Margot: (b.) Feb. 16, 1926 — (d.) March 1945. Anne's older sister, who suffered the same unimaginable fate!

Grimm, (Brothers) Jacob: (b.) Jan. 4, 1785 — (d.) Sept. 20, 1863

Grimm, (Brothers) Wilhelm: (b.) Feb. 24, 1786 — (d.) Dec. 16, 1859. Once upon a fairytale...there were the "Bruder Grimm," two brothers who were born in Hanau and marketed German folklore to the world when they published "Grimm's Fairy Tales" in the mid-19th century. Their works included such legendary fables as "Sleeping Beauty," "Cinderella," "Hansel & Gretel," "Rapunzel," "Little Red Riding Hood," "Rumpelstiltskin," and "Snow White." The brothers were also linguistically inclined, publishing the first volume of the Deutsches Wörterbuch—the standard German dictionary (like Webster's for English)—which has since been revised by contemporary scholars. The brothers are buried side by side in the Berlin suburb of Schöneberg at St.-Matthäus-Kirchhof, section F14 (on street Großgörschenstr.)—ride subway S1 to Yorckstr. _Hours:_ 8:00 until one hour before dusk. _GPS:_ N52° 29.344 - E13° 22.014

Luther, Martin: (b.) Nov. 10, 1483 — (d.) Feb. 18, 1546. Martin Luther, a celebrated theologian who initiated the Protestant Reformation, is recognized as one of the most significant figures in western history. Although his birth and death occurred in Eisleben, he is interred in the Castle Church of Wittenberg (both towns are in the German state of Saxony-Anhalt and hold the commemorative name _Lutherstadt_, or City of Luther).

Richthofen, Manfred von: "The Red Baron" (b.) May 2, 1892 — (d.) April 21, 1918. In the history of aerial combat there is no single name more famous than Manfred von Richthofen, a.k.a. The Red Baron. Not long after the invention of the airplane, Richthofen kicked over the engine of his Albatros, jumped into the cockpit and set a heroic precedent that every future pilot dared to challenge. He mastered the skies with gifted finesse—out of the sun he soared to challenge his opponent, and with each victory The Red Baron became a flyer of legend to both friend and foe.

Richthofen began his WWI career as a cavalry officer on the eastern front in 1914. However, with the advancement of the machine gun came an early exit for soldiers on horseback. Richthofen was soon bored with insignificant combat roles and applied for a position as a fighter pilot. His wish was granted the following year, initially flying reconnaissance missions. It wasn't until some 16 months later that, on September 17, 1916, he scored his first aerial combat victory. Although The Red Baron is best known in the cockpit of his trademark red Fokker triplane, he amassed three-fourths of his aerial victories in a biplane, such as the Albatros DII and DIII. On January 4, 1917, Richthofen scored his 16th aerial victory, making him Germany's top living ace. For his achievements he received Prussia's most prestigious medal: the Pour le Mérite (a.k.a. the Blue Max). He was also given command of Fighter Squadron 11, later dubbed the Flying Circus. On April 21, 1918, less than seven months before the end of the war, The Red Baron impatiently sat in the fabled red triplane while chasing his quarry deep behind enemy lines. The inexperienced pilot in the British Sopwith Camel erratically swayed from side to side as the baron narrowed the gap. Richthofen, about to pounce on his prey, felt a single bullet pass diagonally through his chest. The Red Baron died without celebration as his plane descended gracelessly to the ground and crashed in the French countryside. His body was subsequently retrieved by the British and buried with full military honors. It is commonly believed that the fatal bullet was fired by British ground troops, by reason of the diagonal wound track. *(Note: Hermann Göring, later head of Hitler's Luftwaffe in WWII, succeeded Richthofen as commander of the Flying Circus.)* Manfred von Richthofen, ace of aces with an unprecedented 80 aerial victories, was exhumed from French soil and reburied in his family plot at Südfriedhof in Wiesbaden.

TOMB-LOVERS, WHO'S BURiED WHERE?

A U S T R I A

Beethoven, Ludwig van: (b.) Dec. 17, 1770 — (d.) March 26, 1827. Pianist and composer—considered one of the all-time greats. Among Beethoven's lifetime achievements are one opera ("Fidelio" 1805, revised 1814), nine symphonies, 32 piano sonatas, 10 violin sonatas, and 16 string quartets. He wrote Symphony No. 1 at age 29 and completed his signature composition—Symphony No. 9—in 1824, at age 53, while totally deaf. Beethoven was born in the Rhineland city of Bonn, Germany. His father was a musician who had a weakness for the bottle and his mother was described as a gentle woman with a warm heart. As a young, impressionable teenager, Beethoven set off to visit Vienna, the capital of classical music. It was at this time that he briefly met Mozart. Alas, the trip was cut short when he received a letter explaining that his mother had become deathly ill. Needless to say, he swiftly returned to Bonn. Five years later, in 1792, Beethoven returned to Vienna where he'd remain for the rest of his life. His original intention was to be tutored by Mozart. However, this became impossible with Mozart's death late 1791. Instead, Beethoven became a pupil of Joseph Haydn, the "father of the symphony." During this time, Beethoven first noted his hearing impairment. After the success of Symphony No. 1 in 1800, Beethoven's hearing began to deteriorate and a few years later it was diagnosed as incurable. Mortified by his agonizing disability, he chose not to interact with people and subjected himself, as much as possible, to isolation in the country—he considered his life a wretched existence. He even contemplated suicide, but Beethoven knew he had yet to create his greatest work. By late 1805, accounts of his eccentricities had spread throughout Vienna. He rarely performed in public and he made his last appearance in 1814. With the completion of his first eight symphonies, including the re-release of Fidelio, he was at the pinnacle of his career. The conclusion of Symphony No. 8 marked a 10-year dormant period and the unbearable realization that he had become totally deaf. In 1824, he finished his long-awaited Ninth Symphony. It premiered that May and the crowd reacted as though Beethoven had reached to the heavens and plucked a miracle. A well-received composition usually hailed three standing ovations; Beethoven's Ninth received an unprecedented five rounds of thunderous applause. Completely deaf, he was oblivious to its reception. A nearby musician tugged at his sleeve and directed his gaze to the enthusiastic crowd. He was delighted! Three years later, in 1827, Beethoven died, ending nearly a lifetime of suffering. A testament to the composer's popularity, more than 10,000 people attended his funeral. He is buried in Vienna's Zentralfriedhof (Central Cemetery, page 572). _Hours:_ daily, March-Oct 7:00-18:00 (May-Aug till 19:00), rest of year 8:00-17:00. _Getting There:_ take subway U3 to Simmering, then out front of the station hop on either tram #71 or #6 to "Tor 2" (cemetery's main entrance). Once inside the gate, continue straight some 250 meters to reach Beethoven at Group 32A on the left—look for the small "Musiker" sign. _GPS:_ N48° 09.122 - E16° 26.404. _Drivers_, you can drive through the cemetery for 1.80€.

Beethoven Joke: A grieving family at the cemetery heard some strange noises coming from the area around Beethoven's grave. Concerned, the father sent his son to get the caretaker. When the caretaker arrived, he put his ear to the grave and heard a peculiar melody. Dumbfounded, the caretaker ran off to retrieve the priest.

When the priest arrived, he knelt to the ground and carefully listened. "Hmm... Uh huh... Uh huh..." He uttered, before enthusiastically exclaiming, "I got it! It's Beethoven's Ninth Symphony being played backwards."

He listened a while longer and stated, "There's Symphony No. 8, and it's backwards, too." Mystified, the priest kept listening. "There's No. 7... 6... 5..."

Suddenly, the priest realized what was happening. He stood up and announced to the large crowd that had since gathered: "My fellow brothers and sisters, there's nothing to worry about here...it's just Beethoven decomposing."

Bonaparte, Marie-Louise d'Autriche: (b.) Dec. 12, 1791 — (d.) Dec. 17, 1847. Daughter of (Habsburg) Francis II (last emperor of the Holy Roman Empire) and second wife of Napoleon Bonaparte. With Napoleon's arrival in Vienna came the dissolution of the Holy Roman Empire (formally ending in 1806) and the overthrow of the presiding monarch, Francis II (later Francis I, King of Austria). Moreover, Napoleon forced the hand of Francis II's daughter—Marie-Louise, the beautiful 18-year-old Princess of Austria—in a bid to unify the two former enemy nations. The marriage successfully produced an heir, Napoleon II, a.k.a. the King of Rome, who shockingly committed suicide at the age of 21 in Schönbrunn palace, Vienna. After Napoleon's defeat and subsequent exile (1814), Marie-Louise moved to Parma, Italy, where she remarried. Marie-Louise is buried in Vienna's Imperial Crypt (page 573).

Brahms, Johannes: (b.) May 7, 1833 — (d.) April 3, 1897. Composer, conductor, pianist. Born in Hamburg, Germany, Brahms was considered the second coming of Beethoven. And like Beethoven, Brahms permanently left his native Germany to settle in harmonious Vienna. Shortly after arriving, Brahms put the finishing touches on a score he'd been laboring over for two years: A German Requiem (1868-69), from which he gained continental fame and financial security. With success behind him, he composed his first symphony, which premiered in 1876 to rave reviews. Another three symphonies followed, all of which were warmly accepted. Brahms composed all forms of music except opera, a genre he keenly avoided. Johannes Brahms died of cancer in Vienna at the age of 63. He is buried in the Zentralfriedhof next to Johann Strauss II and meters from Beethoven. For directions, see Beethoven. _GPS:_ N48° 09.122 - E16° 26.404. _Note:_ A colleague of Brahms eulogized the three B's like so: "I believe in Bach, the Father — Beethoven, the Son — and Brahms, the Holy Ghost of music."

Falco: [Hölzel, Hans] (b.) Feb. 19, 1957 — (d.) Feb. 6, 1998. Pop star! A new-age Austrian icon who exploded onto the international charts with blockbusters such as "Rock Me Amadeus" and "Der Kommissar." He surpassed all existing boundaries in Austro-German pop-culture, achieving dizzying new heights that wannabe pop stars could only fantasize about. Falco was born in Vienna to Alois and Maria Hölzel, two lower middle-class wage earners struggling to carve out a living. While Maria was three months pregnant, she began hemorrhaging and was rushed to the maternity ward. She wanted nothing more than to bear a child and was traumatized to learn that she had miscarried her twins. As a result, Maria was kept overnight for observation. After further testing, the doctor miraculously informed her that a baby was still on the way, as she had actually been carrying triplets. Maria could hardly believe her ears. Six months later a superstar was born. In 1986, at 29 years old, Falco was the first German-speaking artist to top the U.S. singles chart, remaining there for three weeks with his smash hit "Rock Me Amadeus." The Amadeus video ran repeatedly on the wildly successful music television network, MTV, while the single saturated the airwaves, played in cinemas, and even gigantic posters notified fans of a Falco hotline they could call. Falco was the first European pop musician to exploit the video culture and conform it to a global audience. During the Amadeus video shoot, filmed in Vienna's Schwarzenberg palace, Falco portrayed Mozart as a modern new wave virtuoso, while bearded bikers acted as his bodyguards. Twelve years later, those same bikers paid him their final respects as pallbearers. On February 6, 1998, Falco died in a car accident in the Dominican Republic. The album he was working on at the time of his death, "Out of the Dark," was released posthumously—two songs from the CD entered the charts: "Out of the Dark" and "Egoist." Falco is buried in Vienna's Zentralfriedhof (Central Cemetery; flip to page 572 for more info). *Plot:* (central part of) Group 40; look for the 9-foot-tall red-marble sphere. Also of interest in Group 40 are memorials to victims of the Nazi regime. *GPS:* N48° 08.855 - E16° 26.622

Habsburg, Empress Elisabeth "Sisi": (b.) Dec. 24, 1837 — (d.) Sept. 10, 1898. Born into the Wittelsbach royal family of Bavaria, Sisi was the beautiful daughter of Duke Maximilian and, most famously, the cousin of the fairy-tale king, Ludwig II. She gained international celebrity status when Austria's Habsburg emperor, Franz Josef I, chose her to be his wife—when she was just 16 years old! They married on April 24, 1854, in Vienna's Augustinian Church. Although Sisi was the First Lady of Europe's most influential dynasty, she lived a depressing life with an uncaring and absent husband—hence she is often referred to as the Princess Diana of the 19th century. After four decades of discontent, Sisi was murdered in Switzerland at the age of 60. She is buried in Vienna's Imperial Crypt (page 573), next to Franz Josef I.

Habsburg, Franz Josef I: (b.) Aug. 18, 1830 — (d.) Nov. 21, 1916. Franz Josef I reigned as Austria's emperor for a whopping 68 years from 1848 to 1916, officially qualifying as the longest governing monarch in Austrian history and the second longest in Europe, after the Sun King, Louis XIV. Franz Josef I is buried in Vienna's Imperial Crypt (page 573), flanked by his (murdered) wife Sisi and their son Rudolf, who committed suicide at the age of 30.

Habsburg, Maria Theresa: (b.) May 13, 1717 — (d.) Nov. 29, 1780. Maria Theresa—Holy Roman empress (1740-80), Archduchess of Austria, Queen of Hungary and Bohemia—became the only female sovereign in the 640-year history of the Habsburg dynasty. Preceding her reign was Charles VI, Maria's father, who shrewdly protected the future of Habsburg rule by declaring the famed Pragmatic Sanction of 1713, which overturned an archaic law that prohibited a female from succeeding her father to the throne. Consequently, the oldest daughter of Charles VI—Maria Theresa—inherited the crown upon her father's death. She achieved her imperial tasks with high praise and is duly noted as one of the great reformists of the 18th century. Surprisingly, though, Maria was pregnant much of the time—giving birth to 16 children. Two of their names may ring a bell: Marie-Antoinette—later queen of France (1774-92)—and Joseph II—co-ruler/successor of the Habsburg throne (1765-90) and who was portrayed in the movie "Amadeus" (near end of film) as the cordial emperor. Maria Theresa is buried with her husband, Francis I, in an elaborate double tomb in Vienna's Imperial Crypt (page 573). In stark contrast, notice the simple box in which their son and emperor, Josef II, rests.

Mozart, Constanze Weber: (b.) Jan. 6, 1763 — (d.) March 6, 1842. Here lies the wife of the great Wolfgang Amadeus Mozart. Initially, Wolfgang was dating the opera singer Aloysia Weber—Constanze's sister—before he attempted the boldly confident switch-a-roo sibling move. Wolfgang's father, Leopold Mozart, loathed Constanze. In a letter to his father, Wolfgang affectionately described Constanze in a plea to inspire a family-like relationship between the two: *"She is not ugly, but at the same time, far from beautiful. Her beauty consists of two little black eyes and a nice figure. She isn't witty, but has enough common sense to make her a good wife and mother.... She understands house-keeping and has the kindest heart in the world. I love her and she loves me..."* The plea fell on deaf ears and the two parties never reconciled their differences. After Wolfgang's death, Constanze met and eventually married Nikolaus von Nissen, a Danish diplomat. Constanze is buried in St. Sebastian's church cemetery, Salzburg—ironically, next to Leopold Mozart. Not only does the placement of these two bitter adversaries side by side drive one's curiosity, but also Leopold must be turning in his grave since Constanze's headstone hugely dwarfs his. *Hours:* (cemetery) daily, 9:00-16:00 (summer till 18:30). *Getting There:* see page 482 for directions. *GPS:* N47° 48.259 - E13° 02.847

Mozart, Leopold: (b.) Nov. 14, 1719 — (d.) May 28, 1787. Respected composer, violin teacher, and father of the great "Wolfgang Amadeus." Leopold was born in Augsburg, Germany, to middle-class parents, Johann Georg Mozart, a bookbinder, and Anna Maria, a homemaker. Leopold left Augsburg at the age of 17 to attend university studies in Salzburg. It is here that he lived for the rest of his life, becoming a court composer and deputy Kapellmeister for the prince archbishop. Having a secure job, Leopold married his true love, Anna Maria Pertl, in 1747. She gave birth seven times while living in their modest third-floor apartment at Getreidegasse 9—only two survived infancy: Maria Anna (Nannerl) and Wolfgang Amadeus. While Nannerl showed signs of a promising career as a musician, Wolfgang left no doubt in anyone's mind that he was a musical genius. Leopold was so proud of his son that he sacrificed his own career as a composer to coach young Amadeus. But as Wolfgang grew older, his desire for individuality and indepen-dence put him at odds with his domineering father. Alas, the two grew apart after the passing of Anna Maria Pertl and Wolfgang's marriage to Constanze. During this trau-matic period, Leopold new he needed his son more than ever. Fortunately, in 1785, he was able to travel to Vienna, where Wolfgang had moved, to see him one last time. Leopold is buried in St. Sebastian's church cemetery, Salzburg—next to Constanze (see previous entry). *Hours:* (cemetery) daily, 9:00-16:00 (summer till 18:30). *Getting There:* see page 482 for directions. *GPS:* N47° 48.259 - E13° 02.847

Mozart, Wolfgang Amadeus: (b.) Jan. 27, 1756 — (d.) Dec. 5, 1791. Regarded as one of the greatest composers of all time, Mozart worked in all musical genres of his era, producing an extraordinary amount of compositions (considering his short life). By the time Mozart died at age 35, he had composed 27 piano concertos, 23 string quartets, 17 piano sonatas, more than 50 symphonies, and six major operas, notably "The Marriage of Figaro" (1786), "Don Giovanni" (1787), and "The Magic Flute" (1791). What is perhaps most amazing of all is that Mozart died penniless and was unceremoniously tossed into a commoner's grave for a large amount of people. Except for the gravedigger and the priest, no one showed up for his funeral, not even his wife! A monument has been erected in St. Marx Cemetery, Vienna, on the approximate spot where he is believed to be buried. St. Marx Cemetery is located in the suburb of St. Marx, 3km southeast of central Vienna—a visit is worthwhile. Unique is the fact that the cemetery was closed to burials in 1874; therefore the graveyard appears as it did in the 19th century, presenting an age-old setting of sunken headstones, worn markings, and spiders tending to their intricate webs. <u>*GPS:*</u> N48° 11.031 - E16° 24.200 (coordinates to cemetery gate). To reach Mozart, ascend main path straight and before the cross follow the "Mozart Grab" sign left. To find St. Marx Cemetery, see page 572 for directions. <u>*Note:*</u> Mozart is the spunky lad depicted on the back of Austria's 1€ coin.

Salieri, Antonio: (b.) Aug. 19, 1750 — (d.) May 7, 1825. Composer, teacher, and self-alleged murderer of Mozart; this is the guy portrayed narrating the movie "Amadeus." Born in Italy, Salieri moved to Vienna and was well respected for his musical prowess. He became the Habsburg court composer as well as an instructor—his list of students included such masters as Beethoven, Schubert and Franz Liszt. Despite his respectable achievements, Salieri is mostly remembered for his rivalry with Mozart. On his deathbed, he allegedly confessed to poisoning Mozart out of jealousy—although, there is no real evidence to support this. Antonio Salieri is buried in the Zentralfriedhof, Vienna. For directions, see Beethoven. <u>*Plot:*</u> Group 0 (upon entering "Tor 2," go left some 200 meters, passing an administration building and following the path paralleling the wall. Once you reach the graves, he is located midway along the wall). <u>*GPS:*</u> N48° 09.214 - E16° 26.680

Schubert, Franz Peter: (b.) Jan 31, 1797 — (d.) Nov 19, 1828. Composer, pianist, violinist, and coffeehouse songwriter. The son of a schoolmaster, Schubert was born, raised, and died in harmonious Vienna. Regardless of his short life, Schubert worked in all musical genres of his era—except opera—producing more than 950 works, including masses, string quartets, piano sonatas, nine symphonies and 600 songs. Despite his impressive achievements, Schubert lived in relative obscurity and his romanticism didn't become fashionable until after his death. At around the age of 25 Schubert picked up a dose of syphilis, which ultimately stole his life. Franz Schubert died at the age of 31 and is buried between Beethoven and Johann Strauss II in the Zentralfriedhof, Vienna. For directions, see Beethoven.

Strauss, Johann I: (b.) March 14, 1804 — (d.) Sept. 25, 1849. Master fiddler and chairman of the "first family of the waltz." The son of a Viennese innkeeper, Strauss acquired his passion for music from the numerous musicians performing at the family inn. At the age of 21 he formed an orchestra, and throughout the 1830s they embarked on a European tour performing in Paris—among other places—and London, where he played for the newly crowned Queen Victoria. Back in his native Vienna, 1846, Strauss was honored with the title K.u.K. Hofballmusikdirektor (Imperial and Royal Court Music Director for Balls), created especially for him. After receiving such an exalted position, Strauss' waltzes and polkas were in high demand. The following year he composed his most famous piece: the Radetzky March. Months later, Johann Strauss I passed away at the age of 45. He is buried in the Zentralfriedhof, Vienna, (left of and right around the corner from his famous son, Strauss II). For directions, see Beethoven.

Strauss, Johann II: (b.) Oct. 25, 1825 — (d.) June 3, 1899. King of waltz! Strauss II was born the first of three boys to a prominent Viennese musician, Strauss I, who had already decided that one artist in the family was enough. Although Strauss the elder went to great lengths to keep his sons from following in his footsteps, all three—Strauss II, Josef (1827-1870), and Eduard (1835-1916)—achieved success as musicians. Credit is due to the boys' mother, who arranged for secret music lessons. In 1844, at the age of 18, Strauss II performed his first concert at Café Dommayer (one block west of Schönbrunn palace). The audience—enthralled by his extraordinary talent—demanded an unprecedented 19 encores, and for the finale Strauss II played one of his father's waltzes. Strauss II maintained throughout his life that his father had always been the motivating force behind his passion for music. There's no greater testimony to the stardom of the waltz king than the buzz around Vienna proclaiming that the Habsburg emperor reigned as long as Strauss II lived. His spirited waltzes and racy gallops mesmerized listeners into a set of swirling revolutions on the dance floor and made Lipizzaner stallions prance at the Spanish Riding School. His legendary waltz, "The Blue Danube," is easily one of the most familiar classical compositions ever written. Other greats include "Vienna Blood," "Emperor Waltz," "Cuckoo Polka," and the celebrated operetta, "Die Fledermaus" (The Bat, 1874). Johann Strauss II is buried next to Brahms, and near Beethoven, in the Zentralfriedhof, Vienna. For directions, see Beethoven.

Vivaldi, Antonio: (b.) March 4, 1678 — (d.) July 28, 1741. Baroque composer, violin maestro, teacher and priest. Vivaldi was born in Venice, Italy, the son of a violinist at Saint Mark's Cathedral. In 1703, the 25-year-old Venetian with cinnamon hair was ordained as a priest and subsequently began teaching music to orphaned girls at the Ospedale della Pietà—a position he held for nearly four decades while simultaneously establishing a reputation in Europe for his heavenly concertos. In 1740—at the twilight of his career—Vivaldi moved to Vienna, where he died the following year at age 63. His burial took place at the Spitaller Gottesacker Cemetery, which neighbored St. Charles' Church. The cemetery was abandoned in 1783, and the Vienna University of Technology was later built on the grounds—thus no one knows exactly where Vivaldi is interred. A plaque on the university building, dedicated in 1978 on the 300th anniversary of his birth, commemorates the approximate burial site (when facing the front of the technical university on Karlsplatz, go left and the plaque is around the corner). Vivaldi's most recognized work is the Four Seasons (1725—Opus 8, 12 violin concertos). However, all of his music is wonderfully divine. _GPS_: N48° 11.928 - E16° 22.250

TOMB-LOVERS, WHO'S BURiED WHERE?

WWII Buffs

<u>Galland, Adolf:</u> (b.) March 19, 1912 — (d.) Feb. 9, 1996. Luftwaffe fighter ace who, at the age of 29, became the youngest general on either side in WWII. Adolf Galland is arguably the most famous of all German pilots in the Second World War, not because of his number of aerial combat victories, which totaled 104, but because of his individual personality and chivalry in combat, earning himself the lasting respect of his comrades and adversaries, as well as a special place in the history of aviation. A testament to Galland's accomplishments was best put by the distinguished U.S. air force general James Doolittle: "Without any doubt the German Luftwaffe produced a lot of skilled fighter aces, however, only one Adolf Galland."

Galland was more proficient in aerial combat, strategy, and tactics than many of the experts twice his age. He was also known for tinkering with the Bf 109 Messerschmitts he flew, e.g. enhancing their firepower, improving the cockpit armor, and even adding a cigar lighter. Since childhood, Galland was fascinated with aviation. He initially built model airplanes, which progressed into physically flying gliders at the age of 16. (Gliders were mega-popular in post-WWI Germany because the Versailles Treaty limited the production of engine-propelled aircraft.) Galland made himself known to the enemy in 1940, during the Battle of Britain, when he scored more than 50 aerial combat victories. At the end of this legendary conflict, Galland bestowed the ultimate praise upon British aircraft designers when Hermann Göring asked him what the Germans needed to muster a victory. Galland replied, "The Spitfire."

During Galland's career he was shot down four times, twice in one day! Near the end of the war, Hitler commissioned Galland to form a squadron comprised solely of the world's first operational jet fighter, the ME 262. With Hitler's blessing, Galland created the legendary fighter squadron "Jagdverband 44," which incorporated the Luftwaffe's cream-of-the-crop pilots. By this time, though, the war was conceivably lost and the fighter squadron achieved only moderate success. Galland was captured at an airfield in Salzburg (May 1945) and subsequently spent two years in prison. In 1948, he was employed by Argentina as an air-force consultant, eventually returning to Germany in 1955. At his funeral (in 1996) air-force officers, past and present, paid their respects, including Galland's American interrogation officer—Captain John Witten—who came a long way to bid farewell to a man he became friends with after the war. General Galland is interred in the town cemetery of Oberwinter, Germany, (4km north of Remagen, 10km south of Bonn). After entering the graveyard (through rusty gate across from bus stop and park area) go left and follow the gravel path until it becomes paved; ascend path and make the fourth left—he's fourth from the end on left. *GPS:* N50° 36.847 - E7° 12.227

Hartmann, Erich: (b.) April 19, 1922 — (d.) Sept. 20, 1993. With an unimaginable 352 aerial combat victories, Erich Hartmann is the world's unrivaled "ace of aces." Most all of his kills were tallied against Russian pilots on the Eastern Front, 1942-45. Due to Erich's snow-white hair and extraordinary aviation skills, he was labeled the Blond Knight of Germany. However, his squadron mates affectionately called him "Bubi" on account of his baby face. After the war, Hartmann was sentenced to 10 years in a Soviet labor camp. Upon his release, he returned to Germany and was reunited with his wife. Afterwards, he took a position in the newly formed German air force, where he served until the early 1970s. Erich Hartmann is buried in the Neue Friedhof, Weil im Schön-buch, Böblingen, Germany, (some 8km southwest of Stuttgart).

Hitler, Alois: (b.) June 7, 1837 — (d.) Jan. 3, 1903. Adolf's parents, Alois and Klara, are buried together in the old church cemetery of Leonding, Austria, a suburb of Linz (90-min drive northeast of Salzburg). If you enter the cemetery at the side of the church you will find the pair midway along the wall on the right beneath the full-grown tree. If you're wondering where Adolf is buried, nobody knows. For more on Alois and Klara, see page 218.

Hitler, Klara: (b.) Aug. 20, 1860 — (d.) Dec. 21, 1907. Klara gave birth six times during her marriage to Alois, only two survived childhood: Adolf and Paula. Klara is buried with her husband, Alois. For more info on Alois and Klara, flip to page 218.

Hitler, Paula: (b.) Jan. 21, 1896 — (d.) June 1, 1960. Adolf's little sister, Paula, seven years his junior, lived in Vienna for many years and later moved to Berchtesgaden in the 1950s under the assumed name of Wolff. She never married or had children. Paula was interred in Berchtesgaden's Bergfriedhof (Mountain Cemetery) until mid-2005, when church administration allowed her remains to be buried over (presumably because nobody paid the "rent" due on her grave, which in Germany means you're evicted).

Jodl, Alfred: (b.) May 10, 1890 — (d.) Oct. 16, 1946. Operations chief for Hitler's Wehrmacht, or armed forces. Alfred Jodl began his long-serving military career in the army as an artillery officer after graduating from Munich's cadet school in 1910. During WWI he saw action on both fronts, eastern and western, and was injured twice. After the war, Jodl remained in the 100,000-strong German military allowed by the Versailles Treaty. In the mid-'20s Jodl met Hitler while the Nazi party was a fledgling band of anti-Semitic radicals. This early relationship paid dividends when Hitler was sworn in as the nation's chancellor on January 30, 1933, from which time Jodl began rapidly accelerating through the ranks. By August 1939, he had risen to the exalted position of operations chief of Germany's armed forces. Jodl proved himself invaluable during Hitler's con-quest of Europe, tirelessly planning campaigns and emphatically keeping the gears of the Nazi juggernaut oiled. A week after Hitler's suicide, Jodl's diligent efforts led him to Reims, France, as Karl Dönitz's representative to sign Nazi Germany's unconditional surrender on May 7, 1945. In the end, Jodl's hear-no-evil see-no-evil approach to Hitler's notorious modus operandi earned him a death sentence in 1946 at the Nürnberg trials. Jodl was accused of conspiracy to commit crimes against peace, crimes against humanity, war crimes, as well as planning, initiating and waging wars of aggression. He was found guilty on all accounts and subsequently hanged. Ironically, seven years later, a German arbitration board posthumously acquitted Jodl of all charges. Alfred Jodl is buried in the church cemetery (adjacent to convent) on the idyllic Fraueninsel (Isle of Women)—adjacent to Herreninsel (Isle of Men), where King Ludwig II built his third and last palace: Herrenchiemsee—in the middle of Lake Chiemsee, 75km south of Munich.

Rommel, Erwin: (b.) Nov. 15, 1891 — (d.) Oct. 14, 1944. General Field Marshal Rommel, renowned military strategist celebrated for leading his Afrika Korps to astonishing victories during the desert campaigns of WWII. He earned lasting respect from his troops and adversaries alike as "The Desert Fox" for his ingenious tactics on the battlefield, successfully driving the inflexible British Army across North Africa from Libya to El-'Alamein, Egypt, in a mere two months (May-July 1942). However, the victories were short lived—Hitler subsequently neglected the North African campaign, absorbing himself instead with the nearly impossible task of conquering Mother Russia. Hitler wastefully threw hundreds of divisions into battle on the Eastern Front when Rommel never had any more than four German divisions at his disposal. After forcibly retreating from North Africa, Rommel was given command of Army Group B in Italy for a short stint before being awarded the hopeless task of fortifying the Atlantic Wall from Denmark to Spain against the impending Allied invasion. After D-Day, June 6, 1944, Rommel urged Hitler to end the war. The Führer wouldn't commit and Rommel allegedly established contact with Stauffenberg's resistance group that planned to snuff out Hitler. When the assassination plot failed on July 20, 1944, Hitler exacted his revenge with the viciousness of 100 enraged lions and sentenced thousands of presumed conspirators to death. Rommel was one of those implicated in the plot and consequently Hitler offered him two choices: (1) commit suicide and be given a state funeral befitting of a field marshal, or (2) face charges of high treason and forgo financial—as well as physical—security for his family. Rommel elected the former: suicide.

Erwin Rommel is buried in the town cemetery of Herrlingen, Germany, 9km west of Ulm. After your visit, ascend the nearby (road) Erwin-Rommel-Steige past his former house and onto the dirt track where his life ended—eventually on the right you'll pass a stone memorial, "Rommel Gedenkstein." On this massive stone is a granite plaque with Rommel's name engraved and a steel hatch from a panzer tank that reads, "He was forced to commit suicide by taking poison in a car on the (road) Wippinger Steige to save his family from the evils of a brutal regime. With this conscious decision inhumanity was defeated."

Schirach, Baldur von: (b.) May 9, 1907—(d.) Aug. 8, 1974. Head of the Hitler Youth and later Gauleiter (district boss) of Vienna. Although born in Berlin, Schirach had a good feel for U.S. culture along with the English language courtesy of his American mother. Despite his democratic upbringing, he joined the radical Nazi party in 1925. Schirach's tight relationship with Hitler was further strengthened in 1932 when he married Henriette Hoffmann, the daughter of Adolf's personal photographer, Heinrich Hoffman. The following year, when Hitler became the chancellor of Germany, Schirach was appointed leader of the Reich's Hitler Youth (HY). Upon the outset of WWII, Schirach briefly parted from his post as HY leader to prove his worth in combat; for his actions he was awarded the Iron Cross 2nd class. In 1940, he fell out of grace with Hitler and was demoted to Vienna as Gauleiter. *(Both Schirach and his wife, Henriette, complained to Hitler about his inhumane policies toward minorities, Jews in particular. Hitler was not impressed! Arthur Axmann subsequently replaced Schirach as HY leader).*

Curiously, a year later (perhaps to get back in with Hitler) Schirach deported 185,000 Jews out of Vienna to the east. During the Nürnberg trials (1946), Schirach adamantly claimed that he did not know of their destiny. The court remotely believed his tale and instead of death, he was sentenced to 20 years in jail. He served his time in Berlin's Spandau prison, built to hold 600 inmates. By special agreement, the prison was reserved to detain the last seven members of the Hitler gang: Rudolf Hess, Albert Speer, Walter Funk, Konstantin von Neurath, Erich Raeder, Karl Dönitz, and Schirach. Spandau prison was ultimately torn down after the last inmate, Rudolf Hess, died (via suicide) in 1987— it is now a parking lot and grocery store.

Baldur von Schirach is buried in the ultra-quaint German Riesling town of Kröv an der Mosel (page 286), in the cemetery behind the church. *GPS:* N49° 58.856 - E7° 05.368 Enter cemetery on right side of church and ascend the steps to the last one; then continue straight to the fourth row on the left and Schirach is the second one in. His grave reads, *Ich war einer von euch.* (I was one of you.) *Note:* Three rows behind Schirach, i.e. the top and last row, are German soldiers who died during WWII—one marker honors three brothers. Lastly, 280 meters down from the church (on same side of road), you'll find the yellow facade belonging to the former Hotel MontRoyal (out of business), where Schirach lived the last years of his life.

Stauffenberg, Claus von: (b.) Nov. 15, 1907 — (d.) July 20, 1944. No WWII burial directory would be complete without Claus von Stauffenberg. He is the heroic symbol of the German resistance movement opposed to the brutal Nazi regime. Stauffenberg was the key figure who organized the ill-fated July Plot to kill Hitler, codenamed *Valkyrie*. Claus von Stauffenberg was born in the country town of Jettingen (25km southwest of Stuttgart) into a long line of devout Catholics and one of the oldest aristocratic families in southern Germany. In the spring of 1926, at 18 years old, he joined the Imperial 17th Cavalry Regiment in Bamberg. After Hitler's rise to power in 1933, Stauffenberg completed a short stint with the SA (storm troops) before transferring back to the cavalry, which later converted to a mechanized division. During WWII, he served with distinction in the east, west and in North Africa (1943) with the (retreating) Afrika Korps, where an Allied aircraft strafed his scout vehicle, resulting in the loss of his right hand, two fingers from the left hand, and his left eye. While laid up for several months in a hospital, Stauffenberg considered his future. He had become disillusioned with Hitler's heavy-handed, unethical policies and concluded there was only one solution: coup d'état! He was burning to act. After his convalescence, he was posted to the War Ministry on Bendlerstrasse in Berlin. This gave him direct access to Hitler; and it was from there that the anticipated coup d'état became a lethal plan of action. Operation Valkyrie, the plan's codename, was really the contingency plan for the Home Army to assume control of the Reich in the event of an unforeseen disaster that severed communications with Hitler's headquarters. Ironically, the plan that Hitler himself had approved to secure order was now the resistance's secret weapon to eliminate him. On the morning of July 20, 1944, Stauffenberg flew from Berlin to the Wolf's Lair—Hitler's HQ—in East Prussia (present-day Poland). Around 12:35, he entered the war room where Hitler was about to conduct a meeting, placed his explosives-laden briefcase under the table next to Hitler and then nonchalantly exited the room. Nearby, he waited (about seven minutes) until the explosion ripped through the war room—he was convinced that no one had survived. *(What Stauffenberg couldn't have known was that someone had coincidently moved his briefcase to the other side of Hitler, behind one of the table's thick wooden legs.)* During the confusion resulting from the bomb blast, Stauffenberg motored out of the compound via a waiting car and flew back to the War Ministry on Bendlerstrasse to mobilize the Home Army and set up the new government. By the time he arrived in Berlin, word was out that Hitler had survived the explosion (24 people were in the room, 4 died). Shocked,

Stauffenberg refused to believe the dubious news. Roughly 30 minutes later (approx. 17:00), Stauffenberg's worst nightmare came true: Hitler broadcasted a live radio message from the Wolf's Lair announcing he was okay and that the traitors were to be apprehended at once. Late that evening Claus von Stauffenberg, along with three co-conspirators, was executed on Bendlerstrasse in the War Ministry's courtyard. On July 20, 1955, for the 10-year anniversary, Bendlerstrasse was ceremoniously renamed "Stauffenbergstrasse." Today, the former War Ministry is the German Resistance Memorial (page 380) and in its courtyard are plaques marking the execution spot to commemorate those who fearlessly confronted the demonic National Socialistic regime. After the execution, Hitler ordered Stauffenberg's body to be cremated and his ashes scattered over a nondescript field.

Notes

AUSTRIA
(Österreich)

Austria (84,000 sq km) is roughly the same size as South Carolina (81,000 sq km).

Capital: Vienna (Wien)

Language: German, with varying dialect from state to state.

Population: just over 8 million (nearly one out of four Austrians live in the nation's capital, Vienna). Austria is divided into 9 Bundesländer, or federal states.

Burgenland: pop. 280,000 — capital is Eisenstadt
Carinthia (Kärnten): pop. 565,000 — capital is Klagenfurt
Salzburgland: pop. 520,000 — capital is Salzburg
Styria (Steiermark): pop. 1.2 million — capital is Graz
Tyrol (Tirol): pop. 670,000 — capital is Innsbruck
Vorarlberg: pop. 350,000 — capital is Bregenz
Vienna (Wien): pop. 1.8 million — capital is Vienna
Lower Austria (Niederösterreich): pop. 1.5 million — capital is St. Pölten
Upper Austria (Oberösterreich): Pop. 1.4 million — capital is Linz

Emergency Telephone Numbers: Known as a *Notruf* (pronounced note roof, meaning emergency call), the following numbers can be dialed free of charge Austria-wide.

Fire dept. (Feuerwehr) = 122
Police (Polizei) = 133
Ambulance/Rescue = 144

Unemployment Rate: 5.15%, or 312,000 (Nov. 2005)

Religion: 78% Roman Catholic, Protestant 5%, other 17%

Elevation: *Highest point:* Gross Glockner—3797m/12,454ft—is Austria's highest mountain, located 100km/60mi south of Salzburg. *Lowest point:* Neusiedler See—115m/377ft—is a lake located 30km/19mi southeast of Vienna, partially bordering Hungary.

National Anthem: *Land der Berge, Land am Strome* (Land of Mountains, Land of Rivers).

Flag: Austria's flag consists of three equal horizontal bands: red, white, red. Bavarians say it's designed that way so Austrians can't make the mistake of hanging it upside down. Actually, the Austrian flag is one of the oldest in the world, dating from 1191, when Duke Leopold V fought in the Battle of Acre during the Third Crusade. The only part of the duke's clothing not stained red by blood was a white band beneath his belt.

Executive Branch:
  President (Heinz Fischer): Largely ceremonial post. Elected by popular vote for a six-year term.
  Chancellor (Wolfgang Schüssel): Traditionally chosen by the president from the majority party in the National Council.

Facts:
- Austria's national holiday is October 26 (independence declared in 1955).
- More than 15 million people fly in/out of Vienna's Schwechat airport per year.
- In 1995, Austria became a member of the European Union (EU).

Austrian Tourist Office: (www.austria.info) P.O. Box 1142, New York, NY 10108-1142. *Tel.#* (USA) 1-212-944-6880, (Canada) 1-416-967-3381

Austrian Rail Authority: www.oebb.at

Calling Austria: (international country code: **43**)
For our example, let's say we are trying to call this tel. number in Salzburg: 0662/123456. *Note:* 0662 is the city code; drop the 0 when dialing from outside of Austria. All area codes in this book are separated from the local number by a back slash (/).
  To call Austria from another country in Europe you must first dial the international access code: 00 (from USA/Canada 011), then the country code: 43. From the USA and Canada you would dial the above number like so: 011-43-662/123456
  From inside Europe, 0043-662/123456
  From inside Austria, 0662/123456
  While in Salzburg, 123456

Austrian (City) Tel. Codes: Bregenz 05574, Eisenstadt 02682, Graz 0316, Innsbruck 0512, Klagenfurt 0463, Linz 0732, Salzburg 0662, St. Pölten 02742, Vienna 01.

Drivers: The law requires that you have an international driver's license to drive in Austria ($10-$15 from your local auto club). The maximum speed limit on the Austrian autobahn is 130 kilometers per hour (kph). And to drive on this efficient motorway you are required to have what's called a *Vignette*, or toll sticker. You can obtain this little decal at most any gas station approaching the border. *Price:* 10 days 7.60€, two months 22€, one year 73€. *Note:* Affix the Vignette to the inside corner of your windshield or behind the rear-view mirror. (Your rental car may already have a toll sticker from the previous renters, but don't be fooled—it's most likely expired.) If you happen to get pulled over without a Vignette, the fine will be upwards of 150€, on the spot!

FM4: Broadcasted nationwide from Vienna, tune in FM4 from early a.m. till early afternoon for English commentary, including news on the hour. "The Morning Show"—from 6:00-10:00 with Stuart Freeman—is a gas. Music can sometimes be out there, but the commentary is interesting. The extended team is Hal Rock, Duncan Larkin and Christine Pawlowsky, who do a reputable, charismatic job. What's more, if you're saddled with a head-pounding hangover on a Sunday morning, listen to "Sunny Side Up" with John Megill from 10:00-12:00 to help ease the pain.
  Frequencies: Salzburg/Chiemsee 104.6, Bad Ischl 105.1, Linz 104.0 & 102.0, St. Pölten 98.8, Vienna 103.8 & 91.0, Graz 101.7, Innsbruck 101.4 & 102.5.

SALZBURG

~ Population: 145,000 ~ Elevation: 450m/1480ft
~ Country/Area Code: +43-(0)662

In 17 A.D. the Romans settled Juvavum (Seat of the Sky God), a majestic outpost on the banks of a jade-green river that bisected the forested Mönchsberg (Monks' Ridge) and the Kapuzinerberg (Capuchins' Ridge). It didn't take long for the Romans to discover the region's most valuable commodity: salt.

They used it abundantly as a medicine — doctoring virtually every illness conceivable — and in their baths as a vaporinhalation treatment. Salt was also used as a food preservative, and the Romans even paid their legionnaires with the "white gold" — hence the term we use today, "salary" (from the Latin "salarium," referring to the salt allotment issued to Roman soldiers for money). Juvavum blossomed and the population swelled to 15,000. By the year 477, the once vast and mighty Roman Empire had collapsed and Juvavum fell to nomadic tribes.

In 696 A.D., the Catholic Church dispatched Bishop Rupert from the German city of Worms to form a diocese on the ruins of Juvavum. He founded St. Peter's monastery, bringing peace and prosperity to the region—from these pious roots came the first archbishop (Virgil) and the community's new name: Salzburg (Salt Castle, first mentioned in 755 A.D.). Appropriately, the jade-green river flowing through Salzburg was also given a name: Salzach, or Salt River—not because of any salt content, but for the prosperous river trade that transported the "white gold" downstream to the Inn River, which flowed into the Danube River and eventually the Black Sea and into the coffers of powerful Asian rulers. Bishop Rupert's city of salt flourished, and Salzburg over the next 1000 years became a wealthy archbishopric, an independent principality ruled by the archbishop.

In 1803, Napoleon's troops arrived and secularized the millennium-old diocese, forcing the last archbishop (Hieronymus) to flee to Vienna. It wasn't until 1816 that Salzburg actually became part of Austria.

More than a century later, Austria joined forces with Hitler's ill-fated Third Reich, consequently attracting swarms of Allied aircraft to the city of salt. From October 1944 till the end of WWII (May 1945), there were 16 bombing raids over Salzburg totaling some 750 bombers (mainly B24s), leaving 46% of the city's buildings either lightly or heavily damaged. However, Salzburg didn't take long to recover and today the antique settlement on the Salt River has never looked better. What's more, since 1996, Salzburg's Altstadt has taken its place alongside the historic Old Towns of Brugge, Belgium • Dubrovnik, Croatia • and Florence, Italy as an esteemed member of UNESCO's World Heritage List. For this reason, Salzburg's Old Town has largely been pedestrianized and its buses are smog-free, powered by electricity. Tourism is the city's No. 1 money-spinner, attracting more than 7 million visitors annually. I—your humble author—have personally escorted some 6000 guests through Salzburg, and *not one was ever disappointed!*

~ **Use Salzburg as your base to tour regional attractions; thus we suggest at least a three-day stay. Mood and weather permitting, divide your time like so,**

Day 1: Begin early; buy the *Salzburg Card and visit "Sights" of interest. (*Note: All attractions listed in the Sights section are *FREE* with the Salzburg Card—see *Salzburg Card*, page 473). Sound of Music fans combine sightseeing with our S.O.M. do-it-yourself walking tour (page 506). Conclude your day on the SteinTerrasse (see *Best Views*, page 484).

Day 2: Travel 23km southwest to the Bavarian village of Berchtesgaden (page 230) to tour the Eagle's Nest, Königssee (King's Lake), and/or salt mines. Pack a picnic lunch, or pop into the hotel-restaurant Watzmann for a yummy meal.

Day 3: Either — head south to the alpine village of Werfen to experience the lofty ice caves and medieval fortress (pages 494-95) or — head east for the day to ogle the Salzkammergut (page 496), arguably the world's most beautiful "lake district".

Day 4: Consider staying an extra day to realize both options listed for day 3. You won't regret it.

Tourist Information: [TI] (www.salzburginfo.at) *Tel.#* 0662/8898-7330
Salzburg has a trio of TIs. *Mozartplatz TI* is the most centrally located, accessible to all. *Hbf TI* is most convenient for Railers, and the *Süd TI* is best suited for Drivers. The TI offers basic maps of the city for free and a detailed, not-so-necessary foldout version for 70¢. Room-finding service, 2.20€.

TI: Mozartplatz. Hours: (closed Sundays in winter—Nov thru March—otherwise) daily 9:00-18:00. This branch has a ticket agency attached.

TI: Hbf (main train station), adjacent to track 2. Hours: daily 8:45-19:30 (mid-June thru mid-Sept 8:15-20:00).

TI: Süd is situated at the Park+Ride about 4km off the A10 autobahn (exit Salzburg Süd). Hours: (may change, call ahead to verify) Easter thru Sept, Advent weekends and New Year Mon-Sat 10:00-16:30, July/Aug daily 9:00-19:00.

Emergency Tel. Numbers: [Austria-wide]
Fire dept. (Feuerwehr) = 122
Police (Polizei) = 133
Ambulance/Rescue = 144

Railers: Salzburg's Hauptbahnhof, or main train station, is smallish and overly scenic upon arrival (especially from the east). The *TI* can be found adjacent to track 2. *Train info* and *ticket purchase* are located in the transit area, street level. (Normal adult price, one way, via rail from Salzburg to Vienna is 40€, 3.5hr—to Innsbruck 32€, 2hr—to Munich with the "Bayern" ticket is 17.50€, 2hr.) *Storage lockers* are located on the street level, 2€-3.50€/24hr. The *post office* (Mon-Fri 7:00-20:30, Sat 8:00-14:00, Sun 13:00-18:00) is situated outside to the right (far side of Burger King). *Internet* is just outside to the right (3€/hr; daily 9:00-24:00; reasonable international calling; burns CDs). *Buses* for local connections—and to Berchtesgaden—are out front. *Taxis* are abundant, and also out front. *Getting to the Old Town* from the station is an easy 20-min walk—exit station left and go straight on Rainerstr., eventually leading under the train tracks. A few streets farther cut (right) through the Mirabell Gardens and cross the river.

Buses: Salzburg isn't big enough to warrant a subway system; therefore an efficient bus network does the trick. Most of the city's attractions can be found in the Old Town, or within walking distance of it, rendering public transportation for many travelers virtually unnecessary. A *Single* (one-way) ticket costs 1.80€ and the *24-hour* ticket is 3.40€ (or 4.20€ from driver). Purchase tickets at multilingual automats labeled Fahrkarten/Tickets or at magazine/tobacco shops. Small groups consider a taxi. *Note:* Stamp ticket in time box on bus to validate (watch locals). An on-the-spot fine of 60€ will be enforced if caught riding "Schwarz" (without valid ticket). Tickets purchased from the driver are pre-validated and cost more money! Holders of the Salzburg Card ride for *FREE!*

Berchtesgaden: Bus #840 to Berchtesgaden departs hourly (from 8:15 until early evening) from Salzburg's main train station at bay (Stand) 4, across parking lot from P.O. (or from Mirabellplatz a few minutes later). The cost is 4.40€ one-way. If you're returning to Salzburg, purchase the day ticket (*Tageskarte*) from the driver for 8€, which will cover all your bus transportation for the day, including to/fro Salzburg and Obersalzberg (bus departure area for Eagle's Nest), as well as to the salt mines and Königssee (King's Lake).

Drivers: *Street parking* pay at nearby automat and leave ticket on dashboard of your car (applicable times Mon-Fri 9:00-19:00, otherwise free). Price: (automat) 10¢/6min, 50¢/30min, max 3€/3hr. Saturdays are free for a max time of three hours, but you must use your "parking dial" (page 450) between the hours of 9:00-16:00. *Parking Garage:* There are a few around town, but tourists should use the Altstadt Garage (1.20€/30min, 2.40€/60min, every 10 min thereafter 40¢; 14€/24hr). Getting there is easy—exit A1 autobahn at Salzburg West and follow signs to Salzburg direction Altstadt. This will eventually funnel you into the *Altstadt Garage (entrance into garage is on right prior to tunnel cutting through cliff face). *GPS:* N47° 47.855 - E13° 02.264. After parking, follow signs "Festspielhäuser" to the Toskaninihof (page 477, *Festival Halls.* S.O.M. fans will find both the Festival Halls and Toscanini Hof in the chapter *Sound of Music*, page 507).

For drivers who wish to avoid the city entirely, leave your car at the Salzburg Süd **P+R (Park+Ride) on the outskirts and ride the bus in. To get there, exit the A10 autobahn at Salzburg Süd and continue in the direction of Salzburg—after about 4km follow TI and Park+Ride signs into parking lot. **GPS:* N47° 46.150 - E13° 04.234. *Note:* Purchase Salzburg Card (page 473) from the on-site TI and the bus ride into town is free. Hours: (TI; may change, call ahead to verify) Easter thru Sept, Advent weekends and New Year Mon-Sat 10:00-16:30, July/Aug daily 9:00-19:00.

Airport: (Flughafen) Salzburg's "W.A. Mozart" airport is idyllically nestled at the foothills of the Alps—a spectacular scene for anyone flying to/fro the city of salt. The reasonably small Mozart airport, moving around 1.7 million passengers annually, is situated 5km west of the Old Town—regular bus connections available (bus #2, 20 min to/fro train station), or a taxi will cost roughly 12€. Aviation aficionados check out Hangar-7 (page 482), an ultramodern structure filled with vintage aircraft.

Horse-Drawn Carriage: (Fiaker) Romantic rides through the Old Town cost 33€ for 20-25 min or 66€ for 50 min (up to 4 passengers, 5 possible—discuss with driver). Carriages can readily be found on Residenzplatz.

Bike Rental: Salzburg is a pleasure to cycle around, and **Top Bike** will help you fulfill this eco-adventure. So get your buttocks in the saddle and feet dancin' on the pedals and ride your very own Tour de Salzburg. Cycle to Schloss Hellbrunn, or along the Salt River, or pedal our do-it-yourself Sound of Music tour (excluding lake district). Rent your wheels from Top Bike—show this book and receive a 20% discount off the below-mentioned prices for bike rental. (www.topbike.at) *Cell.# 0676/476-7259. Getting There:* Top Bike has two locations: **(1)** outside the train station, next to Café Intertreff (follow rent-a-bike signs), or **(2)** at the Staatsbrücke (main bridge in town). *Hours:* daily, April-June and Sept/Oct 10:00-17:00, July/Aug 9:00-19:00 at (1) — or June and Sept, July/Aug 9:00-19:00 at (2). *Price:* (before discount) 6€/2hr, 10€/4hr, 15€/24hr. Audio guides to enhance sightseeing available for rent, or free with lengthy bike rental. *Note:* Bring ID. Closed in bad weather.

Salzburg Card: Fellow travelers, we highly recommend you invest in the huge savings offered by the Salzburg Card. The holder is awarded unlimited use of public transportation within the metro area and *FREE* one-time admission into most attractions in the Old Town, including select discounts on services and entertainment. The Salzburg Card comes in a 1-, 2- or 3-day card—available at the TI, airport, and many hotels. *Price:* (higher price is applicable June-Sept) 24-hour card 20€-23€, 48hr/27€-29€, 72hr/32€-34€. Students, ask for a reduction in the price of the card. **Note:* Every listing in the "Sights" section is *FREE* with the Salzburg Card.

Internet: You can access the World Wide Web at the café just outside the train station (3€/hr; daily 9:00-24:00) or for a cheaper rate ramble across the street from the station to Kaiserschützenstr. 8 (2€/hr, daily 9:00-23:00). Both offer low-priced international calling. Another place to surf is at the petite and outrageously expensive shop a few doors left of the Mozartplatz TI.

Post Office: Salzburg has three central branches. **(1)** When facing the train station, a P.O. is on the left next to Burger King [Mon-Fri 7:00-20:30, Sat 8:00-14:00, Sun 13:00-18:00]. **(2)** The most centrally located P.O. is hidden behind the cathedral. When standing in the middle of Residenzplatz facing the cathedral, wander left around the corner [Mon-Fri 7:00-18:30, Sat 8:00-10:00]. **(3)** Lastly, you'll find a P.O. on Markartplatz. When facing Mozart's Wohnhaus, it's left up the street and on the corner [Mon-Fri 7:30-17:00].

Supermarket: A convenient and centrally located grocery store is Billa, found on busy Hanuschplatz opposite the (Makartsteg) footbridge crossing the river and near the Japanese restaurant Nagano. Hours: Mon-Wed 8:00-19:00, Thur 7:30-19:00, Fri 7:30-19:30, Sat 7:30-18:00.

American Express: Mozartplatz 5 (right of TI on corner). *Tel.#* 0662/843-840. *Hours:* Mon-Fri 9:00-17:30, Sat 9:00-12:00. Emergency toll-free number (only when in Austria): 0800-900-940. I—your humble author—have known the gentleman who works at this branch for more than seven years, but that's nothing...he sold my parents Sound of Music tour tickets some 25 years ago. The gentleman I refer to is Michael, a true asset to the firm and Salzburg! Feb 2006 marks 40 years that he will have worked at this branch.

Holidays in Salzburg, 2006

1. January, Sunday – New Year
6. January, Friday – Epiphany (Three Kings' Day)
14. April – Good Friday
17. April – Easter Monday
1. May, Monday – May Day (Labor Day)
25. May, Thursday – Ascension Day
5. June – Whit Monday
15. June, Thursday – Corpus Christi
15. August, Tuesday – Assumption Day
26. October, Thursday – Independence Day
1. November, Wednesday – All Saints' Day
8. December, Friday – Immaculate Conception
25. December, Monday – Christmas
26. December, Tuesday – St. Stephen's Day (Christmas Day No. 2)

What to do on a Sunday or holiday

The shops are closed but most all attractions will be open. If you've been there done that, consider our Sound of Music do-it-yourself tour. If that's already checked off your list, head to Berchtesgaden, Werfen or the Salzkammergut (see *Excursions*, page 493). Other ideas include renting a bike and cycling along the river or going for a hike (start with *Kapuzinerberg*, page 484). If none of the above appeals to you, how 'bout quaffing a beer under the cooling leaves of a chestnut tree at the Müllner Bräu (page 485).

Church Service, "Gottesdienst"

Note: Hours may have changed—check with staff at your accommodations or at the TI for the latest info, as well as for other religious denominations.

Roman Catholic: (German service) Dom (cathedral) — Mon-Fri 6:30, Sun 8:30, 10:00 and 11:30.

Lutheran: (English service) Christuskirche (located at Schwarzstr. 25, on riverbank a few blocks from the 5-star Hotel Sacher) — Sunday worship 11:00. For more info call the pastor (Richard Solberg) on tel.# 0662/434-314.

FREE Salzburg

1) Capture a grand view from the **SteinTerrasse** (page 484).

2) To relive a movie classic, embark on the most popular outing in this guidebook: The **Sound of Music do-it-yourself tour** (page 504).

3) Though technically not without cost, the **Salzburg Card** (page 473) is mentioned here because it's such a good deal: The holder gains *FREE* admission into everything listed in the "Sights" section.

4) A trip to Salzburg wouldn't be complete without a stroll through the **Mirabell Gardens** (page 481).

5) **Aviation aficionados** must visit Hangar-7 (page 482), an ultramodern structure filled with vintage aircraft.

6) **Grave seekers** will unearth the following two names at St. Sebastian's cemetery (page 482): Mozart, Leopold • Mozart, Constanze Weber (page 461—chapter *Tomb-Lovers, Who's Buried Where? Austria*).

SIGHTS

Note: Everything listed in this section is FREE with the Salzburg Card! Start early to maximize your time.

Fortress, Salzburg: (Festung Hohensalzburg) Never conquered, this must-explore site dominating Salzburg's skyline dates from 1077 A.D. and is the largest preserved fortress in Central Europe. There are two ways to reach its ramparts, via the cable railway (Festungsbahn) or foot (steep, 20 min). The admission ticket includes all the attractions within the complex, and there are plenty. Step inside the World of Marionettes (Welt der Marionetten) and control a puppet on a string. Wander through a wowing maze of museums exhibiting artifacts from the days of the Romans, suits of armor from the Middle Ages and weaponry, medals and uniforms from WWI and WWII. But first, take the 30-min audio-guide tour of the interior to witness a dungeon, explore state rooms formerly belonging to powerful archbishops, and to absorb a breathtaking panorama of Salzburg and beyond to Bavaria from the lookout tower. The tour concludes in the Golden Hall where classical (e.g. Mozart) concerts are held. While in the hall, pay particular attention to the second marble pillar from the left. Midway up its left side you'll see a cavity where a canon ball struck it during the peasants' uprising in 1525. Allow at least two hours for a visit to the fortress. (www.salzburg-burgen.at) *Hours:* daily — Jan-April & Oct-Dec 9:30-17:00, May/June & Sept 9:00-18:00, July/Aug 9:00-19:00.

Price: (includes round trip on cable railway) adult 9.80€, student 8.90€, or *FREE* with Salzburg Card. *Note:* If you walk up to the fortress, admission is 8.60€. Typically, after 18:00 July/Aug, the gate is open and entry into the grounds is free. Visitors in mid-June, check out the medieval festival within the fortress on the weekend of 17-18, 2006.

Mozart's Birthplace: (Geburtshaus) The legendary Amadeus—baptized as Johannes Chrysostomus Wolfgangus Theophilus Mozart—was born January 27, 1756, within the six-story dwelling at Getreidegasse 9 in the heart of the Old Town. Amadeus, as he is so often referred to, comes from Theophilus, which translates to Gottlieb (beloved by God) in German and Amadeus in Latin. He routinely used Wolfgang Amadeus as his signature and is therefore generally known by these two names. Wolfgang was the seventh and last child born to Leopold and Anna Maria Mozart. In 1747, Leopold and Anna Maria moved into this third-floor apartment on Getreidegasse, where they lived for 26 years before relocating across town in 1773 (see *Wohnhaus,* next entry). The Getreidegasse apartment is quite small, consisting of a kitchen, foyer, living room, bedroom and study. Anna Maria gave birth here seven times, only two survived infancy. In 1751, Wolfgang's sister, Maria Anna (a.k.a Nannerl), was born first and five years later came Amadeus. Mozart's birthplace is a world-famous attraction, but bypassing it would be excused if you were not a reasonable fan. If you're carrying the Salzburg Card, definitely check it out. In the museum you'll discover original family documents, paintings and personal belongings, e.g. Mozart's clavichord, viola, concert piano, and the violin he played as a child. Allow at least 30 min for a visit. *Hours:* daily, 9:00-18:00, July/Aug till 19:00. *Price:* adult 6€, student 5€, combo-ticket with Wohnhaus 9.50€/7.50€, or *FREE* with Salzburg Card. *Getting There:* Mozart's birthplace is the mustard-yellow facade conveniently located (on the main shopping street) at Getreidegasse 9; looking much like it did in Mozart's day.

Mozart's Wohnhaus: Since Leopold Mozart had made a name for himself as the arch-bishop's concertmeister, in addition to rearing a child prodigy, the Mozarts could afford to move across the river in 1773 to this *much* bigger, eight-room residence. Here, you'll be given an info-packed audio guide to accompany your journey through the family's former dominions. Wolfgang lived here until 1780, his sister (Nannerl) until 1784, and Leopold until his death in 1787. Near the end of the tour, spend a little extra time at the interactive panel to follow Mozart's concert tours (1762-1790) across Europe. During one of these tours, when Wolfgang was about 6, Leopold covered up the piano keys with a cloth to increase playing difficulty. Much to the astonishment of the crowd, Wolfgang played like a seasoned pro. Allow 60 min for a visit. *Hours:* daily, 9:00-18:00, July/Aug till 19:00. *Price:* adult 6€, student 5€, combo-ticket with Mozart's birthplace 9.50€/7.50€, or *FREE* with Salzburg Card. *Getting There:* Mozart's Wohnhaus is located at Makartplatz 8, across from the Mirabell Gardens and the 5-star Hotel Bristol.

Cathedral (Dom) Museum: At the cathedral's museum you'll witness age-old pious matter dating from the 12th century. A highlight awaits your visit by the principal organ, where you can peer over the cathedral's inner sanctum—this breathtaking sight alone is worth your time. For the general traveler, allow 25 min for a visit. *Hours:* April-Oct & Dec, Mon-Sat 10:00-17:00, Sun 11:00-18:00. *Price:* (*includes audio guide) adult 5€, student 1€, or *FREE* with Salzburg Card. (*Leave ID as deposit.) *Getting There:* Museum is located at the entrance of the cathedral (right and up stairs).

Cathedral (Dom) Excavations: Go subterranean and explore excavations of the medieval cathedral and those dating from Roman times when Salzburg was known as Juvavum. For the general traveler, allow 10 min for a visit. *Hours:* July/Aug, daily, 9:00-17:00. *Price:* adult 2€, student 1.50€, or *FREE* with Salzburg Card. *Getting There:* Stairs descending to the excavations can be found beneath the arches between Residenzplatz and Domplatz.

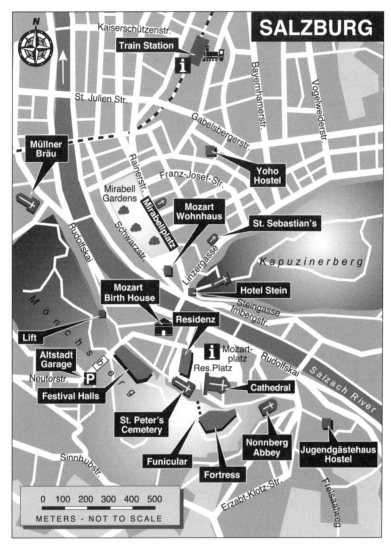

Residenz: Established in 1102 and enlarged during the 17th-18th centuries, the Residenz once accommodated Salzburg's power-wielding archbishops. Alas, the original furniture did not survive the cravings of Napoleon's troops, or the Habsburgs, who chronologically followed. Nonetheless, the city has done a great job of restoring the Residenz to its former glory. It was here that Mozart played his first court concert at the age of 6; where his father, Leopold, was portrayed in the movie "Amadeus" asking the archbishop to retrieve his son from Vienna; and where Emperor Franz Josef on May 1, 1816, administered the oath of allegiance to the Salzburg trades, officially incorporating Salzburg into Austria. Ogle terrific views of Domplatz and Residenzplatz while touring stately rooms. Allow at least 40 min for a visit. (www.salzburg-burgen.at) *Hours:* daily 9:00-16:30, except during official functions, which seem to happen a lot—especially in summer (also closed three weeks before Easter and one week after). *Price:* (includes audio guide) adult

5€, student 4€, combo-ticket with Residenz Gallery 8€/6€, or *FREE* with Salzburg Card. *Getting There:* Residenz can be entered via Residenzplatz or Domplatz. *Residenz Gallery:* On the upper floor of the Residenz you'll find a picture gallery, featuring paintings from the 16th to 19th centuries by European masters, including Rubens and Rembrandt. *Hours:* closed part of Feb/March and Nov, otherwise open Tue-Sun 10:00-17:00 (daily mid-July thru Aug). *Price:* Adult 6€, student 5€, combo-ticket with Residenz 8€/6€, or *FREE* with Salzburg Card. (www.residenzgalerie.at)

Festival Halls: (Festspielhaus) This massive 17th-century structure, formerly the archbishop's stables and riding school, extends the length of the entire block and houses three beloved theaters. **The smallest theater,** far left side when facing building, dates from 1924 and is presently being renovated. Although, the smallest it won't be when the three-year, 29€ million project is completed in May (2006). The theater's seating capacity will be increased by 400 to 1700, and with all the changes comes a new name: House for Mozart. **The middle theater** (Felsenreitschule, or Summer Riding School) boasts 1500 seats, 96 arches (on three levels) hewn into the Mönchsberg cliffs, and a state-of-the-art retractable roof. What's more, it was upon this stage that the Hollywood von Trapps sang their farewell songs before escaping to the cemetery. **The third theater,** the large festival hall, seats 2200 and is one of Europe's largest opera stages (comparable to the Metropolitan in NYC). The only way to see the Festival Halls is by taking the one-hour, multilanguage tour, which we recommend. For Sound of Music fans, the tour is a must! *Tours:* daily — June and Sept at 14:00 & 15:30; July/Aug at 9:30, 14:00 & 15:30; Oct till Dec 20 at 14:00 (closed rest of Dec) and from Jan 7 thru May at 14:00. *Price:* 5€/person, or *FREE* with Salzburg Card. *Getting There:* The Festival Halls are situated at the base of the Mönchsberg cliffs and adjacent to St. Peter's monastery. From the fruit and vegetable market behind Mozart's birthplace, take the lane (Wiener-Philharmoniker-Gasse) running south off the square straight to the halls. *GPS:* N47° 47.890 - E13° 02.564

Museum of Natural History: (Haus der Natur) This fun museum has five levels of everything from outer space matter to sea life (excellent aquariums) and dinosaur displays to reptiles in habitat (third floor). Unfortunately, the museum has few exhibits in English. Nonetheless, a trip here is worthwhile. Don't leave without walking through the astronomy room on the third floor to get your estimated weight (in kilograms) on different planets in our solar system; start with the scale "Erde" (Earth). Allow between one and two hours for a visit. (www.hausdernatur.at) *Hours:* daily, 9:00-17:00 (reptile zoo from 10:00). *Price:* adult 5€, student 3€, or *FREE* with Salzburg Card. *Getting There:* Haus der Natur is located in the northwest part of the Old Town at Museumsplatz 5, between the river and Mönchsberg cliffs. *Note:* Museum is often loaded with raucous school groups.

Boat Rides: (Schifffahrt) In 2002, Salzburg opened its docks to visitors craving a Schifffahrt, or boat ride, on the Salzach River—the first time since 1891. Amazingly, the inaugural craft sunk in the devastating floods that inundated Europe in August 2002. Today, Salzburg's one-boat fleet offers the popular City Highlight cruise (35 min) as well as other appealing excursions. Powered by two jet engines, each thrusting upwards of 350hp, the boat opens up to a respectable 45kph once it's upriver from the Old Town. When we visited, Joe from Huntington Beach, CA, was second in charge of the boat. Maybe he'll be on duty when you arrive? (www.salzburgschifffahrt.at) *Hours:* mid-April thru May and Sept, hourly departures 10:00-17:00, June-Aug 9:30-19:00, and the first half of Oct 13:00-16:00. *Price:* from 12€, or *FREE* with Salzburg Card. *Getting There:* Boat shoves off from Makartsteg, footbridge adjacent to Old Town.

Lift, Mönchsberg: Don't forget to utilize this option with your Salzburg Card. This elevator lifts visitors up to the Mönchsberg (Monks' Ridge) observation terrace, one of Salzburg's most scenic vantage points. Besides a gargantuan view, you'll encounter clean toilets, the Museum der Modern (see next entry) and a casual café/restaurant. The elevator system was originally dug out from inside of the cliffs in 1890, whipping the beguiled visitor up the 60-meter shaft in a record two minutes. Today, the same trip takes a mere 30 seconds and the three elevators transport approximately 1 million guests per year. *Hours:* daily, 8:00-19:00. *Price:* 2.90€ round trip, 1.80€ one-way, or *FREE* with Salzburg Card. *Getting There:* The lift is located at Gstättengasse 13—northwest part of the Old Town. To get an idea of where it is, look above the Old Town for a wood-covered shaft leading up the cliff face; walk towards this and follow the cliff farther to the right to Gstättengasse. Or, outside of the Old Town, ride bus #1, #4 or #7 to Mönchsbergaufzug. *GPS:* N47° 48.039 - E13° 02.356. *S.O.M. Fans:* Maria and the kids sang "Do-Re-Mi" from the observation terrace. *Note:* If the weather is nice, take the elevator up and walk the scenic path down (page 484—*Lift, Mönchsberg*).

Museum der Moderne: (Mönchsberg) At a cost of 22€ million, Salzburg recently (Oct 2004) added a new "Museum of Modern Art" to its bevy of attractions. Located above the Old Town atop Mönchsberg (Monks' Ridge), the museum boasts 3000sq.m/ 32,000sq.ft of exhibition floor space on three levels. (www.museumdermoderne.at) *Hours:* Tue-Sun 10:00-18:00 (Wed till 21:00). *Price:* adult 8€, student 6€, combo-ticket with Mönchsberg Lift (elevator to top of ridge) 9.70€, or *FREE* with Salzburg Card, audio guide available at cashier for a fee. *Note:* Bring a 1€ coin; bags must be stored in a locker. Coin pops back out when locker is reopened. *Getting There:* The museum can be reached via the Mönchsberg Lift (see above entry).

Schloss Hellbrunn: With its generous Baroque gardens, reflecting pools, romantic grottos and trick fountains, Hellbrunn palace was built for Archbishop Markus Sittikus, who reigned from 1612-1619. Sittikus was a passionate man who kept the company of beautiful women. His ornate digs became known as the *Lustschloss*, or palace of plea-sure, where jovial parties and amorous affairs were customary. The trick fountains— specially modified statues, footpaths and walls—were a favorite of the archbishop, who enthusiastically lured visitors into the gardens to run a gantlet of spraying water. The big laugh came when Sittikus invited his guests to the luncheon table, where he seated them onto marble blocks fashioned into stools rigged with water spouts. When Sittikus gave the signal, cold Alpine water shot from the stools—except his, of course—once again saturating his guests, who had to sit unflustered and appreciate that they were the soaking victims of yet another heavenly gag served up by the archbishop.

A visit to Schloss Hellbrunn is a delightful experience. Families will appreciate the open green spaces and fun playground for kids. Sound of Music fans will cherish the famed gazebo (page 511—*Schloss Hellbrunn*). Explorers will pursue the SteinTheater (one-hour trek, signs point the way), where on August 31, 1617, the first open-air opera north of the Alps was performed: "L'Orfeo." And everybody will go wild about the zoo (see next entry) neighboring the palace. Since Schloss Hellbrunn covers many acres and attractions, a visit here could take anywhere from 10 minutes to half a day, depending on your agenda. We recommend you allow at least 30 min to stroll through the gardens (free to enter). Consider packing a picnic. Toilets can be found opposite the gazebo as well as near the palace entrance.

During your visit, you'll notice a canary-yellow structure on the hillside. In 1615, Sittikus required an extra guesthouse for visiting VIPs; thus he ordered one to be built. The archbishop's laborious workforce completed the task within a month, and from this stellar effort the structure originated its name: MonatsSchlössl, or Month Villa. Today, it is a museum housing traditional handicrafts from the region.

(www.hellbrunn.at) *Hours:* (palace and trick fountains; end times denote last tour) daily, April-Oct — April and Oct 9:00-16:30, May/June and Sept 9:00-17:30, July/Aug till 22:00 (after 18:00 fountain tours only). The park and gardens are free to enter and open daily 6:30-17:00, March and Oct till 18:00, April-Sept till 21:00. *Price:* (combo-ticket palace and fountains) adult 8.50€, student 6€, or *FREE* with Salzburg Card. *Tours:* audio guide through palace takes 25 min; guided fountain tour takes 35 min. *Note:* When touring the fountains, if the ground ahead of you is wet, beware of incoming streams of water. However, on a warm summer day, this is a welcome reprieve. *Getting There:* Schloss Hellbrunn is located 5km south of the Old Town. *Cyclists*, ride along Hellbrunner Allee (via Freisaalweg) to Hellbrunn—(consider riding riverside path back into town). *Railers*, take bus #25 from the city to Hellbrunn. *Drivers*, exit the A10 autobahn at Salzburg Süd and follow signs to Salzburg. At the first traffic light, turn left. On the other side of the village (Anif) you'll see the zoo's natural enclosures on the right—continue past the zoo and turn right at the end of the golden wall. Street parking on the immediate left is free (good luck) or 2.20€ in one of the three lots (pick the last one on the right).

Zoo, Hellbrunn: In the early 15th century, the archbishop had a love for animals and consequently established a wildlife habitat 5km south of the Old Town. This evolved into today's Hellbrunn Zoo (next to Schloss Hellbrunn), attracting some 270,000 visitors annually. The zoo is home to 500 animals representing 140 species: zebras, lions, leopards, kangaroos, tigers, wolves, brown bears, rhinos, lemurs, monkeys, flamingos, and a black jaguar, to name a few. Many of the enclosures have been landscaped into the neighboring cliff face, affording the animals a natural-as-can-be environment. Allow at least two hours for a visit. Don't leave the zoo without strolling through the "Tropenhaus" (next to café near main zoo entrance) to see the little monkeys. (www.salzburg-zoo.at) *Hours:* daily, 8:30-16:30 (June thru mid-Sept till 18:30). *Note:* Fri and Sat nights in August the zoo is open till 23:00 (last entry 21:30) allowing visitors a unique look into the nocturnal behavior of animals. *Price:* adult 8€, student 6€, or *FREE* with Salzburg Card, bag of animal food (Futter) 2.60€. *Getting There:* Zoo adjoins Schloss Hellbrunn (see above entry). *Railers*, take bus #25 from the city to Alpenzoo. *Drivers*, exit the A10 autobahn at Salzburg Süd and follow signs to Salzburg. At the first traffic light, turn left. On the other side of the village (Anif) you'll see the zoo's natural enclosures on the right. Free parking out front.

BrauWelt: (Brew World) The folks at "Stiegl" have been brewing Salzburg's beer since 1492, precisely the year Columbus discovered the Americas. To complement Stiegl's 500-year evolution, management has put together Europe's largest beer exhibition, including the world's biggest (43-liter) beer mug. After the tour, enjoy two complimentary beers and a pretzel in Stiegl's rustic tavern. Allow at least 90 min for a visit. *Note:* Before exiting, go back to the cashier and hand he/she your ticket for a free gift. (www.brauwelt.at) *Tel.#* 0662/8387-1492. *Hours:* (end times are last entry) daily, 10:00-16:00, July/Aug till 18:00. *Price:* adult 9€, student 8.30€, or *FREE* with Salzburg Card. *Getting There:* BrauWelt is located at Bräuhausstr. 9, 2km west of the Old Town. *Railers*, take bus #1 from the city to Bräuhausstrasse. Exit bus left and make the next left on Bräuhausstr. The brewery complex is a few minutes farther ahead on the right. *Drivers*, from the city it's tough to find—ask directions. From the A1 autobahn, exit at Salzburg Flughafen and follow signs to Salzburg/BrauWelt. After driving through the airport underpass, make your second right onto Karolingerstr. Follow this straight all the way to the T-intersection (Kendlerstr.), where you'll turn left. Eventually, you'll be making a series of right turns that parallel the brewery—follow the BrauWelt signs to the visitor parking lot off Bräuhausstr.

Catacombs, do-it-yourself tour (allow 20 min). *Hours:* May-Sept Tue-Sun 10:30-17:00, Oct-April Wed thru Sun 10:30-15:30 (Fri-Sun till 16:00). *Price:* adult 1€, student 60¢, or *FREE* with Salzburg Card. *GPS:* N47° 47.801 - E13° 02.689

In the cliffs that rise above St. Peter's cemetery are the catacombs, dwellings dug out by Christians in the 3rd century A.D. Historians don't know a whole lot about these caverns, except that they were used as a hermitage over the past 1500 years. Perhaps Salzburg's founding father, Bishop Rupert, initially resided here in 696.

The dugouts were originally enclosed within the composite rock until a landslide exposed them in 1669. The man-made facade we see today was added later. You won't find any bones in the catacombs as the name suggests. However, at the entrance are the graves of Mozart's sister, Maria Anna (a.k.a. Nannerl), and Michael Haydn (celebrated composer in Salzburg and brother of Joseph Haydn). When viewing the two graves, you're standing on top of an ossuary (oodles of bones), which was positioned here as an "intermediate" depository when no graves were available. The painting at the cross depicts the Virgin Mary, Mary Magdalene, and Jonah flanking Jesus above weak souls praying for absolution in a raging fire. Either side of the painting is the Dance of the Dead (1660), portraying victims of plague.

To your left, ascend 48 irregular steps to reach the first level. Once there, go right and follow the wooden walkway to St. Gertrude's chapel, dating from the 4th century. The monks from St. Peter's monastery (next door) still use this chapel today, along with the consecrated altar (1862). The column in the center of the room dates from the 17th century and is a remembrance to those who died during the plague. Adjacent are the vaulted niches for clergy. In the back of the chapel (through window) is a section hollowed out for those not yet baptized. The fresco above the entrance dates from the 15th century and portrays the martyrdom of St. Thomas Becket.

Head back outside and climb nine more steps to a petite platform affording dramatic views of the cemetery and Salzburg's soaring collection of church steeples. Inscribed on the bell to your left is the year 1681.

Ascend another 36 lopsided steps via a narrow passage to reach Maximus chapel. At the top you'll discover an unconsecrated altar (inlaid tablet is absent), a tiny doorway that once led to further dugouts, and an empty grave with a Latin inscription dating from 1530. It reads: *"In 477, Odoacer, the king of the peoples Ruthenians, Geppiden, Goths, Magyars and Herulians fought against the church of God and threw Maximus and 50 of his followers off the cliffs to their ghastly deaths. Odoacer's men went on to destroy the entire province of Noricum with fire and swords."* (Noricum is roughly the provincial boundaries of today's Salzburgland).

More SIGHTS

St. Peter's Cemetery: This is the oldest active graveyard in Austria, and world famous for hiding the Trapp family in the movie "The Sound of Music." (Actually, they hid in a Hollywood studio but this cemetery inspired the director.) Whether you're a S.O.M. fan or not, St. Peter's cemetery warrants a walk-through. Note the burial chambers encompassing the graveyard: Vault XVI is Lorenz Hagenauer, landlord to the Mozart family. • Vault XXXI is the architect Santino Solari—famous for building the Dom, Schloss Hellbrunn, and many of Salzburg's fortifications constructed during the Thirty Years' War. • Vault IX simply states that the occupant was a Geschäftsfrau, or "business woman"—we're afraid to ask. In the center of the burial ground is St. Margaret's chapel, the only church in Salzburg that still stands as it did in the 15th century (1491). If the entrance doors are shut, the interior may be viewed through two peepholes in the main portal. *Hours:* (cemetery) daily, 6:30-18:00—April-Sept till 19:00. *Note:* The cemetery also accommodates the catacombs; see do-it-yourself tour above.

St. Peter's Church: Neighboring the abovementioned cemetery is St Peter's monastery, where Bishop Rupert founded Salzburg more than 1300 years ago. In the southeast corner of the monastery's courtyard—adjacent to the Stiftskeller, Europe's oldest restaurant—is St. Peter's church, built between 1130-1143. Lavish renovations during the Baroque and Rococo periods (17/18th centuries) have transformed the interior of this must-see church into the region's most spectacular. It is within this hallowed structure that Bishop Rupert is buried (Grab des Hl. Rupertus)—you will find him midway along the right aisle.

Cathedral: (Dom) Salzburg's cathedral is the largest Baroque structure north of the Alps, having the capacity to hold more than 10,000 people. Fittingly, Mozart was baptized here in 1756. Before you enter, hoof it into the middle of the plaza, stand by the statue of the Virgin Mary and face the cathedral. Above its wrought-iron gates are three landmark dates in the Dom's history: **774**, consecration of original structure (long since ruined). • **1628**, rebuilt and reconsecrated (after cathedral was destroyed by fire in the late 16th century) • **1959**, again rebuilt after Allied bombs plastered it during WWII (pictures at back of Dom depict this blasphemous day). Flanking the gates are four figures: (L. to R.) *St. Rupert* (founder of Salzburg/Patron St. of Salt). *St. Peter* (holder of the keys to Heaven). *St. Paul* (holding a sword—assumed beheaded by the Romans). *St. Virgil* (first archbishop of Salzburg and creator of the Dom).

Atop the cathedral is a statue of Jesus, flanked by Moses (right) and Elijah (left). Midway up the facade you'll see the four evangelists: John, Paul, George and Ringo. Um, err, we mean Matthew, Mark, Luke and John. Just above them are two angels holding a crown. Now, walk beyond the Virgin Mary in the direction she is facing and stand beneath the middle archway. Once there, line up Mary's head under the angels. When ready, pace forward and the angels crown her. Neat, huh?

Note: For those who have the urge, **toilets** can be found right of the cathedral underneath the adjoining arches. Ladies, bring small change with you. Additionally, *look for our friend Vlado* who is usually standing immediately right of the cathedral (April-Oct 11:00-18:00, not in bad weather)—he'll masterfully cut out your portrait like Edward ScissorHands on high-octane turnip juice. Price: 4€, but show Vlado this book and pay 3€.

Old Market Square: After clearing the charred houses destroyed by the inner-city fire of 1262, the townsfolk decided to build a firebreak to better protect Brodgasse and Goldgasse. So came about "Alter Markt," where locals flocked to buy and sell their goods. Here you'll find the neighborhood's former water supply, Florian fountain • the oldest pharmacy (1591) • Salzburg's smallest house, 2.2m wide x 8m long (1860, built in a former alleyway) • Café Fürst, home of the original Mozart ball • and Café Tomaselli (since 1703), a historic coffeehouse where Mozart allegedly played cards.

Mirabell Gardens & Palace: Ah, yes…the beautiful Mirabell, everybody's favorite gardens (always open and *FREE* to enter). No trip to Salzburg would be complete without a stroll through its fragrant reserve. S.O.M. fans especially love Mirabell because the von Trapp children, plus one governess, donned specially tailored curtains and frolicked through the gardens singing "Do-Re-Mi." The palace at the back of the gardens came first in 1606, when the crafty Archbishop Wolf Dietrich needed something cozy for his mistress, Salome Alt, and her 15 children. The immaculate Baroque gardens were landscaped a century later, and have been a magnet for locals and tourists ever since. Adjacent to the rose garden, where the path arcs into the grass, you'll behold a wowing view (*GPS:* N47° 48.294 - E13° 02.530). Today, the palace plays host to classical concerts, offices of local government, the Standesamt (marriage registry), and the sumptuous Marble (wedding) Hall. Wouldn't it be nice to say you were married in a palace?

St. Sebastian's Cemetery & Church: Built in late-Gothic style from 1505-1512, St. Sebastian's church fronts an eloquent cemetery conceived not quite a century later under the reign of Archbishop Wolf Dietrich. Buried here is Wolf Dietrich in his fat mausoleum • Philippus Paracelsus, renowned 16th-century alchemist who cured the incurable • Mozart's father, Leopold (>1787) • and Mozart's widow, Constanze (>1842). *Getting There:* From the Old Town, cross the river via the Staatsbrücke (main bridge) and ascend Linzergasse to No. 41 (left). *GPS:* N47° 48.259 - E13° 02.847

Hangar-7: Head over to the airport and check out the really cool Hangar-7, an ultra-modern hangar made of glass and steel housing vintage aircraft, as well as an exclusive restaurant, *Ikarus*; a trendy bar, *Mayday*; and a casual lounge, *Carpe Diem*. Upon arriving, you will be greeted with a boarding pass permitting you access to the hangar to get personally acquainted with a few of history's legendary aircraft, such as the B-25 Mitchell bomber, F4U Corsair, and a DC-6, in addition to some modern jets. From the display floor, look up. Integrated into the hangar's ceiling is the *Threesixty Bar* (open from 18:30 for guests of *Ikarus*), featuring a floor made of glass giving the feel of walking on air. Hangar-7—sponsored by Red Bull, the energy drink—was inaugurated on August 22, 2003, before a crowd of 10,000, including Prince Albert of Monaco, U.S. astronaut "Buzz" Aldrin, and F1 race-car champion Niki Lauda. The event raised nearly $2 million for charity projects.

Other reasons to visit Hangar-7 are its revolving art exhibitions and sparkling restrooms (downstairs), arguably Europe's best. These are equipped with interactive chat screens linked between the male-female restrooms and stocked with nicely wrapped hand towels to enhance your freshening-up experience. (www.hangar-7.com) *Hours:* (aircraft hangar) daily, 9:00-22:00. *Price: FREE* entry. *Getting There:* Hangar-7 is located on the east side of the airport. *Railers*, catch bus #2 direction airport and get off at "Karolingerstrasse"—from there it's a five-minute walk. Exit bus left and march to the forward traffic light. Cross the street, continue straight (on Wilhelm-Spazier-Str) and Hangar-7 is at the end of the road. *Drivers,* free parking opposite entrance. When coming from the city, turn left before the airport underpass into Wilhelm-Spazier-Str. When coming from the A1 autobahn, exit at Salzburg Flughafen and follow signs to Salzburg. After driving through the airport underpass, make the first right into Wilhelm-Spazier-Str. *GPS:* N47° 47.624 - E13° 00.498. *Ikarus:* (fine restaurant; reservations necessary) open daily 12:00-14:00 and 18:30-22:00. *Tel.#* 0662/219-777 (ikarus@hangar-7.com) Pilots, park your aircraft in front of the restaurant. *Mayday:* (semiformal bar) open daily 17:30-03:00. Besides a selection of hand-shaken drinks, Mayday offers flirty intra-bar communications where new acquaintances can be made via high-tech, interactive cartoon aircraft that deliver messages between guests. *Carpe Diem:* (lounge) open daily 9:00-19:00. A hip place to laze about and consume beverages and snacks flown in from around the world.

Casino: Gamblers, try your luck in Salzburg's Baroque casino, located in a fine 18th-century palace—Schloss Kleßheim—once belonging to Archbishop Firmian. Men are required to wear a jacket and tie—however, this dress code can be relaxed in summer. If necessary, you can borrow a jacket and tie from the cloakroom with a deposit. For the ladies—there's no real dress code—presentable is sufficient. Although admission is free, registration is mandatory and a photo ID required (must be at least 18 years of age to enter). *Tel.#* 0662/854-455. (www.casinos.at) *CC's:* VC, MC. *Hours:* open 364 days, 15:00 till 03:00 (slots from noon; closed Dec 24). *Getting There:* Schloss Kleßheim is located 4km northwest of the Old Town. *Railers*, take the free shuttle bus from Hanuschplatz or Mirabellplatz (departs hourly from 11:30 till midnight). *Drivers*, exit A1 autobahn at Kleßheim—parking is free.

Luge Ride, Dürrnberg: Located some 20km south of Salzburg, above the town of Hallein at Dürrnberg (near salt mines, see next entry), is Austria's longest toboggan run, 2.2km/1.4m. Forget all those other so-called toboggan runs—or "Sommerrodelbahn" in German—this exhilarating and wildly scenic luge ride will make the hair on the back of your neck stand on end. No kidding! The course is idyllically set upon the peak of a mountain, thus an enjoyable, quite extensive chair lift will carry you to the summit, where the flora is lush and the views are tremendous. What's more, a short hike from the top station will land you on the German border, complete with frontier signpost (great photo op.). When you're ready to ride the luge down, head to the departure area and the operator will supply your sled. Beware, this is not for the faint hearted—it is steep (57% grade), the corners are sharp, and the track is swift! Those who want to go full-throttle, allow a few minutes to pass before beginning your run so as not to catch the slowpokes ahead of you. _Price:_ one ride 9€, two/15.50€, three/20€ (students ask for discount)—one-ride combo-ticket with salt mines, 21.50€. _Hours:_ daily, May thru mid-Oct 11:00-17:00 (end-June thru mid-Sept 10:00-18:00). _Note:_ Since the price is a bit stiff, take your time at the summit—explore nature, snap memorable photos, have a beverage at the canteen (or, better yet, enjoy a picnic). _Getting There:_ **Railers**, take train from Salzburg to Hallein, then bus to luge (total journey, 40 min). **Drivers**, exit A10 autobahn at Hallein and follow brown signs to Salzwelten (salt mines)—on the other side of town the road will ascend to Dürrnberg. Pass the salt mines and after 1km the chair lift to the luge will appear on the left. If you're coming from Berchtesgaden, ask TI (or a local) for directions because the luge is not far via scenic country roads. _GPS:_ N47° 39.592 - E13° 05.558

Salt Mines, Dürrnberg: Some 2500 years ago, Celtic peoples migrated to Dürrnberg (mountain above the town of Hallein, some 20km south of Salzburg) to quarry salt. The Celts found tons of the so-called "white gold," thus many communities in the region begin with the Celtic word meaning salt: Hall. From this ancient settlement above Hallein developed a prosperous salt mine, featuring a subterranean labyrinth of deep tunnels, crystal galleries, swooshing slides, and a salty lake. For more than a millennium, white gold filled the coffers of Salzburg's archbishops, as well as the Habsburgs who chronologically followed. Today, salt mining on Dürrnberg has gone the way of the buffalo and the only mining still in operation is the extraction of money from tourists, who throw on white overalls and experience the former dug outs like a themed ride at Disneyland. Outside, visitors are treated to a reconstructed Celtic village and distant views of Salzburg. Allow 2.5 hours for a visit. (www.salzwelten.at) _Hours:_ daily, April-Oct 9:00-17:00 (last tour), rest of year tours depart hourly 10:00-15:00. _Price:_ adult 16.50€, student 10€, discount available with valid Salzburg Card, combo-ticket with luge ride 21.50€ (good deal for adults but not for students). _Note:_ Adult Railers purchase the "Salz Erlebnis Ticket" (at any Austrian rail counter), which includes train and bus fare and entrance into mines for circa 21€. _Getting There:_ **Railers**, take train from Salzburg to Hallein, then bus to salt mines (total journey, 40 min). **Drivers**, exit A10 autobahn at Hallein and follow brown signs to Salzwelten. On the other side of town the road will ascend to Dürrnberg, after 3km the mines will appear on the right. _GPS:_ N47° 40.017 - E13° 05.460. _Opinion:_ Some travelers may be wondering which salt mine is better to visit, Berchtesgaden or Dürrnberg? By far the busier mine is Berchtesgaden (page 232), because it's cheaper and practically on the way to the Eagle's Nest. However, unlike Berchtesgaden, the Dürrnberg mine offers dynamite views and a reconstructed Celtic village to ogle. As for the mines themselves, both are virtually the same—offering deep caverns, wooden slides, and a salty lake. So, to answer the question, which mine is better: They both are. Bottom line: Visit whichever mine best suits your travel itinerary, this includes the world's oldest mine in Hallstatt (page 502).

484 *Your Traveling Companion*

Best Views

SteinTerrasse: Atop the centrally located Hotel Stein is the must-see SteinTerrasse, a café on the hotel's terrace featuring jaw-dropping views of the Old Town and fortress, making hotshots out of novice photographers. *Hours:* daily, 9:00-24:00. *Tel.#* 0662/882-070. *Getting There:* Hotel Stein can be found at Giselakai 3, adjacent to the Salzach River and Staatsbrücke (main bridge). Walk straight through the lobby, pass reception, climb the stairs on the right and take the right elevator to floor 7. There is no pressure to buy—simply go for a look or grab a table and order a drink—it's up to you. *Note:* For price info on Hotel Stein, flip to page 491.

Fortress, Salzburg: From the turrets of Salzburg's millennium-old fortress are fabulous views of the Old Town and beyond (page 474).

Kapuzinerberg: (Capuchins' Ridge) This is an excellent option for hikers. Wander up to the monastery—yellowish building—capping the Kapuzinerberg (ridgeline on right bank of river) to reach an abundance of trails and stunning views. The monastery can be accessed via two passageways, one at Linzergasse 14 and the other at Steingasse 9. The latter is best. At Steingasse 9 you'll see a plaque memorializing the birthplace of Joseph Mohr (1792), who penned the world-famous Christmas carol "Silent Night, Holy Night." From here, ascend 256 steps past the adorable St. Johannes chapel to the top (steep, five min). With your legs burning and a shortness of breath, you're only meters away from two lookout points—one is behind you and the other is ahead on the left. For the better view, head to the lookout on the right and behind you (*GPS:* N47° 48.098 - E13° 02.767). Once there, you'll discover a battle-worthy turret from medieval times, tremendously scenic views of the Old Town and its imposing fortress, and the beginning of an intriguing hike (left and down). *Note:* If you go for a lengthy hike, at times you'll feel lost. Just remember, all paths heading west eventually arrive back at the monastery and the other lookout.

Lift, Mönchsberg: Whiz up an elevator to the Mönchsberg (Monks' Ridge) observation terrace for an unforgettable view of Salzburg (page 478—*Lift, Mönchsberg*). If you're keen for a refreshing nature stroll, follow the next set of directions. From the observation terrace (Aussichtsterrasse), ascend the steps and cobblestones straight past the super-zoom telescope and onto the dirt trail. Parallel the iron railing a short distance—don't follow trail leading down—veer right and pass the wooden shack on your left. Fortifications will soon appear on your left and the trail will connect back onto the paved route where you'll see a sign pointing to the Stadtalm. Follow the paved route through the stone archway. (Don't you feel as if you've stepped back into time or you're on a movie set?) On the other side of the archway you'll see the Stadtalm sign directing you left along the wall; ignore this for a moment and notice the plaque in front of you (right of archway). It reads: *"Here the citizens built a defense system consisting of four towers and a wall, as this is the narrowest part of the Mönchsberg. In 1488, citizen watch units were first referred to as the Salzburg Guard, and in 1816 they were dissolved."* Now wander over to the benches behind you and check out the terrific view—that's Bavaria in the distance. When you're done, walk the path along the old fortified wall direction Stadtalm. After a minute you'll reach a narrow portal on the right; go through this... Welcome to the hostel and café Stadtalm (page 489). Are you in awe of the view?

    To reach the fortress, continue on the path. Soon it will fork—go right to the fortress (Festung) or left to the Old Town (Altstadt). The 340-odd steps descending to town are called the 'Clemens Holzmeister' Stiege, named after the famous Austrian architect who created the Festival Halls located at the bottom.

SHOPPING

In need of some retail therapy? Check out Salzburg's contemporary shopping experience at Europark or window shop medieval lanes in the Old Town. Oh, and then there's a store that sells only eggs, lots of 'em.

Europark: This Olympic-sized shopping mall is the pride of retail Austria and a cash cow for Salzburg. If you're ever wondering where all the locals are, come here. Europark boasts more than 100 businesses, including Ikea, Hilfiger, Esprit, Levi's Store, H&M fashion (his/hers), Nike, and a huge Inter Spar supermarket. (www.europark.at) *Hours:* Mon-Fri 9:00-19:30, Sat 9:00-17:00. *Getting There:* Europark is located 3km northwest of the Old Town. *Railers,* catch bus #1 or #20 to Europark. *Drivers,* from the A1 autobahn, exit at Kleßheim. Parking won't be a problem since there are literally thousands of spaces available, many of which are in Europe's largest combined under-ground garages.

Wheat Lane: Located in the heart of the Old Town is "Getreidegasse," Salzburg's main shopping street—an adoringly cute pedestrian thoroughfare chock-a-block full of tourists scampering beneath an eclectic array of gilded wrought-iron signs jutting from retail outlets (even a McDonald's). Getreidegasse gets really congested around the yellow facade at number 9, Mozart's birthplace (Geburtshaus).

Easter-Egg Shop: Yes, those are Easter eggs you saw in the window. Back up, walk by again, just to make sure, but you'll see the same thing: Easter eggs. Trays stacked upon trays of fancifully decorated eggs fill the shop, on two floors no less. And not just chicken eggs, there are quail, turkey and ostrich eggs, too. The owner tells us she has around 110,000 eggs, but not just for Easter, also Christmas! You've got to see this place for yourself. Really! *Hours:* open year round, 365 days, Mon-Sat 9:00-19:00, Sun 9:00-18:00. *Getting There:* The shop is located at Judengasse 13. When standing in front of (and facing) Mozart's birthplace at Getreidegasse 9, go left and continue straight. After passing the Old Market Square (Alter Markt) the lane becomes Judengasse. The shop is ahead and on the left. Or, when facing the Mozartplatz TI, walk left and veer right around the corner. The wide, open area will funnel into Judengasse. The shop will appear on the right.

Judengasse: You'll discover unique, as well as antique, shops on this Jewish Lane and the quaint lanes running off it. While there, pop into the Easter egg shop listed above—use its directions to find this part of town.

Entertainment

As this is written, the pub Dos Dudes mentioned in the adventure novel—*Quest for the Bavarian Cross*—does not exist. However, one day, Jesse would like to turn this dream into a reality. We hope to see you there, soon!

One thing to make clear about Salzburg is the welcomed absence of in-your-face neon signs promoting the latest bar, pachinko parlor, or kitschy shop. Maintaining age-old tradition, this type of advertising is *verboten!* With a little patience you'll discover a wealth of nightlife behind inconspicuous, 19th-century facades—especially along the banks of the Salzach River.

Those who enjoy drinking a beer with history on their side, take note of the following two establishments: Müllner Bräu and Stiegl Keller.

Müllner Bräu—dating from 1621—is Austria's largest tavern. A venerable complex of beer halls and one very leafy, 1500-seat beer garden, situated in the district of "Mülln," named after the umpteen mills that once populated the landscape. In 1605, Augustinian Hermits settled the area, which became a frothy monastic district. Since the 19th century, dry-mouthed citizens have been pouring into Mülln for the Augustinian specialty: beer. One reason for the monks' success is they still store their beer in wooden kegs, giving it an all-natural taste. Inside Müllner Bräu, a row of food counters dish up Austrian fare and a handful of old-world beer halls feature coffee-colored wood paneling, stained-glass windows, and Gothic typeface drafted upon smoke-stained walls. Outside, heady locals bask under a forest of chestnut trees (Kastanienbäume) quaffing liter-sized brews for a paltry 5€ each. (www.augustinerbier.at) *Hours:* daily, 15:00-23:00 (weekends from 14:30). *Note:* Pay for your beer at the cashier, pick out your mug, rinse it in the nearby fountain, head to the *Schenke* (place where beer is served) and hand your receipt to the Kegmeister along with your empty mug. Upon the conclusion of your visit, stop for a moment on the nearby pedestrian bridge—Müllnersteg—for a brilliant view of the Old Town. *Getting There:* (Müllner Bräu) *Railers,* from the Old Town walk along the river (northwest), passing the boat dock and paralleling the Mönchsberg cliffs. Continue straight and the cliff face will taper to a church steeple soaring into the sky—next door is your oasis. *Drivers,* to park in their *lot is free—take a ticket at the gate and have the cashier validate it. **GPS:* N47° 48.336 - E13° 01.978

The **Stiegl Keller** (page 487) is another longstanding institution in Salzburg, situated above the rooftops of Salzburg and below the fortress.

Pub- and club-goers begin your evening in the Old Town on Rudolfskai at either Guinness-inspired tavern: **Shamrock** or **O'Malley's**. Both pubs neighbor each other behind old-fashioned facades on the riverbank. Live music every evening. Pint of Guinness roughly 4.40€. To me Irish mates, "Slainte!" *Hours:* (Shamrock) daily, Mon-Thur 15:00 till late, Fri-Sun 12:00 till even later — (O'Malley's) daily, 18:00 till late.

At St. Peter's Stiftskeller (page 487) don't miss the **Mozart-Dinner-Concert**. Starting at 20:00 (most evenings) in the Stiftskeller's historic Baroque hall, compositions of Mozart are performed by Salzburg artists in traditional costume. Accompanying the music is a multicourse, candlelight dinner prepared according to time-honored recipes from the 18th century. *Price:* (concert and 3-course dinner, drinks not included) adult 45€, student 33€. (www.mozartdinnerconcert.com) *Tel.#* 0662/828-6950. *CC's:* VC, MC, AE. *Note:* Cashier opens 18:45. Dress smart-casual. *Getting There:* St. Peter's Stiftskeller is located in the southeast corner of the monastery's courtyard, adjacent to St. Peter's church and cemetery.

Classical concerts are a dream in the Marble Hall of Mirabell Palace or the Konzertsaal of fortress Salzburg (see *Mozartplatz TI* for ticket details). Folks who are inspired by **organ concerts** check out the latest schedule at the Franciscan church (Franziskanerkirche), where there's usually a pipe sounding a tune (or see TI for schedule around town).

Experience an entrancing evening in the plush, Baroque **Marionetten Theater**. Puppeteers perform from a repertoire of big-time operas and plays, such as Mozart's Don Giovanni and The Marriage of Figaro, Shakespeare's Midsummer Night's Dream, Rossini's Barber of Seville, Tchaikovsky's Nutcracker, Humperdinck's Hänsel and Gretel. (www.marionetten.at) *Tel.#* 0662/872-4060. *Hours:* performances most everyday June thru Sept (less off-season). Box office is open 9:00-13:00 and two hours before every performance. *Price:* 18€-35€. *CC's:* VC, MC, AE. *Getting There:* Theater is located at Schwarzstr. 24, adjacent to Mirabell Gardens and one block from the 5-star Hotel Sacher.

Headline Concerts, Salzburg 2006

Note: Prices, dates, concerts may have changed or been added — query Mozartplatz TI or ticket agency for latest details.

Eros Ramazzotti: April 18, 20:00 at the Arena. Price 59-66€
Simply Red: July 11, 20:00 at the Arena. Price 46-50€

GOOD EATS

We begin this section by making a general statement that will always apply, in our opinion, towards local or national fare in Austria: "It's difficult to find a bad meal." People often ask us, "Where's a good place to eat?" Our answer sounds as if we're shrugging them off: "Most anywhere!" Here are a few appetizing places to kick-start your gastronomic tour of Salzburg.

But first, here's a short description of **Salzburger Nockerl**. Salzburger What? You'll see this term around town posted on signs fronting restaurants and cafés. It refers to a sweet culinary delicacy perfected by the locals: a soufflé-like dessert consisting of eggs, icing sugar, flour, lemon, milk and butter. Served hot out-of-the-oven, Salzburger Nockerl is very filling—enough for three people. Additionally, it is prepared upon your request, never order one if you're in a hurry—it's not uncommon to wait half an hour for your specially made, sweet tasting, puffed-up Nockerl to arrive at your table.

Stiftskeller, St. Peter: *Tel.#* 0662/841-268. This 1200-year-old restaurant undoubtedly needs to be mentioned first because it has been in business a really long time. The court scribe Alcuin first recorded the Stiftskeller into the history books during a visit by Emperor Charlemagne in the year 803 A.D.; therefore it is regarded as Europe's oldest restaurant. Prices are tolerable (15€-23€/meal) and the food is excellent—stop in for a bite to eat, even if it's only for a soup or dessert. (www.stiftskellerstpeter.com) English menu available. *Hours:* daily, 11:00-24:00 (Sun from 10:00). *CC's:* VC, MC, AE, DC. *Note:* Consider spending an evening here listening to Mozart over dinner (page 486—*Mozart-Dinner-Concert*). *GPS:* N47° 47.832 - E13° 02.644

Stiegl Keller: Festungsgasse 10, *tel.#* 0662/842-681. You've probably seen the word "Stiegl" plastered all over town. This is because it's the name of Salzburg's beer company, established in 1492—precisely the year Columbus discovered the Americas. In 1820, the brewery expanded its revenue base by investing in the Stiegl Keller, a delightful restaurant and beer garden nestled above the rooftops of Salzburg and below the fortress (adjacent to cable railway). Here you can enjoy a traditional meal and a thirst-quenching Stiegl beer while absorbing marvelous views. Arrive before sunset to see the Old Town transcend from the sun's golden rays bouncing off church steeples to the mesmeric twinkling of nocturnal lights. *Hours:* May-Sept, daily, 11:00-23:00, (closed Oct-April). *CC's:* VC, MC, AE.

Bistro Nussbaumer: Festungsgasse 2. Located meters from the abovementioned Stiegl Keller, this casual eatery affords easy-on-the-wallet prices and a quaint patio-garden. As you stroll along the cobbled Festungsgasse toward the fortress, look for Nussbaumer's chalk-written sign advertising their lunch special: schnitzel, potatoes and soup, 7€. *Hours:* daily, 10:00-17:00 (summer till 20:00).

Nagano: *Tel.#* 0662/849-488. Are you a sucker for Japanese food? We are. For those of you who have tried it, you know the drill. For those first-timers, order a small sushi to share with your partner and a main course for yourself, e.g. teriyaki chicken. Try any of their beers: Kirin, Sapporo, Asahi—each is amazingly flavorsome. Additionally, order a small sake to share—it tastes like warm water but it's part of the experience. Nagano is centrally located, reasonably priced, and dishes up a healthy meal. *Hours:* daily, 11:00-15:00 & 17:00-23:00 (June-Aug 11:00-23:00). *Getting There:* When facing Mozart's birthplace on Getreidegasse, go right some 50 meters to No. 24. Proceed through the archway and Nagano is beyond the second passage on the right.

Spicy Spices: (Vegetarian!) Wolf-Dietrich-Str. 1 (top of Linzergasse), *tel.#* 0662/870-712. This petite, organic-Indian bistro—run by smilin' Suresh—is an excellent choice for vegetarians or anyone looking for a healthy, pocket-friendly meal. Satisfying are their

5.50€ daily specials with yummy rice and organic salad. Fresh juices, naan bread, and soya with peas are among the items on the menu. Non-smoking environment. *Hours:* daily, 10:00-22:00

Zur Plainlinde: Plainbergweg 30, Bergheim. *Tel.#* 0662/458-557. You may remember this restaurant from chapter 4 in the adventure novel—*Quest for the Bavarian Cross*—where the girls enjoyed dinner and a brilliant sunset. Zur Plainlinde, an award-winning restaurant, dishes up scrumptious food to complement the equally scrumptious views. The prices have increased since the girls last ate here but a visit is still worthwhile for those who have wheels or don't mind the off-the-beaten-path location. Zur Plainlinde is located below the twin-steepled Maria Plain church, 4.5km north of the Old Town. (www.plainlinde.at) *Hours:* Wed thru Sun 12:00-14:00 and 19:00-21:00. *Getting There:* Railers, ride bus #6 direction Itzling West to Plainbrücke—from there, walk back to the main road and turn right. Make the first right on Plainbergweg and ascend this street to the restaurant (20 min). *Drivers,* exit the A1 autobahn at Salzburg "Nord" and head towards Braunau—at the first traffic light turn left. Follow the narrow road (some 2km) as it winds past green meadows and through a pleasant forest. At the end is Zur Plainlinde on the left. *GPS:* N47° 50.104 - E13° 02.437

Café Fürst: Home to the original Mozart ball (Mozartkugel), Café Fürst outshines the bunch. Salzburg is the city of balls. Boxes upon boxes, in all shapes and sizes, filled with little sweets wrapped in shiny foil. People travel to Salzburg from all over Europe for a taste of an authentic Mozartkugel—made of chocolate, nougat, marzipan, pistachio, and more chocolate. Mmm.

There are actually three different companies that produce Mozart balls. However, the original balls come from Café Fürst, established in 1884 by Paul Fürst. Paul created his first ball in 1890 and he soon began winning international awards. It wasn't long before other confectioners copied his idea. Even though Paul's balls were first, they're the ones you won't regularly see around town. The Fürst family believes in quality, not quantity, as a statement by Paul Fürst explains: *"I am of the basic opinion that the Mozartkugel is a sweet, and not a Mozart souvenir to be sold at unsuitably sunlit street stands."* Paul's Mozart balls are still made from the original recipe and are recognizable by their blue-and-silver foil wrapping. *Getting There:* Café Fürst's flagship operation is located in the Old Town on Old Market Square (Alter Markt; open Mon-Sat 8:00-20:00, Sun 9:00-20:00). A second location can be found across the river at Mirabellplatz 5 (Mon-Sat 8:00-18:00)—opposite Mirabell Gardens.

Sausages: Arguably Salzburg's best sausage can be found at the Balkan Grill, a whole in the wall since 1950. You won't find tourists here, only locals waiting in line for a spicy and fatty taste of bliss. The lady working behind the window in cramped conditions proudly serves up the so-called Bosna, two sausages jammed in a hot-dog-like bun dripping with condiments. You can choose from five choices (2.50€ ea.): #1) with onions and curry spice • #2) with onions, curry spice and mustard • #3) with mustard and curry spice • #4) with onions, ketchup and curry spice • #5) with ketchup and curry spice. *Getting There:* When facing Mozart's birthplace on Getreidegasse, go right to No. 33 (left). Proceed through archway into cobbled arcade to find whole in wall.

GOOD SLEEPS

In this pedestrianized city of salt there are more accommodations than you can poke a stick at. Not that we endorse stick poking. Below is an abridged list of restful lodgings to simplify, from *cheap* to *steep*. Unless otherwise stated, all accommodations come with breakfast and have facilities (shower/toilet) in the room (excluding hostels). *Note:* Campgrounds are listed last.

Hostel, Institute St. Sebastian: Linzergasse 41 (www.st-sebastian-salzburg.at) *Tel.#* 0662/871-386. Great hostel, clean facilities, centrally located. Institute St. Sebastian doubles as a home for college students, thus it has all the necessary amenities to sustain long-term occupancy, e.g. elevator, self-service kitchens, laundry facility (by appointment only —book at reception), communal rooms, and one very peaceful rooftop terrace. What's more, St. Sebastian's is oozing with history because it adjoins a late-Gothic church built in 1505. Behind the hostel is an eloquent cemetery, landscaped in 1595 under the reign of Archbishop Wolf Dietrich. Eternal inhabitants of the graveyard include Wolf Dietrich in his fat mausoleum • Philippus Paracelsus, renowned 16th-century alchemist who cured the incurable • Mozart's father, Leopold (>1787) • and Mozart's widow, Constanze (>1842). *Price:* (includes breakfast, sheets) dorm bed 18€ (or 16€ with own sheets), Sgl 37€, Dbl 60€. *CC's:* VC, MC. *Hours:* (reception) 8:00-12:00 & 16:00-21:00. *Note:* Church bells begin ringing at 6:00. *Getting There: Railers*, from the Old Town walk across the Salzach River via the Staatsbrücke (main bridge) and ascend Linzergasse to No. 41 (on left through arch). From the train station it's a 20-min walk, or take any bus direction Zentrum (city center) and get off at Mirabellplatz (3rd stop). Exit bus left and cross the street via the crosswalk into Paris-Lodron-Str. Continue straight 150 meters to the archway on the right, just past the Loreto church. Walk through the archway and continue straight. The door into St. Sebastian's will appear near the end on the left.

Hostel, YoHo: Paracelsusstr. 9 (www.yoho.at) *Tel.#* 0662/879-649. If you're looking for a hostel with a lively atmosphere, one not conducive to restful evenings, look no further. YoHo offers its guests 24-hour Internet, discounted tours, daily screenings (typically 10:30) of the movie "The Sound of Music," cheap meals, and an in-house bar with a very "happy hour" (typically 18:00-19:00). *Price:* (sheets and key included but require a 5€ deposit) dorm bed 16-18€, Sgl 28€, Dbl 42-48€, cheap breakfast. *Note:* Check out 10:00, sharp! *Getting There: Railers,* YoHo is a 15-min walk from the Old Town and 10 min from the train station. Exit station left some 200 meters to the main drag (Gabelsbergerstr.), then go left under rail bridge. Continue straight and the second right is Paracelsusstr. Your digs are on the second block, right side. *GPS:* N47° 48.496 - E13° 02.848

Hostel, Jugendgästehaus: Josef-Preis-Allee 18 (www.jgh.at) *Tel.#* 0662/842-670. This four-story hostel—located within easy reach (five minutes by foot) of the Old Town—has 396 beds, a game room, volleyball area, elevator, basic laundry, inexpensive cafeteria, Internet, discounted tours, fab views of fortress, wheelchair accessibility, and daily screenings of the movie "The Sound of Music." The accommodations are somewhat worn but the location is good and the staff are friendly. *Price:* (includes breakfast) dorm bed 16-18€, Sgl 28-33€, Dbl 60€. *CC's:* VC, MC, AE, DC. *Note:* Check-in 13:00. Must be a member or an extra charge will apply. *Getting There: Railers,* from the station take bus #5 or #25 to Justizgebäude—exit bus left and walk some 50 meters to the crosswalk. On the other side of the road follow green hostel sign pointing into the narrow Josef-Preis-Allee—hostel is at end of lane. *Drivers,* free parking in front. *GPS:* N47° 47.689 - E13° 03.370

Hostel/Café, Stadtalm: (www.diestadtalm.com) *Tel.#* 0662/841-729. Here you'll sleep in a watchtower with first-class views on a pauper's budget. Situated upon the Mönchsberg (Monks' Ridge), Stadtalm is part of the city's historic defense wall built by the citizen guard in 1487. Because of the hostel's inconvenient location and tight confines, we only recommend Stadtalm for adventurers, hikers, or those who are traveling light. However, we do recommend everyone stop by for the views and/or a meal/drink at their popular cliff-side café. To find Stadtalm, look above the Old Town for a wood-covered shaft leading up the cliff face—the structure at the top is the hostel and café. *Note:* open summer only, May thru mid-Sept. *Price:* (includes breakfast) beds from 13.50€ (cash only). *Getting There: Railers*, from the station take bus #1 to Mönchsbergaufzug—then hop on the Mönchsberg Lift (page 478). From the observation terrace, follow directions leading to the hostel listed under *Best Views—Lift, Mönchsberg*, page 484.

Hostel, Eduard-Heinrich-Haus: [HI] Eduard-Heinrich-Str. 2 (www.hostel-ehh.at) *Tel.#* 0662/625-976. The Eduard Heinrich Haus—peacefully located 2.5km south of the Old Town on the edge of a wooded reserve near the river—is a clean hostel for families or the quieter type. On the property is a volleyball area, ping-pong table, cafeteria, sun terrace with BBQ, laundry facility, and a giant-sized chess set. Most rooms have toilet/shower. *Price:* (includes breakfast, sheets) dorm bed 15-19€, Sgl 27-31€, Dbl 38-47€, family discounts available. *CC's:* VC, MC, AE, DC. *Note:* Must be a member or an extra charge (3€) will apply. Members, ask about their *Free Nite* program (www.freenites.com). Property doubles as a learning institute, often attracting groups of students during the day. *Hours:* (reception) someone's always there during the week, Sat/Sun 7:00-10:00 & 17:00-24:00. *Getting There: Railers,* from the station take bus #3 direction Salzburg Süd to Polizeidirektion. Walk to the forward intersection and cross over into Billrothstrasse—follow this street all the way to the end and the hostel is the last right. *Drivers,* exit A10 autobahn at Salzburg Süd and follow signs towards Salzburg. After a few kilometers you'll pass the Park+Ride and TI; soon thereafter turn right at the third light into Billrothstrasse—follow this street until you can drive no farther and the hostel is on the right. *GPS:* N47° 46.852 - E13° 04.353

Etap (Airport) Flughafen: *Tel.#* 0662/857-036 www.etaphotel.com (*hotel code: 5885). Neighboring the autobahn, these accommodations are perfect for drivers who are arriving late into town without reservations (24-hour check-in possible with credit card). Etap is a basic-service, budget hotel with everything a traveler needs, including a TV. Beds are generally a one-piece (triple) unit with a double on the bottom and a single bunk-like bed on top for a child. **Note:* hotel code is compatible with Etap website, creating a shortcut to the property—type hotel code into upper left box and click "OK"; next page click on "The Hotel" (left side). *Price:* Sgl 40€, Dbl 49€, Trpl 49€ (only with child 12 or under), breakfast 6€/person. *Getting There: Drivers,* exit A1 autobahn at Flughafen (5km west of Old Town) and you'll immediately see your digs.

Gästehaus Bonauerhof: Kapellenweg 3, Viehausen (www.tiscover.at/bonauerhof) *Tel.#* 0662/853-361. Drivers, if you're looking for a quiet bed in the 'burbs bursting with fresh country air—this is for you. Gästehaus Bonauerhof is a family run farmhouse run by Helga and Gregor who offer big, apartment-like rooms and big hospitality typically associated with country folk. Located 7km west of the Old Town, Helga and Gregor have plenty of room for you and their stable of horses, 40 cows, and handful of rabbits: Fredi, Tom, Peter, and Fani. Across the street is a quaint chapel—to the left of its front door is a scene depicting the raging infernos that swept through the village in April 1874, charring 12 houses. Right of the chapel door is a memorial to the locals who fell during both world wars. *Price:* (cash only) Sgl 30€, Dbl 48€, Trpl 68€. *Note:* Little English spoken. *Getting There: Drivers,* exit A1 autobahn at Salzburg West. Immediately turn, following the Viehhausen sign—take this road a few hundred meters to your digs on Kapellenweg (left at chapel). *GPS:* N47° 46.985 - E12° 59.252

Pension Junger Fuchs: Linzergasse 54, *tel./fax.#* 0662/875-496. This motherly run pension is clean, cheap, and centrally located on Linzergasse, meters from the Institute St. Sebastian (hostel). Pension Junger Fuchs is an excellent, no-frills choice for those who are looking for a private room close to the sights and indifferent about having to venture into the hallway for the toilet/shower. *Price:* (cash only) Sgl 27-30€, Dbl 38-44€, Trpl 50-55€, Quad with facilities 75€. *Note:* No breakfast. Church bells begin ringing at 6:00. Don't forget to visit the nearby St. Sebastian cemetery (page 482), where Mozart's father and widow are buried. *Getting There:* Railers, from the Old Town walk across the Salzach River via the Staatsbrücke (main bridge) and ascend Linzergasse to No. 54 (right). From the train station it's a 20-min walk, or take any bus direction Zentrum (city center) and get off at Mirabellplatz (3rd stop). Exit bus left and cross the street via the crosswalk into Paris-Lodron-Str. Continue straight some 150 meters to the archway on the right, just past the Loreto church. Walk through the archway and continue straight to Linzergasse and your digs.

Hotel-Pension Chiemsee: Chiemseegasse 5 (www.sbg.at/hotel-chiemsee) *Tel.#* 0662/844-208. This 2-star boutique hotel—situated near Mozartplatz—is so cute that you'll want to call it your own. Incredibly, the building dates from the 12th century. And the marble steps climbing to the rooms were installed around 1540. *Price:* Sgl 43-58€, Dbl 75-96€, Trpl 88-118€, 4-bed apartment available. *CC's:* VC, MC. *Note:* Through the archway at the end of the lane is the Chiemsee Hof (No. 8), an urban palace dating from 1216 presently housing the provincial offices of the governor. *Getting There:* Railers, from the station take bus #6 direction Parsch to Mozartsteg. Exit bus left—walk to the next street (Sebastian-Stief-Gasse) and turn right. This leads to Papaganoplatz. From there, go left. Ahead on the right is Chiemseegasse and your digs will appear on this lane a few doors on the right. *Drivers,* (tough to find) have TI point the way—parking is near hotel and free. *GPS:* N47° 47.867 - E13° 02.967

Hotel Untersberg: St. Leonhard (www.hoteluntersberg.at) *Tel.#* 06246/72-575. Drivers, you'll love Hotel Untersberg, a 4-star rustic retreat with a real Austrian feel that is idyllically nestled at the foot of the mountain after which it was named. Rooms are spacious and feature country-style décor complementing the fresh alpine air. In summer, the hotel's balconies are beautifully ornamented with vibrant geraniums and every half hour a cable car glides by ascending to the snow-peaked mountaintop. *Price:* Sgl 61-79€, Dbl 100-128€. *CC's:* VC, MC. *Getting There:* Hotel Untersberg is situated on the road connecting Salzburg with Berchtesgaden, 13km to either destination. *Drivers,* exit A10 autobahn at Salzburg Süd and head towards Berchtesgaden—after 1km you'll see the hotel's flowering facade on the right (turn at traffic light).

Hotel Gablerbräu: Linzergasse 9 (www.gablerbrau.com) *Tel.#* 0662/88-965 Upmarket but affordable, this classy 4-star hotel—located the proverbial stone's throw from the heart of town—is bursting with European ambiance and exceptional amenities. First documented in 1429 (then under a different name), the property boasts a rich tradition of serving its clientele. *Price:* Sgl 68-102€, Dbl 98-164€, suite 144-198€. *Getting There:* Railers, from the station it's a 20-min walk, or ride any bus direction Zentrum (city center) and get off at Rathaus—walk back across the bridge and straight onto Linzergasse (after two blocks Hotel Gablerbräu will appear on your left). *Drivers,* tough to reach, query reception or TI. Parking 13€/24hr.

Hotel Stein: Giselakai 3 [corner of Linzergasse] (www.hotelstein.at) *Tel.#* 0662/874-3460. Dating from 1399, the 4-star Hotel Stein has a premier location on the right bank of the Salzach River facing the Old Town. The rooms have been recently renovated and are designed in five different motifs: leather, tiger, zebra, stein and Mozart (18C). Plan ahead by picking out your favorite on their website. Make sure it has a city view. Most rooms have been outfitted with a flat-screen TV and for your sleeping comfort you can request the specific height of a mattress. Whether you're staying here or not, visit Hotel Stein's rooftop terrace—the SteinTerrasse—where romantic views of the Old Town and fortress could hardly get better. *Price:* Sgl 99-125€, Dbl 140-185€, suites from 205€. *CC's:* VC, MC, AE, DC. *Getting There:* **Railers,** from the station it's a 20-min walk, or ride any bus direction Zentrum (city center) and get off at Rathaus—walk back across the bridge and Hotel Stein is on the corner. **Drivers,** exit A10 autobahn at Salzburg Süd and follow signs

492 Your Traveling Companion

towards Salzburg. Eventually, after about 8km, you'll arrive at a reasonably congested intersection. Here will be a traffic light then traffic circle—go right on the circle passing the police station and crossing the river. On the other side turn left at the light. At the next intersection (a few meters before the traffic light) are your digs on the right. Pull up to the front door and unload—reception will explain where to park, 13€/24hr.

Hotel Schloss Mönchstein: Mönchsberg Park 26 (www.monchstein.com) *Tel.#* 0662/ 848-5550. "Enchanting" is the first word that comes to mind when pondering Schloss Mönchstein, a luxurious 5-star castle hotel perched upon the cliffs rising above the Old Town. Needless to say, the views are stupendous! The property—wonderfully surrounded by 25 acres of private forested reserve—was first mentioned in the history books as Tetelheimer Tower in 1350. In the coming centuries, aristocrats and celebrities caught wind of this beloved estate and loitered with enthusiasm, including Mozart. Today, overnighters are treated to rooms furnished with antiques and contemporary comforts, creating a uniquely exquisite atmosphere. *Price:* (includes breakfast, parking) Dbl 335-520€, junior suite 535-680€, Schloss suite 635-740€, Mönchstein suite 825-920€, Maria Theresia suite 895-990€. *Note:* Prices are considerably reduced over the winter months.

Hotel Sacher Salzburg: Schwarzstr. 7 (www.sacher.com) *Tel.#* 0662/88-9770. Nestled on the banks of the Salzach River facing the Old Town, Hotel Sacher's posh 5-star digs attract jet-setting tycoons, political heavyweights, and Hollywood movie stars. S.O.M. fans will be interested to know that it was here Julie Andrews and director Robert Wise stayed during filming in 1964 (remainder of cast stayed at the nearby Hotel Bristol). *Price:* (typically their online rate is the cheapest) Sgl 160-290€, Dbl 160-560€, junior suite 415-780€, presidential suite 1130-1700€, breakfast 26€ (or may come with room depending on price category), parking 25€. *Note:* Perhaps the name Sacher rings a bell? Since 1832, according to a secret recipe, Franz Sacher and family have been whipping up the world's most famous torte: a rich chocolate dessert with a hint of apricot. To order Sacher torte, show up in person or go to the hotel's website.

EDITOR'S NOTE: For more stylish living, go to www.schlosshotels.co.at to discover Austria's castle hotels and mansions.

Camping Panorama: Rauchenbichler Str. 21 (www.panorama-camping.at) *Tel.#* 0662/ 450-652. Living up to its name, Camping Panorama boasts views that stretch across Salzburg. Moreover, it has all the necessities a camper would desire, even a Viennese-style kitchen (May-Sept). Need to rent a tent or camper? Call in advance—prices are reasonable. *Hours:* open mid-March thru Oct; office 7:30-23:00. *Getting There:* Camping Panorama is positioned 3km north of the Old Town. *Railers,* from the station take bus #3 direction Itzling to the end of the line (6th stop). Upon exiting bus, walk back to Rauchenbichler Str. and follow signs. *Drivers,* exit A1 autobahn at Salzburg Nord and follow Camping Panorama signs.

Campground, Schloss Aigen: (www.campingaigen.com) *Tel.#* 0662/622-079. Campground Schloss Aigen is situated 5km southeast of the Old Town in a leafy, rural area that epitomizes tranquility—even the drive there is "wunderbar!" Moreover, the distant views to the fortress are mesmeric. Campground operates a beer garden and casual restaurant. *Hours:* office 7:30-22:45, May-Sept, otherwise closed. *Getting There:* *Drivers,* exit A10 autobahn at Salzburg Süd and drive towards Salzburg. After about 4km turn right at the Park+Ride and TI—this is Hellbrunner Verbindungsstr. Cross river and go left at the upcoming traffic circle, then make your first right onto Schießstandstr. Continue straight, which will wind through a quiet residential area for 1km—keep a close eye out for the campground signs. Immediately after the squat bridge over the babbling brook, turn right. *GPS:* N47° 46.791 - E13° 05.470. *S.O.M. Fans:* You're near the former (real) von Trapp villa; page 515—Post Script.

EXCURSIONS

Mauthausen: Consider visiting this concentration camp memorial on the way to Vienna or the Danube Valley (page 547).

Salzkammergut: Outside of Salzburg begins this glorious lake district (page 496).

Berchtesgaden: (page 230) Some 25km southwest of Salzburg (on the German side of the border) is Berchtesgaden, a quite Bavarian village nestled amongst the edelweiss-encrusted Alps. Here you'll discover the Eagle's Nest, salt mines, and Königssee (King's Lake). Departing from Salzburg by bus?—see *Berchtesgaden* top of page 472.

Oberndorf: *(pop. 5500)* Some 22km north of Salzburg is Oberndorf, a cute border town huddled on the Austrian side of the Salzach River (on opposite bank is medieval town of Laufen, Germany). Oberndorf flourished through the ages as a key port along a trade route flushed with merchant vessels hauling salt, known as "white gold." Although Oberndorf has a rich history dating from the 12th century, it is a single incident that transpired over the course of just a few minutes that forever labeled the riverside community as an international tourist attraction. On Christmas Eve, 1818, Joseph Mohr (village priest) required a carol to accompany midnight Mass at St. Nicholas' Church. Mohr handed Franz Xaver Gruber (church organist) a poem that he had written and asked him to compose a simple melody befitting the text. Gruber finished the melody in time for midnight Mass and the two men—along with the choir—sang the newly composed carol to a pleased crowd. The carol was called "Stille Nacht," or more famously, "Silent Night."

Alas, St. Nicholas' Church was swept away by floods at the turn of the last century. Today, the former church grounds consist only of a small museum (explaining history of town, salt merchants, and Silent Night story—daily 9:00-16:00, 2.50€/person) and an even smaller memorial chapel (consecrated 1937), big enough for about 15 people (daily 9:00-18:00). Notice the stained-glass windows of Mohr and Gruber. Allow 20 min for a visit to the grounds. *Note:* See the chapel today via Web cam, go to www.stillenacht.info

Every year on December 24, tour buses usher in thousands of tourists to join locals in a "Silent Night" memorial service, when hot-spiced wine (Glühwein) is sipped from collector's mugs, traditional Christmas shooters chase away evil spirits, and joyous revelers sing the world-renowned carol. The memorial service begins at 17:00 and lasts about 45 minutes (try to arrive no later than 16:45). During the weeks leading up to Christmas, the Silent Night Post Office will be open for business (normal biz hours, daily, from Dec 8 thru Christmas Eve). Bring in your letters/postcards to be mailed and the clerk will strike them with a specially designed "Silent Night" postmark. The temporary P.O. is located in the museum building, where also souvenirs are sold and information given.

Getting There: (*GPS:* N47° 56.736 - E12° 56.200) *Railers,* from Salzburg's central station, trains leave every half hour to Oberndorf (25-min trip). Once in Oberndorf, it's a 15-min walk to the memorial chapel. Exit station left and at the main road go right. Cross the street at the upcoming crosswalk and continue in the same direction. After about 600 meters follow the brown Stille Nacht Kapelle sign left and the chapel will appear on the right. *Drivers,* the scenic drive from Salzburg to Oberndorf is 30 min. Take route 20 on the German side of the border. To find it, head to Freilassing in northwest Salzburg. After crossing the border you'll meet route 20; follow signs to Laufen. Once in Laufen follow signs to Oberndorf, which will lead through the town's medieval gate (circa 1400) and narrow streets. Soon you'll cross the Salt River (Salzach)—halfway across the turn-of-the-century iron bridge is Austria—the other side is Oberndorf. *(This bridge is one of the most attractive in Austria, and was recently commemorated on a stamp marking its 100th birthday. If it's a clear day, notice the picturesque Alps to your distant right.)* Continue straight towards the church in front of you; at the T-intersection, turn left. After 1km look for a parking space (preferably on the curve). The chapel ("Stille Nacht Kapelle") is accessible via a footpath on the left. Or, if there are no spaces, turn left into the lane at Gasthof Bauernbräu for more options (ahead on the left). When heading back to Salzburg, take route 156 on the Austrian side (16km). This is the main road running through Oberndorf, which southbound will land you in Salzburg.

Werfen: *(pop. 3500)* When heading south from Salzburg you'll encounter massive, sheer mountains flanking your journey—an overwhelming sight indeed. Among this chain of Alps is the town of Werfen, 40km from Salzburg. Most of the time it's hard to distinguish one village from another in this region because they all feature an idyllic church steeple lofting towards the stratosphere and a cluster of well-kept houses decorated with vibrant flowers. However, there is one thing that differentiates Werfen from neighboring communities, and that is one hunka-chunka castle: **Burg Hohenwerfen**—kid brother to the Salzburg fortress. It is truly an awesome sight to see this medieval citadel perched above Werfen, hogging its skyline. What's more, Werfen possesses the world's largest **ice cave**: *Eisriesenwelt*. Additionally, moviegoers will be interested to know that Werfen appeared in "The Sound of Music" and in a much bigger role it was the town portrayed in the 1968 movie "Where Eagles Dare" with Clint Eastwood and Richard Burton.

TI: (www.werfen.at) *Tel.#* 06468/5388. *Hours:* Mon-Fri 9:00-17:00 (longer in summer). The TI is located at Markt 24, which is on the main drag in the heart of town. *Railers,* TI is a 10-min walk from the station.

Getting There: Railers, from Salzburg's station, trains depart regularly for Werfen (50-min trip). Once in Werfen, cross bridge over river—then either go straight for TI/town or go right following sign Eisriesenwelt to shuttle bus and castle (path parallels river). *Drivers,* Werfen is a 30-minute drive from Salzburg via the A10 autobahn south, direction Graz-Villach.

Burg Hohenwerfen: Dating from 1078, this imposing castle rests upon a forested bluff overshadowing the village of Werfen. Its powerful bulwarks firmly entrenched into the rock-solid earth represented a strategic outpost along the former trade route linked to Italy. Within the castle grounds you are treated to a tour of its medieval interior as well as a mesmerizing birds-of-prey show—flight demonstrations April-Nov, daily 11:00 and 15:00, duration 30 min. (www.salzburg-burgen.at) *Note:* Time your arrival to coincide with the birds-of-prey show. Allow at least two hours for a visit. *Hours:* (open April-Nov) *April and Oct/Nov 9:30-16:30; May/June and Sept 9:00-17:00; July/Aug 9:00-18:00. *Price:* (includes birds-of-prey show and castle tour): adult 10€, student 8.50€. *Closed Mondays in April.

S.O.M. Fans: In the movie "The Sound of Music" you'll see the abovementioned (castle) Burg Hohenwerfen. Forward to the scene where Maria and the kids are playing in a grassy meadow while wearing curtains and learning to sing "Do-Re-Mi." The significant structure in the background is Werfen's castle. The meadow they are in is called Gschwandtanger. We recommend a visit here if you're in the area—plan your stop around lunchtime to complement the dreamy views with a picnic. To find Gschwandtanger will be either quite easy or somewhat tiring, depending on your mode of transportation. *Railers,* ask TI to point the way up Poststr. and through the woods (steep, 25 min). *Drivers,* at the north end of town turn off the main road (route 159) direction "Dielalm." Ascend the narrow, zigzagging road a little more than one kilometer. Once on the other side of the forest, the view will become familiar—on the left is the S.O.M. meadow. Continue driving and soon you'll see two benches ahead on the left beneath a cluster of maple trees—just beyond them, before the curve, is a good place to pull over. *GPS:* N47° 28.413 - E13° 10.847. *Picnickers,* if you forgot to pack a lunch, there's a deli at Markt 36 (when facing TI, go left several doors—above entrance says Fleischhauerei. The farmhouse-style building doubles as the Weisses Lamm lodge listed below in *Good Sleeps*). *Note:* When absorbing views on Gschwandtanger, look above the castle about three-fourths of the way up the mountain. Now move your eyes left and you'll see a white building, this belongs to the ice cave (see next entry). If you have a fear of heights, you may want to reconsider a visit.

Ice Cave: (Eisriesenwelt) For a chilling experience, visit the world's largest ice cave—more than 40km have been explored. The ice cave is located at a dizzying height upon the mountain opposite Burg Hohenwerfen (other side of autobahn). In 1879, a wandering naturalist discovered the cave. Today, it is a nationally protected landmark and may only be entered with a guide. To reach the mouth of the cave is a serious adventure, not for the faint hearted. First, either by car or shuttle bus, travelers must ascend the mega-steep (21% grade) 4km mountain road to arrive at the parking lot. From there, it's a 20-min walk uphill to the cable car—Austria's steepest cable-car ascent, 500m/1640ft in three minutes—which will lift a dozen passengers (many of whom will see God in the vertical mountain face on the way up) to the elevation of 1575m/5166ft. The views, needless to say, are majestic! From here, one teeters high above the valley floor while trekking another 20 min to reach the mouth of the cave. At this point, most adventurers will be sweating from head to toe, but it is essential to throw on a jacket or sweater, or both. Once the entrance to the cave is exposed, bystanders will be belted by an arctic blast as if being hurled into a giant freezer. Burrr! Inside is pitch black, except for the light emanating from the lamps provided by the guide—a surreal environment of ice, rock, and darkness. (www.eisriesenwelt.at)

Note: Travelers who are out of shape, afraid of heights, or suffer from vertigo—save your money and delete this attraction from your itinerary. • Travelers who are in good health and have a sense of adventure should find the time and money to experience the world's largest ice cave. • Wear good hiking shoes and bring WARM clothes! • Scenic chalet-style (affordable) restaurant located adjacent to cable-car station. • Views are paralyzing! • Photography inside cave *ist verboten!* (That said, your guide might not enforce it.) • Duration of tour 75 min.; usually in German • Overall, expect a visit to take between three and four hours.

Hours: May thru last week of Oct, 9:00-15:30 (last tour), July/Aug till 16:30. *Price:* (includes cable car and guided tour) adult 17€, student 15€. *Getting There: Railers,* ride shuttle bus (5.60€, typically departs 8:20, 10:20, 12:20 and 14:20), or walk 6km (steep, 2hr to cable car). *Drivers,* follow signs Eisriesenwelt. Slip car into first gear and admire the views *after* parking.

Good Sleeps: All three below-listed accommodations are cozy, centrally located, come with breakfast and have facilities (shower/toilet) in the room. Add 2€/person to price if staying only one night. Little English spoken. By far the nicest, as well as the most expensive, place is the Weisses Lamm…

Weisses Lamm: *Tel.#* 06468/5224 (www.obauer.at) Traditional-style accommodations in the heart of town. All room types available, including apart. Check-in at the deli at Markt 36 (when facing TI, go left several doors—above entrance reads "Fleischhauerei"). *Price:* (cash only) 30-35€/person.

Kärntnerhof: *Tel.#* 06468/5214, located at Markt 31, near TI. Basic rooms—nice views. *Price:* Sgl 25€, Dbl 48€, Trpl 65€. *CC's:* VC, MC.

Haus Saller: *Tel.#* 06468/5498, located at Josef Struber Str. 1, which is on the north side of town. Ascend Josef Struber Str. some 100 meters and it's on the left. *GPS:* N47° 28.740 - E13° 11.148. Very reasonable, homely digs in a family run chalet. Great views. *Price:* (cash only) 18€/person.

SALZKAMMERGUT

This strange-sounding name translates to "salt storage estates," referring to the region's rich salt deposits that have been mined since the Iron Age, i.e. Hallstatt. Today, however, the Salzkammergut is better known as the lake district—a collection of glacial lakes strung out like shimmering pearls across three Austrian states: Salzburgland, Styria (Steiermark), and Upper Austria (Oberösterreich). Besides its stunning beauty, what makes the Salzkammergut so unique is that many of the alpine lakes boast crystal-clear, drinking-quality water. It's true! (www.salzkammergut.at)

Within reach of Salzburg, the main lakes of interest are Fuschlsee, Wolfgangsee, Mondsee and Hallstätter See. While reviewing the aforesaid names, you'll notice that they have one thing in common: the suffix "see," which in German (pronounced "szay") means "lake."

S.O.M. fans will be interested to know that a few scenes from the movie were filmed in this region, namely the wedding scene at Mondsee (page 514—chapter *Sound of Music*).

Suggestion: If it's a warm day, bring your bathing suit and pack a picnic. Those who are planning on spending the night, choose between Wolfgangsee and Hallstätter See—either destination is unique and beautiful.

Note: To obtain a discount on most every attraction mentioned in this chapter, including public transportation, purchase the "Salzkammergut Erlebnis Card" (5€)—valid May thru Oct for the duration of your stay—available at most any TI/info stand in the Salzkammergut.

FUSCHLSEE: Situated 15km east of Salzburg, Fuschlsee is the first lake you'll come to after leaving the city limits. Its glistening turquoise-colored waters allure even the most hardcore urbanites. Drivers will parallel the 4km length of Lake Fuschl before reaching the main village upon its shores, aptly named, Fuschl am See. Although petite, Fuschl am See commands a devout loyalty from vacationers who return annually with their campers and tents to claim a sliver of shoreline for another sizzling season.

In contrast to the pocket-friendly joys of camping are the ultra-exclusive digs offered by Schloss Fuschl, a 15th-century mansion converted to a luxury 5-star hotel in 2001 by Sheraton Hotels & Resorts. Originally built in 1450 as the archbishop's summer residence, Schloss Fuschl is idyllically snuggled on the water's edge surrounded by a 35-acre nature reserve. *Note:* Schloss will be closed for renovations until July 1, 2006. *Price:* Rooms from 300€. *Tel.#* 06229/22-530, or toll-free reservations from USA 1-800-325-3589. *Getting There:* To reach Schloss Fuschl, turn left at the Sheraton's second property—Hotel Jagdhof—on the west (Salzburg) side of Lake Fuschl. *WWII Buffs:* In 1938, Hitler's foreign minister, Joachim von Ribbontrop, acquired Schloss Fuschl for his holiday home. After the defeat of Nazism, the property became an R&R resort for Allied soldiers until 1950.

WOLFGANGSEE: This area is so stunningly beautiful that anyone who is planning to travel throughout Austria should adhere to the old adage: "Save the best for last." Those who come here first will dream of the delightful shores of "Lake Wolfgang" for the remainder of their journey—even Austria's Romantic Road has been rerouted to include Wolfgangsee's splendor. The two main resort towns adorning the lake's shoreline are St. Gilgen and St. Wolfgang. The latter is a storybook village dating from the year 976, when Bishop Wolfgang founded a chapel here. Nestled on the far shore, St. Wolfgang is punctuated by a 213-foot-tall steeple belonging to the town's 15th-century pilgrimage church featuring a museum-like interior (modest admission fee). Another celebrated attraction is the pricey Weissen Rössl (White Horse Inn, since 1878), romantically rooted on the waterfront.

Of the two resort towns, **St. Gilgen** is by far the most visited since it's closest to Salzburg and sits at the junction between Fuschlsee, Mondsee and Hallstätter See. What's more, St. Gilgen is the birthplace of Mozart's mother, Anna Maria Walburga Pertl, who is commemorated at the **Mozart Museum**—and many of you have already seen St. Gilgen on the back cover of this guidebook as well as (briefly) in the movie "The Sound of Music" (S.O.M.).

Wolfgangsee is situated 27km east of Salzburg, 7km beyond Fuschlsee and 15km from Mondsee. The lake is 11km long; a recreational paradise encircled by a curtain of majestic peaks. One of these peaks—situated across from St. Gilgen—is **Sheep Mountain** (Schafberg), where a 110-year-old cogwheel train (seen in the movie S.O.M.) lifts tourists to jaw-dropping views. Rising above St. Gilgen, a scenic cable car glides to the (1522m/4992ft) summit of **Zwölferhorn** Mountain, from where hikers can absorb sweeping vistas or adrenaline-pumped junkies can paraglide off the edge and soar like hushed eagles. Farther down the mountainous skyline is the superslick Sommer-rodelbahn, or toboggan run, where speedsters can race down the hillside on an aluminum track (1.3km long) with only a flimsy joystick as a brake, (open April-Oct—one run 5.50€). Other activities include **boat rides**, swimming, or a picnic on an alpine meadow.

TI: (www.wolfgangsee.at) *Tel.#* 06227/2348. *Hours:* (summer) Mon-Fri 9:00-19:00, Sat 9:00-12:00 & 14:00-18:00 — (winter) Mon/Tue and Thur/Fri 9:00-12:00 & 14:00-17:00, Wed and Sat 9:00-12:00. TI has English-speaking staff, plenty of brochures, and an ATM (but remember, to use this money machine may incur a significant withdrawal fee). Clean, free toilets are downstairs. *Getting There:* TI is located on the main road (B158) passing St. Gilgen, adjacent to the "Spar" grocery store—about a 15-min walk to/fro ferry dock. *Railers,* the bus stops within a five-minute walk from TI. *Drivers,* when descending into town from Fuschlsee, go right on the traffic circle (direction Bad Ischl) and the TI is on the right.

Getting There: **Railers,** to get to St. Gilgen from Salzburg catch a bus from Mira-bellplatz (50-min trip). **Drivers,** from north Salzburg follow signs to St. Gilgen (get to Linzer Bundesstr.; after crossing the railroad tracks turn right—this road goes to Fuschl-see and Wolfgangsee). If you're coming from the A1 autobahn, take exit #274 (Thalgau) and head towards Hof then Fuschlsee. *Note:* St. Wolfgang is roughly 20km beyond St. Gilgen—follow signs (direction Bad Ischl). *Parking* automats by the shoreline in St. Gilgen cost (daily, 8:00-18:00) 50¢/30min for a max of 90min or pay 2.50€-3€ for all-day parking in one of the two central lots, or *FREE* parking can be found in the lot on Sonn-burggasse off Aberseestr. (behind hotel Haus Tirol). *GPS:* N47° 45.946 - E13° 22.001

Grocery Store: ^diacent to the TI is a "Spar" grocery store (Mon-Fri 8:00-19:00, Sat 7:30-17:00) but an even bigger selection of victuals can be found at the new "Billa" store (Mon-Wed 8:00-19:00, Thur & Sat 7:30-19:00, Fri 7:30-19:30) located above the main traffic circle at the head of town.

Mozart Museum: This petite "Gedenkstätte" remembers Mozart's mother, Anna Maria Walburga Pertl, who was born at this address on Christmas day 1720. Additionally, Mozart's sister—nicknamed Nannerl—lived here from 1784-1801. Anna Maria's father (Mozart's grandpa) originally built the house, which, today, doubles as the district courthouse. The fountain outside depicts Anna Maria as a young girl. *Hours:* June-Sept, Tue-Sun 10:00-12.00 and 14:00-18:00, (closed remainder of year). *Price:* 1€. *Getting There:* Museum is located in St. Gilgen at Ischlerstr. 15—one-minute walk from ferry dock.

Mozartplatz: In the heart of St. Gilgen is "Mozart's Square," a picturesque platz featuring a statue of Mozart playing violin. Behind him is the three-story town hall (Rathaus), arguably the most beautiful building in town, having an adorable bay window and decorative facade. Opposite is the flower-draped Gasthof zur Post (page 499—*Good Sleeps*), where Mozart's sister was married in 1784. When standing in front of and facing Mozart you can see the summit of Sheep Mountain (page 499). Now move your eyes left and below the town hall's sloping gable—the structure you see is Hotel Schafbergspitze, which presently has a package deal going for 53€/person.

Zwölferhorn: Locally known as Adventure Mountain ("Erlebnisberg"), the Zwölferhorn can be scaled in just 16 minutes by riding one of the colorful cable cars up to its summit. TI has an excellent brochure listing hiking trails here and elevations of the surrounding mountains. *Hours:* daily, 9:15-16:00. *Price:* round-trip adult 17€, student 15.50€; one-way 12€/11.50€. When you're ready to head back to the lake, paraglide down. If you're a novice like most of us, go tandem (110€). *Tel.#* 07612/73-033 or *cell.#* 0664/111-6099.

Boat Rides: A cruise on Wolfgangsee is a summer joy. Hop on a ferry in St. Gilgen and ride it to St. Wolfgang, 50 min. *Hours:* May till mid-Oct, boats depart hourly beginning at 9:15 until early evening. *Price:* round trip from St. Gilgen to St. Wolfgang 11€, to Strobl 13€ (other end of lake), or purchase an all-day ticket (Tageskarte) for 17€. Another way to cruise on the lake is to rent an electric boat (May-Sept; up to five people): 8€/30min, 14€/60min, 36€/3hr supplied by Wassersport Engel at ferry dock. *Cell.#* 0664/585-0891. www.wassersport-engel.at (other watercraft available).

Sheep Mountain: (Schafberg) The Sheep Mountain railway (Schafbergbahn), as it's called, can be found leisurely ascending the 1783m/5848ft high Sheep Mountain across the lake from St. Gilgen, adjacent to St. Wolfgang. The railway operates on old-timer cogwheels that interlock with the grooved track to prevent slippage. Thus the journey to the summit takes 40 minutes to scale the 6km stretch, which was constructed from 1892-93 by 350 Italian workers. *(S.O.M. Fans: The historic steam train [Dampfzug]—is still used and possible for you to ride—was briefly shown in the movie during the "Do-Re-Mi" curtain-wearing sequence.)* Be sure to visit on a good-weather day—from the summit you'll behold magnificent views of pristine lakes, lush meadows and majestic mountains. Catering to the appetite of blissful tourists, Sheep Mountain accommodates two restaurants (one doubles as a *hotel). **Hours:** (railway) May till mid-Oct, hourly 9:00 till 14:50 going up and last train down is roughly 17:00. **Price:** (round trip) 24€, (one way) 14€—add 6€/person to ride the historic steam train (Dampfzug), departing 10:00 and 13:00, but only in good weather, from July 8 thru Sept 10 (best to call ahead for reservations: tel.# 06138/22-320). **Getting There:** (Schafbergbahn) By ferry from St. Gilgen purchase combo-ticket at wharf (32.80€, inclusive of round trip, boat/railway). *Drivers,* follow signs to St. Wolfgang. ***Note:*** worthwhile accommodations package available at Hotel Schafbergspitze, 53€/adult, inclusive of overnight (on summit) with breakfast and roundtrip on railway. Res/info, *tel.#* 06138/3542.

Good Sleeps: The below-listed accommodations come with breakfast and have facilities (shower/toilet) in the room. *Gasthof zur Post, Haus Tirol,* and the *hostel* are centrally located in St. Gilgen, while the *Parkhotel/Resort Billroth* is a 10-min walk from town. The former and the latter are some of the nicest accommodations (for the price) listed in this guidebook—thus, they are written first.

Gasthof zur Post: (www.gasthofzurpost.at) *Tel.#* 06227/2157. Gasthof zur Post, receiving rights to serve beer in 1415, is nearly 600 years old! And nobody is more proud of the fact than the owners—your cordial hosts—Katharina and Norbert Leitner. Catching the eye of all who enter, the mural spanning the front facade dates from 1618 and depicts scenes of noblemen hunting game. The hotel again entered the history books on August 23, 1784, when Mozart's sister (Nannerl) had her wedding reception here in the Gaststube, or dining room. Featuring homegrown décor, the hotel's rustic interior was built using only materials from the Salzkammergut. What's more, each bedroom has its own unique design—and most have a balcony capitalizing on the dreamy views of the lake and Alps. Wine connoisseurs will adore the 16th-century cellar, where Austrian reds and whites are savored. *Note:* Hotel has elevator and offers bike rental, 8€/day. *Price:* (cheaper the longer you stay) Sgl 70-75€, Dbl 98-132€. *CC's:* VC, MC, AE. *Getting There:* Gasthof zur Post is situated in the heart of St. Gilgen on Mozartplatz, a three-minute walk to/fro the ferry dock. *Drivers,* free parking. *GPS:* N47° 46.021 - E13° 21.851

Parkhotel/Resort Billroth: (www.billroth.at) *Tel.#* 06227/2217. This luxury resort hotel located just outside of town sits on a sweeping estate that extends from Austria's Romantic Road to the shoreline of Wolfgangsee. The famous composer Johannes Brahms once stayed here, galvanizing the resort's air of romanticism. Some guests choose to get sweaty in the hotel's sauna before getting comfy on the outdoor terrace, sipping wine and admiring the breathtaking scenery while others take advantage of the resort's recreational amenities, e.g. free paddle boats and swimming area. Those who wish to catch up on business can do so with the complimentary Internet service (in-room access available). *Price:* Sgl 49-112€, Dbl 96-224€. *CC's:* VC, MC. *Getting There:* The resort is situated on the north edge of St. Gilgen. *Railers,* call ahead and they may pick you up at a bus stop in town. *Drivers,* when descending into town from Fuschlsee, go left on the traffic circle (direction Mondsee) and soon you'll see the resort's green signs pointing to the right. *GPS:* N47° 46.385 - E13° 22.196

Haus Tirol: Aberseestr. 9 (www.haustirol.com) *Tel.#* 06227/2317. Basic rooms—most have balcony—with a cozy Austrian touch and a chocolate on the pillow. From Haus Tirol a walk to the lake, ferry dock and boat rental is only the proverbial stone's throw away. *Price:* Sgl 40-68€, Dbl 79-136€. *CC's:* VC, MC, AE. *Note:* Hotel is closed Nov; has restaurant. *Getting There:* Haus Tirol is situated in the center of St. Gilgen. *Drivers,* free parking. *GPS:* N47° 45.946 - E13° 22.001

Hostel, St. Gilgen: [HI] Mondseestr. 7 (www.oejhv.or.at) *Tel.#* 06227/2365. Located meters from the shoreline and a five-minute walk from the ferry dock, this hostel is one Austria's finest in the HI family—a great way to appreciate the aquatic activities and splendor of Wolfgangsee for a cut-rate price. *Price:* (includes breakfast, sheets) dorm bed 16.50-18.50€, Sgl 29€, Dbl 38-42€. *Note:* Reception closed 13:00-17:00. Must be a member or an extra charge (3.50€) will apply. For the price, you can't beat their 6€ dinners (served at 18:00). *GPS:* N47° 46.096 - E13° 22.039

MONDSEE: With a name like "Moon Lake," it has to be romantic. The main town of concern here—and the reason for busloads of tourists—is the lake's namesake: Mondsee. Even though the Romans settled the town nearly 2000 years ago and monks officially established it by building a monastery in 748 A.D., Mondsee didn't make any real headlines until 1965, when the movie "The Sound of Music" premiered. It was in the town's Baroque church (St. Michael's) that Hollywood married Georg and Maria in the wedding scene. Film scouts arrived in 1963 and discovered the location. The following year the cast and crew arrived to shoot the scene. The twin-steepled church was wonderfully ornamented; dignified guests filled the pews while an organ played and the nuns sang, "How do you solve a problem like Maria..." The scene climaxed when Maria—played by Julie Andrews—elegantly paced the nave with her long, white gown to meet her beloved sea captain waiting patiently by the altar.

TI: Dr. Franz Müller Str. 3 (www.mondsee.at) *Tel.#* 06232/2270. *Hours:* Mon-Fri 8:00-12:00 & 13:00-17:00 (June and Sept also Sat 9:00-12:00 & 15:00-18:00) — July/Aug, daily, 8:00-19:00 (Sun from 9:00). TI is located on the town side of the tree-lined road leading to/fro the lake.

Getting There: Railers, to get to Mondsee from Salzburg catch a bus from Mirabellplatz (journey 50 min). *Drivers,* the A1 autobahn skirts Mondsee 25km east of Salzburg—ausfahrt Mondsee.

St. Michael's Church—a distant relative to the 8th-century monastery—is glorious to visit. S.O.M. fans will recognize its movie-set interior; and on hot days fans and non-fans alike will worship its air-conditioned feel. St. Michael's can easily be found in the center of town; aim for the twin spires.

Toilets: When facing the church, from where the long flags are flapping, public toilets are located to the right (other side of building). If you're going to Café Braun for strudel (see next entry), use their facilities.

Strudel: Opposite St. Michael's you can find scrumptious strudel served with vanilla ice cream at Café Braun (mauve facade), locally known as the best. According to the owner, Frau Braun, the S.O.M. film crew used the second floor of her building as a rehearsal/dressing room. Post-strudel, stroll along the tree-lined road to the lakeside promenade. It's time well spent.

HALLSTÄTTER SEE: "Lake Hallstätter" is bendy like a seahorse and, if you didn't know any better, you'd swear you were in Norway. Similar to a Scandinavian fjord, the lake is surrounded by gigantic mountains maintaining sheer cliffs that rise up from the cobalt-blue waters. The main town on this alpine wet dream is **Hallstatt**—a confined but postcard-perfect community nuzzled against a mountain—where time seems to have stood still for centuries. Indeed, this village is mega-old! So old, in fact, an entire epoch has been named after it. The term "Hallstatt" refers to the transitional period from the Bronze Age to the Early Iron Age, constituting the lands of west-central Europe to the Balkans, circa 800-400 B.C. Thus, Hallstatt, the "place of salt," is one of the continent's oldest towns. Prehistoric peoples bore deep tunnels into the mountain and mined salt here; boats sent by wealthy traders and monarchs retrieved the "white gold" for a fee. Salt was vital to survival throughout the ages as the mineral was used to preserve foods, i.e. meat—essentially functioning as pre-refrigeration. Due to this unique history and its diverse natural landscape, the artifact-rich village and surrounding area (Hallstatt/ Dachstein) has since 1997 taken its place alongside such venerated sites as the Komodo National Park in Indonesia and Uluru National Park (Ayers Rock) in Australia as an esteemed member of UNESCO's World Heritage List.

Hallstatt—situated 75km southeast of Salzburg and 45km beyond St. Gilgen—is a petite village of pedestrians (population 950) that doesn't take long to stroll through. *Drivers* will either park in the tunnel or just beyond it. *Railers* will be escorted into town by Stefanie (boat), which will be awaiting your arrival at the station across the lake.

Once in Hallstatt, serendipitous travelers will discover colorfully quaint houses lining the shore; a sleek church spire resembling the tip of a spear defining the skyline; the world's oldest **salt mine** (since 1200 B.C.); and a peaceful cemetery accommodating Michael's chapel, a.k.a. the **Bone House**. Yikes!

Note: Have some bread on hand to feed the ducks/swans. And it's okay to fill your water bottle from the market square's double-barreled fountain.

TI: Seestr. 169 (www.hallstatt.net) *Tel.#* 06134/8208. *Hours:* May-Oct Mon-Fri 9:00-12:00 & 14:00-17:00 (July/Aug no lunch break and Sat 10:00-16:00) — Nov-April Mon-Fri 9:00-13:00. The TI is centrally located one block south of Marktplatz (market square). Here, besides brochures, friendly staff offer a (free) room-finding service and 90-min guided tours of Hallstatt departing July/Aug every Wed & Sat at 10:00— 4€/adult—meet at TI.

Post Office: Next door to the TI is the P.O.; open Mon-Fri 8:00-16:00, Wed till 17:00.

Railers: To reach Hallstatt either catch a train from Salzburg (change in Attnang-Puchheim, total journey 2.5hr) or catch a bus from Mirabellplatz to Bad Ischl and then a train from there (total journey 2hr). Upon arriving at Hallstatt station, you'll soon realize you're on the wrong side of the lake—thus a cute boat named Stefanie will be there to kindly escort you (for 2€) across the lake to Hallstatt. If you have time to kill (at least 15 min), check out the Hanging Bridge (Hängebrücke)—five-minute walk from station. *Note:* Stefanie's last pick up from the station going to Hallstatt is 18:29 (don't arrive after that). Stefanie's first departure from Hallstatt to the station is 6:50 (later on Sun) and its last is 17:50. Double-check times at the dock or with TI in case of changes.

Drivers: Hallstatt is a fair drive from Salzburg, about 75km, but wonderfully scenic—follow signs to St. Gilgen to Bad Ischl to Bad Goisern to Hallstatt. Or, from the A1 autobahn, take exit #224 (Regau) to Gmunden to Bad Ischl to Bad Goisern to Hallstatt. Parking in Hallstatt is tight and restricted. A one-kilometer-long tunnel cuts through the mountain above town, where part way in you'll find parking lot #1 (*GPS:* N47° 33.784 - E13° 38.964). From there, stairs descend to the village. If the lot is full, continue out the other end of the tunnel for more parking options. From May-Oct parking is tight and day visitors will pay 4.20€/day to park (*free for overnight guests); from 14:00-16:30 the price drops to 3€, and after 16:30 it's free. Off-season parking is free. ***Note:*** If you have a hotel reservation, continue through the tunnel and turn left to the boom gate (this leads into town). Tell the control officer where you're staying and he/she will give you a temporary pass. When checking in to your digs, reception will explain the parking details.

Churches: There are two churches in town, Catholic and Protestant. Throughout the centuries the townsfolk have repeatedly changed denominations according to the trend, or who was in power. Today, since most of Austria is Catholic, the majority of locals lean toward Catholicism.

The Protestant church is situated on the waterfront—adjacent to the market square—and is recognizable by its spear-like spire. The much older, 14th-century Catholic church is the significant structure perched above the village. It is here you'll discover excellent views and the Bone House...

Bone House: (Beinhaus) For a spine-chilling experience visit the house of bones in the cemetery behind the Catholic church, 105 steps above the market square. Dating from the early 17th century, an unusual custom permited graves to be recycled every 10-20 years to conserve what little land Hallstatt had available. Skeletons were exhumed and stored in the adjacent chapel (Michaelskapelle, a.k.a. Beinhaus), where oodles of calcium-deficient bones and skulls are presently on display. Of the 1200 skulls exhibited, some with teeth missing and grinning jaw bones, more than half have been ornately decorated with designer-like artwork, including the names of the deceased painted onto the foreheads. Today, this centuries-old custom is no longer in practice, and—allegedly—updated space-saving methods advocate burying the freshly dead standing upright. Whether you're interested in old bones or not, the Catholic church and neighboring cemetery are both must-see sites. *Note:* Don't forget your camera, the lake views are astonishing. *Hours:* daily, 10:30-16:30 (summer 10:00-18:00). *Price:* (entry into Bone House) 1€.

Museum, Hallstatt: This newly opened museum, located meters from the TI, features "a trip through time, 7000 years" of Hallstatt's history: from past epochs to today's village of archeological discoveries. *Hours:* April-Oct, daily, 10:00-16:00 (May-Sept till 18:00); remainder of year Tue-Sun 11:00-15:00. *Price:* adult 7€, student 3.50€.

Salt Mines: (Salzbergwerk) With salt deposits being exploited as early as the 2nd millennium B.C., the Hallstatt mines are recognized as the world's oldest—which, astonishingly, are still worked commercially today. Situated high above Hallstatt, deep in the mountain, the salt mines can be reached via one *steep* funicular (cable railway) and a 10-min walk. Tourists throw on oversized miners' uniforms, ride a bench on wheels into the mountain, explore subterranean cavities dug by prehistoric peoples, meet the "man preserved in salt" (discovered 1734), and slide down a 64-meter wooden banister—said to be Europe's longest—while being clocked by radar. All told, traveling to/fro mines and tour, expect to spend around 3.5 hours. (www.salzwelten.at) *Hours:* April 29 thru Oct 26, daily, 9:00-16:00 (last tour)—closed remainder of year. *Price:* (includes round trip on funicular and tour of salt mine) adult 21€, student 12.60€, discount available with valid Salzburg Card. *Hikers,* salt mine only (without funicular) 15.50€/9.50€, or ride the funicular up (add 5€/3€) and trek down. *Note:* Tours through the salt mine are mainly in German but the guides speak English, so don't be shy if you have questions. *Getting There:* The funicular (called the Salzbergbahn) is located at the south end of town.

Boat Rides: The Hallstätter See Schifffahrt (ferry) co. has been touring the lake's glacial waters since 1862, as well as operating the milk-run between Hallstatt (Markt) and the train station (Bahnhof) since 1881. Today, their fleet has been extended to four boats and you are invited for a cruise. *Price:* Scenic jaunt from Hallstatt to the bottom end of the lake and back 7.50€—other options available, see ferry kiosk for details. *Note:* Those interested in renting an electric or muscle-powered (paddle) boat, look for the sign Bootverleih (boat rental). To give you an idea, the guy next to the ferry dock charges (cash only) 9€/30min for electric and 9€/hr for paddleboat—other options available. Open April-Oct, daily, but only in good weather.

Best Views: Hike above town to capture a stunning view. Or, hop on the funicular to effortlessly ascend the mountain. *Price:* Funicular (Salzbergbahn) only, without salt mine, round trip adult 8.50€, student 5€—or ride the funicular up (one-way 5€/3€) and trek down.

Hiking & Caves: Nature lovers should note the plethora of hiking and cave-exploration opportunities in this World Heritage region of Hallstatt/Dachstein. Inquire at TI for detailed info, or go to www.dachstein.at

Concerts: Every Tuesday (circa 19:00) from mid-June thru mid-Sept Hallstatt will host a series of free concerts (donations accepted) spanning the musical spectrum from Jazz to traditional folk. Query TI for time/location.

Good Sleeps: The following accommodations are listed in order of preference and, needless to say, are excellent choices (otherwise we wouldn't recommend them)—two are located on the market square and the other two are only a chip-shot away. Additionally, they all come with breakfast and have shower/toilet in the room (with the exception of the hostel).

Bräugasthof: Seestr. 120 (www.brauhaus-lobisser.com) *Tel.#* 06134/8221. First mentioned in 1472, the *gasthof* (inn) was a local favorite and before long caught the eye of the emperor who awarded it beer rights—hence the prefix *Bräu*, or brewery. Although the brewery discontinued its frothy trade in 1917, the historic tavern atmosphere remains and their cozy rooms feature antique furnishings and romantic lake views. Nobody knows the Bräugasthof better than the Lobisser family, who have been running it for some 10 generations. Located on the water's edge (50 meters past the TI), within bread-tossing distance of graceful swans, your stay will no doubt be unforgettable. Also a hit with locals and tourists, the Bräugasthof operates a restaurant (May thru mid-Oct) with ample seating on their lakeside terrace. *Price:* (cheaper if you stay three nights) Sgl 45€, Dbl 84€, Trpl 118€. *CC's:* VC, MC. *GPS:* N47º 33.638 - E13º 38.886

Gasthof Zauner: (www.zauner.hallstatt.net) *Tel.#* 06134/8246. Old-world charm meets modern convenience in this quaint gasthof hidden in plain view on the market square. Besides comfy rooms, Gasthof Zauner runs one of the most popular restaurants in town—you'll love its ivy-draped, pine-bedecked dining room. Military buffs notice the mementoes near the top floor. *Price:* Sgl 47-55€, Dbl 86-102€. *CC's:* VC, MC. *Getting There:* When standing in the middle of the market square, with your back to the double-barreled fountain, your ivy-covered digs are in front of you. *Drivers,* continue through the tunnel and turn left to the boom gate. If needed, the adjacent souvenir outlet can give you an entrance card for Gasthof Zauner. Parking is by the hotel and free.

Gasthof Simony: (www.hallstatt.net/gasthof/simony) *Tel/fax.* 06134/8231 Warmly run by Frau Scheutz—a mature, charming woman—Gasthof Simony abuts the shoreline offering its guests lake views and a waterfront garden for relaxing or swimming. *Price:* (cash preferred) Sgl 35€, Dbl 45-75€ (cheaper price means facilities in hallway), extra bed 30€. *Getting There:* When standing in the market square and facing the direction of the lake—with the double-barreled fountain behind you—Gasthof Simony is in the right corner.

Hostel, Gasthaus Mühle: (www.hallstatturlaub.at) *Tel.#* 06134/8318. Arguably dishing up the best pizza in town, Gasthaus zur Mühle also offers the cheapest beds in town. *Price:* dorm bed 12€, sheets 3€, breakfast 3€, pizzas/pastas from 6€. Closed from end of Oct thru first week of Dec. *CC's:* VC, MC. *Getting There:* Hostel (jugend-herberge) is located near the TI and waterfall. Exit TI left and go right around the corner. Look for pizzeria sign over narrow archway next to No. 54 Oberer Marktplatz.

The SOUND of MUSIC
YTC's GPS-enabled do-it-yourself tour

The Sound of Music is arguably the most popular musical film of all time. A guidebook to Austria simply would not be complete without a tribute to its creation. Thus, we composed the first ever GPS-enabled do-it-yourself tour pinpointing the locations made famous by this timeless classic.

So come along, and discover SOM with YTC. But first, before we start our tour, let's begin with the basics.

The Basics, S.O.M. 101

The Movie: In 1963, a Hollywood scouting team began searching locations in the Salzburg region. By the spring of '64, the cast and crew had arrived with a shooting schedule of six weeks. Everything was on cue, a seemingly watertight program, except for the weather—six weeks turned into a slog of 11. Upon completion, everyone returned Stateside to wrap up the interior scenes in the Twentieth Century-Fox studios.

Finally, to the elation of all involved, The Sound of Music was released in March 1965 and theaters everywhere were sold out. Julie Andrews and Christopher Plummer played the starring roles in the Rodgers and Hammerstein production, which won five Academy Awards: Best Picture, Director (Robert Wise), Sound, Film Editing, and Scoring of Music Adaptation.

Main Characters: One of our favorite scenes in the movie is when Maria meets Georg for the first time.

> *Maria:* "You don't look at all like a sea captain, Sir."
> *Herr von Trapp:* "I'm afraid…you don't look much like a governess."

Georg Ritter von Trapp (played by Christopher Plummer) was born on April 4, 1880, in a port town called Zara (present-day Zadar) located some 250 rugged kilometers southwest of Zagreb, the capital of Croatia. Yes, you read it correctly, Croatia! If Georg had been born within the last 85 years, there'd be no Sound of Music and we wouldn't be having this conversation. You see, in those days, most of the Balkan Peninsula was aligned with the Austro-Hungarian Empire. Therefore, Georg had the privilege, as did his father, to be a naval captain serving greater Austria (remember, present-day Austria is landlocked with no access to seaports).

Georg met his first wife, Agathe Whitehead, in 1910. Their marriage produced seven children. Tragically, Agathe contracted scarlet fever and died in 1922—leaving the children motherless.

Maria Augusta Kutschera (played by Julie Andrews) was born on a train en route to Vienna, Austria, around midnight on January 26, 1905. Maria aspired to be a nun and consequently joined Salzburg's Nonnberg abbey—the oldest known convent in the Germanic-speaking world. It was here that she met Georg von Trapp, a widower, when he requested a home tutor for one of his daughters who had become bedridden with rheumatic fever (1926). The mother abbess responded to Herr von Trapp's request by sending him Maria, whom she felt wasn't ready for a sequestered life of chaste and obedience. The following year—on Nov 26, 1927—Maria and Georg tied the knot. (*Note:* It wasn't until 1936 that the von Trapps sang publicly as a family.)

Maria Meets the Children:

> *Liesl*, 16 — She doesn't need a governess.
> *Friedrich*, 14 — He's impossible.
> *Louisa*, 13 — Steps out of line and says she's Brigitta.

Kurt, 11 — He's incorrigible. "What's incorrigible?"…"I think it means you won't be treated like a boy."

Brigitta, 10 — She thinks Maria's dress is the ugliest she's ever seen.

Marta, 7 … on Tuesday and she'd like a pink parasol.

Gretl, 5 — She's practically a lady.

The Anschluss, America & Movie History: On March 12, 1938, Hitler's armies marched into Austria declaring the Anschluss (Germanic unification). Many Austrians dreamed of the day when both nations—Germany and Austria—could unite to form the great Reich, or empire. In contrast, there were others who desired no idealistic fusion of the two nations and were content with their peaceful lives, i.e. the von Trapp family.

Georg—a reserved man possessing immense pride and wisdom—envisioned the harsh realities that lay ahead with the Nazis' tight grip on his beloved Austria. He spoke to each member of the family about their future: What would become of them if they were to remain in the country? Unanimously, they voted to pack up and get out! With only the possessions in their rucksacks, the Trapp family pretended to go on a hiking trip to Italy and slipped through the Nazi web by train. And just like that, in a matter of a few hours, they had left everything behind, becoming refugees without a country.

The family remained in Italy for about five weeks before heading to England, from where they sailed 11 days to New York in September 1938. Dashing from country to country like fugitives was no easy task for the von Trapps, who had since swelled to nine children and Maria was pregnant with another on the way (Johannes, now president of the Trapp Family Lodge).

Although they didn't speak English and only had a few dollars between them, life in America promised a new beginning far from Nazi tyranny. Moreover, the von Trapps were now a family of singers who could possibly strike it rich. Alas, six months later their visitor's visa expired without option for renewal. *"When the Lord closes the door, somewhere he opens a window."* Then, a stroke of luck, instead of having to return to Hitler's Austria, they were invited to perform concerts in Scandinavia.

The family toured Denmark and Sweden and Norway and then it happened: September 1, 1939, Hitler smashed his armies across the Polish frontier, kick-starting WWII. All borders in Europe were sealed shut and foreigners—even those with concerts planned—were asked to go back to wherever they came from. For the von Trapps, this was a possible death sentence.

Again, good luck fell upon the Trapp family as if God had personally dropped a miracle in their lap. Mr. Wagner, their manager in America, sent word that he arranged a new U.S. visa in sync with performances for a multistate tour. In addition to the message, he sent money for a return voyage on the passenger ship SS Bergensfjord. Georg and Maria readily packed up their 10 children and, once again, cruised across the Atlantic Ocean.

On October 7, 1939, the SS Bergensfjord docked safely in Brooklyn. However, New York isn't a city without drama, and Germanic peoples landing on American soil immediately after the Nazi boot stepped into Poland was a sensitive issue with the immigration authorities. As a result, they were detained at Ellis Island while their paperwork was checked, and re-checked. While the von Trapps waited behind bars, they once again pondered their future. Meanwhile, stories circulated of immigrants being detained for weeks on end before being shipped back to Europe, or Asia. One family even had to take refuge on a ship for months while it cruised between ports because no country would accept them.

During their fourth day of confinement, the von Trapps received a final decision from the authorities. A guard appeared at their cell and told them they were free to leave. The jail door opened and outside awaited the great land of opportunity. The recently sprung jailbirds toured America and became reasonably well-known as the "Trapp Family Singers."

They scraped $1,000 together and purchased an old farmhouse on 600 acres in Stowe, Vermont, where the countryside reminded them of Austria. In 1950, they established the Trapp Family Lodge, which now comprises some 2700 acres and 100 rooms (www.trappfamily.com). Sadly, Georg never saw this dream unfold. Herr von Trapp, an extraordinary man whose surname would become as synonymous with Salz-burg as the legendary Mozart, passed away in May 1947—he is buried in the family cemetery next to the lodge.

Two years after Georg's passing, Maria penned the family's enterprising journey, "The Story of the Trapp Family Singers." Not believing it would ever amount to anything, Maria sold all the rights for $9,000. From the book sprang a two-part German film production in the '50s called "Die Trapp Familie." The Germans subsequently sold the rights to the Americans, who (Rodgers and Hammerstein) made it into a long-running, hugely successful Broadway show. Twentieth Century Fox film studios bought the rights for $1.25 million and the rest is history... Ironically, the movie never aired in Austria and most Austrians have never heard of the von Trapp family.

The Tour

To wander around Salzburg perusing age-old attractions is pure bliss. There's hardly a better way to spend a day in Europe, especially if the weather is nice. To complement this superlative ideal, we have composed two do-it-yourself S.O.M. tours: walking and driving. The walking tour, as the name suggests, is easily achieved on foot and embraces all the Old Town attractions seen in the movie. The driving tour, for those travelers with wheels, can venture outside of Salzburg to behold the remainder of sights as well as the must-see Salzkammergut (lake district).

Drivers, depending on your plans and where you're coming from, it may be better for you to do the driving tour first to avoid extra parking hassles in Salzburg.

Railers, you're not completely left out in the cold when it comes to the driving tour, you can do more than half of it (everything except the lake district) on your own by bike. *(To rent a bike, flip to page 472.)* Start early and don't forget to pack a picnic. Although a do-it-yourself bike tour can be tiring, it's more comprehensive, healthier, and much cheaper than the commercial tours on offer for about 35€ a head.

If riding a bike isn't your thing, arrange a bus tour from the TI or through the reception desk of your accommodations. Or, if there are a few of you, consider renting a car.

WALKING TOUR

[Allow 90 minutes.] A good place start our walking tour is in the middle of the Old Town on a square called University Platz, which is situated behind Mozart's birthplace. To get there, go to Getreidegasse (main shopping street) and stand in front of Mozart's birthplace at No. 9. Face its yellow facade and next door (left) is a shop-lined, cobbled arcade—walk through this to...

University Platz: (*GPS:* N47° 47.969 - E13° 02.614) This is a great place to start our tour for two reasons: **(1)** availability of picnic items—vendors offer everything from fruits and vegetables to meats and cheeses to hot dogs (Würste) and pretzels. Regarding the latter, there are seven types: chocolate, apple, cinnamon-sugar, poppy seed, pizza, nut and regular—each costing roughly 2.20€. **(2)** Remember the scene when Maria juggled the tomatoes and Gretl dropped hers? Filmed right here, folks. *Note:* The market is open Mon-Fri early till 18:00 and Sat till 14:30. • The golden facade you see is the back of Mozart's birthplace. • The plaque above the restaurant Zipfer reads: "In this house lived

W. A. Mozart's sister Nannerl (widowed baroness von Berchtold zu Sonnenburg) from Oct 28, 1801, until her death Oct 29, 1829."

~ To reach the next site, take the lane (Wiener-Philharmoniker-Gasse) running adjacent to the restaurant Zipfer. (Note: As you mosey along you'll pass toilets on the right.) The lane will empty into Max-Reinhardt-Platz. Once there, you'll see the elongated...

Festival Halls: (Festspielhaus) This massive 17th-century structure, formerly the archbishop's stables and riding school, extends the length of the block and houses three theaters. The middle theater (Felsenreitschule, or Summer Riding School) boasts 1500 seats, 96 arches (on three levels) hewn into the Mönchsberg cliffs, and a state-of-the-art retractable roof. It was upon this theater's stage that the Hollywood von Trapps sang their farewell songs before escaping to the cemetery. (For more on the Festival Halls, including tour times, see page 477.)

    Optional: At the other end of the Festival Halls you'll find the horse trough (Pferdeschwemme)—erected in 1695 as a bath for the archbishop's horses—briefly seen during the "Do-Re-Mi" curtain-wearing sequence (just before the tomato-juggling scene at University Platz). What's more, a few minutes farther along are the elevators accessing the Mönchsberg (Monks' Ridge) observation terrace, from where they also sang "Do-Re-Mi" (see *Mönchsberg Lift*, page 478).

~ Next stop, Toscanini Hof. Go straight, continuing in the direction you were walking, and amble through the underpass.

Toscanini Hof: In this secluded courtyard—named after one of Italy's great conductors, Arturo Toscanini—Herr Zeller, Hitler's Nazi boss of Salzburg, pulled up in his Mercedes looking for Georg (you'll fleetingly see the two giant-sized doors to your right). Herr Zeller spastically got out of his ride and goose-stepped into the right *corner to enter the staging area. Inside were Max and the children rehearsing for the upcoming folk festival. They informed the Nazi tyrant that Georg and Maria were still on their honeymoon. **Note:* Beyond the Felsenkeller (wine bar) are doors that (when open) really do lead into the middle theater. The picture left of the giant-sized doors is of the middle theater and the stage the von Trapps sang on.

~ From the Toscanini Hof, walk through the gated passage (left) and into the next courtyard (College of St. Benedict). Continue straight through the next passage and straight across the square (St. Peter's monastery), passing St. Peter's Stiftskeller (right), Europe's oldest restaurant (page 487). The other side of the adjacent passage is...

St. Peter's Cemetery: This is the oldest active graveyard in Austria, more than a 1000 years of age. St. Peter's cemetery is where the Trapp family hid during the escape scene. *Watch out for Rolf!* You can see that even if one of the vaults were open, there'd be nowhere to hide. Actually, they hid in a Hollywood studio but this cemetery inspired the director.

    To the right, ascend the gravel path to the entrance of the catacombs. Stand before them and face inside, but don't go in. Now, go left two wrought-iron vaults (LII) and you'll see (on ground, middle right) the name *Canonicus Franciscus Wasner*—this priestly man is the real Max Detweiler. He was not the conceited sponge the movie portrays. "Father Wasner" was the Trapp family's spiritual advisor and musical conductor, who traveled with them every escape step of the way. Without Father Wasner, it's very possible the story would not exist. *Hours:* (cemetery) daily, 6:30-18:00—April-Sept till 19:00. *Note:* For a do-it-yourself tour of the catacombs, flip to page 480.

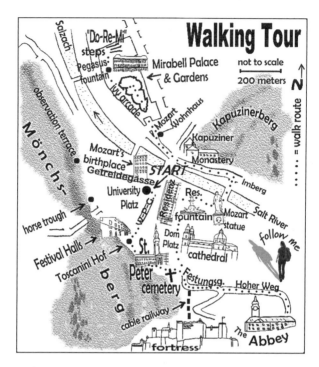

~ *Once you're done visiting the cemetery, face Father Wasner and go left along the path—paralleling the vaults—and out the gate. Keep straight and ascend the cobbled lane (Festungsgasse or Fortress Lane) past the Festungsbahn and Stiegl Keller—the view will develop into a wonder.*

At the top is a crossroads; go left—this road leads to the abbey (two minutes). Eventually you'll come to an archway; above it you'll see St. Erentraud, first abbess, 712 A.D.—hence she's holding the abbey.

Go through the archway; follow the road as it bends right. Continue a bit farther and stop beneath the big maple tree opposite the wrought-iron gate. Spectacular view, no? **GPS:** *N47° 47.741 - E13° 03.096*

Look straight ahead to the forested hill in the valley with the canary-yellow structure nestled amongst the trees—this is the MonatsSchlössl (Month Villa), which belongs to Schloss Hellbrunn (where the "gazebo" is located) and can be seen on the driving tour. Now, move your eyes right and check out Untersberg Mountain, resembling a colossal wave at Waimea.

Untersberg: Soaring (1865m/6117ft) above Salzburg's southern suburbs is Austria's most intriguing mountain: Untersberg. It is upon this landmass in the opening scene of the movie that Maria says she was singing. Maria explained passionately to the mother abbess that Untersberg is her mountain, and as a child she used to climb a tree and peer into the convent's garden (obviously with mega-powerful binoculars) to watch the sisters at work.

Moreover, you'll see the uniquely shaped Untersberg numerous times in the movie with its lengthy plateau (and V-shaped crevice; not seen from this angle. In fact, only half of Untersberg is in Austria and the V-shaped crevice marks the Bavarian frontier). For example, when Maria's singing in the opening scene amongst the birch trees you'll see the V-shaped crevice in the background (from that angle she's actually in Bavaria, which contradicts her narrative to the mother abbess). Also, you'll boldly see it in the background when Georg and Maria are squabbling after the children fall in the lake. However, the most classic time is the final scene, when the von Trapps are supposedly escaping over the Alps into Switzerland—you can't help but notice Untersberg in the background vibrantly framed in panorama scope. Actually, the von Trapps are hiking up the peak adjacent to Hitler's Eagle's Nest. In essence, they are escaping into Nazi Southern Command. Bad move!

Let's get back to the opening scene. When Maria hears the bells chiming while on the Untersberg, we now realize—from our view point, after the distance is calculated—that not only did Maria have bionic hearing, but she also must have been an Olympic athlete in training to even contemplate reaching the convent. No wonder she was late!

~ *Now, turn around and enter through the wrought-iron gate the nuns were twice seen behind talking to visitors.*

Abbey, Nonnberg: (Benedictine) Dating from the 8th century A.D., the Nonnberg abbey is the oldest known convent in the Germanic-speaking world. Together with St. Peter's monastery, the Nonnberg abbey represents the hub of Salzburg's Christian existence. The abbey—true to life—is where Maria really studied, where she and Georg really got married on November 26, 1927 (he was 47, she was 22), and where Hollywood filmed three parts of the movie: *(1)* when Maria left the convent to meet the captain while singing "I Have Confidence," *(2)* when the children were looking for Maria after she went AWOL, *(3)* and during the escape scene, when the Nazis demanded entry to search for the family of nine who seemingly vanished. (It's amazing how sneaky-fast the von Trapps were, going from the Festival Halls to the abbey and to the cemetery in just nanoseconds.) <u>Note:</u> Because the actual convent is off-limits to the outside world, the film crew was only allowed to film externally in and around its church. In front of you, the portal leading into the church dates from 1497. Once inside, angle left through the pillars to see the Romanesque wall paintings (1150 A.D.). If it's dark beyond the glass area, this means 50¢ is required for illumination. If the lights are on and the nuns are singing in their secluded choir above, you've timed it just right. For more info on the church, follow the gravel path (outside portal) around the bend and to the end to find a modest gift shop belonging to the abbey.

~ *Exit the abbey precinct the same way you came, via Festungsgasse. Instead of returning through the cemetery gate, veer right and follow the cobblestones into Kapitelplatz—this is the asphalt square featuring souvenir stands and a huge chessboard. Continue straight through the arches into Domplatz (toilets within arches, left side); bypass the cathedral and exit through the next set of arches. The immense dirt square is Residenzplatz (GPS: N47° 47.918 - E13° 02.812), where you will find...*

Residenz Fountain: Marking the heart of Residenzplatz is the fancifully fluid Residenz fountain—erected in 1658, it is arguably the most beautiful Baroque fountain north of the Alps. You'll recognize it when Maria splashes water in the horse's face while singing "I Have Confidence," and you'll see it again immediately after the wedding scene when Nazi flags are hanging off the Residenz building (left) and German troops are marching through the square. Can you imagine the older locals who went into town that morning to do some shopping? They almost certainly would have dropped their grocery bags and collapsed—*Déja-vu!* <u>Note:</u> Fountain is covered for winter typically from early Nov until the end of March.

☐   *Time to throw on your specially tailored curtains*   ■

~ In the next square you'll see a statue of Mozart—walk past him and angle left towards the traffic light and river. Cross at the light and proceed across the footbridge (GPS: N47° 47.963 - E13° 02.924). This is called the...

Mozart Steg: On this iron footbridge—built in 1903 and named after the legendary Amadeus—the opening scenes of the "Do-Re-Mi" curtain-wearing sequence were filmed. When you're about two-thirds of the way across, turn around for a stunning view. To capitalize on this, the film crew positioned themselves off the bridge half way to forward traffic lights. Once you've reached the end of the bridge, you'll remember the kids bopping from railing to railing with enthusiasm as well as frolicking along the lush riverbanks.

~ To reach the next and last site on our walking tour, cross at the forward lights and go left. Continue straight some distance to the next junction/lights. Once there, the main bridge will be to your left and Linzergasse to your right as well as the Hotel Stein (for an eye-popping view, flip to page 484—SteinTerrasse).

Keep trekking forward on the right side of the street. Ahead on the left, notice the flowered balconies and colorful flags adorning the Hotel Sacher Salzburg. This is where Julie Andrews and director Robert Wise stayed during filming (for price details and a hint of Torte, flip to page 492).

Continue straight. Weave your way past the people waiting at the bus stop and halt on the corner. The building to your right (behind you) is Mozart's Wohnhaus, where his family moved in 1773 (page 475). The Hotel Bristol across the way is where Christopher Plummer and the children stayed.

What you need to do now is rambo the wide-berth road in front of you to the other side, where the bus shelters are. Once it's completely clear, GO!

Great job! Now continue straight ahead; shortly you'll pass two sets of Greek-inspired statues marking the entrance into the...

Mirabell Gardens: Ah, yes...the beautiful Mirabell. Everybody's favorite gardens, where diehard S.O.M.ers go bonkers and we tend to lose guests. Thus, we will end our walking tour here so you can enjoy the splendor at your own speed. But first, we'll explain a few things before bidding adieu.

Maria and the children skipped all through these gardens, as we're sure you will, too. First, you probably recognized those Greek-inspired statues as the scene when Maria and the kids synchronized an arm-raising get-together. Go to the fountain in front of you where you saw them crisscrossing one another. Once there, notice the row of linden trees to the left. On hot days they provide cool sanctuary. Head over to them and continue along the tree-lined path until the dirt changes to pavement; stop there. In front of you (right) is a wrought-iron fence enclosing the rose garden.

At this junction, all points are within striking distance. To your left is the ivy arcade the kids ran through. To your right, where the path arcs into the grass, you'll capture a postcard-perfect view. Straight ahead is the Pegasus fountain they ran around (to its left are steps, climb these and cross the wooden bridge to find the dwarfs they patted), and beyond the fountain are the "Do-Re-Mi" steps (the adjacent unicorns are great to pose on). Have fun! *Note:* In winter the gardens are half closed—you can see the sites but not fully experience them.

DRIVING TOUR

[Allow at least two hours.] There are five sites in this section—four are in Salzburg and the fifth is in the Salzkammergut (lake district). A suggested amount of time to visit is written for each site. The route is fairly simple to navigate and the countryside is delightful to ogle, especially in the lake district. <u>Note:</u> Great picnic spots include Schloss Hellbrunn (second stop) and anywhere in the lake district (last stop). Regarding the latter destination, if the weather's nice, bring your bathing suit.

Railers, you're not completely left out in the cold when it comes to the driving tour, you can do more than half of it (everything except the lake district) on your own by *bike. (To rent a bike, flip to page 472.)* Your route, though, will be different to that of the drivers. You need to get to Freisaalweg, a non-vehicular path southeast of the fortress. This will turn into Hellbrunner Allee, which runs past Schloss Frohnburg and concludes at Schloss Hellbrunn. From there, ride through Anif to reach the Water Castle before backtracking to Schloss Leopoldskron. Start early and don't forget to pack a picnic. Although a do-it-yourself bike tour can be tiring, it's more comprehensive, healthier, and much cheaper than the commercial tours on offer for about 35€ a head. (*Note:* If riding a bike isn't your thing, arrange a bus tour from the TI or through the reception desk of your accommodations. Or, if there are a few of you, consider renting a car.)

~ Okay...Let's begin our driving tour at the Water Castle, located within the suburb of Anif. If you're coming from the city, have the TI or staff at your accommodations point the way. If you're coming from outer Salzburg, exit the A10 autobahn at Salzburg Süd and follow signs to Salzburg/Anif. At the first set of lights turn right, direction Hallein. After 150 meters you'll see (left) a reasonably sized yellow building, a gated entrance and a short cobbled driveway (<u>GPS:</u> N47° 44.768 - E13° 04.049). Park momentarily in the driveway facing the...

Water Castle, Anif: (2 min suggested) Built in the 17th century as a residence for the bishops of Chiemsee, this neo-Gothic "Wasser Schloss" is briefly featured from the air in the opening shots of the movie. Other than its S.O.M. fame, the castle hosted the abdication of the last Bavarian king, Ludwig III (Wittelsbach), in 1918. Since the castle is privately owned, tours are not possible. From the gate you can capture a nice photo. However, make it snappy, notice the golden plaques on either gatepost—they're informing you in three languages to 'beat it!'

~ To reach Schloss Hellbrunn, go back to the traffic light and drive straight through the intersection and into the spick-and-span village of Anif. On the other side of town is the zoo (right), and a few hundred meters farther is the Salzburg city-limits sign—make the next right at the end of the golden wall. Soon you'll pass a small parking area within the walls to your right; continue straight past the second parking area; at the third parking area find a space and cut the engine (2.20€. Stroll through the gardens and unpack your picnic. Salzburg Card holders receive free admission into the schloss, trick fountains and zoo. For more info, flip to page 478). From your car, walk through the palace's back gate (fine view) and turn left into the gardens—the gazebo will be on your immediate right. <u>GPS:</u> N47° 45.790 - E13° 03.847

Schloss Hellbrunn: (15 min to half a day suggested) Some 10 years ago the gazebo was moved here from the gardens of Schloss Leopoldskron, where it was not accessible to the public. More than 300,000 fans visit the gazebo annually to relive the harmonious scene, "Sixteen Going on Seventeen." You may have noticed the gazebo looks smaller; that's because a second, bigger one was used on set in Hollywood. If you're jiggling the door handle to get in to dance on the benches, you'll be disappointed to know that it's always

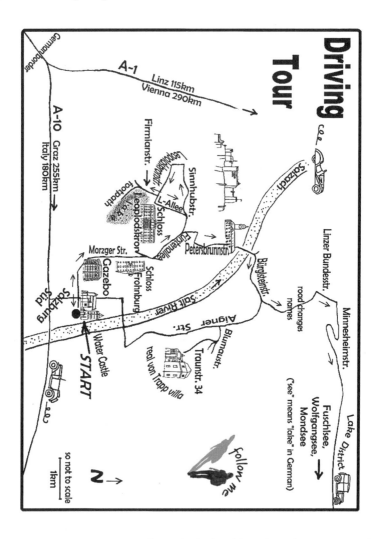

kept locked since previous, equally enthusiastic visitors have been carted off with sprained ankles and broken limbs. *Note:* No part of the movie was filmed at this location. When facing the gazebo, toilets are behind you, the zoo is left down the path and the green shield to your right explains a little more.

~ Return to the main road, go right and continue in the direction of Salzburg. After 1km start looking to your right for Schloss Frohnburg—this is the sizeable estate enclosed within golden walls situated across the meadow behind a row of trees. (Don't confuse it with the yellow estate straight ahead.) Alas, there's nowhere to pull over, so drive slow and have your camera handy. (Cyclists will get a much closer look because the dirt trail, Hellbrunner Allee, passes directly in front of the estate.) What's more, a brief but magnificent view to the fortress will open up in front of you.

Schloss Frohnburg: You'll recognize this estate in the movie as the front of the von Trapp villa. Remember when Maria approached the villa while singing "I Have Confidence" and swinging around those obviously empty bags before peering through the gate? You may also remember when the family silently pushed their vehicle out the gate, only to find Herr Zeller and his Nazi boyfriends there to greet them. (The Gestapo were tipped off by the family's butler.) And, lastly, Georg ripped down a long Nazi flag hanging from the front facade after returning home from his honeymoon. _Note:_ All interior scenes of the von Trapp villa (and abbey) were shot on a Twentieth Century Fox set in Hollywood.

Historically, Schloss Frohnburg dates from the 17th century and was used as a country manor by the archbishops. Today, the estate accommodates students from Salzburg's music academy, the Mozarteum. The academy consists of several properties around Salzburg and affiliates itself with some 400 talented instructors hired to teach an international student body of 1700. Maybe it's something for you? (www.moz.ac.at)

~ *At the upcoming intersection turn right, then make the first left (before crosswalk) onto Fürstenallee. At the next junction merge left (this is still Fürstenallee). Continue to the second set of lights and turn left onto Sinnhubstr. On the right you'll have an impressive view of the fortress. Move your eyes down and you'll see a lone cottage in the meadow. This formerly belonged to the executioner. Perhaps nobody wanted to hang out with him. Pause for laugh. (The last person to wear the noose in Salzburg was in the early 1800s on the knoll behind the cottage).*

Continue straight ahead and the road will narrow into an Einbahnstrasse, or one-way street. At the second traffic light turn left onto an even narrower road (Leopolds-kronstr.). At the forthcoming (tiny) junction merge left and follow the sign Schloss Leopoldskron. Pass the Freibad Leopoldskron (community pool) and make the subsequent right into Firmianstr. After 200 meters either park on the right by the telephone booth or (ahead, left) by the concrete road barriers blocking the lakeside path, which is easiest but illegal! Before getting out of the car, grab some bread for the ducks and swans. Walk the footpath along the lake some 180 meters until you reach the oak tree growing out of the water. Now, to set up a memorable picture, step to right side of the tree and the fortress will be perfectly framed behind the palace. GPS: N47° 47.180 - E13° 02.205. If you happen to be there when a tour group arrives, notice how the guide stops the group well short of this best-picture spot. Time is money, ya know.

Schloss Leopoldskron: (10-15 min suggested) Originally built in 1736 for Archbishop Leopold Firmian, this fabulous Rococo structure represented the back portion of the von Trapp villa (facade facing lake). No doubt you'll remember what scenes were filmed here. Our favorite is just after the kids fell in the lake, when Georg interrogates Maria over children in trees and tailored curtains. After bitter squabbling, Maria exclaimed: "I am not finished yet, Captain!" Flustered, Georg replied: "Oh, yes you are…Captain!"

Today, Schloss Leopoldskron houses the Salzburg Seminar, an international conference center (www.salzburgseminar.org). In winter, the lake freezes over and throngs of locals keenly use it as a giant ice rink. In summer, the lake is a popular place to go for a stroll, jog, or kick back and cast a line (widely caught fish are carp and pike).

~ *To our next and last venue—roughly a 45-minute drive—will deliver us from Salzburg to Mondsee (Moon Lake) in the wonderfully scenic Salzkammergut, or lake district. Note: Supplement this section with the chapter Salzkammergut (page 496).*

1) Head back to Leopoldskronstr. and turn right, then a quick left onto Leopolds-kroner Allee (as you make the turn the gated front entrance into Schloss Leopoldskron will be to your right).

2) At the next junction merge right, passing the executioner's cottage again. (Notice the palatial digs on your right—this is the Altenheim, or old folks' home.)

3) Turn left at the traffic light and follow the road (right) around the bend, then merge left at the junction onto Erzabt-Klotz-Str.

4) At the next set of lights turn left (Petersbrunnstr.), where the abbey's red onion steeple will present itself divinely. Go straight through the forward lights, passing the police station (right) and crossing the Salt River.

5) At the subsequent traffic light turn right and follow signs to St. Gilgen. After 2km you'll come to the major intersection of Linzer Bundesstr., <u>here you must turn right</u> (as a forewarning, the traffic light before is Eichstr.).

6) You'll only be on Linzer Bundesstr. for half a kilometer—get in the right lane— after crossing the railroad tracks follow the St. Gilgen sign to the right (Minnesheimstr.). This road will snake its way above Salzburg and eventually straighten out, escorting you through some of Austria's most charming countryside.

7) After 15km you'll reach the inviting waters of Fuschlsee, the beginning of the Salzkammergut, or lake district.

8) Keep driving towards St. Gilgen, located another 12km on the shore of the next lake: Wolfgangsee. The moment you see Wolfgangsee, pull over at the rest area or just beyond it at the restaurant (<u>GPS</u>: N47° 46.356 - E13° 21.210). From here you can capture a similar image as the one briefly featured from the air in the opening shots of the movie (as well as on the back cover of this guidebook). Another S.O.M. sight is the pointy mountain on the left with a structure planted at the summit. Maria and the children were seen steaming up the side of this mountain during the "Do-Re-Mi" curtain-wearing sequence on the Sheep Mountain Railway (page 499).

9) As you pull away from the rest area, descend towards St. Gilgen. At the bottom, go left on the traffic circle to Mondsee. This is Austria's Romantic Strasse.

10) Along the route you'll pass the privately owned Schloss Hüttenstein, an enchanting mustard-yellow castle perched upon a forested knoll. Behind the schloss is Krottensee, an idyllic lake named "Turtle." Below the castle is Schlossmayrhof, a lovely farmhouse-style bed & breakfast worthy of an overnight(s). Price: (rooms have facilities) Dbl 38-40€, apartment available. Tel.# 06227/2380. (www.tiscover.at/schlossmayrhof)

11) Soon you'll reach the blue waters of Mondsee (Moon Lake). As you get closer to the town of Mondsee, situated on the distant shore, you'll spot what you came for—the twin steeples of St. Michael's church.

12) Upon arriving in Mondsee, follow the sign to Mondsee-Süd. Try and park opposite the Esso gas station (ahead, left). If the lot is full, park adjacent to the lake. (If you park adjacent to the lake, ignore the next step [13] and walk the tree-lined road straight into town/to the church.)

13) After parking, walk toward the Esso—before it you'll see a green sign pointing "Zentrum" down a lane. Follow this into town; you're aiming for the twin-steepled church. The asphalt lane will soon connect with a dirt trail skirting an extensive field. Take this trail to the tree-lined road on the opposite side and go left into town.

Mondsee: (The strudel stop, 30 min to a few hours suggested. If it's warm, consider a swim.) With a name like "Moon Lake," it has to be romantic. Even though the Romans settled the town nearly 2000 years ago and monks officially established it in 748 A.D., Mondsee didn't make any real headlines until 1965, when the movie "The Sound of Music" premiered. It was in the town's Baroque church (*St. Michael's*) that Hollywood married Georg and Maria. When film scouts arrived in Salzburg in 1963, one of their target locations was a church for the wedding scene. However, most churches weren't hip to the idea—only a few would allow filming. Out of their limited choices, film scouts (obviously) chose this one. The following year the cast and crew arrived to shoot the scene. St. Michael's church was wonderfully ornamented and dignified guests filled the pews while an organ played and the nuns sang, "How do you solve a problem like Maria..." The scene climaxed when Maria elegantly paced the nave with her long, white gown to meet her beloved sea captain waiting patiently by the altar.

Toilets: When facing the church, from where the long flags are flapping, public toilets are located to the right (other side of building). If you're going to Café Braun for strudel (see next entry), use their facilities.

Strudel: Opposite St. Michael's you can find scrumptious strudel served with vanilla ice cream at Café Braun (mauve facade), locally known as the best. According to the owner, Frau Braun, the S.O.M. film crew used the second floor of her building as a rehearsal/dressing room.

Post-strudel, consider strolling along the tree-lined road to the lakeside promenade. It's time well spent.

That's all, folks! Thanks for coming along, and we hope you enjoyed the tour.

~ *To get back to Salzburg (25km away) you can conveniently jump on the A1 autobahn, located on the other side of town.* Note: *As a reminder, vehicles traveling on the Austrian autobahn system are required to have a "Vignette," or toll sticker (page 469—Drivers).*

Post Script: If you crave more and would like to have an *external* peek at the real von Trapp villa, head to Traunstr. 34 in the Salzburg suburb of Aigen (3km southeast of the Old Town). *Note:* The villa is privately owned and not on the beaten path, so we beg you to *PLEASE* keep out and be quiet. Sshhhhhh! *GPS:* N47° 47.347 - E13° 04.906

INNSBRUCK

~ Population: 130,000   ~ Country/Area Code: +43-(0)512
~ Elevation: 575m/1886ft   ~ Sister City: New Orleans, Louisiana

Late in the 12th century, a bridge was built over the Inn River — thus originated the settlement and its name: Innsbruck, or "bridge over the Inn." Essentially a crossroads between the German and Italian territories north and south of the Alps, Innsbruck thrived on the heavy influx of merchants and their goods.

During medieval times, members of the dynastic Habsburg family moved to Innsbruck and established it as the imperial capital of the province of Tyrol. Although the monarchy died out nearly 100 years ago, Innsbruck is still the capital of Tyrol, one of Austria's nine federal states.

Innsbruck's Altstadt, or Old Town, is well-preserved and at its core is the city's most ogled site: the Golden Roof (page 522). Tourists flock here within minutes of arriving to snap a picture of its shimmering tiles. Surrounding the Golden Roof is a maze of shop-lined arcades and lanes. The tightly pressed together Gothic-style facades are painted in a rainbow of colors, namely pastels. Even a McDonald's can be found in the collection, denoted by a wrought-iron sign hanging over the door advertising its 40-zillion-served trade. During your explorations you'll notice most all of Innsbruck's buildings are painted in pastels. Tradition dictates that a building cannot be painted any other color than its original shade. Thus if you were to visit Innsbruck again in 'x' amount of years the same building will be the same color.

The water in Innsbruck is alpine fresh, streaming down from the mountains purified and enriched with minerals. Fill up your water bottle at any one of the city's numerous fountains—unless it says "kein trinkwasser" meaning, "not for drinking"!

Ideally living in the heart of Europe, citizens of Innsbruck can readily gallivant across international boundaries. If they desire fresh pasta or a wood-fired pizza for dinner, the Italian border is a mere 35km to the south. If a Swiss watch or an original Swiss army knife is on the shopping list, Switzerland—along with Liechtenstein—can be reached within two hours heading west. And in less than half that time, Innsbruckers can cross the German frontier traveling north.

Referred to as the treasury of the Austrian Alps, Innsbruck is famous for its winter sports and has twice hosted the Winter Olympics: 1964 and 1976. Innsbruck is encompassed by a majestic curtain of mountains and boasts six ski areas totaling some 200km of slopes and 60 lifts. Only 5km from the town center you can ride a cable car up to the ultra-scenic Patscherkofel ski area, which is also popular in summer for wandering trails and mountain hikes (page 522—*Cable Car, Mountain*).

Getting high in Innsbruck is easy, from climbing the City Tower to meeting mountain animals in Europe's highest zoo (←see *Sights*→) and from visiting the Olympic ski jump to hiking and snowboarding alpine summits. But that's not all:

Purchase the Innsbruck Card (page 518) and the city is yours on a platter! This is one of the best value welcome cards offered by any city in this guidebook. To help make your stay cost-effective, everything listed in the *Sights* section (page 519) is *FREE* with this card. To fully experience Innsbruck, allow at least two full days. These GPS coordinates—N47° 15.933 - E11° 23.655—will get you downtown to a world-famous sight.

~ Innsbruck is worth a two-day stay—divide your time like so,
   Day 1: Begin early (9:00) and use your 48-hour Innsbruck Card to start hitting all the "Sights." (*Note:* All attractions listed in the Sights section are free with the *Innsbruck Card*, page 518). The hop-on and -off Sightseer bus will deliver you to each attraction making it almost effortless to see all of Innsbruck.
   Day 2: Visit sights you didn't have time for on day 1.

Tourist Information: [TI] (www.innsbruck.info) Innsbruck has two TIs, one at the main train station *(Hbf)* and the other in the *Old Town*. Either TI sells foldout city maps (1€) with descriptions and history, or you can usually get one free at your accommodations. Those who are interested in getting involved with the recreational side of Innsbruck, ask TI for a copy of their "Activities!" booklet, which is updated biannually for summer and winter. Summer activities include paragliding, rafting, canyoning, bungee jumping, hiking and horseback riding. Winter activities include skiing and snowboarding (www.ski-innsbruck.at) and, of course, schnapps consumption. Cyclists ask TI for their Bike & Fun info map. Culture vultures ask for the Museums booklet.
   TI: Hbf (main train station), located in the central transit hall. *Hours:* daily, 9:00-19:00. *Tel.#* 0512/583-766
   TI: Old Town, located at Burggraben 3—two-minute walk from Golden Roof. *Hours:* daily, 9:00-18:00. *Tel.#* 0512/5356

Emergency Tel. Numbers: [Austria-wide]
   Fire dept. (Feuerwehr) = 122
   Police (Polizei) = 133
   Ambulance/Rescue = 144

Railers: Innsbruck's newly renovated main train station is enormous, non-smoking and arguably Austria's best. Inside, the *TI* (daily, 9:00-19:00) can be found in the main transit hall *(when facing the TI the post office is to your right in the corner and next door is the supermarket)*. The *post office* is open Mon-Sat 7:00-19:30 and the bustling *supermarket* (daily, 6:00-21:00). *Storage lockers*, located right of the post office, can be had for 2€-3.50€/24hr. *Train info* and *ticket purchase* are located in the ÖBB Reisezentrum opposite the TI. (Normal adult price, one way, via rail from Innsbruck to Salzburg is 32€, 2hr — to Graz 45€, 6hr.) *Buses* are out front as well as *Taxis*. *Getting to the Old Town* from the station is an easy and scenic 20-min walk—exit station straight; after the first crosswalk look left for a fab view of the Olympic ski jump (which you will visit later with your Innsbruck Card). Cross at the traffic light and go left to Salurner Str., where you'll go right. Continue straight on Salurner Str.—just past the second cross street you'll see Innsbruck's casino (left). At the third cross street (Maria Theresien Str.) go right, but before you do notice the Triumphal Arch (page 523) on the left. Follow Maria Theresien Str. (page 522) straight past St. Anne's Column towards the majestic curtain of Alps, the Old Town and its gleaming centerpiece: the Golden Roof (page 522).

Buses/Trams: Public transportation in Innsbruck is easy and efficient, combining buses and trams. Tickets cover both and can be purchased at multilingual automats labeled "tickets" or at a tobacco (Tabak) shop. A single (one-way) ticket, or *Einzelticket*, costs 1.60€; the *24hr-Ticket* is 3.50€; the *4-Fahrtenticket* is 5.20€ and good for 4 trips within Innsbruck; and the week ticket, or *Wochenticket*, costs 11€. *Note:* The week ticket is transferable; meaning others can use it. The single (one-way) ticket can only be purchased from the driver, who then validates it. Stamp other ticket-types in the onboard time box to validate, watch locals. An on-the-spot fine of 50€ will be enforced if caught riding "schwarz" (without a valid ticket).

Drivers: *Street parking* pay at nearby automat and leave ticket on dashboard of your car (applicable times Mon-Fri 9:00-19:00, Sat 9:00-13:00, otherwise free). Price: (automat) 50¢/30min, max 90min (on the Innstr. side of the river the max is 180min and Sat is free). *FREE* parking can be found in the suburb of Reichenau, northeast of Old Town—20-min walk or ride bus "O." *Parking Garage:* There are a few around town, charging roughly 2.20€/hr, 15€/24hr. *Note:* As a reminder, vehicles traveling on the Austrian autobahn system are required to have a "Vignette," or toll sticker (page 469—*Drivers*).

Innsbruck Card: With this all-INNclusive card the city is yours on a gold platter. Buy the Innsbruck Card and you'll be awarded unlimited use of public transportation within the metro area and *FREE* (one-time) admission into all the attractions listed in the "Sights" section. What's more, the hop-on and -off Sightseer bus is part of the package and will escort you to (or very near to) each attraction, making your stay really feel like a vacation. The Innsbruck Card comes in a 1-, 2- or 3-day card—available at the TI or major museums and cable cars. When buying the card, ask for the Sightseer bus bro-chure, which lists its tour routes and schedule so you can neatly plan your pick-up connections. *Price:* 24-hour card 23€, 48hr/28€, 72hr/33€. *Suggestion:* We recommend the 48-hour card because one day is not enough time to see everything and three days is perhaps one day longer than you have available. If you do have a third day to spare, buy the 72-hour card. *Note:* You validate the card, which should be done before its first use.

Internet: You can surf at the communications shop at Südtiroler Platz 1 (4.20€/hr)—when facing the train station, look left and it's on the corner. *Hours:* daily, 9:00-23:00. Or, for *FREE*, you can surf at (Innsbruck's newspaper) the Tiroler Tageszeitung in the Rathaus Galerien shopping mall (Mon-Fri 8:00-19:00, Sat 8:00-17:00). To find the mall, enter "Galerien" adjacent to St. Anne's Column. The Tiroler Tageszeitung has about eight computers. Simply go in and sit down at an available terminal. If the screen goes gray, wait two min and it should come back online.

Post Office: The P.O. in the central rail station is open daily 7:00-19:30 and Innsbruck's main P.O. is located at Maximilian Str. 2 (one block from the Triumphal Arch)—Mon-Fri 7:00-21:00, Sat 7:00-15:00, Sun 10:00-19:30.

English Cinema: Moviegoers experiencing popcorn withdrawals can predictably catch an English-speaking flick at the Metropol Multiplex, Innstr. 5, across the Inn River from the Old Town. (www.metropol-kino.at) *Tel.#* 0512/283-310 (reservations). *Price:* Mon-Wed 5.50€, rest of week 8.50€ (students pay 6-7€). *Note:* When browsing the movie listings, look for films labeled "OV" (original version) or "OmU" (original version with subtitles). However—as a word of warning—this doesn't always mean the movie will be in English. For example, if you unknowingly paid to see "Crouching Tiger, Hidden Dragon" labeled "OmU," you'd get a Chinese-speaking movie with German subtitles.

Smallest Shop: One of Innsbruck's must-see and -smell sights is its smallest shop: The award-winning "Speckschwemme," which specializes in the finest Austrian hams and sausages in all shapes and sizes. No need to pull a number here to be served, max two people can fit into this ultra-petite shop at a time. You'll love how the merchandise is literally hanging, or curing, before your very eyes. *Hours:* Mon 9:00-13:00, Tue-Fri 9:00-13:00 & 14:00-18:00, Sat 9:00-15:00. *Getting There:* Speckschwemme is located at Stiftgasse 4. When standing before the entrance of the Golden Roof, go right to the end of Hofgasse; before the archway turn right onto Stiftgasse and it'll be in front of you. Turn your visit into an event and pop into the schnapps shop next door. Eins, zwei, drei...Sample!

SIGHTS

Everything listed in this section is FREE with the Innsbruck Card! Start early to maximize your time. Oh, and your admission tickets double as terrific souvenirs.

<u>Note</u>: Because there is so much to see, buy the 48-hour card and split the sightseeing into two days. The attractions are listed in a suggested touring order, beginning with day 1 and the sites that open first—buy the Innsbruck Card from the cashier at either the Imperial Palace, Court Church or in advance from the TI. The first eight entries (day 1) are located within short walking distance of each other in the Old Town; for all subsequent entries use either the Sightseer bus or public transportation. Additionally, if you start first thing in the morning (9:00), the sights are listed in order to synchronize with lunchtime (picnic or restaurant). Pack a picnic and enjoy it somewhere scenic like (day 1) at the Patscherkofel ski area (6400ft; mountain cable car goes here), or (day 2) at the Olympic ski jump—or, if you're picnicked out, both places have a reasonably priced restaurant.

If you require the use of public transportation to reach the Old Town in the morning to begin your day of touring, or if you wish to visit another sight first that requires the use of the Sightseer bus to get there—instead of paying individually for the bus fare and then buying the Innsbruck Card at the attraction—buy the card beforehand. The seller of the card will explain how to validate it prior to its first use so your bus/tram fare will be covered.

<u>Sightseer Bus</u>: To reach the key sites outside of the Old Town, use the hop-on and -off Sightseer bus. The buses are small but comfortable and are outfitted with headphones providing running commentary in six languages. Be sure to grab the Sightseer brochure, which lists the bus schedule and their tour routes so you can neatly plan your pick-up connections. **Hours:** May-Oct, buses run every 30 min, 9:00-17:30 — Nov-April, buses run hourly, 10:00-18:00. **Price:** Free with valid Innsbruck Card, otherwise (pay driver) 2.50€ one way, 4€ round trip, 8€ day ticket. **Note:** Sightseer bus stops are denoted by a red, circular sign crowning the pole. The acronym "TS" on the schedule board, or on some maps as "S", represents the Sightseer bus.

Day One

Imperial Palace: Wander through the "Hofburg" and relive the imperial days of Innsbruck, when the palace was the seat of provincial sovereigns. Habsburg Empress Maria Theresa (1740-80) refurbished the enormous 15th-century residence into a Baroque super-palace filled with lavish bedrooms, ballrooms and banquet rooms. Of the 25 rooms open to the public, the second room on the tour—the Giant Hall—is the most magnificent ceremonial room in the Alps. Expect a palace visit to take between 25-40 min. <u>Note:</u> Pictures are allowed but without flash. Walk through the palace on your own—there is no audio guide or English descriptions. An explanation booklet is available at the cashier for 2€. Financial titans who are looking to impress, many rooms in the palace are available for hire, including the sumptuous Giant Hall and the subterranean Gothic vault—either venue has the capacity to accommodate some 400 persons. *Tel.#* 0512/587-186. <u>Hours:</u> daily, 9:00-17:00 (last entry 16:30). <u>Price:</u> adult 5.50€, student 3.70€, or *FREE* with Innsbruck Card. <u>Getting There:</u> When standing before the Golden Roof, go right towards the end of Hofgasse—before the archway go left beneath the gilded balcony.

Court Church: Built from 1553-63, the "Hofkirche" is Tyrol's most significant monument, housing the memorial tomb of Emperor Maximilian I (who established the Habsburgs as a pan-European dynasty) and the final resting place of Andreas Hofer—

warrior, Tyrolean hero and Austrian patriot—who fought against Napoleon and was consequently executed by the French. (You will see Hofer depicted in the Third Battle of Bergisel on the Giant Oil Painting and you'll see the actual battlefield [now a memorial] when visiting the Olympic ski jump). Hofer's tomb is located to the right upon walking into the church. Meters away, in true imperial pomp, Maximilian I's tomb is flanked by 28 larger-than-life bronze statues—the so-called black figures—depicting relatives of the emperor, including one of his favorite legends: King Arthur (when facing the altar, he's the eighth figure on the right). You'll see Maximilian himself kneeling atop his memorial tomb. *(The word memorial is used here because he's actually entombed in the city of Wiener Neustadt near Vienna.)* Ascend the steps to the so-called Silver Chapel, the crypt for Ferdinand II. Expect a visit to take around 15 min. (www.hofkirche.at) *Hours:* Mon-Sat 9:00-17:00, Sun 12:30-17:00. *Price:* adult 3€, student 2€, combo-ticket with Tyrolean Folk Museum 6.50€/5.50€, or *FREE* with Innsbruck Card. *Getting There:* When standing before the Golden Roof, go right to the end of Hofgasse and through the passageway. The entrance to the church is off to the right.

Tyrolean Folk Museum: This "Volkskunst Museum," located next door to the Court Church, offers a historical look into Tyrolean culture and customs, from 18th-century Nativity scenes to traditional costume and agricultural tools. One of the museum's foremost highlights is its collection of rooms (kitchen, dining and living rooms) dating from the 16th-century characterizing the lifestyle of farmers and every-day citizens. *Watch your head, low doorways!* Upon reaching the first floor (one level up), notice the handy to-go foldout chairs (on left) for buffs. Expect a visit to take at least 45 min. *Hours:* Mon-Sat 9:00-17:00, Sun 10:00-17:00. *Price:* adult 5€, student 3.50€, combo-ticket with Court Church 6.50€/5.50€, or *FREE* with Innsbruck Card.

St. Jakob's Cathedral: Free a couple of minutes out of your schedule and step inside Innsbruck's "Dom," located in the square behind the Golden Roof. Ogle its stunning interior, which features glorious ceiling murals, the crypt of Archduke Maximilian III (front left), and stuccowork by the Asam brothers. (Remember their eye-popping church in Munich?—page 199.) *Hours:* daily 7:30-19:30—but because of religious services tourists are allowed from 10:15 Mon-Sat and from 12:30 on Sun. *Price:* Free entry.

City Museum: Here, at the "Stadtmuseum," you'll get a comprehensive look at Innsbruck's colorful 800-year history. *Hours:* Mon-Fri 9:00-17:00. *Price:* adult 2.50€, student 1.50€, or *FREE* with Innsbruck Card. *Getting There:* When standing before the Golden Roof, the entrance into the City Museum is 50 meters to the left.

Hölblinghaus: When standing before the Golden Roof, to your left on the corner is an extravagant, Baroque-style facade reminiscent of the sweet decorations seen on a wedding cake. Called the Hölblinghaus after its former owner—Sebastian Hölbling—the structure was originally built in the 15th century featuring Gothic architecture. In the mid-1700s, the Hölblinghaus was refurbished in Baroque-style to its present-day look.

City Tower: Formerly a prison, the 15th-century "Stadtturm" affords a spectacular panorama of the Alps and a bird's-eye view of the Old Town, including a so-close-you-can-almost-reach-over-and-touch-it perspective of the Golden Roof. From street level, look up to the clock tower and you'll see the wrought-iron railing enclosing the open-air observation level, which can be reached via a 148-step work out. Expect a visit to take 20 min. *Opinion:* Those who have a fear of heights, don't deny yourself this opportunity—it's a rather mild affair and the predictably stunning views are worth the anxiety. *Hours:* daily, June-Sept 10:00-20:00, Oct-May 10:00-17:00. *Price:* adult 2.50€, student 2€, or *FREE* with Innsbruck Card. *Getting There:* When facing the Golden Roof, the Stadtturm is the clock tower above you on the right.

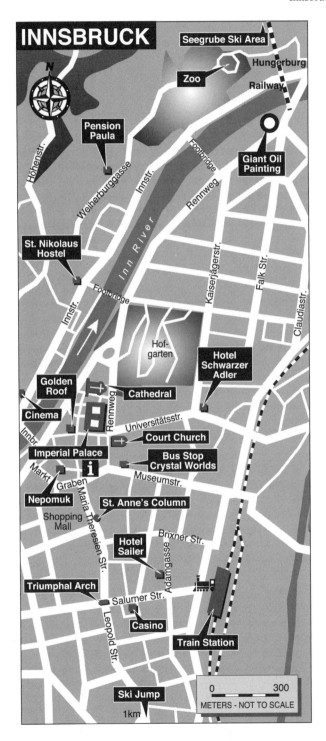

INNSBRUCK

N

Seegrube Ski Area

Hungerburg

Zoo

Railway

Pension Paula

Höhenstr.

Weiherburggasse

Innstr.

Footbridge

Giant Oil Painting

Rennweg

Inn River

St. Nikolaus Hostel

Footbridge

Innstr.

Kaiserjägerstr.

Falk Str.

Claudiastr.

Hof-garten

Hotel Schwarzer Adler

Golden Roof

Rennweg

Cathedral

Cinema

Innbr.

Universitätsstr.

Court Church

Imperial Palace

Bus Stop Crystal Worlds

Markt

Graben

Museumstr.

Nepomuk

Maria Theresien Str.

St. Anne's Column

Shopping Mall

Brixner Str.

Hotel Sailer

Adamgasse

Triumphal Arch

Salurner Str.

Leopold Str.

Casino

Train Station

0	300

METERS - NOT TO SCALE

Ski Jump

1km

Golden Roof: Undeniably Innsbruck's most ogled attraction is the "Goldenes Dachl," dating from the late-15th century. *(Many tourists consider the roof overexaggerated, and we tend to agree, but it's still worth your time.)* To crown the royal residence of Tyrolean monarchs, Habsburg Emperor Maximilian I (1493-1519) commissioned a spiffy veranda—sporting an eye-catching roof comprised of 2657 gilded copper tiles—to serve as a royal box from where he could view the medieval spectacles (e.g. masquerades and jousting tournaments) on the square below. Today, the former royal residence is used for civic purposes (such as the marriage registry) but what concerns you is the Maximilianeum, a small museum on the second floor commemorating Emperor Maximilian I. Before exiting, utilize your ticket to virtually stand on the veranda beneath the golden roof. Expect a visit to take around 35 min. *Hours:* May-Sept, daily, 10:00-18:00 — Oct-April, Tue-Sun, 10:00-17:00. *Price:* (includes audio guide) adult 3.60€, student 1.80€, combo-ticket with City Tower and City Museum available, or *FREE* with Innsbruck Card. *Getting There:* Golden Roof is the heart of the Old Town.

Cable Car, Mountain: Here's your chance to ride a real cable car into the Alps above an Olympic city. In the picture-perfect village of Igls, 5km south of Innsbruck, the Patscherkofel (bahn) cable car will lift you to the (Olympic) Patscherkofel ski area (1952m/6400ft) and incredible views. In summer the mountain comes alive with botanists, nature lovers and hikers. By the docking station is a scenic viewing terrace and a traditional-style chalet that serves yummy Tyrolean food. Picnickers, you will discover plenty of refreshing spots to unpack your goodies. *Hours:* (cable car) daily, 9:00-16:00 (July/Aug till 17:00). *Price:* (round trip) adult 23€, student 19.50€, or *FREE* with Innsbruck Card. *Note:* Igls is also famous for its Olympic Bobbahn, or bobsled and luge track. The track, affectionately referred to as the Ice Channel (in winter), is 1.27km long and has 14 curves. Interested? Like an Olympian you can experience the thrill of this frozen conduit mid-Nov thru Feb with advance reservation, tel.# 0512/377-525 (30€/person) or on a non-frozen track July/Aug Thur/Fri 16:00-18:00 (25€/person)—double check times, prices with TI. *Getting There:* From central Innsbruck catch bus "J" (e.g. from Maria Theresien Str. by Markt Graben) and ride it to Igls (for bobsled track get off at Olympia-express, chair lift near track). Bus J runs approx. every 30 min and takes 25 min between Innsbruck-Igls.

Maria-Theresien-Strasse: This shop-lined thoroughfare—Innsbruck's main drag—extends roughly 1km from the **Triumphal Arch** in the south to the pulsating heart of the medieval Old Town. Midway along it is **St. Anne's Column**, from where tourists congregate to snap majestic views of the Alps.

    Getting There: To get to St. Anne's Column is an easy, keep-going-straight walk from the Golden Roof. At the beginning section of Maria Theresien Str. is a Sightseer bus stop (on right)—in front of you is the column (left of column is another Sightseer bus stop). To reach the Triumphal Arch, continue walking a few minutes farther (on the way you'll pass another Sightseer bus stop). Refer to your Sightseer bus schedule for pick-up times.

    St. Anne's Column: (Annasäule) Dating from 1706, this rose-marbled Corinthian column was erected to commemorate the successful expulsion of Bavarian forces on July 26, 1703—St. Anne's Day—during the War of Spanish Succession. Atop the column is St. Anne and represented at the base is the Virgin Mary. Don't forget your camera; this much-photographed site faces Innsbruck's most-famous view: a grand alpine scene widely flaunted by the media during the Olympics. *GPS:* N47° 15.933 - E11° 23.655

    Note: Adjacent to St. Anne's Column is the **Rathaus Galerien** shopping mall (enter "Galerien"). Besides shops, inside you'll find free Internet at (Innsbruck's newspaper) the Tiroler Tageszeitung (Mon-Fri 8:00-19:00, Sat 8:00-17:00) and for a great view and/or romantic drink take the elevator up to the 7th floor to find the Lichtblick Café/Restaurant as well as the 360° Bar.

Triumphal Arch: Punctuating the southern end of Maria Theresien Str. is the "Triumphpforte," commissioned in 1765 by Empress Maria Theresa to commemorate both joy and sorrow. During the joyous occasion of her son's wedding—Leopold II (brother of Marie Antoinette and later emperor 1790-92)—the festivities were suddenly interrupted and overshadowed by the death of the empress' husband—the groom's father—Francis I. Thus, the north side of the arch (facing church clock tower) mourns the loss of a loved one while the south side (facing ski jump) celebrates matrimony.

Zoo, Alpen: Located at an elevation of 727m/2384ft, this unique zoo is Europe's highest and only accommodates animals from the Alpine region. You can see more than 2000 animals representing some 150 species, from brown bears to an aviary of birds and from bobcats to a cold-water aquarium. Besides an education on mountain nature, the scenic zoo offers one-heck-of-an-exercise program because it's terraced into the hillside—meaning a lot of huffing and puffing to reach the higher enclosures, especially the elks at the top. Whew! The views of Innsbruck, though, are predictably stunning! Now that you've been forewarned, it may not seem so steep. A visit here is worthwhile, allow 60-120 min. Oh, and the ubiquitous sign you'll see throughout the zoo: "Bitte nicht füttern" means, "Please do not feed the animals." (www.alpenzoo.at) *Hours:* (last entry 30 min before closing), daily, 9:00-17:00 (May-Oct till 18:00). *Price:* adult 7€, student 5€, or FREE with Innsbruck Card. *Getting There:* Zoo is located 1.5km north of the Old Town—across river—accessible by foot, car or (your best option) Sightseer bus.

Day Two

Crystal Worlds, Swarovski: In 1895, Daniel Swarovski—as a youthful 33-year-old—believed that "crystal brings joy to man." This being his credo, Swarovski established a crystal works in the Tyrolean village of Wattens—15km east of Innsbruck—where beauty is in abundance; cornfields, pine trees and tall mountains surround the site. Today, the name Swarovski is synonymous with first-rate crystal and his business has developed into an empire, selling some 1.7€ billion worth of product annually and having more than 14,000 employees worldwide with manufacturing sites in 15 countries. As part of the Swarovski centenary in 1995, the Crystal Worlds (Kristallwelten) theme park and exhibition was opened next to the factory in Wattens. This year, around 600,000 people are expected to visit.

A gem of an attraction, Crystal Worlds is a beautifully manicured park containing a labyrinth of glittery rooms located within a grassy knoll designed as face spouting water. Inside, you'll be mesmerized by the three-dimensional world of crystal. The lighting is dim and the exhibitions are psychedelic. Abusers of lucy in the sky with diamonds will have flashbacks here. Toddle through the world's largest kaleidoscope, a crystal forest, the Ice Passage and a trippy dome boasting nearly 600 mirrors. What's more, you'll see the world's smallest crystal stone (.00015 carat) as well as the largest, boasting a whopping 300,000 carats. The go-at-your-own-pace tour concludes in the showroom, or gift shop, where the factory's latest creations are for sale. Beware—this could be costly! If you spend 8€ or more, show your entry ticket and you'll receive 2€ off the price. If you spend 75€ or more, you qualify for Tax-Free shopping. Expect a visit to take at least an hour. If you're coming by bus from Innsbruck, expect a visit to take three hours (30 min to/fro and buses depart every two hours). *Note:* The neighboring Swarovski factory and production line are off-limits to the public—you can only visit the theme park. After picking up your admission ticket, go left around the corner and enter in the left side of the landscaped face. To get an overview of the park, head to the lookout tower behind the face. After, find your way through the hand-shaped maze. (www.kristallwelten.com) *Hours:* daily, 9:00-18:00 (last entry 17:30). *Price:* adult 8€, or *FREE* with Innsbruck Card. *Getting There:* Swarovski is located 15km east of Innsbruck, 2km off the A12 autobahn. From Innsbruck a *shuttle bus* departs four times daily for Swarovski, starting from the main train station at 9:00, 11:00, 13:00, 15:00 and stopping at *two other points within Innsbruck (*Museumstr.: 4 min later, and Hungerburgbahn: 8 min later). Double check pick-up times with TI or staff at your accommodations. Shuttle bus takes 27 min (each way) and costs 8.50€/person round trip (buy ticket from driver; price is for bus fare only; it does not include entry into Crystal Worlds) or *FREE* with Innsbruck Card. *Drivers,* exit Wattens and follow brown Kristallwelten signs. *GPS:* N47° 17.703 - E11° 36.055. *Suggestion I:* Catch the 9:00 shuttle bus there and return with the 11:30 bus. On the way back have the driver drop you off at "Hungerburgbahn," which is near the Giant Oil Painting (see next entry). *Suggestion II:* There is a Swarovski crystal emporium called Crystal Gallery in Innsbruck—some 50 meters from the Golden Roof and two doors right of McDonald's—that will either save you a trip to Wattens or wet your appetite. *Hours:* Mon-Sat 8:00-18:00, Sun 8:00-17:00, open one hour later June-Aug. *Tel.#* 0512/573-100 (www.swarovski.com/crystalgallery)

Giant Oil Painting: Inside the unassuming rotunda-shaped structure on the north side town—adjacent to the Inn River—is the "Riesenrundgemälde," one enormous oil painting, completed in 1896. The painting is a 10,000sq.ft. cyclorama of the Third Battle of Bergisel, when in 1809 some 15,000 Tyrolean freedom fighters—led by Andreas Hofer—defeated an equal number of Napoleon-aligned troops (French, Bavarian and Saxon). Upon arriving, ask the cashier for the English audio and then ascend the steps to the platform positioned in the center of the theater. Soon a narrative will boom through the speakers describing the battle. Expect a visit to take 10-15 min. *Hours:* April-Oct, daily, 9:00-17:00. *Price:* adult 2.50€, student 1.25€, or *FREE* with Innsbruck Card. *Getting There:* The Giant Oil Painting is located 1.5km north of the Old Town—adjacent to the old Hungerburgbahn railway. *Note:* The French executed Hofer in 1810 and you can see his last resting place at the Court Church. From the Giant Oil Painting hop on the Sightseer bus and ride it to the Olympic ski jump (see next entry), which stops meters from the actual Bergisel battlefield (now a memorial).

Ski Jump, Olympic: If you look to the hillside at the south end of town you'll see the brand-new "Bergisel" ski jump. Completed in 2002 by London-based Iraqi architect, Zaha Hadid—who also designed the Contemporary Arts Center in Cincinnati, Ohio—the ski jump was reconstructed (for 15.6€ million) on the same location as the original ski jump used for the 1964 and 1976 Winter Olympics. The new stadium can hold upwards of 28,000 spectators, but on June 27, 1988, some 60,000 Christians packed the stands to hear Pope John Paul II deliver Mass. Walk above the blue painted section in the stadium to find the Olympic rings along with the two dishes that held the Olympic flame. Here are also the names of all the medal winners from both Olympics. If you haven't already noticed, the view from here is amazing, but even more so from atop of the ski jump. After your picnic, head over to the mechanized cabin that ascends to the tower. At the cabin, push the "Kabine Rufen" button to activate it. Once inside, push "Bergstation" to send it to the top. (When you're ready to come back down, push "Talstation".) At the top, hop in the elevator at the base of the tower—press #3 for the panoramic viewing terrace. When finished absorbing the eye-popping views, walk down one level to the Café im Turm. At the back of the restaurant step outside to get an up-close perspective from where the jumpers are unleashed. The track is 98-meters long with a 35-degree slope. Within a handful of seconds the jumper will reach 90kph (56mph). Yikes! Expect a visit to take 45-60 min.

Bergisel—or Mount Isel—is also a hallowed site, locally known as the "hill of heroes," where the freedom fighter Andreas Hofer led some 15,000 Tyrolean militia to victory in 1809 during the Tyrolean War of Independence against an equal number of professional soldiers backed by Napoleon. Near the parking area and bus stop is a memorial to Andreas Hofer on the battlefield site. Across the way is the Kaiserjäger Museum (see next entry). *Note:* Before visiting Bergisel, stop by the Giant Oil Painting to get the gist of what happened here in 1809. (www.bergisel.info) *Hours:* daily, 9:30-17:00 (mid-June thru Oct 8:30-17:00). *Price:* (includes Kaiserjäger Museum) adult 8€, student 6€, or *FREE* with Innsbruck Card. *Getting There:* From Innsbruck, take tram #1 or Sightseer bus—then five-minute walk. *Drivers,* follow signs to Bergisel. Parking available (3.20€)—then five-minute walk.

Museum, Kaiserjäger: A must-see for military buffs, the Kaiserjäger Museum is dedicated to the Tyrolean imperial infantry (1816-1918). Vivid paintings of decorated soldiers in uniform and men in battle adorn the walls. Pistols, medals, rifles, uniforms, flags and bayonets fill the showcases. On the second floor notice the brilliance of (medal No. 28) the Pour le Mérite, a.k.a. the Blue Max, a prestigious medal given for valor. Next to it is an Iron Cross—Germany's Medal of Honor, 1st and 2nd class—from WWI. On the third and fourth floors you'll encounter deadly weapons from WWI. Military buffs allow 60-120 min for a visit; non-buffs can walk through in 15 min. Sorry to say, there are no English translations in the museum. Cashier sells a meager, multilanguage info booklet for 2€. *Hours:* April-Oct, daily, 9:00-17:00 (closed remainder of year). *Price:* adult 3.50€, student 2€, *FREE* with Innsbruck Card, or free with (8€) entry ticket into the Olympic ski jump (go there first). *Getting There:* From Innsbruck, take tram #1 or Sightseer bus. *Drivers,* follow signs to Bergisel. Parking available (3.20€).

Schloss Ambras: Situated 4km southeast of the Old Town, Schloss Ambras was built in the 16th century by Archduke Ferdinand II. The archduke was an avid collector of various arts and weaponry, all of which can be seen today in one of Europe's oldest museum quarters. On display in the Portrait Gallery are walls awash with paintings from European masters, such as Cranach and Rubens. Elsewhere, rooms bursting with medieval armor shed light on the weightiness of knighthood during the Middle Ages. Besides the museums, the Renaissance-style residence is surrounded by 64 acres of manicured gardens and pristine parkland, inhabited by wandering fowl and colorful peacocks. Expect a visit to take anywhere from 1.5hr to 3hr. Shoot for at least 90 min—just to walk through the museums will take an hour and the gardens are pleasant to roam. After touring the first wing of the castle, walk across the gardens to begin part two. To orientate yourself, study the map of museums and grounds on the right before entering the ticket office. *Note:* Although the museums are in English, an audio guide is available at the ticket office for 1€. Gardens are open from sunrise till dusk and are free to enter. *Hours:* daily, 10:00-17:00 (Aug till 19:00 — *closed entire month of Nov*). *Price:* adult 8€, student 6€, or *FREE* with Innsbruck Card—Dec thru March price is halved because Portrait Gallery is closed.

GOOD SLEEPS

Unless otherwise stated, the following digs come with breakfast and have a shower/toilet in the room (excluding hostels). Outlining our Good Sleeps list, *Nepomuk's Bed & Breakfast* offers Innsbruck's best hostel-/budget-type digs; *Pension Paula* is cute like home; *Hotel Schwarzer Bär* adds to the accommodations pool; Mozart once stayed at the delightful *Weisses Kreuz*; and for a bit more money, *Hotel Sailer* and *Hotel Schwarzer Adler* afford 4 stars. *Note:* Ask at your accommodations for the **Club Innsbruck Card**; it's complimentary for all overnight guests and provides various benefits such as a free welcome drink at the casino, free guided hikes (June-Sept) into the Tyrolean Alps (bus ride included, even hiking shoes if you require them) and discounted ski passes in winter — query TI or your digs for details.

Hostel, Nepomuk's Bed & Breakfast: Kiebachgasse 16 (www.nepomuks.at) *Tel.#* 0512/584-118; *cell.* 0650/428-3101. Keenly run by sisters Almut and Anja, Nepomuk's is a renovated apartment on the first floor (one level) above Tyrol's oldest pastry shop (Munding, since 1803) in the heart of the Old Town—90-second walk from the Golden Roof. Nepomuk's is a new venture (2005) for Almut and Anja, whose family has run the (Munding) pastry shop for six generations. We liked what we saw at Nepomuk's and are hats go off to the two aspiring gals busting onto the hospitality scene. We recommend backpackers or cost-conscious travelers book here first—but be early 'cause they only have 10 beds (2 x Dbl and 6 beds in a cozy dorm). *Note:* Has laundry. Check-in at the (Munding) pastry shop. Check out 11:00. *Price:* (cash only) dorm bed 20€, Dbl 50€, cheaper the longer you stay. *Getting There:* From the train station either walk into the Old Town (see *Railers* for directions, page 517) or take tram #3 and get off at Maria Theresien Str. (2nd stop); from there mosey onto Herzog-Friedrich-Str (pedestrian lane leading to Golden Roof) and make the first left (Schlossergasse)—the (Munding) pastry shop will be in front of you. Check-in inside. ***Drivers,*** park in public garage (19€/24hr) or query staff for cheaper options. *GPS:* N47° 16.031 - E11° 23.571

Hostel, St. Nikolaus: Innstr. 95 (www.hostelnikolaus.at) *Tel.#* 0512/286-515. If you can't get into Nepomuk's, let this be your second choice since it's the next best option for backpackers and the location is good (few-min walk from Old Town). Don't expect much more than a cheap bed here, not even a half smile from staff. Okay, breakfast is included, that's a plus. Oh, and they have an unpretentious restaurant and a bar with a happy hour. Also they have an Internet terminal, but don't think about using it unless you're keen on pawn-ing something to pay the pricey surfing fee. *Note:* Check-in 17:00-22:00—if arriving earlier, call ahead to inquire about luggage storage. Beware; they often have a midday lockout! *Price:* [cash only] (includes breakfast, sheets) dorm bed 18€ (second night 17€), 4-bed dorm 19€, 3-bed dorm 20€, Dbl 46€. *Getting There: Railers,* the hostel is a 5-min walk from the Golden Roof and 25 min from the train station; or from the station take bus "D" direction St. Nikolaus and get off at Schmelzergasse—the hostel is opposite bus stop. *Drivers,* free parking in front of hostel. *GPS:* N47° 16.410 - E11° 23.633

Hostel, Innsbruck: [HI] Reichenauer Str. 147 (www.youth-hostel-innsbruck.at) *Tel.#* 0512/346-179. Located 1.5km (25-min walk) from the Old Town and train station; we are only mentioning this hostel because it is cheap and belongs to the traditional HI association, to which some of you are members. Although staff are friendly, the building is old (a concrete block built in 1976 that looks like it was designed by a Communist hardliner) and the dorms are shoeboxes with beds. *Note:* Must be a member or an extra charge (3€) will apply. Check out 10:00. Check-in 17:00-22:00—if arriving earlier, look for sign outside pointing to luggage storage. *Price:* [cash only] (includes breakfast, sheets) 4-bed dorm 17.70€ (second night 15.15€), 6-bed dorm 15€ (second night 12.50€), Sgl 32€, Dbl 48€. *Getting There: Railers,* from the station walk to nearby Sillpark and take bus "O" to Jugendherberge (10-min ride).

Pension "Paula": Weiherburggasse 15 (www.pensionpaula.at) *Tel.#* 0512/292-262. Located on a hill near the zoo, this adorable pension run by the Gunsch family affords great views and a cozy stay for a well-within-the-budget price. If you book early enough, you may get a room with a balcony. *Price:* (cash only) Sgl 28-36€ (←cheaper price means toilet/shower in hallway→) Dbl 49-58€, Trpl 75€, quad 86€. *Getting There: Railers,* from the station take bus "D" direction St. Nikolaus and get off at Schmelzergasse—from there it's a five-minute walk; follow signs Alpenzoo. Ascend Schmelzer-gasse and make your first right (Weiherburggasse). Your digs will soon appear on the left just after the complex of yellow buildings. *Drivers,* free parking in front of pension. *GPS:* N47° 16.622 - E11° 23.681

Hotel Schwarzer Bär: Mariahilfstr. 16 (www.cityhotel.cc) *Tel.#* 0512/294-900. You'll be just fine in these warmly run digs by Werner and Christine Auer. A third generation family business, Hotel Schwarzer Bär is set in a historic building—first mentioned in 1497—facing the river and only a few-minutes walk from the Old Town. *Price:* Sgl from 45€, Dbl 72€, Trpl 95-105€. *CC's:* VC, MC, AE, DC. *Getting There:* Cross the Inn Bridge and go left; soon, on the right, your (green) digs will appear. Parking 5€. *GPS:* N47° 16.109 - E11° 23.362

Hotel Weisses Kreuz: Herzog-Friedrich-Str. 31 (www.weisseskreuz.at) *Tel.* # 0512/594-790. Dating from 1465, the "White Cross" is arguably the most venerated hotel in town. Located a stone's throw from the Golden Roof in the center of the Old Town, many illustrious guests have overnighted here, including a 13-year-old Mozart with his father on their way to Italy in 1769. Although the amenities have since been modernized, the Weisses Kreuz is still in original condition and a stay here is none other than enchanting. *Price:* Sgl 35-60€ (←cheaper price means toilet/shower in hallway), Dbl 90-113€, Trpl also available—query reception. *CC's:* VC, MC, AE. *Getting There:* **Railers,** from the station either walk into the Old Town—or take tram #3 and get off at Maria Theresien Str. (2nd stop)—from there mosey onto Herzog-Friedrich-Str. (pedestrian lane leading to the Golden Roof) and your digs are on the right, next door to McDonald's. A cab from the station will cost around 7€. **Drivers,** hotel parking (10€/day) is located in a garage a few streets away—query staff upon booking.

Hotel Sailer: Adamgasse 8 (www.sailer-innsbruck.at) *Tel.#* 0512/5363. Located 10 minutes by foot from the Golden Roof and three minutes from the main train station, this 4-star hotel combines old world charm with modern amenities for your satisfaction. Hotel Sailer dishes up delicious grub in their traditional Tyrolean restaurant and twice weekly (Nov-March) they host a knee-slappin' Tyrolean Abend show (similar to the Bavarian Heimatabend) with Lederhosen and spoon clangin'—16€/person which includes two drinks and a hat. Yes, a hat! *Price:* Sgl 70-105€, Dbl 110-160€, Trpl 140-220€. *CC's:* VC, MC, AE, DC. *Getting There:* With your back to the main train station, go left to Salurner Str. and make a right. Make the first right on Adamgasse and your digs will appear on the left. *GPS:* N47° 15.810 - E11° 23.883

Romantik Hotel Schwarzer Adler: Kaiserjägerstr. 2 (www.deradler.com) *Tel.#* 0512/ 587-109. With properties dotted across Europe, the Romantik Hotel group offers something unique at each of their locations. With no two rooms designed the same, these 4-star digs are a popular overnight choice. Here, the 15th century tastefully meets the 21st century with themed rooms from the Emperor Maximilian suite to the Versace business suite and the Swarovski crystal room. *Price:* Sgl 101-152€, Dbl 141-215€, Trpl 207-245€, suites 245-475€. *CC's:* VC, MC, AE, DC. *Getting There:* A cab from the main train station will cost around 5€. By foot, exit station right to Brixner Str. and go left. Make the first right on Meinhardstr. Continue straight. After the intersection the road will change to Sillgasse; at the next cross street turn right (on Universitätsstr.) and Kaiser-jägerstr. is on the left along with your digs. **Drivers,** parking costs 9€/day—query staff upon booking.

GRAZ

*~ Population: 245,000   ~ Sister City: Montclair, NJ • Coventry, England
~ Country/Area Code: +43-(0)316   ~ Elevation: 350m/1148ft*

Because it's off the beaten track, Graz is often overlooked by English-speaking tourists. However, it is a wonderful old city that shouldn't be missed. Hopefully, this chapter will convince you to tweak your itinerary to include the southern Austrian province of Styria (Steiermark) and its capital: Graz.

First mentioned in the year 1129 as "Gradec" (Slavic for "little fort"), Graz became a garrison town that bolstered its defenses to guard against an invasion from the east. In the 15th century, Habsburg Emperor Frederick III built a royal residence here together with a cathedral (page 536 — *Burg* — *Cathedral*). The crowned heads of the monarchy encouraged a flurry of trade and Graz boomed.

After Vienna, Graz began the 21st century as Austria's second largest city. Its Old Town sits on the east bank of the Mur River and nestled against Schlossberg—an imposing hill that accommodated the city's massive fortifications until 1809, when Napoleon had them destroyed. Today, Schlossberg (page 532) is a must-visit park boasting eye-popping views of the Old Town and beyond to the Slovenian frontier. Geographically, Graz neighbors Hungary, 75km to the east, and Slovenia, breakaway nation from the former Yugoslav federation, 50km to the south.

During World War II, Graz was the target of 56 Allied bombing raids; more than 1900 buildings were destroyed but less than 2000 people died because they were huddled in the tunnels beneath Schlossberg. Today, tourists stream into the tunnel off Schlossbergplatz on hot summer days for its natural air-conditioning as well as to reach the newly built elevator ("lift") that will rocket them up to the Schlossberg summit in a matter of seconds.

Even though Graz is nearly 900 years old, it still maintains a youthful air with some 50,000 college students—that's one in five of the population. The city established its first university in 1585 and has since added two more: the University of Technology and the University of Music and Dramatic Arts. The latter institution is the only one its kind on the continent specializing in jazz, attracting musicians Europe-wide. In fact, if you stay at the Jugendgästehaus hostel (page 538) around mid-September you will meet a number of these foreign students who are waiting to be accepted for the new school year.

Cities that have large student populations usually have a spirited nightlife, and Graz is no exception. In the evening, throngs of dry-mouthed partygoers descend upon the so-called Bermuda Triangle (Bermudadreieck), a section of the Old Town outfitted with pubs and clubs that gets its ominous name from the frequent disappearance of patrons for hours.

The Old Town is as quaint as can be with its cobbled lanes and mesmerizing squares that lead to intimate courtyards and Mediterranean-inspired passageways. As a testament to its uniqueness, Graz's Altstadt recently joined a select group of Old Towns, such as

Avignon, France; Warsaw, Poland; and Venice, Italy as an esteemed member of UNESCO's World Heritage List. What's more, in 2003 Graz was elected the European Capital of Culture, a prestigious title awarded to a city to represent the continent for the year—marking the first time an Austrian community has held the honor.

To prepare for its new distinction, Graz got a face-lift, adding new landmarks to the cityscape, such as the must-walk-across Island on the Mur (page 532) and the must-ogle Kunsthaus (page 537) dubbed the "friendly alien" because of its biomorphic shape. Positioned in front of many of Graz's attractions you'll find a small-scale model of it for blind people, who use their hands as their eyes.

Picnickers should note that Styria is Austria's breadbasket with regard to pumpkins and apples, growing 80 to 90 percent of the nation's yield. To find these goodies and more (e.g. bread, cakes, sausages, bacon, fruits, vegetables)—homegrown from the farmer—go to the green market (Mon-Sat, early till 13:00) located at Kaiser-Josef-Platz, opposite the opera house.

Some of you have probably never heard of Graz before, and if so, only briefly. However, there's no doubt that you've heard of its favorite son: Arnold Schwarzenegger (see *Grow up with Arnie*, do-it-yourself tour, page 539).

So come along, and discover Graz with YTC. GPSers, these coordinates will get you downtown: N47° 04.440 - E15° 26.123

~ Graz is worth a two-day stay—divide your time like so,

Day 1: All attractions listed in the *Sights* section are within easy walking distance of each other in the Old Town and can be visited in a day. Oh, and don't forget to look up while strolling about town, you never know what you might see.

Day 2: Visit sights/museums of interest that you didn't have time for on day 1, or *Grow up with Arnie* (do-it-yourself tour) beginning on page 539.

Tourist Information: [TI] (www.graztourismus.at) *Tel.#* 0316/80-750
Graz has two TIs; both offer free city maps, helpful brochures in English (e.g. Museums and Galleries, Sights and Attractions, Excursions Around Graz), and both TIs sell bus/tram tickets. *Drivers,* the (often unattended) Hbf branch may be easiest for you since Herrengasse is off-limits to motor vehicles.

TI: Hbf (main train station) — located on street level, right of main entrance before exiting. *Hours:* April-Oct, Mon-Fri 10:00-18:00. *Note:* When TI is closed or unattended, feel free to take one of their complementary city maps sitting on the desk. Also for your use are interactive info screens, free brochures and a free phone connection to the Herrengasse TI.

TI: Herrengasse (No. 16); main drag (pedestrian-only) bisecting the Old Town. *Hours:* daily, Jan-March & Nov Mon-Fri 10:00-17:00, Sat/Sun 10:00-16:00; rest of year Mon-Sat 9:00-18:00 (July/Aug Mon-Fri till 19:00), Sun 10:00-18:00.

Emergency Tel. Numbers: [Austria-wide]
Fire dept. (Feuerwehr) = 122
Police (Polizei) = 133
Ambulance/Rescue = 144

Railers: Graz's refurbished Hauptbahnhof (Hbf), or main train station, is not quite as extensive as Innsbruck's but admissible for being Austria's second largest city. The *TI* is situated right of the main entrance before exiting (April-Oct, Mon-Fri 10:00-18:00). Outside of these hours, see *Note* above under TI: Hbf). *Storage lockers* are below street level and cost 2€-3.50€/24hr. The *post office* is located on street level (Mon-Fri 7:00-22:00, Sat 8:00-20:00, Sun 13:00-20:00) and next door is an *Internet* shop (Mon-Sat 8:00-22:00, Sun 10:00-22:00; 5.80€/1hr). At the end of the hall is a Spar *supermarket* (daily, 6:00-21:00). *Buses, trams* and *taxis* depart from out front. *Train info* and *ticket* *purchase* counter can be found right of the main entrance before exiting. (Normal adult price, one way, via rail from Graz to Vienna is 28€, 2.5hr — to Innsbruck 45€, 6hr.) *Getting to the Old Town* from the station is a long 25-min walk—thus we recommend riding the tram (#3 or #6 by day, #1 or #7 by night) to the main square (Hauptplatz; 8-min ride). *By foot,* (get map from TI and—if possible—have them point the way), exit station right and make a left on Annenstr.—follow this avenue straight to the Old Town.

Buses/Trams: Graz has 7 tramlines—featuring sleek, green streetcars—and a large network of buses to shuttle you efficiently across town. Graz's main transportation hub is Jakominiplatz—a high-octane plaza swarming with people, trams and buses—located at the southern end of Herrengasse in the Old Town (one stop from Hauptplatz). Tickets can be purchased at magazine stands, tobacco (Tabak) shops, the TI, or often directly from the driver. *Die Stundenkarte* (1hr ticket) is valid for 60 min and costs 1.70€. *Die 24-Stundenkarte* (24hr ticket) 3.50€. *Die Wochenkarte* (week ticket) 8.70€. *Note:* Tickets are not pre-validated! To validate you must stamp ticket (*bitte entwerten*) in the time box on the bus/tram—watch locals. An on-the-spot fine of 40€ will be enforced if caught riding "schwarz" (without valid ticket). A valid ticket can be used for the Schlossberg-bahn (funicular up to Schlossberg), but not the "lift".

Drivers: *Street parking* pay at nearby multilingual automat "Parkscheine" and leave ticket on dashboard of your car (applicable times Mon-Fri 9:00-19:00, Sat 9:00-13:00—otherwise free). Price: (automat; prices vary but generally) 60¢/30min, max 3.60€/180min. *Parking garages* around the Old Town are rather expensive; prices vary from 2€-4€/hr to 20€-32€/24hr. *Note:* As a reminder, vehicles traveling on the Austrian auto-bahn system are required to have a "Vignette," or toll sticker (page 469—*Drivers*).

Bike Rental: Graz is a breeze to cycle around. Although, for the general traveler, it's not necessary since everything is so close. But for those who yearn for a healthy ride in the saddle, the cycle shop at Körösistr. 5 has a nice selection of bikes to choose from. *Hours:* Mon-Fri 7:00-13:00 & 14:00-18:00. *Tel.#* 0316/8213-5716. *Price:* (per day) 3- to 7-gear 7.50€, 21-gear 9€, mountain bike 11€. Inquire about special week/weekend rates. *Note:* Bring ID. Return bike by 9:00 next morning. *Getting There:* shop is a 10-min walk north of Hauptplatz (via Sackstr.).

Internet: A good place to log-on is at *Sit'n Surf* at Hans Sachs Gasse 10 (2nd floor)—lane off south end of Herrengasse. Hours: Mon-Sat 8:00-24:00, Sun 9:00-21:00. Price: 2.60€/30 min, 4.50€/hr. Another Internet location is next door to the post office in the main train station. Hours: Mon-Sat 8:00-22:00, Sun 10:00-22:00. Price: 5.80€/1hr.

Post Office: Graz has three central branches. *1)* Hauptbahnhof (main train station) located on street level—Mon-Fri 7:00-22:00, Sat 8:00-20:00, Sun 13:00-20:00. *2)* Anoth-er P.O. is located halfway between the train station and the Old Town at the corner of Annenstr. and Elisabethinergasse—Mon-Thur 8:30-17:30, Fri 8:30-17:00. *3)* Lastly, you'll discover a P.O. just south of the Old Town at Neutorgasse 46—Mon-Fri 7:00-20:00, Sat 7:00-12:00.

FREE Graz

1) Cross the river into the Old Town via the one-and-only **Island on the Mur** (page 532).

2) A trip to Graz wouldn't be complete without a stroll through **Schlossberg** (page 532) high above the Old Town. From its ramparts, soak up the sweeping vistas extending over the red rooftops of Graz into the Styrian countryside and beyond to the distant hills marking the frontier of Slovenia, a Slavic nation once belonging to the former Yugoslav federation.

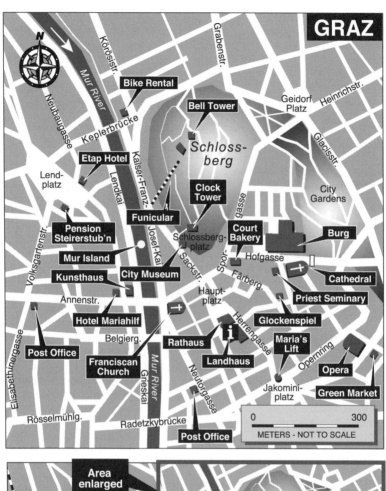

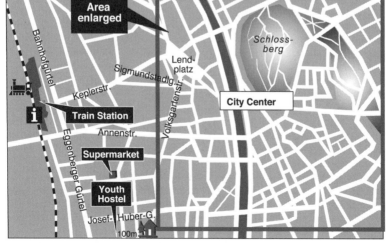

3) For a trippy experience dating from medieval times, visit the double-spiral staircase at the **Burg** (page 536).

4) Grow up with a one of Hollywood's greatest action heroes, "Kaliefornia's" governor and Graz's favorite son: **Arnold Schwarzenegger** (see *Grow up with Arnie*, do-it-yourself tour, page 539).

5) To hear the "Bell's Play," head to the **Glockenspiel** (page 535).

6) For impressions of Italy, visit the **Franciscan Quarter** (page 534).

7) Stop by and sample regal delicacies at the **Court Bakery** (page 536).

SIGHTS

Island on the Mur: (Murinsel) Adjacent to the Old Town and anchored in the middle of the Mur River is an artificial, shell-shaped island that has become one of Graz's signature landmarks. Tourists are often seen crossing the river and back again just to pass through its unique frame. New York artist Vito Acconci designed the island—stabilized by two footbridges connecting it to either riverbank—for Graz's celebration as the Culture Capital of Europe in 2003. On board is a café/lounge, dance club, open-air theater, and a playground for kids. When the theater is not being used, locals and tourists enjoy kicking back on its wave-like benches to read a book, cop a midday rest, or spread out a picnic. Inside, the café is commonly full of patrons sipping a beverage while mesmerized by the river's hefty current. Another island attraction is the café's unusual restroom. Do you feel the urge? (If so, upon entering the café, go straight and it's left around the corner.) *Hours:* (café) Mon-Thur 9:00-24:00, Fri/Sat 9:00-02:00, Sun 10:00-24:00. *Tel.#* 0316/890-335. *Note:* every Fri/Sat from 22:00 a guest DJ spins phat house-tunes.

Schlossberg: Rising (123m/403ft) above the Old Town and dominating the skyline is "Fortress Hill," a wooded peak (formerly) outfitted with massive fortifications that safeguarded Graz from its enemies for centuries. In 1809, Major Hackher defended the hilltop fortress with a mere 900 soldiers against some 3000 Napoleon-backed French troops, who launched no less than eight unsuccessful assaults. Only after the collapse of the imperial Austrian army and the signing of a peace treaty with France did Hackher's men lay down their weapons. To ensure the fortress remained impotent, Napoleon ordered its immediate destruction. In addition to fistfuls of money as a financial sweetener, the people of Graz begged the French to spare Schlossberg's clock and bell towers—thus they still stand. After the Napoleonic wars, the city council decided to landscape the ruins of Schlossberg into a site of eco-beauty for everyone to enjoy. And today, the thousands of locals and tourists who wander Schlossberg each day are a testament to its enduring charm. Attractions include the clock tower, bell tower, casemate stage, garrison museum, 94-meter deep Turkish well (Türkenbrunnen 1558), and the café/bar "aiola." Keeping you up to speed with local history, city workers have thoughtfully erected multilanguage info boards throughout the hill.

Getting There: There are three ways to reach Schlossberg, via the funicular, lift or War Steps. *Suggestion:* Take the funicular up and walk the War Steps down. *Note:* The tunnel running off Schlossbergplatz—beneath the War Steps and from where the lift ascends—was dug out during WWII as an air-raid shelter. On a hot summer day you'll treasure its natural air-conditioning.

1) The **funicular** dates from 1894 and is locally known as the *Schlossbergbahn*. It climbs the hillside at a stiff 61% gradient to its destination at the bell tower. The new funicular (third generation, since Aug 2004)—called the panorama wagon—is a fun and scenic way to reach the summit. For the best views, we recommend the lil' romantic seat at the lowest part of the wagon—upon entering, go down the few steps. *Hours:* daily, May-Sept 9:00-23:00, Oct-April 10:00-22:00. *Price:* Graz's transportation authority runs the funicular, thus the price is included with a valid bus/tram ticket, 1.70€ (page 530—*Buses/Trams*). To find the funicular from Hauptplatz, take Sackstr. to Kaiser-Franz-Josef-Kai and it will soon appear on the right (at No. 40).

2) **Lift:** Built in the year 2000 for some 4€ million, the lift—or elevator—whisks visitors up to the summit in a matter of seconds. *Note:* At the summit you will exit near the clock tower and in front of café/bar "aiola." *Hours:* daily, 8:30-23:30 (Fri/Sat till 01:30). *Price:* 50¢ up or down. To find the lift, mosey into the naturally cool tunnel beneath the War Steps on Schlossbergplatz (off Sackstr.).

3) **War Steps:** From Schlossbergplatz (off Sackstr.) 260 leg-burning steps zigzag up the cliff face to the clock tower. Austrian engineers and Russian prisoners built them during WWI (1914-18), hence their name: the Kriegsteig, or War Steps. To climb them is free and will take roughly 15 min up, 5 min down. We recommend you take the funicular up and walk the steps down. Atop Schlossberg, the entrance to the steps is unmarked and can be found right of the clock tower (look to gate right of info board).

Clock Tower: (Uhrturm) Graz's defining landmark—the clock tower—is also one of its oldest structures, first mentioned in 1265. Originally built as a defense position, the tower was converted to the town's clock in 1712. If you haven't already noticed, the hour and minutes hands are mounted contrary to tradition. The large hand indicates the hour and was mounted first because it could be seen from a distance—the small hand representing the minutes came later. The tower accommodates three significant bells: Graz's oldest bell (1382) rings the hour; the "poor sinner's bell" (Armensünderglocke, 1450) rang during executions, and later to remind night owls of the curfew; and lastly, the town watchman would ring the fire-alarm bell (1645) to alert the fire brigade when flames were spotted. Regarding another kind of flame, romantics should note that the tower is often the chosen setting for local couples to have their first kiss. A romantic setting indeed, the views are tremendous from its base and labeled pictures of the Old Town buildings have been mounted to help you decipher what you're looking at. For people who can't see, their hands are their eyes—and for that reason, nearby is a small-scale model of the tower for visually impaired people. *Note:* The War Steps descending to the Old Town are unmarked and can be found right of the tower (through gate right of info board). Notice how exhausted the people are after arriving at the top. Whew! It makes us dizzy just thinkin' about it.

Bell Tower: (Glockenturm) Standing 100 feet tall and dating from 1588, the bell tower houses one of Austria's largest bells—"Liesl"—cast in 1587 and weighing 4.5 tons (10,000lbs). Liesl clangs 101 strokes thrice daily (7:00, 12:00, 19:00) as it did in former times to announce the beginning and ending of the workday, in addition to a lunch break. After Liesl finishes chiming, it takes some 15 minutes for it stop vibrating. Inside the tower, its multiple levels have been converted into a humble museum (only possible to visit with prearranged group).

Casemate Stage: (Kasemattenbühne) Located above the bell tower, this open-air theater was remodeled out of the ruins to—arguably—Graz's most romantic theater venue. Its retractable roof was added in 1987.

Garrison Museum: Graz from the 17th to 19th centuries was an important garrison town, accommodating troops and training them for battle. Within the museum's small confines you'll see sabers, rifles and uniforms used by these troops along with cannons employed during the Napoleonic wars and rapid-fire weapons from WWI. Also from the First World War notice the "iron soldier," a wooden figure into which nails were hammered to symbolize donations to war victims. *Note:* Museum is partially in English and interesting for military buffs only. Expect a visit to take about 30 min. *Hours:* mid-April thru mid-Oct, Tue-Sun 10:00-17:00. *Price:* adult 2€, student 1€.

Café/Bar Aiola: Near the clock tower is the trendy café/bar aiola, which features glass walls that rise from the floor to close out the elements on bad days and are lowered into the ground on sunny days. *Hours:* Mon-Sat 9:00-02:00, Sun 9:00-24:00—breakfast from 9:00, lunch from 11:30. *Tel.#* 0316/818-797. www.aiola.at (click "upstairs") *Note:* Those who take the lift up to Schlossberg will exit in front of "aiola."

Hauptplatz: Since medieval times, the "main square" has been the pulsating heart of Graz. A lively locale—positioned at the north end of Herrengasse—the square is framed by historic buildings and populated by marketers selling flowers, sausages and crepes. As a major transportation hub connecting all trams, Hauptplatz is popular for people-watching. In the middle of the plaza stands a statue of the Styrian prince, Archduke Johann, whose marriage to the postmaster's daughter put him in good standing with the people. Sticking to the subject of matrimony, many locals have exchanged vows in the impressive-looking Rathaus (town hall) on the south side of the platz. During Advent, the town hall's facade is brilliantly illuminated (from 17:00 till midnight) into a gigantic Advent calendar. Gingerbread permeates the air and gift-wrapped stands decorate Hauptplatz for the Christmas market. However, times weren't always rosy on Hauptplatz. Up to the late-18th century, petty lawbreakers were either locked in stocks and pelted with rotten tomatoes or sentenced to ride a mule around the plaza. For violent criminals, beheadings were not uncommon. *Note:* For impressions of Italy on Hauptplatz, see *Franciscan Quarter* (next entry).

Franciscan Quarter: To see another side of Graz, step into the Mediterranean-soaked atmosphere of the Franciscan quarter. Behind the statue of Archduke Johann on Hauptplatz, slip into the petite (lane) Franziskanergasse (next to "Niedermeyer" shop). The other end of the lane opens into the picturesque Franziskanerplatz, or Square of the Franciscans. The square—and quarter—gets its name from the Franciscan church and adjoining monastery, which is the oldest religious order in Graz and Austria's only continuing hermitage for monks practicing the faith of Francis of Assisi. For an exclusive look into the monastery, go left and after about 25 meters enter through the portal on the right (at No. 14). Follow the hallway straight and then go right. Continue straight and quietly meander through the divine, Gothic-style corridor flanked by 400-year-old headstones. Around the next corner, step through the doorway (on left) into the leafy courtyard and prayer garden. Notice the sword driven into Mary's heart, symbolic of Jesus's pain. Exit the courtyard via the same door you entered and go left. Continue straight—passing headstones displaying skulls and crossbones—to the old wooden door in the right corner, leading into the 16th-century Franciscan church. After ogling the church, exit via its main entrance. To get orientated, the Kunsthaus museum (bluish, alien-looking building) is in front of you and right around the corner is where you began.

Herrengasse: The "Lane of Men" cuts through the Old Town and is really Graz's 'high street,' flanked by well-preserved, historic facades accommodating retail shops and chill-out cafés. Only people and trams are allowed to cruise this drag, no cars. At the north end of Herrengasse is Hauptplatz—at the south end is Maria's Lift (see next entry) followed by Jakominiplatz, Graz's main transportation hub for buses and trams. At only 500 meters long, Herrengasse is a casual 10-min stroll from one end to the other. At Herrengasse 16 you'll find the TI and the **Landhaus** building, housing the Styrian parliament. Its Italian Renaissance-style courtyard is a must-see—enter via the archway right of TI. The courtyard is used as a scenic backdrop for open-air concerts (free, July/Aug) and an ice-sculpted Nativity scene during Advent. Notice the bronze well (1590) with five posts, each featuring a creature that is half-man and half-animal. Your nose may lead you to Herrengasse 8, where you'll sniff out world-famous Sacher torte. Opposite, your eyes can't miss the 14th-century Gemaltes Haus—or Painted House—at Herrengasse 3. Its frescoed facade dates from 1742 and depicts gods from Greco-Roman mythology.

Maria's Lift: (Marienlift) Another project completed for Graz's celebration as the Culture Capital of Europe is Maria's Lift, a glass elevator whisking visitors up to eye-level with a statuette of the Virgin Mary perched atop a column, affording a whole new perspective of the Old Town. The elevator is located at the southern end of Herrengasse (near Jakominiplatz) and costs 1€.

Sackstrasse: A narrow extension of Herrengasse, Sackstrasse means "dead-end street." So there's no truth to the "dead" part, we suggest you be very careful of trams here—they seemingly come out of nowhere!

Midway along Sackstrasse is Schlossbergplatz, from where you can catch the lift up to Schlossberg or climb the War Steps (Kriegsteig). On the corner of Schlossbergplatz and Sackstrasse is the Reinerhof, the oldest documented house in Graz (1164). The Reinerhof has since been renovated and today it houses offices for social services. Next door is the City Museum (page 537), where Francis Ferdinand—successor to the Habsburg throne—was born in 1863. Does his name ring a bell? His assassination in Sarajevo in 1914 sparked World War I. For folks looking for something precious or just plain old, head to the north end of Sackstrasse to discover a handful of antique shops. Opposite Sackstrasse 14 is Admonter Gasse—step into this modern commercial passage and mosey straight through the old archway (1784) to find a picturesque, 18th-century courtyard. On the other side you'll run into a merry piece of Ireland: Flann O'Brien's Irish pub (Mon-Sat 11:00 till late, Sun 15:00-01:00; pint of Guinness 4.40€). Hoist a jar, *Slainte*! Continue past the pub to the busy street ahead; left will take you back to Hauptplatz or right to the river.

Sporgasse: "Spor Lane" gets its name from *Sporer*—blacksmiths specializing in the art of spur making—who lined the street during the Middle Ages. The lane, however, is actually centuries older than Graz, dating from Roman times when a trade route connected the Mur valley with Hungary. When standing on Hauptplatz, with your back to the Rathaus (town hall), Sporgasse is the quaint shop-lined lane running off to the right, between the earth-red structure and the historic facade wonderfully decorated with Baroque stuccowork. As you dawdle up the lane, check out the two cool-lookin' dragon-esque drainpipes above Sporgasse 13. Farther up, at No. 22 (right), wander through the archway into a romantic Romeo-and-Juliet-like courtyard that dates from around 1510 and is paved with Murnockerln, or stones for the Mur River. What's more, the structure was a former district seat of the Teutonic Knights. Across the way—at Sporgasse 21—go through the portal and ascend 67 steps to the Stiegenkirche, or Steps Church, first documented in 1343—but after renovations it's taken on a newer look. Inside the church, notice the craftsmanship of the door and the date above it: 1631. Continuing farther up Sporgasse, look above the archway at No. 25 (left) and you'll see a Turkish warrior protruding from the facade brandishing a saber. He's made of oak wood and dates from the 17th century. In his youth he was used as a target for charging cavalrymen, but has since been relegated to frightening passersby and the odd pigeon.

Glockenspiel: Since Christmas Eve 1905, the carillon's 24 bells on Glockenspielplatz have been chiming to the delight of many. Alas, the bells were silenced during WWII when they were melted down for war materials. A decade after the war—by popular demand—the bells were recast to resume their rhythmic jingles. Today, tourists gather on the quaint square thrice daily (11:00, 15:00, 18:00) to see and hear the Glockenspiel spectacle, which features a wooden couple dressed in traditional Styrian costume dancing in the gable of a house to a select melody. The melodies alternate throughout the year, from alpine folk and yodeling songs to Christmas carols and compositions by famous artists. The show concludes when the golden rooster (above clock) crows "Kikeriki" (German for cock-a-doodle-doo) three times. The Glockenspiel's creator—Gottfried Maurer—loved the rooster atop Munich's carillon so much that he added it to his own design. *Suggestion:* Ten minutes or so before 18:00 consider grabbing an outdoor table at the recommendable **Glöckl Bräu** restaurant (located on the platz, left of Glockenspiel) to get an early start on dinner and to catch the last Glockenspiel performance of the day. The Glöckl Bräu (daily 10:30-24:00; tel.# 0316/814-781—has menus in English) is reasonably priced and serves provincial specialties from Styria, of which Graz is the capital. *Getting There:* The easiest way to find the Glockenspiel is via Sporgasse. Take this lane running off Hauptplatz and make your first right on Färbergasse—continue straight and it will eventually appear on the left. *Note:* Glockenspielplatz is part of the so-called Bermuda Triangle (Bermudadreieck), a lively pub-and-club district. The area gets its ominous name from the frequent disappearance of patrons for hours.

Court Bakery: A must-see (and -taste) in Graz is the imperial "Hofbäckerei," a family run bakery since 1569. "Hof" is an exalted title afforded to only those merchants who were allowed to deliver their goods to the royal court. In this case, the crowned heads were just up the lane at the Burg (see next entry). The bakery is hard to miss with its magnificent wooden (oak and walnut) facade crowned by a gilded double-headed eagle. After snapping a picture, step inside and sample some of the bakery's regal delicacies, such as their sweet hazelnuts. *Hours:* Mon-Fri 7:00-18:00, Sat 7:00-12:00. *Getting There:* Bakery is located at Hofgasse 6, around corner from Sporgasse 22.

Burg: Graz's imperial "residence" dates from 1438 when the duke of Styria, later Emperor Frederick III, erected digs for his family, the Habsburgs. In 1499, Frederick's son—Emperor Maximilian I, of Golden Roof fame in Innsbruck—continued construction on the Burg and added a marvel of medieval stonework: the **double-spiral staircase**. This is one of the coolest staircases you'll ever see; two flights of stairs ascend in opposite directions, spiral and meet one level higher, separate again, spiral and meet one level higher, and so on—all the way to the top floor. Once at the top, you'll capture a nice view of the cathedral (see next entry), which Frederick III had simultaneously built with the Burg. Today, the Burg is home to the Styrian provincial government. There's not much to see here, except the staircase—allow 10 min for a visit. *Getting There:* The Burg is about a 10-min walk from Hauptplatz. Take Sporgasse to Hofgasse, where you'll make a right. At the end of Hofgasse is the Burg (on left, before old-city gate). Upon entering the property, you'll notice it looks rather official. But don't worry; you're allowed to enter. Ramble across the courtyard and step inside the tower (right) adorned by ivy. *Note:* After visiting the Burg, consider sauntering through the Stadtpark, or city gardens. They are beautiful and worth your time (you're in luck if you brought a picnic). To get there, continue on Hofgasse and walk through the Burgtor (old-city gate). After some 70 meters, go left towards the moat-like pond teeming with ducks. When you're done, return to Hofgasse.

Cathedral: Across the street from the Burg is Graz's "Dom," originally constructed in Gothic-style from 1438-62 and later refurbished in Baroque-style. Since 1786 it has been the bishop's chosen church to represent the Catholics of Styria. After ogling its interior, exit via the back right portal and descend the steps to reach the 15th-century wall fresco (right) depicting "God's Plagues." It refers to the year 1480 when Graz was ravaged by three plagues, which were considered to be the wrath of God for its citizens leading immoral lives. The fresco is interpreted as an appeal to God for forgiveness.

Priest Seminary: In 1572, the Jesuit Order of Graz began construction on a college of theology. Today, it is a seminary preparing young men for priesthood. Although this info may seem a little dull, the Renaissance-style structure is anything but, registering as one of the most important examples of Jesuit architecture in Austria. Step into the courtyard and you'll see what we mean. A visit will only take two minutes. *Getting There:* The seminary is located at Bürgergasse 2. If you're visiting the cathedral, it is a must-see because it's just across the street. When facing the "God's Plagues" fresco outside of the cathedral, descend the stairs behind you and cross the cobbled street—continue through the archway and go right.

MUSEUMS

City Museum: At the "Stadtmuseum" you'll get an in-depth perspective of Graz's rich 880-year history. Among the many interesting exhibitions on display, you can see a city model from the year 1800 as well as one of the original Swiss army knives (exhibit 279)—this one having 11 functions and happens to be made in Vienna. From the courtyard you can enter an intriguing example of a 19th-century pharmacy (look to the archway, above which says Apotheke)—if it's closed, let the cashier know you're keen to see it. The museum is largely in English, except for temporary exhibitions. If time allows, view the 25-min film; ask for English. Military buffs will be interested to know that in this building on Dec 18, 1863, Francis Ferdinand was born, whose assassination in Sarajevo in 1914 sparked World War I. Upon entering the museum look to the memorial plaque on the right wall, which is in front of his birth room (there is no cost to see the memorial—simply walk through museum door and look right). *Hours:* Tue-Sat 10:00-18:00 (Tue till 21:00), Sun 10:00-13:00. *Price:* adult 5€, student 1€, groups of 5 or more pay 2€/person. *Getting There:* Museum is located at Sackstr. 18—on right side when coming from Hauptplatz.

Kunsthaus: Unveiled in 2003 during Graz's tenure as the Culture Capital of Europe, the "Art House" is Austria's second largest museum. Because of its funky design, it was dubbed "the friendly alien." Yes, the design is funky and looks extraterrestrial, which totally contrasts the city's red-tiled roofscape. They call its construction "biomorphic"—resembling or suggesting the form of a living organism. See for yourself. Specializing in contemporary art from the past four decades, the Kunsthaus exhibits—among other things—architecture, design, Web art, new media, film and photography. *Hours:* Tue-Sun 10:00-18:00 (Thur till 20:00). *Price:* adult 6€, student 2.50€. *Note:* Tours in English are possible—typically 2.50€/person surcharge—call ahead to see whether any are scheduled: *tel.#* 0316/8017-9200. (www.kunsthausgraz.at) *Getting There: You can't miss it!* The friendly alien is located at Lendkai 1, which is across the river from the Old Town.

Armory, Provincial: For military buffs who are interested in medieval armor and weaponry, this museum is your wet dream! For those folks who are not interested in the subject, do not bother. The Landeszeughaus (as its called in German) is literally jam-packed—from floor to ceiling—with objects to defend, offend, gouge, stab and shoot. In fact, with more than 32,000 objects on five floors, it is the largest collection of historic weaponry in the world. No wonder the Slavic peoples, only 50km to the south, never invaded Austria. From the mid-16th century, nobles, knights and entire armies stockpiled their wares here, such as crossbows, suits of armor, halberds, matchlock rifles, powder flasks and sabers. All are neatly stacked and ready for action, just as they were some 400 years ago. Expect a visit to take around 60 min, but tickets are good all day if you'd like to come back. *Note:* From the top floor is a great view of the Landhaus courtyard (page 534—*Herrengasse*). *Hours:* daily, April-Oct 10:00-18:00 (Thur till 20:00) and Nov-March 10:00-15:00. *Price:* adult 6€, student 2.50€. Tours in English are scheduled twice daily—10:30 and 15:30—at a surcharge of 2.50€/person. *Getting There:* Landeszeughaus is a few doors from the TI on Herrengasse.

GOOD SLEEPS

Hostel, Jugendgästehaus: Idlhofgasse 74 (www.jgh.at) *Tel.#* 0316/708-350
Backpackers will love this hostel as will cost-conscious travelers looking for a private double or triple. This is because much of the hostel has recently been renovated to hotel-like standards. And if that isn't enough, their delicious gotta-get-out-of-bed-for-buffet-breakfast (included in price) is the best we've experienced for a hostel, and better than some hotels. The Jugendgästehaus—located within easy reach of the main train station and Old Town—has laundry facilities, Internet access and a snack bar. *Price:* (buffet breakfast included) 6-bed dorm from 16€, 4-bed dorm from 18.50€, Sgl from 25€, Dbl from 41€. *CC's:* VC, MC, AE, DC. *Note:* Must be member or an extra charge will apply. If staying only 1 or 2 nights, a one-time 3€ fee will be added. A supermarket can be found on the corner of Idlhofgasse and Prankergasse (Mon-Thur 8:00-19:00, Fri 7:30-19:30, Sat 7:30-17:00)—exit hostel left and it's a few blocks along. *Getting There: Railers,* from the station it's a 15-min walk, or take bus #50 a couple of stops to Gürtel-turmplatz (bus stops running around 20:00). From there, cross the boulevard into Laza-rettgasse and then make the first left on Idlhofgasse—after about 150 meters the hostel will appear on the left. *By foot:* From the boulevard out front of the train station go right and continue straight for about 10 min (when convenient cross to the other side of the boulevard). Turn left on Josef-Huber-G. Ahead make the next right—this is Idlhofgasse. The hostel is 100 meters farther on the right. *Drivers,* parking available in front of hostel: 1€/day. *GPS:* N47° 03.903 - E15° 25.436

Pension Zur Steirerstub'n: Lendplatz 8 (www.pension-graz.at) *Tel.#* 0316/716-855, or cell. 0664/184-3257. Located five minutes by foot from the Old Town, this pleasant pension has a traditional-style restaurant and a view of Schlossberg. All rooms have shower/toilet and come with breakfast. *Price:* Sgl 39€, Dbl 70€, apartment 100-160€. *CC's:* VC, MC, AE, DC. *Note:* Looking to rent a bike for the day? Ask staff, they may have one available for free. *Getting There: Railers,* from outside the station catch bus #63 to Lendplatz, or it's a 20-min walk—exit station straight into Keplerstr. and after a handful of blocks go right (just past No. 57 Keplerstr.) onto Sigmundstadl. Take this lane to the end and turn left (on Volksgartenstr.). At the lights—begins Lendplatz—go right and your digs are 4th on the right. *Drivers,* public garage nearby or they may have a free space available—ask in advance. *GPS:* N47° 04.475 - E15º 25.850

Hotel Etap: Neubaugasse 11 www.etaphotel.com (hotel code: 5107) *Tel.#* 0316/764-400. Basic-service, budget hotel with everything a traveler needs, including a TV. Beds are generally a one-piece (triple) unit with a double on the bottom and a single bunk-like bed above for a child. *Price:* Sgl 37€, Dbl 46€. *CC's:* VC, MC. *Note:* Parking, breakfast cost extra. *Getting There:* Since Etap is located across Lendplatz from the above-listed Pension Zur Steirerstub'n, use their GPS and directions. *Drivers,* public garage nearby.

Hotel ibis: www.ibishotel.com (*hotel code 1917) *Tel.#* 0316/7780. Standardized comfort, reasonably priced, and handily located next to the main train station. *Price:* Sgl 62€, Dbl 77€, Trpl 92€. *CC's:* VC, MC. *Note:* Parking, breakfast cost extra. *Hotel code is compatible with ibis website, creating a shortcut to the property—type hotel code into middle left box and click "OK"; next page click on "The Hotel" (left side).

Hotel Mariahilf: Mariahilferstr. 9 (www.hotelmariahilf.at) *Tel.#* 0316/713-163. Above average digs situated behind the "friendly alien" (Kunsthaus Museum) and a short walk from the Old Town. All rooms have shower/toilet and come with breakfast. If staying more than two nights, inquire whether they have a special rate. *Price:* Sgl 45-59€, Dbl 74-102€, Trpl 99-130€. *CC's:* VC, MC, AE, DC. *Getting There: Railers,* query TI for the best bus/tram connection, or 20-min walk. *Drivers,* parking 13€/24hr (public garage). *GPS:* N47° 04.303 - E15° 26.019

Hotel Zum Dom: Bürgergasse 14 (www.domhotel.co.at) *Tel.#* 0316/824-800 If you can afford this upper-end hotel, stay here! Each room is individually designed to the highest standards, comparable to a palace. The finest marble embellishes each bathroom, half of which have a Jacuzzi. Nestled in the heart of the Old Town, your overnight at this exquisite 19th-century hotel will no doubt be a trip highlight. *Price:* (buffet breakfast included) Sgl 80-90€, Dbl 165€, suite 200-322€, extra bed 30€, parking 12€/24hr. *CC's:* VC, MC, AE, DC. *GPS:* N47° 04.249 - E15° 26.541

*   *   *

To commemorate his 57th birthday, the Austrian post office released 600,000 units of a special-edition Arnold Schwarzenegger stamp on July 30, 2004 (see graphic). Demand was so high that within four weeks of its release, the stamp sold out. In the history of Austrian postage stamps—some 155 years—never before has a stamp sold out so quickly!

Grow Up With Arnie,

do-it-yourself tour

He's known affectionately in politics as the Governator, in Hollywood as the Terminator, and in Graz as *der Steirische Eiche*—the Styrian Oak—but for this section, we'll simply refer to the country boy from Austria as Arnie.

Arnie was born on July 30, 1947, in the cutesy-pie village of Thal (pronounced Tall), just outside of Graz, to Gustav Schwarzenegger, a police officer, and his wife, Aurelia, a homemaker who—according to a reliable source—baked the most delicious apple strudel.

In 1953, as a 6-year-old, Arnie was inspired to be a great athlete when his father took him into Graz to the opening of a new swimming pool being dedicated by Johnny Weissmuller, an Olympic gold medalist who became a famous Hollywood actor as Tarzan.

In 1960, at the age of 13, Arnie went with his soccer team to work out at a local gym, where he lifted his first barbell. It was a life-changing experience. Arnie decided his goal was to be the most pumped-up guy in the world and then use his fame to land a gig in Hollywood.

A year later, Kurt Marnul—a professional bodybuilder and former Mr. Austria—met Arnie and invited him to train at his gym, the Athletik-Union in Graz. He trained like a possessed teenager and by the age of 15 he was already a successful bodybuilder. In 1965, at age 18, his agenda was temporarily halted when he joined the Austrian army for mandatory service. The next year, after returning to civilian life, Arnie won the Mr. Europe competition followed by the continent's best-built man contest.

Like many others with dreams of making it big, Arnie set off for California, U.S.A. He landed in 1968 with only a duffle bag containing his belongings, $20 in his pocket, and with hardly any knowledge of the English language. He recently said, "I had empty pockets, but I was full of dreams."

Arnie trained at Gold's Gym in Venice Beach, where all the top bodybuilders of the day worked out. To make a living, he sold training supplies via the mail-order business under the name "Arnold Strong." That same year, he confidently competed for the title of Mr. Universe. He took second place, and he wasn't happy about it. His thoughts relate his mood: "I'm away from home…in America, and I'm a loser." A day later, he recaptured the eye of the tiger and was more determined than ever: "I'm going to pay them back...I'm going to show them who really is best!" The next year, 1969, he won the competition. He was Mr. Universe!

In 1970, he successfully defended his title of Mr. Universe by winning for a second time, as well as winning his first Mr. Olympia title. During this epic year, just as he had planned, his well-defined body opened the door to the movie industry: He was offered the role of Hercules in a low-budget film—although, his voice had to be dubbed because of his hard-to-understand accent. The year 1972 was an emotional roller coaster for the rising star—he added another Mr. Olympia title to his resume; he appeared as a contestant on the popular TV show, "The Dating Game"; and tragedy struck when his father, Gustav, passed away.

In 1974, Arnie won a fifth Mr. Olympia title and he published his first book: "Pumping Iron." Initially, the New York Times refused to review it, citing that the book would have a limited audience. Two months later, "Pumping Iron" was on its best-seller list. The following year, Arnie won Mr. Olympia for a sixth time and he was invited on the Merv Griffin show by Lucille Ball to play an Italian masseur.

From paperback to the silver screen, "Pumping Iron"—the movie—premiered in 1977. For the occasion, there was one person Arnie was determined to have in the audience: his mother. He paid for her airplane ticket and when she landed he taught her some need-to-know English: "I am Arnold's mother."

Another significant event happened to Arnie that same year (1977): He met his future wife, Maria Shriver.

In 1979, he graduated with a B.A. in Business and International Economics from the University of Wisconsin, Superior. In 1980, he won his seventh Mr. Olympia title and starred in the movie "Conan the Barbarian" (released 1982). In 1981, Arnie starred in his signature role as "The Terminator" (released 1984).

The year 1983 was extra-special for the blue-eyed Austrian: he became an American citizen. That day—all day—he traipsed around wearing the American flag on his back. He recently said, "Everything I have — my career — my success — my family — I owe to America."

Life continued to get sweeter for Arnie: In 1986, he wed his long-time love, Maria Shriver. The following year, he was immortalized on the Hollywood Walk of Fame, receiving star number 1,847.

Whether you're a fan or not, there's no denying that Arnold Schwarzenegger is the epitome of the American dream. For an Austrian kid with a vision, his resume reveals one of North America's greatest success stories. Within the last two decades his bio includes multimillion-dollar blockbuster films, a restaurant chain and a governorship: "Red Heat" and "Twins" (1988) • first Planet Hollywood opens (1989) • "Total Recall" and "Kindergarten Cop" (1990) • "Terminator 2" (1991) • "Last Action Hero" (1993) • "True Lies" and "Junior" (1994) • "Jingle All The Way" and "Eraser" (1996) • "Collateral Damage" (2002) • "T3" (2003) • Governor of California (2003).

Oh, and in case you were wondering, according to his autobiography, "Arnold: The Education of a Bodybuilder," Arnie is 6 feet 2 inches tall and at the peak of his career his measurements were — arms: 22 in. — chest: 57 in. — waist: 34 in. — thighs: 28.5 in. — calves: 20 in. — weight: 235 lbs.

OK, you're pretty much up-to-date on the Hollywood blockbuster, now let's hit the road and *Grow Up With Arnie...* First stop, the village of Thal.

~ *Your first—and only—stop on this leg is Thalersee (Lake Thal); from there, Arnie's birthplace and elementary school are reachable by foot. **Note:** His birthplace is privately owned and can only be viewed from outside. No tours!*

Note: If it's lunchtime, Thalersee makes for a nice picnic spot—or there is the reasonably priced Hotel-Restaurant Thalersee nestled on the shoreline.

GPS: N47° 04.291 - E15° 21.935 (coordinates to Thalersee)

Railers, there is no train to Thal—instead, from the main train station take bus #85 to Gösting (15-min ride), then catch bus #48 to Thalersee (9-min ride). *If you're coming from Jakominiplatz, take bus #40 to Gösting (25-min ride) and then catch bus #48 to Thalersee (9-min ride).* **Note:** Buses run regularly to/fro Graz ↔ Gösting (until early evening) and from Gösting about every 40 min to Thalersee. Check connection times in advance to avoid a long wait at Gösting. To signal the driver to stop the bus at your destination, press the stop button located on the handrail in front/behind you or by the exit door. And lastly, to cover all your transportation for the day, buy *Die 24-Stunden-karte* (24hr ticket) for 3.50€—validate it prior to first use.

Drivers, Thalersee is a leafy, 15-minute drive from Graz—query the TI or staff at your accommodations for directions from your departure point. At Thalersee, plan to go for a 60-minute walk (round trip).

Thalersee: (pronounced *Taller-zay*) Congratulations, you've successfully arrived at your first destination, "Lake Thal"—pleasantly framed by a wooded nature reserve—an idyllic spot for (row) boating, fishing, swimming, hiking, or simply lounging on Hotel-Restaurant Thalersee's lakeside terrace with a beverage. In winter, the lake often freezes over providing the perfect rink for a graceful skate or a just-getting-started figure 8.

As a kid, Arnie played and exercised here—that is, before he discovered the gym. Years later, according to a reliable source, he chose the lake's romantic setting to pop the question to his then-girlfriend, Maria Shriver.

Hotel-Restaurant Thalersee is still owned by the same family as in Arnie's day. Inside, some pictures of the movie star adorn the walls. (www.thalersee.at) *Tel.#* 0316/ 582-390. *Price:* Sgl 40€, Dbl 68€, apartment 90€.

~ *With your back to Hotel-Restaurant Thalersee, walk the lakeside path on the right—pass the paddle boats and farther ahead at the fork, go right. (Here is an old-fashioned pump, crank it several times for drinking water.) Ramble up the gravel path to the road, where you'll go left and then immediately right. Ascend this lane. Midway along a mustard-yellow house will appear through the foliage on the left; this is your target. At the top, go left: The mustard-yellow house on the corner block (No. 145) is Arnie's birthplace.*

Birthplace, Arnie's: (*GPS:* N47° 04.334 - E15° 21.763) The house today looks more well-off than it did in the 1947 when Arnie was born. At that time, the house was subdivided and the Schwarzeneggers lived in an apartment on the 2nd floor with no remarkable amenities, not even indoor plumbing. Arnie lived here until 1966, age 19, when he left Austria to live in Munich (and eventually America) to further his athletic career. *Note:* The house is privately owned and can only be viewed from the outside.

~ *Okay, let's walk the route Arnie took every day to/fro school. Face the front door and go left, then left again. Follow the road straight, passing the farmer's shed (left) and the medieval burg (right). Your path will begin to descend and turn to gravel, squeezing between bushes before opening onto a farmer's field bordered by lush trees. Follow the road down, around, and up to the village square. Once there, you'll find (left) the Hans Gross Volksschule—Arnie's elementary school.*

Elementary School, Arnie's: (*GPS:* N47° 04.540 - E15° 21.690) Scholastically, Arnie was an average student but he was motivated and had a thirst for knowledge. He attended this school (built 1838) with his one-year-older brother, Meinhard, who tragically died in an automobile accident in 1971.

~ *Across the square you'll notice the village church, first mentioned in the 14th century. The Schwarzeneggers attended here. Of course the church didn't always look like it does now; some 10 years ago it was renovated. Its funky design will probably be one of the most unique you'll ever see. Walk over for a closer look. Step inside; check out the pews and floor and altar ... Well, you get the point.*

Back outside, where the road begins to descend, you'll see an info board summarizing Arnie's life in addition to listing a walking route (Wanderweg) named in his honor and neatly illustrated within a profile of his head. Geburtsort, by the way, means "birth town." Farther down the road (on right) is a memorial to the local soldiers who died during the two world wars.

Okay, folks, that's a wrap for Thal. For Schwarzenegger devotees, we'll see you back in Graz for the conclusion of our tour.

Drivers, to reach your car (and Graz) retrace your steps.

Railers, to catch the bus back to Gösting-Graz, continue down the street—when you reach the main road at the bottom, go right to the bus stop. This stop is called "Thalkreuz"—the bus departs from here back to Gösting generally as follows (but double check times in advance as they may have changed): Mon-Fri 9:18, 9:58, 10:38, 11:18, 11:58, 12:38, 13:18, 13:58, 14:40, 15:20, 16:00, 16:40, 17:20, 18:00, 18:40, 19:23 and 19:56. Times are quite different on weekends; check in advance. *Note:* If you're coming with us to Graz to continue the tour, from Gösting take bus #40 to Jakominiplatz.

* * *

The next—and final—stop is a gym, located in south Graz. Arnie did not train here but it is significant nonetheless.

Note: The remainder of our tour is recommended for true-blue Schwarzenegger fans, since (to others) the time spent getting there might not be worth the attraction. The gym's hours are typically Mon-Fri 10:00-21:30, Sat 9:00-12:00.

I n 1961, Kurt Marnul—Arnie's mentor and first instructor—invited him to train at (his gym) the Athletik-Union located at Graz's original soccer stadium. With Marnul's guidance, the young athlete got pumped up to take on the world. He was so enthusiastic about weightlifting that he even broke into the gym on weekends, when it was closed. Arnie's father, Gustav, became concerned about his son's obsession with Austria's "least popular sport" and limited his gym visits to thrice weekly. Most teenagers in this situation would've freaked out—but not Arnie, he resolved the issue by building a gym at home.

Some 10 years ago the original stadium was razed. The new 15,000-seat stadium— to honor the birthplace of his career—was named after the star-turned-politician. Regrettably, the giant letters spelling "Arnold Schwarzenegger" above the stadium's main entrance were quietly removed under the cover of darkness late December 2005 due to a difference of political cultures between Austria and the state of California. Even though there's nothing much to see here today, fans may still want to head to the stadium to get an idea of the place where Arnie's pumping-iron career began. Today, the stadium has reverted back to its pre-Arnie name: "Stadion Graz-Liebenau." *Getting There:* **Railers,** from Hauptplatz or Jakominiplatz catch tram #4 to Liebenau/Stadion (end of the line, 10-min ride). **Drivers,** head south on Eggenberger Gürtel (boulevard in front of main train station) and it will change names to Lazarettgürtel. Turn left at the forward intersection onto Karlauer Gürtel; cross the river and turn right (in just under 1km) at the intersection of Conrad-von-Hötzendorf-Str. Go straight and you will arrive at the stadium in just over 1km. *GPS:* N47° 02.744 - E15° 27.340

Athletik-Union: (*GPS:* N47° 03.359 - E15° 26.532) Hanging from the walls of a cramped basement in south Graz is a real cache of Arnie memorabilia and photos. Before the demolition of the original stadium, Kurt Marnul arranged the relocation of the Athletik-Union gym. He packed up his weights and equipment and hauled them some 2km to the north. Compared to today's standards, the gym is raw—almost a throwback to Arnie's day. True-blue fans shouldn't miss a visit here, and if they're lucky: Kurt Marnul himself will be on the premises, in all likelihood instructing the next Mr. Universe. *Hours:* Mon-Fri 10:00-21:30, Sat 9:00-12:00. *Price:* Free entry. *Getting There:* The gym is located at Hüttenbrennergasse 33, in the basement of a clubhouse belonging to a local sports ground. **Railers,** (25-min trip each way) *from the soccer stadium, hop back on the tram heading to Jakominiplatz and get off at Jakominigürtel/Messe (5th stop). Once there, cross the tracks to the other side and wait for tram #5 heading to "Puntigam." Ride this one stop to Josef-Kirche; exit tram right and cross crosswalk right into Schönaugasse—after 300 meters you'll intersect with Hüttenbrennergasse (you'll see a Hofer grocery store on the corner), go left and the entrance into the sports ground (Sportszentrum) will soon appear on the right. Walk through the gate and continue straight to the glass door on the right. Inside, go straight and down the steps to the basement. The gym is at the bottom and to the left. There may be people working out; keep clear of their routine as you ogle the picture-packed walls. (*—or if you're coming from Jakominiplatz, take tram #4 three stops to Jakominigürtel/Messe and follow instructions above.)*

Drivers, **from the soccer stadium, head back to the main train station the way you came. Once on Schönaugürtel, after some 400 meters, turn left on Schönaugasse—after 300 meters you'll intersect with Hüttenbrennergasse (you'll see a Hofer grocery store on the corner), go left and the sports ground (Sportszentrum) will appear on the right. (Follow directions above for *Railers* from "Walk through the gate…")

(***—or if you're coming from the main train station, head south on Eggenberger Gürtel and it will change names to Lazarettgürtel. Turn left at the forward intersection onto Karlauer Gürtel; cross the river and turn right a few blocks ahead onto Schönaugasse—after 300 meters you'll intersect with Hüttenbrennergasse [you'll see a Hofer grocery store on the corner], go left and the sports ground [Sportszentrum] will appear on the right. Follow directions above for Railers from "Walk through the gate…")*

DANUBE VALLEY — The Wachau

40km/25mi—allow one full day and a night

From its source in the Black Forest, the Danube River—"Donau" pronounced *Doe-now* —is the second longest river in Europe, flowing west to east 2840km/1775mi through eight countries, including the capital cities of Vienna, Bratislava, Budapest and Belgrade before dumping into the Black Sea via Romania. In Europe, only the Volga River in Russia is longer, flowing 3700km/2300mi. "What about the Rhine River?" you ask. Well, actually, the Rhine ranks as the seventh longest river in Europe, flowing 1320km/820mi—not even half the size of the Danube.

Besides an economic lifeline, the Donau became an excuse to dance in the 19th century when Johann Strauss II tagged it as the beautiful "Blue Danube," a musical score that waltzed across the imperial ballrooms of Europe. But, today, this chapter is not about dancing or the color blue, it's about the Wachau, a region of the Danube River so culturally unique that it has recently (since 2000) taken its place alongside the central Amazon rainforest in Brazil and the Great Wall of China as an esteemed member of UNESCO's World Heritage List. Beginning 60km upstream from Vienna, the Wachau blossoms with picturesque hamlets, juicy vineyards, ruined castles, orchards of fruit trees, stunning Baroque architecture and dreamy times. Fittingly, Austria's Romantic Road— Romantikstrasse—twists and turns with the river (left bank, route 3) cutting through this slice of heaven. Particularly significant here is the 36km/23mi stretch between the towns of Melk and Krems, which is a joy to cycle. So come on, throw on your shorts, pack a picnic, and let's go for a ride. We'll start in Melk, your pleasant overnight stop.

MELK: *(Pop. 5200 ~ Area Code: -02752)* First mentioned in 831 A.D. as "Medilica," Melk has a rich history, famously as the home of Stift Melk: a big and beautifully Baroque Benedictine monastery nearly 1000 years old. Whether you're traveling by car, train or boat, the monastery is impossible to miss since its elevated mass overshadows Melk, nearly extending the length of the whole town. No kidding; it's humungous!

Positioned on the Danube's right bank—85km/53mi west of Vienna and 220km/137mi northeast of Salzburg—Melk is a quaint settlement; a neat place to visit with many attractions for you to see and do. For starters, stop by the TI and pick up the free town map with self-guided tour. When convenient, ramble up to the monastery and tour God's sanctuary. Whatever you do, save at least half a day for a healthy, enjoyable **bike ride** along the Danube (page 549—*Bike Ride, Melk to Krems*). If cycling isn't your gig, Melk is a good jumping-off point for boat rides on the river—in fact, a combo of the two would be ideal. But don't come here to party, the town is virtually deserted at night. Before leaving Melk, WWII and history buffs should check out the concentration camp memorial (KZ-Gedenkstätte) across town. Oh, and these GPS coordinates (N48° 13.363 - E15° 19.759)—pointing to a spot half way to the memorial—will direct you to an unforgettable view. Don't forget your camera!

TI: Babenbergerstr. 1 (www.niederoesterreich.at/melk) *Tel.#* 02752/523-07410. *Hours:* (closed off-season) April & Oct Mon-Fri 9:00-12:00 & 14:00-17:00, Sat 10:00-12:00; May/June & Sept Mon-Fri 9:00-12:00 & 14:00-18:00, Sat/Sun 10:00-12:00 & 16:00-18:00; July/Aug Mon-Sat 9:00-19:00, Sun 10:00-12:00 & 17:00-19:00. *Note:* If you arrive when the TI is closed, don't despair: maps and other info can be found outside the front door. *Getting There:* The TI is located just off the main pedestrian zone in the Old Town, a short distance from the "Spar" grocery store.

This handy TI has brochures on sights, accommodations, bike rental and more, but most importantly you want to pick up the free town map with self-guided tour—complement this tour with the historical tour (Rundgang) beginning on the first page in the free booklet "Melk an der Donau" (also available from TI). Between the two sources, you won't miss a trick. Pay special attention to the 15th-century *Haus am Stein and its facade adorned by a creeping grape vine. The word "Naturdenkmal" you see means a monument of nature. Not only is the building federally protected, so is the creeping vine because it dates from 1650! *GPS:* N48° 13.655 - E15° 19.757

Railers: Regular trains connect Salzburg and Vienna with Melk. From Salzburg, Melk is a 2.5hr trip (with a change of trains in either Linz or Amstetten), and from Vienna's Westbahnhof it is a 75-min trip. Melk's Bahnhof—or train station—is really small, having that livin'-in-the-country feel to it. The station, though, is outfitted with storage lockers (2€-3.50€/24hr; cheapest size will usually suffice) and typically you can score a free town map at the ticket counter. *To reach the Old Town and TI* is a few-minutes walk. Exit station straight, descend road (Bahnhofstr.) and walk past turn-of-the-(last)-century villas towards a stunning view of the monastery. When the road curves left continue straight, squeezing through the cobbled passage to the pedestrian zone. Once there, go right—the "Spar" grocery store will soon appear on the right and green signs point to the TI farther ahead.

Drivers: Since Melk sits adjacent to the main artery bisecting Austria—the A1 auto-bahn—it is an easy (220km) drive from Salzburg and an even easier (85km) drive from Vienna. Put 'er in cruise control and absorb the rural sights en route. In the Old Town, use your *parking dial (Parkscheibe or Parkuhr) when applicable, usually Mon-Fri 8:00-18:00, Sat 8:00-12:00 (*see page 450, chapter *Traveler's Tips*). Hotel guests query reception about where to park.

Bicyclists: Weather permitting, we recommend you cycle along the Danube (page 549—*Bike Ride, Melk to Krems*). To rent a bike, query your digs or the TI for the latest options. One option is Hotel zur Post, which rents bikes for 10€/day (leave ID as deposit).

Boaters: (boats operate April-Oct) A cruise on the Danube is a summer joy, particularly here! There are two boat companies that do the (100-min) Melk-to-Krems river-run: **DDSG** (www.ddsg-blue-danube.at *Tel.#* 01/58-880) and **Brandner** (www.brandner.at *Tel.#* 07433/259-021). Both companies also cruise the opposite direction, Krems to Melk, but this is not recommended since it's upstream and takes twice as long. Boats depart Melk for Krems, daily, May-Sept 8:25, 11:00, 13:50 and 16:15 (this last boat requires a change in Spitz; first stop) — also boats depart Melk for Krems, daily, April and Oct 13:50, in addition to 8:25 on weekends. *Price:* (both companies charge the same) Krems to Melk 16.50€/person one-way, which allows stopovers. Students, seniors, and rail-pass holders ask for discount. There is no charge to bring a bike on board. *Getting There:* To reach the boat docks from the TI is a 15-min walk. Head towards the river—at the main road, cross it and go right following the canal and signs "Linienschifffahrt, Scheduled Trips Wachau." Soon, veer left with the bike path leading to the docks. *Note:* Confirm departure times with TI or at your digs before setting off. Using your free town map, you'll see the two boat docks on the line between sections B and C, No. 3. The four docks you see just above and left are for the bigger, overnight vessels headed to places like Budapest and beyond. Interestingly, the green space between both sets of docks is the Heiratswald, or Marriage Woods, called so because the town awards newly wedded couples in Melk with a sapling that they themselves plant here to nurture for the rest of their lives. Don't ask us what happens if they get a divorce; that's for the courts to decide. *Combo-Ticket:* ("Bahn-Schiff-Kultur" — Train-Ship-Culture) If you're coming from Vienna for a day trip, buy the Kombi- (combo-) Ticket that includes round-trip train fare, entrance into Stift Melk (monastery), and a Melk-to-Krems boat cruise. Both companies sell this combo-ticket (40€/adult) that is available for purchase at any ÖBB (Austrian rail authority) ticket counter in Vienna.

Grocery Store: In the heart of town—on the pedestrian shopping zone near the TI— is the "Spar" grocery store. *Hours:* Mon-Fri 7:00-18:00, Sat 7:00-17:00. *Note:* Opposite store begins Sechsergasse—the lane climbing (90 steps) to the monastery.

Monastery, Stift Melk: Certainly your open-jawed expression was justified when you first laid eyes on this massive and monumental structure. Benedictine monks have resided here on this ridge overlooking the Danube for more than 900 years, since 1089 when it was a more modest abode. The beautifully Baroque complex you see today was built between 1702 and 1736. Its interior is as striking as its exterior, or as some may say: as stunning as a rainbow. Equally stunning would have been Mozart's melody when he played in the abbey church on Sept. 14, 1767. Tours of Stift Melk are possible and suggested, but you can wander around a decent portion of the building for free (but not the gardens).

To reach the monastery, ascend the lane (Sechsergasse, 90 steps) opposite the above-listed "Spar" grocery store (found at these GPS coordinates: N48° 13.634 - E15° 19.960). At the top of the lane, mosey through the archway into a small courtyard with neatly trimmed hedges and the ticket office (on left). Through the next archway is the main courtyard with fountain and entrance into the monastery (with ticket). Without a ticket, though, you can still forge ahead, if you'd like. Walk across this expanse and go through the archway on the left. Inside this arcade you'll find the gift shop, toilets (from

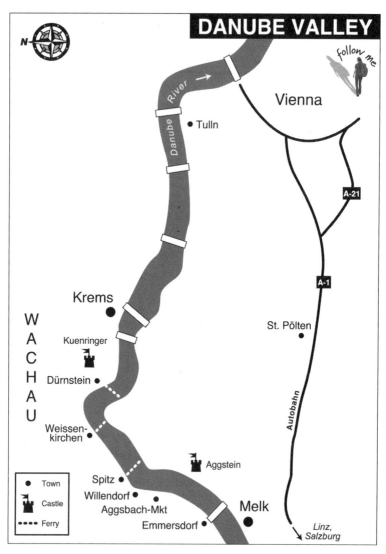

where you can ogle a nice view of Old Town Melk), and the abbey church (go ahead, step inside, you're allowed partial viewing. With your camera, zoom in on a heavenly ceiling fresco. Notice the detail).

   Hours: Stift Melk is open daily year round, April-Oct 9:00-17:00 (May-Sept till 18:00) but last entry is one hour before closing. Rest of year visits are only possible with guided tour (in German) typically at 11:00 and 14:00. To see whether an English tour is scheduled, call ahead: 02752/555-232. (www.stiftmelk.at) *Price:* adult (without tour) 7€, (with tour) 8.80€; student 4.10€/5.90€. *Gardens* are open May-Oct and are included with your entrance ticket into the monastery—separate entrance is also possible, adult 3€, student 2€. *Tours:* The English tour departs April-Oct, daily, at 14:55. For the rest of the year call the above number. The tour is an hour long but you can wander through on your own, April-Oct; generally English translations are found throughout. Or, in the ticket office, buy the monastery guide booklet 4.50€. *Drivers* will find plenty of parking available; follow signs or punch in these GPS coordinates N48° 13.783 - E15° 20.326. *Note:* April-Oct, daily, midday prayers are held in the abbey church 12:00-12:15. *Best View:* For a sweeping, unobstructed view of the Old Town and monastery, head to "Stiege 4" at No. 16 Dorfnerstrasse (*GPS:* N48° 13.363 - E15° 19.759) behind the train station, 10-min walk uphill. These are residential apartments, so please be stealthy and quiet! The best view is up the stairs.

Concentration Camp Memorial: (KZ-Gedenkstätte) Between April 1944 and April 1945, a concentration camp existed in Melk. At the camp's rusted entry gate stands a granite slab with gilded lettering notifying visitors (in German) that thousands of prisoners died here. All told, out of the 14,390 deported to this camp, some 4800 of these perished with more than 3500 being cremated in the oven you'll see inside. On this site you'll find a one-story brick building with a smokestack rising from its slanted roof. This building, among many others that are now part of the neighboring army base, was used by the Nazis to accommodate prisoners who were forced to excavate a deep tunnel safe from aerial bombardment to be used as a makeshift factory for the manufacture of weapons essential to Hitler's war effort. Due to the lack of food and clothing, harsh round-the-clock working conditions and brutal treatment, many prisoners died of starvation, sickness and/or exhaustion. Inside the smokestaked brick building is an emotional exhibition, including pictures, flowers, wreaths, info boards (mainly in German), a crematoria, and a wall chart listing the number of peoples who died here country by country. *Hours:* The camp can be visited Thur thru Sun, 10:00-14:00. However, if the gate is locked (which it most likely will be) you need to walk about 50 meters down the road and knock on the door of Frau Blak's house (right side) at Schiessstattweg No. 8 to get the key. Frau Blak is a sweet, older lady who has been the memorial's caretaker for more than 22 years. She doesn't speak English but just say *Schlüssel*, which means key. She appreciates that foreigners take an interest in visiting the memorial and, if she's not busy, she may offer to guide you around the site. If she does, it's okay to reciprocate the favor by offering her a euro or two afterwards. Interestingly, the Kaserne—or army base—next door dates from 1913, pre-WWI, home to Austrian pioneers. *Getting There:* The memorial is located in the south part of Melk on (street) Schiessstattweg, off Dorfnerstr. Using your free town map, you'll see the camp memorial—listed as KZ-Gedenkstätte—in section B 6 (bottom left). These GPS coordinates (N48° 13.207 - E15° 19.482) will get you there. *Note:* If you arrive in town outside of the camp's opening hours and really want to see it, go ahead and knock on Frau Blak's door anyway. She'll probably be okay with this. Brighten her porch with a big smile; tell her we sent you, and perhaps offer her a donation to the memorial.

WWII buffs with a car consider visiting **Mauthausen concentration camp memorial**, Austria's principal slave-labor camp, located some 20km east of Linz (or 75km west of Melk). The memorial is tremendously poignant—very much worth your time, if you have it. *Hours:* daily 9:00-17:30, last entry 16:45. (www.mauthausen-memorial.at) To get there from Melk, either cross the river and drive the scenic route 3 to the town of Mauthausen (then follow signs KZ-Gedenkstätte) or for a quicker approach hop on the autobahn and get off at exit #151—St. Valentin—then follow signs to Mauthausen and KZ-Gedenkstätte. *Railers,* you can visit, too, it's just tricky. First take the train to Amstetten; change there to St. Valentin, from where you'll pick up a local (and infrequent) shuttle train to the town of Mauthausen. From there—the camp is still 5km away—you can either hike or arrange for a taxi (about 10€ each way; have driver return in, say, two hours). Be sure to coordinate all your return connections. *Suggestion:* If you're headed to Salzburg, visit Mauthausen on the way because you'll pass St. Valentin (just leave early and plan to arrive late in Salzburg). Railers, store your bags at the station).

Good Sleeps: All come with breakfast, per usual.

Hotel-Restaurant zur Post: Linzer Strasse 1 (www.post-melk.at) *Tel.#* 02752/52-345. These 4-star digs are trumps in this town of monks. Run by three generations of the Ebner family—from grandma to grandchild—you'll more than appreciate zur Post's homely rooms, choice of three delicious restaurants, pleasant outdoor courtyard, vintage wine cellar, and free bike rental for guests! Hotel has elevator. *Price:* Sgl 55-60€, Dbl 88-98€, Trpl from 110€, apartment from 135€. *CC's:* VC, MC. *Getting There:* Hotel is located in the Old Town, a five-minute walk from the train station. *Railers,* exit station straight, descend road (Bahnhofstr.) and walk towards a stunning view of the monastery—follow the road as it curves left and after about 50 meters go left on Linzer Str. to your digs on the left. *Drivers,* free parking, query reception. *GPS:* N48° 13.615 - E15° 19.730. *Note:* Hotel zur Post rents bikes to non-guests for 10€/day, leave ID as deposit.

Gasthof Goldener Stern: Sterngasse 17 (www.sternmelk.at) *Tel.#* 02752/52-214. Another excellent choice; Kurt and Regina run the charmingly rustic Goldener Stern, which dates from the 15th century when it was known as the "Stiftstaverne" lodge. Positioned beneath the monastery, these digs register as Melk's oldest inn on the oldest lane in town. Behind its historic walls you'll discover tastefully decorated rooms, with each having its own design—some exceedingly romantic—and fresh flowers on the bed. Rooms boast views of either the Old Town or the monastery. Kurt and Regina also maintain an authentic Austrian kitchen dishing out traditional meals. *Price:* (cash only; cheaper the longer you stay) Dbl 42-100€—lower price means smaller room without facilities—Sgl/Trpl possible. Bike rental available. *Getting There:* Goldener Stern is located on the quiet lane behind the main square (ascend lane running adjacent to cutesy-pie building with twin turrets). *Railers,* from the station follow directions into the Old Town and before the Spar grocery store look left for Sterngasse. *Drivers,* it's possible (but very tight) to pull up to the front door and unload. Limited parking out front; query reception upon booking. *GPS:* N48° 13.644 - E15° 19.844

Pension Weisses Lamm: Linzer Strasse 7. *Tel.#* 02752/54-085 or cell 0664/231-5297. This establishment offers eight big and basic rooms—some with shower-toilet, others with just a shower—at the cheapest prices in the Old Town. Attached is a multi-cultural restaurant serving Mexican, Italian and Greek cuisine. *Price:* (cash only) *Sgl 25€, Dbl 40€, Trpl 60€. *Note:* If things are slow, by late afternoon, the owner may wheel out the advertising board to announce that the Sgl has been reduced to 20€. *Getting There:* Weisses Lamm is located a few doors past Hotel-Restaurant zur Post (see their entry above for directions). *GPS:* N48° 13.595 - E15° 19.696

Hostel, Melk: [HI] Abt-Karl-Str. 42. *Tel.#* 02752/52-681. Friendly staff; decent hostel, it's just getting a bit old now but it has all the basics a backpacker would require. Dorm rooms are small; hopefully it won't be full. No laundry or kitchen; fridge and TV downstairs. *Price:* (includes breakfast, sheets) 4-bed dorm 17€, Sgl 27€, Dbl 44€. *CC's:* MC. *Note:* An extra one-time 2€ fee will be charged if staying less than three nights. Reception is open early till midday and again 16:00-21:00. You can check in early if a bed is available. Check out 10:00. Reception has towels. *Getting There:* Hostel is a 10-min walk from the train station. Using your free town map, you'll see it listed as Jugendherberge on the line between sections C and D, No. 5. *Railers,* exit station straight and make an immediate right onto the tree-lined cobbled lane. At the end of the lane, follow hostel sign left and then right. After walking a few hundred meters more, the hostel will appear on your right. *GPS:* N48° 13.464 - E15° 20.402

Bike Ride, Melk to Krems

Total journey: 36km/23mi between the towns of Melk and Krems. Allow five hours to enjoy a reasonably slow pace with a picnic stop

Here's your chance to cycle along Austria's most beautiful riverscape and a UNESCO World Heritage site to boot. So get your buns in the saddle and feet dancin' on the pedals and ride your very own Tour de Danube. To fulfill this eco-adventure, query TI for latest bike-rental options or you can hire wheels from Hotel-Restaurant zur Post, 10€/day (see *Good Sleeps* above for directions). Before we set off, there are a few things to note:

1) The first 8-9km are nothing special (scenery picks-up after the town of Aggsbach-Mkt), so an idea would be a boat-bike combo: Catch the boat from Melk to Spitz (first stop) and cycle the remaining 20-odd km from there (page 545—*Boaters*). *Note:* Art historians may not want to utilize the boat-bike option; see Willendorf (in bold) below.

2) The path you will be following is called the "Donauradweg" (Danube Bike Route), denoted by little green signs. The route has more slopes than rises, and although it frequently wanders away from the river, it is still scenic.

3) Consider breaking the ride up with a picnic. Also, consider packing a T-shirt or towel to fold and place on the bicycle seat as extra padding for your buttocks. Extended periods of time in the saddle can/will result in backside soreness, especially if you're not used to it.

4) Trains do the hourly milk-run from Krems to Emmersdorf (town across Danube from Melk that serves the left bank), stopping at most every community. Thus, if you want to bug out from the bike ride at any time, pull into one of the stations en route and catch the train back.

5) When returning to Melk by rail, get off at Emmersdorf (town opposite Melk) and cycle (about 30-min) over the river via the bridge. To avoid riding this last stretch back to Melk in the dark, which can be dangerous without proper safety gear, be sure to depart Krems (or wherever) with enough daylight hours ahead of you. From Krems to Emmersdorf by rail takes 60 min and costs around 7€/adult with bike.

6) If bad weather crashes your party, a good rainy-day alternative to biking/boating is to ride the bus from Melk train station to Krems.

OK, that said, let's hit the road! From Melk follow the *Donauradweg* signs to the bridge and cross it. But before you do, you'll have to briefly dismount and walk the bike up to the bridge. On the other side of the river follow the green bike-route signs all the way to Krems. The landscape will develop into a wonder after the town of **Aggsbach-Mkt**, where voluminous vineyards sweeten your path.

Beyond Aggsbach-Mkt is **Willendorf**, a town that art historians will be astonished to read was the site of a famous discovery: The so-called Venus of Willendorf, a small (4.5-inch tall) female statuette that registers as one of the earliest known examples of sculpture, dating from around 25,000 B.C. This prehistoric gal is believed to be a symbol of fertility, which would explain her healthy, Baroque-like figure. Follow signs to Venus to spy the monument marking the spot where she was unearthed (the pocket-sized original can be found in Vienna's Natural History Museum).

Next up is **Spitz**, virtually equidistant between Melk and Krems, first mentioned as "Spitzum" in 865 A.D. Today, Spitz has nearly 2000 inhabitants and is a popular touristic hub in the Wachau. The prominent hill in town is called Tausand-Eimerberg, which dates back centuries ago when the amount of wine it produced from the grapes harvested always totaled "1000 Buckets."

Ahead is the village of **Weissenkirchen**, the largest wine-growing community in the Wachau. You'll adore its picturesque lanes and traditional *Heurigen*—inns run by vintners who serve their own wine together with regional cuisine. Heurigen are recognizable by the sprig of spruce or wreath of hay hanging outside their door. One thing you'll see plenty of en route—besides tourists on two wheels and burgeoning flowers in boxes hangin' from windowsills—is Zimmer, or Bed & Breakfasts, providing you with umpteen options to call home for when you come back.

If you liked Weissenkirchen, you're going to love medieval **Dürnstein**. As you forge ahead, you'll see its brilliantly blue 18th-century Baroque church rising above the rooftops. Amazing sight, huh? To enter this ornate, holy domain will cost adult 2.50€, student 1.50€ (open April-Oct Mon-Sat 9:00-18:00, Sun 10:00-18:00). This includes admittance onto its viewing terrace, perched above the Danube. In town the bike route climbs sharply, but you'll want to dismount anyway to absorb your mesmeric surroundings. Above you are the castle ruins of Kuenringer, named after the Kuenring family who established Dürnstein as their seat of power in the Middle Ages. You can hike to its ramparts for gigantic views. One local writer describes the panorama like so: "All the proud fortresses and monasteries of the Wachau lie at your feet, like precious jewels on a necklace…" To reach the ruins, make the first left after exiting the town's fortified walls. Dürnstein is also renowned for its association with a powerful Englishman: Richard I—or famously, Richard the Lion-Hearted—King of England (1189-99). Shortly after becoming king, Richard made his way to Jerusalem on the Third Crusade. While there, he—allegedly—made fun of the Austrian flag. Consequently, a few years later, Richard was detained while on his way back home to England by the Duke of Austria, Leopold V, and held captive here in Dürnstein until a large ransom was paid for his freedom.

On the other side of Dürnstein is the neighborhood of Loiben, which is separated into two parts: Ober- and Unter-, or Upper- and Lower-. As you cycle by notice the rustic Zimmer nestled amongst the romantic vineyards. Nice, ay? From here, you're only 7km/4mi from Krems.

After pedaling through all those handsome hamlets, **Krems**—with its population of 24,000—will feel like big-city business. First mentioned in 995 A.D. as "Urbs Chremisa," Krems is the home stretch of your Tour de Danube. Continue along the river; the route then cuts into the city passing the Bahnhof, or train station. If you're not too pooped, we suggest one last hoorah on wheels: Explore the Old Town, but first swing by the Bahnhof to get your bearings and check out the train departure time (to Emmersdorf). If you have at least 15 minutes to spare, cycle back to the main road (Ringstr.) and cross over into Dinstlstr. leading to Krems' remarkable Old Town. Cycle around and ogle the architecture. It's like being on a Hollywood movie set, no?

Back at the station, hop on the train and secure your bike on the designated rack. En route, keep an eye out the window to behold the scenic stretches you just rode. That was some trip. Good Job!

V I E N N A (Wien)

~ Population: 1.8 million   ~ Elevation: 180m/590ft
~ Country/Area Code: +43-(0)1

Vienna—Wien in German (pronounced Veen)—is the capital of Austria, accommodating 20 percent of its population and constituting one of the nation's nine Bundesländer, or federal states. The city embodies imperial splendor, voguish coffeehouses and the finest classical music, where Mozart composed his masterpieces, Beethoven penned his symphonies, and "waltz king" Strauss captivated Europe with his twirling melodies.

In the 1st century A.D. the Romans established Vindobona, an outpost by the Danube River to garrison their troops. They brought with them the craft of wine growing, and today Vienna is the only metropolis in the world that has its own wine district. Vindobona flourished and the population swelled to 20,000. However, Vindobona's position on the eastern fringe of the empire made it vulnerable to attack. Marcus Aurelius—Roman emperor and philosopher—came here in the year 180 to bolster its defenses but died during his stay. By the 5th century, repeated incursions by nomadic tribes forced the abandonment of Vindobona.

In the 9th century, the former Roman outpost became part of Charlemagne's Holy Roman Empire and in the year 881 Wenia is mentioned for the first time. In 1278, the German King Rudolf of "Habsburg" acquired Vienna, beginning Austria's 640-year love affair with the royal family.

The most important Habsburgs were Maria Theresa and Franz Josef I. Maria Theresa—Holy Roman Empress (1740-80), Archduchess of Austria, Queen of Hungary and Bohemia—became the only female sovereign in the history of the Habsburg dynasty. Preceding the reign of Maria Theresa was her father, Charles VI, who shrewdly protected the future of Habsburg rule by declaring the famed Pragmatic Sanction of 1713, which essentially stated that there shall be no complaining if the king happened to be a female. Consequently, the oldest daughter of Charles VI—Maria Theresa—inherited the crown upon her father's death. She achieved her imperial tasks with high praise and is duly noted as one of the great reformists of the 18th century. Emperor Franz Josef was the last important Habsburg ruler, reigning for 68 years (1848-1916), Europe's second longest governing monarch—after Louis XIV—corresponding to the office of 18 U.S. presidents, from Polk to Wilson. During his reign, Vienna became a modern city as well as the capital of the Austro-Hungarian Empire (1867-1918), which incorporated 52 million people in the lands that are now Austria, Hungary, Slovakia, Czech Republic and parts of Poland, Romania, Italy and half of the former Yugoslav federation.

After the defeat of Austria in World War I, the Habsburgs were out of a job, the empire was kaput and Vienna's importance declined. And after the defeat of the Axis powers in WWII, the Allies (USA, UK, USSR, France) split Vienna, like Berlin, into four sectors of occupation. In 1955 the Allies went home, giving Vienna its independence.

The city rebounded in the latter half of the 20th century and since 1996 Vienna's Altstadt has taken its place alongside the historic Old Towns of Prague, Warsaw and Jerusalem as an esteemed member of UNESCO's World Heritage List, a United Nations' register of the world's most diverse and unique places.

Vienna has 23 districts (known as Bezirke) and if you think of them as forming the centric rings of a dartboard it's easy to picture the city's layout. The bull's-eye, or 1st district (Bezirk)—bound by the grand Ringstrasse—is Vienna's Old Town, which is surrounded by districts 2-9, with the remaining districts fanning out around them. However, making things easy for you, much of the touristy stuff is located within the 1st district, or Old Town.

Tourists come from distant lands to absorb Vienna's sites, smells and sounds. They gawk at Stephansdom, a medieval masterpiece of Gothic architecture and one of the world's great cathedrals. They ogle the Lipizzaner stallions at the Spanish Riding School. They browse Vienna's world-class museums. They attend the opera and theater and are mesmerized by the great compositions. They drink wine at the Heurige, savor torte bound in boxes and eat Wiener schnitzel by the plate full. And you can, too!

These GPS coordinates—N48° 12.234 - E16° 22.742—will get you downtown before a gilded gent in a green garden grasping his *Geige*.

~ **Vienna is worth at least a two-day stay for the quickest of trips. With umpteen variables as how to divide your time, it is difficult to state a specific itinerary. Here are a few ideas.**

Day 1: Begin early and visit St. Stephan's Cathedral (page 558). From there, wander via the popular pedestrian shopping streets Graben and Kohlmarkt to reach the Lipizzaner stallions (page 567). Then cruise through the Hofburg (page 559) and Heldenplatz. From the adjacent Ringstrasse (page 557) hop on either tram #1 or #2 and do the loop. Culture vultures get off where you got on and cruise across the boulevard to the MuseumsQuartier (page 566). WWII buffs exit the tram closest to the Academy of Fine Arts (page 563). Fans of the performing arts exit at the Opera House for a tour and/or to check the latest program. Behind this historic structure is the TI, Sacher torte, and the main shopping street: Kärntner Str. Before the sun sets, forge a plan for the evening. Consider a Mozart concert, or an opera—3.50€ tickets for travelers on a budget (page 575—*Entertainment*).

Day 2: Spend a few hours at Schönbrunn palace (page 562). The rest of your day visit sights/museums of interest, or search out a grave (page 572—*Cemeteries & Crypts*).

Day 3: The world is your oyster.

Tourist Information: [TI] (www.vienna.info) *Tel.#* 01/24-555. Vienna has one TI, which is packed with English pamphlets and themed booklets (e.g. kids & families, shopping & dining, sports & nature, coffeehouses & concerts). Pick up a city map, they are free and handily illustrate all transportation lines. For a (3€) fee helpful staff will find you a room (or free via TI website). Consider buying the informative "Vienna A to Z" booklet (3.60€ or 2.90€ with Vienna Card). Every important building in Vienna (and there are many) displays a red-and-white banner with an identification number that keys into this A-to-Z booklet, literally placing the history of Vienna in your hands. *Hours:* daily, 9:00-19:00. *Getting There:* TI is located in the Old Town one block behind the Opera House. *Note:* Across from TI is a memorial to "the victims of war and Fascism." (Look for the two white sculptures on granite blocks.) For seven years—1938-1945— Nazism consumed Austria. Smart Austrians left the country the first chance they had. Case in point: the von Trapp family. The location of this memorial was purposely chosen. The granite tablet reads: *"Here stood the Philipphof, where on March 12, 1945, hundreds of people fled to its basement for shelter during a bombing raid. The building was destroyed and the people were buried alive."*

Emergency Tel. Numbers: [Austria-wide]
Fire dept. (Feuerwehr) = 122
Police (Polizei) = 133
Ambulance/Rescue = 144

Railers: Vienna doesn't claim one main train station but three: **Westbahnhof, Südbahn-hof** and **Franz-Josefs-Bahnhof**, which are arguably Austria's least attractive stations of its major cities. Most of you will be coming in from the west—Salzburg/Melk—and therefore arrive at Westbahnhof, the best located of the three. If you're coming in from Graz, your train will terminate at Südbahnhof, but if you want to reach Westbahnhof, get off at Meidling (five minutes before Südbahnhof) and take the subway U6 four stops direction Floridsdorf. *Note:* Austrian rail authority: www.oebb.at

Westbahnhof: On street level you'll find the **P.O.** (Mon-Fri 7:00-22:00, Sat/Sun 9:00-22:00); an **Internet café** (open early till late); **mini mart** (daily, 5:30-23:00—pricey, but on Sundays and evenings it's your only choice); a couple of real **grocery stores** are only one block away at (Äußere) Mariahilfer Str. 135 (and next door), exit station right, (open generally Mon-Thur 7:45-19:00, Fri 7:30-19:30, Sat 7:30-17:00); **storage lockers** are available 2€-3.50€/24hr; and an **info point** is located beneath the clock on street level (daily, 8:30-20:45—which is perfect to book a tour, buy show tickets or reserve a room, but for non-commission-generating queries you'll be lucky to receive a helpful reply. If you have a general question, need train info or a city map, then stop by the info kiosk positioned in the middle of the upper floor). **Taxis and public transportation** are out front. Normal adult price, one way, **via rail from Westbahnhof** to Salzburg is 40€, 3.5hr — to Melk 13€, 85min — to Budapest 3hr, 38€. **Getting to the Old Town**, follow signs U3 down to the tracks (direction Simmering)—get off at Stephansplatz (the heart of Vienna), five stops. *Note:* Westbahnhof is closed mornings 1:15-4:00.

Südbahnhof: If you're coming from the east (e.g. Czech Republic, Poland) or the south (e.g. Croatia, Italy) you'll arrive here—a bigger and emptier station than Westbahnhof. It must have resided smack-dab in the middle of the Soviet sector post-WWII because the main transit hall is big and bland and has an overly communistic feel. Nonetheless, it affords all the useful amenities (on street level) a traveler desires: **TI** (daily, 6:30-24:00; **storage lockers** 2€-3.50€/24hr (in corner past phones); **mini mart** (daily, 5:30-23:00); **P.O.** (Mon-Fri 7:00-20:00, Sat/Sun 9:00-14:00—exit station by mini mart and P.O. is across parking lot, left side). **Taxis and public transportation** are out front. **Getting to Westbahnhof**, take tram #18 (about 10 stops direction Burggasse). **Getting to the Old Town**, hop on tram "O" (direction Praterstern) and ride it to Land-straße—exit tram left and cross the street to the U-Bahn station (U3/U4) or continue farther to the Ringstrasse and Stadtpark. Consider riding the U3 (direction Ottakring) two stops to Stephansplatz, the heart of Vienna. *Note:* For the cheapest price, buy your tram/bus ticket at a touch-screen automat in the transit hall (button for English; one-way 1.50€, or 2€ if purchased on board vehicle; seniors/students check for discounts).

Franz-Josefs-Bahnhof caters more to provincial railers and won't really concern you, unless, for example, you're heading to/fro Krems (Danube Valley). If you do arrive here, out front you'll find the "D" tram heading downtown and a McDonald's. Although, we recommend, if you're heading to/fro Krems, depart from (or get off at) Spittelau station (one stop from Franz-Josefs-Bhf) because it is handily connected to the subway.

Bratislava or Bust: The capital of Slovakia—Bratislava—is only an hour from Vienna and worthy of a visit if you have the time. Make a day trip of it. Ogle the historic Old Town; you'll love its magnetism! *Getting There: By Train:* Trains depart hourly from Südbahnhof and take an hour (11.50€ one way, 14€ round trip). *By Bus:* Buses depart hourly from Südbahnhof and take 1.5hr (9€ one way, 16€ round trip). *(Note: Buy your train/bus ticket at a touch-screen automat in Südbahnhof's transit hall, button for*

English.) **By Boat** (75-min trip)*:* Boats depart June-Oct typically 8:30, 12:30 and 16:30 from the Reichsbrücke (bridge) at the Danube River. *Price:* 15-23€ one-way. The price you pay depends on day and departure time—for example, earlier boats, and weekends, constitute higher prices. *Tel.#* 01/58-880. (www.ddsg-blue-danube.at)

Subway/Bus/Tram: Vienna's integrated and efficient transportation authority (VOR, www.wienerlinien.at) governs an enormous urban network — consisting of 8000 employees, 500 buses, 185km of U-Bahn (Underground) tracks and 445km of tram (Strassenbahn) tracks — utilized by nearly 750,000 commuters per year. The following low-priced tickets are simple to comprehend and easy to use, covering every mode of transportation in the VOR network. *Single Ticket:* (Einzelfahrt) valid for a one-way journey—1.50€, or 2€ if purchased on board vehicle. *24-Hour-Ticket:* (24-Stunden-Karte) good for 24hr from time of validation—5€. *72-Hour-Ticket:* (72-Stunden-Karte) good for 72hr from time of validation—12€. *Week-Ticket:* (Wochenkarte) This ticket is an amazing deal, only costing 12.50€, or 50¢ more than the 72-Hour-Ticket. Beware, ticket is valid from Monday 0:01 (one minute past midnight) until the following Monday 9:00—meaning, if you were to buy the Week-Ticket on a Friday, you'd only get three days use. The ticket is transferable so others can use it. *Note:* All ticket types can be purchased at multilingual vending machines marked Fahrkarten or at tobacco (Tabak) shops. *Tickets must be stamped in the blue box to validate, "Bitte entwerten," watch locals.* Travelers riding without valid ticket risk fines upwards of 50€, on the spot! Plain-clothed officials patrol network constantly!

Drivers: The Viennese don't seem to stress about parking and a testament to their lax attitude is the absence of parking meters. Instead, they offer the strange but lenient pay-and-display ticket ("Parkschein")—applicable Mon-Fri 9:00-19:00, 50¢/30min, max 1.5/2hr—for sale from Tabak (tobacco, newspaper) shops and many banks. Fill out the ticket and put it on the dashboard. Parking is mostly free in outer Vienna (beyond the Gürtel, districts 10-19 and 21-23). For folks who want to avoid the inner city, pull into a P+R (Park+Ride) on the outskirts. Here you park for free and ride public transportation into town (parking lots are next to subway lines or major bus/tram connections). Or, there are a handful of parking garages to choose from in the Old Town—look for the blue "P" sign. One of the most popular downtown garages can be found where Kärntner Str. meets the Opera House (open 24/7; 2.80€/hr or 34€/day; *GPS:* N48° 12.152 - E16° 22.180). *Note:* If staying overnight, query reception in advance about where to park.

Airport: (*Flughafen*; code VIE; www.viennaairport.com) Vienna's Schwechat airport—moving more than 15 million passengers annually—is located 19km east of the Old Town, off the highway to Slovakia and Hungary. Regular connections between the airport and city are available: bus to/fro Schwedenplatz (20min), Südbahnhof (25min) or Westbahnhof (35min) costs 6€/person; the cheapest way is the S7 (Schnellbahn) every half hour airport ↔ subway U3 Wien Mitte (25min, 3€); or faster is the new CAT (City Airport Train) to/fro U3 Wien Mitte (16min, 9€ automat—10€ on board); or the most expensive way is via taxi to/fro Old Town for about 35€ (includes 10€ surcharge). *TI* (daily, 7:00-22:00) is located in the arrivals hall near baggage claim. *Note:* Buy the Vienna Card at the airport to begin savings.

Horse-Drawn Carriage: (Fiaker) Romantic rides through the Old Town cost 40€/20min, 65€/40min, or 95€/60min (up to 4 passengers, 5 possible—discuss with driver). Carriages can readily be found on Heldenplatz (Hofburg), Stephansplatz (behind St. Stephan's Cathedral), and Albertinaplatz (by TI). *Note:* Rides double as a city tour, therefore the better English your driver speaks the better your tour.

Bike Rental: Cyclists will enjoy pedaling around the Ringstrasse and along the Danube River. Bike paths are ubiquitous and well maintained in Vienna—query TI for the latest and greatest deal on a rental.

Vienna Card: The Vienna Card offers a heap of citywide discounts for 72 hours (once card is validated), including unlimited use of public transport and discounts of 10-50% on select attractions, tours, museums and entertainment. The card is available at the TI, a number of hotels and VOR (transportation authority) info counters. *Price:* 17€/72hr. *Opinion:* The card's three-day use of public transport is worth 12€, therefore all you need to do is rack up another 5€ in savings to pay for the card. Pick up the detailed Vienna Card Coupon Book to see whether your movements will compensate the price of the card. You can also gauge your savings by poring over the attractions and museums listed in this chapter, which include the discounted price afforded by the Vienna Card.

Internet: BigNet cafés are a popular downtown surf stop, offering stylish seating and reasonable rates. Austria's largest Internet café (200 terminals) is the BigNet at Maria-hilfer Str. 27 (Mon-Sat 8:00-02:00, Sun 10:00-02:00). BigNet's other two locations— Kärntner Str. 61 and Hoher Markt 8—keep the same hours: daily, 10:00-24:00. But don't fret if you're nowhere near these locations, there's probably a café in close proximity.

Post Office: Handy are the P.O.s in the train stations: *Westbahnhof* (Mon-Fri 7:00-22:00, Sat/Sun 9:00-20:00) and just outside *Südbahnhof* (Mon-Fri 7:00-20:00, Sat/Sun 9:00-14:00). *Note:* Newspaper and tobacco (Tabak) shops often sell postage stamps.

American Express: Kärntner Str. 21-23 (zip: 1010), tel.# 01/5154-0467. *Hours:* Mon-Fri 9:00-17:30, Sat 9:00-12:00. Emergency toll-free number (only when in Austria): 0800-206-840. (fesvienna@aexp.com)

Cinema, English: Moviegoers experiencing popcorn withdrawals can catch an English-speaking flick (original version without subtitles) at English Cinema Hayden, Mariahilfer Str. 57. (www.haydnkino.at) *Tel.#* 01/587-2262. *Price:* 6.60-8.40€, students Mon-Thur 6€, 20% discount with Vienna Card. *Specials:* (except holidays) all movies Mon 6€, Tue/Wed 6.60€.

Embassies and Consulates

USA: [embassy] (www.usembassy.at) Boltzmanngasse 16. *Tel.#* 01/313-390. (embassy@usembassy.at) — [consular section for passport queries, voter registration, etc.] Parkring 12 (consulatevienna@state.gov) *Hours:* Mon-Fri 8:00-11:30. *Tel.#* 01/3133-97535; after-hours emergencies only 01/31-339.

Canada: Laurenzerberg 2 (www.kanada.at) *Tel.#* 01/5313-83000. *Hours:* Mon-Fri 8:30-12:30 & 13:30-15:30. (vienn@international.gc.ca)

Australia: Mattiellistr. 2 (www.australian-embassy.at) *Tel.#* 01/506-740. (austemb@aon.at) *Hours:* [consular/passport] Mon-Fri 9:00-12:30 & 14:00-16:00.

UK: Jauresgasse 10 [embassy and consulate] (www.britishembassy.at) *Tel.#* [all sections] 01/716-130. (visa-consular@britishembassy.at) *Hours:* [consular] Mon-Fri 9:15-10:15. *Tel.#* [consular/passport, available Mon-Fri 14:00-16:00] 01/7161-35151; after-hours emergencies for UK nationals only, cell.# 0676/569-4012.

Holidays in Vienna, 2006

1. January, Sunday – New Year
6. January, Friday – Epiphany (Three Kings' Day)
17. April – Easter Monday
1. May, Monday – May Day (Labor Day)
25. May, Thursday – Ascension Day
5. June – Whit Monday

15. June, Thursday – Corpus Christi 15. August, Tuesday – Assumption Day 26. October, Thursday – Independence Day 1. November, Wednesday – All Saints' Day 8. December, Friday – Immaculate Conception 25. December, Monday – Christmas 26. December, Tuesday – St. Stephen's Day (Christmas Day No. 2)

What to do on a Sunday or holiday

Sundays and holidays are a good time to go for a bike ride since the normal city traffic will be absent from the streets. The shops will be closed (with the exception of convenience stores) but most all attractions will be open. If you've done all the attractions, consider sunbathing by the Danube (page 570—*Parks, Gardens & Sunbathing*) or discovering a grave (page 572—*Cemeteries & Crypts*). But before you do any of the above, check out the **Augustinian Church**'s (page 561) concert-like Mass (11:00 on Sunday), featuring heavenly hits from the choir and organist. After Mass, a clergyman unlocks the door to the hearts of the Habsburgs.

Church Service, "Gottesdienst"

Note: Hours may have changed—check with staff at your accommodations or at the TI for the latest info, as well as for other religious denominations.

Roman Catholic: (English service) Votivkirche (on Ringstrasse) — Sun 11:00. The Votivkirche (Votive Church) is the home base of the Vienna English Speaking Catholic Community. (www.vescc.org) *Tel.#* 01/402-1830.

Roman Catholic: (English service) St. Stephan's Cathedral — Sat 19:00.

Protestant: (English service) Reformierte Stadtkirche (located at Dorotheergasse 16, near the Hofburg in the Old Town) — Sun 12:00.

United Methodist: (English service) United Methodist Church (located at Sechshauser Str. 56, between Westbahnhof and Schönbrunn Palace) — Sun 11:15. *Tel.#* 01/895-8175.

FREE Vienna

1) A trip to Vienna wouldn't be complete without setting foot in—or climbing—**St. Stephan's Cathedral** (page 558).

2) Another must-do is to watch the graceful **Lipizzaner stallions** (page 567) strut from their stalls to the Spanish Riding School.

3) Former residences belonging to **Strauss** and **Beethoven** (pages 564-65) are free to enter if you're in town on a Friday morning or on a Sunday.

4) Nostalgic for Coney Island? Ramble through the **amusement park** at the Prater (page 571).

5) **Culture vultures** should cruise through the MuseumsQuartier (page 566), one of the largest cultural centers in the world.

6) For a relaxing respite from inner-city ruckus, have a spell on a riverside beach or wander into one of the city's fragrant parks, including the must-see **Schlosspark Schönbrunn**. WWII buffs check out the humungous flak towers in the **Augarten** (see *Parks, Gardens & Sunbathing*, page 570).

7) Though technically not without cost, standing-room seats at the **Opera House** (page 576) are a once-in-a-lifetime opportunity at a bargain-basement price.

8) **Grave seekers** will unearth the following names in Vienna: Beethoven, Ludwig van • Bonaparte, Marie-Louise d'Autriche • Brahms, Johannes • Falco • Habsburg, Elisabeth "Sisi" • Habsburg, Franz Josef I • Habsburg, Maria Theresa • Mozart, Wolfgang •

Salieri, Antonio • Schubert, Franz • Strauss, Johann I & II • Vivaldi, Antonio — see *Cemeteries & Crypts*, page 572.

9) **Artist-types** and **WWII buffs** amble through the aged and ornamented hallways of the Academy of Fine Arts (page 563).

10) **Design students** and **art aficionados** check out the colorful facades of the KunstHausWien and Hundertwasserhaus (pages 568-69). Across town, don't miss Otto Wagner's art nouveau (Sezessionstil) facades at Linke Wienzeile 38 and 40 (see Naschmarkt, page 577).

11) Hammer out a winning bid at the **Dorotheum**, Central Europe's leading auction house. Admission is free and worthy of your time (see *Shopping*, 574).

12) For three hot days and nights in June—23-25 (Fri-Sun), 2006—hundreds of entertainers and music bands will perform on 22 stages before more than 2 million people at the **Donauinselfest** (Danube Island Festival), Europe's biggest open-air party (6.5km site). Acts range from hip-hop to country to karaoke. The best part about the festival is it's completely *FREE!* Bring your own food and drink or buy it there from one of the numerous catering stands. Since the festival takes place on a long sliver of land in the middle of the Danube River, bring your bathing suit because there'll be plenty of swimming. Don't miss the mega firework show Sat night (June 24) around 22:00. To get there, take subway U1 to Donauinsel or the U6 to Neue Donau.

13) Every evening in July and August (July 1—Sept 3, 2006) the square facing the Rathaus (town hall) illuminates with the **open-air music film festival**, featuring productions from around the world. Another critical piece of information, the film festival is *FREE* of charge! Bring a bottle of wine and savor it under the stars. Consider having dinner there; numerous foods stands will be dishing up international cuisine.

14) Another summer freebie recalls the original **Hoch- and Deutschmeister** marching band onto the streets, just like in imperial times. The band's history dates from 1741, and even more interesting is the fact that their instruments are custom-made, costing between 3000€-4000€ each. You can see and hear them every Saturday at 11:00 from May until mid-Oct at the corner of (streets) Graben and Kohlmarkt, from where they'll march into the inner courtyard of the Hofburg palace while playing regimental melodies by Strauss and others.

SIGHTS

Opera House: see page 576.

Secession Building: see page 569.

Giant Ferris Wheel: see *Prater*, page 571.

Ringstrasse: Proven to be obsolete by Napoleon, Vienna's medieval walls were razed in 1857 and replaced with a broad circular boulevard—der Ring or Ringstrasse—lined with grand buildings, monuments and parks. Emperor Franz Josef took best advantage of the renovation by showcasing Austria's cultural and political institutions while shining a light on the majesty of the Habsburg monarchy itself. The Ringstrasse—completed in the 1880s—developed into one of Europe's grandest boulevards, orbiting the core of Vienna: the 1st district. Among the more important buildings flanking the "Ring" are Austrian Parliament (1883); Town Hall (Rathaus, 1883); *Burgtheater (1888); University (1883); Votive Church (Votivkirche, 1856-1879); Stock Exchange (Börse, 1877); Opera House (1869); *Museum of Fine Arts (1890); *Natural History Museum (1890); and the Hofburg palace, the oldest part of which dates from the 13th century. Today, the Ringstrasse is as splendid as it was after its completion. Recommended is a cruise around it on either tram #1 or #2 (1.50€/person, or free for holders of the Vienna Card or a valid ticket on Vienna's VOR transportation network). *<u>Note</u>:* Gottfried Semper—creator of Dresden's grand landmark, the Semperoper—designed these buildings.

St. Stephan's Cathedral: If Vienna were a dartboard, and its 23 districts the centric rings, "Stephansdom" would be the bull's-eye. Affectionately called *Steffl* by the locals, St. Stephan's Cathedral is the pulsating heart of the city. Vienna began here, and grew up around it. For more than 850 years a church has stood on this spot (first consecrated in 1147), but all that remains of the original Romanesque structure are portions of the west facade belonging to the Giants' Doorway and Heathen Towers. At nearly 450 feet high, the Gothic-style **south tower**—completed in 1433—provides an excellent vantage point from which to see the city and beyond; that is, if you don't suffer from vertigo and don't mind climbing 343 grooved and dizzying steps that spiral upwards as if to heaven itself. The **north tower**, only 224 feet high, was never completed due to the lack of funds and was capped with a Renaissance-style cupola in 1578. From outside, notice where the construction work abruptly halted and where the modern-day railing encloses the observation terrace, reachable via elevator. Hanging inside the north tower is Pummerin, an enormous 21-ton bell dating from 1711, cast from captured Turkish cannons after their failed siege of Vienna in 1683. Named for its deep "booming" sound, Pummerin can be viewed when visiting the observation terrace. Carved into the cathedral's stone facade (right of main portal) you'll see the insignia "O5," symbolic of Austria's anti-Nazi resistance movement, 1938-1945. Below the insignia is a granite plaque remembering those who died. Inside the cathedral is breathtaking with its ornate Gothic stonework, heavenly high altar and lofty pillars rising to a webbed ceiling. Midway in and on the left is a staircase descending into the so-called **catacombs**, where urns contain the entrails of the Habsburgs and where the great Mozart lay after his death until being carted off to St. Marx Cemetery for a commoner's burial. *Hours:* (cathedral) Although open seven days early till late, portions of the cathedral are closed during religious services, which are frequent. The best hours for visiting are Mon-Sat 8:30-11:30 & 13:00-16:30, Sun 13:00-16:30. *Holy Mass:* (in English) Sat 19:00. *Price:* Newly implemented, there will be an admission fee of 1€ to enter the central part of the cathedral during its busiest months, July-Sept, free rest of year. There is no fee to walk the inside perimeter. *Tours:* Guided tours of the cathedral in English run April-Oct, daily, at 15:45, 4€/person; meet inside at central left stone pillar—or you can buy a quasi-do-it-yourself-tour souvenir booklet (from 4.90€) sold in the cathedral shop (on left after entering). Other options, recently put into action by the cathedral during its busiest months (July-Sept), are 45-min audio-guide tours (from 5€/person). There are three to choose from: **Tour 1** pilots you around the cathedral. **Tour 2** leads you through the cathedral's treasury (Schatzkammer). **Tour 3** is a combo of both (1.5hr). *Catacombs:* Multilingual tours depart daily every half hour Mon-Sat 10:00-11:30 & 13:30-16:30, Sun 13:30-16:30—(overpriced at) 4€/person. *North Tower:* The elevator to the observation terrace and Pummerin is located midway inside the cathedral on the left. Good view of Old Town to the north but the view to the south is blocked by the cathedral. *Hours:* daily, 8:30-17:15, July/Aug till 18:00. *Price:* 4€. *South Tower:* The *entrance is located outside and below the tower. *(*By the doorway are pictures of the cathedral's WWII destruction.)* From the top the views are tremendous but for those who have wobbly legs the height is terrifying! *Hours:* daily, 9:00-17:15. *Price:* 3€. *Note:* Outside the cathedral, midway along its south facade, notice the small-scale model of the holy structure for blind people, who use their hands as their eyes. You can also cop a feel of St. Stephan's by reaching into your pocket to find an Austrian 10¢ coin, on which the cathedral is featured on its flipside.

St. Stephan's Square: The area surrounding the cathedral is "Stephansplatz," an atmospheric plaza bordered by coffeehouses, shops, banks, and filled with wowed tourists, cheerful shoppers, on-the-go locals, and amusing street performers attracting huge crowds. Funneling into Stephansplatz are two influential, pedestrian shop-lined thoroughfares: (1) **Kärntner Str.**; street leading from the Opera House and Ringstrasse — (2) **Graben**, an extra-wide street punctuated by the Baroque-style Pestsäule (column erected by the emperor to commemorate the deliverance of his people from a virulent outbreak of plague in 1679) and accented by moneyed retailers like Hermès, Cartier and Versache.

Hofburg: Dating from the 13th century, the "Imperial Palace" was originally a castle built by the Habsburgs as their seat of power. Their reign developed into one of Europe's most prominent dynasties, ruling the Austrian empire (and often the Holy Roman Empire) for 640 years. Over six centuries the medieval castle grew from a modest bastion to a luxurious, multi-wing palace: the Hofburg, or winter residence of the Habsburgs, a sprawling 59-acre complex consisting of 2500 rooms. The longest reigning monarch to live here was Emperor Franz Josef (1848-1916) with his beautiful but sad wife, Elisabeth, or Sisi, and their children. In 1918, the Habsburgs suffered a political coup and were expelled from their posh digs. Today, the Hofburg accommodates the National Library; the Spanish Riding School; the Vienna Boys' Choir; the Palace Chapel (Hofburgkapelle,

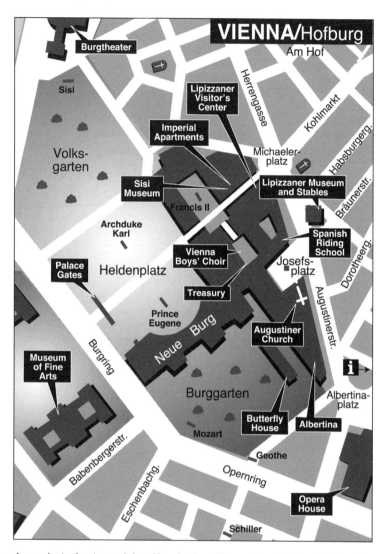

where boys sing); the Augustinian Church; the offices of the President of Austria; a pair of gardens (Volks- and Burggarten); Heroes' Square (Heldenplatz); and a number of museums, namely the Treasury, Imperial Apartments, Sisi Museum and the Silver Collection. (www.hofburg-wien.at)

Vienna Boys' Choir: (Wiener Sängerknaben, www.wsk.at) Since 1498, when Habsburg Emperor Maximilian I (of Golden Roof fame in Innsbruck) commissioned a court choir of six boys, the famed group has endured, expanded and exceeded excellence through the ages. Mozart worked with the singers, and Franz Schubert himself was a choirboy. Today, the choir consists of some 100 boys between the ages of 10-14. With this many boys they are split into four choirs. As a whole, they perform on average 300 concerts per year around the world. Their home venue is the Palace Chapel, or Hofburgkapelle, at the Hofburg, where you only hear them—not see them—sing Sunday Mass. For tickets/info, visit the TI or any ticket office in Vienna.

Treasury: Housed in the oldest part of the palace, the "Schatzkammer" is arguably Europe's most significant Treasury, where you'll discover 1000 years worth of imperial treasures and trinkets, from ceremonial scepters and coronation robes to sparkling jewels and the very large horn of a "unicorn." Witness a 10th-century crown (circa 962) belonging to one of the first Holy Roman emperors as well as the Holy Lance, a spiritual relic from Carolingian times (9C) believed to confer invincibility to its bearer. *Hours:* Wed thru Mon (closed Tue) 10:00-18:00 (last entry 17:30). *Price:* adult 8€, student 6€, Vienna Card holders 7€, audio guide 2€. *Getting There:* The Treasury is located in the Schweizerhof; follow Schatzkammer signs.

Note: The following three attractions—**Imperial Apartments, Sisi Museum,** and **Silver Collection**—share the same hours, entrance and are covered under one ticket for one *price:* (includes audio guide) adult 9€, student 7€, Vienna Card holders 7.50€. *Hours:* daily, 9:00-17:00, July/Aug till 17:30—last entry 30 min before closing. *Getting There:* The ticket office is located in the passageway between the main courtyard and Michaelerplatz.

Imperial Apartments: Within these lavish "Kaiserappartements" you'll mosey through the private chambers of Emperor Franz Josef and Empress Elisabeth, a.k.a. Sisi. Highlights of the 19-room tour include the emperor's study and bedroom as well as the empress' exercise and bathrooms (Sisi was the first Habsburg to have running water).

Sisi Museum: This new addition to the Hofburg opened in April 2004 on the 150-year anniversary of Elisabeth's (Sisi) marriage to Emperor Franz Josef. Explore six rooms dedicated to the beauty and private life of the empress.

Silver Collection: Caterers, restaurateurs, and fans of the metallic element will be awestruck by the extravagant tableware and dining collection amassed by the Habsburgs. Imperial table culture at its finest. Among the collection are exhibits once used by Sisi and Empress Maria Theresa, as well as tableware used in 1815 at the Congress of Vienna (an assembly of the victors of the Napoleonic Wars to reshuffle European borders).

Heroes' Square or "Heldenplatz," as it's called, is an enormous plaza—designed by Gottfried Semper—spread out before the Neue Burg (New Palace, 1913), the last wing added to the Hofburg, now housing the impressive weapons collection (*Rüstkammer,* same price/hours as Treasury). After Hitler annexed Austria in March 1938, he proclaimed the "Anschluss" here on Heldenplatz in front of a packed crowd of 10,000 people. Decades later—at the opposite end of the character spectrum—the square served as an open-air auditorium for Pope John Paul II. The pair of equestrian statues on the plaza memorialize two great Austrian commanders: Prince Eugene von Savoy *(whose military prowess helped save Vienna by defeating the Turks in 1683. WWII buffs note that the heavy battle cruiser Prinz Eugen—of Bismarck and HMS Hood fame—was named after him)* and the other statue is of Archduke Karl (Charles), first commander to defeat Napoleon (1809, Battle of Aspern). Lined up and ready for your business, horse-drawn carriages (called Fiaker) depart from here clip-clopping through town on private tours (40€/20min, 65€/40min, 95€/60min; up to 4 passengers, 5 possible—discuss with driver. *Note:* The better English your driver speaks the better your tour).

Augustinian Church: Formerly the Habsburgs' parish church, the "Augustinerkirche" dates from the 14th century but after renovations it's taken on a newer look. It was here that Emperor Franz Josef married his young 16-year-old bride—Sisi—in 1854. Stop by and worship the church's concert-like Mass on Sunday at 11:00, accented by the choir and a harmonious Baroque organ. After Mass, around 11:45, a clergyman will open the wrought-iron gate to the Loreto Chapel, where silver urns preserve 54 hearts belonging to the Habsburg royal family. Although the hearts are locked away from the public, plain to see are the opulent, low-hanging chandeliers. Also in the church (midway in on right) you'll discover the somber, white-marble memorial to Maria Theresa's favorite daughter, Maria Christina (her remains lie in the Imperial Crypt, or Kaisergruft). *Getting There:* The church's main entrance can be found across Josefsplatz from the Spanish Riding School, or left of (when facing) the equestrian statue in the plaza. *Loreto Chapel:* The "Loretokapelle" is only possible to enter at 11:45 after Sunday Mass, 2€/person. The chapel is located in the front right part of the church. Look through the elaborate wrought-iron portal to the iron door (back left, with two peepholes)—behind it are the hearts. *Note:* The 54 hearts date from 1618 to 1878; the first is from Empress Maria Anna—founder of the Imperial Crypt—and the last belonging to Archduke Franz Karl, father of Emperor Franz Josef.

Schönbrunn Palace: Monarchs typically associated themselves with deity, deserving of supreme power and unlimited wealth. From this arrogant attitude evolved "Schloss Schönbrunn," a vast estate declared the imperial summer residence of the Habsburgs. The royal family desired a residence to rival the great palace at Versailles, France. Molded into its present shape under Empress Maria Theresa in the mid-18th century, Schloss Schönbrunn boasts 1441 rooms—140 more than Versailles—and sculpted gardens that stretch some 457 acres. As a unit, the palace and gardens are so magnificent that in 1996 they were voted onto UNESCO's World Heritage List. Atop Schönbrunn's front gate notice the two gilded eagles; these were added by Napoleon when he resided here in 1805 and 1809. The approach from the front gate to the palace's Baroque facade is stunning, but that's nothing—the real feast awaits you on the other side. Notable within the palace's backyard are two landmarks: the Vienna **Zoo** (world's oldest, 1752) and the **Gloriette**, a divine arcade at the crest of the hill, crowning the gardens and affording an imperial view of the city. Other Schönbrunn highlights include the **Maze** (a journey through a labyrinth of hedgerows) and the **Court Bakery**, where pastry chefs whip up the hourly apple strudel show (free sample included with admission). Schönbrunn palace is highly worth your time, if only to dawdle through the gardens (*free*). But be prepared for crowds, the estate is a major tourist attraction, drawing around 6.7 million visitors per year (1.5 to the palace and 5.2 to the park). For a unique photo opportunity of the back of the palace, head to Neptune Fountain in the middle of the gardens. Climb the first section of the hill to the Gloriette, then cut over to the back of the fountain and stand directly behind the waterfall. *Note:* Mozart, as a 6-year-old child, performed at Schönbrunn Palace in 1762 • Emperor Franz Josef was born here in 1830 • Napoleon's only legitimate son died here in 1832 • and John F. Kennedy met Nikita Khrushchev here in 1961.

(www.schoenbrunn.at) When facing the palace's front facade, the main entrance is the left wing. *Hours:* (palace) daily, 8:30-16:30, April-June & Sept-Oct till 17:00, July/Aug till 18:00—(gardens) sunrise till sunset—(fountains) mid-April thru mid-Oct, daily. *Getting There:* Schönbrunn is located 5km southwest of the Old Town. Ride subway U4 to Schönbrunn and walk five minutes, or take tram #58 from Westbahnhof to the palace (drops off across boulevard). *Drivers* arriving into Vienna from the A1 autobahn will pass right by Schönbrunn's front gate. *GPS:* N48° 11.212 - E16° 18.806

Tours: There are four different tour-types to consider, all come with an audio guide. Of Schönbrunn's 1441 rooms, only 40 are open to the public. The **Imperial Tour** (35 min; adult 9€, student 8€) is a pass into 22 rooms, including apartments belonging to Emperor Franz Josef and his wife, Sisi, as well as the Hall of Mirrors—where Mozart performed as a 6-year-old—and the Grand Gallery, a 40-meter-long Rococo banquet hall that hosted John F. Kennedy and Nikita Khrushchev in 1961. The **Grand Tour** (50 min; adult 11.50€, student or Vienna Card holder 10.20€) is a pass into all 40 rooms, including those belonging to Empress Maria Theresa and the Napoleon Room, where Napoleon's son died at the age of 21. The **Classic Pass** (available April-Oct; adult 15€, student or Vienna Card holder 13€) consists of the Grand Tour, entrance into the Gloriette, Maze and Court Bakery. The **Gold Pass** (valid for single admission to each attraction for one year from date of issue, adult 36€, student or Vienna Card holder 30€) consists of the Grand Tour (immediate admission), entrance into the Gloriette, Maze, Court Bakery, Zoo, Palm House and Carriage Museum (Wagenburg). *Note:* Don't buy this pass outside of the months April thru Oct because some of the attractions will be closed, unless you're planning on coming back to Vienna at a later date.

Opinion: Just being on the grounds is impressive enough, but if you have the time and money we recommend you buy the Classic Pass. Allow a few hours to savor your adventure. Consider packing a picnic for the grounds (by Gloriette) and for dessert (with Classic or Gold Pass) head to the Court Bakery (for your free sample of strudel).

Reservations: To avoid long lines/delays during the summer months, mid-June thru mid-Sept, book your ticket at least 24 hours in advance: online (www.schoenbrunn.at) or e-mail (reservierung@schoenbrunn.at) or call 01/8111-3239 (daily, 8:00-17:00). You will get a start time and reservation number. At least 30 minutes before your start time, pick up your reserved ticket(s) at the little shop immediately left of the front gate after entering. *Note:* Purchasers of the Gold Pass get immediate admission into the palace! Arrive anytime; you do not have to stand in line to get in.

Gloriette: Dating from 1775, this triumphal gate and architectural centerpiece of the gardens affords 360-degree views of the city and estate. *Hours:* April-Oct, daily, 9:00-17:00, April-June & Sept till 18:00, July/Aug till 19:00, closed Nov-March. *Price:* adult 2€, student or Vienna Card holder 1.50€, or free with Classic/Gold Pass.

Maze: Landscaped between 1698 and 1740, the "Irrgarten" is a clever and confusing maze of hedgerows. *Hours:* April-Oct, daily, 9:00-17:00, April-June & Sept till 18:00, July/Aug till 19:00, Nov 10:00-16:00, closed Dec-March. *Price:* adult 2.60€, student or Vienna Card holder 2.20€, or free with Classic/Gold Pass.

Court Bakery: Learn how to make Viennese apple strudel from the pros. Hourly (20-min) demonstrations on the hour in the "Hofbackstube," located on the left side midway between the front gate and palace in the historic vaulted cellar beneath Café/Restaurant Residenz. Free sample of strudel with admission. *Tel.#* 01/2410-0311. *Hours:* (strudel demo) April-Oct, daily, 10:00-16:00, July/Aug till 17:00, closed Nov-March. *Price:* 7.20€ (includes show, coffee and big piece of strudel), or 3.60€ (includes show and small piece of strudel), or free with Classic/Gold Pass.

Zoo, Vienna: Pandas, koalas, cheetahs, lynx, wolves, lions, elephants, giraffes, penguins—to name a few of the animals—beckon your visit in the world's oldest zoo, dating from 1752. (www.zoovienna.at) *Hours:* daily, 9:00-16:30, April-Sept till 18:30, Oct & March till 17:30. *Price:* adult 12€, student 5€, 15% discount with Vienna Card, or free with Gold Pass. *Getting There:* Walk towards the Gloriette (perched upon the hill)—before the path begins to ascend, go right.

Academy of Fine Arts: Though not really a major tourist sight, the "Akadamie der bildenden Künste" is listed with WWII buffs and bohemians in mind. When Adolf Hitler was an aspiring artist living penniless on the streets of Vienna (1907-13, aged 18 to 24), he twice applied to study here—and was twice denied for his lack of talent. It is free and worthwhile to roam the academy's hallowed and historic hallways. Imagine how different the 20th century would have been if Hitler had been accepted into the academy and he pursued a pretentious career as a Viennese artist. Switching gears, culture vultures will find the academy's painting gallery (die Gemäldegalerie) bursting with 15th- to 18th-century masters (e.g. Rubens, Rembrandt, Botticelli, Bosch, Cranach). Price: adult 7€, student 4€, audio guide 2€. Hours: Tue-Sun 10:00-18:00. Fronting the academy is a statue of the German author, Friedrich Schiller. Notice his contemporary, Johann Goethe, seated comfortably across the Ringstrasse. *Getting There:* The academy is located across the Ringstrasse from the Burggarten—follow Goethe's eyes.

St. Charles' Church: "Karlskirche," the jewel of Karlsplatz (Charles' Square), was commissioned by Emperor Charles VI (Maria Theresa's father), who vowed that if Vienna were delivered from the epidemic of plague in 1713 he would build his people a magnificent church. The emperor awarded the design to Fischer von Erlach, the same architect who built Schönbrunn palace. In 1737 the church was completed and the emperor dedicated it to St. Charles Borromeo, a cardinal and the archbishop of Milan noted for his charity work and inspiration to innumerable Christians. Without regard for his own health, Borromeo helped save many lives during the plague of 1576-78. He died a few years later at the age of 46; his last words were "Lord, I'm coming." Borromeo was obviously in good standing with God, because 1713 marked Vienna's last outbreak of plague.

St. Charles' Church is without doubt Vienna's most impressive Baroque house of worship. It's signature turquoise dome (said to be the largest Baroque cupola north of the Alps) and Trajan-inspired columns are unmistakable—a picture worthy of any photo album. Spiraling scenes from Borromeo's altruistic life adorn the two columns. Between the columns, crowning the triangular neoclassical roof, is a statue of Borromeo with outstretched arms. Inside the church you can tour the Museum Borromeo as well as hitch a ride on the new elevator rising more than 100 feet up to a platform for a so-close-you-can-almost-touch-it perspective of the glorious ceiling frescos depicting scenes from the life of St. Charles Borromeo. From there, 118 steps ascend to the observation level boasting terrific views of Vienna. *Hours:* Mon-Sat 9:00-12:30 & 13:00-18:00, Sun 13:00-18:00. *Price:* (audio guide included) adult 6€, student 4€, 15% discount with Vienna Card. *Getting There:* St. Charles' Church is located on Karlsplatz—take subway U1, U2 or U4 to Karlsplatz.

St. Ruprecht's Church: Located in the heart of the Viennese Bermuda Triangle (see *Entertainment*, page 575), "Ruprechtskirche" is the city's oldest church, likely dating from the 11th century. Rather small and unassuming, the church is easily recognizable by its elevated position and blanket of ivy covering its facade and Romanesque tower. The structure takes its name from St. Ruprecht—the patron saint of Vienna's salt merchants—who can be seen in statue form holding a drum of salt on the lower part of the tower. The church and St. Ruprecht overlook the Danube Canal where those merchants once labored, a handful of blocks north of St. Stephan's Cathedral. The church is seldom open; your best shot is in the morning before 11:00.

> *Note,* in Vienna, when you see a street sign, say, like this one: **8., Josefstädter Str**. The number prefix, in this case "8.," means the district, or Bezirk, not the building number.

MUSEUMS

The first five museums listed in this section are run by the city of Vienna and offer *FREE* admission on Friday before noon and all day on Sunday. (www.wienmuseum.at) Four of the five museums are former residences belonging to the great composers Strauss and Beethoven. *(Note: These are small commemorative museums partially in original condition and auf Deutsch—in German.)* The fifth museum in the group, Wien Museum, is dedicated to the history of Vienna.

Strauss (Gedenkstätte) **Residence:** In an apartment at Praterstrasse 54 lived the legendary waltz king, Johann Strauss, for seven years. During this time he penned one of the world's most famous compositions: *An der Schönen, Blauen Donau* (On The Beautiful Blue Danube). Many of his personal belongs are on display, including his violin and organ. When browsing the museum you'll often see the words *Aus Strauß' Besitz*, which means the item/object belonged to Strauss. Note that the elaborate, wood floor is original.

Hours: Tue-Thur 14:00-18:00, Fri-Sun 10:00-13:00. *Price:* adult 2€, student 1€, *free* Friday before noon and all day on Sunday. *Getting There:* Praterstrasse 54 is easy to locate because today it is a McDonald's; the museum is above it. Take subway U1 to Nestroyplatz and exit Rotensterngasse.

Beethoven's "PasqualatiHaus": Named after its long-time owner—Josef Pasqualati—the Pasqualati House was Beethoven's home for some 10 years (1804-1815). After negotiating more than 100 steps to reach the 4th-floor residence, it's amazing to think that Beethoven still had enough energy to author the many great compositions that he did here, e.g. Symphonies 4, 5, 7, and the opera "Fidelio." *Hours:* Tue-Sun 10:00-13:00 & 14:00-18:00. *Price:* adult 2€, student 1€, *free* Friday before noon and all day on Sunday. *Getting There:* PasqualatiHaus is located at Mölkerbastei 8, one block north of the Burgtheater and around the corner from Subway sandwich.

Beethoven's "Heiligenstädter Testament": This two-room museum and former Beethoven residence is located at the top end of Vienna in the suburb of Heiligenstadt, district 19. During Beethoven's era, Heiligenstadt was a village of winemakers far from Vienna. A peaceful life in the country it was not. In fact, the residence is associated with one of the darkest periods in Beethoven's life. He fled Vienna seeking isolation for reasons of despair. In 1802, while living here, he wrote a letter (though never sent) to his two brothers expressing his misery and pain caused by his worsening deafness. The letter historically became known as the "Heiligenstädter Testament," and this petite museum documents its distressing composition along with the music Beethoven wrote here as well as containing a lock of his hair. The mask you will see of Beethoven's face was shaped while he lived. *Hours:* Tue-Sun 10:00-13:00 & 14:00-18:00. *Price:* adult 2€, student 1€, *free* Friday before noon and all day on Sunday. *Getting There:* Museum is located (about 1km due north of the "Eroica House") at Probusgasse 6 (roughly 30 min from central Vienna). Take subway U4 to Heiligenstadt (end station), then out front catch bus 38A to Armbrustergasse. Exit bus left then go right around the corner and at the end of the street go right again. After a short distance Beethoven's former digs will appear on the right. *GPS:* N48° 15.296 - E16° 21.372. *Note:* While you're in the area, consider sampling the local grape juice in a nearby (Heurige) wine tavern.

Beethoven's "Eroica House": At this dwelling in the summer of 1803 Beethoven penned his Symphony No. 3: "Eroica." There's not a whole lot to see here and nothing is original, except the wooden floor—thus it is only open on Fridays for a limited time. It does not qualify for free entry. *Price:* adult 2€, student 1€. *Hours:* Fri 15:00-18:00. *Note:* Outside of these hours hardcore fans flushed with cash can call this number 01/5058-7470 and plead. *Getting There:* Museum is located (about 1km due south of the "Heiligenstädter Testament" residence) at Döblinger Hauptstr. 92—avenue running north of Franz-Josefs-Bahnhof.

Wien Museum: This excellent museum houses an extensive collection on three floors exhibiting Vienna's rich 2000-year history. Highlights include vestiges from Vindobona (Roman Vienna), stained-glass windows from St. Stephan's Cathedral in medieval times, art nouveau by Gustav Klimt, and two large-scale models of Old Town Vienna (in 1800 and 1900). From the top floor is a fine view of St. Charles' Church. *Hours:* Tue-Sun 9:00-18:00. *Price:* adult 4€, student 2€, *free* Friday before noon and all day on Sunday. *Getting There:* Wien Museum is situated on Karlsplatz, adjacent to St. Charles' Church. Take subway U1, U2 or U4 to Karlsplatz.

Mozart's "Figarohaus": Mozart lived in no less than 18 apartments while in Vienna, but the Figarohaus—his 15th residence, located at Domgasse 5—is the only one that has survived the ages. It was here that he lived on the first floor (one level up) with his family from Sept 1784 to April 1787. During this time Mozart composed much of his chamber music, eight piano concertos, and where he penned one of his most famous operas: "The

Marriage of Figaro"; hence the name of the residence. After extensive renovations totaling some 14 months at a cost of 8€ million, the Figarohaus reopened on Jan 27, 2006—the 250th anniversary of Mozart's birth—and now incorporates exhibitions on three floors. *Hours:* daily, 10:00-20:00. (www.mozarthausvienna.at) *Price:* (audio guide included) adult 9€, student 7€, 20% discount with Vienna Card, combo-ticket with House of Music 15€. *Note:* Mozart is the spunky lad depicted on the back of Austria's 1€ coin. *Getting There:* The Figarohaus is located behind St. Stephan's Cathedral. Step through the portal at Stephansplatz 5a; continue straight through the second portal and onto quaint Domgasse (lane). His former digs are ahead on the left.

Museum of Fine Arts: The internationally acclaimed "Kunsthistorisches Museum," as it's called, is one of the nation's most prized possessions, showcasing the artistic treasures assembled by the Habsburg royal family. In the picture gallery you'll encounter walls of paintings from 15th- to 17th-century masters, including Bruegel, Raphael (Raffael), Dürer, Titian (Tizian), Correggio, Rubens, Rembrandt and Vermeer. Additionally, there are rooms of Greek and Roman antiquities as well as the esteemed Egyptian and Near East collections. (www.khm.at) *Hours:* Tue-Sun 10:00-18:00 (Thur till 21:00). *Price:* adult 10€, student 7.50€, Vienna Card holders 9€, audio guide 2€. *Getting There:* Museum is located across the Ringstrasse from the Hofburg palace.

Natural History Museum: Across the plaza and facing the Museum of Fine Arts is its twin, the "Naturhistoriches Museum," where exhibits range from bugs to dinosaurs and gemstones to moon rocks. Its most prized possession, however, is the 25,000-year-old Venus of Willendorf, a small (4.5-inch tall) female statuette that registers as one of the earliest known examples of sculpture. *Hours:* Wed thru Mon (closed Tue) 9:00-18:30 (Wed till 21:00). *Price:* adult 8€, student 6€, Vienna Card holders 6€. *Getting There:* Museum is located across the Ringstrasse from the Hofburg palace.

MuseumsQuartier: Recently fashioned out of the imperial horse stables, the Museums Quartier (MQ) is set within a sprawling Baroque-style complex that registers as one of the largest cultural quarters in the world. To walk through the complex is free and recommended. Inside you'll find restaurants, cafés, dance and theater halls as well as several museums, including the Leopold Museum and Museum of Modern Art and—for fans of architecture there is—the Architekturzentrum. (www.mqw.at) *Note:* Enter the MQ via the (front) main entrance, where an info/ticket center (daily 10:00-19:00) and toilets are located. A combo-ticket to all the museums costs 25€, or there's the Duo-Ticket for the Leopold and Modern Art museums for 16€. *Getting There:* MQ is located across the road from the Museum of Fine Arts—subway U2 MuseumsQuartier. *Drivers,* plenty of underground parking available.

Leopold Museum: Over the course of five decades, Rudolf and Elisabeth Leopold painstakingly and joyously compiled the collections now gracing the interior of their namesake museum, featuring modern Austrian art with more than 5000 works. Interestingly, the Leopold Museum held a special exhibition July-August 2005 called the *Die Nackte Wahrheit* (The Naked Truth), which featured sexually charged artwork by Klimt and Schiele and Kokoschka. It was the middle of summer and warm weather blanketed Vienna. Not all museumgoers, however, were focusing on the artwork but more on the museumgoers themselves. You see, the museum offered free admittance to those who came either wearing their bathing suit or birthday suit. Yes, completely nude, and there were plenty of takers. *Hours:* Wed thru Mon (closed Tue) 10:00-19:00, Thur till 21:00. *Price:* adult 9€, student 5.50€, 10% discount with Vienna Card.

Museum of Modern Art: Widely known as MUMOK, the Museum of Modern Art is Austria's largest museum for contemporary art. *Hours:* Tue-Sun 10:00-18:00, Thur till 21:00. *Price:* adult 8€, student 6.50€.

Albertina: Another one of Vienna's stunning cultural institutions is the Albertina, an extensive museum situated in the historic Hofburg palace that features collections ranging from drawings to paintings to photos, from the Renaissance era to the present day. Highlights include works by Leonardo da Vinci, Michelangelo, Rubens, Dürer, Delacroix, Cézanne, Matisse and Picasso. Exhibitions frequently rotate; double check that your favorite artist is on display before paying. (www.albertina.at) _Hours:_ daily, 10:00-18:00 (Wed till 21:00). _Price:_ adult 9€, student 6.50€, Vienna Card holders 7.50€. _Getting There:_ Albertina is located on Albertinaplatz across from the TI—head up to the imposing terrace above the street. _Note:_ In Albertina's basement is the world's first fully automated storage vault, accommodating the more than one million pieces in its collection. Due to the simplicity of this high-tech system, museum staff can now (via the main computer terminal) click on a painting in the database and have it delivered to the museum in under a minute. It works like so: The artwork's barcode is read by the robot arm in the vault, which then retrieves the item in its sealed container and lifts it to the surface. Presto, painting delivered. Kind of like a modern-day dumbwaiter.

Lipizzaner Museum: From the town of Lipizza in modern-day Slovenia—where the breed originated in 1580—to the establishment of the Spanish Riding School and through two crippling world wars, visitors marvel at the 400-year-old history of the Lipizzaner stallion, chronicled here in the Lipizzaner Museum, located adjacent to their stables known as the Stallburg. Most Lipizzaners are born black or brown, and turn almost white by maturity. Elegant as swans, the Lipizzaners perform intricate maneuvers that are truly amazing, gaining the respect of all who cast an eye on them, even emperors and generals. During the final days of WWII, before advancing Soviets troops, U.S. General George S. Patton ordered a secret operation to evacuate the Lipizzaner stables to ensure the survival of their bloodlines. WWII buffs will remember the end of the movie "Patton," when the general was seen riding one of the stallions he had rescued. (www.lipizzaner.at) _Hours:_ daily, 9:00-18:00. _Price:_ adult 5€, student 3.60€, Vienna Card holders 4€. _Getting There:_ The Lipizzaner Museum, stables (Stallburg), and the Spanish Riding School are all located by each other at (and across from) the Hofburg palace. Opposite the TI, head along Augustinerstr. paralleling the Hofburg—beyond the equestrian statue (on Josefsplatz, left) is the Spanish Riding School and ahead (right) are the stables and museum. _Seeing the Lipizzaners:_ Performances are held every Sunday with few Fridays and Saturdays (March thru mid-June and Sept thru mid-Oct) and seats (25-130€) are booked up months in advance. However, standing room tickets (20-25€) may be available the same day—query ticket office/visitor's center. (www.srs.at) All credit cards accepted. _Tel.#_ 01/533-9031. _Visitor's Center, Lipizzaner:_ Any questions you may have regarding shows, tours, times, or if you would like an info brochure on the horses, stop in at the multipurpose visitor's center (open Tue-Sat 9:00-17:00, Sun 9:00-13:30 [till 15:00 July/Aug], cashier closes one hour before closing). You can find the visitor's center in the Hofburg palace, off Michaelerplatz (see map on page 560). _Training Session:_ (Morning Exercise, _Morgenarbeit_) The next best thing to seeing an actual performance is the training session, adult 12€, Vienna Card holders 11€, students/seniors ask for discount. Query museum or visitor's center for exact days but typically Tue-Sat, Dec & Feb-June and mid-Aug thru Oct, beginning at 10:00. _Note:_ Photography/filming is normally not allowed. _Suggestion:_ Enthusiasts arrive at the museum when it opens at 9:00 and buy the combo-ticket (15€) that includes the museum and a two-hour training session (with music) in the opulent Spanish Riding School. Don't worry if you arrive late to the training session—catching 60-90 minutes will suffice. _FREE_, Lipizzaners: Horse lover or not, it is a delight to watch the stallions strut from their stalls to the Spanish Riding School (during the season) every half hour, Tue-Sun, 8:00-12:00.

House of Music: A big hit with visitors, the "Haus der Musik" allows you to virtually conduct the Vienna Philharmonic, modify sounds to generate your own breed of musical language, compose a waltz with dice, and even record your own music CD. This highly unique, interactive museum contains six floors of high-tech innovations dedicated to the evolution of sound and the feel of music. Participate in the exhibits to experience new tonal discoveries and sensations. *Hours:* daily, 10:00-22:00. (www.hdm.at) *Price:* adult 10€, student 8.50€, 10% discount with Vienna Card, combo-ticket with Mozart's Figaro-haus 15€. *Getting There:* HoM is located at (street) Seilerstätte 30, two blocks northeast of the Opera House.

Belvedere Palace: Just south of Schwarzenbergplatz is the fabulous Belvedere palace, former summer residence of Prince Eugene von Savoy (great commander of his time whose military prowess helped save Vienna by defeating the Turks in 1683. WWII buffs note that the heavy battle cruiser *Prinz Eugen*—of Bismarck and HMS Hood fame—was named after him). In the early 18th century, the prince commissioned sprawling gardens designed in Baroque-style, affording a striking view of Vienna as a backdrop. Today, these are considered among the finest in Europe. Flanking the gardens is the residence, which consists of two palaces: the Upper and Lower Belvedere. Situated at the highest point, the **Upper (*Oberes*) Belvedere** is the more worthwhile and attractive of the two, housing the Austrian Gallery of 19th- and 20th-century art, including works from Monet, Manet, Renoir, and van Gogh's "The Plain at Auvers," as well as an eye-popping collection from Gustav Klimt featuring "The Kiss." What's more, Francis Ferdinand—successor to the Habsburg throne—lived here from 1899 until his historic assassination in 1914 that sparked World War I. In 1955, the Upper Belvedere was the chosen venue by the four Allied powers (USA, UK, USSR and France) to sign the Austrian State Treaty, giving Austria its independence as a republic. The **Lower (*Unteres*) Belvedere**, at the north end of the gardens, accommodates the Museum of Medieval Art and the Baroque Museum. (www.belvedere.at) *Hours:* (both palaces, last entry 17:30) Tue-Sun 10:00-18:00. *Price:* (ticket for both palaces) adult 9€, student 6€, Vienna Card holders 7.50€, audio guide 3€. *Note:* Since there is so much to see, tickets are valid for three months. Heck, you can even get married here. Interested? Call Herr Wodni: 01/7955-7140. *Getting There:* Belvedere is located at Prinz-Eugen-Str. 27—take tram "D" from either Schwarzenbergplatz or Südbahnhof and get off at Schloß Belvedere.

KunstHausWien: While in Vienna, don't miss the work of local artist Friedensreich Hundertwasser. Entire buildings and residence complexes have been transformed by his art, adding new cultural landmarks to Vienna's cityscape. Hundertwasser died in 2002 but his spirited and green legacy lives on. His philosophy: "'Art must meet man's and nature's pace. Art must respect nature and the laws of nature... Art should not endure dogmatic enslavement through negative theories. Art must have a purpose. Art must create lasting values... The taste of KunstHausWien is to achieve these goals.' — Hundertwasser, 1990." Opened in 1991, KunstHausWien displays Hundertwasser's work on two floors; two additional floors are dedicated to rotating exhibitions. *Hours:* daily, 10:00-19:00. (www.kunsthauswien.com) *Price:* adult 9€, student 7€, Vienna Card holders 8€, dogs on a leash are *free*. Mondays are half price. *Note:* Before Hundertwasser and KunstHausWien, the building was Michael Thonet's bentwood furniture factory (see page 320—*Boppard Museum*). *Tours:* Guided tours every Sun at noon—meet at cashier. For a private tour, call 01/7120-49512. *Getting There:* KunstHausWien is located at Untere Weissgerberstr. 13—along the Danube Canal several blocks east of the Old Town. Take subway U1 or U4 to Schwedenplatz, then catch tram "N" to Radetzkyplatz. Exit tram left and go right; follow brown signs. *GPS:* N48° 12.637 - E16° 23.604. *Suggestion:* If you don't fancy wandering through another art gallery/museum, we understand, but at least stop by to externally view KunstHausWien's checkerboard facade. Defying straight lines and cookie-cutter windows, it's unforgettable as well as unmistakable. Afterwards, (when facing its front facade, go right and) walk five minutes along Untere Weiss-gerberstr. to Kegelgasse to externally view the **Hundertwasserhaus**, also designed by the eco-friendly artist—but this one is an actual lived-in (social welfare) housing com-plex. Opposite the *Hundertwasserhaus is the Hundertwasser Village. Step into this unique shopping arcade; notice the uneven floors. Go downstairs and utilize the "Toilet of Modern Art" (.60¢). *GPS: N48° 12.448 - E16° 23.611. If you're ever in north Vienna (suburb of Spittelau), look up to find another Hundertwasser landmark: the district heating plant and its glistening, phallic-like tower.

S e z e s s i o n s t i l

Secession Building: Built in 1898 within six months, the Secession Building was the brainchild of avant-garde artists (like Otto Wagner, Gustav Klimt and Joseph Olbrich) who seceded from Vienna's Association of Austrian Artists (Künstlerhaus) because of its conservative views. Wagner, Klimt and co. formed a new association they aptly called the Viennese Secession and consequently built a showroom (Secession Building) for their work. The artists' signature style became known as *Sezessionstil, or Viennese art nouveau, and the shrine of the movement was the Secession Building. (*Note: Around the same time, Germany had its own art nouveau movement known as Jugendstil, or Youth Style.) Emblazoned on the building's front facade in gilded lettering is the artists' motto: *Der Zeit Ihre Kunst. Der Kunst Ihre Freiheit* (Every Era Has Its Art. Every Art Has Its Freedom). At the turn of the 20th century, traditionalists viewed the new style as radical liberalism but the tolerant-types were inspired by its decorative, fluid design and to this day the structures built during the Secession era are among the most wowing in Vienna. *(See for yourself; nearby examples include the Otto Wagner Pavilion on Karlsplatz and the facades at Linke Wienzeile 38 and 40. For more examples of Sezessionstil, see TI for directions.)* Crowning the Secession Building—and impossible to miss—is an ornate dome consisting of more than 3000 gilded laurel leaves, affectionately referred to by locals as the "golden cabbage." The building today holds around 20 exhibitions of contemporary art per year, but it's largely known for its permanent display of Gustav Klimt's "Beethoven Frieze," a 112-foot-long wall cycle depicting the artist's interpretation of Beethoven's Ninth Symphony. The frieze was created for the Beethoven Exhibition of 1902. You can learn more about it at the museum's Web address: www.secession.at *Hours:* Tue-Sun 10:00-18:00 (Thur till 20:00). *Price:* adult 6€, student 3.50€. *Getting There:* The Secession Building is located at Friedrichstr. 12, a busy inter-section at the forefront of Naschmarkt and across from Karlsplatz—look for the golden cabbage. Take subway U1, U2 or U4 to Karlsplatz. *Note:* Adjacent to the Secession Building you'll see a statue of Mark Antony in a chariot drawn by lions (1899). We're not quite sure what the connection is between Antony and art nouveau but, hey, it's a mighty sight. Maybe Antony is featured here because of his macho character, sym-bolizing power through action. After all, Antony was an influential Roman statesman and general, who defeated Julius Caesar's assassins (Brutus and Cassius) and later took the Egyptian queen, Cleopatra, as his lover. Not a bad gig, while it lasted!

Jewish Museum: Exhibitions at the "Jüdisches Museum" span four floors, consisting of a remembrance to Gustav Mahler, a unique and historical perspective of Viennese Jewry depicted through holograms, and on the top floor you'll behold a priceless array of sacred artifacts in storage (notice many of these have been crippled or defaced from WWII hostilities). Before you leave ogle the Max Berger collection of Jewish ceremonial relics on the ground floor, and, if required, clean toilets are around the corner. (www.jmw.at) *Hours:* Sun thru Fri (closed Sat) 10:00-18:00 (Thur till 20:00). *Price:* (audio guide included) adult 5€, student/Vienna Card holder 3€, combo-ticket with Judenplatz Museum 7€/4€. *Note:* Entry ticket is valid for a 10 % discount into the Sigmund Freud Museum. *Getting There:* JM is located at Dorotheergasse 11, between St. Stephan's Cathedral and the Hofburg palace. Consider visiting the nearby Dorotheum auction house (page 574).

Judenplatz Memorial & Museum: Run by the Jewish Museum, the Judenplatz Memorial is situated on the site of medieval Vienna's one-time thriving Jewish community. Slaughtered and expelled, the community came to an abrupt end in the year 1421. Above ground, dominating the square, sits a mammoth-sized cube-like memorial to the 65,000 Austrian Jews murdered by the Nazis (1938-1945). Below ground, the museum features vestiges of the original synagogue from medieval times as well as a databank containing the names and personal details of the Jews murdered in the Holocaust, and a computer animated walk-through of the Jewish community during the Middle Ages. *Hours:* Sun thru Thur 10:00-18:00, Fri 10:00-14:00, (closed Sat). *Price:* adult 3€, student/Vienna Card holder 1.50€, combo-ticket with Jewish Museum 7€/4€. *Getting There:* Judenplatz neighbors Am Hof, a handful of blocks northwest of St. Stephan's Cathedral.

Sigmund Freud Museum: In 1891, at the age of 35, Sigmund Freud moved into a second-floor apartment at Berggasse 19 with his Jewish family. Until he was forced to leave Austria in 1938 on account of anti-Semitism fanned by the Nazis, Freud lived and worked at this address where he developed the science that fundamentally changed the perception of the human psyche. His former apartment and practice is now a museum exhibiting the life and work of the founder of psychoanalysis. Unlike other museums set in former residences of famous people, many of the furnishings here are original, such as the "waiting room" for patients and his collection of antiques. (www.freud-museum.at) *Hours:* daily, 9:00-17:00 (May-Oct till 18:00). *Price:* adult 7€, student 4€, Vienna Card holders 5€, audio guide 2€, or ask if it's possible to borrow a translation sheet. *Getting There:* Museum is located at Berggasse 19, about five blocks north of the Ringstrasse—catch tram "D" to Schlickgasse, then a short walk.

Museum of Military History: Military buffs will relish the "Heeresgeschichtliches Museum," a fascinating collection of Austria's military history housed in a fortress-like building that dates from 1856 and registers as the city's first museum. Multiple rooms of exhibits (in four enormous halls on two floors) journey visitors through centuries of battle and conflict, from the Thirty Years' War to the war against the Turks, the Napoleonic wars and both World War I and II. Of the many highlights, the one that grabs the most attention is the actual car that Francis Ferdinand—successor to the Habsburg throne—was riding in (plus the blood-stained uniform he was wearing) when he was assassinated on June 28, 1914, which spiraled Europe into WWI. Allow at least two hours for a visit. Oh, and don't leave without viewing the *Panzer Garten* (Garden of Armor), open April-Oct; follow signs outside. (www.hgm.or.at) *Hours:* Sat thru Thur (closed Fri) 9:00-17:00. *Price:* (audio guide included) adult 5.10€, student 3.30€, 35% discount with Vienna Card. *Getting There:* Museum is situated in the extensive Arsenal complex neighboring the Südbahnhof—exit station right and follow signs (10-min walk or take bus 69A one stop to Arsenal, then short walk). *GPS:* N48° 11.107 - E16° 23.221

Parks, Gardens & Sunbathing

Parks and gardens enrich the Austrian capital, providing sanctuary for urbanites to disappear for a while and smell the roses. *(Parks are free to enter and are open from sunrise till sunset.)* For those who wish to hang out in a bathing suit and dig their toes in the sand, Vienna has plenty of beach life and aquatic activities courtesy of the Danube River.

Schlosspark Schönbrunn: a UNESCO World Heritage site—see *Schönbrunn Palace*, page 562.

City Park: Landscaped in 1862, the "Stadtpark" encompasses a huge chunk of the Old Town's eastern boundary. Within its green confines are a number of statues honoring celebrated composers, in particular Johann Strauss II who is immortalized in gold. *Getting There:* subway U4 Stadtpark, or tram #1 or #2. *GPS:* N48° 12.234 - E16° 22.742

Burggarten: Situated on the grounds of the Hofburg palace, the Burggarten originated as a royal park landscaped exclusively for the emperor. Today it belongs to the public and is a peaceful getaway from urbanism, having fewer visitors, more trees but less roses than its counterpart, the Volksgarten (see next entry), across the palace grounds. Moreover, in this shaded oasis, you'll bump into memorial statues of Mozart and Emperor Franz Josef and, the main attraction, the Schmetterlinghaus, or **Butterfly House.** Enchanting and exotic, the elongated turn-of-the-20th-century Butterfly House affords a climate-controlled environment maintaining constant temperatures of 26°C/80°F with 80% humidity. Hundreds of butterflies—representing more than 40 species—thrive here in this tropical rainforest setting. Without natural enemies to contest, most of these live two to six weeks, reasonably longer than in the wild. *Hours:* (Butterfly House) daily, 10:00-15:45 (April-Oct, Mon-Fri till 16:45, Sat/Sun 18:15). *Price:* adult 5€, student 4€, Vienna Card holders 4€. *Getting There:* Burggarten is located on the Ringstrasse, some 200 meters northwest of the Opera House.

Volksgarten: On the northwest side of the Hofburg palace is the "People's Garden," a busier version of the nearby Burggarten. Centrally located in the garden is the Temple of Theseus, a monument named after the Athenian hero celebrated in Greek mythology. Admirers of Empress Elisabeth—a.k.a. Sisi—will appreciate her memorial statue in the garden's northern section.

Schlosspark Belvedere: These stunning gardens are open daily year round—from sunrise to sunset—contrary to the Belvedere palaces, which don't open until 10:00 and are closed Mondays. For info on the palaces and gardens, flip to page 568.

Augarten: Dating from 1712, the Augarten is Vienna's oldest Baroque garden complex. Besides blossoming flowers and perfectly mowed lawns, you'll find a trio of noteworthy sites here: **(1)** The Augartenpalais, where the Vienna Boys' Choir live, rehearse and attend school. **(2)** The Augarten Wien, one of Europe's premier porcelain manufacturers [Mon-Fri 9:30-17:00, www.augarten.at]. **(3)** And two concrete giants called Flaktürme, a stark reminder of Austria's hellish past. These two "flak towers" were built in 1940 by order of the Nazis as part of Vienna's air-defense system. Ominously rising above the 128-acre garden complex, each tower could house hundreds of troops. In case you're wondering, they're too big to implode without causing considerable damage to the community. *Note:* Towers are off-limits and can only be viewed externally. *Getting There:* The Augarten is located on the north side of town and requires some tricky tram planning and extra legwork; query TI or staff at your accommodations for the best route from your starting point. *GPS:* N48° 13.407 - E16° 22.598

Prater: This extensive playground is mainly known for its amusement park and Viennese landmark—the giant Ferris wheel—but that covers just a tiny fraction of the Prater's overall area that extends some 7km from east-central Vienna to the south, paralleling the Danube River. Originally an imperial hunting reserve for the Habsburg royal family, the green Prater was decreed public domain in 1766 by the emperor. Today, it is a popular recreational park teeming with joggers, inline skaters, bikers, tee-toddlers and sunbathers. Highlights of the park include a narrow-gauge railway (Liliputbahn), a swimming complex, tennis courts, harness racing, a golf course, and the 50,000-seat Ernst-Happel-Stadium: home to class-A soccer (football) matches and the stage for A-list concerts. The

Prater's main attraction, however, is the Coney Island-like amusement park, featuring a roller coaster, bumper cars, food stands and the Riesenrad: a 215-foot-tall **Ferris wheel**. Dating from 1897, the giant wheel has been leisurely rotating above Vienna for more than a century, affording wowed visitors a historic and unique view of the Austrian capital. (www.wienerriesenrad.com) To go for a spin will set you back 7.50€, students/ Vienna Card holders 6.50€. *Hours:* (Ferris wheel and amusement park) daily, 10:00-20:00, March/April & Oct till 22:00, May-Sept 9:00-24:00.

Danube Island: Running through the middle of one of Europe's great rivers is the "Donauinsel," a 40km strip of land attracting bikini-clad bathers and au-naturel nudists to its grassy beaches, as well as joggers, inline skaters and bikers to its groomed paths. Adjacent to the subway station U1 Donauinsel is a hip new entertainment zone with riverside bars and cafés. For three hot days in late June the island hosts Europe's biggest open-air party, drawing more than 2 million visitors to its shores (see page 557, *FREE* Vienna, No. 12). *Getting There:* Take the subway U1 to Donauinsel.

Old Danube: Beyond Danube Island and a seashell's throw from the space-needle tower is the "Alte Donau," where Viennese go for the classic bathing experience with riverside promenades, lidos, *boat docks, and the popular Gänsehäufel island. *Note:* Electric and paddle boat rental available. *Getting There:* Take the subway U6 (direction Floridsdorf) to Neue Donau, then 15 min walk (follow signs Strandbäder).

Cemeteries & Crypts

Death is a part of life, and Vienna has its fair share of dead people—many of them house-hold names. In this section we will put you on the right path to the last resting place of the famous and the nameless. On your journey you will often see the word "Friedhof," which is German for "cemetery." *Note:* The three cemeteries are located on the south side of town, with the first two (St. Marx and Central) being reachable via tram #71. The Imperial Crypt is easily found in the Old Town and Vivaldi isn't too far away.

St. Marx Cemetery: Located 3km southeast of the Old Town, "St. Marx Friedhof" is a romantic cemetery renowned for accommodating the mortal remains of an immortal legend: Wolfgang Amadeus Mozart. To read his history and more on the cemetery refer to (page 461) chapter *Tomb-Lovers, Who's Buried Where? Austria*. *Hours:* daily, 7:00-18:00 (winter till dusk). *Getting There:* From Schwarzenbergplatz on the Ringstrasse pick up tram #71 (direction Kaiserebersdorf) and get off at St. Marx (6th stop)—exit tram left and walk to the forward traffic light. From there, follow the "St. Marxer Friedhof" sign right and then make the first left—the cemetery is some 300 meters farther ahead on the right. *GPS:* N48° 11.031 - E16° 24.200. *Drivers,* ample parking in front of gate. *Note:* To get to Central Cemetery (next entry), return to tram #71 and continue in the same direction (Kaiserebersdorf).

Central Cemetery: Dating from 1874 and sprawling some 600 acres, the "Zentral-friedhof" is not only old and extensive but it is the world's elite burial ground for famous composers and musicians. All the heavy-hitters are interred here: Beethoven, Brahms, Salieri, Schubert, Strauss I and II, and pop-icon Falco. All told, Austria's largest burial ground accommodates some 330,000 graves—from commoners to prominent members of Viennese society to presidents of the republic. For histories of the aforesaid composers and musicians, refer to chapter *Tomb-Lovers, Who's Buried Where? Austria*. *Hours:* daily, March-Oct 7:00-18:00 (May-Aug till 19:00), rest of year 8:00-17:00. *Getting There:* If you're coming from St. Marx Cemetery, tram #71 (direction Kaiserebersdorf) will take you to Zentralfriedhof's main gate: "Tor 2." If you're coming from elsewhere in the city, take subway U3 to Simmering, then out front of the station hop on either tram #71 or #6 to "Tor 2." Once inside the gate, continue straight some 250 meters to reach

Beethoven and the others at Group 32A on the left—look for the small "Musiker" sign. *GPS:* N48° 09.122 - E16° 26.404. *Drivers*, you can drive through the cemetery for 1.80€.

Cemetery of the Nameless: Eerie but mystical, "Friedhof der Namenlosen" is the last resting place of numerous unidentified victims who committed suicide, were murdered, or accidentally drowned and landed in the Danube, washing ashore in the area. Moviegoers may remember the cemetery in the film "Before Sunrise" (1995) with Ethan Hawke. *Getting There:* The cemetery is located on the southern fringe of Vienna at Alberner Hafen (Harbor) and can be difficult to reach because of infrequent bus transfers. From Schwarzenbergplatz on the Ringstrasse pick up tram #71 direction Kaiserebersdorf and get off at Hauffgasse (10th stop, or four stops from St. Marx Cemetery). Exit tram left and (to your left) cross the main road—you're heading to the bus stop down the street and on the right, where you'll pick up bus 76A (try to check bus schedule in advance). Alberner Hafen is basically the end of the line some 22 stops away, but don't let this fool you. The driver will only stop the bus when someone onboard pushes the stop button or is waiting at a bus stop, therefore the driver may only stop a handful of times before actually reaching Alberner Hafen. Once there, the cemetery is a seven-min walk. But before you head off, check the bus schedule for pick up times to coordinate your return. Okay, when ready, follow the Friedhof sign down the cobbled road—at the other end of the truck depot is the cemetery. *GPS:* N48° 09.594 - E16° 30.112. Oh, almost forgot, if it's summer, wear your insect repellent; there are scores of mosquitoes!

Imperial Crypt: Beneath the Capuchin Church (Kapuzinerkirche) is the "Kaisergruft," the 17th-century imperial burial vault accommodating the *partial remains of some 145 members of the Habsburg royal family. This is a good time to get their names straight as they lie in orderly rows. For .50¢, invest in the handy, foldout crypt-locating map. The last Habsburg to be interred here was Empress Zita—who died in 1989—the widow of Emperor Charles I, Austria's last ruler (1916-1918). Other names in the vault include Marie-Louise d'Autriche Bonaparte, Elisabeth "Sisi," Franz Josef I, and Maria Theresa (to read their histories, refer to chapter *Tomb-Lovers, Who's Buried Where? Austria*). *Hours:* daily, 9:30-15:30 (last entry). *Price:* adult 4€, student 3€. *Getting There:* Crypt is located two blocks from TI at (street) Tegetthoff 2. *_Note:_ According to tradition, select organs belonging to the Habsburgs have been preserved in two other Viennese locations: Their entrails are interred within copper urns in the crypt below St. Stephan's Cathedral and their hearts (54 of them, dating from 1618-1878) are kept in silver urns at the Augustinian Church (Augustinerkirche) in the Loreto Chapel (Loretokapelle)—the chapel is typically opened to the public (2€/person) on Sundays after Mass at 11:45.

Vivaldi, Antonio: A modest plaque commemorates the death and remains of this heavenly composer—for his history and details flip to page 463. *GPS:* N48° 11.928 - E16° 22.250

Best Views

St. Stephan's Cathedral: Vienna's soaring landmark—"Stephansdom"—affords a choice of fantastic views from its north and south towers (page 558).

Danube Tower: Rising (252m/827ft) above Vienna, the "Donauturm" is Austria's tallest structure. Express elevators whisk thrill-seekers in just 35 ear-popping seconds to the viewing level (150m/492ft) for the most impressive, heart-skipping views in town. Head to the floors above for a cappuccino in the nation's highest café or enjoy a meal in the revolving "Panorama" restaurant. Daredevils can even bungee-jump from the tower. No kidding! *Price:* (elevator) adult 5.30€, student or Vienna Card holder 4.20€, combo-ticket with Ferris wheel 9.70€ — (bungee) April-Sept 140€. *CC's:* VC, MC, AE, DC. *Hours:* daily, 10:00-24:00 (restaurant from 11:00). *Tel.#* 01/263-3572 (www.donauturm.at)

Giant Ferris Wheel: (www.wienerriesenrad.com) Idly rotate some 200 feet above the city on Vienna's landmark "Riesenrad," built in 1897 for Emperor Franz Josef's 50-year jubilee. *Price:* 7.50€, student or Vienna Card holder 6.50€, combo-ticket with Danube Tower 9.70€. *Hours:* daily, 10:00-20:00, March/April & Oct till 22:00, May-Sept 9:00-24:00.

Gloriette: Crowning the sculpted gardens of Schönbrunn palace, the Gloriette was built in 1775 as a triumphal gate for past military victories enjoyed by the imperial Habsburg armies. From its terrace is a grand view of Vienna. *Hours:* April-Oct, daily, 9:00-17:00, April-June & Sept till 18:00, July/Aug till 19:00, (closed Nov-March). *Price:* adult 2€, student or Vienna Card holder 1.50€, or free with Schönbrunn Classic/Gold Pass.

Mount Kahlen: When looking to Vienna's north-northwest skyline you'll see the vine-yard-draped slopes of "Kahlenberg," from where the view of the nation's capital, to put it mildly, is tremendous. If you have time, head up there for memorable photo opportunities and a glass of wine (or two). Hikers and howlers trek back down to the wine taverns (Heurige) of Nussdorf or Grinzing. *Note:* Near Nussdorf is the Heiligenstädter Testament museum (page 565), former Beethoven residence. *Getting There:* Take subway U4 to Heiligenstadt (end station), then out front pick up bus 38A to the "Kahlenberg" lookout. Upon arriving, follow signs "Aussichtsterrasse" (viewing terrace). *Drivers,* from the Old Town head to Grinzing, then climb Cobenzlgasse to the cobbled Höhenstrasse (built 1934-38). Once there, go right to the "Kahlenberg" lookout. After parking, follow signs "Aussichtsterrasse" (viewing terrace). *Note:* The church on the plaza (open daily 10:00-12:00 & 14:00-16:45) originally dates from 1629 and was visited by Pope John Paul II on Sept 13, 1983.

Shopping

Shops in Vienna are typically open Mon-Fri 9:00-18:00, Sat 9:00-17:00, with many staying open till 19:30 on Thur/Fri. The last three listings in this section are weekend bazaars for folks yearning to uncover secondhand treasures and trinkets.

Mariahilfer Strasse: On this mile-long boulevard you can shop from the Westbahnhof to the fringes of the Old Town. Not only can you find just about anything here, but the prices are reasonable, too. The locals picking their way between shops are a testament to the fact.

Old Town: The pedestrian-only thoroughfares of Vienna's historic core attract throngs of people-watchers and jet-setting shoppers. In this colorful setting, the main shop-lined streets to check out are — **Kärntner Str.**; street running between the Opera House and St. Stephan's Cathedral. On this lively drag you'll find Sacher torte, American Express, Vienna's casino and chic boutiques. Clean toilets can be found upstairs at Starbucks coffee, located behind the Opera House. The Ringstrassen Galerien (shopping mall, Mon-Fri 10:00-19:00, Sat 10:00-18:00) next to the Opera House provides a therapeutic shelter for retail addicts. On the lower level of the mall's second building is the Billa food court (Mon-Thur 8:00-19:00, Fri 8:00-19:30, Sat 7:30-18:00), a perfect place to score edibles for a picnic or cook-in dinner. — **Graben**; intersects with Kärntner Str. at the cathedral. Here you'll swing past chillin' cafés, trendy street performers and moneyed retailers like Hermès, Cartier and Versache. — **Kohlmarkt**; joins the other end of Graben, where you'll find more exclusive names, e.g. Gucci, Chanel, Armani and Louis Vuitton.

Auction House, Dorotheum: Ever been to an auction house? How 'bout one that is 300 years old? Here's your chance. The Dorotheum, dating from 1707, is the leading auction house in Central Europe and is within a leisurely two-minute stroll of the TI, Lipizzaner stallions and the Hofburg palace. The building is enormous, taking up half the block at Dorotheergasse 17. Inside are four floors of items for auction and some that are for immediate sale, from antique jewelry to contemporary art to you-name-it. The Dorotheum hosts some 600 auctions per year and you're welcome to join in on the bidding. Stop by and browse the upcoming items to be auctioned; "Ruf Preis" means the starting bid, or opening price. Also, important to know, a hefty (20-38%) tax will be added to the hammer price (depending on the item). But, since you're a foreigner, you can fill out a form to get some or most of that back. There are plenty of staff roaming the floors if you have any questions. Upon entering from Dorotheergasse, toilets are on the left and midway in on the left is an information desk with brochures in English. *Hours:* Mon-Fri 10:00-18:00, Sat 9:00-17:00. (www.dorotheum.com)

Militaria Shop: This pint-sized antique shop is a must-do for military buffs. Here you'll find historic Austrian and German medals and sabers and uniforms from various services and campaigns. Little English spoken. *Tel.#* 01/581-6232. *Hours:* Mon-Fri 10:00-13:00 & 15:00-18:30, Sat 10:00-13:00. *Getting There:* The shop is inconspicuously located at Opernring 9. With your back to the Opera House, cross the Ringstrasse and go right. There is no name advertising the shop's trade, so look carefully for its gold-brown front. If the door is locked, ring buzzer (right of door) to be let in.

Naschmarkt: Every Saturday (6:30-17:30) Vienna's best-known victuals market extends its boundaries to host a flea market offering a wide range of items from antiques to art nouveau to pre-loved clothing to junk. Moreover, Naschmarkt is an outstanding place to buy picnic goodies or have lunch at a sit-in eatery (page 577). *Getting There:* Naschmarkt is a 10-min walk south of the Opera House, beyond the Secession Building, or ride the subway U4 to Kettenbrückengasse (flea market is outside station).

Antique Market, Am Hof: Browse old wares and collectables at the "Antikmarkt" Am Hof (square) in the Old Town, a handful of blocks northwest of St. Stephan's Cathedral. *Hours:* Fri/Sat 8:00-18:00—closed Jan thru mid-March.

Kunst am Kanal: The riverside promenade along the Danube Canal (at Salztorbrücke) comes alive every Sunday, May-Sept, 10:00-20:00 with marketers selling arts and crafts and books and CDs and antiques and things, etc.

ENTERTAINMENT

Vienna has oodles to do, suiting all budgets and tastes, from sipping wines at traditional taverns (Heurige) to headline concerts to evenings at the opera.

Night owls looking to toast new adventures should head to the so-called **Bermuda Triangle**, where rows of bars flank the cobbled streets around St. Ruprecht's Church. We should warn you, though, being the beer connoisseurs that we are, Vienna's brew—Ottakringer—is crap! What say you? We say order another brand, if possible. ("Gösser" beer is not bad.) Fun after dark can also be had (in summer) on Danube Island and/or at club "Flex" on the Danube Canal (by Augarten bridge, next one up from Salztorbr). Many partygoers bring their own drink and sit outside Flex at the picnic tables partaking in the lively atmosphere. Entry into Flex can be free or upwards of 15€/person, depending on what's happening (Tel.# 01/533-7525, or www.flex.at [click on Programm]).

Cheap and amusing entertainment can be found at—and around—St. Stephan's Square (Stephansplatz), where **street performers** are regularly reinventing themselves.

Grapes have been grown here since Roman times and wine lovers will no doubt appreciate the rustic **Heurige** (wine taverns) selling Heuriger (new wine). Vienna is the only metropolis in the world that has its own wine district, more than 1700 acres of vineyards are located within the city limits. Many of these are on the slopes of Kahlenberg (Mount Kahlen; look north-northwest). Traditional Heurige—recognizable by the sprig of spruce hanging above the door—can only be found in the wine-growing districts on the outskirts of the city, essentially west and east of (and beneath) Kahlenberg. Noteworthy towns are Nussdorf, Grinzing and Sievering. Wine served at the Heurige is typically made from grapes picked from the tavern's own vineyard. The grapes are harvested Sept/Oct and the Heuriger—or new wine—can be sold from November 11, when the previous year's vintage becomes "old." If you're not big on wine but you don't want to be left out of the mix, order a *Gespritzter*: half wine and half soda water. Wine can be ordered by the *Viertel* (quarter liter, 8 oz) or *Achtel* (eighth liter, 4 oz).

Vienna is the capital of classical music, claiming more famous composers as residents than any other city. One of these personalities is a man by the name of Mozart, Wolfgang Amadeus. His music is brilliant and the **Mozart concert** being touted around town by people dressed in period costume is actually worthwhile. If you're on a budget, cry poor to the salesperson and you should be able to score a decent seat for 20€. After the show starts, you can move seats if it's not full. Quite often the Mozart concert is held in the **Musikverein**'s Golden Hall (Goldener Saal), from where the Vienna Philharmonic performs its annual New Year's Day concert live on TV to the world.

Another world-class institution is Vienna's ***Opera House**, or Staatsoper, dating from 1863 (***_GPS:_** N48° 12.152 - E16° 22.180). With some 50 operas and ballets performed 300 days of the year, the chances are good something will be on tonight (closed July/Aug). The Opera House has 1709 seats and 567 spots for standing. Show tickets cost 2€/3.50€ for "Stehplatz" (standing room) or 10€-250€ for seats. Travelers who are not keen on the opera or ballet but would like to get the gist of a performance, buy the standing-room ticket for 3.50€ (the 2€ ticket is off to the side on the upper level while the 3.50€ ticket is centered midway up behind 100€ seats). Since it's difficult to stand for an entire three-hour performance, consider having dinner first and arriving for the latter portion to see the finale. The box office for standing room opens 80 min before the performance starts—buy your ticket then (to get there, enter through the side door leading to the Stehplatz-Kasse on the left [Operngasse] side of the building). However, if it doesn't look like it'll be a sell-out, you can buy a ticket even after the curtain opens. Dress is quasi-casual but throw on your best duds. Jackets (of any kind) must be checked at the cloakroom, 1€. _Seats_ can be bought a month in advance via the below-mentioned website or by calling 01/513-1513 (daily, 10:00-21:00. All CCs accepted; have yours at the ready). If seats aren't sold out, check for heavy discounts the day prior to the show. *Note:* After arriving in Vienna, check the program: a ballet may be scheduled one night and an opera the next (or check online at www.staatsoper.at). _Seating, Translations_: *Parkett* = Orchestra • *Logen* = Box • *Parterre* = First level • *Rang* = Balcony • *Balkon* = (upper) Balcony • *Galerie* = (peanut) Gallery, upper deck • *Seite* = Side • *Reihe* = Row. _Tours_ of the Opera House (in English, duration 40 min) are conducted daily, typically in the afternoon on the hour. During July/Aug, when the Opera House is closed to performances, tours normally begin at 10:00. *Price:* (tour and museum) adult 6.50€, student 3.50€, senior 5.50€. *Note:* To beat the price down (to adult 5€, student 2€, senior4€), go on a Monday when the museum is closed. For more info or to check the current tour schedule, go to their website listed above or call 01/51444-2606.

GOOD EATS

Vienna, as the TI likes to put it when concerning its cuisine, is a "melting pot of nations." For the skinny on the hottest dish in town, query TI or staff at your digs. Meanwhile, here are a few tidbits to wet your appetite.

For a sweet taste of Vienna, try the original **Sacher torte**. Since 1832, according to a secret recipe, Franz Sacher and family have been whipping up the world's most famous torte—a rich chocolate dessert with a hint of apricot. Let your nose lead you to the Sacher hotel and café and sweets shop directly behind the Opera House. (www.sacher.com)

Vienna is world famous for its **(Wiener) schnitzel** and the most famous place in town to dish up the breaded (pork/veal) cutlet is Figlmüller—serving schnitzel that overlaps the plate—since 1905. Truly, the portions are huge! Look at the size of the meals coming out from the kitchen. Consider splitting one. Figlmüller has two restaurants, only 70 meters apart. The original, and busier of the two, is located in a quaint passageway at Wollzeile 5 *(daily, 11:00-22:30—closed August. Tel.# 01/512-6177. GPS: N48° 12.543 - E16° 22.469).* The other is around the corner at Bäckerstr. 6 *(daily 12:00-24:00—closed July. Tel.# 01/512-1760).*

Vienna's best-known and liveliest market—**Naschmarkt**—offers a wide, multicultural variety of foods, from tangy tandoori and soft sushi to Turkish döner kebap stands and Asian sit-in eateries to handpicked fruits and vegetables. For a taste of the Mediterranean, try the "Olivenbrot" (olive bread) to snack on while browsing. It comes in big and bigger, so either split one with a friend or ask the vendor if he/she will sell a smaller portion. Besides foods (and wines), Naschmarkt accommodates a patchwork of vendors selling bric-a-brac with emphasis on hippie-type regalia that can be found most anywhere in the world. Every Saturday, however, the southwest end of Naschmarkt transforms into a mecca of marketers hawking an array of secondhand wares amounting to a potentially worthwhile flea market. *Hours:* Mon-Sat 6:30-17:00 (eateries stay open later; stall owners may pack up earlier depending on season and weather). *Getting There:* Naschmarkt is a 10-min walk south of the Opera House, beyond the Secession Building, or ride the subway U4 to Kettenbrückengasse. Exit station Naschmarkt and the Sezessionstil *facades are to your left, the victuals market is in front of you and the marketers are behind you. **Note:* Artists and design students check out Otto Wagner's art nouveau facades at Linke Wienzeile 38 and 40. Classical music buffs will be interested to know that the Theater an der Wien at (street) Linke Wienzeile 6 is where Mozart's last (comic) opera "The Magic Flute" premiered in 1791, just before his death.

Headline Concerts, Vienna 2006

Note: Prices, dates, concerts may have changed or been added — query TI or ticket agency for latest details.

Eros Ramazzotti: April 20, 19:30 at the Stadthalle. Price 55€
   Paul Weller: April 20, 20:00 at the Gasometer. Price 38-43€
Santana: May 28, 20:00 at the Stadthalle. Price 58-68€
   Rolling Stones: June 20, 19:30 at Ernst Happel Stadium. Price 74-96€
Billy Joel: June 26, 20:00 at the Stadthalle. Price 30-105€
   Robbie Williams: August 18-19, 20:00 at Ernst Happel Stadium. Price 70-100€
Pink: December 10, 19:30 at the Stadthalle. Price 46-65€

GOOD SLEEPS

The following accommodations, listed from the least expensive to the most, come with breakfast and have facilities (shower/toilet) in the room, unless otherwise stated.

Hostel, Ruthensteiner: Rob.-Hamerling-G. 24 (www.hostelruthensteiner.com) *Tel.#* 01/ 893-4202. These warmly run digs by Erin and Walter Ruthensteiner and co. provide a homely atmosphere for backpackers far from home. Hostel has a chill-out courtyard, Internet access, bike rental, respectable self-service kitchen, a hip bar/hangout area, but expensive laundry facilities (6€/load). Recent renovations make Ruthensteiner's all the more appealing. *Note:* The hostel is actually set up between three (nearby) buildings. The above-listed address represents the main building where everything is located, including reception, and where you want to stay, if vacancies allow. Check out 10:00! Reception is typically good about holding phone reservations with a credit card. *Price:* dorm bed from

13€ (←plus one-time 2€ linen fee, or free with own sheets), Sgl 26€, Dbl 44-52€, breakfast 2.50€. *CC's:* VC, MC (50¢ surcharge per night). *Getting There:* Hostel Ruthensteiner is an easy five-minute walk from Westbahnhof—exit station (Äußere) Mariahilfer Str. and go right on Mariahilfer Str. Cross the street when clear and after a few blocks make a left on Haidmannsgasse, then go right on Rob.-Hamerling-G. to No. 24 on the right. *Drivers*, street parking available. *GPS:* N48° 11.611 - E16° 20.142

Hostel, Wombats: Grangasse 6 (www.wombats.at) *Tel.#* 01/897-2336. Wombats has fresh amenities, friendly staff, and a hip bar with a very happy hour. If you're trying to get an early night's sleep, this may not be the place. Hostel has laundry facilities, Internet, and all rooms have a built-in shower/toilet. *Price:* (cash only) 4/6 dorm 16-18€, Sgl/Dbl 42-48€, breakfast 3.50€. *Note:* Generally, reception will only hold a phone reservation until 16:00. Wombats is scheduled to open a second, nearby hostel June 2006. *Getting There:* Wombats is about an eight-minute walk from Westbahnhof—exit station (Äußere) Mariahilfer Str. and go right on Mariahilfer Str. Continue straight and after six blocks make a right on Rosinagasse, then second left on Grangasse. *Drivers*, street parking available. *GPS:* N48° 11.667 - E16° 19.855.

Hotel ibis: www.ibishotel.com (hotel code 0796) *Tel.#* 01/59-998. Standardized comfort, reasonably priced, and handily located near Westbahnhof. *Price:* Sgl 67-71€, Dbl 82-86€. *CC's:* VC, MC. *Note:* Parking, breakfast cost extra. Hotel code is compatible with ibis website, creating a shortcut to the property—type hotel code into middle left box and click "OK"; next page click on "The Hotel" (left side).

Pension Nossek: Graben 17 (www.pension-nossek.at) *Tel.#* 01/5337-0410. Hidden in plain view, you'll absolutely adore these inner-city accommodations. Your charming hosts—the Nossek sisters—add a fine touch to an already elegant, 19th-century establishment. Comfy rooms; individually designed. *Price:* (cash only) Sgl 46-69€ (←cheaper price means no facilities in room, or shower only), Dbl 110€, junior suite 136€, extra bed 35€. *Getting There:* Take subway U1 or U3 to Stephansplatz. Two minutes from the Hofburg palace and St. Stephan's Cathedral, Pension Nossek is located in the pedestrian district near the corner of (street) Kohlmarkt. If you're coming from the cathedral or subway, head along (street) Graben and it's on the left some 60 meters past the ornate (plague) column. *Note:* Take elevator to 2nd floor for reception. *Drivers,* parking is difficult, inquire in advance. *GPS:* N48° 12.562 - E16° 22.128

Hotel König von Ungarn: Schulerstr. 10 (www.kvu.at) *Tel.#* 01/515-840. Step back into time in Hotel "King of Hungary," where royalty, artists and celebrities have overnighted since 1815. All rooms boast 19th-century ambiance and are built around a quaint indoor courtyard perfect for a relaxing drink after a day of sightseeing. Situated in the heart of the Old Town, Hotel König von Ungarn is positioned in the same historic building as Mozart's Figarohaus (page 565). *Price:* Sgl 142-162€, Dbl 203€, Trpl suite 280€, Quad suite 330€. *CC's:* VC, MC, AE. *Getting There:* Take subway U1 or U3 to Stephansplatz. Hotel is some 100 meters behind St. Stephan's Cathedral. *Drivers,* a parking garage is 50 meters away, 24€/24hr. *GPS:* N48° 12.487 - E16° 22.525

EXCURSIONS

Danube Valley: (page 543) Consider visiting this unique and diverse locale registered as a UNESCO World Heritage site, 85km/53mi west of Vienna (75-min by train from Vienna's Westbahnhof). Ride a bike (or boat) along the Danube River, from Melk to Krems (page 549).

INDEX

Meet The Author

Brett Harriman grew up in the abundantly appealing seaside town of Dana Point, California, and was fortunate enough to have parents who dragged their kids with them everywhere they went, including on overseas vacations. Thus, the travel bug kicked in early.

Brett has driven across America, trekked around Australia, and explored Europe. He lived in the Australian state of New South Wales for a decade and in Europe for five years, where he was an official tour guide for the U.S. Armed Forces in Germany. In that role he escorted more than 10,000 servicemen and women and their families through many historically rich cities, towns, villages and Alpine hamlets.

When he is not in Europe sleuthing out the latest travel information or on tour promoting *"Your Traveling Companion,"* Brett spends his time between Southern California and Pahrump, Nevada, where his parents have retired. He is single and looking for a lifetime traveling companion.

Notes